Praise for the Pacific War

Pacific Crucible

"Vivid, fast moving and highly readable."
—Ronald Spector, *Wall Street Journal*

"Both a serious work of history . . . and a marvelously readable dramatic narrative."
—*San Francisco Chronicle*

"[A] diligently constructed history of the first seven months of the Pacific War. . . . [Ian] Toll has an affinity for the detailed narrative of military conflict."
—Michael Beschloss, *New York Times Book Review*

"Toll's book does a good job of capturing strategy, tactics, weaponry and, especially, people, on the Japanese side as well as the American. . . . You won't set [*Pacific Crucible*] aside."
—Harry Levins, *St. Louis Post-Dispatch*

The Conquering Tide

"In his masterly narrative, Ian Toll brings clarity and a stinging immediacy to America's long, bitter climb up the island ladder that led to Japan. This is maritime history at its best and most accessible, told with a verve that will leave the reader wondering how such a long book could have sped by so quickly."
—Richard Snow, author of *Iron Dawn* and *A Measureless Peril*

"A beautiful blend of history and prose and proves again Mr. Toll's mastery of the naval-war narrative."
—Jonathan W. Jordan, *Wall Street Journal*

"A gripping narrative of the central Pacific campaign. . . . Toll is strong on the operational details of battle, but he is no less skilled at presenting something that is frequently missing from military histories, a well-rounded depiction of the home front on both sides."
—Walter R. Borneman, *New York Times Book Review*

"Ian Toll takes his place as one of the great storytellers of war. He is equally vivid and commanding describing landing on a carrier at night, making grand strategy in Washington, and brawling in a bar in Australia. Toll is a master; he is writing for the ages."
—Evan Thomas, author of *Sea of Thunder* and *Being Nixon*

"A riveting account of how the US clawed its way back from defeat against initially unstoppable Japanese air, land and sea invasion forces after Pearl Harbor. . . . This is military history at its best."
—Lionel Barber, *Financial Times*

"A lucid and learned exposition of the grand chess match between high commanders in the middle years of the Pacific War, vividly evoking the grit and gristle of its many horrors and triumphs. Ian W. Toll is a superb historian whose writing appeals to both the head and the heart."

—James D. Hornfischer, author of
Neptune's Inferno: The U.S. Navy at Guadalcanal

"Toll's absorbing text flows smoothly and quickly, helped along by anecdotes and stories involving combatants and political leaders on both sides."

—Si Dunn, *Dallas Morning News*

Twilight of the Gods

"[A]n epic masterpiece of military history."

—Nathaniel Philbrick, *New York Times* best-selling author of
In the Hurricane's Eye

"Toll [is] the fitting inheritor of a tradition of writing that began with the naval historian Samuel Eliot Morison. . . . Toll's trilogy . . . is exhaustive and authoritative and it shows the Navy in World War II as it really was, warts and all."

—Mark Perry, *New York Times Book Review*

"[A] magnificent saga of the last year of the Pacific War. . . . A wonderful teller of war stories, Toll is also a shrewd cultural observer."

—Evan Thomas, *AirMail*

"Using meticulous research, including previously untapped primary sources, and a brisk narrative that combines strategic, operational, and personal perspectives, [Toll] presents a very balanced look at the critical decisions and actions on both sides that concluded the war." —Jerry Lenaburg, *New York Journal of Books*

"The Pacific Theater has had entire libraries of histories written about it over the last seven decades . . . Toll has written a trilogy fit to stand with some of the best of them." —Steven Donoghue, *Open Letters Review*

"Combining beautiful prose with the gritty and bloody realities of the island hopping strategy, Toll's third and final volume has been eagerly awaited by scholars and military history aficionados alike." —Claire Barrett, *HistoryNet*

Twilight
of the
Gods

War in
the Western Pacific,
1944–1945

IAN W. TOLL

W. W. NORTON & COMPANY
Independent Publishers Since 1923

For information about permission to reproduce selections from this book, write to
Permissions, W. W. Norton & Company, Inc., 500 Fifth Avenue, New York, NY 10110

For information about special discounts for bulk purchases, please contact
W. W. Norton Special Sales at specialsales@wwnorton.com or 800-233-4830

Manufacturing by LSC Communications, Harrisonburg
Production manager: Anna Oler

Library of Congress Cataloging-in-Publication Data

Names: Toll, Ian W., author.
Title: Twilight of the Gods : War in the Western Pacific, 1944–1945 / Ian W. Toll.
Other titles: War in the Western Pacific, 1944–1945
Description: First edition. | New York : W. W. Norton & Company, [2020] |
Includes bibliographical references and index.
Identifiers: LCCN 2020009619| ISBN 9780393080650 (hardcover) |
ISBN 9780393651812 (epub)
Subjects: LCSH: World War, 1939–1945—Campaigns—Pacific Area. |
World War, 1939–1945—Naval operations, American. |
World War, 1939–1945—Naval operations, Japanese.
Classification: LCC D767 .T653 2020 | DDC 940.54/26—dc23
LC record available at https://lccn.loc.gov/2020009619

ISBN 978-0-393-86830-2 pbk.

W. W. Norton & Company, Inc., 500 Fifth Avenue, New York, N.Y. 10110
www.wwnorton.com

W. W. Norton & Company Ltd., 15 Carlisle Street, London W1D 3BS

1 2 3 4 5 6 7 8 9 0

To Admiral Husband E. Kimmel and General Walter C. Short,
who were dealt a losing hand.

CONTENTS

LIST OF MAPS

AUTHOR'S NOTE AND ACKNOWLEDGMENTS

In 2007, as I wince to recall, I set out to write a single-volume history of the Pacific War. The publisher of my first book, *Six Frigates*, offered a contract and paid me an advance. Two and a half years later, with my deadline six months away, I called my editor, Starling Lawrence, and gave him the good news that I had written almost 800 pages. The bad news, which I also gave him, probably holding the phone away from my ear, was that the narrative had only advanced through the Battle of Midway. I had covered six months of a forty-four-month war, and I had already exceeded the specified manuscript length by 300 pages.

On the same phone call, without pausing to mull it over, or even to demand the 800 pages, Star proposed a solution. Why not convert the project into a trilogy? The contract was amended, new deadlines were extended, and the advance increased (though not, alas, tripled). Volume 1, *Pacific Crucible*, was published in 2011; Volume 2, *The Conquering Tide*, in 2015. The first covered the initial six months of the war, from Japan's surprise raid on Pearl Harbor to the devastating American counterpunch at Midway. The second told the story of the middle two years of the war, from mid-1942 through mid-1944, and the Allied counteroffensives in the south and central Pacific. This volume is the third and last, picking up after the Marianas campaign and covering the last year of the war, through the Japanese surrender in August 1945.

The reader may already have noticed that this book is longer than either of the previous two. That was neither expected nor intended. I had anticipated that the third book would be the easiest of the trilogy to write, perhaps even the shortest. Much of the research was already "in the can," and the period to be covered was only a year, whereas *The Conquering Tide* had covered two years. With reckless confidence I predicted that the final volume would be out in 2018. When that became impossible, I vowed on Twitter that it would be out in 2019 "unless it killed me first." Then 2020 arrived with the book finished but not yet in print. Luckily, tweets can be deleted, and as of this writing I am not dead, but *Twilight of the Gods* turned out to be the hardest book of the trilogy to finish. The reasons are various. The war got very large in late 1944 and 1945, in every dimension, and I found that I could not do justice to the story without giving it the additional time and space it seemed to need. Over the years I had collected a lot of research on subjects that lay along the periphery of the main narrative—for example, military-press relations, naval pilot training, Allied radio and leaflet propaganda, and the lives of evacuated Japanese schoolchildren—and I was determined to get it all into the book. (In the first two volumes, but not in the third, I had the option to say, "I'll pick it up in the next one.") As a result, it took me more than three times longer to produce this three-volume history of the Pacific War than it took the combatant nations to fight it.

In the author's note for *The Conquering Tide*, I made the case for an episodic and discursive narrative, one that colors outside the lines of conventional specialized military history. I won't repeat the manifesto here. Suffice to say that what was true then is even truer now. In the last year of the Second World War, even more than in other years and other wars, grand strategic decisions were an amalgamation of purely military calculations with politics and diplomatic statecraft. In both Europe and Asia, it was understood that the timing, scale, and scope of major operations had downstream implications for the postwar international order. In the United States, moreover, the epochal decisions of 1944 would be made in the glare of a national presidential campaign. Carl von Clausewitz wrote, "War is a continuation of politics by other means," but in a constitutional democracy with a fixed election calendar, the dictum could just as well be reversed: "Politics is a continuation of war by other means." In that spirit, I chose to begin this book with a long first chapter on the Honolulu strategy conference of July 1944, when President Franklin Delano Roosevelt met with his Pacific theater commanders to plan the last phase of the campaign against Japan. The episode was immensely significant, both for the Pacific War and the future of Asia, but it has often been slighted in histories and biographies. I judged that it merited a longer, more nuanced telling, especially since an important new source has recently come to light—the diary of Robert C. Richardson Jr., commanding general of U.S. Army forces in Hawaii, who hosted General Douglas MacArthur during the conference and recorded MacArthur's contemporary firsthand account of his discussions with FDR.

Thanks to all who have assisted my research in various ways: the late Adolphus Andrews Jr., for sharing his recollections of Iwo Jima and postwar Japan; Bill Bell, for forwarding his father William Bell's diary on Task Force 38 air operations; Frank Dunlevy, for his father-in-law's oral history of his service on the destroyer *Johnston*; Ronald Nunez, who gave me the diary of Admiral John Henry Towers; Chet Lay and Captain Michael A. Lilly (USN, ret.), who shared interesting details of Chester Nimitz's friendship with the Walker family on Oahu (since published by Lilly in *Nimitz at Ease*). Colonel Robert C. Richardson IV (USAF, ret.) gave me his grandfather's aforementioned diary, which General Richardson had willed his descendants to keep private until 2015. Ronald Russell, former editor and webmaster of the Battle of Midway Roundtable, reviewed the manuscript and provided valuable feedback, as he did for volumes 1 and 2. Among the Japanese who have assisted me in various ways are Susumu Shimoyama, Kazuhisa Murakami, Yukoh Watanabe, Kiyohiko Arafune, and Yukio Satoh. Eric Simonoff, my agent of eighteen years, has kept the faith through long delays and lapsed deadlines. I am grateful to the whole team at W. W. Norton, including Nneoma Amadi-Obi, Rebecca Homiski, Bill Rusin, and especially Star Lawrence, who has always supported my instinct to stray outside the lanes while also letting me know when I may be straying too far.

The Pacific, 1944

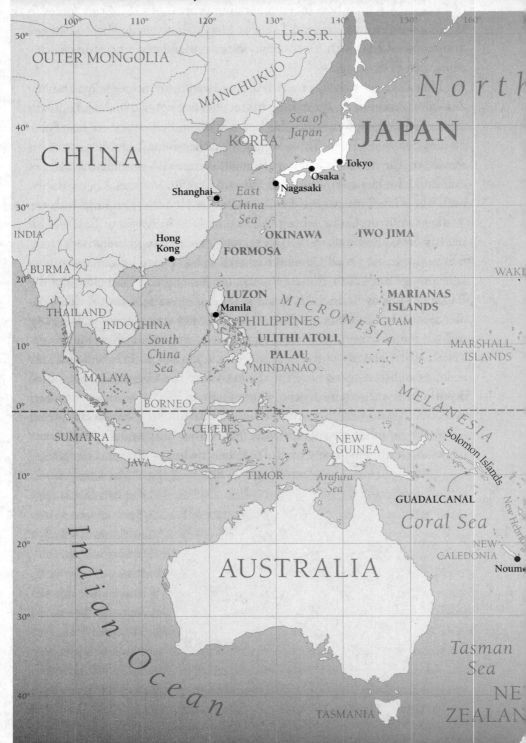

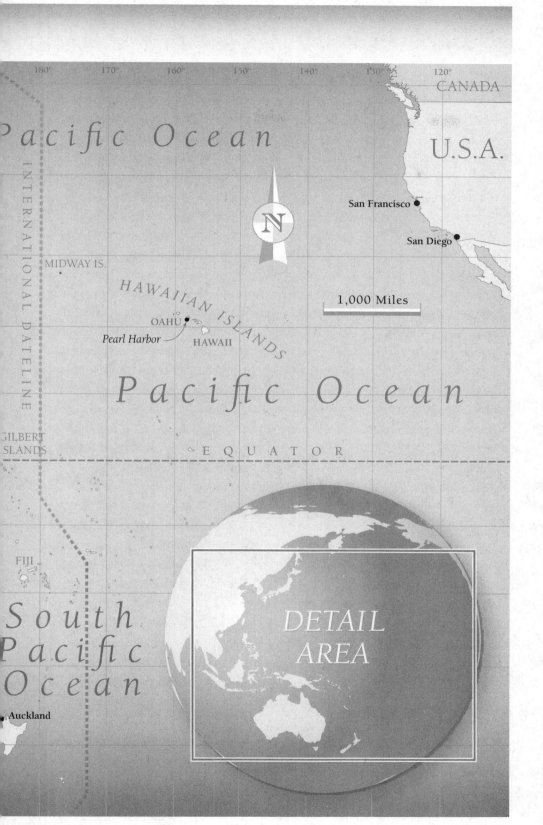

Twilight of the Gods

Prologue

"Don't argue with people who buy ink by the barrel."
—AMERICAN APHORISM, ORIGIN UNKNOWN

Franklin Delano Roosevelt's rapport with the press had deteriorated sharply since his first presidential term in office. Back in those honeymoon days of 1933, the newly sworn president had disarmed reporters with a fond and familiar manner—calling them by their first names, bantering about trivialities, writing birthday notes, and inviting their entire families to White House parties. His twice-weekly press conferences had been freewheeling and uninhibited. Filing into the Oval Office, the reporters were greeted by a cheerful, big-headed man in a well-worn, slightly rumpled suit, seated in his wheelchair behind a large mahogany desk. He was usually clutching a cigarette, and flecks of ash clung to the fabric of his sleeves. He took any question as it came, verbally and off the cuff. He kept the atmosphere light and mirthful. The president might remark that a reporter appeared hungover, for example, and ask the room for its opinion; or he might ask the security detail to confirm that a particular reporter had been frisked. He joked that he was running a "schoolroom," and spoke to the journalists as if they were not especially bright grade school students: "No, my dear child, you have got that all wrong."[1] Listening to a question, he let his mouth drop open in a parody of deep attentiveness. His facial expressions, with vaudevillian exaggeration, conveyed amazement, bewilderment, and alarm. While considering his answer, he gazed up at the Great Presidential Seal—set in plaster in the ceiling overhead—drew in a long breath, puffed up his cheeks, and expelled the air in a long blast. These antics brought forth hearty laughter from the reporters.

The president did not always reply directly—or truthfully, or at all—but he tolerated follow-up questions and engaged in informal back-and-forth exchanges. White House stenographers recorded every word of his 998 press conferences, including the small talk and badinage that opened each session. The transcripts run to many thousands of pages and occupy more than four cubic feet at the FDR Library in Hyde Park, New York.

By 1941, the first year of his third term in office, there were still flashes of that old warmth and wit—but now, more than in years past, White House reporters saw Roosevelt as a quicksilver character, temperamental and even inscrutable, a man of unfathomable depths. In one moment he lit up the room with his famous high-wattage smile; in the next he turned sour and snappish. It was not in FDR's nature to shout, or even to raise his voice, but there was often a cantankerous undercurrent to his banter, and if he did not like a question he was liable to give a reporter the rough side of his tongue. According to Merriman Smith, a United Press correspondent, the president "could be as rough and tough as a Third Avenue blackjack artist, or he could be utterly charming, disarming and thoroughly likeable. It just depended on the question, who asked it and how Mr. Roosevelt felt when he got up that morning."[2]

Calling out individual newsmen to rebut stories they had written, he pressed home his cross-examinations with the zeal of a courtroom litigator. Intolerant of euphemisms such as "error" or "inaccuracy," FDR accused individual reporters of printing "lies"—or if that wasn't clear enough, "plain lies" or "deliberate lies."[3] The term "lie" characterized the motive of the perpetrator, leaving no room for the possibility that an honest mistake had been made, but that was precisely his point. Deploring the trend toward "interpretive journalism," he dogmatically insisted that newspapers should have no role in news analysis or commentary, even in the editorial pages. Syndicated columnists, said FDR, were "an unnecessary excrescence on our civilization." They trolled for gossip—"buzz, buzz, buzz," he called it—and passed those tidbits off as news. He labeled Drew Pearson, the most widely read columnist of the era, a "chronic liar."[4]

At a press conference in February 1939, when questions implied that FDR was attempting to circumvent congressional restrictions on arms shipments to Europe, he launched into a tirade. "The American people are beginning to realize that the things they have read and heard . . . have been pure bunk—b-u-n-k, bunk; that these people are appealing to the ignorance, the prejudice, and the fears of Americans and are acting in an un-American way."

Asked whether he believed the offending papers had deliberately misled their readers, FDR answered with a question of his own.

"What shall I say? Shall I be polite or call it by the right name?"

"Call it by the right name," said one of the newsmen.

"Deliberate lie."[5]

He read four or five newspapers each morning, usually before rising from bed. Roosevelt was a pious man who rarely swore, but the morning editions often put him into a seething fury, prompting a "damn," or in severe cases a "goddamn." As he read, his face darkened, his chin hardened, and his eyes glittered wrathfully. He might tear the offending story from the paper and bring it with him to the Oval Office, where he would thrust it into the hands of his press secretary, Stephen T. Early, complaining: "It's a damn lie from start to finish."[6] He became convinced that most of the American press—85 percent was the proportion he often cited—was functioning as a mouthpiece for the embattled oligarchy. The "Tory press," said Roosevelt, was shrewd, malevolent, and unscrupulous. It was owned and controlled by a cabal of rich conservatives who hated him personally and served up a daily diet of vitriol aimed at him, his political allies, his staff, and even his family.

In the pantheon of FDR's archenemies, four newspaper moguls sat on high pedestals. William Randolph Hearst's national newspaper chain often published identical editorials denouncing Roosevelt and his policies. Media analysts correctly surmised that the invective was orchestrated by the "chief" himself, who wired instructions to his editorial rooms from his garish castle at San Simeon on the California coast. Robert R. "Bertie" McCormick, publisher of the *Chicago Tribune*, openly despised Roosevelt and everything he stood for, and his paper—the second city's leading daily and one of the nation's most widely read newspapers—disparaged the administration without even the pretense of objectivity. McCormick's cousin, Joseph M. Patterson, was founder and owner of the New York *Daily News*, the nation's first tabloid. With its big-photograph format and sensationalist coverage of crime, sports, and sex scandals, the *Daily News* prospered throughout the Depression years, and its circulation eventually overtook that of the *New York Times*. Patterson had once called himself a socialist, and was initially sympathetic to the New Deal, but in 1940 he threw in with the isolationist movement and his paper turned sharply against FDR. Eleanor "Cissy"

Patterson, Joseph's younger sister and Bertie McCormick's cousin, was an eccentric and profane misanthrope who bought two Washington newspapers from Hearst and merged them into one: the Washington *Times-Herald*. By the late thirties, the *Times-Herald* had won the capital's circulation battle and was one of the most profitable newspapers in the country. It was a blatantly partisan broadsheet that attacked the administration nearly every day, and sometimes several times per day in as many as four daily editions. Scurrilous anti-FDR editorials, signed "Cissy Patterson," appeared on the front page. Newsboys hawked the paper on every downtown corner, and one or two were usually found shouting the latest headlines from the sidewalk just outside the White House gates.

None of the four was a stranger to FDR. McCormick and Joseph Patterson had been his Groton schoolmates, and he and Eleanor had been friendly with Cissy Patterson when she was a young debutante on the cotillion social circuit. Earlier in his career, Roosevelt had counted Hearst as an ally and had even called him a "friend." His antipathy toward them, and theirs toward him, was intimate and deeply personal. Since three of the four were blood relatives, and the fourth (Hearst) was linked to the others by long-standing friendships and business dealings, FDR tended to regard the Hearst-McCormick-Patterson newspapers as a united front. But in 1940, as he ran for an unprecedented third presidential term, about three-quarters of all American newspapers opposed his bid for reelection, and FDR's relationship with the press descended to its nadir. On the campaign trail, Roosevelt often went out of his way to denounce the newspapers, charging that they were failing to perform their vital role in American democracy. The press, he said, was a profit-seeking enterprise that found sensationalism and gossip more lucrative than sober, accurate reporting, and was polluting the nation's civil discourse. That fall in the *New York Times*, Arthur Krock cited the president's determination "to preach a class war against the press," and his "steady implications that the press is unreliable and often venal."[7]

After he defeated the Republican candidate Wendell Willkie in a popular and electoral landslide, the attitudes of many newsmen, editors, radio broadcasters, and columnists hardened against the president. FDR had broken 150 years of precedent by running for (and winning) a third term in office. Now more than ever, journalists felt a constitutional duty to defy the powerful president and keep him in check.

Looking back from the present, when his legacy has been engraved in marble, it is difficult to sense how polarizing and controversial a figure FDR was in his own time. It was taken for granted in media circles, even among journalists who liked him personally and were sympathetic to his policies, that FDR was an incorrigible trickster. He had often shown that he could manipulate or circumvent the press. He spoke directly to the American people by radio, and had done so with great success—but radio was still a fairly new medium, and many were concerned that it provided a means to weaponize political demagogy. On several occasions, during the debate between isolationists and interventionists over U.S. involvement in the European war, the president implied that his critics were treasonous. The critics, in turn, worried about the inevitable expansion of presidential powers in the event that the United States joined the war against Hitler. Anyone middle-aged or older could remember the repressive censorship regime imposed during the First World War. The "dignity" of President Woodrow Wilson had been held inviolable, and any criticism of the president or his policies, no matter how mild or well-meaning, had been grounds to prosecute or shut down an offending newspaper. FDR had served in Wilson's administration as assistant secretary of the navy, so he bore a share of responsibility for those earlier abuses. H. L. Mencken, recalling the travesties of 1917–1918, warned his colleagues that it was their duty, in wartime even more than in peace, "to keep a wary eye on the gentlemen who operate this great nation, and only too often slip into the assumption that they own it." If the newspapers did not resist with determination, they would yield to "a squeeze play that politicians have been working on them since the cradle days of the Republic."[8] And there matters stood on December 7, 1941, when the biggest news story of the twentieth century broke in the skies over Pearl Harbor.

TWO DAYS AFTER THE ATTACK, FDR hosted his regular Tuesday press conference, the first of the war. Reporters had been warned to arrive early at the White House, because new wartime security measures would cause long delays. New guard houses and sentry boxes had been erected throughout the grounds. Steel barricades and 10-foot-high sandbag embankments had appeared at every entrance. Machine guns had been set up on the roof. Soldiers in trench helmets carried rifles with bayonets fixed, and plainclothes Secret Service agents carried Tommy guns.

This was to be the largest press conference yet of FDR's presidency.

To accommodate the huge crowd, it was moved from the Oval Office to the East Room. Mike Reilly, chief of the president's Secret Service detail, counted more than six hundred journalists gathered behind a rope line in the lobby, "milling and shoving like so many wild horses in a corral. We let them pass the barrier one at a time, identifying them and asking them to drop their lighted cigarettes as they entered the President's office."[9]

For the previous forty-eight hours, the press had been scrambling to report what had happened in Hawaii. Apart from a small number of specialists who had covered the army and navy, most reporters were largely ignorant of military affairs and could not even name the nation's top-ranking generals and admirals. Press secretary Steve Early had been providing regular briefings since Sunday, but there was much that he could not tell them. Bits and pieces of the truth had filtered back from Pearl Harbor through the rumor mill: hints of sunken battleships, airplanes destroyed on the ground, thousands of servicemen killed and wounded. Hysteria and fear were in the air. The Press Club on Fourteenth Street was humming with rumors. FBI director J. Edgar Hoover had coordinated the first tentative steps toward press censorship. The army had warned newspapers that nothing was to be printed about troop movements, and the navy had taken control of international telephone and telegraph offices. But in those first hectic days of the war, the government had not yet disclosed how and when news from overseas combat theaters would be reported to the American people.

The press conference was delayed for some time as Reilly's security men double-checked credentials. Roosevelt sat behind a desk at the front of the room, with Early hovering nearby, as the last of the journalists and cameramen trickled in. The official stenographer recorded an offhand exchange between them.

"Tremendous crowd," said Early.

"They will get damn little," the president replied.[10]

FDR opened the conference by reading a series of announcements about war mobilization, and gave news of the various agencies involved in rationing and retooling civilian industries for munitions production. The issues of war reporting and censorship were not raised until the second half of the hour. When they were, it was evident that FDR and his advisers had barely begun to think about these issues.

"All information has to conform with two obvious conditions before it can be given out," the president said. "The first is that it is accurate. Well, I should think that would seem fairly obvious. And the second is that in giving it out it does not give aid and comfort to the enemy."

The reporters were evidently more than willing to abide by a censorship regime—the catastrophe at Pearl Harbor had dramatized the need to protect wartime secrets—but they were also eager to separate facts from rumors. If they received information from a nonofficial source, asked one newsman, what should they do with it? FDR said they must withhold it until the military censors could review it: "The papers are not running the war. The Army and Navy have got to determine that."

The president was peppered with a series of questions about Pearl Harbor, and he answered with a minimum of detail. Asked to confirm that thousands of sailors had been granted leave and were in Honolulu on the morning of the attack, FDR shot back, "How do I know? How do you know? How does the person reporting it know?"[11] Rumors were bad enough in peacetime; in wartime they were potentially fatal to the war effort.

That night, FDR addressed the nation by radio in his first wartime "Fireside Chat," reaching a record-breaking audience of 60 million. The speech repeated and amplified the points he had made in his lecture to the White House correspondents a few hours earlier. Rumormongering was an understandable impulse, he said, but it was potentially damaging to the morale of the American people. "Most earnestly I urge my countrymen to reject all rumors. These ugly little hints of complete disaster fly thick and fast in wartime. They have to be examined and appraised." The enemy would spread lies and disinformation aimed at confusing and frightening the American people, and it was their collective responsibility to stand up to such propaganda tactics. Nothing reported by an anonymous source should be believed. He added a direct appeal to the news media:

To all newspapers and radio stations—all those who reach the eyes and ears of the American people—I say this: You have a most grave responsibility to the nation now and for the duration of this war.

If you feel that your Government is not disclosing enough of the truth, you have every right to say so. But in the absence of all the facts, as revealed by official sources, you have no right in the ethics of patriotism to deal out unconfirmed reports in such a way as to make people believe that they are gospel truth.[12]

In those early stages of the war, when the shock of Pearl Harbor was still fresh, leaders in the news media adopted a constructive attitude toward censorship. No editor, reporter, or radio broadcaster wanted to be blamed for harming the Allied cause, whether intentionally or inadvertently. All agreed, at least in principle, that vital military secrets must not fall into the enemy's hands through the medium of a free press. A popular trade journal told its readers: "As between an ethical professional requirement that a journalist hold nothing back and a patriotic duty not to shoot one's own soldiers in the back, we have found no difficulty in making a choice. Freedom of the press does not carry with it a general license to reveal our secret strengths and weaknesses to the enemy."[13]

Mindful that the government had overplayed its hand during the First World War, FDR moved cautiously. He expressed his personal distaste for censorship. "All Americans abhor censorship, just as they abhor war," he said in a statement shortly after the attack on Pearl Harbor. "But the experience of this and of all other nations has demonstrated that some degree of censorship is essential in wartime, and we are at war."[14]

By January 1942, the federal government had established its basic policy. Reporting from overseas would be handled by "war correspondents" accredited by the army or navy, and their stories would be submitted to military censors prior to publication. But newspapers, magazines, and radio broadcasters at home would be subject to a strictly voluntary regime, with no provisions for prior government censorship and no new enforcement mechanisms. They would be asked to abide by a "Code of Wartime Practices for the American Press," which listed categories of information to be withheld from publication for the duration of the war: troop movements, ship departures, war production statistics, the weather, the locations of sensitive military installations or munitions plants. No reference was to be made to information derived from intelligence sources, the effectiveness of enemy defensive measures, or the development of new weapons or technologies. For fear that spies or saboteurs might try to communicate through the American media, newspapers were asked to discontinue "want" ads placed by the public. For the same reason, commercial radio stations were to scrub open-microphone programs, call-in shows, and "man on the street" interviews. They would no longer take musical requests or broadcast local notices concerning lost pets, club announcements, or meetings.

A new federal agency, the Office of Censorship, was charged with implementing these measures. Byron Price, a veteran newsman who had most recently been executive editor of the Associated Press, was appointed director. Upon assuming his new post, Price vowed to resign before he allowed press freedoms to be curtailed, as they had been during the First World War, on such vague or capricious grounds as "public interest" or "national morale." The attorney general retained certain enforcement powers under the Espionage Act of 1917—which remained on the books then, as it does today—but Price's office would have nothing to do with penalizing or prosecuting newspapers. Instead, the agency hired career journalists to act as "missionaries"—that was the term chosen by Price—to travel around the country and persuade editors and broadcasters to abide by the code. The system of voluntary self-censorship, said Price, "put newspapers and other publications on their honor. It enlisted every writer and every editor in the army of the republic."[15]

THE FULL DIMENSIONS OF THE CATASTROPHE at Pearl Harbor were not yet known by the public, but the reports and rumors left no doubt that the Japanese had struck a shattering blow against the Pacific stronghold. Speaking to the press a week after the attack, Secretary of the Navy Frank Knox admitted that several battleships had been destroyed, and others seriously damaged; he also revealed that almost 3,000 sailors and other servicemen had been killed. Investigations were underway, both in Congress and in the armed services. Knox stated that "the land and sea forces were not on the alert," implying that the local commanders had been derelict.[16] Admiral Husband E. Kimmel and General Walter C. Short, the top commanders in Hawaii, were summarily relieved of their commands. They would be reduced in rank, forced to retire, and run through a gauntlet of nine largely redundant investigations that deflected blame away from Washington.

The news from the rest of the Pacific, meanwhile, was confusing and ominous. Hours after hitting Pearl Harbor, the Japanese had launched an aerial *Blitzkrieg* across a 3,000-mile front, striking American and British targets in Micronesia, the Philippines, Malaya, Burma, and Hong Kong. On the third day of the war, torpedo planes sank the British battleships *Prince of Wales* and *Repulse* off the coast of Malaya. Japanese invasion forces had landed at multiple beachheads on the island of Luzon and other islands in the Philippine archipelago. The American commander in the Philippines,

General Douglas MacArthur, was leading his army in a desperate but gallant fight against superior enemy forces—or at any rate, that was the impression given by the sketchy and somewhat baffling early reports from the far side of the earth.

Although the truth would not come out until years later, MacArthur's conduct on the first day of the war had been at least as culpable as that of Kimmel or Short. Receiving nine hours' warning of the attack on Pearl Harbor, MacArthur had remained cocooned at his headquarters and refused to communicate with his air commanders, despite their repeated efforts to reach him. As a result, his main force of B-17 bombers and P-40 fighters was paralyzed for lack of orders, and more than half of the aircraft were destroyed on the ground by the first Japanese air raid on Philippine territory. Leaders in Washington were dismayed by this "second Pearl Harbor," hours after the first, but no one outside a privileged circle even knew that it had happened. Press reports on December 7 only stated that Japanese airplanes had been spotted in Philippine airspace. Three days later, the White House announced that the Japanese had attacked Clark Field, an air base north of Manila, but offered no details: "General Douglas MacArthur thus far has been unable to report details of the engagement."[17]

The different standards of accountability imposed in Hawaii and the Philippines have bothered historians ever since. The latter events were never formally investigated, and MacArthur never answered for errors and derelictions that seemed at least as blameworthy and certainly more avoidable than those in Hawaii. The discrepancy can only be explained as a peculiar result of the way the opening sequences of the Pacific War were reported in the United States. If MacArthur was to be relieved of command, the action needed to be taken immediately, or not at all—and it was not taken immediately. And by the second week of the war, the mood of the American people had changed. Now they seemed eager for a redemptive narrative that would expunge the trauma and shame of Pearl Harbor. MacArthur's beleaguered army, half a world away, with little hope of support or reinforcement, was making a stirring fight against long odds. The man at the head of that army seemed a brave and noble figure, an American paladin straight out of central casting. His daily war communiqués, composed in a style ranging from the lurid to the vainglorious, kept the American people in thrall. "Sartorially he was dashing, physically he was handsome, orally he was spectacular," a press commentator later wrote of

MacArthur. "For all his sixty-two years, he was straight as a ramrod, clear-eyed, rosy-cheeked and only partly bald. His features were even, his expression imperious, and the rake of his braid-encrusted hat added a touch of romance to his elegant facade."[18]

Very suddenly, in those early days of the war, Douglas MacArthur rocketed to superstardom in the American media, attaining a degree of fame, celebrity, and popularity unmatched by any other military commander. His rocket would soar over the Pacific, in a majestic, high-flying trajectory, until Harry Truman shot it down ten years later.

The Philippines were doomed from the outset, and probably would have been even if the Japanese had not hit Pearl Harbor. The initial Japanese assaults on the islands, and many other Allied territories throughout the western Pacific, were executed with great skill and overwhelming air superiority. But MacArthur was willing to fight, and also to make a good show of fighting, and Americans revered him for it. Between December 8, 1941, and March 11, 1942, MacArthur's headquarters issued 142 press communiqués. One hundred nine mentioned only one person by name: MacArthur. Rarely were individual units singled out for praise or credit; the communiqués typically referred only to "MacArthur's army," or "MacArthur's men."[19] Often it was implied that he was personally leading his forces in the field, when he was actually at his headquarters in Manila.

The press-savvy general knew the value of a short, headline-ready remark. "We shall do our best," he told newsmen, on the fifth day of the war.[20] When someone suggested removing the American flag from the roof of his Manila headquarters, so that it would not attract the attention of Japanese bombers, MacArthur replied, "Keep the flag flying."[21] These soundbites were quoted in his communiqués, and appeared the next day as headlines across the United States. He knew just how to pose for photographs, with an erect posture and a certain set of the head, like a white marble statue on a plinth. On the cover of *Time* magazine on December 29, 1941, MacArthur stood proud and resolute, gazing into the distance. Newsreel producers turned up old footage of MacArthur inspecting troops, addressing the cadets at West Point, or being kissed on both cheeks by a French general. Congress voted to rename a conduit road in the District of Columbia, west of Georgetown, as "MacArthur Boulevard." The Red Cross launched a national fund-raising drive during "MacArthur Week." Universities granted him honorary degrees in absentia. A dancing convention in

New York introduced a new dance called the "MacArthur Glide."[22] The Blackfeet Indians adopted MacArthur into their tribe, naming him Mo-Kahki-Peta, or "Chief Wise Eagle." New York publishing houses rushed to publish "instant" MacArthur biographies—actually, hagiographies—and although they were thinly researched and hastily written, they sold briskly: *MacArthur the Magnificent*; *General Douglas MacArthur: Exciting Life Story*; and *General Douglas MacArthur: Fighter For Freedom*.

On the general's sixty-second birthday on January 26, 1942, congressmen and senators on Capitol Hill delivered full-throated birthday panegyrics, each speaker apparently trying to top the sentiments offered by the last.[23] The next day the *Philadelphia Record* told its readers: "He is one of the greatest fighting generals of this war or any other war. This is the kind of history which your children will tell your grandchildren."[24] On February 12, 1942, in a Lincoln's Birthday speech in Boston, Wendell Willkie, the defeated Republican presidential candidate in 1940, urged that MacArthur be recalled to Washington and placed in charge of directing the global war. "Bring home General MacArthur," Willkie thundered. "Place him at the very top. Keep bureaucratic and political hands off him. . . . Put him in supreme command of our armed forces under the president. Then the people of the United States will have reason to hope that skill, not bungling and confusion, directs their efforts."[25]

For FDR and his military chiefs, the nation's breathless absorption in the story unfolding in the Philippines begged the ominous question: How was it going to end? Could MacArthur be reinforced, or even resupplied? General George C. Marshall asked his new deputy, the recently promoted Brigadier General Dwight D. Eisenhower, to investigate the problem from every angle and propose a solution. Eisenhower had served under MacArthur in the Philippines from 1935 to 1939, so he knew as much about conditions in the country as any officer in Washington. He noted that Marshall did not even hint at the "psychological effects" on the American people, but he thought the implication was impossible to miss: "Clearly he felt that anyone stupid enough to overlook this consideration had no business wearing the star of a brigadier general."[26]

In a nutshell, the dilemma was that the Philippines could not be saved, but they could not be abandoned outright. They could not be saved because the Allies could not yet muster even a fraction of the shipping, naval strength, and air power needed to fight across the Pacific. A rescue mission would only increase the scale of the defeat; any ship attempting to run the Japanese blockade to reach the Bataan Peninsula, where MacArthur's army was besieged, would be sunk or captured. No matter how the figures were calculated, Bataan would run out of provisions, ammunition, and other needed supplies long before the Allies could mobilize forces on a scale needed to return to the Philippines. On the other hand, Eisenhower told Marshall, the besieged army could not be "cold-bloodedly" abandoned to the enemy. Even if hard military logic dictated cutting losses, the United States was a great nation with a reputation to uphold. It must try to get at least some supplies into Bataan by submarine, blockade runners, and airplanes. Even if it amounted to little more than "driblet assistance," and even if it prolonged only by a few weeks the inevitable surrender, "we must do everything for them that is humanly possible."[27] Marshall agreed, and authorized Eisenhower to spend virtually any amount of funds to make the token shipments.

MacArthur had given no indication that he wanted to abandon his army. He kept a loaded derringer pistol with him and vowed that he would not be taken alive. But his young wife and four-year-old son were also with him in the Malinta Tunnel on Corregidor Island, off Bataan. To leave the general and his family to their fate would invite a public backlash against the Roosevelt administration. General "Pa" Watson, the influential aide to FDR, had been urging the president to order MacArthur out of the Philippines, arguing that he was worth "five Army Corps." The proposal was to smuggle the general to Australia, and to place him in command of the eventual counteroffensive.

Mulling it over in his diary on February 23, Eisenhower recorded prophetic views about MacArthur: "He is doing a good job where he is, but I'm doubtful that he'll do so well in more complicated situations. Bataan is made to order for him. It's in the public eye; it has made him a public hero; it has all the essentials of drama; and he is the acknowledged king on the spot. If brought out, public opinion will force him into a position where his love of the limelight may ruin him."[28] When FDR finally decided to order MacArthur out of the Philippines, and to appoint him supreme commander of Allied forces in the Southwest Pacific, Eisenhower lamented: "I cannot help believing that we are disturbed by editorials and reacting to 'public opinion' rather than to military logic." Eisenhower would play no role in the Pacific War—he would be busy elsewhere—but in early 1942 he foresaw all of the various headaches that MacArthur would cause for leaders in Washington. MacArthur would use his political influence and his unparalleled access to the American media to demand that more troops, ships, and airplanes be sent to his command. He would reject the "Europe-first" principle as a basis for global strategy. He would meddle in Australian politics. He would insist on running the naval war in the Pacific. He would claim the right to liberate all of the Philippines before any final offensive against Japan. Leaders in Washington would have to reckon with MacArthur's singular influence at every stage of the coming war, Eisenhower predicted, for "the public has built itself a hero out of its own imagination."[29]

ERNEST J. KING, THE HATCHET-FACED SEAMAN who led the U.S. Navy, was determined to have nothing to do with the press. When President Roosevelt had offered to make him commander in chief of the U.S. fleet ("COMINCH") a week after the attack on Pearl Harbor, King had taken the job on the condition that he would not be required to appear at press conferences. He said that his concern was to protect wartime secrets, and his staff batted away interview requests by explaining that King did not want to give "aid and comfort to the enemy."[30] But Washington journalists rightly suspected that Admiral King's hostility ran deeper—that he regarded them as gatecrashers from a contemptible civilian demimonde of hacks and gossips. According to one, King seemed to rank them "somewhat above bubonic plague as something to be avoided at all costs."[31]

This instinct was widely shared among the navy brass. Naval officers tended to regard reporters as pests—dangerous pests, who might spill the navy's secrets. And they were wary of newspapers' tendency to build stories around individuals, particularly those with colorful or forceful personalities. Personal publicity of the kind lavished on Douglas MacArthur, they believed, was incompatible with the navy's team-before-player ethos.

King and his contemporaries had begun their naval careers at the turn of the twentieth century, in the period after the Spanish-American War. In those years, a bitter public quarrel had broken out between William T. Sampson and Winfield Scott Schley, two senior officers who had commanded naval squadrons at the Battle of Santiago de Cuba on July 3, 1898. Each man claimed credit for winning the battle, and each belittled the role of the other. The two officers and their partisans vied for public acclaim and traded accusations and insults in print. A court of inquiry, convened in September 1901, was given headline coverage in the press, especially in the newspapers of William Randolph Hearst; but the court issued a divided ruling, which only inflamed the spectacle. President Theodore Roosevelt attempted to suppress all public discussion of the dispute, fearing that it had tarnished the navy's victory over Spain, but the contretemps continued to echo in the newspapers for years afterward, and was even the subject of one of the earliest American silent films: *The Sampson-Schley Controversy* (1901).

To the midshipmen who passed through the Naval Academy in those years, the unbecoming public spectacle left a lasting impression. The navy's triumphs in the late war had lifted the United States to the status of a global military power. The service should have been basking in acclamation, planning for the future, and consolidating its standing in Washington. Instead, Sampson and Schley and their respective followers, seeming to care only for their own selfish interests, had hung the navy's dirty laundry out on a public clothesline. That generation of young officers, which included King (Class of 1901), William Leahy (1897), William Halsey (1904), Chester Nimitz (1905), and Raymond Spruance (1906), swore to themselves and each other that they would never let it happen again. By the 1940s, most Americans had forgotten the Sampson-Schley affair, if they had ever heard of it. But the admirals of the Second World War remembered it well. They took pride in a culture of teamwork, cool professionalism, and personal modesty, and tended to shun newspapermen altogether if they could get away with it.

But the crucible of war would soon expose the risks and limits of the navy's aversion to publicity. Its failure to provide adequate and timely information about the naval war left a vacuum in the public's understanding of the subject—and inevitably, as if by a law of physics, wild rumors and speculation rushed into that vacuum. No one questioned the need to protect military secrets, but in the early stages of the war, when Japanese forces rampaged across Southeast Asia and the Pacific, influential voices in Washington charged that the navy was abusing its control over war reporting to conceal its fiascos. Worse, leading Republicans accused the navy of carrying water for FDR and the Democrats by managing the news flow with an eye toward the 1942 midterm congressional elections. That was a false charge, but a damaging one, and Admiral King eventually understood that

he would have to refute it, or stand accused of trespassing into the demilita-
rized zone between war-fighting and politics.

Equally pressing was the question of the navy's status in the postwar
defense establishment. After the attack on Pearl Harbor, congressional
leaders of both parties had vowed to streamline the military's organizational
chart. The War and Navy Departments, which had been independent and
coequal since the administration of John Adams, were to be merged into
a unitary department of defense under a single civilian cabinet officer.
Although the specific arrangements remained to be negotiated, the army,
navy, marines, and air forces would be fused into an integrated command
structure. FDR persuaded Congress to postpone those reforms until the war
was won—but anyone could foresee that service unification was destined
to be a political brawl of epic proportions, in which the navy had much
to lose in the way of command autonomy and clout. Secretary Knox and
his undersecretary, James Forrestal, who each had backgrounds in journalism, warned King and the admirals that the struggle had in a sense already
begun, and that the navy had better "tell its story" to the American people.
Forrestal noted that the army was already making its case to congressional
leaders through back channels, and "it is my judgment that as of today the
Navy has lost its case and that, either in Congress or in a public poll, the
Army's point of view would prevail."[32] In August 1944, Forrestal told King:
"Publicity is as much a part of war today as logistics or training and we must
so recognize it."[33]

In the weeks after Pearl Harbor, hundreds of working journalists
applied to the War and Navy Departments to be accredited as war correspondents, the forebears of today's "embedded journalists." According to
the army's *Basic Field Manual for Correspondents*, these frontline reporters
would be subject to military authority and would be required to "submit for
the purposes of censorship all statements, written material, and photography
intended for publication or release."[34] Although they would remain civilians, they were to wear plain khaki uniforms with brass shoulder insignias
identifying them as "Correspondent," "Photographer," or "Radio Commentator." In all, through the end of the war, about 1,600 war correspondents
were accredited by the armed forces.

Journalists shipping out as war correspondents were told to pack their bags and be ready to leave the country with ten hours' notice. Like soldiers and sailors, they were forbidden to disclose sailing dates or destinations, even to their own editors or loved ones. They would travel with the troops, either by air or by sea. Although they had no rank, they were allowed officers' privileges, meaning that they messed with officers and shared the same berthing and living arrangements. As civilians, they were not supposed to salute nor to be saluted—but since they wore khaki uniforms, they frequently *were* saluted by officers and enlisted men. Strictly speaking, if they were to follow protocol, they ought to refrain from returning salutes. On the other hand, none wanted to give offense. No official solution to this dilemma was ever decreed. According to William J. Dunn, a CBS radio correspondent posted to Douglas MacArthur's headquarters in Australia, most of his colleagues adopted the custom of not saluting first, but returning salutes as "a matter of simple courtesy." Whenever coming face-to-face with high-ranking officers wearing "a bevy of stars," however, they found themselves raising their hands to their foreheads quickly and instinctively, protocol be damned.[35]

War correspondents and press liaison officers were natural enemies. In most overseas military headquarters, their working relationship was inevitably fraught with misunderstandings and ill feelings. At the root of the problem was a mismatch between their respective professional cultures and attitudes. Military men of all ranks were accustomed to operating in a chain of command. If an order seemed capricious or illogical, it was not the soldier's first instinct to demand an explanation or justification. The slang acronym SNAFU ("Situation normal, all fouled up"), which gained wide currency during the Second World War, summed up the serviceman's resigned acceptance of regulations and procedures that appeared to defy reason. That stoic attitude did not come naturally to the civilian journalist, who had always felt free to argue with his editor if he thought he was right.

In some overseas headquarters, especially during the first year of the war, press sections practiced a system of "blind censorship." Censors reviewed each story with a red pencil, crossing out whatever sentences or paragraphs they deemed unsuitable, and then cabled the censored version directly back to the United States. The author was not notified of the edits and redactions, nor given any explanation for them, nor allowed to rewrite and resubmit. In some cases, a story vanished into the censor's "kill file," and the reporter who had written it received no word of the decision. Only later would he learn whether his story had "passed" and how much of it had eluded the red pencil. It was galling to see his hard work disappear into such a vortex. Fierce arguments inevitably ensued. The press officer, conscious of his authority and his responsibility to protect secrets, was not inclined to back down. When five war correspondents at a headquarters in New Zealand approached their press censor with a list of complaints, he told them, "I'm not afraid of you any more than I would be of five Japs."[36] Another press office distributed a mimeographed form letter in response to protests:

MY FRIEND:

It is with tears in my eyes and a lump in my throat that I listen to your sad tale of woe. Allow me to offer my deepest and sincerest condolence. However, I do not have the Chaplain's duty and I am short of towels. Please see the Captain of the Head for material for drying your eyes.

PEACE ON YOU, MY FRIEND,
Chief Censor[37]

But it was the press officer's bad luck to be pitted against adversaries who were not cowed by authority, and whose ranks included some of the most lethal polemicists and name-callers in the world. The *New Yorker* correspondent A. J. Liebling profiled the press officers he encountered at General Eisenhower's headquarters in London. As civilians they had been corporate publicity agents or "Chicago rewrite men," Liebling observed—but then the war had transformed them into army majors and colonels who had never been to boot camp or laid eyes on a battlefield. They were feckless "dress extras," immaculately turned out in finely tailored, starched uniforms, who spoke of the army with a practiced "unctuousness." Before the war they had not been respected as journalists; now they were not respected as army officers. Possessing a certain flair for legerdemain and spin, they had "adapted themselves to this squalid milieu and flourished in it." In May 1945, just after V-E Day, when the loss of his press credentials would no longer impose a career penalty, Liebling opened fire in the pages of his magazine. He denounced the use of censorship for "political, personal, or merely capricious reasons" and announced that the time had come to expose "the prodigious amount of pure poodle-faking that has gone on under the name of Army Public Relations."[38]

In Hawaii, where Admiral Chester Nimitz was commander in chief of the Pacific Fleet (CINCPAC), correspondents soon learned to their dismay that the stolid white-haired Texan was determined to give them nothing interesting or quotable. Newspapermen seemed to think that the man sent to avenge the attack on Pearl Harbor ought to look and talk like a salt-stained swashbuckler out of a boy's adventure novel. But Nimitz, as one of them observed, could have passed for a "retired banker."[39] According to *Time* magazine correspondent Bob Sherrod, the CINCPAC was "the despair of his public relations men; it simply was not in him to make sweeping statements or to give out colorful interviews."[40]

Nimitz's first formal press conference, which he gave only after being pressured to do so by Navy Secretary Frank Knox, was held on January 29, 1942, a month after he took command in Pearl Harbor. The war correspondents were ushered into his office at his headquarters, which was housed for the moment at the submarine base in the Navy Yard. They found Nimitz seated behind a standard-issue wooden desk, dressed in plain khaki with no necktie. He did not rise to greet them. The walls were bare but for an analog clock, a calendar, and a map of the Pacific. The journalists sat on folding chairs that had been set up for the occasion. Nimitz read a prepared statement setting out the command arrangements that had been established between the army and navy. All of that information had already been released in Washington, so it was not news. Then he took questions. Yes, he did expect to hold and defend the Hawaiian Islands. No, he did not care to elaborate. *New York Times* correspondent Foster Hailey asked for "some reassuring word for the people back home as to the operations of the Navy since December 7." One imagines the collective sense of letdown as the reply was given: "Admiral Nimitz said that any statement as to the operations of fleet units must come from Washington as part of the grand strategy of the war."[41]

That month, again under pressure from Knox, Nimitz brought on a full-time public relations officer. This was Waldo Drake, a commander in the naval reserve, who had previously been the shipping news correspondent for the *Los Angeles Times*. The practice of commissioning civilian reporters as press officers was based on the premise (as one naval officer put it) that "one hippopotamus can talk to another hippopotamus."[42] Drake made a good first impression with the war correspondents, pledging that the door to his office at Pacific Fleet headquarters would always be open to them. But his job was largely thankless, because his boss continued to regard working with the press as a problem to be managed rather than an opportunity to communicate with the public. Drake's authority did not extend beyond Pacific Fleet headquarters, but there were many other military commands on Oahu—including those of the army, the Army Air Forces (USAAF), and the Fourteenth Naval District—and the various headquarters had their own censorship practices and public relations strategies.[43]

Day after day, the correspondents knocked on Drake's door to air their complaints. News given out by Pacific Fleet headquarters was already generally known, they said. The sluggish pace of Drake's censorship procedures meant that their stories were already stale when they arrived on the mainland. Too few of them had been permitted to go to sea with the fleet. When Wake Island was taken by the Japanese, censors removed the name "Wake" and identified it only as "an island." A correspondent asked, "Is there anybody in the navy who thinks that the Japs are under the impression that they have taken some other island?"[44] As the result of an administrative snafu, correspondents were invited to a press briefing with Admiral Robert English, commander of the Pacific Submarine Force. But Nimitz had decreed a complete news blackout of the submarines, so Drake was obliged to rush into the room and put an end to it. He collected all of the reporters' notepads before allowing them to leave.[45] In an incident that anticipated Joseph Heller's satirical novel *Catch-22*, a news story was passed by both army and navy censors, but the navy censor altered one of the paragraphs. Finding that it did not like the navy's version, the army suspended the credentials of the correspondent who had written it, even though the fellow had not seen the amended version until it appeared in print.

As the number of Pearl Harbor correspondents swelled to more than a hundred, and the chorus of criticism grew louder and more insistent, Drake's "open door" policy was gradually curtailed, becoming a "door sometimes open" policy, and then a "door usually shut" policy. One of Drake's more merciless critics was Bob Casey of the Chicago *Daily News*, who remarked: "The local publicity office should be handled by somebody of decent rank and considerable tact and experience, but most of all by somebody who can look at a clock and tell what time it is."[46]

In the early months of the war, especially, Nimitz could spare little time to think about public relations. He had much bigger problems on his hands. As commander in chief of the Pacific Ocean Areas (CINCPOA), he held authority over all branches of the armed forces within his immense theater. Rivalries between the army, navy, and marines were a constant irritant, and it took all of Nimitz's considerable diplomatic tact and leadership skills to soothe those chronic frictions. In this respect the war correspondents did him no favors, because it was in their nature to investigate controversy. They flitted and fluttered around it, like moths around a porch light. Mesmerized by the various internecine rivalries on Oahu, they did a heroic amount of firsthand reporting. They goaded the marines to complain about the navy, the army to belittle the marines, and the naval aviators to share their feelings about the surface warship officers. They lay in wait at the officers' clubs, where liquor loosened men's tongues, and asked questions shrewdly calculated to elicit frank responses. The censors did not let them publish a word on the subject, but their insights were soon transmitted back to the mainland by word of mouth, where they circulated freely in the newsrooms and the halls of power in Washington. Newspaper stories originating in the United States were not subject to redline censorship. Although bound by the voluntary code to refrain from publishing certain cold hard facts, the papers were free to publish opinions, and much of the press coverage and editorial commentary about the war was informed by the illicit pipeline of information flowing back from the war zones through the correspondents and their remorseless chatter.

By the spring of 1942, in Washington and elsewhere, the post–Pearl Harbor mood of goodwill between the press and military was turning sour. Editorial pages charged that the army and navy were erring too much on the side of withholding information. Many of the officers who made day-to-day censorship decisions were relatively junior, both in age and rank, and anxious not to bring the wrath of superiors down on their heads. A twenty-five-year-old lieutenant would suffer no consequences for killing a story on dubious pretenses—but God help him if he passed a story, and a colonel or general subsequently read it and judged that it had harmed the cause. "The army and the navy felt they owned the news and behaved as if they owned it from the beginning of the war until the end," said David Brinkley, then a cub reporter for a South Carolina paper. "They used it skillfully, as the civilian agencies of government had always used it throughout history—to try to conceal their failures and blunders and to give out fulsome detail on their successes."[47]

In reply to this rising chorus of criticism, FDR created a new agency to coordinate the release of war information across the entire federal government. An executive order of June 13, 1942, established the Office of War Information (OWI), "in recognition of the right of the American people and of all other peoples opposing the Axis aggressors to be truthfully informed."[48] He tapped a veteran newspaperman and radio broadcaster, Elmer Davis, to run it. Four existing federal agencies were merged into the OWI, and Davis said he felt like "a man who married a four-time widow and was trying to raise her children all by her previous husbands."[49] Knowing that he would encounter resistance from the War and Navy Departments, Davis asked that the OWI's charter include authority to review all military operational reports from the war theaters, and to make independent determinations of what news could be released. "But the problem," wrote Brinkley, "was that other agencies, particularly the army and navy, did not read Roosevelt's announcement or, having read it, resolved to ignore it, and did."[50]

Neither the army nor the navy much liked the idea of answering to a new civilian propaganda agency. Asked whether the OWI would be directing the War Department's press functions, Secretary Henry Stimson responded with a question of his own: "Is Mr. Davis an educated military officer?"[51] Navy Secretary Frank Knox was himself a newsman—he had been part-owner and proprietor of the Chicago *Daily News*—but Davis later said that while Knox was always polite, "still all in all I got the polite brush-off."[52] At a daily morning conference in the OWI offices, army and navy officers presented a summary of the reports that had come in from the war theaters during the previous twenty-four hours. Davis and his colleagues then compared those reports to the official communiqués. If they judged that information had been improperly withheld, they pressured the military departments to release it. In extreme cases, as one of Davis's subordinates put it, the OWI claimed the authority "to direct that this information be inserted into a communiqué unless the military could convince us that it had been omitted because of a valid reason of security."[53]

Davis could make little headway with Admiral King. He soon concluded that in the realm of public relations, the navy was the "problem child" among the military services. In a remark that circulated widely in Washington, Davis observed that King's idea of a press policy was to tell the public nothing until the end of the war, and then to issue a two-word communiqué: "We won." King treated Davis cordially, probably because he had been instructed to do so by the president, but remained only minimally cooperative throughout the summer of 1942. At best, during this period, King regarded publicity and press affairs as second- or third-tier problems that could be delegated down the ranks and then ignored.

His attitude was confirmed and hardened by a potentially devastating leak that appeared in print the same week the OWI was created. On June 7, a day after the Battle of Midway, the *Chicago Tribune* ran a front-page story under the headline: "Navy Had Word of Jap Plan to Strike at Sea." The *Tribune* reported that the navy had learned critical details of the Midway operation "several days before the battle began."[54] The story was cagey about its sources, but a discerning reader could deduce that the Americans had broken Japanese radio codes. That was true, but it was also one of the most closely guarded secrets of the war, and disclosing it in a major American newspaper threatened to alert the enemy to the breach. King was livid and ordered an investigation that quickly concluded that the culprit was Stanley Johnston, a *Tribune* war correspondent who had been aboard the aircraft carrier *Lexington* when she had gone down on May 8 at the Battle of the Coral Sea. Picked up by an escorting destroyer, Johnston had berthed with a group of *Lexington* officers while they returned to the American mainland aboard a transport, the *Barnett*. While underway on the *Barnett*, Johnston saw a top-secret dispatch from Admiral Nimitz dated May 31, 1942, concerning details of the pending Midway operation. Commander Morton Seligman, the *Lexington*'s executive officer, was blamed for the leak.*

The question of whether to bring treason and espionage charges against the *Chicago Tribune* dragged on until August, when it was feared that the ongoing imbroglio only increased the risk that the Japanese would notice it. The government convened a federal grand jury in Chicago, but the navy would not provide explicit testimony about its supersecret cryptanalysis programs, and the jury refused to return an indictment against the *Tribune*. The navy eventually concluded that the Japanese had not noticed the story, or had not recognized its significance—and in postwar interrogations, no evidence emerged to contradict that impression.[55]

---

* COMINCH to CINCPAC, June 8, 1942, Message 2050, CINCPAC Gray Book, book 1, p. 559. According to Floyd Beaver, a signalman on Admiral Fitch's flag allowance, Johnston and Seligman were "buddy-buddy," roaming about the ship like "Siamese twins." Author's interview with Floyd Beaver, January 17, 2014. Johnston's book, *Queen of the Flat-Tops*, confirms the impression.

Pressure was building on Admiral King and the navy to be more forth-coming with bad news. On Capitol Hill, according to a Washington reporter, it was taken for granted that "the Navy is throwing a lot of curves in its communiqués. . . . That is to say, they are holding back a number of serious losses. The idea, it seems, is that Admiral King believes the people can't take it."[56] On several occasions in 1942, American ships had been sunk in com-bat, and the public had not been told until weeks or even months after the fact. In each case there were plausible reasons for withholding the news—either because the Japanese did not know the ships had sunk, or because time was needed to notify next of kin—but critics suspected that the news flow was being managed to minimize embarrassment and protect King.

After the Battle of the Coral Sea in May 1942, the first American news-paper stories had reported a smashing victory. The reports exaggerated Jap-anese losses—which in truth included only one small "baby flattop," the *Shoho*—but said nothing of the destruction of the *Lexington*, one of only four U.S. aircraft carriers in the Pacific at that time. King had personally ordered that her loss be concealed from the public, on the grounds that no Japanese airplanes had been in the vicinity when she went down, and therefore the enemy might not know she was gone. News of the sinking of the *Lexington* was held back for more than a month, and then released on June 12, when Americans were celebrating victory at the Battle of Midway. "Holding up this information gave to our Navy security," the communiqué claimed, somewhat defensively, "which was a cornerstone in building for the Midway victory."[57]

Two months later, on the night of August 8—a day after the 1st Marine Division landed on Guadalcanal—four Allied cruisers went down at the Battle of Savo Island. King ordered that news of the awful defeat be strictly suppressed. His reasoning was sensible: the action had occurred at night, and the Japanese fleet had withdrawn immediately toward its base at Rabaul, so one could assume that the enemy did not know what losses they had inflicted. A navy communiqué released a week later emphasized American victories in ground and air combat. But there would be no further details on Allied naval losses "because of the obvious value of such information to the enemy."[58]

But the full dimensions of the disaster at Savo Island could not be kept from trickling back to the mainland through the rumor mill, and by early October—two months after the fact—it was an open secret throughout official Washington. Cynics assumed that King was mainly interested in protecting himself. The Guadalcanal operation had been his brainchild, and he had launched it over the objections of the commanders assigned to carry it out. According to *New York Times* correspondent Hanson Baldwin, King was "on the hot seat because he had been pressing for Guadalcanal right along. He had been the one who said go in, even on a shoestring, and those repercussions, those losses, this naval ineptitude, would not sit well with the American people and wouldn't increase his fame or fortune."[59]

Elmer Davis urged King to tell the public about the losses at Savo Island, and also the sinking of the carrier *Wasp* by submarine attack in September. After a tête-à-tête in King's office in early October, Davis told his wife that the meeting was "acrimonious yet somehow remained friendly."[60] The admiral seemed to realize that his position had become delicate. A media blackout immediately after the sinkings had been defensible, but there was little reason to keep the news out of the papers for a full two months, especially when hundreds of survivors had already returned to the States. In the absence of credible reports, dark rumors were flourishing. Some whispered that a large portion of the Pacific Fleet had been wiped out in the Solomons, and that the Japanese were on the verge of overrunning Guadalcanal. It was a political season—the 1942 midterm congressional elections would take place on November 3—and some suspected that Admiral King and the navy were covering up losses in order to protect FDR's allies in Congress. Under mounting pressure, King conceded that it was time to come clean about the Savo Island debacle, and the navy released a communiqué on October 12: "Certain initial phases of the Solomon Islands campaign, not announced previously for military reasons, can now be reported."[61] The sad story of the four sunken cruisers was told in unsparing detail.

The very next day brought a happy surprise. Another nighttime sea action had been fought in the same waters as the earlier battle, and this one—the Battle of Cape Esperance—had been a smashing American victory. The navy released another communiqué reporting results in full.[62] The timing was genuinely coincidental, but newsmen and Republican congressmen angrily charged that the navy, as in the case of the *Lexington* announcement after Midway, had held back bad news (Savo Island) until it could be paired with good news (Cape Esperance). The episode coincided with the most desperate stage of the Guadalcanal campaign, when many doubted the navy and marines' ability to hold the island, and mismanagement of war news had only exacerbated the tension in Washington. Congressman Melvin Maas, who had recently visited the South Pacific, rose on the floor of the House to declare that the Japanese were winning the war in the Solomons, and charged that the government was trying to cover it up. The press now treated the navy's communiqués with skepticism and derision, and guessed at the magnitude of its yet-undisclosed losses.

King could be pigheaded, but he was experienced enough in the ways of Washington to know that perception and reality often amounted to the same thing. He had many enemies who would like to be rid of him—in the army and navy, in the press, and in Congress—and they had apparently launched a whispering campaign against him. National unity around the war effort was a matter of life and death. He could not afford to become a lightning rod for politically charged criticism; if he did, he would have to go. The time had come for a tactical retreat. He took Davis's advice to clear the accumulated backlog of unannounced sinkings.

On October 26, the navy announced that the *Wasp* had been lost more than five weeks earlier by submarine attack east of Guadalcanal.[63] Later the same day, it reported the first results of the carrier clash known as the Battle of the Santa Cruz Islands, admitting that a U.S. destroyer had been sunk and "one of our aircraft carriers was severely damaged."[64] That was true: the unnamed carrier was the *Hornet*. But the next day, when a subsequent cable reported that the *Hornet* had burned out of control and had had to be scuttled, King hesitated to release the news. The Japanese might not yet know that she was gone, and they might find that information useful. But Elmer Davis warned that if the news were held until after Election Day, Republicans would raise a howl. Davis insisted on releasing it immediately, and felt strongly enough to take his case directly to Secretary Knox and even the president. On the other hand, Admiral Nimitz was equally adamant that the news must be kept from the Japanese, and made his case in a firmly worded cable from Hawaii.

Backed into this corner, with the OWI director threatening to resign over the issue, King decided he had no choice. On October 31, three days before the midterm election, a navy communiqué admitted that the *Hornet* "subsequently sank."[65] The next day Nimitz protested to King that the disclosure was "harmful to us in a very critical situation."[66]

One of King's most trusted confidantes was his personal lawyer and friend Cornelius ("Nelie") Bull, who always addressed the admiral as "Skipper." Earlier in his career, Bull had been a newspaper reporter, and he still had many friends in the Washington press corps. Observing the growing controversy, Bull grew concerned that King's head might be on the block, and he resolved to do something about it. One Friday evening that October, he ran into Glen Perry, assistant bureau chief of the New York *Sun*, at the crowded bar of the Press Club on Fourteenth Street. With their bellies pressed against the bar, the two men sipped Tom Collinses and cooked up a scheme. They would handpick a dozen experienced journalists who worked for major newspapers and wire associations, all with reputations for "absolute integrity and reliability."[67] They would invite them to meet King in a private, nonofficial setting, preferably on a weekend. The newsmen would agree to strict ground rules in advance, tantamount to a latter-day "deep background" briefing—they would agree not to print any of the information given by King, but only to use it to enhance their understanding of the navy's public communiqués. They were not to quote the admiral, either by name or as an unnamed source; and they would not disclose to anyone outside their newsrooms that he had talked to them. Bull would host the gathering at his own home, a place where King would feel comfortable and at ease. Beer and canapes would be served. The reporters would take no notes in the admiral's presence. Bull and his wife would endeavor to provide a relaxed and familiar social setting, an environment that would remind no one (especially King) of an official press briefing.

When Bull proposed the idea to King, the admiral surprised his lawyer by agreeing on the spot. He was aware that his opposite number in the army, General Marshall, had provided off-the-record briefings in his office at the War Department, and that no leaks had occurred as a result. Evidently it was true (as Bull, Knox, Davis, and others had told him) that reputable journalists could be trusted to abide by ground rules. By meeting at the Bull residence, King could pretend that the event was a social occasion, a convenient fiction that allowed him to circumvent the navy's Office of Public Relations, which fell under Secretary Knox's supervision.

King's black sedan pulled up in front of Nelie Bull's house on Princess Street, in Alexandria, Virginia, at eight o'clock on the evening of Sunday, November 1. It was a small house dating back to the Revolutionary War, directly across the street from an old whitewashed nineteenth-century jailhouse that had been a notorious prison for Confederate POWs. Leaving his driver and marine guard behind, King rang the doorbell. The reporters had already arrived and were seated in the living room. A "tall, spare figure in regulation Navy blues" entered and gave Bull his greatcoat and uniform hat. Glen Perry described the scene in a memorandum to his editor:

> He entered the room quietly, and what impressed me right away was that he was alone! No fussing aide or overattentive public relations type to steer him past such reefs as might come up. It was just Ernest J. King, Admiral, USN, perhaps a little tense as one might be who has committed his fate to dubious hands. He was, nonetheless, completely poised, projecting an air of authority, of command, without having to make the slightest effort. Great men may enjoy the ruffles and flourishes, but they do not need them to win instant respect.
>
> Nelie walked the Admiral around the room, presenting each correspondent in turn. He shook hands with each, a quick, firm pressure, repeating the name and accompanying the words with a keen eye-to-eye look. The eyes were not at all unfriendly, but it was no great trick to imagine that under less favorable circumstances they might look as though forged from the same steel that protected his battleships.[68]

After the introductions, all were seated—King in an easy chair in the corner, the reporters arrayed in a rough circle around him. Beer was served from an ice-filled washtub. The men drank directly from bottles.

King began speaking off the cuff, and for the first hour or so the reporters did not interrupt him at all. He gave a complete chronological narrative of the global war, beginning with the problems he had faced in getting convoys across the Atlantic in 1941, and then the attack on Pearl Harbor, the early crises in the Pacific, the victory at Midway, and the vicissitudes of the fight for Guadalcanal.

The journalists hung on every word. Vast strategic and logistical complexities were suddenly made clear to them. King's masterful summary of the big problems of the war was a priceless education in itself—but when he moved to specifics he displayed an astonishing grasp of detail, including technical data. He drank a second beer, then a third; every fifteen minutes or so he lit a new cigarette. Most remarkable, or so it seemed to the newsmen, he spoke with complete candor about the mistakes the navy had made, and did not appear to hold anything back for the sake of security. "He told us what had happened, what was happening, and, often, what was likely to happen next," one recalled. "He reported the bad news as fully as the good news, and in many cases, explained what went wrong on the one hand, and what strategy, weapon, or combination of both, had brought success on the other. Throughout, he was completely at ease and always patient, welcoming the questions that frequently interrupted his narrative, and answering them frankly and easily."[69]

Many questions were asked about the situation in and around Guadalcanal, where it was known that the United States had suffered heavy air and naval losses. Could the Americans hold the island, or would a tactical withdrawal become necessary?

"We'll stick," said King. Explaining that the fighting in the Solomons had been savage and desperate, he admitted that the navy had suffered heavy losses. But there were good reasons to keep slugging it out. The Japanese were suffering too, and they could not easily replace their losses. Geography worked to the Allies' advantage, because the Japanese did not have airbases nearby. King explained how and why the navy chose to announce its losses, and warned that Japanese claims were often inflated by tenfold or more. He noted that Bill Halsey had recently been appointed South Pacific commander, and predicted a pitched sea battle in the coming weeks.*

"Doesn't this mean you're risking losing the fleet?" asked the columnist Walter Lippman.

King replied: "Isn't that what it is for?"[70]

The meeting broke up after three hours, and King departed after shaking every reporter's hand. Some stayed behind to talk among themselves, while others hurried away to commit all they could remember of the discussion to notes. They were stunned by their good fortune and felt as if they understood the Second World War better than they ever had before. One remarked that "King was—above all—a realist; that he did not indulge in wishful thinking or close his eyes to unpleasant problems in the hope that they would go away."[71] As for controversies surrounding the reporting of past sinkings, the journalists accepted King's explanations and concluded that he and the navy had been unfairly maligned.

To his surprise, King had enjoyed every minute of the evening. In a sense he had been talking to himself, telling himself the whole story of the

---

* The Naval Battle of Guadalcanal, which effectively decided the campaign in favor of the Allies, was fought on November 12–15, 1942.

war; and the experience had even helped to clarify some of his own thinking. Upon arriving at his office the next morning, he called Nelie Bull and
asked, "When do we have the next one?"[72]

King's secret Alexandria press briefings continued throughout the
remainder of the war, at an average rate of about one every six weeks. More
correspondents were invited, and their numbers eventually swelled to near
thirty. The journalists nicknamed themselves the "Arlington County commandos," and in good cloak-and-dagger fashion they gave King a codename:
"The Thin Man." When Secretary Knox learned of the briefings, he gave
his hearty approval even though the admiral had subverted his authority by
starting them in the first place. None of the secrets disclosed by King ever
appeared in print.

Admiral King soon realized that he had acquired a fund of goodwill in
the Washington press corps. This was an intangible asset, but it did not
take him long to discover its value. Congressman Maas had been sounding off in Congress and in the media about disunity in the high command,
and was pushing legislation to merge the armed services into one integrated
command structure. King believed that the existing Joint Chiefs of Staff
(JCS) organization was working well enough, and that a service unification
bill should be postponed until the end of the war. He discreetly reached out
to several of the Arlington County commandos. Within twenty-four hours,
major newspapers across the country ran news articles and editorials opposing Maas's views, but without mentioning King's name. Soon thereafter,
with the support of FDR and congressional leaders, service unification was
shelved pending the end of the war.

In 1941, King had arrived in Washington determined to have nothing
to do with the press. Before the first anniversary of Pearl Harbor, he was
manipulating it from behind the scenes like a veteran Washington wire-
puller. On first impression, it was a surprising reversal. But after further
reflection it was not surprising at all, because no one had ever mistaken
Ernest J. King for a slow learner.

AT GENERAL MACARTHUR'S SOUTHWEST PACIFIC AREA (SWPA) headquarters in Brisbane, Australia, the press section was run by Colonel LeGrande
"Pick" Diller, a career army officer who eventually rose (while serving in
that role) to the rank of brigadier general. Diller was a charter member of

the "Bataan gang," the insular circle of MacArthur loyalists who had served in the Philippines before the war and joined him in escaping Corregidor in March 1942. The SWPA press operation never lacked for funds or manpower: Diller eventually had more than one hundred officers and enlisted personnel in his chain of command, including a long roster of captains and majors, many of whom would be promoted to full-bird colonel by war's end. In contrast to the Pacific Fleet headquarters in Pearl Harbor, where Nimitz and his staff were dismayed by the relentless flood of journalists from the mainland, Diller adopted a "more the merrier" attitude and was always delighted to issue a new set of press credentials. The number of accredited reporters, photographers, and radio newscasters in Brisbane eventually surpassed four hundred.

Diller and his team treated the correspondents like valued clients. They replied promptly to all queries; they arranged access to state-of-the-art communications and broadcasting facilities; they looked after the journalists' "creature comforts" when they were touring forward combat areas. They provided regular access to MacArthur himself, albeit in carefully stage-managed press conferences. Diller composed the first drafts of SWPA's near-daily press communiqués, which were then reviewed and often rewritten by MacArthur. Correspondents soon learned that no actual or implied criticism would survive Diller's red pencil, while on the other hand, the thicker they laid on the praise and adulation, the more they would be rewarded with exclusive stories and other desirable privileges.

The newsmen gave Diller and his team high marks for alacrity. In pointed contrast to the situation in Hawaii, news stories submitted to MacArthur's press office were reviewed, censored, approved, and transmitted back to the United States within twenty-four hours, so that the news was still fresh when it appeared in the newspapers. Fresher news was more likely to be treated as front page news, whereas the comparatively stale bulletins from Nimitz's theater were more likely to go into the back pages. That, in turn, contributed to the American public's impression, quite common in 1942 and 1943, that MacArthur was doing most of the fighting in the Pacific.

More than any other American military leader of the war, MacArthur understood the importance of visual imagery. He paid diligent attention to the details of his wardrobe and accessories, which cynics called his "props"—his battered Philippine field marshal's "pushdown" cap, his well-worn leather flight jacket, his aviator sunglasses, and his corn-cob pipes, which tended to grow larger over time. During his first days in Australia, he had experimented with an ornate carved walking stick, but discarded it after someone remarked that it made him look older. He was sensitive about his expanding bald spot, and when it was necessary to be photographed without his hat, he took a private moment to comb his hair across the top of his head, leaving a perfectly straight part about two inches above his right ear—a deftly executed version of the coiffure known as a "combover." Photography, like press copy, was subject to Diller's censorship—and most published wartime photographs of MacArthur were taken at a low camera angle, making him appear taller than he was.

The Brisbane publicity machine often gave the misleading impression that MacArthur was personally leading his forces in battle. As a theater commander, it was not MacArthur's role to lead forces in the field, and his extraordinary valor in the First World War had left him with nothing to prove. Still, it was galling to the men actually doing the fighting, who had rarely if ever laid eyes on MacArthur, to learn from an American newspaper that he had been sharing in the dangers and privations of the front lines. In October 1942, after he made a brief flying trip to Port Moresby, an Allied base in southeastern New Guinea, Brisbane-based war correspondents reported that MacArthur had toured the combat zones around Buna, near the island's north coast. The stories were vetted and approved by the SWPA censors. A photograph of MacArthur watching a field exercise in Rockhampton, Australia, was released to the press with the location falsely captioned as "the front." Newsreel footage depicted him seated in the back of a jeep, bouncing along a muddy jungle road, while the narrator told viewers that the general was touring forward fighting positions. In truth, a towering range of jungle-clad mountains had separated him from the nearest Japanese troops throughout his entire visit.[73]

These blatant fabrications irritated Robert L. Eichelberger, commander of the Eighth Army, who concluded that the SWPA press office was abusing its powers of wartime censorship to indulge MacArthur's personal vanity. General Eichelberger was learning the bitter lesson that Eisenhower and others had learned before him—that if a subordinate officer wanted to get along with MacArthur, he had better keep his name out of the newspapers. After he was quoted and photographed in several press accounts about the Buna campaign, Eichelberger was summoned to Brisbane to be dressed down by MacArthur, who asked: "Do you realize that I could reduce you to the grade of colonel tomorrow and send you home?"[74] Eichelberger took the point, and for the rest of the war he shunned the press. To a visiting public relations officer, he said: "I would rather have you slip a rattlesnake in my pocket than to have you give me any publicity."[75]

From the start of the war, MacArthur always asserted his right to issue his own press communiqués, and he resisted pressure from Washington to tone them down. General Marshall and Secretary Stimson did not like the sensational pronouncements from Brisbane, and they questioned the accuracy of MacArthur's claimed battle results. Truth was often a casualty of the SWPA publicity machine. Action reports were punched up to make them seem more exciting and dramatic, and in many cases not only was the language improved, but new "facts" were liberally added. In some instances, statistics concerning enemy losses were invented wholesale. Moreover, many SWPA communiqués appeared to contain a none-too-nuanced subtext aimed at the navy or at operations in Nimitz's theater. The most notorious of these was issued in March 1943, after a successful air attack on a Japanese troopship convoy off the northern coast of New Guinea, in an action subsequently called the Battle of the Bismarck Sea. Employing a new low-altitude tactic called "skip bombing," Lieutenant General George C. Kenney's Fifth Air Force bombers had sunk a dozen enemy ships, including eight transports and four escorting destroyers. P-38 fighters had shot down about twenty Japanese planes flying air cover over the convoy and driven perhaps twenty more away. The transports had carried about 8,000 Japanese troops, of whom at least 3,000 were killed in the attacks or drowned afterward. (The exact number has never been tallied, as many escaped to nearby shores by clinging to wreckage or were rescued by small craft.)

The bravura performance was a tactical breakthrough for the USAAF, whose land-based bombers had often struggled to hit enemy ships at sea. But the subsequent SWPA communiqués claimed grossly exaggerated results: twelve transports, three light cruisers, and seven destroyers sunk, and 102 Japanese airplanes "definitely observed as put out of action." Furthermore, a communiqué asserted, the convoy had carried an estimated 15,000 Japanese troops, of whom "all perished."[76] In an accompanying statement, also released to the press, MacArthur seemed to draw from this single action the far-reaching lesson that airpower had won strategic dominion over seapower, with the implication that the Army Air Forces had won its ongoing meta-argument with the navy. In the future, he declared, command of the sea would be decided by land-based aviation rather than naval power: "The Allied naval forces can be counted upon to play their own magnificent part, but the battle of the Western Pacific will be won or lost by the proper application of the air-ground team."[77] Flabbergasted admirals demanded that Marshall and Stimson call their man to heel.

The inflated results claimed by MacArthur and Kenney could not withstand scrutiny, and they began to unravel when pilot reports and interrogations of prisoners picked up at sea revealed that the entire convoy was smaller than the number of claimed sinkings. But when General Marshall forwarded corrected estimates to Brisbane, asking that the SWPA headquarters issue a revised communiqué, MacArthur erupted. In a long cable to Marshall that has to be read to be believed, he named twenty-one of the twenty-two ships that his forces had allegedly destroyed, asserted that the results had been conclusively verified by captured Japanese documents and prisoner interrogations, and demanded that Washington revise *its* figures to bring them into line with his previous report. He added that he was prepared to defend his claimed results "either officially or publicly." Moreover, if the War Department intended to issue any public document "challenging the integrity of my operations reports," he wanted to know the names of the men behind it, "in order that I may take appropriate steps including action against those responsible if circumstances warrant."[78]

The moonshine in MacArthur's press communiqués was gratuitous and unnecessary, because his military achievements, in 1943 and 1944, were quite real. His advance up the coast of New Guinea, his landings in New Britain, his bold surprise amphibious landing on Los Negros-Manus, his long jump up the northern New Guinea coast to Hollandia—all those moves were deftly planned and executed. Kenney's bombers *did* wipe out the better part of an important convoy; they *did* improvise a new and lethal tactic to sink ships at sea, a feat that had eluded them in the past. MacArthur's forces had ample cause to take justifiable pride in their achievements, and the controversy surrounding his communiqués only tended to tarnish what should have been regarded, quite properly, as a winning South Pacific counteroffensive.

Critics branded MacArthur a narcissist and a megalomaniac, but his souped-up publicity had a calculated purpose. It was a bid for political influence at home. Diller later said that the general "was trying his level best to get as much help for the Pacific and for our forces as he could, and consequently he tried to keep the story attractive so that people would be sympathetic to his support."[79] In MacArthur's mind, he was pitted against a cabal of enemies in Washington. FDR was his archnemesis, a man he knew well and cordially despised. MacArthur often told his claque that the president had "betrayed" him at the outset of the war by failing to send forces to relieve the Philippines. He was frustrated by the division of the Pacific into two separate theater commands, with the northern realm commanded by Nimitz. He regarded the navy as FDR's pet service—which was not far wrong—and tended to distrust all naval officers as spies or usurpers. But MacArthur's influence in the news media posed a greater problem for the army than for the navy. Marshall, Stimson, and the army leadership in Washington struggled to keep the SWPA commander in line. He was constantly testing the limits of insubordination, often threatening in barely veiled terms to take his case to the public, and any internal disagreement was likely to resonate in the papers and in Congress.

At a visceral emotional level, MacArthur believed that the War Department had failed his army in the Philippines. He ranted about the (mostly) faceless and nameless conspirators—"they"—who had taken control of the army and were plotting to undermine him. "They" had based the global Allied strategy on a principle of "Europe first," a policy he abhorred, and was always ready to denounce as a historic folly. "They" had denied him the forces he needed to turn back the Japanese offensive in the South Pacific. "They" were a clique of deskbound, political generals who were jealous of his public renown, and thus eager to lay him low. "They" were on the spot in Washington, while he was in Australia, half a world away from the seat of power. He had been away a long time—away from Washington, and away from the United States since he had left in 1935; he had even retired from the U.S. Army, serving as Field Marshal of the Philippine Army until appointed U.S. Far East commander by FDR in July 1941. His long physical estrangement had put him at a political disadvantage, or so he believed— and therefore he must do whatever was necessary to make his influence felt in Washington. Only by such means could he hope to obtain the troops, weapons, ships, and airplanes he needed to win the Pacific War, and to win it according to his own playbook. He must beat "them"—his Washington-based antagonists—at their own game, and that meant outbidding them for popularity with the American people.[80] He wanted singular authority over the war, to absorb Nimitz's forces into his own command; but failing that,

he wanted at least to ensure that his theater received the lion's share of
Allied assets in the Pacific. He wanted his own strategic ideas to predomi-
nate over those of the navy, the Joint Chiefs of Staff, and the Allies, which
meant above all that he should liberate the Philippines (including and especially the main northern island of Luzon) as early as possible. Under no
circumstances were the Philippines to be bypassed in favor of a more direct
route to Japan itself.

In private conversations, MacArthur freely admitted that his aggressive
public relations strategy was an instrument to achieve these ends. "They are
afraid of me, Bob," he told Eichelberger in early 1944, "because they know
I will fight them in the newspapers."[81] MacArthur had to "win the war
every morning in his communiqué," observed a correspondent attached to
his headquarters. "He had to convince the public that Roosevelt and the
dastardly Chiefs of Staff were withholding from him the weapons that were
rightfully his."[82]

In his 1964 autobiography, *Reminiscences*, MacArthur maintained that
he never gave a moment's consideration to seeking the Republican presidential nomination in 1944. The truth is that he cooperated willingly with
a "kitchen cabinet" of powerful Republicans, business leaders, and media
owners who shared a zealous desire to be rid of FDR, and regarded Mac-
Arthur as their best and only hope of defeating the popular incumbent in a
wartime election. The SWPA commander discussed the project with various associates and subordinates, including General Eichelberger, who told
his wife in June 1943, "My chief talked of the Republican nomination—I
can see that he expects to get it and I sort of think so too."[83] The first
public inkling of MacArthur's potential candidacy came in April of that
year, when Secretary of War Stimson announced that active-duty officers
could not remain in uniform while running for office. Leading Republicans, including Senator Arthur H. Vandenberg and Congressman Hamilton Fish, interpreted this announcement as a shot across MacArthur's bow.
Each spoke out against Stimson for having meddled in politics, and each
received a letter of thanks from MacArthur for his trouble.

Senator Vandenberg of Michigan, unofficial chairman of the crypto-
campaign, warned that MacArthur must not be seen to lift a finger to
seek the nomination. His opportunity would come only in the event that
the Republican convention, meeting in Chicago in June 1944, found itself
deadlocked between the leading candidates, Thomas Dewey and Wendell

Willkie. In that scenario, the party might nominate MacArthur by general acclamation. Vandenberg planned strategy with other leading supporters, including the newspaper owners Hearst and McCormick; retired general and Sears executive Robert E. Wood; Congressman Carl Vinson; and *Time-Life* publisher Henry Luce and his wife, Congresswoman Clare Booth Luce. The stateside supporters met periodically with senior members of MacArthur's staff during their visits to the United States. (Many leading SWPA staff officers were none too scrupulous in conducting political work while shuttling between Australia and Washington on military aircraft.) As the primary season approached, MacArthur carried on a correspondence with his backers, but he chose his words carefully for fear that his letters might fall into the wrong hands. To Vandenberg, for example, he wrote: "I am most grateful to you for your complete attitude of friendship. I can only hope I can some day reciprocate. There is much more I would like to say to you which circumstances prevent. In the meantime I want you to know the absolute confidence I would feel in your experienced and wise mentorship."[84]

Biographers and historians have debated whether MacArthur really wanted the presidency. Some surmise that his only purpose was to exert pressure on FDR and the Joint Chiefs to put him in charge of the entire Pacific War, and to allocate the resources he needed to win it. Perhaps he was conflicted; perhaps he was flattered by the attention. MacArthur felt a burning desire to return to the Philippines, to free his army from its awful captivity, and to raise the American flag over Bataan. As president he would see those things done, but he would not do them himself. As a student of American history, he must have known that he would risk ending his career as another George B. McClellan, the Union general who had unsuccessfully challenged Abraham Lincoln for the presidency in 1864. Probably MacArthur liked the idea of responding to a groundswell of public acclaim, so long as he did not have to campaign for it. And he must have relished the vision of defeating FDR at the polls. The two men had known one another a long time; they had been colleagues, rivals, and even "friends," in the shallow sense in which the term was sometimes used in Washington. MacArthur had been army chief of staff at the outset of FDR's presidency. He had heatedly opposed FDR's military budget cuts in 1934, and had behaved (even by his own account) with borderline insubordination toward the new president. Like many political conservatives, MacArthur regarded the New Deal as a homegrown strain of Bolshevism. Privately he referred to FDR, with ironic disdain, as "cousin Frank"—or with a crude anti-Semitism common on the political right of that era, as "Rosenfeld."[85] On several occasions, according to Eichelberger, MacArthur said that he would not want the Republican presidential nomination "if it were not for his hatred, or rather the extent to which he despised FDR."[86]

In early 1944, as the Republican primary campaign began in earnest, press reports based on anonymous sources suggested that MacArthur was preparing to return to the United States, where he would campaign full-time for the nomination. Vandenberg went public in an article for *Collier's* entitled, "Why I Am for MacArthur."[87] A report approved for publication by Diller summed up the views prevailing in Brisbane: "It would not be surprising if General MacArthur felt—as do a good many here—that the shortest way to victory would be to place an experienced military man in the White House." When asked on the record about the subject, all of the men around MacArthur gave the same stock answer, a coy nonreply: "Let's get on with the war."[88] The syndicated columnist Raymond Clapper asked MacArthur directly and repeatedly whether he was interested in the Republican nomination, but he never got a straight answer: "Each time he acted as though he didn't hear me."[89] It was noted that MacArthur had been placed on two state GOP primary ballots, in Wisconsin and Illinois—and in neither case did he ask that his name be removed.

A few iconoclastic journalists began to raise questions. Was it proper for a theater commander, in the midst of fighting a terrible war, to flirt with electoral politics at home? Given that MacArthur's image was refracted through wartime media and warped by his own press censors, was it fair that he should compete against candidates who had no such advantage? Few Americans knew how unpopular MacArthur was among the rank and file of his own army. In the glare of the campaign spotlight, a backlash was inevitable. The January 1944 issue of the *American Mercury* supplied it. John McCarten, one of Henry Luce's former editors, had traveled to Australia and returned, thus evading Diller's censorship. In a harshly critical profile, McCarten wrote that MacArthur's performance as a general had been overrated, that he was obsessed to an unbecoming degree with his public image, and that the imposition of heavy-handed censorship in his SWPA headquarters was an intolerable manipulation of the political process. McCarten highlighted the role of the anti-FDR press in creating and sustaining a "MacArthur cult." He suggested that MacArthur was not qualified for the role he sought—that of Pacific Supremo—because he was "a ground general . . . in a predominantly aerial and naval theater."[90] Claims that MacArthur was not personally involved in the presidential campaign were not believable, wrote McCarten, and if he wanted to eliminate speculation, he should quote General Sherman's famous statement of 1884: "If nominated I will not accept, and if elected I will not serve."[91]

MacArthur was infuriated by the *American Mercury* article, even more so because it happened to be included on a reading list distributed to servicemen overseas through the Army War College library service. In a long cable to Marshall, he called the article "scandalous in tone and even libelous" and complained that it parroted Japanese propaganda.[92] But he chose not to refute it directly because (he told Eichelberger) it contained "a thread of truth which prevented his answering it." To be attacked in such terms, he lamented, was a "cross it was necessary for him to bear."[93] He would have been even more chagrined had he possessed the power to see into the future, because on many counts McCarten's "hatchet job" anticipated views that have since become conventional among historians.

In any event, the dark horse candidacy of Douglas MacArthur had entered the home stretch and was about to pull up lame. Tom Dewey, governor of New York, had shown unexpected strength with Republican voters and power brokers, and by late March it was clear that he would defeat Willkie. There would be no deadlock in Chicago, and therefore no chance to draft MacArthur onto the ticket. The shambolic finale was triggered by an unauthorized release of embarrassing letters written by MacArthur to a Nebraska congressman, Arthur L. Miller. Miller had urged MacArthur to accept the party's call to serve: "You owe it to civilization and to the children yet unborn," for "unless this New Deal can be stopped our American way of life is forever doomed." Unwisely trusting to the congressman's discretion, the general had written back directly, stating that he agreed "unreservedly" with the "complete wisdom and statesmanship of your comments."[94] Without asking MacArthur's permission, Miller released the letters to the press on April 14. They were promptly reproduced in full in major newspapers across the country. If Miller had believed they would boost the MacArthur candidacy, he was badly mistaken. Vandenberg regarded the disclosure as a "magnificent boner" and a "tragic mistake." I. F. Stone, writing in *The Nation*, concluded that the letters depicted MacArthur "in a very unsoldierly posture—disloyal to his Commander-in-Chief and a rather pompous and ignorant ass."[95]

According to MacArthur's 1964 autobiography, that was the moment when he first learned that "my name was being bandied about" as a potential candidate on the GOP ticket—and having suddenly been alerted to the ridiculous and dishonorable project, he acted quickly and manfully to put an end to it. He released a statement disavowing presidential ambitions and dismissing any such interpretation of the Miller letters as "sinister."[96] When this first statement was deemed too equivocal, he released a second on April 30, 1944, concluding: "I request that no action be taken that would link my name in any way with the nomination. I do not covet it nor would I accept it."[97]

That ended MacArthur's foray into presidential politics, at least in the 1944 election cycle. The sordid episode would be remembered as a minor footnote in his career. In a larger sense, however, the misadventure left an indelible mark on the last year of the Pacific War. Vital issues of global strategy had been dragged into the arena of partisan politics, and would remain there through the election. Governor Dewey, having accepted his party's nomination, said in a speech on September 14, 1944: "Now that General MacArthur is no longer a political threat to Mr. Roosevelt, it would seem appropriate that his magnificent talents be given greater scope and recognition. . . . General MacArthur has performed miracles with inadequate supply, inadequate airpower and inadequate force."[98] Though innocuous in tone, Dewey's remark contained a serious charge against the president, and by implication against the Joint Chiefs of Staff—that they had allowed politics to guide the allocation of military forces in the Pacific. Dewey did not pursue this line of attack, perhaps because he knew that the Joint Chiefs would refute the charge, but the damage had been done. Roosevelt never forgave Dewey, and the 1944 campaign was the bitterest of his career.

Fundamental questions of grand strategy remained unresolved in the Pacific. Would MacArthur be given the green light to liberate all of the Philippines, including the main northern island of Luzon? Would Ernest King win his case for seizing Formosa? Should the Americans land on the coast of mainland China—and if so, would that lead to a wider direct involvement of U.S. forces in the Sino-Japanese war? More broadly, what was to be the endgame against Japan? Could Japan be persuaded to accept terms of surrender prior to a bloody invasion? What role might Hirohito, the *Showa* emperor, play in the war's final act? These were complicated and immensely important decisions, and they could not be postponed indefinitely. Nor could the presidential election calendar be moved; come hell or high water, the voters would go to the polls on the first Tuesday in November. Inevitably, the big strategic issues looming in the Pacific would be decided in a political season—and they would be viewed through the prism of politics, by contemporaries at the time and by historians ever since.

Chapter One

———————

A FTER DARK ON THE NIGHT OF JULY 13, 1944, PRESIDENT ROOSEVELT
and his traveling entourage were driven to an underground rail siding
on Fourteenth Street in Washington, where they boarded a private train,
the "Presidential Special." With the help of porters and Secret Service
agents, FDR moved into his stateroom on Pullman No. 1, the last car
on the train. Eleanor Roosevelt moved into another stateroom on the
same car, and Admiral William D. Leahy, the White House chief of staff
and an old friend of the Roosevelts, moved into a third. As the train
rolled north through Maryland cornfields, the party slept soundly in their
swaying bunks.

Pullman No. 1 was elegant and sumptuous, with oak panels, plush green
carpets, mahogany furniture, and overstuffed chairs. It was also a virtual
rolling battleship. The car's undercarriage was armored with 12-inch steel
plate, enough to shield it against a large bomb planted in the roadbed. Its
Plexiglas windows were 3 inches thick and would stop a .50-caliber round
fired at point-blank range. The sides carried enough steel to stand up to a
medium-sized artillery shell. Pullman No. 1 weighed 142 tons, almost twice
the weight of a standard car, but it was designed to draw no attention to
itself, and looked no different from any other Pullman private car.

The forthcoming trip would take the president to Chicago and San
Diego, thence by sea to Hawaii, Alaska, and Puget Sound, and finally back
across the continent by rail. The journey would last thirty-five days, one
of the longest of his presidency. Its highlight would be a four-day visit to
Oahu, Hawaii, during which time FDR would tour military installations

and confer with his Pacific theater commanders, General MacArthur and Admiral Nimitz, about their next moves in the war against Japan.

Just two days earlier, FDR had surprised no one with the long-expected announcement that he would seek reelection to an unprecedented fourth term in office. He told the press that he had no choice, because "if the people command me to continue in this office and in this war, I have as little right to withdraw as the soldier has to leave his post in the line."[1] The president's train would stop briefly in Chicago, where the Democratic National Convention was underway. The GOP had met two weeks earlier, also in Chicago, nominating Governor Dewey as their standard-bearer. Given the political season, the forthcoming trip would be denounced by FDR's political rivals as an extended campaign event.

In peacetime, the presidential train had carried up to forty members of the press corps. Now only three correspondents, representing the three major wire services, were permitted to come along on the trip—and their reporting was embargoed until the White House authorized release, usually after about a one-week delay. Wartime security provided the justification for these measures, but the press resented being kept in the dark about the president's whereabouts, especially when he appeared before crowds numbering in the tens of thousands. The president was unmoved by their complaints, even seeming to relish the pretext to get the press out of his hair. "Quite frankly," he told Steve Early, "I regard Freedom of the Press as one of the world's most microscopic problems."[2] When the White House correspondents demanded to know his travel itinerary, FDR relayed his sarcastic reply through Early: "What do you want to do? Watch me take a bath or go with me to the toilet?"[3]

Beginning in the spring of 1944, FDR and his circle had a compelling new reason to keep the press at bay. His health had taken a turn for the worse, and Washington was pulsating with rumors that he did not have the strength to remain in office. His pallor was gray, his eyes sunken and glassy, his voice wan and raspy. He had a nasty hacking cough. His lips and fingernails had a sickly bluish tint. Asked how he felt, the president answered: "Like hell" or "Rotten."[4] In March 1944, a navy cardiologist, Dr. Howard Bruenn, had found severely elevated blood pressure and diagnosed an acute case of congestive heart failure. Given the treatment options available in the 1940s, the patient's chances of living through another four-year presidential term were not good. The median survival rate after such a diagnosis was less than two years. Bruenn later said that if his patient had been anyone other than the commander in chief of a nation at war, he would have insisted on retirement from office and immediate hospitalization. But the only doctor authorized to speak publicly about the president's health was his personal physician, the surgeon general of the navy, Vice Admiral Ross T. McIntire, who told the press that FDR was "in better health than at any time since he came into office in 1933."[5] McIntire's jaunty reassurances were a medical masquerade that would continue until (and beyond) the president's death the following year.

Bruenn later confessed that he and his colleagues had thrust aside medical ethics to answer a higher patriotic calling. FDR was the single most important person in the world. His role in leading the global Allied coalition was seen as indispensable. He was the linchpin of plans and negotiations to create a stable postwar order. Axis propaganda had made a fetish out of physical virility and strength, and had tried to make the wheelchair-bound Roosevelt a symbol of Western democratic decrepitude. His domestic political adversaries had spread rumors that he was in poor health, and would pounce on any evidence that the rumors were true. For all of these reasons, Dr. Bruenn's diagnosis was treated as a state secret, and reporters and photographers were rarely permitted into FDR's presence. On the Presidential Special, the three wire service correspondents (whom the president cheerfully denounced as "cutthroats," "vultures," or "ghouls") were not permitted within three cars of Pullman No. 1. Usually they could be found in the club car, killing time at the bar or the card tables.

AFTER A BRIEF STOP IN THE HUDSON VALLEY, where the Roosevelts spent the day at their home in Hyde Park, they were back aboard the Presidential Special by evening on the fourteenth. That night the train traveled the entire length of the New York Central Railroad. At noon the following day, it came to rest at the Fifty-Fifth Street Coach Yard in Chicago, where it would remain for two hours while Roosevelt met with Robert Hannegan, chairman of the Democratic National Committee.

A majority of the party was determined to be rid of the sitting vice president, Henry Wallace, and Roosevelt bowed to their wishes. The story of how Senator Harry S. Truman landed on the Democratic ticket has been recounted elsewhere, and need not be repeated here. Suffice it to say that it was an odd result, surprising even to the president's inner circle. After a short meeting with Hannegan, FDR signed a letter agreeing to either of two prospective running mates: Supreme Court Justice William O. Douglas, or Truman. The original letter named the two men in that order: Douglas or Truman. But at the last moment before the train pulled out of Chicago, Hannegan emerged from the president's private compartment and asked FDR's secretary, Grace Tully, to retype the letter with the order of names reversed. FDR thus effectively chose his successor in a seemingly spontaneous, seat-of-the-pants exchange with the DNC chairman, even though his doctors had reason to doubt that he could survive another term in office.

This historically momentous stopover in Chicago lasted all of two hours. Before nightfall the Presidential Special was on its way again, bound for Topeka, Kansas, and points west on the Rock Island Railroad. For the next three days, the train meandered through the Great Plains and the desert regions of the Southwest. Its speed rarely exceeded 35 miles per hour, partly because Roosevelt found the ride more comfortable at that imperial pace—but also because he wanted to deliver his speech accepting the party's nomination from a naval base in San Diego, and the exact timing of his nomination was uncertain. At that speed the train's batteries would not recharge, so it stopped often at local sidings to plug into charging stations. FDR was sleeping well each night, a vital consideration for his health. Travel had always done wonders for his spirits. He was invigorated by the peaceful ritual of watching the country roll past while identifying towns and other landmarks on a map he kept in his lap. He impressed his staff and companions by citing esoteric details of local history, and seemed to possess an encyclopedic recall of his past electoral performance in each local voting precinct.

Police and local troops maintained a heavy presence along the route, guarding all trestles, junctions, bridges, and tunnels. Where highways ran parallel to the tracks, army jeeps and trucks motored along in company. Naturally curious, the soldiers stared into the windows of the president's car, hoping to catch a glimpse of the commander in chief, the First Lady, or Fala, their famous little black Scottish terrier. Advance notice of the train's approach spread by word of mouth to the stations ahead. On the sweltering afternoon of July 16, at the train station in El Reno, Oklahoma, Eleanor Roosevelt was seen walking Fala on a leash up and down the platform. Word spread quickly through the town, and a crowd of about five hundred curiosity-seekers converged on the station. More were arriving when the train departed an hour later.[6]

Besides the First Lady and Admiral Leahy, the presidential entourage included a long list of military aides; a medical team, including McIntire, Bruenn, and two other doctors; the speechwriter Sam Rosenman; OWI chief Elmer Davis; Major General "Pa" Watson; Rear Admiral Wilson Brown; and Grace Tully. There was the usual large wartime detail of Secret Service agents, navy porters, railroad employees, and the "three ghouls" of the wire services.

Near the front of the train, behind the locomotive and the baggage car, was a windowless communications car manned by the Army Signal Corps—an intricate warren of cables, tubes, electrical panels, and decoding machines. From here, the signalmen maintained constant secure contact with the White House Map Room through shortwave and radio teletype. Lieutenant William Rigdon, a junior naval aide, spent much of the transcontinental journey walking the fifteen cars between the communications car and the president's private car, a journey of nearly a quarter of a mile. He carried messages through a series of roomette cars, upper- and lower-berth Pullman cars, the club car, the dining car, and more roomette cars; and finally past the armed plainclothesmen who guarded the president's car, always the last on the train.[7]

At two o'clock in the morning on July 19, the Presidential Special pulled up to a siding at the Marine Corps Base in San Diego. The party would spend three days here, at the nation's great West Coast naval bastion, touring local military facilities. The Roosevelts visited their son James and his family, who were living across the bay in Coronado. FDR and his retinue reviewed amphibious training exercises of two marine regimental combat teams of the 5th Marine Division in Oceanside, California, 40 miles north of San Diego. This was a highly realistic "live fire" practice landing, including lots of heavy armor and advanced landing craft. It was a valuable education, both for the president and his senior military aides. The Pacific island-hopping campaign was a new kind of war, and large-scale amphibious maneuvers of the kind they saw in Oceanside had been unknown in peacetime. Leahy was particularly impressed with the close coordination of naval fire and air support with the landing teams.[8]

On July 20, the Democratic Convention in Chicago nominated the president for a fourth term. With the train sitting at the Marine Corps railroad siding, Roosevelt gave a fifteen-minute acceptance speech, which was broadcast to the convention by radio. Afterwards, he reread some of the highlights for the newsreel cameramen. At a little before nine o'clock, Eleanor Roosevelt bid the party good-bye and left to catch a military flight back to Washington. The president, Leahy, and Fala transferred into a car for the short drive to the Broadway Pier, where the heavy cruiser *Baltimore* was berthed. The ship's crew had not been forewarned that President Roosevelt would be a passenger, but some had guessed the truth when wheelchair ramps were constructed in the corridors around the captain's quarters. Roosevelt moved into the captain's cabin, Leahy into the flag officer's cabin.

The president being mindful of the old seaman's superstition against beginning a sea voyage on a Friday, the ship waited until midnight to cast free her lines. Five destroyers followed the darkened cruiser as she headed down the long mine-swept ship channel to the open sea. The formation set a base course of 243 degrees, with cruising speed of 22 knots, and vanished into the offing.

IN MARCH 1944, THE JOINT CHIEFS HAD ORDERED MacArthur and Nimitz to cooperate in seizing Palau, a group of Japanese-held islands in southern Micronesia, with a deadline of September 15; and Mindanao, the big southern island of the Philippines, with a deadline of November 15. But the chiefs remained undecided about the major moves to follow in early 1945. As always, the Philippines were the cynosure of MacArthur's war, and he continued to press Washington to endorse his preferred southern line of attack. He wanted to concentrate all available U.S. forces (including the Pacific Fleet) to liberate the northern island of Luzon, including the capital city of Manila, before undertaking any further amphibious invasions to the north. Admiral King and most of the internal JCS planners preferred to bypass Luzon and aim their next major thrust at the island of Formosa (Taiwan). A March 12 dispatch to the two Pacific theater commanders had laid bare the disagreement, directing both headquarters to prepare contingency plans for "Occupation of Formosa, target date 15 February 1945, or occupation of Luzon should such operations prove necessary prior to the move on Formosa, target date 15 February 1945."[9]

As the *Baltimore* carried the president to Hawaii, invasion forces were in the process of seizing the Mariana Islands of Saipan, Guam, and Tinian. In the Battle of the Philippine Sea (June 19–20, 1944), a naval air battle west of the Marianas, the Japanese had lost about three hundred aircraft and three aircraft carriers. With its sea links to the southern resource areas under increasing assault, the economic and military foundations of the Japanese imperialist project were beginning to crumble. Although the regime in Tokyo was not prepared to face facts, the loss of the Marianas and the destruction of its carrier airpower marked Japan's irreversible strategic defeat in the Pacific War. The final phase of the campaign had begun, and the supreme question loomed: how to force the Japanese leadership to admit defeat, and to accept the terms of peace offered—unconditional surrender? The Americans knew they could take either path at this fork in the road— Luzon or Formosa—and be sure of victory. It was a proverbial high-class problem, but it presented war planners with many-sided strategic and technical complexities, and it had produced a confounding array of opinions both in Washington and in the Pacific. In other words, it was a close call.

In early 1943, the planning arm of the JCS had circulated a "Strategic Plan for the Defeat of Japan." This document envisioned a vital role for China in the last stage of the Pacific War, as a base for bombing raids against Japan and as a source of infantry manpower to destroy the Japanese armies in Asia and (if necessary) the Japanese home islands. To carry it off, the Allies would need to land on the coast of mainland China, and the island of Formosa seemed to offer the key that would unlock the continent's front door. This China-centric vision of the Pacific endgame created momentum in Washington for the navy's preferred central Pacific line of attack, which ran through Micronesia, the Marianas, and Formosa.

The most influential in-house JCS planning body was the Joint Strategic Survey Committee (JSSC), a panel of gray eminences who reported directly to the chiefs. For much of the war the JSSC was chaired by Lieutenant General Stanley D. Embick of the army, who had graduated from West Point in 1899. The four principals of the JCS continued to show a certain degree of deference to the venerable old warriors on the JSSC, who offered advice unfettered by service rivalries or institutional biases. In November 1943, the JSSC had rendered a unanimous and "unequivocal" judgment that the central Pacific offensive was more important than MacArthur's South Pacific campaign, because it offered the shorter route to Japan, and therefore "the key to the early defeat of Japan lies in all-out operations through the Central Pacific, with supporting operations on the northern and southern flanks—using all forces, naval, air and ground, that can be maintained and employed profitably in these areas."[10] MacArthur's impassioned dissent, and his demands for a shift in emphasis to the southern route and the Philippines, had consistently failed to move the JSSC. Each new study tended to reinforce the panel's past conclusions—that MacArthur's South Pacific campaign had become redundant, that the dispersal of effort in the Pacific risked prolonging the war, and that Japan's evident weakness invited a more direct assault upon the enemy's inner ring of defenses. In the committee's considered judgment, that pointed to Formosa.

To his perpetual vexation, MacArthur could never rely on George Marshall to protect the parochial interests of his SWPA theater, or to assign priority to his preferred route of attack through the South Pacific and the Philippines. The previous year, he had expressed himself in remarkably bald terms to his deputy, General Richard Sutherland, who was on his way to Washington: "Emphasize to Marshall that he can control the situation through his allocation of the air and ground forces which are necessary for operations in Pacific. Without these army resources the navy will be helpless. If he will send here the air and ground reinforcements instead of sending men to the navy areas he can accomplish the desired purpose by indirection."[11] It is not known how much of that appeal was conveyed by Sutherland to Marshall, but the army chief of staff was never temperamentally inclined to act by "indirection," defined by *Webster's* as "a lack of straightforwardness or openness." Marshall was not blind to the service rivalries in the Pacific, but he never saw the campaign as a zero-sum struggle between the army and navy, or between MacArthur and Nimitz, and he was always willing to consider the merits of a more direct route of attack on the Japanese homeland. As for leaving the navy "helpless," a mere glance at a map of the Pacific was enough to grasp the likely consequences.

In June 1944, spurred by the JSSC's forceful arguments, Marshall urged MacArthur to let go of outmoded assumptions and to reexamine the entire Pacific chessboard with a fresh perspective. Given signs of Japanese weakness, was it not time to speed the tempo of the campaign? The strategy of bypassing strongly held islands had been a hallmark of MacArthur's successful South Pacific offensive—why not apply the same logic to Luzon? If the Allies would eventually require a port on the coast of mainland China, perhaps it was better to take Formosa sooner rather than later. Marshall was even considering a bolder proposal—then circulating among the JSC planners—a surprise landing on Kyushu, the southern island of Japan. In either case, Marshall told the SWPA commander, "we must be careful not to allow our personal feeling and Philippine political considerations to override our great objective, which is the early conclusion of the war with Japan. In my view, 'bypassing' is in no way synonymous with 'abandonment.' On the contrary, by the defeat of Japan at the earliest practicable moment the liberation of the Philippines will be effected in the most expeditious and complete manner possible."[12] But MacArthur disagreed entirely, arguing that liberating Luzon was necessary, both for strategic reasons and because "We have a great national obligation to discharge."[13]

MacArthur's desire to liberate the Philippines was genuine, honorable, and deeply felt. But in the interest of a full accounting of this history, the following facts should be weighed in the balance. On February 13, 1942, in the command bunker on Corregidor, Philippine president Manuel Quezon signed an order transferring from Philippine commonwealth treasury funds the sums of $500,000 to MacArthur, $75,000 to Sutherland, and lesser amounts to two other senior officers on MacArthur's staff. The payments were described as compensation for past services in the U.S. military mission to the Philippines. The current-day equivalent of the sum paid to MacArthur was a cool $8 million. Because the commonwealth treasury funds were on deposit in New York, in accounts partly controlled by the U.S. government, the payments required the approval of Interior Secretary Harold Ickes. Marshall and Stimson knew what was happening and did not raise objections, or at any rate, did not act to stop the transactions. It is likely, based on the surviving paper trail, that President Roosevelt was informed.[14] Later, after his escape to the United States, Quezon visited General Eisenhower in Washington and offered him an "honorarium"— the sum is not known—to compensate his past services in the Philippines. Eisenhower declined the offer, tactfully explaining that "the danger of misapprehension or misunderstanding . . . might operate to destroy whatever usefulness I may have to the Allied cause in the current war."[15] The future European theater commander judged that the offer was improper under the circumstances, and would be exposed to public scrutiny in the long run. He was right on both counts.

Behind closed doors, in the summer of 1944, Admiral King bluntly questioned MacArthur's competence as a military strategist. In his estimation, the SWPA commander had little knowledge of (or curiosity about) recent advances in amphibious warfare, which had lately proven its capacity to cross long ocean distances to seize strongly fortified enemy islands. MacArthur's past predictions of disaster in the central Pacific had been discredited, but he continued to offer similarly dire prophecies about the Formosa operation. King had championed the South Pacific counteroffensive in 1942—indeed, he had touched it off with his Guadalcanal operation, which had been opposed by MacArthur. But the southern line of attack, in King's view, had been justified only in the early part of the war, when the United States was not yet strong enough to fight across the heart of the Pacific. Now that Australia was secure and Allied forces had smashed through the Bismarcks barrier, it was time to wind down the southern offensive. Mindanao was the logical terminus for MacArthur's campaign. In one of King's regular off-the-record press briefings in Alexandria, he told the reporters that recapturing the Philippines was "sentimentally desirable" but "eccentric," and would likely delay victory in the Pacific by three to six months.[16] To Rear Admiral Daniel E. Barbey, MacArthur's amphibious fleet commander, King acidly remarked that "MacArthur seemed more interested in making good his promise to return to the Philippines than in winning the war."[17]

On July 13, Admiral King flew into Pearl Harbor in his Coronado flag seaplane, trailing a large entourage of staff officers. After two long days of conferences at CINCPAC headquarters, King and Nimitz boarded a twin-tailed Lockheed Lodestar and went island-hopping through the Marshalls, with stops at Kwajalein and Eniwetok, and thence to Saipan on July 17. At Aslito Airfield, where fierce combat had raged just two weeks earlier, they were met on the tarmac by a delegation of military brass, press correspondents, and photographers, including General Holland "Howlin' Mad" Smith, the commander of the Fifth Amphibious Corps (VAC), and Admiral Raymond Spruance, commander of the Fifth Fleet. The island had been declared secure a week earlier, but small-unit fighting was still underway in the more remote areas, and Japanese stragglers and holdouts numbered in the hundreds, perhaps even the thousands. King, who had not personally seen much of the combat zones in the Pacific, was keen to tour the island. Smith was concerned about snipers, but King insisted, so Smith detached three companies of marines to protect the two four-star admirals. King and Nimitz sat together in the back of a jeep and were driven in a long motorcade up the main road on the west coast, through the rubble-strewn ruins of the towns of Garapan, Tanapag, and Chalan Kanoa. Although the burial details had been working in shifts, the sickly sweet reek of rotting corpses was pervasive and inescapable. After a month on Saipan, Smith and his troops had ceased to notice it.

That afternoon, King, Nimitz, and Spruance rode a launch out to the Fifth Fleet flagship *Indianapolis*, which lay about a mile offshore. After a photo session under the ship's 8-inch guns, they went together to the flag mess for an early supper. Spruance sat at the head of the table with King on his right and Nimitz on his left, and about a dozen other officers sat down the length of the table in descending order of rank and seniority. As dessert was served, a great black cloud of flies swarmed into the compartment through the open portholes. They had bred in the decomposing flesh of Saipan's thousands of still-unburied dead, and had wafted out to the fleet on the prevailing breeze. The flies had been a problem for weeks, but the swarm that infested the *Indianapolis* that evening was the worst the crew had seen. They lit upon the table, the food, and the faces and hands of the men. They were hideously engorged, some nearly an inch long. According to Carl Moore, Spruance's chief of staff, the creatures would not buzz away at a waving hand. If they landed on a man's nose they had to be pushed or picked off, and "they'd be in your food and under your spectacles and into your ears and all over the place, and you kept thinking that they'd all been eating dead Japs and coming out to the ship for a little fresh air."[18] The mess stewards closed the portholes, but it was too late. Glasses were knocked over as disgusted officers tried to bat the insects away. Chairs scraped on deck as they stood and retreated from the scene, forsaking the decorum normally observed in the presence of four-star visitors.

At some point that day, King asked Spruance about his preparations for Operation CAUSEWAY, the prospective invasion of Formosa. The Fifth Fleet chief answered frankly: "I don't like Formosa."[19] Instead, he proposed to seize Iwo Jima and Okinawa, in that order. Iwo was on the flight line between the Marianas and Tokyo; possessing it would blunt Japanese counterstrikes by air. Okinawa was smaller than Formosa, and thus more manageable. The island was of ideal size for Allied purposes, said Spruance—small enough to conquer in a matter of weeks, but large enough to serve as a base of operations against the Japanese home islands. It was strategically located along sea routes linking Japan to its southern resource territories. Okinawa offered many potential landing sites, so the defenders would not be able to concentrate their firepower against any one beach. The island could serve either as a stepping stone to the China coast or a launchpad for an invasion of Kyushu.

But Okinawa was just 330 miles from Kyushu, so the amphibious fleet could count on massive and sustained air attacks. The closest bases of Allied support would be more than a thousand miles away. The carrier task forces would be obliged to provide air protection, remaining in the area for a period of several weeks without intermission. Considering these challenges, King asked Spruance, "Can you do it?" Spruance replied that it could be done, so long as the logistics forces perfected the technique of transferring ammunition at sea. That was the one remaining hurdle that the Fifth Fleet had not yet solved. But Spruance was convinced that it could be solved, and as usual he was right.[20]

Because he was the fleet commander who would oversee the invasion, Spruance's view carried exceptional heft. But he was hardly alone. Opposition to CAUSEWAY was coalescing among influential players in the fleet, the amphibious forces, and Nimitz's headquarters. Many doubted whether Formosa was worth the immense effort; the invasion would rival the scale of the D-Day landings in Normandy. And if it turned out to be absolutely necessary to take Formosa, they told King, they would first need the airfields of Luzon and the fleet base at Manila Bay, so bypassing the Philippines was not an option. On the plane back to Hawaii on July 19, King got an earful from Robert "Mick" Carney, Admiral Halsey's chief of staff, who called Formosa "a time-waster."[21] Instead, said Carney, "the buildup should be on Luzon and we should flatten Formosa and bypass it."[22]

King asked, "Do you want to make a London out of Manila?"

"No, Admiral," said Carney. "What I'm thinking of is making another England out of Luzon."[23]

In a last round of conferences at CINCPAC headquarters on July 20, King sat patiently while the Pacific fleet planners registered their various objections to Formosa. Admiral John H. Towers, the deputy CINCPAC, stressed that neither Guam nor Saipan offered sufficient port facilities to mount an invasion force large enough to take the big Chinese island. That was even more true now that the Army Air Forces intended to base at least twelve B-29 air groups in the Marianas. The contemplated preparations for Operation CAUSEWAY, Towers warned, would probably require a "cutback in the VLR [B-29] program."[24] That, in turn, would arouse the ire of General Henry "Hap" Arnold and the USAAF.

In the face of these objections, King remained stubbornly committed to CAUSEWAY. But he did not attempt to use the power of his towering rank to suppress dissent among his colleagues. Contrary to his characterization in much of the historical literature, the CNO was not a caudillo. He insisted on a full airing of views and considered the counterarguments in good faith. As Nimitz was wrapping up the talks, King turned to Carney and asked him to repeat his objections to Formosa once more for the record, to be certain that they were entered into the conference minutes. One can scarcely imagine Douglas MacArthur soliciting the contrary views of a subordinate in such a setting.[25]

King had not been invited to remain in Hawaii for the president's visit. Indeed, he and Marshall had been specifically excluded from the proceedings. It was explained that FDR and Leahy wanted to hear the uninhibited views of the two Pacific theater commanders, and that they were already fully acquainted with the views of the Joint Chiefs. But King resented being barred from this important Pacific command summit. In his postwar memoir, he noted that Roosevelt had kicked off his reelection campaign immediately prior to the conference, and concluded that the president now wanted to "show the voters that he was commander in chief."[26]

In King's absence, Nimitz would have to make the case for CAUSEWAY. King was concerned, with good reason, that Nimitz's heart was not really in the fight. The CINCPAC shared the misgivings expressed by his colleagues in the headquarters and in the fleet. Landing troops on the big Chinese island would not be wise, he warned King on July 24, unless Japanese airpower on nearby Luzon was first neutralized: "Inability effectively [to] reduce or contain enemy air forces on WHITEWASH [Luzon] would render success of CAUSEWAY doubtful."[27] Furthermore, Nimitz added, it might become necessary to occupy all of Formosa, rather than just the northern and southern coasts. If that proved true, he would need more of everything—more troops, more air groups, more shipping, and more naval power. And if the scale of the Formosa operation was to be expanded, the Americans would need larger and more proximate naval and air bases, which in turn pointed back to Luzon.

King did not insist that the CINCPAC parrot his views on Formosa. He knew that FDR and Leahy expected the Pacific Fleet chief to speak for himself. "I tried not to press him too much," said King, "because I was trained to let people think for themselves." But King feared that Nimitz would be overmatched against "two of the shrewdest and most adroit arguers available. Nimitz was a good sound man but he wasn't even in the same class to be pitted with General MacArthur in that way and, of course, Mr. Roosevelt was a 'past master.' "[28]

On July 24, two days before the president's scheduled arrival in Pearl Harbor, King and his party boarded the Lockheed and took off for the mainland. They flew east over the *Baltimore* and her escorts, inbound for Oahu in the opposite direction.

DURING HER PASSAGE TO OAHU, the *Baltimore* observed wartime cruising conditions, which meant constant zigzagging to foil enemy submarines, and darkening the ship between dusk and dawn. The weather was cool with moderate swell and light breezes. Navy fighters and patrol planes were often seen patrolling overhead. The president spent most of the voyage in his cabin, sleeping and reading, replenishing his strength for the punishing schedule that lay ahead. He was briefed each day by Admiral Leahy. Most afternoons, he and Leahy sat for an hour or two on the flag bridge, taking in the sun and salt air. A movie was screened each evening in Leahy's cabin. Fala, as usual, was everyone's friend; members of the crew slipped him snacks and snipped away locks of his hair as souvenirs, until the captain told them to desist. It would not do the *Baltimore*'s reputation any good if the president's dog arrived in Hawaii overweight and looking as if he had the mange.

Bill Leahy was a dignified figure with dark, watchful eyes crowned by shaggy eyebrows, a furrowed brow, and a bald pate. He was discreet, formal, and precise in speech and manner. Even while in uniform, he projected the bearing of a statesman or diplomat. Yet he had risen to serve as chief of naval operations (CNO), the highest rank in the navy, before his retirement from the service in 1939. FDR had thereafter named him governor of Puerto Rico, then ambassador to Vichy France. In 1942, the president had given serious consideration to making Leahy the supreme commander in the Pacific, with authority over both MacArthur and Nimitz. Instead, he was returned to active duty as a four-star admiral and named "military chief of staff" to the president, in which capacity he also served as one of four members of the Joint Chiefs of Staff.

Leahy was the senior American military officer of the Second World War, as determined by rank and date of original commission. He was the first admiral or general in the nation's history to receive a fifth star. His influence shaped every major military and foreign policy decision of the war. But Leahy was also one of Franklin D. Roosevelt's oldest and most trusted friends, a member of his loyal inner circle, who worked in the East Wing of the White House and spent most of his waking hours at the president's side. His role as the president's constant daily companion had recently expanded, because the White House aide Harry Hopkins (who had functioned as Leahy's civilian counterpart, and was likewise personally close to FDR) had been sidelined by terminal stomach cancer.

Before the National Security Act of 1947, the JCS had no statutory charter and no official chairman. There was no formal nominating process, and Senate confirmation was not required. Leahy's role is sometimes described as a "precursor" to that of chairman of the JCS, for he did not possess the formal powers of a modern-day chairman. It appears that Leahy was simply added to the committee by the unanimous concurrence of FDR and his service chiefs. In recognition of his seniority, the other chiefs acclaimed him as their de facto chairman. These decisions were spontaneous and ad hoc.

It is worth dwelling for a moment on these dry particulars, because they illuminate the persistent confusion in the historical literature about Leahy's role in the war. The admiral is alternately named as "White House chief of staff" or "chairman of the Joint Chiefs." Both jobs exist to this day, but they are vastly different, and a single individual would never occupy them simultaneously. So what was Leahy, exactly? Was he a mere staffer? A dependable loyalist? A sophisticated message-runner? FDR's best friend? Or was he really the almighty chairman of the Joint Chiefs of Staff? The answer seems to be that Bill Leahy was all of these things. He was the president's alter ego, especially in the last year of FDR's life; but he was also deeply respected by his fellow joint chiefs as a strategist, a former CNO, and a global statesman. The JCS made policy by consensus, rather than by majority vote. At the very least, therefore, Leahy was one of four equal voices in this powerful quartet. When and if the chiefs failed to muddle through to a unanimous decision, their deadlock would be appealed to the commander in chief, to whom Leahy was the principal link.

Most exchanges between FDR and Leahy occurred behind closed doors, in face-to-face meetings that produced no written record. Consequently, it is not always evident how their minds interacted. The conundrum is exacerbated by Leahy's innate modesty and reserve; he was shy of publicity

and seemingly indifferent to his place in history. In the scholarly and bio-
graphical literature, he tends to vanish into FDR's shadow. No doubt he
would have been pleased.*

On the morning of July 26, lookouts sighted Molokai, a brown lump
of land about 50 miles off the port bow. An aerial escort of eighteen navy
planes droned in from the west and circled low over the *Baltimore*. The
weather was fair, the sea smooth, the breezes light and variable. Diamond
Head, a rugged headland, rose from the sea ahead and marched to eastward,
gradually uncovering the long white arc of Waikiki Beach and the city of
Honolulu. Oahu's steep green mountains soared majestically over the scene.
Off the Pearl Harbor entrance channel, the *Baltimore* lay to while a tugboat
delivered the harbor pilot and a welcoming party of military brass and civilians, including Admiral Nimitz, Lieutenant General Robert C. Richardson
Jr. (commander of army forces in Nimitz's theater), and Hawaii's territorial
governor, Ingram M. Stainback.

As the *Baltimore* crept into the crowded anchorage, it was clear that
Pearl Harbor had been turned out to welcome the commander in chief.
The sky overhead was darkened by hundreds of navy carrier planes flying
in wingtip formation. Warships in the harbor were "dressed"—that is, festooned with pennants on lines that ran from the bow up to the masthead
and aft to the stern. The crews were manning rails—dressed in white uniforms, standing to attention, spaced at 6-to-8-foot intervals and facing outward with hands clasped behind their backs. There had been no formal
announcement of the president's visit, but rumors and speculation had circulated widely. Since secrecy was evidently a lost cause, the presidential flag
was hauled up the *Baltimore*'s main.

At 3:00 p.m., a harbor tug nudged the *Baltimore* into her berth against
a concrete sea wall, just astern of the renowned aircraft carrier *Enterprise*.
On the pier, a party of about two dozen admirals and generals waited by
the gangway. The admirals wore dress whites; the marine generals wore
green; the army generals wore khaki. Rarely, if ever, had so much brass
been concentrated in one place. Behind them, corralled behind barricades, was an immense crowd of military personnel and civilian workers,
numbering perhaps 20,000.

---

* For example, in Max Hastings's half-chapter-length account of the Hawaii conference
in *Retribution* (2008), Leahy's name does not appear.

The officers mounted the gangway and were received on deck without honors. (The ritual had been suspended because it would have caused excessive delays in the afternoon's schedule.) The delegation was escorted up to the bridge deck veranda, where FDR and Leahy had been chatting with Nimitz and Richardson. Introductions, handshakes, and small talk followed. Meanwhile, on the weather deck, navy photographers and a film crew were setting up equipment for a photo shoot scheduled for four o'clock.

General MacArthur's absence was conspicuous. His plane had arrived an hour earlier at nearby Hickam Field. Nimitz's deputy, Admiral Towers, had met the plane before coming aboard the *Baltimore*. But MacArthur had declined to accompany Towers directly to the Navy Yard, choosing instead to go to General Richardson's house at Fort Shafter, where he would lodge during the conference. That bordered upon a breach of protocol. On the *Baltimore*'s bridge, Towers discreetly relayed to Nimitz and Richardson the message given by MacArthur, "to convey to the president that he was at General Richardson's quarters awaiting further instructions as to when he should pay his respects."[29] This message was passed to Leahy and the president. The party waited about twenty minutes, the awkwardness growing palpable. Then FDR turned to General Richardson and asked, "Will you get hold of him?"[30] Richardson agreed and left the ship to fetch the missing SWPA commander.

ACCORDING TO HIS PILOT, Whelton "Dusty" Rhoades, MacArthur had barely slept during the twenty-eight-hour flight from Australia. His aircraft, a new Douglas C-54 Skymaster, was fitted with a comfortable cot, but MacArthur did not use it. He was tense and irritable, but showed no sign of fatigue. He paced indefatigably, up and down the aisle, for hours at a time. During a refueling stop in New Caledonia, MacArthur noted that it was the first time since the start of the war that he had set foot on soil outside his command area. That was true, but only because he had declined all previous invitations to planning conferences in Nouméa or Pearl Harbor.

While the C-54 was flying through inky darkness, Rhoades left the cockpit in the care of his copilot and went back to the main cabin to sit with the general, who started "one of his characteristic monologues, to which I was not expected to reply." MacArthur told the pilot that he had no idea why he was being summoned to meet the president, but "the possible results of the pending conference could run the gamut, all the way from his being removed from his command, to his command's being reduced in order to provide a holding action in New Guinea, to his being given the green light, together with men and equipment, to mount an assault on the Philippines." Assuming that Roosevelt intended to use him as a prop for his reelection campaign, MacArthur grumbled that he would be dragooned into posing for "publicity pictures," and said he hoped that "since he had been ordered to make this long trip and suffered some indignities thereon, the purpose would be more useful than that."[31]

After a second fueling stop at Canton Island before dawn, the plane took off for the final leg into Hickam Field. It arrived over Oahu at 2:30 p.m., just as the *Baltimore* was in the offing. The whole regal scene opened up in a panorama beneath them. Rhoades noted that they "could see the sky literally filled with aircraft that had just become airborne and were maneuvering and assembling to fly a review for the president, approaching in the cruiser off Diamondhead."[32]

On the tarmac at Hickam Field, Admiral Towers met the plane and proposed that they go immediately to the Navy Yard to greet the commander in chief. MacArthur refused, noting that he had traveled a long way and wanted to wash up and change into a clean uniform. He told Towers, "I am going to my quarters! When the president wants me later, he may send for me."[33] Then he walked briskly to a waiting automobile, which took him to Fort Shafter.

MacArthur's tardy arrival on board the *Baltimore* is one of the most familiar scenes of the Pacific War. Sam Rosenman, a longtime FDR aide and speechwriter, recalled that MacArthur's arrival was heralded by a chorus of sirens, "and there raced onto the dock and screeched to a stop a motorcycle escort and the longest open car I have ever seen. In the front was a chauffeur in khaki, and in the back one lone figure—MacArthur. There were no aides or attendants. The car traveled some distance around the open space and stopped at the gangplank."[34]

Every other flag and general officer involved in the ceremony was turned out in immaculate dress uniform. MacArthur, in the heat of a Hawaiian summer afternoon, wore his famous brown leather flight jacket over khaki. The corncob pipe was not in evidence on this occasion, but he wore his familiar aviator sunglasses and his battered Philippine field marshal's cap with a mass of "scrambled eggs" (gold braid) above the visor. "He stood out from his fellows, as he always arranged it," said a naval officer who watched the scene from the patio of a nearby officers' club. "He was truly a caricature of a caricature, but being the ranking officer and popular old hero that he was, he could get away with it."[35]

When the immense crowd behind the barriers caught sight of him, they sent up a roaring ovation. MacArthur waved, climbed the *Baltimore*'s gangway, and then paused a moment to let the multitude have another good look at him. Then he stepped aboard the ship to the whistle of the boatswain's pipe, returned the salute of the officer of the deck (OOD), and went up to meet the president.

On the bridge deck, FDR took MacArthur's hand and greeted him as "Douglas." The general would later say that he was annoyed to be addressed in that familiar manner.[36] Having been away from Washington for so long, MacArthur may have forgotten that the president generally called everyone by their first name, including all of his military chiefs, while expecting to be addressed in turn as "Mr. President." But if MacArthur was offended, he seems to have concealed it well: the bridge was crowded with eyewitnesses, but none noted any sign of strain. Moreover, he reciprocated by addressing the president as "Franklin." Roosevelt did not flinch at this effrontery, and they remained "Douglas" and "Franklin" for the remainder of the conference.

Eyeing MacArthur's careworn leather jacket, Admiral Leahy asked: "Douglas, why don't you wear the right kind of clothes when you come up here to see us?"

"Well," replied MacArthur, "you haven't been where I came from, and it's cold up there in the sky."[37] The reply was a non sequitur, since the general had already returned to his quarters for the stated purpose of bathing and changing into a fresh uniform. But Leahy's remark was friendly badinage, and MacArthur took it in that spirit.*

---

* According to Rosenman, it was FDR who kidded MacArthur about the jacket, observing that "it's darn hot today," to which the SWPA chief replied, "Well I've just landed from Australia. It's pretty cold there" (*Working with Roosevelt*, p. 457). Rosenman's version has been more widely cited, but Leahy's is more credible. He was an old friend of MacArthur's, for whom such teasing would come naturally. He was a fellow officer, senior to MacArthur, and thus more likely to call attention to his uniform. The self-effacing Leahy claimed the words as his own, whereas Rosenman's account was probably an innocent mistake; he witnessed the exchange, but later misremembered who had spoken.

The photo shoot was now running about thirty minutes behind schedule, so the party moved down to the *Baltimore*'s weather deck, where navy photographers and camera crews had set up their equipment. It was customary for cameramen to wait for FDR to be situated before taking pictures or rolling film. But in this case, a brief 16mm film clip captured an image of FDR being pushed in his wheelchair. (The footage is believed to be the only such surviving motion picture image.)[38]

MacArthur was seated to FDR's right, Nimitz to his left, and Leahy to Nimitz's left. The four men posed for a round of photos. Then Leahy withdrew and the president was filmed and photographed with the two Pacific theater commanders. In the silent film footage, FDR chats amiably into MacArthur's left ear, while the general stares impassively back into the camera's lens. For a moment he appears deeply uncomfortable, as if he would rather be anywhere else. But then Roosevelt says something that appears to amuse MacArthur, and the general turns to respond with a warm grin. At that moment, a terrier-shaped dark silhouette ambles into the frame from MacArthur's right, passes under their chairs, and continues out of the frame a few feet to Nimitz's left.[39]

When it was the turn of Governor Stainback to be photographed with the president, MacArthur and Nimitz vacated their chairs. A subsequent film clip caught MacArthur off to one side, chatting with General Richardson. MacArthur uses a handkerchief to mop sweat from his face and neck. He appears uncomfortably hot, but the leather flight jacket stays on. Every great actor knows the value of his wardrobe.

As the photographers and film crews finished their work, the officers began to leave the ship. FDR was wheeled onto a small wooden platform, ringed with rails. The entire platform was lifted from the *Baltimore*'s deck by one of the ship's cranes, and slowly lowered to the pier. A naval officer who watched the process imagined that the crane operator "must have been sweating blood."[40] A marine guard and brass band rendered honors as Roosevelt was helped into the back of the red convertible touring car. In his diary, Leahy described being accompanied off the base by a large police escort, and driving to Honolulu "through lines of soldiers and a cheering populace."[41]

The presidential party was quartered on Waikiki Beach, in a cream-colored stucco villa surrounded by soaring palm trees. The palatial mansion had once belonged to Chris Holmes, heir to the Fleishmann Yeast fortune;

during the war it was leased to the military to provide lodging for VIPs and visiting brass. Security was heavy. A company of marines guarded the walls and gate. Patrol boats hovered offshore. The coming three-day schedule would be long and exhausting, and the doctors insisted that the president go to bed early. After a private dinner with aides, he slept nine hours to the music of surf crashing on the nearby beach.

MACARTHUR AND RICHARDSON DINED at the latter's Fort Shafter residence, and afterward retired to their bedrooms. At 11:45 p.m., however, MacArthur sent word to Richardson, who was already in bed, that he would like to continue their conversation. "We sat up and talked until about 4:00 in the morning," Richardson recorded in his diary: "He did most of the talking, as I was dead tired."[42]

It is worth pausing to note that based upon the contemporaneous diary entries of Rhoades and Richardson, it appears that MacArthur went two consecutive nights with little sleep on the eve of the most important command conference of the war.

Referring to his recent misadventure in presidential politics, the SWPA commander protested "that he had been the subject of such vigorous attacks when he had nothing in God's world to gain now; that he was not at all ambitious and only wanted to do his duty." MacArthur ranged over personal territory, speaking sadly of his first marriage—"doomed to failure"—and sounded melancholy when he reflected that all he had left was his present wife, "a little southern gal," and his "little boy."[43]

Presumably MacArthur must have slept at least a few hours before returning to the Holmes villa on Thursday morning. From there he would accompany the president, Leahy, and Nimitz on a long day of inspection tours around Oahu. The party climbed into a large black hardtop sedan—Leahy in front, Nimitz wedged between Roosevelt and MacArthur in back—and departed at a quarter to eleven. Their route took them west, through the Marine Corps Air Station at Ewa, the naval installations around Barbers Point, and the ammunition depot at Lualualei. They passed a prisoner of war enclosure where Japanese prisoners stared curiously through the wire. At the supply depots, they drove down long, narrow alleys between walls of crates stacked 30 or 40 feet high. The crates were filled with ammunition, provisions, and every conceivable commodity, all awaiting transshipment to new advanced bases in the western Pacific. Oahu had become the ultimate showcase of the phenomenal power and scale of the American military juggernaut.

The president was surprised by how much the island had developed since his previous visit in 1934. It seemed scarcely possible, he later told reporters, that "any place could change as much as the Island of Oahu has."[44] A decade earlier, vacant or cultivated land had been abundant even on the plains surrounding Pearl Harbor and Honolulu. Now, newly built military bases and residential districts abutted one another directly, separated only by chain-link fences.

Escorted by a long motorcade of jeeps and motorcycles stretching to about a quarter of a mile, the car carrying the president and his three companions drove up the sparsely populated Waianae Coast, through green cane fields and native wildflowers. Even here, on the most isolated rural roads of the west Oahu backcountry, they encountered sentries who stood to attention by the roadside, their hands raised to their helmets in salute. At midday, the motorcade climbed a steep, winding blacktop road to Kolekole Pass, high in the Waianae mountains, where they took in a magnificent vista of Pearl Harbor and the many airbases spread out on the plain to the southeast. Here they were met by General Richardson in the red Packard touring car, and the cameras were turned off as FDR was carried by Mike Reilly, head of the Secret Service detail, from one vehicle to the other. The afternoon's itinerary would take them to Schofield Barracks, Oahu's largest army base.

FDR's visit was supposed to have been a secret, but the news had spread widely by word of mouth. The route into Schofield was lined with soldiers—and just behind them, crowded three- or four-deep, a host of cheering civilians. It seemed as if the entire population of Oahu not only knew that the president was on the island, but had somehow learned the route of his motorcade, and had turned out with the enthusiasm of spectators at a tickertape parade. Families brought picnic baskets and folding beach chairs. Young children perched on their fathers' shoulders. School-age boys and girls climbed banyan trees and sat in the branches, where they could see over the heads of those in front. Hawaii was a melting pot of many Asian and Pacific races and ethnicities, as well as *haole* (whites) and various others—but all equally craned their necks for a glimpse of the long red car with the twin American flags mounted on the front fenders, and the man in the backseat wearing a rumpled cream-colored linen suit and Panama hat.

Reilly called the visit "the worst kept secret I have ever known," and half expected one of the warplanes patrolling overhead to skywrite: "Welcome, Franklin D. Roosevelt."[45] He did not like the open touring car, observing that it would pass within 30 or 40 feet of thousands of spectators. Seated among the uniformed officers in the car, Roosevelt was easily identified even from a distance. Japanese-Americans represented Hawaii's single largest ethnic group, with a population of nearly 150,000. Even if the overwhelming majority were loyal—and by 1944 it was abundantly clear that this was so—it would take just one assassin to lob a grenade from the roadside, killing at a stroke both Pacific theater commanders, the chairman of the Joint Chiefs, and the president of the United States. The burly Reilly stood on the Packard's running board, leaned protectively over FDR, and kept his eye on the crowd—but there was no sign of trouble, and Japanese-Americans appeared to cheer as ardently as their fellow citizens.

Despite all that had passed between them, Roosevelt and MacArthur seemed pleased to be in each other's company. Each must have enjoyed the heady novelty of spending the day with the only other American whose national stature and popularity was on a par with his own. The impression is reinforced by the comments of eyewitnesses and by the film footage. Rigdon wrote that FDR was "particularly fond of General MacArthur and seemed genuinely glad to see him again, for the first time in seven years."[46] Dr. McIntire had often heard FDR talk about MacArthur with "sincere admiration," referring to him as a "friend" and "military genius."[47] On MacArthur's part, he recorded in his memoir that they "talked of everything but the war—of our old carefree days when life was simpler and gentler, of many things that had disappeared in the mists of time."[48] Not having seen the president in many years, MacArthur was taken aback by his diminished appearance. He predicted, accurately, that FDR would not survive another term in office. But after watching the president lifted like a child and carried from wheelchair to car and back again, the general "marveled at the spiritual strength Roosevelt obviously possessed in order to retain his mental acumen and wit in the face of evident physical deterioration."[49]

In the silent motion picture footage, the two men appear to evince sincere fondness for one another. Seated in the back of the car on the parade ground at Schofield, they seem lost in private conversation, their faces close together, each grinning broadly, like a pair of mischievous boys cooking up a prank. At some unrecorded quip of the president's, both erupt into full-throated laughter. Perhaps that was the moment (one can only speculate) when MacArthur asked about the upcoming election, and FDR replied, with deadpan earnestness, that he had not given the matter a single moment's thought. "I threw back my head and laughed," MacArthur later told Eichelberger. "He looked at me and then broke into a laugh himself and said, 'If the war in Germany ends before the election, I will not be reelected.'"[50]

At some point in the day, MacArthur remarked that FDR was the overwhelming favorite of U.S. troops in Australia, which was certainly true. Roosevelt told MacArthur that he (MacArthur) would have made a good

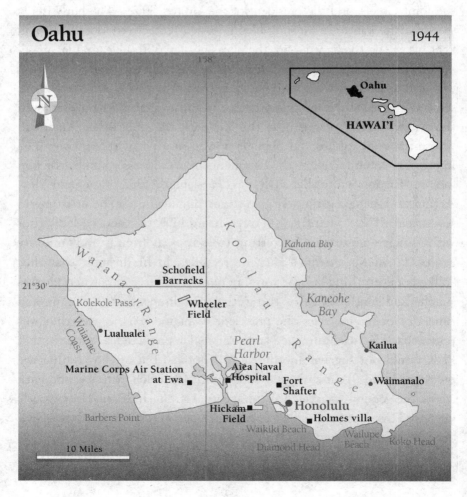

president, if all had gone differently. Now that Dewey was the Republican nominee, it cost the president nothing to pay his rival this compliment.

It is reasonable to infer that the feelings on both sides were mixed. Perhaps they were politicians, merely playing to the cameras. But they may also have been genuinely stirred by the awareness that they were making history, in the heart of America's great Pacific stronghold, amidst the acclamations of thousands, in a summit of warlords who knew that they would soon be masters of the Pacific.

Entering the front gate to Schofield at 12:35 p.m., the motorcade passed through seemingly endless files of tanks and other armored vehicles, through hangars and down the long plane-lined taxiways of Wheeler Field, and past the Post Hospital, where Japanese-American soldiers wounded in Italy saluted from the third-floor windows. The route was lined by soldiers standing to attention, their hands fixed to their helmets in salute. The 7th Infantry Division, 14,000 strong, was drawn up in ranks on the Schofield Parade Ground. The red touring car drove up onto a wooden platform, specially constructed for the purpose, and the president gave a short speech without leaving the vehicle. Fumbling with the microphone, he asked a technician to assist—but the device was already live, so FDR's befuddled queries were broadcast to thousands of men standing in ranks. MacArthur, Nimitz, and Leahy, still seated in the car with the president, wore their best poker faces.[51]

The day's public schedule concluded at 4:30 p.m., and all returned to their respective quarters. But MacArthur and Nimitz were back at the Holmes villa on Waikiki for dinner that evening. They were joined by Bill Halsey, who was preparing to take command of the fleet the following month, and Wilson Brown, who was (like Halsey) a veteran carrier task force commander. The six dined in the mansion's grand dining room, attended by Filipino mess stewards. After dinner, Halsey and Brown departed, and the remaining four discussed the war in a casual way for about two hours. At midnight they adjourned, but the formal conference had been scheduled for the following morning (Friday, July 28) in the same location—so after an overnight intermission, MacArthur, Nimitz, Leahy, and the president reconvened in the mansion's airy parlor, this time with a band of army and navy photographers and a motion picture crew.

The Pacific Fleet intelligence staff had prepared the room with large wall maps of the Philippines and the western Pacific. The session began with a fifteen-minute posed photo session, in which FDR and Leahy looked on as Nimitz and MacArthur took turns holding a bamboo pointer up to the map. Flashbulbs popped, and the film crew moved around in the background, trying different angles. The four men were patient while the cameramen did their work, cooperating willingly in posing for the scene. All were public figures, well accustomed to the ritual. When it was Nimitz's turn with the pointer, he moved it from Saipan, to Guam, to Tokyo, to the lower part of Japan's Inland Sea. But when MacArthur took it, he held it unmoving on the island of Luzon, his supreme objective in the Philippines.[52]

No minutes were kept of this historic debate at Waikiki. Once the film crew and photographers had finished their work and cleared the room, no staff were invited to remain. Accordingly, scholars and historians have been obliged to rely upon first- and second-hand recollections of the four participants. The record is thin. FDR gave a thumbnail synopsis to the historian Samuel Eliot Morison several months after the fact. Leahy recorded a brief summary in his diary and set out the issues in a memorandum to his fellow joint chiefs. Nimitz did not leave any direct account, although his views can be gleaned from cables he sent to King immediately before and after the conference.

MacArthur was the only one of the four to leave a detailed firsthand account of the conference. He reconstructed the entire scene, quoting himself at length, in his 1964 autobiography, *Reminiscences*. This book was published nineteen years after FDR's death, five years after Leahy's death, and two years before Nimitz's death, when the latter was in his dotage. The dialog in the scene appears to have been reconstructed entirely from memory. As a summary of the strategic issues under discussion, MacArthur's account is plausible. But it is characteristically self-serving, and some of its important particulars are at odds with other accounts subsequently given by MacArthur in private conversations.

A few examples may suffice. MacArthur told Bob Eichelberger (six weeks later) and Red Blaik (years later) that he was summoned to Hawaii without being informed of the purpose of his visit and did not learn that the president was there until he arrived. To Blaik he further maintained that George Marshall had deliberately withheld the information from him, so that he would "walk into such a trap."[53] In fact, as we have seen, MacArthur knew that the president would be at the forthcoming rendezvous, and spent much of his flight from Australia ranting to his staff and flight

crew about it. In a yarn he told to a military secretary after the war, Mac-
Arthur maintained that FDR had invited him to Washington for the conference, but "I made him cross over to Hawaii. That was as far as I was going
to leave my work."[54] That, too, was flimflam: MacArthur did not learn of
the president's trip until after it had been scheduled. In the account he gave
to Blaik, the conference took place on board the battleship *Missouri* in Pearl
Harbor, and was attended by Roosevelt's civilian political aides, including
Sam Rosenman and Elmer Davis. But the newly launched "Mighty Mo"
was not in the Pacific at that time, and no civilians or staff took part in
the formal strategy discussions. In presenting the case for a unified Pacific
theater command, MacArthur piously vowed that if FDR "desired a Navy
man as Supreme Commander, I would have willingly accepted the inevitable, as a military victory necessitated such a decision"—and although he
was the senior ranking officer in the Pacific, "I would be willing to accept a
subordinate position, to accomplish the general good."[55] Privately, to General Richardson, he confided that he "would never serve under the Navy."[56]

MacArthur even appears to contradict himself in the relevant passages
of his memoir. He credits FDR for being "entirely neutral in handling the
discussion," but four paragraphs later quotes the president as saying that
invading Luzon "would demand heavier losses than we can stand."[57]

One could go on, but with diminishing returns. MacArthur was a serial
confabulator, and his account of the July 1944 summit should be filtered
skeptically, especially with respect to certain self-serving assertions for
which no corroborating evidence can be found. Alas, his version has been
quoted freely and at length in biographies and histories of the Pacific War,
often without a word of caution. It is not hard to see why. MacArthur gives
us a scene endowed with tension and drama. It soars majestically over the
dreary intricacies of Pacific military planning. It casts MacArthur in the role
of protagonist, facing down a united front of opposition—and in the end
the hero prevails, by dint of genius and force of personality, over the navy
and his rival in the White House. But MacArthur's account does not do
justice to Roosevelt, who was a seasoned military strategist in his own right;
nor to Nimitz, who was already on record as being inclined to agree with
MacArthur that Luzon should precede Formosa; nor to Leahy, who was
looking past these intermediate operations to the ultimate problem: How
was Japan to be conquered without a bloody invasion?

The brief account FDR gave to Morison encapsulates MacArthur's views. After dinner on the twenty-seventh, Roosevelt looked up at a wall map of the Philippines, pointed to the southern island of Mindanao, and asked: "Douglas, where do we go from here?"

MacArthur replied, "Leyte, Mr. President, and then Luzon!"[58]

Morison added a cautionary footnote, noting that the president mistakenly placed the scene on the *Baltimore* rather than at the villa in Waikiki. But any doubt that FDR might have fudged the exact wording of the exchange was dispelled in 2015, when the personal diary of General Richardson was provided to the author. After being debriefed by MacArthur later the same night, Richardson made this entry:

"The president opened a conference after dinner by pointing to Mindanao and saying to General MacArthur: 'Now, Douglas, where do we go from here?' That was the fuse that touched off the discussion and MacArthur then elaborated his point of view and the strategy which he thought should be employed, all of which culminates in the taking of Luzon prior to any action against Formosa, China, or Japan."[59]

MacArthur's case for invading Luzon, which he had been refining for two-and-a-half years, was grounded in conventional principles of logistics and airpower. He championed an orthodox, "by the numbers" amphibious drive, with each new thrust covered by land-based airpower and a fleet train staging from relatively nearby harbors. He maintained that the island-dominated geography of Southern Oceania offered better prospects than regions to the north, where islands were separated by thousands of miles, and could be bombed only by aircraft carrier task forces. In MacArthur's theater, unlike in Nimitz's, land, sea, and ground-based air forces could advance together, coordinated for mutual support. Moreover, he argued, Luzon offered a wealth of potential landing beaches, so that the enemy could not concentrate forces against the initial landing—he had learned this lesson the hard way in December 1941—and terrain suitable for large-scale maneuvers, thus offering the hope of limiting casualties in ground fighting. MacArthur could draw upon intelligence and support from friendly guerillas on Luzon and other Philippine islands, whereas Formosa had been a Japanese colony since the nineteenth century, and much of its population was presumably hostile. Once in possession of Philippine airfields, American airpower would quickly win supremacy over the South China Sea, and could prey upon the shipping lanes linking Japan to its oil supply in the East Indies.

In MacArthur's re-creation of the scene, written from memory two decades later, he hurled these thunderbolts in an uninterrupted monologue, apparently holding the others in thrall. But in Leahy's account, committed to his diary shortly after the event, FDR was the maestro, addressing pertinent questions to both theater commanders, and probing expertly for the bottom line: "Roosevelt was at his best as he tactfully steered the discussion from one point to another and narrowed down the area of disagreement between MacArthur and Nimitz."[60] The president questioned MacArthur closely about enemy troop strength in the Philippines, and tried to nail down his casualty projections. According to the account given by MacArthur to Richardson, FDR asked, "How many Japs are there in the Philippine Islands?"

"About 100,000," MacArthur replied, "scattered all over the archipelago."

FDR said that he had been informed that there were "many more."

"I am in command there," said MacArthur, "and I would like to ask you where you got your information?"

The president did not reply directly, but gave his opinion that "to capture Luzon would be very bloody."[61]

In this version of the exchange, Roosevelt was obviously concerned about casualties, but there is no suggestion that he was leaning against the Luzon operation. He may only have been echoing what he had heard in his recent briefings with General Marshall, whose War Department intelligence staff believed there were at least 176,000 Japanese troops in the archipelago.[62] On that point, as it turned out, the president's doubts were well-founded, because even the War Department's estimates were low. At least 250,000 Japanese troops were in the Philippines in July 1944, and those numbers were swelling as new troopship convoys arrived from China, Manchuria, Burma, and Formosa.[*]

Did FDR arrive in Hawaii with a prior inclination to bypass Luzon? According to the recap given by MacArthur to Richardson just hours after the exchange, FDR had expressed his concern that the operation would

---

[*] MacArthur's G-2 (intelligence) staff consistently underestimated enemy troop strength in the archipelago by wondrous margins. The shortfall was especially striking in January 1945 as the invasion of Luzon began. MacArthur's intelligence chief, General Charles A. Willoughby, said there were 152,500 Japanese troops on the island. General Walter Krueger's subordinate Sixth Army G-2 staff put the number at 234,500. The actual number was at least 270,000.

be "very bloody." But twenty years later, in MacArthur's best-selling and oft-cited memoir, FDR is made to say: "But Douglas, to take Luzon would require *heavier losses than we can stand*" (emphasis added). The discrepancy invites close scrutiny. The implication that FDR was leaning against taking Luzon is not corroborated elsewhere in the historical record. The president had previously backed many invasions and operations bound to incur heavy casualties, including the Normandy invasion seven weeks earlier. For Roosevelt to suggest that the nation could not "stand" heavy troop losses, given the carnage occurring elsewhere in the world, would seem out of character. Questioning the general closely about his casualty projections was simply due diligence; the president asked similar questions of Nimitz about Formosa.

In any event, MacArthur responded to the president's query with a sermon against unwarranted and excessive bloodshed in Nimitz's theater. This was a debating tactic that he had employed since November 1943, when the Marine Corps lost a thousand men killed in action on Tarawa Atoll, the first step in the central Pacific offensive. The cudgels had been taken up by his allies in Congress and the American media—notably in the newspapers of William Randolph Hearst, where MacArthur was often praised for keeping his battlefield casualties in check. In his memoir, MacArthur maintains that he told Roosevelt: "Mr. President, my losses would not be heavy, any more than they have been in the past. The days of the frontal attack should be over. Modern infantry weapons are too deadly, and frontal assault is only for mediocre commanders. Good commanders do not turn in heavy losses."[63] According to Richardson's diary, MacArthur also predicted that a Formosa operation would be at least as bloody as Luzon, and added that "there had been less bloodshed in his area in all the campaigns—that there were less dead than in any other theater."[64]

Nimitz suffered these gibes with his customary German-Texan equanimity, letting them pass without rebuttal. But the implied criticism must have rankled, especially since his forces were suffering heavy combat losses in the Marianas at that very moment, and Douglas C-54 "flying ambulances" filled with wounded soldiers and marines were landing on Oahu each passing hour. Later, in a postwar analysis, Nimitz granted that the butcher's bill had generally been higher in the central Pacific than in the south, but called it a "common fallacy" to assume that the Japanese "would have acted as they did even had the Allies acted otherwise than as they did." Operations north of the equator had diverted enemy forces from the south—and if they had not done so, "the Southwest Pacific forces would have met far greater resistance in the New Guinea area."[65] Had he been inclined to bicker, Nimitz might also have pointed out that MacArthur had argued long and hard in favor of attacking Rabaul, the strongest Japanese position in his theater, until being ordered by the JCS to bypass it. And he could have added that a direct comparison of casualty figures in the two theaters was beside the point. What mattered was the cost in American casualties relative to the *inherent strategic value* of captured territory—and the seizure of islands north of the equator, closer to Japan, offered a more decisive contribution to victory.

On the morning of July 28, Nimitz took the floor and presented Admiral King's case to bypass Luzon in favor of Formosa. No doubt he made a competent presentation, but it seems to have been largely pro forma. Under FDR's close questioning, Nimitz did not disguise his reservations. Both Leahy and MacArthur noted that he was not wholly committed to CAUSEWAY.

Nimitz offered two specific concessions to the case for Luzon. First, he acknowledged that he could support the Luzon operation with existing forces, whereas he would likely need reinforcements to take Formosa. And second, as recorded by Leahy in his diary: "He admits that developments may indicate a necessity for the occupation of the Manila area."[66]

With that, Luzon was comfortably ahead of Formosa on points, even before taking into account the moral, political, and psychological dimensions of the issue. But MacArthur's knockout argument, which he had been rehearsing since departing Corregidor in March 1942, was that liberating "17 million loyal Christian Filipinos" was an American responsibility, tantamount to a blood-oath. "I argued that it was not only a moral obligation to release this friendly possession from the enemy, now that it had become possible, but that to fail to do so would not be understandable to the Oriental mind. . . . I felt that to sacrifice the Philippines a second time could not be condoned or forgiven."[67]

Bypassing Luzon, said MacArthur, would vindicate Japanese propaganda, which had always maintained that white men would not spill their blood for Asians. Luzon was home to about 7,000 American prisoners of war and thousands more Allied civilian internees. With each passing month, hundreds died in the camps, and bypassing the island would require a cold-blooded decision to let many more perish in abysmal captivity. As for the notion that bypassing Luzon might spare the island needless bloodshed and destruction, MacArthur was unmoved: "We had been thrown out of Luzon at the point of a bayonet and we should regain our prestige by throwing the Japanese out at the point of a bayonet."[68]

MacArthur's March 1942 declaration—"I shall return" to the Philippines—was one of the most famous public utterances of the war. But FDR's promises had been every bit as explicit, and the SWPA chief was not going to let him forget it. During the crisis of early 1942, as Japanese forces overran the Philippines, President Quezon had considered giving himself up to the enemy and suing for peace. MacArthur had half-endorsed this proposal on the grounds that it might alleviate the Filipino people's suffering. But FDR had rejected it categorically. In a letter to President Quezon he had pledged: "Whatever happens to the present American garrison, we shall not relax our efforts until the forces which we are now marshalling outside the Philippine Islands return to the Philippines and drive the last remnant of the invaders from your soil."[69] The wording of that oath would seem to leave little room for maneuver.

When Admiral King subsequently learned that MacArthur had strayed from the straight-and-narrow path of debating military strategy, he cried foul. He seemed to believe that the broader moral or foreign policy elements of the decision lay wholly outside any military officer's professional ambit. In postwar notes, he complained that MacArthur had "started in talking *not* of the military problem in the Pacific . . . but about the poor Philippines whom the United States had promised to free from the Japanese."[70] But here King diminished himself. If ever a commander had earned the right to petition for a decision on such grounds, MacArthur was that man. Since December 1941—and even since the Spanish-American War, one might say—American honor, prestige, and credibility had been at stake in the Philippines. Since the administration of Theodore Roosevelt, the chief aim of U.S. policy had been to assist the Filipino people in constructing a functioning democracy capable of repelling aggressors. The Philippines had been promised independence by 1946, and that commitment remained in force. For FDR, the successful decolonization of the Philippines was to set a righteous example for the world, and especially for the British. In this terrible global war, no major strategic decision could be separated from its long-term political or foreign policy consequences. In both Europe and the Pacific, the campaign against the Axis had entered its endgame, and a new postwar order was struggling to be born.

According to another anecdote that has become familiar through frequent repetition, MacArthur took FDR aside and bluntly warned that bypassing the Philippines would imperil the president's hopes of reelection. This hearsay can be traced to Courtney Whitney, a lawyer and reservist army officer who served under MacArthur during and after the war. In 1956, a dozen years after the Hawaii conference, Whitney published a MacArthur hagiography rife with myths and invented dialogue. In one passage, he has MacArthur tell FDR: "Mr. President, if your decision be to bypass the Philippines and leave its millions of wards of the United States and thousands of American internees and prisoners of war to continue to languish in their agony and despair—I dare to say that the American people would be so aroused that they would register the most complete resentment against you at the polls this fall."[71] This prolix tongue-lashing would have been, at the very least, a breach of protocol. Considering MacArthur's recent caper in party politics, it might even have been interpreted as a threat. Lacking corroboration, Whitney's anecdote is best understood as a fabulist's retelling of a story he had heard from another fabulist.

Others have gone even further, speculating that a clandestine bargain might have been struck in Hawaii, with the understanding that FDR would greenlight the Luzon operation in return for MacArthur's pledge to supply favorable headlines before the election. Proponents of this theoretical "secret handshake" admit that they can find no shred of evidence to support it.[72]

Whatever the truth, there seems little doubt that MacArthur gave Roosevelt an earful. According to Dr. McIntire, the president told him, "Give me an aspirin. In fact give me another aspirin to take in the morning. In all my life, nobody has ever talked to me the way MacArthur did."[73]

After lunch on the twenty-eighth, Roosevelt, Leahy, and Nimitz accompanied MacArthur to Hickam Field, where his C-54 was fueled and ready to take off. It seems that whatever was said in the car, MacArthur concluded that he had won his case. Leahy told him, as they parted, "I'll go along with you, Douglas."[74]

As MacArthur strode across the tarmac toward his waiting plane, the pilot Dusty Rhoades fell into step beside him. He asked the boss whether the conference had been a success. MacArthur glanced around to be sure no one was in earshot, then replied in a low voice: "Yes, everything. We are going on."

"To the Philippines?" asked Rhoades.

"Yes. It will not be announced for a few days yet, but we are on our way."

Nine hours later, when the Skymaster touched down on the airfield at Tarawa for a refueling stop, Rhoades entered the exchange into his diary. He noted that MacArthur was in a euphoric mood, "like a child with new toys."[75]

WITH MACARTHUR ON HIS WAY BACK TO AUSTRALIA, one might have expected FDR to retreat to his bed at the villa on Waikiki, or to his cabin on the *Baltimore*. But he had another day and a half remaining in Hawaii, and he was determined to see as much of Oahu as time would permit. For a man with terminal heart disease, FDR was exhibiting seemingly phenomenal powers of recuperation. This had been his pattern in the past: intervals of deep rest (as on the *Baltimore* during her passage from the mainland) followed by torrents of astonishing vitality. "Throughout this period of hectic activity," Dr. Bruenn observed in his clinical notes, "the President moved without obvious fatigue or difficulty of any kind."[76] That impression is confirmed in the film footage. He appears gaunt and frail, with large dark bags under his eyes; yet he somehow remains cheerful and animated while greeting scores of high-ranking officers, civilian VIPs, and servicemen. On Friday afternoon, the presidential motorcade drove up and over the rugged Koolau range to the east, to a jungle combat training program in the wild country around Kahana Bay on the island's windward coast. FDR remained seated in the back of the red touring car, hat pushed back on his forehead, and watched an hour-long live firing demonstration through binoculars. Green-clad infantrymen crawled under wire, then rose and advanced across a field in a line abreast, firing machine guns and flamethrowers from the hip. The finale was a coordinated practice assault on a plywood mockup of a Japanese village. Then the motorcade headed south on the coast road, stopped at the Naval Air Station at Kaneohe Bay, and returned to Waikiki (as the White House daily log noted) by way of "Kaialua, the Amphibious Base at Waimanalo, Koko Head, the Coast Guard Base at Wailupi and Diamond Head."[77]

The last day of the president's visit was largely devoted to visiting wounded servicemen recently returned from combat in the Marianas. The motorcade rolled into downtown Honolulu, where the narrow streets were flanked by packed crowds of spectators held back by national guardsmen. The president's car pulled to a stop outside the army's 147th General Hospital, where doctors and nurses were drawn up in ranks on the front steps. Patients stood on crutches or sat in wheelchairs, and a camera caught one earnest serviceman saluting the president with an arm wrapped in a plaster cast. After an hour touring the wards, FDR was back in the car and off to Naval Air Station, Honolulu—now the Honolulu International Airport— and then to Hickam Field, where one of the big four-engine Douglas "flying ambulances" had just touched down and taxied to a stop. As stretchers were lowered from the plane, patients were carried directly to the side of the president's vehicle. To their astonishment, wounded men just evacuated from Guam suddenly found themselves face to face with Franklin Delano Roosevelt. The presidential daily log noted, "What a surprise and cheer those boys showed on unexpectedly facing FDR."[78]

Among servicemen in the Pacific, there had been a pervasive feeling that the "folks back home" had forgotten them. The struggle against Nazi Germany had dominated print, radio, and newsreel reporting—and that was doubly true during that summer of 1944, when Allied forces were pouring into France and driving toward Paris. Since the start of the war, they had seen FDR touring military bases and war plants in every corner of the mainland United States, and they had seen him in exotic international locations such as Morocco, Egypt, and Persia. Until now, perhaps, they had not expected to see the president of the United States in the Pacific. His visit told them that they were not forgotten. The point deserves emphasis, because FDR's trip to Hawaii has often been framed as a publicity stunt to boost his reelection campaign.

At the Navy Yard, long rows of sailors stood along the route, saluting in unison as the motorcade hove into view. Men drawn up in ranks were under orders to gaze dead ahead—but as the president's car swept past, many could not resist stepping forward, wide-eyed and gaping, to try for a better look. Thousands of civilian yard workers were gathered three or four deep along the route. More were hanging out of the second- and third-story windows of administrative buildings. The motorcade drove into and through several cavernous workshops, then paused briefly at the submarine piers, where submarine crews stood to attention and saluted in unison. Stopping abreast of the battleship *Maryland*, then in drydock, the president received a short briefing on the ongoing repairs to her hull, which had been damaged five weeks earlier by an aerial torpedo off the coast of Saipan.[79]

The last stop of the day's inspection tour was the new Aiea Naval Hospital, which sat atop a hill east of Pearl Harbor. The motorcade pulled up shortly after three o'clock to find an expectant crowd gathered on the front steps. The staff and about fifty ambulatory and wheelchair patients were drawn up in ranks to greet the president, and the upper-story windows were crowded with more doctors, nurses, and patients who seemed eager to see the spectacle. A row of men standing on crutches saluted together, in unison. The president was to speak directly from the back seat of the open touring car, as he had been doing these past three days, and the communications team stepped forward to set up two microphones. One was for the public-address system, the president was told, and the other for the motion picture crew. As at Schofield two days earlier, FDR's befuddled queries were broadcast through the loudspeakers: "Which is which, that one or this one?" The crowd tittered; the nurses appeared especially entertained. Nimitz, seated next to FDR, smiled tolerantly. "I never can get accustomed to these new contraptions," the president told his audience. "I'm doing it twice, once for the movies and once for you good people."

Judging by the three minutes of rambling, unscripted remarks that followed, FDR had not given a single moment's thought to what he might say. He chatted with the assembly in a relaxed, conversational tone. He was glad to see them, he said; he had brought greetings ("at least in theory") from their families at home. He mentioned his personal role, together with that of Dr. McIntire, in conceiving and designing the Aiea hospital. He lauded the great gains that had been made since the First World War in caring for battlefield casualties, assuring his audience that "the whole country is very, very proud."[80] Whatever the state of his health, the president's voice was strong, and its familiar velvet tone was intact. Smiling warmly, he tossed his head and put the microphone down. The crowd's applause seemed wholehearted.

As always, the cameras were turned off before Mike Reilly lifted the president from the car and transferred him into his wheelchair. The photographers and film crews were not permitted to follow the president as he toured the 5,000-bed hospital, but several witnesses recorded their impressions. The wards were filled with young men who had been maimed in the fighting on Saipan and Guam. Many had lost limbs, or the use of limbs, or had suffered other grievous wounds from which they would never fully recover. To them, the handicapped Roosevelt embodied the possibility of a successful and fulfilling life. Dr. McIntire recalled that the president "wheeled through every ward, stopping at bedsides for chats, maybe a pat on the back, his voice as warmly affectionate as though the broken soldiers and sailors were his own sons. Always there was a kindling of new light in dull, despairing eyes."[81] In one ward, McIntire went ahead and was talking to a marine who "did not seem to have a whole bone left in his body."

> His face, ravaged by pain, was set in lines of utter dejection, but when
> he looked around and saw who was approaching, the youngster's mouth
> flew open in the widest and most delighted grin I have ever seen.
> "Gee!" he exclaimed. "The President!" So it was down the whole long
> line of beds in every ward. Not one of us but felt, actually *felt*, the wave
> of hope that swept the hospital as shattered men saw before them not
> merely the President of the United States but another human being,
> once struck down as they themselves were stricken, who had triumphed
> over physical disability by force of will and invincibility of spirit.[82]

McIntire, Leahy, and Rosenman each individually attested that they were deeply moved by the scene at Aiea. So indeed was the president. "I never saw Roosevelt with tears in his eyes," Rosenman recalled; "that day as he was wheeled out of the hospital he was close to them."[83]

THE PARTY WAS DUE TO SAIL from Pearl Harbor on the *Baltimore* that evening, but one last chore awaited the president. The "three ghouls" of the wire associations had not been invited on the various inspection tours—they had not been permitted anywhere near the president—and had been complaining about it with rising vehemence to Nimitz's press officer, Waldo Drake. At last, Steve Early (from his office in Washington) agreed to schedule a press conference. It took place on the manicured lawn of the Holmes villa on Waikiki Beach, with FDR seated on a wicker garden couch and the journalists drawn up in a semicircle. The three wire service men were joined by about two dozen war correspondents accredited by Pacific Fleet headquarters. The coconuts on the palm trees that towered overhead had been removed, lest one should fall and strike the president.

In the film footage, Roosevelt appears physically exhausted. His shoulders are visibly slumped and his head sags as he speaks. But he offers a genial smile as he greets the reporters and shakes several hands. Leahy and Nimitz stand at the end of the couch, the latter with his arms folded over his chest; both admirals appear to listen with intense interest.[84]

FDR began off-the-cuff, speaking of his admiration for the military personnel and civilians of Oahu, who had recovered so dramatically from the carnage of December 7, 1941. He called the conference with MacArthur and Nimitz "one of the most important we have held in some time." Seeing General MacArthur again, after an interval of seven years, had been personally gratifying. It had been essential to hear his and Nimitz's firsthand views in advance of the big strategic decisions that lay ahead. So valuable was the conference, said FDR, that it would have been "awfully hard to get along without it."[85]

Questions followed, but the president gave the newsmen little of substance. Was another major offensive being planned in the Pacific? Yes, he replied, but that could be deduced from the pattern of the war up to that point, so it should not be considered news.

Was there to be any new "emphasis or speedup" in the Pacific offensive? "Neither one nor the other."

Would General MacArthur liberate the Philippines, as he had pledged to do?

"We are going to get the Philippines back, and without question General MacArthur will take a part in it. Whether he goes direct or not, I can't say."

The remaining half of the press conference was devoted to the Allied doctrine of "unconditional surrender." A reporter (not identified) asked, "Are we going to make that our goal out here in the Pacific?"[86]

Defining "unconditional surrender" had been a recurring nuisance since FDR had first articulated the controversial formula—suddenly and rashly, it seemed to many—at a press conference in Casablanca in January 1943. Although the doctrine had been discussed in Allied conferences, British prime minister Winston Churchill had not agreed to it before the president blurted it out to an audience of international newsmen. The president's public statement made it a *fait accompli*, however, and Churchill was left with no choice but to affirm British support. FDR was determined to avoid a reprise of the peace that followed the First World War, when a German "stab in the back" myth ignited the rise of the Nazi party. But many Allied military and civilian leaders privately believed that broadcasting a demand for unconditional surrender was a costly blunder—that the Axis nations would seize upon the announcement as evidence that the Allies intended to destroy and enslave them, thus reinforcing the determination of their military forces and civilians to fight to the last ditch. Some historians of the Third Reich have concluded that FDR's announcement undercut anti-Hitler plots within the German army, and may have prolonged the European war.

Apart from the immediate boost it provided to Nazi and Japanese domestic propaganda, the "unconditional surrender" formulation was troublesome because it was ambiguous. It was easier to define it in the abstract than to explain how it would be applied in practice. Efforts to clarify it only tended to raise more questions. Whatever answers were given in public could be (and were) seized upon and distorted by the Axis propaganda mills.

FDR drew his inspiration from an apocryphal version of the meeting between Ulysses S. Grant and Robert E. Lee at Appomattox Court House, Virginia, at the close of the American Civil War. Because the formula would assume great importance in the last phase of the Pacific War, it is worth quoting FDR's response to the journalist's question in full.

"Back in 1865," he told the newsmen, "Lee was driven into a corner back of Richmond, at Appomattox Court House. His army was practically starving, had had no sleep for two or three days, his arms were practically expended."

> So he went, under a flag of truce, to Grant. Lee had come to Grant thinking about his men. He asked Grant for his terms of surrender.
> Grant said, "Unconditional surrender."
> Lee said he couldn't do that, he had to get some things. Just for example, he had no food for more than one meal for his army.
> Grant said, "That is pretty tough."
> Lee then said, "My cavalry horses don't belong to us, they belong to our officers and they need them back home."
> Grant said, "Unconditional surrender."
> Lee then said, "All right. I surrender," and tendered his sword to Grant.

Grant said, "Bob, put it back. Now, do you unconditionally
surrender?"

Lee said, "Yes."

Then Grant said, "You are my prisoners now. Do you need food for
your men?"

Lee said, "Yes. I haven't got more than enough for one meal more."

Then Grant said, "Now, about those horses that belong to the
Confederate officers. Why do you want them?"

Lee said, "We need them for the spring plowing."

Grant said, "Tell your officers to take the animals home and do the
spring plowing."

There you have unconditional surrender. I have given you no new
term. We are human beings—normal, thinking human beings. That is
what we mean by unconditional surrender.

As Civil War history, the account was badly mistaken. Twice during his earlier campaigns in the West, but not at Appomattox, Grant had demanded
the "unconditional surrender" of a rebel force. In each case (Fort Donelson
and Vicksburg), Grant subsequently engaged in face-to-face negotiations
with the opposing commander, and agreed to a surrender with conditions.
At Appomattox, Grant did *not* insist that Lee surrender unconditionally,
even as a formality, and he readily agreed to put the Confederate general's
conditions into the surrender document.

But the factual errors did not matter so much as the themes Roosevelt
intended to emphasize in this parable of Grant and Lee. He was determined that the Axis powers should recognize that they had been utterly
and permanently defeated. No doubts or ambivalence on this score could
be permitted to intrude into the proceedings, either at the time of surrender
or in the long lens of history. Therefore, it was necessary to insist upon the
formality of an unconditional surrender. Behind that formality, however, lay
the implied promise of a magnanimous peace. It might even be said that the
lesson of FDR's parable was that if the Germans and Japanese would first
agree to surrender unconditionally, they could anticipate that all reasonable
requests would subsequently be granted. But what requests were reasonable?
And how could the defeated nations know in advance, without appearing
to bargain? Therein lay the intractable problem with the "unconditional
surrender" formulation. It was, in a sense, a paradox. In plain terms, it stated

that the victors would treat the vanquished as they chose, without regard to their wishes or interests. But its tacit meaning, according to FDR, was very nearly the opposite.

A reporter at Waikiki laid his finger on the problem when he asked a follow-up question. Would the Allies, like General Grant, offer to feed the defeated Axis armies? FDR dodged the question—rather curtly, it seems from the transcript. But such questions would continue to be asked, and the answers would continue to flummox Allied leaders. Every attempt to clarify the formula only prompted more questions, and that irksome cycle would continue even after FDR's death, literally until the last week of the Second World War.

As the *Baltimore* put to sea that evening from Pearl Harbor, Admiral Leahy collected his thoughts and committed them to his diary. General MacArthur, he observed, "seems to be chiefly interested in retaking the Philippines," and had not yet given much thought to the endgame in the Pacific. But both MacArthur and Nimitz had expressed agreement in principle that "Japan can be forced to accept our terms of surrender by the use of sea and air power without an invasion of the Japanese homeland."[87] In the long run, Leahy believed, this consensus of the two theater commanders—that an invasion of Japan should be avoided—was to have greater significance than the immediate question of whether to strike first at Luzon or Formosa.

The potential use of atomic bombs had not yet entered the calculation. FDR and Leahy were among the handful of Allied leaders who were fully briefed on the Manhattan Project. MacArthur and Nimitz knew nothing of it, and would not be informed until the following year. In the summer of 1944, it was not yet clear whether the bomb could be built at all, or whether it would be ready in time for the war's final act. Admiral Leahy, who had once been a naval explosives specialist, doubted that it would work. Still, he was absolutely sure that the war could be (and must be) won by some combination of a sea blockade and aerial bombardment, followed by a truce and a peaceful occupation of Japan by Allied forces.

But if the Pacific War was to end with a bloodless surrender, someone in Tokyo would have to speak for the Japanese regime. Who was that to be? A prime minister, a general? Or was it to be Hirohito, the putatively divine *Showa* emperor? With victory in sight, the "old Japan hands" in the Allied governments were debating a critical unknown. What exactly was

Hirohito's status? Was he a figurehead, a puppet controlled by the military? Or did he wield real power? Could he play the part of Lee to FDR's Grant? The answers bore heavily on strategic and diplomatic choices that Allied leaders would have to confront well before the end of the Pacific campaign.

FDR and his representatives had repeatedly asked Josef Stalin for assurances that the Soviet Union would join the war against Japan after the defeat of Nazi Germany. In mid-1944, this was the American government's single greatest objective in its diplomacy with Moscow. But would the Red Army really be needed against Japan? That obviously depended on the relative durations of the Pacific and European campaigns. But even putting that dimension of the problem aside, another vital uncertainty loomed ahead. In the event that the regime in Tokyo *did* surrender, would Japan's vast overseas armies—in Manchuria, Korea, China, and elsewhere—also lay down arms? Or would they fight to the last man, as they had done in every battle of the war? Many Allied military commanders stated flatly that no Japanese ground force would ever willingly surrender, even if the government in Tokyo gave up—and predicted that they would have to be eradicated root and branch in whatever territory they occupied. If that was the case, the Americans badly wanted the Soviets to invade Manchuria and destroy Japan's million-man Kwantung Army. Likewise, they wanted the Nationalist forces of Chiang Kai-shek to do most of the fighting (and the dying) in China. On the other hand, if Hirohito could be persuaded to order his far-flung armies to capitulate, and if those armies would obey the distant man-god's command, the Pacific War might be won more quickly and with less bloodletting than the pessimists anticipated. In that case, the Russians might not be needed in the war against Japan, which meant that the Americans need not horse-trade with Stalin for his commitment, which would alter the balance of power in the complicated global struggle that was not yet called the Cold War. These various and perplexing considerations would come to bear on vital decisions in the year to come.

THE BALTIMORE AND HER ESCORTING DESTROYERS headed north from Oahu, and once safely beyond the offing (far enough so that they could not be observed from land) they set a base course of 353 degrees at speed 22 knots. FDR retreated to his cabin and was rarely seen in the following week, sleeping long hours and seeming to do little work. Their destination was the Aleutian Islands, where the president would inspect the region's naval and air bases.

At home, where the sound and fury of the election campaign was at full blast, Republicans and opposition newspapers had charged that FDR, his entourage, and his dog were on a Pacific pleasure cruise at the taxpayers' expense. In his diary, Admiral Leahy wrote that the Hawaii conference had been justifiable and necessary, but he was skeptical of the value of this Alaskan side-jaunt. As a former chief of naval operations, he was sensitive to the insinuation that American warships had been deployed solely for the president's comfort or recreation, especially in wartime. But there is no evidence that he shared these misgivings with his friend and boss.

On August 9, with the ship engulfed in pea-soup fog in Alaska's Inside Passage, FDR wrote a warm personal note of thanks to MacArthur, declaring that "to see you again gave me a particular happiness." Regarding the Philippines, the president wrote, "As soon as I get back I will push on that plan for I am convinced that on the whole it is logical and can be done. . . . Someday there will be a flag-raising in Manila—and without question I want you to do it."[88]

On the strength of this letter, and a second "Dear Douglas" the following month, many scholars and biographers have asserted categorically that the president granted MacArthur's wish to liberate the Philippines. But the facts are more nuanced, and the story more convoluted. The ultimate decision to send MacArthur back to Luzon was not confirmed until the end of September, more than two months after the Honolulu conference. In the interim, it seemed entirely possible to all concerned that Luzon might be bypassed, at least momentarily, in favor of an all-out assault on Formosa.

On August 1, two days out of Pearl Harbor, news had arrived on the *Baltimore* that President Quezon of the Philippines had died in a hospital in Saranac Lake, New York. Both MacArthur and Roosevelt had made many promises to Quezon and his countrymen. MacArthur's had been more public, but FDR's were no less clear and binding. In the long run, both men knew, FDR's promises would be laid bare in the historical record. In MacArthur's mind, a decision to bypass Luzon would constitute a disgraceful betrayal, and he would do his utmost to convince posterity to censure FDR. It is fair to infer that Roosevelt, as a keen student of history, perceived this latent threat to his posthumous reputation. In writing to pledge support for a "flag-raising in Manila," FDR knew that his secretary, Grace Tully, would deposit a carbon copy of the letter into his outgoing correspondence file, which would eventually find its way (under the heading "MacArthur") into his presidential library at Hyde Park, where it would serve as a flashing neon billboard for future historians.

But what exactly did Roosevelt promise MacArthur? Just as in his earlier letters to Quezon, the president chose his words carefully, and they should be parsed carefully—not only for what they say, but for what they do not say. "I will *push on that plan*." As commander in chief, FDR possessed the undisputed constitutional authority to order MacArthur into Luzon, either before or instead of the contemplated Formosa invasion, regardless of what the Joint Chiefs advised. But he held that power in abeyance. "*Someday* there will be a flag-raising in Manila." The president said nothing of timing, and such a pledge could even be fulfilled in a postwar ceremony. To the correspondents in Waikiki he had said, "We are going to get the Philippines back, and without question General MacArthur will take a part in it. Whether he goes direct or not, I can't say."[89] The newspapers were barred from printing that statement, but it seemed to leave the door open to all options under consideration. His slapdash conflation of "the Philippines" with the main northern island of Luzon was shrewdly ambiguous. In fact, the JCS had already authorized (in March 1944) the capture of Mindanao, the big island at the southern end of the archipelago, so MacArthur had already received orders to liberate a major portion of the Philippines.[90]

It is not known precisely what FDR and Leahy said to MacArthur on their last day together in Hawaii, but the SWPA chief told his C-54 pilot that he had received three specific verbal commitments. His troops would be brought up to full strength with fresh replacements from the United States, his Fifth Air Force would be reinforced with new fighters and bombers, and the Pacific Fleet's carrier task forces would be deployed to support his amphibious landings in the Philippines (wherever and whenever they might occur).[91] He was in an ebullient mood during the flight from Oahu to Brisbane. One can only imagine his outrage, then, upon arriving at his SWPA headquarters to find a new cable from Washington confirming an intention to bypass Luzon and land troops in Formosa at the "earliest practicable date." The message had been sent by the planning staff of the JCS, and was dated July 27, the same day FDR and MacArthur had first met in Hawaii. The Washington planners warned that "Some SoWesPac air, ground, and service forces would be necessary in CAUSEWAY (Operation against Formosa)"—and added that those assets would not be returned to MacArthur afterward, but retained by Nimitz for "post–CAUSEWAY operations." MacArthur should plan for the "eventual complete reoccupation" of Luzon and the rest of the Philippines, but—here was a twist of the knife— "These operations would be conducted without the direct support of the Pacific Fleet."[92]

It was a planning-level message, meaning that it did not have the imprimatur of the four JCS principals. But it directly contradicted the conclusions MacArthur had taken away from Hawaii, and he must have wondered if he had been bamboozled. He wrote directly to General Marshall, expressing his "strongest nonconcurrence" with the assumptions of the JCS planners, and insisted that liberating all of the Philippines was essential from the "highest point of view of national policy." Condemning the proposed invasion of Formosa as a course "fraught with the gravest danger of disaster," he noted that President Roosevelt had already stated that the Philippines would be recovered. Worse yet, MacArthur wrote, the bypass proposal carried a "more sinister implication"—it would impose a complete sea blockade on the Philippines, leading to a famine that might starve millions of innocent Filipinos, as well as Allied prisoners and internees, and such an outcome "would exceed in brutality anything that has been perpetrated by our enemies."[93]

But this jeremiad made little impression on the planners in Washington. They were under instructions to consider purely military factors. Political or foreign policy arguments lay outside their scope of authority. The in-house JCS planning apparatus has received negligible attention in most histories, and none at all in most FDR and MacArthur biographies, but it held great sway over strategic decisions in the Pacific. The subject is somewhat dismal, requiring the researcher to descend into a labyrinth of committee memoranda and planning studies. Much of the relevant material was not declassified until the 1970s, when some of the most widely read histories of the war had already been published. For that reason, the point needs emphasis: whatever passed between Roosevelt and MacArthur in Hawaii, the gears of the JCS planning machine continued to turn in Washington, and influential voices (especially on the JSSC) continued to argue that the Pacific campaign should be consolidated on the northern line of attack. To MacArthur's disgust and frustration, this remained the governing assumption even after the Hawaii conference.

Those internal mechanisms of the JCS would have been irrelevant if FDR had peremptorily overruled his military chiefs, as he had done at least a dozen times before. The Constitution gave him the power to put his finger down on a map and tell his generals and admirals to attack. Most dramatically, the president had decided in favor of Operation TORCH, the November 1942 invasion of North Africa, over the unanimous resistance of his service chiefs. But most such presidential overrulings had occurred in the first year of the war, and a lot had changed between 1942 and 1944. The in-house planning and study committees of the JCS organization had barely existed in 1942; by 1944 they were fully staffed-up, and included some of the best strategic minds in the armed forces. In the later stages of the war, FDR allotted more of his time and attention to postwar planning and diplomacy, and less to the brass tacks of strategy and military operations. He trusted Leahy to act as his agent on the JCS, and although Leahy backed MacArthur's "Luzon-first" policy, he did not move to preempt the ongoing planning and preparations for CAUSEWAY. At a special meeting of the JCS on August 22, the admiral argued that Luzon would be "less costly in life and resources and not more costly in time" than the alternatives, but he did not say that Formosa should be ruled out, and did not press for an immediate decision.[94] That was hardly a resounding endorsement of MacArthur's position. Assuming that Leahy and Roosevelt were in harmony, as they generally were, it appears that the president chose to allow the JCS planning process to continue without his interference.*

Out in the Pacific, meanwhile, the naval and ground commanders to whom it would fall to execute CAUSEWAY remained skeptical of the operation. The more they studied Formosa, the less they liked it. Admiral Forrest Sherman, the forty-seven-year-old wunderkind who served as Nimitz's deputy chief of staff—in 1949 he would become the youngest CNO in the navy's history—told colleagues that it was "ridiculous" to propose an amphibious landing on Formosa while "leaving Luzon with all its airfields and available supplies and everything on the flank."[95] Sherman said he

---

* Samuel Eliot Morison, who was in direct touch with several of the principals, concluded of the Honolulu conference: "Actually no firm decision was made—that was for the J.C.S.—but an agreement was reached on major strategy. . . . The J.C.S. do not seem to have been particularly impressed by this top-level accord, since they continued to argue the questions 'Luzon, Formosa, or what?' for months afterward." Morison, *Leyte*, vol. 12, pp. 10–11.

intended to sabotage CAUSEWAY by writing a draft operations plan that was "so obviously bad that they would cancel the idea."[96] Richmond Kelly Turner, the Pacific Fleet's leading amphibious specialist, to whom it would fall to command the amphibious fleet in the operation, threw his influence against CAUSEWAY on similar grounds.

Each new draft of the army's CAUSEWAY plan called for more troops. The Joint Chiefs planners had assumed that American forces could seize and defend a handful of strategic ports on the coast, but the Pacific commanders concluded that they would probably have to conquer and garrison the entire island. Formosa was a large, rugged landmass populated by people who might be loyal to the Japanese, so the job would be long and bloody. On August 18, 1944, Nimitz estimated that the operation would require 505,000 army troops, 154,000 marines, and 61,000 navy shore personnel.[97] Those were huge numbers, and delivering them would be difficult, especially as it became clear that the war in Europe would last into 1945. CAUSEWAY would be comparable in size to the Normandy invasion (OVERLORD), but instead of staging it across the English Channel, the fleet and amphibious forces would have to leap from the Marianas across a thousand miles of open ocean. The Herculean shipping and logistics effort would divert scarce resources from other priorities, such as the development of B-29 bases on Saipan and Guam. Admiral Towers called King's attention to this problem, noting that "the Army Air Force would fight any change" in the scheduled airfield development program.[98] Thus, by late August 1944 the Formosa operation had earned another powerful enemy on the JCS—General Henry "Hap" Arnold of the Army Air Forces, who foresaw that the Marianas (rather than China) would serve as the major launch pad for strategic bombing of the Japanese homeland.

Most importantly, perhaps, Admiral Spruance remained implacably opposed to the Formosa operation and was determined to substitute his preferred Iwo Jima–Okinawa one-two punch. Upon returning to Pearl Harbor in August 1944, Spruance began building a case against CAUSEWAY. Like Sherman, he assumed that the disadvantages of Formosa were so obvious that the plan would be cancelled, and told his staff to pay no attention to it.

At a planning conference in early September, General Simon Bolivar Buckner of the army was briefing Nimitz and the CINCPAC staff on his preparations for CAUSEWAY. Spruance apparently concluded that Buckner's presentation was a waste of time. He stood up, begged pardon to interrupt, walked to the back of Nimitz's office, pulled down a wall chart of the western Pacific, and began speaking. The other officers turned their chairs toward Spruance, leaving Buckner seething with indignation, and listened as the admiral laid out his grand vision for the final phase of the Pacific War. Marine Major General Graves B. Erskine said it was "one of the most professional off-the-cuff estimates of the situation for an operation that I think I've ever heard."[99] Spruance demolished the assumptions underlying the CAUSEWAY operation, arguing that Okinawa was a better target in every respect. Okinawa could not be taken before the following spring—another six months was needed to build up the necessary fleet, air, and logistics capabilities—but he anticipated that he could do it by March or April 1945. That timetable would leave ample time for MacArthur to secure the Philippines, including Luzon. Formosa could be safely bypassed.

Spruance was a reserved figure who did not normally speak so forcefully to Nimitz, especially in the presence of others. By deviating from his usual phlegmatic style, he must have made a powerful impression. Nimitz trusted Spruance more than any other officer in his chain of command, and since it would fall to him to execute the operation, his opinion was uniquely influential.

Even then, CAUSEWAY died a lingering death. On September 9, 1944, the JCS ordered MacArthur and Nimitz to cooperate in seizing the island of Leyte, in the central Philippines, with a target date of December 20. But the chiefs directed that planning should continue for subsequent landings on both Luzon and Formosa, and "A firm decision as to whether Luzon will be occupied before Formosa will be made later."[100]

In a meeting at his Brisbane headquarters three days later, MacArthur told General Eichelberger, "At the present time . . . all I have won out on is the agreement that we will go up to and including Leyte. The question of whether or not the route will be by Luzon or Formosa has not yet been settled in Washington."[101] Upon his return from Hawaii six weeks earlier, MacArthur had led his staff to believe that he had secured a presidential decision to liberate all of the Philippines. Evidently, he had not understood that FDR intended to leave the matter in the hands of the JCS. That week MacArthur received another letter from the president, written from the Allied OCTAGON conference in Quebec. FDR told him that "the situation is just as we left it at Hawaii though there seems to be some efforts to do bypassing which you would not like. I still have the situation in hand."[102] The elusive phrasing again begged the question: If FDR had already decided for MacArthur, why didn't the president simply issue orders for the invasion of Luzon?

Meanwhile, events in the Pacific were quickly rendering past planning assumptions obsolete. In mid-September, the Third Fleet's carrier airstrikes in the Philippines revealed that enemy air strength throughout the region was surprisingly weak. On September 12, an American fighter was shot down near the island of Cebu. The pilot ditched his plane at sea, got ashore, and was told by local natives that there were only about 15,000 Japanese troops on Cebu and none on Leyte. Admiral Halsey radioed this intelligence to Nimitz, recommending that American forces be landed on Leyte as soon as possible. Nimitz passed the message up the chain to Admiral King and the JCS, who were in Quebec with FDR. By the end of the day on September 16, the chiefs had moved the landing date for Leyte up by a full two months, to October 20, 1944.

Five days later, in a long cable to the JCS, MacArthur laid out his overall vision for the future course of the Pacific War. From Leyte he proposed to jump directly to Luzon, landing four amphibious divisions at Lingayen Gulf by December 20. This operation would require "support by the full resources of the United States Pacific Fleet," but once ashore on Luzon, MacArthur would recover Manila and its bay by the end of February. "This will permit of the launching of contemplated operations to the northward on the schedule now projected with the great advantage of [Luzon] bases and land-based air support. The [Formosa] operation will then be unnecessary and, particularly with a prior attack on [Iwo Jima], a direct move may be made on [Kyushu]."[103]

MacArthur's vision had obvious merit. His proposed chronology of operations could be achieved with forces already in the Pacific, and did not call for redeployments from Europe. It would keep MacArthur *and* Nimitz's forces continuously engaged against the enemy, while avoiding the one operation (Formosa) that virtually no one in the theater liked. Subsequent events would show that it matched up closely to the actual course of the war, omitting only the invasion of Okinawa. Even MacArthur's projected dates were close to the mark: in the end, he landed in Lingayen Gulf on January 9, 1945, and secured Manila in early March. Thus it can be said that in mid-September 1944, MacArthur and Spruance—who did not know one another and had scarcely any direct contact—had together provided a final blueprint to win the Pacific War.

Now it remained only for Admiral King to admit defeat. He was due to meet Nimitz in San Francisco at the end of September at one of their periodic COMINCH-CINCPAC conferences. CAUSEWAY's opponents in Pearl Harbor prepared their chief for the upcoming rendezvous. General Buckner, the prospective ground commander for CAUSEWAY, signed a letter stating that service troops allocated to the operation were "far short of the forces required," and added that the army could take Okinawa with existing resources.[104] Forrest Sherman prepared a paper recommending that MacArthur's recommendations for the Philippines and Spruance's for Iwo Jima and Okinawa be approved by the JCS. After taking about three minutes to skim it, Spruance handed it back to Sherman and said, "I wouldn't change a word of it."[105]

In San Francisco, Spruance recalled, King continued to argue the case for CAUSEWAY, "but finally gave in and said he would recommend [Luzon-Iwo Jima-Okinawa] to the Joint Chiefs of Staff in Washington, which he did."[106] On October 3, the JCS issued new directives sending MacArthur into Luzon in December 1944, the marines into Iwo Jima in January 1945, and a large combined navy-army-marine force into Okinawa in March 1945. That fixed the sequence of major operations for the last year of the Pacific War.

Up to this point, Ernest J. King had been accustomed to getting his way in the Pacific. In April 1942 he had bargained successfully with General Marshall for a dual-theater command, with the northern half of the Pacific under naval authority. He had stood up to the British, who had wanted to demote the Pacific campaign to a defensive holding operation pending the defeat of Germany. He had championed an early invasion of Guadalcanal over the objections of the South Pacific commanders who would carry it out. Against MacArthur's ardent opposition, King had won JCS approval to seize the Gilberts in 1943, the Marshalls in early 1944, and the Marianas in mid-1944. He had crushed MacArthur's hopes of obtaining command of the Pacific Fleet and dominion over the entire Pacific theater. But in arguing for an invasion of Formosa, King had finally met his match.

Later, reflecting on the triumph of Mao Zedong's communists in the Chinese Civil War in 1949, King regretted that neither he nor anyone else had offered an effective rebuttal to MacArthur's political arguments for Luzon. China was the most populous nation in the world, with the potential to become the dominant power in Asia. China's political future was of vital interest to the United States and the world. That was not necessarily true of the Philippines. If it was fair game for MacArthur to argue for Luzon by referring to the "highest point of view of national policy," an even stronger case might have been made for Formosa on the same grounds.

Could the course of Asian history have been diverted by a different strategy in the last phase of the Pacific War? Posterity can only speculate. Alas, wrote King, the chance was fumbled away, because "little was said about the other basic idea of arranging to help the Chinese help themselves. . . . It seemed to me that Mr. Roosevelt was fated to decide for the 'poor' Philippines, although in the long view he was misled by the short view."[107]

Chapter Two

IN EARLY 1942, AS THE UNITED STATES WAS IN THE THROES OF WAR
mobilization, Alexander P. de Seversky published a manifesto entitled
Victory Through Air Power. Seversky's argument, that strategic bombing
would do most of the work of winning the Second World War, appealed to
Americans, who dreaded the specter of another bloody ground campaign
in Europe. The book topped the bestseller lists and sold 5 million copies.
The following year, Walt Disney adapted it into an animated documentary
feature film, and the same creative team that had made *Dumbo* and *Bambi*
turned their talents to rendering hand-drawn technicolor scenes of burning
and desolated Axis cities.

Seversky was a true believer and an evangelist. He was also a leading aircraft manufacturer, an entrepreneur who had sold thousands of airplanes to the U.S. Army Air Forces (USAAF) and hoped to sell tens of
thousands more before the war was won. His book earned him plenty of
goodwill with his clients, who adopted it as their secular bible. But the
Seversky Corporation had done no business with the navy, a fact that may
explain the author's comments on aircraft carriers: "Ship-borne aviation
is necessarily helpless against the enemy's land-based aviation, and the
'bases' themselves are extremely vulnerable. Navies have been disqualified
for what used to be one of their primary jobs: to take the offensive initiative against enemy shores."[1]

By 1944, that portion of Seversky's argument had been debunked by
the exploits of Task Force 58, the main carrier striking force of the Pacific
Fleet. Nothing like it had ever been seen on the high seas, nothing like it
has existed since 1945, and it is unlikely that a fighting fleet will ever again

be built on such a scale. The mighty armada typically comprised twelve to sixteen aircraft carriers with a screen of battleships, cruisers, and destroyers. Its great size rendered it omnipotent in whatever part of the ocean it occupied. Task Force 58 could put more than a thousand warplanes into the air in thirty minutes, send them to attack an enemy 200 miles away, and recover them safely when they returned. The planes attacked with bombs, torpedoes, rockets, incendiary .50-caliber machine-gun fire, and napalm. They punched craters in runways, killed pilots and mechanics in their beds, strafed and bombed parked planes, and turned airfield hangars and machine shops into smoking rubble. Vice Admiral Marc Mitscher, commander of Task Force 58, told a colleague, "There are just so many Jap planes on any island. We'll go in and take it on the chin. We'll swap punches with them. I know I'll have losses, but I'm stronger than they are. . . . I don't give a damn now if they do spot me. I can go anywhere and nobody can stop me. If I go in and destroy all their aircraft, their damned island is no good to them anyhow."[2]

The standard American carrier fighter of this era was the Grumman F6F Hellcat, a machine that weighed 9,000 pounds unloaded and was powered by a muscular 2,000-horsepower Pratt and Whitney engine. The Hellcat outflew and outfought its chief adversary, the much lighter Mitsubishi Zero. It matched the Zero's climbing speed below 14,000 feet and climbed faster at higher altitudes; in level flight or a dive it was *much* faster. "I was amazed at how much power the engine produced," said a veteran pilot who had flown the previous-generation F4F Wildcat. "It seemed like the airplane just leaped off the ground; the take-off roll was so short compared to the Wildcat's. And once airborne, the Hellcat seemed to want to climb and climb and climb."[3] Its six .50-caliber machine guns could literally tear the Zero wing from wing. With steel armor plating and self-sealing fuel tanks, the brawny Grumman could stand up to considerable punishment in air combat. Often the Hellcats recovered safely on their carriers with wings and fuselage thoroughly perforated by bullets and shell fragments.

On a typical "strike day," reveille sounded at 3:00 a.m. A bugler played flight quarters through the ship's loudspeakers, and the boatswain's mates shouted: "Reveille! Reveille! Reveille! All hands! Up all bunks!"[4] Throughout the ship was heard the dogging down of hatches and the slamming of doors, and hundreds of pairs of feet scampered across steel decks. On the hangar deck, in a hot, stifling cavity reeking of fuel and oil, ordnance gangs carted bombs and torpedoes to the underbellies of the bombers. Planes were coaxed into the elevators and brought up to the flight deck. Wooden chocks were placed in front of the wheels. The planes were gassed up and their bombs were fused. As launch time approached, a voice on the loudspeaker commanded: "Pilots, man planes!"

The airmen swarmed up the ladders from their squadron ready rooms, festooned with gear and parachutes, goggles pushed up on their foreheads. Hooded deck crewmen led them through the maze of parked planes, each to their assigned machine. They climbed onto the wings, slid down into their cockpits, and buckled their shoulder straps. In the predawn darkness the cockpit was a black hole, with only the instrument gauges dimly lit, and the pilot felt blindly for the stick and pedals. At the order "Start planes!" the cartridge fired and the engine sputtered, coughed, backfired, and roared to life. The propeller turned, missed, and then dissolved into a blurred disk; the engine settled into a throaty, throbbing purr, and blue clouds of exhaust wafted down the deck. The carrier heeled sharply as the ship turned into the wind. The red and white "fox" flag went up at the yardarm, signaling the start of flight operations. With the actual wind added to the apparent wind created by the ship's forward momentum, a powerful gust swept aft along the flight deck. Flight deck crewmen armed with light wands braced themselves, taking care not to be blown into the propellers. They coaxed each plane forward to its takeoff spot.

The wand twirled. The pilot pushed the throttle forward while standing on the brakes, causing the engine to ascend to a savage, quaking roar. He checked the magnetos, the fuel mixture, and the propeller pitch; he glanced at the engine instruments and confirmed that oil temperature and pressure were good; he ran the engine up to 2,700 rpm and watched his manifold pressure. Tongues of blue flame licked out of the exhaust pipes and threw a faint glow over the engine cowling. The flight deck officer, satisfied with the sound of the engine, lowered his wand and pointed down at the deck. The pilot lifted his feet from the brakes and was immediately shoved into his backrest. The dark shape of the carrier's island flashed by on his right. The tail lifted from the deck, then the wheels, and the Hellcat was airborne and climbing. The pilot pulled a hydraulic lever to raise the landing gear and banked left, keeping an eye on the needle and ball to avoid dropping into the dark sea below.

Strikes commenced with a fighter sweep comprising dozens or even hundreds of Hellcats, intended to clear the skies of enemy planes ahead of the arrival of the SB2C Helldiver dive-bombers and TBM Avenger torpedo planes. The outbound fighters performed a "group grope," a running rendezvous into formation. The eagle-eyed pilots studied the faint blue exhaust flames that were the only visible trace of the planes ahead. Formation flying in darkness required constant adjustments to airspeed, course, and altitude, and sustained concentration to fight off the vertigo and disorientation that could easily lead to crashes. They put on their masks and climbed to altitude, 20,000 or 30,000 feet. Soon the cockpits were as cold as meat lockers. They clapped their gloved hands and danced in their seats to keep warm. They relaxed a bit as dawn broke and they could see the horizon and the planes around them. Since the first days of their training they had been told to "keep their heads on a swivel," and they continually shifted gaze, scanning the sky for enemy aircraft—ahead, above, below, to the left, to the right, ahead again, and repeat.

As they approached the target, they lowered their noses and picked up speed to fly through antiaircraft bursts. If there were enemy planes in the sky, they were usually at lower altitude. David McCampbell, one of the most prolific F6F aces of the Second World War, noted that they almost always spotted their Japanese adversaries beneath them, which allowed for diving attacks. The Hellcats peeled off the formation, "zoomed down and would shoot a plane or two. . . . We'd make an attack, pull up, keep our altitude advantage and speed, and go down again. We repeated this over and over."[5]

In 1944, the Hellcat was the best carrier fighter in the Pacific, but it was also versatile enough to be employed as a bomber. Experiments soon proved that the F6F could carry and deliver bombs almost as effectively as a purpose-built dive-bomber—but unlike a dive-bomber, once relieved of its bomb the Hellcat could defeat any rival in air-to-air combat. The plane was sometimes armed with six HVARs—high-velocity aerial rockets, nicknamed the "Holy Moses"—which proved more effective than bombs against certain ground targets. Each HVAR carried a 5-inch shell as its warhead, matching the destructive power of a 5-inch naval gun, and so a Hellcat firing six rockets in one salvo packed a punch equivalent to a destroyer's full broadside. In time another rocket was introduced—the 10-foot-long "Tiny Tim," which matched the destructive power of a shell fired from a 12-inch naval gun. These air-to-ground weapons grew increasingly effective in the later stages of the war, as the aviators gained more experience with them.

As the campaign moved into the western Pacific, F6Fs increasingly struck Japanese ground fortifications with napalm bombs. Napalm was a simple incendiary composed of gasoline thickened by a gelatinous chemical. It tended to cling to whatever surface it landed upon—a pillbox, an anti-aircraft battery, a parked aircraft, human skin—and burned intensely until the fuel was exhausted. A napalm blaze atop a concrete bunker would drive the occupants out into the open, where they could be cut down by strafing Hellcats that followed close behind the napalm-armed leader.

The versatility of the F6F made it the most valuable aircraft in the carrier task forces, and commanders lobbied for a higher proportion of Hellcats on the carriers. In turn, that led to shrinking bomber squadrons. By war's end, a typical Essex-class complement of ninety-six planes included a dozen SB2Cs, a dozen TBMs, and seventy-two Hellcats.

A long-accepted tactical catechism—reiterated by Seversky in his bestseller—had held that aircraft carriers were no match for shore-based air power. Like many old orthodoxies, this one had been unseated by convergent advances in radar, antiaircraft gunnery, and communications technologies. The task forces could now confidently fight off even the heaviest air attacks, and commanders like Mitscher were increasingly emboldened to hover in the offing near an enemy-held island. According to Arleigh Burke, Mitscher's long-serving chief of staff, operations were "gradually evolving from the hit-and-run tactic to stay-and-slug-it-out tactic. The stay-and-slug-it-out business meant that we had to get rid of the enemy air permanently."[6] Aerial counterstrikes on the task force were inevitable, but much-improved radar systems could "see" inbound enemy planes when they were a hundred miles out, with accurate readings of altitude, speed, and heading. IFF ("Identification, friend or foe") technology could now reliably discern friendly and enemy planes on the radar screens. All these data were channeled into the Combat Information Center (CIC) on each carrier, from which a Fighter Director Officer (FDO) and his assistants radioed the orbiting Hellcats and directed them to intercept the approaching threat. In the later stages of the Pacific War, the CICs and the defending fighters routinely performed near-flawless interceptions. Often the crews of the ships did not even lay eyes on a hostile plane.

If an intruder managed to run the gauntlet of defending Hellcats and penetrated into the heart of the task force, it flew into a storm of antiaircraft fire. The screening battleships and cruisers bristled with antiaircraft weapons, ranging from the powerful long-ranged 5-inch/.38 guns, to the newer 40mm quad Bofors batteries, to the last-ditch 20mm Oerlikons that were aimed and fired by a single man strapped into the gun. Anticraft shells became much more lethal with the introduction of the VT (variable time) or "proximity" fuse, which used a miniaturized Doppler radar to detect the target aircraft and detonate in close proximity. In the carrier duels of 1942, ships had relied on aggressive high-speed maneuvering to dodge air attacks—the "snake dance," as it was called—but in 1944, when task forces were larger and the risk of collisions greater, new tactical doctrines placed less emphasis on the helms and more on the guns. It was thought better to stay on course and let the gunners wrap the ships in a protective screen of deadly flak.

Task Force 58 was built for speed. It could lace up its "seven-league boots" and travel thousands of miles in any direction before the enemy suspected it was on the move. The big *Essex*-class fleet carriers (CVs) and the smaller *Independence*-class light carriers (CVLs) could carve a track through the ocean rollers for days without dipping below 23 knots, and could ring up more than 30 knots for combat. During the *Yorktown*'s shakedown cruise in 1943, she achieved a peak speed of 34.9 knots—a breathtaking pace, the fastest of any carrier in history up to that time. The fast carriers were escorted by new *Iowa*-class "fast battleships," 45,000-ton leviathans that had no trouble keeping the pace. There were no lame horses in Mitscher's cavalry; all older and slower classes had been banished to the amphibious or logistics fleets. Task Force 58's speed lent it mobility and range, a vital consideration in the Pacific's blue immensities. It was a great nomadic air base, racing headlong from one part of the ocean to another, crossing and recrossing the equator, climbing up and down the latitudes. One day, sailors wore wool hats, fur-lined gloves, and heavy watch coats; a day or two later, they sweated through their dungarees and stripped to the waist under the pitiless equatorial sun. The great fleet plunged deep into enemy waters, remaining incognito by practicing strict radio silence. It hid itself in weather fronts and chased north behind tropical storms. It snuck over horizons in darkness, undetected, and attacked with complete surprise and overwhelming force. Perhaps it would stay and fight for a while—or perhaps it would vanish back into the interminable ocean wastes, from which it might suddenly reemerge a thousand miles away to devastate another enemy target. The Japanese could only guess.

They cruised in circular formation, with three or four carriers at the center and the screening ships arrayed in concentric rings by descending order of size. In a typical setup, two heavy and two light carriers would cruise in a staggered formation at the center. Battleships were close aboard to starboard and port, with cruisers at the cardinal points. On the outer rings were the destroyers, the versatile little "tin cans" that performed variously as radar pickets, message-runners, antiaircraft platforms, pilot-rescue guards, and submarine hunters. As a tactic to confuse and thwart enemy submarines, the fleet followed a zigzagging course, making sudden radical turns at precisely scheduled intervals. All ships turned together, their white wakes carving synchronous arcs through the sea. In a minute and a half, they could execute a 90-degree turn and steady on a new course. The finely choreographed maneuver required deft seamanship on every ship, down to the humblest destroyer or auxiliary vessel. Conning officers kept their ships on station with slight corrections to course and speed, always with a wary eye on the vessels ahead, to either side, and astern.

In daylight, these turns could be executed by "seaman's eye"—but on a dark night, or in thick weather, when visibility was cut to zero, the only way of discerning the position of neighboring ships was by watching the circular scopes in the radar shacks. A radius line swept around the scope, like the long hand of an analog clock, leaving a trail of fading light green "snow" and darker green "blips." While the ship was turning, it was a matter of watching those adjacent blips and sending constant steering and speed corrections to the bridge, in order to prevent them creeping toward the center of the screen. In such conditions, the radar shack was a pressure cooker. At night, with portholes and hatches sealed to prevent light from leaking out, it was a sweltering, airless cavity. Cigarette smoke hung heavily in the air and men sweated through their uniforms. On the night before a strike, when the task force sprinted through darkness at 30 knots, radar scope operators could not afford to pull their eyes away from the scopes, even for a moment. Many struggled to keep their wits together. A sailor on the destroyer *Dale* recalled a barely averted calamity on such a night. When another destroyer executed an unexpected turn, a high-speed collision seemed inevitable, and the *Dale*'s conning officer ordered both engines astern one-third to take the way off the ship. Her propellers bit deep into the water; her hull quaked and shuddered as if coming apart at the rivets; her stern dug into her wake; and she reared up out of the sea like a bucking bronco. The other ship crossed her bow with 300 feet to spare.[7]

BECAUSE TASK FORCE 58 WAS SO BIG, and because it grew steadily as newly commissioned ships arrived in the Pacific, it was too unwieldy to operate in a single circular formation. The force was cleaved into component "task groups," each a small circular fleet in itself. Each task group sailed as a unit and operated semi-independently under the local command of a rear admiral. It could break away to refuel or conduct air operations; or it might be dispatched by Admiral Mitscher to raid a target several hundred miles away. It was also possible to form a conventional surface warship force consisting of battleships and cruisers of the several task groups, which could then be sent ahead to engage Japanese warships in a conventional naval gunnery battle, or to bombard enemy shore fortifications. Usually, however, the task groups (varying from three to five in number) remained at full strength in adjacent positions, spaced at a distance of fifteen to twenty miles, so that they could provide mutual support.

When this great "fleet of fleets" operated as a unit, it could not be seen all at once by any one pair of eyes, even from an airplane high above it. From the bridge of a carrier in one of the circular formations, a witness could look in every direction and see gray steel ships of various sizes and classes stretching to the horizon and beyond. The rectangular silhouettes of the carriers at the center of a neighboring task group might be visible in the far distance, or perhaps only their superstructures would be peeking over the horizon. Search planes flew wedge-shaped patterns to a radius of 200 or 250 miles, allowing the fleet to "see" over the horizons to either side; on a clear day it would miss nothing in a 500-mile-wide swath of blue ocean. At night, the mighty turbines stirred up microbes for miles in every direction, and the sea was lit by a greenish phosphorescent glow—bright enough to read a newspaper by, as some claimed. The antiaircraft gunners were always at their weapons, eyes peeled for hostile planes, steel helmets pushed back on their heads, and life vests cinched up around their necks. Now and again a blinker light flashed silently as one ship messaged another.

The fleet's unprecedented mobility was multiplied by its capacity to remain at sea for weeks or even months at a time. Supporting and resupply-

ing Task Force 58 was the job of the Pacific Fleet logistics command, which
operated on a previously undreamed-of scale. Like war correspondents
before them, historians have never had much success in making logistics
interesting for readers. But logistics was the drivetrain that propelled overwhelming military force into the far precincts of the western Pacific, a basic
prerequisite for Allied victory. Logistics (as naval professionals constantly
reminded war correspondents during the war, and historians afterward) was
the bedrock foundation of the entire Pacific campaign.

By the spring of 1944, the war had moved a long way west of Hawaii,
and Pearl Harbor was too distant to serve as the Pacific Fleet's main operating base. The fleet was obliged to shelter in secluded mid-Pacific atolls,
thousands of miles from any proper naval shore establishment. Eniwetok,
Kwajalein, and Majuro in the Marshall Islands were huge oblong rings of
low-lying coral sand, the remnants of prehistoric volcanoes. They enclosed
shallow lagoons large enough to accommodate hundreds of ships at anchor.
Rising 10 or 15 feet above sea level, the long, narrow islets functioned as
natural breakwaters, shielding the fleet against the Pacific's long swells. But
they lacked enough landmass to block gale-force winds, so the lagoons were
rough in a storm, and vessels often tore loose of their moorings and ran
aground on a lee beach.

The islands supplied little in the way of food, freshwater, or raw materials
except coral rock, which could be crushed and made into high-grade concrete for airfields, roads, and piers. But little new construction was needed
ashore, because "floating logistics" supplied the basic needs of an advanced
fleet base. An ungainly flotilla of oil-streaked transports, tankers, and auxiliary ships swung on rusty anchors in the roadsteads, ready to provide all
essential repair and supply services to the fighting fleet. All but the most
critical battle damage could be repaired in floating mobile dry docks. An
umbilical cord of shipping linked these outposts to Pearl Harbor and the
west coast of North America. The peripatetic "fleet train" included cargo
ships, commercial tankers, troopships, fleet oilers, ammunition ships, hospital ships, minelayers, minesweepers, refrigeration ships, submarine tenders,
floatplane tenders, and escort or "jeep" carriers (CVEs). They came heavily
laden with fuel, ammunition, provisions, spare parts, replacement aircraft,
and newly trained relief personnel.

Task Force 58's awesome range and mobility owed much to the strategic proximity of these Micronesian anchorages, but perhaps even more

to the practice known as underway replenishment. The fleet refueled at sea, reprovisioned at sea, and eventually even loaded ammunition at sea. In April 1944, the "At Sea Logistics Service Group" set up shop in Eniwetok, the westernmost atoll in American hands, comprising thirty-four 25,000-ton fleet oilers, eleven escort carriers, nineteen destroyers, and twenty-six destroyer-escorts. A column of a dozen or more oilers departed Eniwetok regularly, escorted by destroyers, to rendezvous with Task Force 58. A destroyerman recalled coming over the horizon to find a row of oilers ready to service the fleet, arrayed in a line abreast like "tollgates on a bridge."[8] A fetid stench of brown bunker oil could be picked up a mile downwind. In 1942, refueling in rough seas had been the bane of carrier operations, often causing costly delays—but now, after more than two years of wartime experience and training, the crews had become considerably more adept. The vessel to be fueled crept up alongside the oiler from astern and steadied on a parallel course at 9 or 10 knots, with a 30-foot gap between the ships. Hawsers and phone lines were thrown across, hoses were hauled back and fastened to intake valves, the pumps were switched on, and oil began to flow. In a rolling swell, both ships pitched heavily, and the hoses were jerked here and there, always threatening to tear free. "Hauling a hose from one ship to another is like hauling a boa constrictor out of a tree," a witness wrote. "It writhes and clings and jerks with live resistance, and even after it has been made fast to the intake pipe, it struggles to break away."[9] Helmsmen in both vessels made constant corrections to remain on precisely parallel courses. The two bows acted as a funnel, sending wild seas surging down the gap between them. When the refueling ship's tanks were full, she cast free the hoses and gradually increased her speed to pull away, and another ship crept up from astern. The procedure was repeated until the entire fleet had drunk its fill.

Between fall 1943 and spring 1944, Task Force 58 grew steadily as newly commissioned fast carriers and screening ships arrived from the United States. The burgeoning force demonstrated the possibilities of unprecedented tactical mobility, roaming far and wide throughout the central and southern Pacific and attacking Japanese targets across a 5,000-mile front. Carrier fighters and bombers provided air cover for every major amphibious invasion of the period, including those in both Nimitz's and MacArthur's theaters, sometimes striking targets north and south of the equator in the same week. In November 1943, a single task group detoured south to hit

Rabaul, on New Britain, while the rest of the force covered the invasions of Tarawa and Makin in the Gilbert Islands. Then the reunited carrier force stormed into the heart of the Marshall Islands and launched a series of punishing airstrikes, culminating in the FLINTLOCK landings of February 1944. Later that month saw Task Force 58's boldest gambit to date— Operation HAILSTONE, a surprise attack on Truk Atoll, the largest Japanese naval base outside the home islands. In a two-day raid the American carrier planes destroyed 249 Japanese aircraft (most on the ground) and sank about 200,000 tons of shipping. While returning north, the force struck opportunistically at Guam and Rota in the Marianas, then veered south again to hit targets in the Palau Islands, which lay a full 1,200 miles west of Truk and only 575 miles east of the Philippines. In April, elements of Task Force 58 again dipped below the equator to support General MacArthur's move into Hollandia on the north New Guinea coast, striking and neutralizing Japanese airfields throughout the region. While returning north, almost as if on a whim, the force made a westward detour and poured another two days' worth of abuse down on Truk and the Palaus.

Admiral Spruance, the big boss afloat, was a reticent figure, phlegmatic and somewhat shy. He was of average height, always fit and trim, dressed in pressed khakis and well-shined shoes. His close-cropped blond hair was flecked with gray; his eyes were pale blue. He had the bronzed skin of a man who spent long hours under the sun. He was fifty-seven years old but could have passed for forty-seven. Some thought him a dead ringer for the late humorist Will Rogers.[10]

At the beginning of the war, Spruance had been an anonymous rear admiral commanding a cruiser division in Admiral Halsey's carrier task force. In June 1942, two momentous developments sent his career up a steep upward trajectory. First, he was lifted to temporary command of Task Force 16, centered around the *Enterprise* and the *Hornet*, when Halsey was laid low by a skin disorder. In that role, Spruance fought the Battle of Midway (June 4–6, 1942) and was credited for the immortal victory. Immediately afterward, he was recalled to shore duty as Nimitz's chief of staff, a powerful job that he would hold for more than a year. During this period, from June 1942 to July 1943, he lived in a small, austere bedroom on the second floor of Nimitz's house on Makalapa Hill in Pearl Harbor. The two admirals grew close, professionally and personally, and when Spruance's tenure at Pacific Fleet headquarters drew to a close, Nimitz selected him as commander of the

Fifth Fleet, the biggest and most important seagoing command in the U.S. Navy. (By a wide margin, it was the largest fleet command in the history of *any* navy.) Nimitz trusted Spruance to act as his surrogate—to render the same decisions that he, Nimitz, would make if he had been commanding the fleet at sea. As a CINCPAC staff officer remarked, "The admiral thinks it's all right to send Raymond out now. He's got him to the point where they think and talk just alike."[11]

Though he stood above Admiral Mitscher in the chain of command, Spruance was usually content to let his Task Force 58 chief exercise tactical command of the fleet. His humble flagship *Indianapolis* sailed as part of the circular defensive screening formation in Mitscher's Task Group 58.3, centered on the *Essex*-class heavy carrier *Lexington* (CV-16). For days at a time, when Task Force 58 was steaming at high speed across the Pacific expanses, Spruance did little or no work, rendered no important decisions, and did not communicate at all with Mitscher, though their two flagships were only a quarter of a mile apart.

The Fifth Fleet chief of staff, Charles "Carl" Moore, later gave a frank account of the boss's eccentric personality and working habits. Spruance did not fit the conventional mold of a wartime fleet commander. He was aloof, introverted, and monkish. He often described the Pacific War as "interesting." A physical fitness zealot, Spruance said that he could not think clearly or get a decent night's sleep unless he walked at least 5 miles a day. On an average day at sea, Spruance paced for three to four hours around the forecastle of the *Indianapolis* while dressed in a garish Hawaiian floral-print bathing suit, no shirt, white socks, and his regulation black leather shoes.

Spruance paid little attention to administrative details, preferring to let his subordinates worry about them. When Moore tried to engage Spruance about some pending matter, and the admiral did not think it merited his attention, he brusquely refused to reply. He walked off the flag bridge and returned to his customary deck circuit, or barricaded himself in his cabin with a paperback book. "He never gets ruffled or excited, never gets exasperated with me when I get disagreeable," Moore told his wife in a letter of early 1944. "When he doesn't want to do business, he just pretends not to hear and goes to bed or walks off and doesn't answer."[12]

Spruance was deadly serious about his sleep. He aimed for eight or nine hours a night, and was often in bed by eight o'clock. Even when the *Indianapolis* was roaring into enemy waters at 30 knots, and his shipmates were tense and restless, the admiral slept soundly. One night, Moore shook him awake to give him the news that a strange plane had been picked up on radar.

"Well," Spruance asked, without rising from his bunk, "is there anything I can do about it?"

"No," Moore replied.

"Then why wake me up? You know I don't like to be awakened in the middle of the night." He turned over and fell back asleep.[13]

The Fifth Fleet staff enjoyed telling stories about their chief's compulsive daily rituals, which he practiced with devout attention to detail. Spruance began each day with a cold shower. He did not speak a word until he had drunk his morning cup of coffee, but he turned up his nose at the navy "joe" that sat in Pyrex carafes in the mess. He insisted on fresh coffee brewed with premium Hawaiian Kona beans. Not trusting the mess stewards to do the job properly, the admiral made his own coffee, grinding the beans with his personal hand-crank grinder, and then brewing it in a percolator at the table. He drank three small cups at breakfast, but no more for the rest of the day. He was a disciplined and abstemious eater. "He had a few pieces of toast, grapefruit if we had it," said his flag lieutenant, Charles F. Barber. "Lunch was a bowl of soup and an ample salad. I often warned guests before lunch that that was all they would get."[14] Dinner was hearty, as Spruance had normally worked up an appetite by trekking around the ship. He ate beef and raw sliced onions, which he believed were good for his health.

Spruance insisted upon neatness and cleanliness, especially in his personal space. Once he rebuked Moore for putting his feet up on a chair in the flag cabin.

"The deck is perfectly clean," Moore replied. "It's just as clean as the chairs are."

Spruance made a show of brushing off the seat before sitting down, remarking, "I don't want my trousers to get all dirty sitting where you had your feet."[15]

In private conversations, the admiral faulted his old friend Bill Halsey for talking too freely to newspaper reporters. Believing that Halsey had allowed himself to be "exploited" by the press, Spruance was determined not to repeat the same mistake. Upon first taking command of the Fifth Fleet in the fall of 1943, he had refused to allow war correspondents on board the *Indianapolis*. But his tenure as fleet commander coincided with a renewed push in Washington to upgrade the navy's public relations. Undersecretary Jim Forrestal, in particular, was pressuring all major naval commands to improve the quality, quantity, and timeliness of press coverage. The Pearl Harbor–based press corps took an increasing interest in the enigmatic four-star admiral. Interview requests poured in. "He refused to see any war correspondents at all," said Moore, "until I succeeded in making him believe it was his duty."[16]

When finally cornered by the newsmen, Spruance was cool and matter-of-fact. He dwelled on the minutiae of logistics, a subject that did not much interest them. He did not speak in soundbites; he gave them nothing that they might have used to sketch his personality or style of leadership. Some reporters used their imaginations to fill the void. A January 1944 issue of *Collier's Weekly* depicted Spruance as a hard-driving workaholic: "When Admiral Spruance isn't walking he's driving—driving himself, his subordinates, his ships and the enemy. He's a demon for work."[17] Moore teased the admiral by repeating the phrase on the bridge of the *Indianapolis*. A demon for work! Years later, in a postwar interview, Moore burst out laughing as he reread the *Collier's* story: "The laziest man you've ever seen! He hated to work. He hated to write anything. He was no driver—you can see, he didn't drive me, he tried to keep me from working, and the same thing with everybody else. He didn't drive his ships. He *did* drive the enemy, when it came to that point, but this fellow gives the impression that you've got a tough, hard-boiled, driving man here, which he wasn't at all."[18]

In June 1944, while the Fifth Fleet was spearheading the invasion of the Marianas, Spruance's bronzed face appeared on the cover of *Time* magazine under the headline: "The Mechanical Man." *Time* depicted him as a "cold, calculating, mechanical man," more technician than warrior. When the magazine was delivered to the flag bridge of the *Indianapolis*, Spruance tried to hide it. The subterfuge failed, as Moore found another copy and read excerpts aloud over the ship's public-address system. Later, in a more reflective mood, Moore wrote his wife (who was, like himself, a dear old friend of Raymond Spruance) and concluded that *Time* had simply fabricated an identity for the Fifth Fleet commander. "If they had come to me, I could have given them a much better picture of him, but I think it is just as well that the public and the thousands of men in this fleet look on him as *Time* had pictured him. He has the fine military qualities *Time* credits him with, but he is shy and diffident rather than hard-boiled."[19]

If Spruance deliberately tried to avoid work, as he freely admitted in at least one postwar letter, he achieved the singular feat of turning his indolence into a virtue.[20] His insistence upon delegating authority down the line of command tended to bring out the best in subordinates. He kept his mind clear of details in order to focus on the big picture; he refused to consider minor issues because he was storing up his mental energy for the major ones. His daily 5-mile deck hikes kept him healthy and fit. The physical exercise helped him sleep soundly at night, even while under the strain of prolonged operations in enemy waters. As others in the fleet grew exhausted and edgy, Spruance remained fresh and well rested. He told his wife in a letter from sea, "If I don't exercise, I don't feel as well and I get nervous and mentally depressed . . . I am in tip-top condition and intend to stay that way in order to do my job, which, after all, is an important one."[21]

This wisdom of this philosophy was apparent as the new seakeeping capabilities lengthened the duration of the fleet's blue water cruises. Military and medical authorities were confronting the rising costs of "command fatigue." More than ever before, seagoing commanders were rated according to their mental and physical stamina. When a visitor went aboard the *Indianapolis* in the summer of 1944, he noted that the Fifth Fleet staff officers were "dog-tired and showed it." They seemed overdue for a long leave on dry land. But Spruance, who was older than any man on his staff, appeared rested, healthy, and alert.[22]

A COLLEAGUE HAD REMARKED TO SPRUANCE, at the outset of the Marianas campaign: "Every commander must be a gambler." If that was so, Spruance retorted, he intended to be a gambler of the "professional variety," because he wanted "all the odds I could get stacked in my favor."[23] He did not believe in running unnecessary risks, especially at this late stage of the Pacific War, when American forces enjoyed a large and growing margin of superiority. Above all, he intended to protect the beachhead on Saipan and the vulnerable amphibious fleet that lay offshore. When a powerful Japanese fleet approached on the night of June 18, 1944, Admiral Mitscher asked permission to take Task Force 58 west to intercept it. Wary of the risk (however remote) of an end-run attack on the beachhead, Spruance denied the request. On the morning of June 19, the Japanese carriers launched three large airstrikes against the Fifth Fleet. In a daylong aerial battle nicknamed the "Great Marianas Turkey Shoot," F6F Hellcats met and slaughtered the attackers, sending more than three hundred Japanese aircraft down in flames. But Task Force 58 was too far east to launch a counterattack on the Japanese fleet. After a twenty-four-hour stern chase, Mitscher's carrier airmen finally managed to sink two enemy fleet oilers and an aircraft carrier on the night of June 20, but the greater part of the Japanese fleet survived to fight another day.

Following this two-day "Battle of the Philippine Sea," Spruance's conservative tactics came under harsh scrutiny. Critics charged that he had forgotten or ignored the cardinal principle of carrier warfare—to *strike first*. In this case, according to the naval aviators, it had been doubly important to move west on the night of June 18, because the prevailing trade winds in those waters blew from the east, and the carriers would therefore be obliged to steam east throughout the daylight hours to conduct flight operations. By tethering Task Force 58 to Saipan, Spruance had made the calculated decision to allow the Japanese to strike the first aerial blow, while simultaneously placing his carriers out of range for a counterstrike. In the (admittedly short) history of carrier warfare, the decision was unprecedented.

To Spruance's critics, his tactics had seemed not only wrong but *obviously* wrong, and therefore unpardonable. Arleigh Burke, Mitscher's chief of staff, later recalled that he and his colleagues were "heartbroken" by the decision. The Americans had grasped the chance to wipe out the entire striking arm of the Japanese navy, and let it slip through their fingers. The debate exposed a rift in the ranks of the U.S. Navy between traditional naval line officers who had served chiefly in battleships and other surface warships ("blackshoes") and an insurgent cadre of professional naval aviators ("brownshoes"). The brownshoes argued that a blackshoe like Spruance was not qualified to command the fast carrier task force because he lacked an innate feeling for the new capabilities of carrier aviation. The controversy was freighted with biases and warped by personal ambitions, but it was remarkably virulent. A rising cohort of brownshoe captains and rear admirals insisted that Spruance must go, and they were willing to test the limits of propriety (or even mutiny) in aiming criticism against their chief. Spruance's performance in the battle was endorsed by King and Nimitz when they visited the Marianas the following month, silencing chatter that he might be ousted from his job. But the hullabaloo continued to reverberate noisily in Pearl Harbor and Washington.

August 1944 brought an important command transition. Admiral Halsey, who had held a sub-theater command (COMSOPAC) in the South Pacific since October 1942, was brought north to relieve Spruance. The changeover would occur at the conclusion of the Marianas campaign. Spruance and his staff would take a well-deserved leave in the States, and then return to Pearl Harbor to plan future operations. Halsey would command the fleet until January 1945, and then be relieved in turn by Spruance. The cycle would repeat every five to six months until the end of the war. One admiral and his staff would be at sea while the other was ashore, planning the next round of invasions and carrier strikes. Somewhat confusingly, the Fifth Fleet would be designated the Third Fleet when Halsey commanded it, and Task Force 58 would become Task Force 38. Upon Spruance's return, they would again become the Fifth Fleet and Task Force 58. The numbers would change, but the two fleets were one and the same. This ruse was intended to dupe the Japanese into believing that two independent fleets were roaming the Pacific. There is evidence that it succeeded, at least at first. Japanese commercial radio broadcasts sometimes referred to both the Fifth and the Third Fleets, speculating on their respective locations and missions.[24]

The "two-platoon" command scheme offered clear advantages. Spruance might possess exceptional stamina, but he and his team could not be expected to remain at sea indefinitely without a breather. The war had moved so far to the west that it was no longer practicable for the fleet to return to Pearl Harbor after each successive operation. When the Americans penetrated into the inner perimeter of Japan's empire, it was thought essential to keep the Pacific Fleet continuously engaged against the enemy. The air assault would be unremitting, with one strike following close upon another. But it was also necessary that fleet commanders and their staffs be directly engaged in planning new operations. As a practical matter, one team would need to be working in a shore-based headquarters while the other was at sea.[25]

Some had doubts about the wisdom of this rotating fleet command. Two analogies lent themselves to describing the new arrangement, and both gained wide currency at the time and in postwar accounts. The first was: "Two drivers, one team of horses." The second was the inescapable football metaphor: "Two backfields, one offensive line." In either case, the horses or the linemen had reason to be concerned, because no provision was made for *their* rest. According to Rear Admiral Arthur Radford, who commanded one of the carrier task groups in 1945, "the horses sometimes wondered whether the returning drivers, rested from their earlier exertions, really were aware of the nerve-wracking, day-in-day-out months at sea put in by the single crews of the ships."[26]

There was also the sensitive question of whether Halsey's team was ready. Spruance and his outfit had grown into the job during a year of hard-earned experience. Halsey and his close-knit staff had been in a shore-based headquarters in Nouméa, New Caledonia, for nearly two years. Halsey had not commanded at sea since the comparative dark age of 1942. Far-reaching technological and doctrinal changes had occurred in the intervening period. He and his squad would have a great deal to learn, but naval combat was a hard and unforgiving school.

While commanding in the South Pacific, Halsey had made a name for himself as a charismatic, swaggering, limelight-loving warrior, the navy's answer to George S. Patton. His nickname among the rank and file, quickly adopted by the newspapers, was "the Bull." He was obliging with reporters and always quick with a quotable line. His bloody-minded tirades against the Japanese had been received with enthusiasm, not only by Allied servicemen in the Pacific but also civilians in the United States. Like many celebrities, he had a famous tagline. "The way to win this war," he said, "is to kill Japs, kill Japs and kill more Japs."[27] He signed off his messages: "Keep 'em dying." Referring to atrocities against American prisoners, he declared ominously, "They'll be properly repaid." He told the press he intended to ride the emperor Hirohito's famous white horse through downtown Tokyo, and had addressed himself directly to the emperor, declaring: "Your time is short."[28] Halsey's tendency to speak first and think later had caused embarrassment in the past, most notably when he had rashly predicted that the Allies would achieve complete victory in the Pacific by the end of 1943. Three months later, he had been forced to retract that sensational forecast, and the retraction was gleefully highlighted in the Japanese state-controlled news media. Halsey regretted that he had "made a monkey out of myself many times" in the newspapers, and pledged to learn from his past mistakes.[29] But Spruance privately feared that "Halsey's publicity had actually turned his head," and wondered (prophetically, it turned out) whether his brassy colleague would feel pressured to "live up to a glorified public image, rather than be guided by his best military judgment."[30]

A war correspondent who got to know Halsey's inner circle of staff officers in mid-1944 noted that the gang was always in high spirits. "Halsey kept up a running banter; all the Halsey men seemed always to be having a hilarious time."[31] Their leader set the tone. He was a profane, rowdy, fun-loving four-star admiral who laughed at jokes at his own expense and fired provocative verbal salvos against the enemy. The staff, led by Robert "Mick" Carney, called itself the "Dirty Tricks Department." They were intensely loyal to Halsey, and he reciprocated their loyalty. Naturally they all wanted to come along with "Admiral Bill" on the next adventure, especially since the Third Fleet command was a plum assignment for any ambitious officer, and Halsey did not want to break up his band. That undoubtedly played into his decision to take a large cohort of his SOPAC staff with him when he left Nouméa for Pearl Harbor on June 16, 1944. As they moved into their temporary Third Fleet headquarters in the Navy Yard at Pearl Harbor, they numbered more than a hundred officers and enlisted men, and more were due to arrive from the South Pacific before the intended command turnover in August. Few had served in the fleet since the arrival of the *Essex*-class fast carriers the previous year. Halsey's Third Fleet staff was nearly twice the size of Spruance's team, and it would have been even larger if Admiral Nimitz had not insisted on limiting its headcount.

Personnel reshuffling was occurring at the task group level as well. Mitscher had been ruthless in purging weaker performers, forcing out three task group commanders since assuming leadership of Task Force 58 in January 1944. A new generation of recently promoted aviation admirals coveted those jobs, which were among the most prestigious in the navy. Career ambitions, personal rivalries, and the ongoing brownshoe insurgency came into play as they jockeyed for the prized billets. Most of the new task group commanders had graduated the Naval Academy between 1916 and 1919. That made them considerably junior to the blackshoe admirals who commanded the battleships and cruisers in the fleet. Vice Admiral Willis "Ching" Lee, who had administrative command of the battleships, had graduated in the Class of 1908, just two years behind Spruance. He had a decade of seniority over the men running the several task groups, to whom Lee and his battleship skippers would have to answer. That sort of arrangement was virtually unknown in the prewar period, but the blackshoes had acknowledged the ascendency of the aircraft carrier, and with a war to win they did not stand on the niceties of the class-year pecking order.

Admiral King was determined to maintain control of top personnel assignments in the Pacific. His practice was to rotate officers from the fleet back to administrative and planning jobs in Washington, and to send others from the headquarters out to the fleet. The policy was sensible and just, but it meant that men who had been "flying desks" in Washington were suddenly thrust into important seagoing commands even though they had no recent experience in the fleet. Given the breakneck pace of technological and doctrinal evolution, they would have much to learn and absorb. When the Fifth Fleet put into Eniwetok Atoll on August 10, after more than two months of uninterrupted combat operations supporting the invasion of the Marianas, several newly appointed task group commanders flew in and relieved their predecessors. Vice Admiral John S. "Slew" McCain, who had most recently served as King's deputy chief of naval operations for air, relieved Joseph "Jocko" Clark as commander of Task Group 58.1. His flagship was to be the *Wasp.* Frederick "Ted" Sherman relieved Alfred Montgomery in command of Task Group 58.3, hoisting his flag in the *Essex.* Gerald Bogan retained command of Task Group 58.2, with his flagship *Bunker Hill*; Ralph Davison rode in the *Franklin* as commander of Task Group 58.4. All were briefed on the impending fleet command turnover, which would occur midday on August 26. Spruance would take the *Indianapolis* back to Pearl Harbor, and the battleship *New Jersey* would bring Halsey out to the western Pacific by the first week of September.

Sooner or later, Admiral Mitscher would also need a spell of rest. The fleet surgeon had noted the telltale signs of nervous exhaustion: Mitscher had lost about 15 pounds in six months, and since he had been scarcely bigger than a horseracing jockey to begin with, he could hardly afford it. But replacing Mitscher presented a dilemma. Several ambitious brownshoe admirals were angling for the job, both in Washington and in Pearl Harbor. Few naval aviators in the service possessed Mitscher's rank and seniority, and none had seagoing experience with the new carriers. Mitscher favored promoting one of the existing task group commanders into the role: he nominated Ted Sherman. But Sherman had begun the war as a captain, and promoting such a junior admiral into the exalted command would excite jealousy and resentment.

King eventually selected John McCain for the job. McCain was a very senior vice admiral, having graduated Annapolis in 1906. He had been one of King's most trusted deputies in Washington. He had been the air commander in the South Pacific during the Guadalcanal campaign, and then ran the aeronautics bureau of the Navy Department. Like King and Halsey, he was a latecomer to aviation—all three officers had done their flight training when they were captains over the age of fifty, solely in order to earn the qualification needed to command an aircraft carrier. The "real" brownshoes, who had come up through the ranks as flyers, did not regard these "Johnny-come-latelys" as genuine members of their guild. Many were perplexed and even unsettled by the news that McCain would take over Mitscher's role as commander of Task Force 38.

Mitscher was slated to remain with the fleet until November, during which time McCain would undergo a three-month break-in period in the subordinate role of a task group commander, one of four in Task Force 38. His predecessor in that job, Jocko Clark, would remain at sea in the *Hornet*, making the short flight from the *Hornet* to the *Wasp* to consult with the new boss whenever necessary. "Makee-learnee," a term derived from pidgin English, was the navy's nickname for this sort of on-the-job training arrangement. McCain would not inherit Mitscher's experienced staff, so he faced the difficult task of building a new team from scratch. But many of the officers possessing essential know-how were due for leave, or already attached to other admirals, or both.

Noting that he was senior to Mitscher by a margin of four years, McCain remarked to John Towers that he felt as if someone were trying to "cut his throat."[32] In any previous era of American naval history, a four-year gap in seniority would have decided all such wrangles in McCain's favor. But under the pressure of a vast and bloody war, many old traditions were being set aside. Pragmatic solutions were the order of the day. After giving him a respectful hearing, Nimitz told him to do his best under the circumstances.

While the fleet rested at Eniwetok, sailors and officers took liberty ashore. Two different islets had been designated as recreation zones, one for officers and one for enlisted men. Beer was rationed, two cans per man, but there was plenty of black-market liquor available as well, especially on the islet designated for officers' recreation. One day in mid-August, a group of well-oiled *Hornet* aviators was standing on the dock, waiting for a launch to take them back to their ship. Horseplay ensued. An ensign was shoved into the lagoon. He swam back to the beach and charged down the dock, intent on revenge. Dozens more went into the water. Before long, any man wearing a dry khaki uniform was a fair target. Even Commander Harold

L. "Hal" Buell, the *Hornet*'s air group leader, was seized by his feet and arms and swung into the lagoon. He did not mind. "After all," he wrote, "it was good clean fun, and the water helped to shake off the effects of an afternoon of imbibing."[33]

Returning dripping wet to the dock, Buell glimpsed a small, white-haired man being pitched headlong into the lagoon. The victim was already airborne when Buell recognized him as Admiral McCain. Naval etiquette gave leeway in certain circumstances, but in general, drunken aviators were not permitted to lay hands on a three-star admiral and heave him into the sea. Buell shouted a warning, but too late. He and several others dove after McCain immediately:

> As we got hold of him and helped him to his feet, he was gasping and wheezing and said: "Get my hat, boys, get my hat." The hat, a special version of a field fatigue hat with the gold band and scrambled eggs almost all green from salt air, was his lucky hat and well-known among the fleet pilots. We retrieved the hat, got the admiral back up on the dock, and expressed our deepest regrets for our conduct. . . . He was a small man, almost fragile, and looked like a strong wind could blow him away. Dripping salt water, seaweed, and coral sand, he kept grinning as he shook hands with each of us while we continued making our apologies. He asked for a dry cigarette, lit up, and started telling us how good it was to be back with his "fighting men." With blue eyes twinkling from a wrinkled face, dominated by both a nose and ears of heroic proportions, McCain looked for all the world like a leprechaun.
>
> As the boats began to arrive, one of the first was McCain's motor launch. Completely white, spotless, with brass gleaming and three-star blue flag flying, it was a beautiful sight. The admiral was now having fun with his boys, and didn't want it to end. So he asked us to join him on the boat; he would take each of us to our ship. To the dismay of the spotless boat's crew, a dozen or more dirty, bedraggled pilots came aboard with the admiral. We then wound our way through the mass of warships in the harbor delivering each pilot to his ship.[34]

Task Force 38, as it was now redesignated, sortied from Eniwetok on August 28. As always, the departure was a long and intricately choreographed procedure: destroyers and cruisers went out through the deepwater exit channel just before the carriers and immediately commenced sonar-ranging for enemy submarines. All ships dialed up high speed—the better to get away from the perilous approaches, where Japanese submarines were known to lurk—and coalesced into a cruising formation without breaking the pace. Mitscher's force was at full strength, comprising eight *Essex*-class carriers and eight light carriers divided into four task groups, embarking more than a thousand airplanes altogether. This cruise was to be the longest and most ambitious in the year-long history of the fast carrier task force.

On a map of the Pacific, a 3,000-mile-long arc of island groups reached from Japan through the Bonins, the Marianas, the Carolines, and the Palaus, terminating in the southern Philippines. Having taken the Marianas, American forces would now extend control southward down that long arc. Task Force 38 would cover the impending Operation STALEMATE amphibious landings on islands in the Caroline and Palau archipelagoes. By November, if all went as planned, they would occupy or otherwise neutralize every important island in the chain from the Marianas in the north to Mindanao in the south. The forthcoming cruise would take the carriers to the front door of the Philippines, where they would reduce Japanese airpower in the region ahead of MacArthur's planned invasion of Mindanao on November 15. Photo reconnaissance flights had identified no fewer than sixty-three Japanese airfields in the Philippines, and according to the best intelligence estimates, they were supplied with about 650 aircraft of various types.

Up the crescent, between the Marianas and Japan, were the little islands known as the Bonin and Volcano groups, called the *Nanpō Shotō* by the Japanese. The Americans had nicknamed them the "Jimas."[35] They had become a strategic hot spot since the Americans had landed in Saipan ten weeks earlier. Iwo Jima was especially significant as a way station for enemy air reinforcements headed south. Jocko Clark's Task Group 58.1, which included the *Essex*-class flattops *Hornet* and *Yorktown*, launched five big carrier raids against the Bonins between June 15 and August 5. Again and again, the American carrier planes returned to pulverize the airfields, ammunition dumps, antiaircraft batteries, fuel tanks, and ground complexes. They had shot down nearly a hundred planes over the Jimas and destroyed another hundred on the ground; they had dive-bombed Japanese shipping in the harbors, strafed fishing sampans offshore, and torpedoed Japanese convoys at sea. Although the rank and file of the fleet did not know it, Admiral Spruance was arguing strenuously for an invasion of Iwo Jima, and the relentless carrier raids were providing useful intelligence about the state of Japanese defenses on the island.

Clark later said that he "regarded those islands as my special property," and his aviators nicknamed them the "Jocko Jimas." Upon returning to Eniwetok the previous month, they had drawn up stock certificates in an imaginary real estate investment company, the "Jocko Jima Development Corporation," which advertised its business as the acquisition and development of "exclusive sites in the Bonin Islands." Designated "shareholders" were presented with colorfully illustrated stock certificates, which entitled the owner to a share in "choice locations of all types in Iwo, Chichi, Haha, and Muko Jima—only 500 miles from downtown Tokyo." As "president" of the make-believe firm, Clark signed each certificate in his own hand. Share No. 1 was issued to Admiral Mitscher. The certificates soon became prized collectors' items and were traded (in some cases for real money) throughout the Pacific and as far afield as Washington.

Now, as Task Force 38 went to sea again, the force divided into its component subunits. Three groups turned south to strike assorted targets in the Caroline and Palau islands, and one (Task Group 38.4, under Ralph Davison) went north to call on the Bonins yet again. In a three-day strike, Davison's airmen flew 633 sorties over the islands, returning with claims of forty-six Japanese planes shot down or destroyed on the ground and six ships sunk.[36] In his report to Halsey and Mitscher, Davison remarked: "Shares in Jocko JRIC development corporation selling at new high after brisk turnover in airfield and industrial sites."[37]

Davison's carriers lost only five airplanes in the operation. One of the downed planes was a Grumman TBM Avenger piloted by Lieutenant (jg) George H. W. Bush, a future president of the United States. His plane was hit and damaged by antiaircraft fire over Chichi Jima. Bush parachuted into the ocean and was later rescued by a submarine, the *Finback*—but his two aircrewmen, and six other aviators from other downed planes, were captured, tortured, and executed by Japanese military personnel on the island. Four of the prisoners were partly eaten by Japanese officers in an episode of ritualistic cannibalism. These ghastly events and the war crimes trials of the perpetrators were documented by James Bradley in his 2003 book *Flyboys*.

Halsey and his staff had left Pearl Harbor in the *New Jersey* on August

24. Halsey had brought an enormous staff with him, nearly two hundred officers and sailors, amounting to about 10 percent of the ship's crew. The superstructure of the 45,000-ton battleship had been extensively reconfigured to serve as the fleet command center. Two decks under the captain's bridge were occupied by "flag country," which included a new flag plot retrofitted with state-of-the-art communications and radar technology, a spacious flag bridge with verandas to starboard and port, berthing compartments for officers and bluejackets, and a cavernous wardroom that doubled as a conference center.[38] This region of the ship was considerably larger than the corresponding arrangements on Spruance's smaller flagship *Indianapolis*. The newly updated wardrooms and mess facilities were sumptuous by navy standards. Lieutenant Carl Solberg, an intelligence officer, recalled that the junior officers were pleasantly surprised by the quality of the meals served in their wardroom, on white linen tables—"fresh steaks and chops, tossed salads and not just ice cream every evening but Baked Alaska every Sunday."[39]

Before falling in with Task Force 38, Halsey wanted to confer with MacArthur's leading naval and air commanders in Manus. During the ten-day passage from Hawaii, the *New Jersey* and her three escorting destroyers conducted daily antiaircraft gunnery drills, with the gunners firing at target sleeves towed behind the battleship's floatplanes. The *New Jersey*'s 16-inch guns were also fired in practice. To the satisfaction of the Third Fleet communications staff, the powerful concussions of the big weapons did not interfere with the workings of their equipment, a problem that had plagued previous flagships. Mick Carney put the flag plot staff through a series of high-pressure drills known as "simulated battle problems."[40] At this point Halsey and his flagship were separated from Task Force 38 by thousands of miles, and Mitscher remained in tactical control of the carriers—but Halsey sent him frequent instructions from the towering radio antennae of the *New Jersey*. Even now, before the flagship had fallen in with the fleet, it was clear that Halsey would take a more hands-on approach than his predecessor.

Halsey and his "Dirty Tricks Department" had their own ideas about how to fight and win the Pacific campaign, and they did not hesitate to propose major revisions to existing plans. During the interim period before taking command of the fleet, Halsey had argued that most of Operation STALEMATE was unnecessary. In his view, the remote equatorial archipelagoes of the Carolines and Palaus were prime candidates to be bypassed, and he recommended transferring the troops slated for those landings to MacArthur's control for use in an accelerated invasion of the Philippines.[41] Nimitz had countered by ordering the bypass of one major STALEMATE objective (Babelthuap in the Palaus) and agreed to consider bypassing Yap in the Carolines—but the CINCPAC was firm that invasions in the western Palaus (Peleliu and Angaur) would proceed as planned. Halsey's staff also proposed a major redeployment of the Pacific submarine force, aimed at shifting its targeting priority from Japanese merchant vessels and tankers to Japanese warships. This gambit was firmly rejected by the Pacific Submarine Force commander, Admiral Charles A. Lockwood.

In Pearl Harbor there was a feeling that Halsey and his Third Fleet staff were spending too much time and energy trying to revise the basic blueprint for winning the Pacific War. Nimitz's deputy, Forrest Sherman, sat down with Mick Carney in mid-August and delivered a blunt message. The Third Fleet's job was to execute operations planned by the Joint Chiefs and the Pacific Fleet headquarters. "It was made very clear to us that we were not to concern ourselves with strategic planning," recalled Carney, "that this was a function of the C-in-C Pacific headquarters, taking its directives from Admiral King and the Joint Chiefs of Staff. This was specifically not the business of the tactical fleet commanders. Now, this was driven home to us very, very clearly and very, very forcefully."[42] Even while at sea, however, Halsey continued to indulge what Lieutenant Solberg called "his penchant for improvisation," frequently radioing bold suggestions to Nimitz—most of which the CINCPAC rejected.[43] During the same period, Nimitz gently reprimanded Halsey on several occasions for exceeding his authority or failing to comply with prior orders.[44] The Fifth to Third Fleet transition, it is fair to say, got off to a rocky start.

On September 8, the *New Jersey* fell in with Task Force 38 north of the Caroline Islands. Halsey and several senior staff officers transferred via highline to Mitscher's flagship, the *Lexington*. According to the Third Fleet War Diary, the crew of the *New Jersey* was "thrilled to see four stars go over the side at sea."[45] In a long conference in flag country on the *Lexington*, they refined their plans to strike the Philippines.

A week's worth of carrier airstrikes on Yap, Palau, and Mindanao had revealed that Japanese air power in the region was surprisingly feeble. Over many targets the carrier airmen had encountered little or no resistance. They had blown craters in airfields; demolished buildings, storage dumps, and defensive structures; and attacked whatever enemy shipping and small craft they found in the harbors. The full strength of three task groups tore into the Palau group for three consecutive days from September 6 to 8, reporting "extensive damage to ground installations, ammunition and supply dumps, the radio stations, barracks, buildings, and warehouses on Peleliu, Angaur, Ngesebus, and Babelthuap."[46]

Moving west to hit Mindanao on September 9, Task Force 38 expected a much hotter reception, but again encountered only weak and scattered Japanese resistance. Attacking planes were met by only a handful of defending Japanese fighters, all of which were quickly shot down. The carrier airmen claimed about sixty Japanese planes damaged or destroyed on the ground. They bombed and strafed shipping and small craft in Davao Gulf and Sarangani Bay, returning with claims of about forty vessels sunk or set afire. Only a dozen U.S. planes were lost in these strikes—eight to flak, four to accidents. One F6F fighter was lost when it made a low-altitude run over a river barge. The plane's .50-caliber incendiary strafing fire set off a cache of ammunition on the barge which exploded and engulfed the aircraft.

At their postflight debriefing sessions with the air intelligence officers on the carriers, aviators complained that they were not finding enough worthwhile targets. In aerial photos taken during and after the raids, many of the Mindanao airfields appeared deserted, and the ground facilities were primitive and minimal. The Third Fleet War Diary generously gave credit to General Kenney's Fifth Air Force B-24s for their previous bombing runs over the island: "Evidence that the Fifth Air Force had already done a thorough job of reducing Japanese installations on Mindanao was found and that carrier strikes on this area were not wholly needed."[47]

The carriers and their screening ships now moved east, over the horizon, to rendezvous with a squadron of fleet oilers. The ships topped off fuel and collected their incoming mail. Conferring by low-frequency short-range radio, Halsey and Mitscher agreed that further aerial attacks on Mindanao would be a waste of time. Intelligence analysts on Halsey's staff were boldly speculating that Japanese airpower might be verging on complete collapse. A strategic estimate published on September 9 considered the possibility that the Japanese fleet might sortie against the American fleet in a suicidal naval *banzai* charge. The analysts speculated that Japanese leaders might even deliberately seek complete destruction of their own fleet, reasoning that "an early defeat would permit greater salvage from the wreck of the

Empire than a defeat of the fleet when we were ready to land troops in the homeland."[48] This was an extraordinary theory—that a faction within the Japanese naval command had already concluded that defeat was inevitable, and was attempting to force the Tokyo regime to an early surrender. The supposition was wrong, but the stunning lack of enemy resistance in the southern Philippines seemed so bizarre and incomprehensible that even far-fetched speculation was given a fair hearing.

Halsey called off the Mindanao strikes and took most of the fleet north to the central Philippines, where it would hit targets on the islands of Leyte, Cebu, and Negros. (Davison's Task Group 38.4 remained in the Palau area, several hundred miles to the east, in order to provide air support for the pending amphibious landings on Peleliu and Angaur.) Third Fleet air and intelligence analysts were giving serious consideration to an even more audacious gambit—a surprise carrier airstrike on Manila and the big Japanese air complexes on central Luzon. Halsey wanted to destroy bulk fuel storage tank farms near Manila, a blow that he believed might hobble Japanese fleet units passing through the area.[49]

After a high-speed overnight northbound run, three task groups arrived in the waters off Leyte Gulf at dawn on September 12. The sea was mild, with light breezes. As the first light came up, sailors on the decks of the ships could see the green mountains of Samar on the northwest horizon. Eight flight decks launched more than 350 fighters and bombers. They flew away to the west, gradually joining up in a big vee-of-vee pattern as they climbed to altitude. They were still climbing as they flew over Leyte, where an American soldier who had escaped capture in 1942 was awakened by the drone of engines overhead. "I got a case of goose pimples I had been saving for three years," he later wrote. "Yeah, guess my biggest thrill came right then." Filipino villagers and guerillas cheered savagely for the attacking planes: "People dragged American flags out of mothballs and waved them and hollered, 'Kill the Japs! Kill the Japs!' That was the best thing they could shout. It was what they wanted most in life."[50]

Hal Buell, the *Hornet* air group leader, was among the first over Cebu airfield, one of their principal objectives. From altitude he could see dozens of Japanese aircraft parked along the taxiways and aprons. Dust was kicking up from the ground and men could be seen running among the planes; the Japanese appeared to be rushing to scramble their interceptors. F6F Hellcats flew low over the field and strafed parked and taxiing enemy planes before they could take flight. Buell, flying an SB2C Helldiver, pushed over into his dive and aimed for the end of the runway. Two Japanese Zeros were taking off in a wing-to-wing formation. Selecting an aiming point between them, Buell released his entire bomb load, consisting of one 1,000-pound bomb and two 250-pounders: "The bombs struck among the two fighters just as they were leaving the ground. The leader veered right into the jungle in a flaming arc; the other exploded at the end of the runway."[51]

Rookie F6F pilot Bill Davis, who flew with the Lexington's VF-16, made his first kill over Cebu that morning. A Zero banked sharply away to the left as Davis dove from above. He lined the target up in his sights and pressed the trigger. A quick burst was enough to tear the Zero to pieces. "I was aware of someone screaming over the radio," Davis recalled. "I listened for a moment, but it had stopped. Then I realized that that screaming had been me. As I had fired my guns at the Zero, I had automatically screamed at the top of my lungs. That scream had come from somewhere deep in my brain, from the primordial lizard part of my brain."[52]

On a second strike that day, Davis flew low over an oil refinery on an island near Cebu City. Almost on a lark, he fired into the heart of the complex. Assuming that a few .50-caliber rounds would do minimal damage to the big complex of tanks, towers, and pipelines, Davis was startled when an explosion rocked his aircraft. He instinctively banked away and pulled up. Corkscrewing back to altitude, "I could see the entire refinery going up in flames. Explosions erupted all over the island as the refinery went up in a gigantic fireball."

Upon returning to the Lexington, Davis told the story of what he had done. One of his fellow pilots grimaced. "That refinery was the property of Texaco Oil Company," he said, "and I hoped it would survive the war. I own stock in Texaco."[53]

The American flyers would remember the September 12 raid as the "Cebu Barbeque." More than 1,200 sorties were flown that day. It was the most one-sided aerial slaughter since the Marianas Turkey Shoot two months earlier.

Masatake Okumiya, a senior Japanese air commander, had ordered about 150 Zero fighters from Luzon to Mindanao to reinforce the airfields that had been battered in the raids of the previous week. They staged through Cebu on their way south, and most were on the ground that morning when the armada of American carrier planes came over the eastern horizon. Okumiya happened to be on a transport aircraft inbound for Cebu just as the airstrike began. The pilot banked sharply away to avoid the attacking Hellcats, giving Okumiya a bird's-eye perspective of the "dive-bombers plunging from the sky, and the fighter planes as they screamed back and forth over the field, their wing guns spitting tracers into the parked Zeros. Within minutes Cebu became utter confusion. The American pilots were remarkably accurate, and the flames and black smoke boiling from the burning Zeros reminded me of a crematorium . . . ours."[54] Okumiya said the Third Fleet airstrikes of this period dealt a crippling blow against his effort to establish a fighter line capable of repelling an invasion of the Philippines.

Even after discounting the exaggerated claims of their returning pilots, the Third Fleet air intelligence officers reckoned that the strikes had destroyed 75 enemy planes in the air and another 123 on the ground. At least five ships had been sunk, another seven damaged. The sampans and small craft strafed, burned, or sunk were too many to count, probably at least forty or fifty. Ground installations at the airfields had been flattened or gutted. The carriers and their screening ships had braced for aerial counterstrikes from Japanese airfields in the Philippines, but no more than a handful of enemy planes had appeared on radar, and all had quickly turned away rather than challenge the orbiting Hellcats of the combat air patrol. Halsey reported to Nimitz on September 14: "Enemy's non-aggressive attitude unbelievable and fantastic. . . . No airborne opposition and only meager AA encountered. . . . No shipping left to sink. . . . This area is wide open."[55]

One of the few American planes lost was piloted by Ensign Thomas C. Tiller of the *Hornet*, whose Hellcat was struck and badly damaged over Leyte Gulf. Tiller made an emergency water landing and inflated his rubber raft. Local Filipino tribesmen paddled out to him in an outrigger and took him ashore. They treated him well, gave him food and shelter, and made contact with local pro-American guerillas who managed to radio the American fleet offshore. Tiller was picked up by a floatplane from the cruiser *Wichita* and returned to the *Hornet*, where he debriefed Admiral Jocko Clark.

The natives on Leyte had given Tiller some remarkable intelligence. There were no Japanese troops on Leyte, they said, and no airbases on the island except bare dirt or grass strips. The enemy garrison on neighboring Cebu numbered only about 15,000 troops. American intelligence estimates had been badly mistaken. An amphibious landing on Leyte would meet little or no opposition, if it could be executed quickly. Clark passed Tiller's information on to Halsey and Mitscher.

For more than two months Halsey had been pressing Nimitz to cancel interim operations in favor of an accelerated invasion of Mindanao in the southern Philippines. Now he considered an even bolder proposal. Perhaps MacArthur should bypass Mindanao and strike directly at Leyte, as soon as the invasion force could be mounted. Carney and others on the Third Fleet staff agreed. Still, Halsey hesitated; he sat in a corner of the *New Jersey's* bridge and mulled it over. Nimitz had rebuffed most of his prior suggestions, and he knew that "Such a recommendation, in addition to being none of my business, would upset a great many applecarts, possibly all the way up to Mr. Roosevelt and Mr. Churchill."[56] Finally he decided to go ahead. The urgent dispatch was addressed to Nimitz with MacArthur and King as coaddressees. Halsey renewed his proposal to cancel the pending amphibious landings in Yap and the Palaus, as they did "not offer opportunity for destruction of enemy forces commensurate with delay and effort involved in STALEMATE." The forces slated for those operations should be transferred to MacArthur's command, where they could be deployed in seizing Leyte "immediately and cheaply without any intermediate operations."[57]

Nimitz responded by suspending the landing on Yap, and he told King that he was willing to endorse an earlier landing on Leyte if MacArthur responded favorably. But Nimitz continued to insist that American forces must take the islands in the southern part of the Palau group. Noting that invasion fleets were already underway for Peleliu and Angaur, the CINCPAC ruled that these forces "will be sailed as planned."[58] In a separate cable to King later that day, Nimitz wrote that possession of those islands was "of course essential and it would not be feasible to reorientate the plans for the employment of the Palau attack and occupation forces as rapidly as Halsey's 130230 appears to visualize."[59] However—and here Nimitz raised a tantalizing possibility—if MacArthur resisted the proposal to accelerate the Leyte operation, "it may be feasible to take Iwo Jima in mid-October using the Yap force. . . . Am preparing plans along these lines for use if required. The foregoing represents concepts which may or may not eventuate but which are submitted now to keep you fully informed of possibilities."[60]

Peleliu was a bloody island fight that was, in retrospect, probably unnecessary. Iwo Jima was an even bloodier island fight that might have been less so if it had occurred earlier, before the Japanese had time to reinforce the island and dig a network of underground fortifications. If Nimitz had been willing to cancel the landing on Peleliu as Halsey had suggested, and had authorized a surprise assault on Iwo Jima in October using the same troops, the two decisions in combination might have saved thousands of American lives.

MacArthur was at sea on the cruiser *Nashville* with the Morotai invasion force. Due to radio silence requirements, he could not immediately reply. But he was "jubilant" about the prospect of an accelerated invasion of the Philippines, and as soon as the beachhead at Morotai was secure he flew back to his headquarters in Hollandia and drafted his affirmative reply to Halsey's proposal, stating, "I am prepared to initiate at once the execution of KING TWO [Leyte] with target date of October 20."[61]

The Joint Chiefs were in Quebec with Roosevelt, Churchill, and the British military chiefs. MacArthur's message arrived on the evening of September 15, when they were dining with their British counterparts. Excusing themselves, the four chiefs stepped out of the dining hall and into a nearby conference room to discuss it. None dissented. If Halsey, Nimitz, and MacArthur were all in agreement, they did not feel the need to give it much thought. Ninety minutes after receiving MacArthur's cable, the new orders were on their way back to the Pacific: "The Joint Chiefs of Staff authorize MacArthur to execute LEYTE Operation target date 20 October. . . . MacArthur and Nimitz arrange necessary coordination. . . . Inform Joint Chiefs of Staff of your plans."[62]

The American military leadership of the Second World War had resolved to spurn the creeping inertia that would lock them into existing plans and operations. In principle, they were ready and willing at all times to throw out their plans and adopt new ones, to move quickly to exploit changing circumstances. Adhering to this principle required steady pressure from the top of the command ladder, because large organizations tended to resist or even sabotage sudden changes in direction. The transpacific campaign was the largest and most complex multiservice amphibious war in history. Major changes in planned operations required a corresponding run of smaller changes across geographically far-flung units. In retrospect, then, it was remarkable that such momentous shifts in strategy could be and often were decided in the eleventh hour. The overnight decision to bypass Mindanao and hit Leyte in October 1944 was the most dramatic and far-reaching of all such changes. The Dirty Tricks Department had earned the right to congratulate itself, as it did in its war diary entry of September 14: "The Third Fleet suggestion had been approved and the Pacific War advanced three months."[63] FDR indulged in a spot of well-deserved boasting in his State of the Union address the following January, when he told Congress: "Within the space of 24 hours, a major change of plans was accomplished which involved Army and Navy forces from two different theaters of operations—a change which hastened the liberation of the Philippines and the final day of victory—a change which saved lives which would have been expended in the capture of islands which are now neutralized far behind our lines."[64]

But Nimitz nixed Halsey's urgent appeal to cancel the invasion of Peleliu, a sun-scorched patch of mangrove swamps and limestone badlands at the southern end of the Palaus. Peleliu hosted the most important Japanese airfield in the region, although most of its ground installations were destroyed by aerial and naval bombardment before American forces landed on the island. Initially the CINCPAC noted that the invasion forces earmarked for Peleliu were either at sea or had nearly finished combat-loading, which seems a rather threadbare rationale. Nimitz was not the sort of man to let interservice or inter-theater rivalries influence a decision when the lives of his troops were on the line. Nevertheless, a full accounting of this history must include the following facts. The main force slated to take Peleliu was the storied 1st Marine Division of Guadalcanal fame. The CINCPAC staff had quarreled heatedly with MacArthur's staff over control of that division. Halsey's proposal would require returning it to MacArthur's command. Without the Palau operation, there would be no major amphibious invasions in Nimitz's theater until 1945, and Nimitz would be obliged to transfer much of his idled amphibious shipping, landing craft, and troops to MacArthur for deployment in the Philippines campaign.

More than any major commander in the Pacific, Admiral Nimitz had preached the virtues of nimble and opportunistic decision-making. He had championed bold bypass maneuvers in the past—most notably during the FLINTLOCK operation the previous winter, when he had insisted upon bypassing the eastern Marshalls atolls over the opposition of his naval and ground commanders. In this instance, however, he insisted on taking Peleliu without providing a convincing justification for his decision. Samuel Eliot Morison, one of Nimitz's greatest admirers, was gently critical on this score. Until the end of his life, Nimitz continued to insist that the Palau landings had been indispensable—just as, for example, Spruance never conceded that the invasion of Tarawa in November 1943 had been unnecessary. In each case, time and experience showed that bypassing the islands could have been accomplished without loss of momentum in the broader offensive.

This axiom generally held true throughout the Pacific War—that each time American commanders considered and debated the option to bypass an island, and finally decided to go ahead and take it, their decision would seem tragically mistaken in hindsight. But they were naturally loath to admit error, either to historians or to themselves, because the blood spilled in those sands could never be unspilled, and no one wanted to hear that young men had died for a mistake.

Chapter Three

THE "OLD BREED," ALSO KNOWN AS THE 1ST MARINE DIVISION (1stMarDiv), was back in the vicinity of Guadalcanal—the island they had invaded, defended, and made famous two years earlier. Now they were stationed on Pavuvu, a 50-square-mile blotch of fetid green jungle that lay 30 miles west of Guadalcanal. They had been sent to this island for rest and training after their most recent campaign, a landing at Cape Gloucester on New Britain.

The Guadalcanal veterans, who comprised about a third of the division in September 1944, reminisced about their 1943 sojourn in the paradise of Melbourne, Australia, with its fine weather and complaisant women, and wondered why they could not go back. The others, replacements who had joined after Guadalcanal and before Cape Gloucester, or freshly trained boots who had just shipped in from the States, listened to the stories and cursed their bad luck for being sent instead to this godforsaken boondock.

From the day the Old Breed stepped onto the little wooden pier at Pavuvu, they reviled the place. Living conditions were primeval. The main "road" inland was little more than a muddy footpath, which led into a clearing between symmetric rows of soaring palms, the last remnants of an abandoned British coconut plantation. There they were told to pitch camp. Rummaging around in the underbrush, they found their tents, cots, and blankets piled on the ground, rain-soaked and filthy. Since no one had harvested the plantation in two-and-a-half years, the ground was covered with layers of fallen, rotting coconuts and palm fronds. Clearing the campground was a labor of the damned. The accumulated debris emitted a putrid stench that grew stronger as they excavated the layers. Rotten coconuts fell apart and spilled foul-smelling juice on the handlers. As they dug, they exposed nests of corpulent rats. Resolving to drive the creatures from their camp, the marines attacked with flamethrowers. Burning rodents scurried in every direction, and the tart scent of burning rat hair blended with the earthy reek of decomposing coconuts.

Before they could begin training in earnest, the marines could look forward to weeks of pick and shovel work in the stultifying heat and humidity. They dug drainage ditches and latrines. They built wooden boardwalks through mangrove swamps. They cleared and widened the old roadways by hacking at the jungle with machetes. In many areas the ground was too soft and wet to accommodate the weight of trucks, so they carted in crushed coral rock and poured it into the roadbeds. Each afternoon, with clocklike regularity, came a short, heavy tropical downpour. Since the island had no shower facilities, the marines stripped off their fatigues and ran soap over their bodies. They hurried, hoping to be clean and rinsed before the rain let up.

Without a proper mess hall, they ate C-Rations heated over sterno canisters. They slept in six-man pyramid tents, in a camp lit by makeshift torches made of empty ammunition cans and gasoline. Each night, an army of land crabs invaded and occupied the camp. The marines soon learned to shake the little bluish-black crustaceans out of their boots before putting them on each morning. Every few days, a private recalled, "we reached the point of rage over these filthy things and chased them out from under boxes, seabags, and cots. We killed them with sticks, bayonets, and entrenching tools. After the action was over we had to shovel them up and bury them, or a nauseating stench developed rapidly in the hot, humid air."[1]

They trained as best they could on Pavuvu, within the limitations of time, geography, and equipment shortages. Each morning they did calisthenics and ran a three-mile track around the island. After clearing a rifle range, they practiced marksmanship and refreshed their skills in the use of field weapons, including the Browning Automatic Rifle (BAR), the carbine, the Thompson submachine gun, the bazooka, the flamethrower, and the new 60mm shoulder mortar. Because the island was small and covered in dense undergrowth, there was little room to maneuver, and field exercises were necessarily done at the company level. But there were 15,000 marines on the island, more than one hundred companies; troops marching in column were constantly running into one another, and one had to stand aside to let the other pass. At first, there were scarcely any amphibious landing vehicles available to the division, and no tracked LVTs ("amtracs"). An urgent call went out to nearby islands to borrow any type of landing craft, including the army DUKWs and ordinary Higgins boats (LCVPs). Small-scale amphibious exercises followed, with individual companies landing in live-firing drills on one of Pavuvu's beaches. The rifle squads landed first, followed closely by machine gunners, bazooka gunners, and mortar squads. The sergeants shouted at them to race up the beach and take cover in the palm groves: "Get off the damn beach as fast as you can and move inland. The Nips are going to plaster it with everything they've got, so your chances are better the sooner you move inland."[2]

On August 28, they embarked on transports and LSTs anchored off Pavuvu, shuttling to the anchorage in landing craft. During a two-week westward passage through the South Pacific, marines killed time by writing letters, playing cards, reading books and magazines, or repacking their gear. They stripped their rifles, oiled them, and reassembled them; they sharpened their Kabar knives; they painted camouflage patterns on bazookas and flamethrowers. "I liked to stand at the railing and watch the porpoises play in the wake of the ship, the flying fish glide over the crests of the waves," recalled R. V. Burgin, a mortarman with K-Company, 3rd Battalion, 5th Marines. "We were all zigzagging as we sailed along, changing direction every fifteen minutes or so."[3] Belowdecks was stifling, as the heat surging up from the engines merged with the heat radiating down from the equatorial sun, but the navy crews attempted to limit the number of marines who could come up on deck for a breath of fresh air.

As usual, men in the ranks had no idea of their destination until they were at sea and underway. Informed that they were bound for Peleliu, they shrugged. No one had heard of it, but that was no wonder—their whole war to date had been a blur of indistinctive look-alike tropical islands, one after another. A foam rubber scale model of the island was distributed to each ship, and platoons were briefed by officers who used pointing sticks to indicate terrain features and landmarks. On Peleliu's flat southern half was the airfield—two runways and a taxiway making a figure "4," with broad tarmac and parking aprons. The landing beaches were on its southwest coast, designated White Beaches 1 and 2 and Orange Beaches 1, 2, and 3. The northern part of the island was dominated by limestone massifs covered by a thin jungle scrub. The division would establish a beachhead on D-Day, take the airfield and bisect the island on D-Day plus one (D plus 1), and overrun the hilly country to the north on D plus 2 and 3. That was the plan.

The commanding officer of the 1stMarDiv was Major General William H. Rupertus, who had been second-in-command (after Alexander Vandegrift) during the Guadalcanal campaign and had led the detachment on Tulagi, on the northern side of Ironbottom Sound. Rupertus was confident that the Peleliu operation would be bloody but quick, much like past invasions in the central Pacific such as Tarawa in the Gilbert Islands or Roi-Namur in the Marshalls. He expected that a massive preinvasion aerial and naval bombardment would kill many of the Japanese defenders, demolish their fortifications, and perhaps take the fight out of the survivors. If all went as hoped, the enemy infantry would launch reckless *banzai* charges, allowing the marines to mow them down with rifle and machine-gun fire. Rupertus was full of bravado during the passage to the Palaus, telling his subordinates that he expected one of them to bring him the Japanese commander's samurai sword.

The army's 81st Infantry Division ("Wildcats") was also headed to Peleliu, where it would be held in reserve in transports offshore. The overall Third Amphibious Corps commander for Operation STALEMATE was Major General Roy S. Geiger, who had succeeded Holland Smith in that role a month earlier. Geiger would decide whether to land the reinforcements on Peleliu; if they were not needed, they would be diverted to the smaller island of Anguar, a few miles to the southwest. Rupertus did not want the army on Peleliu and did not think it would be needed. He told war correspondents who sailed on his command ship, "It will be a short operation, a hard fought 'quickie' that will last for 4 days, 5 days at the most."[4]

On the night of September 14, D-day minus one, the 1st Division marines hit the sack early. Most did not sleep much, however; a good night of sleep was never assured in those cramped, stifling conditions, and many were too nervous and adrenaline-charged even to close their eyes. At 3:00 a.m., sergeants went through the sleeping compartments and rousted the marines from their bunks. They rose and began their D-Day ablutions—a last shave, a sink wash, and (critically) a bowel movement. Men stood in long lines for a turn at the sink or the head. They filled their canteens and drew three days' field rations. They broke out their battle dress—green dungarees with black Marine Corps emblems on the breast pockets. The ships' galleys served the traditional "condemned man's" breakfast of steak and eggs, but many marines had no appetite and did not eat a bite. They stuffed their personal belongings into canvas seabags, folded them into U-shaped bundles, and stowed them forward. Machine guns were test-fired into the ocean. Tins of black and green camouflage skin paint were passed through the ranks, and the men smeared their faces and hands with it.

Emerging on deck in the predawn darkness, they heard the *crump crump* of naval guns and glimpsed flickering lights on the northern horizon. Baritone reverberations rolled across the sea to a great distance, but out of sync with the distant flashes. As the ships surged onward toward the island, the explosions grew brighter, the thumping louder, and the time lag between them shrank. One sailor was reminded of "a summer storm in the Rockies."[5] As dawn broke in the east, it revealed a clear blue sky, without a cloud in sight—but Peleliu was enshrouded in smoke and haze, and all that could be seen was a vague purple shape, slightly humped at one end. Through and above the layer of smoke was a near-continuous lightshow of orange and pink flashes followed by spurts of yellow smoke. Every now and then came a glimpse of shredded palm trees, or ivory-hued razorback ridges in the island's central highlands. A gunnery officer on the cruiser *Portland*, studying the limestone ridges through binoculars, watched as a steel door slid open, a gun fired, and the door slammed shut. He trained his ship's 8-inch batteries on that door, and fired several projectiles at it, but could not destroy the target. He commented, "You can put all the steel in Pittsburgh on that thing and not get it."[6]

Like many amphibious troops before them, the marines were awed by the scene. Even half a mile from the battleships and cruisers, men had to shout to be heard over the thunderclaps made by the great guns. The 1st Marine Division had made two previous amphibious landings—Guadalcanal and New Britain—and neither had been opposed. Would it be three for three? They had heard enough about the landings on Tarawa, Saipan, and Guam to know that appearances could be deceiving, but still they wondered how anyone on Peleliu could survive such a monstrous barrage. About 1,400 tons of naval ordnance were dropped on the island in the hours before the landing. The panorama of destruction certainly improved their mood. One remarked, "It was beyond your imagination how anything could be alive, so we were beginning to feel pretty good."[7] Another wondered whether "the island would still be there by the time we arrived."[8]

On an LST (Landing Ship, Tank) that carried elements of the 1st Marine

Regiment, a voice on the loudspeaker commanded: "Now all marines lay to your debarkation stations!"⁹ The men buckled their packs and felt to confirm that their gear was hanging loosely in place. They went down the ladders in single file to the tank deck, a harshly lit enclosed cavity crowded with amtracs. Engines fired to life with an ear-piercing roar, and the air was choked with blue, swirling exhaust fumes. The marines climbed into their assigned vehicles and took their places. They closed their eyes against the fumes, but could not avoid breathing them, and some grew nauseous. "Beads of sweat broke out on our faces, and our jackets were already soggy wet and clinging to us," recalled Captain George P. Hunt, commanding officer of K Company, 3rd Battalion, 1st Marines. "The exhaust was pouring over us in spite of the great fans which whirred over our heads. The palms of my hands were hot and slippery."¹⁰ Hunt wondered whether his men would be poisoned before they had a chance to fight, but at last the clamshell bow doors separated, the steel ramp slid forward and down, and the first row of amtracs moved forward with a sudden lurch. They clattered down the ramps and into the sea, and the passengers filled their lungs with fresh air.

The LSTs were arrayed in a long row, their bow bays open and their ramps extending into the sea like long steel tongues. The crowded amtracs wallowed on the tide and awaited the signal to start toward the beach. Swells broke over the gunwales and soaked the men. Soon hundreds of amtracs were circling behind the line of departure. With no breeze, the blue exhaust fumes hung thick in the air. Naval patrol craft darted busily among the landing craft, their crews setting out buoys and shouting instructions through bullhorns. The battleships continued to fire on the island, punching temporary craters into the sea beneath their guns' muzzles. Marines in the boats had to shout to be heard over the relentless salvos. At 8:30 in the morning, right on schedule, came the order to launch the first wave.

The amtrac drivers opened up the throttles, the boats surged and rode higher on the water, and the engines threw up fan-shaped plumes of spray. Marines in other boats shook their fists and shouted encouragement as the first wave left the line of departure, but the roar of the engines and the guns drowned out their voices. The naval barrage ascended to a new pitch: the rockets whooshed overhead, the blasts of the big guns seemed to crack open the heavens, and the naval projectiles roared overhead like freight trains. When the drivers shifted gears, the transmissions responded with violent thuds that shook the hulls. They hit peak speed of 7 knots, rooster tails flying off the rudders. Men who peered over the bows could see little—Peleliu remained enshrouded in smoke and dust—but they might catch a glimpse of F6F Hellcats flying low over the beach and pouring out orange tracer fire, or carrier dive bombers hurtling down from overhead and planting bombs on unseen targets.

As they approached the reef line, it became apparent that the Japanese were firing back. Artillery and mortar rounds began falling among the boats, sending up impressively large columns of spray that caught the morning light and momentarily split into a rainbow of colors. The enemy could not see them; they were firing blindly through the smokescreen. Few boats were hit, but the barrage confirmed that the enemy was alive and full of fight. The beach remained hidden behind a curtain of flame and smoke. "It seemed as though a huge volcano had erupted from the sea," recalled Eugene B. Sledge, a twenty-year-old private, "and rather than heading for an island, we were being drawn into the vortex of a flaming abyss."[11]

The LVTs slowed as they approached the reef line. They bumped; the treads bit into the coral; the bow tilted sharply upward, and they began lurching and trundling across the top of the reef. Marines were thrown from their feet. They could not sit in the boats without fracturing their tail bones, so they crouched and held on to one another for support: "We grabbed and lurched and swore."[12] Many of the LVTs had been fitted with 75mm pack howitzers, and these fired back at the beach, also blindly. Inside of the reef, the sea was shallow and green, the sandy bottom visible from the gunwales. A line of broken, blasted palm trees loomed out of the white murk. The sun overhead was dimmed in the overcast, appearing as a silver disk, but its heat beat down relentlessly.

The earthshaking explosions made by the naval shells moved inland as the first boats scraped ashore on Orange Beach. The treads of the amphibious tractors bit into the sand; the engines raced; they trundled some distance up the beach, then jerked to a stop. Rear tailgates fell open with a slam, and sergeants shouted, "Let's go!" The marines rushed out the back, made a quick U-turn, and dashed up the beach. Chattering machine-gun and rifle fire came from unseen positions beyond the tree line. Rifle shots snapped and whined around their ears. The enemy was firing bigger weapons, too—antiboat guns and field artillery. Many marines in that first wave died on the open beach. Others sprinted into the palm groves and looked for the first opportunity to take cover—behind a tree, into a shell crater, or flat on the ground. Blackened and splintered palm trees soared over their heads. Their eyes and mouths were choked with dust; their nostrils filled with the acrid scent of cordite. The terrain had been blasted into a wild jumble of craters and fallen palm logs and tilting slabs of earth. The ruined landscape provided cover for advancing marines, but also for Japanese snipers.

The officers and sergeants kept shouting to push forward; they had to clear the beach for the succeeding waves of landing craft. They cut through barbwire entanglements. They moved forward from one covered position to another. Many fell to sniper fire. On the far side of the palm groves were machine-gun nests, log firing walls, and a long antitank ditch. The marines took them by frontal assault, at full sprint, "hollering like a bunch of Indians"—the leatherneck version of the *banzai* charge.[13]

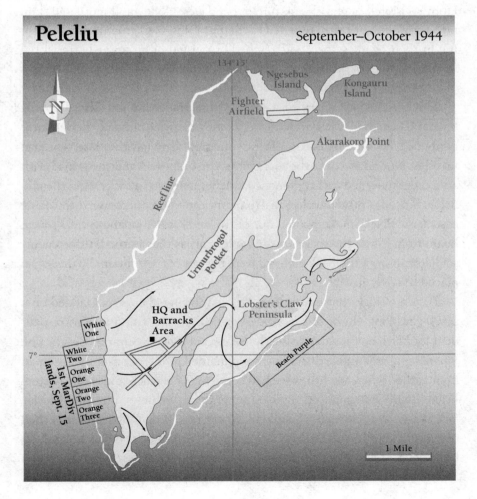

Peleliu　　　　　　　　　September–October 1944

Hunt's company landed at the northern end of White Beach, where a rocky headland jutted about 200 yards out into the sea. Strong pillboxes and cunningly hidden firing embrasures were built into the southern face of that rock. A 47mm antitank gun in an unapproachable firing position knocked out several amphibious vehicles before they reached the beach. K Company marines found themselves under a hailstorm of enfilade fire, without any good options for cover. They tried to dig in as best they could, but the ground was hard coral rock. The heat built up by mid-morning and became awful; everyone was soaked through with sweat. As Japanese mortar fire found the range, the marines' wounded multiplied. They were strewn across the beach, seemingly too many to evacuate. Constantly came the cry: "Corpsman!" Stretcher-bearers were cut down by enemy sniper fire. Captain Hunt registered "a ghastly mixture of bandages, bloody and mutilated skin; men gritting their teeth, resigned to their wounds; men groaning and writhing in their agonies; men outstretched or twisted or grotesquely transfixed in the attitudes of death; men with their entrails exposed or whole chunks of body ripped out of them."

Smoke grenades provided a respite from the murderous fire. Lobbing several to the base of the rock face, Hunt's marines blinded the Japanese gunners, who were reduced to firing randomly through the haze. A squad was sent around to cover the rear exit of the pillbox. A marine armed with a shoulder-mounted rocket grenade launcher managed a lucky shot; the grenade glanced off the muzzle of a 47mm antitank gun and entered the firing casement. Black smoke poured out of the embrasure. Japanese voices were heard from inside the rock, screaming in pain as they burned; three enemy soldiers ran from the back exit and were put out of their misery by the squad placed to cover it.

By ten o'clock that morning, three infantry regiments had landed on a 2,500-yard-long chain of beaches. Tom Lea, an artist and war correspondent for *Life* magazine, landed with the second wave on Orange Beach. The Japanese mortar and artillery barrage remained as intense as it had been an hour earlier, when the first wave had come in. The beach and shallows were littered with burning and disabled amphibious vehicles, and marines lay face down on the beach, "huddled like wet rats." Lea took cover in a shell crater and kept his head down as mortar blasts tore up the beach. Looking back out to sea, he watched as marines waded in through the surf, rifles held above their heads, pillars of whitewater erupting around them. He saw several killed: "One figure seemed to fly to pieces. With terrible clarity I saw the head and one leg sail into the air."[14]

Lea had not brought his sketchpad to the island, but he took mental photographs and stored the images to be retrieved from memory. Later he drew or painted several scenes for *Life*, including a provocatively graphic painting entitled "The Price," which depicted a mortally wounded marine staggering up the beach in the moment before he fell dead. The left side of the man's face was completely gone, "and the mangled shreds of what was left of an arm hung down like a stick, as he bent over in his stumbling, shock-crazy walk. The half of his face that was still human had the most terrifying look of abject patience I have ever seen. He fell behind me, in a red puddle on the white sand."[15] After publishing the image months later, *Life* received a flood of complaints and subscription cancellations. Some accused Lea of embellishing the scene, a charge he angrily denied. He had painted exactly what he had seen, he said, no less and no more.

In a palm grove inland of the beach, Lea found a large shell crater that had been commandeered for a temporary field hospital. Corpsmen, four to a stretcher, were arriving continuously and setting the stretchers down in rows. Plasma bottles hung from a broken tree stump. Corpsmen gave morphine shots and applied tourniquets. A chaplain held a canteen in one hand and a bible in the other. "He was deeply and visibly moved by the patients' suffering and death," Lea wrote. "He looked very lonely, very close to God, and he bent over the shattered men so far from home. Corpsmen put a poncho, a shirt, a rag, anything handy, over the gray faces of the dead and carried them to a line on the beach, under a tarpaulin, to await the digging of graves."[16]

The Americans now held a two-mile-long beachhead, with an average depth of about 500 yards, encompassing the southwestern shore of the island. Mine disposal squads were digging up Japanese artillery shells that had failed to detonate. Men carried spools of telephone wire and were draping it haphazardly across the plowed-up ground and charred underbrush behind the beach. Scattered everywhere was the debris of battle, a jumble of discarded packs, helmets, rifles, boxes, clothing, and rubber life belts. A long antitank ditch that had been dug by the Japanese had been commandeered as the 1st Division command post. Nearby were regimental and battalion CPs for the 5th Marines. These areas remained under heavy mortar fire throughout D-Day. One battalion CP (3/5) took a direct hit that injured the regimental commander and several of his staff.

The division command was still struggling to form an accurate picture of what was happening on the island. Radiomen could not establish contact with forward units. The relentless artillery fire chewed up the field telephone systems. Message runners were forced to rush across exposed positions, and many were wounded or killed. General Rupertus committed his reserve battalions, and then told his staff that he had "shot his bolt." As reports came in, his staff tallied D-Day casualties of 1,111, including at least 209 killed.[17]

That evening, as darkness fell, the naval vessels offshore fired parachute flares and star shells to keep the contested ground illuminated. The spectral orange and yellow light gave the blasted-out landscape an eerie, otherworldly appearance. Shadows veered and danced. The gnarled stumps of blasted trees reached up from the earth. A sailor offshore was reminded of a "moonscape," or "the photos I had seen of no-man's land during the trench warfare of World War I."[18] Japanese artillery and mortars fired periodically, and infiltrators and small unit attacks continued intermittently until dawn. Company K, holding the rocky point at the northern flank of the beachhead, kept their fingers on their triggers while listening for any sound that might portend a new attack—"a shout, a rustling, a jabbering, a scraping of feet on the rocks."[19] The marines threw hand grenades blindly at those sounds. The Japanese fighters on Peleliu did not rush forward pell-mell in the style of a *banzai* charge, but crossed from one covered position to another. They fought shrewdly, attacking in much the same manner as the marines would attack if the circumstances were reversed. "Japs were bobbing in and out of the rocks," Hunt recalled. "I could see their flat, brown helmets. At times it was hard to distinguish them from my men, so quick were the movements."[20] Unseen snipers fired from the tops of high palm trees, hitting marines who were keeping their heads down and had assumed they were out of the line of fire. There was no rest or respite for the men of Company K; the enemy kept coming, all night long, from three directions. "The fight became a vicious melee of countless explosions, whining bullets, shrapnel whirring overhead or clinking off the rocks, hoarse shouts, shrill-screaming Japanese."[21]

An hour before dawn on the sixteenth, the ground was still warm to the touch, and the temperature was 80 degrees Fahrenheit. A low mist rode over the airfield, but when the sun came up it soon dissipated and was replaced by a shimmering heat haze. The temperature that day would reach 105° in the shade, but few marines on Peleliu had the luxury of shade. The air was heavy and still. Sweat ran down their faces and left streaks in their camouflage face paint. Gray coral dust stuck to the sweat and paint and made them look as if they were wearing ivory-colored masks.

Most marines had landed with two canteens of drinking water. By the second day the canteens were empty, or nearly so. A platoon on the edge of the airfield found a pool of milky-looking water at the bottom of a pit. It was full of grit, but the men were too thirsty to care, and drank from it. At a little after seven, carriers brought five-gallon cans of water to the front lines, and the men dipped their tin cups into it. It had a brownish tint and smelled of fuel. A blue film of oil rode on top of the water. R. V. Burgin recalled: "Guys would take a mouthful and spit it out. Those that swallowed it would throw up a few minutes later. Some of them had the dry heaves all morning."[22] They subsequently learned that the freshwater reserves had been loaded onto the transports in fifty-five-gallon fuel drums, and some of these drums had not been properly cleaned and sanitized.

The 5th Marines had been given the job of driving straight across the airfield to Peleliu's eastern shore. They would bisect the island and cut off the Japanese fighters in the south. As they prepared to advance, they looked up at the sheer rock face directly north of the airfield, the forbidding feature someone had named "Bloody Nose Ridge." Japanese artillery and mortar fire had been pouring down from that ridge since they had landed the previous day. Some attested that they could "feel" the gaze of unseen enemy soldiers from that soaring vantage point, and it gave them a sensation of powerlessness.

The jump-off signal came a few minutes after ten. The marines rose to their feet and began jogging toward the center of the airfield. They spread out as they had been trained to do, with 8 or 10 feet between them. They moved fast, but kept their heads down. Artillery and mortar shells landed among them, but they did not stop because they knew a stationary target was easier to hit. Blasts gouged chunks of soil out of the ground and flung it up into the sky. A constant shower of shrapnel and coral pebbles fell upon them as they ran. Smoke and dust got in their eyes, noses, and mouths. Corporal Burgin recalled: "Everything was coming at us—mortars, artillery, machine-gun and rifle fire. You heard hiss and zing of shrapnel and bullets all around you. We were as exposed as bugs on the breakfast table. I kept yelling, 'Keep moving! Keep moving!'"[23]

In his peripheral vision, Sledge saw men fall to his right and left. His field of vision was partly concealed by smoke, and he felt grateful for that. The ground seemed to tilt beneath his feet. His ears rang from the repeated concussions. The big blasts seemed to grow closer and more numerous:

> I felt as if I was floating along in the vortex of some unreal thunder-storm. Japanese bullets snapped and cracked, and tracers went by me on both sides at waist height. This deadly small-arms fire seemed almost insignificant amid the erupting shells. Explosions and the hum and the growl of shell fragments shredded the air. Chunks of blasted coral stung my face and hands while steel fragments splattered down on the hard rock like hail on a city street. Everywhere shells flashed like giant firecrackers. . . . The farther we went, the worse it got. The noise and concussion pressed on my ears like a vise. I gritted my teeth and braced myself in anticipation of the shock of being struck down at any moment. It seemed impossible that any of us could make it across.[24]

The airfield was a burned-out scrapyard, littered with the blackened wrecks of more than one hundred Japanese planes. All the buildings had been bombed out, but heaps of rubble and the remains of concrete walls provided cover for enemy soldiers. Whatever their plans, the marines had to stop and take cover as they approached these positions. As soon as they stopped running, they realized how great a toll the heat was taking. They had sweated entirely through their field uniforms, and their boots were full of sweat. Several men were suffering heat prostration. Their faces were mottled and scarlet-colored, and they shivered as if freezing cold. Sledge lay on his back and lifted his feet, one and then the other: "Water literally poured out of each shoe."[25]

After a five-hour firefight on the airfield, the first echelons of the 5th Marines reached the eastern shore at 3:00 p.m. They set up a semicircular perimeter in a mangrove swamp, with their backs to the beach, and prepared for the inevitable long night of shelling, infantry attacks, and infiltration tactics.

By the afternoon of September 16, D plus 1, Orange Beach had assumed the appearance of a busy ship-to-shore depot. The beachmasters had taken over, and an abundance of cargo, equipment, and vehicles was coming ashore in a constant relay of pontoon barges.[26] Men were pounding signs into the ground to indicate where incoming cargo should be dumped. One part of Orange Beach was so congested with crates and vehicles that it had to be closed to foot traffic. Dead marines were laid out in rows on the beach; presently a burial detail would collect their dog tags and bury them in long trenches. There were also many hundreds of Japanese dead, mostly uncovered. Their pockets and other belongings had been thoroughly rifled, and all valuables or interesting souvenirs claimed. One marine recalled "glossy red tripe boiling from naked bellies. Those arms and legs that are still attached are curiously bent akimbo. . . . The eyeballs are deflated, dehydrated, collapsing in on themselves."[27] Their skin was beginning to turn brown, and flies were buzzing around them. The odor of death soon became overpowering in the heat, and the marines put in an urgent demand for bulldozers so that the dead could be buried as quickly as possible.

General Rupertus had wanted to come ashore on D-Day, but he had been injured in a training accident, his foot was in a cast, and he was walking with a cane. His staff convinced him to wait a day. On D plus 1, he put ashore and took command at the division CP inland of Orange Beach. His mood was upbeat. The 5th Marines had taken possession of the airfield, Peleliu's only real strategic asset, and had stitched up their lines across the waist of the island. Convinced that the worst of the fight was behind them, Rupertus radioed Geiger (in his command ship offshore) to say that he would not need the reserve force. General Geiger, in turn, released the 81st Infantry Division to land on nearby Anguar. Rupertus's recommendation and Geiger's decision would subsequently draw close scrutiny and censure.

On the third day of the battle, assuming that victory was imminent, Rupertus ordered the 1st Marines to take the high terrain north of the airfield, the limestone massif they had nicknamed Bloody Nose Ridge. On old maps of Peleliu, it was designated Urmurbrogal Mountain. The route of attack was a narrow, rocky valley they called the Horseshoe Bowl. From the airfield, the Horseshoe was approached by a serpentine footpath leading through rubble-strewn remains of concrete blockhouses and pillboxes. Marines advanced carefully, flanking and attacking the blasted-out fortifications, where Japanese machine gunners and snipers had taken cover. It was slow, bloody work. The heat and humidity were unremitting, and often the men had to stop and wait for water carriers to haul five-gallon cans up to the lines. Obstacles and debris were cleared to make way for tanks. Lea, who visited the scene, described the path as a "trail littered with Jap pushcarts, smashed ammunition boxes, rusty wire, old clothes, and scattered gear.

Booby traps kept us from handling any of it. . . . There were dead Japs on the ground where they had been hit, and in two of the pillboxes I saw some of the bodies were nothing more than red raw meat and blood mixed with the gravely dust of concrete and splintered logs."[28]

By the end of the day, advance patrols of the 1st Marines reached the base of the Horseshoe. They did not like the look of it. Every inch of the rock-strewn canyon was swept by mutually supporting Japanese firing ports and embrasures. Some could at least be seen, high in the cliffs, but many others were well concealed behind scrub brush. How to attack such a fortress? Climbing a rock face to get at one Japanese firing port would only expose the marines to deadly fire from another. And the Horseshoe was only the beginning of a labyrinth of badlands implanted with fiendishly ingenious fortifications. Beyond it lay one razorback ridge after another. The craggy topography had previously been covered by jungle foliage, and aerial reconnaissance photographs had given the impression of gently rounded hills. But the bombing and shelling had exposed a sinister landscape of half-blackened ridges, knobs, pinnacles, canyons, gulches, and sinkholes. The marines named each feature as they drew their maps and devised their plan of campaign. The Horseshoe was overlooked by Walt's Ridge to the east and the Five Sisters to the west, joined to the Five Brothers to the north. Running parallel to the Horseshoe was another canyon they named the Wildcat Bowl, enclosed by a sheer escarpment they named the China Wall—and on the far side of that, a boulder-strewn corridor they called Death Valley. The contested area was only about a single square mile—but for the men who fought in it, the Urmurbrogal pocket was like a planet unto itself, a seemingly interminable and unconquerable maze of karst.

THE JAPANESE GARRISON, 11,000 MEN STRONG, was drawn from the crack Fourteenth Division of the Kwantung Army. The commanding officer was Colonel Kunio Nakagawa, a heavily decorated "star" officer who had commanded the division's Second Regiment. The force had shipped in from Manchuria after the sudden loss of the Marshall Islands earlier that year. Tokyo did not expect the Peleliu garrison to survive, and had made no plans to evacuate survivors. These seasoned veterans were expected to sell the island as dearly as possible, and then die to the last man.

Since their arrival in May, the Japanese had worked tirelessly to improve and extend Peleliu's underground fortifications. Colonel Nakagawa was a leading champion of defensive *fukkaku* ("honeycomb") tactics, which relied on burrowing under the ground into bunkers and tunnels. Foreseeing that the enemy would win absolute naval and air supremacy and would reduce all above-ground positions to rubble, the colonel kept most of his troops in reserve in caves deep in the massifs. He intended to make the Americans come to him, in the high terrain of the island's interior. This "defense-in-depth" concept would allow the Japanese to hold out over a longer period of time and exact a higher price from the attackers.

Peleliu was better suited to those tactics than any other Pacific War battlefield. The ridges in the heart of the island, and the great honeycomb of caves that lay beneath them, were products of millions of years of geological processes. A thin topsoil clung to the ivory-colored rock, enough to support a sparse green scrub that concealed cave entrances and firing embrasures—but the rocky ground was impervious to picks and shovels, which meant that the attackers could not easily dig themselves into foxholes. The Japanese had expanded and improved nature's handicraft. In September 1944, on the eve of the American landing, the greater part of Nakagawa's garrison force inhabited a great subterranean labyrinth connecting more than five hundred natural and manmade caves. Some of the entrances were fitted with steel doors built flush into the slopes, well hidden by camouflage netting or vegetation. Some were so small that men could enter only by crawling on their hands and knees, but one great underground cavern was large enough to accommodate a thousand men at once. The system had been fitted with wooden stairways, electric lights, telephone lines, storerooms, ventilation shafts, interior decks, mess cooking facilities, hospitals, command posts, and built-in bunks. Freshwater had collected in cisterns, enough to sustain a long siege. The tunnel network went on for miles. Nakagawa could move reinforcements from one part of the hills to another, even over a distance of half a mile, without exposing them to enemy fire. Deep in the rock, the temperature was cool and comfortable, giving the defenders respite from the furnace-like heat outside.

The garrison was well armed and amply supplied. Nakagawa had 75mm artillery pieces, 81mm mortars, 141mm heavy mortars, .50-caliber machine guns, dual purpose antiaircraft guns, rocket launchers, and plenty of ammunition of all types stored deep in the caves. In many instances, cave entrances doubled as high-ground firing ports. The larger guns were mounted on rails and could be moved through subterranean passages from one position to another. An ingenious system of hoists and small railcars moved ammunition up from the magazines. At the mouth of the larger cave entrances, Japanese engineers had blasted deep bays into the sides of the tunnels; troops could take cover here when the mouth of the cave came under artillery fire. Hidden passageways and firing ports were left in place, so that even if a cave was breached by the enemy, it might still remain a threat.

In early September, Peleliu came under heavy and repeated aerial attacks by Third Fleet carrier planes and Army Air Forces B-24 bombers. The attackers flattened virtually every structure above ground, including all of the buildings adjacent to the airfield. During a September 6 fighter sweep, the aviators found "no airborne aircraft or shipping and meager AA. Few operational aircraft seen on ground."[29] Dozens of Japanese planes were destroyed, including many on the ground. Repeated carrier strikes hit the airfield and beach fortifications with bombs, rockets, and napalm. On September 12, the American battleships and cruisers had appeared in the offing and began raining high-explosive projectiles down on the island. The bombardment destroyed most remaining structures and blockhouses above the landing beaches and especially around the airfield. The cumulative onslaught began to burn and strip away the jungle foliage in the central hills, revealing the unexpectedly steep and rocky terrain, crowned with soaring palisades of coral spires and columns that might have been considered beautiful in a different context. A few Japanese guns fired back, but not many.

In his command post under one of those ridgelines, Colonel Nakagawa remained in radio contact with the Japanese headquarters on Koror, another island to the north. His post was comfortable, efficient, and well constructed. The cavern was equipped with an elaborate array of decks and stairways, a refrigerated storeroom, and comfortable quarters partitioned by bulkheads for Nakagawa and other senior officers. The CP was furnished with desks, conference tables, file cabinets, wall maps, and communications equipment. From deep in their underground lair, the concussions of the big naval shells seemed distant and muffled. They had suffered only negligible casualties in the bombing and shelling, and had conserved the better part of their strength to meet the enemy on the ground of their choosing—the high ground.

Four battalions of the 1st Marines mounted the first attack up the Horseshoe Bowl. The terrain funneled them into a sector approximately 1,000 yards wide, enclosed on both sides by ridges and enfiladed by high firing positions. Marines moving up the rock-strewn corridor had to climb and crawl. They were constantly under fire from different directions, by weapons of various types and calibers—rifles, machine guns, grenades, rockets, mortars, and field artillery. Their entrenching tools made no impression on the rocky ground, so they could not dig for cover. The unseen enemy fired from one slot, withdrew into the subterranean network as the marines returned fire, and then fired from another. A rain of mortars blasted coral dust and pebbles from the ground, augmenting the shrapnel effect of each shell. Tanks and other armored vehicles were stopped by boulders and rock piles.

Colonel Lewis Burwell "Chesty" Puller, the regimental commander, intended to take high ground, one ridge at a time, and he was willing to suffer heavy losses to do it. But gaining possession of a ridge would avail the marines nothing if they could not hold it. On September 20, a company (B-Company, 1st Battalion) led by Captain Everett P. Pope seized the summit of Hill 154 at the edge of Horseshoe Valley, only to find itself exposed to overpowering crossfire from Japanese positions on even higher ground. Lying flat, the unit held on until nightfall, but darkness brought waves of ferocious infantry counterattacks. The company defended its position not only with rifles, machine guns, and grenades, but also with bayonets, knives, rocks, and their bare hands. Their numbers diminishing, their wounded accumulating, they ran low on ammunition. At dawn they still held the ridge, but only eight men were healthy enough to fight. They had no option but to withdraw, and received permission to do so. But the company had to evacuate their wounded, no easy task; they lowered them down the ridge with ropes. The dead were left where they lay, and the bodies would bake in the tropical heat for another two weeks until they could be removed and buried in a cemetery near the beach. The ordeal of Pope's marines was a bitter foretaste of the fighting to come as the Americans pushed farther into the pocket.

Marines who had fought on multiple Pacific island battlefields agreed that Peleliu was the worst. The pitiless equatorial sun beat down on a lifeless moonscape of ivory-colored coral rock, and temperatures routinely surpassed 110 degrees. After three days on the line, the men looked like wraiths: lips blistered, hair matted, coral dust caked on unshaven faces. Sweat ran into their eyes, which already ached from the glare of the sun. The acrid smell and biting taste of cordite stung their noses and throats. Their hands were raw and abraded from crawling on the rocks. No one could escape the all-pervading stench of putrefying bodies, rotting rations, and their own excrement. Clouds of large greenish-blue flies fed off the unburied dead and tormented the living. Sudden torrential rainstorms came in the late afternoon, and sometimes at night. There was no escape from the relentless artillery and mortar barrages. Even among those who were not directly injured by the blasts, the accumulating concussions sapped their strength and spirit. At times the roar and thud of artillery continued from dusk to dawn, making it difficult to get a wink of sleep—but a man who was exhausted enough could sleep even under the muzzles of a 155mm howitzer, which made a sound, said Sterling Mace, another man in Sledge's platoon, "commensurate to having a subway tunnel running between your ears."[30] When the guns paused, the marines could hear wounded and dying Japanese crying out in the night. Often they cried out for their mothers, as did dying men of all races.

Down on the island's southern lowlands, the rear-echelon engineering and logistics forces were already hard at work converting Peleliu into an advanced operating base. Three navy construction battalions ("Seabees") had come ashore on D plus 3. They had improvised an ingenious quarter-mile-long causeway made of pontoon barges, allowing vehicles to drive directly out of the LSTs and over the reefs to Orange Beach. By D plus 4, the airfield and bivouac areas were teeming with trucks and bulldozers. Tent camps were springing up in the palm groves inland of the beaches. The Seabees had orders to extend and grade the main runway to a length of 6,500 feet so that it could accommodate B-24s.[31] Bulldozers pushed the wrecked remains of Japanese aircraft to the margins of the airstrips. Trucks carted away debris and brought in crushed coral rock to be turned into concrete. Japanese artillery and mortars on the Urmurbrogal ridges could still hit the northern part of the airfield, so the engineers were obliged to work under fire, and new craters were punched in the runways even as they were filling in the old ones. The air was heavy with dust kicked up by explosions and heavy machinery, and the engineers wore masks to avoid choking on it. "In the north, over Bloody Nose Ridge, I could see the red-orange glare of fire and hear the rumble of war, like continuous thunder," said Charles S. McCandless, a Seabee lieutenant. "The whole vista was like a scene from *The Inferno.*"[32]

A squadron of Marine F4U Corsairs flew into the airfield on September 19 and commenced ground-support operations against Japanese positions on the nearby ridgeline. They dropped 500-pound bombs and napalm, often from very low altitude. These may have been the shortest bombing runs of the entire Pacific War. The Corsairs took off, banked right immediately, and flew low over enemy-held positions in the hills. They dropped their payloads, banked right again, and landed. A typical bombing run lasted less than two minutes; the pilots did not even bother to retract their landing gear.

Ordinary bombs seemed to make little impression against the Japanese subterranean positions, but napalm at least stripped away remaining vegetation, exposing the Japanese firing ports to view. The jellied gasoline incendiary sometimes penetrated into the mouths of the enemy caves, forcing the Japanese to withdraw deeper into their network of underground tunnels.

General Rupertus, failing to grasp the full dimensions of what his division was up against, issued unduly optimistic reports to General Geiger. The Americans now held firm control of the landing beaches, the eastern beaches, the eastern "Lobster's Claw" peninsula, and the airfield. Elements of the 5th Marines were pushing up the West Road against light and scattered resistance. The 7th Marines had overrun the southern end of the island and were methodically hunting down and killing all Japanese stragglers in that area. Most of the remaining Japanese troops on the island were hemmed in to a shrinking pocket in the Urmurbrogal. One last big offensive push should do it, or so Rupertus and his division staff believed. Constant forward momentum was their governing ideal. Rupertus told Colonel Puller to "hurry up" and break the stalemate. Puller, a famously belligerent warrior who did not need to be cajoled, passed those exhortations down the line to his company commanders, and detached several of his 1st Marines staff personnel for frontline duty. The regiment charged up the Horseshoe again and again, with infantrymen advancing behind tanks and supported by artillery barrages; again and again they were repulsed with heavy casualties. The regiment suffered 1,749 casualties in the first eight days of the battle for Peleliu. Attacking units had suffered 56 percent casualties, including a staggering 71 percent in the 1st Battalion. They had little to show for those awful losses, having made barely any progress into the enemy-held badlands.

When General Geiger first toured Peleliu on September 21, he was alarmed by what he saw. Rupertus and his division command staff showed signs of fatigue and self-doubt, but they were not yet ready to admit that new tactics were needed. At the 1st Marines regimental CP at the base of the Horseshoe Bowl, many of the unit commanders looked to be in a state of physical, emotional, and spiritual exhaustion. They wore gaunt, hunted expressions. Colonel Puller was monosyllabic, virtually catatonic. He and his staff had no ideas other than to bring in reinforcements and attack in greater numbers. Geiger concluded that the 1st Marines were done, that their losses had been too heavy, and that the regiment should be pulled off the line. He decided to bring in part of his corps reserve—a regimental combat team of the army's 81st Infantry Division. Rupertus objected strenuously, but Geiger had made up his mind. He ordered Puller's marines to prepare to ship out, and summoned the army RCT to land on Peleliu.

As Gene Sledge's King Company (3rd Battalion, 5th Marines) moved up the West Road on September 21, they passed a column of 1st Marines coming the other way. Sledge saw immediately that the regiment's numbers had been severely culled. "What once had been companies in the 1st Marines looked like platoons," he wrote, and "platoons looked like squads."[33] Sterling Mace, marching in column with Sledge, was thinking along the same lines. One glance at the faces of the men in the shattered regiment was enough to tell him that Peleliu had worse to offer than what his unit had encountered so far. Their brothers coming down from the Horseshoe stared back at them with "eyes glazed and distant . . . they looked like hell, with battered dungarees salted white with sweat, unshaven and filthy from powder burns, blood-stained and near emaciated." Aware that his regiment was likely to be sent up into those same ridges, Mace wondered if they might be catching a glimpse of "our future selves."[34]

Tom Lea, the *Life* combat artist, sketched a portrait of a marine who had just returned to the bivouac area near Orange Beach after frontline combat. The term "combat neurosis" was just then entering into the medical-military lexicon, and the man in Lea's painting exhibits the symptoms. He appears gaunt, haggard, and hunted; his pupils are dilated, his jaw hanging open, his eyes lifeless. It is a wretched and inconsolable portrait, analogous to Edvard Munch's 1893 painting *The Scream*. Lea's painting, entitled *That*

2,000-Yard Stare, ran in the June 1945 issue of *Life*. It remains one of the most famous (or infamous) artworks of the Second World War.

Eight days after D-Day on Peleliu, Operation STALEMATE was threatening to live up to its name. The Japanese had beat back every concerted thrust into their "pocket" in the ridges. With possession of the high ground, they could and did harass the airfield with intermittent mortar and artillery fire. Navy patrols discovered that enemy reinforcements carried by barges and small craft were landing on the northern shore of the island. Division command insisted on securing northern Peleliu, which meant driving up the West Road in force and securing it against artillery and sniper fire. Two regiments, one army and one marine, began probing attacks up the road. In a section designated "Sniper's Alley," the rugged cliffs of the Urmurbrogal protruded toward the coast, funneling the American forces into a narrow pass between a mangrove swamp and enemy-held high ground. Snipers fired from the ridges on the right and the swamps to the left, killing or wounding many dozens of soldiers and marines. The road was mined and booby-trapped with tripwires and other devices. These impediments inevitably slowed any progress, but getting control of the West Road was deemed essential, and Rupertus continued to push them hard. Given the bloody stalemate in the Horseshoe Bowl, he hoped to find a more profitable route into the Urmurbrogal pocket from the north.

On September 23, the army's 321st RCT launched a general attack on the ridgeline from a staging point just south of Garekoru Village. With the close support of naval gunfire from warships offshore, the soldiers made good initial progress.[35] Under cover of jungle vegetation, they penetrated inland to a distance of about 1,200 yards, cleaning out several caves and pillboxes, killing about thirty enemy soldiers, and seizing much more territory than they had anticipated. The sudden advance took the Japanese by surprise; they had not deployed strong forces to defend that part of their perimeter. Nightfall brought punishing counterattacks, however, and by midday on September 24 the attackers were wondering whether they had bitten off more than they could chew. The front line having been pushed far up into the ridges, the supply line from the coast was long and precarious, over rocky and uneven ground. Ammunition, fresh water, and rations had to be carried in by hand, over a half-mile route that led up and over steep slopes and down through deep ravines. The Japanese counterattacked vigorously. Artillery and mortar fire continued unabated. The wounded had

to be brought out on stretchers, a painstaking effort that caused great pain
to the injured men, and many stretcher bearers were struck down by snipers.
The Americans dared not leave their wounded behind, knowing that they
were liable to be tortured to death.[36]

As always, the Japanese came at night, either singly or in small parties.
In the nocturnal stillness, every sound was dramatically amplified. Captain Hunt wrote of the nearly unbearable strain of those nights on Peleliu:
"When one lies in a hole peering intently into die black, listening, smelling,
hearing only the sound of one's breathing, waiting, expecting, the stillness
may become appalling, dead objects may rise slowly and live, the motionless
may move, sounds of leaves stirred by the breeze may become the sneak-
ing movements of human feet, a friend may be an enemy, an enemy a
friend, until, unless controlled by toughness of mind, one's imagination may
become haunted by the unseen and the unheard."[37] Some men went mad,
and began shouting in their madness. They were pulled off the line immediately, because a marine who could not stay quiet endangered his comrades.
Japanese night-infiltrators wore split-toed canvas *tabi* shoes that made no
sound, and attacked silently with knives, swords, or bayonets. According to
Corporal Burgin, a Japanese soldier snuck into a firing nest on a ridgetop
one night and began choking a marine in his squad. The man woke up and
jammed his fingers into the Japanese soldier's eye sockets, then threw him
from the cliff. "I heard the Jap screaming all the way down, from the second
his eyes were gouged until he hit the bottom," Burgin wrote. "I've never
heard such a bloodcurdling sound in my life."[38]

As on Saipan two months earlier, clouds of bloated metallic greenish-
blue flies rose from the rotting, unburied bodies of the dead. They buzzed
loudly in the air, though they seemed to prefer to crawl rather than fly.
They fed on the remains of discarded food, on excrement, on blood and
bodies; they crawled into the men's canteen cups and lighted down upon
their ration cans. They were lazy and seemingly stubborn. Unintimidated
by a waved hand, they had to be shaken or plucked away from a spoon or
fork. After the experience on other Pacific killing fields, this fly infestation
had been anticipated. Experts from the U.S. Department of Agriculture
were flown in to run an island-wide extermination campaign. Hundreds
of barrels of DDT were stored in the holds of the transport fleet offshore.
The chemical was mixed with diesel oil and sprayed throughout the island,
especially over corpses. More than three hundred sanitary squads, with

tanks of the mixture strapped to their backs, sprayed it over the dead, over pools of standing water, and around "kitchens, messes, and latrines."[39] Truck-mounted sprayers coated much of the area around the beaches. The sanitation teams even found a way to cover the contested ground in the ridges. A TBM Avenger was fitted with gasoline-powered aerial sprayers, and an aircraft refueling pump system was used to pump the solution from belly tanks. The system sprayed about one hundred gallons per minute. By these means the insecticide was spread widely over the Urmurbrogal, settling indiscriminately on both enemy and American positions, coating the living and the dead. These efforts appeared to reduce—but did not eliminate—the fly population.[40]

By the first week of October, most of the front-line infantrymen were nearing the end of their endurance. Three weeks might as well have been three months or even three years. Sledge remembered Peleliu as "a nether world of horror from which escape seemed less and less likely as casualties mounted and the fighting dragged on and on. Time had no meaning; life had no meaning. The fierce struggle made savages of us all."[41] Lieutenant McCandless had compared Peleliu, as did many others who served and fought there, to Dante's vision of hell in *The Inferno*. But a closer fictional likeness was found in J. R. R. Tolkien's *Lord of the Rings*. Like the "black land" of Mordor, the battleground was a foul, evil-smelling wasteland— stripped of its greenery, shrouded in haze, and sealed off by forbidding razor-back ridges. An army of cunning troglodytes had burrowed deep into the earth, and could cross beneath mountains through elaborate subterranean networks of tunnels and caverns. To their opponents, these foes seemed every bit as cruel and scarcely more human than Tolkien's orcs. Even the vile realm's name, Urmurbrogal, might have been borrowed from a map of Middle Earth—and like Tolkien's fictional battle for Middle Earth, this was a war to be won by total extermination of the enemy.

On D-Day, Sledge had been taken aback to witness a veteran of his company "field-stripping" a dead Japanese soldier for valuables and souvenirs. But he and the other fresh "boots" of the 1st Marine Division were soon inured to far more ghastly scenes. On much of the battlefield it was impossible to dig graves in the rocky ground. Bodies rotted in the heat for weeks. They bloated, darkened, and broke open like rotten fruit. Sledge's unit found their way around the terrain by using familiar corpses as landmarks. "It was gruesome to see the stages of decay proceed from just killed, to bloated, to maggot-infested rotting, to partially exposed bones—like some biological clock marking the inexorable passage of time."[42] Sledge watched a young marine pass the time by tossing rocks into the rain-filled broken skull of a dead Japanese, "as casually as a boy casting pebbles into a puddle on some road back home; there was nothing malicious in his action."[43]

The Americans would take deadly risks to remove their own dead from the battleground, to be buried near the beach. But it was not always possible to do so immediately. Mutilation of enemy dead was an offense committed on both sides. Sledge recalls finding the remains of dead marines whose corpses had been hideously dismembered: heads and hands cut off and penises severed and stuffed into their mouths. "My emotions solidified into rage and a hatred for the Japanese beyond anything I ever had experienced," he wrote. "From that moment on I never felt the least pity or compassion for them no matter what the circumstances."[44] Japanese dental practices of that era used gold to fill cavities, so many of the enemy soldiers had gold-crowned teeth. Some Americans made a practice of "harvesting" those prizes from the enemy dead. In a scene witnessed by Sledge, a marine attempted to extract a gold tooth from the mouth of a wounded enemy soldier by cutting it out with his kabar knife:

Because the Japanese was kicking his feet and thrashing about, the knife point glanced off the tooth and sank deeply into the victim's mouth. The Marine cursed him and with a slash cut his cheeks open to each ear. He put his foot on the sufferer's lower jaw and tried again. Blood poured out of the soldier's mouth. He made a gurgling noise and thrashed wildly. I shouted, "Put the man out of his misery." All I got for an answer was a cussing out. Another Marine ran up, put a bullet in the enemy soldier's brain, and ended his agony. The scavenger grumbled and continued extracting his prizes undisturbed.[45]

Trophy-taking and mutilation of enemy dead were prohibited by standing orders. But in that disordered environment, amidst such unremitting brutality, it seemed beside the point to object directly on moral grounds. The infantryman who wanted to dissuade a comrade from engaging in such practices offered practical objections. He appealed to field sanitation standards, for example, or the risk of being caught and punished, or a desire to keep the stench of decaying flesh at bay. Taking teeth from Japanese corpses, he warned, might expose the taker to dangerous germs. As a last resort, he might point out that the people back home would never understand. Another marine in Sledge's platoon carried a Japanese hand with him for a time. He wrapped it in wax paper and kept it in his pack, intending to take it home with him when they left the island. Sledge and several others objected. The officers would bring him up on charges, they told him. The hand would stink up the ship. It gave them the creeps. Finally, and reluctantly, the man threw his souvenir away. "The war had gotten to my friend," Sledge reflected. "He was a twentieth-century savage now, mild mannered though he still was. I shuddered to think that I might do the same thing if the war went on and on."[46]

Belatedly Rupertus recognized that his hoped-for quick hard fight was not to be. The Urmurbrogal pocket was a sophisticated fortress, shrewdly embedded in the terrain, and designed to inflict maximum casualties on attackers. The enemy's elaborate cave-and-tunnel system had been constructed over many years with the aid of miners and mining engineers. Patience and new tactics were required. The last phase of the battle would be a painstaking battle of attrition. Progress against the defenders came slowly, in fits and starts. Territory was to be taken yard by yard. Armored vehicles advanced into the ridgelines and fired back at Japanese positions. Their main objective was to discover the location of all Japanese guns and firing ports, and to strip away all remaining vegetation. The Americans mapped the entire battlefield, down to minute detail, including the position of every known enemy firing port. A day's progress might be measured by five or ten yards. Perhaps the marines might lift a heavy artillery piece to some new promontory, using steel cables run through a block and tackle rig. The newly placed gun might then manage to land direct hits on troublesome cave entrances or embrasures higher up the ridge. The 155mm howitzer was large enough to take the ridges down, chunk by chunk—and with the use of these weapons they began destroying and blasting out cave entrances.

On October 12, the division command declared an end to the "assault phase" of the campaign. The announcement was greeted with scorn by the troops still battling the enemy in the ridges. The Japanese were far from finished; they had plenty of fight left in them, and Americans were still dying. One marine remarked, "Somebody from the Division CP needs to come up here and tell them damned Nips the assault phase is over."[47] But it was true that the remaining Japanese, penned into their shrinking perimeter,

posed little threat beyond their lines. The southern plain of Peleliu was
functioning as an advanced operating base. USAAF bombers were taking
off from the airfield to support the invasion of the Philippines. Cargo ships
were running supplies in to the island on a regular schedule. By the second
week of October, the pocket had shrunk to an area measuring about 400
by 800 yards, and there were not many more than a thousand unwounded
Japanese fighters remaining. Someone suggested, only half-jokingly, that
the marines should string barbed wire around the area and call it a prisoner of war enclosure. Planes dropped leaflets around the battlefield and
Japanese-language specialists began broadcasting surrender appeals through
loudspeakers. There were few takers. Nakagawa's headquarters must have
had a printing press somewhere in the caves, because they responded with
a leaflet of their own, addressed to "Poor Reckless Yankee-Doodle." In the
strange music of Japanese-translated English, it told the Americans that
they had been sent to Peleliu because FDR needed a Pacific victory to seal
his reelection campaign. It accused the Americans of fighting dirty, but
pledged that the Japanese would still win in the end. The leaflet is quoted
here with original spelling and diction errors:

> The fraud Rousevelt, hanging the president election under his nose
> and from his policy ambition, worked not only poor Nimmit but also
> Maccasir like a robot. Like this, what is pity. Must be sacrifice you pay.
> Thanks for your advice notes of surrender. But we haven't any reason
> to surrender to those who are fated to be totally destroyed in a few
> days later. Add to you, against the manner of your attack paying no
> heed to humanity, your god shall make Japanese force to add retalia-
> tive attack upon you. Saying again, against the attack paying no heed
> to humanity contrary to the mutual military spirits, you shall get a
> very stern attack. We mean cruel attack. Japan Military.[48]

Marines were gradually pulled off the line and replaced by the army's 81st
Infantry Division (the "Wildcats"). On October 15, when they finally
received orders sending them back to Pavuvu, the 5th Marines were the
last Marine Corps regiment remaining on Peleliu. They were trucked to the
north end of the island, where a new bivouac area had been prepared for
them. They burned their old uniforms and boondockers and drew new ones,
and enjoyed the small pleasures of showers, sleeping tents, and a proper

Quonset mess hall with hot meals. A few days later they filed down to the beach, where they would board landing craft and be ferried out to a waiting transport. Peleliu had knocked three marine regiments out of action; they would have to be rebuilt over time with a large proportion of replacements.

A few days later, Geiger turned command of all forces remaining on the island to Major General Paul J. Mueller, the Wildcats' division commander. The 1st Division had suffered casualties of 6,786, of whom more than 1,300 were killed in action. Many survivors would suffer the effects of long-term post-traumatic stress disorder, although the condition was not yet known by that name. Their efforts and sacrifices were recognized in a message from Admiral Halsey: "The sincere admiration of the entire Third Fleet is yours for the hill blasting, cave smashing extermination of 11,000 slant-eyed gophers. It has been a tough job, extremely well done."[49]

On many Pacific battlefields—most infamously on Saipan—the differing tactical concepts of the army and the marines had caused serious friction between the services. Geiger and Rupertus had wanted to snuff out Japanese resistance before turning the island over to the army, and they regretted their failure to do it. But it would take seven more weeks of hard fighting to dig the enemy out of their caves. In this final stage of the battle for the Urmurbrogal badlands, the Wildcats showcased the advantages of go-slow siege tactics. They needed a wide, well-graded road up the Horseshoe Bowl in order to get tanks, trucks, armored bulldozers, and heavy artillery to the front lines, so they built one. They kept the Japanese perimeter under constant heavy artillery fire and airstrikes, dropping tons of napalm each day. They erected enormous sandbag embankments to provide cover for infantry. The sandbags were filled at the beach and transported to the front lines in amtracs or other armored vehicles. Eventually, the army engineers even built an aerial tramway, similar in appearance and function to a primitive ski lift, which moved sandbags directly from the beaches up into the hills. These walls of sandbags were pushed inward, closer and closer to the Japanese firing positions; in some cases, soldiers crawled forward while using poles to push sandbags ahead of them. Cave openings and firing ports were sealed off. The Japanese responded with their customary skill, shrewdness, and determination. Even when the Wildcats held peaks and ridgelines above their heads, the Japanese might yet hold the interiors of the hills. The Americans sometimes heard Japanese voices in the rock beneath them, or smelled Japanese cooking rising through hidden air vents. Cave openings sealed by artillery might later be blasted open from within, and a party of Japanese fighters sneak out to attack from unexpected directions. Small-unit attacks were most frequent at night, so the army engineers set up floodlights to keep the battlefield brightly illuminated. The sandbags marched inexorably toward the heart of the pocket. A pipeline was constructed, and diesel fuel was pumped up from the coast to be poured into the cave entrances. "With the aid of a booster pump and nozzle at the end of the pipeline, the effect of a garden hose was obtained. White phosphorus grenades were used to ignite the fuel which settled in crags and crevices in the area covered."[50]

On November 24, 1944, Colonel Nakagawa radioed his final report to the division headquarters on Koror. He burned the regimental colors. He had fewer than one hundred men remaining; they would form small infiltration squads and launch one last round of night attacks. Nakagawa apparently committed ritual suicide, but no one who witnessed it survived to tell the tale. Nor did the Americans notice any final assault—indeed, small numbers of Japanese went on fighting for months, and many dozens of stragglers continued to live in the caves until the end of the war and beyond. In March 1947, a full eighteen months after V-J Day, a group of thirty-three Japanese stragglers under the command of a lieutenant were discovered and persuaded to surrender.

The battle for Peleliu passed mostly unnoticed in the United States. A few brief press accounts appeared in the back pages of newspapers. The news from Europe in those weeks was more stirring and sensational: Allied armies had liberated Paris and were sweeping across France toward Germany. In the Pacific, there was more interest in MacArthur's march toward the Philippines. The Palau Islands were remote and obscure even by Pacific standards, and it was difficult to convey how this fight differed from a hundred other island battles. Nor was Peleliu a particularly large battle on the scale of the ongoing global carnage. But it was a milestone of a kind, and also a foreshadowing of what was to come in the Pacific, especially in the later and better-known island battles on Iwo Jima and Okinawa. In proportional terms, from the American point of view, Peleliu was the costliest battle of the Pacific campaign. Of the 28,000 marines and soldiers who fought on the island, nearly 40 percent were casualties, including about 1,800 killed and 8,000 wounded. Nearly the entire Japanese garrison of 11,000 perished. Even accounting for the disparity in the numbers killed—inevitable given the customary Japanese refusal to surrender—those results gave a casualty ratio of nearly one to one.

Nakagawa had effectively used his underground network to vitiate American advantages in offshore firepower and command of the air. His forces had mostly eschewed the tactically futile *banzai* charge. They had made shrewd use of the terrain, fighting on ground of their own choosing. Those tactics would be repeated on a larger scale on islands nearer Japan in the battles to come in 1945.

U.S. infantrymen had come to regard their enemy as a vicious and sadistic creature, barely human, who had to be rooted out of the ground and exterminated. All the same, they could not help but admire the enemy, even while hating him from the bottom of their hearts, for his tenacity, his cunning, his stamina, and his implacable courage in the face of certain defeat and death.

THE THIRD OBJECTIVE OF OPERATION STALEMATE (after Peleliu and Anguar) was Ulithi Atoll, 345 miles northeast of Peleliu. This oblong loop of palm-crowned sandspits would serve as a new fleet anchorage, almost exactly midway between Guam and the Palaus. With a lagoon measuring 209 square miles, Ulithi was large enough to shelter the entire Third Fleet and its supporting mobile logistics forces. Eniwetok, which had served a similar function for the prior six months, would be reduced to the status of a way station linking Pearl Harbor to the Marianas.

The Japanese had abandoned Ulithi some months earlier, so no blood was shed in the capture of the great atoll. On September 21, minesweepers swept and buoyed the main entrances into the lagoon, and a small reconnaissance force of army Wildcats went ashore on one of the larger outlying islets. They were greeted by timid Polynesian natives who turned friendly the moment they understood that the strangers were enemies of the Japanese. The advance units spread through the atoll, hopping from one islet to the next in rubber boats. They found some abandoned Japanese equipment, but no enemy troops. According to the 81st Division report, they found only "2 Japanese, both dead."[51] Ulithi was declared secure at sundown on September 23.

The native Ulithians were led by a kindly, paralytic chieftain called "King Ueg." Like the big American chief in Washington, Ueg had been

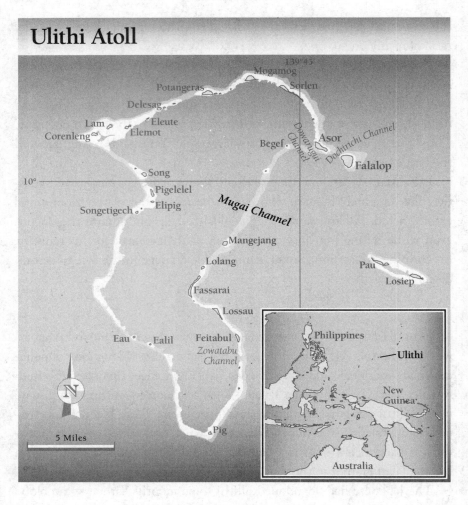

Ulithi Atoll

Mogamog
Potangeras   Sorlen
Delesag
Lam   Eleute
Corenleng   Elemot
Begef   Asor
Dowangui Channel   Dochitrichi Channel
Falalop
Song
10°
Pigelelel
Songetigech   Elipig
Mugai Channel
Mangejang
Lolang
Pau
Fassarai   Losiep
Lossau
Eau   Ealil   Feitabul
Zowatabu
Channel
Pig
N
5 Miles

Philippines
Ulithi
New
Guinea
Australia

crippled by polio. His subjects carried him around in a sedan chair constructed of palm logs and hand-woven fiber. The Ulithians lived in simple
native villages spread across six or seven different islets, in graceful platform
huts built of split palm logs and platform floors carpeted with soft fibers, and
they were topped with soaring, steeply canted roofs thatched with pandanus
fronds. Men and boys wore loincloths; women and girls wore grass skirts;
all wore flowers in their hair and smeared their bodies with oil. Portuguese
and Spanish explorers had made first contact with the Ulithians more than
four hundred years earlier, and Jesuit missionaries had visited in the early
eighteenth century. Since that time, the natives had practiced an exotic
form of Christianity in isolation, with the doctrines and practices brought

by the Jesuits gradually merging into their own ancient myths and religious traditions. In 1944, they lived much as their ancestors had lived for millennia, fishing in the lagoon and tending small plots of taro. They traveled and fished in hand-carved outrigger canoes—paddling through the surf, raising triangular sails of woven fiber, and speeding away "like a flock of gulls skimming the incredibly blue floor of the lagoon."[52]

A navy civil affairs officer persuaded King Ueg to relocate all of his subjects to a single island in the southern part of the atoll. In return, the occupiers would provide food, medical care, and other desired goods for the duration of the war. After initial hesitation, Ueg agreed. Straggler lines were set up to guard the island and prevent U.S. personnel from approaching it without authorization: "These steps proved effective in eliminating molestation of natives by our troops."[53]

The press of time was heavy. The Third Fleet would need to shelter in this anchorage before the end of the month; it did not have time to return to Eniwetok, given the new October timetable for the Leyte operation. The first echelon of the 51st Seabee Battalion disembarked and began working around the clock in twelve-hour shifts. Beachmasters set up landing areas and depots. Piers were erected quickly by filling pontoons with sand and coral rock, which were then sunk and anchored into the bottom. In three days, the engineers unloaded more than 3,000 tons of supplies, including water, rations, fuel, medical supplies, and ammunition, and about three hundred vehicles, including trucks, bulldozers, and half-tracks. They cut down palm trees with gasoline-powered saws. Stumps and roots were blasted out with demolition charges, and the debris was winched out to the cleared areas alongside the airstrip and the roads. Trucks hauled crushed coral rock to be fed into cement mixers. A fleet of exhaust-belching diesel bulldozers began working over the existing Japanese airstrip on Falalop Island, which would be lengthened, widened, and resurfaced. A prefabricated steel fuel tank farm was linked to a fueling dock by five pipelines; a beach was suddenly displaced by a concrete seaplane ramp; an air traffic control tower shot up amongst the palms; and coral taxiways, aprons, and hardstands extended out from the edges of the airfield. One island, Mog Mog, was set aside as a fleet recreation area; in time it would support a network of baseball diamonds, basketball courts, barbeque pits, outdoor amphitheaters, and mess halls. The service and logistics fleet would have to sail on its own steam from Eniwetok, a voyage of more than 1,500 miles.

It would be a long and hazardous journey, because the service vessels could not make more than 12 or 14 knots at sea, and the barges and drydocks had to be towed at 6 knots.

Before dawn on October 1, two carrier task groups filed into the lagoon and dropped their hooks in the north anchorage: Admiral Bogan's Group 38.2 (which included Halsey's flagship *New Jersey*) and Admiral Sherman's Group 38.3. That amounted to about half of Task Force 38, an armada of sixty steel ships with blue-gray camouflage patterns and soaring masts. They seemed to dwarf the adjoining islets. Lieutenant McCandless of the Seabees woke up that morning and walked down to the beach: "As I emerged from the palm trees and looked across the lagoon, I could hardly believe my eyes. It was full of warships—all sizes and types. Aircraft carriers, battleships, cruisers, tankers, destroyers, ten or twelve submarines, etc., all riding peacefully at anchor. They had slipped in during the night. I have no idea how they could have done it so silently, and I realized then why we were on Ulithi. It was a great protected hiding place into which the big powerful American task forces could rendezvous."[54]

The fleet had counted on a few days of rest and replenishment at anchor, but it was not to be. On October 2, its second day in Ulithi, seas were rough even in the protected waters of the lagoon, and loading was difficult. The barometer was sinking, and fleet meteorologists warned of an approaching typhoon. As in other mid-Pacific atolls, the low-lying islands did not provide much protection against storm winds. Reluctantly, Admiral Halsey led the fleet back out to sea to ride out the typhoon. On October 3, the two task groups were buffeted by high seas and 50-knot winds. Reentering the atoll by Mugai Channel on the morning of October 4, they learned that the storm had thrown sixty-five Higgins boats and fourteen LCMs onto the beach. Most were deemed unsalvageable. But there was no time to pause; the fleet had to get back to sea for another round of carrier strikes in support of the impending invasion of Leyte. The Third Fleet had many promises to keep.[55]

The two task groups were at sea again on the afternoon of October 6, forging north in the tail of the typhoon. They would rendezvous with the rest of Task Force 38 at sea, then proceed to the Ryukyuan archipelago between Japan and Formosa, where they would hit targets on Okinawa and adjacent islands. The seventeen-carrier force, totaling one hundred ships with nearly 100,000 seamen, would approach closer to Japan than any other Allied warship (except submarines) had since the Doolittle Raid in April 1942.

The 1,300-mile voyage was rough and tumble, with gale-force winds and seas breaking over the decks.[56] At flag plot on the *New Jersey*, Carney and the staff designated the typhoon "Task Force Zero." Since it was moving north, ahead of the task force, it performed the useful service of suppressing Japanese air activity and keeping the enemy's long-range patrol planes at bay. The four groups of Task Force 38 rendezvoused at sea on October 7, about 375 miles west of Saipan, and began a long, frustrating day of refueling. The ships lurched and rolled in sickening fashion, with green water breaking over decks, and even many of the old hands fell seasick. The Third Fleet Diary noted that the "seamanship of the fleet was given a severe test. Fueling was terminated at 1915, and was completed except for a few of the large units which had not received full quota of fuel."[57]

At noon on October 9, the fleet rang up flank speed for the all-night run to Okinawa. The ships roared through the night, but no patrol planes appeared on radar; the Japanese did not expect them. Carney remarked that "we caught the boys on Okinawa utterly unprepared, because I suppose they figured nobody in his right mind would be at sea during anything of this sort. We arrived unheralded and in full force."[58] Arriving at its planned launch point northeast of Okinawa at dawn on October 10, the fleet turned into the wind and began launching planes. The initial fighter sweep found few enemy planes airborne, but plenty parked on the ground. At Yontan Airfield, the largest on Okinawa, the attackers strafed parked planes, leaving about a dozen ablaze. Then followed four waves of bombers, escorted by additional fighters armed with bombs and rockets; they targeted airfields, barracks, ammunition dumps, fuel tanks, and defensive installations all up and down the Ryukyus. In the last of the day's strikes, they worked over targets still burning fiercely from the earlier raids. Fires engulfed the ancient central district of Naha, Okinawa's prefectural capital, killing about six hundred civilians and leaving four-fifths of the town in ashes. The fire destroyed much of the art, architecture, and cultural patrimony of the old Ryukyuan kingdom. Even now, older Okinawans remember the disaster by the date it occurred: 10/10.

For the day, Mitscher's airmen had flown a total of 1,396 sorties against Okinawa and other nearby islands. Twenty-one American planes were lost, but most of the downed flyers were rescued by lifeguarding submarines.[59]

Task Force 38 turned south toward Formosa. Japanese snoopers shadowed the Americans all night long and into the next morning. When confronted by U.S. fighters flying combat air patrol (CAP), the ubiquitous Japanese patrol planes turned away and fled, often escaping into clouds.[60] But they were clearly tracking the position of Task Force 38, so the odds of achieving surprise in the upcoming airstrike on Formosa did not look good. The destroyers were already low on fuel—an inescapable consequence of high-speed maneuvers—so on October 11, with the fleet continuing to make way to the south, they refueled directly from the tanks of battleships, including the *New Jersey*. Throwing a head fake intended to fool the enemy on Formosa, Halsey ordered a sixty-one-plane fighter sweep over Aparri Airfield on northern Luzon. The ruse did not succeed, however—radar screens revealed many Japanese scouts headed out from Formosa in wedge-shaped search vectors. The aviators would have to fight their way into Formosan airspace, where the Japanese would be ready and waiting for them. Halsey realized that he had erred in hitting Okinawa first; he should have aimed the first strike at Formosa.

After sunset on October 11, with Task Force 38 again fueled up, the ships turned onto a north-northwest course and began their high-speed night approach. At first light on October 12, the snow-capped peaks of the East Formosan mountains were seen to the west. The first fighter sweep was airborne as the sun peeked over the eastern horizon. More than two hundred outbound Hellcats climbed over the mountains to reach their targets, the big air complexes on the island's western plain. Descending through cloud cover, the Grummans found about forty Japanese fighters circling at 25,000 feet. Even the greenest of the Hellcat pilots had little to fear from Japanese Zeros, especially at that altitude; in the ensuing fight, all of the defending planes were shot down, or dove into clouds to escape.

This aerial melee was witnessed by the local air commander, Admiral Shigeru Fukudome, commander of the Second Air Fleet, who watched from his headquarters building at the Takao Air Base in southern Formosa. At first, craning his neck to observe the black dots high above, he could not distinguish between American and Japanese planes. When aircraft began falling in flames, he mistook them for Hellcats, and concluded that his pilots were getting the better of the attackers. He clapped his hands and shouted in exultation: "Well done! Well done! A tremendous success!" Moments later, when he saw that all of the falling planes were Japanese, his heart sank: "Our fighters were nothing but so many eggs thrown at the stone wall of the indomitable enemy formation."[61] Fukudome had scrambled all available fighters (about 230 altogether) when coastal radar had picked up the incoming wave of American carrier planes. About half would be shot down by the end of the day. The island's main airbases were badly mauled in follow-on strikes, and many aircraft were destroyed on the ground. Fukudome's own headquarters building was reduced to rubble. After the morning's initial fighter sweep, he had prudently ordered his entire Second Air Fleet staff into an underground bunker, so none was injured or killed.

Counting up the day's losses, Fukudome reckoned he had fewer than 150 operational aircraft remaining on Formosa. But his Second Air Fleet command also encompassed airbases in the Ryukyu Islands and Kyushu, where he had about four hundred more planes; and he could always call upon Tokyo for reinforcements. Should he throw everything he had at the American fleet offshore, or was it better to conserve his strength to fight another day? Upon assuming this command in June 1944, Fukudome had found most of his aviators "in the training stage."[62] Four months later the situation was only marginally better, and Fukudome had little faith in any but his most elite flyers. The bomber and torpedo plane squadrons were led by veterans, but most airmen in those units had little experience in overwater navigation and had never attacked enemy ships at sea. He did not like their chances of getting through the screen of defending Hellcats and the wall of antiaircraft fire that the Third Fleet warships would erect to defend themselves.

Admiral Soemu Toyoda, commander in chief of the Combined Fleet, happened to be in Formosa at that moment on an inspection tour. He had left his chief of staff, Rear Admiral Ryūnosuke Kusaka, with instructions to order the air forces into action if it appeared that the Americans were making another concerted thrust into the western Pacific. When carrier planes struck Okinawa on October 10, Kusaka ordered all forces on alert. Toyoda concluded that a "general decisive battle" was at hand, and he decided to direct the battle from his temporary advanced headquarters on Formosa. That took the matter out of Fukudome's hands.

As the Japanese high command saw it, they had little choice in the matter. The carrier strikes on Formosa might presage an invasion of that island; or perhaps the next big amphibious landing would occur to the south, in the Philippines. In either event, the big fight was upon them. Given the deteriorating logistical situation, and their ignorance of the enemy's intentions, they had to move quickly just to ensure they had the opportunity to fight at all, let alone to win. Having long since lost the initiative, the Japanese were now, once again, compelled to react to the enemy's moves. On October 12, at 9:45 a.m. Tokyo time, Admiral Kusaka issued orders to execute *Sho*-1 and *Sho*-2, the Imperial Japanese Navy's contingency plans for an enemy attack on the Philippines or Formosa.

Given the sorry state of his air forces, Fukudome issued orders to "approach the target with a large number of torpedo planes and bombers under the strongest possible escort of our fighter planes and to resort to a simultaneous attack with that large formation." In other words, the Japanese dive-bombers and torpedo planes would not fly together in formation as trained, and would not even attempt to carry out choreographed attacks. They would simply make a beeline toward the Third Fleet in a disorderly massed aerial armada, with hopes of overwhelming enemy defenses by sheer weight of numbers. Fukudome later explained, "We had to content ourselves with the hope that we had somehow cast a mold for a large formation attack."[63]

Mick Carney monitored the incoming strike on the *New Jersey*'s radar screens. It was a large blip, encompassing about seventy-five to one hundred planes. Combat air patrol fighters were vectored out to intercept. When the Hellcat pilots looked over the incoming formation, "they began to report a great many different kinds of planes. In other words, this was not a homogeneous, well-integrated tactical outfit, but it was very much of a heterogeneous air mob coming up there, composed of all kinds of damn things."[64] Carney and his colleagues wondered whether this higgledy-piggledy airstrike was a sign that Japanese airpower was nearly finished. Most of the attackers were shot down, others lost to flak, and some shied away and turned back toward Formosa. But smaller formations arrived after dark, almost continuously, skimming in at wavetop altitude.[65] Lieutenant Solberg of the Third Fleet intelligence staff saw one enemy plane after another illuminated in the glow of red tracer fire: "Before our eyes they cartwheeled one after the other in flaming arcs and exploded spectacularly in black geysers of smoke and seawater."[66]

Task Force 38 came through the night unscathed except for a single destroyer, the *Pritchett*, which was slightly damaged by friendly antiaircraft fire. Of the approximately one hundred Japanese planes that attacked the American fleet that night, twenty-five returned safely to Formosa. Those who returned reported, optimistically and wrongly, that they had sunk two U.S. warships, including an aircraft carrier, and had damaged two more. [67]

But the Americans were not yet done with Formosa. At 6:14 a.m. on October 13, with dawn's gray light rising in the east, Task Force 38 carriers launched the first of four huge fighter sweep-airstrikes against airfields and other installations on the island. The attackers encountered thick cloud cover down to 2,000 feet over most of eastern Formosa, with fogs and mists hugging the ground. The bombers had been told to plaster anything that might be militarily useful to the enemy—runways, hangars, docks, barracks, warehouses, fuel tanks, shipping—but they also targeted the island's basic infrastructure, including bridges, railheads, power plants, a dam, and even a sugar refinery.[68] Kent Lee, a Hellcat pilot with VF-15 of the *Essex*, dropped through the cloud ceiling to find a swarm of Japanese Zeros waiting to give battle. It was a confused general melee, with both American and Japanese planes weaving in and out of cloud banks. When they shook their aerial adversaries, the Hellcats strafed ground targets. Lee recalled, "Our mission was to destroy everything that was movable—tank trucks, vehicles, people, airplanes—on these airfields. That we did."[69]

Bill Davis of the *Lexington*'s VF-16 dove from 12,000 feet and found himself in a high-speed head-on run with a Zero. Davis knew he should turn away, because the Zero's 20mm cannon was powerful enough to take down his F6F Hellcat, but his blood was hot and he kept boring in even as the Zero's guns began winking like strobe lights. "Finally," he wrote, "after what seemed like an eternity, I raised the nose of the plane slightly and opened up with all six guns. Immediately I could see large pieces flying off the Zero. He kept coming for a few more moments, then slid under my left wing and blew up."[70] Another pilot in Davis's squadron returned to the *Lexington* with chunks of Japanese aircraft debris embedded in his F6F, including "five square feet of Zero wing wedged in [his] wing."[71]

The Americans flew a total of 947 sorties that day, with not-inconsiderable losses of forty-five planes to combat and accidents. Clearly the Japanese had flown in air reinforcements overnight, but the newcomers' average skill was noticeably lower. The American airmen also discovered many Japanese airfields that had not been on their briefing maps and had been overlooked the previous day. Task Group 38.3 aviators reported that they had found fifteen airfields in their assigned sector, when they had been briefed to expect only four.[72]

As expected, aerial counterattacks began shortly before sunset, as the last of the CAP were recovered aboard the carriers. At sundown (6:26 p.m.), radar indicated low-flying bogeys approaching simultaneously from several directions. Hellcats poleaxed several intruders as the last light drained out of the western sky, but more of the low-flying twin-engine torpedo planes appeared as darkness fell. Leaders dropped floating flares to mark a path for following planes. "The enemy seems quite determined and came in whenever they found us," noted the Task Group 38.3 war diary. "There were approximately 40 to 50 bogeys in the sector, and judging by gunfire on the horizon the other groups were not overlooked."[73]

Aboard the command ships, air staffs lamented that their pilots had apparently left many Formosan airfields in operation. In fact, most of these latest attackers had flown all the way from Kyushu. They were Mitsubishi G4M (Allied codename "Betty") bombers, which had often proven their effectiveness as night torpedo bombers. They were elements of an elite Japanese mixed navy-army squadron known as the "T" Attack Force. Among the leaders were some of the most seasoned and skilled airmen remaining in the Japanese military. Admiral Toyoda, still commanding from his temporary advanced headquarters on Formosa, had personally ordered the "T" force into action, and he expected them to deal a heavy blow against the American fleet.

Crewmen in Task Force 38 would remember that night as one of the hairiest of the war. Air attacks continued for hours. Green phosphorescent torpedo tracks passed through the heart of the task groups' circular formations, narrowly missing their intended targets. Antiaircraft fire brought enemy planes down just as they were reaching a position to make torpedo drops. An officer in the *Lexington*'s hangar recalled a moment shortly after dark when "all hell broke loose. Every antiaircraft gun in the fleet opened fire. Looking out through the open doors on the side of the hangar deck, I saw Japanese planes everywhere."[74] He heard an earsplitting cacophony of large- and small-caliber fire. The sea and sky were lit by tracers and flak bursts. Enemy planes were torn apart and went flaming into the sea.

Four G4Ms penetrated into the heart of Group 4 and attacked the carrier *Franklin*. Two went down in flames before they could drop their fish, but two actually made good drops, and the *Franklin*'s crew considered it a miracle that she was not hit. A torpedo missed ahead only because the ship's skipper ordered her engines backed at maximum. Another passed directly under the ship and was seen to emerge on the far side. A G4M flew low over *Franklin's* flight deck and was shot down while attempting its getaway; another was set afire by anticraft fire, but the pilot aimed a suicide crash at the ship's island. He missed and crashed into a catwalk. Flaming wreckage skidded across the deck and was carried by its own momentum into the sea on the far side.

Only one U.S. warship was struck that night. A G4M attacking Admiral McCain's Group 38.1 shortly after sunset aimed a torpedo at the carrier *Wasp*. The weapon missed narrowly but continued on its track and struck the heavy cruiser *Canberra*, sending flames to the height of her masthead. The blast tore a great, jagged hole in the cruiser's bow, beneath her armor belt; 4,500 tons of seawater poured into the ship, flooding her engine and fire rooms, and killing twenty-three of her crew. Her engineers judged that there was no chance whatsoever that the *Canberra* could make way under her own steam.

Halsey now confronted a high-stakes decision. Should he order the *Canberra's* crew taken off and the crippled ship scuttled? Or could she be towed out of the combat zone? No one would have faulted him for choosing the first, more conservative option. The Third Fleet could afford to lose a single cruiser, and trying to bring her to safety might expose other ships to risk. But Halsey was obstinate, and he chose to save her. He ordered the cruiser *Wichita* to take the *Canberra* under tow. Soon the pair were underway, but at the heartbreaking pace of 4 knots. The distance to Ulithi was 1,300 miles. The retreating ships would be subject to daily and nightly air attacks launched from more than one hundred Japanese airfields in three directions for more than a week.

To suppress the airstrikes that were sure to follow, Halsey ordered another round of fighter sweeps against Formosa on the morning of October 14. Task Group 4 was sent to hit the Japanese airfields on the north coast of Luzon, a defensive measure that would also reassure MacArthur. From his headquarters in Pearl Harbor, Nimitz summoned land-based air units from all over the Pacific to get into the act against Formosa, Luzon, and the Ryukyus. The Army Air Forces launched one hundred B-29s from airfields in China to hit the Takao complex on Formosa.

A force of three cruisers and eight destroyers, mordantly nicknamed "Cripple Division 1," was detached to accompany the damaged *Canberra* in her withdrawal. A task group built around the light carriers *Cowpens* and

Cabot was assigned to provide close air protection. Japanese planes dogged this new "CripDiv" throughout the daylight hours of October 14. Ships screening the crippled cruiser dodged aerial torpedoes and fought off strafing attacks.[75]

Getting the flooded *Canberra* under tow was no mean feat of seamanship. The *Wichita* first took her in tow with a 1 1/8-inch plow-steel towing wire, rigged with manila mooring lines, snubbing gear, and chafing gear to take up the strain of sudden jerks without breaking or tearing out the reels. Both ships struggled against wind and sea with a dangerous corkscrewing motion, leading to near-collisions and injuries as sailors were pinned to the deck by the wire. By the early hours of October 14, the crippled ship was pointed in the right direction (southeast) and underway. With a partly flooded cruiser under tow, the salvage group made a fat target. Rainsqualls and a low ceiling worked in the Japanese planes' favor by enabling them to hide from the orbiting Hellcats. The attackers came in low, under the radar, from many directions at once. Leading planes dropped parachute flares to mark the way for the planes winging in behind them. As on the previous two days, the Japanese suffered heavy air losses, but still threatened to overwhelm the Americans by sheer numbers. The screening ships, circling the lumbering *Wichita-Canberra* pair at about four times their speed, put up a barrage of antiaircraft fire to protect the two nearly immobilized cruisers.[76]

At dusk on October 14 came the day's worst attack. At 6:45 p.m., the new light cruiser *Houston* took a devastating torpedo hit amidships that flooded her engineering spaces, cut her power, and seemed likely to break up the ship. The main deck was underwater, said one of the ship's crew, and "waves were 14 feet high."[77] As she listed heavily to starboard, her captain ordered abandon ship, and destroyers began picking up swimmers. But an hour later, the captain changed his mind, summoned his crew back on board, and called for a tow.[78]

Several hundred miles east, on the *New Jersey*'s flag bridge, Halsey paced the deck, chain-smoked, and wondered whether he had made the right call. The day's air attacks had been much heavier than expected. Now he had two cruisers crippled and under tow. The navy had not taken such a severe beating since 1942, in the Solomons. Radio intelligence (informally designated "Ultra," short for "Ultra-secret") had confirmed that the Japanese were pouring air reinforcements into Formosa. Every fifteen minutes or so, Halsey looked at the pin on the chart table that represented the salvage group and confirmed that it was barely moving. The crippling of the *Houston*, he later wrote, "reawakened my fears that an attempt at salvage would mean throwing good ships after bad."[79]

No one could have faulted Halsey for making the conservative decision to "scuttle and skedaddle"—that is, to send the two cripples to the bottom and get the undamaged ships out of the area. But the Dirty Tricks Department had been monitoring news broadcasts by Radio Tokyo, and what they heard piqued their interest. The Japanese were reporting, to their own public and to the world, that their Formosa-based air forces had scored an annihilating victory over the American fleet. The newscasters claimed, in giddy tones and with apparent sincerity, that the Japanese planes had sunk between eight and eleven U.S. aircraft carriers. Successive bulletins added to the chimerical tally until early on the morning of October 15, when Radio Tokyo proudly declared that no fewer than *seventeen* American carriers had been sent to the bottom. Altogether, it asserted, the Americans had lost thirty-six ships sunk and another seventeen "seriously damaged."[80] The broadcasts included vivid firsthand accounts drawn from interviews with returning Japanese airmen. Military experts provided color commentary. The extraordinary claims had been corroborated by other evidence, they said—such as the diminished intensity of American carrier raids in the area, the "fact" that many castaways had been seen in rafts, the silence of Nimitz's headquarters concerning results of the battle, and the appearance of China-based B-29s over Formosa, which was interpreted as an act of desperation on the part of the Americans. The tremendous victory off Formosa, said one expert, proved that "the Japanese hold undisputed supremacy in that area. . . . Action of the past few days has given truth that the nearer the enemy approaches Japan proper and Japan's formidable ring of defenses, the greater will be the losses to the enemy."[81] Radio Tokyo reported that Vice Admiral Marc Mitscher's flagship had been sunk, and therefore "it is highly probable that the commander of the American task force would by this time be enjoying eternal repose in his watery grave together with many other men under his command."[82]

Halsey also came in for some personal taunts. Commentaries in the newspaper *Mainichi Shinbun* recapped Halsey's past boasts and threats to take revenge on the Japanese people. The sinking of his fleet, said a front-page editorial, was "Heaven's punishment to the Yankees who have human faces but beastly minds with an insatiable greed for world domination."[83]

Halsey was amused to learn from the radio that a zookeeper at Ueno Zoo in Tokyo had prepared a cage for the admiral in the monkey house. "The Japs are losing their grip," he commented to his staff, "even with their tails."[84]

Why did the returning Japanese pilots report such risibly inflated results? The "T" Force airmen had attacked in darkness on the night of October 13, when they could not closely observe the results. Double- and triple-counting of apparent torpedo hits was a problem even in daylight; at night it was endemic. A dozen pilots might see the same "pillar of fire" and count it as a torpedo hit. Flying into a maelstrom of antiaircraft fire, the flyers were temporarily blinded by the colorful bursts. Many Japanese planes shot down among the ships of the American task force remained afloat and burning before sinking. These fires were easily mistaken for burning ships. Local air commanders took their reports at face value, and passed them along to IGHQ in Tokyo. Fukudome wrote after the war: "Airmen, aspiring to fame, were likely to exaggerate their achievements. Night attacks resulted in universal exaggeration."[85]

Most interesting to Halsey and his staff were references to a mopping-up operation. Radio Tokyo reported that the Japanese fleet was in pursuit of the beaten and retreating remnants of the U.S. fleet, intending to sink them before they could get to safety: "The Japanese air force, in close teamwork with surface units, are now attacking the doomed enemy task force. . . . The remaining enemy warships are now all doomed to perish at the bottom of the Pacific Ocean."[86] All the hullabaloo might be nothing more than propaganda. But the voices on the radio seemed convinced of the truth of their own reports. Moreover, new "Ultras" from Pearl Harbor confirmed that a fleet of surface warships was preparing to put to sea via the Bungo Strait to chase and mop up whatever was left of the Third Fleet.

It dawned on Halsey's staff that they might have an opportunity to exploit the enemy's misguided optimism. Carney said of the crippled *Canberra*: "She was really a dry fly, in my book. She was a fine floating lure."[87] He and Captain Ralph Wilson, the fleet operations officer, devised a plan and sold it to Halsey. The crippled ships would be dangled as bait. With a little luck, the American carriers might spring a trap on the pursuing Japanese naval force, scoring a wipeout victory before MacArthur's forces even hit the beaches on Leyte. Halsey assented, and new orders were transmitted to the fleet from the *New Jersey*'s soaring radio masts. Task Groups 38.2 and 38.3 were positioned about 100 miles east of the cripples, far enough to evade detection by Formosa- or Okinawa-based search planes but close enough to ambush a Japanese naval force should it come into range. The rest of the Third Fleet withdrew to a safe distance and commenced refueling from fleet oilers. Halsey advised Nimitz of his plans, and the Pacific Fleet chief ordered all available patrol planes in the region to search for the enemy ships: "Suspicion exists [that] enemy surface force may have departed Empire area to mop up on Blue [U.S.] cripples withdrawing [from] Formosa strikes. Extend search to . . . cover assumed enemy approach from Bungo Channel to approximate position."[88] Halsey also let MacArthur know that he was preparing to come to grips with a major portion of the Japanese navy, and that in view of that contingency, "all strikes on the Philippines were withdrawn until further notice."[89] Halsey told Admiral DuBose in the *Wichita* to send out a series of mock distress signals. CripDiv 1 was given an even more telling nickname: BaitDiv 1.

Saving the two flooded, dead-in-the-water cruisers would have presented a challenge even if waves of attacking planes had not been descending upon them from hour to hour. The officers and men of BaitDiv 1 knew they were expendable. Watching the slothlike pace of the towed ships, one skipper of the division remarked, "Now I know how a worm on a fishhook must feel."[90] For the towing ships, absorbing the shock of 16,000 tons bucking and lurching on long swells required a mastery of "old-fashioned marlinspike seamanship," with sophisticated rigs of towing chocks and pelican stoppers.[91] The work was perilous, and several crewmen were badly injured. The cruiser *Boston* first began towing the *Houston* during a night so dark that the *Houston* could not be seen from the *Boston*'s stern even while under tow. The ocean tug *Pawnee* rendezvoused with the group on October 15 and took over the job of towing the *Houston*. Miraculously, it seemed to the crews of the salvage group, no Japanese warplanes bothered them that day, or the night following. But on the sixteenth their luck ran out, as a flight of 107 fighters and bombers from Formosa attacked at midday.

The combat air patrol F6Fs of the *Cabot* and *Cowpens* shot down about fifty enemy planes, but a few managed to get through the screen. One dropped an aerial torpedo aimed at the *Houston*'s stern. The fish ran down her wake and struck almost directly between the rudder posts, flipping the hangar hatch up into the sky like a bottle top. Twenty sailors were lifted off their feet and pitched into the sea. The aviation gasoline tanks in the hangar bulkheads ignited, and fires raged on the fantail. The tug *Pawnee* continued towing throughout the attack and its aftermath, the slack never leaving the cable. The *Houston*'s captain chose to keep fighting for his ship's life. The 12,000-ton ship was flooded with about 6,300 tons of seawater, but she kept crawling toward Ulithi. All but about one hundred men of her crew were taken off. She was down very deep in the water, with a draft of 32 feet and an 8-degree starboard list.[92] She rolled sickeningly, almost onto her beam-ends, as green seas washed across her decks.

Admiral Toyoda had given initial orders to dispatch a cruiser-destroyer squadron from the Inland Sea, under the command of Vice Admiral Kiyo-hide Shima, to hunt down the American cripples. In the end, however, the naval high command refused to swallow its own codswallop. On the morning of October 14, as search flights blanketed the area east and south of Formosa, reports confirmed that many undamaged American war-ships remained in the vicinity. Moreover, the punishing carrier airstrikes launched against Luzon that day proved that the American fleet must be largely intact. Sensing a trap, Toyoda recalled the Shima force to the Amami Islands north of Okinawa, where it would refuel and put to sea again on October 18 to fulfill its role in the pending *Sho*-1 operations to defend the Philippines.

That concluded the four-day "Air Battle of Formosa." According to Fukudome's figures, he had lost 329 Formosa-based aircraft. Of these, 179 had sortied to attack the U.S. fleet and failed to return; the others had been destroyed on the ground or in the air over Formosa. At Takao Air Base, the main air installation on the island, barely a structure was left standing and barely a single airplane was left undamaged. At least two hundred additional planes based on Kyushu, Okinawa, and Luzon had been destroyed, for a total of more than five hundred Japanese warplanes lost between October 10 and October 17. Since the start of Halsey's Third Fleet operations six weeks earlier, the Japanese had lost approximately 1,200 aircraft in the region.

After a grueling ten-day passage, the *Canberra* and *Houston* and their salvage group limped into Ulithi Atoll on the morning of October 27. Both cruisers were returned to the United States for extensive repairs, and both would be returned to service in the postwar navy.

The final day of the Formosa battle was followed, one day later, by the arrival off Leyte of the first elements of MacArthur's invasion fleet. At dawn on October 17, lookouts at the Suluan lighthouse (at the entrance to Leyte

Gulf) radioed a sighting report: a squadron of minesweepers was entering the channel. When the report reached Toyoda about an hour later, he sent a *Sho*-1 alert to all commands. The various elements of the Japanese fleet, flung across an axis of several thousand miles between Japan and Malaya, began hurried preparations to put to sea.

Plan *Sho* had been conceived in desperation, but even the most pessimistic planners at Imperial General Headquarters in Tokyo had not anticipated the loss of so much Japanese airpower immediately prior to the arrival of the U.S. invasion fleet. Replacement airplanes and aircrews were pouring into the Philippines from Japan and China, but what chance did they have against the American carrier airmen, given the fate of their recently slaughtered comrades? Though they could not afford to admit it, either to their subordinates or perhaps even to themselves, the Japanese admirals knew that the last big naval confrontation of the Pacific War was upon them. They would fight it without effective air support, and therefore they would lose it—but at any rate their real mission was not to win at all, but to go down fighting in a final blaze of glory.

Chapter Four

Throughout the summer of 1944, Tokyo was hot, dirty, and discontented. The city's once vibrant commercial districts were shabby, colorless, and half-deserted. Michio Takeyama, a teacher during the war years who later became one of Japan's most celebrated novelists, recalled that "suffocating winds blew through town, and ash-like dust piled up on rooftops. Even around Shibuya whole rows of shops were closed and roads dug up, and few people were to be seen, except that here and there, in front of food stores, there were long lines."[1]

Food had become a universal preoccupation. Famine had not yet touched the country, but for ordinary citizens it took planning and effort to find enough to eat. One could see it in one's neighbors' faces: many Japanese had grown visibly emaciated. Takeyama noted that his school headmaster appeared to be wasting away week by week, so that he scarcely looked like the same man. "His jaw narrowed; his neck shrank, pathetically. With unruly white hair, eyes glittering beneath baggy eyelids, gradually wrinkling skin, he often looked like an old carved mask."[2] People tired easily and had less energy to face the day; at the same time, however, the daily effort required to obtain food began to crowd out other concerns. One source estimates that the average Japanese family spent five hours per day shopping for food or standing in ration lines. Shops remained shuttered all week, until an occasional delivery of rationed food arrived—and then they would open only until the inventory gave out. People who had waited in line for hours were often sent away empty-handed. The practice of begging had been virtually unknown in prewar Japan, but now even well-dressed people were seen imploring their fellow citizens to share a morsel. The struggle to put food on the family table taxed the time and energy of women, especially—and many of those same women ate less in order to feed their children and husbands, which in turn deprived them of energy to brave the shops and ration lines.

City dwellers traveled out to the country in hopes of buying food directly from farmers. But the commuter trains were groaning under the crush of a much-enlarged wartime ridership, so the journey was always an exhausting struggle. Train stations looked like refugee camps. People waited hours to catch a train, perhaps bribing a station attendant for a ticket. Once aboard, they found themselves squashed into a seething throng. Broken ribs were common, and in a few widely reported cases, infants suffocated to death. The compartments were shabby and filthy, the upholstery threadbare and ripped open, hanging straps gone from the overhead rails, windows broken, floor tiles torn up. Overcrowded trains charged through stations without stopping, for fear that those waiting on the platforms would try to fight their way into the cars.

An urbanite who braved the ordeal and reached the countryside entered a bucolic landscape of hills and rice terraces arranged in jigsaw patterns around sleepy hamlets. In this serene, picturesque setting, she detected no visible sign that the nation was waging a war for its survival. But she found the farmers insolent and brazen. They charged scandalous prices and expected the buyers to make signs of exaggerated gratitude. Then it was straight back to the train platforms and the desperate and degrading struggle to return to the city.

White rice had been the foundation of the Japanese diet since time immemorial, but now it could rarely be found even at inflated prices. Wartime rationed rice was adulterated with dried noodles, barley, soybeans, or sweet potatoes, and as the war dragged on those inferior substitutes grew steadily as a proportion of the allocation.[3] To stretch this rice-like farrago, people tossed it with wheat flour and sautéed it in oil to make a much-despised dish called "nukapan." Fresh meat and fish were vanishing from the rationing rolls, to be replaced by tofu, vegetables, and crispy dried sardines called "niboshi." For dietary variety, people made do with whatever they might find in the markets on any given day—descending the culinary scale, eggplants, fresh radishes, dried radishes, bean sprouts, pumpkin squash, bamboo shoots, and chrysanthemum leaves. Fresh eggs were almost never to be found; instead they mixed powdered "shanghai eggs" with water to make a sickly egg-like gruel. Ham was replaced by something called "whale ham," and when bakers could not obtain wholesale flour, they produced a breadlike substitute using sweet bean paste. Thus the popular Japanese lunchtime sandwich, a tidy square of white bread and ham, was supplanted by an imposter that contained neither ham nor bread.

As the quality and quantity of rationed food declined, the black market became essential to sustain the lives of ordinary Japanese. By the last year of the war, "Mr. Black" probably represented about half of the nation's retail sales. The disparity between official and black-market prices widened considerably in mid-1944, so that nearly every category of foodstuff commanded tenfold its official listed price. In March 1944, black-market rice commanded fourteen times the legal listed price; in November 1944, it fetched *forty-four* times the official price.[4] For certain rare items, the prices quoted were so astronomical that people wondered whether *any* of their fellow citizens could afford them. In Tokyo, in late July 1944, tomatoes were offered for the previously unimaginable price of fifty-seven sen, and peaches fetched the breathtaking price of 1.25 yen.[5] Skyrocketing costs inevitably aroused class resentments. Rich or well-connected Japanese were visibly better fed than their poorer neighbors. The amount of extra flesh on a person's face and body was a measure of his privilege, and perhaps of his corruption. Tsune-jiro Tamura, a seventy-four-year-old man living in Kyoto, complained in his diary: "The rich can do anything with the money they have, and they buy up the lower classes' goods and food and circulate them back to the black market. . . . It's the age of the strong eating the weak."[6]

Under the close scrutiny of an omnipotent police state, the Japanese people offered no organized resistance during the war, and precious little public dissent of any kind. Indeed, they gave signs of continued support for the war and its aims. Since the nation's invasion of Manchuria in 1931, the great mass of Japanese had grown accustomed to war as a natural and quasi-permanent condition. Many did not think it strange or immoral to conquer and subjugate foreigners, and they took hotblooded pride in the overseas triumphs of their military forces. But by the late summer of 1944, they were beginning to grasp that the Pacific War was essentially different. As the Allies advanced westward across the Pacific, anyone who could read a map could see that Japan was losing territory. One by one, entire island garrisons had been annihilated as *gyokusai*, "smashed jewels." This was nothing like the war in China. It was a total war against an enemy resolved to occupy and disarm Japan, an enemy who possessed the power and will to do so—and the only alternative to complete destruction might be an appeal to the conqueror's mercy. As that realization dawned on the population, defeatist sentiments proliferated. The process hit an inflection point in July 1944, with the simultaneous fall of Saipan and the ouster of Prime Minister Hideki Tojo.

In low voices or secret diaries, ordinary citizens were asking hard questions about the reliability of official reports. In the quest to separate fact from propaganda, they inevitably traded in rumors. The police went to great lengths to suppress rumormongering, but their efforts were largely futile, because the public now had every reason to fear for their safety and the nation's future. While outright defiance was rare, there were increasing signs of passive resistance to the regime. Ordinary citizens were more likely to complain about official corruption and the rapacity of the black markets. They mocked local authorities during the mandatory civil defense and air-raid drills, and gave only the minimum effort required. Tardiness, absenteeism, shirking, and "calling in sick" were common syndromes both in the workplace and at mandatory neighborhood events. According to the Japanese industrial journal *Diamond*, the daily absentee rate in munitions factories was 10 percent in 1943, rising to 15 percent in 1944.[7] Crime, vandalism, and juvenile delinquency were on the rise: many Japanese noted and lamented the corrosion in basic manners, kindliness, and honest dealing. Enthusiasm waned at the quasi-obligatory patriotic rallies, parades, and send-off parties for departing military recruits. A mother whose son had died in the war refused to visit Yasukuni Shrine in Tokyo, where the spirits of the nation's war dead were laid to rest. "When those who have lost a precious child go to the Yasukuni Shrine, they're made to squat on the white sand like beggars, and they have to bow their heads," she declared. "I will never go to that stupid place!"[8]

Prime Minister Kuniaki Koiso, who had replaced Tojo in July, privately expressed concern about the brittle morale of the Japanese people. There was talk in his cabinet of relaxing censorship measures in hopes of restoring the regime's fading credibility. With great fanfare, the Board of Information announced a policy of "free speech" and the "enlightenment of public opinion" in the press and broadcast media.[9] On October 13, 1944, an NHK radio commentator explained that the new measures would "open the way for the people to express publicly what they are thinking. . . . There is no necessity anymore to exchange their opinions secretly in low voices." Frank and truthful war reporting was intended to lift the morale of the Japanese people, to make them "feel happy and jolly."[10]

The very next day brought the first reports of the phantasmal sea victory off Formosa. At the Imperial General Headquarters in Tokyo, a press liaison officer burst into the press room with a bottle of sake in hand. "Here comes a torpedo," he shouted, and held up the bottle to represent an aerial torpedo speeding toward the hull of an American ship: "The moment we've been waiting for has come! It's the Divine Wind, the Kamikaze!"[11] Reports were still coming in, he said, but the returning Japanese flyers were unanimous— they had scored a sensational victory, the greatest yet of the war. The bottle was opened and the reporters and officers shared a toast.

The next morning, a headline in the *Asahi Shinbun* reported "Great Battle Results Rare in History." The paper reported that the Americans had lost 500,000 tons of shipping and 26,000 sailors killed in action.[12] The triumphant voices of NHK newscasters resounded through the streets and alleys of Tokyo's densely packed neighborhoods. The estimated tally rose steadily throughout the day, until at 3:00 p.m. the IGHQ stated definitively that Japanese warplanes had sunk ten aircraft carriers, eleven battleships, three cruisers, and a destroyer; they had also damaged three aircraft carriers, a battleship, four cruisers, and eleven other warships of unknown type.[13]

Even an unschooled civilian could understand that these were extraordinary claims, but the authorities seemed sure of themselves, and the reports were backed up by the quoted testimony of Japanese pilots who had fought in the battle. Formosa would go down as the greatest victory of the war, they said—greater even than Admiral Togo's victory over the Russians at Tsushima, perhaps even the most annihilating naval victory of all time. Radio correspondents were sent out to collect the views of Japanese civilians in "man-on-the-street" interviews. Every few hours, official announcements added new and exciting details. Newspapers put out late-day "extras," and citizens waited in long lines at every newsstand. Prime Minister Koiso intoned that the great victory vindicated the "drawing-in" strategy that had been discussed in public for more than a year. Grand Admiral Karl Donitz of Germany sent a congratulatory telegram on behalf of Adolf Hitler. The *Showa* emperor proclaimed a public holiday to commemorate the "glorious victory" and announced that a special ration of "celebration" sake would be distributed to every home in the country. The Japanese people were given license to relive some of the euphoria of the early war—to party like it was the spring of 1942 again, when news of electrifying victories had come once or twice a week.[14]

Within less than twenty-four hours after the first Formosa victory reports, senior military leaders knew that the claims had been (at the very least) grossly exaggerated. They would not know the full truth—that two American warships had been torpedoed, but none sunk—until after the war, but air reconnaissance reports on October 14 confirmed that the Third Fleet was largely intact. Fukudome said he knew by the end of that day that "the damage done to the enemy was slight, and I was convinced that a major invasion of the Philippines would soon be launched."[15] Admiral Matome Ugaki commented in his diary: "There are occasions when exaggeration may be necessary to uplift morale, but those in a position to direct operations mustn't kid themselves by exaggerating the results achieved."[16] At IGHQ, on October 18, naval planners openly admitted to their army counterparts that the Japanese fleet was unlikely to survive (let alone win) another pitched naval battle against the Americans—but they wanted to fight it anyway, so that the Combined Fleet could "die a glorious death."[17]

Insofar as the Japanese public was concerned, however, the cat was out of the bag. The government and news media had chosen their story, and now they were stuck with it. Hirohito had given his imprimatur to the victory announcements, and official communiqués issued over the man-god's seal were sacrosanct. Moreover, the supposed wipeout of the hated U.S. fleet had fed the nation's collective emotional need for any sort of good news. All concerned—military leaders, reporters, editors, the public at large—desperately *wanted* to believe the thrilling reports. For the moment, at least, the news alleviated potent and potentially toxic internal pressures, and allayed concerns about the state of public morale. Looking back on the episode from a postwar perspective, a journalist who had covered the IGHQ concluded: "Theirs weren't intentional lies, but rather signs of the acute anxiety, the desire everyone felt for something good to happen."[18]

On October 20, Koiso led a celebratory rally in Hibiya Public Hall, a ten-story terracotta building in Hibiya Park, near the heart of Tokyo. A tremendous crowd, probably more than 100,000 people, filled the park and adjacent streets and signaled their approval with raised fists and hats tossed in the air. The prime minister's speech was carried live over the radio.

He delivered a long philippic against American military forces, citing the bombing and strafing of civilians by American warplanes and the mutilation of dead Japanese soldiers on the battlefield; he charged that the Americans had abandoned all pretense of civilized warfare, and were no better than "mere beastly murderers, and nothing else. . . . The gods certainly will deal upon them a crushing blow of punishment."[19]

Koiso, whose government was three months old, had previously served as the governor-general of Korea. He was bald, with a feline, martial bearing; his imposing looks had earned him the nickname "Tiger of Korea." Because Koiso had not commanded troops in the field during the present war, there was no stain of defeat on his hands. Having been away from Tokyo for two years, he had taken no part in the political intrigue and factional struggles that had led to the ouster of his predecessor, General Hideki Tojo, the previous July. Koiso had been selected as prime minister by a coterie of senior statesmen, not because he was thought to be an especially promising leader, but because objections were raised against all of the other candidates. His premiership was the product of a fragile consensus; he was little more than a figurehead. Having retired from active duty in 1938, he was not eligible to hold the post of army minister and was largely excluded from discussions of military strategy. Later, Koiso maintained that he was not even privy to much of what was happening during his nine-month stint in office: "I didn't know what was really going on inside the military."[20]

Getting rid of Tojo had not corrected the root deficiencies of Japan's wartime political regime. The forms and protocols of the Meiji Constitution were outwardly maintained, but the parliamentary parties had been sidelined, and real power was apportioned among a few staffs and departments in the military and bureaucracy. Army and navy leaders distrusted one another, and often backed irreconcilable strategies. The cabinet and various liaison bodies met to exchange views, but no one possessed the authority to implement a coherent policy across the entire regime. Under Tojo, the supreme decision-making body had been called the "Imperial Headquarters-Government Liaison Conference." With Koiso's succession, that committee had been dissolved and replaced with a panel of six called the Supreme War Direction Council—the "SWDC"—including the prime minister, the foreign minister, the army and navy ministers, and the respective chiefs of the army and navy general staffs. Later, and subsequently in the historical literature, this inner cabinet was nicknamed "the Big Six"—

and although there were changes in personnel, it was this panel that would render major decisions until the end of the war.

Big policy changes could be achieved only with the unanimous support of these six men—and even then, only so long as they had the backing of the court aristocracy, the imperial household staff, and the emperor himself. As always, decisions were achieved by the plodding and painstaking method of *nemawashi,* or "digging around the roots for a consensus." In the event of a deadlock, nothing could be done. Often in such cases, the army and navy would pursue their own lines of action, but for the sake of appearances pretend that they were coordinated elements of a grand strategy. Admiral Mitsumasa Yonai, a former prime minister who returned to government as navy minister and vice premier in Koiso's government, explained that not even a vote of the council could break an impasse. "It isn't a question of a majority vote," he told interrogators after the war. "If they can't obtain agreement on a question, it means there is a lack of unity."[21] When consensus did not exist, inertia prevailed. Whatever its prior direction had been, Japan would continue in that direction.

Hirohito, the forty-three-year-old *Showa* emperor, had given his personal support to General Tojo, and had long resisted efforts to oust him from power. Toward the end of Tojo's tenure, Prince Takamatsu, the sovereign's younger brother, had begun to criticize Hirohito in imperial court circles, suggesting that he was allowing national affairs to drift out of control. The emperor's role in government was limited by prevailing interpretations of the constitution, but he wielded great intangible authority even over those who knew he was not actually a god. The degree of his responsibility for the war and its miseries remains the subject of spirited debate among scholars and historians. Before December 1941, Hirohito had resisted the drift toward war, urging the maintenance of stability both at home and in international affairs. He had demanded that army hotheads and insurgents be suppressed and punished. But such exhortations did not carry any real constitutional weight, and were not binding except in the rare circumstance that a deadlocked cabinet sought a "sacred decision." In finally acquiescing to the ouster of Tojo in July 1944, Hirohito pressed his new government to lay the groundwork for a diplomatic initiative to end the war. But he did not propose establishing direct contact with the Allied governments to seek an armistice. He believed that Japan must first score a smashing victory against the Americans, perhaps in the impending Philippine campaign, before the time would become ripe for diplomacy. In his postwar "Soliloquy," Hirohito stated that he had wanted to pour all of Japan's remaining military power into the defense of Leyte Island: "Then, with America staggering, we would have been able to find room for a compromise."[22]

No one in government dared talk of surrender, or even a treaty settlement that would require Japan to give up the overseas territories it had held before 1941. At a minimum, the Allies would have to abandon their demand for unconditional surrender and consent to sit down at a negotiating table. Still, the men who ruled Japan understood that diplomacy must play a role in the war's final act, and Foreign Minister Mamoru Shigemitsu had several irons in the fire. Tentative peace feelers were sent out from Japanese embassies in neutral European countries, including Sweden, Portugal, and Switzerland. Hoping to end the war in China, Shigemitsu's envoys had approached Wang Jingwei's collaborationist regime in Nanjing, offering to withdraw Japanese forces from the country if Chiang Kai-shek would sever his relationship with the Allies and pledge a "benevolent neutrality." This overture led nowhere, partly because the intermediaries approached by the Japanese government did not have much influence with Chiang, and partly because the Chinese could see that Japan was on its way to defeat in the Pacific.[23]

The linchpin of plans for a diplomatic "off-ramp" involved enlisting the Soviet government to act as a mediator between Tokyo and Washington. This scheme, never especially realistic, had been discussed at length prior to the attack on Pearl Harbor, and Shigemitsu now hoped to bring it to harvest. His ambassador to Moscow opened a dialogue with the Kremlin, offering to arrange peace talks between Russia and Germany. With peace restored on the eastern front in Europe, Moscow might then mediate a negotiated settlement of the Pacific War. But when the proposal was put before Soviet Foreign Commissar Vyacheslav Molotov in September 1944, he rejected it firmly. The idea would have been far-fetched at any point during the Nazi-Soviet War—but at that late date, when the Allies were advancing against Nazi Germany from east and west, it was a nonstarter. When the Japanese proposed extending the Japanese-Soviet Neutrality Pact beyond its scheduled expiration in the spring of 1946, Molotov replied that the issue could be addressed in good time. Shigemitsu and his colleagues had no inkling that Josef Stalin had hinted broadly to FDR that he would turn his forces loose on Japan as soon as Germany was defeated, or that he would make that commitment explicit at the Yalta conference in February 1945.

Japanese diplomats continued to nurture futile hopes of a Stalin-assisted armistice until the last week of the war, when the Soviets suddenly declared war on Japan and the Red Army charged into Manchuria.

In truth, political conditions in Japan would not permit a concerted bid to end the war through diplomacy, and all the leading figures in and out of government knew it. Getting rid of Tojo had been a necessary first step toward a diplomatic exit, but a sudden turn toward peace in the fall of 1944 would arouse the fervent resistance of army hardliners. The military police (*Kempetai*) kept cabinet ministers and other leading figures under surveillance, vigilant to the prospect of a back-channel bid for peace talks. Tojo continued to exert influence over this state security apparatus even after leaving power, and many suspected that the deposed leader was preparing the ground for a coup d'etat. With good reason, the ruling group feared a return to the military factionalism, insurrectionary violence, and targeted assassinations of the 1930s. Civil war did not seem beyond possibility. According to Admiral Kichisaburo Nomura, the last prewar ambassador to the United States, the regime's habit of celebrating make-believe victories was self-defeating, because Japanese public opinion was never prepared for a negotiated settlement. "If we had stopped the war any earlier the people would not have understood. They had never been told the truth about the situation and there would have been civil war in Japan among the people . . . it seems to me that it was the destiny of our country to continue this very unwise war to the very end."[24]

From the start, Koiso's public statements echoed those of his predecessor. There was no discernible shift in tone, certainly no hint that his cabinet might be exploring options to end the war. The new prime minister declared that the conflict was approaching a furious new stage, when the Japanese people must unite to resist the enemy with fanatical zeal. The week the new government took power, the Tokyo papers were full of references to American "beasts," "butchers," and "demons." A photograph published in *Life* magazine, depicting an American woman admiring a Japanese skull collected as a battlefield souvenir, was given wide publicity. It was reported that the United States had emptied its prisons to fill the ranks of its army. "We cannot but feel shocked with disgust," remarked an NHK radio commentator in August 1944. "Unless they take advantage of the brutal spirit of criminals, Americans cannot fight as normal brave fighters. This proves they are nothing but gangs of wild animals."[25] In a speech to the Diet (Japan's national parliament) on September 8, 1944, Koiso warned: "We must do well to consider the possibility of the enemy landing on our home soil."[26] His home ministry announced plans for nationwide training of civilians in hand-to-hand combat. Women, children, and old men would join the ranks of a homeland defense force: they would resist the hated barbarian with homemade weapons and bamboo spears whenever he set his filthy barbarian's boots on the divine shores of Japan.

With the U.S. conquest of the Marianas, large-scale aerial bombing of the homeland was to be expected, and the government ordered new civil defense measures. On August 16, 1944, the transportation ministry announced a series of measures to "counteract the disrupted conditions resulting under air raids, naval bombardment, and other forms of enemy attacks," which would include "first aid, emergency commodity distribution, patrol, evacuation, prevention of epidemics, water supply, cleaning of debris, and emergency restoration to normalcy."[27] Long swaths of houses and buildings were razed to create urban firebreaks. Schoolchildren were put to work building the fantastical weapons known as "balloon bombs," which would be launched into the jet stream to be carried some 5,000 miles across the North Pacific to strike random targets on the U.S. mainland. Speeches, newspaper articles, and radio broadcasts dwelled on overtly religious and mythological themes. Koiso, a devout Shinto practitioner, made a publicized visit to the Ise Grand Shrine shortly after taking office, declaring a new national slogan: "National Responsibility Must Be Returned to the Highest Commander."[28] This purposely ambiguous reference was best read as a prophecy: when the moment of supreme crisis arrived, the *Showa* emperor would summon the ancient gods to protect the homeland.

The next major American offensive, whether it fell on the Philippines, Formosa, or the Ryukyus, would likely sever Japan's economic lifeline to the oil fields and other natural resources of the East Indies. That could trigger a collapse of the Japanese economy at the same time that it immobilized the fleet and cut Japanese island garrisons off from seaborne support. More than two years of sedulous lying would be exposed for what it was. At the same time, Japan's only real ally appeared to be losing the war in Europe. Any citizen with a rudimentary understanding of the global conflict knew that by launching its war in the Pacific, Japan had placed an enormous wager on the ascendency of Nazi Germany. If trends held, the great pile of chips would soon be swept from the table.

Every ominous development in the war to date had occurred when the Japanese people were hungry, but not yet starving. In the fall of 1944, the food situation looked to be on the verge of becoming much more serious. Domestic rice production had declined by more than 10 percent since the start of the war, even though the homeland had not yet been subjected to heavy bombing. Food imports had declined, and were likely to shrink further as Japanese merchant shipping succumbed to the depredations of American airpower and submarines. An internal government report in July 1944 warned that production of nearly every category of food was on the decline, and "the national standard of living in 1944 will become a good deal more stringent compared with last year."[29] That left a smaller margin for bad weather, and the 1944 rice harvest was threatened by persistent strong driving rains. Moreover, domestic food production might suffer a catastrophic decline in 1945, due to a foreseeable combination of shipping losses, an energy crisis, and the disruption of road and rail transportation by aerial bombing.

Hunger was one thing; famine was another. Famine, the Japanese leadership feared, might cause a breakdown in civil order and threaten the foundations of its authority. The Japanese people had supported overseas imperialist aggression with the understanding that it promised a higher standard of living at home. But life had grown much harder since the attack on Pearl Harbor, and it remained to be seen how much deprivation they would endure. In the prewar era, young officers of the army had threatened to take direct action to alleviate the economic suffering of the Japanese people, and had nearly achieved a coup d'etat in 1936. Some in the ruling circle pointed to the example of the Bolshevik revolution of 1917, which had likewise been fueled by empty stomachs and the disruptions of a catastrophic foreign war. Keeping a lid on internal tensions became a prime consideration of all Japanese policy-making—domestic, political, diplomatic, and strategic—right up to the hours before the surrender in August 1945.

IN SEPTEMBER 1944, Hirohito reviewed and approved military plans for the next stage of the war. These were designated "*Sho*," after an old Chinese ideogram meaning "victory." Plan *Sho* ("*Sho*-go") came in four versions, based on four contingencies thought most likely after the American conquest of the Marianas. *Sho*-1 through *Sho*-4 would counter

amphibious landings against targets in four zones stretching in an arc from
south to north: the Philippines; Formosa and the Ryukyu Islands; Honshu;
and Hokkaido. From the beginning, however, Japanese planners considered the Philippines the most likely target of the next major operation,
and gave the most thought and planning to *Sho*-1. Their thinking on this
score was influenced by MacArthur's famous public pledges to return to
the Philippines.[30]

Sho-1 bore many of the familiar hallmarks of previous Japanese naval
operations. It was intricately choreographed, with widely separated forces
approaching the enemy from several directions. It relied on precise timing
between different fleet elements, and was therefore vulnerable to disruption. Many previous Japanese campaign plans had included feints, lures, and
other acts of deception: likewise, *Sho*-1's only real hope of success depended
upon a *ruse de guerre*. Admiral Takeo Kurita's "First Striking Force," comprising most of the surface strength of the Combined Fleet, would start
north from Borneo. Off the island of Palawan, in the southwest Philippines,
one part of the fleet would break away and head southeast, under the command of Admiral Shoji Nishimura, while the main force continued north
under Kurita. The two subdivided fleet elements would pass through the
Philippine archipelago by two different straits, Surigao in the south and
San Bernardino in the north. Meanwhile, Admiral Jisaburo Ozawa's "First
Mobile Force," comprising all of Japan's remaining aircraft carriers, would
sortie from the Inland Sea and descend on the battle zone from the north,
in hopes of luring the bulk of Halsey's Third Fleet away from the beachhead.
If all went as hoped, Kurita and Nishimura's columns would debouch from
the straits and attack MacArthur's invasion fleet in a naval pincer movement. This force, the Japanese knew, would include some 100,000 enemy
troops and hundreds of cargo ships loaded with weapons, equipment, and
supplies to support the invasion. The crux of the Japanese plan was to get
Kurita's battleships, cruisers, and destroyers into short-range action against
this amphibious fleet as it lay off the invasion beaches.

It was a grand and glorious vision. But in fact, as all senior officers knew,
Sho was really shaped by the mobility and range limitations imposed by the
stringent fueling situation, and the difficulty in keeping the fleet properly
supplied. The fuel supply was far to the south, in the oil fields of Borneo and
Sumatra—but the shipyards and repair facilities were in the Japanese home
islands, as were the myriad provisions, ordnance, ammunition, and reserve

manpower required to keep the fleet in fighting trim. It was no longer possible to transport enough oil to Japan to meet the thirsty fleet's needs, and the shortfall was growing steadily worse as American submarines and airplanes hunted down and sank the country's remaining oil tankers. The bulk of the fleet must therefore remain in anchorages far to the south, near the empire's fueling wellspring. But Ozawa's carriers had been almost entirely denuded of airplanes and trained carrier aviators at the Battle of the Philippine Sea (June 19–20, 1944), and he needed to acquire and train replacement air groups. Given the pitiable state of Japan's flight-training pipeline and aviation plants, he would need to keep his flattops in Japanese waters for some time, probably at least three or four months.

Since it was necessary for these fleets to be separated by thousands of miles, Kurita was detached from Ozawa's command and placed under the direct control of the commander in chief of the Combined Fleet, Admiral Soemu Toyoda, who had recently moved his headquarters from a command ship anchored in Tokyo Bay to a bunker under Keio University's Hiyoshi campus in Yokohama. Ozawa and Kurita would now receive their orders separately, by long-range radio broadcast from Hiyoshi. This scattershot deployment of Japan's major fleet elements was far from ideal. Given the retrograde logistical situation, however, it was inevitable.

If MacArthur's amphibious force could be attacked at all, it would have to be attacked by surface warships and land-based air forces, because no one expected much of Ozawa's neutered aircraft carriers or the much-reduced Japanese submarine fleet. Plan *Sho*'s chief concern was to move Japan's widely separated naval and air forces into position to give battle. Twelve fleet oilers had been assigned to fuel Kurita's fleet. This fueling group had planned to conduct underway replenishment exercises that October, but those exercises had been cancelled. Every single remaining oil tanker was important now; there was no room for error in the management of the fuel situation. It was not even certain that Kurita's ships would have enough fuel remaining at the end of the battle to withdraw to safety. Ozawa's contribution to the battle would depend on the state of his carrier air forces at whatever moment the Americans chose to make their next move. No one expected the Japanese carrier forces to meet their adversaries on anything like equal terms, and Ozawa knew he was likely to suffer another mauling while inflicting scant punishment in return. Given that dismal outlook, it was decided that the once-mighty Japanese carrier striking force should function as a lure, to provide Kurita with an opening to get at the invasion fleet. Ozawa was willing to serve in this lowly role. "A decoy, that was our first primary mission, to act as a decoy," he said. "The main mission was all sacrifice. An attack with a very weak force of planes comes under the heading of sacrifice of planes and ships."[31]

After July's political upheaval, army and navy leaders had pledged to work more closely together. But as late as the third week of October, when MacArthur's invasion fleet was underway for Leyte, the two services were reading from different playbooks. Japanese army commanders had still not decided whether to move troop reinforcements to the island. Some wanted to concentrate the army's strength on Luzon, even if that meant conceding Leyte to the Americans.

On October 18, at the Officers Club in Tokyo, a group of four officers (one each from the army and navy ministries and the army and navy general staffs) met to hammer out a joint strategy for the defense of the Philippines. Having reviewed Sho-1, General Kenryo Sato of the army ministry raised an eleventh-hour objection. Acknowledging that the Japanese people were "crying" for the fleet to do battle with the enemy, Sato insisted that the high command must keep its "coolness" and not act rashly to appease public opinion. If the Combined Fleet fought now, he said, it was likely to suffer an annihilating defeat. Better to keep Ozawa's ships in port, where they would have some deterrent value in simply keeping the enemy from approaching the home islands. Moreover, Sato pointed out, the fleet would have to burn a lot of precious fuel just to get into battle. At that moment, a column of six oil tankers was inbound from the south, carrying about 60,000 tons of oil. That fuel was needed to keep the Japanese war economy running. Sato asked his navy counterparts, "What can the Combined Fleet do going out for battle now? The 60,000 tons of oil is more important."[32]

The speech brought the entire room, including Sato, to the brink of tears. He had put Japan's predicament into stark relief. The honor of the once-mighty Imperial Japanese Navy now mattered less than six tankers and the oil they carried. Even a general could see that the fleet's diminished status was a portent of doom. "This was the saddest feeling I had ever experienced," Sato wrote.

Sobbing freely, Rear Admiral Tasuku Nakazawa of the Naval General Staff replied on behalf of the navy. He was grateful to the general for his kindness, but "now the Combined Fleet of the Empire of Japan wishes to be given a place to end her life." Because of the oil shortage and the enemy's growing dominance in the air, Plan *Sho* offered the "last chance" for the fleet to "die a glorious death." Nakazawa concluded: "This is the navy's earnest wish."[33]

After a choked silence, with tears streaming down his face, Sato agreed that the 60,000 tons of oil should be offered as a "parting present" to the navy. As the meeting broke up, an air-raid siren wailed in the streets outside, and he prayed silently for "the heroic end of the Combined Fleet."[34]

The moving scene underscores a point often neglected in western histories of the Battle of Leyte Gulf. Plan *Sho* was virtually a naval *banzai* charge. Its unstated purpose was to ensure that the Japanese fleet put up one last good fight before the war came to an end. According to Rear Admiral Toshitane Takata of the Combined Fleet staff, "questions were beginning to be asked at home as to what the navy was doing after loss of one point after another down south, such as Marianas and Biak."[35] Japan's surface warships had done barely any fighting since the previous year's action in the Solomons. Its splendid line of battleships had seen no surface action at all since the Naval Battle of Guadalcanal, a full two years earlier. The superbattleships *Yamato* and *Musashi* had never come within gunshot range of an enemy ship. The sister behemoths had been built at monumental expense, in Kure and Nagasaki; they were the two largest warships in the world, and Japan had invested great hopes in their war-winning potential. But they had spent most of the war at anchor, mainly because they required so much fuel to operate at sea. Both had served as sumptuous floating headquarters for fleet commanders and their staffs. Their inactivity and virginal combat status had provoked grumbling in the ranks of the fleet, where they were derisively tagged as "Hotel *Yamato*" and "Hotel *Musashi*." To end their careers at anchor, without having once fired their 18-inch main guns at an enemy ship, would be an intolerable disgrace. Admiral Kurita, whose command included both of the great ships, asked his officers on the eve of the battle for the Philippines, "Would it not be shameful to have the fleet remain intact while our nation perishes?"[36]

In postwar interrogations, naval leaders confirmed that they had not entertained any real hope of saving the Philippines, and expected to suffer cataclysmic losses, perhaps even a complete wipeout. They chose to fight anyway, because they judged that nothing could be gained by saving the fleet to fight another day. If and when the Americans took the Philippines, they would strangle the sea routes linking Japan to its oil supply. In that case, said Takata, "even though the fleet should be left, the shipping lanes to the south would be completely cut off so that the fleet, if it should come back to Japanese waters, could not obtain its fuel supply. If it should remain in southern waters, it could not receive supplies of ammunition and arms." With no good options, they decided to "take the gamble," understanding that "if the worst should happen, there was a chance that we would lose the entire fleet."[37] Admiral Kurita said he was prepared to lose half his ships in exchange for "damaging one-half of all your ships in Leyte Bay." Even that result, he added, would not defeat MacArthur's invasion but only "delay the landing for two or three days. . . . It was then a limited objective, to delay that particular landing for two or three days. We could do nothing about succeeding landings, not having enough strength."[38] As for Ozawa, whose defanged carriers would be offered as bait for Halsey, "we expected complete destruction."[39]

ONE INCIDENT DURING THE AERIAL FIGHT off Formosa was singled out for special attention in the Japanese news media. It had occurred on October 15, when Halsey was withdrawing to the east, and the crippled *Canberra* and *Houston* were in slow retreat. Rear Admiral Masafumi Arima, commander of the Twenty-Sixth Air Flotilla on Luzon, had removed his rank insignia, climbed into the cockpit of a Mitsubishi G4M bomber, and led a one-way suicide crash attack against the enemy fleet. His airplane was either lost at sea or destroyed in a failed attack on the carrier *Franklin*; at any rate, it did not return to base. But Tokyo reported that the "hero god" Arima had deliberately crash-dived into an American aircraft carrier, and that the target had been sunk. Fulsome media coverage of the flight signaled that the regime was preparing to launch suicide tactics on a mass scale. The curtain had been raised on the last act of the Pacific air war, when Japanese planes would become deadly missiles piloted by men resolved to die in a ball of fire.

The term kamikaze, "divine wind," was not yet associated with suicide planes—it was still reserved for the mythological heaven-sent typhoon that had destroyed a Mongol invasion fleet seven centuries earlier. Instead, the Japanese spoke of "sure-hit weapons" and "body-crashing" tactics to be carried out by "special attack" (*tokko*) corps. These *tokko* operations would include aviators and aircraft, but also a range of other purpose-built suicide weapons including speedboats, scuba divers, manned rockets, and small submersibles.

Pacific War histories have tended to underplay the controversy created in Japan, and even in the military ranks, by the introduction of organized suicide tactics. Many Japanese resisted strongly, arguing that it misconstrued traditional samurai warrior ideals (*bushido*). Some naval officers associated the concept with a pathological "death cult" that held sway in the Japanese army, and they argued that it had no place in the navy. Veteran aviators, recalling the victories they had won in the skies earlier in the war, tended to regard kamikaze attacks as essentially defeatist. Now and again, Japanese pilots had crash-dived into Allied ships, or rammed Allied bombers in flight—but before the fall of 1944, such attacks had been sporadic and opportunistic, often occurring when an airplane was damaged and could not return to base. When first ordered by a unit commander to fly a suicide mission, the great fighter ace Saburo Sakai was stunned. "A great roaring sounded in my ears," he recalled. "What was he saying? I was in a turmoil. I had a cold, sinking feeling of revulsion in my brain."[40] A pilot must always be ready to die in battle, said Sakai, but that did not include "wantonly wasting one's life."[41]

After the war, a damaging charge was leveled against Japan's military leaders. They were accused of luring thousands of young men into flight training under false pretenses. It was suggested that by early 1944, the military secretly planned to train most of its new pilots as kamikazes, but concealed the fact until it was too late for the trainees to back out. Potent taboos governed (and still govern) discussion of the subject. The historical record is spotty—especially concerning the question of who knew what, and when—but there appears to be considerable evidence behind the charge. In the early stages of the kamikaze recruitment program, no references to suicide tactics were permitted to appear in writing; only verbal orders were given. Naoji Kozu, a reserve naval ensign, agreed to volunteer for the manned torpedo program before he knew that it was a suicide weapon. He and his fellow recruits were told only that they must be "willing to take on a dangerous job" and "willing to board a special weapon." Looking back on the episode after the war, Kozu concluded: "Today, I know they deceived us! I know it with all my heart!"[42]

In postwar interrogations, several senior Japanese naval officers falsely asserted that kamikaze tactics were first proposed and championed by pilots in front-line fighting squadrons. Captain Rikibei Inoguchi, chief of staff of the First Air Fleet, said that the idea had arisen spontaneously among airmen based in the Philippines, and was "purely and simply a policy of that base."[43] Confronted with evidence that kamikaze operations had been planned in Tokyo well before MacArthur's landing on Leyte, Inoguchi remained adamant: "This sort of thing has to come up from the bottom and you can't order such a thing. At no time were kamikaze tactics ordered . . . initially the kamikaze concept was a method of coping with local situations and not the result of an overall policy handed down from GHQ."[44] The record shows those claims to be false. Similarly, Admiral Toyoda told his American interrogators that the first kamikaze flights were an "unexpected result of the decision to send the Second Fleet into Leyte Gulf."[45] He credited the idea to local air commanders in the Philippines, who argued "that if the surface units are taking such desperate measures we too must take similarly desperate measures, and started the first operation of the so-called Special Attack Force."[46] That was false: Toyoda's Combined Fleet staff had been debating and planning suicide operations long before the Battle of Leyte Gulf. Admiral Ozawa's account was equally shifty. At first he maintained that "the first time I heard of kamikaze attacks was when Kurita's fleet went through San Bernardino Strait." Confronted with contrary evidence, he suddenly remembered that in June 1944 "it was recommended to Toyoda. Toyoda said that the time wasn't ripe yet, it was too early to use it."[47]

In fact, kamikaze operations had been studied, debated, and planned for more than a year prior to their first appearance in the Pacific. Captain Eiichiro Jo, a carrier commander who had previously served as the emperor Hirohito's naval aide-de-camp and as a naval attaché in the Washington embassy, had proposed a "Special Attack Corps" in a plan circulated in June 1943.[48] In March 1944, before his fall from power, Prime Minister Hideki Tojo had approved preliminary plans for dedicated suicide units. Admiral Koshiro Oikawa, who served as chief of the Naval General Staff in late 1944, pushed to institutionalize such tactics throughout the naval aviation corps.[49] References to "sure victory weapons" and the "body crashing spirit" were common in newspapers and radio broadcasts after the fall of Saipan in July 1944. On October 6, several weeks before the first suicide air corps was organized in the Philippines, a Japanese admiral told a radio interviewer that the naval air corps would shortly commence "body-crashing" tactics to "ram an enemy plane or ship." He expected such attacks to turn the tide of the war: "This method of warfare, I am sure, will never become ineffective. On the contrary, its possibilities are inexhaustible—it will become better and better."[50]

By the fall of 1944, an arsenal of purpose-built suicide weapons was in advanced production. These included a manned rocket, the *Oka* ("cherry blossom"), which was dropped from a larger aircraft and dove on enemy ships at velocities approaching the speed of sound. A one-man suicide submarine called the *Kaiten* ("heaven shaker") was released by a larger "mother" submarine; its pilot would drive it into an enemy hull like a torpedo. A small wooden speedboat called the *Shinyo* ("ocean shaker") carried a two-ton warhead, and could charge into the midst of an enemy fleet at 50 knots. *Fukuryus*, "crawling dragons," were scuba divers who would carry mines underwater and attach them directly to the hulls of American ships. There were others as well, including gliders that could be launched from mountain peaks, and explosive vests redolent of a more recent era. Some such weapons and vehicles would prove more effective than others in combat. But the time and resources dedicated to these programs belied the myth that the kamikaze era began as a spontaneous, grassroots movement in October 1944.

Some scholars, both Japanese and Western, have argued that the kamikaze phenomenon was an innate expression of Japanese ideologies and traditions, including *bushido* (the way of the samurai), State Shinto, Zen Buddhism, and the custom of suicide to expunge shame. In a rival view, the kamikaze was a grotesque perversion of Japanese ideals, foisted upon a bewildered and prostrate people by the militarist regime and its propagandists. Elements of truth are probably found in both views. Shinto and Buddhism held that the self was an illusion, and therefore death was not to be feared. Shinto's myriad gods (*kami*) revolved around the divine emperor, with whom every individual Japanese was said to be essentially cosubstantial. To die in combat was a purifying rite, burning or washing away the detritus and corruption accrued in earthly life. Only the slain warrior's undefiled essence remained, and it was subsumed into the emperor's divine essence. Practitioners of Zen and other schools of Buddhism offered a harmonious theology rooted in the precept that life and death were essentially one and the same. Meditation tended toward the annihilation of the ego. According to Goro Sugimoto, an army officer and influential writer: "Egolessness and self-extinction are most definitely not separate states. On the contrary, one comes to realize that they are identical."[51] A Buddhist scholar linked kamikaze tactics to the revealed truth of Zen: "The source of the spirit of the Special Attack Forces lies in the denial of the individual self and the rebirth of the soul, which takes upon itself the burden of history. From ancient times Zen has described this conversion of mind as the achievement of complete enlightenment."[52]

To die by one's own hand had long been associated with samurai ideals of honor and fidelity. Suicide offered a solution to the loss of face (*giri*, or honor). That was a chief theme of Japan's national epic, the story of the 47 Ronin. As defeat loomed in late 1944, the entire nation was poised to suffer a cataclysmic loss of face. The combat-suicide of the kamikaze pilots, the flower of Japanese youth, could be seen as a ritualistic collective sacrifice that redeemed some portion of the national *giri*.

Beginning in the early 1930s, with the start of the era the Japanese call their "dark valley," an increasingly repressive ultranationalist regime choked off dissent and took control of all sources of information. In this benighted environment, academic charlatans were encouraged to conjure up a self-serving mytho-history that fit the domestic and foreign priorities of the imperial militarist agenda. For centuries of Japanese history, the samurai had ruled the country and its people. Even more than in medieval Europe or other feudal societies, the elite warrior caste had dominated and shaped the nation's culture. After the Meiji Restoration, and especially in the decades before the Second World War, it was thought that samurai ideals might serve as a template for national development, and the nation transmuted into a master race of warriors—thus giving Japan hegemonic strength among nations, just as the samurai had once wielded uncontested power over their fellow Japanese. But *bushido* had always been an elite, class-bound creed, and was not necessarily suited to mass adoption across the population. In the transition, it underwent subtle but significant distortions. The ancient *bushido* of the sword-bearing samurai had emphasized zealous loyalty to a local feudal lord—but not to the emperor, who had been an obscure and little-thought-of figure before the Meiji era. *Bushido* meant stoicism, self-discipline, and dignity in one's personal bearing; it emphasized mastery of the martial arts through long training and practice; it lauded sacrifice in service to duty, without the slightest fear of death; it demanded asceticism and simplicity in daily life, without regard to comforts, appetites, or luxuries. The samurai was "to live as if already dead," an outlook consonant with Buddhism; he was to regard death with fatalistic indifference, rather than cling to a life that was essentially illusory. Shame or dishonor might require suicide as atonement—and when a samurai killed himself, he did so by carving out his own viscera with a short steel blade.

But traditional *bushido* had not imposed an obligation to abhor retreat or surrender even when a battle had turned hopeless, and the old-time samurai who had done his duty in a losing cause could lay down his arms with honor intact. That was the last of the *Thirty-Six Strategies*, a Chinese classic studied by twenty generations of Japanese warriors: "When overwhelmed, you don't fight; you surrender, compromise, or flee. . . . As long as you are not defeated, you have another chance to win."[53] Nor had suicidal tactics played an important role in previous eras of Japanese warfare. After the Russo-Japanese War (1904–05), the Japanese army had implemented sweeping changes in its culture and doctrine. The infantry manuals were rewritten to emphasize the importance of "fighting spirit" over such factors as technology and mechanical power, and the massed fixed-bayonet *banzai* charge was adopted as a preferred tactic in close combat. The "no surrender" ethos was codified after the First World War, and later amplified into an absolute injunction in the Japanese army's revised field manual of 1928. The army and its publicists did not explicitly glorify suicide tactics until the fighting in and around Shanghai in 1932, when reports of "human bombs" and "human bullets" received headline coverage in Japanese newspapers. In the middle years of the Pacific War, this evolved into an exaltation of death *in defeat*, embodied in the expression *gyokusai*, "smashed jewels." The lyrics of "Umi Yukaba," which became tantamount to a national anthem, even seemed to celebrate death for its own sake, quite apart from the question of victory or defeat:

> If I go away to sea,
> I shall return a corpse awash.
> If duty calls me to the mountain,
> A verdant sward will be my pall.
> Thus for the sake of the Emperor,
> I will not die peacefully at home.[54]

Frequent repetition on the radio and at patriotic rallies might have left the impression, especially to younger Japanese, that "Umi Yukaba" and the sentiments it contained had an ancient lineage. Actually, the lyrics dated back to an eighth-century poem, but that poem had previously been obscure, and had only been set to music in 1937. The explicit glorification of death in battle—death as an end in itself—was a recent phenomenon in Japanese culture, as were the "no surrender" principle, massed suicide attacks, and the master race ideology of imperial *bushido*. None of those ideas was anchored in the samurai tradition. The pre-Meiji samurai had fought only his fellow Japanese. He had no occasion to indulge in racial chauvinism, and he did not think at all of foreign conquest. He would have been puzzled by the suggestion that he and other Japanese were somehow cosubstantial with the divine emperor. Traditional *bushido* extolled humility, and the virtues of knowing and respecting one's enemy. It did not preach an attitude of thickheaded truculence, or an expectation of heaven-sent victory. But those elements of the ancient warrior codes did not serve the purposes of the ultranationalist junta, so they were simply whitewashed out of history, education, and civic discourse.

In 1944, there was a simple, pragmatic case for aerial suicide tactics. The new crop of Japanese aviators was simply not good enough to hit the enemy fleet using conventional bombing or torpedo attacks. Air formations dispatched to hit American ships offshore were suffering disastrous losses, and enemy carrier planes were roaming the skies over the Philippines unchallenged. The Japanese had lost nearly a thousand airplanes in October alone, and the replacement aviators flying into Philippine airbases had only rudimentary skills. Pilot cadets were being rushed through truncated programs and sent to frontline units having logged just a few dozen hours of flight time. Most received no formal gunnery or navigation training. If these new aviators were going to die in their cockpits anyway, as seemed inevitable, perhaps suicide tactics offered the only realistic hope of scoring a valedictory blow against the enemy.

Captain Inoguchi, in charge of training the new aviators for kamikaze attacks, said that the problem was essentially spiritual—to inculcate the will to carry it out. As for tactics, he said, "the ordinary technique of the pilot is sufficient; no special training methods are necessary." Compared to dive bombing, torpedo bombing, or dogfighting, diving a plane into a ship was a relatively simple maneuver. Even pilots with only basic flying skills should be able to manage it. Therefore, said Inoguchi, it was possible to use aviators "who have had short training and least flight experience."[55] Moreover, as the revised *Sho* plans were distributed to commanders throughout the region, it was evident that if the Japanese stood any hope of repelling MacArthur's landings, their air forces must knock out at least a portion of the American fleet. They were under intense pressure to deliver results in the impending battle.

The kamikaze corps was inaugurated on October 20, 1944, on the same day (virtually in the same hour) that General MacArthur waded ashore on Leyte behind his amphibious invasion forces. The catalyst for this momentous development was Vice Admiral Takijiro Onishi, who flew in from Japan to take command of the First Air Fleet on October 19. Onishi was a fierce-looking character—moonfaced, with close-cropped hair and an athlete's wiry physique. He was an intimidating figure, with a reputation among his colleagues for sudden rages; as a younger man he had often been reprimanded for lashing out violently at colleagues and others, especially after he had been drinking. He had risen from humble provincial origins in Hyugo Prefecture, near Kobe, and spoke in the round vowels of the regional Kansai dialect. Like Isoroku Yamamoto, his late friend and mentor, Onishi had cast his lot with naval aviation early in his career. He had held a series of important aviation jobs, ashore and afloat, since the pioneering days of the early 1920s, and he deserved an important share of the credit for building the naval air corps that had launched a successful aerial blitzkrieg across a 6,000-mile front in December 1941. Onishi had opposed the decision to attack the United States (as had Yamamoto), but he had helped to plan the attack on Pearl Harbor, and he had personally commanded the Formosa-based air groups that had decimated American airpower in the Philippines in the first week of the war.

When suicide tactics were first proposed in 1943, Onishi had sharply opposed the concept, and for more than a year he had maintained his opposition to this "heresy."[56] Undoubtedly, the subject was personally trying for Onishi, whose first team of aviators had worn the laurels of so many remarkable victories just two-and-a-half years earlier. As he assumed command of the First Air Fleet in October 1944, however, he was obliged to face up to the grave realities in his new command. Philippine air bases could muster only about fifty planes in flyable condition. Reinforcements would soon be pouring in from China and the homeland, but the enemy fleet was already in the offing. Except for a handful of veterans, his pilots were greenhorns. Conventional bombing tactics were ineffective, and most airplanes sent out on such missions did not return to base.

On October 19, the night after his arrival in Manila, Onishi was driven in a black Packard limousine to the main air complex on the island of Luzon—Mabalacat Airfield, which the Americans had called Clark Field. Because American fighters sometimes made strafing attacks on roadways, it was thought safest to make the two-hour-long drive after dark. On the other hand, driving at night could also be dangerous, because anti-Japanese guerillas sometimes staged roadside attacks. Even now, when the Americans had not yet landed forces in the Philippines, the Japanese must have had the distinct sense that they were already losing control of the islands.

Arriving in Mabalacat, he found the local air staff of the 201st Air Group in a command tent alongside a pockmarked airstrip and a row of dilapidated airplanes, which were kept in barely flyable condition by the efforts of the ground crews. Spare parts had been scavenged from the junked planes that littered the edges of the field. Local staff officers and squadron commanders were rounded up and convened at the headquarters building in town. According to a flight officer who was there, Onishi's pitch was succinct, impassive, and matter-of-fact: "In my opinion, there is only one way of assuring that our meager strength will be effective to a maximum degree. That is to organize suicide attack units composed of Zero fighters armed with 250-kilogram bombs, with each plane to crash into a carrier. What do you think?"[57]

At first, no one uttered a word in response: the inner turmoil and confusion can only be imagined. No one raised an objection, however, and the only questions had to do with the tactical niceties of converting a Zero fighter into a man-guided missile. The aviators and their officers agreed that the suiciders should approach the enemy fleet at high altitude, about 18,000 feet. When the American radar detected them, they would descend quickly to about 200–300 feet in hopes of slipping under the radar screen. They would drop "window"—aluminum strips—in order to thwart the radar operators. On the final approach to their targets, the pilots would drop the noses of their planes and descend in a 45-degree dive.[58]

When the assembly broke up, the various squadrons huddled and conferred among themselves. One by one, the leaders came back and reported that their flyers were unanimous: they would do it. Many were inspired by the example of their recently deceased base commander, Admiral Arima, who had sacrificed himself just five days earlier. They were likewise spurred to action by the news that the entire Japanese navy was charging toward

Leyte Gulf at risk of total annihilation. Their collective mood was resolute and even giddy. "At the time," remarked one pilot ruefully, "this seemed the only option we had."[59] It was thought best to name a Naval Academy graduate as leader of the new corps. After some discussion among the staff and commanders, Lieutenant Yukio Seki was nominated for the job. When the idea was put to him, Seki responded without hesitation: "You absolutely must let me do it."[60]

The newly formed suicide air group comprised only twenty-six Zero fighters, divided into four sections. Three sections were based at Mabalacat; the fourth was on the island of Cebu, to the south. One-half of the planes were designated as escorts and observers; the others would crash-dive the enemy. Thus, this first kamikaze unit amounted to only thirteen aircraft slated for an actual suicide dive. The command staff gave a name to this corps: "*Shimpu*," an archaic pronunciation of the Chinese ideographs for "god" and "wind." An alternate vernacular pronunciation was "kamikaze," but that term did not come into common currency until later; the original name of the suicide corps was *Shimpu Tokkotai*, or "Divine Wind Special Attack Force."*

Upon these thirteen suicide planes, the Japanese high command hung great hopes. It was even thought that they might all score, perhaps sinking as many as thirteen American aircraft carriers, a blow devastating enough to repel the coming invasion of the Philippines. Thus, this new *Shimpu* outfit, as small as it was, hoped to make a major contribution to the impending confrontation.

However, there was another dimension to this first introduction of organized suicide plane tactics, which does not always receive the emphasis it deserves. The kamikaze program was at the heart of a public relations and propaganda campaign aimed at Japan's fighting forces and simultaneously at the Japanese population. On October 21, and again in subsequent days, Admiral Onishi presided over a lugubrious send-off ceremony in which the departing suicide pilots stood to attention as he bid them good-bye, then raised cups of ceremonial sake in a final toast. They sang "Umi Yukaba," saluted the admiral, and climbed into their cockpits. The ceremony was

---

* The term "kamikaze" may have originated in an Allied translation error. In any case, "kamikaze" caught on with the Allies during the last year of the war, and has since become the commonly accepted term in Japan as well. See Sheftall, *Blossoms in the Wind*, pp. 59–60, footnote.

attended by a platoon of war correspondents, photographers, and motion picture crews, leaving no doubt that the new kamikaze tactics were to receive wide publicity at home. The purpose of this public relations offensive was much the same as that of the pretended victory off Formosa the previous week. It was propaganda aimed at shoring up the self-confidence of the air groups themselves, who had begun to despair of doing anything to contest American air supremacy—for as Inoguchi remarked, "Nothing is more destructive to morale than to learn of the enemy's superiority."[61]

It was also propaganda aimed at the home front. Obsessed with the specter of war-weariness among the Japanese public, the Tokyo regime wanted to provide a shot in the arm to the general mood. The spectacle of young warriors immolating themselves in battle might spur the people to work harder, to sacrifice more, to band together for the climactic stage of a war for national survival. Those themes had already been introduced into the Japanese news media. After his recent suicide attack on the American fleet, Admiral Arima had been lifted up as a "hero god," and it was suggested that Japanese civilians should be inspired by his example and do more for the war effort. There was even an implicit suggestion, in much of the editorial commentary, that civilians should be shamed by the sacrifices of their fighting forces, and must arouse themselves to work harder, eat less, and give more of themselves to the war effort. Arima's colleague, Admiral Kichisaburo Nomura, went on the radio to urge Japanese workers to "attack in the field of production with the spirit of 'bodily crash.'"[62]

Finally, and perhaps most importantly, the kamikaze was a propaganda weapon aimed at the enemy. It was the culmination of what might be called Japan's "theory" of the Pacific War—a line of reasoning behind its seemingly reckless decision to attack the United States in December 1941, a decision taken in full awareness that American industrial capacity was some ten times larger than Japan's. The unique collective "fighting spirit" of the Japanese people—the "Yamato spirit," as it was often called—explained why Japan had never been conquered, and why it had never lost a war. After the war, General Torashirō Kawabe told his American interrogators: "I wish to explain something which is a difficult thing and which you may not be able to understand. The Japanese, to the very end, believed that by spiritual means they could fight on equal terms with you. . . . We believed our spiritual confidence in victory would balance any scientific advantages."[63]

This was religious dogma, rooted in the divinity of the emperor and (through him) the Japanese race. If the Americans were still fighting in 1944, and still demanding unconditional surrender, it was because they had not yet fully grasped the potency of this spirit. And how could they? They were a mongrel people, hopelessly decadent and self-seeking, without any real unity of spirit or purpose. Their great material wealth, industrial base, and technological aptitude would count for nothing if they could not summon the will to fight to the end on Japan's terms. It was no accident that the kamikaze was introduced to the world in the final weeks of the U.S. presidential campaign, when FDR and Governor Dewey were at one another's throats, and American political disharmony was on display for the entire world to see. A typical view was expressed by Admiral Ugaki, who commented on the new kamikaze corps in an October 21 entry in his diary:

> Oh, what a noble spirit this is! We are not afraid of a million enemies or a thousand carriers because our whole force shares the same spirit. . . . If 100 million people set out for production and defense with this spirit now, nobody need worry about the future of the empire.
>
> In the United States they are said to be all crazy about the presidential election and Dewey is a little ahead. I dare say they can't match us, as their objective in war or their policy of operations are all based on personal benefit.[64]

For the nine remaining months of war to come, this was to be Japan's guiding strategic vision: to display to the Americans the full force and fury of their Yamato spirit. A nation willing to turn its young men into guided missiles was a nation that would fight to the last man, woman, and child—and a nation willing to fight on such terms could not be conquered. If the Japanese raised the stakes high enough, the Americans would flinch. Their leaders, beholden to American voters, lacked the stomach to fight to the point of civilizational annihilation. Perhaps the Pacific War was already lost; in private councils, among themselves, the junta's leaders were increasingly willing to admit it. But there was a difference between defeat and surrender, between losing an overseas empire and seeing the homeland overrun by a barbarian army. The man-guided missiles were never a realistic bid for victory, but rather a talisman to ward off the horror of total defeat. Even if the official propaganda would not yet admit it, the battle for the sacred islands of Japan had already begun, and the kamikazes were its first line of defense.

Chapter Five

THE LEYTE INVASION WAS NOT QUITE AS LARGE AS THE NORMANDY invasion four months earlier, but the fleet was obliged to cross a lot more ocean. Thirteen hundred miles lay between Hollandia, MacArthur's major port of embarkation on northern New Guinea, and the landing beaches at Leyte Gulf. But the invasion fleet amounted to more than seven hundred ships, too many to squeeze into Hollandia—so a major portion of the force sailed from Manus, in the Admiralties, which lay another 500 miles to the east. The various elements of the great armada would rendezvous at sea along the way. By now, it was an old story. Hundreds of landing craft had been borrowed from the Pacific Fleet, but that was another old story—the two theaters had been sharing these specialized vessels and their crews since 1943. After more than two years of amphibious campaigning, the Americans had the game well in hand. They had honed their techniques the hard way, in some thirty landings north and south of the equator. There was the typical last-minute rush to get forces ready, the distribution of bulky plans, the hurried last-minute fueling and provisioning, the communal spasm of effort required to get the ships to sea on time—and all of this, too, was by now an old and familiar story to the thousands of veterans of this largest amphibious campaign in history.

A *Gambier Bay* pilot, patrolling overhead, called it "the largest force I'd ever seen gathered. Ships stretched all the way to the horizon."[1] The various semiautonomous task forces sailed in circular cruising formations, doing no better than 9 or 10 knots, so that even the most sluggish vessels could stay on station—a baroque array of attack transports, ordinary transports, landing craft, patrol craft, minesweepers, ammunition ships, oil tankers, and various other service ships. The transports carried 174,000 troops. Each type of landing craft was designated by an acronym beginning with the letter "L," for "landing"—LSTs, LSDs, LCIs, LCTs, and half a dozen more. Destroyers knifed through the formations, as graceful as greyhounds and as vigilant as sheep dogs. Nine out of ten vessels in this force had not even existed when the Japanese had taken the Philippines in 1942. Indeed, many had just recently arrived in the Pacific, manned by freshly trained crews who had never fought in combat.

After the war, an interviewer asked Vice Admiral Thomas Kinkaid, commander of the Seventh Fleet, how he had coordinated the movements of those hundreds of ships. "I didn't quite do it with my own little fingers," he replied. "It was a question of organization, that's the thing."[2] The byzantine timetables were devised by working backward from the moment each vessel was wanted in Leyte Gulf. The slowest ships departed first, some as early as October 4, when the plans were still being written. Then ships left in staggered departures, sailing from their various ports of origin, separated by hundreds or even thousands of miles. The fleet had to refuel while underway, given the great distance, so fleet oilers were found waiting at predetermined times and coordinates.

MacArthur jokingly referred to "my three K's"—his troika of senior naval, air, and ground commanders, who all happened to have surnames beginning with that letter. Kinkaid led the Seventh Fleet, colloquially known as "MacArthur's navy." Lieutenant General George C. Kenney of the USAAF had served as Southwest Pacific air commander since July 1942. The Sixth Army, the principal ground force for the Leyte operation, was commanded by Lieutenant General Walter Krueger. Covering air support for the first stage of the invasion would be provided by the Third Fleet. Halsey would remain in Nimitz's chain of command, as he (and Spruance) had in prior joint operations. The Joint Chiefs did not attempt to decide how the commands would mesh, merely instructing Nimitz and MacArthur to "arrange for coordination of mutual support."[3]

After an unprecedented run of carrier air strikes throughout the western Pacific, the Third Fleet and its Task Force 38 airmen were overdue for a long rest in port. Pilot fatigue was evident in all of the carrier air groups, and its toll was beginning to be counted in more frequent operational accidents. Flight surgeons had noted the debilitating effects of this dread syndrome— the gaunt, hunted look on the faces of the pilots, brittle nerves, rapid weight loss. Halsey had only taken command of the fleet in August, but many of the rank and file had been at sea for ten months, with only brief liberties in remote central Pacific atolls. Even Halsey was tired, as Mick Carney had noted. The fleet needed a long spell of rest and replenishment while swinging peacefully at anchors in Ulithi lagoon. Alas, the invasion of the Philippines was only beginning, and the fast carriers of the Third Fleet had a leading part to play. For the first time, MacArthur's ground forces would wage a sustained campaign beyond the radius of USAAF fighter protection. On Leyte, it was hoped that the Americans could capture and quickly upgrade Tacloban Airfield, so that it could receive Kenney's interceptors as soon as possible. But until that happened, Halsey's aviators would need to do most of the work of beating back the Japanese air response. When Halsey queried MacArthur on October 21, asking for an estimate of when Task Force 38 could pull back to Ulithi, the SWPA commander responded firmly: "Basic plan for this operation in which for the first time I have moved beyond my own land-based air cover was predicated upon full support by 3rd Fleet. . . . I consider that your mission to cover this operation is essential and paramount."[4]

One of the looming "known unknowns" about the pending operation was the scale and depth of Japanese air resistance. Another was the question of whether the Japanese fleet would contest the landings. Halsey's recent rampages had exposed the frailty of Japanese airpower, it was true— but the Philippines were home to hundreds of enemy airfields and feeder strips, and its geographic position was such that it could be reinforced quickly from China, Formosa, and the home islands. The Leyte operation differed from all prior Pacific amphibious landings in that the enemy could rely on depth and dispersal of his air reinforcements. In the pessimistic scenario, the Americans might find themselves in a protracted and grinding air campaign, fighting off waves of enemy planes incoming from the south, west, and north. That was a grim outlook for the carrier force, given that aviator fatigue was already a critical problem. Halsey might have reflected, ruefully, that the Leyte invasion had been moved up by two months on his own bold recommendation. He had made his own bed, and now he was compelled to lie in it.

As for the enemy fleet, cryptanalytic intelligence and sighting reports had correctly placed Kurita and the surface warships in Lingga Roads near Singapore, and Ozawa and the carriers in the Inland Sea. Prevailing opinion in MacArthur's shop, and also in the Third Fleet and at Pearl Harbor, was that the Japanese navy would not come out to fight. But there were dissidents to this view, and all could agree that a major fleet action was at least possible. If Kurita's surface ships moved against the Americans, they would have to come through one of the navigable straits that pierced the island barrier of the central Philippines—Surigao Strait to the south of Leyte, or San Bernardino Strait north of Samar—or else pass south of Mindanao, or the long way around the north coast of Luzon. All were considered, but in the rush to meet the October 20 deadline, the Third and Seventh Fleet commanders and their planners never agreed on detailed contingency plans for each scenario.

Kinkaid's Seventh Fleet was far from defenseless, and could do much of the work of protecting itself against any enemy thrust. The shore bombardment and fire support group included six battleships of the older and slower classes—among them several leviathans damaged in the attack on Pearl Harbor—and an ample number of cruisers and destroyers. This force was designated Task Group 77.2, and commanded by Rear Admiral Jesse Oldendorf, a veteran of several previous amphibious operations. Kinkaid's fleet also included sixteen small escort carriers, whose planes would be deployed mainly in the role of bombing and strafing ground targets on the invasion beaches, and flying protective cover over the amphibious fleet. This was Task Group 77.4, commanded by Rear Admiral Thomas Sprague. His flotilla of small, slow flattops and their screening destroyers was divided into three sections, remembered in history by their radio call-signs: Taffy 1, Taffy 2, and Taffy 3.

Mick Carney, Third Fleet chief of staff, recalled that Halsey had inculcated this dictum into everyone in his chain of command—"that if major action could be provoked, that this was always your primary purpose, to bring about that climactic action. . . . And it was his intention that we go in and slug it out with them, if we could get anybody to slug with, no matter what the hell we took. This was firmly fixed in the minds of all of us, on the basis of his personal instructions to us and conclusions from all the discussions that we had leading up to operations."[5]

ON OCTOBER 17, advance elements of the fleet landed U.S. Army Ranger commando teams on three small islands that guarded the mouth of the gulf. The rangers swiftly overpowered the Japanese garrisons, and then set up navigation lights to aid the amphibious convoys. Minesweepers began the painstaking work of finding and sweeping up about two hundred floating and fixed mines, clearing a broad channel to the landing beaches. Elite frogmen of the "Underwater Demolition Teams"—progenitors of today's navy SEALs—hunted for undersea obstacles, but found none. Before dawn on October 19, Admiral Oldendorf's fire support ships filed into the gulf and opened fire on the beaches, commencing a thirty-six-hour-long bombardment. Japanese shore batteries returned fire, landing a few hits on American ships. In firing, however, they advertised their positions, and all were quickly put out of action by the fleet's superior firepower.

On October 20, a dark and moonless night, the transport and amphibious fleet filed into the gulf unseen, like ghost ships, and maneuvered to their preassigned positions. Admiral Oldendorf's bombardment group continued to pour destruction down on the beaches. At 6:00 a.m., as the new day dawned on the eastern horizon, the gunfire climbed in volume and intensity to a thunderous din.

Watching the spectacle from the bridge of the cruiser *Nashville*, MacArthur did not mind admitting that he was awed. The barrage made a terrestrial mincemeat out of the shoreline; it was literally reshaping Leyte's coastal topography. Great shells streaked into shore, chugging like freight trains and tracing long red arcs through the sky. Rockets made bright white vapor trails that remained etched against the sky in latticelike patterns. Coils of smoke rose from the beaches, and the hills above the beaches. Through binoculars, a witness on a transport offshore watched a destroyer aim 5-inch salvos at a Japanese pillbox on a high promontory. "The pillbox was split open like a walnut shell. We could see a few men attempting to climb out when the second salvo hit. That was all. What had once been a well-built fortification was now nothing but a white scar on the hillside."[6] Repeatedly throughout the morning, the naval guns fell silent just seconds before carrier planes swooped over the shoreline, pouring out bombs and rockets and .50-caliber tracers. The beaches themselves were all but invisible under the continuing assault. Layers of yellow and brown smoke hung heavily in the humid air; there was little or no breeze that morning to carry it away. Even on the decks of transports far behind Oldendorf's ships, men had to shout to make themselves heard. Their khaki uniform shirts fluttered against their chests, and they could feel the stupendous concussions down low in their viscera. Distant detonations on the hills made a penetrating and resonant sound: *crump, crump, crump.* The entire horizon to the south and west was a ring of strobe-like flashes.

At exactly 10:00 a.m., the first wave of landing boats departed for shore. The barrage rose to a new pitch. The air, the ground, and the decks of the ships seemed to vibrate like harp strings. An observer offshore noted in his log, "It is impossible to distinguish one explosion from another; it is just a roar."[7] The LCVPs and LCTs were led by a vanguard of rocket-mounted boats that fired continuously—the rockets going off with a *whoosh, whoosh*—and these deadly little missiles fell upon the beaches and the terrain around the tree line. Timing and coordination had been refined to such a degree at this stage of the war, that the assault troops peeking over the gunwales of their boats witnessed a sight that none would ever forget. Seconds before the first boats scraped ashore, the curtain of destruction moved suddenly inland about half a mile, like a thunderstorm sweeping across a prairie, and came to rest on positions safely above their landing beaches.

Out of the boats, racing up the beach, the assault troops threw themselves flat on the sand, or in the craters made by the great blasts. But they quickly realized that they were not under fire. A few isolated Japanese snipers remained among the burned and blasted remains of palm trees, and here and there one heard the rattle of machine-gun fire from a surviving pillbox, but opposition was otherwise negligible. Most enemy troops on the island had apparently pulled back into the mountainous country to the west. The first echelons pressed inland quickly, taking territory and clearing the beaches for the successive waves of boats. In less than an hour, the attackers had secured a beachhead to a depth of about a thousand feet along most of its length. To the extent that they were held up at all, it was more by the wet terrain than by enemy resistance.

Many thousands of troops—four divisions overall—landed on their heels, and soon the shoreline was converted into a burgeoning supply depot, with vehicles driving on mud tracks, crates stacked in rows, and men standing and walking upright. Farther inland, infantrymen were digging foxholes and trenches. There was such a concentration of troop strength in the area that the holes directly abutted one another. Many had carried life jackets from the boats to use as pillows, and had laid palm fronds across their foxholes to keep out the rain. The Third Amphibious War Diary noted, "Troops generally 1000 to 1400 yards inland. Resistance is fairly light. Troops are still advancing except where enemy is entrenched and using mortars. Casualties are light on landing beaches. There is little evidence of enemy movement."[8] Without any concerted enemy resistance, units on the northern sector swung north and quickly seized possession of the island's most important strategic asset: Tacloban airfield, near the town of that name on the island's northeast coast.

From the bridge of the *Nashville*, MacArthur swept his binoculars from White Beach near Dulag on the south end of the long arc, up to Red Beach near Tacloban on the north. There were so many ships standing between the *Nashville* and the invasion beaches that it was actually difficult to see the beach at all. He paused often to relight his corn cob pipe, and chatted amiably with the war correspondents assigned to his ship. He regaled them with stories of his first posting in Tacloban when he was a newly commissioned officer out of West Point.

A few minutes after one o'clock, MacArthur descended a ladder to his landing barge. He was followed by leading members of his staff, his air commander General Kenney, and a handful of his favorite war correspondents. The barge stopped at another transport to embark Sergio Osmeña, who had succeeded the late Manuel Quezon as president of the Philippines, and Brigadier General Carlos P. Romulo, resident commissioner to the U.S. House of Representatives. As the barge ran in toward Red Beach, MacArthur sat upright on a bench near the stern. He slapped Dick Sutherland on the knee and said, "Believe it or not, Dick, we're back!"[9] After two-and-a-half years, the scene seemed dreamlike. He said it again to Romulo, grasping both of his Filipino friend's hands: "Well, here we are!" They were all saying it, recalled Romulo: "All said it over and over again, with different inflections, as if it were the newest and profoundest of expressions. It didn't sound trite to us. It sounded like Washington's Farewell Address, or Lincoln at Gettysburg. We couldn't hear it enough."[10]

The coxswain ran the barge gently aground with a thud, and dropped the ramp. They were about fifty yards from shore. Two Signal Corps photographers stepped off the ramp and waded ashore, so they could capture the scene on film. Sutherland, at MacArthur's arm, repeated, "We're here!"—and MacArthur agreed: "Well, believe it or not, we're here."[11] The party waited patiently until the photographers had their cameras ready. Then MacArthur, wearing aviator sunglasses under his gold-braided field cap, stepped down into the knee-deep water and began wading in to shore. He was followed at a short distance by Osmeña, then by the others in his party. The photographs capturing this scene would be published in newspapers around the world.

Wading through the surf onto a beach congested with supplies, the smell of cordite and burning palm trees thick in his nostrils, MacArthur strode inland at a brisk pace. A company of troops assigned to guard him hurried forward, suddenly anxious, because for a moment the SWPA chief seemed determined to head directly toward the tree line, where Japanese snipers might still be lurking. Then he did an about-face and went back to shake hands with Osmeña again. "Mr. President, how does it feel to be home?" Osmeña, tears welling in his eyes, could not find his voice.[12] Carrier planes droned low overhead. The roar of not-so-distant artillery and rifle fire rang in their ears. Emaciated Filipino civilians milled about the scene, many waving American flags that had been kept in hiding during the years of Japanese occupation. They greeted the American soldiers with wide smiles, saying, "Lovely Americans!"

Another Signal Corps crew was preparing a radio broadcast unit and mounting up a transmitter. MacArthur and Osmeña sat together on a fallen palm log. On a tree nearby, the American and Filipino commonwealth flags fluttered side by side. The crew let them know the broadcast team was ready.

After a short delay, MacArthur took up a handheld microphone. A soft rain began falling as he spoke. The broadcast was carried live in the United States, an extraordinary feat at the time; it was also broadcast throughout the Philippines via the mobile transmitter, although it seems that very few Filipinos heard that initial broadcast.

As was his usual practice, MacArthur employed the first-person singular pronoun to refer to the forces under his command. "People of the Philippines," he declared: "I have returned! By the grace of Almighty God, our forces stand again on Philippine soil." He instructed the Filipino people to rise up and strike the enemy, and "Rally to me!"[13]

The speech was met with eye-rolling among many of the troops under his command, who saw it as another instance of MacArthuresque grandstanding. Hadn't they *all* returned? But there was no arguing with the electrifying effect on the Filipino people. Even if they did not hear the speech on the radio, most soon learned of it from leaflets or word of mouth. The following day, on the steps of the State Capitol in Tacloban, MacArthur would preside over a more formal ceremony with President Osmeña—a symbolic transfer of sovereignty back to the Philippines. He had not cleared this declaration with the U.S. State Department or the Department of the Interior, which held commonwealth authority over the Philippines. MacArthur was making his own U.S. foreign policy in Asia—not for the first time, and certainly not for the last.

LATE ON OCTOBER 20, Kurita's powerful column of battleships, cruisers, and destroyers entered Brunei Bay in North Borneo. Two oil tankers were waiting; all ships would drink their fill. The following afternoon, launches from throughout the fleet delivered captains and senior officers to the heavy cruiser *Atago*, Kurita's flagship. There they were briefed on the final *Sho* operations order, just arrived from Combined Fleet headquarters in Hiyoshi. Their faces told the tale; the officers were unsettled by the plan, and some ventured to ask blunt questions. If the situation was as dire as the high command believed, shouldn't the commander in chief personally lead them into battle? Why was Admiral Toyoda holed up in his safe underground bunker in Yokohama? If this sortie amounted to a naval *banzai* charge, shouldn't they aim for the American battleships and carriers, rather than the transports in Leyte Gulf? And why were they to attack in daylight, after training intensely for a night action?

Kurita finally rose and answered these objections with a short speech. The surprise attack on the transport fleet offered their best hope of dealing a serious blow to the invasion, he said. This might be the last opportunity for a concerted fleet battle; if they did not fight now, they might never have another chance. It was now or never. Moreover, he said, orders were orders. The officers stood and gave a unified cheer of "Banzai!" Then they drank a toast of cold sake and returned to their ships.[14]

Kurita's force of thirty-one warships sortied from Brunei at 0800 on October 22 and shaped a northerly course for Palawan Island. Having studied the charts and considered all the factors, he had decided that his force would take a middle route through the Palawan Passage, and thence to the Sibuyan Sea and San Bernardino Strait. Kurita was followed seven hours later by Nishimura at the head of the "Section C" force, which would take a more direct southerly route to Leyte Gulf via Balabac Strait, the Sulu Sea, and Surigao Strait. Far to the north, Admiral Shima's "Second Striking Force" sortied from the port of Mako in the Pescadores Islands, and started south with vague orders to follow Nishimura through Surigao Strait. Ozawa's threadbare carrier fleet had hauled their anchors out of mud at the bottom of the Inland Sea and headed for a rendezvous at the Bungo Strait, putting to sea on the afternoon of October 20. By nightfall on October 22, all of the various elements of Plan *Sho* were in motion.*

Before the battle, the Americans had forty-four submarines at sea, many of which were specifically placed to intercept and observe Japanese naval units headed for the waters off the eastern Philippines. More than a dozen had been deployed to observe and guard the sea approaches to Leyte Gulf. The region's complex island geography tended to limit the routes that any deep-draft ship could take through the barrier formed by the central islands of the Philippines. Submarines were stationed at various navigational bottlenecks: the Balabac Strait, Mindoro Strait, Verde Island Passage, Palawan Passage, and seas west of Luzon. After studying the charts and considering all the factors, Kurita and his staff chose to traverse Palawan Passage, a navigable corridor running northwest between Palawan Island and the "Dangerous Ground." The latter was a poorly charted region of the South China Sea, rife with shoals, cays, and reefs—a four-hundred-year graveyard of shipwrecks. Kurita and his staff knew that their chosen route would likely bring them into the crosshairs of American submarines, but they had no other alternative, given their rigid orders and the limitations imposed by a tight fuel budget.[15]

At midnight on October 22–23, two American *Gato*-class submarines waited near the southwest end of Palawan Island. The *Darter* (Commander David McClintock) and *Dace* (Commander Bladen Claggett) were surfaced, idling side by side, separated by only about 200 feet. At 1:16 a.m., blips began appearing on the *Darter*'s SJ radar scope. They were in the southeast, at a range of about 17 miles. At first the operator thought it must

---

* The Japanese order of battle has been identified by a confusing array of names. Kurita's old Second Fleet was now designated the First Striking Force, subdivided into Sections A (Kurita) and C (Nishimura), but some Japanese sources called them the First and Second Diversionary Attack Forces. Ozawa's carrier fleet was formally the First Mobile Force; now the Japanese called it the Main Body. Shima's column was designated the Second Striking Force, but it had previously been the Fifth Fleet, and some sources cite the earlier name. Following the convention in most Western histories, this account will call them the Southern Force (Nishimura), the Center Force (Kurita), and the Northern Force (Ozawa), in some cases substituting only the commander's name. Shima's ten ships will simply be called "Shima's force."

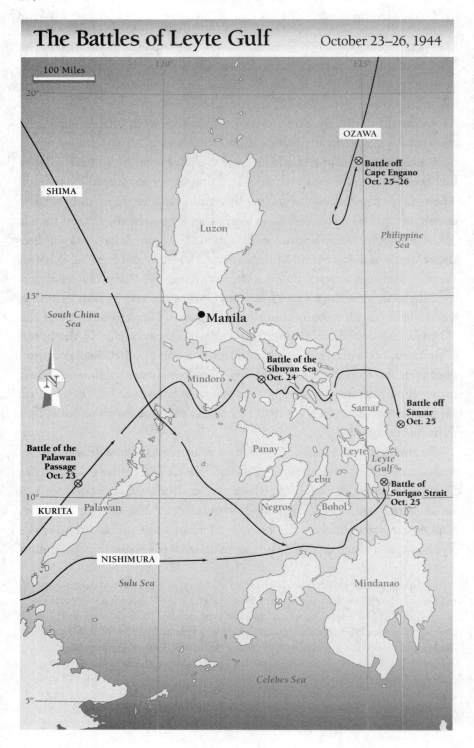

The Battles of Leyte Gulf

October 23–26, 1944

100 Miles

120°

125°

20°

OZAWA

⊗ Battle off
Cape Engano
Oct. 25–26

SHIMA

Luzon

*Philippine
Sea*

15°

*South China
Sea*

● **Manila**

Mindoro

**Battle of the
Sibuyan Sea**
⊗ Oct. 24

Samar

**Battle off
Samar**
⊗ Oct. 25

N

Panay

Leyte

*Leyte
Gulf*

**Battle of the
Palawan
Passage
Oct. 23**
⊗

Cebu

⊗ **Battle of
Surigao Strait
Oct. 25**

10°

KURITA

Palawan

Negros

Bohol

NISHIMURA →

Mindanao

Sulu Sea

Celebes Sea

5°

be a weather front, but soon they resolved into many blips, moving together across the scope. They could only be heavy warships, northbound for the Palawan Passage. With a handheld megaphone, McClintock called across the water to the bridge of the *Dace*: "We have radar contact. Let's go!"[16] The two subs ran at four-engine speed on the surface, making about 19 knots, hoping to reach an interception point ahead of the enemy force.

Cloaked by darkness, the two submarines radioed reports of a Japanese fleet northbound through the Palawan Passage, correctly estimating that it included at least three battleships.[17] *Darter*'s first flash report went to Admiral Christie in Australia, who promptly passed it along to Halsey and other commands. Each of the *Darter*'s follow-up contact reports raised the number of ships estimated in the column. In his last report before submerging, McClintock reported: "Minimum 11 ships. Same course, speed."[18]

Supposing that the enemy fleet was traveling at 22 knots, the *Darter*'s tracking party was pessimistic about their chances of getting into an attack position. But as the range closed it became apparent that the fleet was making no better than 18 knots. And it was being funneled into a narrow passage, so its defensive zigzagging would be limited. "We had them now!" exclaimed the *Darter*'s log.[19] As the pallid dawn rose over the jungle-covered mountains of Palawan, both U.S. boats submerged.

The big ships in the Japanese fleet were arrayed in two parallel columns, with a few destroyers on the flanks. *Atago* led the port column. *Darter* moved into position to attack that group; *Dace* continued a few miles northeast and set up an ambush on the starboard column. Their crews manned battle stations.

In the conning tower of the *Darter*, Commander McClintock held his eye up to the periscope glass and turned it by grasping the two handles on the shaft. Through the lens, the enemy warships loomed out of the mist, appearing as gray cathedral-like shapes evenly spaced in two lines. The *Darter* was almost directly ahead of the port column. McClintock watched the *Atago* as she closed the range, until she grew so large in his crosshairs that he could not see her entire length in the circular field. At 6:32 a.m., he fired six bow-tube torpedoes at the "can't miss" range of 980 yards, then turned sharply to port and fired four stern tubes at the following ship, the cruiser *Takao*.

The *Atago*'s lookouts did not spot the incoming torpedo tracks until they were nearly home. In any case, the flagship had no hope of evading.

Four columns of fire and whitewater erupted along the length of her starboard side. Several hundred of her crew were killed immediately, probably before they knew what was happening. Her bow plowed under, and she listed heavily to starboard. Through the *Darter*'s periscope, McClintock saw black smoke boiling up from a searing mass of orange flames. The stricken cruiser's superstructure was entirely concealed behind the oily plume. He saw Japanese sailors gathering on deck, preparing to abandon ship.

On the *Atago*'s bridge, Kurita knew right away that his flagship was finished. He did not hesitate. He told her captain, "It's time to go."[20] Then he removed his shoes, dropped into the sea, and began swimming for the nearest destroyer, the *Kishinami*. By his own account, Kurita was the first man to leave the ship.

The *Takao* caught two torpedoes near her fantail about a minute later. The blasts broke two shafts and flooded her boiler rooms, leaving her dead in the water. Her crew rushed into damage control mode as the rest of the column overtook and passed around her.

The entire formation now turned sharply to starboard, away from the unseen enemy submarine. But the coast of Palawan was not far to starboard, leaving little room for evasive maneuvers. With *Atago* foundering, command passed temporarily to Admiral Ugaki in the *Yamato*. Both columns increased speed and steadied back onto the base course of 40 degrees, but that took them directly into the sights of the *Dace*. Commander Claggett watched the starboard column as it bore down on him. The *Dace* was low on torpedoes, so he had to be selective. He decided to let the first two ships pass unmolested with the memorable order, "Let them go by—they're only heavy cruisers."[21] Mistakenly he identified the third ship in column as a *Kongo*-class battleship: actually she was another heavy cruiser, the *Maya*. When she was broadside-on at 1,800 yards, he fired a six-fish salvo.

Minutes later, the *Dace*'s crew heard the unmistakable sounds of four torpedo hits, followed seconds later by an explosion so deep and terrible that the soundman wondered whether "the bottom of the ocean was blowing up." Then they heard a big ship tearing herself apart, rivet from rivet. Claggett called it "the most gruesome sound I have ever heard."[22] He rightly surmised that the *Maya*'s magazine had detonated. The ship went up in a soaring tower of whitewater and flame; debris rained down in every direction, and it kept raining for the better part of a minute. Admiral Ugaki, watching in dismay from the *Yamato*'s bridge, saw a pall of yellow smoke hanging over the *Maya*'s final position, and "nothing was left after the smoke and spray subsided."[23]

The other big ships dared not break the pace, so they kept on to the north. But the escorting destroyers scattered depth charges throughout the area, forcing the two submarines to remain submerged for several hours. The Japanese destroyers also rescued hundreds of survivors of the *Atago* and *Maya*. Admiral Kurita struggled through gelatinous oil-covered seawater to the *Kishinami*, where he was hauled aboard and given a shot of whiskey and a pair of white sneakers to replace the shoes he had left behind. Looking across to the *Atago*'s last position, he noted that she was already gone—she had sunk in nineteen minutes. Kurita signaled to Ugaki that he intended to come aboard *Yamato* and take her as his new flagship. But he and his staff could not transfer to the battleship until nine hours later, because the surviving ships needed to clear Palawan Passage in a hurry.

The *Atago* and *Maya* were gone; the *Takao* was seriously damaged but could still make way at reduced speed, so she was sent back to Singapore with an escort of two destroyers. (She was later judged beyond repair, and would never fight again.) As a result, this opening blow in the Battle of Leyte Gulf had subtracted five ships from Kurita's thirty-one-ship fleet.

Darter and *Dace* stalked the retreating *Takao*, but were forced to give up the hunt when *Darter* ran hard aground on an uncharted shoal. Every effort was made to haul her free, but to no avail. *Dace* took *Darter*'s entire crew aboard and returned to Fremantle, abandoning the grounded submarine after placing demolition charges in her control room and conning tower. To this day, the rusted remains of the wreck of the *Darter* are perched on a reef off Palawan Island, serving as a navigation aid and tourist attraction.

McClintock and Claggett's radioed contact reports may have even been more valuable than their attacks on Kurita's fleet, because they gave the first definite indication that the Japanese navy intended to contest the invasion of Leyte. On the other hand, the sinking of the *Atago* had dumped the fifty-five-year-old Kurita into the sea and forced him to swim for his life. It had done the same to his entire Center Force staff. They would pass nine hours on the cramped bridge of a destroyer—during which time the ship was constantly evading phantom submarine contacts, with the crew expecting to be torpedoed at any moment—before going aboard the *Yamato* in late afternoon. In *The Art of War*, Sun-Tzu had written, "If your enemy is rested, cause him to exert himself." After the war, when interviewed by

American interrogators, Kurita was too proud to say that the experience had exhausted or demoralized him. But he privately admitted to colleagues that physical strain, sleep deprivation, and high tension had diminished his performance in the ensuing battle.

ADMIRAL HALSEY HAD DOUBTED that the Japanese fleet would contest the Leyte invasion, but at the end of the day on October 23 he was forced to conclude that he had been wrong. The day's accumulated sighting reports, and clues derived from top-secret radio intercepts ("Ultras"), pointed to a "violent reaction" by the enemy. The *Darter* and *Dace* had revealed that a major surface force was advancing into Visayan seaways, and a subsequent flash report from the submarine *Guitarro* put that same force near the entrance of Mindoro Strait. No one had spotted the Japanese aircraft carriers, but Nimitz's headquarters warned of indications that Admiral Ozawa's First Mobile Fleet had sortied from the Inland Sea and might be closing in from the north. (These intelligence estimates were based on radio traffic patterns and a stray intercept discussing movements of fleet oilers to a rendezvous between Japan and the Philippines.)

As night fell, the northernmost of Halsey's three carrier task groups, Group 38.3, was shadowed by low-flying Japanese night patrol planes, presumably from airfields on Luzon. The fighter squadrons spent a tense and mostly sleepless night, expecting to be launched in darkness to fight off a night attack. No such attack came, but the ubiquitous night snoopers seemed to presage a big airstrike the following morning, as indeed they did.

Halsey had hoped for a brief reprieve, so that he could rotate his carrier groups back to Ulithi for rest and replenishment. He had already dispatched Group 1 (McCain) to the atoll, which lay 800 miles east, and had hoped to send Group 4 (Davison) the following day. But there was to be no rest for the weary. Halsey ordered McCain to pause, refuel, and await further orders, and he summoned his three other carrier groups to concentrate close inshore, in waters off southern Luzon and the San Bernardino Strait, and to keep their boilers on the line, ready to make maximum speed. At first light on the twenty-fourth, Task Force 38 launched a huge aerial "reconnaissance in force." Two-plane sections, comprising one Hellcat and one Helldiver, would each cover a 10-degree "slice of the pie" to a distance of 300 miles. Climbing to altitude, they fanned out in a great arc on diverging headings, ranging from southwest to northwest, taking them over the Visayan Sea, the Sibuyan Sea, the Mindoro Straits, and all the multitude of other seas, straits, bays, and gulfs of the central Philippine archipelago. Another dozen Hellcats were dispatched as "relay planes" to circle at altitude about 100 miles west of the task force, their purpose to serve as radio links to aircraft at or near the far western end of their search vectors. In a pinch they could also defend the task force against enemy airstrikes approaching from the west.

The morning was clear and beautiful, with scattered high clouds and a thin layer of broken cumulus at 1,500 feet. From 8,000 feet above the earth, the searchers could see nearly a hundred miles in every direction. Below them unfolded a majestic tropical panorama, a repeating pattern of azure shallows, white sandy cays, and mountainous jungle-clad islands. Broad white beaches merged into lush coconut palm groves, lighter greens darkened to deeper greens inland, and steep slopes rose to brown peaks six or seven thousand feet high, or to black volcanic cones with gaping, smoking calderas. The sea was lighter here and darker there, varying by depth, bottom, and angle of light, with lighter cerulean bands running parallel to the beaches, the shallows strewn with coral reefs that went on for miles, and the sea darkening as it deepened in the straits between the islands, its surface glistening in the morning sun. The carrier airmen had no problems matching the landmarks and channels to the charts they carried in their cockpits. Having flown so many missions over the Philippines during the past six weeks, they knew the region well—and they knew precisely where to look for Japanese warships in the relatively few navigable passages through the intricate archipelago.

Approaching the island of Mindoro at 7:46 a.m., an *Intrepid* SB2C pilot noted a cluster of blips on his airborne radar. They were about 10 miles south of the island. He turned toward the contact and soon spotted parallel white wakes, the first indication of a big fleet on the move. In another minute he could estimate the composition of the fleet: thirteen destroyers, eight cruisers, and four battleships. The contact was received on the *New Jersey* at 8:10 a.m. Monitoring the VHF circuits in flag plot, Halsey and his team awaited confirmation and soon had it: a pilot from the *Cabot* reported: "I see 'em. Big ships." Two minutes later, the *Intrepid*'s Bombing Squadron Eighteen commander came on the circuit, loud and clear: "Four battleships, eight heavy cruisers and 13 destroyers, course east, off the southern tip of Mindoro."[24]

That left no doubt: this could only be Kurita's Center Force, rounding the southern cape of Mindoro and entering Tablas Strait. Kurita's armada was a bit smaller than it had been before crossing paths with *Darter* and *Dace*, but it remained formidable by any measure. Judging from his location and heading, it was a good bet that Kurita intended to force the San Bernardino Strait and sweep down on Leyte Gulf from the north. Halsey was preparing to order an airstrike against him when another contact report arrived, this one from an *Enterprise* search group about 200 miles south, in the Sulu Sea, southwest of the island of Negros: a column of seven surface warships, including two battleships. This was Nishimura's Southern Force. Based on its location and northeasterly course, it was easy to surmise that it was bound for Surigao Strait.

Having gotten off their contact reports, and summoned aerial reinforcements from adjacent search sectors, the *Enterprise* planes prepared to attack the Southern Force. They climbed to 12,000 feet, the ideal push-over altitude for the SB2Cs. The 14-inch batteries of the two Japanese battleships, elevated to maximum angles, threw up antiaircraft shells that made spectacularly large bursts. These commanded the American aviators' respect, but none was close enough to bother them. The Hellcats dove first, fired their 5-inch aerial rockets from 2,000 feet altitude, then pulled out of their dives and flew strafing runs over the enemy ships. Behind them were the Helldivers, hurtling down at 70-degree dive angles and releasing 500-pound bombs. Several narrowly missed the *Yamashiro*, exploding close aboard; one near-miss caused the starboard hull to buckle slightly, and tons of water entered the ship through the ruptured seams, causing her to list to starboard. The flagship's pagoda superstructure was shot up by the F6Fs' rockets and strafing runs, and about twenty crewmen were killed. The battleship *Fuso* was hit by two bombs. The first hit near her No. 2 turret and exploded two decks down; another struck near her stern, smashing through her armored deck and exploding in the wardroom. An aviation fuel tank ignited and started a raging fire that devoured her floatplanes on their catapults. For a time, it looked as though the *Fuso* might not survive, but her crew contained the damage, and she resumed her station in the formation. The destroyer *Shigure* was also hit by a 500-pounder, but the bomb glanced off her forward turret and exploded in the sea alongside the ship.

During this brief, vicious air attack, Admiral Nishimura watched impassively from the bridge of the *Yamashiro*. A shipmate later recalled, "He looked as cool as a cucumber, and was not perturbed at all. He was completely fearless and had iron nerves. Such a commander instilled composure and bravery to his men."[25] First blood had been drawn against his force, but no ship was forced to turn back, and all remained in column with speed undiminished.

Judging that the Southern Force was small enough to leave to Kinkaid, Halsey decided to concentrate on the Center Force. Bypassing Mitscher, the Task Force 38 commander, he got on the low-power TBS ("Talk Between Ships") circuit and gave the order in his own voice: "Strike, Repeat: Strike! Good luck!"[26] Here was Halsey as the attention-seeking thespian, putting his own personal stamp on the battle. Circumventing the chain of command that had been set up by his self-effacing predecessor, he chose a phrase that would be recognized throughout the fleet as a callback to his electrifying order at the Battle of the Santa Cruz Islands two years earlier: "Attack, Repeat: Attack!"

At just that moment—8:27 a.m.—a wave of incoming planes appeared on the Task Force 38 radar scopes, approaching from the direction of airfields on Luzon. As expected, the American carriers were going to have to fight off air attacks throughout the morning. As a result, only Admiral Bogan's Task Group 2 managed to put an outgoing strike into the air: a forty-five-plane formation of dive bombers, torpedo bombers, and fighters from the carriers *Intrepid* and *Cabot*.

Strike leader Bill Ellis led the flight on a slightly circuitous northwesterly course, skirting the island of Cebu (where Japanese airbases were thought to have been reinforced) and then turning south toward Tablas Strait. After a flight of less than an hour, the Americans spotted their quarry in clear weather. From the air they could see the whole fleet—visibility remained excellent over the Sibuyan Sea—but every airman's eyes were drawn to the two superbattleships, the largest warships in the world, steaming at high speed near the hub of a concentric-circular array of smaller battleships, cruisers, and destroyers.

There were no Japanese airplanes in the vicinity, so the American aviators circled overhead and took their time preparing their attacks. The torpedo-armed TBM Avengers would make "anvil" attacks on both bows of their targets, to be timed closely with the dive-bombing runs of the SB2C Helldivers. Earlier in the war the Americans had struggled to get this cho-

reography right, but in 1944 they had learned to coordinate their attacks
with split-second timing.

On the Japanese ships, buglers sounded general quarters and men hurried to their stations. The Japanese cursed their lack of air protection, but
at least their ships had been reinforced with dozens of new antiaircraft batteries. The *Yamato* and *Musashi* each mounted about 150 individual AA
weapons; collectively, the guns of each ship could throw up 12,000 shells
per minute. The smaller battlewagons had about 120 AA guns, the cruisers 90, the destroyers between 30 and 40. In Lingga Roads they had trained
intensively to improve their aim and rate of fire. New *sanshikidan* shotgun-
type "beehive" antiaircraft shells had been designed for the 18.1-inch main
batteries of the two superships. As the U.S. planes descended and started
their attack runs, Kurita distributed a message to all ships: "Enemy attackers
are approaching. Trust in the gods and give it your best."[27]

Bill Ellis said it was the greatest volume of antiaircraft fire he had ever
seen. The huge main batteries of the battleships had been raised to maximum elevation. As the SB2Cs and Hellcats rolled into their dives, the big
naval weapons erupted into fire. The flak bursts were weirdly colorful, Ellis
recalled—"pink with streamers, purple with white tracer, and an abundance of white phosphorus and one shell that burst and ejected silvery
pellets."[28] The Helldivers dove from the east, the sun behind them; they
hurtled down at near-vertical angles, flying through the antiaircraft bursts,
turning as the Japanese ships turned, keeping their bombsights fixed on
their targets, and releasing their 1,000-pound bombs from a height of about
2,000 feet. Both the *Yamato* and *Musashi* were momentarily hidden behind
curtains of spray thrown up by near-misses. The *Musashi* took a hit on
her No. 1 main battery turret, but the bomb did little damage to the well-
armored weapon, only removing a circular patch of paint. The near-misses
apparently loosened the hull plates slightly, causing a sudden surge in leaks,
but as the spray subsided, it was clear that the *Musashi* was forging on with
undiminished speed.

The Avengers made full-power descents from 15,000 feet to about 200
feet above the sea, collecting speed in the process, so that they leveled off
at about 300 knots. They bore in toward the *Musashi* at this great velocity,
from both sides simultaneously. "I saw that damned pagoda," said the torpedo section leader. "But it was the size of the ship that got me. It was so

long and you couldn't miss."[29] From a range of 900 yards, the TBMs dropped their fish and turned to escape. The *Musashi* maneuvered to evade, and two tracks passed narrowly ahead of her, but the third tore into her starboard hull amidships, throwing up a 200-foot tower of whitewater. The shock of the explosion threw hundreds of her crew off their feet. The ship listed to starboard slightly, but counterflooding quickly returned her to an even keel.

As the American planes droned away to the east, the *Musashi* reported that she could still make 24 knots. She and her sister, the *Yamato*, had been designed to stand up to twenty or more torpedo hits; one was just a pinprick. But the Avengers had also sent a torpedo into the heavy cruiser *Miyoko*, a more serious blow; she was forced to drop out of the column and turn back for Brunei Bay.

BACK AT THE U.S. TASK FORCE, the orbiting Hellcats of the CAP had been fighting off Japanese airplanes since early that morning. Three successive waves of planes launched from Luzon airfields, each comprising fifty to sixty aircraft, fell upon Admiral Sherman's Task Group 3, the northern-most of the Third Fleet's carrier units. The defenders managed to prevail in a series of one-sided aerial dogfights throughout the morning. The Hell-cats were also needed elsewhere—to accompany outgoing airstrikes on the approaching Japanese fleet, and to fly fighter sweeps over enemy airfields—but the attacking swarms were numerous, persistent, and dangerous. If even a single intruder slipped through the fighter screen, it might score a lucky hit on a carrier, and the American fleet was a long way from any friendly port. "Bogies came early and stayed late during this day," noted Sherman's war diary.[30]

David McCampbell, commander of Air Group 15 on the *Essex*, was pre-paring to accompany an outbound airstrike when his squadron received an emergency call to scramble. McCampbell rushed out of the ready room and climbed into his F6F Hellcat, which was being fueled on a catapult. The hoses were disconnected when his tanks were about half-filled, and McCampbell was catapulted off the deck. He did not circle for a rendezvous with the rest of his squadron; he just pointed his nose west and climbed. Seven more F6Fs followed him to 14,000 feet altitude, gradually executing a "running rendezvous" that left them in a workable flight formation. Pres-ently they spotted their adversaries, a composite group of torpedo bombers,

dive bombers, and Zero fighters, about fifty planes all told, flying a reciprocal heading at slightly lower altitude. McCampbell radioed the sighting call,
"Tally Ho!" Then he climbed, his wingman Roy Rushing climbing with
him, to about 18,000 feet. They prepared to make diving attacks on the
enemy, but the Japanese now slipped into an old-school defensive maneuver
known as a Lufbery Circle, a merry-go-round flight pattern in which each
aircraft guarded the plane ahead.

McCampbell and Rushing waited patiently, circling about 2,000 feet
above this whirlpool of enemy planes, "figuring that some were apt to come
out of this Lufbery circle, and then we could go to work on them."[31] The
standoff lasted almost a full hour. The two men actually smoked cigarettes
in their cockpits as they waited. Now and again a Japanese plane unwisely
broke out of the formation or tried to climb to altitude. "It was simply a
question of watching for an opening, knocking them down, converting
into altitude the speed we had obtained in the dive, and then waiting for
a couple more to lay themselves open."[32] Eventually the circular formation
began to unravel, as Japanese planes turned west and fled the scene. The
Hellcats gave chase and continued making kills. Concerned that he might
lose count, McCampbell made pencil marks on his dashboard: "I'd cross
them when I got to five, and that way kept score."[33] When Rushing ran out
of ammunition and McCampbell's fuel needle was bouncing on empty, they
turned for home. There were eleven pencil marks on McCampbell's dashboard. Just as he landed on the *Essex*, his engine conked out, and the deck
crew had to push his plane forward of the crash barrier.

Asked how the flight had gone, McCampbell was "almost embarrassed"
to answer. He was certain he got nine, maybe as many as eleven. Based
on his gun camera footage, he was credited with nine, a single-flight kill
record. The seven *Essex* Hellcats that had sortied with him were credited
with twenty-four kills overall. For that remarkable flight, McCampbell was
awarded the Medal of Honor.

But the enemy warplanes kept coming, all morning long. The network
of Japanese (once American) airfields north of Manila had become an aerial
cornucopia, having been reinforced heavily from other airbases on mainland China and Formosa. The Japanese must not have been aware of the
existence to the south of two more carrier task groups, because the whole
weight of this day's airstrikes fell on Ted Sherman's four flight decks off
the east coast of Luzon—the big carriers *Essex* (his flagship) and *Lexing-*

ton, and the light carriers *Princeton* and *Langley*. Sherman worried that the Japanese might eventually wear down his overworked CAP by sheer weight of numbers.

By mid-morning, dawn's clear skies gave way to transient weather fronts and rainsqualls. Poor visibility at sea level was a joker in the deck, a capricious factor that could work to either side's advantage. After a chaotic aerial melee shortly after nine that morning, half a dozen surviving Japanese warplanes eluded the defending American fighters by diving repeatedly into low-lying cloud banks. These enemy strays could be tracked on radar, but the F6F pilots could not shoot what they could not see. The intruders remained in the vicinity, circling the task force at low altitude, presenting an omnipresent danger. This was white-knuckle warfare, in which fortunes could turn suddenly and blindly in any direction. Helmsmen steered into every passing squall, which could hide ships as well as airplanes. Antiaircraft gunners sent up terrific volleys whenever an enemy aircraft appeared in a break in the clouds, and falling shell casings roiled the sea like a steel hailstorm.

At 9:49 a.m., the light carrier *Princeton*'s luck ran out. She was turning into the wind for flight recovery operations when a lone D4Y *Suisei* ("Judy") dive bomber dropped out of the cloud ceiling overhead. The plane was already in a high-speed dive, lined up perfectly on the centerline of the ship. Captain William H. Buracker called for hard left rudder, but there was no time to evade. The 250-kilogram bomb descended like a missile from 1,500 feet and struck dead center amidships. It penetrated the flight deck and the hangar deck, and detonated in the bakeshop and the adjoining scullery on the second deck, killing the men stationed there.[34]

At first, Buracker was hopeful. "I wasn't too much concerned," he said. "I thought it was a small bomb and we could patch up the damage quickly."[35] But a fire in the aft part of the hangar deck fed upon gasoline spilled from a destroyed TBM Avenger. Firefighting and damage control teams were on the job, and the captain maneuvered the *Princeton* to put the wind on her port bow, intending to contain the blaze in the aft part of the ship. Fire main pressure was soon lost, and firefighters could not keep hoses on the fire. The inferno engulfed five more TBM Avengers on the hangar deck: one by one, their fuel tanks ignited, and at 10:10 a.m., the torpedoes in their bomb bays went up all at once. The tremendous blast caused the forward and aft elevators to pop free of their wells, and black smoke boiled out of the aft hangar bays and flight deck. Smoke spewed out of ventilation shafts in the island and pilot ready rooms. No one could remain in the hangar without masks and oxygen tanks. Hundreds of crewmen stumbled up the ladders and poured out onto the flight deck, their faces and clothing blackened by smoke. They pressed up toward the forward end of the flight deck and out onto the port catwalks, seeking relief from the heat, flames, and smoke radiating from the hangar.

Princeton was adrift, broadside to the wind, seemingly helpless to contain her fires. The captain ordered all crew except damage control parties to evacuate. Her faithful escorts—light cruiser *Birmingham*, destroyers *Morrison* and *Irwin*—drew in close and began taking men off the ship. The *Birmingham*'s fire hoses poured water and Foamite on the *Princeton*'s fires, in high-arching streams from one ship to the other—and several dozen brave volunteers of the *Birmingham*'s firefighting team boarded the *Princeton* and joined the fight to save her. The *Irwin* nosed up against the *Princeton*'s bow and began taking men directly off her flight deck. Badly wounded men were tossed from one ship to waiting hands on the other, with the tosses timed to the rise and fall of the two decks. Others went down lines and swam across to the *Morrison*'s and *Irwin*'s cargo nets, but the sea chop was rising and several dozen men drowned. For a time, the *Morrison*'s superstructure became fouled in the *Princeton*'s overhanging air intakes and was fastened in that position, unable to pull free. A gasoline vapor explosion on the *Princeton* hurled one of her plane-pulling tractors into the air—the vehicle fell end-over-end and struck a glancing blow on the *Morrison*'s bridge, then came to rest on the destroyer's forecastle. Later, her skipper dryly remarked that this was something he had never expected to witness during his naval career.

Buracker remained on the bridge of the *Princeton*, stepping out onto the veranda when the ambient heat became unbearable. He was accompanied by John Hoskins, another captain who had come aboard as his prospective replacement. Buracker had one serious concern, which he shared with Hoskins. A load of 100-pound aerial bombs had been stored in a ready stowage compartment under the aft part of the hangar. The compartment was roasting in the flames. Would it go up? There was no way to be certain, but Buracker reasoned that if the bombs were going to cook off, they would have done so at the time of the earlier explosion. He still hoped to quench the fires and save the carrier.

Between noon and 1:00 p.m., the situation seemed better. The blaze was again corralled in the aft part of the ship, and several screening ships were providing firefighting support. But at half past one came the first of several untimely submarine sonar contacts and air warnings, and all ships were ordered to pull clear and maneuver evasively. For about an hour the *Princeton* lost the benefit of her escorts' hoses. When they returned, the wind had risen to 20 knots and the flames were gaining. The *Birmingham* nudged up against the *Princeton*'s weather (port) quarter and passed spring lines across to make the two ships fast. The cruiser's hoses again began working on the carrier's fires, and stretchers on the *Princeton* were carefully transferred across. Topside, the *Birmingham* was now teeming with men, including firefighters, sailors handling lines, medical corpsmen, antiaircraft gunners, and officers directing these various operations.

That was the scene at 3:23 p.m., when the *Princeton*'s ready bomb stowage detonated, just as Buracker had feared. According to the war damage report, the monster explosion was caused by the simultaneous "mass detonation of four hundred 100-pound GP bombs. . . . which blew off the entire stern aft of frame 120 and the structure above."[36] The aftermost quarter of the *Princeton* was simply gone. Debris and chunks of steel, some very large, soared above the ship in high-arching parabolas. Bodies and parts of bodies rained down in every direction. "I saw the explosion and remember seeing ten or fifteen bodies fly through the air," recalled John Sheehan, a sailor on the destroyer *Porterfield*. Some soared over the destroyer *Casson Young* and splashed down into the sea on the far side. "We went to see if there were any survivors, but couldn't find any. I guess they were just blown to pieces."[37]

Later, when talking to a reporter for the *Cleveland Plain Dealer*, Buracker choked up. "It was as surprising as it was terrifying, that explosion," he said. "It was the worst I've ever heard in my life. I can't describe it to you."[38]

Shrapnel cut across the *Birmingham*'s exposed forecastle like a scythe, killing or wounding 229 of her crew. According to the ship's war diary, "the spectacle which greeted the human eye was horrible to behold. . . . Dead, dying and wounded, many of them badly and horribly, cover the decks." A surviving officer recalled, "Blood ran freely down our waterways." Many of the ship's crewmen were burned so badly that it seemed unlikely that they could survive, or would even want to survive. Some declined medical treatment, urging that aid be redirected to shipmates with better odds of survival. A petty officer said to the *Birmingham*'s executive officer, "Don't waste morphine on me, commander; just hit me over the head."[39]

Lee Robinson, below when the explosion occurred, worked for two days straight to help his wounded shipmates. "I can get on a crying jag real easy talking about that," he said in an oral history recorded decades later. "So many people died so fast, and the blood was just running off the sides of the ship. We had to spread sand around on the decks to keep from slipping on it." He and his unwounded shipmates ran the ship's laundry continuously for days to provide clean bandages for the wounded. Robinson recalled of the *Birmingham*'s sick bay, "None of us would go in there alone. We went in in pairs because of what we had to look at when we went in."[40]

Captains Buracker and Hoskins were on the *Princeton*'s flight deck when the bomb compartment went up. Buracker suffered only superficial wounds in the blast, but Hoskins was struck in the leg by a piece of shrapnel, and the limb was almost entirely severed below the knee. He told Buracker to attend to the other wounded. When the skipper returned a few minutes later, he saw that Hoskins had cut away the remaining flesh with his own knife, completing an auto-amputation, and applied his own tourniquet. Realizing that his tenacious bid to save the *Princeton* had come at a dreadful cost, Buracker ordered abandon ship. At 4:40 p.m., he was the last of her crew to go down the line.

KURITA HAD BEEN TOLD to expect air cover while passing through the seaways of the central Philippines, but he and his men saw only five or six Japanese airplanes during the entire three-day battle. He radioed the Philippine air commanders repeatedly and plaintively, but to no avail. Admiral Fukudome, interrogated after the war, admitted that he had "turned a deaf ear to those requests, and decided that the best protection I could give to Kurita's force would be to concentrate my entire air force in attacking your Task Force which was waiting outside beyond the channel."[41]

The Center Force was continually set upon by U.S. carrier bombers and torpedo planes throughout the afternoon of October 24. The crews fought back with the only weapons they could muster against this onslaught— their antiaircraft guns—and advanced across the Sibuyan Sea expecting that the attacks would only grow worse as they closed the range. Task Force 38 made a total of 259 aerial sorties against Kurita, including airplanes from no fewer than seven different carriers: the *Intrepid, Essex, Lexington, Franklin, Enterprise, San Jacinto,* and *Belleau Wood.* The Americans lost only eighteen planes in this "Battle of the Sibuyan Sea," a mercifully low cost considering the volume of flak thrown up by the Japanese ships.

The second wave of attackers arrived shortly after noon: about one hundred bomb-armed F6Fs and torpedo-armed TBMs from the *Intrepid*. The Avengers scored again on the *Musashi*, sending three (possibly four) torpedoes into her port side; at the same time, Hellcats performing as dive bombers hit the ship with two bombs. One put the No. 1 main battery turret out of action, and another penetrated into her outer port-side engine compartment, destroying steam lines and forcing one of her boilers off line. Deprived of one of her four propellers, and with a hole gouged into her port-side torpedo blister, *Musashi* could do no more than 22 knots. At that speed, she threw up an unnaturally large bow wave on her port side, caused by the torpedo damage below the waterline. Kurita slowed the rest of the fleet so that the injured supership could stay in company, but a slower speed would make her more vulnerable to dive bombers and especially torpedo bombers.

The third wave was devastating. Planes from the *Essex* and *Lexington* again targeted the *Musashi*, planting two bombs near the No. 3 turret and sending four more torpedoes into her starboard side. The bombs spread carnage among her antiaircraft gunners and other topside crew, and the torpedoes cut critical power lines and flooded many of her engineering spaces. The impacts caused the length of the great ship to shake intensely: sailors were thrown off their feet, and cascades of seawater carried dead and wounded men through her scuppers. Below, the sick bay was filled to capacity with bleeding and burned men, and stretchers lined the bulkheads of adjoining corridors. Bomb damage released toxic gases into that part of the ship, requiring an emergency evacuation of the medical staff and wounded. Damage control efforts were hindered by the death or injury of personnel, the flooding of critical regions of the ship, and the frequent arrival of new airstrikes. As compartments housing the ship's hydraulic pumping units were flooded or damaged by bombs, it grew increasingly difficult to keep her on an even keel. As the *Lexington* and *Essex* planes headed back over the eastern horizon at 1:50 p.m., the *Musashi* was listing noticeably to port and riding 13 feet deeper than she had been before the day's first attack. Full of seawater and unable to remain in company with the rest of the Center Force, she fell behind, accompanied by a lone heavy cruiser, the *Tone*.

When the final wave approached the Center Force at 2:55 p.m., *Enterprise* and *Franklin* airmen saw that *Musashi* was trailing a long oil slick and making only about 8 knots. The attacking planes circled high above with impunity, well out of reach of even the battleship's 18-inch *sanshiki-dan* shotgun-type "beehive" antiaircraft shells. The torpedo planes waited patiently, planning their attacks; they would all target the ship's port side, the direction of her list.

Separated from the rest of the fleet (except *Tone*), full of seawater, hobbled, down by the bow, the great battleship was a proverbial sitting duck. Her surviving crew, with rising sun ("*hachimaki*") bandanas tied around their foreheads, continued the fight with desperate ferocity. Stepping over and around the remains of dead and dying shipmates, they manned the remaining antiaircraft guns. The 18.1-inch main batteries filled the sky with the multicolored bursts of their *sanshikidan*. American aircrews felt the blast waves emanating from the big weapons. "Even at a distance," recalled Jack Lawton, an Avenger pilot with VT-13, "I felt the muzzle blast each time they fired. I could swear the wings were ready to fold every time these huge shockwaves hit us."[42] The flak rounds were dye-marked with various bright colors, an expedient to aid the Japanese gunners in spotting fire and correcting aim. As blooming multihued salvos rocked their planes, the pilots had the odd impression of flying through a celestial florist's shop. "Some of the explosions were blue, some red, some were pink, and some were yellow," said Lawton. Another VT-13 pilot, Bob Freligh, was reminded of "the sight and sounds of the Fourth of July Celebration at the Lenawee County Fair in my home town of Adrian, Michigan."[43]

The torpedo flyers descended in full-powered glides to wavetop altitude, throttles at the firewall, airspeed indicators pinned on the dial's red line. The best defense against flak was velocity. Lawton felt his machine "shimmer and shudder with every impact of every round." Red tracers reached up toward his windshield. He jinked his Grumman to avoid the columns of water erupting in his path, because "running into one of these geysers would be like running into a mountain."[44] Main and secondary batteries fired into the sea in the path of the TBMs, sending up 200-foot columns of colored seawater. The Japanese had employed this technique since the early days of the Pacific War—placing shell splashes in the path of low-flying torpedo planes, hoping to knock them down or at least force them to turn away from their attacking runs. Dropping his torpedo at 600 yards, Lawton turned sharply across the *Musashi*'s bow to make good his escape. Freligh also made a good drop, but "while taking evasive action to get away from the fire of the ship's guns, I ran into tracer bullets that got my fuel line. Oil started spurting out all over my windshield." Freligh ditched the plane off a nearby island and got ashore with his two aircrewmen. Taken in by friendly Filipinos, they were rescued several weeks later.[45]

With the *Musashi* sluggish and down in the water, she was an easy target. The TBMs hit her with at least seven torpedoes, all striking her vulnerable port side. At the same time came a well-synchronized diving attack by SB2Cs and Hellcats, which rained armor-piercing bombs along her length. A 500-pound bomb struck the ship's superstructure and destroyed the bridge; a second struck lower on the tower, setting it ablaze. These blows killed many of the ship's senior officers. Rear Admiral Toshihira Inoguchi, the skipper, was injured in his right shoulder, but could still move on his own feet. He and his executive officer set up a new command post on the lower (flag) bridge, but there was not much more they could do to save the ship. She was ablaze all along her length, her port list increasing, and sea chop was breaking over her bow. At least one and possibly two torpedoes had penetrated the protective outer hull through the jagged holes left by earlier attacks, exploding against the inner hull and flooding the No. 4 engine room. According to the executive officer (XO), "Pumping was hindered due to the cumulative bomb damage above, so it was impossible to check the flooding."[46]

The rest of the Center Force had drawn about 30 miles ahead of the *Musashi*, and was entering the western approaches to the San Bernardino Strait. Kurita radioed several more urgent requests for air cover, and for airstrikes against Task Force 38, but received no encouraging replies.[47] After the previous morning's fiasco in Palawan Passage, he and his staff were mindful of the risk of a crippling submarine ambush in the chokepoint formed by the strait. They had only eleven destroyers remaining as escorts, after sailing from Brunei with fifteen. Commander Tonosuke Otani, the operations officer, predicted that the Center Force would have to fight off three more big airstrikes before nightfall, and he warned Kurita against being caught in confined waters that would make evasive maneuvering difficult. Forcing the strait would be safer after dark. He proposed that they retire temporarily to the westward. The delay might buy more time for air attacks on the American carriers, he reckoned. It might also serve as misdirection, to trick the enemy into concluding that Center Force was in retreat.

Evidently, many on the *Yamato*'s bridge agreed with Otani's reasoning.

They cursed the missing-in-action Japanese air forces, and muttered sarcastically about their headquarters colleagues. A Japanese journalist who later interviewed several officers cited "the anger and anguish of every man on the Kurita force . . . it seemed to the men of the fleet that their ships were being offered to the enemy for target practice."[48] That afternoon, Combined Fleet radioed a warning. Enemy submarines were probably lurking in the San Bernardino Strait, and therefore: "Be alert." This message prompted derisive murmurs on the bridge; it was considered "ludicrous and infuriating."[49] The Center Force had already lost two cruisers to submarine attack, and had spent the past forty-eight hours reacting to periscope sightings. Did the imbeciles at headquarters suppose they were anything less than alert?

Kurita gave the order at 3:30 p.m., and the fleet executed a 180-degree turn. Another thirty minutes elapsed before he advised headquarters. Owing to "the frequency and numerical strength of these enemy attacks," Kurita told Admiral Toyoda, he was pausing his advance so that land-based air forces would have time to strike a blow against the American flattops. "If we continue our present course our losses will increase incalculably, with little hope of success for our mission."[50] He was retiring westward "temporarily," he said, and would "return to the action later."[51]

For an hour the force steamed westward, returning to within visual range of the stricken *Musashi*. The Japanese had expected several more rounds of heavy air attacks, so they were pleasantly surprised when none came. A reconnaissance plane was spied circling high above, obviously marking the fleet's westward progress, but after 4:20 p.m. no more enemy aircraft appeared.

At 5:15 p.m., having not heard from Toyoda in reply to his last message, Kurita decided that his duty lay on the other side of San Bernardino Strait. "All right," he said simply, "let's go back."[52] The order was apparently greeted with surprise and consternation by certain members of the staff. The *Yamato*, her escorts in formation, made two right angle turns and resumed their eastward course. They were now six or seven hours behind schedule, which meant that a coordinated pincer attack on the amphibious fleet in Leyte Gulf was not going to happen, unless Nishimura's Southern Force was equally delayed.

Congested radio communications were to blame for the delay in the Combined Fleet's reply. (The problem was similarly acute on the American side.) Finally, at 7:15 p.m., Kurita heard from Admiral Toyoda. It was a peremptory order, with quasi-religious overtones: "With confidence in divine guidance, all forces resume the attack." The original Japanese wording of this message, Operations Order No. 372, was: *"Tenyu wo kakushin shi zengun totsegeki seyo."* A literal translation was: "Trusting in heaven's assistance, all forces charge!"[53] But it had a between-the-lines meaning that does not translate readily into English. Its author was Toshitane Takata, the Combined Fleet chief of staff, who drafted it for Admiral Toyoda's signature. Takata later told American interrogators that the order carried a connotation understood by every Japanese officer, to mean that "damage could not be limited or reduced by turning back, so advance even though the fleet should be completely lost. That was my feeling when sending that order; consequently I am safe in saying that the Second Fleet was not restricted in any way as to the damage it might suffer."[54]

Kurita was being ordered to annihilate himself and his fleet, while trying to inflict some compensatory blows on the American fleet. The survival of Japanese naval forces was not supposed to figure at all in his calculations. He was not to consider, for example, that his destroyers might run out of fuel and be left defenseless against American counterattacks. He was to lead the naval *banzai* charge that was to secure the Imperial Navy's honor in defeat.

This thunderbolt arrived more than an hour after Kurita had already turned back toward the strait. According to Masanori Ito, it was greeted with "jeering remarks" aboard the bridge of the *Yamato.* Kurita's staff mocked the presumption of those senior officers, safely tucked away in their underground bunker at home, who dashed off such orders while "ignorant of enemy attacks." The impression given by this account is that the collective mood on the bridge was mordant, contemptuous, perhaps even a bit mutinous. One officer remarked, "Leave the fighting to us. Not even a god can direct naval battles from shore." Another translated the meaning of Toyoda's order: "Believing in annihilation, resume the attack!"[55]

Steaming again to the east, the Center Force passed a few miles south of the smoking, listing, foundering wreck of the *Musashi.* As one of the two most heavily armored ships in the world, she could take a great deal of punishment, and she had—more than twenty bomb hits topside, and about nineteen or twenty torpedoes below the waterline, including fifteen in her port side. No warship in history had ever suffered such punishment and survived. From the *Yamato*'s bridge, binoculars brought the scene right up close to Admiral Ugaki's eye—the 72,000-ton colossus was listing heavily to port, her towering superstructure smashed and blackened by bomb damage, a column of black smoke unspooling thousands of feet into the air. Her long sleek bow was swamped, her weather deck awash to her forward main turret, and the sea was lapping up against her gold chrysanthemum bow crest. The sun was nearly down, so the pitiful spectacle was suffused in low-angle light that cast long shadows across a violet sea. Ugaki told his diary that the *Musashi*'s "miserable position was a sorrowful sight."[56]

The *Musashi*'s fate was an ill omen for the *Yamato*. The two behemoths were twin sisters, built on identical lines. Both had been advertised as unsinkable. Japan had poured immense reserves of money, manpower, raw materials, and engineering expertise into their design and construction. An officer in the naval ministry had estimated that for the cost of both superbattleships, the Japanese navy could have built 2,000 state-of-the-art fighter planes and trained top-flight pilots to fly them.[57] The program had required major expansions of the two shipyards where they were born, at Nagasaki (*Musashi*) and Kure (*Yamato*). Their 2,700-man crews were elite, handpicked from among the navy's top performers at every level of the chain of command, from skippers to the humblest ordinary seamen. They were the sister-queens of the fleet, whose symbolic importance far surpassed their actual value as weapons. Both had served as flagships to commanders in chief of the Combined Fleet; Ugaki had previously been billeted in both ships as chief of staff to the late Admiral Isoroku Yamamoto. With his expert eye, Ugaki did not need a full report to know that nearly all of the *Musashi*'s available starboard "pumping in" compartments had already been flooded, so there was little more that could be done to correct the list. As he scrutinized the dying *Musashi*, the implication was clear—if that ship was sinkable, so was the ship under his feet.

Ugaki transmitted orders by blinker light: if there was no hope of reaching Colon Bay, Admiral Inoguchi should try to reach any nearby harbor. Failing that, he should beach his ship on the nearest island. But Ugaki did not really expect the *Musashi* to survive, and told his diary that she had "sacrificed herself for the *Yamato*." He added that he expected the *Yamato* to meet the same fate the following day: "I therefore finally made up my mind to share the fate of my ship without reservation, having decided to have *Yamato* as my death place."[58]

The *Musashi*'s port list gradually increased until men had to brace themselves against bulkheads to keep their footing. On the bridge, Inoguchi informed his executive officer, Captain Kenkichi Kato, that he intended to remain with the ship. He penned a quick note to Admiral Toyoda, commander in chief of the Combined Fleet, declaring that he had been wrong to place so much faith in the power of big-gun battleships, and admitting the supremacy of naval aviation. He gave the note to Kato and ordered the younger man to save himself. In a ritual that had become all too familiar, the emperor's portrait was removed from the wardroom and transferred lovingly to a launch. The enormous "Sun and Rays" battle ensign, some 20 by 10 feet in area, was lowered and folded while a bugler played "Kimigayo," the national anthem.

Meanwhile, the remaining crew worked frantically to arrest the ship's increasing list. Everything that could be moved was transferred to the starboard side of the ship, including wounded men and dead bodies. Their efforts were to no avail. At half past seven, the *Musashi* rolled past 30 degrees, through her point of secondary stability, and capsized. Scores of men went over the starboard rail and climbed the barnacle-encrusted bilge and keel as the ship rolled over. Some fell into the holes left by Task Force 38 torpedoes earlier in the day. The *Musashi*'s bow slid under and her stern lifted from the sea, water falling in cataracts from her four great propellers. Sailors retreated aft as the ship went down, climbing the rails and deck fittings, some falling as the quarterdeck rose nearly vertical; others jumped from the stern railing, and were seen to strike and glance off the screws as they fell. When the sea finally closed over the stern, an enormous whirlpool sucked down debris and swimmers. Men wearing life vests were lifted back to the surface, where they filled their lungs in relief, but many were quickly pulled down again by this implacable suction, and then surfaced again—and so on, repeatedly, as if the ghosts of dead shipmates were reaching up to clutch their ankles. The farther they swam from the sinking colossus, the greater their odds of survival. A few prevailed and lived to tell the tale. Many others were lost, dragged down into the abyss with their beloved *Musashi* as she voyaged to the floor of the Sibuyan Sea, 3,000 feet below.

FLAG PLOT, OCCUPYING A DECK in the *New Jersey*'s superstructure, was crowded, tense, and noisy. Cigarette smoke hung thick in the air. Voice radio transmissions of pilots in flight were piped into the room on loudspeakers.

New data continually streamed into this teeming brain center of the Third Fleet, from many disparate sources. It was the job of the "Dirty Tricks Department" to make sense of it all.

The situation was fluid, and immensely complex. Two separate enemy naval task forces were threading the island barrier of the central Philippines, evidently bound for the Surigao and San Bernardino Straits, respectively. This splitting of forces was a familiar tactic of the Japanese; Halsey had seen it in several naval battles of 1942. No brilliant deductions were needed to see that the enemy intended to force the two straits and launch a pincer attack against the amphibious fleet in Leyte Gulf.

As the afternoon's last big airstrike on the Center Force turned for home, their radioed reports were upbeat. The returning pilots were confident that they had wrecked both *Yamato*-class battleships, as well as two other smaller battleships of the *Nagato* or *Kongo* classes; they also claimed to have pulverized two or three heavy cruisers with torpedoes and bombs. Moreover, reconnaissance flights had sighted remnants of the Center Force on a westerly course. Perhaps they had given up the fight and turned away for good. At any rate, Halsey assumed that Kurita's surviving ships had been so thoroughly mauled that they "constituted no serious threat to Kinkaid."[59] Even if the Center Force managed to run the strait, "its fighting power was considered too seriously impaired to win a decision."[60]

The emerging mosaic suggested that the Japanese were making an all-out attempt to contest the Leyte invasion. But if that were so, where were their aircraft carriers? Intelligence shops in Washington and Pearl Harbor were unanimous in agreeing that Ozawa's carrier force had been in Japanese waters until at least mid-October. In the past two days, decrypted radio intercepts ("Ultras") gave circumstantial evidence that Ozawa had sailed from Japan, and was now in the Philippine Sea somewhere north of Luzon. It was a good bet that he was approaching from the north, and that his arrival would be timed to coincide with those of the other enemy task forces. Halsey and key subordinates were alert to the likelihood that Ozawa would attempt to employ "shuttle-bombing" tactics by linking up to airfields on Luzon. They were determined to find and strike the Japanese carriers before they could be brought into action.

Earlier that morning, Halsey had ordered Mitscher to launch a reinforced air search to the northward. But radio circuits were so congested that the directive had not reached the *Lexington*'s flag bridge until 11:30 a.m. At that hour, Task Force 38 was busy fighting off waves of aerial attackers from Luzon. Therefore, the searches were not sent off until 2:05 p.m., and two hours later they still had not found Ozawa.

In the interim, at 3:12 p.m., Halsey distributed a housekeeping order that was fated to play an outsized role in the next day's events. Designated as a "battle plan," it directed that six battleships, five cruisers, and fourteen destroyers currently deployed as screening vessels throughout the carrier groups "will be formed as Task Force 34 under Vice Admiral Lee, Commander Battle Line."* Its purpose would be to "engage decisively at long ranges."[61] The message was addressed to all subordinate Third Fleet commanders and copied to Nimitz and King. Halsey intended it as a "preparatory dispatch," or a warning order, to be executed if and when an opportunity for a surface engagement arose. To drive home the point, he subsequently informed his forces by TBS: "If the enemy sorties [through San Bernardino Strait], TF 34 will be formed when directed by me."[62]

Halsey later stressed that the first message was not intended for anyone beyond his own Third Fleet. But since all U.S. naval commands could intercept radio traffic, and were privy to the same codes, it was possible for others to eavesdrop on such message traffic. Indeed, it was the usual practice to do so. Halsey's message was copied by the Seventh Fleet communications team and delivered to Admiral Kinkaid aboard the *Wasatch*. The subsequent clarification by short-range voice radio was not copied (and could not have been copied) by Kinkaid, nor by Nimitz or King. Given the stilted phrasing common in military dispatches, the words "will be formed" were ambiguous, especially without benefit of the second, clarifying message. They could be read as a present-tense imperative, meaning that Halsey was telling his subordinates to form the new task force right away, in preparation for the planned battle. Or his use of the future tense "will" might merely signify that the various ships, deployed in three widely separated carrier task groups, would need several hours to rendezvous under Admiral Lee. That was the sense in which Kinkaid understood Halsey's order, and it was similarly misconstrued in Pearl Harbor and Washington.

---

* Willis "Ching" Lee, the veteran battleship division commander who had been serving in that role for several years. Lee had led U.S. forces in the second phase of the Naval Battle of Guadalcanal (November 14–15, 1942), the only battleship gunfight prior to this point in the Pacific War.

At 4:40 p.m. came news from one of the search planes up north. A large enemy carrier force was sighted about 190 miles off Cape Engano, on the northeast coast of Luzon: speed 15 knots, course 210 degrees.[63] That could only be Ozawa, and he appeared to be inbound. Given the late hour, he was far out of air-striking range.

In flag plot on the *New Jersey*, Halsey and his staff studied the charts and analyzed the position. Three enemy naval forces were converging (or had intended to converge) on Leyte Gulf from three different directions. Significantly, or so it seemed to Halsey and his team, all three formations were traveling at the "deliberate" speed of about 15 knots, well short of their best cruising speed. As the Third Fleet action report put it, "it was inferred that there was a pre-determined focus of geographical location and time. The movements indicated that a carefully worked-out coordinated Japanese plan was in motion, with 25 October as the earliest date of concerted action."[64] The Southern Force was headed for Surigao Strait, south of Leyte; it was relatively weak, and could be safely left to Kinkaid. The Center Force had suffered a savage day-long beating from Task Force 38's air groups, and appeared to be in retreat. The Northern Force, newly discovered, was the only enemy naval task force with aircraft carriers. It was fresh, unscathed, its striking power unimpaired. Ozawa probably intended to shuttle-bomb the American fleet—meaning that his bombers would strike Task Force 38 at dawn, fly to Luzon to refuel and rearm, and then strike again before returning to their carriers.

Halsey could be fairly certain of winning the air battle, given the comfortable margin of superiority possessed by American carrier airpower at that stage of the war—but he wanted to annihilate the Northern Force, to cripple it with multiple airstrikes and finish it off with his surface warships. To be sure of a total wipeout, he would need to close the range. Several officers of the close-knit "Nouméa gang," who had served under Halsey since the fight for Guadalcanal, advised taking the whole fleet north.[65] Halsey put his finger down on the chart, indicating the reported position of Ozawa's fleet, and told Carney, "Here's where I'm going. Mick, start 'em north."[66]

At 8:22 p.m. on October 24, the *New Jersey*'s radio transmitters summoned Bogan and Davison to raise steam and head north at 25 knots, to fall in with Sherman's Group 3. The *Princeton*, gutted by fire and abandoned by her crew, was ordered scuttled; the job was carried out by a salvo of torpedoes fired by one of her own escorts. Significantly, all three available carrier groups would join the run north, including the fast battleships and other surface warships that would otherwise have been detached as Task Force 34 and left to guard the eastern mouth of the San Bernardino Strait. The entire armada, sixty-five ships altogether, would join the northbound charge. Kurita's much-weakened Center Force, should it pull itself together and traverse the strait, would be left to the guns and escort carriers of Kinkaid's Seventh Fleet.

Halsey informed Kinkaid that he was "proceeding north with three groups to attack carrier force at dawn."[67] Much was left out of this missive, and perilous misapprehensions crept into the resulting voids. Halsey did not mention Task Force 34 at all. He did not inform his colleague that the fourth carrier task group had previously been sent away to the east, and was too distant to provide direct support. Kinkaid's attention was not directed to the vital fact that no part of the Third Fleet was guarding (or even watching) the San Bernardino Strait.

Having given his orders, Halsey went down to his sea cabin and turned into his bunk. He was bone-weary, having barely slept during the previous forty-eight hours. He needed shut-eye and would take it now, while he could get it.

Among certain members of his intelligence staff, and on flag bridges throughout the Third Fleet, there was an outbreak of second-guessing. Halsey's decision to leave none of his considerable force to guard the San Bernardino Strait seemed peculiar, even inexplicable. Did he know something that others did not?

As Halsey's chosen battle plan was being set in motion, new sighting reports cast doubt on the premise that Kurita was in retreat. The light carrier *Independence*, in Admiral Bogan's Task Group 2, was equipped with a night flying squadron. Several night patrol flights had been sent over the western approaches to the San Bernardino Strait. Some of their reports were garbled and confusing, but taken together they suggested that the Center Force was eastbound at high speed. At 6:35, the enemy column was spotted about 6 miles north of its previous position, apparently headed northeast. Another *Independence* plane reported it adjacent to the middle of Burias Island, which put it 25 miles farther northeast than at the previous point of contact. Then came a report that the Japanese ships were between Burias and Masbate Islands, which meant that Kurita had turned east and was making an imputed speed of 24 knots. If Kurita could cruise at that pace, his force must be in better condition than earlier supposed. Finally came news that navigation lights marking the channel in the San Bernardino Strait had been turned on.

Admiral Bogan got on the voice radio and spoke directly to the skipper of the *Independence*, who told him that the Japanese fleet was traveling on a northeasterly course at high speed. They would soon reach the western approaches of the San Bernardino Strait, where the navigation lights had been turned on. Bogan then hailed the *New Jersey* directly and was connected to an unknown officer in flag plot. Passing on what he had learned, Bogan proposed that Task Force 34 and one carrier group (his own) be left in charge of the strait. With a "rather impatient voice," the other man cut him off, saying, "Yes, yes, we have that information."[68]

Bogan said later, "I thought that Admiral Halsey was making one hell of a mistake."[69] He regretted that Lee's battleships were not matched against Kurita's, a fight he believed the Americans would have won handily. "It could have meant the end of Japanese naval power right there," Bogan concluded. "Completely. It was extremely frustrating."[70]

Admiral Lee was thinking along the same lines. He tried to reach the *New Jersey*, first by blinker light and then by TBS. He asked whether the Third Fleet command had noted the latest sighting reports, and was answered simply, "Roger."[71] Like Bogan, he concluded that there was no more he could do.

Ralph Davison, commander of Group 4, told his chief of staff, James Russell: "Jim, we're playing a hell of a dirty trick on the transports in Leyte Gulf." Russell agreed and asked if Davison would like to contact Admiral Mitscher to recommend a different course of action. Davison declined, remarking, "He must have more information than we do."[72]

On the *Lexington*, the Task Force 38 staff asked for and received confirmation that Halsey had taken direct tactical command of the carriers. Since August, Admiral Mitscher had grown accustomed to riding sidecar in this fashion. He was obviously very tired, physically and mentally, having served continuously since the beginning of 1944; now he seemed resigned to whatever Halsey and his posse were cooking up. Mitscher was crawling into his bunk when his chief of staff, Arleigh Burke, popped his head into the admiral's sea cabin. He wanted to radio the *New Jersey* to warn that the Northern Force was a decoy. "I think you're right," replied Mitscher, "but

I don't know you're right. I don't think we should bother Admiral Halsey. He's busy enough. He's got a lot of things on his mind."[73]

Later, Burke returned with the Task Force 38 operations officer, Jim Flatley. They awakened Mitscher and renewed the appeal, citing the news that the navigation lights in San Bernardino Strait had been illuminated. Mitscher asked: "Does Admiral Halsey have that report?" Flatley admitted that he did. In that case, said Mitscher, it was not their job to second-guess the fleet boss: "If he wants my advice, he'll ask for it."

Several officers of the Third Fleet intelligence staff believed that the carrier force to the north was a lure, and worried that Halsey was about to swallow it. They had not been consulted before the decision to head north. Mike Cheek, the fleet intelligence officer, argued "furiously" with Doug Moulton, the air operations officer who was a long-standing member of Halsey's inner circle. Raising his voice, which he was not wont to do, Cheek declared that he *knew* Kurita was coming through San Bernardino. Moulton was unmoved.

Cheek retreated in defeat, but two of his juniors later convinced him to take his case up the chain of command to Mick Carney. Carney said that if Cheek wished to wake Halsey to plead his case, he (Carney) would not stand in the way. However, said Carney, he doubted Halsey would be moved by Cheek's reasoning, and added that Halsey "has had little or no sleep in the past 48 hours."[74] Cheek could not bring himself to wake the admiral, and that was that.

Halsey and his inner circle were determined not to repeat the blunder they believed Spruance had committed the previous June, during the naval battle off the Marianas, when he had refused to let Task Force 38 (then designated 58) chase Ozawa into the west. They were primed, in other words, to run the Japanese carriers to ground and destroy them, and they were willing to gamble heavily to accomplish that goal. According to Mick Carney, in an interview given two decades after the war: "Halsey and Moulton particularly felt very strongly and early expressed the view that if the Japanese fleet was deprived of its tactical air arm, whatever the plan was for the future, that the effectiveness of that fleet was hamstrung for all time, because we had been convinced that they could replace nothing.

"Out of these discussions came a determination that night, in Halsey's flagship, that the principal objective should be the carrier air. It became practically—well, I would say it was almost an obsession."[75]

Destroying the Japanese carriers was Halsey's "obsession." That was the judgment of his long-serving and loyal chief of staff, the majordomo of the Dirty Tricks Department, who later climbed to the top rung of the navy's command ladder (chief of naval operations, 1953–1954). Carney's admission was damning, to Halsey as well as to himself, but it shed light on the breakdown that night of the Third Fleet's tactical decision-making machinery.

Halsey and his team seem to have been feeling the effects of prolonged mental and physical fatigue. Many in flag plot were recovering from a recent round of the flu. In six weeks of almost uninterrupted carrier combat operations, they had taken virtually no rest.

But fatigue and the flu did not tell the whole story. Since Halsey had taken command of the fleet in August, relieving Raymond Spruance, there had been a pattern of confusion, sloppiness, and impulsiveness in basic procedures. The Third Fleet staff was considerably larger than the Fifth Fleet staff, but it gave the impression of being far less efficient. The new outfit generally did not produce detailed operations plans, as Spruance's staff had done; they preferred to operate through frequent dispatches to the fleet. But communications were often late, ambiguous, or countermanded by eleventh-hour changes. Carrier task group commanders were kept in suspense about their next moves. The slapdash habits of the new fleet boss caused headaches even in Pearl Harbor. Nimitz frequently reprimanded Halsey for exceeding his authority or failing to make clear and timely reports. Of one such mishap in early October, Halsey begged the CINCPAC's pardon: "I am most apologetic for the present mix-up. I can assure you that my intentions were excellent, but my execution rotten."[76]

Halsey was in the habit of relying on officers who had accompanied him from SOPAC, men he knew personally, even though none had recent experience in carrier operations. According to Admiral Arthur Radford, a carrier admiral and future chairman of the Joint Chiefs of Staff, Halsey "either suffered from poor advice in connection with carrier air operations or insisted on making his own decisions, which could be worse."[77] Similar opinions were widely heard in the fleet, even before the most controversial episodes of Halsey's career. The historian Clark Reynolds judged that Halsey "did not enjoy the keen professional respect" that Spruance had earned, even if he was "loved dearly" as a leader.[78] Roland Smoot called him "a complete and utter clown . . . but if he said, 'Let's go to hell together,' you'd go to hell with him."[79]

THREE HUNDRED MILES TO THE SOUTH, in Leyte Gulf, the Seventh Fleet was preparing to meet and repulse Nishimura's Southern Force as it came through Surigao Strait. Kinkaid signaled Admiral Oldendorf, commander of the bombardment and fire support group: "Enemy can arrive Leyte Gulf tonight. Make all preparations for night engagement."[80]

Oldendorf's force included most of the U.S. Navy's older battleships with supporting cruisers and destroyers, including five battleships that had been knocked out of action in the Japanese strike on Pearl Harbor. Two of those five survivors, *West Virginia* and *California*, had been gutted by Japanese aerial torpedoes, causing them to sink to the harbor floor. With a herculean salvage effort, they had been raised and repaired. While in drydock at Pearl Harbor, they had been reconstructed from keel to topmasts, and equipped with state-of-the-art gunnery, fire control, and radar systems. Even their crews were new: the *West Virginia*, especially, was manned by well-trained greenhorns, most of whom had never been to sea before coming aboard in June. According to the ship's action report, "Only twelve enlisted men had ever had previous sea experience. Two of the turret officers had never been to sea before, the third came from submarine duty, and the fourth from small craft. Yet, in a short three months, these had gone through a grueling shakedown period and had joined the fleet as a fighting unit."[81]

Oldendorf deployed these resurrected battlewagons in a single file across the northern mouth of Surigao Strait. On the flanks, two miles south, the cruiser divisions would steam in diagonal lines, in effect creating a semicircle of big guns trained on the enemy's expected line of advance. It was a straightforward and conventional arrangement, faithful to the centuries-old naval concept of the "battle line." Oldendorf deployed his destroyers farther south, down the strait, with orders to hug the shores; they would take cover in the radar shadows created by the hills and cliffs along the coasts of Panaon and Dinagat Islands. When the moment came, they would make torpedo attacks on the Southern Force as it came up the strait.

Oldendorf also had the use of all of the Seventh Fleet's forty-five PT-boats. He deployed them in the southern part of the strait and the western approaches to it. The boats were to serve mainly as early warning pickets. After radioing contact reports, they were at liberty to attempt torpedo attacks.[82]

With several times Nishimura's aggregate "weight of metal," Oldendorf's forces seemed more than sufficient to score a knockout. The Southern Force would run a long, deadly gauntlet of night torpedo attacks on its way up Surigao Strait. At the head of the strait, if they got that far, the Japanese warships would encounter the massed naval gunfire of six battleships and eight cruisers. Oldendorf's big ships would be positioned on an east-west axis, while Nishimura's column must approach on a northerly heading. That meant the Allied fleet would have the opportunity to "cross the T" of the Japanese fleet—that is, bring their full broadsides to bear on ships that could return fire only from their forward turrets. It was an old and venerated tactical concept, dating back to the first mounting of cannon on ships. In effect, the geometry of the action promised to augment Oldendorf's (already decisive) margin of firepower superiority.

Knowing they held the high cards, the Americans were confident of victory. Still, there remained some uncertainty about the composition of the approaching Japanese fleet, and moderate concern about the type of ammunition in Oldendorf's ships. Aerial sighting reports did not agree on the number of battleships in the Japanese column: some had reported two, but at least one pilot thought he saw four. The Americans would hold an advantage even against four Japanese battleships, but it would be a more closely matched fight. Prior to the landings on Leyte, the fire support group had loaded a high proportion of the high-explosive (HE) ordnance preferred for shore bombardment, so their reserves of armor-piercing (AP) ammunition were relatively limited. That would not become a vital factor except in a prolonged fight, but Oldendorf did not want to tempt fate. To conserve AP ammunition, he told the battleships to hold fire until the enemy had closed to medium range, between 17,000 and 20,000 yards, "where their percentage of hits and their fire effect would both be high."[83]

During these final preparations, Admiral Kinkaid engaged in delicate negotiations with MacArthur. Under ordinary circumstances, the battle group assigned to Oldendorf would include the cruiser Nashville. But the Nashville had also brought General MacArthur from Hollandia, and for the moment she was still serving as his command ship. He had gone ashore every day since the invasion, but had returned each night to the ship. The situation ashore seemed well enough in hand that MacArthur could have moved his headquarters to Leyte; in fact, he had planned to do so the following day. Kinkaid wanted to send the Nashville down to Surigao, and her officers and crew were certainly keen to join the action. But MacArthur was still aboard, and he wanted to go along on the adventure. He told Kinkaid, "There is every reason why I should be present during such a crucial engagement. Besides, I've never been in a major naval action, and I am anxious to see one."[84] But Kinkaid saw no reason to put the SWPA commander at risk by sending him into a naval battle. He offered MacArthur the use of another noncombatant ship, and then invited him aboard his own command ship, the *Wasatch*. When MacArthur declined both offers, Kinkaid detached the *Nashville* from the battle group and left her in Tacloban anchorage.

Oldendorf's ships were on station before sunset. The battleships and cruisers catapulted their floatplanes, sending them to land on Leyte airfields, in order to clear their turrets' arc of fire. The battleships joined up in column at 6:30 p.m. An hour later, the fleet went to general quarters and set "readiness condition one easy."[85]

In Leyte Gulf, all eyes, ears, minds, and hearts were directed south, toward the impending fight in Surigao Strait. No one in the Seventh Fleet suspected that Halsey had taken his whole enormous force north, or that he had left the gate at San Bernardino standing wide open, without so much as a destroyer picket to raise the alarm. While preparing to ambush Nishimura to his south, Kinkaid was about to be ambushed to his north, and he would not learn the awful truth until Kurita's big guns opened fire a few minutes after dawn.

Chapter Six

Throughout the afternoon of October 24, Nishimura's Southern Force had forged on doggedly through the Mindanao Sea, still on course for Surigao Strait. After that morning's brief, violent encounter with the Third Fleet's patrol planes, it had been left unmolested. The *Yamashiro*'s damage had been contained, her starboard list corrected.

Concerned by aerial reports placing many American PT-boats in the approaches to Surigao, Nishimura decided to send ahead the cruiser *Mogami* with four destroyers to scout the area before bringing his two battleships into Surigao. The *Mogami* reconnaissance force separated from the battleships at 6:30 p.m. and forged ahead to sniff around the northern part of the Mindanao Sea. Shortly after the scouting force left, Nishimura received Toyoda's message, addressed to all Japanese commanders but implicitly aimed at Kurita: "With confidence in divine guidance, all forces resume the attack."

This strangely worded message must have puzzled Nishimura, because he did not yet know that Kurita had turned west. Three more hours passed before he got word directly from Kurita that the Center Force was delayed and could not arrive in Leyte Gulf until about eleven the next morning. Undeterred by the discouraging news, Nishimura pressed on at undiminished speed, intending to attack on the original timetable. He must have known that his hopes of penetrating into Leyte Gulf had never been good, but now he could be sure of running into the concentrated gunfire of the entire American fleet, undistracted by the northern prong of the planned pincer attack. His decision to press on also guaranteed that Admiral Shima's "Second Striking Force," a stepchild fleet comprising two cruisers and several destroyers, would not have time to fall in with his force. Trailing behind by about 45 miles, Shima would simply charge into the fray, with no prior plan to synchronize operations or tactics with Nishimura.

Because so few senior Japanese officers lived to tell the tale of what happened in Surigao Strait that night, historians have necessarily relied on inference and speculation. No one can know what was in Nishimura's mind as his flagship *Yamashiro* plunged into the unpromising battle. He must have suspected that he was leading his seven-ship column into an ambush. Perhaps he supposed that the Japanese retained some vestige of their superior skill in night surface combat, for which they had trained so intensively before the war, and which they had put on display in several night actions in the Solomons. A naval gunfight under cover of darkness would also cut the risk of air attack.

But all such tactical considerations overlook the more important point about Nishimura's mission: no part of his force was expected to survive. Nishimura knew he was leading a naval *banzai* charge, and he was evidently resigned to die. In one sense his Southern Force was a decoy, intended to divert some portion of U.S. forces south in order to improve Kurita's odds in the north. In a deeper sense, his little flotilla was to serve as a sacrificial offering to the gods of war. Nishimura's real duty was to suffer glorious annihilation, guns blazing to the last, thus sustaining the Japanese navy's honor in defeat.

Such an assignment could not be spelled out in plain writing, and it was not explicitly communicated in the text of Plan *Sho* or Toyoda's subsequent orders. In his postwar account of the battle, Masanori Ito stressed that Western critics had failed to understand these "particular circumstances of [Nishimura's] assignment." But the accounts of surviving officers and crew confirmed this understanding of their role. Captain Tomoo Tanaka of the destroyer *Michishio* said that "all officers in this force considered that they were engaged in a suicide mission and none of them expected to return."[1] An operations officer on the battleship *Fuso* told the sailors of his division that they would dash into Tacloban Anchorage, where under the superior guns of the American fleet, the ship would run aground on the beach so that she could continue firing her main batteries even while in a sinking condition. "We are going to participate in a surface special attack," he told his men.[2] In this context, "special" (*tokko*) referred to a one-way suicide attack. During a prebattle briefing, according to another witness, Admiral Nishimura had "emphasized the need for spiritual readiness as much as combat readiness. Nishimura was reconciled to death. His attitude permeated the ranks, and Nishimura's men went along with him willingly on this suicidal duty."[3]

American PT-boats lay in wait along the route of Nishimura's advance. Thirty-nine boats were deployed in thirteen sections, hugging the shores of islands in the Bohol Sea and the southern approaches to Surigao Strait. They lay to in the calm, unruffled sea, their Packard engines rumbling in idle, exhaust fumes floating away on the breeze, waves slapping languidly against their wooden hulls. The night was sultry and mostly clear. A quarter moon hung low in the west, casting a glistening yellow trail across the sea.

The vanguard section was stationed about 60 miles from the southern mouth of the strait, close inshore to the islands of Bohol and Camiguin. At 10:36 p.m., PT-131 registered two large blips on her radar scope, closing from the west at 20 knots. Scanning the horizon with night binoculars, Ensign Peter Gadd soon caught sight of the enemy: a double column led by four destroyers, followed by the two battleships with their distinctive towering pagodas, and finally the cruiser *Mogami*.

While Gadd was radioing the contact report, the Japanese sighted the PT-boats in turn and fired illumination rounds in their direction. Starshells burst overhead, bathing the scene in searing red light. Gadd's three PTs opened their throttles. Their engines roared, their hulls lifted up out of the sea, and long, white wakes stretched away astern. The destroyer *Shigure* caught them in her searchlights, and her 5-inch guns opened fire. White-water columns shot up around the little wooden vessels as they closed the range at better than 30 knots. "The first thing I knew, the boat was hauling ass," said a PT-152 crewman. "We were caught in a searchlight. The noise was incredible."[4]

The 40mm gun crew on PT-152 fired on the *Shigure*, hoping to take out her searchlight, but to no avail. The *Shigure* and several other ships in the Japanese column turned toward the attackers, reducing their target profiles and preparing to "comb" torpedoes. The boats launched their fish and turned away to flee. All torpedoes missed—probably widely, because the Japanese lookouts saw no tracks.

While speeding away in retreat, zigzagging and laying smoke, PT-152 took a direct hit astern. The boat's 37mm gun was destroyed, the gunner killed instantly, and fires flared up in her aft compartments below. PT-130 was also struck, probably by a six-inch projectile fired from one of the *Yamashiro*'s secondary batteries, but the armor-piercing shell punched "through and through" the boat's plywood and mahogany without detonating. For an anxious moment it appeared that the damaged PT-152 would be overtaken by the *Shigure* and blown out of the water, but the destroyer turned back into column, giving up the chase. The Japanese had bigger fish to fry.

By a stroke of bad luck, all three of the boats in Gadd's section discovered that their radios were disabled. PTs 130 and 131 turned southeast and raced toward Camiguin, where they fell in with another section. Boarding PT-127, Gadd radioed his contact and action report to Admiral Oldendorf at the head of the strait. Now Oldendorf knew that Nishimura was just south of Bohol, about 90 miles southwest of his position, and he would continue to receive position updates throughout the evening. The Allied battleships and cruisers continued to pace the strait at 5 knots, guns trained south, and waited for the enemy to come into range.

Passing Limasawa Island, the Japanese force re-formed into a double column with destroyers on the flanks. They were observed closely, first on radar and then visually, by the three boats of PT-Squadron 12, commanded by Lieutenant Dwight H. Owen. As Nishimura reached the southern tip of Panaon Island, Owen's boats swarmed out of the inshore darkness and attacked. PTs 151 and 146 advanced into the searchlights, water spouts leaping up around them, and launched torpedoes from a range of 1,800 yards. Both missed widely. The boats turned away and fled, zigzagging for their lives. In the melee's confusion, the battleship *Fuso* mistook the cruiser *Mogami* for an enemy and briefly fired on her, but did not inflict serious damage.

As it rounded Panaon Island and turned north into Surigao Strait, the Japanese force was suddenly beset by a swarm of attackers on all sides. Lieutenant Commander Robert Leeson's three PT-boats (134, 132, and 137) charged the center of the Japanese column and found themselves in the blinding searchlight of a battleship, probably the *Yamashiro*. Closing to 1,500 yards, they launched seven torpedoes, then veered sharply away to escape. Zigzagging erratically, they were chased by the *Yamashiro*'s big guns and a storm of machine-gun fire. "Her 40-millimeter batteries and her 14-inch main batteries turned night into day," said a PT sailor who felt lucky to have survived the encounter. "There was considerable 5-inch gunfire as well. The destroyers must have opened up too, and tracers, smoke, exploding shells and fire were everywhere."[5]

As the Japanese guns reached out for Leeson's three retreating boats, another trio charged in from the darkness in the southeast. PTs 523, 524, and 526 found their targets perfectly silhouetted by their own muzzle flashes and starshells. They launched torpedoes, then sheared away to run for the cover of Sumilon Island. It is not clear that the Japanese even saw these three starboard attackers, however, because at nearly the same moment PTs 490, 491, and 493 sped in from the north in a virtual head-on attack. This section broke out of a covering squall to find itself just 700 yards from the nearest enemy destroyer. The enemy ships were engaged with PTs on the other side, therefore momentarily inattentive. This trio of boats made the boldest torpedo run of the night, closing to within 400 yards before being illuminated by searchlights; they launched fish and veered away, chased by whitewater eruptions. All three were hit by enemy fire while zigzagging away to the north. PT-493 took the worst beating of any boat that night: one 5-inch shell struck the stern, a second punctured the hull below the waterline, and a third hit just aft of the chart house, killing two men instantly and wounding seven more. With no one left at the helm, PT-493 turned randomly and threatened to head back toward the enemy, until one of the survivors got to the wheel and straightened her out. She escaped into a passing squall, but she was a wreck, in sinking condition, with most of her crew immobilized by injury. The survivors ran her aground on Panaon Island and carried the wounded men ashore, where they were rescued the next morning.

Thus far, the PT attacks had been nothing more than a nuisance to the Japanese. More than two dozen torpedoes had been launched, but none had scored. The PT crews, it was later agreed, needed more training in torpedo tactics. Undoubtedly they had made many wild launches while under fire, or had declined to court their own annihilation by advancing into point-blank range. Some of their weapons had probably malfunctioned; some might have actually hit their targets but failed to explode. Still, the PTs had executed their prime assignment, to provide an early warning of the enemy's approach. As the Japanese ships fought off successive swarms of "devil boats," they lit up the night with gunfire and illumination rounds that could be seen a very long way away. At 2:06 a.m., noted the log of the *West Virginia*: "Saw starshells to southeast far distant." Two minutes later: "Gunfire sighted bearing 180° true."[6] Nishimura had blown his cover with this traveling fireworks show.

That did not stop him, however, or even slow his progress. Turning into the center of the strait, Nishimura's ships sped on toward the waiting American fleet on a course of zero degrees, dead north. The moon had set at 11:00 p.m., and the night was very dark. The sea remained calm, but frequent squalls of rain swept through the area, obscuring visibility. Japanese lookouts could barely make out the looming masses of the islands of Panaon to port and Dinagat to starboard. They could not see their soaring, heavily forested ridgelines at all, except in sporadic flashes of distant sheet lightning. The familiar shape of Ursa Major, the Big Dipper, was low in the northern sky.

Captain Jesse Coward's Destroyer Squadron 54 was closing quickly from the north. Coward had arrayed his destroyers in two parallel sections, intending to envelop the Japanese column on two flanks. Closing the range at a combined speed of 40 knots—with Coward's destroyers roaring south at 20 knots and Nishimura's charging north at the same speed—the two adversaries made visual contact simultaneously when separated by about 5 miles. Coward's eastern column was closing almost head-on, just 10 degrees off the starboard bows of the leading Japanese ships. They laid smoke on their approach, obscuring visibility further—but the owl-eyed Japanese lookouts could make out the distinctive shape of their funnels moving against the formless backdrop of Dinagat.

The Japanese opened fire at long range, but their first shots were wild, the splashes falling about 2,000 yards short of their targets.[7] By hugging the shorelines of Surigao Strait, Coward's ships kept within the "radar shadow" cast by the hilly island terrain. According to Commander Shigeru Nishino, skipper of the destroyer *Shigure*, this tactic served its purpose. The frustrated Japanese gunners, peering at their radar scopes, "could not differentiate between the ships and the land. We just got one merged reaction on the screen. We fired regardless but I think it was very ineffective."[8]

The American ships did not return fire, lest their muzzle flashes serve as aiming points for the enemy. Coward had instructed his squadron to attack only with torpedoes. At 3:00 a.m., the three destroyers in his eastern section launched twenty-seven torpedoes, then turned sharply away to port, chased by naval shells of many calibers. Lookouts on the Japanese ships spotted incoming torpedo tracks and the green phosphorescence they churned up—and the Japanese column steered to evade. The *Fuso*'s 14-inch guns opened fire on three retreating destroyers, straddling the *McGowan* but scoring no hits. At nearly the same moment, however, the *Fuso* caught two torpedoes, possibly three, on her starboard side amidships. Her boiler room flooded, she listed heavily to starboard, and abruptly lost power. She fell out of formation. The cruiser *Mogami*, following in her wake, had to execute an emergency turn to avoid colliding.

The second half of Coward's destroyer force—the western group, comprising the *Monssen* and *McDermott*—launched a spread of twenty torpedoes at ranges between 8,000 and 9,000 yards. These arrived just as Nishimura's force was turning back onto its base course, dead north. The results were devastating. Three of four Japanese destroyers in the column were struck in three minutes. The *Yamagumo* was struck amidships by two torpedoes simultaneously. The blasts detonated two of the ship's own torpedoes, primed into their tubes. The combined explosions virtually blew her apart, and she sank in about two minutes. Commander Nishino recalled that she went down with a hissing sound, "like a huge red-hot iron plunged into water."[9] The *Michishio* was crippled by a hit that struck her port engine room. She began foundering, dead in the water, and only by heroic efforts of her surviving crew was she kept afloat. The third, the *Asagumo*, was struck forward. Her entire bow was torn away, but her crew managed to seal off the damage.[10] The ship turned around and limped south.

The crippled *Fuso* could barely make way. She was fighting for her life, "entirely enveloped in flames from her waterline to her masthead."[11] For the ensuing hour, she drifted helplessly on the current. The captain ordered abandon ship, and her crew began leaping into the warm water of Surigao Strait. At about 4:00 a.m., she rolled onto her starboard beam ends, her huge superstructure striking the sea with a great splash. Her bow went under; her stern stood out of the sea to a height of 150 feet, her screws still turning, and she slid under. Oil spread across the sea and the fire spread around her to a distance of several hundred feet, engulfing many men attempting to swim to safety. It is not known how many survived her sinking, but very few survived the hours that they would spend as castaways at sea. Only about ten of the *Fuso*'s crew returned to Japan after the battle.

Now there was a tremendous amount of confusion on the Japanese ships. Some thought that the column was surrounded by PT-boats. Commander Nishino was under the impression that the flagship *Yamashiro* had been hit, rather than the *Fuso*. The *Yamashiro* continued pressing north at 25 knots, but Admiral Nishimura and his officers did not know that the *Fuso* and three destroyers had been hit, and that more than half of the column's combined tonnage was disabled or destroyed. Only the *Mogami* remained in company with the flagship. *Shigure*, the only remaining seaworthy Japanese destroyer, raised speed to get clear of the torpedoes, but then lost contact with the rest of the force. For a time, Nishino was unable to raise any friendly ship on the radio. He turned south "to find out what had happened to *Yamashiro* and to get orders if possible; then made a second turn and proceeded north again."[12]

At the northern end of the strait, meanwhile, Oldendorf's battleships and cruisers tracked the approaching Japanese ships on radar. They intercepted oddments of Japanese chatter on low-power radio frequencies. The lookouts spied distant starshells and gunfire and heard the rumble of far-off explosions. Admiral Oldendorf saw the beam of an enemy searchlight sweep across the horizon, which he compared to a "walking stick of a blind man being waved through the night, though what it touched we could not see."[13] When the *Yamagumo* blew up, the explosion could be seen clearly from the top of the strait—and a few seconds later, a corresponding "pip" vanished from the radar scopes.

The gunners were locked on target and ready to open fire, but they held back in obedience to Oldendorf's prior instructions. First the northernmost destroyer group—Destroyer Squadron 56—must have its turn to strike the enemy. At 3:34 a.m., Oldendorf ordered them forward, to "get the big boys."[14]

This final destroyer attack was led by Captain Roland Smoot in the *Newcomb*. His Destroyer Squadron 56 destroyers were arrayed in three sections, with three *Fletcher*-class ships in each column—one to attack Nishimura's left flank, one his right, and one head-on. They tore down the strait at 25 knots. Mindful that Oldendorf's big guns were about to open fire, and that he had better have his destroyers out of the line of fire when they did, the commander of the middle column radioed: "This has to be quick. Stand by your torpedoes."[15] When the range had closed to 6,000 yards, each column turned their broadsides toward the enemy and launched torpedoes—five from each ship, forty-five altogether. Then they continued at peak speed toward the edges of the strait, blowing copious amounts of funnel smoke and racing to clear the field of fire.

The big guns around the northern horizon erupted just as the last of Smoot's torpedoes shot from their tubes and slapped down into the sea. The 6- and 8-inch guns of the right-flank cruisers were first, followed quickly

by the 14- and 16-inch main battery salvos of the battleships. Red tracers soared overhead in long, lazy arcs. The big projectiles seemed to hang
patiently in the air during their 12-mile journey toward their targets. Captain Smoot called it "the most beautiful sight I have ever witnessed. The
arched line of tracers in the darkness looked like a continual stream of
lighted railroad cars going over a hill."[16]

At 3:53 a.m., the *West Virginia*'s first salvo struck home. The gunnery
officer chuckled over the intercom and announced "hit first salvo." Captain
Herbert V. Wiley, studying the target through binoculars, saw the target
flare up as the second salvo landed.[17] Although he did not yet know it, the
target was the *Yamashiro*, Nishimura's flagship, which soon absorbed the
concentrated shellfire of at least a dozen American cruisers and battleships.
The *Denver*'s action report remarked: "Almost from the time of commence
firing at 0350 the enemy ships appeared to observers in this ship to be a
continual mass of flame and explosions."[18]

The *Yamashiro* advanced stubbornly into this maelstrom. For the next
seven minutes, all of the naval gunfire of the entire Allied fleet was concentrated upon this one ship. Vertical whitewater columns leapt up close
aboard to starboard and port. Her heavily armored deck shuddered under a
rain of armor-piercing shells. Wounded men were carried down to the wardroom and laid out on tables, but a direct hit obliterated the compartment
and killed everyone in it, including the medical staff. Even after all internal
communications were lost, and the turret gunners were cut off from the
bridge, they kept pumping salvos from her main and secondary batteries,
and splashes leapt up around the U.S. destroyers and cruisers on the right
flank.[19] Without fire control radar, the *Yamashiro*'s shooting was wilder than
that of her adversaries, but several shells fell uncomfortably close to the
Allied cruisers. One salvo landed wide of the Australian cruiser *Shropshire*,
a second landed closer, and a third went over and sent up big splashes on
the far side. Columns of water shot up around the *Phoenix* and the *Louisville*,
Oldendorf's flagship. The admiral ordered the line of cruisers to raise speed
for evasive maneuvering.

On the *Mogami*, following about a quarter of a mile behind the *Yamashiro*,
a crewman recalled that the shriek of incoming shells was "an awfully gruesome sound, which passed from left to right." As the first salvo straddled the
ship, "a towering wall of whitewater suddenly appeared in the darkness."[20]
Six- and 8-inch shells connected topside, disabling a gun turret and flood-

ing the engine rooms. The captain ordered a starboard turn to bring her broadside to bear on the enemy. The *Mogami* launched four torpedoes, aiming roughly at the muzzle flashes up the strait. They were set for a high-speed run, which would limit their range.

As she turned, the *Mogami's* main guns came to bear on three retreating American destroyers, the *Daly, Hutchins,* and *Bache.* She fired a broadside. The captain of the *Daly* watched in dismay as the red tracers reached out for his ship: the salvo looked to be on target. "It was definitely *on* in deflection, for it gave the sensation of standing in center field waiting for a fly ball which will land in one's glove," the skipper later remarked. "Fortunately this salvo passed overhead, landing from 200–300 yards over."[21]

The *Yamashiro* suffered two more torpedo hits on her starboard side, probably fired by the destroyers *Newcomb* and *Bennion.* That brought the total to four. She listed to port and her speed was cut to 6 knots. Fires raged along her length, and her pagoda blazed like a torch. But Nishimura and his chief officers survived, behind the armored steel of their bridge high in the superstructure. He told his chief of staff: "Report to the commander of the Main Body. We proceed to Leyte for *Gyokusai.*"[22]

The *Mogami* had continued through her starboard turn until she was southbound, headed away from the enemy guns. On the bridge, an argument broke out among the officers. Some wanted to continue down the strait, considering the battle as lost; others were resolved to fight to the end. The captain, won over by the firebrands, ordered the ship back into the fray. Before the turn could be executed, however, two 8-inch shells fired by the cruiser *Portland* ended the argument by scoring a direct hit on the *Mogami's* bridge. For a time the ship continued on course, no one at the helm and no one giving orders. Surviving members of the crew finally climbed the ladder and found the bridge a charnel house. This sudden decapitation left the ship's gunnery officer in command. The *Mogami,* continually pummeled by shellfire, was in no condition to fight. The new commanding officer resolved to head south in hopes of saving the ship.

The *Shigure,* having long since lost contact with the *Yamashiro,* was straddled by 6- and 8-inch shells. The repeated near-misses took a heavy toll on the lightly built ship; Commander Nishino said that the close detonations caused the hull to lurch out of the water by at least a meter. "I was receiving a terrific bombardment," he said. "There were so many near misses that the gyro compass was out. The ship was constantly trembling from force of

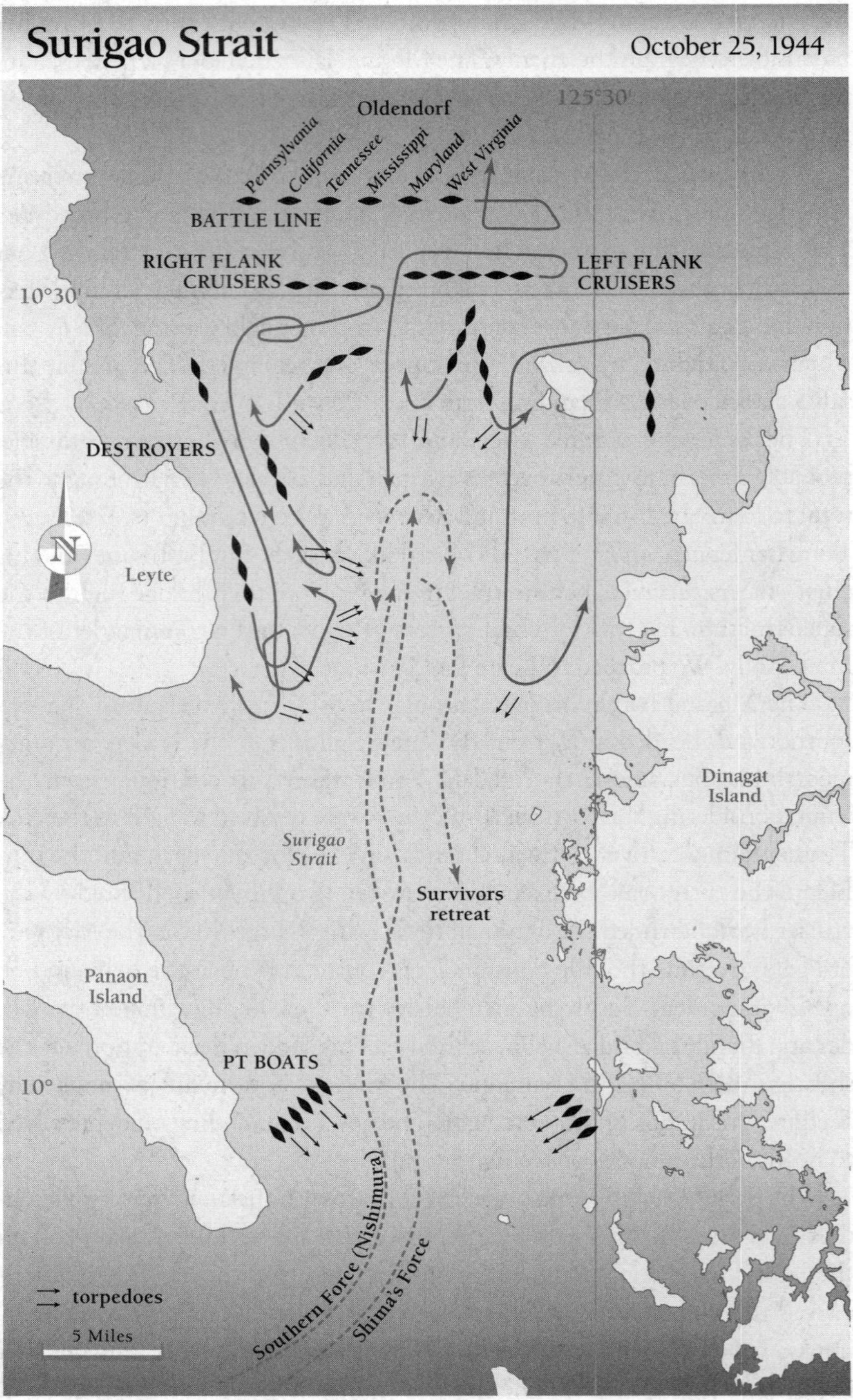

Surigao Strait

October 25, 1944

Oldendorf

Pennsylvania   California   Tennessee   Mississippi   Maryland   West Virginia

BATTLE LINE

125°30'

RIGHT FLANK
CRUISERS

LEFT FLANK
CRUISERS

10°30'

DESTROYERS

N

Leyte

Dinagat
Island

Surigao
Strait

Survivors
retreat

Panaon
Island

PT BOATS

10°

Southern Force (Nishimura)

Shima's Force

→→ torpedoes

5 Miles

near misses, and the wireless was out."[23] Without radio communications, Nishino could not know whether he was expected to press on or retreat. He turned east, hoping to get within signaling range of the *Yamashiro*, but saw no sign of her or the *Mogami*, and wondered whether they were still afloat. As on the *Mogami*, there was a mutinous outbreak of democracy among the ship's officers. Some believed the *Shigure* to be the last survivor of the Southern Force. The gunnery officer questioned whether it was their duty to "simply die a dog's death." At 3:15 a.m., Nishino judged that the *Yamashiro* and *Mogami* were probably gone, and so "I decided to withdraw without receiving orders from anyone."[24]

An American destroyer, the *Grant*, had failed to clear the field of fire and found herself taking heavy fire from two directions. The *Yamashiro*, firing from a range of about 3 miles, dropped shells all around her. But the most punishing fire was friendly, from the right-flank cruiser line. *Grant* was pulverized by about twenty hits, most probably fired by the cruiser *Denver*. Thirty-four of her crew were killed, ninety-four wounded. The commander of the right-flank cruisers, Admiral Russell S. Berkey, got on the circuit to warn that a destroyer lay dead in the water and was taking friendly fire. At 4:09 a.m., Oldendorf warned the entire force: "*Grant* is hit and lying dead in the water. All ships take special precaution."[25]

As the American fleet complied, the guns fell quiet, and the strait was suddenly eerily serene. The respite was extended when the American battleships turned north in order to avoid torpedoes fired by *Mogami*.

Notwithstanding Nishimura's brave pledge to keep charging the enemy, the crippled, burning *Yamashiro* turned south shortly after the Allied guns ceased fire. Perhaps he intended to fall in with Shima, perhaps to retreat to safety: no one can know, as neither he nor any other bridge officer survived to tell the tale. Somehow the engineers managed to bring the *Yamashiro*'s speed back up to 12 knots, but that only increased the inward press of water through the wounds in her hull. At 4:19 a.m. she began keeling over to port, and Nishimura's chief of staff ordered abandon ship. Then she rolled all the way onto her beam ends, and her great pagoda lay down on the sea. She sank quickly, stern first, taking all but a few of her crew down with her.

To the south, meanwhile, visibility had worsened. Rainsqualls swept through the Mindanao Sea and the lower part of the strait. Charging east through dirty weather at 25 knots, Shima's little fleet had nearly run aground on Panaon Island; it had turned sharply at the last possible moment, when the island's mountainous ridgeline had suddenly loomed out of the mist.[26] While Shima's squadron was making this emergency turn, PT-137 fired a torpedo at the destroyer *Ushio*. The weapon ran under its target but continued on and struck the deeper-draft cruiser *Abukuma*, 3,000 yards away. That was the only torpedo fired by a PT-boat to score in the battle. *Abukuma*, badly damaged, fell out of column and limped away at 10 knots.

Entering Surigao Strait, and steaming north through darkness at 28 knots, Shima's lookouts caught a distant glimpse of the sinking *Fuso*. Smoke added to rain and haze made for poor visibility, and Shima's men mistakenly thought they saw two burning battleships, not one. This may have been because the *Fuso*'s bow had been torn from the ship, and was still afloat; it is also possible that the lookouts had mistaken a large oil fire for a second ship. At any rate, the newcomers did not pause, but continued up Surigao Strait at high speed.

At 4:22 a.m., Shima's column turned right and began firing torpedoes. The missiles raced away at 49 knots. Just as the flagship *Nachi*'s torpedoes were away, her lookouts spotted the *Mogami*. To their eyes she appeared dead in the water, still burning; but as the range closed the bridge officers realized that the ship was underway on a fast-converging course. The *Nachi*'s captain ordered full reverse power, but it was too late to avoid the head-on collision. The *Mogami*'s steering room was flooded and her speed cut in half. The *Nachi* was also badly damaged, with her top effective speed cut to 19 knots. The *Nachi* turned south, the crew investigating the damage.

During this interval, the Fifth Fleet torpedo officer, Kokichi Mori, conferred with Shima on the *Nachi*'s bridge. Considering the damage to the ship, the near-annihilation of Nishimura's force, and the deteriorating visibility at sea level, Mori argued that it would be suicidal to keep advancing. A trap had been laid for them: "Admiral," he said, "up ahead the enemy must be waiting for us with open arms."[27] Shima, convinced, decided to call it a night. He radioed Toyoda: "This force has concluded its attack and is retiring from the battle area in order to plan subsequent action."[28] Samuel Eliot Morison called Shima's decision "the most intelligent act of any Japanese commander in the entire battle."[29]

At 5:00 a.m., with a pale gray dawn budding in the east, the surviving remnants of the two Japanese fleets limped down Surigao Strait. Leaving the battleships on station, Admiral Oldendorf led a group of cruisers and destroyers (including his flagship *Louisville*) south to pursue and "polish off enemy cripples."

Wary of blundering into a torpedo attack, Oldendorf held his speed to a cautious 15 knots. Visibility at sea level remained poor, hindered by squalls, mists, and persistent smoke from burning ships and floating oil fires. The sea was polluted by spilled bunker oil and littered with debris and floating bodies. Hundreds of Japanese sailors were seen among the flotsam, treading water or clutching wreckage. As usual, nearly all refused offers of rescue, even attempting to drown themselves when American ships approached. The pursuers came upon the floating wrecks of what they took to be four different Japanese ships in a sinking condition, but these vessels "could not be identified because of the heavy oil smoke and flames surrounding them."[30] Part of the *Fuso* remained afloat, possibly her bow: the passing *Louisville* fired several salvos at this remnant and apparently sank it.

At first, the damaged *Nachi*, *Mogami*, and *Shigure* managed enough speed to stay ahead of Oldendorf. Off Kanihaan Island, however, they were slowed by a swarm of pesky PT-boats. The *Mogami*, still afire and barely able to steer, traded blows with the little attackers. She scattered 8-inch shells around the boats and drove them off, and even scored a direct hit on PT-194, which destroyed three of the boat's engines and killed a 40mm gunner. Oldendorf's cruisers sighted the distant *Mogami* at 5:29 a.m. and opened fire at long range, scoring about ten hits. The captain of the *Columbia*, observing the target through binoculars, reported that she was "completely ablaze and burning worse than the *Arizona* burned at Pearl Harbor."[31] Admiral Shima took the hard-hearted decision to keep moving, leaving the *Mogami* behind to divert the American pursuers. The *Nachi*, the *Shigure*, and the rest of the Second Striking Force slipped away and rounded Panaon.

Incredibly, however, the *Mogami* refused to die even when left behind in this desperate condition. Her intrepid engine crew got her moving at 12 knots again, and she escaped to the Mindanao Sea.

The last Japanese ship left afloat in Surigao Strait was the crippled destroyer *Asagumo*, which had earlier been shorn of her bow by Coward's torpedoes. She lay dead in the water, her foredeck awash. One gun turret still had life in it, and fired gamely back at a swarm of PT-boats that attempted to sink her with torpedoes. The captain had ordered abandon ship sometime before 7:00 a.m., and the men were transferring into boats when the pursuing American ships came into range. *Asagumo* came under fire at 7:04 a.m., first by a destroyer, followed minutes later by many more cruisers and destroyers: in all, ten American ships participated in the final pummeling of the dying destroyer. Ripped open at the waterline, flames bursting from all of her hatches, the *Asagumo* rolled over and went down by the bow. Someone on her bridge radioed a valedictory report to Admirals Toyoda and Kurita: "I went down under attack."[32] By some accounts, her single operative turret kept firing even as the ship sank. James L. Holloway III, gunnery officer on the *Bennion*, saw the last of this plucky little warrior: "When we had closed to about 2,000 yards, the Japanese destroyer slid beneath the gray, choppy waters, bow first, her screws still slowly rotating as we passed close aboard."[33]

Carrier airstrikes would chase the fleeing ships, and the nine-lived *Mogami* would finally succumb to air attack later that afternoon. The *Shigure*, the only surviving unit of Admiral Nishimura's Southern Force, would reach Brunei on October 27. Aerial pursuit and mopping-up operations would continue in the days that followed, eventually chasing Shima all the way to Manila Bay, where his flagship *Nachi* would be sunk by air attack on November 5.

But Oldendorf's part of the battle was finished. At 7:25 a.m. on October 24, he received the first of several urgent distress calls summoning him north. The Seventh Fleet escort carriers, stationed north of Leyte Gulf, were under attack by a powerful Japanese surface fleet that had seemed to materialize out of nowhere.

SAN BERNARDINO STRAIT being a narrow and precarious passage, Kurita's Center Force was compelled to pass through it in single-column formation. Fearing a reprise of the devastating submarine attack in Palawan Passage, the 13-mile-long file of ships rushed through at a breakneck 20 knots. An 8-knot current was running, and the danger of grounding seemed high. But the night was clear, with visibility unimpeded—and as Halsey's night patrol planes had earlier noted, the channel buoys and lighthouses were illuminated. The fleet emerged intact, debouching into the Philippine Sea at half past midnight. Six hours behind schedule, its crew still had no word of Nishimura's fate.

Assuming that they were being tracked by radar, night reconnaissance planes, and Filipino coastwatchers along the shores of the strait, Kurita and his officers could hardly believe their good fortune. No enemy submarines had bothered them. They had expected to find the massed guns of U.S. battleships blocking their exit from the strait—the same sort of T-crossing ambush that had just walloped Nishimura 300 miles south. Operations officer Tonosuke Otani later said that such a scenario would have given the Center Force a "hard time," and the expectation caused "grave concern" on the bridge of the *Yamato*.[34] But here they were, safely through the strait, with nothing standing in their way.

For two hours the force ran east, straight out to sea. The single column re-formed into a night-search disposition, six columns covering a swath of ocean nearly 20 miles wide. The Japanese had no intelligence of Halsey's whereabouts; they were merely guessing at where they might find him, based on the headings the American carrier planes had flown the previous afternoon. At 3:00 a.m., the *Yamato* blinkered orders to alter course to the southeast, toward Leyte Gulf. For the next three hours the fleet charged south, keeping Samar's distant mountains broad on the starboard beam.[35]

At half past five, the *Yamato* received Admiral Shima's report that the *Yamashiro* and *Fuso* were gone, the *Mogami* was in flames, and all surviving Japanese forces were retiring from Surigao Strait. The dismal news could not have come as a great surprise, but it confirmed that the envisioned pincer attack would not come off. If the Center Force managed to push through to Leyte Gulf, it would do so alone. At 6:14 a.m., the new day broke with a characteristically vivid tropical sunrise. The northeasterly wind was gentle and the sea was docile, but a gray ceiling of broken cumulus drifted overhead, and dark rainsqualls swept low over the sea.

Standing between Kurita and his objective were the escort carrier groups of the Seventh Fleet. This force amounted to sixteen small flattops with twenty-two destroyers and destroyer escorts (DEs) as screen. Together they were designated Task Group 77.4, under the command of Rear Admiral Thomas L. Sprague. The group was subdivided into three task units, "Taffy 1," "Taffy 2," and "Taffy 3." The northernmost unit, Taffy 3, was led by Rear Admiral Clifton A. F. ("Ziggy") Sprague.

The two Spragues were not related. By an improbable fluke, these two Naval Academy classmates (class of 1917), who shared a relatively uncommon surname but not a bloodline, had landed together as rear admirals in the same little section of the Seventh Fleet.

The escort carriers, "CVEs," were small auxiliaries sometimes known by their nicknames, "jeep carriers" or "baby flattops." They were about one-half the length and one-third the weight of the *Essex*-class fleet carriers. They were 500 feet long, displaced about 10,000 tons, and carried just twenty-five to thirty aircraft. Their greatest virtue, from the navy's point of view, was that they could be built and launched quickly and cheaply. They were deployed in limited roles: to provide air cover for merchant convoys and transport fleets, to support amphibious landings, and to ferry replacement aircraft across the Pacific. They were too slow to keep company with the big fighting carriers of Task Force 38: most could do no better than 18 knots. They were considered too frail to stand up to a concerted air or submarine attack, because their thin steel skin was too easily pierced by bombs or torpedoes. The crews joked that "CVE" stood for "combustible, vulnerable, and expendable," and their mordant appraisal was accurate on all three counts.

The first CVEs had been improvised by throwing a flight deck over the hull of a cargo ship or oil tanker, but a subsequent generation was purpose-built by Henry Kaiser in his Vancouver, Washington shipyard. The Kaiser-built units (hull numbers 55 through 104) were disparaged as "Kaiser's coffins." Of the sixteen escort carriers in Task Group 77.4, thirteen had been built by Kaiser.

Thus far, the Leyte operation had been fairly uneventful for the Taffy units. The ships had been on station off Samar and Leyte for nearly a week. The air groups had been busy flying combat air patrol over the transport fleet and reconnaissance flights over the central Philippines, and attacking ground targets on the beach. But the ship's crews had barely seen any enemy airplanes. There had been a few submarine scares, but no sign of Japanese warships. The destroyers had faithfully executed their screening functions, hunting the perimeter for submarine intruders and lifeguarding downed aviators. The Taffy units had not expected to participate in the sea fights raging to the south, the east, and (prospectively) the north. So it came as a rude surprise when the pagoda masts of Kurita's giant battleships and cruisers first peeked over the northwest horizon, shortly before seven o'clock that morning.

The first hints of the intruders' presence had arrived half an hour earlier, when Taffy 3's antisubmarine patrol planes had catapulted from the flight decks. Japanese voices were overheard on a short-range low-power radio channel. The nearest enemy ships were thought to be more than 150 miles away, but the transmissions could have originated on an island of the nearby Philippines. An unidentified SG radar contact seemed to reveal something approaching from the north, but the blips had not resolved into anything resembling a fleet. It could be a portion of Halsey's force, or perhaps just a weather front. At 6:46 a.m., lookouts in Taffy 3 sighted distant antiaircraft bursts over the northwest horizon. That was definitely strange, and Ziggy Sprague was about to tell his orbiting planes to investigate when a pilot radioed: "Enemy surface force . . . 20 miles northwest of your task group and closing at twenty knots."

Assuming that "some screwy young aviator" had foolishly misidentified elements of the Third Fleet, Admiral Sprague was irritated. He shouted into the squawk box, "Air Plot, tell him to check his identification."

The reply came back a minute later. "Identification of enemy force confirmed," said the pilot. "Ships have pagoda masts."[36]

Sprague and his officers scanned the northwest horizon with disbelieving eyes. More flak bursts mottled the sky. The dark shapes of Japanese topmasts emerged above the horizon. The nearest pursuers were 17 miles away and bearing down quickly.

On the *Franks*, a destroyer in the nearby Taffy 2 screening group, breakfast was interrupted by a hair-raising call to general quarters. "We ran to the battle stations," recalled sailor Michael Bak Jr. "I ran to the bridge and looked out, and I saw what looked like toothpicks on the horizon, right across the horizon—many, many ships."[37]

Blindsided by the sudden emergency, Sprague reacted quickly. He broadcast a contact report and called for air support from the neighboring Taffy groups. He turned his carriers east, into the wind, and ordered them to work up to maximum speed. All airplanes spotted on the flight decks were launched immediately, even if they were not armed with antiship ordnance. The destroyers were told to zigzag astern of the fleeing CVEs while laying down the heaviest smoke screen they could manage. The carriers, too, were instructed to blow as much smoke as possible from their stacks, and to deploy chemical vapor units ordinarily employed by aircraft.

The Japanese were almost as surprised as the Americans. Lookouts caught sight of Taffy 3 only minutes before they were sighted in turn, at about the maximum distance permitted by the curvature of the earth. Even before the Americans began laying smoke screens, visibility was less than ideal. The sky was overcast, with gray mists at sea level. The strange ships were hull-down in the southeast, and at first it was not obvious that they were aircraft carriers. Some on the bridge of the *Yamato* even said that they must be Japanese ships. Had they found Admiral Ozawa's Northern Force? Soon the masts of the second escort carrier group, Taffy 2, peeked over the ocean rim to the south. As the range closed, lookouts saw planes launching, and the rectangular profiles of the CVEs rose above the horizon. They *were* carriers, and not Ozawa's. But what sort of carriers? The Japanese did not know that the U.S. Navy had deployed a large force of small auxiliary aircraft carriers in the Pacific. The officers on the *Yamato*'s bridge concluded that they must have stumbled upon part of Task Force 38.

In any case, victory seemed within their grasp. "This was indeed a miracle," said Tomiji Koyanagi, Kurita's chief of staff. "Think of a surface fleet coming up on an enemy carrier group! We moved to take advantage of this heaven-sent opportunity."[38] Their prime objective was to overtake and destroy the American flight decks before they could launch planes to attack their pursuers. The tactical circumstances called for making an all-out chase—and also, if possible, maneuvering to windward of the quarry so that they could not conduct flight operations while running away. Kurita ordered "General pursuit," which meant that each Japanese ship was to give chase at its best individual speed, not bothering to remain in fleet cruising formation. At 6:59 a.m., he ordered, "Ready for surface battle."[39] In deference to custom and tradition, the other ships waited for the flagship to fire the first salvo. The *Yamato*'s 6-inch secondary batteries spoke first, followed quickly by her two forward 18-inch main battery turrets.

At that great range, the long barrels of the *Yamato*'s mammoth main guns were trained forward and elevated to 23 degrees. Propelled by six great jets of flame and smoke, six armor-piercing projectiles spun out of the muzzles and began climbing toward the distant target. Each shell weighed 3,200 pounds. After twenty-five seconds of flight, midway to impact, the shells reached the apex of their trajectories, about 20,000 feet above sea level. Then they began descending at a terminal velocity of about 1,500 feet per second— significantly less than initial muzzle velocity, but still much faster than the speed of sound. From the American point of view, therefore, no whining or whistling announced the incoming salvo. They did not learn that they were under fire until six whitewater towers suddenly erupted off the starboard beam of the carrier *White Plains*. Each matched the height of a twenty-story building. The towers dissolved only gradually, as cataracts of spray fell away to leeward; half a minute after impact, six ghost-columns of vapor still hovered over the spots where the monstrous shells had struck.

No ship in Taffy 3 was armed with weapons greater than 5-inch caliber, so the Americans could not return fire at this range: they could only run for their lives. But they could not run especially fast. Even with all boilers on the line, some of the CVEs in the group could barely make 17 knots. Sprague later admitted, "I didn't think we'd last fifteen minutes."[40]

The *Yamato*'s second salvo, fired less than a minute after the first, bracketed the *White Plains* with a close straddle. The baby flattop vanished momentarily behind a wall of spray. She surged ahead, seemingly intact, but the *Yamato*'s near-misses sent destructive shock waves through the lightly constructed ship. Rivets tore loose, welds ripped open, electric power cut out, interior lighting was doused, radio transmitters and receivers were disabled, radar screens flickered out, and a table on the bridge fell over when one of its legs buckled.

As sheets of spray fell across the *White Plains*'s flight deck, the *Yamato*'s third salvo arrived. The six-shell pattern fell "microscopically close," according to Captain Dennis J. Sullivan, who added: "The vessel was shaken and twisted violently, throwing personnel in some parts of the ship from their feet and much gear to the deck from normal horizontal storage."[41] One of the shells burrowed into the sea and detonated beneath the ship, on the port side near the keel. According to the after-action report, "The ship twisted and lifted, crushing and tearing expansion joints at frame 101 and 146 port and starboard."[42] The shock of the blast tore hull plates asunder beneath the waterline, cut the steering control leads, warped interior decks and bulkheads, and sprung oil and aviation gasoline leaks throughout the ship. On the flight deck, a Wildcat preparing to launch jumped its wheel chalks and lurched forward, where its propeller took a bite out of the wing of the next aircraft ahead. Two of the ships' four boilers suffered a sudden reduction in steam pressure. If the submerged projectile had exploded a few feet aft, it might have flooded the engineering spaces and left the *White Plains* dead in the water, in which case the ship would have been left to the mercy of the fast-approaching enemy.

The Type 1 armor-piercing projectile fired by the *Yamato* had been purposely designed to dive under a ship, if it landed in the sea short of the target. This round had functioned as intended, maintaining a linear underwater trajectory and detonating 0.4 seconds after surface impact. Though it did not make physical contact with the ship, its blast force was directed upward into the vulnerable part of the hull. In this respect, the Type 1 projectile had behaved like a mine or an American torpedo fused with a magnetic detonator, designed to trigger the warhead when the weapon was directly beneath the ship. In his meticulous analysis of the Battle off Samar, *The World Wonder'd* (2014), Robert Lundgren proposes that the *Yamato*'s third salvo should be credited as a hit on the *White Plains*.[43] If the claim is accepted, the *Yamato* holds the singular honor of scoring the longest-ranged naval gunfire hit in history—34,587 yards, or nearly 20 miles.

Edward J. Huxtable, air commander on the *Gambier Bay*, was eating breakfast in the wardroom with fellow aviators when the shattering alarm for general quarters blared from the loudspeakers. He dashed up to the flight deck, ignorant of the sudden developments. His aircraft, a TBM Avenger, had not yet been armed with either bombs or torpedoes, but the plane captain seemed eager to launch him anyway. Huxtable was perplexed as he slid into his cockpit, wondering why he would be sent aloft in a disarmed plane. Suddenly, "I heard what seemed to be a rifle shot next to my left ear. I looked and saw a salvo of heavy caliber stuff splashing alongside the *White Plains*. Until that instant I had no idea the enemy was so near. I was more than ready to get on that catapult!"[44]

Huxtable catapulted and climbed, followed by several more Avengers. They zoomed through a layer of gray overcast at 1,200 feet. Admiral Sprague came onto the circuit and told them: "Attack immediately." Visibility from the air was very poor, and Huxtable could barely make out the enemy fleet through the lowering gloom. He noted that four Japanese cruisers were closing in on Taffy 3's port quarter, and resolved to make strafing runs in hopes of slowing their pursuit. Huxtable flew low along the axis of their advance, passing over each ship in turn. Flak bursts rocked his plane, but he kept his finger depressed on the trigger and poured a stream of .50-caliber tracer fire onto the enemy decks. Then he banked around for another low-altitude run, this time opening his Grumman's long, narrow bomb bay doors. He had no torpedo in the bay, but the Japanese would see the open doors; perhaps they could be tricked by a simulated torpedo attack into taking evasive maneuvers that would buy time for the fleeing carriers.[45]

Dozens of other airmen had similar ideas. Aircraft of many squadrons orbited the Japanese fleet and dove through the overcast to strafe, bomb, or torpedo Kurita's fleet, or to pretend to strafe, bomb, or torpedo it with unarmed "dummy runs." Antisubmarine and combat air patrol aircraft of the *St. Lo*, *Fanshaw Bay*, and *Kitkun Bay* made effective attacks in the early stage of the action, scoring topside hits or damaging near-misses on the battleship *Kongo* and the heavy cruisers *Haguro*, *Chokai*, and *Chikuma*. Antiaircraft fire was heavy, and many U.S. planes were damaged by flak bursts. Few were taken down by antiaircraft fire, however, and one Japanese skipper lamented that his gun crews would have done no worse if they had been "shooting blanks."[46] At 7:27, the heavy cruiser *Suzuya* came under simultaneous bombing attack by a swarm of TBMs: one bomb landed just off the port quarter, and the resulting blast wrenched the port outer propeller shaft out of alignment. The *Suzuya*'s top speed was cut to 20 knots; she dropped behind and gave up the chase.

A few airplanes recovered on Taffy 3 carriers early in the morning's action, when they were steaming directly into the easterly breeze. At 7:15 a.m., however, Sprague turned south to seek cover in a passing rainsquall. That shut down air operations on the Taffy 3 flight decks. The sister carriers of Taffy 1 and 2, farther south, took up part of the load, and some airborne planes headed over to nearby Tacloban airfield on Leyte to refuel and rearm. More American aircraft converged on the Japanese fleet, often without suitable ordnance, and did their best to bluff the enemy into turning away from the escaping carriers.

Visibility was compromised by wet weather. Periodically the sun broke through the clouds and shone down on the battle, but more often the sea horizon was obscured by low-lying clouds, squalls of rain, and a copious mass of black funnel smoke and pale yellow chemical smoke laid down by the destroyers zigzagging across the sterns of the jeep carriers. The sea was a gloomy, gunmetal gray, with a mild chop flecked by whitecaps. The Japanese lookouts persistently overestimated the size of the enemy ships, mistaking the destroyers for cruisers and the CVEs for *Essex*-class carriers. It was a deadly game of cat and mouse, with the prey appearing momentarily and then vanishing into smoke and haze. Firing windows were fleeting, and the Japanese gunners rarely saw the fall of their shots, so they could not make targeting corrections in consecutive salvos.

American destroyers, trailing astern of the carriers and laying smoke, took heavy fire from the Japanese battleships and cruisers. Dye-tinted splashes made a kaleidoscope of colors: yellow, red, blue, pink, and green. A sailor shouted, "They're shooting at us in technicolor!"[47] The destroyer

Johnston, laying smoke across a half-mile-wide front, found herself in the precarious rearguard position. She was nearer to the enemy than any other American warship, and therefore came in for special attention from the enemy gunners. She was straddled repeatedly by 14-inch and 8-inch salvos. "The red, green, purple and yellow colors might have been pretty under different circumstances," said Bob Hagen, the *Johnston*'s gunnery officer, "but at this moment I didn't like the color scheme."[48] When a right-side formation of Japanese cruisers closed to within 18,000 yards, the *Johnston* returned fire with her 5-inch main batteries.

At 7:16 a.m., Sprague ordered his destroyers and destroyer escorts to turn back toward the enemy and launch a torpedo counterattack in hopes of breaking up the pursuit. The *Johnston*'s skipper, Commander Ernest E. Evans, had begun preparations for such an attack even before receiving the order. "Stand by for a torpedo attack," he ordered: "Left full rudder." The 2,700-ton *Fletcher*-class destroyer turned back and began a lone frontal charge against the pursuing battleships and cruisers.

Born and raised in Pawnee, Oklahoma, Evans was three-quarters Native American. His mother was a full-blooded Cherokee, his father one-half Creek. He had first entered the navy in 1926 as an eighteen-year-old enlisted man, but won an appointment to the Naval Academy the following year and graduated with the class of 1931. Most of his fourteen years of service had been aboard destroyers. Evans was not the type of officer who had been marked for promotion into the navy's upper ranks; he was considered a steady and dependable performer. Like every other man in Taffy 3, he had not begun the day expecting to wage a life-and-death struggle against an overpowering enemy fleet at cannon shot range. But here he was, and here was the *Johnston*. "I can see him now," Hagen recalled, "short, barrel-chested, standing on the bridge with his hands on his hips, giving out with a running fire of orders in a bull voice."[49]

The little two-funneled ship heeled radically as she turned toward the enemy, then surged ahead like a greyhound. She was making flank speed, more than 30 knots. Multicolored splashes rose around her, and Evans ordered steering adjustments to "chase salvos"—that is, to steer toward each falling shot in order to evade the gunners' targeting corrections. The 5-inch turrets fired back, throwing out more than two hundred rounds, and began scoring hits as the range closed. At 7:20, when the *Johnston* was 9,000 yards from the leading Japanese cruiser, the *Kumano*, she let go of a ten-torpedo spread. The weapons were set to low speed to give them range, with a spread of one degree between them. They fanned out as they sped toward the enemy, all running "hot, straight, and normal." Then Evans ordered a sharp turn to starboard, and the ship heeled far to port as she came around, vanishing into the protective cover of her own smokescreen. The crew could not see the results, being obscured in smoke; much later the survivors would learn that one of their torpedoes struck the *Kumano* head-on and gouged a terrific hole in her bow, forcing her to drop out of formation. The *Kumano* limped away to the north, licking her wounds: she would play no further part in the battle.

For the next few minutes the *Johnston* withdrew to the east, safely veiled behind her own smokescreen. When she emerged briefly, at 7:25, gunners on the *Yamato* let fly with salvos from the superbattleship's main and secondary batteries. The range was 20,313 yards, much closer than the earlier salvo that had struck "microscopically close" to the *White Plains*. This time the *Yamato*'s gunners did not miss: three 18-inch projectiles struck the *Johnston*'s port main deck amidships. "It was like a puppy being smacked by a truck," recalled Bob Hagen.[*] The massive blasts pushed the little ship over to starboard, penetrated down into the lower decks, and gutted the portside engine room. A boiler in the after fireroom ruptured, filling the compartment with superheated steam and scalding several men to death.

Seconds later, a salvo fired by the *Yamato*'s six-inch secondary guns hit the *Johnston*'s forward stack and the port side of her bridge, where the ship's senior officers were lifted off their feet and hurled against bulkheads. Hagen's helmet, telephone, and binoculars were blown off his head and neck. The stool he was sitting on broke and he was thrown to the deck, injuring his knee. The gunnery officer was fortunate, however: two other men stationed nearby were killed outright, and two more eviscerated by shrapnel. Commander Evans, knocked to the deck a few feet away from Hagen, was suddenly bare-chested—his uniform khaki shirt had been torn from his body

---

[*] Hagen believed his ship was hit by a 14-inch salvo fired by a *Kongo*-class battleship. Most accounts have endorsed this view, crediting the *Kongo*. Based on his analysis of Japanese action reports, and the *Yamato*'s log entry at 0725 claiming a fatal hit on a cruiser, Robert Lundgren builds a persuasive case that the *Yamato* fired the salvo. (Lundgren, *The World Wonder'd*, pp. 69–74.) In 1944, the Americans did not know that the *Yamato* mounted 18-inch guns, or even that such weapons existed. If Hagen had known, he might have concluded that the puppy had been hit by a train instead of a truck.

by the shock of the blasts. The skipper's hair was singed, his face blackened and bleeding, and he was missing two fingers on his left hand. In that condition he rose to his feet and continued bellowing orders as if nothing had happened. He wrapped a handkerchief around the stumps of his severed fingers. When the doctor approached, Evans declined medical attention, saying, "Don't bother me now."[50]

At this point it looked bad for the *Johnston* and for the rest of Taffy 3. But a timely rainsquall was sweeping in from the east, and it suddenly enveloped the ship. Admiral (Ziggy) Sprague had been running directly toward it, so his six baby flattops were likewise shrouded from view just as a column of fast Japanese cruisers closed on their port quarter. That provided a providential respite from the enemy's alarmingly accurate naval gunfire. Visibility in the squall fell to a few hundred feet, but the Japanese continued firing nonetheless, and American crewmen noted the familiar tightly grouped colorful geysers erupting from the sea in their midst. The *Johnston* fired back at the unseen adversaries, using only modified radar control—and although the gunners could not visually confirm that they were hitting their targets, several Japanese cruisers were struck by 5-inch fire during this interval.

Sprague did not like his chances. The squall would pass over quickly, exposing his ships to view again. The enemy cruisers and battleships could make peak speeds over 25 knots; his CVEs could barely reach 17 knots. While hidden from the enemy's view, Sprague altered course to the southwest. He hoped to draw his pursuers south, toward Leyte Gulf and the big guns of Oldendorf's force. He also reasoned that if he lured the enemy fleet farther from San Bernardino Strait, it was less likely to escape a counterattack by other Allied air and naval forces. As for Taffy 3, "there appeared only one possible outcome of the encounter—complete annihilation."[51]

HALSEY'S SIXTY-FIVE-SHIP ARMADA HAD CHARGED north through the night, intending to ambush Ozawa at dawn. Tactical command was passed back to Mitscher, who kept the three carrier groups on slightly different headings and speeds, so that they would arrive at optimum launch points at first light. All carriers were instructed to arm and fuel up their strike planes and spot them on deck; they would launch right after the first F6Fs of the combat air patrol, whether or not the enemy's position had been pinpointed. Task

Force 34 was formed under Ching Lee and sent to the vanguard of the three carrier groups, about 10 miles ahead. As the first faint glow of dawn rose in the east, airplanes began roaring off the decks and climbing into the sky. Heavily reinforced searches departed the fleet on diverging headings to the north and east. The attack groups, dive-bombers, and torpedo bombers with Hellcat escorts were ordered to circle about 50 miles north of the American fleet, awaiting clarity on the enemy's exact whereabouts.

Aboard the *Wasatch*, 300 miles to the south, Admiral Kinkaid and his officers were celebrating Oldendorf's knockout victory down in Surigao Strait, and debating how aggressively to pursue the retreating remnants of the Southern Force. An operations officer reminded Kinkaid that they had not yet received explicit confirmation that Halsey had left his heavy ships behind to guard San Bernardino Strait. It seemed prudent to ask for confirmation. At 4:12 a.m., therefore, Kinkaid queried Halsey directly: "Question. Is TF 34 guarding San Bernardino Strait?"[52]

Given the scale of operations underway throughout the region, the navy's radio communications net was badly congested. Kinkaid's dispatch did not reach the *New Jersey* until 6:48, more than two-and-a-half hours after it was sent. It flummoxed Halsey, who called it his "first intimation that Kinkaid had intercepted and misconstrued the preparatory dispatch I had sent to my fleet the preceding day."[53] He replied in the negative, reporting that Task Force 34 was far to the north with the Third Fleet carriers off Cape Engano, hunting the Japanese carrier force.

The search planes did not take long to find Ozawa's fleet. One division of the *Essex* combat air patrol was sent on an impromptu reconnaissance flight to the northeast, where they found the enemy flattops a few minutes after Halsey had received Kinkaid's message. They were 130 miles away, on a true bearing of 15 degrees from Task Force 38. Ozawa was northbound, apparently running away. But this would be no reprise of the Marianas Turkey Shoot four months earlier: now the Americans held the high cards. The distance was manageable; visibility was clear; and a fresh breeze was blowing about 45 degrees off their starboard bows, which meant that they could launch and recover planes while closing the range on the enemy. The initial strike planes were already airborne, circling north of the American fleet, so they had only a short distance to fly.[54]

A pitifully small number of fighters rose to defend the Japanese fleet against the waves of incoming planes, and all were quickly massacred. For the rest of the day, Ozawa had no fighters in the air at all. The attackers took their time, circling over the enemy fleet like vultures, safely above the reach of Japanese antiaircraft guns. Designated strike coordinators remained at altitude, organizing and directing the attacks, and ensuring that they did not fall disproportionately on only the largest ships. In all, the U.S. carriers launched 527 sorties against Ozawa's ships throughout the course of the day.

Lieutenant Edwin John Weil, flying a Curtiss SB2C from the carrier *Franklin*, dove on the light carrier *Zuiho*. Pushing over at 14,000 feet, he descended through "unbelievable" antiaircraft fire, the hands on his altimeter spinning counterclockwise, and fought the stick to keep the flight deck's red disk in the center of his bombsight. He dropped his bomb from 600 feet above the target, well below standard release altitude. As he pulled out of the dive, his rear gunner shouted over the intercom, confirming a direct hit. The Curtiss dropped to low altitude, 100 feet above the sea. Jinking his airplane, flak bursting all around him, Weil flew directly alongside a heavy warship, noting that "its pagoda masks and varieties of firepower were awesome."[55]

The antiaircraft fire thrown up by Ozawa's fleet was the most intense the American pilots had ever seen. Bill Davis, flying a Hellcat from the *Lexington*, dove through a storm of flak so dense that he could not see the sea beneath him. "At 10,000 feet there was a black cloud of bursting shells from the 40mm and 5-inch guns . . . a second deadly cloud was forming at 4,000 feet from the exploding 20mm shells."[56] Knowing that velocity was his friend, Davis firewalled the throttle. Pulling out of the dive, he estimated that he was flying more than 500 miles per hour, significantly faster than Grumman's recommended maximum. He was low over the sea, and a Japanese heavy cruiser loomed ahead. Rapidly it grew larger in his windshield; he did not have time to turn away. Davis pulled up and banked hard to the right, passing between the superstructure and the forward gun turret. "I was perhaps three feet from the windows on the bridge and could see the Japanese officers and enlisted men commanding the ship," he said. "There was an admiral in dress whites, complete with sword. The other officers and men were also in dress whites. I was going 530 miles an hour, and I only got a glimpse, but that image is impressed on my mind forever."[57]

The first wave of attackers scored against the *Chitose*, *Chiyoda*, *Zuiho*, and *Zuikaku*. The *Zuikaku*, Ozawa's flagship, was the sole surviving aircraft carrier of the six that had hit Pearl Harbor in 1941, and the Americans

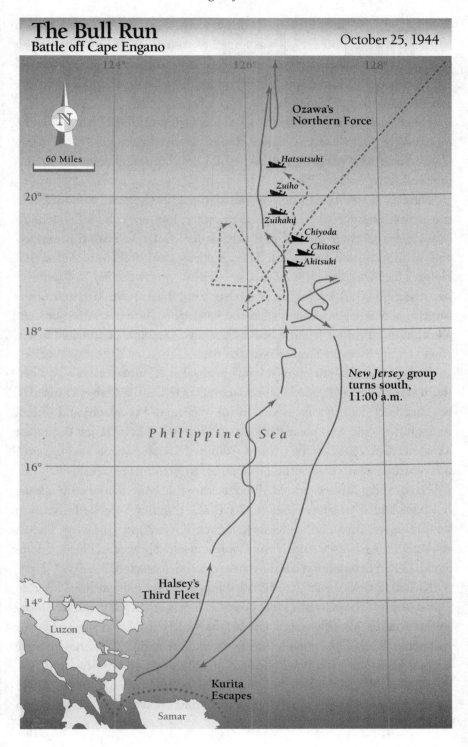

The Bull Run
Battle off Cape Engano

October 25, 1944

N

60 Miles

Ozawa's
Northern Force

Hatsutsuki

Zuiho

Zuikaku

Chiyoda

Chitose

Akitsuki

New Jersey group
turns south,
11:00 a.m.

Philippine Sea

Halsey's
Third Fleet

Luzon

Kurita
Escapes

Samar

were especially determined to send her to the bottom. She was crippled by the first wave, and Ozawa was forced to transfer his flag to the cruiser *Oyodo*.[58] The *Chitose* was pulverized by three torpedo hits and several 1,000-lb bomb hits; she was left burning out of control and dead in the water, and sank at 9:37 a.m.[59]

Halsey did not learn of the situation off Samar until 8:22 a.m., when he received the first of several urgent dispatches from Kinkaid: "CTU 77.4.3 [Ziggy Sprague] reports enemy battleships and cruiser 15 miles astern his unit and firing on him."[60]

Halsey later wrote that he was "not alarmed" by the news, assuming that the escort carriers could hold the enemy at bay long enough for Oldendorf's heavy ships to come up and join the battle.[61] But that has an unmistakable whiff of false bravado. Intelligence officer Carl Solberg recorded that Halsey's face was "ashen," and that he seemed "pretty dashed."[62] Whatever he thought of Taffy 3's chances, Halsey must have realized that Kurita's surprise appearance cast doubt on the wisdom of his earlier decisions. At a minimum, it meant that he had exaggerated the damage inflicted by his planes in the Sibuyan Sea the previous day.

Eight minutes later came Kinkaid's next salvo, a blunt demand: "Fast battleships are urgently needed immediately at Leyte Gulf."[63] Halsey claimed to be "surprised" by this suggestion. In his reading of his operational orders, it was not his job to protect Kinkaid's fleet; it was Kinkaid's job to protect Kinkaid's fleet. However, he radioed Admiral McCain, whose Task Group 1 was refueling at sea east of the Philippines, to "strike as practicable."[64]

Ziggy Sprague now butted directly into the conversation, by adding "COM3RDFLT" (Halsey) and "CINCPAC" (Nimitz) as coaddressees on several urgent dispatches to Kinkaid.[65] Strictly speaking, this was a breach of protocol, as Halsey and Nimitz were outside Sprague's chain of command. Given extenuating circumstances, no one objected.

Kinkaid's next dispatch reached the *New Jersey* half an hour later, at 9:00 a.m. Now the Seventh Fleet boss was repeating himself, but in a more agitated tone: "My situation is critical. Fast battleships and support by air strike may be able [to] prevent enemy from destroying CVEs and entering Leyte."[66] But Halsey believed he had already done all that he could do. He radioed McCain again, this time ordering him to make best possible speed to intercept Kurita. Then he let Kinkaid know that McCain was on the way.[67]

Twenty-two minutes later, a message from Kinkaid reported that the enemy fleet "evidently came through San Bernardino during the night. Request immediate air strike. Also request support from heavy ships. My old battleships low in ammunition."[68]

This last bit of information was a new factor, said Halsey, "so astonishing that I could hardly accept it." He wondered why Kinkaid had not told him earlier. Then he read the time-date stamps, and realized that he had been receiving Kinkaid's dispatches out of order. The last message was the third to be sent by Kinkaid, but the sixth received. It had been sent almost two hours earlier, at 7:25 a.m. During that two-hour interval, the *New Jersey* had traveled about 40 miles farther from the scene of action off Samar. The overloaded radio net was playing havoc with communications between the two fleets. A coding officer later explained that all messages were transmitted on the "Fox broadcast schedule" based on Oahu, and a spike in volume "imposed a terrific burden on that schedule because it was transmitted at a fairly low rate of words per minute, because all of the ships in the fleet were expected to copy most of the messages, or at least be able to copy them."[69] Various originators, frustrated by backed-up radio circuits, had resorted to sending ordinary communications with "high priority" designations. This practice tended to spread like a contagion, inevitably slowing the pace of genuinely urgent radio traffic.

Halsey replied: "Am now engaging enemy carrier force. TG 38.1 with 5 carriers and 4 cruisers has been ordered to assist you immediately."[70] He added his Lat-Long position, which showed that the issue was moot. The Third Fleet was almost 400 miles away, too far north to help the Seventh Fleet even if Halsey had wanted to do so.

Several of Kinkaid's prior messages had been sent "in the clear"—that is, in plain language, without encryption. That laid them bare for the enemy to intercept, but it also tended to hurry them through the coding rooms and reach their recipients faster. In this instance, the transmissions were delayed nonetheless, but Kinkaid told a colleague that he had radioed in plain language for another reason—"to give it an electrifying effect, which it certainly did have."[71]

In the eyes of at least one subordinate on the *New Jersey*'s bridge, Halsey's famous bravado appeared to be waning. The admiral sat alone on a leather transom, brooding silently. He was overheard to mutter, "When I get my teeth into something, I hate to let go."[72]

The dialogue between Kinkaid and Halsey was being monitored in real time at military headquarters throughout the Pacific, and even on the U.S. mainland. Admirals King and Nimitz were copied as "information address-ees" on several messages in the thread. Even when they were not, they were generally privy to all transmissions, because their communications depart-ments eavesdropped on the radio net. Enlisted men plotted each updated Lat-Long position on charts laid out on tables, allowing the admirals to visualize the locations of various fleet elements. In Pearl Harbor and Wash-ington, therefore, Halsey's only two direct superiors were paying close atten-tion to the unfolding drama, and rendering spot judgments upon his every move. Neither was pleased.

Jocko Clark, the once and future carrier task group commander, was visiting the Navy Department on Constitution Avenue in Washington. Stepping into Admiral King's office, he found the CNO in a towering fury. King was pacing the floor "like a tiger," and cursing Halsey for leaving San Bernardino Strait unguarded. "I've never seen Ernie King madder in my whole life," Clark recalled, "and I've seen him mad a good many times, and I've seen him awfully mad, but this was one that was for the storybooks. He was pacing up and down and the air was blue with what he had to say about Halsey."[73]

At Pacific Fleet headquarters in Hawaii, meanwhile, Nimitz was pacing the floor of *his* office. That was strange, said Bernard Austin, the assistant chief of staff, because "Admiral Nimitz was not one to pace the floor. He faced many problems calmly and without any outward manifestation of the difficulties that he was having mentally coping with the situation. But on this occasion, he was pacing up and down. So I knew that this was an index of a very high order of perturbation on the part of the Fleet Admiral."[74]

Nimitz would later say that he spent most of this period on the horse-shoe court behind his house on Makalapa Hill. "I was on pins and needles, but couldn't show it. So I went to my quarters to pitch horseshoes, telling my staff, 'if word comes, you can reach me there.' Most of the dispatches from that great battle in which the Japanese fleet was destroyed reached me on the horseshoe court."[75] That was undoubtedly true, but according to several staff officers, Nimitz was in his headquarters during the critical hours of Halsey's run north to Cape Engano. He repeatedly pressed a buzzer to summon Austin into his office, each time asking whether any incoming radio dispatches indicated whether Halsey had left his heavy ships guarding San Bernardino Strait. Austin combed through the dispatches, finding nothing to shed light on the question. He suggested that Admiral Nimitz simply ask for confirmation that the strait was guarded. Nimitz refused, avowing that "he did not wish to send any dispatch which would directly or indirectly influence the responsible tactical commander in the tactical use of his forces."[76]

Several other senior staff officers were in and out of Nimitz's office during this interval, including Forrest Sherman and Truman Hedding. When Kinkaid reported that Taffy 3 was under fire, they raised the question again. Should Nimitz ask for the location of Task Force 34?

It was a sensitive question. Nearly three years into the war, Nimitz had never inserted himself into a battle by demanding information or prodding a fleet commander to act. Often he had been tempted to do it, or was lobbied to do it by members of his staff—during the Battle of the Coral Sea, the Battle of Midway, several of the naval battles around Guadalcanal in late 1942, and most recently at the Battle of the Philippine Sea the previous June. In each instance, Nimitz had refrained from needling his fleet commanders, preferring to trust their tactical judgment.

Pearl Harbor had not copied Halsey's message to Kinkaid reporting that the battleships were up north, with the rest of the Third Fleet. So the question was put to the chief again, for a third time, by Sherman, Hedding, and Austin. Why not simply ask Halsey for the location of Task Force 34? At last Nimitz relented.

The brief dispatch was composed by either Sherman or Austin—the accounts vary—and approved by Nimitz for transmission: "Where is Task Force 34?"[77] King and Kinkaid were copied as "for your information" addressees.

Down the message went, with a whoosh of the pneumatic tube, to the coding room in the CINCPAC headquarters basement, where occurred the most notorious snafu in the history of encrypted radio communications. When an outgoing dispatch was enciphered, it was standard procedure to add a few nonsensical words to the beginning and end of the text. This gibberish was called "padding," and its purpose was to confound enemy codebreakers. Padding was separated from the message text by a two-letter "null," and the receiving communications officer was supposed to remove it before passing it to its recipient. A short message was considered more vulnerable to cryptanalysis, so it was common practice to repeat part of the text solely in order to lengthen it. In this instance, the outgoing dispatch was transmitted as:

TURKEY TROTS TO WATER GG FROM CINCPAC [Nimitz]
ACTION COM THIRD FLEET [Halsey] INFO COMINCH [King]
CTF SEVENTY SEVEN [Kinkaid] X WHERE IS RPT WHERE IS
TASK FORCE THIRTY FOUR RR THE WORLD WONDERS.[78]

On the other side of the Pacific, the dots and dashes were gathered out of the atmosphere by the *New Jersey*'s towering radio masts. In the coding room below, a teleprinter spat out a short tape with the decrypted text. In normal circumstances the communications staff would copy out the message on a dispatch form. But when a message was urgent, as this one plainly was, they tore off the padding and rushed the raw decode tape directly up to flag plot. Lieutenant Charles Fox, a communications officer, recognized the initial padding as obvious gibberish, and tore it off. But the final three words presented a dilemma. Though they were separated from the prior text by a two-letter null, it was at least possible that "RR" was garble. In cases of confusion or ambiguity, if there were any doubt whether a phrase constituted padding or message text, the standard practice was to leave it on the tape and let the recipient judge whether it belonged.[79]

Fox handed the decode tape to a subordinate, who placed it into a cartridge and inserted it into the pneumatic tube, which took it with another whoosh three decks up to flag plot. A communications officer removed it from the tube, saw that it was from Nimitz, and handed it directly to Halsey, who glanced down and read what he took to be a sarcastic mock-question: "Where is, repeat, where is Task Force 34, the world wonders?"

Halsey erupted. According to various eyewitnesses, he turned purple with rage, threw his cap to the deck, crumpled the dispatch, threw it down, and trampled it. By some accounts, tears welled up in his eyes and he let out a plaintive bleat, akin to a sob. "I was as stunned as if I had been struck in the face," he later wrote.[80] He shouted: "What right has Chester to send me a goddamn message like that?"[81]

Mick Carney, alarmed by the specter of a four-star meltdown in full view of the Third Fleet staff, moved quickly to confront Halsey: "Stop it! What the hell's the matter with you? Pull yourself together!"[82]

Halsey stormed off the bridge and down to his quarters, Carney on his heels. The two men remained sequestered there, behind a closed door, for nearly an hour. During that time, the Third Fleet continued north at high speed, toward Ozawa's stricken force and away from the desperate fight off Samar.

According to Charles Fox, the message was broken and rebroken, several times, and the specious inclusion of "the world wonders" was quickly corrected.[83] Given its importance, the error and correction would have been brought to Halsey's attention right away. Soon after his initial shock, therefore—if not while in his sea cabin with Carney, then immediately upon returning to flag plot—Halsey learned that he had misconstrued the last part of the message. Neither Halsey nor Carney disclosed details of their hour-long private discussion, but as long-serving sailors they could deduce that the "Where is, repeat, where is" wording was a coding convention, and not intended to lend the message a peremptory tone. Halsey knew Nimitz well enough to be sure that the Pacific Fleet chief was not capable of sarcasm, certainly not in this context. "I was infuriated by what appeared to be an insulting message," he told a historian years later. "After my rage had cooled off and I had time to think, I realized that something was wrong. I also realized that Admiral Nimitz could not possibly have sent me a message such as this."[84] It is reasonable, therefore, to infer that the initial misunderstanding was short-lived.*

That last point deserves emphasis, because it has often been obscured. However mundane the phrasing, even stripped of the errant padding, Nimitz's query amounted to a humiliating reprimand that undercut Halsey's authority. Never before had the CINCPAC intervened while a battle was in progress. Even if "Where is Task Force 34?" was taken as a simple question, rather than as a prod to action, it implicitly faulted Halsey for failing to report his movements clearly and unambiguously. If Nimitz could not make sense of Halsey's prior dispatches, how could Kinkaid be expected to have done so? In effect, Nimitz was fixing blame on Halsey for letting the Japanese sneak up on the Seventh Fleet. The inclusion of King and Kinkaid as addressees was a twist of the knife.

---

* In Halsey's memoir, he contends that he did "not know the truth for several weeks." He may have meant that he did not receive Nimitz's personal assurance that no insult was intended until the latter visited the fleet in late December. Halsey and Bryant, *Admiral Halsey's Story*, p. 220.

Under the circumstances, Nimitz's dispatch was not really an inquiry at all. It was an order, politely phrased as an inquiry. The CINCPAC no longer doubted the whereabouts of Task Force 34; he could easily deduce that it was up north with the rest of the Third Fleet. Halsey's flagship *New Jersey* was herself a component of Task Force 34. In other words, the task force was wherever Halsey was—and the admiral had employed the first person in several messages to Kinkaid, as in "Am proceeding north with three groups," and "Am now engaging enemy carrier force." Halsey would not have left his battlewagons without air cover, but he had clearly stated that all three carrier groups had gone north; therefore, the battleships must have gone too. More directly to the point, Kurita was now known to have traversed San Bernardino Strait and traveled far enough south to shoot at the Seventh Fleet. Since Task Force 34 had not been there to intercept it, and no reasonable third alternative existed, it must have gone north. Years after the war, Nimitz told his biographer, "I knew perfectly well where Task Force 34 was."[85]

Returning to flag plot shortly before 11:00 a.m., Halsey and Carney wore brave faces. Carney began issuing orders. Task Force 34 was to reverse course and race south at peak speed to relieve the Seventh Fleet. One carrier group, Bogan's Group 2, would come along; the two others would be left behind to finish off the Northern Force. When the big ships began turning around, they were only 42 nautical miles from the nearest cripples of Ozawa's fleet, almost close enough to see them on the horizon. It was a woeful anticlimax. Halsey later wrote, "I turned my back on the opportunity I had dreamed of since my days as a cadet."[86] But Nimitz had forced his hand. He notified Kinkaid, "Am proceeding toward Leyte with Task Group 38.2 and six fast battleships."[87] He added that he did not expect to arrive before eight the following morning.

"A STERN CHASE IS A LONG CHASE," was an old sailor's maxim—and in the running battle off Samar that morning, the principle held. Kurita's Center Force battleships and cruisers were about ten knots faster than Taffy 3's escort carriers, but Sprague maneuvered his ships deftly, altering course to keep his pursuers astern, and making good use of smokescreens and wet weather. For twenty minutes he hid his six baby flattops in a rainstorm, and while they were so hidden he turned south, and then southwest. The

Japanese did not cut across the arc of his turn, as he had feared, but kept turning behind him, traveling a longer distance. Kurita's loose echelon formation was continually harassed from the air, by Taffy 3's own aircraft and by those of the neighboring Taffy groups to the south. Most unforgettably, the little "tin cans" of the Taffy 3 screen—a handful of destroyers and destroyer escorts—fought a ferocious and desperate rearguard action, buying precious time for the carriers by forcing the Japanese ships to dodge torpedoes.

At 7:50 a.m., the *Hoel*, *Hermann*, and *Raymond* made a tight starboard turn at flank speed and charged the enemy. The destroyers worked up to thirty knots, their sterns pushing down as their screws bit into the sea and their bows rising, and steered directly for the middle column of the Japanese fleet—the battleships. The wounded *Johnston*, on emergency steering, managed to fall in behind the attacking destroyers and fired her 5-inch main batteries at the closest Japanese cruisers. The Japanese were also making close to thirty knots, so the range closed quickly. When the lead destroyer *Hoel* passed through 18,000 yards range, her torpedomen prepared to launch. They set the weapons to intermediate speed. One-half of the salvo was aimed head-on, at the battleships; the other half was aimed to starboard, at the cruisers. The *Hoel* launched her fish at a range of 9,000 yards, then turned hard starboard to retire.[88]

The Japanese made this bold little destroyer pay for her temerity. As the *Hoel* showed her broadside to the enemy, a rain of shells smashed through her port side and laid waste to her bridge. The helmsman and several officers were killed, and all voice radio communications cut out. Her after fireroom and after turbine took direct hits, killing her port engine. A stern hit jammed the rudder in place, keeping the *Hoel* locked in a clockwise turn. A quick shift to emergency manual steering kept her on course, away from the enemy.[89]

Meanwhile, the *Hoel*'s torpedoes ran north in a spreading fan. At 7:54, the *Yamato*'s lookouts sang out and pointed to incoming tracks off the starboard bow, and the giant battlewagon turned hard to port to evade the threat. Now she was running north, away from the enemy. Four torpedo wakes ran roughly parallel on her starboard beam, two more to port. The *Yamato* was traveling at 26 knots, about the same speed as the torpedoes: she was trapped on this course until the weapons ran out of steam and sank. Admiral Ugaki recorded that the *Yamato* was forced north for about ten minutes, "but it felt like a month to me. After the traces disappeared we finally could turn to starboard and put all our power into the chase."[90]

The *Hoel* still had hot torpedoes loaded in her tubes, but the torpedo crews had been decimated by shellfire. An officer on one of the bow mounts made his way aft and took over, aiming the tubes by sight, and fired five torpedoes at the Japanese heavy cruiser column, which was closing on the port quarter at a range of 6,000 yards. "With our ten fish fired we decided that it was time to get the hell out of there," said a surviving member of the *Hoel*'s crew.[91] But with one engine out of action, her speed was cut to 17 knots. With battleships closing on her starboard quarter, and cruisers closing on her port quarter, the *Hoel* was out of options. The ship fishtailed and "chased salvos," but the incoming fire was heavy on both quarters, then

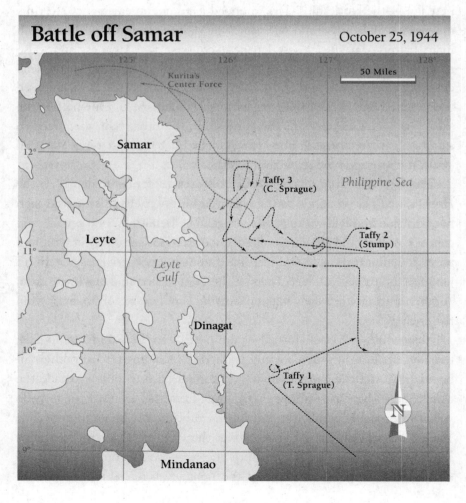

Battle off Samar   October 25, 1944

on both beams. The *Hoel* crumpled under a rain of hits along her length. The torpedo shack, the signal bridge, the sick bay, and two 20mm antiaircraft mounts were demolished. She was hit several times at or below the waterline on the port side, causing her lower regions to flood quickly; she listed heavily to port with fires blazing out of control. The bridge ordered abandon ship, and runners were dispatched to pass the word to crewmen at their posts below. Men came up the ladders, coughing, eyes shut against the smoke. They stumbled over the bodies of dead and dying shipmates, then stepped into the sea. The *Hoel*'s forward turrets continued firing gamely even as her stern was awash, and a messenger was sent forward to tell the gunners to cease fire and get to safety.[92] At 8:55 the *Hoel* rolled onto her beams ends and her stern went under. Her bow lifted up and then slid gradually into the sea, taking 253 of her crew of 300 down with her.

Survivors treaded water and clung to a floater net, helping their wounded as best they could. The Japanese fleet passed at pistol shot range, but no one fired on the men in the water. Americans looked up and made eye contact with Japanese sailors watching silently from the rails of the passing warships. Four battleships went by, and eight cruisers: one giant ship after another, all flying red and white "Sun and Rays" battle ensigns. Admiral Ugaki, staring down at the *Hoel*'s castaways from the *Yamato*'s bridge, wondered: "What did they think of the magnificent sight of our fleet in pursuit?"[93] The American sailors were awed by the sight of the colossal *Yamato* and her soaring gray pagoda. One shouted, "My God, look at that thing!" They were even more enchanted when an American fighter descended through the cloud ceiling and strafed the passing fleet. "We were so close to the ships that we could hear the .50 caliber bullets hit the hard wood decks," said Glenn Parkin, survivor of the *Hoel*. "The Japanese were shooting about every small gun they had. The F6F came down, strafed and was back into the clouds in less than 30 seconds. My God what a sight—with a front row seat."[94]

Now the Taffy 3 carriers were out of the rainsquall and fleeing on a south-southwesterly course. Sprague's flagship *Fanshaw Bay* led the formation, with *White Plains* and *Kalinin Bay* following astern, *St. Lo* to starboard, and *Kitkun Bay* and *Gambier Bay* to port.

A quartet of Japanese cruisers—*Chikuma*, *Chokai*, *Haguro*, and *Tone*— was gaining steadily on Taffy 3's port quarter. These powerful warships had peak speeds surpassing 30 knots. As the race entered its second hour, they had closed the range to about 14,000 yards, and the carriers were frequently straddled by 6-inch and 8-inch salvos. The fragile little ships shuddered violently at the impacts of close detonations—throwing crew members off their feet, shorting out electrical systems, and opening fissures between the hull plates. The *Fanshaw Bay* took four direct hits, and may have been saved by her light construction, because at least two armor-piercing projectiles passed "through and through" multiple decks and bulkheads and exploded outside the ship.

Destroyers continued zigzagging astern and laying as much smoke as they could muster. Michael Bak Jr. of the destroyer *Franks* recalled, "We were going right full rudder, left full rudder, right full rudder, left full rudder, and the shells were coming all around us."[95] The flamboyantly colorful splashes fell steadily closer to the *Franks* as the pursuers gained. During one close barrage, Bak crawled under the chart table and kept his head down. He wondered how the enemy had managed to sneak up on the American fleet without being detected by air patrols: "I couldn't believe you could see these ships so close. I made out a flag on one of the ships, it was so close. I couldn't believe they got so close to us without our admirals knowing about it. And it was just one of those things that during war everybody is looking the other way, and they come in from the rear."[96]

Sprague was repeatedly obliged to turn away from his speedy pursuers, gradually altering course to the southwest, and eventually steering almost dead west, toward the green mountains of Samar. The long turn disrupted the American formation, leaving the six carriers arrayed in a long, ragged column. The *Kalinin Bay* and *Gambier Bay* trailed behind their sisters, leaving them most exposed to the enemy's guns. They fired their 5-inch "peashooters" back at the nearest Japanese cruisers, which now crept up on their port beams. The *Kalinin Bay* was hit more than a dozen times, and suffered perhaps twice that number of destructive near-misses; her skipper thought it a miracle that the ship was not overtaken and destroyed.

The *Gambier Bay*, trailing astern of the others, took the worst of it. For the better part of an hour, the carrier had avoided direct hits by "chasing salvos." But at 8:20 a.m., she took a bad hit on the port side amidships, at the waterline. Tons of seawater rushed into the ship, flooding the forward port engine room. She lost an engine, which cut her speed to 11 knots. Since the Japanese were already nipping at her heels, that left no possibility of escape. Captain Walter V. R. Vieweg informed Admiral Sprague that his ship was dropping out of formation. She was quickly overtaken by the Japanese cruisers, which commenced pouring fire into her at close range. At the same time, the battleships *Yamato* and *Kongo* found the range from astern and sent a rain of large-caliber salvos down upon the luckless *Gambier Bay*.

The *Johnston*, having already suffered the wrath of the *Yamato*'s 18-inch guns, was still underway at reduced speed. Her steering machinery had been smashed beyond repair, so the rudder was handled manually (as in bygone eras) by four strong sailors who had to be relieved in ten-minute shifts. Evans at first ordered course changes by telephone, but he was soon forced to quit the ruined bridge and move back to the fantail, where he could shout directly down to the helmsmen. The ship's fire control equipment was out of action, so the guns could fire only "in local control," but the *Johnston* kept up the fight as best she could.

At 8:10 she emerged from a dense smokescreen and discovered her sister the *Heermann* speeding toward her on a collision course, only 200 yards away. Both skippers ordered "all engines back," though in the *Johnston*'s case that meant only one engine. Bob Deal, standing by the *Johnston*'s deck charge racks astern, was thrown from his feet: "Our stern dug deep into the sea and the ocean boiled over the after deck."[97] The *Heermann*, backing full on both engines, came to a complete stop, and then pulled away in reverse (sternway) at 15 knots. Even so, the two sisters missed one another by a margin of only 10 feet. Both crews sent up a spontaneous cheer. Then Evans threw his one working engine forward, turned away from the *Heermann*, and returned to the fight.[98]

At 8:20 the *Kongo* loomed out of the smoke on *Johnston*'s port beam, 7,000 yards away. The *Johnston* fired about forty 5-inch rounds at the bigger ship, observing several hits on the pagoda superstructure. "As far as accomplishing anything decisive, it was like bouncing paper wads off a steel helmet," Hagen admitted, and when the *Kongo*'s 14-inch guns turned on the *Johnston* and began shooting back, the American ship again sought refuge in her own smokescreen. When the smoke cleared ten minutes later, the *Gambier Bay* came into view a few miles ahead. She was dead in the water, taking heavy fire from a Japanese cruiser, probably the *Chikuma*. Hagen recalled: "Commander Evans then gave me the most courageous order I've ever heard. 'Commence firing on that cruiser, Hagen,' he said. 'Draw her fire on us and away from the *Gambier Bay*.'"[99]

The *Johnston* now traded salvos with the cruiser *Yahagi*, and took several damaging 6-inch hits. A column of five enemy destroyers approached on the opposite beam, apparently headed toward the crippled *Gambier Bay*. For the moment, the *Johnston* was the only American destroyer in the vicinity, so she fired on all of the enemy ships in turn, training her guns from one to another as they came into range. Now the *Johnston* was pounded by 5-inch gunfire from one side and 8-inch gunfire from the other. Her forward mount was silenced; fires broke out throughout the ship; the 40mm ammunition ready locker was engulfed in flames; and the antiaircraft shells began cooking off and exploding. Engineering compartments filled with smoke and forced crewmen up to the main deck, which was painted red with blood and strewn with their dead shipmates.

Two miles south, the *Gambier Bay* was a derelict, dead in the water, listing heavily and threatening to capsize. An Avenger in the hangar deck exploded, and fires fed on spilled aviation fuel. Black smoke boiled up from the lower decks and forced men up the ladders to the flight deck. An explosion blew the elevator out of its well. An avalanche of shells tore through the ship, ripping out her bowels and killing scores of her crew. Many penetrated through-and-through, entering the port side and exiting the starboard side of the ship: some of the Japanese ships then switched to high-explosive shells with instantaneous fuses, which blew up at the moment they made contact with the hull. At 8:45 a.m., the captain ordered all codebooks and other classified materials jettisoned, and then told the men to get off the ship. Shortly after 9:00 a.m., the *Gambier Bay* rolled over and sank quickly. She was the only American aircraft carrier ever destroyed by naval gunfire.

Japanese destroyers now closed in on the *Johnston* and pumped salvos into the burning wreck. The wreck's single remaining operable turret fired back obstinately. At 9:45 a.m., after three hours of savage combat, Commander Evans passed the word to abandon ship. As survivors stepped into the sea or took to the rafts, the enemy destroyers closed to point-blank range and fired into the *Johnston* until she slipped beneath the waves.

Tadashi Okuno, a twenty-five-year-old sailor on one of the Japanese destroyers, later recalled the scene. "Men were floating on the water's surface or sinking beneath it, while half-naked crew members jammed themselves into lifeboats and rowed away, escaping. We were close enough to see their unkempt beards and the tattoos on their arms. One of our machine gunners impulsively pulled his trigger. He must have been overflowing with feelings of animosity toward the enemy. But it was checked by a loud voice from the bridge saying, 'Don't shoot at escaping men! Stop shooting, stop!' "[100] American survivors confirmed that the Japanese held fire, and one witnessed a Japanese skipper salute the *Johnston* as she went down.

By that time, Kurita's fleet formation had come almost completely unglued. Visibility remained poor, obscured by low-lying clouds, squalls of rain, and tactical smokescreens. The Japanese ships lost sight of one another, and commanders struggled to remain in radio contact because of technical failures and the loss of key personnel. Traveling at various speeds, diverging onto different courses to chase different ships, dodging torpedoes, and repelling air attacks, the Japanese fleet was losing its cohesion and unity of purpose. It was no longer gaining appreciably on the five surviving escort carriers of Taffy 3. "We were making a stern chase on your ships which were zigzagging and that made it difficult to get the range," Kurita later said. "Also, the major units were separating further all the time because of your destroyer torpedo attacks."[101] The Japanese lookouts had trouble identifying the ships they were chasing, and assumed that they were 30-knot *Essex* carriers, which could keep ahead of the Japanese guns even in a daylong chase. Chief of staff Koyanagi judged that the "pursuit would be an endless seesaw, and that we would be unable to strike a decisive blow. And running at top speed, we were consuming fuel at an alarming rate."[102] For all of those reasons, Admiral Kurita signaled his ships to break off the chase and follow him north.

Amazed that the *Fanshaw Bay* had not already been run down and destroyed, Ziggy Sprague had begun to hope that some part of his force might escape. At 8:15, having run from the enemy for an hour, he turned to his chief quartermaster and said, "By golly, I think we may have a chance." Then the picture grew darker, as the *Gambier Bay* was overtaken and gunned down. When the Japanese guns finally fell silent and the enemy turned away to the north, the Americans could scarcely believe their good fortune. A *Fanshaw Bay* signalman exclaimed in pretended distress, "Goddammit, boys, they're getting away!"[103]

UNTIL THIS MORNING, Admiral Onishi's new kamikaze suicide unit had met only frustration and failure. On three consecutive days, beginning on October 21, Lieutenant Seki had led sorties from Mabalacat Airfield on Luzon; in each instance, the warplanes had failed to find suitable fleet targets and returned to base in shame. On the twenty-fourth, the weather over the airfield was socked in, and the planes did not even leave the field. The kamikaze observer planes were manned by experienced pilots who could be trusted to fly in thick weather, but most of the designated suicide pilots possessed only rudimentary flying skills, and Onishi did not want them to get lost, or perish in operational accidents. Better to wait for clearer weather, when they would stand at least a puncher's chance.

Now and again, since the first days of the war, individual Japanese pilots had spontaneously decided to turn their airplanes into man-guided missiles. The Allied fleet in Leyte Gulf had suffered a few such "unofficial" suicide attacks in the early days of the invasion. The worst fell upon the Royal Navy cruiser *Australia* on October 21, when a lone Aichi D3A1 bomber approached the starboard bow at wavetop altitude, then banked suddenly toward the ship's superstructure, its machine guns strafing viciously as the range closed. The plane flew into the *Australia*'s mainmast just beneath the crow's nest, disintegrating in a ball of orange fire. The interior spaces of the superstructure were flooded with burning aviation fuel, and shrapnel cut a path through the bridge, killing or badly wounding many of the ship's senior officers. The captain, struck in the abdomen, was rushed down to sick bay, where he died a painful death. The fires were brought under control and the *Australia* survived with only moderate damage, but the attack offered a grim sample of what the Japanese might achieve with aerial suicide tactics on an organized scale.

The first massed suicide attack fell on Thomas Sprague's Taffy 1, southernmost of the three escort carrier groups, at the most hectic stage of the running battle off Samar. The Taffy 1 carriers were maneuvering into the wind to launch aircraft—which would fly north to attack Kurita's force—when four Japanese Zeros dropped out of the overcast and dove on the *Santee* and *Suwannee*. One crashed the *Santee*'s flight deck just forward of her after elevator; its bomb penetrated into the hangar deck. The crew had the fires under control when the unlucky *Santee* took a torpedo hit fired by a Japanese submarine, *I-56*. In the confusion, the *Santee*'s officers believed that the ship had been damaged by one of her own depth charges, jettisoned by the damage control team; not until she went into dry dock a month later did the Americans realize that she had been hit by a Japanese torpedo. Meanwhile, several of her sisters suffered near-misses as would-be suicide gods crashed into the sea close alongside. The *Suwannee* was hit by two kamikazes over the course of twenty-four minutes, the second making a wreck of the hangar deck and shutting down the *Suwannee*'s flight operations for the rest of the afternoon.

Another wave of kamikazes arrived three hours later, soon after Kurita's Center Force had broken off their pursuit and turned north. As if Ziggy Sprague's group had not had a rough enough morning already, this deadly swarm fell directly on Taffy 3. The crews had just secured from general quarters and were celebrating their unexpected reprieve when many bogeys appeared on radar scopes, approaching from the north. At 10:40 a.m., the sky filled with flak as six Japanese planes winged in from astern. Two struck the *Kalinin Bay*, which erupted in blossoms of flame: the explosions and fires killed five of her crew and wounded fifty. Another aimed for the *Fanshaw Bay* but was poleaxed by antiaircraft fire, crashing alongside the ship. The *White Plains*'s gunners likewise destroyed an attacker at point-blank range, but the aircraft's bomb detonated near enough to the ship that men were wounded by debris raining down over her flight deck. A Zero narrowly missed the bridge of the *Kitkun Bay* and crashed into her forward port catwalk; fires sprung up, but they were quickly subdued.

On all but one of the stricken carriers, damage control teams managed to contain the fires and the ships could at least withdraw from the battle under their own steam. The exception was the *St. Lo*, which was hit at 10:53 a.m. A Zero banked sharply away from a wall of flak thrown up by the *White Plains* and flew over the bow of the *St. Lo*. The kamikaze nosed down directly above the flight deck and crashed the centerline amidships. The attacker's 250-kilogram bomb exploded in the hangar, starting an aggressive fire that quickly swallowed up the ready bomb and torpedo stowage magazines. Torn apart by a series of blasts, the lightly built ship began rolling to port. Though the *St. Lo* still had normal two-engine propulsion, the captain stopped the engines and ordered abandon ship, and men began going over the side. Listing heavily to port, the ship suddenly righted and then kept rolling over to starboard. She capsized and went down at 11:25 a.m. The screening ships, which had just finished their heroic action against Kurita's battleships and cruisers, moved in close to rescue survivors. Most of the crew, 754 of 800, were saved.

This attack had been led by Lieutenant Yukio Seki, the pilot anointed by Admiral Onishi to head the first dedicated "*Shimpu*" suicide unit based at Mabalacat on Luzon. The observer planes were led by Chief Warrant Officer Hiroyoshi Nishizawa, one of the most renowned Zero aces in the Japanese navy. Nishizawa returned with a thrilling report: four of Seki's suicide planes had scored, sinking one carrier and a light cruiser, and damaging another carrier. The news was radioed to Tokyo, and a public communiqué reported those same results.

For once, the public reports were not exaggerated. No cruiser was in the vicinity, but Seki's planes had hit three carriers, not two, destroying one and damaging the others badly enough that they had to be withdrawn to rear bases for major repairs.

This small cadre of suicide airplanes, whose attack came as an addendum to the great naval battle that was just winding down, presented a baleful foretaste of what was to come. The lesson was taken to heart on both sides: if Japanese pilots were willing to trade their lives for sure hits on Allied ships, they could draw blood.

———

HALSEY'S DETACHED WARSHIPS RACED SOUTH through the night, but arrived too late to catch the retreating Kurita. The admiral and his staff waited with drawn breath for news that the enemy fleet had entered Leyte Gulf, and for a time Kinkaid's dispatches gave conflicting indications. A confusing run of radio updates flowed into flag plot on the *New Jersey*. Tommy Sprague first allowed "situation looks better," but forty-five minutes later added, "Enemy surface forces returning to attack CVEs."[104] When it was clear that Kurita really had broken off the attack, Halsey decided to make flank speed for the mouth of San Bernardino Strait, hoping to head him off at the pass. He subdivided his forces again, sending his fastest ships ahead. The chase group included his own flagship *New Jersey* and her sister *Iowa*, with light cruisers and destroyers; they worked up to 30 knots and shaped course for San Bernardino. Kurita got there first, and was safely through to the other side two hours before Halsey's force arrived shortly after at 1:00 a.m. A single straggler was in range of the American guns, a crippled destroyer, the *Nowaki*. The cripple was too piddling a target for the *New Jersey*'s 16-inchers, so Halsey sent one of his destroyers ahead to finish her. That was the only action directly witnessed by the Third Fleet staff in the course of the battle. The mighty *New Jersey* had chased 300 miles north, turned around, and chased 300 miles south. Her part in the battle was finished, and her guns were cold. "And the rat got back to his hole before the cat could get there," Carney ruefully concluded, "and all we could do was make a quick scratch at his tail as he went through."[105]

Off Cape Engano, meanwhile, the two Third Fleet carrier task groups that had remained (38.3 and 38.4) continued to fly strikes against the retreating remnants of Ozawa's fleet. Four Japanese aircraft carriers were sent to the bottom, including the *Zuikaku*, the sixth and last surviving carrier that had attacked Pearl Harbor in December 1941. With a spirit of friendly competition, the various air units singled her out for special attention; all wanted the honor of delivering the killing blow. As Admiral Frederick C. Sherman recalled, the third strike launched from his Task Group 38.3 flight decks "put the finishing touches on the *Zuikaku* with nine direct 1000 and 2000-pound bomb hits." Previously she had been hit by an estimated seven aerial torpedoes. The burning wreck listed heavily to port, then rolled over and sank bow-first at 2:14. The target coordinator, watching from altitude, pronounced it "a very gratifying sight."[106]

That afternoon, a cruiser-destroyer squadron under Rear Admiral Laurance T. DuBose was sent ahead to sink enemy cripples with naval gunfire. DuBose's ships caught up to the *Chiyoda* and fired into her until she was gone. A fighter pilot overhead relayed a report back to the task force: "Splash one CVL at 1701—4 down and none to go."[107] Three hours later, the same force sank the destroyer *Hatsuzuki*. At nightfall, however, Dubose was summoned back, and the two carrier groups turned south to fall in with Halsey the next day.

Now all remaining Japanese naval forces were in headlong retreat. Carrier planes chased the fugitives into the Mindanao Sea, the Sulu Sea, and the Sibuyan Sea. The Taffy carriers launched pursuing airstrikes on the last of Nishimura and Shima's retreating ships, finally putting an end to the *Mogami* on the afternoon of the twenty-fifth. The *Abukuma*, which did not have sufficient propulsion to maneuver effectively, was hit by a tight pattern of 500-pound bombs dropped by army B-24 Liberators; she went down off Negros Island. Kurita's retiring survivors were attacked repeatedly from the air throughout the day of October 26; many suffered serious additional damage, including the *Nagato*, the *Haruna*, the *Kumano*, and the *Yamato*. The cruiser *Noshiro* was sunk at 11:37 a.m. in Tablas Strait. Of Nishimura's Southern Force, only the *Shigure* survived; she returned alone to Brunei Bay, and her captain was the only surviving commanding officer of that force. The U.S. submarine *Jallao* knocked off the retreating cruiser *Tama*, lately of Ozawa's force, northeast of Luzon. By outpacing his own cripples, Admiral Shima managed to get away from Surigao Strait in the *Nachi*—but she was later set upon by Task Force 38 planes in Manila Bay and sent to the bottom. The carrier planes strafed survivors in the water; 807 of her crew perished.

Some of those later mopping-up actions fell outside the time boundary set by historians to mark the end of the Battle of Leyte Gulf. Even so curtailed, however, the sprawling contest had been the largest naval battle in history. It had involved nearly three hundred ships with combined displacement of about 3 million tons. The contending fleets were manned by about 200,000 men, enough to populate a midsized city. Combined losses were thirty-four ships, more than five hundred airplanes, and more than 16,000 casualties. The contest had included every conceivable variety of naval fighting, by every kind of vessel—carrier strikes, gunnery and torpedo duels between surface warships, submarine attacks, swarming PT-boat attacks, and suicide air attacks. The action included history's last "battle line" at Surigao Strait, the consummate David versus Goliath fight of the "tin can" sailors at Samar, and the official opening blow of the kamikaze campaign. Lasting four days, the "battle" was really a series of widely separated actions fought over a theater covering 100,000 square miles. Four were large enough to qualify as major battles in their own right, and named accordingly: the Battle of the Sibuyan Sea, the Battle of Surigao Strait, the Battle off Cape Engano, and the Battle off Samar. No fighting (except air attacks) occurred in Leyte Gulf, so the name given to the whole battle was really a misnomer. At first the navy called it the "Second Battle of the Philippine Sea," and some early histories actually used that name. MacArthur preferred "Leyte Gulf," which emphasized his beachhead as the enemy's intended point of convergence, and the name stuck. (Better than either would have been the "Naval Battle of the Philippines," but the issue was settled long ago.)

The battle effectively brought the naval war for the Pacific to an end. Given the much-weakened state of the Imperial Navy before the battle, its losses at Leyte Gulf were ruinous: four aircraft carriers, three battleships, ten cruisers, and twelve destroyers. Aircraft losses had been heavy in the weeks before the battle, but the Japanese managed to lose some five hundred more. It would take many weeks to count up the losses in officers and sailors, but the figure would eventually surpass 12,000. Surviving remnants of the Japanese fleet limped away, but they would never again sortie in force. As both sides had foreseen, an American foothold in the Philippines rendered Japan's north-south sea links untenable, which meant that its remaining heavy warships were starved of fuel and thus largely immobilized. According to Admiral Ozawa, the fleet's survivors "became strictly auxiliary . . . there was no further use assigned to surface vessels, with the exception of some special ships."[108] What little remained of the carrier air corps was deployed to terrestrial airfields, and most remaining airmen and airplanes were merged into kamikaze units.

The U.S. and Allied side had suffered as well. The Americans had lost one light carrier (*Princeton*), two escort carriers (*Gambier Bay* and *St. Lo*), two destroyers, and a destroyer escort. Many other ships were seriously damaged and had to be sent back to Manus, Hawaii, or North America for major repairs. The Americans suffered casualties of about 1,500 men killed or missing and twice that number wounded. Those losses were not inordinate relative to the scale of the victory, but they left a sour aftertaste in the mouths of the victors. A tone of recrimination could be detected in radio messages between the Third and Seventh Fleets. The near-debacle off Samar was exacerbated by a botched air-sea rescue response, which left more than a thousand Taffy 3 survivors adrift at sea for almost two days after the Japanese fleet left the scene. As a result of mistaken position reports, the initial rescue efforts covered an area too far south. Late on October 26, a squadron of LCI landing craft picked up 700 *Gambier Bay* survivors, then found the last survivors of the *Johnston*, *Roberts*, and *Hoel* the next morning. Many of their shipmates had drowned, died of exposure, or been taken by sharks. Commander Evans of the *Johnston* was among those who had perished during the long delay; he would receive a posthumous Medal of Honor.

In the immediate aftermath of their victory, the victors seemed frustrated, embittered, and exhausted. After arriving off San Bernardino to find that Kurita had already made his escape, Halsey radioed a victory cry to all commands: "It can be announced with assurance that the Japanese Navy has been beaten, routed, and broken by the Third and Seventh Fleets."[109] Although that was true, it was a dollop of bravado to salve a festering wound. In a heated and defensive 480-word message composed in the small hours of October 26, and radioed that morning to King, Nimitz, MacArthur, and Kinkaid, the Third Fleet commander set out to explain and justify his decision to take his entire fleet north. The harangue included some passages that could only be explained as the product of acute mental and emotional fatigue. "To statically guard San Bernardino Straits until enemy surface and carrier air attacks could be coordinated would have been childish," Halsey wrote. Kurita's Center Force had been "crippled" by his carrier airstrikes in the Sibuyan Sea on October 24, and was "so badly damaged that [it] constituted no serious threat to Kinkaid." By turning away from the fight off Engano, Halsey complained, he had missed "my golden opportunity" to wipe out the enemy's northern carrier force.[110]

This was the first of Halsey's post hoc rationalizations for his decisions at Leyte Gulf. They would continue, adamant and unyielding, until his death in 1959. Allowances should be made for clumsy phrasing in a message hastily dashed off at the end of a grueling three-day battle. But the word "childish" seemed especially ill-chosen, and prompted concern among Halsey's colleagues. Deploying the battleships to guard San Bernardino Strait would not have been "static," much less "childish," but rather active and manful. The idea that Kurita's force had been "crippled" in the Sibuyan Sea, and thus presented no threat to Kinkaid, had already been resoundingly debunked by that morning's Battle off Samar. "My golden opportunity" did not sit right, either. It cut against the navy's team-before-player ethos, and hinted at a MacArthuresque longing on Halsey's part to secure his place in history.

As THE LAST, LARGEST, and most closely studied naval battle in history, Leyte Gulf is a subgenre unto itself. Generations of scholars have had their say, but pioneering new contributions appear year after year, and various controversies remain the subject of vigorous debate. This is particularly true of the two controversial decisions by Halsey and Kurita—the former to take his entire force north on the night of October 24, and the latter to break off his attack on the morning of October 25. C. Vann Woodward, author of the first major history of the battle, judged that "the two colossal failures at Leyte Gulf are reasonably attributable to an American Hotspur and a Japanese Hamlet."[111] In the American view, Kurita's decision to turn back providentially neutralized Halsey's failure to cover San Bernardino Strait. Like corresponding terms in an algebra equation, the two blunders cancelled each other out.

After breaking off pursuit of the escort carriers at 9:25 a.m., Kurita had summoned his ships to regroup in circular battle formation. This was more easily ordered than accomplished. Visibility remained deplorable, radio communications were spotty, and relentless air attacks continued to fall upon the Center Force. Reassembling into fleet formation took a full two hours, during which time a flood of new contact reports and radio intercepts only added to the impression of chaos. Persistent reports of another American task force to the north left the Japanese with the sense that they were surrounded, but no enemy ships materialized in that direction. At 11:20, Kurita set course to the southwest, momentarily intending to break into Leyte Gulf. Half an hour later, lookouts reported seeing the masts of a *Pennsylvania*-class battleship and four other ships hull-down to the south at an estimated range of 39 kilometers. This could not have been Oldendorf, who was still south of Leyte Gulf, and no other battleships were in the vicinity—evidently, it must have been another apparition. (Kurita dispatched a *Yamato* floatplane to investigate, but it was apparently shot down.) At 1:13 p.m., Kurita again changed his mind and reversed course to the north, this time intending to run up the coast of Samar in hopes of finding another American carrier group, whose presence was surmised by Kinkaid's intercepted plain-language transmissions. For several hours the Center Force headed north, fighting off several more waves of airstrikes while underway. Kurita had expected to make contact with the enemy task force within two hours, but as masthead lookouts scanned the horizon in every direction, no enemy ships were to be seen. Fuel considerations began to weigh more heavily on his mind. Soon he would not have enough fuel to make Colon Bay, or even to maneuver against American airstrikes. If he was going to withdraw, it was now or never. At 6:30 p.m., with dusk looming, he decided to call it a battle and head for San Bernardino Strait.

Kurita had been directly ordered, in no uncertain terms, to charge into Leyte Gulf and attack the American transport fleet and beachhead. He had been expressly instructed to press on even at the risk of complete annihilation. Why had he chosen not to do so? The various explanations and justifications given by the admiral and his acolytes were confusing and incongruous from the start. He said he believed the air attacks upon his ships were growing in intensity and effectiveness, and "In the narrow confines of Leyte Gulf I couldn't use the advantage that ships have of maneuvering, whereas I would be a more useful force under the same attack with the advantage of maneuver in the open sea."[112] His communications team had intercepted American transmissions calling for air support, so he expected the airstrikes to grow fiercer and more numerous. Moreover, he had not budgeted fuel to get home: "Therefore, the fuel was a very important consideration; the basic one."[113] Kurita added that he believed most of the American amphibious fleet had probably already pulled out of the gulf, "and I therefore considered it not so important as it would have been before."[114] The *Yamato* had received a mysterious report placing an American task force 113 miles north of the Sulutan lighthouse. Kurita thought it better to steer toward this contact, which he presumed to be another Third Fleet carrier group, in hopes of bringing it under his guns before it could launch an airstrike against him.

Western histories of the battle have leaned heavily on postwar interrogations of Kurita and his senior staff officers. In the months after the surrender, the U.S. Strategic Bombing Survey, working with the U.S. Navy, rounded up leading Japanese officers and questioned them closely about their major decisions in this and other battles. The result was an invaluable resource for historians. Not surprisingly, however, not all of the Japanese were equally forthcoming under interrogation. Whenever sensitive or potentially embarrassing topics were raised, evasion, misdirection, and outright lies were to be expected. Naturally, these proud men did not wish to air their dirty laundry in the conqueror's presence. After a long interview with Kurita in November 1945, USSBS interrogators described the admiral as "somewhat on the defensive, giving only the briefest of replies. . . . In some instances his memory for details such as times, cruising dispositions, etc. appeared to be inaccurate."[115]

Kurita became somewhat more animated when invited to explain his decision to turn north on October 25. He gave several reasons, some contradictory. Asked if he had turned north in order to avoid a destructive air attack, he replied: "It wasn't a question of destruction, that was neither here nor there. It was a question of what good I could do in the bay. I concluded that under the heavy attack from ship and shore-based planes, I could not be effective. Therefore, on my own decision, I concluded it was best to go north and join Admiral Ozawa." But joining up with Ozawa was never a realistic proposition, and Kurita soon contradicted himself: "My intention was not primarily to join Admiral Ozawa but to go north and seek out the enemy. If I failed to find the enemy, having reached here [indicating a position on the chart, about 13°20′N] my intention was to go north and seek out the enemy but to be able to retire through San Bernardino Strait at dark." Kurita seemed to mean that he wanted to keep the escape hatch at San Bernardino within reach, but only as a last resort in case he could not find the enemy. But he added a stray remark suggesting that his main intention was always to get away that night, because "if I did not get into the Straits by night, the next day was hopeless for me because I could be brought under attack by land planes and by [Halsey's] force."[116]

Taken together with the interrogations of the Center Force chief of staff (Tomiji Koyanagi) and operations officer (Tonosuke Otani), as well as the diary of Admiral Ugaki, an extraordinary concatenation of reasons was offered to justify the decision to turn north. Koyanagi alone enumerated six reasons, counting them out one by one. (First, they could not catch the Taffy 3 carriers; second, they were too far behind schedule to coordinate attacks with Nishimura; third, they expected a heavy air attack based on Kinkaid's plain-language transmissions; fourth, they did not want to be caught in confined waters under heavy air attack; fifth, they hoped to fight a pitched battle with Halsey's force to the north; and sixth, they were running short of fuel.)[117] What emerges is a mosaic picture, a decision made under great stress and driven by several interconnected factors. Koyanagi and Otani both affirmed that the decision to turn north was supported unanimously by the staff. In his diary, Ugaki remarked, "I felt irritated on the same bridge seeing that they lacked fighting spirit and promptitude." But Ugaki also believed that the phantom American carrier force to the north was real, and even recorded that he had seen "takeoffs and landings of planes far over the horizon" on a bearing of 20 degrees. Since no such carrier force was in that location, the apparition recorded by Ugaki only adds to the impression of chaos and bewilderment on the *Yamato's* flag bridge that morning.[118]

Perhaps the whole story will never be known, but this much is clear: Kurita was exhausted. Since leaving Brunei three days earlier, he had not slept at all. His flagship *Atago* had been shot out from under him in Palawan Passage, dumping the fifty-five-year-old vice admiral into the sea and forcing him to swim for his life. His ships had suffered under the most sustained air attack ever encountered by a fleet at sea, with no friendly air protection at all. To Americans, journalists, and other outsiders, Kurita was loath to admit that fatigue had played any role in his decision to break and run. In private conversations with colleagues, he was more candid. He told Tameichi Hara, the veteran destroyer skipper, "I made that blunder out of sheer physical exhaustion."[119] The staff must have been similarly weary, for they had shared in the long ordeal and did not oppose the decision.

Kurita had held a smashing victory in his grasp, and let it slip through his fingers. That was an egregious command failure, never convincingly justified by the array of rationales offered later. Some have charged him with timidity; many others have implied it. At the very least it would seem that his heart was not in the fight. From the start, Plan *Sho* had encountered resistance in the fleet. Voices had been raised against it during the command conference in Brunei. The plan to attack transports and troopships in Leyte Gulf had offended the sensibilities of many Japanese officers, who had been trained to believe that warships should fight warships. Others faulted Admiral Toyoda for ordering the operation but failing to lead it in person. While advancing through the Sibuyan Sea against relentless air attacks, with no sign of the air support they had been promised, officers on the bridge of the *Yamato* uttered quasi-mutinous remarks about the stupidity and rigidity of Combined Fleet headquarters. Kurita turned away from the battle not once but twice, temporarily on the twenty-fourth and permanently on the twenty-fifth—and in the first instance, some of his staff had preferred to keep heading away from the enemy. And while the point is often forgotten, several of Kurita's fellow commanders also turned back prematurely. Ozawa turned north briefly on the afternoon of October 24, after his Northern Force was sighted by Halsey's search planes, until instructed to turn south again by radio dispatch from the Combined Fleet command bunker in Hiyoshi. Admiral Shima hightailed it out of Surigao Strait on the morning of October 25, after launching a single salvo of torpedoes. He radioed Toyoda to report that his retirement was only temporary, but American warplanes chased him all the way back to Manila Bay. The samurai Shoji Nishimura carried out his naval *banzai* charge more faithfully than any of his fellow fleet commanders. Even so, every ship in his Southern Force turned back, or at least attempted to do so, once it became clear that the cause was lost. Even Nishimura's own flagship *Yamashiro* turned away at the last moment, after trying in vain to advance alone into the concentrated gunfire of the Allied fleet.

In truth, the officers and men who manned the Japanese fleet had never really bought into Plan *Sho*, because it did not offer a realistic prospect of success. They understood that the staff officers who had written the plan did not really expect them to win, but to fight one last glorious battle to crown the Japanese navy's career. They were being asked to offer up the still-mighty Combined Fleet as a sacrificial lamb. But the Japanese navy differed from the army in this respect: its culture, training, and traditions offered no precedent for a mindless, headlong *banzai* charge. While the naval air corps was eventually given over to kamikaze tactics, that development was a last resort, long delayed by opposition in the ranks. It involved sacrificing airplanes and novice pilots who lacked the skills to fly and fight using conventional tactics. But the emperor's ships were major capital assets, state-of-the-art weapons, beloved national icons, built and manned over many decades at monumental expense. It had never been intended that they should immolate themselves for the sake of abstract considerations of honor.

Throughout its history, the Japanese navy had always tried to win. Winning was its prime objective: "dying well" was an ancillary virtue. If a ship's fate was to be destroyed in battle, she was expected to go down with guns blazing. If a man's fate was to die in battle, he was expected to die willingly, and afterward his spirit would rest eternally at Yasukuni Shrine. But the overriding purpose had always been victory. Now, in October 1944, the ironically named "Plan Victory" inverted that order of priorities. The Tokyo admirals had foreseen that if the Americans gained possession of the Philippines, the fuel supply problem would become impossible to solve. In that case, the fleet would be immobilized, left to end the war while riding at anchor, or to sink in port under a rain of enemy bombs. *Sho*'s driving purpose was to avoid that ignominious finale, to ensure that the Japanese navy went out with a bang rather than a whimper. If it was possible to win, so much the better, but the battle must be fought no matter how long the odds.

The point had often been obscured in Western histories of the Battle of Leyte Gulf, partly because the "between the lines" meaning of Tokyo's operational orders and subsequent dispatches was lost in English translation, and partly because Japanese officers were cagey on the subject with their postwar USSBS interrogators. But the truth shone through in contemporary sources and postwar accounts. Kurita had rallied his officers in Brunei with the remark: "You must all remember that there are such things as miracles."[120] Koyanagi, writing after the war, pointed out that the fleet had been obliged to travel almost 1,000 miles to the scene of battle, through waters known to be infested with enemy submarines and under skies dominated by enemy airplanes. "This was a completely desperate, reckless, and unprecedented plan that ignored the basic concepts of war," he concluded. "I still cannot but interpret it as a suicide order for Kurita's fleet."[121]

Perhaps it was not cowardice so much as sagging morale that best explains Kurita's equivocation and retreat. He and his fellow officers knew better than their civilian countrymen that the war was already lost, and that the high command had tried to hide the truth behind a skein of lies. They could not acknowledge it openly, but the incubus of defeatism was spreading through their ranks. And how could it have been otherwise, when the ludicrously named "Plan Victory" was itself a token of the regime's defeatism?

HALSEY WENT TO HIS GRAVE refusing to concede that he had erred in leaving San Bernardino Strait undefended on the night of October 24, 1944. His only error, he told anyone who would listen, was in reversing course when Ozawa's carrier group was nearly under his guns. Carney and the Third Fleet staff upheld this party line, but virtually all carrier group and task force commanders were convinced that their chief had blundered, and their whispers quickly circulated back to Guam, Ulithi, Manus, Pearl Harbor, and Washington. Moreover, keen observers noted discord even among the dirty tricksters. Rear Admiral Arthur Radford, who would soon take command of a task group, reported on board the *New Jersey* on November 17, having just arrived in the theater. He wanted to discuss the recent battle with Mick Carney, his old friend and Naval Academy classmate. "To my surprise," said Radford, "the usually garrulous Mick was rather noncommittal, and the same was true of Admiral Halsey and several other members of the staff. The impression that remained with me was definite: they did not want to talk about those days in October. I felt distinctly that all were displeased with their performance but had not yet agreed on the reasons for it."[122]

For one reason or another, often bad luck, Halsey had missed all of the Pacific War's previous carrier-versus-carrier battles. In May 1942, his *Enterprise*-centered task force had arrived too late for the Battle of the Coral Sea, because he had been sent north to cover the Doolittle Raid against Japan. The following month he was laid low by a skin disorder, and ordered to the hospital by Nimitz, thus missing the Battle of Midway. (His trusted understudy, Raymond Spruance, stepped into Halsey's shoes and won the immortal victory.) Halsey was not in the South Pacific for the Guadalcanal landing in August 1942, or the clash of carriers later that month at the

Battle of the Eastern Solomons. In October 1942, during the Battle of the Santa Cruz Islands, he was shorebound at his SOPAC headquarters in New Caledonia. Then followed an eighteen-month hiatus, during which the Japanese carriers did not come out to fight. When they finally reappeared in June 1944, at the Battle of the Philippine Sea, Spruance was commanding the Fifth Fleet.

In the South Pacific, Halsey had earned a reputation as a "rough brush"—that is, an artist who painted in big, sweeping strokes, rather than a draftsman who drew fine, precise lines. Tactical subtleties did not much interest him; he simply gathered up his forces and hurled them at the enemy, trusting to the fortunes of war. His more famous nickname, "Bull," got at the same trait. Since taking over the Third Fleet in August 1944, Halsey's major ambition had been to destroy the enemy's carrier task force—not simply to meet it in battle, not just to defeat it, but to annihilate it, to wipe it out, to burn and sink every remaining Japanese flattop with all their airplanes and screening vessels. He was proud to declare himself a naval meleeist in the tradition of Horatio Nelson, who won several such wipeout victories against the enemies of England during the Napoleonic Wars. In his memoir, he quoted Nelson's instructions before the Battle of Trafalgar: "No captain can do very wrong if he places his ship alongside that of an enemy." Halsey added, "If any principle of naval warfare is burned into my brain, it is that the best defense is a strong offense."[123]

His friend Spruance had allowed most of the Japanese fleet to escape after the Battle of the Philippine Sea four months earlier. Task Force 58 commander Marc Mitscher had wanted to move west against the enemy on the night of June 18, to be in position to launch airstrikes the next morning. Spruance had declined, for fear of an end-run attack on the beachhead at Saipan. That conservative decision was decried by many of the navy's influential brownshoes (aviators), who charged that the blackshoe (non-aviator) Spruance was fundamentally ignorant of the capabilities of modern carrier airpower. During this period, Halsey was encamped at Pearl Harbor, preparing to assume command of the fleet. He and his staff received an earful from the aviators, who begged them to avoid another such letdown. Carl Moore, Mick Carney's counterpart in the Fifth Fleet, believed that Halsey "was among those who sat around and panned Spruance during those first few days. And I think that the idea got into his head that he would never get himself into that kind of a position. . . . Now, I have no proof of it. I think Carney would deny it. And Halsey certainly, in hindsight, describing everything, denied it. But there you are."[124]

As usual, Nimitz allowed his seagoing commander broad latitude to handle his forces as he chose, depending on tactical circumstances. His operations plan charged Halsey with "covering and supporting the Leyte Gulf-Surigao operations." But it also specified: "If opportunity for destruction of major portion of the enemy fleet is offered or can be created, such destruction becomes the primary task."[125] A critical ambiguity lay in the seam between these two clauses. Ruses, feints, and lures were familiar hallmarks of Japanese strategy. In several previous naval battles, including all four carrier duels prior to the Battle of the Philippine Sea, the Japanese had divided their forces and approached the scene of action by different routes. What if several "major portions" of the enemy fleet advanced from different directions, as they did at Leyte Gulf? How to weigh the impulse to chase and destroy one part of the enemy fleet against the competing mandate to "cover and support" the Seventh Fleet and beachhead? Those contingencies were left to Halsey's judgment.

The clause concerning "destruction of major portion of the enemy fleet" was boilerplate: versions of it had been included in the operational orders for amphibious operations since GALVANIC, the invasion of the Gilbert Islands in November 1943. Still, orders were orders, and the designation of such destruction as the "primary task" would seem to justify Halsey's aggressive mindset. Facing a dilemma comparable to the situation in the Marianas four months earlier, Halsey's instinct was to reverse the order of priorities. Spruance had refused to risk an end-run attack on the beachhead, even if it meant letting the enemy carriers get away. Halsey would refuse to let the enemy carriers get away, even at the risk of allowing an end-run attack on the beachhead.

When Ozawa's Northern Force appeared off Cape Engano, Halsey was confronted with a high-stakes decision. Broadly speaking, he had three alternatives. He could stay where he was, he could divide his forces, or he could chase north with his entire fleet. He rejected the first option, keeping his entire force off San Bernardino Strait, for sound reasons: he wanted to sink the enemy carriers before they could link up with airfields on Luzon and "shuttle-bomb" him. But his justifications for rejecting the second option (leaving Task Force 34 off San Bernardino) in favor of the third (taking everything north and leaving the strait unguarded) persuaded

Chester W. Nimitz, Ernest J. King, and Raymond A. Spruance under the 8-inch guns of the USS *Indianapolis*, Fifth Fleet flagship, on July 18, 1944. Immediately after this photo was taken, the three admirals sat down to dinner in Spruance's messroom, where they were beset by an infestation of flies from nearby Saipan. *Naval History and Heritage Command.*

General Douglas MacArthur, President Franklin D. Roosevelt, Admiral William D. Leahy, and Admiral Chester W. Nimitz pose for a photograph at the Holmes villa on Waikiki Beach on the morning of July 28, 1944. Their formal strategy discussion began immediately after the photographers and film crew had left the room. *U.S. Navy photograph.*

Task Force 38, the main carrier striking force of the U.S. Navy. "All ships turned together, their white wakes carving synchronous arcs through the sea. In a minute and a half, they could execute a 90-degree turn and steady on a new course." *U.S. Navy photograph, now in the collections of the U.S. National Archives.*

U.S. aircraft carriers of Task Force 38 entering the fleet anchorage at Ulithi Atoll on December 12, 1944. *National Archives*.

First wave of amphibious assault boats hits the landing beaches at Peleliu, September 15, 1944. Photograph taken from a floatplane belonging to the battleship *Pennsylvania* (BB-38). *National Archives*.

A column of marines advances into a devastated landscape in the Urmurbrogal pocket, Peleliu. *U.S. Marine Corps Archives.*

Two LSTs unload vehicles and gear onto the beach near Tacloban, Leyte. *National Archives.*

Admiral William F. Halsey Jr., official portrait taken shortly after the war, following his promotion to fleet admiral with five stars. *U.S. Navy photograph, now in the collections of the National Archives.*

Vice Admiral Takeo Kurita, official portrait circa 1942. *U.S. Naval History and Heritage Command.*

Crew of the *Zuikaku* give a valedictory "banzai" cheer as the carrier sinks at the Battle off Cape Engano, October 25, 1944. She was the last survivor of the six Japanese carriers that had attacked Pearl Harbor in December 1941. *Courtesy of Mr. Kazutoshi Hando, 1970. U.S. Naval History and Heritage Command.*

Kamikaze pilots preparing for their final mission. One young flyer is securing the Rising Sun *hachimaki* headband for a comrade. *Naval History and Heritage Command.*

The USS *Wahoo* (SS-238) returns to Pearl Harbor from her historic third war patrol on February 7, 1943. She has a broom fixed to her periscope shears, signifying a "clean sweep," and a banner with the motto "Shoot the Sunza Bitches." Skipper Dudley W. "Mush" Morton is visible on the bridge, in right center. Standing to left (with foot on stanchion) is the executive officer, Lieutenant Richard H. O'Kane. *U.S. Navy photograph, now in the collections of the National Archives.*

A Japanese cargo ship, later identified as the *Nittsu Maru*, sinking in the Yellow Sea. Periscope photograph taken from USS *Wahoo* (SS-238), which had just torpedoed her. *U.S. Navy photograph, now in the collections of the National Archives.*

A portion of the Third Fleet at anchor in Ulithi Atoll, Caroline Islands, November 6, 1944. *National Archives.*

Enlisted men on liberty, drinking rationed beer on Mog Mog Island, Ulithi Atoll, November 1944. *U.S. Navy photograph by Charles Fenno Jacobs, now in the collections of the National Archives.*

Nimitz (center) confers with Halsey (left) aboard the Third Fleet flagship *New Jersey* in Ulithi lagoon, December 1944. This was shortly after the fleet had been mauled in a typhoon in the Philippine Sea. At right is Nimitz's deputy, Rear Admiral Forrest P. Sherman. *U.S. Naval History and Heritage Command.*

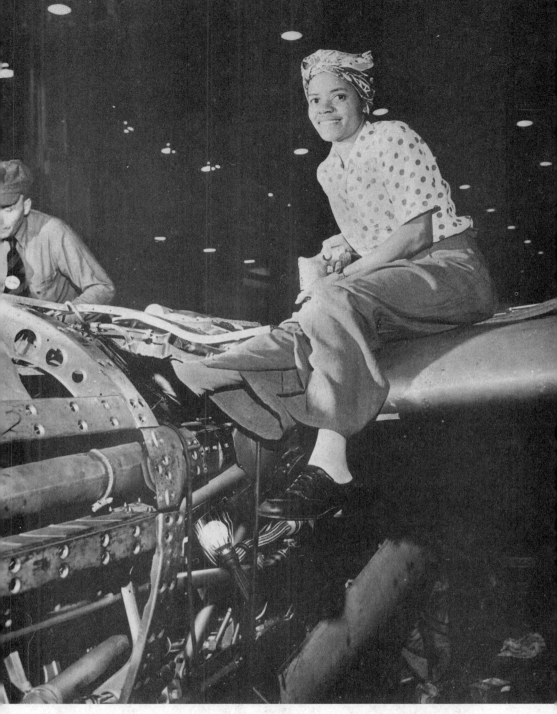

A riveter at the Lockheed Aircraft Corporation, Burbank, California. *National Archives*.

Aviation cadets check flight boards at the Naval Air Training Center in Corpus Christi, Texas. A hand-lettered sign warns: "Don't get caught above clouds." In hangar to rear is a Boeing-Stearman N2S, colloquially known as the "Yellow Peril." *Photograph by Charles Fenno Jacobs, U.S. Navy photograph.*

Task Force 58 pilots are briefed on their impending strike on Tokyo, February 15, 1945. More than half of the fighter pilots on this unprecedented mission were fresh out of training programs, and had never flown in combat. *National Archives.*

Stretcher party evacuates a wounded U.S. soldier from Intramuros, the Walled City in the ruins of Manila, on February 23, 1945. *National Archives.*

Civilian Filipinos massacred by the Japanese, February 1945. It was like this all over the city. *National Archives.*

Amtracs, tanks, and supplies lay smashed and awash on the beach at Iwo Jima. Observing the scene from the command ship offshore, General Holland Smith compared it to "a row of frame houses in a tornado." *National Archives.*

A TBM Avenger torpedo plane over Mount Suribachi, Iwo Jima, shortly after the island was secured in March 1945. Note extensive development of the area north of volcano. *U.S. Navy photograph, now in the collections of the National Archives.*

B-29s of the 462nd Bombardment Group on a taxiway at West Field, Tinian. *U.S. Air Force photograph.*

General Curtis E. LeMay,
U.S. Army Air Forces.
*National Museum of the
U.S. Air Force.*

virtually no one beyond the handful of staff loyalists who took part in the decision. The reasons offered in the Third Fleet action report were too nebulous to be convincing. Taking the whole fleet north, it argued, "maintained the integrity of the Blue [U.S.] striking fleet; it offered best possibility of surprise and destruction of enemy carrier force."[126] To say that the decision "maintained the integrity" of the fleet was true, inasmuch as the fleet stayed together as an undivided whole, but that only rephrased the decision without explaining or justifying it. It was a tautology, disguised by a semantic sleight of hand. Fleet concentration for its own sake was Mahanian orthodoxy, which had reigned supreme when Halsey's generation had passed through the Naval Academy. By 1944, advances in radio, radar, and aviation had changed the game, and the old rule of concentration was as obsolete as a square-rigger.

Halsey had no compelling reason to concentrate his entire sixty-five-ship fleet against the nineteen-ship carrier force to his north, but he had urgent reasons to guard the strait. Moreover, he did not have to pick between alternatives, because he had more than enough strength to deal with Kurita and Ozawa simultaneously. His action report described the Northern Force as a "fresh and powerful threat," deserving the Third Fleet's full attention. It was fresh in the sense that it had not yet been attacked, while the Center Force had suffered a terrific thrashing from the air. But the Japanese carrier force had already been emasculated by the loss of its leading aviators, a fact widely known and understood in American aviation and intelligence circles even before the Battle of Leyte Gulf. "We all knew at that time the Japanese had very little carrier aviation," said Truman Hedding, a former Task Force 58 chief of staff now posted to Nimitz's CINCPAC headquarters. "It was practically nothing . . . and any one of our carrier task groups could have overwhelmed them."[127] Hedding's judgment was corroborated by many other authorities at the time and after the war.

As for the Center Force, Halsey considered it "so heavily damaged that it could not win a decision . . . with battle efficiency greatly impaired by torpedo hits, bomb hits, topside damage, fires, and casualties."[128] But that assessment was based solely upon the reports of Task Force 38 pilots returning from the day's strikes in the Sibuyan Sea. Three years of war had revealed that such claims were generally exaggerated, often to a prodigal extent. The various task group commanders were amazed that Halsey would bet so much upon their accuracy, especially after new air patrols confirmed that the Center Force was again headed toward San Bernardino Strait, where the navigation lights had been turned on. On this point, Halsey convicted himself with his own pen, or rather his yeoman's typewriter. He thought it so vital to take his whole enormous fleet north that he would risk letting Kurita's battleships have their way with the transports in Leyte Gulf:

> Jap doggedness was admitted, and Commander Third Fleet recognized the possibility that the Center Force might plod through San Bernardino Straits and on to attack Leyte forces, a la Guadalcanal, but Commander Third Fleet was convinced that the Center Force was so heavily damaged that it could not win a decision. . . . Finally, it was calculated that the Third Fleet forces could return in time to reverse any advantage that the Center Force might gain. . . . It was a hard decision to make, and having made it, Commander Third Fleet was gravely concerned until he received word that the Center Force had given up in the face of the valiant efforts of the Seventh Fleet CVE groups.[129]

Not surprisingly, General MacArthur saw the matter in an entirely different light. It is not known whether he read the lines just quoted from the Third Fleet action report, but this is how he imagined the same scenario:

> Should the naval covering forces allow either of the powerful advancing Japanese thrusts to penetrate into Leyte Gulf, the whole Philippine invasion would be placed in the gravest jeopardy. . . . It was a dramatic situation fraught with disaster. . . . Should the enemy gain entrance to Leyte Gulf, his powerful naval guns could pulverize any of the eggshell transports present in the area and destroy vitally needed supplies on the beachhead. The thousands of U.S. troops ashore would be isolated and pinned down helplessly between enemy fire from ground and sea. Then, too, the schedule for supply reinforcement would not only be completely upset, but the success of the invasion itself would be placed in jeopardy. . . . Now I could do nothing but consolidate my troops, tighten my lines, and await the outcome of the impending naval battle.[130]

If Kurita had been more steadfast, precisely such a calamity might have occurred. The long-term consequences might not have been quite so dire as MacArthur predicted—it is difficult to see how the invasion could have failed, given the state of Japanese air and ground strength. But the reverberations would have reached all the way back to Washington. Every journalist in the Pacific would have pounced on the story, and MacArthur's censorship apparatus would have let it be told. Regardless of censorship, the facts would have quickly spread to stateside newsrooms, and the story would have broken during the final two weeks of a hotly contested presidential campaign—a campaign in which the challenger had already criticized the incumbent for splitting the Pacific into two commands. On Capitol Hill, where there had been much caterwauling about command disunity in the Pacific, lawmakers would have scheduled hearings. Halsey and the navy would have been blamed for the disaster, justifiably. The massacre of MacArthur's transport fleet would have been offered as Exhibit A in his case for a unified command in the Pacific. The JCS would have been obliged to revisit the perennially quarrelsome issue under the glare of intense public scrutiny.

Privately at the time, and publicly after the war, Halsey blamed his misunderstanding with Kinkaid on a faulty command setup. He told Nimitz in a private "My dear Chester," written a week after the battle, that "two autonomous tactical fleet commands cannot be justified from a naval viewpoint. Cooperation can never be a substitute for command in a naval action, and the further employment of the Seventh Fleet in conjunction with but separate and independent from the Pacific Fleet has all the elements of confusion, if not disaster."[131]

Nimitz made no reply to these remarks, or at any rate none can be found. But one can imagine what he must have been thinking. None of Halsey's errors on October 24 could be directly attributed to the command setup. Having often skirmished with MacArthur during his eighteen-month stint as SOPAC commander, Halsey was aware of the obstacles to a unified Pacific command. The situation remained precisely as it had been in April 1942, when the two-theater system had been negotiated by King and Marshall. MacArthur would resign before being subordinated to any admiral, but the admirals were equally unwilling to be subordinated to MacArthur, considering him unqualified to command the Pacific Fleet. The dual-command arrangement was inelegant and even wasteful, but it had functioned adequately for two-and-a-half years, and it still seemed to offer the "least worst" solution to the impasse. Halsey was officer-class—four-star flag officer-class—which meant that he was expected to act as a caretaker of the navy's institutional interests, to show finesse in managing rivalries with other services and theaters, and to leave no opening for political mischief. The higher dimension of Halsey's failure at Leyte Gulf is revealed in that light—he nearly wrecked the consensus that had secured the navy's control of its own crown jewels, the Pacific Fleet.

In the end, of course, no such crisis occurred, because Kurita's retreat had saved the day. There was some grumbling against Halsey in the Seventh Fleet, and even in the Third Fleet—but those sour notes were muffled by the louder celebrations of a historic Allied victory. MacArthur issued a triumphant communiqué on October 26. Secretary Forrestal, determined that the navy should share the next morning's headlines, released Halsey's earlier message of that date declaring that the Japanese fleet had been "beaten, routed, and broken by the Third and Seventh Fleets."[132] At a White House press conference, FDR read Halsey's message aloud, and it was quoted in hundreds of American newspapers the following day. In the eyes of the American people, Halsey now loomed larger than ever before.

No one was interested in letting a public feud ruin the moment. Kinkaid scrubbed his action report of any direct criticism aimed at Halsey. When one of Nimitz's subordinates drafted a report critical of Halsey's decisions, Nimitz brusquely instructed the man, "Tone it down." When a number of SWPA officers disparaged Halsey's performance at a meeting that week, General MacArthur cut them off: "That's enough. Leave the Bull alone. He's still a fighting admiral in my book."[133]

Many have contended that Halsey kept his job because his fame and popularity were valuable to the navy. No direct evidence for this claim can be found in communications between Nimitz and King, or in their later interviews and writings. So far as is known, it was never cited by Secretary Forrestal, Admiral Leahy, or any other member of the Joint Chiefs. Nevertheless, it is plausible. The Leyte battle and its aftermath coincided with Forrestal's drive to upgrade the navy's public relations. For the rest of the war, Halsey's blustering personal style and his "Kill More Japs" sloganeering were featured widely in press accounts and newsreels. At a Washington press conference in February 1945, Halsey boasted that the Third Fleet had wrested command of the sea from the "bestial apes." He added: "We have knocked down their planes, we have burned them, we have drowned them. And they're just as pleasant to burn as they are to drown."[134]

Halsey retained a fund of goodwill with his colleagues and superiors, for whom the disasters and emergencies of 1942 remained fresh in memory. Often in the past, his fearless and rousing leadership had seemed reckless, but it had succeeded. He had earned the right to a few mistakes. Relieving him of command would only draw unwelcome attention to the near-disaster in Leyte Gulf. And who would replace him? Four-star officers who possessed the requisite seniority and were qualified for the job were vanishingly few. Mitscher could have been fleeted up, but he was overdue for a long rest, and his replacement (John McCain) was still learning the ropes. King and Nimitz apparently discussed the possibility of relieving Halsey, at least temporarily, but quickly discarded the idea. The two-platoon rotation system, alternating every few months between Halsey and Spruance, would remain intact through the end of the war—and Halsey (but not Spruance) would eventually receive a fifth star.

THE COMMAND CONTROVERSIES of Leyte Gulf had a long and tortuous postwar afterlife. Halsey could never quite bring himself to acknowledge that the Japanese had deliberately set out to lure him north, and that the aircraft carriers of Ozawa's Northern Force had been nothing more than bait. That self-serving conviction somehow persisted even after copies of Plan *Sho* were recovered and translated, and even after Ozawa, Kurita, Toyoda, and others told the whole story to U.S. interrogators after the war. The role of the Japanese carriers, Ozawa told the U.S. Strategic Bombing Survey, was strictly limited: "A decoy, that was our first primary mission. . . . The chief concern was to lure your forces further north; we expected complete destruction."[135] More than six years after that important disclosure, Halsey still claimed to be perplexed by the failure of Ozawa's carriers to put up a better fight. In an article for the U.S. Naval Institute journal *Proceedings*, he wrote: "A curious feature of this engagement is that the air duel never came off. Our strikes found scarcely a handful of planes on the enemy carriers' decks and only fifteen on the wing."[136]

A little humility would have gone a long way at this late stage of Halsey's distinguished career. He was a five-star fleet admiral, one of only four in history, a position that entitled him to active duty status with full salary, an office, lodging allowance, and a car and driver until the end of his life. Through the sale of his memoirs and a lucrative tour on the public speaking circuit, he became rich. Seats on corporate boards added another generous source of income. "Bull" Halsey was a major celebrity with a devoted public following, often appearing on television in the 1950s. He could have remained aloof from the judgments of historians. It would have cost him little to acknowledge error at Leyte Gulf—indeed, it probably would have enhanced rather than diminished his legacy. He might have said publicly what he once admitted privately—that he wished Spruance had been in command at Leyte Gulf, and he (Halsey) in command at the Battle of the Philippine Sea.[137] But until his death in 1959, the proud old fleet admiral fought a losing rearguard action against the hardening judgment of history.

During the war, he had counted Samuel Eliot Morison a friend. In 1950, however, Morison delivered a lecture to naval officers in which he called Halsey's decision to leave San Bernardino Strait unguarded a "blunder." Halsey heard about the remark through the grapevine and confronted Morison in an angry letter. The historian agreed not to use the term "blunder" again, but he did not back off his thesis. In future lectures, he told Halsey, he would substitute the term "error of judgment." Considering this reply unsatisfactory, the admiral called Morison a "splendid Monday morning quarterback."[138]

A frosty silence followed until 1958, when Leyte—the twelfth volume of Morison's series on the naval operations of World War II—appeared in print. In it, Morison bluntly concluded that Halsey had fallen for the Japanese ploy to lure him north, and that he was chiefly responsible for the near-debacle at Samar. The admiral, incensed, tried to rally his old Third Fleet officers to launch a counterattack. "My idea is to get the son of a bitch's cojones in a vice and set up on them," he wrote one of the Dirty Tricksters. "I hope you will join me."[139] Some were willing to join in such a campaign, but Mick Carney (who had subsequently risen to the navy's top rung, chief of naval operations) threw cold water on the project. Morison's reputation was unassailable, warned Carney, and "No blast of yours, however justifiable, will destroy that structure; it would far more likely boomerang."[140] He suggested that Halsey instead file a statement of refutation with the Naval History office.

The old fleet admiral apparently took his former chief of staff's advice. But a few months later he added another leading scholar to his blacklist. E. B. Potter, a professor at the Naval Academy, had asked Halsey to read the manuscript of a forthcoming book. Not liking the professor's account of the Battle of Leyte Gulf, the admiral sent this peevish and even menacing reply: "I do not intend to allow grossly wrong statements about my thoughts to go into a book which will be used to teach midshipmen, without making trouble for you."[141]

In Halsey's declining years, the nickname "Bull" gained wider currency. Halsey had never much liked it, even when it was fixed upon him by an adoring press and public in 1942. It had never caught on in his Nouméa headquarters or among his Third Fleet staff. MacArthur must never have received the word, because he had used the nickname almost exclusively when referring to Halsey, and even when addressing Halsey directly. The admiral had let it stand, probably because MacArthur seemed to mean it with sincere respect and affection. But now, in his later years, Halsey refused to answer to the "fake, flamboyant" nickname.[142] He told a friend, "Only those people who don't know me call me Bull."[143]

It was no wonder that Halsey rejected the nickname. It was decidedly double-edged, and grew more so on reflection. The bull is respected for its size, strength, and aggression, but not for its tactical acumen. The bull is stubborn, unreasoning, "bull-headed." It goes about its work heedlessly, "like a bull at the gate." Other large beasts are clumsy in tight quarters, but it is the bull that is most dreaded by the world's china shop proprietors. Every mammal leaves its feces on the ground, but it is the bull's that has a revered place in American slang, signifying "nonsense, lies, or exaggeration."

The bull chases the matador's cape while failing to notice his sword. Seeing red, the bull lowers its horns and charges, confident of striking down this feeble antagonist. But in the end, it is almost always the bull's bloody carcass that is dragged from the bullring, while the matador leaves on his feet.

Chapter Seven

In an award-winning essay for the U.S. Naval Institute published after the war, Captain J. C. Wylie Jr. argued that Japan had been beaten by a synergetic combination of "sequential" and "cumulative" operational strategies. The first was represented by the westward naval-amphibious offensive, a *sequence* of battles and invasions carrying Allied forces ever closer to Japan. The sequential campaign could be diagrammed with arrows on a map, indicating the territorial gains of fleets and armies. It lent itself to a conventional chronological narrative. It was intuitively graspable, even to laymen without formal military training or education. To those who had followed the war in the newspapers, or read the early campaign histories, the sequential campaign was *the* story of the Pacific War.

By contrast, according to Wylie, a cumulative operational strategy does not involve territorial offensives and pitched battles, but a "less perceptible minute accumulation of little items piling one on top of the other, until at some unknown point the mass of calculated actions may be large enough to be critical."[1] It weaponizes the logic of "death by a thousand cuts." In the Pacific, cumulative strategies chipped away at the economic and political foundations of Japan's imperial empire. One example was propaganda, sometimes called "psychological warfare," aimed at foreign peoples under Japanese occupation, Japanese civilians, the rank and file of Japan's armed forces, and eventually even the senior leadership circle in Tokyo. Another was strategic bombing. Beginning in November 1944, a sustained bombing campaign was launched against Japan's industrial heartland, aimed at crippling major war industries. Eventually it laid waste to most of the nation's urban areas. Most tellingly, U.S. air and naval power (especially submarines) were deployed against Japan's overseas shipping routes, in a campaign that cumulatively throttled the nation's warmaking potential. By 1945, quite apart from the sequential territorial gains of MacArthur's and Nimitz's twin offensives, the Japanese economy was running on fumes and sputtering toward a final breakdown.

More than any other industrial nation, and certainly more than any other major combatant of the Second World War, Japan lacked self-sufficiency in raw materials. The home islands were all but destitute of natural resources, offering little or no oil, iron ore, bauxite, or other useful minerals, and only limited reserves of timber and low-grade coal. Since the Meiji period, when Japan had first aspired to become the leading power in Asia, the chief aim of its foreign policy had been to secure access to these basic commodities. Through the 1920s, foreign trade had met the requirements, and Japanese diplomacy was shaped by the need to protect and sustain that trade. But in the 1930s, the era of Japan's "dark valley," the ascendant militarist-imperialist regime was determined to seize and colonize overseas territories that could supply the necessary inputs to its industrial economy and war machine.

In 1931, the invasion of resource-rich Manchuria locked down a copious supply of iron ore and coking coal for Japanese steel mills. But Japan had remained helplessly dependent on the United States and certain European colonial territories in Southeast Asia for imports of crude oil, rubber, bauxite, copper, zinc, and other ferro-alloys and nonferrous metals. Japan's most important foreign suppliers—the United States, Britain, and the Netherlands—were aligned against Nazi Germany. Even so, in September 1940, Tokyo joined with Berlin and Rome to form the Axis alliance, a rash decision that triggered an onslaught of trade sanctions. Prior to 1940, the United States had supplied 74 percent of Japan's scrap metal imports, 93 percent of its copper imports, and (most vitally) about 80 percent of its oil imports. In 1940, the Roosevelt administration began imposing embargos on these and other goods, and these measures escalated steadily in scope and severity. In August 1941, the West Texas crude oil spigots were entirely shut off. With no other viable source of oil, Japan was forced to tap into a finite and diminishing domestic stockpile. More than any other single factor, that crisis prompted the Tojo cabinet's fateful decision to launch the Pacific War.

In the opening phase of the conflict, Japan had fixed its resource problem by launching a *Blitzkrieg* offensive against Allied colonial territories to the south. By April 1942, just four months after Pearl Harbor, the conqueror was digesting the resource-rich prizes of Malaya, the East Indies, and the Philippines, among others. Above all, Japan had seized control of Borneo and Sumatra, erstwhile Dutch and British colonies that were home to the region's most productive oilfields and refineries.

But there was no way around the bothersome fact that the captured oil-fields were a long way from home. The lifeblood of the Japanese economy flowed through a long and tenuous sea link, a 3,000-mile-long femoral artery. If this artery was severed, the Japanese war machine would quickly bleed out, and defeat would become inevitable. The threat was clearly foreseen in Tokyo, even before the nation's reckless lurch into an unwinnable war, but the ruling junta had persuaded themselves that the sea lanes could be safe-guarded long enough to attain victory. Even so, they knew the margins were narrow. Japan's merchant marine was hard run, at nearly 100 percent utili-zation. At the end of 1938, just 0.3 percent of Japan's merchant fleet was laid up in ordinary (idled), while comparable ratios for the British and American merchant fleets were 3 percent and 10 percent, respectively.[2] Shipping was needed not only for the importation of raw materials, but to supply overseas armies, fleets, and bases. Moreover, only 3 percent of Japanese territory was arable land, and food imports were needed to stave off famine. Shipping was imperative even to Japan's domestic transportation system. The nation's rail system was generally too light to haul heavy freight, and most industrial trade was carried from port to port in coasting vessels.

After an intensive shipbuilding drive in the late 1930s, the merchant fleet (comprising steel ships of at least 500 gross tons) had grown to an approximate total of 6 million tons. Of this quantity, about 4.1 million tons was claimed by the army and navy for their own shipping pools, leaving just 1.9 million tons for civilian and industrial purposes.[3] The Cabinet Plan-ning Board insisted that at least 3 million tons of shipping was needed to keep the Japanese economy turning over, but the military services refused to allocate more ships to civilian uses. The regime expected shipping losses of between 800,000 and 1.1 million tons in the first year of war, declining to 700,000–800,000 tons in each of the two following years. Wartime con-struction was expected to offset these losses, at least partially. Japan's war-time shipbuilding effort was heroic in scale, rising from 238,000 tons of new cargo shipping launched in 1941, to 1.6 million tons launched in 1944. But sinkings ran much higher than forecast, and net losses remained critical in every year of the war.[4]

The Japanese army and navy largely neglected to cooperate with one another, or with the civilian merchant marine. Military cargo vessels carried troops, weapons, and supplies to overseas bases, then returned to Japan in ballast (empty). Shipping efficiency might have been improved by diverting them to nearby ports, to embark cargoes for the return passage. But the Japanese regime possessed no single controlling authority to impose such an arrangement on the rival military services.

If Japan's overseas shipping routes were vulnerable to air and submarine attack, its urban and industrial areas were virtually defenseless against strategic aerial bombing. Japan's industrial base was new and emergent, having been conjured up from almost nothing in thirty or forty years. Bureaucrats and capitalists, working in partnership, had set out to bootstrap an industrial economy centered on munitions production, with priority given to the steel, shipbuilding, automotive, aircraft, tank, and machine tool industries. The results were astonishing, even unique in history. In 1940, a year before the attack on Pearl Harbor, heavy industrial production had increased by fivefold in a dozen years. Seventeen percent of the Japanese economy was devoted to war production, as compared to 2.6 percent of the U.S. economy.[5] Munitions production rose sharply as a share of Japanese GDP after 1941, approaching 50 percent in 1944. At that stage, Japan's civilian population was more or less immiserated, and most of the remaining (nonmunitions) share of the economy involved agriculture and food production. There was simply no room for further growth in the war industries; all slack had been wrung out of the system. Plant utilization ran just short of 100 percent during the war, except when production lines shut down for lack of requisite materials. Industries relied on an elite cadre of trained machinists and engineers who could not be easily replaced. Production was concentrated in a few large plants served by comparatively retrograde logistics. For example, most Japanese steel production, which undergirded the entire economy, was concentrated in six major steelworks whose location was known to the Allies. The supply might be disrupted by a few well-executed bombing raids, targeting either the steelworks themselves or the transport infrastructure that served them. Without spare plant capacity to fall back upon, the effects would quickly ripple through the economy.

It was plain, therefore, that Japan's power to make war could be undermined, perhaps fatally, by sea and air attacks on merchant tonnage and war industries. But how to weigh opposing Allied priorities in a vast and intricate war? The struggle between (if you like) "sequentialists" and "cumulativists" colored every phase of Pacific strategy. Allied commanders in the field or at sea were instinctively inclined to think first about their immediate tactical problems, and cast doubt on the value of long-term "cumulative" operations against the enemy's economy. "Marus"—Japanese merchant cargo vessels—were seen as secondary targets, or consolation prizes, by army and navy aviators. Theater commanders were inclined to direct air power to the latest hot spots, and questioned the value of open-ended strategic bombing missions against the enemy's distant homeland. Submarines were used in sundry roles and missions, often with no overarching strategic rationale: not until late 1943 were they deployed in a single-minded drive to destroy Japanese merchant tonnage.

In August 1944, as Admiral Halsey took command of the Third Fleet, he and his Dirty Tricksters proposed a basic change in the deployment of Pacific Fleet submarines. They called it the "Zoo plan." Mick Carney and Rollo Wilson worked out the details. About two dozen zones, in seas bordering the Philippines, Formosa, and the Ryukyu Islands, were designated by the names of different animals (thus "zoo"). Submarine wolfpacks would be positioned across the sea lanes in each zone, with orders to intercept and sink Japanese warships in the aftermath of a major fleet engagement. No matter what the outcome of the expected naval battle, Carney later explained, the Japanese fleet would afterward "retire to refuel and go back to their bases, and at that time they would be forced to go through a tight line of submarines deployed against the line of retreat."[6]

In a private letter to Nimitz on September 28, 1944—less than a month before the Battle of Leyte Gulf—Halsey made the case for "Zoo." Acknowledging the value of sinking merchant tonnage, he argued that "every weapon in the Pacific should be brought to bear if and when the enemy fleet sorties."[7] Halsey proposed that the submarines be placed under his direct tactical command, at least until the impending naval showdown, so that they could be properly coordinated with the Third Fleet.

After giving this proposal "thorough consideration," Nimitz rejected it. He let his friend down tactfully, in a "Dear Bill" dated October 8. Submarines would attack enemy warships whenever the opportunity arose, he said, but their chief mandate would remain commerce-destroying operations. Nimitz and his submarine force commander, Vice Admiral Charles A. Lockwood, would retain direct tactical control of the boats. He urged Halsey to "accept my decisions as resulting from full consideration of all the factors involved, usually in light of more information than is available to you and always with the background of my wider responsibilities."[8]

In an ironic twist, Nimitz found himself on the other side of an analogous dispute concerning the new B-29 "Superfortress" bomber, which was being deployed in large numbers to airfields in the Mariana Islands, and would commence bombing missions over Japan the following month. The weight and range of this giant Boeing airplane was unprecedented—it could haul a 10,000-pound payload to a radius of 1,600 miles. The USAAF brass, led by General Arnold, was determined that the entire fleet of Superforts should be deployed in a strategic bombing campaign against Japan. But the theater commanders had designs on the new bombers, and were bursting with ideas about how they might be deployed in tactical roles. Nimitz's headquarters was interested in their capabilities for long-range reconnaissance, search-and-rescue operations, and minelaying in Japan's inland waters. MacArthur expected *all* of the B-29s to be sent to his SWPA domain, warning George Marshall that "the initial employment from the Marianas of this untried airplane would subject it to the most difficult operating conditions for its first combat employment."[9]

But Hap Arnold outmaneuvered both Nimitz and MacArthur. He persuaded his fellow Joint Chiefs to create a new unified air command, the Twentieth Air Force, dedicated solely to a strategic bombing campaign against Japan's home islands. Unlike any other air force, the Twentieth would be controlled directly by the JCS from Washington. Orders would be given by Arnold, acting as the "agent" for his fellow chiefs. It would include two bomber commands, the 20th and the 21st, based in India-China and the Marianas, respectively. Although the 21st Bomber Command would be based in Nimitz's theater, the CINCPAC would hold no authority over it, except in an emergency. The atypical command setup was necessary, General Arnold maintained, to ensure that the Superfortresses stuck to their primary mission of hitting industrial targets in Japan.

When Nimitz learned of this development, he was not pleased. Brigadier General Haywood S. "Possum" Hansell Jr., the first B-29 air commander in the Marianas, visited Pacific Fleet headquarters on October 5, 1944. Nimitz told him bluntly: "I must say to you that I am in strong disagreement with these arrangements. . . . This is an abrogation of the chain of command." But since the Joint Chiefs had already acted, his hands were tied, and he pledged to do his utmost to support Hansell: "I will give you all the help and cooperation in my capability. You have my very best wishes for success."[10]

The record does not show whether Nimitz noted the parallel to his disagreement with Halsey over the "Zoo plan," which the CINCPAC vetoed three days later. Nimitz kept the submarines out of Halsey's hands in order to safeguard their "cumulativist" mission to cut Japan's overseas shipping links. The Joint Chiefs kept the B-29s out of Nimitz's hands in order to safeguard their "cumulativist" mission to bomb Japan.

WITH RARE EXCEPTIONS, the submarines were kept out of the public eye. Press reporting was minimal, especially during the early stages of the Pacific War. The nickname given to the submarine force, the "Silent Service," was well earned: submarine warriors were instinctively tight-lipped, even in the presence of their colleagues in other branches of the navy. Their base at Pearl Harbor seemed enigmatic, even ominous. Low, sleek, coal-black boats, tucked behind finger piers on East Loch, were distinguishable only by stenciled numbers on their bridge towers. In the Navy Yard, just behind the piers, sat a plain three-story concrete office building. A discreet street-level sign identified it as "ComSubPac" headquarters.

One of those rare exceptions was the arrival in Pearl Harbor of the *Gato*-class submarine *Wahoo* on the morning of February 7, 1943. Someone in Pacific Fleet headquarters had decided that the submarine force was due for a dose of public acclaim. The *Wahoo* came up the channel under escort, wearing a broom fixed (bristles up) to her periscope shears and a long banner inscribed with the motto: "Shoot the Sunza Bitches." A crowd of hundreds was waiting on the pier, including war correspondents, photographers, and newsreel film crews. As the *Wahoo* inched into her berth, a brass band struck up a tune. A delegation of senior officers in gold braid came up the gangplank, followed by a battery of newsmen who had been cleared to take photographs and interview members of the crew. The *Wahoo*'s sailors, habituated to secrecy, were collectively gobsmacked. One marveled in his diary: "I had my picture taken in the aft engine room. It will be in the *Time* magazine."[11]

This burst of publicity was occasioned by the *Wahoo*'s sensational third war patrol, just ended, in which the submarine was credited with sinking five ships totaling 32,000 tons. (The broom, abovementioned, symbolized a "clean sweep.") Under the aggressive and eccentric Captain Dudley W. "Mushmouth" Morton, the *Wahoo* had proven that a submarine could take risks previously deemed imprudent, that it could stay on the surface for long hours in daylight, and that it could hunt with impunity on the surface at night, even in the presence of Japanese escort ships. With his trusty understudy, executive officer Richard O'Kane, Morton had pioneered new procedures for approaching and attacking targets. O'Kane was designated "co-approach officer," and made all periscope observations during torpedo attacks, thus freeing Morton to consider all other sources of incoming data while making decisions. The most spectacular feat of the *Wahoo*'s cruise had occurred in Wewak harbor, New Guinea, where she had fought off a charging Japanese destroyer with an unprecedented "down the throat" torpedo shot. Asked how he had felt during that tense encounter, Morton replied: "Why do you think I made O'Kane look at [the destroyer]? He's the bravest man I know!"[12]

Morton was a big, irreverent, swaggering Kentuckian with the accent to prove it, who roamed around the ship in a disgraceful red bathrobe and provoked spontaneous wrestling matches with surprised shipmates. He colored his patrol reports with wry little commentaries that had little or nothing to do with the business of submarining. His attitude toward the enemy was ruthless. Morton seemed to regard it as his personal duty to sink every Japanese ship that floated, and felt no compunction about slaughtering their crews. He was the type of personality whose career might have languished in the peacetime navy—but under the peculiar pressures of war, his buccaneering attitude and risk-seeking tactics made him a star.

The *Wahoo*'s third patrol had been only twenty-four days long, among the shortest on record (only because she had turned home after expending all of her torpedoes). The customary interval between submarine patrols was two weeks, during which time the crews—officers and bluejackets alike— enjoyed a swanky R&R at the Royal Hawaiian Hotel, queen of Waikiki Beach. But since the *Wahoo* had come home so quickly, Admiral Lockwood decided that a single week's liberty was long enough.

The submarine was given a stem-to-stern overhaul. She was dry docked, and her bottom scraped and repainted; she was cleaned, reprovisioned, and armed with new torpedoes. Her 4-inch deck gun was transferred forward, and a third 20mm machine gun was mounted aft. All American submarines were being modified to augment their on-deck firepower, because experience had shown that "surface and destroy" tactics were delivering results.

On February 17, with the crew aboard, and a delegation waiting to see her off, the *Wahoo* made ready for sea. Her engines rumbled in idle. Sailors uncleated her mooring lines and heaved them back onto the pier. She crept into the fairway at half-knot speed, blue clouds of her own exhaust wafting along with her. With the help of a pilot, she edged out of the congested harbor and passed down Pearl Harbor's long, narrow entrance channel shortly before noon.

The *Wahoo*'s fourth patrol would take her into waters not yet penetrated by American submarines—the East China Sea and the Yellow Sea, close inshore to China and Korea. Morton had asked for the mission, and Lockwood had granted it. Morton knew those waters well, having passed through the region as a young officer in the mid-1930s. Some of the busiest shipping routes in the world lay in those waters, including links between Tsingtao, Darien, the mouth of the Yellow River, and Shimonoseki Strait (the western entrance to Japan's Inland Sea, between Kyushu and Honshu). Morton told O'Kane and the crew that the *Wahoo* was headed for "virgin territory" and should "make a killing" in the forthcoming cruise.[13]

The boat forged across the cold gray wastes, bucking through nasty head seas day after day. She ran on the surface, except for a standard daily training dive. Not a single patrol craft or plane was sighted. *Wahoo* made a quick refueling stop at Midway, where she took aboard a crate of improvised Molotov cocktails, a gift from the island's marine garrison. (It was thought that they might come in handy during close encounters with sampans and other small craft.) With seas building in the first week of March, she throttled back to one-engine speed in order to conserve fuel.

On the morning of March 10, a high periscope observation revealed the rugged green mountains of Yakushima, an island south of Kyushu. Many other islands of the "Nansei Shoto" archipelago came into view, including some that could be readily identified by volcanoes or other landmarks. The *Wahoo* ran through the Colonet Strait, the main passage through the Nansei Shoto, on the night of the eleventh. The next morning before dawn, she battle-surfaced in the East China Sea, her assigned patrolling area.

For the next several days, the *Wahoo* remained submerged throughout the daylight hours, hunting fat targets along the shipping route between

Formosa and Kyushu. The area was crowded with "small fry"—fishing sampans, junks, and trawlers of less than 500 tons, often lit up at night, indicating that they were not military vessels. The skipper and executive officer (XO) took turns at the periscope, and debated whether various targets merited a torpedo. On March 13, they fired the first of the boat's twenty-four torpedoes at a large trawler. But the weapon ran under the target's stern, and Morton would not risk wasting another torpedo; he preferred to keep his powder dry for the bigger game he expected to find farther north. In the following four days, the *Wahoo* passed near hundreds of sampans, and the crew nicknamed the area "Sampan Alley." On March 17, the patrol report noted, the *Wahoo* "had some difficulty in dodging all of the junks and trawlers to prevent being sighted."[14]

She pushed north, into the heavily trafficked waters of the Yellow Sea—a shallow inshore lobe of the Pacific, enclosed on three sides by China, Manchuria, and Korea. Prevailing northerly winds swept an Arctic cold front into the region, and men standing watch on the bridge at night wore heavy wool coats, hats, and gloves. They could see their breath in the moonlight; they stamped their feet and clapped their hands; the skin on their faces grew red and raw, and they were relieved frequently by their shipmates.

Morton had cruised in these waters before the war, and had studied the charts and intelligence reports. He expected to find a wealth of targets on the routes linking Tsingtao and Darien to Nagasaki and Shimonoseki, and he was not wrong. In a five-day romp between March 19 and March 25, the *Wahoo* sank five cargo ships of more than 2,000 tons. The new torpex warheads packed a terrific wallop: several of the targets were observed to simply disintegrate when hit. Debris was ejected hundreds of feet into the air, and the remaining intact sections of hull usually sank in two minutes or less. Survivors were often seen clinging to wreckage. Since the sea was only a few degrees above freezing, few of the castaways would survive. But Morton was determined not to leave witnesses who could "tell on us."[15] On March 21, after sinking the freighter *Nitu Maru* off the Shandong peninsula, Morton ordered the *Wahoo* up to the surface and the deck guns manned. He conned the ship to run over one of the lifeboats, knocking the survivors into the frigid sea. A 20mm gun quickly killed the swimmers. A *Wahoo* sailor recorded in his diary: "So the *Nitu Maru* & her entire cargo & crew are now where the rest of the Jap Navy will soon be."[16]

About one-third of all torpedoes fired by the *Wahoo* in the Yellow Sea failed to function as intended. This was an endemic problem throughout the first two years of the Pacific War—American torpedoes ran off course, or ran under their targets, or bounced off an enemy ship's hull without exploding, or exploded prematurely, or sank, or circled back toward the submarine that had fired them. At dawn on March 25, partly because of Morton's frustration with malfunctioning torpedoes, the *Wahoo* surfaced and took on a small freighter with the submarine's 4-inch deck guns. Morton enjoyed using his deck guns in this way, and certainly they were much more reliable than the torpedoes: but the weapon was arguably a bit too large to be mounted on a 1,500-ton submarine, and its muzzle blast played havoc with the topside works. One sailor remembered watching as the deck planking was torn away by the concussions. Nonetheless, the gun systematically tore the 2,500-ton freighter to pieces, until it sank from sight. Some of the *Wahoo*'s crew taunted the surviving Japanese sailors, as they clung to the wreckage of their ship, shouting, "So solly, please!"[17]

The *Wahoo*'s patrol report observed of this encounter: "Anyone who has not witnessed a submarine conduct a battle surface with three 20mm and a 4-inch gun in the morning twilight with a calm sea and in crisp and clear weather, just ain't lived . . . it was truly spectacular."[18]

Staying on the surface even as the light came up in the east, the *Wahoo* ran down and destroyed another freighter and several smaller vessels. Speeding away to the south and submerging, the *Wahoo* tracked a 7,000-ton naval auxiliary and fired three torpedoes at it. One struck near the bow, crippling the ship but not sinking it.[19] Morton did not claim a sinking; but postwar analysis showed that this victim had indeed sunk after fleeing to the north.

The *Wahoo*'s rampage set off alarm bells in Tokyo. IGHQ assumed that an American wolfpack must be operating in the Yellow Sea. Patrol craft converged on the site of the recent sinkings, and reconnaissance airplanes crisscrossed the sky overhead. For all his bravado, Morton was not a cowboy. O'Kane was a voice of reason, urging prudence in light of the dangers inherent in this patrol. The Yellow Sea was really just a flooded continental shelf, too shallow to accommodate the deep-diving evasive maneuvers that were a submarine's best defense against depth-charge attacks. Morton referred to the sea as a "wading pond," and his patrol report noted, "we have to be careful with our angle on dives to keep from plowing into the bottom."[20] Some of the ubiquitous sampans and junks were probably military patrols; several were observed to mount large radar arrays and radio transmitters that one would not expect to find on a fishing boat. Surface-and-destroy was a fine tactic when it worked, and thus far it *had* worked—but any harmless-looking trawler might have a deck gun concealed under a tarp, and a direct hit by a mid-caliber shell might be enough to destroy a submarine.

Firing faulty or dud torpedoes often served only to announce a submarine's presence. On the afternoon of March 25, after *Wahoo*'s run of sinkings earlier in the day, a Japanese destroyer bore down on the submarine. The angle on the bow was manageable, and the *Wahoo* might have maneuvered for a good torpedo attack on her adversary. She had two torpedoes left. In Wewak, two months earlier, she had destroyed an enemy destroyer with an audacious "down-the-throat" torpedo shot. In this case, Morton and O'Kane agreed to play it safe. The *Wahoo* crash-dived to 150 feet, rigging for depth charge. The destroyer passed out of range, apparently unaware of the submarine's presence. According to the patrol report, the *Wahoo* "did not dare tackle this fellow with only two torpedoes aboard from late experience would likely be prematures. It hurt our pride to have to hide in our shell and crawl away."[21]

Farther south, the next day, the *Wahoo* fired a single torpedo at a 4,000-ton freighter laden with coal, probably bound for the steelworks in Kyushu. The fish struck amidships and the ship went up with a mighty thunderclap, launching a mushroom cloud of coal dust that left the air unbreathable for a few minutes. The *Wahoo* continued working south, stalking the main shipping route to the southern territories, and let her last fish loose at a freighter on March 28. She sank in two minutes.

With all torpedoes expended, Morton ordered the *Wahoo* to the surface. She charged back into Sampan Alley, terrorizing small craft with her deck guns. On the morning of March 27, the *Wahoo* ran down a trawler with a large radio antenna, which Morton suspected was a Japanese military patrol craft. Three deck guns blasted away as the trawler began to founder. The 20mm guns overheated, and their barrels were dunked in barrels of seawater. One crew member noted that the guns were so hot that they boiled off the water in the barrels. A "commando team" of divers went across to the sinking wreck to search it for documents, but found none. They finished her off with a few of the Molotov cocktails contributed by the marines on Midway.

That night, as the *Wahoo* withdrew toward Colonet Strait, the crew listened to Radio Tokyo, and were amused to hear the announcer declare that no American submarines would dare approach Japanese waters.

The *Wahoo*'s fourth patrol had been another triumph. In nineteen days in the Yellow Sea, often remaining on the surface, she had sunk nine ships, a trawler, and two fishing sampans. She had penetrated into waters that the Japanese had previously thought safe, taking full advantage of the element of surprise. Morton claimed eight ships, and was credited for eight; the postwar reckoning raised the score to nine, which made it the best single cruise of the war as measured by the number of enemy ships destroyed. His rampage through the Yellow Sea confirmed Morton's status as the "most valuable player" in the Pacific submarine force.

The *Wahoo* had run up her fearsome tally despite the malfunctioning of at least six torpedoes, one-quarter of her total. Her failure to sink a fat oil tanker on March 24 was especially galling. Morton had fired four torpedoes at this high-value target, and none had functioned as intended. Two had detonated prematurely; a third was knocked off course by those two untimely neighboring blasts; and the fourth had begun "porpoising"— diving and surfacing in a sine-wave pattern—and gone careening off course. Morton gave Admiral Lockwood an earful about the problem, and Lockwood did not doubt a word of it. By the summer of 1943, he was convinced that the Mark 14 steam torpedo was a lemon, and he was raising a ruckus in Washington about the problem. On June 24, he received Nimitz's permission to deactivate the magnetic exploder on all torpedoes, pending further investigation. That same week, Lockwood told Admiral King that torpedo failures had probably reduced the effectiveness of his Pacific submarine fleet by at least 50 percent through the first eighteen months of the war.

The trouble was aggravated by the scandalously slow response of the navy's Bureau of Ordnance, which had designed and built the Mark 14. The weapon had not been adequately tested prior to the war, partly owing to a lack of sufficient funds. Certain influential officers and engineers at the Naval Torpedo Station in Newport, Rhode Island seemed to take all complaints about the weapon personally, and insisted that any failures must be attributed to mishandling and poor maintenance practices at Pearl Harbor and aboard the submarines themselves. Confronted with such a response, the submariners redoubled their commitment, "babying" the weapons while on patrol, and firing them only in ideal conditions. Many boats began keeping the torpedo tube doors closed until moments before firing, so that the weapons would not be prematurely exposed to saltwater.

But the failures continued. The causes were numerous, and one cause tended to mask others, which tended to make them more difficult to identify and correct. Many were related to the "magnetic influence" detonator, a device intended to trigger a torpedo's warhead by detecting a target ship's magnetic field. This technology, highly advanced in its time, was a product of one of the most secret U.S. weapons programs of the prewar period. It was designed as a countermeasure to the hull "blisters" that were a common feature of most heavy warships. (Blisters were double hulls that bulged out at the waterline, shielding the inner hull against conventional torpedoes fired on the surface.) The idea was that a torpedo would run *under* the ship and explode directly beneath the keel. Such a blast, directed upward into the unprotected bottom, would do much greater damage to the target. But the magnetic influence trigger often went haywire in combat, resulting in a high percentage of duds and prematures. Eventually it was found that the designers had failed to account for magnetic variability in different regions of the world, and that the technology needed fine-tuning for longitude and latitude.

It was also found that the Mark 14 tended to run deeper than set, by a margin of about 10 or 11 feet. This problem was relatively easy to correct, but it was not finally identified until June 1942, six months into the war, when more than eight hundred of the weapons had already been fired in combat. Moreover, the problem was not uncovered by the Bureau of Ordnance, despite many complaints—it had fallen to Lockwood himself, then commander of the submarine force in Western Australia, to conduct a series of tests in King George Sound. The tests showed that the weapons were running (on average) 11 feet deeper than their settings. At first the Bureau of Ordnance held that Lockwood's tests were unauthorized and the results inaccurate. Only two months later, after Admiral King had "lit a blowtorch" under the bureau, did it concede (based on tests conducted in Newport) that the Mark 14 was indeed running deep and that the mechanism had been inadequately tested prior to the war.

Yet a third problem was masked for over a year by the other defects. The Mark 14's contact exploder, a conventional alternative to the magnetic influence exploder, had an excessively fragile firing pin that was often crushed on impact, failing to trigger the warhead. This problem was not identified until 1943, when Lockwood ordered the magnetic detonator deactivated on most boats. Soon came reports of torpedoes running directly into the hull of a target ship, striking at the optimal 90-degree angle, and simply bouncing off without detonating. The most notorious episode of the war came on July 24, 1943, when Captain Dan Daspit of the submarine *Tinosa* attacked a Japanese cargo ship west of Palau. With Daspit watching through the periscope, *Tinosa* fired eleven consecutive torpedoes at close range in near-perfect conditions. Torpedo after torpedo struck the ship and then sank out of sight. One bounced off the hull, leapt up out of the sea like a fish with a hook in its mouth, and then dove back into the water and vanished, like a fish that had spit out the hook. With one torpedo remaining, Daspit gave up trying to sink the target; he would carry that last weapon back to Pearl Harbor for a close examination.

Lockwood had done the Bureau of Ordnance's job a year earlier, with his tests in Australia. Now he repeated the act with a series of tests in Pearl Harbor. The faulty contact exploder was quickly identified, and the problem was easily corrected by reengineering the firing pin using a sturdy aluminum alloy. "This at last broke the back of the torpedo bureaucracy," said Edward Beach, a submarine officer of the era, "which was now willing to concede that expending a few extra torpedoes in laboratory tests was better than expending them impotently in combat."[22]

In September 1943, the Pacific submarine force was informed that the Mark 14 was finally "fixed," and aggregate statistics pointed to improving performance in the following months. However, reports of misbehaving torpedoes continued through the end of the war. The most dreaded malfunction was the "circular run," when a weapon's rudder jammed and caused it to turn back, fully armed, toward the submarine that had fired it. Several U.S. submarines experienced this horrifying mishap, and escaped narrowly by diving or maneuvering evasively on the surface. Two boats were known to have been destroyed by their own torpedoes, because someone on the crew survived to tell the tale. It stands to reason that others were sunk in the same manner, with the loss of all hands, but posterity can only wonder.

The next-generation Mark 18 Westinghouse electric torpedo, which left no visible wake of bubbles or exhaust, was being introduced into service just then, in the fall of 1943. The weapon was sent to the NTS in Newport for testing and trials—but the "Newport guys," as one submariner observed, were largely uncooperative. Having designed and built the Mark 14, the NTS engineers resented the Westinghouse product as a usurper. Goat Island (the island in Newport Harbor that was home to the NTS) was possessed by a "not invented here" syndrome. Officers of the submarine *Lapon*, supervising trials in Newport, were dismayed by the attitudes they encountered. "Maybe sabotage is too strong a word," said Eli Reich, the *Lapon*'s executive officer, "but they weren't helping one bit."[23] Reich told Lockwood's deputy in Pearl Harbor: "I don't think these people are war-minded."[24]

WAHOO RETURNED FROM HER FIFTH PATROL, which had taken her up into the icy northern latitudes of Japan's Kurile Islands, on May 21, 1943. She had sunk three ships, a good score given the nature of her mission—but Morton told Lockwood that he could have sunk six, and would have done so had the torpedoes behaved properly. The *Wahoo* was overdue for a major overhaul, so she was ordered back to Mare Island, California, the place where she had been born eighteen months earlier. Dick O'Kane was promoted to command his own boat, a *Balao*-class submarine to be called the *Tang*. She was under construction, also at Mare Island, just a short stroll down the riverfront from the *Wahoo*'s berth. The *Tang* would be launched in August 1943; O'Kane and a skeleton crew would oversee the final stages of her building and fitting out. Meanwhile, the *Wahoo* was considerably rebuilt, to the extent that her profile was dramatically different when she left for Pearl Harbor in July 1943. Morton had taken on several new officers and a largely new crew aboard the new *Wahoo*. As she maneuvered into the Napa River on July 21, the skipper bid his friend and long-standing executive officer good-bye. It was the last time they would meet.

Morton wanted to take the *Wahoo* into the Sea of Japan, the nearly landlocked body of water separating Japan from the Asian mainland. Lockwood granted his star skipper's request. This represented, in a sense, the "last mile" of the undersea campaign; it was the only major area that had not yet been penetrated by U.S. submarines. It was full of ships plying the waters between Japan and its Asian territories. Because it was so self-contained, the Japanese had not previously taken any special antisubmarine measures in it. If the Yellow Sea had been "virgin territory," the Sea of Japan was almost as inviolate as the sacred soil of Japan itself.

There were only three viable routes into and out of the Sea of Japan: the straits of Tsushima, between Kyushu and Korea; Tsugaru Strait, between Honshu and Hokkaido; and La Perouse (or Soya) Strait, between Hokkaido and Sakhalin. All were potentially deadly chokepoints. All had been mined; all were guarded by coastal artillery; and all were heavily patrolled

Last Four Patrols of the *Wahoo* (SS-238)

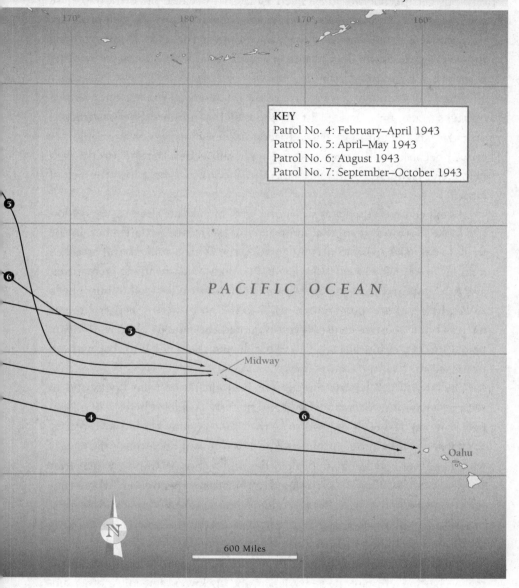

February–October 1943

170°   180°   170°   160°

KEY
Patrol No. 4: February–April 1943
Patrol No. 5: April–May 1943
Patrol No. 6: August 1943
Patrol No. 7: September–October 1943

PACIFIC OCEAN

Midway

Oahu

N

600 Miles

by antisubmarine patrol boats and airplanes. Getting in would be dangerous, but getting out would be even more so—because once the Japanese
were tipped off to the presence of enemy submarines in the Sea of Japan,
they would redouble antisubmarine measures at the exits. After studying
the problem, Lockwood and Morton agreed that La Perouse Strait was the
best option, both for entry and escape.

The *Wahoo* ran the La Perouse Strait on August 14, 1943. She went in
on the surface, on a dark night, at about eighteen knots. She was tracked
on radar, and a lighthouse flashed recognition signals, which she could not
answer because she did not know the applicable codes. But she was through
before the Japanese could react, and vanished like a ghost into the Sea of
Japan.

As expected, the sea was swarming with high-value shipping, and Morton looked forward to another rampage. But her torpedoes failed her. In the
week between August 15 and August 22, the *Wahoo* stalked and attacked
a dozen freighters, but she was plagued by duds, deep runners, prematures,
and fish that ran off course and disappeared. Morton decided to hurry back
to Pearl Harbor and demand attention to the problem. In his patrol report
for this brief, abortive cruise, Morton quoted the famous old naval slogan,
first coined by Admiral David Farragut during the Civil War, but with an
ironic twist: "Damn the torpedoes."

On August 28, having already received clearance from Lockwood to
return to base, the *Wahoo* surfaced and fired shots across the bow of a Japanese sampan. When it did not stop, the *Wahoo's* guns blasted it to pieces.
Six Japanese fishermen surrendered and were taken aboard as prisoners of
war. They were given clean, dry clothes and a shot of brandy, which they
seemed to relish. They were confined to the after-torpedo room, where they
slept on mats on the deck. Relations between the *Wahoo's* crew and the prisoners were cordial, even friendly. The prisoners did their own mess cooking
and willingly pitched in with routine cleaning jobs.[25]

At Pearl Harbor, the *Wahoo* made a quick turnaround. Morton wanted to
make a beeline return to the Sea of Japan, and Lockwood agreed. Another submarine, the *Sawfish*, would sail in company. The *Wahoo* took on a load of the
new Mark 18 torpedoes and the two submarines put to sea on September 10.

In a recorded debriefing session at SubPac headquarters that morning,
Morton had given a long, chatty interview. In the transcript, his characteristic cheerfulness and irreverence jump off the page. At 11:50 a.m. he broke

off the interview, explaining that his ship was due to "shove off" at 1:00 p.m. Morton promised to sit down again at the end of his next patrol—"and when he returns," the interviewer says at the end of the transcript, "we will have more of the story of the adventures of the *Wahoo*."[26]

But Mush Morton never returned to Pearl Harbor, and the rest of the story of the *Wahoo* will never be told. Her seventh cruise was to be her last. She remains, as submariners say, "on eternal patrol."

Events of the *Wahoo*'s last patrol can be partly reconstructed from Japanese sources and educated guesswork. She left Pearl that afternoon, with the *Sawfish* in company. Two days later, she put into Midway Atoll and topped off her fuel. A seven-day run brought her back to La Perouse Strait. The *Wahoo* ran it again, at night, probably on the surface; the *Sawfish* followed two nights later. Morton had said that he intended to prey upon shipping in the southern basin of the Sea of Japan, around the western approaches to Shimonoseki Strait, the main western gateway to Japan's Inland Sea. On October 5, Japan's Domei News Service in Tokyo reported that a "steamer" had been sunk that day by an American submarine, with the loss of 544 lives. The *Wahoo* was the only submarine in those waters. The Domei report did not identify the ship, or whether the dead were civilians or military personnel. Postwar records revealed that it was the *Konron Maru*, an 8,000-ton passenger ship that had been taken into the army as a troop transport. Her loss prompted the Japanese to cancel night ferry service between Japan and Korea.

Postwar analysis concluded that the *Wahoo* destroyed three more enemy ships of at least 1,000 tons in the week that followed. They went down in locations that could only have been reached by the *Wahoo* on the given dates.

The *Sawfish* exited through La Perouse Strait on October 9, two days ahead of the *Wahoo*'s scheduled passage. Her captain noted that Japanese antisubmarine measures had been intensified considerably; the *Sawfish* was chased and hunted by several patrol boats and an aircraft. Diving to 200 feet, she was kept down for several hours by echo ranging. Several bombs and depth charges were dropped, but none was close. She transited the strait while submerged and was safely through by the following morning.

The *Wahoo*, following two nights later, was fired upon by a coastal artillery battery on northern Hokkaido. She may have been damaged by a near-miss. She crash-dived, but could not dive quickly enough to evade a circling floatplane of the Ominato air fleet, which dropped three depth charges on her location. Patrol boats, probably the same ones that had gone after the *Sawfish*, surged into the strait and scattered depth charges through the area. No Japanese craft obtained a sonar fix on the *Wahoo*, but they remained in the area for four hours. That part of La Perouse Strait was too shallow to allow for a deep dive. An enormous oil slick, 3 miles long, marked the *Wahoo*'s final descent to the sea floor, just 213 feet below the surface. Her wreck was located and identified in 2008.

The Americans knew nothing of the circumstances of *Wahoo*'s demise until after the war. She might have been depth-charged to oblivion in La Perouse Strait, but she could just as well have been done in by an accident, a mine, or a faulty torpedo. On November 9, 1943, SubPac headquarters declared her "overdue, presumed lost." The news sent a ripple of grief through the submarine force. Morton was the most revered submarine captain in the fleet, and his colleagues had been urged to study and adopt his bold methods. Should they now interpret the loss of the *Wahoo* as a warning sign that he had been reckless? The possibility was unsettling, but it could not be dismissed. Then again, they all knew that submarine warfare was a perilous business, and that any boat might be lost at any time, regardless of tactics. For the moment, Lockwood put a stop to all penetrations into the Sea of Japan, and that line of attack would not be renewed until late in the war.

When statistics were compiled and revised by postwar analysis, Morton and the *Wahoo* stood near the top of the submarine force's "league tables." His wartime record was given as seventeen enemy ships sunk; postwar accounting raised the figure to twenty, and more recent evaluations have concluded that the figure may have been as high as twenty-four. Despite having been killed at the war's midpoint, and having been handicapped by faulty torpedoes (a problem much alleviated after his death), Morton was tied for second place in the rankings by number of ships sunk, and again tied for second place in the rankings of the best single war patrol. Perhaps it was a further tribute to Morton's leadership that his erstwhile executive officer, Dick O'Kane, eventually surpassed him in both categories.

THE FALL OF 1943 SAW A SHIFT in American thinking about submarine deployments. Previously, Lockwood and the submarine admirals in Australia had kept many fleet boats patrolling the sea approaches to Truk Atoll, in the Caroline Islands, which served as the Japanese navy's largest overseas fleet anchorage. They provided valuable sighting reports and warnings of major naval movements, and had seized opportunities to attack enemy warships as they entered or exited the atoll. Submarines had also been positioned in the Solomon Islands and the South Pacific in support of Halsey and MacArthur's offensives in the region. As always, subs were also sent yon and hither on various special missions, such as reconnaissance, aviator lifeguarding, and smuggling agents and intelligence into and out of the Philippines. Between October and December 1943, more boats were sent to attack Japan's interior sea routes in the western Pacific, including the waters pioneered by the *Wahoo*: the East China Sea and the Yellow Sea. By that time, American submarines were routinely destroying more than 100,000 tons of Japanese shipping each month.

Admiral Ralph Christie's Western Australia command, based in Fremantle, devoted nearly its entire strength to hunting and sinking Japanese oil tankers plying the waters between Borneo and Truk. Many tankers on this route were double-hulled, which made them tough to sink; but they were slower than warships, which made them easier to hit. The new torpex warheads packed a heavy punch, and the tankers were often filled with relatively volatile unprocessed crude oil, which made them vulnerable to devastating secondary explosions and fires. In the last quarter of 1943, boats operating out of Fremantle sent a dozen tankers to the bottom, enough to disrupt the supply line and arouse serious fears in Tokyo that the fleet would be immobilized for lack of fuel.

In 1944, the submarines achieved peak effectiveness in the tonnage war. Total sinkings of merchant ships (not counting warships) more than doubled, from 1.2 million tons in 1943 to 2.5 million tons in 1944.[27] As new *Balao*-class units entered service, the size of the Pacific submarine force expanded from forty-seven boats in February 1943 to more than a hundred in June 1944. Lockwood and his team began experimenting with wolfpack tactics, deploying three to six boats under one commander. The submarines were equipped with better sonar, radar, optical, and communications systems, more powerful deck guns, and torpedoes that finally worked as designed. The Mark 14 torpedo gave way to the Mark 18, which became a lethal weapon as its defects were corrected. A new breed of younger, more daring skippers followed Mush Morton's example by keeping their boats on the surface for most of their patrols. They were sent on long missions into coastal waters off mainland Asia and Japan, to prey upon the enemy's busiest shipping lanes. At night, using the much-improved SJ radar, they pin-pointed the location, speed, and heading of their quarry, and then charged into attack positions at four-engine flank speed, often touching twenty knots. Cryptanalysts in Pearl Harbor broke Japanese shipping codes, and could accurately predict the locations and routes of Japanese merchant con-voys. This valuable "Ultra" data was used in assigning patrol locations, and was regularly transmitted by long-range radio to submarines already at sea.

Dick O'Kane and his new *Balao*-class submarine *Tang* made her maiden passage from Mare Island to Pearl Harbor in January 1944. During the nine-month career of this deadly boat, with O'Kane as skipper, the *Tang* would rise to the top of the submarine force's league tables for total tonnage destroyed, surpassing even the record of Morton in the *Wahoo*. According to the postwar conclusions of the Joint Army-Navy Assessment Committee (JANAC), she destroyed twenty-four ships. Her skipper and others insisted that the total was actually higher, perhaps as many as thirty-three. In any case, there is no doubt that *Tang* was one of the three most productive boats in the Silent Service during the Second World War.

O'Kane seemed to be on a personal mission to avenge the death of Mush Morton and the eighty souls who had gone down with the *Wahoo* in La Perouse Strait. His three patrols as the *Wahoo*'s executive officer had pro-vided the best possible education in this business. Like Morton, O'Kane was a champion of night surface attacks. He considered the crash dive to be a last resort, to be used only in case of emergency. Operating on the surface at night provided exceptional visibility, not only through the SJ radar but also by sending eagle-eyed young sailors to the top of the periscope shears with powerful binoculars. Before each sequence, O'Kane calculated the odds; if he liked them, he initiated daring, slashing attacks. Again and again, the *Tang* evaded Japanese destroyers and penetrated into the inner ring of an enemy shipping convoy, often sinking multiple ships in a single salvo.

On *Tang*'s first patrol, to the waters between the Caroline and Mariana island groups, she stalked a large convoy through rainsqualls for two days, sinking three big ships. Two nights later her radar picked up another north-bound convoy, and in a two-day game of cat and mouse, *Tang* sank two more valuable targets, including a big naval fuel tanker, the *Echizen Maru*. After this red-letter patrol, *Tang* served as lifeguard submarine during the Fifth Fleet's first carrier air raid on Truk (Operation HAILSTONE, February 17–18, 1944), and distinguished herself by rescuing seven downed carrier airmen, more than any other boat participating in the operation. Her third and fourth patrols took her into the East China Sea—waters O'Kane knew well, having patrolled there in the *Wahoo* a year earlier—where the *Tang* behaved like a one-boat wolfpack. On the night of June 24, 1944, not far out of Nagasaki, she ambushed a column of six large cargo ships with escorts, firing a six-torpedo spread. O'Kane believed and claimed that two torpedoes had found their mark, sinking two ships. According to postwar accounting, however, the salvo had knocked down four big freighters with a combined weight of 16,000 tons. Four ships down with a six-torpedo spread made it the single most lethal submarine salvo of the war. *Tang* followed that performance with an August 1944 rampage south of the main Japanese island of Honshu, boldly intruding into shallow inshore waters off the most populous coastline in Japan, and destroyed (at least) two more large merchantmen with combined weight of 11,500 tons.

Several other standout submarines and captains were making their names that year. The superbly named Slade Cutter, a former Naval Academy 1935 football star, was a bold, risk-taking captain in the mold of Mush Morton. In four brilliant patrols, culminating with a June 1944 rampage in Luzon Strait, Cutter's submarine *Seahorse* sank nineteen enemy ships totaling 72,000 tons. At the end of the war, he was tied for second with Mush Morton in the table of total sinkings (O'Kane was first). Sam Dealey, who made six war patrols as captain of the *Harder*, sank sixteen Japanese ships totaling 54,002 tons. The *Harder*'s most famous contribution to the war came in June 1944, just before the Battle of the Philippine Sea. Stalking the main Japanese battle fleet at its anchorage at Tawi Tawi, in the southern part of the Sulu Sea, the *Harder* sank three Japanese destroyers in three days. Reuben Whitaker was captain of the *Flasher*, with Chester Nimitz Jr. as third officer; in four patrols around the Philippines and South China Sea, the *Flasher* sank fifteen ships of 60,846 tons. Gene Fluckey, skipper of the *Barb*, compiled an exceptional record over seven war patrols in the Luzon Straits and the East China Sea, sinking seventeen ships totaling 96,628 tons. The highlight of *Barb*'s career came in July 1945, when she landed a party of commandos on the coast of Sakhalin Island, then Japanese territory. The attackers blew up a railroad train. This was the only mission of its kind in the Pacific War, and the only Allied ground operation in the Japanese home islands.

But the Pacific tonnage war did not only depend on the champion performers of the U.S. submarine force. In a "death by a thousand cuts," each little cut did its part to kill the subject. Most captains and submarines stood well down the scoring tables. But even the middling players, whose names are mostly forgotten, were doing their part. To the Japanese, it mattered little whether their precious remaining oil tankers were sent to the bottom by superstars like the *Wahoo*, *Tang*, or *Seahorse*, or by unsung boats such as (to pick a few at random) the *Cod*, the *Kingfish*, or the *Barbero*. The total number of U.S. submarines on patrol in the Pacific doubled in 1944, from an average of twenty-four boats in June 1943, to forty-eight in June 1944.[28] At Imperial General Headquarters in Tokyo, it was said that a man could walk from Japan to Singapore on the periscopes of American submarines. What mattered in the end was the cumulative result of their efforts.

By late 1944, the submarines were sinking more than a quarter of a million tons of Japanese merchant shipping each month. Sinkings peaked in October 1944, when the eyes of the world were on MacArthur's return to the Philippines and the great naval Battle of Leyte Gulf. That month, undersea predators destroyed 328,843 tons of Japanese merchant shipping, including 103,903 tons of oil tankers.[29] Thereafter, monthly totals declined, but only because there was a relative scarcity of targets. American submarines patrolling the busiest maritime routes found the sea littered with oil slicks and the flotsam and jetsam of previous sinkings. Many skippers increasingly turned their attention to sinking junks and trawlers with deck guns.

The *Tang*'s last patrol, which began the last week of September 1944, took her to the Strait of Formosa. The cruise coincided with Halsey's Third Fleet carrier strikes in the area, and the opening moves in the Battle of Leyte Gulf. For two days, Captain O'Kane stalked Admiral Shima's task force as it headed south (where it would arrive late to the Battle of Surigao Strait). Taking 8-inch fire from one of Shima's cruisers, the *Tang* crash dived to safety. O'Kane's sighting report was received at Pearl Harbor and relayed to Halsey and Kinkaid. On October 23, the *Tang* intercepted a northbound convoy of three tankers flanked by two cargo ships, heavily escorted by destroyers. Evading the destroyers, O'Kane maneuvered his submarine in for a point-blank night torpedo attack, and sank all three tankers in a single close-range salvo. The explosions momentarily illuminated the *Tang*, and the remaining cargo ships turned directly toward the submarine, apparently intending to ram her. O'Kane ordered "All ahead emergency," and with a sudden lunge the boat bolted ahead of the two ships, which were closing in from both sides. The two Japanese ships found themselves on a collision course as both turned in the same direction; they collided, and a moment later both were struck by another salvo of torpedoes fired from the *Tang*'s stern tubes. The two ships went up in spectacular twin explosions. *Tang* did not even bother to dive. She had destroyed five valuable targets in the space of ten minutes, one of the most astonishing feats of the war.

O'Kane still had eleven torpedoes, and he intended to make them count. On October 24, as the Battle of Leyte Gulf was raging to the south, the *Tang*'s SJ radar picked up another northbound convoy. It was a big one, perhaps as many as ten ships with escorts. Another slaughter ensued: O'Kane maneuvered the *Tang* in close and fired a six-torpedo salvo. Two fish connected with two different targets, and both went down quickly. A four-torpedo stern tube shot hit a tanker, which limped away crippled. When a destroyer suddenly loomed off to *Tang*'s port, O'Kane crash-dived and ran away from the scene, silent and deep. Later, he brought the submarine back to the surface and went after the cripple. The *Tang* had two remaining fish for the purpose. O'Kane, standing on the bridge, ordered two bow-tube torpedoes prepared and trained on the nearly immobilized, still-burning tanker. The first ran hot, straight, and normal, and hit the target near the bow, sending another pillar of fire into the sky. It was probably enough to be sure of her, but the *Tang* had only one torpedo remaining, and O'Kane chose to fire it as the *coup de grâce*.

It *was* the *coup de grâce*, but in the wrong sense. As soon as that final torpedo was away, it began porpoising spasmodically and veered left. Its track, a long slick speckled with bubbles and lit by a phosphorescent glow, turned toward the *Tang* in a wide counterclockwise arc. O'Kane shouted down the hatch: "All ahead emergency," and "Right full rudder," but there was not enough time. The torpedo's rudder had jammed, or its steering engine had malfunctioned; either way it was on target to hit the *Tang* dead amidships, right under the bridge where O'Kane was standing with eight other men. As the submarine's engines flared, she bucked forward and began swinging away from the oncoming track in a fishtail maneuver, but the weapon hit and detonated, tearing the *Tang*'s hull open near the after-torpedo room. The aft compartments flooded immediately, the stern sank, and the bow lifted clean out of the sea. O'Kane shouted down to the conning tower to close the hatch, but it all happened too quickly. The sea poured over the bridge and down the hatch; O'Kane and the other men were swept to sea; and the *Tang* wallowed helplessly, her stern down and her bow pointed to the heavens. Now the best-case scenario for the eighty men left on board was that the *Tang* would float long enough to give them a chance to escape, in which case they could look forward to spending the rest of the war as prisoners of the Japanese.

The men treading water—O'Kane and nine others, including one who had come up through the conning tower hatch—watched the boat slip beneath the surface. She sank to a depth of about 180 feet, then leveled off. About thirty men in the forward torpedo room had survived, and they managed to seal off the hatches. They burned all confidential papers, but the smoke fouled the air and made their predicament even more desperate. Four parties, thirteen men in all, managed to exit the submarine through the forward escape trunk, and ascended to the surface using the crude breathing apparatus known as the Momsen Lung. Eight died in the ascent, or after reaching the surface, possibly from decompression trauma ("the bends"). After a long night adrift on the surface, a total of ten of the *Tang*'s crew, including O'Kane, were picked up by a Japanese destroyer.[30] They served the rest of the war as prisoners of war, shuttled between various camps in Honshu. Only four came home at war's end. O'Kane, one of the survivors, was awarded the Congressional Medal of Honor.

IN 1932, THE AIRPOWER VISIONARY BILLY MITCHELL, a retired army aviator, had called for the development of a heavy bomber with a flying range of 5,000 miles, a bomb-load capacity of 10,000 pounds, and a service ceiling of 35,000 feet. At the time, the idea had seemed futuristic and fantastic, like a machine conjured up in the imagination of Jules Verne or H. G. Wells. But the 1930s was a decade of long strides in aviation. By 1940, as Hitler's armies rampaged across Europe, aeronautical engineers believed that a very heavy, very long-ranged pressurized bomber had become feasible. With FDR's backing, Army Air Corps leaders persuaded Congress to reach deep into the taxpayers' pockets to fund a new Boeing-designed bomber with twice the range and twice the payload capacity of the B-17 "Flying Fortress." Three billion 1940 dollars later, the B-29 "Superfortress" was born.

The program's advocates, being keen to the political climate of the times, did not advertise the plane as an instrument for strategic bombing. The very heavy or very long-ranged bomber ("VHB" and "VLR" were the acronyms, used more or less interchangeably) was to be a keystone of the "hemisphere defense" strategy cherished by prewar isolationists. With its awesome range, the B-29 would watch over the Atlantic sea lanes, detecting any approach of enemy (presumably German) shipping. The aircraft would win uncontested mastery in the skies over those mid-ocean zones, intercepting and repelling enemy invasion forces before they could gain a foothold on the North or South American continents. If the Nazis did manage to secure a beachhead in South America, the B-29 could hit the enemy from bases in Florida or the Caribbean. In this way, the giant airplane would serve as watchdog and guard dog for "Fortress America." So it was said.

As the specter of global war loomed in 1941, the War Department pressured Boeing to accelerate the development timeline and put the new bomber into production before it had been properly tested and modified. Boeing received an initial order for 250 units in May 1941, six months before the attack on Pearl Harbor. A year later, the company was under contract to deliver 1,644 of the planes, even though none had yet taken flight.[31] Boeing dedicated two large plants to the B-29, in Renton, Washington, and Wichita, Kansas. Many other leading aviation firms were enlisted to produce components or engines, including Bell, Fisher, Martin, and Wright. The Army Air Forces set up a major new command and administrative organization based on future deliveries of this aircraft, at a time when just a handful of experimental models existed. Pilots and aircrews were recruited and trained in B-17s and B-26s; most did not fly (or even see) the Superfortress until they were already proficient in the smaller bombers. An early prototype B-29 crashed during a test flight in February 1943, demolishing a meatpacking plant in downtown Seattle and killing the program's most seasoned test crew and engineers, as well as twenty-one civilians on the ground. But the pace of the program did not slacken. When the first B-29 was delivered in July 1943, it had many flaws, and thousands of alterations were incorporated into the design even as assembly lines around the country were ramping up.

It was, by far, the largest aircraft that had ever been put into general production. Ninety-nine feet long, it had a wingspan of 140 feet. It weighed 74,500 pounds unloaded, but its combat-loaded takeoff weight was generally at least 120,000 pounds, and routinely exceeded 140,000 pounds. The immense thrust required to lift the Superfortress from the earth was supplied by four Wright R-3350 radial engines of 2,200 horsepower.

When first introduced to the new plane, pilots and aircrewmen gawked.

They marveled at the long, sleek fuselage, the enormous Plexiglas "green-house" nose, the immense wings and flaps, and the towering tail section, which rose to the height of a three-story building. With its "tricycle" landing gear, the airplane stood proud and level on the asphalt. The airframe was flush-riveted with an aluminum alloy that shone brilliantly in the sun, like polished silver. Most recruits had trained in the B-17, and regarded that aircraft as a big, heavy bomber. The Superfortress was far bigger in every dimension, and about twice as heavy. The airmen knew their lives would depend on those four mighty eighteen-cylinder engines, with their canoe-sized propellers stretching 16 feet from tip to tip.

Climbing inside, they found much to like about their new airplane. Two spacious compartments, connected by a crawl tube over the bomb bay, offered plenty of elbow room for the eleven-man crew. The cabin was heated and pressurized. Even at 30,000 feet, where the temperature outside might be a hundred degrees below zero, they could sit comfortably in their shirtsleeves. While cruising, they would wear no oxygen masks and could smoke freely. The waist and tail-gunners sat in Plexiglas bubbles providing good visibility, from which they controlled multiple .50-caliber turrets simultaneously through electrical remote systems. Engine noise was pleasingly muffled, and the machine guns did not roar in the ears as they did in the unpressurized B-17. The cockpit, perched forward in the conical Plexiglas nose, provided magnificent visibility in every direction, especially above and below. Pilots and copilots had the odd sensation of being thrust out into space, almost ahead of the long fuselage; one remarked that piloting the Superfortress was like "flying a house while sitting out on the front porch."[32]

Straining against gravity to lift a 70-ton airplane, the Wright R-3350 engines were prone to overheat, leak oil, blow cylinder heads, swallow their own valves, and spread molten debris into their highly combustible magnesium crankcases. The original air-cooling system had to be rebuilt after hundreds of B-29s had come off the assembly lines. A burning engine trailed fire and smoke behind it, like an asteroid entering the atmosphere—but this asteroid was bolted into the wing of the aircraft, and threatened to burn into the aluminum skin and spars of the wing itself. A misbehaving engine had to be shut down quickly, preferably before it burst into flames. That was accomplished by "feathering" the propeller. A hydraulic system, controlled from the cockpit, turned or "feathered" the four rotor blades until they stopped and spun in the reverse direction, stopping the engine's rotation. If the crew reacted too slowly, or the feathering mechanism failed, the propeller would begin to "windmill," creating terrible drag; within a few minutes it would burn free of its shaft and fly right off the engine, sometimes taking a bite out of the wing.

If an engine failed and was properly shut down, the surviving three would bring the B-29 home, even over a long distance. But the three working engines would consume much more fuel than before, so it was vital to redistribute fuel from tanks and lines serving the dead engine. That might require an intricate rebalancing of the entire fuel reserve. The margin of error was narrow; any setback and the flight was likely to end in calamity.

Even the most experienced B-17 pilots needed weeks of classroom instruction before taking the B-29 up for a check-out flight. Every stage of a mission required meticulous attention to a long checklist. Takeoffs involved a long run, more than a mile, and the engines strained audibly to lift the giant machine from the ground. Once airborne, however, the B-29 was surprisingly nimble. "It was the biggest, heaviest, and most powerful airplane I had ever flown," recalled one USAAF pilot of his first flight in the B-29. "Yet it responded beautifully, with a gentle and precise handling of the controls."[33] And it was fast, with a ground speed easily surpassing 300 miles per hour. Its combination of speed, altitude, and well-placed .50-caliber turrets vindicated the airplane's name: the Superfortress would be a tough nut to crack, for both enemy fighters and antiaircraft batteries.

Pressure to rush the B-29 into service forced the government to take unprecedented measures. The War Department signed contracts to purchase more than a thousand airplanes before they had been properly tested, intending to modify them as necessary once they were on the flight line. The design-testing-manufacturing cycle was accelerated to about double the peacetime pace. This practice was risky and grossly wasteful, but it was the only way to get the B-29 into action by the spring of 1944, as no less a figure than President Roosevelt had insisted it must be. In a sense, the B-29's introduction into service was a microcosm of the whole saga of American mobilization for the Second World War. At every turn, leaders chose velocity of production over efficiency, thrift, safety, or even prudence.

Before the first echelon of B-29s departed for the long flight to Asia, they were flown by their aircrews into Wichita, to an airfield adjacent to the Boeing plant, to undergo several hundred modifications. USAAF leaders nicknamed this operation the "Battle of Kansas," or the "Kansas blitz." Several other modification centers or "mod shops" were set up at airbases in every region of the United States. Rookie pilots and aircrews flew their newly issued B-29s into the centers for modifications. These flights were incorporated into their training regimens, and provided opportunity to build up their flight hours before overseas deployments. But that was not the end of it: many hundreds of new modifications were ordered even after many planes had left the United States. In such cases, modification and repair "kits" were flown out to distant foreign airfields in Egypt or India, with necessary parts and engineers. Modifications were made to the propeller feathering system, the fire control system, the electrical system, and most importantly, the troublesome Wright engines. Two of the largest overseas B-29 modifications centers were established in Cairo and Karachi. Even after major operations commenced in China and (later) the Marianas, ground mechanics were constantly engaged not only with routine maintenance, but with correcting the original deficiencies of the Superfortress. USAAF general Curtis E. LeMay observed that his airmen were forced to conduct a test program while flying live combat missions. It was a difficult and dangerous job, because the B-29 "had as many bugs as the entomological department of the Smithsonian Institution. Fast as they got the bugs licked, new ones crawled out from under the cowling."[34]

At the Allied command conference in Cairo, Egypt (SEXTANT, November 1943), FDR had pledged to Generalissimo Chiang Kai-shek that hundreds of B-29s would be based in China, and would launch a sustained bombing campaign against the Japanese home islands. Chiang had complained stridently about a perceived lack of support from the Allies, and had threatened (in only slightly veiled terms) to seek a truce with the Japanese. FDR often told his military chiefs that bombing Japan from Chinese airfields would catalyze and reinvigorate Chinese morale. Neither the B-17 nor the B-24 possessed the range to do the job. From the beginning, therefore, B-29 deployments to the China-Burma-India (CBI) theater were a political gambit, intended to placate the Nationalist regime and keep it in the war. The operation was given the code name MATTERHORN.

From the start, however, Operation MATTERHORN was hobbled by wretched logistics. The new Superforts with their balky engines were flown into the theater by recently trained aircrews. Their round-the-world odyssey began at Morrison Field, Florida and continued across a daisy chain of refueling stops in the Caribbean, Brazil, Ascension Island (in the mid-Atlantic), Liberia, Cairo, Baghdad, Karachi, and Kharagpur, India (near Calcutta). Along the way, the Wright engines often overheated, leading to crashes and groundings. With dozens of planes stranded in Cairo and Karachi, it was found that ambient ground temperatures surpassing 110 degrees were causing the engines to fail on takeoff, and the Wright engines' air-cooling mechanisms had to be rebuilt by engineers flown in from the United States.

In April 1944, B-29s began arriving at their permanent rear-bases at Kharagpur. From there they would stage into advanced Chinese airfields at Chengdu, in Sichuan Province. This involved a grueling and treacherous flight "over the hump" of the Himalayas, the world's loftiest mountains. The Superfortresses soared over a forbidding landscape of sawtoothed peaks and plunging gorges, tossed by vicious turbulence and sudden downdrafts, with winds surpassing 100 miles per hour and visibility often falling to zero. Every so often, through a clear patch of sky, the aircrews might glimpse the summit of Mount Everest, just 150 miles north of their flight path.

Their destination, at the end of the 1,200-mile flight, was one of four new airfields south of Chengdu, where construction work was ongoing. More than a quarter of a million Chinese peasants had been enlisted to build the 8,000-foot runways almost entirely by hand. Newsreel footage depicts an immense throng of laborers, many barefoot and wearing conical hats, hauling dirt and gravel in baskets and wheelbarrows. Boys aged eight or nine smashed rocks with hammers to make gravel. Stones from a nearby river were carried to the site in sacks hanging from carrying poles slung over the workers' shoulders. These were laid in tight patterns on the runway beds, and then paved over with gravel and dirt and compacted by a great stone roller hauled by fifty men. When an approaching B-29 entered the landing pattern, a loud horn sounded and the workers dashed to the edge of the runway. After the plane landed, the mass of humanity swarmed back onto the field to resume their labors.

Early plans for MATTERHORN had contemplated basing two B-29 combat wings (150 bombers each) at Chengdu. But the aircraft's teething problems, and the uneconomical supply line through India, required scaling back to a single bomb wing. The 20th Bomber Command was supposed to have been self-sufficient, logistically speaking, which meant shuttling in its own parts, supplies, bombs, and aviation fuel from India. For this purpose, the command was assigned a fleet of C-109 fuel tankers and C-87 transports. The Superfortresses also performed double-duty as their own transports, with guns and extraneous equipment stripped out of the aircraft and fuel tanks fitted into the bomb bays. But the sheer tonnage of fuel and matériel that had to be hauled over the Himalayan "hump" was daunting. An average of twelve round-trip cargo flights to India was required for each bombing mission flown during MATTERHORN. For every eight barrels of aviation fuel airlifted from Kharagpur to Chengdu, seven were burned in the round-trip flight. It was soon evident that the 20th Bomber Command could not possibly feed itself its own needed fuel and supplies, and the existing Air Transport Command would have to pick up the slack. That meant reallocating scarce fuel and other resources from Chinese and American ground forces in China, and from General Claire Lee Chennault's Fourteenth Air Force.

The B-29's combat debut came on June 5, 1944, when ninety-eight planes departed Kharagpur to hit Japanese-controlled railheads in Bangkok, a thousand miles away. The raid dropped 368 tons of bombs on the target, an encouraging result. Ten days later, the Superforts paid their inaugural visit to the Japanese homeland. As U.S. amphibious forces stormed the beaches of Saipan in Operation FORAGER, fifty B-29s lifted off from Chengdu to bomb the Imperial Iron and Steel Works at Yawata, Kyushu. This raid, the first on Japan since the Doolittle Raid in April 1942, received headline coverage in the United States, China, and Japan. General Marshall released a war communiqué announcing that the mission had introduced "a new type of offensive" against the Japanese home islands. Chiang Kai-shek and his allies were exultant. Publicly, the IGHQ in Tokyo brushed off the raid on Yawata, falsely claiming that dozens of the bombers had been downed by Japanese fighters and antiaircraft fire. As always, however, the appearance of enemy warplanes over Japanese soil stirred panic among the public. It seemed to matter little that the raid had done negligible damage.

In the weeks that followed, the MATTERHORN B-29s hit enemy targets all around the periphery of the China theater: coke ovens in Manchuria and Korea, oil fields in the Dutch East Indies, steelworks and port facilities in northeast China, piers and depots in Shanghai, airbases on Formosa, shipping at Hong Kong, railroads and depots in Burma. Eventually, the 20th Bomber Command launched eight more raids against military and industrial targets on Kyushu. But long intervals were needed between missions to replenish fuel, bombs, and other matériel. Bombing results were often disappointing, and operational losses heavy. From Chengdu the B-29s could (just) reach Kyushu, 1,500 miles away—but they could not reach Tokyo or other high-priority targets on Honshu. To launch a full-scale strategic bombing campaign against Japan, more airbases were needed in eastern China. But the Allies did not control any seaports on the Chinese coast, which meant that the cargo airlift from India would have to be extended even farther. Moreover, no one had any confidence that airfields in eastern China could be defended against the Japanese army, which was expanding its footprint on the mainland with a brutally successful ground offensive called "Ichi-Go" (Plan One). Indeed, "Ichi-Go" even threatened the Allied airbases around Chengdu and Kunming. General Joseph "Vinegar Joe" Stilwell, the U.S. Army commander in China, gave his opinion that fifty trained Chinese infantry divisions were needed to guarantee the safety of the airfields. But no one (including Stilwell) believed that Chiang could supply forces on that scale.

For all of those reasons, Operation MATTERHORN never fulfilled its promise. From the beginning it had been driven by FDR's concern to keep the Allied coalition together in the CBI theater, and to preserve the possibility of drawing upon China's bottomless manpower reserves in the final invasion of Japan. By mid-1944, it was becoming clear that the logistical and security challenges confronting MATTERHORN were too great to overcome. Meanwhile, a better alternative had presented itself: the Marianas, which U.S. forces seized between June and August of that year. Saipan, Guam, and Tinian offered terrain suitable for large B-29 airbases, security against enemy ground assault, and (most importantly) a seaborne rather than an airborne supply line. They lay within a 1,500-mile flight radius of Tokyo. In July 1944, the Joint Chiefs confirmed that the new 21st Bomber Command in the Marianas would receive priority allocation of new Superfortresses and supporting matériel, and after November of that year, no new B-29s flew into India or China. MATTERHORN closed up shop in January 1945.

Looking back on the China misadventure, LeMay concluded: "It didn't work. No one could have made it work. It was founded on an utterly absurd logistic basis. . . . The scheme of operations had been dreamed up like something out of the Wizard of Oz."[35]

Still, the difficulties presented by the Marianas were daunting. Fuel and supplies would be brought in by sea, but the maritime umbilical cord was long—5,800 miles from San Francisco Bay—and the B-29s would have to compete with hundreds of other Allied military units for scarce shipping and other resources. The heavily loaded bombers would operate from bases that had not yet been built, on islands where enemy holdouts were still fighting in the hills. From Saipan, Tinian, or (especially) Guam, targets in Japan lay near the outer limit of the B-29's operating radius. Relatively inexperienced aircrews would have to navigate over 3,000 miles of trackless ocean, partly at night, in round-trip missions lasting fifteen hours or longer. There was not a fighter plane in the world with the range for such missions, and the Allies possessed no airfields nearer to Japan: consequently, all B-29 missions would be unescorted. In spite of its name, the Superfortress was rather lightly constructed (due to weight-saving requirements), and it made a very large flying target. Some USAAF planners warned of prohibitively high losses over Japan.

"Possum" Hansell was tapped by Arnold as the first chief of the 21st Bomber Command. Hansell had distinguished himself as a section chief on Arnold's Washington-based planning staff, and had most recently served as chief of staff to the Twentieth Air Force. (Asked why her husband was nicknamed "Possum," Mrs. Hansell said that it was because he looked like one. Based on the photographic evidence, she had a point.) Like most other USAAF line commanders, Hansell was a comparatively young man (forty-one) and a skilled flyer in his own right. He piloted the first B-29 into Saipan while handling the controls from the left-side seat. The *Joltin' Josie*, as the aircraft was called, flew from Mather Field, California (near Sacramento) in three hops to Honolulu, Kwajalein, and Saipan, landing at Isley Field on October 12, 1944. Crowds of servicemen, most of whom had never laid eyes on a Superfortress, were gathered along the runway. As the *Joltin' Josie* approached, one witness recalled, "a great cheer went up, and all work stopped as men shaded their eyes to watch the plane pass over. . . . The thrill that went through all was almost electric in effect."[36]

Hansell was dismayed by the conditions he found on Saipan. Plans had called for two parallel runways, both 8,500 feet long, and eighty hardstands (paved parking areas abutting the taxiways). He found one runway, 7,000 feet long and only partly paved, and a parallel strip of land that had been cleared and graded but not yet paved at all. Only forty hardstands had been completed, and when B-29s of the Seventy-Third Bomb Wing flew in later that month, they had to be double-parked. Aviation gasoline was stored in tank trailers lined up in a nearby parking lot. The base was scheduled to receive 180 aircraft and 12,000 men by the end of the year, but there were no barracks, no administrative offices, and no warehouses. As advance echelons of the 21st Bomber Command arrived, they moved into tent cities around the edges of the airfields. Even General Hansell was quartered in a canvas tent perched on a cliff overlooking the sea to the east. The mess hall was a Quonset hut, and even the brass stood in the "chow line." "I had no shops and no facilities except tents," Hansell later remembered. "I had a bomb dump, a vehicle park and gasoline storage, but the rest of it was the most miserable shambles I have ever seen."[37]

The delays were not for a lack of effort. Bulldozers had started working over Isley Field on June 24, when combat was still raging and the Japanese lines were only a mile north. Aviation engineering battalions had worked in shifts, around the clock, under floodlights at night, sometimes harassed by artillery or sniper fire. Bucketing rains had turned the unpaved segments of runways and hardstands into mud baths. The islands offered functionally limitless reserves of coral rock, which was crushed and converted into high-quality concrete for asphalt. But the roads linking coral pits to airfields were generally too narrow, and unpaved in many places; frequently they were jammed by traffic, or swamped by tropical downpours. Thousands of tons of crushed coral were needed to pave the runways and service areas—but first the roads had to be widened, graded, and paved, which likewise required thousands of tons of crushed coral.

Desperately short of necessary equipment and spare parts, Hansell sounded an urgent call to the mainland for logistical support. When a ship laden with vital cargo put into a dysfunctionally congested harbor in Guam, the navy harbormaster declared, "I'll give you 24 hours to get that goddamned ship out of here."[38] In the rush to unload, the cargo was dumped in a field at the edge of the jungle, where it was exposed to rain, humidity, and plunder. Most of it was lost or judged unsalvageable. With shortages threatening to delay bombing missions, an air cargo route was opened all the way back to California. Once again, B-29s were hauling their own stores into a combat zone. It was the "hump" again, but this hump was the curvature of the earth over 94 degrees of longitude.

In the weeks following Hansell's arrival, an average of three to five new Superfortresses flew into Saipan each day. Most were staged out of the training and modification centers of Kansas and Nebraska by their own recently trained aircrews. They followed the route taken by Hansell in *Joltin' Josie*: over the mountains to Mather Field, California; over the eastern Pacific to John Rogers Field in Honolulu, formerly a civilian airport; thence across the International Date Line to Kwajalein Atoll in the central Pacific, losing a day on the calendar; and the final 1,500-mile leg to Isley Field, Saipan. The long transoceanic flight was unfamiliar to most young airmen. It was a trial by fire of their overwater navigation skills, and a worthwhile training exercise in itself. When flying above a cloud ceiling, the navigator peered down through gaps in the overcast and caught glimpses of the wrinkled blue seascape. Now and again he might see a coral reef, or a tendril of sand, and he tried to match those features to the chart on his desk. At night, the navigator tracked his aircraft's position by taking star sightings with a sextant, like an ancient mariner. Mostly he relied on dead reckoning, keeping meticulous track of airspeed and compass heading, adding corrections for the wind, until he could pick up a LORAN signal or a radio homing beacon.

A typical B-29 aircrew comprised eleven men ranging in age from nineteen to thirty. On many planes, the captain and oldest member of the crew was a twenty-five-year-old lieutenant who had learned to fly in a single-engine trainer about eighteen months earlier. Not even youth or peak physical condition spared them the fatigue of long flights at high altitude. After a fifteen-hour mission, one pilot wrote in a letter home, "my legs and back were stiff and I can still feel it! We took off at dawn and landed several hours after dark. That's a point lots of folks miss. Bombing the target takes only a short time. It's that workout going to the target and returning home to your destination that gets you."[39]

As new planes and airmen crowded into Saipan, Hansell judged that more indoctrination and training was needed in formation flying, rendezvous, communications, navigation, and precision bombing. There was no better training, he reasoned, than live combat missions against relatively weak enemy positions. On October 27, Hansell personally led a tactical bombing strike against the once-formidable Truk Atoll, targeting Japanese submarine pens on Dublon Island. (The USAAF brass was normally barred from flying combat missions; to his chagrin, this was the last such flight that Hansell was cleared to lead.) Three more break-in missions against Truk followed, and two against Iwo Jima. Hundreds of tons of bombs were dropped during these raids. Those on the receiving end might have been surprised and disheartened to learn that they were only training runs.

A Superfort specially configured for long-distance photo reconnaissance flights, designated the F-13, arrived on October 30. By a stroke of luck, the following day dawned with unusually clear skies over Tokyo and its environs. Captain Ralph D. Steakley proposed to fly a photographic mission right away, hoping to capitalize on the rare favorable weather, and Hansell agreed. The lone F-13, sardonically named the *Tokyo Rose*, soared over the Japanese capital at 32,000 feet, its four cameras snapping continuously. Steakley circled in lazy figure-eight patterns around Tokyo, Tokyo Bay, Yokohama, then west over Mt. Fuji to the Tōkai region and the industrial heartland of greater Nagoya. This was the first Allied airplane to penetrate Tokyo airspace since the Doolittle Raid, two-and-a-half years earlier. Japanese army fighters scrambled to intercept, but to the air defense command's toe-curling mortification, they were unable to catch the fast, high-flying intruder. Above 30,000 feet, the Nakajima KI-44 fighters (Allied codename "Tojo") could climb only with a significant loss of ground speed, allowing the *Tokyo Rose* to sail away, serene and untouchable. Antiaircraft batteries put on a dazzling fireworks show, but the bursts were low and wild.

After a fourteen-hour flight in freakishly clear weather, the F-13 touched down on Saipan with thousands of aerial negatives covering major industrial and aviation plants in the Tokyo and Nagoya regions. A photo lab unit, housed in a Quonset hut, worked around the clock for several days to turn out 7,000 high-resolution prints. These served as the basis for future mission planning. Steakley's pathfinding flight was of incalculable value to the entire strategic bombing enterprise.[40]

At the time, target selection decisions were shaped by the USAAF's recent experiences in the air war over Germany. The first step in the bombing campaign against Japan, planners believed, should be to win supremacy in Japanese skies. That meant breaking down enemy air strength at its source by targeting the aviation industry, including the major Japanese engine plants and airframe assembly centers. For years before the war, little by little, Allied military attachés and intelligence analysts had accumulated data about this secretive industry. A handful of big firms dominated: Mitsubishi, Nakajima, Kawasaki, Aichi, and Tachikawa. Most of their major plants were located in or around Tokyo, Nagoya, Osaka, and Kobe. It was known, for example, that an important Nakajima plant was in Musashino, a suburb of Tokyo. The Mitsubishi complex in Nagoya was said to be the second largest aircraft manufacturing plant in the world. The approximate whereabouts of many other such factories were known to the Allies. The photos taken by *Tokyo Rose* filled in the gaps, allowing analysts to pinpoint the sites and dimensions of high-priority targets.

Current doctrine in November 1944 favored massed, high-altitude, precision bombing raids. Missions were to be conducted in daylight, preferably in clear conditions, so that the bombardiers could aim at the targets through their bombsites. Radar-based targeting was a less desirable contingency, to be employed only in overcast conditions. Low-altitude night bombing was not yet deemed a viable alternative. Hansell wanted at least a hundred Superforts to participate in the first mission against Japan. He was reluctant to launch them until the weather was clear enough to allow for visual bombing. A massed attack in favorable weather would take full advantage of the element of surprise. On the other hand, he had committed to launch his inaugural mission against Tokyo by the end of November, so time was short. By November 18 there were enough B-29s, ordnance, and aviators on Saipan to make the flight, but the weather over Japan was overcast that day, and it remained so for a week. Night after night the aircrews attended pre-mission briefings, only to be told to stand down. It was hard on the nerves. "Talk about tension-builders!" one young airman exclaimed in his diary: "You can put this down; whoever said he wasn't afraid, wasn't exactly telling it like it was!"[41]

The weather broke on November 24, Thanksgiving Day. The airmen were out of their cots at 0300. As dawn broke, long columns of Superforts warmed their engines on the taxiways. Aiming for a publicity splash, the 21st Bomber Command had brought in twenty-four war correspondents representing every major newspaper and wire service in the United States. Film crews rolled and flashbulbs popped as Brigadier General Emmett "Rosie" O'Donnell, commander of the Seventy-Third Bombardment Wing and mission leader, climbed into his cockpit. O'Donnell's plane, the *Dauntless Dotty*, was first to lift off, followed at thirty-second intervals by 110 more Superforts. They climbed into the east, over Magicienne Bay, and banked left for the long run north. Each plane was loaded to the absolute limit, 140,000 pounds. (Wright engineers had recommended that the limit be set at 120,000 pounds: they were overruled.) Straining to lift themselves to altitude while performing a running formation rendezvous, the airmen watched their engines carefully. Fires and other mechanical mishaps forced seventeen planes to turn back. The remaining ninety-four pushed on toward the primary target, the Musashino Works of the Nakajima Airplane Company at Kichijoji, west of Tokyo.

The Japanese knew of the buildup of Superfortresses on Saipan. They were expecting this raid and had taken measures to prepare for it. China-based B-29s had hit Kyushu in eight missions since June, so they were not unfamiliar with the big bomber and its capabilities. After their failure to intercept the *Tokyo Rose* weeks earlier, Japanese fighters were modified to improve their climbing speed and raise their service ceiling. Engine tweaks helped, as did fitting the planes with fatter propellers that provided more thrust in thin air. The most radical measure—and the most characteristically Japanese—was the creation of an air-to-air ramming squadron. Fighters in this unit were stripped of all guns, ammunition, and armor plating. That enabled them to perform well at higher altitudes, but it obviously left them with no way to shoot at the enemy. The pilots, kamikazes by a different name, had practiced high-side ramming maneuvers aimed at a Superfortress's vulnerable tail section.

When coastal radar stations detected the incoming flight, about 125 Japanese fighters scrambled to intercept. Among them were ten Nakajima Ki-44 *Shoki* aircraft of the Japanese army's Forty-Seventh Sentai air group, all dedicated to attempting ramming attacks on the enemy bombers.

Catching the high-flying Superfortresses would have been difficult in any conditions. The intruders entered Japanese air space at altitudes between 27,000 and 32,000 feet, and most of the defending fighters needed a full hour to climb to that lofty height. The jet stream was fierce that day, with 150-mile-per-hour tailwinds pushing the B-29s' ground speed to above 400 miles per hour. Formations came apart in those buffeting conditions, spoiling any pretense of precision bombing. The Nakajima factory was obscured under a fleecy blanket of clouds. Only twenty-four planes dropped bombs on Musashino, and nearly all fell outside Nakajima's perimeter fence. Sixty-four planes hit the Tokyo dockyards, the designated secondary target.[42]

Corporal Yoshio Mita of the Forty-Seventh Sentai scored the only kill of the day with a spectacular ramming attack. Approaching a formation of B-29s from above and behind, this indomitable samurai snapped into a hard diving roll and flew his Nakajima into the tail section of the "A-26," piloted by First Lieutenant Sam Wagner. Mita's plane exploded in a ball of fire and fell to earth trailing a long tail of smoke. "A-26" flew on, but the collision had torn away its vertical stabilizer and left elevator. Wagner tried to turn for home, but could not keep the crippled bomber airborne. It crashed about 20 miles from Tokyo Bay. None of the crew survived.

For the other Superforts, the return to Saipan was a long ordeal. A low cloud ceiling blanketed the sea south of Japan, obscuring landmarks, and darkness descended when the returning planes were still several hours north of Isley Field. The runway was marked only by smudge pots. If an accident should foul up the strip, many B-29s would probably be forced to crash-land. But ninety-one landed safely, bringing the mission to a successful conclusion. Everyone breathed a sigh of relief.

Reflecting upon it afterwards, Hansell admitted that the November 24 mission to Tokyo was risky to the point of rashness. The bombing had achieved little of value, inflicting scant damage at Musashino and no direct hits on the Tokyo docks. He considered it fortunate that only three planes were lost. (Two went down in the ocean south of Honshu; submarine lifeguards searched for them but found nothing.) Hansell had dreaded failure, he later wrote, "but I was so afraid that the command situation would erode and rob us of our independent operations against the Japanese islands that I offered to go ahead."[43] In other words, Hansell had felt pressure to demonstrate the feasibility of hitting Tokyo from the Marianas—to silence the doubters, and to firm up the autonomy of the Twentieth Air Force. It was felt that so long as the Superforts fulfilled their promise to bombard the industrial heart of Japan, Hap Arnold could resist pressure to disperse them for other purposes.

A DOZEN U.S. SUBMARINES had been positioned south of Honshu on lifeguard duty. One was the *Archerfish,* a *Balao*-class boat skippered by Lieutenant Commander Joseph F. Enright. She was patrolling in waters informally called the "Hit Parade," where other submarines (including the *Tang*) had found a wealth of shipping inbound to or outbound from Tokyo Bay. When a B-29 was forced to ditch at sea on the evening of November 24, *Archerfish* searched for three days. Finding no plane, no rafts, and no wreckage, Enright finally radioed Pearl Harbor to report "that the state of the seas was unfavorable for a water landing and it is presumed that the bomber crashed and sank quickly."[44]

On November 27, a radio dispatch from SubPac headquarters reported that there would be no more B-29s over Japan for forty-eight hours. That meant that the *Archerfish* and the other lifeguard submarines were free to resume the hunt for enemy shipping. Enright took his boat in close to the coast of Honshu, running submerged during daylight hours and making frequent high periscope observations. The great cone of Mount Fuji often passed through the crosshairs of the scope's circular field, but Enright saw no vessels except trawlers and other assorted small craft, which he considered "too small for torpedoes."[45]

Enright, born and raised in Minot, North Dakota, had graduated the Naval Academy with the class of 1933. Earlier in the war he had captained the *Dace*, but after a disappointing forty-nine-day patrol in the fall of 1943, Enright had concluded that he was not cut out for submarine command and had asked Lockwood to relieve him.*

For eight months he had performed shore duty at the Midway submarine base. In August 1944, he had felt the urge to try again, and Lockwood had granted Enright the rarest of gifts: a second chance as a submarine captain. Even more than the average Pacific submarine skipper, therefore, Enright was under pressure to score. Thus far in the patrol, he was empty-handed. The *Archerfish* had not yet fired any of her twenty-four Mark 18 electric torpedoes.

At 8:48 p.m. on the twenty-seventh, the *Archerfish*'s SJ radar revealed a contact at 24,700 yards, bearing 28 degrees true. A lookout climbed to the periscope support platform and trained his binoculars toward the northeast horizon. Conditions favored a visual search: the weather was clear and mild, and the moon nearly full. Enright first assumed that the contact was an island, but radar sweeps soon indicated that it was moving closer, and the lookout reported a "dark shape on the horizon two points off the starboard bow."[46]

Through binoculars, Enright soon made out a slight "bump" on the sea horizon. Comparing the visual fix to the range given by radar, he could deduce that it was a big ship, perhaps an oil tanker, which would make it a top-priority target.

Archerfish remained on the surface and took a westerly course, hoping to circle around to the "down-moon" side of the target. About an hour after first

---

* Five weeks earlier, it will be recalled, the *Dace,* under a different skipper, had ambushed Admiral Kurita's Center Force in Palawan Passage, striking the opening blow in the Battle of Leyte Gulf.

contact, a lookout called down from the shears to say that the distant shape
had the rectangular profile of an aircraft carrier. At first Enright was skeptical,
but after taking a long look he was persuaded. The shape grew more distinct
as it approached, and the carrier's huge island and funnel stood out on the
horizon. She was on a base course of 210 degrees with a speed of 20 knots. [47]

THE MYSTERIOUS FLATTOP WAS THE *SHINANO*, the world's largest aircraft carrier, a 65,000-ton behemoth built on a hull originally intended as the third
Yamato-class battleship. She had been built in the shipyard at Yokosuka
Naval Base in Tokyo Bay, launched on October 8, and commissioned just
eight days earlier. Since the previous June, when Japan had lost three carriers in the battle for the Marianas, her crew and 3,000 yard workers had
been working fourteen hours a day, seven days a week. Upon this huge new
ship rested Japan's last and only hope of resurrecting her once-formidable
carrier striking force.

The *Shinano* was bound for Kure, where she would complete her
fitting-out and embark her air group. Her skipper, Captain Toshio Abe,
was concerned about her readiness for sea. Under the strain of impossible deadlines, many shortcuts had been taken. Much of her vital inboard
works had not yet been installed and tested, including watertight hatches,
pumps, fire mains, and ventilation ducts. Abe had warned his superiors
that the ship and crew were not yet ready for sea, even for an overnight
run down the coast. But headquarters was unyielding, all the more so after
that week's B-29 raids. They had to assume that the big aircraft carrier
had been sighted and photographed, and the high-flying enemy bombers
might return at any time to hit the shipyard. The Tokyo admirals overruled Abe's request for a postponement and ordered the *Shinano* to sea no
later than November 28.

As in the case of her half-sisters *Yamato* and *Musashi*, the ship's existence
during construction had been wrapped in a shroud of fanatical secrecy. On
the waterfront at Yokosuka, ambitious measures were taken to hide the project from prying eyes. Towering fences made of corrugated tin panels stood
around the perimeter of Dock No. 6, where the *Shinano* was built. Thousands of shipyard workers were sequestered on base, and never permitted to
leave for the duration of the project. Military police would arrest, imprison,
interrogate, and torture any worker who so much as uttered the ship's name.

She was a titan: 872 feet long, 119 feet on the beam, with a full-load displacement of 71,890 tons. Like the two superbattleships, the *Shinano* was powered by four gigantic steam turbines that drove 150,000 horsepower to her propellers, giving her a peak speed of 27 knots. Her flight and hangar decks were armored, designed to withstand hits by 1,000-pound bombs. Her island, starboard amidships, was the size of an office building. It was integrated into an immense smoke funnel that was canted sharply outboard, giving the ship an idiosyncratic profile. The *Shinano* was fitted with hundreds of antiaircraft guns, more than had been mounted on any other aircraft carrier. "When I stood at the stern on the paved flight deck, the people standing at the bow looked as small as peas," recalled Oshima Morinari, a yard worker at Yokosuka. "I remember crying out in admiration. The *Shinano* was the greatest aircraft carrier in the world."[48] If by "greatest" he meant largest, Morinari was not wrong—none larger would exist until 1954, a decade later, when the first *Forrestal*-class aircraft carrier was launched by the United States.

True to her orders, the *Shinano* departed Tokyo Bay shortly after sunset on November 28, accompanied by three destroyers. She had about 2,475 men on board, including her crew of 2,175 officers and men and about three hundred shipyard workers. She carried no airplanes. In her hangar were fifty *Oka* guided suicide missiles, of the type designed to be dropped from planes, and six *Shinyo* suicide speed boats. It was intended that she would put the suicide crafts ashore in Kure, or perhaps deliver them to Okinawa at some point in the future.

After conferring with his superiors, Captain Abe had plotted a roundabout, offshore course. This would simplify navigation somewhat, and also (it was hoped) evade waters known to be infested with American submarines. The first stage of the passage would take the carrier and destroyers well south, out to sea. Before dawn the next morning they would turn west and make a dash for the Inland Sea. The final stretch would occur in daylight, without air cover, but there was nothing Abe could do about it; Tokyo had given him no choice. He believed he had chosen the safest possible route in the circumstances. The *Shinano* and her escorts surged through the calm, moonlit sea, making twenty knots and zigzagging erratically to foil enemy submarines.

THE U.S. NAVY'S RECOGNITION MANUAL did not have any silhouette matching the profile of the *Shinano*. Enright and his officers concluded that the stranger must be a *Hiyo-* or *Taiho-*class carrier. They did not suspect that their quarry was twice the tonnage of an *Essex*-class fleet carrier. No one in the Allied camp had a clue that such a ship existed.

Three escorting destroyers emerged on the radar scopes, and as the range closed they became faintly visible from the *Archerfish*'s periscope platform. Enright assumed, mistakenly, that there was probably a fourth on the far side of the target.

Attempting a surface approach against an enemy carrier escorted by four (or even three) destroyers would not do, especially under that bright moon. Such a thing had never been done. To attempt it, Enright believed, "would be practically suicidal."[49] But diving would deprive the *Archerfish* of most of her speed, rendering it impossible to maneuver into an attack position. The situation was not promising. Enright turned south, about nine miles ahead of the *Shinano* on a nearly parallel course, and raised speed to 19 knots. He would need a stroke of luck. The enemy ships were traveling at 20 knots, slightly faster than the *Archerfish*. The sub would have to dive once the range had closed to three or four miles, or risk detection. The firing window would be narrow, and it would not open at all unless the *Shinano* and her escorts happened to "zig" toward the *Archerfish*.

Enright radioed a contact report. Perhaps another submarine could be guided into position to intercept the unknown carrier, or Halsey's Third Fleet could take care of her. He had not given up hope for the *Archerfish*, but he was not sanguine: "Our only chance was to maintain our best surface speed, keep running on a parallel track, and pray for the carrier to make a course change in our direction."[50]

Aboard the *Shinano*, radar-finding instruments had detected the *Archerfish*'s probing surface search radar. Its frequency and pulse rate indicated that it was American, but the *Shinano*'s radar technicians were unable to establish a bearing. The radio signature of *Archerfish*'s contact report was also picked up aboard the *Shinano*—but again, no bearing was obtained. Captain Abe inferred that at least one enemy submarine was in the vicinity, but he had no idea of its location. An intelligence bulletin that week had reported that a group of U.S. submarines, perhaps as many as seven, had departed Guam together five days earlier. Putting one and one together, Abe concluded that an American wolfpack was stalking his ship. He passed the word to his lookouts—twenty-five had been posted around the flight deck and superstructure—and urged them to look for submarines running on the surface.

At 10:45 p.m., a sharp-eyed lookout reported "an unidentified object off the starboard bow." The visual contact was barely perceptible, even with the aid of the *Shinano*'s most advanced optical devices. A low-profile, black-painted submarine, five miles distant, would have been hard to see even in daylight. The curvature of the earth concealed all but the top of her bridge structure. Moreover, she was running well ahead of the *Shinano* on a parallel course, which shrank her profile. Dozens of pairs of Japanese eyes scrutinized the distant dark lump on the southwest horizon. The *Shinano*'s navigator thought it might be a "small ship."

One of the destroyers, the *Isokaze*, left the formation without orders. She raced toward the *Archerfish* at more than thirty knots, leaving a long, foaming, phosphorescent wake behind her.

On the bridge of the *Archerfish*, Enright watched the enemy destroyer as she bore down from astern. He correctly identified her as a *Kagero*-class destroyer—one of the fastest warships in the world, capable of doing better than 35 knots. He ordered the lookouts down from the platform and the bridge cleared. He checked his watch; it was 10:50 p.m. He trained his binoculars on the oncoming destroyer, noting that she was "looming larger and larger as she closed on *Archerfish*. Boy, was she coming fast!"[51] Enright was about to drop down the hatch and order a crash dive, when to his surprise the *Isokaze* turned away and returned to her station off the *Shinano*'s starboard beam. The *Archerfish* held course and stayed on the surface.

Abe had summoned the *Isokaze* back to her place in formation. Still assuming that the *Shinano* was being shadowed by an enemy wolfpack, he feared that the unknown contact to the south was deliberately attempting to lure away one of his escorts. "She's a decoy, I'm certain of it," he told the other officers on his bridge. He ordered a turn to the east, away from the *Archerfish*.[52] Running at more than twenty knots, Abe knew he would have no trouble outrunning the stranger.

Enright assumed he had missed his chance, but he kept the *Archerfish* knifing through the sea at flank speed, on a course roughly parallel to the base course of the *Shinano* group. The Japanese ships were traveling at least one knot faster than the *Archerfish*, so there was little chance of getting into attack position unless they turned back to the west. Captain Enright fingered his rosary beads while silently praying for such a turn.

At 11:40 p.m., it happened. "Looks like big zig in our direction," noted the log.[53] The *Shinano*'s sharp starboard turn put her on a westerly course, crossing the *Archerfish*'s stern. If her "zig" was followed by a timely "zag," the giant carrier might blunder directly into the submarine's firing window.

For the next three hours, all concerned held their relative courses. The *Shinano* and her three escorts gradually passed astern of the *Archerfish*, from the submarine's port quarter to her starboard quarter. It was an odd sort of chase, with the hunter leading miles ahead of her prey. The *Archerfish* was charging headlong toward a speculative location several miles south— a spot where, if Enright had guessed right, the paths of the *Shinano* and *Archerfish* would converge.

On the submarine's bridge, lookouts pointed their night binoculars at the distant behemoth, whose towering island and canted funnel rose above the sea horizon astern. The *Archerfish*'s bow rose and fell as she sprinted south across the moonlit sea. Her long hull throbbed with the guttural power of four engines running at full bore. Flumes of spray leapt back from the bow and pelted the lookouts' faces. Another stroke of luck was needed now, and Enright kept busy with his rosary beads.

At 2:56 a.m., his prayers were answered. The *Shinano* and her escorts turned again, this time to port, and steadied on a southwesterly course that would bring them directly into the *Archerfish*'s wheelhouse. The newest and largest aircraft carrier in the world was offering herself to the *Archerfish* as if gift-wrapped. The log noted, "Range closing rapidly and we are ahead."[54]

Eight minutes after the *Shinano*'s "zag," with the range closing to 12,000 yards, Enright ordered the *Archerfish* down. The lookouts dropped into the conning tower; the captain followed; the diving alarm sounded ("Ah-ooooooh-ga"); a sailor yanked the lanyard to close the hatch and secured it with a half-dozen turns of the handwheel. The *Archerfish* dived and leveled off at 60 feet. Enright raised the No. 2 periscope, the night scope, and trained it on the target. He fixed the crosshairs on the *Shinano* and murmured softly to himself, "Just keep coming, sweetheart. Don't turn away."[55]

The submarine crept west, maneuvering for an ideal firing position: 1,000 to 2,000 yards directly abeam of the carrier, where the *Shinano* would present the longest possible target for the *Archerfish*'s torpedoes. Several times Enright raised the night scope for a quick peek, confirming the target's course and speed. The tracking party fed his estimates into the torpedo data computer (TDC) and planned possible angles of attack. Passive sound bearings confirmed the skipper's periscope observations. He told the forward torpedo room crew to prepare six bow tubes. The weapons were set to a depth of 10 feet, providing a margin in case they ran deeper.

Again Enright raised the night scope and grasped the periscope handles. The *Shinano* was growing large in the circular field, and Enright took in details of her moonlit superstructure and distinctive canted funnel. She did not match anything in the recognition manual. Perhaps she was an older carrier that had been completely rebuilt? He made pencil sketches on a piece of scrap paper. Then Enright made out a blinker light on her bridge, apparently signaling one of the escorting destroyers. He swung the night scope until the destroyer came into the field, and noted with some alarm that she was bearing directly down on the *Archerfish* at high speed.

Enright now confronted the single most important decision of his career. If the *Archerfish* had been detected, he needed to crash dive and rig for a depth-charge attack. But that would take her out of attack position, ensuring that the *Shinano* would pass out of range. It seemed unlikely that the periscope could have been sighted. Enright asked his sonar man: was the destroyer sound-ranging? No, came the reply—no pinging. Since everything was riding on the question, however, Enright demanded confirmation. "Scanlon," he told the man, "look me in the eye and tell me whether that destroyer is pinging."[56] Scanlon checked all possible frequencies, turned to Enright, and repeated his answer. No pinging.

The captain took the sub down a few feet lower, to a keel depth of 62 feet. If the destroyer passed directly overhead, as seemed likely, her keel would pass over the *Archerfish*'s upper periscope support with about 10 feet of clearance. Not daring to raise the scope again, Enright and a very tense conning tower crew listened to the approaching ship. Passive sound bearings confirmed she was headed directly toward the submarine. The thrum of her engines became audible, and then the swish of her propellers. The rhythmic noise grew louder. "She thundered overhead like a locomotive," wrote Enright. "The whole submarine vibrated and rolled from the shockwaves."[57] Then she passed over, and the noise began diminishing. The Japanese had dropped no depth charges; evidently, they had had no inkling of the submarine's silent presence just beneath their keel.

Enright raised the night scope and centered the crosshairs on the *Shinano*'s great island, pale in the moonlight. "Mark, bearing," he called; "Standby . . . fire one."[58]

A rumble-shudder-hiss sounded from the bow, and the submarine recoiled as the first torpedo rocketed out of its tube. In the periscope field Enright saw the track stretch away toward the target, "hot, straight and normal." Eight seconds passed, then: "Fire two." Another blast of compressed air, and the *Archerfish* "jerked as if she had been smacked by a whale."[59] Then the third and fourth at eight-second intervals. The tracking party hurriedly entered a setup, and the *Archerfish* jumped again as the fifth and six torpedoes rushed out of their tubes.

The six torpedoes had been fired with 150 percent spread, meaning that four had been aimed to strike the *Shinano*, one to pass ahead, and one to pass astern. That was consistent with doctrine for big, high-value targets—the idea was to provide a margin of error in case the TDC solution was wrong, ensuring that at least one fish struck home. In this case, however, the *Archerfish* could scarcely have missed. She lay directly abeam of the 872-foot-long carrier, at what amounted to point-blank range for a torpedo attack: 1,400 yards. It was like firing at the broad side of a barn.

Seconds ticked away as the torpedoes ran toward the target. Tension in the conning tower rose. Enright kept the circular periscope field trained on the *Shinano*. As the first torpedo's estimated runtime ticked down to zero, he feared it must have missed, or was a dud. But then: "In the glass I saw a huge fireball erupt near the stern of the target. Then we heard the noise of the first hit, carried to us through the water. Then *Archerfish* felt the shockwaves created by the 680 pounds of torpex explosive."[60] Shouting in exultation, Enright kept the scope up for eight more seconds and was rewarded with the sight of a second fireball, fifty yards forward of the first.

Swinging the scope, Enright saw one of the destroyers turning toward the *Archerfish*. He slapped the handles against the shaft, ordered down scope, flood negative, and rig for depth charge. As the ballast tanks flooded, the bow grew heavy, and the deck tilted forward as gravity pulled the boat down. The hydroplanes bit into the water as her forward momentum increased, forcing her down at an even steeper angle. The *Archerfish* passed through 400 feet depth before leveling off.

The depth charges began: sharp blasts, loud and unnerving but not especially close. Enright estimated that the nearest detonation was 300 yards away. The Japanese seemed to be guessing. After fifteen minutes of scattering "ash cans" at random, they gave up the counterattack. The submarine's sonar tracked the destroyers as they headed away to the southwest.

For three hours the *Archerfish* crept through the depths, running slowly and silently. Dead-reckoning back to the location where he believed he had sunk his target, Enright brought her up to periscope depth. It was 6:10 a.m. Raising the scope and sweeping all the way around the horizon, he saw nothing but sea. It was a bright, sunny morning with moderate breezes. The *Archerfish* submerged again and remained down all day, surfacing again at 5:22 p.m. to radio the heady news to Pearl Harbor: she had torpedoed an enemy aircraft carrier.[61]

SINCE 11:00 THE PREVIOUS NIGHT, it had been clear in Captain Abe's mind that the *Shinano* was being shadowed by an enemy submarine wolfpack. Submerged predators might be anywhere, in any direction, or in every direction. There was nothing to do, he concluded, but maintain brisk speed and keep zigzagging erratically. He had been on the verge of ordering another "zig" just as the *Archerfish*'s torpedoes tore into the starboard side of his ship.

The first hit just forward of the stern, about 10 feet beneath the waterline, tossing up a pillar of orange-red fire. Three more struck in quick succession, raising three more spikes of fire, each one forward of the last. The blasts flooded compartments on three decks, including three boiler rooms, and killed dozens of sailors asleep in their bunks. Fuel lines ignited and an oil tank ruptured. Damage control parties rushed to put hoses on the flames, but the blaze obstinately traveled into nearby regions of the ship. Hundreds of stretchers were rushed to the sick bay, quickly overwhelming the medical staff. Within minutes of the impact, the *Shinano* was listing 10 degrees to starboard.

Like her half-sisters the *Yamato* and *Musashi*, the supercarrier had been built to withstand torpedo hits. A month earlier, in the Sibuyan Sea, the *Musashi* had absorbed almost twenty before sinking. Abe was a bit surprised at how quickly the *Shinano* had listed to starboard, but he assumed that the list could be corrected by counterflooding, and was confident of keeping her afloat so long as she suffered no fresh blows. Wary of the imagined wolfpack, the skipper rang up the engine room and told his engineers that he needed every possible knot of speed to clear the submarine-infested area. The *Shinano* and her destroyers did not pause; they forged ahead with speed undiminished.

Below, along corridors adjoining the stricken area of the ship, a fearsome keening sound rang out from watertight doors, pipes, and ventilation ducts. It was the song of compressed air being forced through watertight seals, caused by the unstoppable pressure of tons of seawater entering the ship through the four gaping breaches in the hull. "As we worked we could hear squeaks and shutters from the tortured metal under at least one hundred tons of pressure," recalled a member of the crew. "The rivets were shaking and appeared almost ready to burst free from their holes."[62] Jets of water shot through cracks in the seals of watertight hatches. Piping and ventilation ducts burst open. The *Shinano*'s mighty engines, driving her forward at better than twenty knots, were working indirectly to force thousands of tons of the Pacific Ocean into the starboard side of the ship. Even after pumping 3,000 tons of seawater into port-side bilges, the *Shinano* leaned farther to starboard. When the list reached 15 degrees, sailors were forced to brace themselves against starboard bulkheads.

Captain Abe's reassuring voice came on the loudspeakers. He informed the crew that there was no danger of capsize, but exhorted the pumping teams to do everything they could to correct the list.

Speed fell gradually until the *Shinano* was making only ten knots. Flooding and fires spread wantonly, threatening to overwhelm hydraulic pumping stations. Hundreds of men, standing by their posts as ordered, were trapped behind jammed hatches and crushed bulkheads. As the sea broke into their compartments, they drowned. Belatedly realizing that the *Shinano* was in a desperate fight for her life, Captain Abe sent an S.O.S. signal to Yokosuka. Then he turned the crippled ship north, hoping to run her aground on the nearest island.

The first faint glow of dawn rose above the eastern horizon. The moon set in the west. The wounded carrier limped north, her three escorts hugging her close. Her great superstructure and funnel leaned drunkenly to starboard, and a pall of smoke trailed to leeward. At 7:00 a.m., her engines shut down for lack of steam. The *Shinano* lay dead in the water, in the trough of the ocean; each time she rolled, her list increased. Abe ordered two destroyers, *Hamakaze* and *Isokaze*, to take the 65,000-ton carrier under tow, but the physics of such an arrangement were out of the question. When a steel cable snapped, the effort was halted.

Abe was slow to order a general abandonment, and hundreds of the crew paid with their lives. Refugees from the flooded regions of the ship milled about on the hangar and flight decks. Discipline threatened to break down, at least in parts of the ship. Sailors panicked and leapt into the sea without orders. At half past nine, the *Shinano* rolled over to starboard, slowly but inexorably. The sea flooded into the main elevator wells on her flight deck, sweeping sailors off their feet and hurling them down into the hangar. As the funnel submerged, many scores of swimmers were sucked back into its black maw. When at last Abe passed the word to abandon ship, many of his crew had already done so, but for others it was too late. Around the capsized leviathan, to a radius of about half a mile, castaways clung to debris and awaited rescue by the escorting destroyers.

Captain Abe did not intend to survive, and a retinue of his officers insisted on remaining with him. He and his followers hiked up the steeply canted flight deck to the bow, which they knew would be the last part of the ship to go under. As the stern dipped, the ship rolled back onto an even keel. Her bow lifted clear of the sea and reared up until the flight deck was nearly vertical. The *Shinano* hung in that position for a time, seemingly immobile, as the sea invaded from astern. From the interior came the roar of explosions, the hiss of jetting gases, and the crashing of heavy equipment and debris as it tore loose and fell along the longitudinal axis of the ship. She slid under, gradually, until the ocean swallowed her sixteen-petal gold chrysanthemum crest. Captain Abe rode her into the abyss, accompanied by 1,400 other souls.

That concluded the maiden voyage of the *Shinano*.

Upon *Archerfish*'s return to Guam on December 15, Joe Enright ran into a wall of skepticism concerning his claimed sinking. Naval intelligence had no idea that such a ship even existed, and his description of the target's superstructure and canted funnel did not correspond to any known aircraft carrier in the Japanese fleet. On November 28, Pacific listening posts had intercepted a Japanese message, which the cryptanalysts quickly broke: "*Shinano* sunk." There was no record of a Japanese ship of that name, but "Shinano" was the name of a major river in northeastern Honshu. Based upon the Japanese navy's rigid naming conventions, such a name suggested that the target was probably a cruiser. On that basis, Admiral Lockwood leaned toward crediting the *Archerfish* with sinking a heavy cruiser of unidentified class, probably an older ship that had been thoroughly rebuilt.

But Enright was certain that he had sunk a carrier, and he backed up his contention with the pencil sketches he had made while studying the *Shinano* through his periscope. The analysts in Pearl Harbor were forced to agree: the detailed sketches depicted a carrier. Meanwhile, someone in Sub-Pac headquarters pointed out that "Shinano" was also the ancient name of a province in the Nagano region, which meant that it was a plausible name for an aircraft carrier. On those grounds, Lockwood credited the *Archerfish* with sinking a 28,000-ton *Hiyō*-class carrier.[63]

Not until after the war was the entire truth known. U.S. Strategic Bombing Survey interrogators confirmed that the *Archerfish* had sunk a 65,000-ton aircraft carrier, which meant that she had earned the distinction of the single most productive submarine patrol of the war as measured by tonnage sunk. The self-effacing Enright always emphasized that he had been lucky, that blind chance had delivered the zigzagging *Shinano* into a narrow firing window. That was undoubtedly true: fate had dealt the *Archerfish* a winning hand. But Enright had played the cards flawlessly, and for that he was awarded the Navy Cross.

Chapter Eight

THE SEAS AROUND LEYTE WERE LITTERED WITH DEBRIS, THE REMNANTS OF U.S. and Japanese ships sunk in the great naval battle. Oil slicks polluted the beaches along Surigao Strait. Bodies, mostly Japanese, drifted with the tides and washed ashore. A Seventh Fleet officer noted that the entire area was choked with "the odor of decaying flesh."[1] According to an American intelligence officer embedded with anti-Japanese guerillas on Samar, much "treasure" was found on the beaches in the days after the battle between Kurita's fleet and the Taffys. Crates of rations floated ashore, containing crackers, cheese, jam, dehydrated potatoes, spam, cigarettes, and coffee. Clothing and mattresses were salvaged by civilian Filipinos. A waterlogged paperback copy of *Gone with the Wind* was laid out in the sun to dry. Drums of gasoline were carried away and stored in hidden caches.[2] A headless body washed ashore, probably Japanese: it was cremated atop a pile of driftwood.

In the enclosed waters of Leyte Gulf, some 650 ships of Kinkaid's transport and amphibious fleet settled in for a long stay. The work of unloading cargo onto the landing beaches would require many weeks. The sea grew fetid, an open sewer for a floating city with a population exceeding 100,000. "The water in the bay is a sickly green, filthy with the toilet wash of many, many ships," a sailor reported in a letter home.[3] To protect itself against Japanese air raids, the fleet produced screens of chemical gray, brown, and yellow smoke. Smoke pots were mounted in the stern racks of landing craft; smoking floats were anchored to windward of transports; Besler fog oil generators mounted on larger ships spewed out vast clouds of the stuff for hours at a time.[4] Every dusk and dawn, when the threat of air attack was greatest, a gossamer veil descended over the gulf.

The east coast of Leyte was well suited to amphibious logistics. Long white-sand beaches shelved abruptly to navigable water, and no coral reefs blocked the approaches. Larger vessels, LCTs and LSTs, could nose up onto the beaches and unload supplies directly over ramps and pontoon causeways. Jeeps, trucks, and tanks drove ashore directly from the landing ships. Aerial photos of the coast near Tacloban depicted dozens of these big amphibians, bows wedged securely on the beach, ramps extended like tongues from gaping clamshell doors. The white wakes of hundreds of small craft were seen plying the waters between the beaches and the transports anchored offshore. In the two months after "A-Day," Kinkaid's amphibious forces unloaded a daily average of 11,000 deadweight tons of weaponry, ammunition, provisions, vehicles, and miscellaneous supplies onto those beaches.[5]

But the heroic pace of unloading left a disorderly pileup of cargo in the landing zone. By October 1944, this was an old and familiar headache. As usual, amphibious commanders blamed a shortage of labor on the landing beaches, while ground commanders replied (not unreasonably) that their troops were preoccupied with fighting an actual battle ashore. The flat country just inland of the beaches was soon a teeming supply dump, covering many square miles of terrain. It was roughly laid out in a grid pattern, with dirt tracks running between stacks of crates, fuel drums, and parked vehicles. This great concentration of war matériel was exposed to attack from the air, and much of it was destroyed in the first week of the campaign. On the evening of October 25, for example, a Japanese bomb struck a 4,500-drum gasoline dump. The fire was still burning twenty-four hours later. But an even greater aggravation was the relentless, hammering, monsoonal rains, which turned roads and footpaths into hog-wallows and drainage ditches into swollen brown rivers. General Eichelberger described the coastal region south of Tacloban as "a swamp and a mud hole and nothing more."[6]

A ground echelon of the 308th Bomb Wing of the Army Air Forces worked over the Tacloban airstrip, racing to turn it into a major air base. But circumstances conspired against them. The ground was soft and soggy, and no amount of bulldozing and grading could tame its muddy expanses. Trucks dumped dirt and gravel along its length, but there were no coral deposits within easy reach, and thus no suitable materials for making concrete or asphalt. Frequent emergency landings of carrier planes forced the construction teams to clear the field. Brave men stood out on the strip with flags and flares, marking the locations of treacherous spots to be avoided by the planes. Crashes were a near-daily ordeal. Bulldozers shoved the wreckage to the edges of the field. Rain and enemy air raids interrupted the work, as they did everywhere else on Leyte. Marston steel mats were brought ashore and laid over the surface, but that did not entirely solve the problem, as the soft soil underlying the mats caused them to become misaligned. Similar problems dogged the airfields to the south, in Dulag, Bayug, Buri, and San Pablo. General Kenney's Fifth Air Force did not operate in force from Leyte until December 1944, when the Philippine campaign was already moving on to Mindoro and Luzon.

In the early days of the Leyte campaign, U.S. forces took more territory than they had expected with fewer casualties than they had feared. The U.S. Sixth Army, commanded by the German-born Lieutenant General Walter Krueger, had four fully equipped divisions lodged on the island's eastern coastal plain, and the great naval battle offshore had secured their seaborne supply lines. Dirt tracks through the lowlands climbed into a long spine of high rugged country, roughly arrayed on a north-south axis, with heavily forested mountains ascending to peaks of 4,000 feet. Tanks and heavy equipment could run up those roads, though the weather was always a joker in the deck, and Japanese troops occupied strong positions on the commanding heights. Near the northern end of the island, the eastern Leyte Valley connected to the western Ormoc Valley by Highway 2, a steep and winding mountain road. This road continued south down the island's west coast to the port of Ormoc and farther south to the town of Baybay. There the road turned inland and climbed into the mountains, crossing the central range and terminating at Abuyog on the east coast.

Sixth Army made steady early progress inland, while Japanese forces generally moved back in fighting retreats. Advance patrols crossed the mountainous waist of the island, taking possession of Baybay without running into any serious enemy resistance. X Corps, commanded by Major General Franklin C. Sibert, cleared the northern Leyte Valley and began pushing north along the coast of the San Juanico Strait. On the 24th, units of the 8th Cavalry Regiment crossed the strait in landing craft to land at La Paz, on Samar, and held that position in order to guard against Japanese small-craft incursions into the strait. With firm control of the waterway, the Americans could now lift troops and supplies up the coast by sea.

On November 7, elements of the U.S. 24th Division stormed ashore on the western side of Carigara Bay, on the northern coast of the island. The roads leading south from Carigara were steep, winding, and frequently washed out by heavy rains. Pushing south into high country, the Americans ran into a stout line of defense in a horseshoe-shaped circle of heavily forested hills which they called "Breakneck Ridge." The elite Japanese First Division was well entrenched in a network of log-lined trenches and firing positions. Here the fighting grew hard and heavy, stalling the American advance for nearly two weeks.

JAPANESE ARMY COMMANDERS HAD DEBATED their strategy to meet the U.S. invasion right up until the eve of MacArthur's landing. Field Marshal Count Hsaishi Terauchi, commander in chief of the South Asia Army, had dominion over all army forces in the South Pacific and much of Southeast Asia. Six months earlier, in April 1944, he had transferred his headquarters from Singapore to Manila. To oversee the defense of the Philippines, he tapped Lieutenant General Tomoyuki Yamashita, who had earned his name by conquering Malaya and Singapore in early 1942. Yamashita arrived in Manila in early October, only two weeks before the American invasion of Leyte, to find that no firm strategy was in place to meet the coming threat. Japanese commanders in the Philippines had expected an American landing around October 1, but no one knew where it would come. The southern island of Mindanao presented one obvious possibility, and Leyte another—but a bolder thrust directly at Luzon could not be discounted. Their dilemma was identical to that faced by MacArthur in December 1941—the vast archipelago offered hundreds of possible entry points to an invader with local naval and air superiority.

Fundamental disagreements over strategy had riven the Manila headquarters. Some argued that air supremacy was the only sure defense, and wanted to pour the army's collective manpower and resources into building and improving airfields. Through the end of August 1944, the Japanese army had devoted most of its major effort to building and improving airstrips throughout the theater, particularly in Luzon. Wide dispersal was the keystone of this strategy, with airplanes distributed to a network of many small dirt strips in remote and heavily forested regions. But other commanders wanted to pour their efforts into preparing fixed fortifications facing the most likely invasion beaches, or constructing strongholds on high ground, where the terrain would favor the defenders. Here again, there were two rival schools of thought, summed up by one senior officer as "annihilation at the beachhead" versus the "battling withdrawal."[7]

But the more pressing question, in mid-October 1944, was whether the Japanese army would maintain its principal strength on the main northern island of Luzon, or whether it would attempt large-scale troop transfers to meet the invaders on Leyte. On October 18, when U.S. warships first began shelling Leyte's beaches, and special forces seized the small islands at the entrance of Leyte Gulf, the question remained unresolved. General Yamashita wanted to fight a limited, delaying battle on Leyte. He was opposed to transferring large numbers of troops from Luzon, presuming that many would be lost at sea. U.S. air and submarine attacks on troop transports had extracted an exorbitant cost in the South Pacific. But others were swayed by the Japanese navy's accounts of the punishment inflicted on the U.S. Third Fleet off Taiwan between October 12 and October 15. That was compounded by the navy's subsequent report that it had scored another major victory in the Battle of Leyte Gulf. Field Marshal Terauchi insisted upon pouring reinforcements into Leyte, overruling Yamashita. The latter, vexed by what he regarded as a disastrous policy, nonetheless ordered the mass transportation of Japanese troops from Mindanao, Luzon, and other islands in the Visayas into Leyte by the back door at Ormoc Bay.[8]

Approximately 43,000 Japanese troops were on the island as the invaders came ashore, about double the number estimated by U.S. intelligence. But the Japanese managed to bring an additional 34,000 reinforcements ashore during the campaign. Nine major reinforcement convoys sailed from Manila, and countless smaller troop movements from Mindanao and the Visayas arrived by boat or barge. About 10,000 Japanese troops were lost while in transit to Leyte when their transports were attacked. Many who landed safely on Leyte did so without their equipment and heavy weaponry, limiting their effectiveness once ashore. Nevertheless, the arrival of the crack First Division in the first week of the campaign did much to fortify the confidence and morale of the Japanese. "We had hopeful discussions of entering Tacloban by the 16th of November," said General Tomochika, the division's chief of staff. Moreover, there was serious talk of taking MacArthur alive, and ransoming him at the price of "the surrender of the entire American army."[9]

Early plans had envisioned deploying the First Japanese Division in the vicinity of Carigara and the Twenty-Sixth Division a few miles south, at Jaro. A supply line would be run up the coast in sea lifts from Ormoc. But on November 1, island headquarters at Ormoc learned that American forces were already crossing the Carigara range, which was separated by much difficult terrain from their landing beaches. The power and speed of the American armored ground attack, so far from their initial landing point on the island's east coast, came as a nasty surprise. Many battalion-sized units were decimated, and island headquarters found it difficult even to maintain communications with their forward lines. The Japanese army was forced back into the mountains southwest of Carigara, where the terrain was more favorable for defense. But that move cut them off from the coast, which complicated the logistical picture, because it was difficult to maintain overland supply lines from Ormoc.

In the immediate aftermath of the Battle of Leyte Gulf, the victorious Third Fleet was worn out. Pilots had flown near-daily combat operations since early October. Air group leaders warned that symptoms of acute fatigue were spreading through the ranks. A flight surgeon on the *Wasp* judged that only 30 of the carrier's 131 airmen were fit for continued daily flight assignments.[10] Most of the ships' crews had not felt solid ground under their feet for two or three months. Halsey wanted to pull his fleet back to Ulithi Atoll for a brief rest before Operation HOTFOOT, a carrier raid on the Japanese homeland, tentatively planned for the third week of November. Just four minutes after his dispatch to all commands boasting that the Japanese navy had been "beaten, routed, and broken," Halsey radioed Kinkaid: "For future planning it must be understood that fast carriers require rearming and air groups are exhausted after 16 days unprecedented fighting."[11]

That suggestion did not go down well with Kinkaid, or with MacArthur, who expected Task Force 38 to remain in the area until the Fifth Air Force was ready to take over air defense of the Leyte beachhead. Kinkaid reported details of the mauling suffered by his escort carriers in the Battle off Samar. They were in no condition to maintain air cover over the transport fleet and beachhead: "CVEs have been doing splendidly in keeping planes in air but may shortly become inoperative." The army planes could not yet assume responsibility for air cover because the Tacloban and Dulag airfields were in no condition to receive them. For the time being, at least one of Halsey's carrier groups must stay behind "for support and protection [of] Leyte Gulf area and possibly CVEs."[12]

Kinkaid did not have to spell out what was clearly implied: that Halsey must do penance for his recent sins. Since the Third Fleet boss was at fault for having allowed the Taffys to be ambushed by Kurita, it was only right that he make up the deficiency in airpower. In the days that followed, Halsey renewed his urgent entreaties to be released, and Kinkaid insisted upon continued air protection. It was not just the airmen: Halsey and his staff were feeling the strain of prolonged combat operations at sea. Later he admitted, "I was tired, in mind, body, and nerves. So were we all."[13]

Late on October 26, Halsey put his case directly to MacArthur: "After 17 days of fighting, the fast carrier force is virtually out of bombs, torpedoes, and provisions, and pilots are exhausted. I am unable to provide any extended direct air support. When will your shore-based air take over air defense at the objective? Halsey."[14]

From his headquarters in Pearl Harbor, Nimitz monitored the situation with mounting concern. He knew that the Third Fleet had been pushed to the limit, but the navy had agreed to provide carrier air cover to support the Leyte operation. The near-calamity off Samar had raised the stakes. Issues of interservice and inter-theater coordination, if not resolved in the Pacific, would be kicked up to the Joint Chiefs. Worse, influential voices in Congress and the press had taken aim at the two-theater command setup in the Pacific. Governor Dewey had raised the issue on the presidential campaign trail, and the election was just two weeks away. If a major setback occurred in the Pacific, MacArthur's powerful backers would insist upon consolidating the entire campaign under his singular authority.

The naval high command had remained aloof from politics, as its professional code required. But Nimitz, King, and Leahy had each served many years in Washington, and they were wise to the city's ways. Command unity in the Pacific was a cause célèbre of the political opposition. The threat was real. The dual-theater command model must be made to work.

When Nimitz intercepted Halsey's importunate query to MacArthur (261235), he moved quickly to intervene. Halsey had reported a shortage of provisions as one factor dictating his retirement to Ulithi. Nimitz did not believe it, and challenged his fleet commander's accounting in a message copied to King and Vice Admiral William L. Calhoun, the Pacific Fleet logistics chief: "Your 261235 reference to provisions not understood. Report approximate average number days supply of dry provisions in each type of combatant ship in company with you and list controlling items which are sufficiently short to affect combat operations."[15] As for the question of air protection over Leyte Gulf, the CINCPAC put Halsey in his place with this peremptory order, adding Kinkaid and MacArthur as coaddressees: "My OpPlan 8–44 remains in effect. Cover and support forces of the Southwest Pacific until otherwise directed by me."[16]

Thus chastened, Halsey arranged to rotate his carrier groups back to Ulithi Atoll in a "round robin." Two carrier groups, 38.1 (McCain) and 38.3 (Sherman), retired to Ulithi for rest and replenishment, while the remaining two—38.2 (Bogan) and 38.4 (Davison)—remained off Samar to provide air cover for Leyte Gulf. But Sherman's task group, anchoring in Ulithi on October 30, was urgently recalled by Halsey two days later. The Japanese were putting up an unexpectedly spirited fight in the air. Luzon's airfields were being reinforced by replacement planes from Formosa, China, and the Japanese homeland. Furthermore, massed aerial suicide attacks presented a new, perpetual, and bloodcurdling threat. The era of the kamikaze had arrived.

Bogan's flagship *Intrepid* caught it on October 29. An outgoing afternoon strike had bombed and strafed Japanese airfields north of Manila. Several kamikazes apparently tracked the American planes as they returned to their carriers. One dove out of the overcast, striking the *Intrepid*'s starboard 40mm gun gallery. The carrier's battle efficiency was not impaired, but the attack killed six men and injured ten.

The following afternoon, Davison's group was targeted by a swarm of kamikazes, and this time the butcher's bill was higher. Jim Russell, chief of staff to Admiral Davison, watched the attack from the *Franklin*'s flag bridge. Five enemy planes eluded the combat air patrol and dove into the heart of the task group: "The first thing we knew, they were coming down in these long slanting suicide dives."[17] Every antiaircraft battery on every ship opened fire. Gunners on the *Enterprise* sawed the wing off one attacker, which splashed into the sea about 30 feet from the ship. *San Jacinto*'s gunners shot down another, sparing their carrier. The *Belleau Wood*'s gunners knocked down one kamikaze but could not hit the second—and that one hit aft, penetrating the flight deck and setting off a destructive fire in the hangar. The fifth hit the *Franklin*, dead center on her flight deck. It gouged a 40-foot hole just forward of the No. 3 elevator and exploded in the elevator pit. More than an hour was needed to bring the fires under control.

Personnel losses were heavy: ninety-two killed on the *Belleau Wood*, fifty-four on the *Franklin*. A dozen planes on the *Belleau Wood* and thirty-three on the *Franklin* were incinerated or damaged beyond repair. They were jettisoned.

On the *Franklin*, according to Russell, the Japanese pilot's body was recovered intact. "You know," he said, "despite the explosion, that fellow's body was recognizable. His silk flying suit held him together enough so you knew he was a human, at least. Of course, he was well smashed."[18]

JAPAN'S STATE-RUN NEWS MEDIA had reported yet another spectacular victory in the Battle of Leyte Gulf. The Imperial Japanese Navy had deliberately bided its time, said the reports, "in order to pile training upon training." It had waited patiently for the Americans to cross the wide Pacific, where they would be disadvantaged by lengthening supply lines. Finally, the U.S. fleet had blundered heedlessly into the flight-radii of powerful Japanese air bases in Formosa and the Philippines, and had suffered two back-to-back thrashings in the space of just two weeks. A commentator on NHK radio assured listeners that the end must be near:

> One thing is now clear: America has lost the war. Japanese forces have now complete air and sea superiority on and around Leyte, and powerful additional Japanese forces are moving up for the attack. All the Japanese have to do in future operations is to project their indomitable spirits at the enemy and they will suffer internal fear that will defeat them before they get into the fight. The Occidental mind, of course, will not understand the great Oriental power.[19]

Reports dwelled especially on the kamikaze attacks off Samar on the afternoon of October 25. Oblique references to "special attack forces" and "body-crashing" had been heard before—but from that date to the end of the war, the kamikazes were the single biggest story in Japanese newspapers and radio broadcasts. By one estimate, stories about suicide pilots occupied about one-half of all column inches in the Tokyo papers during the period. Although references to discord between the army and navy were forbidden to appear in print, it was clear to anyone who could read between the lines that the two services were competing to lay claim to the *tokko* ("special attack") phenomenon.[20] The navy had been the first mover, with the sacrifice of Admiral Arima on October 15—but the army responded just five days later, trumpeting the creation of its "Banda Unit" at the Hokota Flight Training Center in Ibaragi Prefecture. IGHQ directed the new suicide units to "disrupt the reinforcement and replenishment at sea of the enemy landing forces (including the destruction of transports near anchorages) and destroy the enemy carrier striking task force (including naval vessels supporting the landing operations)."[21]

Kamikazes were both a tactical and a propaganda expedient. The militarist junta was alarmed by the public's waning spirits and its rising doubts about the veracity of domestic war reporting. Faith in ultimate victory must somehow be restored. The suicide air corps and other novelties—such as the *oka*, *kaiten*, and intercontinental balloon bombs—were analogous to the "miracle weapons" (*wunderwaffe*) advertised by the Nazis during the same period. To a certain extent, all were propaganda gambits aimed at shoring up the Axis regimes' deteriorating credibility and consolidating their grip on power. In Japan, where shame always offered a practical lever for social control, the kamikazes were held up as exemplars for ordinary civilians. In reporting the suicide attacks on Task Force 38 in late October, the editors of the *Mainichi Shinbun* reflected: "All of us should learn from the serene spirit of these youths."[22] Prime Minister Koiso urged munitions workers to follow the example of "the valiant men of the Special Attack Corps, [and] demonstrate even more spirit of sure victory in the field of production."[23]

With remarkable speed, the kamikaze corps was expanded and institutionalized in both the navy and the army. Entire air groups were redesignated as special attack units with new highfalutin literary or mythological names. Hundreds of planes and airmen designated for *tokko* missions flew into the Philippines in November 1944, so that the kamikaze corps expanded rapidly even while many suicide planes were immolated in combat. Two hundred army planes flew into Negros Island, west of Leyte, to join Lieutenant General Kyoji Tominaga's Fourth Air Army. At training centers in Japan, entire classes of pilot-cadets, some with only rudimentary flying skills, were merged into the nascent kamikaze corps. Many were sent to fly directly to the Philippines for attacks that might occur within weeks or even days. Recent inductees who had not yet started primary flight training were informed that they would train from the outset as kamikazes. That established a training pipeline, ensuring that a freshet of suicide pilots would become available in the spring of 1945.

Vice Admiral Fukudome had at first resisted Onishi's suggestion that the navy's two air fleets in the Philippines adopt massed suicide tactics, and his Second Air Fleet continued to fly conventional missions during the Battle of Leyte Gulf. But Fukudome was impressed by the apparent success of Lieutenant Seki's October 25 mission, and swayed by mounting evidence that conventional aerial tactics were no longer effective. The next day, October 26, the two air fleets were combined into one, with Fukudome in charge and Onishi as his chief of staff. From that date, Fukudome said, "the kamikaze or special attack planes constituted the nucleus of my air force."[24] He had personal misgivings about sending young men to their certain deaths, as did other senior commanders, especially when word arrived from Tokyo that the *Showa* emperor had been briefed on Seki's attack. Hirohito had asked the navy chief of staff, "Was it necessary to go to this extreme? They certainly did a magnificent job."[25] Admiral Onishi interpreted the man-god's query as implied criticism, and was deeply troubled by it. But he and Fukudome agreed that no realistic alternative existed.

Some defiance persisted down the ranks. Lieutenant Commander Iyozo Fujita, a veteran squadron leader, was asked to select twelve pilots for suicide missions. "I refuse to do this," he told his superiors. "If you want to do it, I have nothing to do with this decision; you select the pilots." Then he returned to his quarters and lay down in his bed. Fujita added, after the war, "At this time in the war I believe that the high command was going crazy. In the end the group of fighters still went on their mission, and nothing was ever heard from them again."[26] Some pilots were privately horrified, but did not feel free to voice their objections. One aviator-in-training, a university student, recalled that he was "bowled over" by the news that his training class had been designated for kamikaze operations. But he dared not speak up, even to his fellow cadets. "We couldn't share our doubts with each other. We were all drawn from different universities. If I had expressed my disquiet, my university could have been disgraced. I had to keep my own counsel."[27]

Yet anecdotal evidence suggests that a majority of Japanese airmen were not only willing but eager to give their lives as kamikazes. When volunteers were solicited, unanimous acquiescence was typical. One squadron leader recalled that his men crowded around him and clutched at his arms, crying, "Send me! Please send me! Send me!" He snapped at them: "Everyone wants to go. Don't be so selfish!"[28] According to air commander Rikihei Inoguchi, pilots designated for future kamikaze flights lobbied fervently to be assigned to each upcoming mission. "Why don't you let me go soon?" they implored, and "How long must I wait?"[29]

Kamikazes were a privileged caste. Exalted as "gods without earthly desires," they were treated with respect and deference even by colleagues whose rank, experience, and skill surpassed their own. While standing by for assignment to a *tokko* mission, they lodged in separate quarters, typically the best and cleanest on the base, and ate meals fit for high-ranking officers. They received expensive gifts from conventional aviators and other military units. Civilian groups at home, including primary school students, wrote fan mail and sent "care packages." War correspondents and photographers sought them out for interviews and photo shoots. They were feted at lavish banquets where geishas sang and danced for their entertainment, and rare delicacies were washed down with high-shelf sake. Distinctions of rank faded. Commander Inoguchi recalled an exchange with kamikaze airmen at the airfield on Cebu, an island in the central Philippines. One pointed out that the order of precedence for dead spirits at Yasukuni Shrine, the Shinto Valhalla, was fixed by date of arrival rather than by military rank.

"I will outrank you then, Commander," he said, "because you will have to send out many more pilots before you can go yourself."

"Say," said another, "what shall we do with the Commander when he reports in at Yasukuni?"

"Let's make him the mess sergeant!"

The remark elicited a lusty roar of laughter.

Inoguchi, playing along, beseeched his subordinates: "Can't you do better by me than that?"

"Well, then," one replied, "perhaps mess officer." More laughter.[30]

New kamikaze flyers arriving in the Philippines underwent a seven-day indoctrination program, including classroom instruction and basic flying drills. A typical outgoing flight consisted of a small formation, generally four to six planes, including one or two escort-observer planes. (The escorts, piloted by experienced aviators of superior skill, were not to attack. Their role was to lead the kamikazes to the target, observe the results, and return safely to base.) Two approach and attack methods were employed: one at high altitude and one at sea level. In the former, the planes approached the enemy fleet at 25,000 feet or higher. Closing to forty miles, they dropped copious amounts of "window"—aluminum strips—to confuse the U.S. radar systems. When the ubiquitous F6F Hellcats swarmed up to intercept, the escorts tried to lure them away with showy defensive maneuvers, while the kamikazes dove for speed and sought cloud cover, hoping to get to within attack range of the U.S. fleet. The low-altitude approach involved skimming 20 or 30 feet above the wavetops. U.S. radar systems generally did not detect low-altitude attackers beyond a range of about ten miles, owing to the curvature of the earth and interference caused by ocean swell. Drawing to within five or six miles of the enemy fleet, the low-altitude kamikazes suddenly pulled up and climbed to about 2,000 feet. If there was a cloud ceiling, they attempted to hide in it while selecting a target.[31]

For the final attack—this applied to both high- and low-altitude approaches—the kamikazes were told to bear down on the target at a steep angle, like a dive-bomber. They were to aim for the enemy's topside deck. The steeper their angle of attack, the greater their penetrating power. When attacking an aircraft carrier, they were to aim at one of the elevator pits on the flight deck. That was believed to offer the best hope of smashing through into the hangar, where the potential for secondary fires and explosions was greatest. (At the very least, putting an elevator out of action would impair a carrier's flight operations.) If a steep-diving impact on the flight deck was not possible, the kamikazes were told to aim for the carrier's island superstructure, with hopes of killing the senior officers and destroying the ship's brain center.[32]

On the first day of November, waves of suicide planes descended on Admiral Kinkaid's Seventh Fleet in Leyte Gulf. Attacks started up in late morning and continued through the early evening. Many ships narrowly avoided direct hits with aggressive maneuvering; antiaircraft guns destroyed perhaps twenty planes. One attacker struck a glancing blow on the main stack of the destroyer *Ammen*. At about 1:30, radar scopes revealed a small formation of inbound attackers, gliding down from altitude at high speed. No American fighters were in the air to intercept them. The destroyer *Abner Read* maneuvered violently as an Aichi dive-bomber broke through the cloud ceiling. The *Abner's* 40mm and 20mm antiaircraft guns blazed fiercely, actually tearing the attacker's port wing cleanly away, but the wrecked plane's momentum carried it down to strike the destroyer starboard amidships.

Fires raged throughout the forward part of the *Abner Read*, threatening to engulf the depth-charge racks and torpedo mounts. Sailors raced to jettison the depth charges and launch the torpedoes before they cooked off. A witness on the destroyer *Claxton*, patrolling near the stricken ship, watched in astonishment as a nameless torpedoman charged directly into the flames to reach the torpedo tubes. "The power apparently was knocked out; so, with his whole body engulfed in flames, he manually cranked the tube mount out to starboard and, with a hammer, manually fired all five of the torpedoes."[33] That saved the ship from its own torpedoes, but the fires soon spread to the ammunition lockers and magazines, setting off a chain of devastating explosions. As the *Abner Read*'s crew began to abandon ship, the *Claxton* moved in to pick up survivors. At that moment another kamikaze descended in a steep trajectory. It missed the *Claxton* narrowly, but its bomb detonated as it struck the sea close aboard, killing five men and flooding the lower regions of the ship. The *Claxton* nonetheless managed to pick up 187 survivors of the *Abner Read*.

Fresh waves of kamikazes arrived over Leyte Gulf throughout the afternoon, often diving and missing by frightfully small margins. That evening a third destroyer, the *Anderson*, took another direct hit. Kinkaid was forced to send six warships back to Manus for drydock repairs.

Multiple threats seemed to be converging on the Leyte beachhead that day. A Fifth Air Force patrol plane reported a powerful Japanese naval task force in the Mindanao Sea, headed east. This might herald a second Battle of Leyte Gulf, only now the Allied naval presence in the area was much weaker. Halsey doubted the accuracy of the report, but he could not afford to ignore it. He detached a force of battleships and cruisers to guard Surigao Strait.[34] (By the next morning it was clear that the sighting report had been in error.) Meanwhile, relentless Japanese airstrikes fell upon the landing beaches. The attackers came in at low altitude, their approach concealed by the surrounding hills. They bombed and strafed the supply dumps, the beached LSTs, the airfield at Tacloban, and the various embryonic military headquarters established in tents and huts along the beach. P-38 Lightning fighter planes of the 308th Bombardment Wing of the Fifth Air Force had begun operating from Tacloban on October 27, but not yet in great numbers because of "difficult field conditions."[35] Many USAAF fighters were destroyed on the ground, including twenty-seven in a single raid. During the first week of November, conventional (non-kamikaze) air attacks on the Leyte beachhead destroyed 2,000 deadweight tons of gasoline and 1,700 tons of ammunition.[36]

Kinkaid was at his wit's end. He sent a dispatch to MacArthur that evening (November 1) warning that the situation in Leyte Gulf was critical. The enemy's air strength had rebounded alarmingly. Air attacks on the beachhead were virtually unchecked and threatened to throttle the army's supply lifeline, and the kamikaze attacks on the fleet offshore were an intensifying nightmare. He warned that the delay in establishing a strong USAAF presence at Tacloban and Dulag threw the entire campaign into jeopardy.[37]

At the same time, the Seventh Fleet chief renewed his entreaties for more carrier air support over Leyte Gulf. Halsey replied that he preferred to meet the air threat at its source, by hitting Japanese airfields on Luzon. On November 5 and 6, Task Force 38 airplanes pummeled the enemy's big air bases north of Manila. They also attacked shipping in Manila Bay, where their victims included the heavy cruiser *Nachi*, Admiral Shima's flagship that had survived the Battle of Surigao Strait. On the fifth, however, several small formations of kamikazes and their escorts tracked the returning American planes back to the task force, east of Samar. They broke away as they encountered the patrolling American fighters, then sought cloud cover and skulked around the fringes of the task force. At 1:39 p.m., seven or eight planes penetrated into the heart of Task Group 38.3. Most were shot down by short-range antiaircraft fire while diving on carriers at the hub of the circular formation. One missed the *Ticonderoga* by about 30 feet to starboard, exploding on the sea in a ball of fire. Another dove determinedly through a wall of antiaircraft bursts and crashed the *Lexington*'s signal bridge. Fires raced through the island superstructure, gutting the bridge and destroying much of its communications and radar technology. Flight operations were not interrupted, but casualties were heavy—42 killed and 126 wounded. Among the wounded was a large proportion of the carrier's gunnery department and signal force, many of whom suffered grievous burns. The *Lexington* was sent back to Ulithi for repairs, where she would be seventeen days at anchor. She buried her dead at sea on the sixth, during which time her colors (and those of Task Group 38.3) stood at half-mast.[38]

Among officers and crewmen of the American fleet, the kamikazes inspired dread, horror, loathing, and (not least) fascination. They seemed to confirm a prior suspicion that the Japanese were fundamentally different from other "races"—that they were weirdly fanatical and not quite human in their zeal for guaranteed death. This impression of exotic, dehumanizing "otherness" inspired fanciful rumors about the kamikazes—that they wore green and white religious robes, or black hoods, or were manacled into their cockpits. Some called them "green hornets." They inspired a new kind of terror. A destroyer sailor wrote his wife: "I have never in my life seen such a vicious scene as a wicked monster driving a plane straight at me at 200 miles an hour with six wing guns going full blast. It looked as if he was after me personally."[39] Bob Sherrod, a *Time* magazine correspondent, noted that American sailors in the Pacific were obsessed with kamikazes and spoke of almost nothing else. "Nothing could have been more awesome than to see a human being diving himself and his machine into the enemy," wrote Sherrod. "Nobody except the Japanese could have combined such medieval religious fervor with a machine as modern as the airplane."[40]

Others offered more cold-blooded evaluations. Raymond Spruance, still on leave in the United States, immediately grasped that suicide attacks were a "very sound and economical" use of Japan's diminishing air power, and that the Allied fleets would be dealing with them until the end of the war.[41] Jimmy Thach, a legendary fighter pilot now serving as Task Force 38 operations officer, regarded the kamikaze as a weapon "far ahead of its time." A pilot in a terminal suicide dive could make last-minute adjustments to hit the target, like a man-guided missile. The kamikaze was especially deadly against aircraft carriers, because he could aim right at a carrier's exposed bridge, and strike it; or he could aim for penetration into the hangar, where explosions and fires would feed upon fuel, explosives, and other combustible material. "It was actually a guided missile before we had any such things as guided missiles," said Thach. "It was guided by a human brain, human eyes and hands, and even better than a guided missile, it could look, digest the information, change course, avoid damage, and get to the target."[42]

Throughout Task Force 38, a cry arose for more fighters. The argument had been brewing for months; now it rose to a new pitch. With most of the Japanese navy sunk, the U.S. fleet had limited use for traditional carrier bombers. The brownshoes wanted a radical rebalancing of the standard air group complement in favor of Hellcats and F4U Corsairs. "In this kind of war," argued Gerry Bogan in a strongly worded dispatch addressed directly to Nimitz and King, the SB2C Helldiver "complicates plane handling, and occupies vital space which should go to invaluable VF [fighters]." The training pipeline was not an obstacle, he added, because current dive-bomber pilots, and those in training, could simply be transferred into fighters. Bogan said he knew that the planes were available, and that they could be shifted to the western Pacific immediately: "Our preparations have had in mind hitting the enemy at his source of power. The time is not in the future."[43]

This dispatch flouted established communications protocols, and its tone was borderline mutinous. As Bogan certainly knew, a task group commander had no business addressing himself directly to the CINCPAC, let alone the chief of naval operations. Nimitz reproved Bogan for submitting a message "improperly addressed direct to higher authority," and told him to resubmit his views in a letter to Halsey.[44] But the tense exchange underscored the sense of urgency in the fleet. For months the carrier bosses had been begging for more fighters; the sudden threat posed by kamikazes only exacerbated the shortfall.

Naval leaders were doing all they could to send more Hellcats and Hellcat pilots out to the Pacific, but they were also wary of disrupting future plans. If they accelerated the deployment of fresh F6F squadrons in late 1944, they risked a shortage in 1945, when the fleet was needed at full strength for the planned assaults on Iwo Jima, Okinawa, and Japan itself. The brownshoes countered that bomber pilots could be placed directly into fighter cockpits. They would not become fighter aces overnight—but under current conditions in the Pacific, even middling F6F pilots were more valuable than SB2C pilots. Bogan maintained that a two-hour checkout flight was sufficient, given the emergency.

Furthermore, the F6F Hellcat made a fine bomber in its own right, even if it had not been designed for that purpose. It had the horsepower to carry a 1,000-pound bomb, and it remained stable in a steep dive. Equipped with rockets, as it often was, it could hit ground targets with better accuracy than a dive-bomber. "This is one of those rare miracles where you get something for nothing," said Thach, "you drop your bomb, then you've got the world's best fighter."[45] Thach also wanted to bring in Marine Corps aviators and their F4U Corsairs, which had recently begun operating from escort carriers in support of amphibious operations. If they had learned to recover aboard a small jeep carrier, they should have no trouble landing on the much larger flight deck of an *Essex* carrier.

Nimitz and King gradually gave way to these persistent entreaties from the frontline aviators. They had already revised the standard carrier complement from eighteen torpedo bombers (VT), thirty-six dive-bombers (VB), and thirty-six fighters (VF) to eighteen VT and twenty-four VB, "with VF to capacity."[46] On November 29, King approved a new standard *Essex*-class complement of seventy-three Hellcats, fifteen Helldivers, and fifteen Avengers. Executing the change was another question, however. Carrier fighters were in high demand, but the supply was tight.[47] Nimitz told Halsey that he intended to retain a replenishment pool of F6Fs in Guam, but the CINCPAC was moved by Halsey's beseeching reply: "Urgently request [that] you reconsider. Time is short and things are already moving. . . . The suicide attack is a grave menace to our carriers and to your future operations if not countered. More fighters are needed to counter it, and they cannot be found except by reducing number over target or adding to complement."[48] The next day Nimitz reversed his decision, releasing the entire existing pool of replacements for immediate deployment to Task Force 38. But he remained gravely concerned that a shortfall in carrier fighters loomed in early 1945.

In the fleet, air staffs cooked up creative new tactics to deal with the kamikaze threat. Task Force 38's four task groups were consolidated into three, so that each could operate at full strength. More carriers at the center of a formation meant more defending fighters overhead; it also meant a bigger screening force and a greater concentration of antiaircraft fire. A defensive measure called the "Moose Trap" was devised to counter the Japanese tactic of sending kamikaze formations to track U.S. planes returning to their carriers. Two picket destroyers ("watchdogs") were stationed about 60 miles from the carrier task force, on the direct flight line to the strike objective. As the U.S. airstrikes returned, they were to head directly for these "watchdogs," and take a full 360-degree turn over them before returning to the carriers. Fighters ("tomcats") patrolled overhead, and examined the returning planes closely as they made their turns. They shot down any Japanese planes they discovered. This process was called "delousing."[49] American pilots were instructed to steer clear of the zone between the picket destroyers, which was designated "fair game." Any radar contacts appearing in that area were presumed enemy, and attacked right away. The picket destroyers also provided early radar detection of low-flying kamikazes, and a low-altitude CAP (called "jacks") was vectored out to intercept them. "We told the pilots that they were just likely to get shot if they didn't come back and delouse themselves over the picket," said Thach. "Just leave the area clear, and if any attack was coming straight out, like they usually did, we picked him up very much quicker. So that worked."[50]

To these defensive tactics they added an offensive, air-striking system called the "Big Blue Blanket." On strike days, the carriers sent big formations of F6F Hellcats to patrol over enemy airfields on Luzon, and rotated replacements into the area all day long, thereby maintaining a continuous daylight presence directly over the enemy's bases. Enemy planes taking off or attempting to land were shot down. Thach arranged a three-strike rotation, with launch and recovery times carefully staggered to keep the "blanket" in place, and "we rolled up quite an impressive total of aircraft destroyed, some in the air but mostly on the ground."[51]

At first, the new tactics seemed to pay off. On November 19, a round of airstrikes on Luzon encountered little opposition. As the final strike returned to the task force, about twenty "bogeys" were intercepted and shot down outside the strike pickets, about 70 miles from the task force. None got through the screen.

After withdrawing to the east to refuel, Task Groups 2 and 3 made another high-speed predawn approach to Luzon five days later, and launched a strike shortly after sunrise. A few minutes after noon, bogeys appeared on the Task Group 2 radar screens. A layer of broken cumulus clouds at about 6,000 feet gave cover to the attackers. At 12:52 p.m., a swarm of Zeros dropped through the cloud ceiling and dove on the *Intrepid*, the *Cabot*, and the *Hancock*. One crashed the ill-fated *Intrepid*'s port gun tubs, killing ten and wounding six of her crew. The damage was severe but containable, and the *Intrepid* surged on with undiminished speed. Six minutes later, however, another Zero bore in from astern, machine guns blazing, and crashed the port side of her flight deck. Wreckage skidded all the way to the bow, but the bomb smashed through the flight deck and exploded in the hangar. Admiral Halsey, who witnessed the attack from the nearby *New Jersey*, wrote that the *Intrepid* "went through hell. An instant after she was hit, she was wrapped in flames; blazing gasoline cascaded down her sides; explosions rocked her; oily black smoke, rising thousands of feet, hid everything but her bow."[52] The *Intrepid* lost sixty-nine men killed and seventeen planes destroyed. Once again, this proud but unlucky ship was obliged to pull out of the war zone and head back to Pearl Harbor for repairs.

While this vicious attack was unfolding, Group 3 radar screens detected another wave of bogeys approaching from the southeast at range 55 miles.

Many were intercepted by the CAP, but others escaped into cloud cover. The intruders orbited the task group for about twenty minutes, playing cat and mouse with the American fighters, then commenced fast gliding approaches. A 40mm antiaircraft gun on Admiral Sherman's flagship *Essex* opened fire on one attacker, a D4Y *Suisei* ("Judy") bomber, hitting its port wing root. The war diary noted, "While this did not stop him, it at least turned him to the left causing him to miss the after-flight deck which was crowded with planes gassed and armed. He crashed about 15 feet inboard on the port side of flight deck amidships just forward of #2 elevator, bursting into intense flames with great heat and heavy smoke, which appeared worse than it actually was."[53] The explosion tore a hole in the flight deck approximately 16 feet across, and started fires which gutted (among other things) the admiral's cabin. But damage and casualties were slight in comparison to those suffered by the *Intrepid*, and the *Essex* soldiered on without pause, even taking aboard eleven *Intrepid* fighters that were unable to recover on their own carrier.

The next day Halsey shot off a dispatch to Nimitz, warning that the air situation in the Philippines was perilous. The Japanese had managed to disperse their airplanes widely across many small dirt fields on Luzon, and had camouflaged them effectively under foliage and netting. Often, individual planes were hidden miles away from the airstrips, and pushed or hauled to the runways under cover of darkness. A steady flow of replacement aircraft and pilots were flying in from Japan and Formosa. The Third Fleet was destroying hundreds of planes, but it was also suffering. Many carriers had been badly damaged, including the *Cabot*, *Intrepid*, *Lexington*, *Franklin*, and *Belleau Wood*. Many others had taken hits that did not inflict serious damage, but the threat was omnipresent. The delay in establishing land-based airfields on Leyte, combined with the introduction of deadly suicide tactics, must inevitably lead to delays in the planned invasions of Mindoro and Luzon.

Meanwhile, the Seventh Fleet was catching it in Leyte Gulf. At midday on November 27, a battleship-cruiser-destroyer task force under Rear Admiral T. D. Ruddock was attempting to refuel from a 14,000-ton tanker. At 10:50 a.m., radar scopes detected about thirty unidentified planes approaching from the north and east. They were stacked at various altitudes, some well above a loosely fragmented cloud ceiling and some skimming the wavetops. A handful of army P-38 fighters patrolled overhead, but not enough to intercept all of the intruders. The *West Virginia*, alongside the tanker, disconnected her fueling hoses in a hurry and got underway. The deep repeating thuds of the 5-inch antiaircraft guns started up, and brown-black flak bursts mottled the sky.

At 11:25, three kamikazes plunged on the battleships at the hub of the circular formation. One narrowly missed the *West Virginia*. Two dove simultaneously on the *Colorado* and one scored, striking the battleship's portside secondary 5-inch battery. Nineteen of her crew were killed and seventy-two wounded, but the damage was negligible. Another targeted the cruiser *St. Louis* and buried itself in her hangar astern. The gasoline in the plane's tanks started a fire, and the ship trailed a plume of black smoke that appeared to attract more kamikazes as the action developed. Four more suicide planes were shot down while lunging at the *St. Louis*; one crashed her port side just above the waterline.

According to the diarist James J. Fahey, seaman first-class aboard the cruiser *Montpelier*, the enemy planes seemed to attack from every direction at once. At 11:25 a.m., the height of the action, "Jap planes were falling all around us, the air was full of Jap machine gun bullets. Jap planes and bombs were hitting all around us. Some of our ships were being hit by suicide planes, bombs and machine-gun fire."[54] For more than an hour, the 40mm and 20mm antiaircraft guns blazed away with barely a pause. The sea around the task force was roiled by flak and spent casings, as if a heavy rainstorm was pouring down. Shrapnel and fragments of destroyed Japanese planes fell along the length of the *Montpelier*, injuring many of Fahey's shipmates. Three kamikazes were blown away at point-blank range. Wreckage from one attacker rebounded off the sea and crashed into a 40mm mount on the ship's port side. Several crewmen were injured by flying debris or burning gasoline. Fahey noticed that one of the gun captains was shouting into his headphones, not realizing that shrapnel had cut through the wires. "It looked like it was raining plane parts. They were falling all over the ship. Quite a few of the men were hit by big pieces of Jap planes."[55]

Peace returned with jarring suddenness. At 2:10 p.m., the last of the enemy planes was gone or shot down. The sea around the task force was littered with aircraft wreckage and floating gasoline fires. None of *Montpelier*'s crew had been killed, but eleven were wounded, some seriously. Wreckage and the bloody remains of Japanese pilots were scattered across the ship. Lifeboats were smashed, cables down, and steel stanchions bent over, and empty shell casings were still hot to the touch. The deck near Fahey's battle station was strewn with "blood, guts, brains, tongues, scalps, hearts, arms etc. from the Jap pilots." As hoses were brought out to wash the mess off the deck, souvenir hunters stooped to sift through the grisly mélange. A marine cut a ring off the finger of a dead enemy airman. A sailor picked up a scalp. "One of the men on our mount got a Jap rib and cleaned it up," Fahey wrote. "He said his sister wants part of a Jap body. One fellow from Texas had a knee bone and he was going to preserve it in alcohol from the sick bay."[56]

The following day brought a respite, but the twenty-ninth was another long day of intermittent air attacks. The claxon kept ringing, calling men back to their battle stations. Just after sunset, the radar screens grew busy with many "blips." A kamikaze darted through the cloud ceiling and dove on the *Denver*, but was deterred by a storm of antiaircraft fire. It banked sharply away and climbed back into the clouds. Several other planes were seen weaving in and out of cloud cover, dodging flak bursts and looking for a target. One plane performed a number of acrobatic maneuvers, almost as if taunting the Americans. Then it pushed over into a throttle-stop dive, aiming for the battleship *Maryland*. There was no time for the ship to change course, and the gunners could not take the rocketing plane down. It hit the *Maryland*'s forecastle, dead center between the forward 16-inch turrets. "You will never see a stunt like that again," wrote Fahey, who watched the attack from the nearby *Montpelier*. "Something like that happens only once in a lifetime. One thing about these suicide pilots there is never a dull moment, they go all out to kill themselves."[57]

The diving kamikaze was probably traveling at more than 500 miles per hour, a velocity that gave it fearsome penetrating force. Its bomb pierced two of the *Maryland*'s heavily armored decks and laid waste to much of the third deck between frames 26 and 52. Smoke filled the stricken area, forcing damage-control parties to retreat. Thirty-one men were killed; thirty more were wounded. The sickbay was gutted by the blast, so emergency medical stations were set up in the junior and warrant officers' wardrooms. The dead were identified and placed in bunks in a screened-off compartment, to be buried at sea later. Crew morale, according to the *Maryland* cruise book, fell to a low ebb: "The terrific heat, the persistent air raids, the tense living and the recent disaster put many men almost at their breaking point." The crew was "overjoyed" to learn that the *Maryland* would return to Pearl Harbor for extensive repairs.[58]

TAKING STOCK OF THE AIR, NAVAL, and ground campaign at the end of November, Admiral Kinkaid concluded that the planned invasion dates for Mindoro (December 5) and Luzon (December 20) were out of the question. In a long memorandum to MacArthur on November 30, Kinkaid urged that the invasions of Mindoro and Luzon be "cancelled." (He did not say "postponed.") To attempt landings on these islands before General Kenney's Fifth Air Force had taken control of the air, he wrote, "could result in a disaster seldom equaled in the annals of warfare."[59]

Kinkaid tapped his staff liaison to the SWPA headquarters, Lieutenant Commander Arthur McCollum, to act as his emissary to MacArthur. He told McCollum to deliver the message that the campaign must be delayed indefinitely, given the current state of U.S. naval and airpower in the Philippines. McCollum was thought to have a good personal rapport with MacArthur. The two had joked about their common nickname: "Mac."

Perhaps thinking of the fate of the messenger who had brought bad news to an ancient Armenian king, McCollum replied: "Well, I think that's a hell of a thing, Admiral, for you to do to me. I mean, to send me in there."[60]

Kinkaid told him, "You're the only guy that I know who can go up there and maybe talk to him face-to-face without getting into a big hassle over something, army-navy relations, or what have you. God damn it, get on in there and go see the general and then tell me."

McCollum thought the assignment was "a dirty trick to play on a junior guy," but he went ashore and made his way to SWPA headquarters, near Tacloban.

In the weeks since the invasion of Leyte, fierce monsoonal storms had battered the island's eastern coastal plain. Twenty-five inches of rain had fallen since A-Day. Seventy-mile-per-hour winds had uprooted trees and swept tents and shacks up into the ether. Engineers had excavated deep drainage ditches in an attempt to control the relentless flooding, and laid wooden boards across muddy footpaths. Plans had called for temporary field hospitals providing 9,000 beds, but due to the deplorable state of access roads, construction lagged. (The deficit was met by Seventh Fleet hospital ships anchored off Tacloban.) DDT was sprayed throughout the area, but mosquitos bred abundantly in the soggy, fecund soil—and "in the evening," recorded General Eichelberger, "we went to bed amid a cloud of insects."[61]

Japanese air attacks often targeted the complex of relatively well-appointed buildings that served as SWPA and Sixth Army headquarters. On November 3, MacArthur had been in his headquarters office when a Japanese plane flew low overhead and strafed the building. A .50-caliber round blasted a hole in the wall behind his head. As others rushed into the room, MacArthur was grinning. Gesturing to the hole, he exclaimed: "Not yet!" The incident was described in an SWPA press release, and made headline news in the United States the following day.[62]

When McCollum arrived and delivered Admiral Kinkaid's message, MacArthur reacted as expected. "Let me tell you something, Mac," he said. "I came in here on the assurances of your damned navy admirals that they would support me all the way, and now you come in and tell me this." He charged that the admirals were "welshing" on their commitments.

"General," McCollum replied, "that's not the way it is. I mean, Heavens, General Kenney has welshed on you. He was going to have all those damned airfields built around here."

To which MacArthur replied, "Yes, I reckon that's true."

The general summoned Dick Sutherland into the office. "McCollum has come here to tell me that the god-damned admirals aren't going to carry me any farther!" The SWPA chief of staff, McCollum observed, was always ready to "light a fire" under McArthur's wrath. The conversation continued, with MacArthur booming his disapproval. McCollum held his ground, recounting the hard realities. The ground campaign on Leyte had taken longer than expected, the Japanese were still landing reinforcements on the west coast, and the kamikazes were raising havoc with the Sixth Army's seaborne supply line. Admiral Halsey shared many of these concerns and had said so.

At last MacArthur gave way. "I don't give a damn what you tell [Kinkaid], but go on up there and tell him it's okay," he said. "I don't like it, but I understand, and there we are."[63]

Providing logistical support to U.S. ground forces grew more difficult as they advanced into the onerous terrain of Leyte's "cordillera," or mountainous interior. Roads running inland were often washed out, or petered out into the jungle. Fighting bogged down in high country the Americans called Breakneck Ridge. The entrenched positions on the ridge were manned by elite, hand-picked units of the First Japanese Infantry Division, recently shipped in from the Kwantung Army in Manchuria. For days the lines did not move at all. Units trudged up steep paths, sometimes losing their boots in the muck. In flooded rice fields, the water came up to their waists. Other American forces seized Limon, at the head of the valley lead-ing down to Ormoc Bay, on November 5. However, further progress in that direction was stymied by the deplorable supply situation.

Anxious to break the bloody stalemate, and conscious that Japanese reinforcements were arriving on the west coast by sea, General Krueger convinced MacArthur to release the infantry reserves. With more than 120,000 troops on the island, he intended to overwhelm the Japanese with a huge pincer attack in the Ormoc Valley. Japanese positions on Breakneck Ridge were finally broken down by a double-envelopment, as one battalion bushwhacked to the east around Hill 1525, and another was sealifted up the coast in eighteen LVTs, to land near the southward turn of Highway 2. The maneuver left local Japanese forces in untenable positions in remote jungle terrain, cut off from their sources of resupply on the west coast.

Belatedly, the Americans grasped that the enemy was determined to pour reinforcements into the island at any cost. MacArthur and his com-manders had started with the assumption that Leyte was an interim fight, a stepping stone to Luzon. At first, they had guessed that columns of trans-ports putting into the port of Ormoc were there to evacuate Japanese troops, rather than to deliver fresh ones. But the Japanese headquarters in Manila was committed to win the battle for Leyte, and continued to push reinforce-ments into the island through the first week of December 1944. "By the end of November," wrote MacArthur, "despite large convoy losses and severe combat attrition, there were many thousand more enemy troops on Leyte than there had been at the end of October."[64]

Japanese supply runs into Ormoc touched off a series of ferocious air and sea battles in the Camotes Sea. In many respects, it was a reenactment of the Guadalcanal campaign, when the combatants had fought to isolate an island and to dominate the sea lanes around it. Several long convoys of troop transports and cargo ships escorted by destroyers left Manila Bay between November 3 and 9. They traveled 600 miles through the inland seas of the Philippines, and debarked more than two full divisions at Ormoc Bay. American carrier warplanes attacked those convoys, sinking more than a dozen Japanese ships. Fifth Air Force B-24s and B-25s, flying from airfields on Morotai, hit and sank two large transports on November 8. Still the convoys continued. Since Manila Bay was under constant air attack, the Japanese judged that there was no point in trying to save the ships for

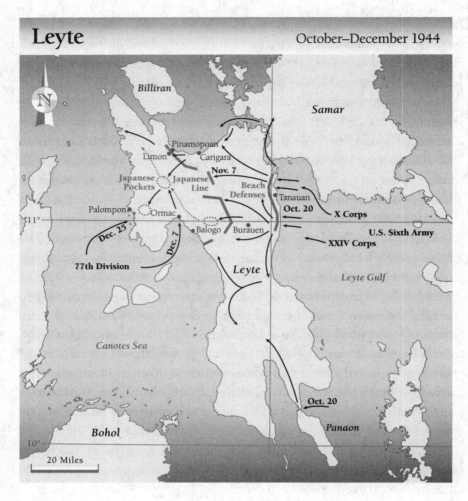

Leyte   October–December 1944

some future purpose. If they were not sent out immediately, they were likely to be destroyed at anchor.

On November 11, a major reinforcement landed at Ormoc Bay and debarked most of the Twenty-Sixth Japanese Infantry Division. But while the division's heavy weapons and supplies were still unloading, a wave of American carrier planes descended on the scene, sinking four large transports and four destroyers. The Task Group 38.3 war diary noted, "The Nips spent a hapless day as TF 38 methodically set about eliminating the convoy."[65] According to Japanese sources, the division got ashore with minimal casualties, but carrying only their rifles and about ten units of ammunition.[66]

In the first week of December, Seventh Fleet destroyers ventured through Surigao Strait and up through the Canigao Channel to sweep the west coast of Leyte. These naval attacks took the Japanese by surprise. They had mined Canigao Channel heavily and did not believe the mines could be swept while aerial patrols were overhead. On December 2, a three-destroyer task force led by Commander John C. Zahm left Leyte Gulf at dusk, charged around southern Leyte, and arrived at Ormoc Bay shortly before midnight. A Japanese convoy was unloading troops and supplies onto the piers. With complete surprise, Zahm's three "tin cans" poured out 5-inch fire and launched torpedoes at the Japanese ships and dock areas. An American destroyerman recalled, "Shortly into the battle, the night began to light up like a huge fireworks display from the red and green tracers going in all directions, from ships and shore installations burning and exploding in multi-colored fireballs, and from winks of fire coming from the many guns firing at us. It was just hell!"[67] The destroyers demolished two enemy ships and laid waste to valuable war matériel in supply dumps ashore. At 12:22 a.m., the destroyer *Cooper* was hit by a torpedo that tore the ship in two; she sank immediately with the loss of 191 lives. Under heavy enemy fire, the other two destroyers cleared the area without stopping to pick up survivors. Three PBY "Black Cat" float planes landed in Ormoc Bay and picked up dozens of survivors of the *Cooper*. One managed to take off with no fewer than fifty-six survivors aboard, in addition to the nine crew members—a PBY record never surpassed or equaled.[68]

Having finally cleared the Breakneck–Kilay Ridge area, X Corps launched an unstoppable drive down the Ormoc corridor. The 32nd Division joined forces with the 1st Cavalry Division to overrun well-prepared Japanese positions. Remaining elements of the elite First Japanese Division fought desperately and well, but they could not resist the sustained energy and violence of the American ground attack. Infantry and tank attacks were preceded by long, heavy, and accurate mortar and artillery barrages. The Americans attacked Japanese pillboxes and bunkers with tanks, flame-throwers, and hand grenades. A westward advance across the rugged middle of the island was spearheaded by the 11th Airborne Division, assisted by elements of the 32nd Infantry. At the same time, the southern pincer pressed north from Baybay. On that front, the Japanese were surprised. Scouts had assured General Suzuki that the one road leading into that area from Dulag, on the east coast, was impassable. Nor had the Japanese anticipated the ease with which enemy forces in that area were resupplied by sea.

At the Japanese headquarters near Ormoc, basic command and control was disintegrating. Contact with frontline units was intermittent, and then lost. Orders continually went out urging that Japanese forces attack, when they were barely able to maintain their defensive positions. On December 6, a staff officer of the First Division reported that it had "reached the stage of collapse."[69] The headquarters staff was vexed to hear Japanese radio broadcasts predicting an imminent triumph on Leyte. Press offices in Manila and Tokyo rewrote the frontline dispatches to conform to the sanctioned version of events. "The enemy is now on the defense," one such bulletin declared. "Our reinforcements coordinating with the main strength advanced toward the western part of Carigara. They opened hostilities with the American 24th Division. On 7th November a portion of our units using enveloping tactics advanced rapidly over rough terrain, and cut off the avenues of retreat and dealt a severe blow. Under our pressure the enemy vainly struggled to escape."[70]

At dusk on December 6, American troops and engineers stationed near San Pablo airstrip, near the main beachhead at Leyte Gulf, were surprised to see a formation of transport airplanes pass overhead at medium altitude. White parachutes began to blossom in the sky behind them. The alarm was raised, and antiaircraft guns, artillery, machine-gun, and small arms fire was directed upward. It was an audacious paratrooper attack, involving about four hundred "Takachiho" paratroopers of an Airborne Raiding Brigade based on Luzon. The Japanese troopers returned rifle fire from aloft, and threw hand grenades as they approached the ground. Several Seabee engineers were in the shower as the enemy paratroopers hit the ground, and "bolted, buck naked, for their guns."[71] Fierce firefights continued late into the night. Squads of attackers set demolition charges in parked airplanes and fuel storage dumps, and fires blazed through the area. Fighting continued for three days. The 11th Airborne Division, supported by Seabees and miscellaneous other units, took back the airfield on December 9. The attack had accomplished some material damage, but otherwise failed.

The fight for Leyte had entered its endgame. But victory could not be secured until the island was completely cut off from its sources of reinforcement and resupply. That meant shutting the enemy's "back door" to Leyte, the port of Ormoc. On December 7, the 77th Division under Major General Andrew D. Bruce stormed ashore at Desposito, four miles south of Ormoc. The surprise amphibious assault included the same basic features of previous landings, such as those on Saipan, Guam, or Leyte's east coast, but on a miniature scale. The landing caught the enemy by surprise, and two regiments of Bruce's division got safely ashore and dug into entrenched positions before the Japanese could muster a counterattack.

Japanese air forces arrived too late to interfere with the landing, but they dealt a severe beating to Admiral Arthur D. Struble's amphibious convoy. Kamikazes hit the destroyer *Mahan* and the high-speed transport *Ward*. On both ships, the damage was so grave that the ships were abandoned and scuttled. During the long withdrawal to Leyte Gulf by way of Canigao Channel and Surigao Strait, the force suffered under a relentless series of air attacks. The transport *Liddle* took a bad hit on her bridge, which killed most of her senior officers, but she managed to continue under her own power.[72]

The newly landed troops attacked north, taking heavy casualties, and fought their way into Ormoc City on December 10. The 7th Division pushed north from Baybay, overcoming scattered but fanatical resistance. With American forces in possession of Ormoc's bay and port facilities, the last big Japanese convoy from Manila was forced to divert to San Isidro, thirty miles up the coast. American airstrikes sank five large transports. About two Japanese battalions managed to get ashore, but they were quickly surrounded and overpowered by U.S. forces already in the area.

On December 15, MacArthur declared that organized resistance on Leyte had come to an end. Small unit fighting would continue in the rugged highlands, but the battle for the Philippines was already moving west: the amphibious landing on Mindoro occurred that same day. "The enemy fought valiantly," the SWPA chief wrote, "but found it impossible to cope with our three-way offensive. His forces were chopped into isolated segments, either struggling in small pockets or being scattered into the mountains."[73]

HALSEY AND HIS CARRIER ADMIRALS had been asking for at least ten consecutive days at Ulithi, for an extended period of "three Rs"—rest, repairs, and replenishment. On December 1, three Task Force 38 task groups dropped their anchors into the sandy holding ground at the bottom of Ulithi lagoon.[74] The service and logistics fleet had completed its move from Eniwetok, so the roadstead was more congested than ever before. Boats and barges plied the waters to and fro between the fleet and the main islets of Asor, Falelop,

Potangeras, Sorlen, and Mog Mog. Occasionally, through binoculars, one might catch a glimpse of native fishermen, clad only in loincloths, gliding over the sapphire lagoon in their hand-carved outriggers.

That week an aerial photographer snapped a photo of "Murderers' Row"—a long row of Task Force 38 aircraft carriers riding at anchor. All were painted in blue-gray camouflage "dazzle" patterns. They were surrounded by flotillas of cruisers, battleships, and destroyers—and beyond, to the north, the innumerable service ships of the logistics fleet. It was an unprecedented concentration of naval power, more ships than had ever squeezed into Pearl Harbor at one time.

Measures were taken to conceal the fleet's presence. For the duration of the war, the word "Ulithi" was never permitted to appear in the press. The fleet observed strict radio silence. All outgoing dispatches were flown to Guam, 400 miles northeast, for transmission from that island. The Japanese were not fooled, however: they knew that the U.S. fleet had adopted Ulithi as its new homeport. On November 20, several *kaitens*—one-man suicide submarines—were released by a large "mother" submarine north of the atoll. At least two of the stealthy little boats penetrated into the lagoon by secondary entrance channels. At dawn on November 20, one struck the tanker *Mississinewa*. Laden with tens of thousands of tons of avgas, diesel, and bunker oil, the ship erupted in flames. Tugs put hoses onto the burning wreck, but nothing could be done. At 10:00 a.m. she turned over and sank, taking sixty of her crew to the bottom.[75] Destroyers scattered depth charges through the area, and at least one other *kaiten* was sunk.

From that day to the end of the war, the Americans never felt entirely secure at Ulithi. Admiral Sherman recalled, "We felt that we were sitting on a powder keg which might go off at any time. Far from enjoying a rest, we felt we might be safer in the open sea."[76]

Even so, fleet recreation at Ulithi was serious business. A new movie was screened on every ship in the fleet, every night. A destroyer designated as the "movie exchange ship" kept a library of hundreds of films and thousands of reels, which rotated around the fleet according to a published calendar.[77] USO musical revues travelled from ship to ship, as the entertainers often performed four or five identical shows per day. Admiral Halsey especially liked Eddie Peabody, "King of the Banjo," and his "All Navy Band." On Mog Mog, a picturesque island at the north end of the lagoon, Seabees had been hard at work building a fleet recreation area. Footpaths led inland from the piers to a network of picnic grounds, tennis courts, volley-ball courts, boxing rings, baseball diamonds, bandstands, barbeque pits, and beer gardens. For thousands of war-weary and sea-weary men, it was the first opportunity in months to feel solid ground under their feet. Sailors were rationed beer at two cans per man, but some finagled harder stuff by back-handed means. Officers arranged to have cases of liquor put ashore at the officers' club on Mog Mog, located in a native-built canoe shed in a quiet corner of the island. One recalled, "it was just a hog-killing."[78] In that first week of December 1944, noted the Third Fleet war diary, Mog Mog "was crowded daily with from 10,000 to 15,000 enlisted men and 500 to 1,000 officers."[79] In the evenings, as the western sky blazed with majestic tropi-cal colors, boats loaded to capacity pulled away from the piers and motored slowly back to the fleet anchorage.

On December 11, the fleet staged another grand sortie through Mugai Channel, bound for another round of airstrikes on Luzon to support MacArthur's invasion of Mindoro. Beginning on the fourteenth, Halsey recalled, "We struck with all our strength, for three days running."[80] The "Big Blue Blanket" was thrown over Luzon once again, as large formations of F6Fs kept watch over ninety known or suspected enemy airfields. Return-ing pilots claimed sixty-two kills in the air and another 208 enemy planes destroyed on the ground. The "Moose Trap" and other defensive measures seemed to pay off, as no enemy planes got within 20 miles of the task force. On December 14, the day's first outgoing strike ran into a flight of eleven Japanese aircraft on a reciprocal heading, "and splashed 100 percent near the east coast of Luzon."[81]

The Mindoro landing, delayed ten days at Kinkaid's insistence, involved a deep foray into waters easily reached from Luzon's airfields. Japanese ground forces on Mindoro were not expected to give the invaders much trouble, but the approach would be dangerous, and the amphibious trans-port fleet would have to pull out quickly. The invasion convoy was com-manded by Rear Admiral Struble, whose force had been roughed up just a week earlier in the Ormoc Bay operation. At 2:57 p.m. on December 13, in the channel between Negros and Mindanao, Struble's flagship *Nashville* took a bad kamikaze hit. The admiral was unharmed, but the *Nashville* was forced to turn back. Struble transferred his flag to the destroyer *Dashiell*. On December 15, U.S. ground forces landed on Mindoro and quickly overran the small Japanese garrison.

Capture of Mindoro's two small airfields changed the complexion of the entire Philippines campaign, as it put nearby Manila and its environs into the crosshairs for General Kenney's USAAF fighters and bombers. The island's capture also left Leyte in the position of a strategic backwater. On the eighteenth, General Yamashita radioed General Suzuki to advise that Leyte would receive no further reinforcements or material support. As Yamashita had feared, the fight for that island had consumed a major portion of Japanese strength in the Philippines, darkening the outlook for the pending fight for Luzon. Based on a methodical attempt to count bodies during the last week of December, the Americans estimated that 60,809 Japanese troops had perished on the island. Just 434 had been taken prisoner.[82] U.S. Sixth Army losses were just 2,888 killed and 9,858 wounded.

Task Force 38 withdrew to the east for a fueling rendezvous, intending to return for a second round of airstrikes on Luzon. On the morning of December 17, about 500 miles east of Luzon, the fleet fell in with its trusty at-sea logistics support group and commenced its familiar refueling ritual. As usual, the destroyers were especially low, and many sidled up to the battleships and carriers to drink from their cavernous tanks. But a heavy swell was on the make, with winds gusting from twenty to thirty knots, and the smaller vessels were pitching and corkscrewing hazardously. Fuel served as ballast for the lightly built "tin cans," so a destroyer whose tanks were mostly empty was intrinsically unstable. The problem was exacerbated as new radar and communications devices were mounted on the masts and topsides of the little ships, raising their center of gravity. While fueling from larger ships, an officer recalled, deballasted destroyers "bucked and twisted like mustangs."[83] When they collided with their larger neighbors, as they often did in heavy seas, the impacts damaged their superstructures and tore equipment from their rigging. Fueling hoses broke, pouring cataracts of brown bunker oil over their decks and into the sea between them. On that tempestuous morning of the seventeenth, Admiral Halsey watched from his flag bridge as the destroyer *Spence* attempted to fuel from his flagship *New Jersey*. After it had taken on only 6,000 gallons of fuel, the hoses broke and the *Spence* was forced to sheer away.[84]

The barometer was falling, winds were backing into the north, and seas were building. Wisps of high cirrus sped across the sky, and the sun wore a menacing halo. The fleet meteorologists had noted a "tropical disturbance" forming about 500 miles to the southeast, headed north at about 12 to

15 knots—but they were not ready to call it a tropical storm, much less a typhoon. At any rate, they were fairly confident that it would collide with a cold front and recurve away to the northeast. Many veteran seamen in the fleet were not so sure. This was typhoon season, and the fleet was near the heart of the region known as "typhoon alley." The navy was not yet doing any systematic long-range weather reconnaissance flights, and was thus obliged to rely on intermittent reports from aircraft, ships, and submarines. Judging whether a "disturbance" would develop into a full-scale tropical witches' brew was as much an art as a science. So was predicting the path that a storm would travel. On bridges across the fleet, officers consulted their charts and instruments. Some thumbed through old copies of Bowditch's *The American Practical Navigator*. As the afternoon wore on, the wind and seas continued to build. Admiral Radford, sailing as an observer on the *Ticonderoga*, judged that "we were in for it." The carrier's skipper agreed and issued orders to secure for a typhoon.[85] Many others throughout the fleet, including all of the task group commanders and many senior captains, reached similar conclusions.

The safest move would have been to turn south. But that would have taken Task Force 38 out of position to launch the planned airstrike on Luzon two days later, and Halsey was determined to keep his promises to MacArthur. Given that his meteorologists were forecasting that the storm (if such it was) would turn right rather than left, the admiral kept the fleet on a northwesterly heading. "Halsey felt that we should live up to that commitment to the last minute, rather than retreat before a situation which really had not fully developed as a threatening typhoon situation," Mick Carney later explained. "So we did." The chief of staff emphasized that the boss was calling the shots: "This was his decision and nobody was disposed to argue with it."[86]

The sea was lumpy and disgruntled. The sky was painted in freakish colors, a dull coppery glow beneath a purple scudding murk. Gale-force gusts blew streaks of spindrift off the wave crests. At 2:37 p.m., noted the fleet diary, "the seas were getting heavy and the winds were now 40 knots from 020." Halsey suspended fueling and fixed a new fueling rendezvous for 6:00 a.m. the next morning, 200 miles to the northwest. Many ships found it difficult to keep station, and Halsey approved Admiral McCain's request to slow the task force from 17 to 15 knots and cease zigzagging.[87] As the hours wore on, conditions worsened and the weather predictors revised their forecasts. It was a cyclonic storm building to typhoon strength, and its track had swerved to the west. A report from an aircraft tender placed the storm only 200 miles away. According to Carney, the storm seemed to be chasing after them, as if "imbued with some intelligence of its own."[88] Halsey ordered a course change to the south and changed the location of the next morning's rendezvous. Even now, he had hopes of refueling at dawn and getting the carriers into position to launch the promised airstrikes on the nineteenth.

At dawn the wind was gusting to fifty knots, and barometric pressure was sinking like a stone. Sailors on deck reached for handholds and bent their heads against the driving sheets of spray. All around the horizon, the ocean was gray, torn, and tormented. From high in the superstructures of the bigger ships, one could see ranks of tall, forbidding combers marching down from the north. Unaccountably, given those raging conditions, Halsey signaled the fleet to come north to a heading of 60 degrees, with speed ten knots, and commence fueling operations. But it was soon clear to all that no fueling was possible, and the fleet turned south again.

An hour after sunrise, the sun could not be seen and the sky had barely lightened. Visibility deteriorated, the seas grew mountainous, and the winds gusted higher—to 60 knots, then to 70 knots. The PPI radarscope in the *Wasp*, on the northern flank of Task Force 38, depicted a tightly constructed circular storm-eye passing only about 35 miles to the north.[89] Halsey and his team could no longer deny it; the fleet was caught in the "dangerous semicircle" of a proper typhoon, and could do nothing but run before the wind and seas and hope for the best. At 8:18 a.m., Halsey radioed MacArthur and Nimitz to report that he was cancelling the next day's raids on Luzon.[90]

The storm mounted in strength and malevolence. The distance between the crests lengthened as the waves grew. At the top of each sea the wind howled in their ears and the rain and spray blasted them like buckshot. In the troughs between the crests, the noise and wind fell to almost bearable dimensions, but white water broke across their decks and cascaded through the scuppers. Orders were given and then countermanded by both Halsey and McCain, but it was soon clear to every skipper that he was alone, and must do whatever he could to save his ship. At 11:49 a.m., Halsey instructed McCain by short-range radio to "take the most comfortable course with the wind on the port quarter."[91] But the smaller vessels, especially the destroyers, could do nothing but steer for their lives, regardless of heading.

Visibility continued to fall until most ships could not see their neighbors at all, and the danger of collision was added to the violence of the storm. Sometimes another ship loomed suddenly out of the maelstrom, then turned away and vanished. The gusts grew more violent, eventually surpassing 100 knots. Barometer readings fell below 27 inches. Halsey informed Nimitz that the fleet was fighting through "heavy confused seas, ragged ceiling, heavy rains, wind west northwest, 70 knots . . . typhoon of increasing intensity."[92]

The destroyers, still deballasted by low fuel, suffered the worst. No combination of engine and steering would keep them on course, so they wallowed helplessly in the troughs between the great seas. The storm reached its zenith at about noon, when the gusts touched 120 knots and the waves measured about 80 feet from trough to crest.[93] According to the captain of the *Dewey*, the rain and scud was so thick that men on the bridge could not see the bow. If a man was exposed to it, "it felt like a barrage of thousands of needles against the face and hands," and it "removed the paint from metal surfaces in many places like a sandblaster." Again and again the little ship was knocked down almost onto her beam ends. In the pilot house, men seized handholds and hung with their feet swinging free of the deck until she righted herself. One astonished sailor found himself standing on a stanchion that was normally vertical. Holding up his palms, he shouted to his shipmates, "Look! No hands!" On an especially deep roll, with the inclinometer against the stop (73 degrees was the maximum on the gauge), the starboard wing of the *Dewey*'s bridge dipped under the sea and scooped up solid green water. "None of us had ever heard of a ship righting herself from such a roll," noted the skipper, "but this one did!"[94]

Big ships were better able to withstand the storm, but even the *Iowa*-class battleships labored precariously in those gigantic seas. Mick Carney had feared for the survival of the *New Jersey*. "It's difficult to describe the sickening lurch of that ship when she went way over, very close to her critical stability angle, and brought up at that particular point and then would hang there until she went back."[95] Even from his high perch on the *New Jersey*'s flag bridge, Carney had to tilt his head up to see the crests of oncoming combers. On the *Ticonderoga*, a 27,000-ton *Essex*-class carrier, Arthur Radford watched the storm in awe from the flag bridge veranda. As the *Ticonderoga* rolled to starboard, and the slope of a great wave rose up toward the ship, he had the odd feeling that if he stretched out his arm, he might actually touch the sea. The *Hancock*, one of *Ticonderoga*'s sisters, shipped tons of green water over her flight deck, nearly 60 feet above her waterline.[96]

Being narrower on the beam than their larger counterparts, the *Independence*-class light carriers (CVLs) rolled even more radically in the typhoon. On the *Monterey*, four F6F Hellcats parked on the flight deck broke loose and skidded into the sea, carrying away port-side safety nets and the landing signal officer's platform. With the wind increasing, the captain ordered all hands to clear the flight deck and seek shelter. But the real emergency was below, on the hangar deck, where airplanes were heaving and straining alarmingly at their mooring lines. The airedales raced to tighten and redouble the lashings, but as the rolls surpassed 34 degrees, they found it hard to keep their footing. Shortly after 9:00 a.m., a Hellcat fighter tore free and was suddenly a 5-ton combustible battering ram. It thrashed back and forth, port to starboard to port to starboard, crushing ventilation ducts, electrical lines, water pumps, and other airplanes. Though it had been drained of gasoline, the residual fuel in its tanks and engine lines burst into flames, and soon an explosion ripped through the hangar. Several more planes tore loose and multiplied the mayhem. Smoke entered the ruptured ventilation ducts and poured down into enclosed spaces on the lower decks, forcing crewmen out of the engine rooms until they could return with portable breathing gear.

Scenes on the *Monterey*'s sisters *Cowpens* and *San Jacinto* were much the same. Planes tore loose of their cables, ripped steel eye bolts out of the deck, crashed into neighboring planes and tore them loose, and rocketed back and forth across the hangar with an accumulating bulk of wreckage. According to the *San Jacinto*'s poststorm report, "Spare engines, propellers, tractors, and other heavy equipment were all scrambled into the violently sliding mass, and smashed from side to side, ripping open and carrying away the unprotected flimsy air intakes and ventilation ducts. Repair parties and volunteers tried valiantly to secure the ungovernable and destructive heavy pieces item-by-item, and finally succeeded at about 1600, but not before a series of small electrical and oil fires had broken out."[97]

With the *Monterey*'s engine spaces abandoned, the captain was forced to stop the engines. That left the carrier dead in the water, at the mercy of mountainous seas. Everything that might catch fire was jettisoned, including ammunition in the ready service magazines. Hoses were rushed to the hangar and jets of water aimed into the fires, and after a delay the sprinkling system was finally restored to operation. The ship was saved, but two-thirds of her hangar was completely gutted by fire. On the *San Jacinto*, fires were doused sooner, but the sheer quantity of loose wreckage precluded sending crewmen into the hangar on foot. According to the captain's report:

> To the uninitiated, the loud sound of crashing and tearing airplanes, and the banging and tearing of the flimsy metal of the ventilation ducts, and the avalanche of heavy weights being thrown violently from side to side, and the presence of much boiling water on the deck, plus a large volume of steam escaping from the ruptured atmospheric exhaust within the enclosed hangar deck space, created a wholly frightening situation. However, regardless of these frightening surroundings, men on the hangar deck were lowered from the overhead, and skidded on the deck in pendulum fashion on the end of lines into this violently moving pile of rubble, and succeeded in securing it and holding the damage to a minimum when to do so appeared to them to be almost certain death or very serious injury.[98]

As the storm reached the peak of its fury, the wind was a maniacal shrieking darkness of rain and spume. Visibility closed in to 30 or 40 feet. Men stationed topside could make no meaningful distinction between sea and sky, or even between up and down, and their only remaining sensation of the enormous seas was felt in the rollercoaster motion of the decks beneath their feet. The sea captain-turned-author Joseph Conrad had once described a ship's ordeal in a nineteenth-century typhoon in these same waters: "Her lurches had an appalling helplessness: she pitched as if taking a header into a void, and seemed to find a wall to hit every time. . . . At certain moments the air streamed against the ship as if sucked through a tunnel with a concentrated solid force of impact that seemed to lift her clean out of the water and keep her up for an instant with only a quiver running through her from end to end. And then she would begin her tumbling again as if dropped back into a boiling cauldron."[99]

When *Farragut*-class destroyers rolled past 45 degrees, their engines lost lubricating oil suction and shut down.[100] Without steerageway, wallowing at the base of tremendous seas, they were pinned down like defeated wrestlers. Radio masts, radar antennae, searchlights, whaleboats, davits, and depth-charge racks were carried away into the maelstrom. Heavy steel covers were ripped from ammunition lockers. Lieutenant Commander James A. Marks, captain of the *Hull*, was concerned that his ship's smokestack might be uprooted from the deck. As a 100-knot gust knocked the ship down, "the junior officer of the deck was catapulted from the port side of the pilot house completely through the air to the upper portion of the starboard side of the pilot house."[101] Gradually, after a "breathless eternity," the ship righted herself. On the *Dewey*, the cables and eye pads securing the smokestack tore loose, and the stack came down, hanging loosely over the starboard side of the ship. By lowering her center of gravity and reducing her wind profile, this seeming disaster might actually have saved the *Dewey*. "Almost immediately," her skipper concluded, "there was a perceptible change for the better in the way the ship rode."[102]

Aboard the *Aylwin*, the engine room blowers failed and the temperature in the engineering spaces shot up to 180 degrees, forcing all personnel to evacuate. Water sloshed around below, rising to several feet above the floor plates. At about 11:00 a.m., the *Aylwin* lay down on the sea, nearly on her beam ends, and remained there for twenty minutes. Without her engines she could not steer out of her predicament—but somehow, using the hull as a sail, her captain managed to maneuver her stern far enough into the wind to take pressure off the ship. That brought her back to an incline of "only" 60 degrees, and she remained afloat in that desperate condition until the storm abated.[103]

The *Hull* was not so fortunate. Shortly before noon she was knocked down onto her starboard side, pinned down at an angle of about 80 degrees, and stayed there. Water flooded into the pilot house and poured down her stack. There was no coming back from such a blow. Lieutenant Commander Marks stepped off the port wing of the bridge and swam away. Held up by his kapok life vest, he turned and caught a last glimpse of the *Hull* as she was swallowed by the sea. "Shortly after, I felt the concussion of the boilers exploding underwater. . . . I concentrated my efforts thereafter to trying to keep alive in the mountainous seas which pounded us."[104] A similar fate was suffered by the destroyers *Spence* and *Monaghan*.

That evening, as the wind and seas abated, Halsey directed McCain to detach a search-and-rescue force to head north, along the track the fleet had taken. The rest of Task Force 38, licking its wounds, headed northwest to attempt another round of airstrikes on Luzon. But conditions remained foul, with heavy swells from the north. At midday on December 21, Halsey canceled the strikes and ordered the fleet to retire toward Ulithi.[105]

The search-and-rescue force kept up their efforts for seventy-two hours. The vessels spread out in a broad scouting line, destroyers on the flanks, and scanned the sea ahead with searchlights at night. The fleet diary noted, "numerous empty life rafts, cork rafts, and floating debris were sighted and investigated for personnel during the search."[106] Many whistles were heard. Life rafts were dropped into the ships' wakes. On December 21, the destroyer escort *Tabberer* (which had suffered badly in the storm) discovered a raft with ten survivors of the *Spence*. Maneuvering upwind of the rafts and swimmers, the *Tabberer*'s skipper let the wind blow his ship gradually down toward the castaways, so that the hull shielded the swimmers from wind and waves. Two large cargo nets were lowered over the leeward side of the ship, and life rings with long lines attached were thrown out to the swimmers. Several of the *Tabberer*'s own crewmen, attached to lines and wearing kapok life vests, leapt into the sea and swam out to the castaways, hauling them back into the cargo nets.[107] The *Tabberer* kept at it, fishing out a total of fifty-five survivors of the *Spence* and *Hull*.

The typhoon had claimed 790 American lives. Three destroyers were gone and several others severely damaged. Ninety-three castaways were rescued in the search operations after the storm. The highest mortality rate was among the crew of the *Monaghan*, of whom just six men survived. One hundred forty-six carrier aircraft had been destroyed or blown overboard, mostly from the CVLs. The *Monterey*, *Cowpens*, and *San Jacinto* were badly damaged and would require major overhauls.[108]

On Christmas Eve morning, the *New Jersey* entered Ulithi and maneuvered carefully into her designated "berth." A long procession of heavy warships arrived by Mugai Channel, including dozens of carriers, until "Murderers' Row" once again dominated the north anchorage.

Admiral Nimitz had flown into Ulithi for a planned conference with Halsey and the Third Fleet staff. The CINCPAC, recently promoted to the new five-star rank of "fleet admiral," was piped aboard the *New Jersey* at 1:50 p.m. For the first time in the navy's history, a five-star flag was broken out at the masthead. After niceties, the brass convened in flag country wardrooms to review recent operations and plan for the future.

Christmas Eve dinner was held aboard the flagship in Admiral Halsey's mess. Nimitz and his entourage had arrived from Pearl Harbor carrying a

Christmas tree decked with ornaments. This kind gesture, noted the war diary, "contributed to the Christmas spirit on the occasion."[109] But Halsey later confessed that he found it difficult to enjoy the festivities, considering that the holiday marked "four consecutive Christmases away from home, four Christmases of sea and sand instead of snow and holly."[110] Though he did not admit it, either at the time or later, Halsey must have known he bore grave responsibility for the beating the fleet had just suffered. His subordinates were comparing notes and opinions, and many agreed that Halsey had erred by failing to dodge the storm when there was still time, on the afternoon of December 17. The brownshoe admirals were typically outspoken in their criticism. Admiral Gerry Bogan "felt that it was just plain goddamn stubbornness and stupidity."[111] Jocko Clark, on standby status aboard the *Hornet*, was similarly harsh, as was Arthur Radford. Ted Sherman attested that the appearance of sky and sea on December 17 had been a sure sign that a typhoon was brewing.

Halsey had done what he had done because he was determined to keep his promises to MacArthur. That motive was admirable, but the end result was no airstrikes on Luzon and a storm-mauled fleet. For the second time in two months, Nimitz was forced to question Halsey's fitness for the critically important job he held. According to Truman Hedding, a senior member of Nimitz's staff (and a former Task Force 58 chief of staff to Mitscher), the CINCPAC found it "difficult to understand taking the task force right into the dangerous semicircle of the typhoon . . . he was very concerned about it and very upset about it, because that is a reflection on your seamanship. That is something that officers usually pride themselves on—being good seamen."[112] Hedding also heard, through the grapevine, that Admiral King was furious, and he "practically tore the Navy Department apart about it."[113]

Nimitz spent most of Christmas Day aboard the *New Jersey*, holding numerous conferences. He and Halsey faced the press together that afternoon, refusing to entertain any questions about the typhoon. But Nimitz ordered a court of inquiry to investigate the loss of the three destroyers. Halsey gave testimony on December 28.[114]

The court's formal report, issued in early January 1945, placed a "preponderance of responsibility" on Halsey for failing to dodge the storm, and faulted him for "errors of judgment under stress of war operations." Although the court did not recommend any specific sanction, its ruling was sufficiently critical that it might have justified relieving Halsey of his command. Spruance was due to return as commander in chief of the Fifth Fleet later that month; he could simply have been recalled a few weeks early. But after conferring privately, Nimitz and King decided not to do it. Truman Hedding believed, as did many others, that Halsey's popularity with the press and public saved his command, "because Admiral Halsey was a national hero, and in time of war you don't do that."[115]

The Pacific Fleet chief took the extraordinary step of addressing himself to the entire fleet on the subject, in a long and detailed memorandum entitled "Lessons of Damage in Typhoon." In bygone eras, Nimitz wrote, before the advent of radio, naval fleets encountering storms had had no means of maintaining formation or command unity. In such conditions, every captain became his own master, and did whatever he thought best to save his ship, regardless of the wishes of the fleet commander. In 1944, the case was somewhat different, in that a fleet commander could and did continue to issue commands even at the height of a violent storm. In such conditions, still relatively new in the long annals of maritime history, "It is most definitely part of the senior officer's responsibility to think in terms of the smallest ship and most inexperienced commanding officer under him." He must not take their capabilities for granted, or assume that they will "come through weather that his own big ship can." In the same spirit, it was every skipper's responsibility to do what he must to save his own ship, and when confronted with a "fatal hazard," he must take it upon himself to break formation. Moreover, he must not wait too long to take such measures, because "Nothing is more dangerous than for a seaman to be grudging in taking precautions lest they turn out to have been unnecessary. Safety at sea for a thousand years has depended on exactly the opposite philosophy."[116]

Chapter Nine

WITH ALLIED VICTORY IN SIGHT, BOTH IN EUROPE AND THE PACIFIC, minds were turning to the postwar future and the challenges of demobilization. Many expressed growing concern about a wide psychological gulf that had opened between men fighting overseas and the "folks back home." Among veterans, feelings of bitterness and alienation were common. Their resentments were complicated, sometimes ambivalent or inchoate—but in general, veterans felt let down by their fellow citizens. Their anger tended to flare up suddenly and unexpectedly, often taking civilians by surprise. Any mention of industrial strikes aroused their fury, as for the sailor who wrote his wife to condemn the "union devils and high wage workers that I loathe so intensely."[1] Rumors of corruption, profiteering, hoarding, and black-market chicanery reached their ears. They scowled at the shrill caterwauling of Washington politicians, who bickered over issues that the servicemen would have considered frivolous even in peacetime. Infantrymen in foxholes sometimes even mused that it would be a good thing if an American city were bombed by the enemy, because it might shock the civilians and awaken them to the reality of war.[2]

Servicemen were keenly aware that the home economy was booming—that there was lots of money to be made, lots of ways to spend it, lots of single women, and a favorable (to men) gender ratio. They could not stand to hear civilians complain about such trivialities as rationing, high rents, blackouts, carpooling, long lines, overcrowded trains, or the price of meat. They assumed, as did many professional economists, that the war would bankrupt the nation and peace would return it to the immiseration of the 1930s. Just in time for their return to the chilly embrace of American capitalism, all those once-in-a-lifetime "big money" jobs would vanish. So they pessimistically assumed and believed.

Civilians fed on a three-year diet of censored press coverage presumed to know what was happening in the war. And indeed, in a sense, a well-read civilian might be better informed than the average soldier, sailor, or marine about the intricacies of global military strategy. He might be able to recite details and statistics about the progress of Allied forces in various foreign theaters. But a civilian who had not fought in combat never really *knew* what he was talking about, and it irked the veteran to hear him speak so glibly. "Talk, talk, talk, that's all they do," said one American GI of the chatty civilians he met at home, "and what they have to say about the war is stupid or it doesn't matter."[3] When a mother visiting her wounded son at a veterans' hospital began talking about the war, he turned sour and asked, "Did you read that in some newspaper?"[4] Servicemen grimaced to hear radio announcers speak in the first-person plural—"We"—when referring to American forces fighting overseas. They snorted at the expression "home front." As if scrap metal drives and victory gardens could turn a peaceful republic into a battlefield! Posters on factory walls told workers to think of themselves as "soldiers of production." Soldiers! With their eight-hour shifts and fat paychecks! Everywhere on this so-called home front, servicemen encountered billboard patriotism and war bond sales kitsch. They shook their heads in sorrow at the appropriation of the American flag for commercial advertising. When films were screened for fighting men, and Old Glory unfurled to the accompaniment of swelling orchestral music, they sometimes even groaned and jeered: "Boo, wave that flag!"[5] Their scorn was not aimed at the flag itself, which they revered, but at the gross machinations of Hollywood and Madison Avenue. A marine officer observed of his troops, in late 1944: "The great illusion of fighting a glorious war they had forgotten or had never known. Although they might have been stirred once by a parade, a cheering crowd, and a brass band, they knew now that fighting was a dirty business in which the glamour that had existed once in their imagination was lost."[6]

But to civilians who had lived through the hardscrabble years of the Great Depression, their newfound prosperity was exhilarating. In 1944, the U.S. unemployment rate fell to 1.2 percent—the lowest ever recorded, probably the lowest that *will* ever be recorded. Gross national product grew by more than 60 percent in real terms from 1940 to 1944.[7] The gains were broadly distributed: indeed, they were proportionally greatest at the low end of the income scale. The war boom completed what the New Dealers had started—it lifted the fortunes of the poorest Americans, including blacks, Latinos, and poor rural whites. In 1944, 19 million women of all races were working outside the home, including about 2 million in the munitions industries. Surging wages ran up against rationing and the enforced unavailability of certain big-ticket goods, such as automobiles and major household appliances. The result was unprecedented savings and a near-quintupling of household wealth. Personal savings, deposited in banks or invested in war bonds, grew from $8.5 billion in 1940 to $39.8 billion in 1944.[8]

Most remarkable of all, perhaps, wartime inflation was kept in check by effective price- and wage-control measures, so that the consumer's real buying power rose even as the government preached the virtues of wartime austerity. On December 7, 1944, the third anniversary of Pearl Harbor, Macy's department stores rang in the largest single day of sales in the company's history. Shoppers were not deterred by shortages of certain luxury and consumer goods. "People want to spend money," said a store manager, "and if they can't spend it on textiles, they'll spend it on furniture, or we'll find something else for them."[9] In the opinion of the economist John Kenneth Galbraith, "Never in the history of human conflict had there been so much talk of sacrifice and so little sacrifice."[10]

Rich as it was, said the critics, this "home front" America had grown meaner, colder, and less charitable. About 4 million families, or 9 million people altogether, picked up and moved to a different part of the country in pursuit of war work. Trains and intercity buses were jammed to capacity, with passengers sitting on suitcases in the aisles. Scalpers roamed through the stations offering tickets at steep markups. Everywhere one saw young military wives with infants and small children, doggedly following their husbands from post to post. Many migrated to the West Coast to find a home nearer to the Pacific War. Sailors on ships deployed in the Pacific might put into San Diego or San Francisco at any time, without advance notice, and be given a three-day liberty pass. If they wanted a reunion, the families had better be living nearby. In California, however, there were millions of new migrants—the Golden State's population grew by more than one-third during the war—and never enough housing. A city official in San Francisco reported: "Families are sleeping in garages, with mattresses right on cement floors and three, four, five to one bed."[11]

Marjorie Cartwright married a sailor a week before he shipped out with MacArthur's Seventh Fleet. She accompanied him to San Francisco, his ship's home port, and promised to wait there for his return. It was the first time she had traveled beyond the borders of West Virginia. "I was on my own, living in a city I didn't know and where I knew very few people. It was like being an orphan. I felt completely alone." She found a furnished room in an apartment and took a job as a keypunch operator for Standard Oil. "I learned to knit at that time and spent many nights knitting socks for my husband and listening to the radio for war news," she recalled years later. "I lived alone for four years during the war, and they were the most painful, lonely years I think I will ever spend. I look back and wonder how I ever got through those years, but when you're young you can do a lot of things that you can't do as you grow older. I spent many nights by myself in my room, crying because I was so lonely."[12]

In a normally functioning market economy, the great population movements of 1941–1945 would have touched off a residential building boom. But to guide labor and materials into the munitions industries, the federal government clamped down on new housing construction. In 1941, $6.2 billion had been invested in residential construction. The figure plummeted to a low of $2.0 billion in 1943, recovering only to $2.2 billion in 1944.[13] Wartime boomtowns were overrun with newcomers who could not find a place to live, and the landlords were rapacious. Around Ford's Willow Run factory in Ypsilanti, Michigan, one of the largest aircraft manufacturing plants in the country, there was almost no residential housing at all. The workforce was bused in from Detroit or crowded into squalid trailer camps along the roads. Shantytowns of tar paper shacks sprung up in the Michigan mud. In existing dwellings, owners made a killing by renting out their spare rooms. Old Victorian homes became overcrowded bunkhouses, with beds rented out by the hour. Two or three people alternated in the same bed—"hotbunking"—with their sleeping schedules synchronized to their work schedules at the plant.

With thousands of workers leaving the factories at midnight, retail and entertainment businesses found it profitable to stay open all night. Bars were open around the clock and crowded even in the small hours of the morning. Long lines stretched down the sidewalks outside nightclubs, where "swing shift" shows featured C-list entertainers between midnight and dawn. One could go bowling at three o'clock in the morning. Movie theaters screened films back to back, twenty-four hours per day, and were always full. Homeless workers bought a ticket for a midnight showing and tried to sleep in their seats. Parents dropped their children off at a movie theater, worked a shift at the plant, and then returned to pick them up. The journalist Max Lerner described the all-night cinemas of wartime New York: "They are always long and narrow and smell to high heaven, and there is a tough character who patrols them to see that the ranker forms of murder, arson, mayhem, and rape are not carried out successfully. You have not really seen a movie until you have seen it in an all-night theater."[14]

Mass migration squeezed Americans of different races, classes, and ethnicities into congested cities, where they suddenly found themselves living and working in each other's pockets. The war industries, by executive order, were integrated. The war accelerated the exodus of African Americans from the American South to the industrial North and Midwest; about 700,000 blacks picked up and moved during the war. The promise of high-wage jobs also enticed hundreds of thousands of rural whites into the cities, where they found a new and unfamiliar way of life.

In the hot summer of 1943, an epidemic of racial violence swept through many American cities. The largest and most infamous riots of the war broke out in Detroit, where the population nearly doubled between 1940 and 1943. An early flashpoint was the construction of a public housing project, the Sojourner Truth Homes, on the border of a predominantly Polish-American neighborhood in February 1942. Demonstrations and counterdemonstrations turned violent, and the National Guard was called in to protect black residents as they moved into the newly opened homes. That dispute eventually simmered down, but in June 1943, a wider conflict erupted on a sweltering Sunday afternoon, as racially charged fights broke out in the Belle Isle Park on the Detroit River. At dusk, as thousands of citizens walked back across the bridge connecting the city to the island, dozens of individual fights began to merge into a general melee pitting blacks against whites. Rumors and incitements to violence spread quickly through the city by word of mouth. Thousands of young men of both races headed into downtown Detroit, looking for trouble. Violence, vandalism, arson, and looting spread and continued all night and into the next day, when white mobs were seen accosting, beating, and murdering black men at random while the police looked the other way. A newspaper photographer caught a mob dragging a black man from a streetcar and beating him in the street. Many whites caught in the wrong place at the wrong time got similar treatment at the hands of black rioters. The Detroit Police Department arrested a few whites and shot dozens of blacks. According to reports, the police declared an unofficial curfew in black neighborhoods and executed many young black men caught outdoors after hours.

After three days of rioting, federal troops poured into the city and restored order, but the city would never be the same. Afterward, a sixteen-year-old white boy boasted of what he had done: "There were about 200 of us in cars. We killed eight of them. I saw knives being stuck through their throats and heads being shot through. They were turning over cars with niggers in them. You should have seen it. It was really some riot."[15]

In the same month, violence broke out in Los Angeles, in the predominantly Mexican-American neighborhood of Chavez Ravine (near the present-day site of Dodger Stadium). The riots were touched off by simmering tensions between sailors posted to a nearby naval reserve training center and local Latino youths who wore "zoot suits" and broad-brimmed hats. The zoot suiters, as they were called, resented the influx of thousands of servicemen to their "barrio." Angry confrontations on the streets were common. Los Angeles newspapers, especially the two local Hearst dailies, began campaigning against the zoot suiters in 1942, accusing them in sensationalistic terms of violence, theft, rape, indolence, draft-dodging, and smoking marijuana. On June 4, 1943—the first anniversary of the Battle of Midway—a rumor swept through the naval and military bases of the region. It was said that a gang of zoot suiters had attacked a sailor and then retreated into a local movie theater. Carloads of sailors wielding baseball bats converged on Chavez Ravine. They stormed into the cinemas, forced the projectionists to turn on the lights, strode up and down the aisles, and dragged anyone wearing a zoot suit out into the street. The victims were beaten and the suits ripped from their bodies. The Los Angeles Police Department and navy shore patrol stood by, for the most part, and did not intervene. On the second day of the riots, when a new crop of sailors and marines arrived from San Diego, the attackers targeted all young Latino males, whether or not they wore zoot suits. The mayhem spilled into downtown and East L.A. The Hearst papers blamed the violence on the Mexican-American community. "A lot of people got hurt, a lot of innocent people, a lot of these young Mexican kids," said Don McFadden, an eighteen-year-old who witnessed the riots. "I saw a group of servicemen stop a streetcar. They spotted one zoot-suiter on it. They got on, he couldn't get off. They carried him off unconscious. Here's a guy riding a streetcar and he gets beat up because he happens to be a Mexican. I actually saw that happen."[16] A serviceman who did not approve remarked, "I could find nothing to distinguish the behavior of our soldiers from the behavior of Nazi storm trooper thugs beating up outnumbered non-Aryans."[17]

In the South, where the federal desegregation edict collided with Jim Crow laws, rioting broke out in several cities—most infamously in Mobile, Alabama, where savage violence followed the promotion of twelve black workers at a local shipyard, and in Beaumont, Texas, where a predominantly African American residential district was burned to the ground. At Camp Stewart in Georgia, a gun battle broke out between white and black MPs; one was killed and four others wounded. Racially charged disputes escalated into riots in El Paso and Port Arthur, Texas. Lawlessness and violence spread across northern and midwestern cities as well, including Philadelphia, Indianapolis, St. Louis, Baltimore, and Springfield, Massachusetts. In Harlem, New York, in August 1943, rioting broke out after a police officer shot a black soldier.

In the hard-fought presidential election campaign of 1944, Republican candidate Thomas Dewey was heavily disadvantaged. His challenge, which would have been daunting even in peacetime, was to keep his party's voting base together while also peeling away a slice of FDR's thrice-victorious New Deal voting coalition. The GOP was fractured by internal arguments over both domestic and foreign policies. Many Republicans remained unyielding in their determination to roll back all of the New Deal—but repealing Social Security, labor protections, or banking reform laws were unpopular propositions. Leading Republican officeholders, such as Senator Robert A. Taft of Ohio, retained their isolationist instincts of the prewar era, and wanted to limit U.S. participation in postwar treaties and multilateral organizations. But isolationism had earned a bad name on December 7, 1941, and a clear majority of Americans now favored international engagement to prevent another global war. Anti-Roosevelt animus was the glue that held the Republican coalition together, but Dewey sounded a "me too" message on the leading issues of the campaign, promising to retain most New Deal reforms while also pledging to win the war faster and at a lower cost in American lives. Dewey wanted to charge the administration with negligence in missing advance signs of the attack on Pearl Harbor, but doing so would disclose that the U.S. military had broken Japanese diplomatic codes prior to the war. General Marshall persuaded him to hold his fire, warning that Americans would lose access to that message traffic if the Japanese were tipped off to the breach. Dewey had also heard (accurate) reports of FDR's failing health, and considered making it an issue in the campaign, but finally concluded that such attacks might backfire by arousing the public's sympathy for the president. He was reduced to making obscure allusions to the "tired old men" of the Roosevelt administration, a line of attack that probably hurt more than helped his chances.

The highlight (or lowlight) of the campaign was a speech given by the president on September 23 at the Statler Hotel in Washington. The occasion was a banquet hosted by the International Brotherhood of Teamsters. FDR was seated at a long dais at the head of the great ballroom, flanked by some twenty teamster leaders, including (to his immediate left) the Brotherhood's Irish-born president, Daniel J. Tobin. He spoke into a forest of radio microphones, and his remarks were carried live to a national radio audience. The "Fala speech," as it came to be known, was a partisan stemwinder—the angriest, most caustic, most hard-hitting philippic of FDR's long political career. Referring to Dewey's attempts to disassociate his party from its long history of opposition to popular labor laws, he said: "We have all seen many marvelous stunts in the circus but no performing elephant could turn a hand-spring without falling flat on his back." (At this, Tobin appears to have almost fallen backward out of his chair in laughter.) The president refuted his opponent's charge that he had failed to prepare the nation adequately for war—"I doubt whether even Goebbels would have tried that one"—by reviewing the history of Republican opposition to military spending prior to 1941. Dewey and other leading Republicans had recently given speeches blaming FDR's policies for extending and deepening the Great Depression. With his eyes widened in theatrical incredulity, the president feigned amazement at this new line of attack. "Now, there is an old and somewhat lugubrious adage which says: 'Never speak of rope in the house of a man who has been hanged,'" he intoned. "In the same way, if I were a Republican leader speaking to a mixed audience, the last word in the whole dictionary that I think I would use is that word 'depression.'"

Wine and liquor flowed freely in the Statler ballroom that night. One guest, a journalist employed by the OWI, feared that the teamsters might erupt into violence. Again and again they leapt to their feet and thrust their fists into the air with savage glee. One pounded a silver tray with a soup ladle, and another smashed wine glasses to punctuate each of FDR's attack lines.

The president's parting shot, and the one that his audience would remember best, concerned a rumor that had circulated during his sea voyage to Hawaii and Alaska that summer—that Fala, the president's dog, had accidentally been left behind on an Aleutian island, and that a navy destroyer had been dispatched from Seattle to retrieve him. The story was nonsensical on its face: How could the dog have been forgotten by the entire presidential entourage? How could his absence have gone unnoticed until the party returned to Seattle? Why send a ship instead of a plane? But it was repeated widely in the anti-FDR press. As the rumor snowballed, the destroyer was upgraded to a cruiser, then to a battleship, and the cost of the imagined rescue operation rose as high as $20 million. After a week or so, Admiral Leahy felt compelled to deny the story publicly, causing it to vanish from the headlines. But FDR knew that his opponents had overreached, and he was not going to let the opportunity pass. With deadpan earnestness, and long pauses to accommodate the audience's lusty roars of laughter, he delivered his cornball *coup de grâce*. "These Republican leaders have not been content with attacks on me, or my wife, or on my sons," he told the teamsters. "No, not content with that, they now include my little dog, Fala."

> Well, of course, I don't resent attacks, and my family doesn't resent attacks, but Fala does resent them. You know, Fala is Scotch, and being a Scottie, as soon as he learned that the Republican fiction writers in Congress and out had concocted a story that I had left him behind on the Aleutian Islands and had sent a destroyer back to find him—at a cost to the taxpayers of two or three, or eight or twenty million dollars—his Scotch soul was furious. He has not been the same dog since. I am accustomed to hearing malicious falsehoods about myself—such as that old, worm-eaten chestnut that I have represented myself as indispensable. But I think I have a right to resent, to object to libelous statements about my dog.

In a nation of dog lovers, this attack drew blood. A member of the Democratic National Committee concluded afterward that the race was between "FDR's dog and Dewey's goat."[18]

As the dinner broke up at 10:30 p.m., two young navy lieutenants were unlucky enough to be caught on the mezzanine outside the ballroom. Suddenly they found themselves engulfed in a crowd of well-lubricated and belligerent teamsters who demanded to know whether they were Democrats or Republicans, and whether they were for Roosevelt or Dewey. Lieutenant Randolph Dickins Jr., a 23-year-old veteran of the Battle of Midway, replied that it was "none of their business."[19] A scuffle broke out. According to Dickins, the teamsters demanded to know what servicemen overseas thought of unions, and accused the two officers of being "disloyal to the service and to our commander-in-chief."[20] Punches were thrown. According to some reports, Dickins landed a blow on Daniel J. Tobin himself, knocking the teamster boss to the floor. Dickins was held from behind by two goons while a third punched him repeatedly in the face, "blackening his eyes so badly that several stitches were required to close the wound."[21] Bellhops intervened and were roughly handled for their trouble. The hotel manager called in the shore patrol, who finally put a stop to the brawl. As Dickins was hauled away, a teamster allegedly told him that he had knocked down a personal friend of the president of the United States, and would suffer the consequences.

This "Battle of the Statler Hotel" was featured prominently in the anti-Roosevelt press. The teamsters denounced the story as a libel calculated to defame organized labor, and flooded Washington with more than a hundred sworn affidavits blaming the two officers for provoking the fight.

After the Fala speech, campaign oratory grew vitriolic on both sides. Dewey's running mate, Governor John W. Bricker of Ohio, charged that unions and big-city political machines were in the grip of "forces of communism linked with irreligion." Dewey declared that FDR was "indispensable to Earl Browder," leader of the American Communist Party.[22] But as polls hardened in the incumbent's favor, those attacks had the whiff of desperation. Allied forces continued to advance victoriously against the Axis on all fronts, and FDR dispelled concerns about his health with a show of vigor on the campaign trail. On November 7, Roosevelt won reelection with 53.4 percent of the popular vote, securing an electoral landslide of 432–99.

With peace in sight, an "over the hump" mentality took hold among the American people. War industries were winding down. Rationing measures were gradually relaxed on such goods as canned foods and meat. The War and Navy Departments issued hundreds of cancellation notices to contractors. Tens of billions of dollars previously appropriated by Congress were held in reserve accounts to be returned to the treasury. In June 1944, the total number of workers employed in the munitions industries had declined by about a million in six months. Newspapers were full of news about the unwinding of complex procurement contracts, with attendant legal wrangling over such details as contract termination fees, low interest financing for plant retooling, accelerated depreciation schedules for tax purposes, and the disposition of inventories. Jeeps and other surplus military assets were sold in civilian markets. Refrigerators and other large household appliances were advertised for sale for the first time since 1941. The U.S. Mint resumed production of copper pennies. Blackout restrictions were eased in major cities and then eliminated altogether. Newly discharged servicemen were coming home. People began dressing in formal clothes again for Broadway premieres and other such events. The race tracks reopened and the betting windows took in unprecedented sums. Strikes were threatening to hit critical industries, as union leaders concluded that such stoppages could no longer cripple the war effort.

From the top to the bottom of the economic ladder, most assumed that the end of the war would bring a return to the Depression conditions of the early 1930s. The syndrome was even given a name: "depression psychosis." At the height of the war, the economy employed 55 million civilian workers. Another 12 million were in uniform. Demobilization of the armed services and the cancellation of munitions contracts would occur simultaneously. Together, these shocks might eliminate as many as 20 million jobs. The immense army and navy surpluses would have to be reabsorbed into the economy without disrupting existing markets. Many economists warned that a postwar employment crisis was inevitable. New Dealers demanded a return to mass publicly funded employment programs. Business leaders wanted the federal government to subsidize the cost of "reconversion" to civilian industries.

The timing of the end of the war was thought to be a critical variable. Germany was expected to collapse in early 1945, but the generals and admirals freely admitted that they had no idea how long it would take to subjugate Japan. According to one panel of economists, if Japan unexpectedly threw in the towel, "the United States would find itself largely unprepared to overcome unemployment on a large scale."[23] A war correspondent wrote that a sudden and early end to the Pacific War would be "a Pearl Harbor of peace."[24] In strictly economic terms, therefore—without reference to the human costs—it was considered desirable that the war in the Pacific should continue at least several months after the fall of Nazi Germany. One even heard such sentiments among ordinary civilians. Peggy Terry, who worked in a munitions plant in Kentucky, recalled hearing a coworker say that she hoped the war "didn't end until she got her refrigerator paid for. An old man hit her over the head with an umbrella. He said, 'How dare you!' "[25]

In November 1944, in the wake of FDR's reelection, Secretary of War Henry Stimson warned that American civilians on the home front were relaxing prematurely. A disappointing harvest brought calls to reimpose rationing. A national service bill, introduced in Congress but not enacted, would have empowered the federal government to draft civilian workers and to impose employment freezes in war industries. The German counteroffensive called the Battle of the Bulge had set back hopes for an early termination of the war in Europe. General Eisenhower wrote FDR to warn against expectations of a "clean-cut military surrender of the forces on the Western Front."[26] The letter was promptly released to the press. In a joint letter to the president in January 1945, Marshall and King warned of looming manpower shortages in both the army and navy, and asked for 900,000 more draft inductions to replace "casualties and war-fatigued men."[27] Stimson grew alarmed by signs of deteriorating morale in the military ranks. If the war was to last longer than expected, would servicemen demand to be brought home? He lobbied the president to reimpose austerity on the home front, even if such measures were largely symbolic.

On January 3, 1945, a federal order shut down the operations of all horse and dog tracks. The stated purpose was to reduce the burden on roads and mass transit systems. But the real purpose, as government officials acknowledged in off-the-record comments, was to eliminate the unseemly spectacle of war-enriched civilians betting their newfound wealth at the tracks. The following month, a midnight curfew order was imposed on bars and nightclubs. In this case, the ostensible purpose was to save electricity and fuel oil, but the measure was really "an instrument for meeting what is perhaps officially felt to be a shortage of 'war awareness' by civilians."[28]

By early 1945, servicemen overseas and civilians at home were in broad accord on at least one point: all were heartily tired of the war, and yearned for a return to the ordinary routines of peacetime. Newspaper columnist Robert M. Yoder looked forward to the day when "It will be all right to suggest to a few thousand volunteer morale builders and duty-explainers that they go soak their heads. And you can uproot the victory garden and throw the turnips at the block captain."[29] In a similar spirit, a 1st Marine Division corporal just wanted to "go home to my wife, get my job back driving the mail truck, and be left alone."[30] Postwar expectations were modest. For millions of homesick servicemen, paradise was a simple, ordinary, boring life in a free country where no one was ordering them around or trying to kill them. When they dreamed of home, commonplace amenities and rituals assumed exaggerated significance—privacy, leisure, a cup of coffee at a dime store counter, a walk in the park, the company of women, pushing a child on a swing, physical safety, a soft mattress, and a good night's sleep. Whatever their pent-up resentments against the "folks back home," the fighting men had learned to love and appreciate their country more than they ever had as civilians. They conjured up elaborate visions of their futures—of the wife they would marry, the house they would live in, the children they would raise. "A very smart man I once knew said that anticipation was sixty percent of life," said the soldier Elliot Johnson. "There was this anticipation of returning to this beautiful girl. And fantasies of kids and jobs. It was absolutely sustaining."[31] In the same spirit, Marjorie Cartwright passed her idle hours daydreaming about life after the war, when her husband would return from the Pacific and be mustered out of the navy. They would build a two-story brick house with a grand entrance hall, a winding stairway, and enough bedrooms upstairs for five children: "I just loved that house and carried those plans around in my mind for years and years."[32]

AT THE START OF 1944, the U.S. Navy had 27,500 airplanes in service, a tenfold increase since 1940. As the assembly lines at Grumman, Douglas, Martin, and Curtiss reached peak production between March and June of that year, the navy's inventory of new planes swelled so rapidly that it threatened to become an unmanageable glut. The service accepted delivery of 24,000 new combat aircraft during the 1944 fiscal year, a figure that exceeded the totals for the previous three years combined.[33] That was a high-class problem, one that any other combatant nation of the Second World War would have been glad to face. But the admirals faced an immediate decision: How to resolve the mismatch between surging production and a bloated inventory? In February, Admiral King signed an order fixing an upper limit of 38,000 planes in service, and adamantly refused to relax that edict.[34] The production lines began ramping down steeply in the summer of 1944—but the plants could not be permitted to shut down entirely. To preserve the physical capital and know-how of this strategically vital industry, it was thought necessary to keep them turning over at a reduced rate. Admiral McCain, then serving as deputy CNO for air, proposed a plan to assign only the newest aircraft to frontline service, and to return older units to the United States for training or other purposes. In September 1944, the navy adopted a more radical plan—to junk thousands of older planes, including those already deployed in the Pacific, to make room for newer units. The word went out to all commands: get rid of older aircraft by any means necessary.

As a measure of the industrial might of the United States in 1944 and 1945, the subsequent whirl of destruction told a better story than a thousand pages of statistics. If a plane needed minor repairs, it was pulled off the flight line and junked, and a shiny new replacement unit flew in to take its place. Hundreds of airplanes were flown into remote Pacific island airstrips, parked in a vacant clearing, and abandoned. Many such aircraft "boneyards" were later used for target practice by U.S. bombers on training missions. Scrapped airplanes were bulldozed into pits, and the wreckage compacted by running tanks over them. Marginally damaged carrier planes were pushed off the flight decks into the sea, and new replacement units flown in from escort carriers. This mass-junking of perfectly serviceable warplanes occurred *at the height of the war*, when the Japanese were falling well short of aircraft production targets and struggling to keep their assembly lines in operation at all.

Mass-producing pilots was an entirely different sort of challenge, one that the navy was never willing to outsource to private industry. Admiral Towers and his fellow brownshoes had anticipated the problem in the 1930s, laying the groundwork for a training command that could scale up rapidly in the event of war. And so it did: the navy awarded "wings of gold" to 3,112 new flyers in 1941, 10,869 in 1942, 20,842 in 1943, and 21,067 in 1944. This phenomenal growth was accomplished without compromising training standards. Indeed, the reverse was true—the rookie crop of 1944 arrived in frontline squadrons with an average of six hundred flight hours, including two hundred hours in the service planes to which they were assigned, and the veterans rated them as more skilled and combat-ready than any previous generation of aviators. This feat was made possible by the expansion of the navy's main training complex at Pensacola, Florida, and the establishment of twelve new naval air stations around the country. The largest, which would rival Pensacola's in size, was constructed on flat scrub land south of Corpus Christi, Texas, on the Gulf of Mexico. Texas congressman Lyndon B. Johnson worked behind the scenes to have an initial $24 million cost-plus-fixed-fee building contract awarded to his major campaign contributor, the Brown & Root construction company of Houston. The cost of building NAS Corpus Christi would eventually balloon to $100 million.[35] The massive project had the indirect effect of supercharging Johnson's political career and sending him on a trajectory for higher office.

In earlier eras, Annapolis graduates had provided most of the navy's flight students. But as the threat of war loomed in Europe, new recruitment channels were opened. The Naval Aviation Reserve Act of 1939 aimed to train 6,000 new pilots; a supplementary law in 1940 raised the goal to 15,000 new navy and Marine Corps pilots of all types. Recruiters fanned out to universities across the nation, setting up tables with brochures in classrooms and quadrangles. The navy wanted engineering students but would even settle for an English major, provided that the man was in excellent health, with perfect 20–20 vision, unmarried, not a father, no shorter than five feet four inches tall and no taller than six feet two inches, and had completed at least four semesters of coursework. (Later the navy began accepting qualified high school graduates.) Vision tests and physical examinations were provided on the spot. Would-be recruits took a math-heavy intelligence test and were questioned closely by a psychiatrist. If they made the cut, they signed induction papers and were sent to a small rural airfield called an "E-base," where they received thirty days of basic instruction in a small, single-engine Piper Cub.

"E" stood for "elimination," and that was precisely the point. At the cockpit controls of the little fabric-covered Cub, which one trainee compared to a "kite with a small engine in it," the recruits either demonstrated basic flying aptitude or were eliminated from the program. Samuel Hynes did his elimination flying in Denton, Texas, at a grass airfield that was barely distinguishable from the surrounding farmland. There was a small hangar, a post and rail fence, and a pole with a wind sock. Sheep grazed on the airstrip, which doubled as a pasture. As the Cub taxied out to the field, the pilot maneuvered the aircraft to chase the animals out of the way.

Natural flyers took quickly to the controls, and were soon flying the little plane confidently and well. Others were washed out of the program, as the instructors judged that they would not provide a good return on Uncle Sam's training investment.

E-base survivors went on to preflight school, where they would undergo several months of basic training and classroom instruction. Most were placed in programs established at civilian colleges and universities around the country—the largest were at the Universities of North Carolina, Iowa, Georgia, and St. Mary's College in California. But any notion that the pre-flight trainees were college students was quickly set aside. They were issued uniforms and shorn of most of their hair. They had enlisted as seamen, second class, placing them at the bottom of the navy's pecking order. Wash-outs would be sent to the fleet as ordinary whitehats and "mop jockeys." Dormitories leased by the navy were converted into barracks where the trainees slept in bunk beds with their personal belongings in a foot locker. Boot camp discipline was enforced by chief petty officers who turned them out of bed at 0600 for calisthenics, close order drills, and a long run. Every-where they went—to the mess hall, the classroom, the parade ground, the pool—they marched together in column. On their first day at the pool, they were told to climb to the top of the high dive and jump in. To a trainee who explained that he could not swim at all, an officer replied, "I didn't ask you if you thought you could swim. I said jump in, and we'll tell you if you can swim or not."[36]

At night, the petty officers put them to work scrubbing their barracks until all was spotless. They swabbed the "decks" (floors) until they were as clean as unused dinner plates. Robert Smyth recalled scrubbing a toilet while a CPO stood over him and shouted, "Get your arm down in there and scrub the bottom of that crapper—and when you get this one polished, go back and redo the ones you finished!"[37]

About half their time was spent in classrooms, where they completed courses on aeronautical engineering, mathematics, physics, communica-tions, navigation, and aerology (the science of the earth's atmosphere). Much of the work involved rote memorization, with frequent tests to mea-sure their progress. They learned to communicate by semaphore and Morse code until they could receive thirteen words per minute. Working with photographs, silhouettes, and small toy-like airplane models, they learned to recognize and identify every type of aircraft flown by every combatant nation in the world. They studied the fundamentals of aircraft engines and how air flowed over an airplane's control surfaces. Hal Buell estimated that preflight school crammed the equivalent of one full year of college study into four months. He called it a "grueling grind."[38] Many aspiring navy fly-ers were shipwrecked on those classroom shoals, and flunked out of the pro-gram before reaching primary flight training.

At Pensacola, a graceful old Spanish town at the western tip of the Flor-ida panhandle, buses carrying each new crop of aviation cadets entered the base by a grand stone entrance gate. They drove along avenues of elegant officers' houses, where moss-draped live oaks were evenly spaced on mani-cured lawns. On the flat scrublands to the west were more than a dozen airfields, large and small, lined by handsome red brick hangars. Throughout the daylight hours, and often at night, the skies above were crowded with low-flying airplanes. Fatal accidents were unexceptional, and empty pine coffins were stored in stacks against the walls of the hangars. At the height of the war, there was an average of one crash per day at Pensacola. Planes lost altitude on takeoff and crashed at the end of runways. Planes collided in midair. Cadets died because they flew too tentatively and stalled out, or they died because they flew recklessly—for example, by skimming treetops and hitting a power line. When a body was recovered, the medical corpsmen tied cords around the sleeves and cuffs of the flight suit, explaining, "That's to keep him from sliding out of his flight suit. . . . The body is like jello, not a bone left; it'll slide right out."[39]

The navy's primary training aircraft was the Boeing-Stearman N2S, an open cockpit biplane covered with bright yellow fabric. It was known by its nickname, the "Yellow Peril." It had two cockpits, fore and aft. The instructor sat in front and spoke to the student, to his rear, through a one-way communication line called a "gosport." In the air, the instructor dem-onstrated basic maneuvers—stalls, recoveries, spins, glides, climbing, and diving. Then he let the cadet take control of the plane and shouted instruc-tions through the gosport. Matt Portz recalled the instructor's monologue as he took the control stick for the first time: "You're climbing too slow. Get that nose down. Stop making flat turns. Do you want to spin us in? Your control work is jerky. How come you don't have any confidence?"[40] Since the device did not allow the cadet to speak back to the instructor, he could not ask questions or offer excuses.

The Stearman was a forgiving machine, easy to fly—but it was also acrobatic enough to perform the basic maneuvers a pilot would need to handle a fighter, including loops, wingovers, snap rolls, Immelmanns, split-S's, and the "falling leaf." Cadets practiced precision turns by flying a figure-eight pattern around two pylons spaced in a field, maintaining an altitude of just 500 feet. This taught them how to bank sharply without losing altitude, a vital skill for any aviator. They learned to land in a strong crosswind. And so it went on, one flight after another. After ten or twenty flights, the cadet was permitted to solo for the first time. It was a milestone that none would ever forget.

Russell Baker, an eighteen-year-old from Baltimore (and a future *New York Times* columnist), was told that flying an airplane was like driving a car. Baker had never driven a car, but he did not dare to admit it, fearing that the instructor would think less of him, or perhaps even expel him from the program. Later, after a bumpy flight in the Stearman, the instructor told him to ease up on the control stick. "Baker," he said, "it's just like handling a girl's breast. You've got to be gentle." Baker did not dare to admit that he had never touched a woman's breast, either.[41]

As the weeks passed, the ranks of the aviation cadets were steadily thinned. Some concluded that flying was not for them, and asked to be transferred to another officer training program. Others were killed in crashes. Many more were washed out by the instructors. Washouts left quickly and quietly, usually without saying good-bye to their fellow cadets. To do so would be awkward, recalled one: "It was too embarrassing for both of us."[42]

Survivors advanced into secondary flight training, where they flew in progressively more advanced training planes. The North American SNJ "Texan" and the Vultee SNV "Vibrator" were low-wing closed-canopy airplanes that looked and performed almost like service aircraft. Compared to the "Yellow Peril," they were more demanding and dangerous. "Everything happened at higher speeds," Bill Davis said, "and everything happened faster, with much less room for error."[43] In these intermediate trainers the cadets were introduced to basic bombing tactics, dogfighting, and gunnery. They shot at target sleeves towed by another aircraft. They acclimated to dogfighting in a device called the Simulated Aerial Combat Machine, which Samuel Hynes compared to "a booth at a fun fair." It consisted of a mock-up of a cockpit facing a movie screen, on which was projected film footage of attacking enemy planes. As the cadet moved his control stick, the planes on the screen moved. When one swam into the crosshairs, the cadet pulled the trigger and was rewarded by a bell indicating a "hit." To Hynes, it made "the business of shooting men out of the sky seem a harmless game of skill, something you might do in a pinball palace to pass the time, and win a Kewpie doll."[44]

The cadets were first introduced to instrument flying on the ground, in an early flight simulator called the Link Trainer. This involved climbing into the "Iron Maiden," a stifling, claustrophobic cavity designed to resemble a cockpit. A lid was closed on the cadet from above. He used simulated controls and monitored simulated aircraft instruments. The instructor, talking through a gosport, told him to fly designated courses and altitudes. His performance was measured by a primitive computer that spat out pages of data. Natural pilots who had excelled in previous training flights were sometimes disoriented in the motionless Link, which provided no sense of "feel" in flight. But it was critical to master the art of flying by instruments alone, because every naval aviator would sooner or later fly at night, or in zero visibility weather. They learned to trust their instruments—airspeed, altimeter, compass, attitude indicator, needle and ball. They learned how to "fly the beam"—that is, to follow navigational beacons to a destination. Later, their skills were tested in flight by flying "under the hood." A canvas curtain was drawn around the canopy of a training aircraft, so that the pilot could not see outside, and he was forced to fly the plane using his instruments alone. Many found this drill to be a holy terror. Smyth said that his first such flight was like "trying to balance a beach ball on the tip of a stick."[45]

After nearly a year of hard work, cadets were awarded their coveted gold wings. They stood in ranks on a quadrangle at Pensacola, while an admiral came down the line and pinned the wings to each man's starched white blouse. They were commissioned as ensigns. Now they could properly call themselves naval aviators. It was an important milestone, but it was not the end of their training. In 1944, newly "winged" aviators would fly another three hundred to four hundred hours with an advanced carrier training group (ACTG) before being deployed to a frontline unit. Many were sent to Opa Locka Field, northwest of Miami, "an area of sand, scrub brush, and rattlesnakes under a blazing tropical sun."[46] They flew service-type planes—Hellcats, Helldivers, Corsairs—the same machines they would fly in combat. For the first time, they trained with veteran pilots recently back from the fleet. They practiced formation flying, gunnery, bombing, night flying, and overwater navigation. Dive bombing tactics were refined by dropping smoke bombs on a plywood bull's-eye deep in the heart of the Everglades. They were told not to use the radio except in dire circumstances—"Stay off the air!"—and learned an elaborate hand signaling system so that they could communicate using visual cues from cockpit to cockpit.

Most ACTG air group and squadron leaders were veterans of carrier operations in the Pacific. They knew the ordeals and challenges the rookies would face when deployed to the fleet. "We flew and flew and flew," said Hamilton McWhorter, a famous Hellcat ace who returned to the United States to lead a fighter squadron in Air Group Twelve, a full composite carrier group in training. "If my students were catching on, then we flew some more. And after they caught on, we flew some more anyway—lots of formation tactics, and air-to-air and air-to-ground gunnery, some instruments and night work, and, of course, dogfighting and the usual tail chases on the way back to the airfield."[47]

Air Group Twelve was stationed for several weeks at Naval Air Station Astoria, on the Oregon coast. Most mornings, the planes took off in "zero-zero" conditions: solid fog. They climbed through an opaque white gloom, peering ahead for a glimpse of the faint blue exhaust flames on the plane ahead. At 4,000 feet they emerged suddenly into a bright sunlit sky, with a carpet of white, fleecy clouds beneath them. That sort of flying could put gray hair on a young man's head, and it often did. But as McWhorter never tired of telling them, it was the kind of flying they would do in the Pacific war zones. There would be mornings when the carrier task force was wrapped in impenetrable murk. There would be days when the pilot would have to rely on his instruments or a homing beacon, because he could see nothing through his windshield. There would be late-afternoon flights when he would have to return at dusk, eyes peeled for a darkened flight deck, as his fuel needle bounced on empty. There would be flights when he was bone-weary, nodding off in the cockpit, and flights when he would have to find his way home in a shot-up airplane, perhaps while injured and bleeding. His training would give him the skills and instincts he needed to face those coming trials.

The young pilots often broke regulations, sometimes with the tacit approval of their leaders. "Flathatting"—flying very low to the ground—was prohibited by standing regulations, especially in populated civilian areas. But in wartime, especially, many aviators flouted the prohibition. Navy planes flying from NAS Corpus Christi flew low over the nearby King Ranch, driving herds of cattle, while the cowboys shook their fists. In Southern California, flathatting flyers flew ten or fifteen feet over beaches, or down the centerlines of highways, sometimes forcing motorists off the road. The rookies quickly adopted the after-hours habits of the more senior aviators, which meant heavy drinking and late nights at local bars and nightclubs. The dive-bomber pilot James W. Vernon did his advanced training at Naval Air Station Wildwood, near the southern end of the New Jersey shore. The experience was a blur of flying and partying in the nearby beach town, with the "phony exhilaration of booze, smoke-filled clubs, inane talk, sloppy dancing, clumsy caressing, tacky hotel rooms, empty late-night streets, roaring hangovers, and worries about VD. . . . It must have had something to do with hormones and peer group approval that made us squirm so pathetically in the sweaty grip of war."[48] He and his fellow pilots routinely slept only three or four hours before awakening to 0600 reveille. Breathing pure oxygen through their cockpit masks helped relieve the throbbing pain in their heads.

Venereal diseases hit the advanced pilot training squadrons especially hard. Medical authorities distributed films exhorting servicemen to practice safe sex. Bill Davis especially liked one entitled: "Flies Breed Germs, Keep Yours Closed." In it, a doctor informs a sailor that he has contracted venereal disease. "I must have gotten it in a public toilet," said the sailor. "That's a hell of a place to take a date," replied the doctor.[49]

In early 1945, as victory loomed, many young aviators in training squadrons were frantic to get into the war. They feared a sudden peace that would spoil their chances of flying in combat. The veterans told them that their zeal would fade after three or four weeks of continuous daily combat flying; the syndrome known as pilot fatigue was real and universal. Flying was a job; it was work. The cockpit was often an inhospitable place, too hot or too cold. A man forced to sit for hours grew cramped and uncomfortable. Flying required sustained concentration, and the mental strain took a toll. The persistent nearness of death ate away at their nerves. Even so, the most jaded pilot was occasionally reminded of why he had wanted to fly in the first place. For Samuel Hynes, one such moment came during a training flight at dusk, when the ground below fell into shadow: "The surface of the plane seemed to absorb and hold the light and color of the sunset; brightness surrounded me. It was as though the earth had died, and I alone was left alive. A sense of my own aliveness filled me. I would never die. I would go on flying forever."[50]

ON NEW YEAR'S DAY, 1945, the Third Fleet was back at sea again, northbound from Ulithi Atoll. Its mission was familiar—yet another round of carrier strikes on the archipelago of islands lying between Japan and the Philippines, this time in support of MacArthur's planned invasion of Luzon on January 9. The objective was to isolate the beachhead at Lingayen Gulf by disrupting the flow of air reinforcements from Japan into the combat zone. Photoreconnaissance planes would take thousands of high- and oblique-angle photographs of Okinawa, to be used in planning the forthcoming invasion of that island, to begin in three months' time.

On January 3 and 4, dirty weather made for abysmal visibility over Formosa, so Admiral McCain cancelled about half of the planned strikes on the island. Returning pilots described it as some of the worst flying weather they had ever encountered. Lieutenant William A. Bell, an air intelligence officer on the *Essex*, noted "sinister grey clouds as thick as pudding from 700 feet altitude to 10,000 feet, rain squalls everywhere, and a slate-colored, wind-whipped sea."[51] Operational losses were heavy; Task Force 38 lost twenty-eight planes on January 7 alone. But the airmen kept at it, bombing and strafing airfields on Formosa, Luzon, and the Pescadores Islands.[52]

Down in Lingayen Gulf, MacArthur's bombardment and minesweeping groups were fighting off waves of kamikazes, and the SWPA chief repeatedly urged Halsey to suppress the threat. Aerial photos exposed the source of the deadly attacks: the Japanese had gone to extraordinary lengths to camouflage their planes on the ground, concealing them under foliage and brush, and parking them miles away from the airfields. January 7, 8, and 9 were long, busy days for the carrier force, with pilots making as many as four "hops" each day, and flying audacious treetop-altitude search-and-strafing runs over central and northern Luzon.

Since taking command of the Third Fleet in August, Halsey had been hoping to lead a carrier raid into the South China Sea, west of the Philippines. He expected to find a wealth of high-value targets in harbors along the coasts of south China and Indochina (Vietnam). No Allied warships except submarines had dared enter those waters since December 1941, when the British battleships *Prince of Wales* and *Repulse* had been sunk by Japanese air attack off the coast of Malaya. In October and again in November 1944, Halsey had asked for permission to enter the South China Sea, but Nimitz and King had deemed it too risky. (Halsey was right when he said: "I am afraid that my superiors worried about my judgment in the presence of a juicy target."[53]) Now Halsey renewed the request. He was especially keen to destroy two older Japanese battleships, the *Ise* and *Hyuga*, believed to be at anchor in Camranh Bay, Indochina. Nimitz finally assented.

Late on January 9, the same day that MacArthur's troops went ashore on Luzon, Task Force 38 passed through the Bashi Channel, south of Formosa. This route took the great fleet only 80 miles south of Koshun Airfield, a major Japanese base in southern Formosa. At the same time, a logistics fleet, comprising thirty fleet oilers with escorting CVEs, destroyers, and ammunition ships, passed through the Balintang Channel, the second of the two main navigable passages through the chain of islands between Luzon and Formosa. Neither force was detected by the enemy. As the sun rose on January 10, the main striking force of the U.S. Navy was in the heart of the South China Sea, an enclosed body of water surrounded on all sides by enemy air and naval bases. The fleet's situation, Halsey later wrote, was "extremely ticklish," because Japanese planes could attack from any direction, or several directions simultaneously. Task Force 38 was amply capable of defending itself, but Halsey also had to worry about the vulnerable logistics fleet train. On the other hand, from this position the U.S. carriers could launch powerful airstrikes in any direction, hitting targets that had been untouchable for nearly three years.

After topping off fuel, the force began a high-speed overnight run toward the coast of Indochina. Halsey flashed a message to the aviators: "You know what to do. Give them hell. God bless you all. Halsey."[54] The next morning, more than a thousand carrier planes laid waste to targets between Camranh Bay and Saigon. They pulverized airfields, destroyed planes on the ground, knocked out bridges, derailed and overturned freight trains, bombed wharves, warehouses, and fuel dumps, and sank enemy ships at their moorings. A convoy of eleven unescorted Japanese merchantmen was caught in open water near Cap Saint-Jacques (Vung Tau), and all were sunk. No fighter planes rose to intercept the incoming strikes, and antiaircraft fire was negligible; it appears that the Japanese in the region were caught completely by surprise. Aerial photographs depicted a panorama of destruction along the coast—according to Lieutenant Bell's diary: "Flaming, smoking vessels everywhere you look. Sunken vessels, too, their masts and stacks jutting from the calm water. Or lying on their sides in death."[55] The *Ise* and *Hyuga* had left for Singapore two weeks earlier, but the day's score was good enough that Halsey did not mind. Local Free French agents later reported that the airstrikes sank forty-one ships of 127,000 tons, damaged twenty-eight ships of 70,000 tons, and turned the entire coast into "a shambles."[56]

This was the height of the northeast monsoon season, and the weather was turning ugly. The sky was hazy, the seas were rough, and a gale-force wind blew out of the north. After the ordeal of the typhoon three weeks earlier, Halsey and his subordinates were inclined to be cautious. As the task force withdrew from Indochina, it slowed to 16 knots in order to prevent storm damage. The destroyers were low on fuel, and would have to top off before the next round of strikes against the China coast. But fueling was downright dangerous in those conditions. Coming alongside the fleet oilers, the destroyers pitched like seesaws. Their bows reared up high, exposing thirty or forty feet of their keels—and then they crashed down into the troughs of the oncoming seas, their propellers exposed to view, ejecting sheets of spray, green water sloshing over their decks and pouring in jets through their scuppers. Drenched crewmen hung on like rodeo bull-riders. Watching the unnerving scene, Admiral Radford was thankful to be aboard a 27,500-ton fleet carrier. Lieutenant Bell, watching from the flight deck of the *Essex*, noted that the little ships rolled so far from side to side that "it seemed as if their masts, swaying like poplars in a gale, would dip into the turbulent water."[57]

Fueling operations continued throughout January 13 and into the morning of January 14, draining six fleet oilers of every last drop they carried, at which point all of Task Force 38 had been brought up to at least 60 percent fuel.

The next day, the force launched strikes against Hong Kong, Canton, Hainan Island, Amoy, and (again) Formosa. Over Hong Kong they encountered the heaviest antiaircraft fire that many veteran airmen had ever seen, with the multicolored bursts forming three solid layers between 3,000 and 15,000 feet. One pilot described the flak as ranging from "intense to unbelievable."[58] But it was another red-letter day for the attackers. They destroyed many tens of thousands of tons of shipping and laid waste to waterfront facilities, drydocks, piers, and oil refineries in Canton, Kowloon, and Stonecutters Island. The returning pilots claimed to have destroyed or derailed ten trains in Formosa. But plane losses that day were heavy—thirty in combat and thirty-one in operational accidents. A handful of errant American Hellcats mistakenly bombed and strafed ground targets in Macao, a colony of neutral Portugal. The Portuguese government lodged an angry protest in Washington, and the State Department offered a formal apology and restitution.[59]

On January 18, it seemed as if the weather were conspiring to keep the task force bottled up in the South China Sea. A low-pressure area was funneling through the Luzon Strait, and seas were rising. Halsey was not keen to take the Third Fleet through those narrow and confined waters in such conditions. He considered withdrawing to the east, through the interior waters of the Philippines—Mindoro Strait, the Sulu Sea, the Mindanao Sea, and Surigao Strait. It would be a high-speed transit of narrow seaways, the same route that Nishimura's Southern Force had taken during the Battle of Leyte Gulf two months earlier. The individual task groups would be obliged to use a special and unfamiliar cruising formation, and the risk of running aground would be high. The move would likely be discovered by the Japanese, and although enemy airpower in the region had been much reduced, the kamikaze threat could not be ignored. When Halsey proposed the idea to Nimitz, the CINCPAC nixed it, directing that the force remain in the South China Sea until the weather moderated.[60] The fleet exited by the Balintang Channel on January 20. Halsey's foray into the South China Sea had lasted eleven days, during which time the fleet had steamed 3,800 miles.

MacArthur's forces were safely ashore on Luzon, and driving south toward Manila. But the air attacks on the amphibious fleet in Lingayen Gulf had continued, and as usual the SWPA commander wanted more direct air support from the Third Fleet. January 21 was another long day of strikes against now-familiar targets on Formosa and the Ryukyus, but the Japanese air forces responded furiously, launching waves of counterattacks on the fleet. The Japanese planes approached unseen through the overcast skies, apparently tracking U.S. planes returning from the morning strike, and vanished into clouds when challenged by orbiting Hellcats. Between noon and one o'clock, many enemy planes descended through the cloud ceiling. One dropped a small bomb on the carrier *Langley*, and a kamikaze hit the destroyer *Maddox*, killing four of her crew. The *Hancock* was badly damaged when one of her own airplanes landed with a bomb that detonated, killing forty-eight sailors. Two kamikazes devastated the *Essex*-class carrier *Ticonderoga* (CV-14). Her signal bridge was destroyed, the flight deck was rendered inoperable, and the hangar deck was gutted by fire.[61] One hundred forty of her crew were killed, including many senior officers. The fires destroyed thirty-six planes, more than one-third of her complement. Lieutenant Bell, watching the floating inferno from the nearby *Essex*, noted in his diary: "This kamikaze business is the biggest story in the Pacific, but few people at home even suspect it. With a small number of planes manned by a small number of mad little savages, the Japs can seriously damage or sink as many surface ships as we have in combat. . . . In the kamikaze the Japs have the most effective secret weapon of the war. Certainly the most sinister and the most terrifying to contemplate."[62]

The Third Fleet's work was done, at least for this round. It had been at sea for twenty-eight consecutive days, steaming more than 12,000 miles. Its airplanes had destroyed 300,000 tons of Japanese shipping. On January 25, the task force was back in "the barn" at Ulithi. The lagoon anchorage was more crowded than ever before, including major elements of both the Third and Seventh Fleets. Admiral Spruance's flagship *Indianapolis* was present; he was scheduled to take command of the Third Fleet the following day. Spruance and an entourage of senior staff officers visited the *New Jersey* that evening to confer with Admiral Halsey. The two four-star admirals met alone for more than an hour in Halsey's flag cabin. Neither left a record of their conversation.

At midnight on January 26, command automatically passed from Halsey to Spruance. The Third Fleet became the Fifth Fleet, and Task Force 38 became, once again, Task Force 58. Admiral Mitscher returned as commander of Task Force 58, relieving McCain in that role. Halsey flew back to Pearl Harbor and then on to the United States for a long and well-deserved leave.

Chapter Ten

Lingayen Gulf, a horseshoe-shaped indentation on the northwest coast of Luzon, had provided the main entry point for the Japanese invasion in December 1941. Three years and three weeks later, history repeated itself, but on a far grander scale. The greatest invasion fleet yet assembled in the Pacific, comprising more than eight hundred combatant and transport ships, began arriving in the gulf on January 6, 1945. Its mission was to land the U.S. Sixth Army on Lingayen's southern beaches. "Sierra Day," the designated landing date, was set for January 9.

As new ships arrived, they maneuvered carefully through the congested roadstead, following channels marked by buoys to their preassigned "berths." Mountainous terrain framed the shoreline. To the east, darkly forested hills and ridges rose toward the craggy green peaks of the Cagayan Range. Crewmen on the warships and transports were on edge, for good reason. The fleet was too big, and the gulf too small, to allow for high-speed evasive maneuvering. Most ships were obliged to remain at anchor throughout the operation. They were close-packed and stationary. Japanese aerial attackers could disguise their approach by hugging the radar shadows cast by the rugged coastal topography. Radar operators kept their noses pressed to their scopes, antiaircraft gunners kept their eyes peeled, and carrier planes of the CAP circled protectively overhead. Smoke generators churned out a chemical haze that clung to the surface of the gulf, and even seemed to defy the breeze.

For the first time in the war, the Americans now encountered the fearsome *Shinyo* ("Ocean Shaker") suicide speedboats. These little wooden vessels sallied out from beaches along the western shore of Lingayen Gulf and bore in toward the fleet at high speed. After several American ships and landing craft took bad hits on the night of January 6, the 20mm machine gunners kept their fingers on their triggers and opened fire on anything they could not identify. From dusk to dawn, the shoreline was kept illuminated by starshells and searchlights. Suicidal Japanese swimmers even attempted to carry explosives to the hulls of American ships, concealing their approach by hiding under floating debris. Others disguised themselves as Filipino fishermen and approached the fleet in native canoes laden with hidden explosives. One such attack blew a hole in the side of a transport, killing several of her crew.

During the week-long passage from Leyte Gulf, the Allied invasion force had been hit by the worst kamikaze attacks of the war to date. The ordeal had commenced with a vicious strike on Vice Admiral Jesse Oldendorf's fire support group as it threaded narrow inshore channels west of Panay. At 5:12 p.m. on January 4, a lone Yokosuka P1Y ("Frances") bomber plunged through the cloud ceiling and buried itself in the deck of the CVE *Ommaney Bay*. The attack came so suddenly and unexpectedly that the antiaircraft gunners did not even have time to open fire. Two bombs pierced the jeep carrier's thin steel flight deck and exploded in her hangar. Fires raged out of control, engulfing the bomb and aerial torpedo storage lockers and setting off internal explosions. The little flattop was torn apart; ninety-three of her crew were killed. Survivors leapt into the sea and were picked up by escorting destroyers. The burning wreckage was scuttled in the Mindoro Strait.

Although the Americans did not yet know it, Japanese air strength in the Philippines was down to its last gasp. The 201st Air Group, headquartered at Mabalacat, could muster only about forty aircraft in flyable condition. Throughout all of the Philippines, there were probably no more than two hundred remaining planes. In the last week of December, the Imperial Headquarters had decreed that the Philippines would receive no further air reinforcements. The flight route north of the archipelago was no longer tenable. Since the Battle of Leyte Gulf, approximately three of every ten Japanese planes sent into the Philippines from Formosa or Japan had been lost in operational accidents, or shot down by Third Fleet carrier planes.[1] Now, by Tokyo's order, all remaining aircraft were to be launched against the American fleet in suicide attacks. Surviving personnel at the air bases would withdraw to the mountains and join up with Japanese army forces. Senior officers at the 201st Air Group headquarters would evacuate to Formosa by air, under cover of darkness. That last order was kept secret, for fear that the news would undercut morale among those to be left behind.

Airfields on Luzon were visited almost daily by U.S. bombers and strafing fighters. Unless parked well away from the airfields and hidden under camouflage nets or brush foliage, Japanese airplanes were quickly destroyed on the ground. The young, inexperienced kamikaze pilots were briefed to take off quickly, as soon as their planes were uncovered and pushed into position, and to climb to altitude before being intercepted by American fighters. They would need skill and good luck just to reach the enemy fleet, let alone to score in a diving attack on a ship. But there was never any shortage of volunteers to fly suicide missions. At Clark Field, where there were more pilots than flyable planes, young men mobbed their air commanders and begged to be chosen to fly. On the evening of January 5, only thirteen aircraft were available for the next day's strike, and thirteen pilots were chosen. Those who had been disappointed hunted among the grounded and disabled planes on the airfield, and "begged mechanics to put the best parts of condemned planes together into something that would fly."[2] After a gallant overnight effort by the ground crews, five derelicts were patched up to the extent that they could take off.

At dawn, a solemn departure ceremony was held on the edge of the airfield. The pilots took a cup of sake from a white linen-covered table and were saluted by their comrades before climbing into their cockpits and taking off for the last time.

Later that morning, as Oldendorf's 164-ship shore-bombardment group took position off Lingayen Gulf, kamikazes swarmed in from the east. Oldendorf's flagship, the Pearl Harbor survivor *California*, was hit on her starboard side near the mainmast; the blast killed 32 men and wounded dozens more. A plunging bomber hit the portside bridge of the battleship *New Mexico*, flagship to Rear Admiral George Weyler, and blew up in a tremendous ball of fire. Among the thirty men killed was the skipper, Captain Robert W. Fleming, and two prominent guests—Lieutenant General Herbert Lumsden of the British Army, and *Time* magazine correspondent William Henry Chickering. Admiral Sir Bruce Fraser, the highest-ranking British officer in the Pacific, was riding aboard the *New Mexico* as an observer; he survived the attack. Late that afternoon, a lone kamikaze flew through a storm of antiaircraft fire to strike the cruiser *Louisville*. The plane's two bombs detonated, igniting a fierce fire around Turret No. 2 and the pilot house. Rear

Admiral Theodore E. Chandler, commander of Cruiser Division 4, suffered grievous burns and died the next day. When the headless, naked body of the kamikaze pilot was recovered, the *Louisville*'s damage control party simply heaved it over the side.

In the five days before the first amphibious landings in Lingayen Gulf, kamikazes struck or near-missed thirty Allied vessels. Three warships were destroyed, fourteen heavily damaged, and thirteen lightly damaged. A witness on the attack transport *Doyen* described a "grotesque-looking procession" of ships with smashed superstructures and "blackened and torn spaces that had once been gun turrets."[3] General MacArthur, riding on the cruiser *Boise*, personally witnessed several attacks that might easily have killed him. Brusquely refusing all suggestions to take cover below, he watched the action from the rail of the quarterdeck while coolly puffing on his pipe. In his memoir, he described a "blazing barrage of antiaircraft fire as every ship opened in a deafening blast of flak."[4]

On January 7, in response to urgent requests from Kinkaid and MacArthur, Halsey threw his "Big Blue Blanket" over Luzon. The carrier airmen returned to their ships with claims of at least seventy-five Japanese planes destroyed on the ground. In the following days, mercifully, the kamikaze threat abated significantly.

The command roster for the Luzon invasion was much the same as it had been for the Leyte operation. General Krueger remained in command of the Sixth Army, consisting of two army corps of two divisions each—I Corps under Major General Innis P. Swift (the 6th and 43rd Divisions), and XIV Corps under Lieutenant General Oscar W. Griswold (the 37th and 40th Divisions). A fifth division, the 25th, was to be kept in "floating reserve" offshore. Admiral Kinkaid's Seventh Fleet would blockade Manila and Subic Bay and protect the long seaborne supply line. General Kenney remained in charge of the Fifth and Thirteenth Air Forces. His USAAF fighters and bombers would fly into Clark Field and other Luzon airfields as soon as they were secured. The Eighth Army, still under General Eichelberger, would employ deceptive measures in hopes of convincing the Japanese that the main landings would occur in southern Luzon. On "S-Day," Krueger's four assault divisions would land abreast on a 20-mile-wide beachhead at the foot of Lingayen Gulf, then drive inland to take control of the Luzon Central Plain. I Corps, on the left, would keep Japanese forces bottled up in the Cagayan Mountains, while XIV Corps raced south to descend on

Manila. Later, an Eighth Army force would land on the island's south coast. The Sixth and Eighth Armies would envelop Manila and its bay in a pincer movement. If all went as planned, the bulk of Japanese ground forces would be isolated in the island's mountainous north, cut off from the capital and other Japanese army detachments to the south.

On the night before the landings, the bombardment flotilla put on a pyrotechnic extravaganza as they showered the beaches with heavy naval shells. In a letter to his wife, James Orville Raines of the destroyer *Howorth* described the projectiles as they raced into shore on their long, high-arching trajectories. "You know, they seem to travel very slowly when you watch them. They seem to float across the sky like slowly falling stars. We were shooting seven miles and between were layers of clouds and smoke. I stood on the wing of the bridge and watched the red balls disappear and reappear in and out of the layers. It was so far away, I could see only a very few tiny red flashes when they hit."[5] Fire was directed against suspected Japanese shore positions along the entire shoreline of Lingayen Gulf, especially on the designated landing beaches at the lower bend of the horseshoe, around the towns of Lingayen, Dagupan, Mabilao, and San Fabian. There was little counterfire from enemy shore batteries, and none at all from the vicinity of the southern landing beaches. In the town of Lingayen, at dawn, a crowd of civilian Filipinos was seen marching under an American flag. After surveying the scene through binoculars, Oldendorf ordered that fire be shifted away from that area.

As the assault troops descended the rope nets into their landing boats, the weather was calm and mild, with light breezes, scattered clouds, and barely any swell in the gulf's enclosed waters. Crux, the Southern Cross, hovered directly over the landing beaches, which were shrouded in a low haze. The boats milled around the transport zone, engines rumbling in idle, while awaiting the signal to land. A few *Shinyo* speedboats made desperate runs from the western shore, but all were destroyed or driven away before they could strike home.

At 9:30 a.m., the first wave was away. More than 1,000 landing craft motored in toward the beaches, their long wakes carving parallel white lines. By 9:40, nearly 20,000 troops were ashore; by noon, 68,000. They stormed ashore along a 12-mile stretch of beaches at the southern end of the gulf, adjacent to the towns of Lingayen, Dugupan, and Mabilao. The beach was wide and continuous, large enough to accommodate two full army corps (four infantry divisions abreast) and the gigantic amount of heavy equipment, vehicles, weaponry, and supplies scheduled to come ashore in a matter of hours. Resistance was scant. Joyful Filipinos greeted them with handshakes and kisses. Japanese defenses were concentrated along the eastern part of the gulf, where General Masaharu Homma's invasion force had landed three years earlier. On the right flank of the American lines, the 40th Division met no enemy opposition at all: no artillery, no mortars, no small arms fire, and no Japanese to be seen. Advancing patrols found a few pillboxes and blockhouses, and inspected them cautiously—but not a single enemy soldier was to be found. The division moved inland and captured a working airstrip in Lingayen.

To the east, the 6th Division landed on Blue Beaches 1 and 2 near Mangaldan, while the 43rd Division landed on White Beaches 1, 2, and 3 near San Fabian. They took some desultory long-range artillery and mortar fire from Japanese positions in hills to the east, above San Fabian. This fire was an irritant rather than a threat; it was not heavy or accurate enough to inflict heavy casualties, but cargo unloading was diverted farther down the coast to the west. Among the handful of casualties was a soldier who had been knocked down by a stampeding water buffalo.[6]

General MacArthur went ashore at noon, trailing an entourage of staff officers, war correspondents, and photographers. His barge motored toward the center of the beachhead, where the engineers had rigged a temporary pier by anchoring a pair of pontoon barges into the sand. The helmsman intended to go alongside this pier, but veered away at MacArthur's signal. The general instead disembarked in knee-deep surf and waded ashore. This ritual had become something of a trademark. Now, as at Leyte and Mindoro, the event was documented by photographers. In his familiar field marshal's cap and aviator sunglasses, MacArthur walked erect and unflinching, even when a lone Zero flew low overhead. He watched in approval as the enemy plane was destroyed in a "solid wall" of antiaircraft fire.[7]

Northeast of the beachhead, in the I Corps sector, advance patrols of the 43rd Division ran into stiff artillery and mortar fire coming from the hills and ridges above the towns of Damortis and San Fernando. General Swift's I Corps headquarters ordered the division to drive inland and seize these grassy heights. One regiment was assigned the job of clearing Hill 470, directly east, while another seized the ridgeline above Mabilao. Other elements of the force were put "on wheels" to drive up the coastal road. Japanese field artillery and mortars took a steady toll of casualties throughout the afternoon, but the invaders encountered only scattered infantry resistance on the ground. By sunset on January 9, the Americans had expanded the beachhead by 4 miles up the coast, to San Jacinto and Binday.

On the second and third day of the invasion, the 43rd Division launched probing attacks up the valley roads east of San Fabian and Damortis, and along the ridgeline running south to Rosario and the Cabaruan Hills. Everywhere in this sector, the invaders encountered stiffening Japanese resistance on the roads leading into the mountains. Intelligence had revealed that the senior Japanese army commander on the island, General Tomoyuki Yamashita, had established his headquarters in the resort town of Baguio, about 20 miles inland, high in the Cagayan Mountains. The mountain roads were defended by strongly entrenched and well-camouflaged firing positions, caves, and mines. The Americans hit back with heavy artillery, naval call fire, and airstrikes, but the Japanese would not be dislodged except by a concerted attack into that treacherous high ground. It was not to be. Manila, MacArthur's prime objective, lay in the other direction. According to the boss's playbook, the main thrust was to the south, into the heart of the Luzon Central Plain and on to the capital. Therefore, General Krueger could do nothing but reinforce his left-flank lines and hope that the Japanese were not preparing an armored counterattack from the mountainous region to the northeast.

By the third day of the operation, the Sixth Army's beachhead was 20 miles long and 5–7 miles deep, encompassing the entire southern base of the gulf. The equivalent of about fifteen army divisions was on the island, arrayed in lines stretching about 30 miles in length. The placid beaches of Lingayen had been converted into a ship-to-shore depot with the cargo-handling capacity of a large urban seaport. LSTs had nosed onto the beach and opened their clamshell bow doors, and were unloading bulk cargo at an industrial pace. Fully loaded trucks, tractors, and jeeps were driving ashore over pontoon causeways. The beachhead was a teeming maze of stacked crates, fuel drums, parked vehicles, tent cities, and antiaircraft batteries ringed by sandbags. Cantankerous navy beachmasters shouted through bullhorns. Lingayen was to be the only seaport under U.S. control until Manila Bay itself was captured and opened to Allied ship traffic.

The once-pristine cerulean waters of Lingayen Gulf were stained by the accumulated effluent of eight hundred ships. Garbage and debris littered the sea and shore. Distended corpses, nearly all Japanese, floated among the anchored transports. Periodically, cleanup details on garbage scows gathered up the debris and enemy dead and burned it all together on the beach.

Inland of the XIV Corps sector was a lush wetland, crisscrossed by streams and dotted with commercial fish ponds. This sodden terrain presented logistical and engineering difficulties. Around Lingayen town, large sand dunes proved impassable for wheeled vehicles, so bulldozers were pressed into service to clear a level road. Most of the bridges in the area had been destroyed—either by the enemy, friendly Filipino partisans, or U.S. bombing and bombardment. Columns of soldiers waded across streams with their rifles held above their heads. Amphibian tractors were put to work as ferries, crossing swollen streams that were too deep to ford. Engineers built timber bridges to span the deeper crossings. Once properly anchored, they could support the weight of thousands of men, trucks, and tanks. Twenty miles of railroad track on the Damoritas-Rosario line was torn up, and the roadbed was converted into a highway for heavy equipment. On D plus 3, advance patrols reached the Agno River, the first major natural barrier on the army's route of advance. The engineers quickly assembled two modular steel frame bridges that would support 35 tons of weight.

The route to Manila led through the heart of the Luzon Central Plain, a flat, fertile region of rice paddies, pasturelands, and canefields, watered by a network of streams and irrigation ditches. Enclosed by mountains on either side, it was about 120 miles long from north to south, ranging between 30 and 50 miles wide. It was one of the most productive agricultural regions of the Philippines, dotted with grand plantation houses and little market villages with stone churches overlooking Spanish plazas. It had the best-developed road net in the Philippines, including a two-lane macadam highway intersecting every mile or so with gravel roads running east and west, and two railroad trunk lines. It was a placid, bucolic landscape, bursting with many shades of green: alternating meadows of cogon grass and sunken rice fields, serpentine streambeds flanked by groves of durian and mangosteen trees, elevated huts on riverbanks, thatched with dun-colored nipa palms; grazing black *carabao* water buffalos, some with white herons perched on their backs; and bamboo-framed sheds with rusty corrugated tin roofs, garlanded with hibiscus and bougainvillea.

At first, the Japanese army offered only token resistance in the low country. Small units armed with light weapons and artillery fired on American scouting parties, then withdrew farther south or east up into the hills. These interim firing positions were set up in irrigation ditches or in clusters of plantation buildings improved with banks of sandbags. Firefights were brief and spasmodic, and they barely affected the tempo of the offensive. Anxious to keep the Sixth Army's lines stitched up in a single wide front, General Krueger grew concerned at the headlong pace set by Griswold's XIV Corps in its race toward the capital. Swift's I Corps had the job of defending the army's left flank, by keeping Japanese troop concentrations bottled up in the mountains to the northeast. But that meant that Swift had to match Griswold's pace of advance—and that was proving difficult, because there were not many Japanese standing in XIV Corps's way. The 37th Division tore down the Lingayen-Bayambang Road, meeting no one but throngs of ebullient Filipino civilians, while the 40th Division thundered south along Highway No. 13, which ran parallel about 10 miles to the west. Progress in the I Corps zone was stymied by stiffer Japanese defenses on the Damortis-Rosario road, where 43rd Division engineers were laboring to clear roads and build bridges while under intense artillery fire—and in the Cabaruan Hills, where the 6th Division ran into heavy fire from well-entrenched positions on a soaring promontory. Eyeing the risk of a Japanese counterattack on his elongated lines, Krueger deployed his reserve force, the 25th Division (less one regiment), to reinforce the 43rd Division.

MacArthur had set up his initial headquarters at Dagupan on Lingayen Gulf, but he spent most of his days on or near the front lines. His jeep drove along long columns of marching soldiers, and soldiers did double-takes as they glimpsed the familiar figure wearing the field marshal's cap and aviator sunglasses. No fixed timetable had been agreed for the advance, but MacArthur was eager to take Manila as early as possible, partly because he was mindful of the dangers to American prisoners of war and civilian internees held in camps in the city limits. He suspected that Krueger's concerns about the danger of a counterattack were overblown. On January 12, at a conference of senior commanders on the *Boise*, still anchored in Lingayen Gulf, MacArthur pressed his Sixth Army chief to speed the advance toward Manila. If XIV Corps was not suffering heavy losses, it should move faster. He interrogated Krueger: "Where are your casualties? Where are they?"[8] MacArthur insisted on an early capture of the big airbase that the Japanese called Mabalacat—and the Americans still called Clark Field—so that the Fifth Air Force could begin operating heavy bombers on

Luzon. But Krueger remained wary of an armored counterattack from the mountainous northeast, maintaining that "I considered that a precipitate advance toward Manila would probably expose [XIV Corps] to a reverse, and would in any case cause it to outrun its supply—a serious matter, since all bridges had been destroyed."[9]

GENERAL YAMASHITA WAS PESSIMISTIC. The U.S. submarine and air cordon had effectively severed links between Japan and the Philippines, so he could count on no further supplies or reinforcements. He had expected MacArthur to land at Lingayen Gulf, but he had not expected the landings to come so soon. Yamashita had been forced against his will to send his best troops by sea to die on Leyte Island. He still had impressive numbers under his command—about 270,000 Japanese troops and other military personnel were on Luzon—but his forces were scattered widely and fragmented into various and overlapping army and naval commands. The bulk of Japanese ground forces on Luzon were immobilized in defensive pockets in three widely separated mountain ranges. Transportation links were crippled by shortages of vehicles, rolling stock, and fuel—and the situation was exacerbated by Filipino guerilla attacks and sabotage operations against roads, vehicles, and railways. It was only a matter of time before the greater part of the Japanese army would be reduced to semiautonomous conditions, with small units roaming around the country and foraging in the jungles for whatever they could find to eat.

Under these dire circumstances, Yamashita was forced to adopt a static defense. His objective was to hold out for as long as possible, to slow the tide of American conquest as it washed toward the homeland. But Luzon and Manila would sooner or later fall to the invader, no matter what he did, and he knew it.

The largest Japanese troop concentration, the "*Shobo* Group," numbering 152,000 men, was in the Cagayan Mountains, northeast of Lingayen Gulf. General Yamashita commanded it directly from his headquarters at Baguio, a resort town located 5,000 feet above sea level. A second group occupied Clark Field, north of Manila, with detachments on Bataan and Corregidor. A third, numbering about 80,000, was entrenched in mountains east of Manila. Smaller detachments were scattered in outlying areas. Yamashita rejected proposals to counterattack MacArthur's forces in the plains west of the Agno River, reasoning that the attacking columns would be destroyed by superior U.S. artillery and airpower. Instead, he deployed his forces to plug all feasible invasion routes into the Cagayan Mountains. Local commanders elsewhere were told to establish defensive positions in high ground in hopes of "containing the main body of the American forces on Luzon and destroying its fighting strength, and at the same time, [to] prepare for protracted resistance on an independent, self-sufficient basis."

That left the road to Manila wide open, but Yamashita did not intend to defend the city or its bay. He directed that some 65,000 to 70,000 metric tons of supplies, stockpiled on the Manila waterfront, should be moved to caches in the mountains, where they could supply existing Japanese detachments. After this transfer was completed, the remaining garrison force was to evacuate Manila and withdraw into the more defensible high country east of the city. That was the plan.

As I Corps pushed south and east during the second week of the campaign, the terrain continued to favor the defenders. Japanese artillery was positioned in caves in the sides of hills and ridges, cunningly positioned to keep the advancing columns under enfilade fire from several angles. In towns and road junctions, the Japanese had dug shallow trenches and set up banks of sandbags to protect their machine and antitank guns. In some places, they had buried medium tanks up to their turrets, converting them into fixed artillery emplacements. The Japanese fought with their habitual tenacity, and hard fighting was required to take these positions. The 25th Division encountered fierce resistance in the village of San Manuel, where the Japanese Seventh Tank Regiment launched several armored counterattacks. After two weeks of bloody fighting, the Americans finally took the town and cleaned out the remaining enemy.

MacArthur moved his headquarters down to a sugar refinery in San Miguel, near Tarlac, about 75 miles north of Manila. From there, near the front lines, he continued to press his field commanders to speed the pace of the campaign. On January 17, he ordered Krueger to attack Clark Field. Krueger relayed the order to General Griswold, whose XIV Corps had enough running room to reach and cross the Bamban River on January 23. But the following day, Griswold's forces ran into an entrenched defensive line north of Fort Stoltenberg, where the ominous shape of Mount Arayat, an inactive volcano, loomed over the plain to the east. Admiral Takijirō Onishi had personally directed the construction of a series of concentric defensive lines around Clark Field. His forces had dug trenches and tank traps; they had extracted machine guns from wrecked planes and transferred them into firing nests; they had set up strong points overlooking Highway No. 3 as it climbed into the foothills to the west.[10] On January 27, the 37th Division smashed through the Japanese lines with a tank and infantry attack and captured the airbase, while the 40th Division fought to take out one pillbox and cave at a time in the difficult terrain north and west of Fort Stoltenberg. Retreating Japanese troops left behind a wealth of provisions, supplies, and weaponry. In a communiqué dated January 29, MacArthur enumerated the captured assets, including "200 new aircraft engines, many radio transmitters and receivers, great quantities of miscellaneous equipment, several months' stores of ammunition, food and equipment, and over 40 artillery pieces of various calibers."[11]

Filipino guerillas had alerted MacArthur's headquarters to the existence of a POW camp at Cabanatuan, about 60 miles north of Manila. Several hundred American prisoners were being held there in a barbed-wire stockade. In aerial reconnaissance photographs, the facility appeared to be only lightly guarded. MacArthur authorized a rescue operation. The mission was assigned to the 6th Army's Ranger Battalion. An Alamo Scouts team was sent on a 14-mile overland trek, traveling light—rifles, BARs, grenades— with orders to conceal themselves in the jungle. The camp guards had withdrawn from the scene, leaving the prisoners alone, but hundreds of other Japanese troops were encamped in the area. At 8:00 p.m. on the night of January 30, the scouts staged a surprise attack on the Japanese camp and quickly killed over two hundred enemy, losing only two rangers killed and one wounded.

Assuming that they were about to be slaughtered by the Japanese, many of the POWS at Cabanatuan were too shocked to celebrate. Their evacuation required traveling nearly 10 miles over open country. Many of the prisoners were too weak or sick to walk, and were loaded into carts pulled by water buffalos. The rangers and 512 liberated POWs returned to American lines on January 31. The former prisoners were placed in care of a 1st Cavalry field hospital that had been set up in a Filipino schoolhouse. Many seemed timid or self-conscious, and flinched when doctors, nurses, or war correspondents tried to engage them in conversation. They ate heartily and gained weight quickly. But their full recovery, physical and psychological, would take time.

To the south, elements of General Eichelberger's Eighth Army were getting into the fight. On January 29, an amphibious force designated the XI Corps went ashore on the Zambales coast, north of Subic Bay. The landing encountered no opposition, either on the beaches or during its initial inland advance. At Zigzag Pass on Highway No. 7, the Japanese finally made a stand against this new prong of the American offensive. After several days of heavy fighting, the road was cleared and opened. XI Corps poured through the pass and secured the area north of Manila Bay, sealing off the route into the Bataan Peninsula. South of Manila, meanwhile, two regiments of the 11th Airborne Division landed unopposed at Nasugbu and seized a strategic bridge before the Japanese could destroy it. A third regiment, the 511th Parachute, parachuted onto Tagaytay Ridge on the north shore of Lake Taal. The 11th Airborne took control of the southern part of Manila Bay and began advancing north through the capital's southern suburbs. The force encountered only token Japanese resistance until reaching the town of Imus on February 3. There, a small but determined party of Japanese in a stone building carried on a daylong firefight. Finally a sergeant scaled the building and poured gasoline down through the roof, and then ignited it with a phosphorus grenade. Most of the Japanese were killed; those who attempted to escape the burning building were gunned down as they emerged.

To the north, MacArthur continued to hector Krueger to pick up the pace. His long motorcade of jeeps was often seen racing ahead to the front lines, where he toured advanced positions and conferred with division and regimental commanders. On January 30, after visiting the 37th Division on the road between San Fernando and Calumpit, MacArthur radioed his Sixth Army chief to complain of a "noticeable lack of drive and aggressive initiative."[12] He predicted that an early attack on Manila would surprise the Japanese forces in the city, prompting them to evacuate in haste. In the best-case scenario, the Japanese would declare the capital an open city—as he, MacArthur, had done in December 1941. He was concerned about the fate of thousands of American and Allied prisoners of war and civilian internees in camps at Santo Tomas University, Bilibid Prison, and Los Banos. In December, at a POW camp on the long narrow island of Palawan, Japanese guards had herded 150 starving prisoners into trenches and burned them alive. MacArthur was understandably anxious to prevent more such enormities. The issue was not abstract; he personally knew many of the military

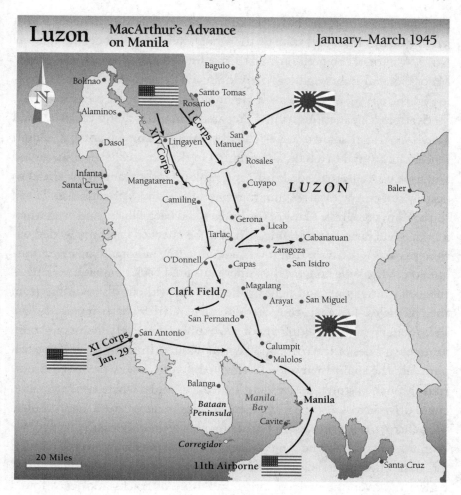

Luzon MacArthur's Advance on Manila — January–March 1945

and civilian prisoners in and around Manila. At the new SWPA headquarters in Tarlac, General Dick Sutherland made sure that the war correspondents knew where he and the boss stood on the matter. In off-the-record remarks, Sutherland panned Krueger's cautious attitude, and added: "If I were commanding the Sixth Army, we'd be in Manila right now."[13]

With Clark Field and Fort Stotsenburg in American hands, XIV Corps gathered its strength for the final push into the capital. The reserve 1st Cavalry Division, under Major General Verne D. Mudge, was landed in Lingayen Gulf and trucked south to the front lines, where it would form one of two prongs of XIV Corps's southern offensive. In a morning visit to Mudge's command tent in the town of Guimba on January 30, General MacArthur said he expected the "1st Cav" to move quickly: "Go to Manila, go around

the Nips, bounce off the Nips, but go to Manila." Plentifully supplied with
jeeps, trucks, tanks, and trailers, the whole division rolled down Highway
No. 5. A spirit of competition fired their spirits. Mudge was eager to outpace
Major General Bob Beightler's 37th Infantry Division, which was converging on the city along the route of Highway No. 3 to the west.

Scattered Japanese units had prepared ambushes along the road, and
a few American soldiers were felled by snipers. The advancing column
repeatedly ground to a halt, as personnel in the exposed jeeps dismounted
and took cover in roadside brush, and tank-infantry teams went ahead to
destroy the enemy or drive him to retreat. Rivers and streams also slowed
the column's progress. Many of the bridges had been blown, and even when
a bridge had been left standing, it had to be checked carefully by demolitions experts to confirm that it was not mined. When small Japanese units
fired on the passing convoy, the Americans fired back in greater volume—
rifles, machine guns, and light artillery, often without dismounting from
their vehicles. *Life* magazine correspondent Carl Mydans reported: "We
shot them up with racketing fire of everything from everyone in our train,
firing both sides of the road, and kept moving."[14] In many places, the column left the main highway and traveled by dirt roads, or blazed a new
trail through pasturelands. Scouts looked for "fords" where heavy vehicles
could drive across a stream. Long cavalcades of jeeps, trucks, and trailers
drove across, with brown water surging above their axles and sometimes
even their hoods. At the Angat River, the water was found to be too high
for most wheeled vehicles. The problem was solved by creating "trains,"
with a tank serving as locomotive and a file of trucks and jeeps towed
behind. Afterward, the vehicles had to pause for an hour as their engines
dried in the sun.

As American forces passed through villages, they were greeted by
crowds of jubilant Filipino civilians. Barefoot boys ran alongside the jeeps
and trucks, arms held above their heads in triumph. Men held their hats
above their heads and wept with joy. American flags were already flying
above houses and public buildings. Filipino guerilla units were drawn up in
ranks under American and Philippine colors. In the little city of Baliuag,
recalled Bill Dunn, the 1st Cavalry Division was met by thousands of Filipinos "who thronged the streets, screaming, singing, and dancing around
our column, oblivious to danger, until it became almost impossible to move.
In the heart of the city our jeep finally was completely surrounded and we

were forced to stop. As soon as we did, women and children threw flowers at us and fought to touch our hands, and the same was true of every vehicle in the column."[15] The Americans were offered fruit, fish, eggs, and roasted yams. Two young Filipinos had climbed to the top of the church tower and were pounding the bell with stones. General Mudge's "flying column" was brought to a complete halt while local police and troops worked to move the crowds out of the streets so that the advance could resume.

Anticipating the problems of sanitation and drinking water for the city of nearly one million inhabitants, the U.S. commanders took steps to secure Manila's water supply. XIV Corps was ordered to seize the vital reservoirs, dams, and aqueducts on the city's northern outskirts—the Novaliches Dam, the Marikina Dam, the Balara Water Filters, and the San Juan Reservoir. U.S. commanders also intended to secure the major electrical power installations, including the steam power plant on Provisor Island in the Pasig River.

On February 3, the 1st Cav reached Novaliches, on the north bank of the Tullahan River. An advance squadron reached the main bridge crossing just as the Japanese were preparing to dynamite it. In the midst of a fierce firefight, a navy lieutenant and demolitions specialist rushed out onto the bridge to cut away the burning fuse. That intrepid action saved the bridge, gaining at least a day for the advance. Once across the river, the division encountered very little resistance at all. Later that afternoon, the cavalrymen met the 37th Division at the junction with Highway No. 3 and joined forces. The combined force crossed into the Manila city limits on February 4.

Three battalions moved to surround Santo Tomas University, whose walled campus had been converted into an internment camp for some 4,000 American and other Western civilians, including the U.S. Army nurses known as the "Angels of Bataan." A Sherman tank smashed through the front gates and led an infantry battalion into the grounds. The Japanese guards, under the command of Lieutenant Colonel Toshio Hayashi, were not inclined to put up a fight. After a few shots were exchanged, Hayashi signaled that he was willing to release most of the internees. More than 3,000 liberated Western civilians, emaciated but elated, began streaming out of the gates. But Hayashi had ordered the remaining 221 internees into a single large building near the center of the campus, intending to hold them as hostages and to bargain for their lives. Fearing a massacre, the U.S. commanders offered a ceasefire and parley. Hayashi agreed to free the internees in exchange for a guarantee of safe conduct to Japanese lines. In a scene that was not repeated at any other point in the Pacific War, Hayashi led his prison guards out of the building and through the university's main gates, directly past the glowering stares of thousands of American soldiers. Civilian internees hurled verbal abuse at the Japanese as they marched. "Small bands of men and women followed them through the encampment jeering and hooting—the women loudest of all—until the Japanese plodded out of the camp and the gates clanged shut."[16] But the contract was honored. No shots were fired on either side, and Hayashi's men were permitted to head south, where they would join the main concentrations of Japanese ground forces. As they parted ways with the Americans, each Japanese officer and soldier either saluted or bowed.[17]

General MacArthur visited Santo Tomas later that afternoon. He was mobbed by a grateful, tearful crowd. They pressed toward him from all directions. He greeted those he knew by name. Some of the younger children, having spent three years in the camp, remembered little of their prewar lives. "One man threw his arms around me, and put his head on my chest and cried unashamedly," MacArthur recalled. "It was a wonderful and never to be forgotten moment—to be a life-saver, not a life-taker."[18] As the prisoners were interviewed, the stories they told vindicated MacArthur's insistence upon speed in liberating the camps. The food allocations to the prisoners had declined sharply in the past month, and many were verging on starvation. If the liberators had arrived thirty days later, said Bill Dunn, the CBS radio correspondent, "the results might have been completely tragic."[19]

As American forces advanced into the built-up districts of northern Manila, an ominous pall of smoke hung over the city. Retreating Japanese units had started more than a hundred fires in the northern business and commercial districts. Lacking tools to do the job properly, they did it like two-bit arsonists, with gunny sacks, matches, and 5-gallon cans of gasoline. Entire city blocks were gutted by fire. On the bayfront to the west was the densely populated residential neighborhood known as the Tondo, where the close-built wood-frame stucco houses burned like tinder. The XIV Corps report noted, "the smoke and the dust were so intense, and the heat from burning structures so terrible, that little progress could be made."[20] Forlorn refugees streamed north on the major boulevards, passing the American soldiers headed in the opposite direction: young mothers carrying babies, families with belongings piled into pony carts, children begging the American soldiers for food or cigarettes. Looters were hard at work stripping everything valuable from the ruins of burnt-out buildings and houses abandoned by their owners.

General Griswold sent the 2nd Squadron, 5th Cavalry to secure control of the Quezon Bridge, the last remaining bridge spanning the Pasig River, which ran through the heart of Manila. But at the intersection of Quezon Boulevard and Azcarraga Street, between the large edifices of Old Bilibid Prison and Far Eastern University, the Americans came under heavy machine gun and antitank gunfire. The squadron was pinned down in a deadly crossfire from several directions, including windows on upper floors of the university, a sandbag emplacement on the street to the south, and an improvised battlement comprising four derelict trucks wired together and guarded by steel spikes pounded into the pavement. The Americans retreated quickly, intending to return with reinforcements. Meanwhile, other units of the 1st Cavalry Division cleared out the streets and alleys to the east, along the north bank of the Pasig, and occupied Malacañang Palace.

In the Tondo District, advancing patrols came upon hideous scenes of civilian massacres. Hobert D. Mason of the Medical Corps discovered forty-nine bodies strewn across the floor of a cigarette factory, including many women and children as young as two years old. Their wrists had been tied tightly behind their backs. Most had been butchered by bayonets and samurai swords.[21] Nearby, at the Dy-Pac Lumber Yard, U.S. soldiers counted 115 murdered civilians. Children and even infants had been beheaded. In a sworn affidavit provided to war crimes investigators, Major David V. Binkley described what he took to be a mother who had tried to save her two children: "A woman lay face down with an arm around each child. This woman had been slashed to death by a sabre-like weapon. One child had part of its skull sliced off."[22]

Filipino guerillas, who could move freely through the streets disguised as ordinary *Manileños*, had risen up as U.S. forces approached the city. They had ambushed Japanese units, sabotaged equipment, blown up trucks and railcars, cut phone lines, and transmitted valuable intelligence to the invading army, right down to the locations of individual pillboxes, armories, and mines. Guerilla bands brazenly radioed information from Manila to MacArthur's headquarters, often in plain English. The Japanese intercepted these broadcasts, but they could rarely pinpoint their origin. In China, Manchu-

ria, Malaya, and elsewhere, the Japanese army had summarily wiped out
entire communities suspected of aiding guerilla or enemy forces, a practice known as *Genju Shobun* ("Harsh Disposal") or *Genchi Shobun* ("Local
Disposal"). For more than three years, Japanese forces in the Philippines
had given proof of their capacity for wanton violence and sadism directed
against innocents. But the stinging humiliation of defeat, combined with
signs of jubilation among ordinary Filipinos, incited an unprecedented
series of savage reprisals.

Scattered and intermittent firefights continued in pockets of north
Manila, and the rattle of machine gun fire could be heard here and there,
but by February 6 it was evident that the Japanese were only fighting delaying actions to cover their withdrawal south of the river. U.S. tanks and
infantry units worked to clear each barrio of enemy, block by block and
even house by house. That afternoon, the Americans resumed their drive
on the Quezon Bridge, this time with tanks and heavy artillery support.
The Japanese staged a fighting retreat across the bridge and then blew it up.
This development brought the 1st Cav up short. With no remaining bridges
spanning the Pasig, they had no means of driving trucks and tanks directly
across the river. The advance would have to pause until a new plan could
be devised.

Meanwhile, a thousand U.S. and Allied POWs were liberated from Bilibid Prison, including many troops captured on Bataan and Corregidor in
1942. MacArthur was there to meet the prisoners as they exited the compound. "As I passed slowly down the scrawny, suffering column, a murmur
accompanied me as each man barely speaking above a whisper, said, 'You're
back,' or 'You made it,' or 'God bless you.' I could only reply, 'I'm a little late,
but we finally came.'"[23]

To the south, the 11th Airborne Division had seized Nichols Field and
was advancing into the city's southern precincts. Manila was bracketed by
superior forces to both north and south, and on both sides the invaders had
arrived within the city limits while encountering only scattered resistance.
XIV Corps had thundered into Manila with orders to liberate Allied prisoners of war and civilian internees before they could be harmed, and to
secure the city's water system. The two divisions had completed both missions with commendable speed and efficiency.

Suddenly in possession of the entire city north of the Pasig, General
Griswold had no clear idea of how many enemy troops remained on the

opposite bank, or whether they intended to put up a last-ditch fight. At this uncertain moment, General MacArthur decided to declare victory. His headquarters, still located well north of the city in San Miguel, issued a statement implying that the fight for Manila was in its closing phase: "Our forces are rapidly clearing the enemy from Manila. Our converging columns . . . entered the city and surrounded the Jap defenders. Their complete destruction is imminent."[24] Across the world, the following day, newspapers heralded the triumphant recapture of Manila. MacArthur's staff began planning a victory parade through the heart of the city. In fact, another month of hard fighting lay ahead.

Subordinate field commanders were irked by the rash announcement. This was not the first time that MacArthur's press operation had jumped the gun. In his diary, Griswold recorded his view that MacArthur was "publicity crazy." Eichelberger, more tactfully, called the announcement "ill advised." Men who had yet to fight the largest and fiercest urban battle of the Pacific War did not like to be told that they were only "mopping up."[25]

MANILA WAS A CONTRAST of old and new, rich and poor, grand and humble, Asian and European. Many rated it as the most beautiful city in Asia. It was a college town, with more than a dozen secular and Catholic universities. Its many modern hospitals provided the best medical care in Asia. Before the Japanese invasion, it had been a banking and commercial hub, where leading international firms had maintained major offices. It had broad boulevards, verdant parks, first-class hotels, grand public buildings, spacious plazas, and the spires of many Gothic churches. Manila had a Spanish character, with something of the grace and grandeur of Madrid or Seville.

As XIV Corps took possession of the tall commercial and residential buildings along the north bank of the Pasig, the Americans set up observation posts on high floors and rooftops. Griswold's command post, on the eighth story of a partly burned-out hotel, offered a sweeping view to the south. An evil pall of smoke hovered over the skyline and blocked out the sun. The city was burning, north and south alike. The bodies of fallen soldiers and civilians roasted as the fire advanced, and the stench of burning flesh wafted on the air. At night, the domes and spires of churches and cathedrals were illuminated by a spectral, copper light thrown off by sheets of flame. The Japanese perimeter included several of the capital's major gov-

ernment buildings, including the Legislature, the Departments of Finance
and Agriculture, city hall, the post office headquarters, the Manila Police
Department, and the Metropolitan Water District Building. These colossal
neoclassical edifices, built of steel, masonry, and concrete, were designed to
withstand major earthquakes. The Japanese had converted them into fortresses. Their doors and windows had been sandbagged, and Japanese artillery and mortars were mounted on the rooftops.

Studying these defenses through binoculars, General Griswold concluded that his forces had a long and brutal fight on their hands. The Japanese were going to fight to the end, as usual, and it was difficult to see how
the city could be saved. If MacArthur believed otherwise, he was delusional.
"He does not realize, as I do, that the skies burn red every night as they systematically sack the city," Griswold told his diary on February 7. "Nor does
he know that enemy rifle, machine gun, mortar fire and artillery are steadily
increasing in intensity. My private opinion is that the Japs will hold part of
Manila south of the Pasig River until all are killed."[26]

The Pasig was not really a river, but a placid estuary connecting Laguna
de Bay to Manila Bay. It was a deep, wide basin, a chasm in the heart of
the city, with the "river" usually running about 20 feet below street level.
Six bridges had recently spanned the Pasig, but the Japanese had destroyed
them all. XIV Corps would have to cross in boats. It was to be another
amphibious invasion, but in the heart of one of the largest cities in Asia.

General Yamashita, from his isolated headquarters in the mountainous north, had ordered Japanese forces to evacuate Manila after destroying
or carrying away all stockpiles of supplies and ammunition. But due to a
combination of factors—spotty radio communications, the press of time, a
fragmented command, service rivalries—those instructions were not carried out. The transport situation was so retrograde that no more than a
trickle of supplies could be moved up into the mountains. Rear Admiral
Sanji Iwabuchi, the garrison commander in Manila, had earlier activated
plans to demolish all installations that might be put to profitable use by the
invaders, including wharves, warehouses, factories, fuel tanks, and power
stations. Derelict ships had been sunk at the city's piers, in order to prevent
U.S. ships from berthing. All buildings and installations at Cavite Naval
Base had been burned or blown up. An order of February 3 had specified
that the destruction should be done discreetly, in secret if possible, "so that
such actions will not disturb the tranquility of the civil population nor be

used by the enemy for counter-propaganda."[27] Japanese communiqués subsequently blamed the explosions and fires on U.S. aircraft or artillery, or Filipino guerillas.

Lieutenant General Shizuo Yokoyama, whose headquarters was at Montalban in the mountains east of Manila, was subordinate to Yamashita. But he told the garrison to stand and fight: "They must revenge their countless comrades in arms who have perished since Guadalcanal, and must block the hated enemy's plans for a northward advance. . . . We must believe in the power of the gods until the very end."[28] Yamashita may not even have known that these contradictory orders had been issued by Yokoyama; there are indications that he did not even know that a Japanese force remained in the capital. But when President José P. Laurel of the collaborationist regime begged Yamashita to declare Manila an open city, as MacArthur had done in 1941, Yamashita refused. He explained that it would reflect poorly on the fighting reputation of Japanese forces.[29]

It appears that Admiral Iwabuchi never intended to leave Manila, whatever his orders. He had been captain of the battleship *Kirishima* when she was sunk at the Naval Battle of Guadalcanal more than two years earlier. Some among his colleagues deemed it less than honorable to survive such an event, and that may explain the admiral's determination to keep his forces in place until the city came down around their heads. A *gyokusai* fight for Manila offered a chance for redemption, or payback, or both. His Manila Naval Defense Force consisted of four battalions of naval base troops, another four battalions of provisional infantry troops, and a sundry assortment of other army and navy units, amounting altogether to about 16,000 fighting men. Iwabuchi seems to have lingered in the capital on the pretense that more time was needed to complete the destruction of installations, until the Americans arrived and evacuation was no longer possible. During the delay, he oversaw the construction of strong fixed defenses in the heart of the old city, south of the Pasig River. Roadblocks and steel barricades were set up in the streets; mines and booby traps were laid in the pavement and among the ruins. The forbidding ancient masonry of Intramuros, the Walled City on the south bank of the river, was honeycombed with tunnels, pillboxes, and artillery emplacements. The Japanese would fight block to block, building to building, room to room; there would be no escape, no surrender, and no survival.

The first U.S. patrols across the Pasig drew intense Japanese mortar and small arms fire from the massive stone walls of Intramuros. So Griswold decided to land his XIV Corps forces farther east, in a flanking maneuver. At dawn on February 7, two battalions of the 148th Infantry crossed the river between the Malacañang Palace and the San Miguel Beer Brewery Company, and took the fortified southern embankment by direct assault. Fighting off fierce counterattacks, the Americans consolidated their foothold south of the river, and began expanding it rapidly as troops moved across. Elements of the 1st Cavalry Division followed. The plan was to strike south into the once-serene neighborhoods of Pandacan and Paco, then launch a westward attack on the Walled City.

Meanwhile, elements of the 129th Infantry stormed Provisor Island in the Pasig, home to the largest power plant in the city. A Japanese garrison had converted the facility into a fortress. A ferocious three-day fight ensued, involving room-to-room fighting in the dark interior of the facility. The battle claimed 285 American casualties, including thirty-five killed and ten missing. The steam turbine plant was completely destroyed in the fighting, guaranteeing that most of the city would be without electrical power in the weeks ahead.

On February 8, combat raged through the burning streets of Pandacan and Paco. Japanese forces in the area staged a fighting retreat to the Paco Railroad Station, a neoclassical edifice built in 1915.[30] The 148th Infantry closed the ring around the station. Three companies of elite Japanese army troops had prepared their defenses with care. Machine gun nests, antitank guns, and heavy mortars were protected by sandbag walls. Pillboxes commanded sweeping fields of fire on all the street approaches. Field artillery took the beautiful old station down stone by stone, but the Japanese were resilient, and reinforcements managed to slip through the U.S. lines to enter the station on foot. A platoon (of Company B) was pinned down on a broad boulevard about 100 yards north of the station. Two privates, Cleto "Chico" Rodriguez and John N. Reese Jr., advanced into heavy enemy fire and took cover in a house about sixty yards from the station, and then took turns providing covering fire as they advanced to within thirty yards of the nearest pillbox. In an hour of extraordinary combat, the two soldiers killed about thirty-five Japanese soldiers and wounded many more. Running low on ammunition, they staged a fighting retreat back to the American lines. Reese was killed by a burst of machine gun fire. Later that night, their battalion stormed the station and killed all remaining enemy soldiers in the vicinity. In recognition of their outstanding valor, both Rodriguez and Reese received the Congressional Medal of Honor.

As U.S. forces turned west toward the Walled City, they encountered some of the most vicious urban fighting of the entire Second World War. Every structure in their path, every half-collapsed ruin, had to be searched and cleaned out. They encountered a variety of fiendish defenses, including barricades improvised by steel spikes driven into pavement, overturned trucks and automobiles, stacks of fuel drums filled with rubble, coils of barbed wire, and antitank and anti-personnel mines. Pillboxes of concrete guarded the approaches to those barriers. Snipers' perches were set up on rooftops and on the high floors of buildings. The infantrymen employed small-team tactics to advance upon and destroy those formidable defenses. The location of every mine was detected and mapped, and it was hauled out of the ground with a chain attached to a Sherman tank or half-track. Light mortars threw smoke shells to blind the enemy. Machine guns provided suppressing fire as the squads advanced and attacked pillboxes at point-blank range with grenades, explosive charges, and flamethrowers. When a team entered a house or building, they rushed up to the roof and the top floors first, then descended the stairways and searched each room carefully. When in doubt, they threw hand grenades ahead, or filled a room with flames and roasted their enemies alive. They blew holes in walls rather than passing through doorways. If enemy resistance was too severe, they withdrew and knocked the entire structure down with artillery and demolitions.

On February 12, a remaining core force of six Japanese battalions (four naval, two army) were corralled into an area of about one square mile, bounded by the Pasig River on the north, a line running between Luna, Paco Market, and Paco Creek to the east, and a line running from the Polo Club to the bay front on the south. Japanese defenses between Fort McKinley and Nichols Field had collapsed under the relentless pressure of the Eighth Army, and remaining Japanese forces in the area were cut off in isolated pockets. "Destruction and chaos marked the path of our drive into Manila," wrote Edward Flanagan of the 11th Airborne Division. "Houses and shops, flanking both sides of the highway which leads to the heart of the city, were torn up by both Jap and American artillery. Tin-roofed houses looked as though a giant can-opener had sliced through them, while once pretentious mansions gauntly displayed charred chimneys and trash piles of rubble."[31]

But the hardest fighting of the battle for Manila still lay ahead. The enemy pocket included several of Manila's major government buildings, whose steel-reinforced concrete walls stood up to all but the heaviest artillery. The doors, porticos, and windows were sandbagged, and gun emplacements swept all approaches. They were surrounded by broad plazas, parks, and boulevards—which meant that they could only be approached over open ground, where the attacking U.S. infantry would find little natural cover. A belt of well-camouflaged and interconnected pillboxes guarded each building. In the interiors, the corridors, stairwells, and rooms had been barricaded with sandbags and ordinary furniture, with a few feet of clearance left at the top, so that grenades could be lobbed at the attackers. These strongpoints together formed an outer ring of defenses around the old Spanish walls of Intramuros.

Hoping to spare the city, both its physical infrastructure and its inhabitants, MacArthur strictly prohibited aerial bombing of Manila. For the same reasons, he had restricted the use of heavy artillery; in the early stages of the battle, the big guns were limited to counterbattery fire (shooting back at enemy artillery) and to "observed fire on known enemy strong points."[32] But the enemy's formidable defenses left the U.S. ground commanders with limited options. As their casualty rates climbed, they fell back upon their tried-and-true practice of pulverizing all structures from which enemy fire was detected. As the infantry advanced against Japanese strongpoints in the heart of the city, prolonged heavy artillery barrages razed entire blocks. Civilian refugees streamed out of the stricken areas and passed through the American lines, desperately trying to get to safety.

Some major buildings could be isolated and bypassed, but others had to be totally destroyed before U.S. forces could advance past them safely. They were shelled by 105mm and 155mm howitzer fire until they began to crumble to the ground, slab by slab. The regimental commander of the 148th Infantry told a reporter, "I can see little hope of saving many of Manila's famous buildings. This is a full-scale artillery battle and you know what that does to a city."[33] Tanks closed to within point-blank range and added their guns to the cumulative punishment. Mortars were showered down on the outer walls and arcades. Eventually, the structural integrity of the great buildings failed, and their roofs caved in. Infantry squads then entered through breaches in the walls (not through the doors, as these would be guarded by rifle, machine guns, and booby traps) and killed all remaining enemy soldiers.

The National City Bank of New York Building, north of the Pasig River, served as an artillery observation post. Officers armed with binoculars studied the fall of their shells and spoke to spotters on the ground and in spotting planes circling overhead. City maps were spread out on tables, and coordinates were passed on to the gunners. In a suite on the sixth floor, journalists sat in comfortable armchairs while eating canapes and drinking cold beer. They watched the spectacle in open-mouthed awe, shaking their heads in sorrow at the obliteration of the old city center. One by one, Manila's major landmarks crumbled under the onslaught. The Japanese had lashed Filipino civilians to the outer walls of strategic buildings, perhaps expecting them to serve as human shields. The American guns did not spare them. The 155mm gun, nicknamed the "Long Tom," threw a 95-pound shell to a maximum range of 9 miles. The correspondent John Dos Passos was jolted by the concussive shockwaves made by the weapon, even at a distance of several hundred yards: "Each time the Long Tom shoots, it's like being hit on the head with a baseball bat."[34] Bill Dunn, the radio broadcaster, believed that he suffered permanent damage to his eardrums. From that day forward, he wrote, he was "increasingly hard of hearing."[35]

The Rizal Memorial Baseball Stadium, near Harrison Park and La Salle University, hosted a fierce battle on the morning of February 16. U.S. artillery blasted an opening in the outer walls near right field. Sherman tanks advanced into the overgrown outfield, with infantrymen of the 5th and 12th Cavalry Regiments advancing in a crouch behind them. Three or four companies of well-armed Japanese troops were dug into the stands, dugouts, and tunnels behind home plate and the first base line. All openings had been barricaded with sandbags, and firing slots had been cut into the walls. The visiting team advanced into the infield behind their tanks, firing mortars and bazookas. A daylong firefight ended when every Japanese soldier in the ballpark was killed.

Japanese troops had been ordered to stem the tide of civilian refugees toward the American lines. Soldiers were systematically destroying all boats and canoes that might carry people across the Pasig or into the bay. Sentries were posted at each of the four arcaded gates of Intramuros. As the battle for Manila entered its terminal phase, Japanese soldiers began rounding up civilians all over the city. They began with men and teenage boys above the age of eleven or twelve. Innocent Filipinos and expatriate civilians were kept as hostages against U.S. airstrikes. This brutal practice accomplished its purpose, inasmuch as MacArthur never acquiesced to aerial bombing in Manila. In the end, however, massive and sustained artillery barrages did the same work that the bombers would have done. No one knows how many innocent souls perished in the Battle of Manila, but the figure was certainly enormous—perhaps more than 100,000. Some were buried under the rubble of their dwellings, hiding places, and prisons, but many more— again, reliable statistics are elusive—were murdered by the Japanese in one of the most iniquitous atrocities of the twentieth century.

Mass execution orders were distributed in writing to Japanese troops. Roundups and executions of "guerillas" became steadily less discriminate as U.S. forces had crossed the Pasig River. Documents captured on the battlefield refer to "disposals" on a large scale. A Japanese soldier's diary, translated and submitted to a postwar tribunal, included the following entries:

> Feb. 7, 1945: 150 guerillas were disposed of tonight. I personally stabbed and killed 10.
> Feb. 8: Guarded over 1,184 guerillas which were newly brought in today.
> Feb. 9: Burned 1,000 guerillas to death tonight.
> Feb. 10: Guarded approximately 1,660 guerillas.
> Feb. 13: Enemy tanks are lurking in the vicinity of Banzai Bridge [Jones Bridge]. Our attack preparation has been completed. I am now on guard duty at guerilla internment camp. While I was on duty 10 guerillas tried to escape. They were stabbed to death. At 16.00, all guerillas were burned to death.[36]

On February 13, Admiral Iwabuchi directed his army forces to kill all civilians remaining in the Japanese lines: "Even women and children have become guerillas. . . . All people on the battlefield with the exception of Japanese military personnel, Japanese civilians, and Special Construction Units will be put to death."[37] Two days later, a Manila Naval Defense Force order added more detailed instructions, with an eye toward conserving manpower and ammunition. Civilians to be killed should be rounded up and driven into houses or buildings which could then be burned or blown up. This would alleviate the "troublesome task" of disposing of corpses. For the same reason, "They should also be thrown into the river."[38]

Between February 11 and February 15, the reign of terror turned darker and more feral. Mass murder escalated into a wild abandon of pillage, arson, rape, torture, and mutilation in churches, universities, hotels, and hospitals. The city's Spanish and mestizo elite were especially targeted, as were expatriates of various nationalities who had lived and worked in the heart of the international capital. Entire families were wiped out. Disposal squads targeted anyone who had once worn a police or military uniform, or had shown compassion to Western civilian internees or prisoners of war.

Many of Manila's most famous religious, medical, and educational institutions were host to notorious war crimes. Priests, nuns, and other Christian ecclesiastics were murdered in their churches and on their altars. Hundreds of civilians were driven into the cathedral at the corner of Santo Tomas and General Luna Streets. Bands of drunken soldiers roamed the aisles and pews, bayoneting innocents and dragging young women and girls from the arms of their sobbing families to be raped in a nearby chapel. In a lecture hall at La Salle College, according to the testimony of Father Francis J. Cosgrave, twenty Japanese soldiers entered and "began bayoneting all of us, men, women, and children alike." The dead and wounded, including children as young as two years old, were piled in a heap at the foot of a stairway. A woman's breasts were cut off. The soldiers departed for an hour and were heard drinking in a courtyard outside. Later they returned, and "laughed and mocked at the sufferings of their victims." Cosgrave, bleeding from two bayonet wounds, crawled among the dying and administered the last rites. He noted with approval that some of the victims were "actually praying to God to forgive those who had put them to death."[39]

Walter K. Funkel, a professor at the University of the Philippines, kissed his wife farewell as they and six others were bound in the center of a room and doused in gasoline. She was killed instantly by a hand grenade, and "I was thankful in my heart that my beloved wife was spared from being burned alive."[40] Dr. Funkel was one of two in the room who managed to escape after the Japanese left the scene. In a classroom at Saint Paul's College, Cayetano Barahona tried to shield his family as a band of soldiers began bayoneting everyone in the room. A soldier wrested a baby boy from his mother's arms and tossed him in the air. "Another Japanese with a fixed bayonet came in and just stuck the baby right in the middle of his stomach," said Barahona. He noted in horror that the infant did not immediately perish: "I could see how the baby dangled moving his hands."[41]

At the Philippine General Hospital, some 7,000 civilians were herded into the wards and corridors and kept there as hostages. At night, drunken Japanese soldiers prowled through the crowds, shining flashlights into faces, and dragged young women and girls away to be raped. Atrocities continued even while the hospital was under attack by U.S. artillery and tanks, and the walls began to come down around the captors and captives alike. At St Paul's College, Japanese soldiers separated the men and boys from the women and girls. The females were driven through streets at the point of bayonets to the Bayview Hotel on Dewey Boulevard. Terrified and sobbing, clinging to one another, they were forced up the stairs to the third floor. Groups of fifteen or twenty were placed in separate guestrooms and forced to sit on the floor. There they remained for days without water or food. Again and again, Japanese naval troops entered and inspected each of the women. Victims were dragged away to be raped elsewhere in the hotel. The women did their best to make themselves unattractive, or to hide their faces. "Everyone in the room knew what was going to happen to us," one victim recalled. "Everyone in the room was crying and trying to hide under mattresses and nets."[42]

Manila's German inhabitants, being citizens of an Axis ally, had been left alone during the three-year occupation. As U.S. forces drew closer, many took refuge at the German Club in the Ermita district. But if the Germans had supposed that their national status would shield them from the rampaging Japanese, they were mistaken. A squad of soldiers stormed into the club on the morning of February 10. The occupants frantically explained that they were allies. A woman with an infant in her arms stepped forward to beg mercy, perhaps believing that the child would deter the intruders' aggression. A soldier plunged his bayonet through the infant's body and into that of his mother. Others began tearing young women away from their families, ripping their clothes off and dragging them away. The club was later set on fire, and crowds rushed to the doors in panic, to find themselves barricaded from the outside.

At the Red Cross headquarters on Isaac Peral Street, the doors opened to all civilian refugees of any nationality, with promises to provide sanctuary and medical care. Every corridor, every room, every stairwell in the building was teeming with refugees, seated on every part of the ground.

On February 10, a party of Japanese arrived and demanded to see a roster of occupants. They spurned the staff's references to the protections of international law. Later in the day, larger groups of soldiers converged on the building and entered by the front and back doors simultaneously. They began killing wantonly with bullets, knives, swords, and bayonets. When a registered nurse asked to speak to the commanding officer, she was butchered on the spot. A mother attempted to save her baby daughter, who had been bayoneted in the abdomen. "I tried to put her intestines back in her stomach. I did not know what to do."[43] The infant died.

A familiar pattern of escalation was seen in the behavior of Japanese troops. At first, before U.S. forces crossed into the Manila city limits, they were menacing but otherwise disciplined. Small parties of Japanese soldiers, led by an officer, might visit a home or premises and demand to know the names and ages of all civilian occupants. The information would be entered into a notebook. A day or two later they might return, explaining that they were under orders to search for guerillas or contraband. Soldiers might pocket valuables found in cabinets or dressers, but otherwise leave the occupants unharmed. On a third visit they might demand to search the occupants as well as the premises, and the robberies would become more brazen. Women might be groped in the course of these searches. Men and older boys might be arrested and led away. On a fourth visit, a single rape might occur. As American forces entered the city, and the din of artillery was heard in the distance, the mood of the Japanese became more wanton and vindictive. Men and women were separated, and gang rapes became more common. In the final stages, with U.S. forces closing in on the perimeter and artillery raining down, the attacks became more frenzied and the cruelty more imaginative. Now it was not enough to rape and kill the women—instead they must mutilate them, cut off their breasts, douse their hair in gasoline, and set them on fire. Survivors reported instances of attempted necrophilia. Sometimes the murderers attempted to cover up their crimes, perhaps by burning down the house or building in which they had occurred. In the later stages, as American forces closed in, the Japanese were more likely to put their execrable handiwork on display—for example, by hanging tortured and headless civilians from lampposts.

The sack of Manila exposed the worst pathologies of Japan's military culture and ideology. It was a glaring indictment of the "no surrender" principle, revealing the depraved underside of what the Japanese glorified as *gyokusai*, "smashed jewels." Iwabuchi's troops knew that they only had a few more days left to live. They were under direct orders, by officers whose authority was absolute and even godlike, to execute every last man, woman, and child within their lines. Many were instructed to perform the ghastly work with bayonets, or by burning their victims alive, in order to save ammunition. Trapped in this lurid nightmare, stewing in their own fear and hatred, they went berserk and abandoned themselves to a primordial blood orgy that the world will not soon forget.

FROM HIS *SHIMBU* GROUP HEADQUARTERS in Montalban, General Yokoyama urged Admiral Iwabuchi to attempt a breakout before it was too late. But no such maneuver was possible, certainly not by that point. The remnants of Iwabuchi's six battalions were besieged on all sides, hunkered down in their bunkers, buildings, and tunnels under a rain of mortars and artillery shells. The U.S. 37th Infantry Division was closing in from the north, the First Cavalry from the east, and the 11th Airborne from the south. Nearly all remaining Japanese artillery pieces had been silenced, either because the weapons had been destroyed or captured, or their ammunition was exhausted. In a radio signal of February 15, the admiral explained his situation to Yokoyama:

> The headquarters will not move. . . . It is very clear that we will be
> decimated if we make an attempt. We can hold out another week if
> we remain entrenched as we are. What is vitally important now is
> to hold every position and inflict severe losses on the enemy by any
> means. Fixed positions are our strong advantage. If we move, we will
> be weak. Therefore, we will be able to hold out as long as possible and
> then make a desperate charge with all our strength. We are grateful for
> your trouble.[44]

Then Iwabuchi signaled the headquarters at Baguio:

> In anticipation of disruption of communications, I hereby submit this
> message to you. I am overwhelmed with shame for the many casual-
> ties among my subordinates and for being unable to discharge my duty
> because of my incompetence. The men have exerted their utmost

efforts in the fighting. We are glad and grateful for the opportunity of being able to serve the country in this epic battle. Now, with what strength remains, we will daringly engage the enemy. 'Banzai to the Emperor!' We are determined to fight to the last man.[45]

About 2,000 Japanese fighters remained barricaded in prepared defensive positions behind the Walled City of Intramuros. Built by the Spanish in the late sixteenth century, this massive stone edifice ran about two-and-one-half miles in circumference; it was 25 feet tall and varied in thickness from ten to twenty feet. Its walls looked similar to the medieval walls that were common in Europe, especially in Italy, Spain, and southern France—but there was nothing quite like it anywhere else in the islands of the Pacific. The walls had once been ringed by a moat, but the moat had since been drained and converted into a city park and a nine-hole public golf course. The four arched gates were all heavily sandbagged and swept by Japanese machine and antitank guns. The Japanese had carved gun emplacements and tunnels into the old masonry, linking them to other defensive positions.

Within those walls were thousands of starving civilian hostages, many packed into ancient dungeons beneath the riverbed, others actually hanging from the outer walls in full view of the American besiegers. Surrender appeals were broadcast by loudspeaker, and leaflets were dropped by spotter planes, but no answer was given. On the morning of February 23, as XIV Corps prepared its assault on the Walled City, it was clear that the Americans would have to storm the fortress and slay every last defender.

Again, General Griswold asked for airstrikes; again, he was denied. It seemed that MacArthur still hoped for a stroke of providence that would preserve the beloved old barrio. Again, the Americans brought in massed heavy artillery to do the same job that the bombers would have done. At half past seven on the morning of February 23, more than a hundred 105mm and 155mm howitzers opened the most concentrated artillery barrage yet seen in the Pacific War. Some of the weapons were positioned at short range, about 300 yards, with the projectiles fired at a flat trajectory. In a single hour, the artillery and tanks fired a combined total of 7,896 high-explosive rounds.[46] The entire Walled City disappeared from view amidst sheets of flame, smoke, and dust. It was as if Mount Pinatubo had erupted in the heart of Manila. George Jones, a *New York Times* correspondent, described "great geysers of black smoke, showering rubble and shrapnel.

The air filled with smoke and dust and quickly Intramuros was obliterated from sight. The only thing to be seen through this curtain were flashes of exploding shells."[47]

In the catacombs beneath Fort Santiago, Japanese soldiers obeyed orders to slaughter all prisoners remaining in the dungeons. Many were stabbed, slashed, shot, or bayoneted. In the larger cells, jammed with prisoners who had received no food or water for days, gasoline was poured through the bars and onto the floors, and then ignited. According to the later-recovered diary of a Japanese navy lieutenant, Admiral Iwabuchi exhorted his last surviving forces to kill as many Americans as possible before falling in battle: "If we run out of bullets we will use grenades; if we run out of grenades, we will cut down the enemy with swords; if we break our swords, we will kill them by sinking our teeth deep in their throats."[48]

When the artillery barrage lifted at 8:30 a.m., and the smoke and dust cleared, large sections of the old ramparts had been reduced to hills of rubble. Troops of the 145th Infantry and the 129th Infantry launched a coordinated assault, with soldiers climbing those hills and shooting their way into the streets on the other side. Armored bulldozers moved in to clear a path for Sherman tanks. A flotilla of about one hundred assault boats crossed from one muddy bank of the Pasig River to the other. Artillery fire had deliberately carved "steps" in the masonry between the river and the walls, so that troops could climb the embankment. Throwing smoke grenades ahead to blind the enemy, platoon-sized units passed in single file through breaches in the walls.[49]

The rattle of machine guns and rifle fire was heard as the assaulting units spread out into the narrow, labyrinthine streets at the hub of the citadel. The soldiers resumed the street-fighting tactics they had honed in the districts to the east. They took their time, preferring to contain their own casualties rather than to score a quick victory.

Iwabuchi and his principal staff officers, with field headquarters in the Agricultural Building, are believed to have taken their own lives before dawn on February 26.

A few enemy holdouts held the tunnels and catacombs under Fort Santiago. Entrances to these subterranean lairs were sealed with heavy demolition charges. Gasoline was poured into tunnels and white phosphorus grenades thrown after them, converting the interiors into kilns.

Until the very end, MacArthur appeared to be in denial about the unfolding tragedy in Manila. Between February 7 and February 19, he remained at his headquarters in Tarlac, visiting the capital only briefly. Even after seeing the devastation in the northern barrios, and confronted with evidence of fires and destruction south of the river, he continued to issue upbeat opinions to his colleagues. He refused to let his press team describe the full scale of the fighting and carnage in their near-daily communiqués, perhaps because he was embarrassed by his earlier premature victory announcement. Pressuring his field commanders to hurry the reconquest of the city, MacArthur ignored evidence that the Japanese were strongly fortified in the old city.

When the SWPA chief finally entered the wrecked capital on February 23, he was driven in an armored motorcade to his prewar home at the Manila Hotel. The once-elegant landmark building had been gutted by fire. Large sections of the outer masonry had collapsed, exposing the remnants of guestrooms on the upper floors. Accompanied by soldiers armed with submachine guns, MacArthur climbed a rubble-strewn stairway to his old penthouse apartment. To his sorrow, he found it burned out and littered with debris. A Japanese colonel lay dead in the foyer. None of his possessions had survived. His large personal library of military histories was a complete loss. A pair of ancient vases presented to his father by the former Japanese emperor lay in shards. "It was not a pleasant moment," MacArthur recalled. "I was tasting to the last acid dregs the bitterness of a devastated and beloved home."[50]

Four days later, in a formal ceremony at Malacañang Palace, a crowd of khaki-clad U.S. Army officers, Filipino legislators, and war correspondents assembled in the elegant Reception Hall, with its ornate carved woodwork, Persian carpets, and crystal chandeliers. The Philippine commonwealth government was restored to its full prewar authority. Standing behind a battery of microphones, General MacArthur recounted three years of "bitterness, struggle, and sacrifice" to recover the Philippines. He angrily denounced the Japanese for failing to evacuate Manila and declare it an open city, as he had done in 1941: "The enemy would not have it so, and much that I sought to preserve has been unnecessarily destroyed by his desperate action at bay—but by these ashes he has wantonly fixed the future pattern of his own doom."[51] Speaking for another minute or so, the general finally choked up and found that he could not go on. Without concluding his prepared remarks, MacArthur yielded the lectern to President Osmeña.

In newsreel footage, he is seen standing in the background, behind the president, dabbing at his face with a handkerchief.[52]

There was no more talk of a victory parade. Much of Manila was simply gone. In the western districts south of the Pasig, shells of gutted buildings and hillocks of charred rubble stretched away to the horizon in every direction. Blackened, gnarled stumps were the only remains of mature trees that had once lined the boulevards. Most landmarks had vanished, as had the street signs; even native Manileños lost their way while navigating through the ruins of their once-familiar city. Strewn among the debris were the unburied dead—brown and bloated in the sun, features unrecognizable, with blank, staring eyes and hideous grinning rictuses. At massacre sites, dead civilians were piled together in heaps—men, women, and children together, with swollen hands tied behind their backs, shot, bayoneted, or beheaded. The vile stench of putrefying flesh was inescapable, except by traveling well upwind of the city limits.

Refugees camped amidst the rubble and erected pop-up ghettos. Rudimentary shacks were assembled with whatever materials could be salvaged from the wreckage—boards, pipes, bricks, blankets, and sheets of corrugated tin. Looters sifted through the ruins of burned-out buildings or houses abandoned by their owners. Army medics and Red Cross workers distributed distilled water, food, clothing, blankets, and other supplies. Wounded civilians received medical treatment in hastily established field hospitals. A sanitation emergency threatened; the city's water supply had been secured, but the water and sewage mains in the stricken areas were ruptured. Many districts would have no running water at all for more than a year, and the gutters were open sewers. Prostitution rings were doing a brisk business even before the last pockets of Japanese resistance were eliminated. Street urchins accosted American soldiers and quoted a price for their older sisters. But even in this squalid wasteland, amidst such misery and despair, many Filipinos celebrated their liberation by dancing in the streets while shouting: "Mabuhay!" ("To life!").[53]

Manila Bay was an abattoir, polluted by floating corpses and greasy coils of fuel from sunken ships. Of the latter there were at least fifty of various types and sizes, including gutted cargo ships half awash on a mud flat, and several large Japanese warships whose pagoda topmasts protruded above the surface. The wharves had been bombed for six months, by Halsey's Third Fleet carrier planes and by USAAF bombers operating from points south.

At Cavite Naval Base, south of Manila, not a single structure remained intact. The Japanese had taken care to demolish or burn everything left standing after the air raids. They had deliberately scuttled cargo ships at the wharves, in order to render them unusable. At one important berth, according to the U.S. Navy's salvage command, three small ships had been sunk one atop another, so that the steel wreckage was stacked up and would have to be removed section by section. Clearing the harbor and getting the seaport into working condition was a stupendous salvage job—but it had to be done quickly, as Manila would be one of the major staging bases for the invasions of Okinawa and Kyushu.

For the Filipino people, the price of losing Manila was incalculable. In the old, historic city center, it was not even a question of rebuilding—they would have to cart off the rubble and begin anew, with a blank slate. Much of the nation's cultural patrimony had been obliterated: architecture, libraries, museums, archives, the history of several centuries. Even the destruction of official government records was a problem with far-reaching consequences, because it destabilized the legal and civil foundations of the nation's post-war recovery. Manila, the elegant and functional city, "Pearl of the Orient," had been the single most valuable asset possessed by this emerging Asian democracy. It was the nation's singular political, commercial, and cultural capital. Losing it was a cruel setback to the Filipino people's hopes for economic recovery and a successful transition to independence.

General Carlos P. Romulo, who represented the Philippines as a nonvoting delegate in the U.S. House of Representatives, had been forced to leave his wife and four sons behind after the Japanese had put a price on his head in April 1942. Now, returning to his home in the Ermita district, he found it in ashes. The site was deserted. On the edge of his property he found a badly decomposed corpse that had been bayoneted. He recognized the dead man as his next-door neighbor. Exploring the stricken neighborhood, Romulo ran into many people he knew. He rejoiced in their survival, but no one had word of his family, except that they had fled the capital. Inspecting the bodies strewn in the streets, Romulo found to his horror that he recognized many of their faces: "These were my neighbors and my friends whose tortured bodies I saw pushed into heaps on the Manila streets, their heads shaved, their hands tied behind their backs, and bayonet stabs running them through and through. This girl who looked up at me wordlessly, her young breasts crisscrossed with bayonet strokes, had been in school with my son."[54] (A week later, Romulo was reunited with his wife and children, who had all survived without injury.)

Even while fighting was still raging in the city, teams of lawyers, photographers, stenographers, translators, and doctors began the painstaking work of collecting documentary and eyewitness evidence of war crimes. Witnesses were interviewed, sworn testimony was recorded, prisoners were interrogated, survivors were examined, photographs were taken of the massacre sites, and captured Japanese documents were translated by the Allied Translator and Interpreter Section. In some cases, the perpetrators had attempted to cover up their handiwork with fire, but the atrocities were so numerous and widespread that there was much more evidence than could be practically collected. The files were soon bulging with damning evidence of systematic war crimes, collected with an intention of building a case that "the sack of Manila and its attendant horrors are not the act of a crazed garrison in a last-ditch, berserk defense but the coldly planned purpose of the Japanese high command."[55] (That case was not proven, but Yamashita would hang nonetheless.)

If it had all gone differently—if the Japanese had committed no atrocities and released the civilians unharmed—a last-ditch fight for Manila might have aroused the begrudging admiration of their enemies. After all, the Americans had their own anti-surrender traditions and lore—the Alamo, Captain James Lawrence's "Don't give up the ship," and (much more recently) General Anthony McAuliffe's one-word reply to a German surrender demand at Bastogne: "Nuts." But the systematic rape, torture, and massacre of innocents stripped the fight of its honor. Three-quarters of a century later, the Japanese performance in Manila is admired by no one in the world, save a handful of unregenerate mythmakers on the Japanese right.

The Meiji emperor's "Imperial Rescript to Soldiers and Sailors," issued in 1882, was Japan's official code of ethics for military personnel. It was one of two founding documents of Imperial Japan. (The other was the "Imperial Rescript on Education," 1890). It does not go too far to say that the two Meiji rescripts were tantamount to scripture in World War II–era Japan, and the "Imperial Rescript to Soldiers and Sailors" was held to be the singular basis of all Japanese military authority. Every man in uniform was required to memorize and recite it. The most famous line, often quoted in Western histories, is: "Duty is heavier than a mountain, while death is lighter than a feather." More noteworthy, however, is the following passage, included in the Rescript's third article:

> To be incited by mere impetuosity to violent action cannot be called true valor. The soldier and the sailor should have sound discrimination of right and wrong, cultivate self-possession, and form their plans with deliberation. Never to despise an inferior enemy or fear a superior, but to do one's duty as soldier or sailor—this is true valor. Those who thus appreciate true valor should in their daily intercourse set gentleness first and aim to win the love and esteem of others. If you affect valor and act with violence, the world will in the end detest you and look upon you as wild beasts. Of this you should take heed.[56]

For four decades, the soldiers and sailors had taken heed. In wars of the late nineteenth and early twentieth centuries, Japanese forces met and often surpassed the standards of discipline and chivalry prevailing in Western armies. When Japan joined an international coalition to suppress the Boxer Rebellion in China (1901), neutral journalists documented the professional conduct of Japanese troops, who were reported to be more conscientious than their Western allies in the treatment of civilians. During the Russo-Japanese War (1904–1905), civilians in the combat zone feared the Russians more than the Japanese, and the Japanese met exemplary standards in their treatment of Russian prisoners of war—a fact confirmed by International Red Cross observers. Thereafter, within the span of a single generation, for reasons that are still puzzled over and debated by scholars, Japan's military culture took an abrupt turn toward the barbarous. By the early 1930s, the behavior of Japanese troops was attracting international notoriety, and the trend only grew worse through the end of the Second World War.

Meiji's warning thus became prophecy. In throwing away their lives like so many feathers, Iwabuchi's forces in Manila unshouldered the burden of a mountain. Forsaking the "true valor" prescribed in the rescript, possessing no sound discrimination between right and wrong, the soldiers and sailors abandoned themselves to feral violence against defenseless innocents. And in the end, as Hirohito's grandfather had foretold, the world came to detest them and to look upon them as wild beasts. As one surviving witness to the Manila atrocities commented afterward, "They were like mad, wild dogs. They were not even human beings—they acted like animals."[57]

ACROSS MANILA BAY TO THE WEST loomed the green mountains of Bataan and the low gray lump of land that marked the island of Corregidor. XI Corps was responsible for reclaiming those hallowed territories, and their drive down the Bataan Peninsula had kicked off on February 15. Two strong columns attacked southward along the two coasts of the peninsula, quickly overrunning the inferior Japanese forces in the area. Bataan was secured in a week. On heavily fortified Corregidor, a garrison of about 6,000 Japanese troops held out stubbornly under a rain of naval shells and bombs dropped from the air. The 503rd Parachute Infantry Regiment dropped on the western heights of the island, on the peak called "Topside," and joined up with amphibious troops landing on the east coast near the mouth of Malinta Tunnel. The defenders put up a typically desperate to-the-last-man fight, demolishing the tunnels as they retreated further into the interior of "the Rock." The island was declared secured on February 28, but there remained hundreds of holdouts and stragglers to be hunted down.

On March 2, MacArthur collected a delegation of officers who had left Corregidor with him in March 1942. For the sake of tradition, they crossed Manila Bay in a flotilla of new navy PT-boats. Accompanied by reporters and newsreel crews, they climbed the rock to "Topside" for an emotional flag-raising ceremony. Colonel Jones of the 503rd Parachute Infantry saluted MacArthur and said, "Sir, I present to you Fortress Corregidor."

Many more months would be required to complete the conquest of Luzon, a large and mountainous island. From his mountain headquarters at Baguio, 150 miles north of the capital, General Yamashita told Japanese press correspondents that the fight for Luzon was still in "merely the initial phase of the operations." The Americans, he said, had suffered 70,000 casualties. (The actual number at that point was about 22,000.) MacArthur had not yet come to grips with the main strength of his forces on the island. "It was and remains our deliberate strategy to lure the American landing troops into the Central Luzon plains and the Manila area, and then to bleed them from many sides," Yamashita told the Japanese newsmen. "Thus, the fighting on Luzon is going wholly according to our plans."[58]

This was standard-issue propaganda, but it was true that the great bulk of Japanese forces on the island—and throughout the rest of the Philippines— were still at large. Yamashita had avoided a reprise of MacArthur's strategic blunders of 1941–1942, when the defenders had waged an untenable battle on the plains while failing to make adequate preparations for a siege until it was too late. In the earlier campaign, the American-Filipino army had been forced to surrender Bataan less than four months after the Japanese invasion at Lingayen Gulf. Three years later, when the tables were turned, the core of Yamashita's *Shobo* Group held out in Luzon's northern mountains for more than eight months, until Japan's official surrender in August 1945.

Krueger's Sixth Army attacked north and east in three simultaneous offensives—I Corps toward the Cagayan Valley and Yamashita's redoubt at Baguio, XI Corps to the Sierra Madre range east of Manila, and XIV Corps to the island's southeast provinces. Pressure on the remaining pockets of Japanese resistance was unrelenting. U.S. forces made full use of their superiority in air power, artillery, tanks, mobility, field engineering, and logistics. Filipino guerilla units provided valuable intelligence concerning the locations, numbers, armament, and even the plans of Japanese forces. Yamashita gradually lost touch with his subordinates in other parts of the island. On May 23, the 25th Division broke through a strategic chokepoint at Balete Pass and poured up the Cagayan Valley.

During those same months, without authorization from the Joint Chiefs of Staff, MacArthur ordered a series of smaller amphibious invasions to recapture islands to the south. On February 28, elements of the Eighth Army landed on Palawan Island, quickly driving the Japanese into inaccessible mountains. A landing on Mindanao followed on April 17, followed by smaller landings on Panay, Cebu, Negros, and smaller islands to the south. Casualties were minimal, as Japanese forces generally retreated into mountainous terrain and then wasted away for lack of provisions and support. Surviving Japanese troops dispersed into the backcountry, roaming around in small bands like jungle hoboes, gradually starving or succumbing to tropical diseases. Native guerillas hunted the stragglers, often torturing them to death and mutilating their corpses. Discipline collapsed. Enlisted soldiers turned against their officers. Men fought over food, even to the point of murder and cannibalism. Takamaro Nishihara recalled that a fellow soldier, dying of disease, invited him to prolong his life by eating his buttocks. The starving Nishihara exclaimed that he could never do such a thing, "but I couldn't take my eyes off the flesh on his rear."[59]

A young naval officer, Kiyofumi Kojima, struggled to keep his little squad together in the mountains of Luzon as starvation culled their numbers. He and his men came to fear their fellow Japanese as much as they feared the Filipinos and Americans. "Weak stragglers became the prey of stronger ones. It was horrible. Surrounded, we just wandered in circles in the jungle in worn-out clothes looking for food. Fighting the enemy was the last thing on our minds."[60] Kojima finally broached the heretical idea of surrendering to the Americans. At first the idea was shouted down by his men, but the intensity of their resistance gradually abated, and at last the survivors acquiesced to the once-unthinkable disgrace. Eight men managed to evade the ferocious Filipino guerillas on their trek to the American lines, where they were taken prisoner and given cigarettes and canned rations.

Observing his captors, Kojima was astounded by their racial and ethnic diversity: "Blond, silver, black, brown, red hair. Blue, green, brown, black eyes. White, black, skin colors of every variety. I was stunned. I realized then that we'd fought against all the peoples of the world. At the same time, I thought, what a funny country America is, all those different kinds of people fighting in the same uniform!"[61]

On June 28, MacArthur declared the end to the "major phases of the Luzon campaign," noting that American forces now occupied all the plains, towns, and strategic passes throughout the island: "The entire island of Luzon, embracing 40,420 square miles and a population of 8,000,000, is now liberated."[62] Luzon had been the first battle of the Pacific War in which the U.S. Army had fought at corps strength, with the ability to maneuver across broad expanses of terrain. In other words, the fight for Luzon had been more like the war in Europe than any other chapter of the Pacific War. It was the largest ground campaign in the Pacific, excepting only the Battle of Okinawa, which it rivaled in size. In some respects, MacArthur's arguments in favor of Luzon had been vindicated—in particular, his points concerning the terrain advantages to an attacker, and the value of allied guerilla units as scouts, spies, saboteurs, and partisan fighters.

In the end, the Japanese lost the great bulk of their forces on Luzon, with only token resistance remaining at the end of the war. Two hundred thousand Japanese troops died on Luzon; just 9,000 were taken prisoner prior to Tokyo's surrender in August 1945. Only about 40,000 Japanese troops who fought on the island eventually returned to their homeland after the war. Overall, according to Japanese government statistics, the army suffered cumulative losses of 368,700 dead in the Philippines.[63] American forces had destroyed nine of Japan's elite army divisions and reduced another six to a condition in which they could no longer fight effectively. The campaign had caused, directly or indirectly, the destruction of more than 3,000

Japanese airplanes, and had forced the Japanese to adopt kamikaze suicide tactics as their main aerial tactic for the remainder of the war. American combat losses amounted to about 47,000, of whom 10,380 were killed—but casualties to causes other than combat, especially to diseases, ran to 90,400 American servicemen.

Chapter Eleven

IN JUNE 1944, TWO DAYS BEFORE U.S. FORCES HAD STORMED ASHORE ON Saipan, a new commanding general flew into Iwo Jima. Lieutenant General Tadamichi Kuribayashi was a stout man of medium height, aged fifty-three, with a small, trim moustache. He was one of the star officers of the Japanese army, having distinguished himself in staff jobs and in the field. While serving as military attaché in Washington in 1928–1929, he had mastered English and traveled widely through the United States. He had commanded a cavalry regiment at Nomonhan, Manchuria, during the undeclared war between Japan and Russia in 1938–1939. After 1941, he had served as chief of staff of the South China Expeditionary Force in Canton. More recently, he had transferred to Tokyo to command the Imperial Guard, a prestigious posting that brought him into direct contact with the emperor. His new command gave him dominion over the 109th Division and the Ogasawara Army Corps, which included all garrison forces in the Bonin Islands. Upon his departure from Tokyo, Prime Minister Hideki Tojo had instructed Kuribayashi to "do something similar to what was done on Attu."[1] That amounted to a suicide order: that Kuribayashi must defend the island to the last man.

Iwo Jima was eight desolate square miles of sulfur-volcanic ash, dusty canefields, and rocky cliffs. It was the largest of the barren little islands of the Volcano archipelago, a sub-group of the Bonin Islands. The pork chop–shaped island lay almost directly on the flight line between Saipan and Tokyo, 625 nautical miles north of Saipan and 660 nautical miles south of Japan. Much of its coastline was steeply angled beaches—but instead of sand, the beaches consisted of volcanic cinder that would not support the weight of heavy vehicles. Mt. Suribachi, a dormant volcano rising to a height of 550 feet, anchored the southern point of the island. On the plain north of Suribachi were two working airstrips, Motoyama Airfields No. 1 and No. 2. A third, No. 3, was under construction. To the north, the island widened as the terrain rose in rocky terraces and alternating ridges and ravines to a dome-shaped rock, 350 feet above sea level, called the Motoyama Plateau. Everywhere on the island, sulfur festered just beneath the ground, and steam vents brought geothermal heat and gases to the surface. It was a dark, desolate, evil-smelling place, but it was the only island in the region with terrain suitable for airfields to accommodate heavy bombers such as the B-29. That made Iwo Jima a prize worth possessing, and Kuribayashi decided to establish his headquarters here, rather than on the more populous and pleasant island of Chichi Jima, which lay 168 miles north.

Immediately upon his arrival, General Kuribayashi toured the island on foot, carrying a wooden walking staff and a canteen slung over his shoulder. At the southern edge of Airfield No. 1, just inland of the beaches, he lay prone on the ground and sighted along his wooden staff, as if it was a rifle. He told his aide-de-camp, Major Yoshitaka Horie, to approach from different directions. Kuribayashi then diagramed the sightlines in a notebook. Within two hours of his arrival, he knew precisely how he would arrange his forces and construct his defenses. Anticipating that the Americans would possess total naval and air supremacy, the general abandoned any hope of meeting and destroying their amphibious force on the beaches. He would concentrate his troops and artillery well inland, in high rocky ground. His army would burrow deep into caves, tunnels, and subterranean bunkers, firing at the enemy through heavy embrasures, blockhouses, and encasements carved into the rock. Mt. Suribachi would be converted into a fortress, and an independent fighting detachment deployed to guard it. The bulk of his forces would be arrayed to the north, in heavily fortified lines bisecting the island from coast to coast—one between Airfields No. 1 and 2, and the second immediately north of Airfield No. 2. At the top of the Motoyama Plateau would be the *Fukkaku Jinchi*, the "honeycomb defensive position"— Iwo Jima's supreme citadel.

That summer, U.S. attacks on the island increased in frequency and severity. Task Force 58 carrier planes struck five times in seven weeks. As B-24 bombers began operating from Saipan, they commenced regular "milk runs" over Iwo Jima; eventually, in late 1944, they began visiting the island every day. Japanese cargo ships and troop transports, attempting to bring supplies and reinforcements from the homeland, were intercepted by American submarines. In July, a U.S. cruiser-destroyer task force appeared in the offing and rained 8-inch and 5-inch naval projectiles down on the island. Planes were demolished on the ground; tents were shredded; the headquarters buildings and barracks were leveled. "There was nothing we could do, there was no way in which we could strike back," recalled a pilot whose Zero was destroyed on the ground. "The men screamed and cursed and shouted, they shook their fists and swore revenge, and too many of them fell to the ground, their threats choking on the blood which bubbled through great gashes in their throats."[2]

Kuribayashi was the ranking officer on the island, but army and navy personnel lived in separate camps, and the interservice politics were as contentious as ever. Naval commanders haggled brazenly with Kuribayashi's headquarters for allocations of food, water, and other supplies. Shortages grew more severe as reinforcements arrived and the size of the garrison swelled. When Kuribayashi arrived in June 1944, there were 6,000 military personnel on the island; nine months later, when the Americans landed, there were almost four times that number. The most pressing issue was water. Digging wells was pointless, because the ground water was salty and sulfurous: the soldiers called it "devil water" or "death water."[3] Cisterns collected rainwater, but not nearly enough to meet the needs of 20,000 men. Thirsty men drank directly from puddles on the ground, a practice that caused outbreaks of paratyphoid and dysentery. Rationing was strict. Bottles were shipped in from Chichi Jima on wooden barges, and the empty bottles shipped back to be refilled. Kuribayashi set an example for his men by shaving, washing his face, and brushing his teeth with a single cup of water.[4]

Naval officers on the island, backed by their superiors in Tokyo, argued for a "waterline defense" strategy. They wanted to build a chain of 250 to 300 pillboxes around the perimeter of the No. 1 Airfield, with the hope of repelling an American invasion on the beach. The navy would ship the needed construction materials and weapons from Japan, including cement, steel-reinforcing rods, dynamite, machine guns, and ammunition. The waterline defense scheme was at odds with Kuribayashi's preferred defense-in-depth strategy, but the general badly wanted the materials and arms, so he hesitated to overrule his navy colleagues. At a command conference in October, he presented his arguments. The Japanese garrison, he said, was solely a ground force. It would be pitted against the enemy's combined ground forces, air forces, and naval forces. A beach-facing strategy would expose the defenders to overwhelming U.S. naval firepower and aerial bombing, ensuring their early destruction.[5] But the naval camp was unmoved. Its offer of construction supplies was contingent on its policy of defending the airfield. If the airfield was not to be defended, the navy would not ship the materials from Japan.

Major Horie brokered a compromise. Half of the materials sent to the island by the navy would be employed in building its desired pillboxes above the beaches. The rest would be allocated to Kuribayashi's fortifications on higher ground. Reasoning that half of something was better than all of nothing, General Kuribayashi agreed.

Kuribayashi brought in a team of military and mining engineers to oversee his excavations. Much of Iwo Jima's terrain consisted of "tuff," a porous rock formed by compacted volcanic ash, which was susceptible to picks and shovels. Digging parties worked seven days a week in round-the-clock shifts. They set a pace of three feet per day; if they had dynamite, they could achieve twice that pace. Excavated dirt and debris was hauled up to the surface in rucksacks. It was a labor of the damned. As the workers tunneled deeper into the island, they were tormented by geothermal heat and sulfur fumes. Wearing nothing but loincloths and *tabi* rubber-soled shoes, they could dig for no more than ten minutes in a shift, before being forced to retreat to the surface for fresh air and a rest. "Our hands were covered in blisters, our shoulders got stiff, and we gasped and panted in the geothermal heat," recalled an army private. "Our throats would smart, but there was no drinking water to be had."[6]

In the fall of 1944, as the great effort progressed, an intricate honeycomb of tunnels, stairways, and bunkers was bored into the rock. Natural caverns could accommodate as many as five hundred men at once. Electrical lighting and ventilation systems improved habitability. Bare rock walls were plastered over. Command posts were interconnected by radio links or underground telephone lines. Eventually, some 1,500 subterranean bunkers were connected by 16 miles of corridors, with widely scattered entrances and exits to the open ground above. In this sunless subterranean city, one found hospitals, bunkrooms, mess halls, and communications centers filled with state-of-the-art technology. The island's main naval command post, called the *Nanpo Shoto* bunker, was ninety feet beneath the surface. On the surface, the navy's labor teams built hundreds of dome-shaped concrete blockhouses around the perimeter of the airfields. Sand was piled around them, both to conceal them from view and to protect them against naval bombardment. Small slit firing ports provided overlapping fields of fire on the landing beaches. Antitank ditches doubled as infantry trenches. The naval engineers also cannibalized aircraft wreckage for improvised fortifications along the runways. Wings, bomb bays, and tail sections were salvaged for use as construction materials. Wrecked fuselages were buried halfway into the ground, and then covered with stones and sandbags to serve as makeshift pillboxes. One officer, inspecting the work, gave his approval: "Good job. These aircraft are serving the country twice."[7]

In order to reduce the number of mouths to be fed, General Kuribayashi ordered the entire civilian population of Iwo Jima evacuated to Japan. Between July 3 and July 14, a thousand civilians living on the island were repatriated to the mainland. All men between the ages of sixteen and forty without dependents were conscripted into the army. When Kuribayashi learned that senior officers were lingering at headquarters, with pretended bureaucratic and administrative tasks, he ordered them to "get out on site as much as possible and devote themselves to leading from the front." Some resented the endless labor, and criticized the general behind his back: "We came here to make war, not to dig holes."[8] Kuribayashi, who had a ruthless streak, purged the dissidents and malcontents. He dismissed several senior officers from their posts, including his own chief of staff, a brigade commander, and two battalion commanders. He promoted younger officers into their jobs, or brought in replacements from the mainland.

Some called Kuribayashi a tyrant, but the general showed genuine concern for the welfare of his subordinates. When visitors from the mainland brought gifts of food or vegetables, he ordered them distributed among his men. He was a family man who doted on his wife and each of his four children. Kuribayashi wrote them each separately, often dwelling on small details of their domestic life, and reminding the children of their particular duties around the house. He prophetically warned of the devastation to come in the bombing raids on Japan. To his wife, Yoshii, in a letter of September 12, 1944, he wrote: "When I imagine what Tokyo would look like if it were bombed—I see a burned-out desert with dead bodies lying everywhere—I'm desperate to stop them carrying out air raids on Tokyo." Two months later, when the Superfortresses began operating from bases in the Marianas, Kuribayashi and his troops could see the big silver bombers soaring high overhead on their way to Japan. But the garrison could do nothing to stop them, because they were well out of range of the antiaircraft guns. "In this war, there's nothing we can do about soldiers like me out here on the front line dying," he wrote Yoshii on December 8. "But I can't stand the idea that even you, women and children on the mainland, have to feel that your lives are in danger. No matter what, take refuge in the country and stay alive."[9]

In January 1945, Kuribayashi and his officers concluded that an invasion was imminent. They had weeks left to prepare, perhaps less. Plans had envisioned linking the Motoyama Plateau to Mt. Suribachi by a long tunnel running deep under the airfields, but there was not enough time or manpower to dig it. The shipping lanes to Japan were no longer safe, and it was even becoming dangerous to navigate small craft between Iwo and Chichi Jima. Renouncing his earlier bargain with the navy, Kuribayashi ordered a halt to pillbox construction around the airfields, and reassigned all laborers and materials to completing defensive fortifications on the Motoyama Plateau. He wanted more effort to camouflage the entrances of both underground bunkers and firing embrasures for guns. Kuribayashi also stepped up the training regimen, with exercises devoted to refining techniques for sniping, night infiltration attacks, and antitank tactics.[10]

In his radiograms to Tokyo, Kuribayashi lobbied for more arms, ammunition, and supplies, asking that they be flown into the island by air freight. He wanted small craft and even fishing boats to be pressed into service to carry freshwater and provisions from Chichi Jima. But in February, as the island garrison surpassed 22,000 men, working and living conditions degenerated. Underground bunkers were hot, overcrowded, and filthy. Ventilation shafts were added, but subterranean temperatures often surpassed 140 degrees Fahrenheit, and sulfurous vapors made it extremely difficult to breathe. There were not enough latrines on the island, and men with uncontrollable diarrhea had to relieve themselves on the spot. Clouds of blowflies rose from open cesspools near the tunnel entrances. To protect the garrison's supplies against relentless American air raids, everything had to be moved down into the tunnels and bunkers. Corridors were lined with 55-gallon drums containing freshwater, fuel oil, kerosene, or diesel fuel. Men laid thin mattresses or blankets across the tops of the drums and used them as beds. Infestations of flies, ants, lice, and cockroaches drove men to the ends of their wits. Body odors permeated the airless underground cavities. A soldier wrote in his diary, "In the air raid shelter it is just like staying in the hold of a ship. It is so stuffy from cooking etc. and the temperature rises so, one cannot remain inside for a long period of time without getting a headache."[11]

During those same weeks, U.S. intelligence analysts in Guam and Pearl Harbor marveled at the Japanese garrison's apparent disappearing act. Iwo Jima had been bombed, strafed, and blasted for eight months; it had been shelled from offshore, bombed by B-24s and B-29s based in the nearby Marianas, and visited a dozen times by carrier task forces. Craters upon craters had been punched into the island's soft volcanic ash. The B-24s alone had hit the island for the past seventy consecutive days, dropping thousands of tons of bombs. But during this same period, Iwo Jima's underground fortifications and artillery encasements had only grown stronger and more extensive. The bombing and bombardment had made little impression on the island's defenses; nor had it interrupted the pace of the garrison's work. Every square yard of Iwo Jima had been photographed by U.S. planes and submarines, producing thousands of high-resolution images from every possible angle. The photos revealed that the Japanese had vacated their exposed barracks and bivouac areas and moved underground. Daily reconnaissance overflights confirmed that virtually no buildings or tentage remained on the island, and scarcely any troops could be seen from the air. Captain Thomas Fields of the 26th Marines put it succinctly: "The Japanese weren't *on* Iwo Jima. They were *in* Iwo Jima."[12]

On the eve of the invasion, Iwo Jima was well prepared to receive the enemy. Suribachi and the Motoyama Plateau had been converted into natural fortresses. Implanted in the rocks were a variety of weapons, from big coastal defense guns in sunken casements, to mortars, light artillery, anti-tank guns, and machine guns. Mortar tubes and rocket launchers were concealed under steel or concrete covers that could be retracted and closed quickly. The best marksmen in the garrison were armed with sniper rifles and positioned in cave entrances with the best sightlines onto the beaches and airfields. Baskets of hand grenades were stashed near bunker entrances. The lanes leading up from the beaches to the terraces and airfields were sown with anti-personnel mines, and the roads and flats were riddled with heavy antivehicular mines that could destroy or disable tanks, bulldozers, and trucks. Food was stockpiled to feed the garrison for two months.

Although General Kuribayashi had encountered stubborn resistance in his ranks, he had finally imposed his will on the garrison, and indoctrinated all of his subordinate commanders into his plan. There would be no massed counterattacks over open ground. *Banzai* charges were strictly forbidden. The Japanese would blanket the landing beaches with artillery and mortar fire when the attackers were most vulnerable, but they would not stage an all-out fight to hold the airfields.

General Kuribayashi did not hold out hope that his men could *win* the battle for Iwo Jima. They were to fight a delaying action, to inflict maximum casualties on the Americans, and (eventually) to die to the last man. In the final days before the invasion, from his subterranean command bunker near the rocky northwest shore, Kuribayashi wrote out a list of six "courageous battle vows." These were mimeographed and distributed to every unit on the island, and every soldier was compelled to memorize and recite them. The vows were posted on the walls of bunkers, pasted to the barrels of weapons, neatly copied into notebooks, and kept on folded pages in soldiers' pockets:

1. We shall defend this place with all our strength to the end.
2. We shall fling ourselves against the enemy tanks clutching explosives to destroy them.
3. We shall slaughter the enemy, dashing in among them to kill them.
4. Every one of our shots shall be on target and kill the enemy.
5. We shall not die until we have killed ten of the enemy.
6. We shall continue to harass the enemy with guerilla tactics even if only one of us remains alive.[13]

On February 16, 1945, as the American invasion fleet gathered offshore, radioman Tsuruji Akikuisa was in an observation bunker near the lower airfield. Peering through a 3-foot-long firing slit, he saw concentric rings of warships surrounding the island, stretching to the horizon and beyond: "It looked like a mountain range had risen up out of the sea."[14] When the distant battleships opened fire, he saw the flash before he heard the report. A whoosh of warm air came through the slot and blew in his face, and the acrid scent of cordite stung his nostrils. As the first shells struck home, they ejected great mounds of earth and rock. The ground trembled, and the walls of the bunker quivered as if made of marmalade. Corporal Toshiharu Takahashi of the First Mixed Brigade of Engineers was awestricken: "On the island there was a huge earthquake. There were pillars of fire that looked as if they would touch the sky. Black smoke covered the island, and shrapnel was flying all over the place with a shrieking sound. Trees with trunks one meter across were blown out of the ground, roots uppermost. The sound was deafening, as terrible as a couple of hundred thunderclaps coming down at once. Even in a cave thirty meters underground, my body was jerked up off the ground. It was hell on earth."[15]

WHEN TASK FORCE 58 LEFT ULITHI on February 10, 1945, about half its pilots were rookies, recently deployed to the fleet. Many of the veteran aviators who had fought through the Philippines campaign had been rotated out of service for a badly needed rest. The newcomers were superbly trained, with an average of six hundred hours of "stick time" in their flight logs, but they had yet to test their skills in air combat.

As the fleet steamed north through gentle seas and mild breezes, rumors abounded. All could guess that another big invasion was in the cards; that much was clear by the multitude of troop transports and amphibious vessels they had seen anchored in Ulithi lagoon. On February 15, the electrifying news was announced on every ship: Task Force 58 was headed for Tokyo, where it would raid airbases and aircraft manufacturing plants before turning south to support an amphibious landing on Iwo Jima. No U.S. carrier task force had attempted to hit Japan since the Doolittle Raid, nearly three years earlier. Attacking the enemy's capital would be like kicking over a hornet's nest: hundreds of Japanese fighters would likely challenge them, and antiaircraft fire would be heavy. One young Hellcat pilot began applauding, then stopped, turned to his squadron mates, and asked, "My god, why am I clapping?"[16]

As the force pushed north into higher latitudes, the weather turned wet, cold, and blustery. Bucketing rainsqualls washed across the decks and splattered against the Plexiglas windows of the bridges and pilot houses. Ships reared and plunged, heaving and shuddering as they smashed through the gray winter seas. Admiral Spruance called it the "damnedest, rottenest weather that I could think of."[17] Heavy wool watch coats, caps, and gloves were distributed to all crewmen with duty topside. But the inclement weather offered a compensating benefit: the task force managed to sneak into Japanese coastal waters without raising an alarm. The enemy's patrol planes were grounded, or if they were airborne, they could not see the approaching fleet through the overcast. Radar operators kept their eyes fixed on their scopes, but no enemy planes approached. NHK Radio and Radio Tokyo, whose frequencies were monitored continuously in the American radio shacks, continued to broadcast their normally scheduled programs.

On the eve of the strike, Admiral Mitscher distributed a memorandum to all air groups. "The large majority of the VF [fighter] pilots in Task Force 58 will engage in air combat for the first time over Tokyo. This fact will not be too great a handicap if pilots will remember the fundamentals and keep calm. . . . Try not to get too excited. Remember that your plane is superior to the Jap's in every way. He is probably more afraid of you than you are of him." Mitscher stressed the importance of sticking together in section formations, and resisting the instinct to peel away to chase individual Japanese planes. That was particularly true at lower altitudes, where the margin for error was smaller and the Zeros could exploit the advantages of their tight turning radius. "When you sight your first Jap resist the impulse to follow your first individual reaction," Mitscher wrote. "If you are a wingman follow your section leader and never leave him."[18]

That night the aviators gathered in their ready rooms. Seated in comfortable reclining leather armchairs, they were briefed by their squadron leaders and air intelligence officers. The target selectors had identified two dozen airfields and aircraft plants in and around Tokyo, and assigned primary and secondary targets to each squadron. Among the top-priority targets were two important factories that the B-29s of the Twentieth Air Force had tried to destroy, without success, for the past ten weeks: a Tachikawa aircraft engine plant in Tama, west of the city, and a Nakajima airframe plant in Ota, southern Tokyo, near the bay.

During the final overnight run-in toward the Japanese coast, the weather remained abysmal, and speed was throttled back from 25 knots to 20 knots. Even so, it was a rough ride. The ships lurched sickeningly, and expansion joints creaked and groaned under the strain. Aboard the *Randolph*, the young ensigns of VF-12 lay awake in their bunks, staring at the overheads, trying in vain to get some sleep before the big day. A chain was banging against the *Randolph*'s hull and making an awful racket. One later recalled: "I must have finally dozed off for a while, being suddenly awakened to the blare of 'General quarters. Man your battle stations.' This is what we trained two years for."[19]

At dawn on the sixteenth, the task force was 60 miles off the coast of Honshu and about 125 miles southwest of Tokyo. A freezing wind gusted out of the north at 30 knots. Hard rain lashed the carrier flight decks. In the bone-chilling cold, the precipitation included sleet and even snow. Visibility was "zero-zero."[20] The plane crews, bundled up in wool coats and hoods, wielding red and green flashlights, guided the pilots through the maze of parked planes. At the Fox signal, the starter cartridges fired and the engines spun to life; they coughed and backfired, and then settled into their familiar throaty roar. An officer watching from the bridge veranda of the *Yorktown* imagined the scene as "a cross-section of the bottommost level of hell—black, cold and roaring. The thunder of the engines shakes the ship. Pale blue flames flicker from their exhausts and are reflected from the wet deck, until the propellers blast the puddles dry."[21]

Task Force 58 launched 1,100 warplanes from seventeen aircraft carriers. They climbed north through the damp gray gloom, each pilot attempting to keep his eyes fixed on the faint blue exhaust flames of the planes ahead. Lieutenant McWhorter of VF-12 recalled: "I had the canopy pulled shut against the icy wind, and I shivered instinctively as blowing rain and sleet splattered noisily against my airplane. The white-capped waves, only a few hundred feet below, had a steely gray, angry look to them—inhospitably cold."[22] At 14,000 feet, the forty-seven *Randolph* Hellcats suddenly popped out of the clouds into clear sky. Beneath them lay a gray, fleecy carpet stretching to the horizon in every direction. They could see nothing of Japan except the snowcapped circular caldera of Mt. Fuji, about 70 miles to port. It offered a useful point of reference for navigation.

As they crossed the Japanese coastline, the overcast began to break up. Through gaps in the clouds they caught their first glimpses of enemy soil—a snow-covered landscape of hills, rice terraces, and clusters of dark tiled rooftops. McWhorter spotted a Japanese Zero above and to his left. Ignoring the preflight instructions to remain in formation, he banked hard left and gave chase. The enemy plane, evidently not keen to fight, turned away and dove toward the clouds. But the lightly built Zero could not match the Hellcat's speed in a dive, and McWhorter quickly overtook his quarry. He fired one long burst into the Zero's engine and wings. It was trailing fire and smoke as it disappeared into the overcast.

Southern Tokyo was socked in, so most of the attacking squadrons diverted to their secondary targets. Diving through gaps in the clouds, they hit airfields north and east of the city. Hellcats fired salvos of 5-inch high-velocity air-to-ground rockets, striking hangars, machine shops, and parked planes. Then they banked and returned for low-altitude strafing runs. Hundreds of Japanese planes were airborne, but many showed little appetite for combat, and weaved in and out of clouds to avoid their pursuers. Evidently, they had taken off only to avoid being destroyed on the ground.

Off the coast, visibility remained poor, and the returning pilots were obliged to follow their respective carriers' YE/ZB radio homing beacons. Descending through solid overcast, eyes fixed on the instruments in their cockpit panels, many of the young rookies gave silent thanks for the long hours they had logged in the Link Trainer and flying "under the hood" of their training aircraft. The Task Force 58 commanders had expected heavy operational losses, but only thirty-six airplanes failed to return on February 16. Some of those that did return had been badly shot up. One Grumman Hellcat had lost about ten feet of its port wing, but still managed to make a perfect recovery. On the *Randolph*, sailors clustered around a badly chewed-up Hellcat and marveled at the punishment it had suffered. They counted fifty-four bullet holes in one wing, and "the fuselage appeared as though it had been used for target practice, target practice for the Japs."[23]

At first light on the seventeenth, the weather had improved only slightly from the previous day, with intermittent rain showers and a cloud ceiling ranging from 300 to 700 feet. Spruance authorized the morning fighter sweep, but told Mitscher that he expected conditions to remain unfavorable and "if early operations for the day were considered unprofitable, we should retire in order to support the landings at Iwo Jima."[24]

The skies over Tokyo were clearer than on the previous day, and Japanese air defenses were on full alert. Air Group Twelve, flying in a single large "vee of vee" formation, was tracked by about a dozen Japanese fighters. The air group leader, Commander Charlie Crommelin, told his fighters to stay in formation; their priority was to deliver the Helldivers and Avengers to their primary target, the Tachikawa plant in Tama. Dive-bombers hit the complex with fifty 500-pound bombs; the Hellcats added another forty-two aerial rockets. The installations at the heart of the complex were reduced to a seething mass of flames. Ensign John Morris, an SB2C pilot, pulled out of his dive and flew a treetop escape route, which seemed safer than climbing back to altitude where the antiaircraft fire was more intense. He flew low over Tokyo Bay, "jinking left and right and up and down. We strafed any ships that happened to be along our flight path, but we didn't go out of our way looking for something."[25] He returned safely to the *Randolph*.

At Konoike Airfield, northeast of Tokyo, a dozen Mitsubishi G4M bombers were lined up wingtip to wingtip on the flight line. Konoike was an *"Oka"* (manned suicide missile) training center, and the bombers were the mother planes that carried and dropped the little rocket-propelled suicide craft. The G4Ms were fully fueled up, as they had been scheduled to fly a training exercise that morning. A squadron of Corsairs flew a low strafing run over the field and riddled the parked planes with .50-caliber incendiary fire. All twelve of the Mitsubishis were destroyed on the ground. One of the Japanese trainee pilots recalled: "The flames lit up everything. Everything that had been bluish-gray a second before was now yellow and orange. If the scene hadn't been so horrible, I would be tempted to call it beautiful."[26]

At 11:00 a.m., Spruance pulled the plug. He told Mitscher to recover all planes and retire to support the landings on Iwo Jima. By 4:00 that afternoon, the task force was speeding away to the south.

Despite the challenges presented by the weather, the Tokyo raids had been a smashing success. Task Force 58 airmen had shot down about one hundred Japanese planes and destroyed another 150 on the ground. Many critical airfield installations and air depots were left in smoking ruins. The carrier bombers had taken the Tachikawa plant off line and demolished about 60 percent of the structures at the Nakajima airframe plant in Ota. Task Force 58 had lost sixty carrier planes in combat and twenty-eight in operations, but the carriers and screening ships were unscratched. The strikes were held up by naval aviators as Exhibit A in their ongoing meta-argument with the USAAF. The navy had argued that dive bombing and low-altitude strafing and rocket attacks could hit targets on the ground more reliably than the high-altitude precision bombing practiced by the Superfortresses. The results at the Tachikawa and Nakajima plants appeared to justify their claims. Mitscher probably had that interservice debate in mind when he called the two-day attack "the greatest air victory of the war for carrier aviation."[27] Task Force 58 (and 38) would return again and again to hit Tokyo and other points in Japan with increasing frequency and ferocity, literally until the last day of the war.

More than half of the fighter pilots who had flown the February

16–17 strikes had had no prior air combat experience. They had acquitted themselves like veterans. Mitscher's action report concluded: "Too much credit cannot be given to the naval aviation training organization and its methods."[28]

THE BOMBARDMENT FORCE, which had arrived off Iwo Jima the same day the carrier planes hit Tokyo, buried the island under an avalanche of high-explosive shells. Wrapped in a shroud of smoke and flame, nothing of Iwo Jima could be seen from the fleet, except (sporadically) the peak of Mt. Suribachi. The projectiles arced toward the island in parabolic trajectories, high and low, according to the caliber of the gun and the distance that each warship lay offshore. The successive explosions merged into a solitary, unbroken roar. Men watching from the rails of the ships felt the blast concussions in their viscera. Warm puffs of wind caused their shirts to flutter against their chests. A formation of B-24s soared overhead, and diagonal glints of steel fell away from their open bomb bays. A series of explosions walked across the heart of the island, and spikes of orange and yellow flame shot above the boiling smoke and dust.[29] War correspondent Bob Sherrod, who had witnessed the landings on Tarawa, Kwajalein, and Saipan, called it "more terrifying than any other similar spectacle I had ever seen."[30]

The troopships of Task Force 53, embarking the 4th and 5th Marine Divisions, arrived after midnight on D-Day. Minesweepers had cleared the lanes to the beaches, and the frogmen of the underwater demolition teams (UDT) mapped the sea bottom and demolished all obstacles placed there to deter landing craft. As usual in such operations, the assault troops had a front row seat for the climax of the preinvasion bombing and bombardment. To Lieutenant Ronald D. Thomas of the 5th Marine Division, "It didn't seem possible that anything could be alive. The dive-bombers filled the sky and as they dove, the place was a big dust bowl."[31]

The invasion force carried 111,000 troops, including 75,000 troops in the landing force (nearly all of whom were marines) and another 36,000 in the army garrison force. The transports and landing ships carried 98,000 tons of supplies. Many of the smaller amphibious landing craft, such as the amtracs (LVTs) and amphibious trucks (DUKWs), had been preloaded in Pearl Harbor with rations, ammunition, fuel, and other supplies. Surface warships that had been lent to MacArthur's Seventh Fleet for the Luzon invasion had been obliged to hurry north in time for Iwo Jima. The *West Virginia*, for example, had put into Ulithi Atoll on February 16, after thirty-five straight days in Lingayen Gulf. She was fueled and loaded in twenty-four hours. The venerable old battleship, a resurrected survivor of the attack on Pearl Harbor, made the 900-mile run to Iwo Jima in fifty hours, her best speed. Arriving off the island at 10:30 a.m. on D-Day (February 19), an hour and a half after the invasion had started, she provided counterbattery and call fire for eleven straight days, exhausting all of her 16-inch ammunition.

As awesome as the naval bombardment seemed, it fell far short of what the marines had wanted. While planning Operation DETACHMENT, Major General Harry Schmidt had requested a minimum of ten consecutive days' bombardment before landing. He had been backed by Lieutenant Colonel Donald M. Weller, the naval gunfire officer on Admiral Turner's staff, who had made a systematic study of the effects of naval gunfire on Tarawa, Saipan, and Peleliu. Targeting and firepower were important, said Weller—but the time duration of shore bombardment was an equally critical factor. Nothing compared with day after day of relentless big-gun shelling of defensive positions ashore. But Schmidt's request was rejected by Turner as logistically unworkable; the navy had never attempted such a prolonged bombardment. After several rounds of arguments and bargaining, Admiral Spruance had ruled that the island would receive three days' bombardment before D-Day. In explaining his decision, he referred to the risk of submarine and air counterattacks on the stationary fleet, and the difficulties involved in replenishing ammunition at sea. Lieutenant General Holland "Howlin' Mad" Smith, the top marine in the Pacific, later vented in his postwar memoir: "We had to haggle like horse traders, balancing irreplaceable lives against replaceable ammunition. I was never so depressed in my life."[32]

The command lineup was largely unchanged from that of prior operations in the Gilberts, the Marshalls, and the Marianas. Spruance remained the big boss afloat, in charge of the entire Fifth Fleet, with Mitscher as commander of Task Force 58. Admiral Turner commanded the Amphibious Expeditionary Force, as he had done since the Tarawa operation sixteen months earlier; and in that role he gave orders to the marine ground commanders, as he had done before. Smith commanded the expeditionary troops, comprising the 3rd, 4th, and 5th Marine Divisions and an army garrison force that would land after the island was secured. But Smith would not command the Fifth Amphibious Corps (VAC) directly, as he had done in prior operations; that job would fall to General Schmidt. This arrangement, which raised eyebrows among many of the subordinate field commanders, inserted a new layer into the tried-and-true command table. Smith was shoehorned between Schmidt and Turner, even though Schmidt would really be doing the same job that Smith had done in previous operations. The sixty-two-year-old Smith was facing mandatory retirement from frontline service, and Iwo Jima would be his last battle. As the only senior marine with a track record of working effectively with the irascible Kelly Turner, his job was to remain aboard the admiral's command ship *Eldorado*, representing the views and safeguarding the interests of the Marine Corps, while Schmidt went ashore and oversaw the battle on the ground.

Turner was considered irreplaceable, the leading amphibious warfare expert in the U.S. armed forces—and therefore, the world—but he did not always play nicely with others. It was an open secret that Turner had been drinking heavily every night—even while on duty at sea, in violation of standing regulations. "Admiral Turner had great difficulty with liquor," said Charles F. Barber, flag secretary to Spruance. "And yet he had a great capacity to be inoperative at night and fully operational in the morning. . . . Admiral Spruance stayed with him and valued his services."[33]

The 4th and 5th Marine Divisions would land on the island's southeast beaches. The 4th Division would drive directly inland to take control of the larger of the two airfields, Motoyama No. 1, and then turn north to take Airfield No. 2. The 5th Division would push across the relatively narrow and flat neck of the island, and then turn south to isolate and seize Mt. Suribachi. Once the volcano was in U.S. hands, the 5th Division would advance north up the west coast and form a continuous line across the island with the 4th Division. The 3rd Marine Division would be held aboard the transports offshore as a floating reserve, but Schmidt and Smith expected that it would probably be summoned ashore on the third or fourth day of the battle, to be inserted into the middle of the line. Then the three marine divisions would drive north in a line abreast to overwhelm Japanese defenses in the Motoyama Plateau.

No one expected a walkover. The Americans were braced for a bloodbath on Iwo Jima. In a press conference a week before D-Day, Admiral Turner had told the correspondents: "Iwo Jima is as well defended as any other fixed position in the world today."[34] Another officer judged that storming Gibraltar would be easier. General Smith expected his assault forces to suffer a minimum of 15,000 casualties. The fleet had converted four tank-landing ships (LSTs) into floating medical triage centers, where wounded men would be assessed and treated before being evacuated to the hospital ships *Samaritan* or *Solace*. The hospital ships would shuttle casualties back to Saipan and Guam, where 5,000 beds were available in newly built army and navy hospitals. As soon as the airfields on Iwo Jima were made available, Douglas Skymaster "Flying Ambulances" would evacuate the most gravely wounded men to the Marianas, or even directly to Oahu.

On the transports, the first-wave marines climbed down the rope-nets into the Higgins boats and amtracs. The flat-bottomed landing craft pitched and plunged on the rolling swell, and each man had to time his last step carefully, letting go when the boat was at the height of its motion. There were a number of "rough dismounts," as marines lost their footing and went sprawling into the bottom of the boats.[35] Picking themselves up, they took their seats on benches, huddled closely to make room for the others coming down the nets.

Conditions were about as favorable as one could hope for. The wind was moderate, from the northwest, and the sea was as calm as it had been in the three days since the advance elements of the task force had arrived. The naval barrage ascended in pitch, and the 16-inch battleship shells rumbled overhead, sounding like freight trains passing through a tunnel. At least a few Japanese shore batteries were firing back, because whitewater towers erupted periodically around the transport group as the first wave boats assembled behind the line of debarkation. At 8:40 a.m., at the sound of a horn, the coxswains opened their throttles and started their long run into the beach. The boats bucked and reared through the swells, so that from the point of view of those watching from the rails of the transports, they seemed to disappear entirely into the sea before rising to become visible again. It was a rough ride. Men struggled against seasickness, their tailbones bumping uncomfortably on the wooden benches, their dungarees soaked and their eyes stinging from the cold salt spray. Passing the cannonading warships, they felt the blast concussions radiating from the big naval guns. As Lieutenant Thomas's boat passed near the battleship *Tennessee*, he noted that the sea directly beneath the muzzles was flattened and smoothed each time the weapons fired.[36]

As the boats drew closer to Iwo Jima, the steep, sable-colored beach loomed ahead. On the terraces at the top of the beach, a row of wrecked

Iwo Jima
February–March 1945

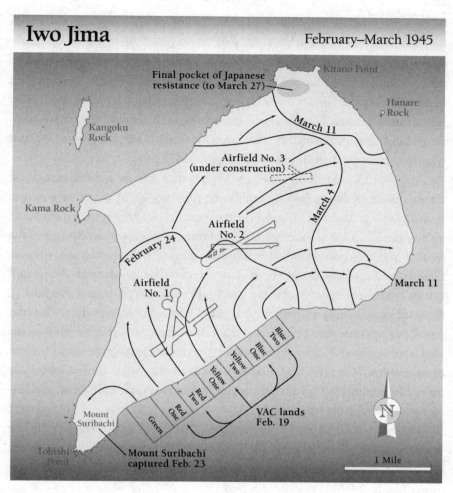

Final pocket of Japanese resistance (to March 27)

Kitano Point

Hanare Rock

Kangoku Rock

Airfield No. 3 (under construction)

March 11

Kama Rock

Airfield No. 2

March 4

February 24

March 11

Airfield No. 1

Blue Two

Blue One

Yellow Two

Yellow One

Red Two

Red One

Green

VAC lands Feb. 19

Mount Suribachi

N

Mount Suribachi captured Feb. 23

Tobishi Point

1 Mile

Japanese aircraft marked the southern end of Airfield No. 1. Towers of whitewater erupted among the incoming boats, as the Japanese mortars opened fire. The marines heard the rattle of Japanese machine gun fire and the deeper reports of heavier caliber weapons. Two files of F4U Corsairs flew low over the beach, strafing the pillboxes just inland of the terraces. These were Marine Fighter Squadrons 124 and 213, flying from the carrier *Essex*— the first Marine Corps aircraft that most of the infantrymen had ever seen. They approached on opposite headings from north and south, then peeled off at the last moment before colliding, to east and west—a "razzle-dazzle" maneuver, as the marine air coordinator recalled, which might have been "more spectacular than effective."[37] One Corsair took a direct flak hit, burst into flames, and crashed in the sea.

Nearing the beach, the coxswains struggled to keep the little flat-bottomed craft from broaching. Six-foot waves lifted the boats and set them down hard, with a crunch of coarse sand under the hull. The ramps dropped with a bang and the marines trudged up the steep-sided beach. It was a hard climb. The "sand" under their boots was soft volcanic cinder, and their boots sunk to the laces. On the steeper sections, they found themselves slipping and sliding backward. A rifleman with the 4th Marine Division said it was like "trying to run in loose coffee grounds."[38]

At first, the situation on the landing beaches seemed manageable. Unit commanders ashore radioed encouraging reports: "Light machine gun and mortar fire. . . . Light opposition on the beach. . . . Only sporadic bursts of mortar fire."[39] Colored flares went up, signaling a successful landing, and the second and third waves of boats followed quickly behind the first. On the Green and Red Beaches, at the southern end of the beachhead, the assault troops overran enemy blockhouses and pillboxes and advanced inland to a distance of 300 yards, taking only minimal losses. Some speculated that the naval barrage and air support had done the trick; Holland Smith guessed that the Japanese "lay stunned under the terrific explosive shock of our naval gunfire."[40] In the first ninety minutes of the battle for Iwo Jima, the marines put eight battalions ashore, including two tank battalions and elements of two artillery battalions.

The hardest fighting that morning was in the craggy terrain at the far northern flank, above Blue Beach 2, in an area the marines called the "Rock Quarry." Here the gorges and rock faces were seemingly impervious even to direct hits by 1,000-pound bombs and large-caliber naval weapons. The terrain had been improved with prolific use of concrete and rebar, and all possible approach lanes were swept by machine guns. From the moment they landed, the 3rd Battalion, 25th Marines were under punishing machine gun and mortar fire. As they advanced over the first terrace, they drew a crossfire from pillboxes inland and to the south. To Lieutenant Colonel Justice M. Chambers, the battalion commander, the Japanese seemed to be targeting them from every direction: "You could have held a cigarette and lit it on the stuff going by. I knew immediately we were in for one hell of a time."[41] The Rock Quarry was the hinge upon which the entire U.S. line would turn. The 25th Marines had a critical job to do, and they knew it. They could do nothing but take the casualties and keep fighting, so they did.

At 11:00 a.m., the Japanese mortar and artillery barrage suddenly intensified. The weapons had been preregistered to hit the invasion beaches, between the surf line and the top terraces, where the American troops were densely concentrated in exposed positions. The naval task forces and support planes did their best to silence this fire, but the Japanese gun emplacements on Suribachi and the Motoyama Plateau were well camouflaged, and many could not be seen even from overhead. Sherman tanks, put ashore from LSMs in the third and fourth waves, struggled to climb the beaches, and they made fat targets for the Japanese artillerymen. Marines landing behind Chambers's 3rd Battalion on Blue Beach were cut down by machine gun fire as they left their landing boats. Heavy mortar fire also descended on the Red beaches north of Suribachi, where the going had been easier that morning. The marines lay prone in the soft cinder, digging for cover with their entrenching shovels, their helmets, and their bare hands. But the cinder lacked cohesive consistency, and their foxholes collapsed inward. "God damn!" one exclaimed. "It's like digging a hole in a barrel of wheat."[42]

By noon, the landing beaches looked like junkyards. Surveying the scene through binoculars from the *Eldorado*, about two miles offshore, General Holland Smith compared it to "a row of frame houses in a tornado."[43] Tanks and amphibious tractors failed to surmount the steep beach gradient, or were swamped in the surf, or took direct artillery hits, or ran over mines, or fell into tank traps, or stripped their treads, or could not find a path between other wrecked, stranded, and burning vehicles. Bodies and debris were scattered across the congested beach, and tanks were driving directly over the remains of slain marines. The pileup of wreckage posed a hazard for incoming landing boats. The coxswains steered toward an unobstructed patch of sand between the burning wrecks, but many boats broached in the surf. Pontoon causeways became unmoored and went rogue, surfing uncontrollably on the incoming breakers, colliding with boats or striking marines from behind as they trudged up the beach. But since the marines ashore desperately needed more men, tanks, artillery, ammunition, and supplies, Admiral Turner had no option but to keep sending more boats to attempt landings.

Entire platoons lay immobilized, pinned down in the dark volcanic cinder. The whine and blast of the mortars was earsplitting, and men had to shout to make themselves heard. Those who stood and advanced to a new position risked being cut down by machine gun or rifle fire from the pillboxes at the top of the terraces. But those who remained in their hastily dug holes risked taking direct hits from the relentless mortars. The Japanese

were using a giant 320mm "spigot mortar," which lobbed a 675-pound shell
to a distance of 1,440 yards. The marines called it the "flying ashcan," or the
"screaming Jesus." They could look up and watch the ugly black specks as
they approached in high-arching trajectories. One officer recalled, "I'd hold
up my finger out in front of my eye, and if it moved left or right I'd know it
wasn't coming down near me. But if my finger blocked it for more than a
split-second, then I knew I was in trouble."[44]

Medical corpsmen rushed across exposed ground to assist the wounded,
but for the men worst hit by mortar shrapnel, there was little that could
be done. Flesh was slashed and shredded, limbs severed, faces disfigured,
and wounds contaminated by the ubiquitous volcanic cinder. The corpsmen administered morphine shots, applied tourniquets, bandaged wounds,
inserted intravenous needles for blood plasma, and dragged the wounded
men to cover. Often they were hit by artillery or snipers while crouched
beside their patients. On Red Beach, a badly wounded marine—blinded,
with both hands blown off—was stumbling back toward the beach through
a hail of artillery and machine gun fire. A lone corpsman rushed out over
open ground to guide the man to an aid station. Many corpsmen on Iwo
Jima paid the price for such selfless service. In the 4th Marine Division, the
casualty rate among medical corpsmen was 38 percent.

On the ships offshore, pitching and rolling on the whitecap-flecked swell,
the expressions on the faces of senior commanders told the tale. The situation was dire. The later waves were taking heavier losses than the earlier
waves. A backlog of casualties on the beach awaited evacuation to the fleet.
Warships offshore and carrier planes circling overhead were doing their
best to identify and destroy the Japanese mortars and guns, but the enemy's
weapons were mounted in deep embrasures. Nothing but a direct hit could
silence them, and sometimes not even that. Carrier planes dropped napalm
bombs on the positions they could see, hoping to kill the Japanese gunners
or drive them underground. But the rain of mortars continued unremitting,
and each successive blast ejected ash, debris, and bodies high into the air.
It was vital to get more troops and tanks ashore before dark, because all
dreaded a night counterattack in force. The marines on the beach had to
push inland as quickly as possible, even if it meant taking heavy casualties,
to make space for succeeding waves.

At nightfall, the Americans had 40,000 troops ashore. They held about
10 percent of the island, from the northeast corner of Motoyama Airfield

No. 1 to a point farther south where the 5th Division had bisected the narrow isthmus north of Mt. Suribachi. The Japanese held high ground to the north and south, and looked down on the marines from lofty observation posts. All night long—indeed, for every night in the month to come—the battlefield was kept brightly illuminated by starshells fired by the warships offshore. An average of a thousand illumination rounds were expended each night of the campaign. The marines credited the searing, spectral light for deterring Japanese small-unit infiltration attacks. In a letter home, a destroyer sailor described the strange visual effect: "It was interesting watching the shells float downward through a thick white cloud. They would burst in the midst of the cloud and cause it to glow like snow and then drift downward through the layers and finally through the bottom and light up the whole island."[45]

Few slept a wink that first night, and lookouts kept their eyes peeled for any sign of the enemy. The night was chilly, even cold—a reminder that this was winter and they were north of the tropics. But no attack came, and by dawn the American commanders were beginning to understand that they were up against a shrewd infantry tactician. There would be no major counterattacks over open ground, where the Americans could bring their superior firepower and air support to bear. The defenders would remain underground, out of sight, and out of range, and make the attackers pay for every inch of territory they gained.

To the south, the 28th Marines looked up at "Hot Rocks"—the name they had given to Mt. Suribachi—a steep-sided mass of brown ash, barren of vegetation, whose sulfuric steam vents jetted foul vapors. The regiment, led by Colonel Harry B. Liversedge, had orders to isolate the little volcano, seal off its caves and bunkers, root out its defenders, and secure the summit. Around the base, at ground level, was a girdle of seventy earth-covered concrete blockhouses manned by the soldiers of Iwo Jima's southern defense sector, led by Colonel Kanehiko Atsuchi. Before Suribachi could be scaled, the fortifications at the base would have to be cleaned out. They could not be flanked; they would have to be taken by direct infantry assault.

On the morning of D plus 1, under a cold drizzle, a tremendous combined onslaught of field artillery, naval gunfire, and carrier bombers fell upon Mt. Suribachi, and the volcano momentarily vanished behind a mantle of smoke, flames, and dust. At 8:30 a.m., the appointed "jump-off time," the shelling and bombing abruptly halted. The marines advanced in a running crouch, crossing from rocks to shell craters to rocks. The 2nd Battalion attacked to the left, and the 3rd to the right. Advancing into machine gun and 47mm antitank gunfire, many fell. The 2nd Battalion took the worst casualties of the day. The last 200 yards of their advance was over flat volcanic soil, offering little or no cover. Throwing smoke grenades to blind their enemies, they advanced directly against the enemy firing ports. Private Donald J. Ruhl of Company E fell on a Japanese grenade, trading his life to shield others in his platoon. In recognition of this ultimate sacrifice, he was awarded a posthumous Medal of Honor.

At Camp Pendleton, in Southern California, the marines had learned and practiced their system. They executed it patiently, meticulously, with devout attention to detail: heavy naval gunfire, napalm bombs dropped by planes, tanks and 75mm halftracks advancing to point-blank range, smoke grenades to blind the Japanese, phosphorus grenades and demolition charges thrown into firing ports, flamethrowers fired into rear exit doors, hand-to-hand combat with bayonets, knives, and even fists. Where the terrain prevented tanks from advancing on the Japanese defenses, 37mm guns were hauled into an advanced position, from which they could take a concrete structure apart, little by little—killing, stunning, or otherwise neutralizing the occupants, so that infantry squads could move in and finish the job. One by one, the blockhouses were converted into tombs. Armored bulldozers pushed mounds of earth against them, so that they could not be reoccupied by the Japanese.

The third day of the battle was gray and blustery, with scattered rain showers. The 3rd Battalion attacked in the center of the line, through broken terrain that stopped the U.S. tanks. To the left, the 2nd Battalion worked to clean out its rear areas, where snipers and individual Japanese fighters had mysteriously appeared. By nightfall, the 28th Marines had surrounded the mountain and silenced all but a few of the enemy firing positions around the base. According to Lieutenant Colonel Robert H. Williams, the regimental executive officer, the fighting tailed off sharply once the regiment overran the enemy lines at the base of Suribachi. He told Major General Keller E. Rockey, commander of the 5th Marine Division: "We figure we've killed about 800 Japs down there, but we'd have a hard time finding 100. We must have blown up 50 caves."[46]

With the Americans in control at the base of the hill, Colonel Atsuchi now attempted a breakout, ordering his remaining organized forces to try a dash for the northern lines. Nearly all the Japanese were cut down as they came into the open, but about twenty-five somehow crossed through the American lines to the Motoyama Plateau, where the bulk of Japanese fighting forces remained. Kuribayashi was disappointed to learn that his Suribachi detachment had not held out longer. He asked his staff, "I had imagined the fact that the first airfield should fall into the enemy's hands. But what is the matter that Mt. Suribachi would fall within only 3 days?"[47]

On the fourth day of the fight, the marines took the summit. The morning was gray and drizzling, as the previous days had been—and it began as the previous days had begun, with a prodigious naval and air bombardment that pummeled Mt. Suribachi until it was enveloped in smoke and dust. Two scouting patrols reconnoitered a footpath to the crater, up the steep and menacing east face. A forty-man patrol followed, reaching the summit a few minutes after ten. Resistance was scattered. A few Japanese emerged from tunnels and caves, including an officer who waved a samurai sword as he charged; all were quickly killed. Wielding flamethrowers and explosive charges, the marines sealed off all cave entrances they could locate. Many Japanese took their own lives, by holding grenades against their chests or inserting their rifles into their mouths and pulling the triggers with their toes. A revolting stench emerged from some of the interior cavities on Suribachi, where the remains of Japanese soldiers were scattered thickly on the ground.

From the peak, the Americans took in a panoramic view to the north: the airfields, the landing beaches, the naval task force offshore. Their fellow marines were heavily engaged in a firefight on the flat terrain between the two airfields. For the first four days of the battle, the Japanese had commanded this tactically useful observation post. Now the roles were reversed; the Americans owned Suribachi, and they had a flag to prove it. Marines of Company E, 2nd Battalion pulled a 10-foot length of lead pipe out of the rubble—it had connected a water cistern to a bunker beneath the summit—and rigged it as a flagpole. At 10:20 a.m., they raised their battalion flag. Observers to the north, and on ships offshore, were overjoyed. Lieutenant Ronald Thomas recalled, "Everyone yelled and I suppose some cried."[48] Brigadier General Leo Hermle, assistant commander of the 5th Division, called it "one of the greatest sights that I remember in my whole life . . . a terrific cheer went up from the whole island, as far as you could see."[49]

Jim Forrestal, the secretary of the navy, had been observing Operation DETACHMENT from Admiral Turner's command ship *Eldorado*. Forrestal was a spare man of medium height, with a pug nose and a straight, wide mouth. His sandy brown hair was slicked back and parted high on his head. He was an intense, hard-driving former Wall Street bond salesman who had become one of FDR's most trusted and influential cabinet advisors. The secretary had chosen this morning, D plus 4, to come ashore for a brief tour of Red Beach. Wearing a helmet and plain green fatigues without insignia, escorted by General Holland Smith and a platoon of marines, he disembarked from a Higgins boat just as the tiny flag was spied atop the southern peak. Forrestal turned to Smith and said, "Holland, the raising of that flag on Suribachi means a Marine Corps for the next 500 years."[50]

The navy secretary had been pushing for more fulsome publicity in Nimitz's theater. He had taken a direct hand in streamlining censorship functions, and had pressured the admirals to guarantee overnight transmission of press copy and photographs to newsrooms in the United States. During his current tour of the Pacific, Forrestal had often reminded the navy and marine brass that an epochal political struggle lay ahead over the reorganization and unification of the armed services, and the postwar status of the Marine Corps was not yet decided. The "500 years" remark thus had a contemporary context and subtext: Forrestal meant that the stirring image would strengthen the corps' claim to an autonomous role in the postwar defense establishment.

According to the scene recounted by General Smith in his postwar memoir, Forrestal sauntered among wrecked boats, tanks, and tractors on the crowded beach, shaking hands with surprised marines, while artillery shells and mortar blasts blanketed the area. Twenty men were killed or wounded within a hundred yards of where they were standing, Smith wrote—"but the Secretary seemed utterly indifferent to danger."[51] Perhaps Forrestal seemed indifferent because the situation was not as the general described it. In his diary entry that day, Forrestal recorded only that "the beach received some shelling during the morning but it was not considerable, although one burst did inflict casualties an hour before we were there."[52]

A second and more famous flag-raising occurred three hours later, when a subsequent patrol of the 28th Marines carried a larger "replacement" flag to the summit of Mt. Suribachi. Associated Press photographer Joe Rosenthal was on hand to record the scene. As six marines raised the flagpole, with the flag snapping smartly in the breeze, Rosenthal pressed the shutter button on his camera without even looking through the viewfinder. He sent his undeveloped film roll to Guam, where it was developed by an AP photo editor and sent on to the United States. The hastily snapped photograph, an accidental masterpiece of composition, became the single most iconic image of the Pacific War. Transmitted through copper telephone wires to newsrooms throughout the United States, it appeared simultaneously on hundreds of front pages and magazine covers. Rosenthal received a Pulitzer Prize. The flag-raising was adopted as the thematic showpiece of a national war bonds campaign, and three surviving marines in the photo were recalled to the United States for a publicity tour. The image was re-created as a bronze sculpture at the Marine Corps War Memorial in Arlington, Virginia.

The 28th Marines reported 510 men killed and wounded in the fight for Mt. Suribachi. Including its losses on D-Day, the regiment had suffered 895 casualties in five days. As bad as those losses were, they were no worse than those suffered over the same period by other regiments fighting to the north. At home, many Americans assumed that the flag-raising in Rosenthal's photograph must have marked the triumphant climax of a victorious campaign. In fact, the conquest of Suribachi was just one early phase of a long and costly battle. The fight for the Motoyama Plateau would eventually claim twenty American lives for every one lost on Suribachi. On D plus 6 (February 25), the 28th Marines were returned to the V Amphibious Corps reserves, and they began moving north to join their brothers on the bloody line bisecting the midsection of the island.

GENERAL SCHMIDT ESTABLISHED his V Amphibious Corps (VAC) headquarters north of the now-pacified Mt. Suribachi. That entire portion of the island, half a mile behind the front line, was gradually assuming the appearance of a working base. The unfavorable weather of past days gave way to lighter winds and calmer surf, allowing cargo unloading to proceed. Supply dumps, assembly areas, motor pools, fuel dumps, administrative command tents, and field hospitals were set up by rear-echelon troops, even while the enemy's mortars and artillery kept raining down. Bulldozers were improving the road net, and clean-up details were hauling wreckage away from the main transportation arteries. Seabees of the 31st Naval Construction Battalion were at work on Motoyama Airfield No. 1, clearing the runway and revetments of mines and bringing concrete mixers and heavy construction equipment ashore. Schmidt told a reporter that five more days of heavy fighting would extinguish enemy resistance on Iwo Jima: "I said last week it would take ten days, and I haven't changed my mind."[53]

The major combat line now ran through Motoyama Airfield No. 2, which was at slightly higher elevation than No. 1. The runway and taxiways were strewn with airplane wreckage that the Japanese infantry units had adopted as rough and ready pillboxes. The marines called down naval gunfire, heavy artillery fire, and airstrikes on these positions, and then attacked across the open field with tanks and infantry. The dark domed rock of the Motoyama Plateau loomed ahead to the north. Taking it would require ascending a staircase of lava terraces honeycombed with fearsome defenses. Holland Smith described it as a "deep belt of fortifications running from coast to coast, a mass of mutually supporting pillboxes, many of them almost buried underground."[54] The terrain did not offer many prospects for flanking attacks, so the marines were left with no option except direct frontal assault by brute force. Lieutenant Colonel Joseph L. Stewart called it a "grunt and crunch-type operation."[55] Another officer used the inevitable football metaphor: "You can't run the ends up there. Every play is between the tackles."[56]

Schmidt called in the rest of his floating reserve: the 3rd Marine Division (less one regiment), commanded by Major General Graves B. Erskine. This veteran outfit was inserted into the center of the line, with the 5th Division on its left and the 4th on its right—and assigned the tough task of driving directly north through the remains of Motoyama Village and the unfinished Airfield No. 3, up into the tableland at the center of the Motoyama Plateau. Schmidt ordered that 50 percent of VAC artillery fire be directed into this area, with the remaining 50 percent to be divided equally between the flanks facing the 4th and 5th Divisions. With three divisions abreast, the renewed northward offensive was commenced on D plus 5, one day after the flag-raising on Suribachi.

The Americans possessed a three-to-one advantage in troop strength over the defenders, a ten-to-one advantage in artillery firepower (if the naval guns were counted), and total control of the air. But Kuribayashi's ingenious subterranean defenses effectively vitiated those advantages. Often the tanks had to be left behind, at least in the first stages of an attack, because all routes up to higher terraces had been heavily mined or blocked by tank traps. The infantry led the way, attacking with small arms, flamethrowers, and demolitions. In the center of the line, the 3rd Division took heavy casualties as it drove into some of the most heavily fortified ground anywhere in the Pacific.

For men on the line, the din of battle was inescapable. The rattle of machine gun fire and the ululating roar of artillery and mortars never paused. They kept their heads down, knowing that Japanese snipers posted in higher ground were constantly watching through their rifle scopes. The Japanese even sniped with their larger weapons, particularly their 47mm antitank guns, which could be aimed accurately enough to hit a single man at several hundred feet range. With so many heavy weapons firing, men became fatalistic about mere rifle shots, and even demonstrated their indifference when the bullets snapped through the air nearby. Captain William Ketcham of I Company, 24th Marines, was hit in one arm and one leg, but after having the limbs bandaged, he remained on the line with his company. He scoffed: "Shot at me twelve times and barely broke the skin with two bullets."[57]

The infantrymen learned to hate the island almost as much as they hated the enemy. Iwo Jima was "ghastly," recalled Ted Allenby of the 4th Marine Division: "It was almost like a piece of the moon that had dropped down to earth."[58] Digging into the ground for protection against the relentless enemy fire, the marines released vents of foul sulfurous steam. The sulfur merged sickeningly with the odor of burning and rotting flesh, a stench that could not be escaped anywhere on the island. Land crabs emerged from the cinders at the bottom of their foxholes and scuttled across their bodies as they tried to sleep. Fine volcanic dust, stirred up by wind and explosions, got into men's eyes, ears, noses, and mouths. The ground was warm to the touch, and it grew warmer the deeper they dug. Elton Shrode buried his canned rations in the ground at the bottom of his foxhole. Half an hour later, he dug up the can and "would have a steaming hot C-ration to consume. This was the only advantage that I could come up with for this miserable rock."[59]

With about 80,000 troops concentrated into less than eight square miles, Iwo Jima was one of the most densely populated battlefields in history.

Given the amount of firepower on both sides, the carnage was hideous. The worst of it was on the front lines, but there was really no such thing as a rear area on Iwo Jima. Each combatant had the power to direct heavy artillery and mortar fire to any location on the island; consequently, everywhere on the island was in one sense the front line. Rolling barrages raked the beaches, the foxholes, and the command posts. Letups were brief. The marines grudgingly praised their enemy's diabolical skill. "The Japanese were superb artillerymen," said Colonel Stewart: "Somebody was getting hit every time they fired." There was no safe ground, no rear area, and—for the Americans—little natural cover. General Schmidt's VAC headquarters, a short distance north of Mt. Suribachi, was a cluster of tents surrounded by sandbags. According to Colonel Edward Craig, Schmidt's operations officer, the post came under intermittent heavy shelling throughout the battle. The sandbag embankments grew steadily higher, but the concussions were still a terror. Whenever it started up, Craig recalled, "we were three-deep on the floor of a small C.P. tent, and there we remained until it stopped."[60] Half a mile north, at the 4th Marine Division command post, the huge 320mm spigot mortars crashed down on every side, the sky glowed an unearthly red, and a fine mist of ash particles hung in the air. The marine howitzers and the warships offshore answered with counterbarrages, but the Japanese seemed unfazed, and their heavy weapons kept at it with undiminished ferocity.

The headquarters remained in touch with the division commands and the front lines by radio or message runners. Insights offered by regimental and company commanders influenced the tactical decisions of General Schmidt and his staff. Many officers and NCOs in the VAC and division CPs were detached for combat duty and sent forward to replace those killed or wounded in action. The wounded were transported south in jeep "ambulances" or by hand-carried stretchers. Trucks, tanks, and bulldozers headed north. Mines were buried all over the island, posing an omnipresent peril. Marines walking along tracks learned to take care to set their boots into the treads made by vehicles. Large antitank mines were buried deep, so that the minesweeping teams did not always find them. They were triggered when a tank or another heavy vehicle passed over. Shrode saw it happen to a heavy DS Cat bulldozer that was widening a road south of the No. 2 Airfield. "There was a terrible explosion and the DS disappeared right in front of my eyes, so I ran for cover. Pieces of that tractor rained down all over the area.

Some of those parts weighed at least a thousand pounds. The driver, God rest his soul, landed about ten yards from me."[61]

In the first five days of the battle, the marines suffered an average of more than 1,200 casualties per day. The beaches and the flat terrain around the airfields were strewn with dead. Shell craters left records of direct hits; some contained the mashed-up remains of ten or twelve marines. Exploring the terraces above Red Beach, Bob Sherrod observed: "Nowhere in the Pacific War had I seen such badly mangled bodies. Many were cut squarely in half. Legs and arms lay fifty feet away from any body. In one spot on the sand, far from the nearest cluster of dead, I saw a string of guts 15 feet long."[62] Losses were proportionally higher among officers and NCOs. Gunnery Sergeant John Basilone, a nationally famous marine who had received the Medal of Honor for his heroics on Guadalcanal, was killed on D-Day as he led his men onto Motoyama Airfield No. 1.

Armored bulldozers were digging long trenches to serve as mass graves. "We buried fifty at a time in bulldozed plots," said Chaplain Gage Hotaling. "We didn't know if they were Jewish, Catholic or whatever, so we said a general committal: 'We commit you into the earth and the mercy of Almighty God.' "[63]

Warships patrolled off the coast, the destroyers and gunboats close inshore and the cruisers and battleships farther in the offing. Marine coordinators on the front lines could call down accurate naval gunfire on any target, via an open radio net linking them to gunnery officers on the ships. The ships often fired by radar direction alone, as the crews simply entered coordinates into the fire directors. The navy's guns could not always be employed to good effect on Iwo Jima, because of the close proximity of friendly and enemy troops. Nevertheless, as Admiral Turner reported, there were an "unprecedented number" of naval call fire missions during the operation. High-explosive shells ranging in caliber from 16-inch to 5-inch rained down upon targets across the Motoyama tablelands. Small gunboats—modified landing craft armed with rockets, light mortars, and 20mm guns—patrolled close inshore around the northwestern part of the island, delivering harassing fire on enemy positions. They also deterred movements of Japanese troops along the shores, and intercepted boats attempting to land from Chichi Jima or other islands to the north.

On the destroyer *Howorth*, the voice of a marine officer ashore was broadcast through the ship's loudspeakers, so that every man aboard could follow the action. Because the island was often obscured by smoke and dust, the crew could rarely see their 5-inch salvos strike home. Yeoman James Orvill Raines felt proud when the voice on the radio link confirmed that the *Howorth* was hitting her assigned targets: "Look at those bastards run!" And later, "It might interest you to know your shooting is very good. The results are very gratifying." Raines peered through binoculars, trying to make out what was happening ashore. When the smoke cleared, he caught a glimpse of a Sherman tank advancing into heavy machine gun fire, with an infantry squad crouching behind it. In a letter to his wife, Raines wrote that he was thrilled to know that the *Howorth*'s guns were hitting the enemy. "I'm glad, in spite of the sacrifice I feel that you and I are making, that I had something to do with killing some of them. I feel really grand about it. I get a special kick out of killing them. I only wish I were in close enough to see their bodies and parts of bodies go sky high when our shells hit." On the other hand, Raines admitted that he preferred to watch the action from his relatively safe vantage point on the *Howorth*: "You couldn't have dragged me on the beach with a winch."[64]

The Japanese air response to the invasion of Iwo Jima was fairly weak, due to a combination of inclement weather and Task Force 58's suppressing airstrikes on Tokyo airfields. Few Japanese warplanes appeared over the island, and when they did, most were quickly downed by the U.S. carrier fighters patrolling overhead. Only one massed kamikaze attack was attempted. At twilight on February 21 (D plus 2), about fifty twin-engine Mitsubishi G4Ms accompanied by Zeros attacked the fleet in the offing. The carrier *Saratoga* was hit by three planes, suffering casualties of 123 killed and 192 wounded, and was forced to return to Pearl Harbor for repairs. The escort carrier *Bismarck Sea* was hit aft by a suicide plane, causing fatal secondary explosions in her hangar. Her fires burned out of control, and she rolled over and sank, taking 218 officers and men down with her. A second CVE, the *Lunga Point*, was slightly damaged after fighting off four kamikazes. A cargo ship and an LST were also hit and badly damaged.

U.S. ground forces on the island never lacked for close air support. Bombing, reconnaissance, and strafing missions were flown by aircraft of three services—the navy, the marines, and the Army Air Forces. At times, American warplanes were so thick over Iwo Jima that collisions appeared inevitable. Hour after hour, formations of Grummans, Voughts, and Curtiss bombers winged in from the carriers, sun flashing off their wings. The dive-bombers plunged down at 70-degree angles and released their bombs on unseen targets behind enemy lines, causing spurts of flame to leap up from boiling masses of smoke and dust. Low-flying fighters walked .50-caliber tracers across Japanese gun emplacements, or fired 5-inch rockets from 2,000 feet altitude. The flyboys put on an impressive show, the marines agreed. But the effectiveness of strafing, bombing, and rocketry was limited by the same factors that dogged naval gunfire. Much of it had little effect on the island's brawny caves and sunken casemates, and the pilots were wary of hitting friendly troops—as well they should have been, given the nearness of the opposing lines. The carrier planes provided other useful services, of course, such as aerial spotting for artillery, and deterring Japanese troops from moving over open ground. But the tactical situation on Iwo Jima called for unprecedented teamwork between ground forces and aircrews, a paradigm that took time and experience to refine.

Colonel Vernon E. Megee, the marine air coordinator, came ashore on February 24. He set up his communications tent in the VAC complex north of Suribachi. Eventually he would take over as air commander, Iwo Jima. Megee pioneered a system in which air liaison officers on the front lines could call down airstrikes on Japanese positions as close as 300 yards away. Marine tactical observers flew in the rear cockpits of TBM Avengers, with open radio links to artillery battalions on the ground. Japanese anti-aircraft fire was generally moderate, but it burst forth at unexpected times and places. In the course of the month-long battle, it claimed twenty-six American planes destroyed and nine seriously damaged.

On March 6, the USAAF's Fifteenth Fighter Group—including a contingent of P-51s (Mustangs) and P-61s (Black Widows)—flew into Airfield No. 1. The army airmen had not been trained for close support of ground combat operations, but they were crackerjack pilots with an "eager-beaver attitude," and they were willing to try whatever Megee asked them to do. The P-51s had the horsepower to carry and deliver 1,000-pound bombs, which had much greater effect than 500-pounders against the sandstone pumice of Iwo's rocky northern heights. Approaching their targets in a 45-degree glide, the Mustangs flew parallel to the front lines, in order to reduce the risk of misses that would endanger the marines. Half-ton bombs with delayed-action fuses, when dropped into enclosed canyons or recesses in the rocky terrain, exploded with amplified destructive force. In a few memorable instances, said Megee, a bomb dropped by a P-51 "blew the sides of entire cliffs into the ocean, exposing enemy caves and tunnels to direct fire from the sea."[65]

When talking to battalion and regimental commanders, Megee stressed that the 1,000-pounders posed a serious hazard to their troops, especially in case of a wide miss in the direction of U.S. lines. As a rule of thumb, he proposed that target distances should be one yard for every pound of bomb, meaning that the 1,000-pounders should be aimed at targets no less than 1,000 yards from the marines: "A 1000-pound bomb going off two or three hundred yards in front of you is no toy." But the 4th Marine Division, engaged in a bitter, bloody struggle against cave fortifications on the northeast coast of the island, wanted the Mustangs to hit enemy positions directly opposite their lines. One battalion commander told Megee, "Well, you can't hurt us any worse than we're being hurt." With a radio link directly to the cockpits, the marines would take cover just before the bombs were released. "So I went up there and ran all these strikes," Megee said, "and we jarred the back teeth of a lot of people, including mine, but we didn't hurt anybody but Japs."[66]

GENERAL SCHMIDT'S TEN-DAY VICTORY FORECAST had been far too optimistic. On Sunday, March 4—the two-week mark—major combat remained as intense as it had been at any point in the campaign. The marines held about two-thirds of Iwo Jima, including all three airfields, and had smashed through Kuribayashi's outer line of defenses on the Motoyama Plateau. V Amphibious Corps had taken 13,000 casualties, including 3,000 dead. The worst-hit units had lost their commanders, their officers, and their NCOs, and then adjusted to the arrival of new commanders, officers, and NCOs, and then lost the replacements. On the eastern anchor of the lines, the 4th Marine Division finally overran the craggy coastal inlet they called the "Amphitheater." The 5th Marine Division on the west was driving toward Nichi Ridge and Hill 362-B, and running into tough resistance in the rocky cliffs along the coast. In the center, the 3rd Marine Division had fought a punishing offensive into high, broken terrain, advancing by 3,000 yards in nine heartbreaking days. The dark, menacing shape of the "Motoyama honeycomb" loomed directly ahead. This zone of action was only about one square mile in area, but it included a thousand different cave or tunnel entrances to the sophisticated labyrinth that lay beneath.

To the south, in the plains around the airfields, rear-echelon troops were building an advanced operating base. Beach unloading was now progressing with little interference, except an occasional long-range mortar or artillery shell. A cemetery, marked by lengthening rows of white crosses, had been established in the shadow of the pockmarked slopes of Mt. Suribachi. The Seabees of the 133rd Naval Construction Battalion had erected six water distillation units. The energy-hungry machines converted saltwater into potable processed water, which was trucked to the front lines in five-gallon cans. By March 6, the distillers were producing enough drinking water to fill three canteens per marine on the island each day. Meanwhile, in the Japanese caves and bunkers, water stockpiles were rapidly diminishing and men were beginning to succumb to the ravages of thirst.

On March 4, the Superfortress *Dinah Might* (1st Squadron, 9th Bombardment Group) made an emergency landing at Motoyama No. 1, which the Americans had named South Field. Heavily damaged in a bombing mission over Japan, the aircraft would have been forced to ditch at sea if not for the runway on Iwo Jima. As it taxied to a stop and shut down its four engines, a crowd of perhaps two hundred marines and Seabees gathered around it. Photographers and a motion picture crew recorded the historic scene. The arrival of the big silver bomber was an unforgettable milestone in the campaign, and a timely boost to morale. It dramatized the larger purpose of the bloody island fight—to secure an airbase within easy striking range of Tokyo. A month later, P-51 Mustangs of VII Fighter Command would begin joining up with northbound formations of B-29s, providing fighter escort during their bombing missions. A squadron of navy B-24 (PB4Ys) patrol bombers would begin operating from Iwo Jima on March 16. While fighting still raged a mile and a half north, South Field was beginning to assume the appearance of a major working airbase.

After a command conference at the VAC headquarters, Schmidt ordered a renewed offensive by all three divisions across the line, to be prefaced by a massed artillery bombardment. On March 5, the most worn out and battle-scarred units were pulled back to the rear assembly areas for a short rest, and to integrate replacement troops into the decimated battalions. They were back on the line before dawn on March 6, when the artillery "preparation" started up. This was the heaviest barrage of the battle, a prolonged onslaught by all available field howitzers combined with support from the big guns offshore. The artillery battalions reported the day's ammunition expenditure as 2,500 155-millimeter "Long Tom" rounds and 20,000 75mm and 105mm rounds. A battleship, two cruisers, three destroyers, and miscellaneous gunboats added 22,500 naval shells. Target coordinates were set at least 200 yards ahead of the U.S. lines, but many shells fell uncomfortably close to the marines, and a few strays fell directly into their lines. The airplanes also did their part, bombing and strafing with exquisite timing. As usual, amateur witnesses doubted that anyone or anything could have survived under the monstrous punishment; as usual, they were mistaken.

As the barrage lifted, the assault echelons advanced against the enemy lines. Where the terrain allowed it, the Shermans led the infantry. The Japanese opened murderous volleys of machine gun and rifle fire; their resistance was seemingly just as stiff as it had been before. Deadly fire poured out of pillboxes and cave entrances, catching the advancing marines in enfilade. White phosphorus shells fell around them, forcing them to fall flat on the ground and dig for cover. New Japanese firing positions, previously undiscovered, opened fire from inconvenient angles. Given the broken and rocky character of the terrain, the tanks could not advance in many places, and the infantry was obliged to go ahead. The forward momentum of the coordinated attack quickly petered out, but the marines did not withdraw; the fighting continued at a fierce pitch throughout the rest of the day. In hopes of breaking stalemates, forward unit commanders called down artillery strikes on positions as close as 100 yards from their own positions. A few caves were sealed off, some pillboxes were taken out by flamethrowers and demolitions, and scores of Japanese were killed. But the defenders rarely exposed themselves by attacking over open ground. They stuck to their entrenchments and fortifications, and circulated through their underground networks, as they had been told to do by General Kuribayashi.

By the end of the day on March 6, the marines had advanced by about 250 yards in the draws and gorges along the coasts, but in most places their forward progress was limited to 50 yards. Against the toughest part of the line, the marines might have gained only 30 yards—but that was something, after all. Differing rates of advance left exposed flanks and salients on both sides, which offered the prospect of flanking attacks (and even attacks from overhead) against previously unassailable Japanese firing positions. Armored bulldozers cleared paths through the broken terrain, so that the tanks and 75mm armed half-tracks could move forward with the infantry. But it took time and patience to blaze new tank trails, and to sweep out the mines, and all of it had to be done while under enemy fire. General Clifton B. Cates, commanding the 4th Marine Division, summed up the sense of resignation that had taken hold among the brass. "Well, we'll keep on hitting them," he told Bob Sherrod. "They can't take it forever. We've got to keep pressing 'em until they break. Don't let up."[67]

On March 7, General Schmidt told the artillery battalions to conserve ammunition, which was running dangerously low after the previous morning's pyrotechnics. He ordered the 5th Marine Division to turn its attack inland and seize high ground overlooking the sea and the chain of formidable defenses around Kitano Point. But the 27th Marines came under devastating mortar fire just as they were preparing to jump off for battle. Company E of the 2nd Battalion took a direct mortar strike that killed or wounded thirty-five men. Not surprisingly, the attack in that area bogged down almost immediately. To the east, in the 4th Division zone of action, much rearguard cleaning up had to be done behind the lines, in the Amphitheater and Turkey Knob features, where new Japanese fighters suddenly materialized as if by some dark sorcery. The division was in rough shape. Leadership had been compromised by the death of so many officers and NCOs. Symptoms of combat fatigue were observed. The division had encountered problems integrating replacement marines at the company and platoon levels. A report noted that "the result of fatigue and lack of experienced leaders is very evident in the manner in which the units fight," and estimated that the 4th Division's combat efficiency was about 40 percent of its D-Day baseline.

The ground north of the Amphitheater was a series of jagged rocky ridges alternating with ravines clustered with heavy underbrush. The 25th Marines continued pressing inland, enveloping the enemy and closing a tighter cordon around a shrinking pocket occupied by the Second Mixed Brigade, commanded by Major General Sadasue Senda. Eyeing the risk of a breakout attack, perhaps even a massed *banzai* charge, the marines strung coils of barbed wire and planted hundreds of anti-personnel mines between them. They set up weapons of various types and calibers to sweep the terrain over which the Japanese must attack, and registered their pack howitzers and light mortars to hit the no man's land in front of their lines.

In the 3rd Marine Division's sector, there had been insufficient progress toward Hill 362C, a promontory of special tactical value, and a key link in the chain of defenses across the high part of the plateau. The only route led through some of Iwo Jima's most jumbled and rocky ground, where the Japanese had prepared fiendishly strong defenses. It was an ominous landscape, smelling strongly of sulfur. The ground was warm underfoot—so much so that it was uncomfortable to lie flat and even more so to dig a foxhole. Yet the troops who advanced into this killing zone would need to dig for protection against the enemy's machine guns, knee mortars, and antitank guns. With little prospect of bringing its rolling armor into that broken and confused terrain, the division would have to do it the old-fashioned way, by direct infantry assault.

Never before in the Pacific War had the marines attacked at night. It was not in their doctrine or training to do so. But General Erskine had been arguing for some time that a battalion-sized night infiltration attack would catch the Japanese by surprise. Erskine requested and received permission from General Schmidt to launch his attack before dawn on March 8. At first, the flamethrower-demolition squads moved quickly and silently, penetrating about 500 yards behind the Japanese lines. With the benefit of complete surprise, they sealed off pillboxes and cave entrances before the occupants were prepared to react. Many Japanese soldiers were killed in their sleep, sometimes with bayonets. As dawn broke, the marines lobbed smoke shells into the area, drawing a veil across all sightlines. The 3rd Battalion, 9th Marines had been assigned the job of taking Hill 362C, and at first they believed they had done it. But the smoke could confuse the Americans as well as their enemies, and at about 0600 Company K's officers discovered to their distress that they had taken Hill 331—not Hill 362C, which lay another 250 yards north. And those were long yards, across an exposed salient swept by Japanese machine gun and small arms fire. Fierce fighting continued throughout the day, with two marine companies trapped and taking heavy losses. However, Colonel Boehm, leading the attack, decided to push on toward the original and correct objective. It was a bloody struggle, consuming all of the morning and the early afternoon, but by nightfall the battalion had established defensive lines around the summit of Hill 362C.

On the same day, also before dawn, General Senda's besieged forces staged their attempted breakout. This was not a massed *banzai* charge, but rather a clever series of small unit infiltration attacks all along the line, preceded by a massed mortar, rocket, and artillery fire demonstration. The attackers came stealthily, under cover of darkness, making cunning use of the jumbled terrain. But the 4th Division marines benefited by their defensive preparations. Their pack howitzers poured down shellfire on the advancing force, and many of the attackers detonated mines or were killed while trying to cut through the barbed wire aprons. About a dozen Japanese penetrated as far as the 2nd Battalion, 23rd Marines command post, where they were killed quickly. The next morning, 650 dead Japanese were counted on the battlefield. According to Lieutenant Satoru Omagari, one of a handful of Japanese survivors of the battle, the area around the Turkey Knob and the Amphitheater was a charnel house. "I saw torsos with no limbs, dismembered legs, arms and hands, and internal organs splashed onto the rocks."[68]

It was a battle pitting men above against men below, an army of surface dwellers against an army of troglodytes. Many Japanese on Iwo Jima did not see the sun at all for the last several weeks of their lives. They heard the rumbling of the tanks overhead; they heard the gaseous thrust of flames even before they felt the heat. A Japanese commander reported that the Americans were "making a desert out of everything before them. . . . They fight with a mentality as though exterminating insects."[69] When the marines seized terrain above their bunkers, the Japanese sometimes set charges and blew themselves and their enemies to Kingdom Come. It was a horror reminiscent of the "mining" attacks along the Western Front during the First World War, or the siege of Petersburg in the American Civil War. Elton Shrode witnessed one such event, on a hill north of Nishi Village: "I saw many bodies blown into the air like rag dolls."[70] Forty-three marines were killed or injured in the titanic blast.

DURING THE FIRST TWENTY-ONE DAYS of the fight on Iwo Jima, the medical corps handled an average of 1,000 casualties per day. By D plus 33, a total of 17,677 cases had been evacuated to hospital ships offshore or to hospitals in the Marianas.[71] All took justifiable pride in the outstanding efforts of medical personnel, from the corpsmen on the battlefield, to the forward aid stations, to the field hospitals, to the hospital ships offshore, to the hospitals on Saipan and Guam. Corpsmen and litter bearers, the battlefield's indefatigable first responders, rushed across terrain exposed to enemy fire. Crouching beside stricken marines, shells bursting nearby and bullets snapping over their heads, the corpsmen reached into their "Unit

3" pouches for morphine syrettes, called "Hypos," to ease a man's pain and relieve the symptoms of shock; sulfanilamide powder, to be sprinkled directly into wounds as a disinfectant; hemostat clamps, sutures, bandages, and tourniquets to control bleeding. If a man was losing too much blood, he might receive an intravenous infusion of plasma—a life-giving fluid that mitigated the deadly effects of hypovolemic shock. The plasma bottles were held aloft or perhaps slung from a rifle staked in the ground. If the wounded man was fortunate, four litter bearers arrived quickly and carried him back to his battalion aid station, where his wounds were inspected and redressed by a medic. Here, amidst the roar of nearby artillery, he might also receive a shot of penicillin to cut his risk of infection. A chaplain, wearing ordinary fatigues and a helmet, provided a kind word, a sip of water, a prayer, or the sacrament of last rites.

Stretchers were loaded onto the back of an ambulance jeep, or perhaps a halftrack or tractor, to be transferred down the island to a field hospital. They bounced painfully over rutted roads, plasma bottles swaying on their racks. Field hospitals on Iwo Jima were located on main roads well behind the lines, most in sunken terrain or revetments adjoining South Field—complexes of low, unobtrusive dark green tents surrounded by sandbags. Wounded marines were carried through heavy double-blackout flaps into a long tent serving as the receiving ward, where their stretchers were laid on portable plywood operating tables. Doctors and corpsmen made notations on clipboards affixed to each stretcher. Plasma bottles were often swapped for whole blood intravenous feeds. Bloody or dirty clothing was cut away; wounds were cleaned; preoperative patients were washed and shaved. It was a stifling environment, particularly at night, when the tents had to be sealed against light leakage. The air was stuffy, smelling of blood and antiseptic compounds, and choked with cigarette smoke. Even so, the field hospitals were extraordinarily well equipped, by the standards of mid-twentieth-century medicine—probably the most sophisticated military field hospitals that had ever existed. They were stocked with operating tables, X-ray machines, oxygen masks and tanks, refrigerators for serums, electrical generators, flake ice machines, and banks of whole blood donated by civilians in the United States and flown into the island packed in ice. The more urgent cases were moved directly back into the operating rooms, where surgeons of various specialties went to work immediately. The worst, the doctors agreed, were the "belly cases"—the men who had been shot through the stomach, intestines, or other vital organs. The damaged organs had to be removed, resected, and returned to the wounded man's abdomen. Such wounds required long, intricate surgeries, often consuming four or five hours, followed by extended postoperative care. Even so, about half of all patients died after surgery, often from sepsis or infection. A sheet was pulled over their heads and they were placed on the ground outside, to await transport to one of the cemeteries.

More than 9,000 wounded marines were evacuated from Iwo Jima by sea. Their stretchers were loaded into specially configured Higgins boats or LVTs, which carried them to one of four LSTs that had been established as floating triage centers. A corpsman in each boat looked after the wounded while they were in transit. The passage was often rough, as swells tossed the boats and spray arced over the side. Hanging plasma bottles swung on their racks, and some of the wounded men became seasick, compounding their other miseries. Those who died while underway were returned to the beach to be buried in the cemetery.

More serious cases were taken farther offshore to transports, or to the dedicated hospital ships *Samaritan* and *Solace*, which shuttled patients down to Guam and Saipan in relays. Large red crosses were painted on their sides, with a green stripe around the hull—and unlike virtually all other ships in wartime, they were kept brightly illuminated at night. Stretchers were taken aboard by block and tackle rigs, and moved immediately to a spacious hall serving as a receiving ward. The treatment wards produced prodigious amounts of medical waste—bloodstained bandages and washrags, empty plasma bottles, strips of cut-away clothing, discarded casts and splints—and the cleanup crews moved through frequently, gathering it all up to be jettisoned. Sailors pushed mops over bloodstained decks, stopping frequently to wring the red-tinted water into a bucket.

Yet somehow, most of the wounded marines remained brave and even cheerful. A man whose leg had been blown off told a doctor on the *Solace*, "Doc, I think I'm going to be all right if I get enough blood." The doctor replied, "Son, we've got all the blood anybody needs."[72] Many deprecated the seriousness of their wounds and urged the doctors and nurses to look after others who had been more seriously hit. Some apologized for having earlier shouted in pain, disturbing the peace. Some joked. A man who had lost his right arm remarked, "Well, anyway, I won't have to write any letters now."[73] Marines whose pallor was blanched and corpselike could be revived by an infusion of whole blood. Color returned to their faces and they regained consciousness. Some patients were frankly elated, reveling in the knowledge that they had done their duty and survived the war.

Beginning on March 4, Skymaster "flying ambulances" began evacuating about two hundred cases per day from South Field, Iwo Jima. By March 21, D plus 30, a total of 2,393 medical casualties had been flown out of the island.[74]

Battlefield medicine had taken long strides in the quarter century since the First World War. In the earlier conflict, about eight of every one hundred wounded soldiers evacuated to a U.S. field hospital subsequently died. In World War II, that figure fell to under 4 percent. It was a superb improvement, attributed by medical authorities to better first aid on the battlefield, quick evacuation of the wounded, including by air, and the widespread availability of fresh, type-matched whole blood.[75] But despite the excellent capabilities of the medical corps on Iwo Jima, the mortality rate of casualties evacuated from the island was nearly 8 percent. In other words, it was double the mortality rate for all theaters in World War II, and about the same average as for U.S. infantry forces in the First World War.

The disparity is explained by a horrific feature of the Battle of Iwo Jima. Relentless mortar fire literally tore men apart, creating a high proportion of especially grievous wounds. Often they were contaminated by the island's fine volcanic ash, and could not be easily cleaned. A doctor on one of the transports said: "I was on this ship in the Normandy invasion, and not more than five percent of our cases required major surgery; here, I swear I believe it will run 90 percent. I never saw such nasty wounds."[76] And unlike that in most other Pacific island fights, the carnage continued almost unabated into the second, third, and fourth weeks of the battle. Units involved in the hardest fighting suffered cataclysmic losses. Officers and NCOs were killed or wounded at such a rate that young lieutenants were left in charge of entire companies, and buck privates led platoons. For officers of the 2nd Battalion, 26th Marines, the casualty rate was a staggering 108 percent. The pool included fourteen replacement officers, sent forward from the reserves to take the place of those killed or wounded in the line. Of those fourteen replacements, ten were subsequently killed or wounded.[77] Company B of the 1st Battalion, 28th Marines lost eight consecutive company commanders. Company I, 3rd Battalion, 24th Marines landed on D-Day with 133 riflemen; when the company departed the island thirty-five days later, nine remained alive and unwounded.

DURING THE CLOSING STAGES OF THE BATTLE, Japanese artillery and mortar barrages slackened noticeably. The last big shells fell within American lines on March 11. But for units in the vanguard, driving into the northern reaches of the island, the fighting remained as bitter and costly as ever. The terrain was unforgiving, and largely inaccessible to tanks, with alternating boulder fields, rocky outcrops, and plunging gorges. Sulfur steams hung like shrouds over the angry, scarred landscape. Infantry squads with flamethrowers took out pillboxes one by one, advancing to point-blank range and filling the enclosures with fire, then finishing the job with demolition charges. Getting to the northern coast of the island was an important psychological goal, and the breakthrough came on the morning of March 9, when a six-man advance patrol of the 21st Marines climbed down the northern cliffs and plunged into the sea. They filled a canteen with seawater and sent it back to General Erskine marked: "For inspection, not consumption."[78]

By nightfall on March 9, Erskine's forces controlled about 800 yards of contiguous coastline at the northeastern corner of Iwo Jima. That had the effect of cleaving the remaining Japanese forces into two pockets, on the northeast and northwest coasts of the island. The eastern salient was contained by the 4th Division, which had consolidated its grip on the area after the bloody failure of General Senda's counterattack. A tougher prospect was presented by the rugged coastal terrain around Kitano Point in the northwest, where General Kuribayashi's command center was in a deep bunker. This strongpoint was well defended, and the natural terrain advantages of the area precluded direct assault. Naval gunfire and airstrikes were directed against it for days, with seemingly little effect. Kuribayashi had anticipated and planned that Kitano Point and the rocky cliffs and ravines to its south would be the final pocket of organized resistance on Iwo Jima. The cave entrances and firing ports were high in a sheer rock face, sweeping a 200-foot-wide rocky gorge. Perhaps 3,000 Japanese troops remained alive and well enough to fight.

Holed up in their caves and bunkers, the defenders were relatively protected from the unending violence of the artillery barrages and aerial bombs.

But the noise and blast concussions took a steady toll on their nerves, and many were reduced to a catatonic stupor. Their subterranean world grew steadily more fetid and unlivable. There was no way to bury the dead, so the living simply laid them out on the ground and stepped around them. The stench was unspeakable; the ovenlike heat and the lack of ventilation did not help. Nor did the shortage of drinking water, which grew critical in the fourth week of the battle, as the last of the cisterns was emptied. Men spoke endlessly of water, of the fresh mountain streams and springs of Japan. Whatever water collected on the floors of the caves was quickly lapped up by parched soldiers. They were not above licking moisture off the walls. Some drank their own urine. One soldier of the 20th Independent Artillery Mortar Battalion said, "I don't think I will ever be able to forget the memory of how sweet the rainwater that formed puddles in the tunnels in the night tasted when we got down on all fours to drink it."[79]

General Kuribayashi's bombproof headquarters was about 300 yards inland of Kitano Point, and about 75 feet beneath the ground. The command bunker was a spacious cave with 9-foot ceilings, large enough to accommodate a conference table, desks, and communications equipment. His personal wardroom, a short walk down a narrow tunnel, was a small stone cavity with a cot, a desk, and a chair. Electric lighting was provided throughout the complex. A labyrinth of tunnels spread out from this nexus, leading by many different routes to the world above, and to pillboxes and firing ports manned and armed with machine guns and other small arms. Directly above, fused into the rock, was a massive steel-reinforced concrete blockhouse, 150 feet long by 70 feet wide, with a roof 10 feet thick.

Final radio signals were received from one outpost after another, as the marines sealed up caves and tunnels. Many subordinate units announced plans for a last *banzai* charge against the enemy, but Kuribayashi firmly told them to remain in their positions and fight to the last bullet. He said that "everybody would like to get an easy way to die early," but it was the duty of every Japanese soldier on the island to stay alive as long as possible, to "inflict heavy casualties to the enemy."[80]

The Americans set up loudspeakers and began broadcasting surrender appeals in Japanese, including personal appeals aimed directly at Kuribayashi. There was no response, except bullets. General Erskine's 3rd Division staff sent two Japanese POWs back into the Japanese lines to carry a message to the commanding officer of the 145th Infantry Regiment. The messengers somehow managed to return to the U.S. lines with the report that General Kuribayashi was still alive, and did not intend to surrender.

In a final valediction to Tokyo on March 16, Kuribayashi wrote that "the gallant fighting of the men under my command has been such that even the gods would weep." His forces had been "utterly empty-handed and ill-equipped against a land, sea, and air attack of a material superiority such as surpasses the imagination."[81] These sentiments transgressed powerful taboos, and the text published in the Tokyo newspapers was heavily edited. The phrase "utterly empty-handed and ill-equipped" was redacted. The last line was changed to a vow that Kuribayashi would launch a final attack "with all my officers and men reverently chanting *banzais* for the emperor's long life."[82]

Radio contact with Tokyo and other islands became spotty and intermittent. Major Horie, from his post on Chichi Jima, tried to get a message through to Kuribayashi informing him that he had been promoted to full general, but it was not clear that the message was received. A March 21 transmission informed Horie that the remaining force had had nothing to eat and no water to drink for five days. The last word from Iwo reached Chichi Jima on March 23. It said simply, "All officers and men of Chichi Jima, goodbye."[83]

Before dawn on March 26, about 300 Japanese troops emerged from their caves and crept down the island's west coast toward Mt. Suribachi. They surprised a bivouac of marines and USAAF personnel on Hirawa Bay, near South Field. After a firefight of nearly three hours, all the Japanese were killed. The Americans, unprepared for the sudden predawn onslaught, lost 170 killed and wounded. An official Marine Corps history concluded, "This attack was not a banzai charge; instead it appeared to have been a well-laid plan aimed at causing maximum confusion and destruction."[84]

No one witnessed Kuribayashi's death, and his body was never identified. Some Japanese sources maintain that the general led this final attack, and was killed in action; others suggest that he took his own life before leaving the bunker. The Americans searched the Japanese dead at Hirawa Bay, but all rank insignia had been removed, and none carried any documents.

The marines had commenced "loading out"—departing the island—on March 14, 1945. They left in echelon, with the 4th Division first to go, followed by the 5th and the 3rd Divisions. Permanent garrison duty was assumed by the army's 147th Infantry Regiment, which arrived on March

20. The army took command of the island on March 26, at virtually the same hour that the surprise attack at Hirawa Bay was defeated.

It is safe to assume that not a single American regretted leaving Iwo Jima. A Seabee vowed that he would take no souvenirs from the island: "All I want to take away from this place is a faint recollection."[85] For many, of course, the island was impossible to forget.

The victors had paid dearly for their victory. The marines and naval personnel on the island had sustained 24,053 casualties, representing approximately one of every three men who had landed. Of that figure, 6,140 died. Save a few hundred Japanese taken prisoner, the entire defending garrison was wiped out, numbering about 22,000 men. Taking the sum of killed and wounded on both sides, Kuribayashi's forces had inflicted more casualties than they had suffered. In view of the many advantages possessed by the attackers, that was a remarkable feat. His troglodyte army had remained disciplined and organized to the very end, making the marines pay for every yard of captured territory. But if any doubt had remained after Tarawa, Roi-Namur, Saipan, and Peleliu, the Japanese now knew with absolute certainty that their enemy could take any Pacific island they wanted, no matter how strongly fortified or zealously defended. Even when the fighting was at its worst, the marines had never doubted that they would win. On Guadalcanal, recalled Lieutenant Colonel Robert E. Galer, they had often wondered, "Can we hold?" But at Iwo Jima, "The question was simply, 'When can we get it over?'"[86]

In the five remaining months of the war, B-29s of the Twentieth Air Force would make 2,251 emergency landings on Iwo Jima. Possession of this vital way station, almost directly on the flight line between the Marianas and Japan, effectively added to the range and payload of the Superforts. It also saved untold numbers of lives. In April, P-51 squadrons based on Iwo would begin providing fighter escort for the B-29 formations as they hit Japan. Approximately 20,000 USAAF aircrewmen made at least one emergency landing on the island; many would otherwise have perished at sea. A B-29 pilot spoke for all of his fellow airmen when he said, "Whenever I land on this island I thank God for the men who fought for it."[87]

THE HEAVY CASUALTIES ON IWO JIMA touched a nerve with the American public, and prompted an outbreak of recriminations and second-guessing.

Holland Smith, who had commanded the expeditionary troops in the earlier bloodbaths on Tarawa and Saipan, was accustomed to being denounced as a "butcher," a "coldblooded murderer," and an "indiscriminate waster of human life."[88] Now more of the same epithets were flung at him and the entire Marine Corps. Letters poured into Washington, and congressmen asked the usual questions. Was the island worth the cost? Could it have been captured with fewer American casualties?

MacArthur, whose Luzon campaign was underway at the same time, did not let the opportunity pass. On February 26, a week after the marines had landed on Iwo Jima, MacArthur's forces completed the recapture of Corregidor. A garrison of about 6,000 Japanese troops had been almost completely wiped out, at a cost of just 675 Americans killed or wounded. An SWPA communiqué proudly declared: "A strongly fortified island fortress, defended to the point of annihilation by a well-equipped, fanatical enemy . . . was reduced in a period of twelve days by a combination of surprise, strategy and fighting technique, and skill, perfectly coordinated with supporting naval and air forces."[89] No one missed the insinuation. MacArthur was saying that superior generalship could have won the Battle of Iwo Jima with fewer American casualties. The issue was especially salient at that particular moment, because the two prongs of the Pacific offensive must soon merge into one. MacArthur was bidding for supreme command in the Pacific, and his backers in the United States were quick to pick up his cues. At his hilltop castle at San Simeon, on the central California coast, William Randolph Hearst picked up the telephone and dictated an editorial about Iwo Jima to the managing editor of the San Francisco *Examiner*. On February 27, it ran on the *Examiner*'s front page: "The attacking American forces are paying heavily for the island, perhaps too heavily. . . . Plainly, what we need in all our Pacific operations is a military strategist." Hearst nominated MacArthur, because "he saves the lives of his own men."[90]

That afternoon, a group of about one hundred off-duty marines filed into the *Examiner*'s newsroom in the Hearst Building at Third and Market Streets. A flustered employee called the police, but then called back a few minutes later to say that the police were not needed. The marines were calm and law-abiding. They did not threaten the staff or premises, but only wanted to look the editor in the eye as they explained that he did not have the facts.

In the end, however, the Marine Corps won its case in the court of public opinion. Secretary Forrestal, who had once worked as a Hudson Valley beat reporter, had compelled the navy and marines to adopt more press-friendly policies. By February 1945, his efforts were bearing fruit. Dozens of war correspondents reported from Iwo Jima, and their stories were transmitted back to the mainland in less than forty-eight hours. Lavish press coverage ensured a high degree of public interest in the battle, and a better understanding of the unprecedented tactical problems posed by the enemy's subterranean fortifications. Hap Arnold and other USAAF leaders publicly emphasized the absolute necessity of securing Iwo Jima to support the B-29 campaign. Joe Rosenthal's stirring photograph of the flag-raising on Suribachi was worth a million newspaper column inches.

MacArthur's implied criticism had been grossly unjust. The tactical options for seizing Iwo Jima had always been limited, and Kuribayashi's preparations had been brilliant. For all his undoubted talents as a field commander, MacArthur had never confronted such a challenge as Iwo Jima, and one fails to imagine what he could have done differently. Dwight D. Eisenhower, who had served as MacArthur's protégé in the Philippines, and who had led the largest ground campaign of the war, briefly visited the island (as president-elect) in 1952. As he stepped off his plane and looked around, Eisenhower was astounded to learn that the marines had brought more than 60,000 troops ashore. Comparing the barren little island to the "wide open spaces of Normandy," Eisenhower said that he could barely visualize a battle on such a scale, in such constricted terrain: "It was just very difficult for him to comprehend."[91]

Chapter Twelve

AT THE 21ST BOMBER COMMAND HEADQUARTERS ON GUAM—A COMPLEX of modest Quonset huts perched on a northern bluff—"Possum" Hansell and his team were frustrated to the point of gloominess. Start-up problems and growing pains had plagued every aspect of their operations, including maintenance, training, supply, housing, and airfield construction. Even as new B-29s and aircrews flew into the Marianas, Hansell's organization struggled to put a larger number of bombers into action against Japan. The cumulative "abort rate"—the percentage of planes forced to turn back due to engine trouble or other technical problems—stood at 21 percent. Their largest mission had been their first, on November 24, 1944, when 111 B-29s had taken off and 94 had reached Japanese airspace. That figure was not surpassed until three months later.

Until the capture of Iwo Jima, Japanese fighters based on that island flew regular low-altitude bombing and strafing raids against the Marianas airfields. The most spectacular of these had occurred on November 27, when fifteen Zero fighters flew south from Iwo Jima at wavetop altitude, ducking under Saipan's radar screens, and appeared without warning over Isley Field. Achieving complete surprise, the Zeros strafed B-29s parked on the hardstands, destroying three and damaging eight more. General Hansell witnessed this audacious attack personally, and was nearly killed by it. He was riding shotgun in a jeep when a Zero roared overhead and strafed the vehicle. Hansell and his driver rolled out and took cover in the bush. When the Japanese pilot had expended his ammunition, he cranked down his wheels and actually landed on Isley's main runway. To Hansell's amazement, the pilot leapt out of his cockpit with a pistol in his hand and fought a gun battle with American soldiers, who quickly killed him.

More such attacks followed, and the toll of damaged and destroyed Superforts rose, until Hap Arnold demanded an upgrade to the island's air defenses: "Our B-29 raids on Japanese homeland will continue to provoke desperate and fanatical counteraction."[1] New fighter patrols were scheduled, and B-24 raids cratered the airfields on Iwo Jima. Searchlights and a Microwave Early Warning (MEW) radar system were installed at the north end of Saipan, and destroyers were positioned north of the island to act as radar pickets. These measures helped, but the threat was not entirely eliminated until February 1945, when the marines stormed Iwo Jima.

To build airfields and supporting ground facilities for a fleet of 1,000 Superfortresses, on islands nearly 6,000 miles from the U.S. mainland, was a task of colossal proportions. A single bombardment wing required two parallel runways, each 8,500 feet long and 200 feet wide, with adjoining hardstands, taxiways, and maintenance aprons. Great expanses of land had to be graded and paved, but the bulldozers and steam shovels could not even break ground until a basic island infrastructure had been established. Airbase construction was only one of many priorities; the Marianas were simultaneously hosting a rapid buildup of naval and ground forces for operations against Iwo Jima and Okinawa. Guam and Saipan required electrical power, water systems, sanitation, housing, and modern seaport facilities. Work could not progress without advanced road networks linking the airfield sites to seaports and coral rock quarries. At Isley Field, the first active B-29 base in the Marianas, all arming, fueling, and maintenance was done in the open air, on congested hardstands, in scorching heat and driving rain. Tools and spare parts were stored in outdoor supply dumps, stacked in crates on the ground, and covered with tarps. A fleet of Douglas C-54 transports shuttled spare parts from California on a twice-weekly schedule. The mechanics worked around the clock, under floodlights, or with penlights between their teeth. They were still learning the big Boeing airplane's many complex systems, especially its temperamental 2,200-horsepower Wright Duplex-Cyclone engines. Often they were required to complete an engine transplant at night, hours before a Superfort was due to depart on another fifteen-hour bombing mission.

In the early days, each new B-29 bombardment wing arriving in the Marianas was obliged to commence operations with a single runway. That meant that a limited number of B-29s could take off in a given interval of time, requiring the lead planes to burn fuel while the trailing planes were still on the ground. Returning from their mission, with their fuel tanks running dry, the aircrews faced another perilous bottleneck. There might be two dozen B-29s circling above the field, awaiting their turn to land. This state of affairs required a larger fuel reserve, which in turn meant a smaller bomb load, and a corresponding reduction in the total bomb tonnage dropped on Japan. That latter statistic was closely monitored by Hap Arnold and his staff in Washington, and they were not pleased. Hansell and his team were under intense pressure to produce a return on Uncle Sam's sizable investment in the B-29 program.

From its first mission in November through the end of 1944, the 21st Bomber Command launched ten raids against the Japanese homeland. The missions targeted aircraft factories and urban installations in Tokyo, Yokohama, Hamamatsu, Numazu, and Nagoya. Some were more successful than others. Bombs dropped from 30,000 feet often missed the aircraft plants they targeted and fell into nearby residential districts. A November 29 raid touched off destructive fires in the Kanda and Nihonbashi districts of Tokyo, killing about one hundred civilians and destroying an estimated 2,500 homes. In the heavily industrialized Tokai region, southwest of Tokyo, a major earthquake (magnitude 8.1) and tsunami struck on December 7, 1944. The natural disaster killed 1,223 people and destroyed almost 30,000 homes. The Mitsubishi Aircraft Engine Works, a giant airframe production center east of Nagoya Harbor, was severely damaged. As Mitsubishi struggled to get its production lines up and running, three large B-29 raids struck on December 13, 18, and 22. The weather was clear, and the bombing more accurate than usual. An assembly shop and seven auxiliary buildings were destroyed. The raids persuaded Mitsubishi and the government to shut down production at the site, and to attempt to disperse the assembly lines to underground sites and outlying locations. Meanwhile, the Americans attacked the psychological foundations of the Japanese war effort by dropping leaflets over Nagoya, asking, "What shall we offer you next, after the earthquake?"[2]

In the 1930s, the U.S. Army Air Corps had poured funding into technologies for high-altitude precision bombardment—most notably, the vaunted Norden bombsight, which proponents advertised as a potential war-winner. The Superfortress had been conceived as a weapon that could fly 30,000 feet over enemy territory and drop bombs "into a pickle barrel." In Europe, even as the RAF had pioneered nighttime area bombing and incendiary attacks, true believers in the USAAF had kept the faith with their precision-bombing orthodoxy, and B-17 Flying Fortresses had achieved a certain degree of success in bombing German industrial targets from high altitudes. When the Twentieth Air Force was set up under the aegis of the JCS, its chief mission was to employ precision-bombing techniques to destroy the "war-making industrial structure of Japan," starting with the aircraft industry.

But clear weather was a rarity in Japan, especially in the winter months, when coastal Honshu was often concealed under thick cloud cover. The best weather forecasters in the Pacific could not predict when the skies over the target area would be clear. Reconnaissance B-29s could be sent ahead to scout the weather, but during the seven to eight hours required for a formation of bombers to reach Japan from the Marianas, conditions might change completely. High winds often scattered the northbound B-29 formations before they even made landfall. Over Japan they encountered the jet stream, a factor that had not figured in the bombing campaign over Germany. At the high altitudes flown by the B-29s in those early raids, winds typically surpassed 100 miles per hour, and sometimes reached 200 miles per hour. The Superfortresses flew downwind, pushing their ground speed above 500 miles per hour. The bombardiers despaired of correcting for the ballistic errors produced by those hurricane-like conditions.

Over Germany, the B-17s had usually been accompanied by a fighter escort. But no friendly fighters could escort the B-29s to Japan until April 1945, when P-51s began joining up from Iwo Jima. Without fighter protection, daylight missions required an ample supply of gas and guns—gas to climb to altitude, gas to fly in formation, and guns to ward off Japanese interceptors. Fuel, machine guns, and ammunition were heavy, requiring weight-saving trade-offs. In the first three months of the 21st Bomber Command's operations, bomb loads averaged 3 tons per aircraft—less than one-third of the 10-ton bomb loads that backers of the Superfortress had been advertising for years. There was talk of radar bombing at night, a technique that promised better accuracy and higher bomb loads, but the development of radar-based bombing was slow. That was partly due to the slow adoption of the latest radar bombsight, the APQ-7—which had been issued to only one of the 21st Bomber Command's wings, the 315th, by the end of 1944.

Japanese fighters gave the unescorted B-29s more trouble than the

USAAF planners had anticipated. The B-29 missions followed a predictable pattern—the bombers repeatedly arrived in daylight over the same regions (Tokyo and Nagoya), at the same altitude (30,000 feet). In time, the Japanese army and navy fighter commands recognized these patterns and made tactical adjustments to counter the raids. As soon as their coastal radars detected an inbound strike, the fighters scrambled to altitude. Often the Japanese were able to put more than two hundred fighters into the air to meet an incoming formation of fifty to seventy-five unescorted B-29s. Air defense of the Kanto region was concentrated at Atsugi Air Base, near Yokosuka. The elite 343rd Kokutai, based at Matsuyama Air Base on Shikoku, was recruited and organized by the famous Japanese naval pilot Minoru Genda, who had developed the tactical plans for the attack on Pearl Harbor. Southern air defenses were organized under Vice Admiral Matome Ugaki, who took command of the newly activated Fifth Air Fleet, the largest remaining naval air flotilla, with headquarters at Kanoya Air Base in southern Kyushu. The navy concentrated its best remaining fighter planes and veteran flyers at these bases.[3]

The homeland air defense squadrons consisted of a hodgepodge of different aircraft types, including many older-model Zeros, but also a few newer designs that performed much better at higher altitudes. The Mitsubishi A7M "Reppu," successor to the Zero, had a rate of climb rivaling that of the Hellcat and the Mustang, and a service ceiling of 40,000 feet. Its Allied codename was "Sam." The Kawanishi N1K2-J Shinden-Kai, developed from an earlier floatplane fighter, was a fast, powerful, maneuverable aircraft with brawny defenses and almost twice the standard firepower of the Zero. The Americans had seen a few Shinden-Kais over the Philippines and Formosa, and given it the identification codename "George," but they were not yet fully aware of the new fighter's capabilities. The J2M "Raiden" ("Thunderbolt") was a powerful Mitsubishi interceptor designed to take on American heavy bombers. Its speed in level flight surpassed 400 miles per hour, and it was armed with four 20mm cannon, more than enough firepower to bring down a B-29. The Allies called it "Jack." Sam, George, and Jack were high-powered machines that needed skilled pilots, of whom only a few remained in the Japanese air corps. One of the last great Japanese aces of the war was Lieutenant Sadaaki Akamatsu, a hard-drinking hellion who lived at a brothel near Atsugi. "He often came racing to the air base in an old car," one of his colleagues later recalled, "driving like a demon with one hand,

drinking from a bottle held in the other. The sirens were screaming a warning as he bolted from the car to his fighter plane, already warmed up by the
mechanics. He took off the moment the cockpit canopy was closed."[4] Log-
ging more than 8,000 hours of stick time in China and Japan, Akamatsu
was eventually credited with twenty-seven kills. Improbably, he survived
the war and died in 1980, at age seventy.

For the B-29s of the 21st Bomber Command, January 1945 was the deadliest month of the war. Pilots and aircrewmen described the Japanese fighter
interceptions as "hairy." Enemy planes made head-on and high-side passes,
guns blazing, apparently indifferent to the Superforts' .50-caliber machine-
gun turrets. If the Japanese flyers could not bring down a B-29 with their
guns, they sometimes resorted to suicidal ramming attacks. John Ciardi,
manning a .50-caliber gun on a side blister, shot down several Japanese
fighters as they attempted to strike his B-29. He saw many other bombers
from his squadron go down. "One of the saddest things I ever saw, when we
were flying wing on a plane that got hit, was the barber's chair gunner in the
big bubble at the very top. He was right there beside us in plain sight, beginning to go down. He just waved his hand goodbye. There was nothing you
could do. You couldn't reach out to touch him. Of course, that got you."[5]

So long as no major control surface was shot away, and at least two
engines were running, a Superfortress had a chance to get home. But when
a damaged Superfort commenced its long return flight, the tyranny of
Pacific distances came into play. Until Iwo Jima fell into American hands,
there was no safe runway within 1,400 miles of Japanese shores. Inexperienced crews made navigation errors in thick weather or in darkness, and
had to burn extra fuel to get back on course. On nearly every mission, B-29s
were seen to crash at sea, or their crews radioed to report that they were
attempting a controlled water landing. But recovering the castaway crews
was a low-percentage proposition. Searching for little yellow rubber rafts in
those blue immensities was like trying to find a needle in a haystack, especially when the weather was less than perfectly clear. The navy floatplanes
employed for air-sea rescue operations lacked the range or endurance to
search thoroughly in waters so far from base. Lifeguard submarines were
always stationed south of Japan, but their chances of finding downed aircrews were slight, unless the planes ditched in clear weather at designated
coordinates. A damaged Superfort might fly all the way back to the Marianas only to crash on the runway, breaking apart and bursting into flames.

In January 1945, an average of four to five B-29s failed to return safely from each bombing mission over Japan, for an average loss rate of 5.7 percent. The worst-hit squadrons were devastated. The 873rd Bomb Squadron lost ten of seventeen B-29s, and eighty of the ninety-nine aircrewmen who went down on those planes had died. The USAAF had tentatively fixed a tour of duty at thirty-five combat missions. The airmen could do the math. With per-mission losses topping 5 percent, they could expect to survive, on average, fewer than twenty missions. Worse, the pipeline of newly trained B-29 relief crews did not appear to be large enough to allow for regular rotations out of the theater, which meant that they might be required to fly *more* than thirty-five missions. If their loss rate did not improve, all of the B-29 pilots and aircrews could expect to keep flying missions until they died. "We were playing a lottery," said Ciardi. "A certain number of planes had to be lost. We were just hoping that by blind chance ours would not be."[6]

Morale deteriorated. The B-29 crews were conscious of having fallen short of the high expectations set for them. Bombing accuracy had been consistently disappointing, due in part to abominable winter weather over Japan. Their losses had been heavy, and they seemed to be getting worse. Hansell told his superiors in Washington that the airmen were being driven too hard; symptoms of pilot fatigue had been reported by the flight leaders and doctors. One B-29 pilot told a war correspondent: "We feel it has been worthwhile; we have to believe that. But the cost has been high. We've lost a lot of good men, especially key men like group and squadron commanders."[7]

Between missions, the airmen did very little. Many just lay on their folding canvas cots, sleeping or staring at the ribbed steel arches of their Quonset hut ceilings. They stored up rest between missions, and they needed it. Even for young men in peak physical condition, the nervous energy they expended on a round-trip combat flight to Japan took four to five days to replenish. On nights before missions, many could not sleep at all. They lay awake, grimly wondering whether they would survive the day.

By January 1945, USAAF planners and analysts were raising doubts about the suitability of daylight precision tactics against Japan. After more than ten missions aimed at Japanese aircraft manufacturing targets, only the Mitsubishi plants in Nagoya had been seriously disrupted, and that was owed partly to the December earthquake. Nakajima, Tachikawa, and Kawasaki production centers had been attacked without evident success. A Nakajima engine plant in Musashino, Tokyo had been visited five times by Hansell's

B-29s, but remained largely intact. Hap Arnold and his headquarters planners wanted to experiment with mixing incendiaries into the standard high-explosive "iron" bombs in the payloads. Some argued for a more radical shift in tactics, employing full-scale firebombing raids on Japanese cities—that is, to burn them down, more or less indiscriminately. Such missions could be flown at night, when Japanese fighters would be less dangerous.

Hansell resisted the shift to firebombing, maintaining that precision bombing could be refined with practice: "I believed in it."[8] He argued that the situation called for patience. Time was needed to hone the techniques, to develop the airfields and supporting infrastructure, and to bring more B-29s and aircrews from the United States.

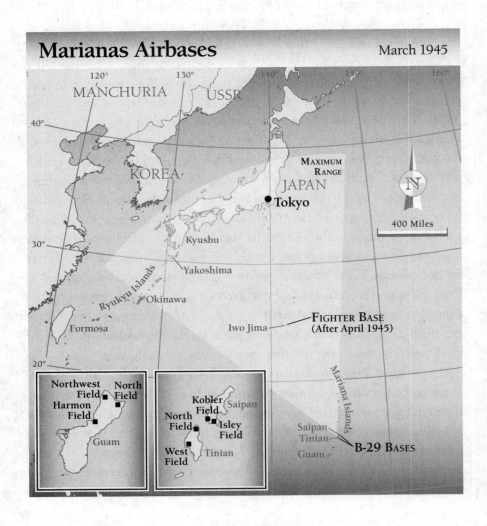

In the China-Burma-India (CBI) theater, the 20th Bomber Command had been dissolved, and was rapidly winding down. All B-29s in China and India were to be shifted to the Mariana Islands, and the commanding general of the 20th Bomber Command had received orders to shift his headquarters to Guam. Major General Curtis LeMay had previously served under Hansell in Europe, but he had since been promoted and was now senior to Hansell. Arnold decided to put LeMay directly in charge of the 21st Bomber Command; Hansell, in turn, would act as LeMay's vice commander. Hansell was one of Arnold's star protégés, and the USAAF chief took pains to emphasize that he had not lost confidence in him. But given the trend toward new tactics, and Hansell's clear reluctance to implement a shift to massed incendiary raids, his relief may have been inevitable.

A disappointed Hansell swallowed his pride and expressed his full confidence in LeMay, but he declined to remain as his second-in-command, judging that LeMay "needed no second string in his bow . . . and I would have been unhappy as a figurehead."[9] Hansell flew back to the United States and took command of a B-29 training program. LeMay flew back to Kharagpur, India, to tie up loose ends in the CBI theater, then returned to Guam on January 18 to assume command of the newly consolidated Twentieth Air Force.

JAPANESE CIVILIANS REGARDED the B-29s with curiosity, fascination, and even admiration. Whenever the tiny silver crosses appeared overhead, they crowded out into the streets, craning their necks and pointing to the sky. "We went through those early bombings in a spirit of excitement and suspense," wrote a Tokyo journalist. "There was even a spirit of adventure, a sense of exultation in sharing the dangers of war even though bound to civilian existence."[10] Police and civil defense authorities shouted at the spectators, but many were too excited to retreat into their underground shelters. They wanted to see what was happening. With a touch of irony, perhaps, civilians spoke of the "honorable visitors" and referred to the Superfortress as "B-san" ("Mr. B"). A man in Tokyo watched a "splendid" formation of B-29s through his telescope, describing details of their design and operation to awestruck neighborhood children.[11] Michio Takeyama, the teacher and future novelist, described a formation of Superforts that flew over the capital on a late afternoon in January: "The brilliant violet shining cross shapes came floating from among the clouds, in regular patterns, beautiful. In the winter, with their tails of frozen vapor, they looked like slender jellyfish trailing transparent white tentacles."[12]

The air raids presented a dilemma for the regime's propaganda authorities. Witnessed by millions, they could not be censored out of existence. News coverage veered between competing impulses—to belittle the raids as feeble and ineffective, or to whip up popular anger. The newspapers tended to downplay the damage inflicted by the bombers, while exaggerating the number of U.S. planes shot down by antiaircraft fire or Japanese fighters. "Funeral Procession of B-29s," shouted a front-page headline in the *Asahi Shinbun* on January 1, 1945. The story reported that 550 of the big bombers had gone down in flames since they had started raiding the Kanto region five weeks earlier.[13] (The actual number at that point was fewer than fifty.) The damage caused by air raids was often described as "slight," but scant detail was reported. Assurances were often given that the Imperial Palace had not been hit and that the emperor and empress were safe.

Other reports aimed to arouse the public, to incite a desire for revenge, and to inspire civilians to work harder for the war effort. According to the *Mainichi Shinbun*, "There is no other way to awaken the Japanese except by bombs falling dead center in Tokyo."[14] It was reported that the American bombers were targeting hospitals and schools. On January 14, 1945, a high-explosive bomb dropped by a B-29 struck near the Toyouke Shrine at Ise, one of the most venerated of all Shinto sites. The shrine had not been targeted, and was not damaged in the raid, but the *Asahi Shinbun* exploded in rage at the "enemy's tyrannical barbaric behavior" and "real demonic nature." A headline screamed: "God Damn You! From Now On Watch Out!"[15]

For the first time since the Doolittle Raid, almost three years earlier, citizens of Tokyo could compare the news reports to the evidence they took in with their own eyes. Peering out of the windows of passing trains and streetcars, they saw smashed and burned remnants of homes and buildings. Chinaware, clothing, and tatami mats were strewn among the debris. People sifted through the ruins, digging out their bedding, shoes, and crockery. Refugees carried their last worldly goods on their shoulders, or offered them for sale to their neighbors: hibachis, books, baskets, futon mattresses, blue and white ceramic pots. Others were made homeless by government fiat, as demolition crews razed entire neighborhoods to create urban firebreaks.

A witness recalled: "The families being forced from their homes stood in small groups on the street, watching with sorrowful faces as the labor gangs ripped their homes to pieces."[16]

On January 27, 1945, seventy-two B-29s were diverted from their primary targets by cloudy weather. They dropped their payloads on the heart of downtown Tokyo, and bombs fell among Saturday shoppers in the tony Ginza district, killing several hundred. For urbanites who witnessed such scenes of devastation, the regime's appeals to "fighting spirit" inspired bitter sarcasm. In his diary, Kiyoshi Kiyosawa commented that "the Japanese spirit encourages the idea that when one sees B-29s, they can be dealt with [by] bamboo spears or judo."[17]

After the war, the U.S. Strategic Bombing Survey (USSBS) conducted extensive interviews with a cross-section of Japanese at every level of society. The results led the USSBS analysts to conclude that aerial bombing was the "most important single factor" in undercutting the morale of the Japanese people. More than any other development—including military reverses overseas and the reduction in food rations at home—the appearance of enemy planes in Japanese skies prompted ordinary citizens to doubt their chances of victory, and to desire an early termination of the war. Strategic bombing of Japanese cities "produced great social and psychological disruption and contributed to securing surrender prior to the planned invasion."[18] Moreover, the Japanese were more inclined to blame the air raids on their own leaders than on the enemy. "Now was the time when Japan's history of geographical isolation, abetted by centuries of cultural isolation, became a liability," wrote the USSBS authors. "The insularity of leaders and people, bred by isolation, was reflected in feelings of remoteness from attack, and invulnerability of the home islands. The B-29s rudely awakened them from the dream of security."[19]

Devastating fires had been a recurring horror in Japanese cities since time immemorial. The worst of all was the 1923 Great Kanto earthquake and fire, which had destroyed 700,000 buildings and killed more than 100,000 people in Tokyo and Yokohama—but there had been several others only marginally less severe in the years leading up to the Pacific War. Like every other big Japanese city, Tokyo was a tinderbox. Commercial buildings and factories were surrounded by densely built residential districts. Houses were built of wood, paper, and thin plaster walls, with floors covered by straw mats. Many were still lit by kerosene lamps and paper lanterns, and cooking was done over open charcoal fires. Flammable gas was piped through shallow and easily disrupted gas mains, and electricity was transmitted through low-slung power lines. For all of that, Japanese firefighting brigades were undermanned and ill-equipped, and organized into sclerotic local outfits. The war had further weakened them by drafting the fittest and youngest men out of their ranks. Most firefighters still on the job in 1945 were older men, past their prime, and their numbers were far short of what would be needed in a major emergency.

With B-29s appearing regularly in Japanese airspace, the authorities redoubled their emphasis on civil defense preparations. Citizens were required to take solemn oaths promising to "follow orders, refrain from selfish conduct, and cooperate with one another in air defense."[20] All were required to carry gas masks and padded cloth hoods to protect them against sparks and falling debris. Every household was obliged to keep a steel bucket of sand, a ladder, two shovels, tanks of water, mops, and wet blankets. Community councils organized efforts to dig trenches and backyard bomb shelters. Inspections and drills could occur at any time, even in the middle of the night. The director of Ueno Park Zoo ordered that lions, tigers, and other large predators be euthanized, lest an air raid destroy their enclosures and set them loose in the streets of Tokyo. Students drilled in their schoolyards. Younger children learned the routines by singing and clapping with their teachers:

> Air Raid. Air raid. Here comes an air raid! Red! Red! Incendiary
>   bomb!
> Run! Run! Get mattress and sand!
> Air Raid. Air raid. Here comes an air raid! Black! Black! Here
>   come the bombs!
> Cover your ears! Close your eyes![21]

Resentment grew as drills and inspections become more frequent and intrusive. Civil defense routines sapped people's energy at a time when many were not getting enough to eat. A disgusted Japanese woman said, "Running uphill with pails of water seemed to me a silly and tedious way to fight a war."[22] Every third or fourth night, air-raid sirens called them out of their futon beds to sit in dank, subterranean air-raid shelters. The shelters, dug by civilians wielding picks and shovels, were cramped and poorly constructed, often without lighting or even seating. If there was any rain at all, they flooded. False alarms were common, and when the sirens and wooden clackers started up, people were inclined to pull a pillow over their heads and ignore them. Noncompliance spread even as the threat of air raids grew.

In late 1943, the regime had begun promoting the idea that noncombatants and nonessential workers should evacuate the cities. Mass evacuation was a partial solution to the danger of air raids, but also a means to relieve pressures on mass transit, and to ease the logistical problem of importing food from rural areas. The campaign began with public service messages encouraging the very old, the very young, the pregnant, and the physically infirm—anyone who was not actively contributing to the war effort—to move in with their country cousins. According to the Cabinet Board of Information, in an official statement of December 1943: "Urban evacuation does not mean only fleeing and dispersion from the city," but was a "positive contribution toward strengthening our fighting power."[23] Those working in munitions factories or other jobs deemed essential to the war effort were not permitted to go, unless entire factories were relocated, in which case workers were compelled to move with their employers and fellow employees. Special "evacuation trains" were run out of Tokyo, full of morose-looking urbanites carrying whatever worldly goods they could manage and leaving everything else behind.

Children were evacuated from cities on a voluntary basis beginning in early 1943, but in December 1943, the Japanese Ministry of Education stepped up pressure on urban schools and parents to send all primary school students to rural areas. On June 30, 1944, as the Americans invaded Saipan, the government announced the compulsory evacuation of 350,000 children from a dozen of the nation's largest cities. They were resettled in country inns, meeting halls, Buddhist monasteries, and abandoned resorts.[24] As the B-29 raids began in November, entire schools left the cities under the supervision of their teachers, on trains bedecked with Rising Sun flags, while their parents bid good-bye from the platforms. Arriving at their destinations, the children were quartered in overcrowded dormitories, with twenty-four-hour-a-day communal living and working arrangements. Allotted rations were often insufficient, and the children grew emaciated and malnourished. A teacher who accompanied her students from Tokyo to Nagano recalled, "It was pitiful to see the children lament when they took off the covers of their lunch boxes, to find them only half full."[25] To supplement their meager diet, they were sent out to forage for wild food, much of it barely edible:

weeds and bracken ferns, dandelion greens, bamboo shoots, bog rhubarb, persimmons, chickweed, mugwort, and dropwort. They hunted frogs and snakes to be skinned and roasted. They fished local streams for freshwater shrimp, carp, and loaches. They ate grasshoppers, sparrows, snails, and beetles sautéed in oil. By the end of the war, according to a government medical report, evacuated children were consuming an average of 1,000 calories per day, far short of their minimal dietary requirements.[26]

The daily routines were strictly regimented, with classroom instruction and hours of hard physical labor. Students wore military uniforms and marched in ranks behind their teachers. Those of lower "rank" were required to salute their superiors, and all could be promoted or demoted according to their performance, attitude, personal bearing, and obedience to orders. They attended send-off ceremonies for departing servicemen and kamikaze pilots, sent letters and "comfort" packages to servicemen overseas, and greeted the returning ashes of fallen Japanese soldiers and sailors.

As the war progressed, evacuated children spent less time in the classrooms and more contributing to the war effort. In September 1944, Prime Minister Koiso announced a total mobilization of the population: "Facing this grave situation, we cannot permit even one idle person or one spectator within the country regardless of age and sex. . . . Every Japanese is a soldier."[27] An edict issued by the regime ruled that work in the factories was "equal to education," but by 1945 the factory managers were beset with absenteeism, and demanded that their child workers spend more hours on the job. Children as young as eight were put to work in munitions factories. Others were detached as farmhands to help harvest crops. In forested areas, legions of children went out to gather pine cones for the improbable purpose of converting pine oil to aviation fuel. By the end of the war, some 3.4 million students had been mobilized, and many were getting no more than an hour of traditional classroom study per day.[28] "We no longer had many classes at school," recalled Hideo Sato, an evacuated sixth grader in Ibaragi Prefecture. "The main thing we did was dig an antitank ditch in the corner of the schoolyard." It was an onerous task, especially for children, who did not have the strength to haul much earth. "It took three days to hollow out a single foxhole deep enough so that when the teacher jumped in, it would be over his head. We were assigned the task in groups, and each group was responsible for completing theirs."[29]

In this isolated and confined rural environment, the children were told only what the Ministry of Education decreed that they should be told. Teachers were monitored for any sign of defeatism. In late 1944, a new "National Defense Thought Drive" aimed to ensure that "those entrusted with the mission of education have resolved that they will firmly maintain a conviction of certain victory and devote themselves to bolstering the fighting spirit."[30] Evacuated children were required to keep diaries, both to practice their writing skills and to record their innermost thoughts and feelings. The diaries were submitted to the teachers, who graded them based upon conventional measures of grammar, diction, calligraphy, and writing style, but also upon the sincerity and ardor of their sentiments. Mihoko Nakane, a nine-year-old girl whose entire primary school was evacuated from Tokyo to Toyama Prefecture in 1945, often expressed a wholehearted desire to learn, to improve, and to please her teachers. In her diary she pledged to be a "good child," or an "even better good child," and to do her best to "become a splendid citizen." Mihoko's enthusiasm was irrepressible, whether she was gathering firewood, completing a "fun" training march, foraging for wild mugwort, seeing off new army recruits, singing war songs, or honoring the spirits of returning war dead: "It was a truly sad affair. . . . I really feel grateful to them." She recorded her obligatory hostility toward the enemy: "Hateful, hateful Americans and English! How hateful the Americans and English are! That's what I thought." Mihoko never complained about her meager rations, even when they were infested with weevils, and often recorded that her lunch or dinner was "really delicious." When she was promoted to the rank of squad leader, she was mindful of her grave duty: "Because of this, I want all the more to be a good child and to act like a squad leader."[31]

Innocent, trusting, and adaptable by nature, children tended to maintain their zeal for the war even as their parents and teachers grew disillusioned. They did not expect to eat well because they could not remember a time when they had not been hungry. They did not mind working in munitions plants because the experience was a novelty, and provided a relief from tedious classroom routines. Producing weapons for the war effort made them feel important. Gathering pine cones for aviation fuel gave them the sense that they were personally helping to lift the Japanese warplanes that flew overhead. Those who worked in the balloon bomb factories were told enthralling stories of how their creations would soar around the earth to smite the demonic Americans. They enjoyed the pageantry of the war, the singing and marching, the invitation to trample and spit on American

and British flags, the monthly reading of the Imperial Rescript on Education, and the group calisthenics each morning, when they all stripped to
the waist (girls included) and chanted: "Annihilate America and England!
One-Two-Three-Four! Annihilate America and England! One-Two-Three-
Four!"[32] They were the last to suspect that the glorious victories reported on
the radio were fabrications.

"I was born in war," Hideo Sato explained in an oral history recorded
half a century later. "Boys like war. War can become the material for
play. . . . It almost becomes a sport. It's just an extension of naughty games
they all play anyway." He was eleven years old when his class was evacuated to Ibaragi Prefecture. They were put to work on an airfield that was
repeatedly attacked by American carrier planes. Hideo and his classmates
were thrilled whenever the Hellcats and Corsairs arrived, and tried to prove
their courage by standing erect without flinching for as long as they could
stand it:

> If you were watching, you might be able to roll away and escape at
> the last moment. The plane comes in low, a cannon on each wing,
> right toward you, at enormous speed, but still it takes time. You can
> tell if they're aiming at you. Then you see sparks fly. The sound comes
> afterwards. You learn to judge from experience the angle of the sparks.
> When they flash at forty-five degrees, they're most dangerous. Then
> you closed your eyes instinctively. They often called it strafing, but it
> wasn't with machine guns. They were machine cannons, twenty mil-
> limeters, and they had explosives in each shell. It wasn't like in the
> movies, when you see those little puffs of smoke. Across the rice pad-
> dies the dirt flew up, and at the root sparks shot up, and explosions
> went off, "Boom!-boom!-boom! boom!-boom!"
>
> The instant you knew they'd missed, you'd stand up and start run-
> ning. They were so low that the pilot sometimes opened his cockpit
> window and leaned out—American pilots, looking out at us, wearing
> airplane goggles. I even waved at them. This happened to me more
> than ten times.[33]

In line with Prime Minister Koiso's national policy to "Arm the 100 Million," evacuated children were trained in hand-to-hand combat, so that
they could do their part in the looming battle for the homeland. Mihoko

Nakane, the nine-year-old evacuee in Toyama, described this "spiritual training" with her usual brio: "It was lots and lots of fun." Her class trained with spears, wooden swords, and mock grenades. The drills were interspersed with their ordinary recreational routines, such as dodgeball, piggyback rides, war songs, and scavenger hunts. The children stripped to their underwear and put on Rising Sun headbands. In a "hand grenade-throwing class," they threw small balls at a large ball, which was said to represent an enemy soldier's head. Then they trained with wooden swords: "We faked to the left and faked to the right." While Mihoko practiced thrusting with a bamboo spear, her teacher shouted, "Spear them! Spear them!" Later she told her diary: "It was really fun. I was tired, but I realized that even one person can kill a lot of the enemy."[34]

EIGHT MONTHS AFTER ITS RECAPTURE, Guam was home to 200,000 American servicemen, 24,000 Guamian civilians, and untold hundreds (perhaps thousands) of Japanese stragglers hiding out in the jungle. A list of major construction projects underway in February and March 1945 filled six pages of small print in the Guam Island Commander's war diary.[35] Seabees of the Fifth Naval Construction Brigade were widening and extending the roads, improving the seaport, and installing a power, water, and sanitation infrastructure worthy of a major American city. Apra Harbor had been expanded with pontoon jetties, breakwaters, and a 3,900-foot-long causeway, and was now able to handle 265 cargo ships per month—a tenfold increase over its prewar capacity. A new four-lane asphalt highway, the backbone of the island's road network, ran between Sumay and Agana. Sixteen thousand civilians (mostly Chamorros) were living in three refugee camps along the island's west coast. The civil affairs department intended to return them to their farms and villages as soon as possible, but a certain amount of rebuilding was required, and Japanese stragglers still posed a security threat in outlying areas.

Guam was nicknamed the "Pacific Supermarket," and the nickname was well earned. Describing the cavernous arch-ribbed warehouses he found on Orote peninsula, the war correspondent Ernie Pyle had observed: "You could take your pick of K rations or lumber or bombs, and you'd find enough there to feed a city, build one, or blow it up."[36]

Most of the U.S. troops on Guam were idle, pending their deployment in forthcoming campaigns, and considerable efforts were made to keep them occupied and entertained. During the month of March 1945, for example, 64 servicemen's baseball teams played a total of 256 games, and 50 basketball teams played 220 games. The sporting leagues were slickly organized, with professional umpires and referees, colorful uniforms, large wooden scoreboards, and bleachers for spectators. Movies were projected on four hundred different screens each night, to an estimated nightly audience of 80,000. A newspaper, the *Island Command Daily Press News*, was circulated to more than 100,000 readers. Station WXLI of the Armed Forces Radio Service (AFRS) was on the air nine-and-a-half hours per day. An estimated 30,000 spectators watched a series of exhibition boxing matches between two former middleweight champions, Georgie Abrams and Fred Apostoli. About a dozen USO musical variety troupes were touring the island at any one time; the smash hit *Girl Crazy* was performed twice a day between March 12 and March 30. Four beaches had been set aside for recreational swimming, with dressing tents and lifeguards; they were visited by an average 4,000 swimmers per day. Major league baseball stars, flown in from the United States, played four exhibition games attended by an estimated 40,000 troops. According to the Red Cross field headquarters, "plans were made for the construction and operation of an 8-operator beauty shop for service women on the island, and four to five bowling establishments for military personnel."[37]

In January, after long discussion and study, Admiral Nimitz had approved the expansion of the B-29 airbase development program on Guam. Work was advancing on two enormous airfields on Guam's rugged northern plateau, North and Northwest Fields, each with two runways and ground facilities for two bombardment wings. By the first week of February, one runway at North Field was in operation, serving 180 Superfortresses of the 314th Bombardment Wing. The second runway had been cleared and partly graded, but was only 50 percent surfaced. Northwest Field was not yet in operation, but bulldozers, steam shovels, concrete mixers, and graders were working around the clock.

The war correspondent John Dos Passos, touring Guam that month, visited a stadium-sized coral pit where steam shovels were loading crushed stone into dump trucks. The workers wore masks against the fine white dust kicked up by the machinery. One told Dos Passos: "They used to load a truck every forty seconds, now it's every twenty seconds."[38] The seemingly endless column of trucks descended a winding road to the Sumay-Agana highway, drove 4 miles north, and then ascended a series of switchback roads to the "muddy tableland" of Northwest Field. It was well after dark when Dos Passos and his driver arrived, but they found the work proceeding at a vigorous pace. The trucks dumped their loads of crushed rock directly onto the runway bed, and bulldozers immediately began spreading it out. "Scrapers, graders, sheepsfoot rollers, machines we didn't know the names of, moved evenly behind them. The glistening bodies of the men, dark from the tanning sun, were highlighted with streaks of white dust in the glare of the floodlights."[39]

Allocation of resources and labor support aroused constant acrimony between Admiral Nimitz's CINPAC headquarters and General LeMay's Twentieth Air Force. Since LeMay was outside Nimitz's chain of command, their disputes were often bucked up to the Joint Chiefs for resolution. LeMay took the view that the Marianas had been captured in order to launch a B-29 campaign against Japan, and that all construction and development efforts should be channeled to that end. The navy countered that the Marianas were also a staging base for the huge amphibious invasions to come in 1945. Resources were scarce all around, requiring difficult tradeoffs that satisfied no one. Spring brought tropical downpours—sixteen wet days in March alone, when 6.5 inches of rain fell on the island, causing the engineers no end of grief at the airfield construction sites.[40] When the island command transferred two aviation engineer battalions from construction on Northwest Field to other projects of "higher priority," the reverberations reached Washington immediately.

LeMay was exasperated by the lavish recreation and entertainment facilities he found on southern and coastal Guam. "They had built tennis courts for the island commander; they built fleet recreation centers, marine rehabilitation centers, dockage facilities for inter-island service craft, and every other damn thing in the world except subscribing to the original purpose in the occupation of those islands." He joked that Guam would probably have a "roller-skating rink" before 21st Bomber Command had a proper headquarters.[41]

Shortly after his arrival, LeMay was invited to dinner at Nimitz's house on the Fonte Plateau, a hill overlooking Apra Harbor. The fine white house had four bedrooms, a spacious screened porch, and a dining room suitable for entertaining ranking officers and visiting VIPs.[42] The grounds had been handsomely landscaped, planted with flowers and native shrubs, and a horseshoe court had been built for Nimitz's recreation. The dinner was attended by many other senior army, navy, and marine officers stationed on Guam. "I went in to find chandeliers glowing and all the lights ablaze, the dinner table set with the white tablecloth, sparkling silverware, and so forth," LeMay wrote in his memoir. "Everyone was standing around in starched white uniforms having a drink."[43] They were served cocktails in highballs and hors d'oeuvres "such as you might find at an embassy in Washington." A multicourse dinner included soup, a fish course, a beef roast, and dessert, followed by demitasses, brandy, and cigars.[44]

In the story he never tired of telling, LeMay reciprocated by inviting the navy brass to dinner at his camp, where they stood in line at a Quonset hut mess hall and ate canned rations. That got the point across, "and eventually they came up with the facilities we needed."[45]

Feeling intense pressure from the JCS, Nimitz took steps to accelerate the B-29 airbase program. He granted Hap Arnold's request to ship new aviation engineer battalions into the islands, even if they arrived in advance of their heavy equipment.[46] The Seabees were obliged to transfer a certain amount of *their* equipment, forcing a reordering of other priorities. Shipping was a critical bottleneck, including such prosaic considerations as berthing time at the cargo loading docks. On March 28, Pacific Fleet headquarters ordered a "sharp curtailment" of shipping into the Marianas for all other purposes, in order to free up cargo space for the materials needed by the Twentieth Air Force. Cargo allocations would henceforth be reserved "to the maximum practicable limit for munitions and other supplies needed for the Superfortresses."[47] The order aroused resentment in many other quarters of the navy and Marine Corps. Admiral Richard S. Edwards, King's deputy in Washington, observed that General Arnold "wants to run the whole thing [the Twentieth Air Force] from Washington until his people in the field get into trouble, then expects the theater commander to rush in and save the situation."[48]

There was some compensation in the discovery that the island of Tinian, which was largely flat, would be able to accommodate as many as eight B-29 runways, rather than the four that had been planned before the capture of the island. Six naval construction brigades were put to work taking down about half of a long coral ridge, with the double purpose of leveling the ground and mining the rock within. Four operational runways were built at North Field, Tinian, a base that was completed and made operational more quickly than any other in the Marianas. In January 1945, it was decided to push forward with the development of Tinian's West Field as well, which would allow this smallest of the three occupied Mariana islands to accommodate two full bombardment wings. The first runway at West Field was activated on March 22, 1945. Meanwhile, the surveyors discovered that Isley Field on Saipan could be expanded to accommodate four groups of the Seventy-Third Bombardment Wing on two parallel 8,500-foot runways.

Taking stock of his command in early March, General LeMay was not pleased, and he did not mind who knew it. High-altitude precision bombing missions were consistently failing to achieve their hoped-for results. Of the eleven top-priority Japanese aircraft plants targeted by the USAAF, none had been destroyed (although production had been cut significantly at several). Eight missions had attempted to bomb the Nakajima engine plant in Musashino, but recent reconnaissance photography indicated that the complex had suffered only 4 percent damage. Due to operational problems, including engine failures and navigational problems, the Twentieth Air Force was failing to put enough planes over Japan. There were now 350 B-29s operating from the Marianas, but in an average mission, only 130 planes were actually crossing into Japanese airspace.[49]

To LeMay's chagrin, American newspapers were giving the impression that the B-29s were inflicting tremendous punishment on Japan. That was not necessarily the fault of the USAAF press offices, which had stuck closely to the facts in their press communiqués. The American papers seemed to want to tell their readers what they dearly wanted to hear—that the Superforts were spreading biblical carnage from one end of Japan to the other. On March 6, 1945, General LeMay told his public relations officer, Major St. Clair McKelway: "This outfit has been getting a lot of publicity without having really accomplished a hell of a lot in bombing results."[50]

Since taking over in January, LeMay had been considering a revolutionary change in tactics: low-altitude, high-intensity nighttime incendiary attacks. Such missions would involve sending the B-29s over their targets at night, at an altitude of 5,000 to 7,000 feet, far below their typical operating altitudes of 25,000 to 30,000 feet. They would avoid the jet stream and the strain on the engines created by the long climb to altitude. The fuel savings would allow for a higher bomb load—6 to 8 tons, whereas previous missions had averaged 3 to 4 tons. By scattering napalm incendiary clusters over a wide area, bombing accuracy would be moot. The Japanese fighter defenses were considered far less dangerous at night. Assuming that the B-29s would not encounter much resistance in the air, all .50-caliber guns and ammunition could be removed from the planes. That would save weight, and "at least our folks won't be shooting at each other."[51] With the element of surprise, LeMay reasoned, the Americans might get away with it.

LeMay, a natural-born self-promoter, later gave the impression that the low-altitude firebombing attacks were his idea. In fact, planners at the USAAF headquarters in Washington had already shown a great interest in incendiary attacks on Japanese cities, and had debated the potential advantages of sending the Superforts in at night and at lower altitudes. General Arnold, acting for the JCS, had issued orders for a series of "maximum effort" B-29 missions over various urban centers of Japan. (A "maximum effort" mission was defined as one in which every single airplane that the maintenance personnel had said was fit to fly *would* fly.) For the first time since the B-29s had begun operating from the Marianas, stockpiles of incendiary bombs were sufficient to allow for about five or six max-effort missions. The Seventy-Third Bombardment Wing had already received extensive training in night operations, with the intention of bombing by radar at night. At the Dugway Proving Ground in Utah, a model "Japanese Village" had been erected, duplicating the known materials and techniques of Japanese construction. Bombing tests employing a mix of napalm and magnesium incendiaries had quickly burned the model to the ground. Japanese cities were known to be much more vulnerable than German cities to firebombing, because the population densities were higher, and the close-built wooden houses were more susceptible to fire.

The workhorse of the firebombing raids was the M69 napalm incendiary submunition, clustered in a 500-pound E46 cylindrical finned bomb. Nearly all had been produced at a remote and secret plant in the Pine Barrens of New Jersey, about 15 miles inland from Atlantic City. Each M69 submunition or "bomblet" was essentially a cheesecloth sock filled with jellied gasoline, inserted into a lead pipe. Thirty-eight M69s were clustered together in an E46, bound by a strap that burst open on a timed fuse. The clusters were timed to open at 2,000 feet above the ground. Three-foot cotton gauze streamers trailed behind each bomblet, causing them to disperse over an area with a diameter of about 1,000 feet. On impact with the ground, a second fuse detonated and an ejection charge fired globules of flaming napalm to a radius of about 100 feet. Whatever these globules hit—walls, roofs, human skin—they adhered and burned at a temperature of 1,000 degrees Fahrenheit for eight to ten minutes, long enough to start raging fires in the teeming, close-built wood and paper neighborhoods at the heart of all Japanese cities.

In the 1930s, and in the early years of the Second World War, American leaders had staunchly opposed the practice of bombing cities from the air. In September 1939, as Europe had plunged into war, President Roosevelt had called upon all belligerent nations to forswear "the bombardment from the air of civilian populations or of unfortified cities."[52] Even within the ranks of the Army Air Corps, there were persistent objections to the "area bombing" of cities. In 1940, Hap Arnold had avowed: "The Air Corps is committed to a strategy of high-altitude, precision bombing of military objectives. Use of incendiaries against cities is contrary to our national policy of attacking only military objectives."[53] Five years of global savagery, and the behavior of the Axis nations, had prompted a gradual revision of these views. The Japanese and Germans had been the first to launch aerial attacks on civilian populations—the Japanese in raids against Shanghai, Nanjing, Chongqing, and other Chinese cities, and the Germans against Rotterdam, London, Coventry, and many other English cities. The Luftwaffe's "Blitz" of 1940 provoked British demands for retribution, which the RAF Bomber Command began supplying that year.

Indiscriminate terror bombing of German cities had culminated in the firebombing of Dresden on the night of February 13–14, 1945, killing an estimated 35,000 German civilians. Dresden prompted a certain amount of criticism in the American press, and even in the British House of Commons, as the bombing seemed to have no obvious military purpose. An Associated Press story reported: "Allied air commanders have made the long-awaited decision to adopt deliberate terror bombing of the great German population centers as a ruthless expedient to hasten Hitler's doom."[54] But Secretary Stimson denied the AP report, and justified the bombing of Dresden as a military necessity. He added: "Our policy never has been to inflict terror bombing on civilian populations . . . our efforts are still confined to the attack of enemy military objectives."[55]

Even now, in the late stages of a war of unprecedented brutality, American leaders were loath to admit that they had abandoned their policy against terror bombing. Firebombing Japanese cities demanded a plausible military pretense. USAAF target selectors argued that much of Japanese industrial production occurred in residential districts, where a cottage industry of small "feeder" or "shadow" workshops produced components for major plants. These were said to be the real target of the mass incendiary raids. But after the burning of Dresden, which occurred just three weeks before the first big firebombing raid on Tokyo, the moral objections seemed rather quaint. If the Germans had invited such retribution, so had the Japanese. Later, LeMay acknowledged that Japanese war crimes had provided a justification, at least in his own mind: "I was not happy, but neither was I particularly concerned, about civilian casualties in incendiary raids. I didn't let it influence any of my decisions because we knew how the Japanese had treated the Americans—both civilian and military—that they captured in places like the Philippines."[56] It was no coincidence that the world learned of Japanese atrocities in Manila just two weeks before the start of the firebombing campaign.

The new tactic entailed heavy risks. A bombing mission flown at 5,000 feet over Germany would draw devastating fighter attacks and heavy antiaircraft fire—as LeMay put it, "a low-level formation like this would have been cut to ribbons by the Luftwaffe."[57] But he was willing to gamble that the Japanese night fighters were not skilled or numerous enough to shoot down the B-29s in darkness, and that the flak would be wild and ineffective, especially given the element of surprise. Japanese radar-directed AA guns were thought to be crude and inaccurate in comparison with those in Germany. But that was an unproven supposition; no B-29 mission had flown over Japan at lower than 8,000 feet, and the only missions that had flown *that* low were those over the Yawata steelworks in Kyushu. The antiaircraft batteries defending Tokyo, Nagoya, and Osaka were more numerous, and possibly more advanced. It was known that the Japanese had trained at least two night-fighting squadrons. If LeMay was wrong, the price could be catastrophic losses of airplanes and aircrews.

According to Major McKelway, the press officer, flak experts from the various bombardment wings warned LeMay that he was courting disaster. They told him that Tokyo's antiaircraft batteries would shoot the low-flying bombers down like plywood ducks in a shooting gallery. Even Japanese machine guns on the ground might be able to hit the planes. One predicted losses of seven out of ten Superforts. "If you are right," LeMay replied, "we won't have many airplanes left if we go in low."[58] LeMay was one of history's most prolific killers, but he felt a "natural inborn repugnance" against sending his airmen to their deaths. He would have liked to lead the mission in person, but Washington had barred officers of his rank against flying over enemy territory. Losing aircrews to inevitable circumstances was bad enough, but losing them to poor tactical decisions by a ground-based commander was different: "That's when it really comes home to you."[59] If the mission failed, LeMay was likely to be relieved of his command, and could have been reduced to his permanent rank. He might have ended his career in the USAAF as a humble captain.

Critically, however, LeMay won the backing of his wing leaders, the brigadier generals who piloted lead aircraft for each of the 21st Bomber Command's three bombardment wings—Emmett "Rosie" O'Donnell, Thomas S. Power, and John H. Davies. The three brigadiers were quick to see the advantages of the proposed mission. The ferocious jet stream winds would be far above them. Winds at 5,000 feet would be no more than 25 to 30 knots, so bombing drift would not be a problem. The most capable and veteran pilots and crews (including the wing leaders) would fly the lead "pathfinder" planes, which would drop their incendiaries in an "X" pattern to mark the target. Those initial fires would serve as aiming points. For the planes that followed, navigation would be a cinch. The land-sea contrast of the Japanese coastline showed up clearly on airborne radar scopes, so that even the least experienced aircrews would have no trouble navigating to Tokyo Bay, regardless of visibility. At that point, they would simply "turn on the heading we give them, continue so many seconds, and pull the string."[60]

For the first time in the B-29 campaign, weather would not be a factor. As LeMay put it, "We could say forget the weather. We've proved that even the stupidest radar operators can get us over that land-water contrast up there at Tokyo. If we send some veterans in ahead, they're bound to get on the target, and they're bound to start the fires. We really get a conflagration going, the ones that come in later can see the glow. They can drop on that."[61]

The area to be targeted was Tokyo's Shitamachi district, the "lower city" or "undercity" of the Sumida River basin, a predominantly working-class district of close-built neighborhoods. In selecting this part of Tokyo, USAAF planners had consulted maps produced by the Office of Strategic Services (OSS)—predecessor agency to the CIA—which had ranked Tokyo's thirty-five wards by their susceptibility to fire. The OSS analysts had considered the density and nature of construction, and had even collected risk assessments produced by Japanese fire insurance companies before the war. The Shitamachi was chosen, in short, because it would burn better than any other part of the capital.[62]

The pilots and aircrewmen were briefed the day before the mission, in crowded Quonset huts at the various airbases throughout the islands. For purposes of secrecy, none had received advanced word of the new tactics. As the operations officers spelled out the particulars, silence fell over the gatherings. One colonel told his pilots: "We are throwing away the book. This time we will not fly formations."[63] They would carry much larger bomb loads, but leave their .50-caliber guns and gunners on the ground. According to a pilot of the 498th Bombardment Group on Saipan, "a dead silence" followed the news that they would be hitting Tokyo at night. But when the briefers told them that they would fly over the heart of Tokyo at altitudes of between 5,000 and 7,000 feet, "a huge gasp was then heard from the crew members."[64] Compared to past missions, that was nearly 5 miles closer to the ground.

Taking their cues from the wing commanders, the operations officers explained why the new tactics had been chosen, and why they were expected to succeed. Tactical surprise would be the Americans' friend, and it would permit them to get through the flight without excessive losses. Not all the airmen were persuaded, however, and as they returned to their quarters that night, some predicted losses of at least one-third of all planes on the mission. With that happy thought, they crawled into their cots and tried to get a decent night's sleep.

THE FOLLOWING AFTERNOON, AT NORTH FIELD, the pilots and aircrewmen of the 314th Bombardment Wing were driven in canvas-covered trucks to their planes on the hardstands. The crews boarded their aircraft and began their meticulous gear inventories and checklists. Mechanics rotated the great propeller blades, flushing excess oil from the engines. Thirty minutes before the first scheduled takeoff, the Wright Duplex-Cyclone engines began firing to life. They coughed, caught, whirred, and backfired thunderously, expelling clouds of exhaust smoke. Then the doors, hatches, and bomb bays were slammed closed, and the lead planes began inching out of their hardstands and trundling down the taxiways. Dust whipped up by the propellers got into the eyes, mouths, and noses of the ground crews and the many sightseers gathered along the length of the runway. The commingled roar of so many great engines caused the air and ground to vibrate. One witness was reminded of the Indianapolis 500.[65] Soldiers and marines sat on hillocks along the runways, as if they were spectators at an outdoor concert.

At 6:15 p.m., when the sun was very low in the western sky, a green flare shot up from a control tower, and the lead Superfortress began its takeoff run. The pilot eased the four throttles forward and lifted his feet from the brakes. He balanced on the rudder pedals to keep his machine accelerating down the centerline of the runway. He held the yoke tight, keeping the plane down so that it would gain more speed. At a certain point, the aircraft was moving too fast to stop, and must either take off or crash. At 160 miles per hour, the nose wheel tilted up, and the rear wheels lifted clear of the asphalt. The copilot hit the gear switch, and the struts and wheels folded neatly upward into their wells. No sooner had the first plane lifted off than the next one began its run. And so it continued, for more than an hour.

Once over the bluffs, the pilot nosed down just slightly in order to gather speed, and then raised the flaps very slowly. The heavy aircraft dipped low over the ocean, and the prop wash made four visible white wakes on the sea. Then it began climbing, ever so slowly. The takeoff weight of most B-29s on the March 9 mission was the maximum allowable 140,000 pounds—70 tons.

The first planes to take off were those of the nineteenth and twenty-ninth groups of the 314th Bombardment Wing, based on North Field, Guam. Forty minutes later, the lead planes on Saipan and Tinian began their takeoff runs. The interval between the first planes to take off from Guam and the last to take off from Saipan was a full two hours and forty-five minutes. Finally, well after dark, 334 Superforts were airborne and on their way to Tokyo.[66]

Since they were not flying in formation, there was no rendezvous. Each pilot simply turned north, climbed to his assigned altitude, and flew a course heading. During the seven-hour flight to Japan, they encountered some overcast and air turbulence, but the conditions were not severe enough to be dangerous. Flying just 5,000 to 7,000 feet above the ocean, the engines hummed along at low power settings. The crews kept a careful watch at the windows and blisters, peering out into the darkness for any sign of planes that might stray too close. One pilot recalled that he was constantly on edge as he scanned the sky through his greenhouse nose canopy—left and right, ahead, below, and above, peering into the darkness and imagining another B-29 suddenly looming into his field of vision. "The chances of collision seemed very high. It was spooky."[67]

In the lead "pathfinder" planes, the radar operators hunched over their APQ-13 radarscopes and tracked the approaching land mass of southern Honshu. Even in complete darkness, the coastline showed up clearly on the green circular screens: the Boso Peninsula, Cape Nojima, and the deep coastal indentation represented by Tokyo Bay. As the pathfinders made landfall, they flew dead north over the heart of Tokyo Bay, the Sumida River estuary, and the dockyards. Cloud cover was less than expected, varying from about 10 to 30 percent over the target, so the lead bombardiers had no trouble identifying their aiming points.

The bombing run was at full throttle, in a shallow dive for speed, the better to spoil the aim of the antiaircraft gunners and the attack maneuvers of pursuit planes. The engines ascended to a higher pitch, and speed inched up to 300 knots. The bomb bay doors fell open. The radar men watched their scopes and communicated through headsets with the bombardiers. At a quarter past midnight, the first M47 bombs fell clear. Bursting open at 100 feet above the ground, they ejected searing white magnesium. The blazes formed a large iridescent "X," marking a target area of about 10 square miles. One of the leaders radioed back to Guam: "Bombing the target visually. Large fires observed. Flak moderate. Fighter opposition nil."[68]

When the following planes arrived over Cape Nojima, the fires in Tokyo cast a pink glow over the northern horizon. As the "T-Square 12" passed over the Sumida estuary, Captain Charles L. Phillips Jr. saw a swirling mass of pyrocumulus clouds, illuminated from below by spectral reddish-orange light. The city's street plan could be seen, a network of dark lines crisscrossing a blanket of fire. Phillips and his crew could smell smoke and even the sickly sweet reek of burning flesh. "Those of us in the forward crew compartment could actually see pieces of window and door frames flying by the airplane."[69]

As the T-Square 12 entered the cloud, it lurched upward. Caught in a buffeting thermal updraft, the plane rose more than 6,000 feet in four minutes. Phillips throttled all four engines back to idle, but the T-Square 12 was still climbing and "bouncing around like a leaf in a windstorm."[70] Phillips called it "the wildest flight with the most severe turbulence I've ever experienced in over 7,000 hours of flight. It seemed certain the wings would be torn off our B-29."[71]

For a plane caught in that incredible updraft, there was nothing to do but climb. A pilot could attempt to hold his airplane down at his assigned altitude, but that would mean diving steeply through the updraft, resulting in airspeeds well above the recommended maximum "placard speed" of 300 miles per hour. A few B-29s were actually tossed onto their backs, fully inverted, with airmen hanging in their straps and loose gear pinned to the overheads. If they held together, they did a complete loop and came out of the dive. One pilot reported that he had surpassed an airspeed of 450 miles per hour—which the Boeing engineers had reckoned as fatal to a B-29—and gained control only 200 feet over Tokyo Bay.[72]

The T-Square 12 released its full load of M69 clusters. Suddenly 6 tons lighter, the aircraft lurched upward at an even greater velocity, and the altimeter needles raced clockwise around the dial. Phillips and his copilot were not wearing their shoulder straps. At 14,000 feet, the updraft abruptly ceased and the plane suddenly began diving again. Both pilots were lifted bodily from their seats and floated up toward the overhead, as if they were astronauts in zero-G space. "We both held on for dear life," wrote Phillips. "The situation lasted for several seconds. Then we sank back into our seats and regained control of the airplane. After a rather steep left turn we headed out toward the Pacific Ocean and our route home."[73]

THE AIR-RAID SIRENS HAD STARTED UP about an hour before the first planes had arrived, when Japanese coastal radar stations had first detected the incoming raid. Civil defense wardens ran through the streets and cobblestone alleys, using wooden clackers to call the citizens to their assigned posts. At first, many refused to leave their beds and homes, assuming that it was another false alarm. But as the first pathfinder B-29s arrived over the city, flying so much lower than ever before, the drone of their engines drew people out into the streets. Looking up, they saw the big silver bombers, their bellies reflecting orange, pink, and violet light from the fires below. They were four or five times closer than they had been in previous raids. A witness recalled: "It was as if we could reach out and touch the planes, they looked so big."[74] Searchlights reached up for them, and bursts of flak appeared above them. Some saw the M69s, twisting and turning as they fell, with long cotton gauze streamers flapping behind them.

A strong, dry wind was gusting that night, and the initial fires spread quickly. Thirty minutes after the first pathfinder bombs had fallen, according to the Tokyo fire chief, the situation was "completely out of control; we were absolutely helpless."[75] The fire brigades went into action, but their efforts were pitifully inadequate, especially as a shower of new napalm incendiaries fell from newly arrived Superforts. Wind-fanned fires spread and merged, engulfing the densely built wood-and-paper neighborhoods, from Asakusa in the northwest to Honjo in the northeast, from Fukagawa in the southeast to Nihonbashi in the southwest—advancing like a storm, leaping from house to house, wall to wall, roof to roof, across the narrow cobblestone alleyways, growing in heat and intensity as it devoured the mother lode of fuel that it found in its path. The workshops and small factories, stocked with combustible grease, lubricating oil, and gasoline, exploded as if they had been bombed. Walls of fire raced over rooftops and down streets, and roasted people where they stood, or consumed their homes with such speed that they never had a chance to get out. An air defense manual published by the home ministry had advised that "the first minute is the most crucial for dealing with firebomb attacks," which was certainly true—but the manual had told citizens to stay and fight the fires, rather than flee. They were to "throw water on flammable things near you to prevent a fire from spreading if it breaks out."[76] Against a disaster of this magnitude, such measures were futile. Their only real hope of survival was to run, and to be lucky in the direction they chose.

Survivors attested that they were surrounded by a constant, crashing pandemonium, so loud that they had to shout to be heard. The fire crackled, howled, hissed, and roared. Sparks, embers, and firebrands swirled in wind eddies and landed on their heads and backs. The ambient temperature rose and kept rising, as if the door of a giant oven had opened. The fire radiated waves of infrared heat that desiccated all material in its path, and caused flammable material to ignite even ahead of the flames. The asphalt under their feet was sticky and bubbling; eventually, it would liquefy completely. The instinct was to run blindly from that heat, but those who survived often made choices based on a plan—to get to the widest streets, or to a swimming pool, or the river, or one of the parks. Takeshi Nagamine, a student at Waseda University, believed that he and his family survived because his father was aware that a strong wind was blowing from the west, and knew the fires would advance upon them from that direction. He led them to Sumida Park, calculating that the fire would circumvent it. They lived. Others ran toward the schools, which doubled as disaster shelters—but for many civilians that decision proved fatal.

Kazuyo Funato, a sixth grader who lived above her father's toy shop in Asakusa, followed her parents and five siblings into the street. They ran downwind, toward Sunamachi, but the fires seemed to advance upon them from every direction at once. Her father led them toward a local park, but they found their way blocked by a mass of people coming the other way across a narrow footbridge. Forced to turn back, they ran blindly, and in the maelstrom the family was unable to stay together. "The wind and flames became terrific," said Kazuyo:

We were in Hell. All the houses were burning, debris raining down on us. It was horrible. Sparks flew everywhere. Electric wires sparked and toppled. Mother, with my little brother on her back, had her feet swept out from under her by the wind and she rolled away. Father jumped after her. "Are you all right?" he screamed. Yoshiaki shouted, "Dad!" I don't know if his intention was to rescue Father or to stay with him, but they all disappeared instantly into the flames and black smoke.[77]

Michiko Okubo, twelve years old, came across another girl aged four or five, who must have been separated from her family while running from the fires. Michiko took the girl's hand, saying, "Let's get away from here together." Hand in hand, they ran. She looked up and saw an incendiary falling toward them, "spewing flames and making a shrill noise." The younger girl's hand slipped from hers. She turned and saw several people engulfed in flames: "A fragment of the little girl's padded hood drifted high into the sky." Recalling the scene decades later, Michiko wrote, "I have never been able to forget the feeling of her soft, little hand, like a maple leaf, in mine."[78]

Many thousands ran toward the canals, or the Sumida River. On the narrow old bridges, great masses of people tried to flee in both directions at once, creating a stalemate, and all were immobilized before the advancing fires. Walls of flame swept over them, sucking the oxygen from the air and killing them all together. They gasped for breath, but the air was too hot to breathe, and then they choked, coughed blood, and convulsed. Many leapt from the bridges, and found momentary relief in the water, until other jumpers dropped on top of them, and they drowned. Survivors recalled a seething mass of people flailing in the water. "It was a hellish frenzy, absolutely horrible," said firefighter Isamu Kase. "People were just jumping into the canals to escape the inferno."[79] In the smaller and shallower canals, the water boiled over, leaving the dead exposed in heaps.

The Asakusa Kannon Buddhist Temple, one of the largest and most famous in Japan, had survived the 1923 earthquake and fire even as the surrounding neighborhood had burned to the ground. Thousands now ran to the temple and its spacious plaza, hoping to find refuge. Throngs entered the building, until it was jammed full. More came, trying to push into the doorways, while those inside fought to keep them out. As the fires closed around the structure, sparks and embers fell on the panicked crowd outside the big wooden doors. More napalm incendiaries fell from the B-29s passing overhead, and some landed directly on the tile roof of the temple. The great wooden edifice began to burn, and the flames advanced quickly. Burning timbers fell from the ceiling onto the heads of those trapped in the temple. The mob clamoring to get in was opposed by a surging mass of panicked people trying to get out. As the heat grew intolerable, many were crushed or trampled. The temple burned to the ground.

At the Sumida Telephone Exchange, one of Tokyo's six major switchboards, regulations required the staff to remain at their posts and fight the fire. The switchboards were operated by young women, many still in adolescence. They had been trained to defend the facility with wet mops and buckets of sand and water. As the B-29s roared overhead and fires engulfed the surrounding neighborhoods, the operators remained at their posts. Women carried water in buckets from the bathrooms, and even the teakettle in the kitchen. A row of sturdy telephone poles had been set up as buttresses to keep the building from collapsing if hit by bombs. But the poles burst into flames, and the fires spread to the walls. Without orders to evacuate, the workers felt obliged to remain and try to fight the fires. "When everything was burning, there was no order issued to evacuate the office," recalled Hiroyasu Kobayashi, a maintenance worker. "No order came releasing you. You must defend your position to the death! That's it."[80] The night supervisor finally gave the order to evacuate the building, but for most of the staff it was too late. Only four switchboard operators survived; thirty-one died in the fire. Most were between the ages of fifteen and eighteen. Kobayashi was one of the few employees to escape the telephone exchange. Later, he was asked by his employer to explain why he had fled. "But when they investigated, they found that even the coin boxes on the public phones had melted completely. Then they understood."[81]

A few in the heart of the burned-out districts managed to survive by sheer luck. They found a route of escape early, and got upwind of the fires. They found an open space, where a ditch or a concrete structure provided just enough shelter against the heat and flames, or a safety lane beneath an elevated railway. They stayed low, where there was still enough oxygen to breathe, and endured the heat long enough to outlast the fires. Kazuyo Funato, the sixth grader, found shelter in a trench behind a school. Her younger sister kept crying, "It's hot, hot!"[82] But they stayed put, wisely, and survived. A boy survived by lying down in a gutter on a wide street, with the curb interposed between himself and the flames. Several hundred headed for the expansive rail yards of the Ryogoku Railroad Station, where they found open ground surrounded by concrete and steel structures that did not burn.

Tomoko Shinoda, a housewife, was hurrying past Oshiage Station when she was told to stay there. "It was so hot and suffocating that I pressed my cheek to the ground. The air was cool and clean down there."[83] She remained all night, wedged against a stranger. Around dawn, she stood up, and the stranger toppled over. "I shook him, but he was dead. They said he died from smoke and the heat of the flames."[84] Hidezo Tsuchikura, a factory worker, made his way to the roof of the Futaba School with his two young children. As the fires approached, embers and burning debris dropped on their heads, and the children wailed in pain and begged to be taken home. Tsuchikura pried open the rooftop water tank and scooped water over his children, putting out fires on their clothing. Then he plunged them into the tank, one at a time, repeatedly. "For the next ninety minutes or so we kept repeating this procedure. The air was so hot that as I doused the children and put them back on the roof the water steamed almost immediately from their clothes." Tsuchikura and his children survived without serious injury.[85]

Burning with such intensity, and on such a scale, the fires burned themselves out fairly quickly. By dawn on March 10, they had mostly subsided. The stricken area was choked with smoke so thick that the survivors found it painful to keep their eyes open. People shuffled pitifully through the streets, skin burned and blistered, smeared with grime, clothes partially burned, eyes red and raw. Some squatted on the ground, not wanting to sit because the ground was still too hot. The city was a smoldering wasteland—mounds of ashes and rubble, interspersed with a few blackened and gutted concrete walls, brick chimneys, and steel safes. Those middle-aged or older were reminded of the 1923 disaster. Survivors gravitated toward their homes, or the sites where their homes had once stood, but some neighborhoods were so thoroughly razed that the landmarks were gone, and they could not find their way. They noticed distant city vistas, faraway buildings that they could not have seen the previous day.

The authorities began the macabre task of counting, collecting, and disposing of the dead. Corpses were stacked like cordwood. They looked like charcoal mannequins, shrunk to three-quarters of their size, their facial features burned beyond recognition. Men could not be distinguished from women; smaller figures, children, died alongside their parents. The bodies were burned on the spot, or loaded into trucks to be buried in mass graves, or cremated in bonfires on the outskirts of the city. Walking back through the carnage toward her home, Tomoko Shinoda saw a pair of black work gloves on the ground. Stooping to inspect them, she saw that they were human hands. She came across a fire truck, once red, now blackened; the firemen, also blackened, had all burned to death in the vehicle. Sumida Park, recalled Sumi Ogawa, was "a graveyard with lumps of earth piled up in rows. People dug large pits and poured kerosene on corpses to incinerate them."[86] Michiko Kiyooka, a twenty-one-year-old woman living in Asakusa, warmed herself by a still smoldering heap of dead. "I could see an arm," she said. "I could see nostrils. But I was numb to that by then. The smell is one that will never leave me."[87]

The authorities pried open the doors of the various schools and other buildings that had served as shelters, to find hundreds of dead. In a swimming pool by the Futaba School, people had leapt into the water to escape the heat and flames. "It was hideous," a witness recounted. "More than a thousand people, we estimated, had jammed into the pool. The pool had been filled to its brim when we first arrived. Now there wasn't a drop of water, only the bodies of the adults and the children who had died."[88]

According to the Tokyo Metropolitan Police, the air raid killed 88,000, injured 41,000, and left almost a million homeless. About 267,000 houses were completely burned down. Sixteen square miles of the city lay in ashes.[89] In later revised estimates, the Japanese government put the death count at more than 100,000; other estimates ranged as high as 125,000. The actual number is not known, partly because the fires consumed most official registration records for the districts that were destroyed, and partly because the police and army personnel despaired of making an accurate body count. One Tokyo official told USSBS interrogators after the war, "The condition was so terrible I could not well describe it. After a raid I was supposed to investigate, but I didn't go because I did not like to see the terrible sights."[90] It seems likely that the March 9–10 firebombing of Tokyo killed more people, at least initially, than the atomic bombings of either Hiroshima or Nagasaki. If the highest death toll estimates are accurate, the Tokyo raid may have killed more people (initially) than Hiroshima and Nagasaki *combined*. It was the most devastating air raid of the war, in either Europe or the Pacific. It left more dead than any other single military action in history.

The Japanese press downplayed the scale of the catastrophe. Coverage dwelled on the fact that the Imperial Palace had not been hit, and the emperor was unharmed. Headlines accused the Americans of "blind bombing" or "slaughter bombing." Editorials expressed confidence that the spirit of the Japanese people would be aroused to new heights by the enemy's atrocious conduct. The *Asahi Shinbun* assured its readers: "Our accumulation of war power for the final battle in the homeland will not be blocked by such an enemy attack. Rather, it will stir our fighting spirit and our resolve to destroy the enemy."[91]

AT HIS OPERATIONS CONTROL HUT IN GUAM, LeMay paced the floor and awaited news of the mission. Most of the staff had gone to bed, but LeMay stayed up, smoking cigars and drinking Coca-Colas. He told Major McKelway that he could not sleep: "A lot could go wrong."[92]

The first bombs-away radio messages arrived shortly before two in the morning, Guam time. The news was encouraging; plane losses seemed to be lower than expected. Seven hours later, when the first returning B-29s landed, the airmen rendered their verdict: "Tokyo caught fire like a forest of pine trees."[93] General Power, the mission leader, returned with photographs of the fires in progress. A U.S. submarine south of Honshu reported heavy smoke at sea level, a full 150 miles off the coast. Three B-29 photo reconnaissance planes flew over Tokyo at midday on March 10, snapping thousands of photos in clear weather. Later that night, when the poststrike photographs were delivered to the operations control hut on Guam, they were laid out on a table under electric lights. They depicted an ugly whitish-gray scar running along both sides of the Sumida River, covering about 16 square miles of the city. LeMay, a cigar clamped in his teeth, his face "expressionless," leaned over the table and put his hand down on that part of the photograph. "All this is out," he said. He ran his hand down the whitish-gray band. "This is out—this—this—this."[94]

Just fourteen Superfortresses failed to return, out of the 334 that had taken off. That was a loss rate of 4.2 percent, lower than the cumulative average in past missions. Given that LeMay and his airmen had dreaded much higher losses, the safe return of 320 planes was a welcome surprise, vindicating LeMay's theory that the Japanese would be caught by surprise. (After the war, the Americans learned that the Japanese fighter planes had been uncontrollable in the wild thermal updrafts created by the fires; they could not even get near the B-29s, let alone attack them.) Morale among the pilots and aircrewmen soared, especially after they saw the aerial photos depicting one-fifth of the enemy's capital in ashes. The photos were blown up to large scale, marked up with arrows and comments, and pinned to corkboards in the administrative offices and briefing huts on Saipan, Guam, and Tinian.

LeMay was eager to continue the blitz immediately, before the Japanese could take countermeasures. He had hoped to turn his planes around the same day to hit Nagoya on the night of March 10, but that was not feasible. The first planes took off on the afternoon of March 11, just thirty hours after the last B-29s had returned from the Tokyo mission. The Nagoya strike was another "maximum effort" mission: 313 B-29s were launched, and 286 reached the target. Tactics were much the same as over Tokyo two nights earlier. The attackers dropped 1,790 tons of incendiaries, slightly more than had been dropped on Tokyo. For a combination of reasons—less wind, lower building density, a better firefighting response—Nagoya was spared the holocaust suffered by Tokyo. Hundreds of fires failed to merge into a general conflagration, and they burned out "only" two square miles of the city. By any standard other than the disaster in Tokyo, however, the Nagoya fires were devastating. Several of the city's most important industrial targets were damaged or destroyed.

After flying two fifteen-hour missions in forty-eight hours, Charles Phillips was as tired as he had been since he had learned to fly. "We had seen tremendous fires two nights before," he wrote in a letter home, "so the sight of a big city like Nagoya burning fiercely was nothing really new. It is still just as awesome as the last time. Again, we could look down and count the very blocks in the city that we had touched off. The city had become an inferno. Smoke billowed up something awful and again we could actually smell Nagoya burning from inside our aircraft."[95]

Osaka, the nation's second largest city, was the objective on March 13. Two hundred four Superforts reached the city, dropping 2,240 tons of incendiaries from low altitude. Cloud cover obscured the city, but radar bombing proved accurate, with a "thicker and more uniform pattern" than in past missions.[96] Nine square miles of Osaka were burned to the ground. Among the important targets destroyed was the Osaka Arsenal, which provided about one-fifth of the Japanese army's total artillery shells. Thermal updrafts over the city were even more severe than over Tokyo four nights earlier. One pilot described "a great mushroom of boiling, oily smoke, and in a few seconds we were tossed 5,000 feet into the air." A 313th Wing B-29, the aptly named *Topsy-Turvy*, was flipped onto an inverted position, with the crew hanging upside down from their shoulder straps.[97] It plunged 10,000 feet—almost to the ground—before the pilot was able to regain control and turn for home. The *Topsy-Turvy* returned safely to base. Remarkably, only two B-29s were lost on this mission and thirteen damaged.

On the night of March 16, an armada of 307 B-29s hit Kobe, a major seaport and industrial hub, the sixth largest city in Japan. Twenty-three hundred tons of incendiaries burned down three square miles of the city. The Japanese fighter response was heavier than in past raids, but the intercepting planes were unable to make effective attacks, and only three B-29s on the mission failed to return.

The fifth and last mission of the blitz was a return to Nagoya on the night of the nineteenth. Two hundred ninety Superforts dropped 2,000 tons of bombs on the city. The raid targeted a smaller district with tight patterns of incendiaries and high-explosive bombs. Virtually all remaining incendiaries in the Marianas bomb dumps were loaded into the planes. The raid destroyed three more square miles of Nagoya, damaging or destroying high-priority targets such as the Nagoya Arsenal, the freight yards, and an Aichi aircraft engine plant.

That concluded the March 1945 firebombing blitz, at least for the moment. Everyone involved—including the pilots, aircrews, administrative staffs, and ground support personnel—was completely worn out. A pause was needed, or operational accidents would become critical. Moreover, the entire stock of Marianas incendiaries had been expended in the five missions, and the supply would have to be replenished by sea. In the meantime, the B-29s would have to return to conventional bombing with general purpose "iron bombs." It would not be possible to resume firebombing raids on Japanese cities until mid-April. In the interim, the B-29s would be pressed into service to support Operation ICEBERG, the invasion of Okinawa.

In five "maximum effort" firebombing missions flown in ten days, the B-29s had completed 1,595 sorties and dropped nearly 10,000 tons of bombs on Japan. The raids had burned down 32 square miles in four large Japanese cities. The 334 planes launched on the first incendiary night mission against Tokyo were almost double the number launched in any previous mission. Almost overnight, the Twentieth Air Force had progressed from fifty-plane raids to three-hundred-plane raids. Flying a 3,000-mile round trip that took them just a mile above some of the most heavily defended airspace in Japan, U.S. plane losses had amounted to only 1.3 percent, and aircrew losses to 0.9 percent. In May and June, new firebombing raids would be launched on an even larger scale, and loss rates would decline steadily.

The success of the incendiary raids vindicated and consolidated the autonomy of the JCS-controlled Twentieth Air Force. The B-29s would be enlisted in future tactical missions—most notably, bombing Kyushu airfields in support of the pending Okinawa operation—but LeMay now insisted with greater confidence that he should be allowed to get on with the task of wiping out Japanese cities. He planned to run his airmen and airplanes to the outer limits of their endurance, telling his superiors in Washington that his command could surpass a rate of more than 6,000 sorties per month by August 1945. Years later, he speculated that if the navy had provided sufficient logistical support to keep his B-29s flying uninterrupted maximum-effort missions against Japan, the nation might have surrendered sooner than August 1945: "I think it might have been possible."[98]

For eighteen months, the Japanese government had been encouraging evacuations from Tokyo and other cities. Now the trickle became a flood. Hundreds of thousands had no home, and had no choice but to leave; many others joined the exodus for fear of future such disasters. The population of

Tokyo dropped by more than one-half between January and August 1945. Nationally, the total number of urban refugees who moved out of the cities (and what remained of the cities) probably exceeded 10 million by war's end. At urban factories, worker absenteeism spiked. The Tokyo fire chief gave his confidential opinion that the capital was indefensible against such raids. The principle that people should stand and fight the fires was abandoned, both by the citizens and by the authorities. Now it was recognized that the best tactic for survival was to run, as soon as the air-raid sirens started up.

One afternoon in late March, an armed motorcade carried Hirohito beyond the moats of the Imperial Palace, and the emperor inspected the scorched ruins of the stricken "low city." Press reports, with doughty understatement, conceded that the damage was "not small" or "considerable."[99] But the regime had informers everywhere, and most Japanese citizens knew enough to guard their tongues. Within earshot of neighbors and strangers, it was considered safest to say, "It doesn't seem too bad."[100]

Chapter Thirteen

W̲ITH ITS MISSION AT IWO JIMA COMPLETED, TASK FORCE 58 RETURNED to Ulithi for a short interlude of rest, repairs, and replenishment. The great fleet filled the northern anchorage, almost to capacity. At night, in spite of wartime blackout procedures, a witness could see many lights showing on the anchored warships. On the islands around the periphery of the spacious lagoon, movies were screened each night in outdoor amphitheaters. With the war moving north, all had grown heartily tired of blackout restrictions, and were increasingly inclined to let them slide.

On March 11, about an hour after sunset, Admiral Jocko Clark was on the flight deck of his flagship *Hornet* when he heard aircraft engines overhead. Looking up, he saw a green twin-engine bomber with red disks under its wings. It was descending rapidly toward the *Randolph*, another *Essex*-class carrier anchored a quarter of a mile away. The kamikaze crashed the *Randolph*'s starboard quarter, just beneath her flight deck, gouging a 40-foot hole in the deck and starting fires in the machine shops and after hangar spaces. Twenty-seven of her crew were killed and fourteen aircraft destroyed. Half an hour later, a second Japanese plane crashed and exploded on nearby Sorlen Island, injuring fourteen men and damaging ground installations. The pilot may have mistaken the brightly lit island for an anchored ship.[1]

The attackers had flown all the way from Kyushu, a distance of more than 1,600 miles, in a Fifth Air Fleet suicide mission designated "Operation TAN." Twenty-four Yokosuka P1Y "Galaxy" bombers (Allied codename "Frances") had lifted off that morning from the main runway at Kanoya Air Base. Ten had suffered engine problems and were forced to turn back, or made emergency landings on other islands. Several others disappeared while en route. At 6:52 p.m., after a nine-hour flight, the lead pilot radioed Kanoya to report that the remaining planes had achieved complete surprise over Ulithi Atoll. Based on an overoptimistic assessment of that report, the Fifth Air Fleet staff concluded that eleven American aircraft carriers must have been struck.[2] In fact, the *Randolph* was the only victim.

The ultra-long-range attack highlighted a tactical advantage possessed by the kamikazes: without need to conserve fuel for the return flight, their flight radius was effectively doubled. Admiral Clark called it "a feat of great daring, quite characteristic of our Japanese adversaries."[3]

Three days later, Task Force 58 returned to sea. The grand sortie took the better part of the day, with five semiautonomous carrier task groups filing out of Mugai Channel one at a time. They forged north through an intertropical front, bucking rough seas under thick cloud cover. The task groups were commanded by the brownshoe admirals Jocko Clark, Ralph Davison, Ted Sherman, and Arthur Radford; a smaller fifth group (58.5), specializing in night operations, was led by Rear Admiral Matt Gardner. Task Force 58 commander Marc Mitscher rode in the carrier *Bunker Hill* as part of Sherman's Task Group 58.3. Their mission was to hammer Japanese airbases in Kyushu, Shikoku, and southern Honshu, in hopes of blunting the Japanese air response to Operation ICEBERG, the invasion of Okinawa, scheduled to begin two weeks later.

On the night of March 17–18, as the task force approached the southern coast of Kyushu, Japanese reconnaissance planes dropped floating flares around the perimeter of the task force. *Enterprise* night fighters shot down two snoopers, but radar scopes revealed many more skulking around the edges of the American fleet. Tactical surprise, in this round, was a lost cause.[4]

Admiral Matome Ugaki, the Fifth Air Fleet commander, monitored the various sighting and radar reports from his headquarters at Kanoya Air Base. Long distance patrols had confirmed that the bulk of the American fleet had left Ulithi on March 15. After sunset on March 17, night patrols made contact with the leading elements of the American fleet. Ugaki was not in doubt: he expected heavy raids to fall on his airfields on the morning of March 18.

Two weeks earlier, the army and navy sections of the Imperial General Headquarters in Tokyo had established a conservative policy for the deployment of air power in the homeland. The best and most experienced squadrons were to be held back until an invasion force approached Japanese shores. They were not to be sent to repel a mere "carrier raid." Even if U.S. carrier planes appeared over the homeland, Japanese pilots and airplanes should avoid contact to the extent possible, and "positive operations will be avoided to preserve strength."[5] In other words, the Japanese aviators were to survive to fight another day, even at the cost of allowing uncontested raids on their airfields: "Anti-fighter plane combat for the purpose of air defense of strategic points will not be carried out, in principle, with combat strength, except when the situation is particularly favorable or when it is urgently needed."[6]

But Ugaki had never accepted the logic of this tame, self-protective strategy. He anticipated that American fighter sweeps would fall heavily upon the air bases of southern Japan, making it impossible to carry out the offshore scouting and reconnaissance that would determine whether or not an invasion was coming. As Task Force 58 moved into its launch position east of Kyushu, Ugaki worried that the American carrier strikes would "be so relentless that we wouldn't be able to preserve our strength even if we tried to do so. I couldn't stand to see [aircraft] destroyed on the ground." Therefore, Ugaki took the decision, upon his own authority, to counterattack with the Fifth Air Fleet's "whole strength."[7]

Before dawn on March 18, from a position about 90 miles off the southern tip of Kyushu, the American carriers launched 130 Hellcats and Corsairs. The initial fighter sweep encountered scant opposition in the air, and the pilots saw few planes on the ground, so they contented themselves with shooting up ground installations. A bombing strike followed about forty minutes later, consisting of sixty dive and torpedo bombers escorted by forty fighters. That afternoon, a second round of strikes was sent farther inland, to airfields in northern Kyushu. The flyers returned with claims of 102 enemy aircraft shot down and 275 destroyed or damaged on the ground.[8]

The task force offshore found itself under a low thick cloud ceiling, with the overcast suspended just 500 feet above the flight decks. That was a tactically dangerous situation, because it permitted Japanese planes to evade the combat air patrol and descend suddenly through the clouds before the antiaircraft guns could react. The Enterprise was struck by a large bomb on its forward elevator, and the Intrepid was slightly damaged when a G4M bomber hit the sea close aboard. A few minutes after 3 p.m., the carrier Yorktown (Admiral Radford's flagship in Task Group 58.4) was hit on the starboard side of her signal bridge. All three carriers managed to contain the damage, but the crews were unnerved by these determined and surprisingly skillful conventional (non-kamikaze) bombing attacks, which seemed to prove that the Japanese had conserved some of their best and most seasoned aviators for the climactic phase of the war.

That impression was confirmed the following morning, when a large airstrike was launched against Japanese warships anchored in the harbors of Kure and Hiroshima in the Inland Sea. The outgoing strike had a rough time of it. Over Matsuyama, an airbase on the north coast of Shikoku, two squadrons of Hellcats were ambushed from above and behind by Japanese fighters of the elite 343rd Kokutai, flying fast and powerful Kawanishi N1K2-J Shinden-Kais. The number of U.S. planes shot down in the dogfight over Matsuyama on March 19, 1945, is unknown, but the Japanese claimed more than a dozen kills. The surviving U.S. planes went on to suffer additional heavy losses over Kure, where the antiaircraft fire was severe. The SB2C and F6F pilots planted bombs on seven different Japanese warships, but sank none. For the day, the Americans lost sixty planes.

Meanwhile, a Japanese airstrike was on a reciprocal heading for the task force, and found it just a few miles off the south coast of Shikoku. Once again, the partial overcast at 2,000 feet allowed the attackers to elude the CAP; Mitscher described the conditions as "perfect for the enemy. . . . Radar again was unable to compete."[9] A swarm of well-handled bombers descended on the big carriers at the hub of Admiral Davison's Task Group 58.2. The *Wasp* took a bad hit at 7:10 a.m. The bomb penetrated three decks before detonating and killing about one hundred crewmen. Minutes later, a Yokosuka D4Y *Suisei* dive-bomber plunged through the base of the clouds, about a thousand yards directly ahead of the *Franklin*, and dropped two 250-kilogram bombs before the gunners could react. The deadly missiles punched through the *Franklin*'s flight deck and plunged into the heart of the ship. The results were calamitous. The fires and explosions aboard the "Big Ben" were worse than those suffered by any aircraft carrier that survived the Pacific War. Hundreds were killed instantly, probably before they were even aware that the ship had been hit.

The attack was so sudden that Captain Leslie Gehres, on the bridge, never caught a glimpse of the plane or the bombs it had dropped. The *Franklin* had been in the process of launching planes. The ordnance and ready service ammunition in the antiaircraft mounts was cooked off by the explosions, which in turn caused more explosions. Several F6F Hellcats were armed with "Tiny Tim" rockets, which ignited and began launching from the disabled planes. According to Commander Joe Taylor, the executive officer, "Some screamed by to starboard, some to port, and some straight up the flight deck. The weird aspect of this weapon whooshing by so close is one of the most awful spectacles a human has ever been privileged to see. Some went straight and some tumbled end over end. Each time one went off, firefighting crews forward would instinctively hit the deck."[10] Firefighters were forced to seek cover, interrupting their efforts to control the fires.

On other ships of the task force, witnesses trained binoculars on the exploding carrier. Admiral Radford, whose ship was at least 15 miles away, noted a series of mushroom clouds and the largest pall of smoke he had ever seen emerge from a single ship. "We could not believe that anyone remained alive on a ship undergoing such travail," he said. "I mentally said goodbye to my classmate Admiral Davison and to *Franklin*'s skipper, my friend, Captain Leslie Gehres."[11] On the *Yorktown*, 12 miles away, an officer on the bridge counted nine huge explosions. A shipmate remarked: "That's all, brother! We can tell 'Big Ben' goodbye."[12]

But Gehres chose to fight to save his ship. The cruiser *Santa Fe* came alongside and took off many of the surviving crew, including Admiral Davison and his staff. (He shifted his flag to the *Hancock*.) The fire control parties kept at it for four hours, until by 11:00 a.m. the fires had subsided to the point that the cruiser *Pittsburgh* managed to take the *Franklin* in tow. Soon the badly wounded carrier was making 3 knots on a southerly course.[13] At three o'clock the next morning, after a twenty-hour fight for her life, the "Big Ben" regained power and was able to make 20 knots under her own steam. Spruance sent her back to Ulithi, and then to Pearl Harbor. From there, she made a 12,000-mile voyage to New York, also under her own steam.

At every port on her voyage, witnesses gaped. The *Franklin* was a pitiable wreck, blackened and gutted. Deformed lumps of charred steel on her flight deck were the only remaining traces of her aircraft. (The fires had burned so hot that the wreckage had fused onto the ship, and could not be jettisoned.) The *Franklin*'s casualty list included 807 killed and more than 487 wounded, amounting to nearly half her complement. As Chester Nimitz later concluded, "No other ship in World War II, and possibly in history, suffered such extensive injuries and yet remained afloat."[14]

In two days of strikes off southern Japan, Task Force 58 had hit Japanese airfields, ports, and warships, and destroyed about four hundred planes in the air or on the ground. But it had suffered a cruel thrashing in return. Six carriers had been hit and damaged, of which three (*Enterprise*, *Wasp*, and *Franklin*) needed major repairs at a rear base. On March 20, Mitscher decided to pull out of the area without launching a third day of strikes. The wounded ships were sent down to Ulithi, with strong screening escorts, while the others rendezvoused with a service squadron 150 miles southeast of Okinawa for refueling and rearming. There would be no rest for Task Force 58. The carrier air groups were needed to support Operation ICEBERG, the invasion of Okinawa, to commence on April 1.[15]

AS A RULE, EACH SUCCESSIVE AMPHIBIOUS OPERATION in the Pacific was larger than the last. Okinawa was the last amphibious operation of the war; accordingly, it dwarfed all previous landings. The ground force included 183,000 combat troops drawn from the army and marines, with an additional 120,000 service troops and engineers. The transport and logistical fleet consisted of more than 1,200 ships. That figure did not include the roughly two hundred warships of Task Force 58 and the British Pacific Fleet, which would furnish air protection. Okinawa was 6,100 miles from San Francisco, 850 miles from Iwo Jima, 920 miles from Manila, 1,400 miles from Guam, almost 1,400 miles from Ulithi—but only 330 miles from the Japanese home islands. Allied forces would be operating at the end of an unprecedentedly long supply line, in waters exposed to constant enemy air attack, for almost three months. "The fleet that came to stay," as the sailors called it, would burn 6 million barrels of fuel oil per month. All of it had to be transported into the combat zone in commercial tankers and fleet oilers.

For the sake of secrecy, only senior commanders and their staffs actually knew how many ships were involved in the operation. Men down the ranks could only guess, and trying to count the ships around the horizon was almost as futile as trying to count the stars on a clear night.

Beginning on March 23, 1945, a week before the invasion, Task Force 58 planes were constantly in the air above Okinawa. They flew bombing and strafing missions, photo reconnaissance missions, and combat air patrols. Looking down through broken cloud cover, a crewman on a *Yorktown* TBM Avenger saw "a dainty island with crumpled hills, thickly wooded, sloping down to a neat crazy quilt of tan and green farmland."[16] The island's economy was chiefly limited to fishing and agriculture; the important crops were sugarcane, rice, sweet potatoes, beets, barley, and cabbages. Cane fields, terraces, and sunken rice paddies took up almost all of the island's central plains, and a fair portion of the hills. Only the hilltops remained thickly wooded with live oaks and evergreen pines. The roads were little more than dirt paths, wide enough for horse-drawn carts. Here and there was a humble little hamlet, with close-built thatched stone houses. West-facing slopes were dotted with stone burial tombs, in the shapes of lyres or keyholes; many had evidently been incorporated into Japanese defensive fortifications.

Okinawa was about 60 miles long, varying in width from about 15 miles to 3 miles, and took in about 480 square miles of territory. The northern half of the island was rugged, heavily forested, and sparsely populated. About 80 percent of the prewar population had lived in the southern third of the island, which included the cities of Naha and Shuri. Task Force 58 planes attacked the island's major airfields, at Yontan, Kadena, Machinato, and Naha. All of the runways were badly cratered, and the Japanese seemed to have stopped trying to defend or repair them. There were few Japanese planes to be seen, except wreckage. Naha had been devastated by a Third Fleet carrier raid in October 1944, and it was largely burnt out and depopulated. In the southernmost area, the island was rugged, a region of broken terrain, soaring ridges, plunging ravines, rocky escarpments, and natural caves. Along the southern coast, sheer cliffs abutted rocky beaches. The island's only paved road was a two-lane highway connecting Naha and Shuri.

The U.S. carrier airmen took thousands of photographs. Okinawa was a populous island, they knew, with a 1940 population of 800,000—but now, as they looked down, they saw few people at all. Nimitz's intelligence analysts had estimated Japanese troop strength on the island at 65,000. The actual number was closer to 100,000—but from the air it was difficult to pinpoint the locations of blockhouses and gun emplacements.[17] Circling over the southern hills around Shuri, eagle-eyed pilots gradually discerned a continuous line of well-camouflaged fortifications from the east coast to the west. Mitscher radioed Vice Admiral Richmond Kelly Turner on March 25: "From photos, [the] whole island of Okinawa appears to be honeycombed with caves, tunnels and gun positions, particularly along roads. Tanks and armored cars seen entering caves. It will probably be tough."[18]

Although Okinawa was a fully incorporated prefecture of Japan, the island's people were culturally, racially, and linguistically distinct from the Japanese. On average, they were shorter of stature and more round-faced than their neighbors to the north. For centuries, the island had been the monarchical seat of the "Great Loochoo" kingdom, which had spanned the Ryukyuan archipelago. Younger Okinawans had learned Japanese in school, and spoke it fluently, but older and less educated inhabitants spoke only Okinawan. Japanese soldiers tended to treat the locals as members of an inferior caste. Since the start of the Pacific War, the Japanese had required hundreds of thousands to evacuate to Formosa and the Japanese home islands, but tens of thousands of Japanese troops had arrived during the same years, so that the net population in 1945 was between 450,000 and 500,000, of whom 100,000 were Japanese military personnel or local militias under Japanese army command.

As the largest and most important island in the archipelago known as the *Nansei Shoto*, which stretched almost 800 miles from Kyushu to Formosa, Okinawa sat at a strategic crossroads. It was roughly equidistant to Formosa, the coast of China, and Kyushu, and within an easy flight radius of them all. In Allied hands, Okinawa would provide a logistical backstop for the invasion of Japan, as well as ample terrain suitable for large airfields and harbors. Its airfields would allow Allied air forces to control the skies over the East China Sea. The island would serve as the principal operating base and springboard for an invasion of Kyushu.

American forces were organized under the overall command of Admiral Spruance, Fifth Fleet commander, whose arguments for the Okinawa invasion had persuaded Nimitz and King to back the operation. Admiral Turner commanded the transport fleet and joint expeditionary forces. Collectively designated Task Force 51, it included the old battleships, the escort carriers, screening cruisers and destroyers, hundreds of attack transports, thousands of landing craft, minesweepers, hospital ships, and innumerable other auxiliary vessels. As the navy's indispensable amphibious expert, who had led one landing after another since Guadalcanal in 1942, "Terrible Turner" could not be spared. But the admiral was worn out, physically and psychologically, and his temper was more volatile than ever before. It was an open secret that Turner was drinking heavily each night, in breach of standing regulations. Spruance, Nimitz, and King knew about the drinking but judged that Turner would do the job better than anyone else, sober or otherwise.

The invasion force was organized as the Tenth Army. It was under the overall command of Lieutenant General Simon B. Buckner Jr. of the U.S. Army. Major elements of this force were the army's XXIV Corps, including three infantry divisions (the 7th, 77th, and 96th) commanded by Major General John R. Hodge, and the III Amphibious Corps, comprising the 1st and 6th Marine Divisions, under the command of Major General Roy S. Geiger. Two additional divisions, one army and one marine, were kept in floating reserve. The British Pacific Fleet, designated Task Force 57, was assigned to cover the region to the south, between Okinawa and Formosa. It included four aircraft carriers, two battleships, and fifteen screening warships, making it about the same size and strength as one of the American carrier task groups. Its commander, Admiral Sir Bruce Fraser, reported directly to Admiral Spruance. Because the British fleet had not yet refined its capabilities for underway refueling and replenishment, it would lean heavily upon the Americans for logistical support.

The sea around Okinawa was generally less than 100 fathoms deep, and therefore easy to mine. More than a thousand fixed and floating mines guarded the approaches to the island, a threat dramatized by the sudden sinking of the destroyer *Halligan* west of Naha on March 26, 1945. Prior to "L-Day" ("Love Day," the scheduled landing date of April 1), minesweepers cleared 250,000 square miles of sea around Okinawa, including six major minefields in shoal water off the island. Working close inshore, the minesweepers were potentially vulnerable to shore batteries—but for the most part, the Japanese refrained from firing upon them, probably to avoid unmasking the position of their coastal artillery pieces. As the minesweepers completed their work, they set out radar buoys to mark the safe channels.

On March 26, Love Day minus 5, three battalions of the 77th Division landed in the Kerama Islands, 15 miles west of southern Okinawa. The small Japanese garrison, numbering about five hundred troops, was quickly overpowered. The hilly islands of this little archipelago offered no terrain suitable for airfields, but a semienclosed interior waterway ran north to south between its largest island (Tokashiki) and five smaller islands to the west. This "Kerama Roadstead" would function as an advanced fleet anchorage, large enough to accommodate about seventy-five large ships in depths of twenty to thirty fathoms. Its narrow entrances could be guarded against enemy submarines. West of the main anchorage was a zone that would serve as a seaplane base, where the long ocean rollers would not interfere with takeoffs or landings except in the roughest conditions. On March 27, dozens of auxiliary and repair ships began dropping their hooks in the roadstead. From here, in sheltered waters just a few miles from the

Okinawa beachhead, a floating logistics task force would provide fueling and ammunition replenishment for the duration of the long campaign. A salvage and repair group provided emergency ship repairs in this advanced position, less than an hour's steaming time to Okinawa. An unexpected dividend of the Kerama landings was that the Americans captured 350 *Shinyo* plywood suicide speedboats before they could be launched against the American fleet.

On March 31, another force was put ashore on the islands of Keise Shima. Just 8 miles west of Okinawa, this allowed 155mm artillery pieces to be directed to hit targets on Okinawa.

Throughout this week before the invasion, the Japanese continued to launch intermittent air attacks against the American fleet from bases in southern Kyushu and Formosa. Allied intelligence and aviation analysts were trying to understand the scale and resilience of the remaining air threat posed by Japan. Opinions were divided. Estimates of the number of Japanese warplanes remaining in the homeland ranged widely, from a low of about 2,000 to an upper bound of about 5,000. The one-way flight from Kyushu to Okinawa was less than 400 miles. No one in the Allied camp even pretended to know how many proficient veteran Japanese aviators were still alive and flying, but the aerial skirmishes of March 18 and 19 had proved that at least a few remained. While Task Force 58 was retiring from that fight, on March 19, Ugaki's Fifth Air Fleet had launched its first major effort to attack the enemy with the manned suicide missiles called the *Oka* ("cherry blossom"). Nineteen G4M bombers took off from Kanoya, each carrying one rocket-propelled *Oka*, with a pilot seated in the cockpit. The bombers were to carry them to within 40 miles of the U.S. fleet, where they would be dropped from the fuselage and plunge into an American ship. But the flight was tracked on radar, and Hellcats intercepted and shot down all of the G4Ms when they were still 60 miles away, before the craft could be launched. Each *Oka* weighed more than 2 tons, a burden that made the bombers slow and sluggish, and thus easy to shoot down. This tactical Achilles Heel of the *Oka*—that its sluggish, overloaded mother plane could be intercepted and shot down before reaching launch range—had never been seriously considered by the Japanese.

On March 26, just after midnight, the destroyer *Kimberly* was attacked by two diving Aichi D3A dive-bombers. Her antiaircraft guns took down one plane, but the other crashed her aft gun mounts, killing or wounding more than fifty of her crew. After being patched up in the Kerama road-stead, she was dispatched to California for repairs. The following day brought intermittent kamikaze attacks all day long, resulting in hits on the battleships *Nevada* and *Tennessee*, the light cruiser *Biloxi*, and several other destroyers, transports, minesweepers, and minelayers. On March 31, a day before the landings, Admiral Spruance's longtime flagship *Indianapolis* was attacked by a Nakajima Ki-43 ("Oscar") fighter. The diving plane released its bomb a split second before crashing the ship on her port side aft. It pen-etrated through the condenser room and mess deck before exploding next to one of the ship's fuel tanks. The ship was patched up in Kerama and sent home for repairs. Spruance shifted his flag to the battleship *New Mexico*, another ship that was no stranger to kamikaze attacks. According to flag lieutenant Charles Barber, Spruance was characteristically stoic: "I did not observe any reaction except that he was very disappointed that the *India-napolis* was lost to the bombardment prior to the landing and would not be in place where he could observe the operations."[19]

In the seventy-two hours before Love Day, the naval bombardment group rained high-explosive projectiles down on the landing beaches, which lay along Hagushi Bay on the island's west coast, 11 miles north of Naha. As in previous amphibious landings, the workhorses of this fire support mission were the venerable "OBBs"—the "old battleships"—sev-eral of which had been knocked out of action in the raid on Pearl Harbor, and later salvaged and rebuilt. Too slow to operate with the carrier task forces, but still packing a tremendous punch, they were commanded by Rear Admiral Morton L. Deyo, whose fire support group included nine cruisers, twenty-three destroyers, and 117 LCI gunboats armed with rockets and mortars. As the minesweepers cleared the waters near the beaches, the smaller craft moved closer to the coast. In the last twenty-four hours before the landings, Deyo's ships fired 3,800 tons of naval shells at targets on Okinawa. They kept it up day and night, systematically and relentlessly, sometimes not aiming at any target in particular, but simply firing into ran-domly chosen zones. A destroyerman who wondered why it was necessary to keep up this scattershot bombardment all night long was told "it was to keep the Japs awake."[20] Those ashore, suffering under the immense barrage, called it the "typhoon of steel."

In hindsight, much of the effort was wasted. Nearly every village in the southern part of Okinawa was flattened in the onslaught, and the airfields inland of the landing beaches had been converted into a barren moonscape—fresh craters on top of older craters on top of even older craters—even though they had been abandoned by the Japanese, and were no longer working at all.

The assault troops had been briefed to expect a savage reception on the landing beaches. According to the Tenth Army operations plan, the Japanese had prepared field fortifications for one regiment in the landing zone, and enemy reinforcements could be brought into the area quickly. The first wave of U.S. landing craft would come under heavy artillery, machine gun, and mortar fire. Just above the high tide mark on the beach stood a 6-foot seawall. The attackers would have to climb over it using wooden ladders. On the other side, they would run into pillboxes and covered trenches with "intense machine-gun fire."[21] Love Day at Okinawa, which happened to fall on both Easter Sunday and April Fool's Day, was expected to be a heartbreaker. Men in the 1st Marine Division were told to expect 80–85 percent casualties on the beach.[22]

A separate fire group and assault division (the 2nd Marine Division) was sent around to the southeast coast of the island, as part of a sham "demonstration"—a simulated landing intended to dupe the Japanese into moving reinforcements to that part of the island. It was the largest and most realistic feint of its kind in the entire Pacific War, a feat made possible by the unprecedented wealth of transports and landing craft now deployed in the theater. The Japanese commanders apparently bought the ruse, because they subsequently reported that they had repelled a major landing attempt on that part of the coast.

Before dawn on the 1st, the landing troops rose from their bunks and began their familiar D-Day routines—squaring away their packs, carbines, ammunition, canteens, and other gear, oiling rifles, sharpening knives, standing in line at the heads, and bolting down their traditional "condemned men's breakfast" of steak and eggs. Each unit, army and marines alike, was a blend of new rookie replacement troops and combat veterans. Virtually all of the NCOs had fought in at least one previous amphibious invasion, and many had two or more under their belts. They knew what to expect, and they shared their knowledge with the novices. The big guns of the heavy warships were plastering the area behind the beaches, including the Yontan and Kadena airfields. Even the old hands were awed by the epic bombardment. Despite what they had seen in previous operations, they wondered whether any living creature could survive such monstrous violence. They gaped at the seemingly infinite number of ships in the offing, to the horizon and beyond in every seaward direction. A marine remarked, "The immensity of our fleet gave me courage."[23]

It was a mild day, with partially cloudy skies, northeasterly breezes, and gentle swells. The temperature was 75 degrees Fahrenheit. Troops who had fought in the tropical heat and humidity of the South Pacific welcomed the cooler weather. While en route from Ulithi on their troop transports, stargazers had watched the Southern Cross sink toward the southern horizon night after night, until it had finally vanished. (The constellation was featured on the shoulder patches of the 1st Marine Division.) The landing troops had been issued wool-lined field jackets with zippers, an article of battle dress that would have been worthless in the Solomons or the Palaus.

As the first traces of dawn were seen over the island to their east, the assault troops went down the rope nets into the waiting Higgins boats, each man taking a seat on a bench snug against his neighbor. The coxswains maneuvered the loaded boats into an area seaward of the line of departure, engines rumbling in idle, exhaust fumes drifting over the sea. With the craft sitting low in the sea, swells broke against the gunwales and sometimes into the boats. Carrier planes patrolled overhead. The landing troops marveled at the scale and balletic sophistication of the operation.

At 8:30 a.m., flags went up on the control boats, and the coxswains of the first-wave landing craft opened their throttles. Passing around the battleships and cruisers, the boats steadied into straight, narrow lanes, separated by about 100 feet from beam to beam, each boat following in the wake of the one ahead. Gunboats led the way, firing rockets and 3-inch bow guns. Next came the guide boats, flying colored banners corresponding to different sectors of the landing beach. Their long white wakes were exactly parallel, like the teeth of a comb. An observer noted that the first wave "possessed something of the color and pageantry of medieval warfare, advancing relentlessly with their banners flying. In the calm sunlight of the morning, it was indeed an impressive spectacle."[24] Samuel Eliot Morison, watching from the deck of the *Tennessee*, described the 40mm tracer fire as "clusters of white-hot balls, which looked as if they would fall among the boats, but their flat trajectory carries them clear to the beach."[25]

Sixteen separate assault landing zones had been designated along a seven-and-a-half-mile stretch of the coast. Large coral reefs stood between

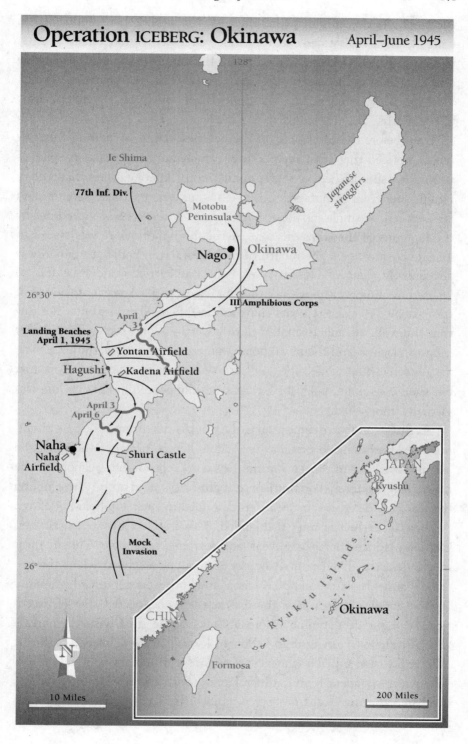

Operation ICEBERG: Okinawa
April–June 1945

128°

Ie Shima

77th Inf. Div.

Motobu
Peninsula

Nago

Okinawa

Japanese
stragglers

26°30'

April
3

III Amphibious Corps

Landing Beaches
April 1, 1945

Yontan Airfield

Hagushi

Kadena Airfield

April 3
April 6

Naha
Naha
Airfield

Shuri Castle

Mock
Invasion

26°

N

10 Miles

JAPAN

Kyushu

CHINA

Ryukyu Islands

Okinawa

Formosa

200 Miles

the amphibious fleet and the beaches, but the landing had been timed to coincide with high tide, and the underwater demolition teams (UDTs) had cleared navigable channels through the coral. As the first boats came ashore, the assault troops set up large colored banners to mark each zone. The marines landed north of the mouth of the Bisha River, the army to the south.

Even before the first boats hit the beaches, the boat crews and assault troops noticed that they were taking scarcely any enemy fire. A spike of whitewater shot up here or there, signifying the fall of a mortar or artillery round—but compared to previous amphibious assaults, these were few and far between. A single Japanese machine gun was quickly knocked out by the big guns of the ships offshore. A trickle of mortar fire was traced to a firing position near the mouth of the Bisha River, but that weapon was also quickly silenced. The first wave boats had carried wooden ladders, to be used in climbing the seawall they had been told to expect at the top of the beaches. But as the boats came ashore, the soldiers and marines saw that the wall was much smaller than advertised—no higher than 3 feet in most places—and the naval bombardment had mostly flattened it. The assault forces had braced for small arms fire and long-range artillery fire, but there was none. Hagushi Bay was weirdly peaceful. The landing was virtually unopposed.

As the second wave came ashore, the troops walked up the beach upright, not even bothering to crouch. On Yellow Beach, north of the river, the assault battalions of the 1st Marine Division crept inland, weapons at the ready, but encountered no hostile fire at all. They found nothing resembling the fearsome defensive fortifications described in their shipboard briefings. An hour after the first wave had landed, 16,000 U.S. troops were ashore on Okinawa, advancing against weak and scattered resistance. The area was mostly deserted. The Japanese did not even put up a fight to defend the two critical airfields of Yontan and Kadena, and both were captured by noon.

The landing forces gave thanks for their unexpected stay of execution. An hour after coming ashore, a soldier of the 7th Division remarked: "I've already lived longer than I thought I would."[26] Gene Sledge of the 1st Marine Division called it "the most pleasant surprise of the war."[27] The *New Yorker* correspondent John Lardner, landing with the 6th Marine Division, compared the invasion to a "fierce, bold rush by cops, hunting gunmen, into a house that suddenly turned out to be only haunted."[28] After the first hour, the assault troops were stepping gingerly from the landing craft, hopping over the surf to avoid soaking their boots, and strolling up the beach as if on a weekend outing. The regimental and division command echelons went in earlier than scheduled, and set up temporary CPs on the beach. Bulldozers were already leveling the sand dunes at the top of the beaches in order to clear paths inland to the airfields and supply dumps. At the medical aid stations, the corpsmen were squatting on their heels, chatting aimlessly; they had nothing to do. A few Okinawan civilians were found among the fishermen's shacks along the beaches. They bowed deeply and displayed their native Okinawan tattoos, explaining, "No Nippon." They were not Japanese, and they wanted the Americans to know it.

At sunset on Love Day, the landing forces possessed a beachhead more than 8 miles long, reaching inland to a maximum distance of 3 miles, and encompassing the two airfields. Fifty thousand American troops were ashore. Casualties were mercifully light—28 killed, 104 wounded, and 27 missing.[29]

ON A GREEN HILLTOP 12 MILES SOUTH OF HAGUSHI, Lieutenant General Mitsuru Ushijima and a group of staff officers watched the American forces come ashore. The men smoked, talked, and took turns studying the amphibious panorama through a pair of binoculars. Observing the intense naval bombardment of the largely deserted area above the beaches, they took pleasure in the sight of so much wasted enemy ammunition. But the sheer size and scale of the invasion was awesome and alarming. One thought it was "as if the sea itself were advancing with a great roar."[30]

As on Iwo Jima and Peleliu, the Japanese had chosen a defense-in-depth strategy, concentrating their major forces in high rocky terrain well back from the beachhead, and digging deep into the earth against superior U.S. airpower and offshore naval gunfire. The defenders planned to concede the initial landing, and wait patiently for the Americans in ground of their own choosing. Unlike on Iwo Jima or Peleliu, however, the Japanese on Okinawa would not bring their own heavy artillery into action until the invaders had advanced well inland, into the main zones of ground combat. Keeping their powder dry, and their guns concealed in the mouths of caves or under camouflage netting, they would conserve ammunition until it could be employed to best effect.

Ushijima's plan of campaign was controversial. It had been implemented only recently, at the end of 1944, after feisty debates between staff officers and unit commanders, and against the wishes of higher command echelons in Formosa and Tokyo. Earlier plans had emphasized an air defense, relying on strong and well-supplied airfields and a steady flow of airplanes flying in from nearby Kyushu. For the first ten months of 1944, the military construction program on Okinawa had been devoted to expanding and improving the island's airfields. At one point, work was proceeding simultaneously on eighteen separate airfields on Okinawa and smaller adjacent islands. The Imperial General Headquarters had envisioned Okinawa as a 60-mile-long "unsinkable aircraft carrier." But the high command never came to grips with the obvious flaws and contradictions in this concept. How could this network of island airfields be defended against the relentless American naval-air-amphibious juggernaut, which had never failed to capture any island it had targeted, and which was growing steadily larger, stronger, and more proficient with each passing month? The U.S. carrier task forces would take control of the sky over the airfields. The flat, low-lying terrain was impossible to defend against superior ground forces, especially when they were supported by overwhelming naval gunfire from offshore. Investment of manpower and construction materials in improving airfields would only raise their value for the Allies, who would inevitably capture them and turn them against the Japanese. As one of General Ushijima's staff planners concluded: "It was as if our ground forces had sweated and strained to construct airfields as a gift for the enemy."[31]

Japanese ground forces on the island fought under the banner of the Thirty-Second Army, commanded by Ushijima from an elaborate underground command bunker under Shuri Castle, an ancient stone edifice in the hills east of Naha. It included the Twenty-Fourth Infantry Division, the Sixty-Second Infantry Division, the Forty-Fourth Independent Mixed Brigade, the Twenty-Seventh Tank Regiment, and the Fifth Artillery Command. The Thirty-Second Army headquarters force included many independent and elite units specializing in artillery, mortars, antiaircraft fire, and antitank guns. Approximately 9,000 naval base troops were stationed on the Oroku peninsula, just south of Naha; they operated independently of the Thirty-Second Army until the American invasion on April 1, at which point (by prior agreement) they fell under Ushijima's command. With miscellaneous other units and personnel, total regular Japanese troop strength on the island amounted to about 76,000. Local Okinawan militias and draftees, some trained for combat and others mainly for labor, raised the total number of uniformed troops on the island to about 100,000.

In late 1944, as Allied power grew and an invasion seemed more likely, leading officers on the Thirty-Second Army staff pushed for a basic revision to operational plans. Colonel Hiromichi Yahara, the senior operations officer, argued that the Thirty-Second Army did not have the strength to defend the beaches, the plains, and the airfields as Tokyo wanted. He preferred to fight a battle of attrition in Okinawa's more defensible southern hills. Major General Isamu Cho, the chief of staff, supported Yahara's proposal and passed it up the chain to Ushijima, who gave it his peremptory approval. The revised operational plan was distributed on November 26, 1944, even though it had not been authorized by IGHQ. This defiant act bordered on insubordination, but a mutinous spirit seems to have spread through the ranks of the army on Okinawa. Among soldiers in the line, as well as elite staff officers in Ushijima's command bunker, one heard angry muttering against their higher-ups in Tokyo, who remained cosseted in their comfortable offices, too afraid of American airplanes and submarines to risk traveling to Okinawa to inspect the situation for themselves. Or perhaps they had no reason to come, as one officer commented sardonically, because Naha's red-light district had been burned down in American carrier bombing raids.[32]

The bulk of all available labor and materials was redirected to southern Okinawa. There, in the rugged country east of Naha, an ambitious program of building and excavations set out to create a huge system of interconnected tunnels, bunkers, pillboxes, trenches, tank traps, artillery emplacements, and spider holes. The fortifications spanned the island in a continuous line, coast to coast, across a forbidding landscape of ridges, ravines, and sheer escarpments. The region was honeycombed with natural limestone caves, which were expanded and interlinked by tunnels, so that nearly the entire Thirty-Second Army could hunker down in subterranean shelters, with their weapons, ammunition, provisions, and freshwater cisterns, impervious to bombing, strafing, or shelling by even the largest caliber guns of the American battleships offshore. The heart of this natural citadel was at Shuri, the ancient seat of Ryukyuan kings, where the old stone castle and walls stood on a rocky promontory, looming over the remains of a bombed-out town. The entrance to General Ushijima's underground headquarters was on the reverse slope of a ridge near the castle. Around Shuri in three directions lay concentric rings of heavy fortifications, placed on high ground with sweeping fields of fire on all possible approaches, and interconnected with covered trenches and tunnels. It was a Pacific Verdun.

Each unit of the Japanese army was assigned responsibility for digging and preparing its own part of the line. Grasping that their efforts provided the key to surviving intense naval and air bombardment, soldiers on the line poured their energy into the backbreaking toil. Their slogan, promulgated by the Thirty-Second Army headquarters, was "Confidence in victory will be born from strong fortifications."[33] As on Iwo Jima, the army lacked mechanized tunneling equipment or demolitions, so the troops were obliged to do the job with picks and shovels. They also lacked cement, or the equipment to make it, so the tunnels had to be shored up with raw pine timber. Much of it was lumbered in the forests of northern Okinawa, and shipped south along the coast in small native craft. The heavy artillery of the Fifth Artillery Command was concentrated near the center of the defensive lines, so that the guns could be directed to whatever position was heavily engaged. The firing embrasures were well camouflaged, and the wheeled guns could be retracted into caves and moved through tunnels to other firing positions, limiting their exposure to counterbattery fire. The artillerists on Okinawa were among the best-trained and most experienced in the Japanese army.

Okinawa's large civilian population was a complicating factor. During the war, the prefectural government had first encouraged, and then compelled, mass evacuations to Formosa and the Japanese home islands. But those measures were unpopular, and resisted by many Okinawans, especially after a ship loaded with hundreds of evacuees was sunk while en route to Kyushu in August 1944. In March 1945, the Japanese army issued orders to evacuate most remaining Okinawan civilians to the northern part of the island, but that measure was also resisted. Writing in the *Okinawa Shinpo*, the island's daily newspaper, General Cho warned that all civilians must act as members of a militia, following the army's orders. In the event of invasion, each civilian should try to kill ten enemy soldiers before being killed in turn. Cho added that all women and children should "move to a safe area so that they will not be operational obstacles," because it was "not acceptable to lose in battle to save civilian lives."[34] Hundreds of middle school and high school students, boys and girls, were mobilized as a student corps, serving as messengers, cooks, laborers, or nurses. As for the men, a general call-up was announced on the first day of 1945. All Okinawan males aged 17 to 45 were conscripted directly into a local "defense corps." Most would never be seen by their families again.

In the last weeks before the invasion, the army and the government continued efforts to relocate noncombatants to northern Okinawa. But many civilians had been frightened by Japanese propaganda, which had asserted that any who fell into American hands would suffer death by torture. As the American fleet appeared offshore in the last week of March, about 300,000 civilians remained in the southern half of the island, and many were desperate to get behind Japanese lines. Without sufficient food stockpiled to feed them, a humanitarian catastrophe was set in motion even before the battle was joined.

AT IMPERIAL HEADQUARTERS IN TOKYO, army and navy staff officers hammered out an agreement on their air strategy for the Ryukyus and the East China Sea. Navy planes would target enemy warships, and army planes would go after the transport convoys. Both services would launch conventional bombing and kamikaze attacks, but the "emphasis will be placed on build-up and use of the special attack strength."[35] Flight cadets would be rushed through training programs and sent directly to active striking units, where they would be invited to volunteer as kamikazes. With ground forces on Okinawa engaged in a prolonged campaign of attrition, the Allied fleet would be forced to remain in the area for several weeks, where it could be attacked repeatedly from the air. Japan's last hope was to degrade the enemy's "preponderance in ships, aircraft, and men, to obstruct the establishment of advanced bases, to undermine enemy morale, and thereby to seriously delay the final assault on Japan."[36]

Most of the work would be done by the Fifth Air Fleet, headquartered at Kanoya Air Base in southern Kyushu. This "fleet" was a heterogeneous assortment of naval air units, including many types of aircraft, scattered across two dozen airbases on Kyushu and Shikoku. The Fifth Air Fleet mustered about six hundred planes, including about four hundred in dedicated kamikaze units. Under constant threat of B-29 and U.S. carrier airstrikes, personnel at Kanoya and other air bases were working to move the repair shops, ammunition dumps, and fuel reserves to underground bunkers and tunnels. Excavations were underway in fields around the runways. As on Okinawa, much of the work was done with picks and shovels, and even the aviators lent a hand. Smaller airfields were disguised as simple rural dirt roads. Abandoned barracks and hangars were left standing to serve as decoys for the American bombers. As for the Fifth Air Fleet's airplanes, "emphasis will be laid on the thoroughgoing dispersal, protection and camouflage of the planes and on the setting up of dummy planes and revetments."[37]

In his private diary, Ugaki often lamented the deplorable state of his air forces. He lacked the pilots, planes and fuel even to conduct sufficient daily air patrols over the waters south of Japan. Crashes and other operational losses were distressingly frequent, and he was forced to cancel many training exercises due to weather and other factors. His Fifth Air Fleet was receiving priority allocations of aviation gasoline, but no more than a trickle of oil imports was reaching Japan, and the parsimonious fuel budget was beginning to impinge on operations. On February 27, Ugaki had received a briefing on the process of extracting biofuel from pine roots: Japanese schoolchildren were being sent into the country's forests to forage for pine cones, roots, and needles by the bushel. This effort was ingenious but futile, requiring more than a thousand labor-hours to produce enough fuel for a single hour of flight. The headquarters at Kanoya, in a barracks building near the runway, was deemed too vulnerable to air raids, so on February 28, Ugaki and his staff moved into an underground bunker. There was even talk of transferring airplanes to Korea or Manchuria, to prevent their being destroyed on the ground. A March 17 entry in the Fifth Air Fleet war diary reflected the staff's darkly pessimistic outlook: "In our attack against the enemy task force, the picked strength of our air units will be lost immediately."[38]

Spring came early in southern Kyushu, and short walks in the woods and fields around the base lifted Ugaki's spirits. On quiet afternoons he took his shotgun and hiked alone up into the hills, hunting the green pheasants native to that region. After one outing, he told his diary, "Nature's great progress in a few days' time seem to laugh pityingly at the silly little human world, where we were making a fuss about war and enemy task forces and so on."[39]

In the actions of March 18 and 19, the Japanese conventional dive-bombing squadrons had performed unexpectedly well. As usual, however, the estimated results were grossly exaggerated. On March 21, after a conference at the Kanoya headquarters, it was announced that the Americans had lost five aircraft carriers, two battleships, and four cruisers.[40] These reports were trumpeted in the headlines with the customary rhapsodies. The loss of an entire flight of G4M bombers carrying *Oka* manned suicide missiles was withheld from the press, and Fifth Air Fleet analysts concluded that such an attack could not possibly succeed unless the Japanese were first able to obtain temporary air supremacy over the objective. Given the state of Japanese air forces, the only method that might succeed was to overwhelm the U.S. air defenses with sheer mass, which meant launching hundreds of airplanes at once, in the hope that at least a few would get through the fighter and antiaircraft defenses to score.

On March 25, as the U.S. invasion force gathered off Okinawa, Combined Fleet headquarters in Hiyoshi issued orders to initiate the "Ten-Go" Operation. This plan called for all-out massed suicide and bombing attacks on the U.S. fleet. After the heavy losses suffered during the recent carrier raids over Japan, time was needed to move the forces into position. New kamikaze squadrons and planes were flown to Kanoya and other airfields in preparation for the first full-scale *Kikusui* ("floating chrysanthemums") attack. After delays in moving the air and naval forces into position, the date chosen was April 6. On that same day, the Japanese army on Okinawa would launch a counterattack on American lines, and the last remaining Japanese surface warships (including the superbattleship *Yamato*) would sortie from the Inland Sea in a naval *banzai* charge. Several hundred suicide gods would take off from Kyushu airfields, with orders to "exterminate the enemy ships off Okinawa."[41] In his diary, Admiral Ugaki confessed feeling wretched and guilty about sending so many flyers to their certain deaths, and he swore to "follow the example of those young boys someday. I was glad to see that my weak mind, apt to be moved to tears, had reached this stage."[42]

TASK FORCE 58 HOVERED IN THE OFFING southeast of Okinawa, providing continuous daily and nightly air support for the troops ashore and the amphibious fleet on the other side of the island. It was hard going for all concerned, airmen and crewmen alike. Gale-force winds and rough seas interfered with flight operations. On the gray, misty morning of April 4, an officer on the *Yorktown* recorded that the carrier had "bucked like a rogue stallion all night long. When I shaved this morning, I had to hold on to the basin with one hand; and when I crossed the compartment, half the distance was a climb, the other half a charge."[43] The previous night, blinded by foul weather, the battleship *New Jersey* had collided with a screening destroyer, the *Franks*. Given the mismatch in size and mass, the battleship was barely scratched while the *Franks* was smashed and gutted along the length of her port side, and her skipper was severely wounded.[44] Enemy air attacks were few and far between during this period, a blessing that Spruance attributed to the air raids against Kyushu two weeks earlier. Each carrier group conducted flight operations for three days, and on the fourth day retired some distance to the southeast to rendezvous with the refueling and replenishment ships.

The sixth of April was a cool and windy day, with choppy seas. Arthur Radford's Task Group 58.2 was refueling and replenishing, so Sherman's Task Group 58.3 and Clark's 58.1 were the only ones on the line. An hour after dawn, picket destroyers north of Okinawa detected radar bogeys inbound from the north. Japanese planes in the vanguard of the attack scattered copious amounts of "window"—aluminum strips—to confuse the U.S. radar systems, but the raid was too big to hide. Mitscher sent word to the carriers to stow all bombers in the hangars, freeing the flight decks for fighter operations. More Hellcats and Corsairs were launched to fortify the CAP, and others were vectored on a course to intercept. The fighter control circuits rang with chatter. The American fighters tore into the Japanese air formations, sending at least sixty planes down in flames in the first stages of the long day's battle. But given the size of this first "floating chrysanthemums" attack—about seven hundred planes, of which more than half were kamikazes—more than two hundred got through the fighter screen to attack the American fleet.

They came in waves, morning through dusk, with the heaviest strikes arriving in the late afternoon. "How they came!" a junior officer aboard a transport recalled, "in singles, twos and bunches, gliding, diving, swooping, some hugging the water. . . . It seemed they never stopped coming."[45] Admiral Clark called the swarming attacks "almost overpowering."[46] The sky was mottled with the bursts of antiaircraft shells, and tracers cut across the twilight sky, making red and yellow lattices of light. On many ships, the radio transmissions between the fighter control officers (FDOs) and fighter pilots were transmitted through the loudspeakers, leaving the crew with the uncanny sense that they were listening to the live broadcast of an athletic competition. The *Time* and *Life* correspondent Bob Sherrod, on Admiral Turner's command ship *Eldorado*, watched a Japanese plane dive on an LST off the Hagushi beachhead. "Terrific streams of ack-ack poured toward the plane from every ship within two miles," he wrote. "When the Jap was 300 feet from his target he flamed, winged over, and fell into the shallow water."[47]

By the end of the day, twenty-six American ships had taken kamikaze hits. Six had been sunk, including two Victory ships; a minesweeper; an LST; and two destroyers, the *Bush* and the *Colhoun*. Others were badly mauled and suffered heavy casualties, including by friendly antiaircraft fire striking nearby ships in formation. Critically, however, the sacrifice of picket destroyers and other ships in the outer screens had helped shield the aircraft carriers at the heart of Task Force 58. A few flattops took some nerve-racking near-misses, but none was hit or damaged. The carrier air groups, working with FDOs on the picket destroyers, had shot down more than two hundred planes during the day. The *Essex* air group nearly broke the single-day carrier air-kill record by shooting down sixty-five planes.[48]

Earlier that day, an American submarine on patrol off the Bungo Suido (the channel between Kyushu and Shikoku) had detected a column of Japanese warships headed out to sea. This was the battleship *Yamato* with her screening group of one light cruiser and eight destroyers, the last seaworthy remnant of the Imperial Japanese Fleet. The *Yamato* force had been under regular aerial observation for the past week, with B-29 and U.S. carrier planes reconnoitering and photographing the ships at anchor south of Kure, and tracking their progress down the Inland Sea, so their sudden appearance at sea was no surprise. Before dawn on April 7, PBM seaplanes lifted off from the Kerama Islands and flew north to track the enemy ships. At 8:23 a.m., search planes from the carrier *Essex* spotted the *Yamato* force at 30°44′ north by 129°10′ east, traveling at 12 knots on a course of 300 degrees. The formation had rounded the southern tip of Kyushu and was now headed west-northwest, almost as if bound for Korea.[49]

Spruance, Mitscher, and Turner each separately deduced that the Japanese were attempting to evade detection and interception. The *Yamato* and her escorts hoped to take a roundabout course through the East China Sea, doubling back to sneak up on the U.S. fleet from the west. Spruance detached a powerful battleship-cruiser-destroyer squadron under Admiral Deyo, and sent it to intercept. But Mitscher and the Task Force 58 aviators wanted to finish the *Yamato* with carrier air power, and their airplanes could get there faster. Their range to the target was 238 miles, a flying time of less than ninety minutes. Sherman's Task Group 58.3 had rejoined the two others, so the Americans had plenty of air-striking power to spare. Beginning at 10:18 a.m., three carrier task groups launched an armada of 386 planes, including 180 fighters, 75 dive-bombers, and 131 torpedo planes. Jocko Clark told his Avenger pilots that he expected them to sink the supposedly unsinkable *Yamato*, because their torpedoes would rip open the mighty battleship's hull and "let the water in."[50]

THE OFFICERS AND CREW OF THE *YAMATO* and her nine escorts held no illusions. Their mission was a naval *banzai* charge, a futile suicide rush that served no real tactical purpose. Without air cover, they would be left to fight off waves of American planes with their antiaircraft guns alone. Just as in the earlier case of *Sho*, the Japanese "victory" plan for the Battle of Leyte Gulf, the fleet was being asked to immolate itself for abstract considerations of honor. Unlike in the earlier battle, however, there was not the slightest hope of surprising the U.S. fleet. One senior officer remarked that it was "not even a kamikaze mission, for that implies the chance of chalking up a worthy target."[51]

This operation, like Plan *Sho*, was ordered by Admiral Toyoda, commander in chief of the Combined Fleet, from his command bunker at Hiyoshi. Now, as before, Toyoda chose not to lead the mission in person, a failure that inspired quasi-mutinous grumbling among the cynics on the *Yamato*'s bridge. Vice Admiral Ryunosuke Kusaka, Toyoda's chief of staff, had flown into Kure with a mission to sell the plan. Vice Admiral Seiichi Ito, who had succeeded Takeo Kurita as commander of the Second Fleet, was stiffly opposed to the suicidal assignment, and he did not hesitate to say so. The one-way sortie was a pointless sacrifice of ships, fuel, ammunition, and trained fighting men who were needed to defend the homeland. Tamechi Hara, skipper of the light cruiser *Yahagi*, called it a "ridiculous operation . . . just like throwing an egg at a rock."[52] Kusaka countered that the plan was a "decoy mission," whose real purpose was to divert the attention of the American aircraft carriers while hundreds of kamikazes attacked the enemy fleet from airfields on Kyushu. But Kusaka also admitted that the Imperial Headquarters was keen to avoid the disgrace of seeing the *Yamato* end the war at anchor. After long discussion, it became clear that no matter how gently Kusaka presented his case, the suicide mission was an order, not a request.

The night before the *Yamato* put to sea, a generous ration of sake was distributed to the entire crew, and each division held its own riotous bacchanal. The executive officer bellowed through the ship's loudspeakers, "Kamikaze *Yamato*, be truly a divine wind!"[53] In the first wardroom, Captain Kosaku Aruga stood at the center of a packed crowd of lieutenants and ensigns, drinking sake directly from a large bottle. Amidst "boisterous singing and wild dancing," with empty sake bottles rolling around on the deck underfoot, many hands reached in toward the skipper and patted his bald head. Some even gave it a hard whack. The executive officer, locked in a wrestling scrum with other officers, tore his uniform jacket.[54]

The next day, as the crew nursed hangovers and wrote final letters to their families, the *Yamato* sucked every last remaining drop of bunker oil out of the fuel depot at Tokuyama. All cigarettes and other treats remaining in the canteen were distributed free to the crew. At 6:00 p.m., a general assembly was convened on the foredeck. The *Yamato* broke out the flag of the Second Fleet. As evening fell, the cruiser *Yahagi* led the formation into the Bungo Suido. The column slipped down the coast of Kyushu at 12 knots. In the gathering dusk, crewmen noted that some of the cherry trees along the coast had blossomed. Officers sipped from illicit flasks of liquor. The antiaircraft gunners ate at their posts, rice balls washed down with green tea. On deck, sailors were sharpening bayonets and assembling combat gear to be distributed to the crew, in case they managed to beach the ship on Okinawa and join the army forces on the island.

A waning crescent moon rose in the east, ahead of the sun. Dawn broke shortly after the column rounded the southern tip of Kyushu. The green mountains of Kagoshima receded into their wakes. A few Japanese fighters were seen patrolling overhead, but they soon returned to their bases on Kyushu. Ensign Mitsuru Yoshida, a radar officer stationed on the *Yamato*'s bridge, noted grimly that "not a single escorting plane could be seen; nor was one to be seen from this time on. We were literally abandoned."[55]

The *Yamato*'s radio monitors had intercepted transmissions, some in plain English, reporting the task force's position and progress. As expected, they had been reconnoitered by enemy submarines off the Bungo Suido. PBM seaplanes circled high above the *Yamato*, tracking her progress. They were careful to remain just beyond the range of the antiaircraft guns. Occasionally one of the ship's main guns fired a salvo, and flak bursts appeared overhead, but always well below and behind the American planes.

The first wave of incoming carrier planes showed up on the *Yamato*'s radar scopes at 12:20 p.m. The *Yamato*'s navigator shouted: "Over 100 hostile planes are headed for us!"[56] An alert was flashed to the other ships in the task force. Ten minutes later, lookouts sighted the first clusters of black specks, high above and beyond the range of even the *Yamato*'s mammoth 460mm antiaircraft guns.

The Americans took their time, circling counterclockwise over the task force like buzzards over carrion, waiting for the trailing squadrons to fall into formation. Visibility from altitude was poor. Peering down through a layer of broken overcast between 3,000 and 5,000 feet, Ensign Harry D. Jones—an Avenger pilot with the *Hornet*'s Torpedo Squadron Seventeen— could not see the enemy fleet at all. Then, through a break in the clouds, he glimpsed the *Yamato*. Jones thought the superbattleship looked like "the Empire State Building plowing through the water. It was really big."[57]

With fuel to spare, and no enemy planes to bother them, the strike leaders were patient and methodical in planning the attack. The Hellcats and Corsairs would dive on the *Yamato*, dropping their smaller bombs and then strafing the decks; the SB2C Curtiss dive-bombers would follow closely, dropping their 1,000-pounders, and the Avengers would time their torpedo runs to coincide with the dive-bombers. Most of the torpedoes would be aimed at the great battleship's port side, in hopes of forcing her to capsize in that direction.

As the first attack sequence began, the *Yamato*'s antiaircraft guns opened fire, throwing up colorful bursts of flak. The fire was heavy but inaccurate, and the planes held steady in their dives. A *Yorktown* Hellcat pilot thought, "Jesus, they'll never get through that AA! It's murder!"[58] But the attackers maintained their velocity and flew through the bursts. Lieutenant Commander Chandler W. Swanson, who led the *Bunker Hill*'s torpedo squadron, was most concerned about the risk of hitting other American airplanes. "Our planes were crisscrossing over the target from all directions. That was the most dangerous part of it. We had to keep from running into our own planes. There were so many of them and so little room to maneuver. It was surprising we had no collisions."[59]

The Japanese ships were tearing through the sea at 27 knots. The *Yamato* maneuvered violently, and a "forest of geysers" sprung up around the ship as bombs dropped by the Helldivers missed narrowly. The towers of whitewater sent powerful cataracts of water down on deck, knocking men off their feet and even wrenching equipment from the rigging. Four heavy bombs struck in short order, silencing antiaircraft batteries and tossing debris and bodies into the air. Strafing fighters riddled the ship's superstructure with .50-caliber machine-gun fire, striking and killing several men on the bridge. Fires raged aft, and a column of smoke trailed away in the *Yamato*'s wake. Yoshida saw "silvery streaks of torpedoes" converging on the ship from several directions.[60] Captain Aruga conned his ship deftly, steering toward the tracks and evading several, but the *Yamato* could not avoid them all. Three hit portside amidships in quick succession, then a fourth hit farther aft. The great ship leapt and shuddered with each blow, then began listing to port.

To the *Yamato*'s left, the destroyer *Hamakaze* was hit by bombs and dropped out of formation. She began going down by the stern; in a few minutes she was gone, "leaving only a circle of swirling white foam."[61] The cruiser *Yahagi* vanished behind a curtain of spray, and fighter planes flew low strafing runs over the ship, Captain Hara recalled, "fanning us with bullets and propwash as they pulled out at masthead level." Watching the TBMs boring in through heavy bursts of antiaircraft fire, he thought, "the enemy pilots certainly had guts."[62] A torpedo struck the starboard engine room, killing the engineering crew and knocking out her propulsion. Six or seven bombs rained down along her length. The 8,000-ton *Yahagi* could not withstand much of that kind of punishment. She was reduced to a burning, listing wreck, incapable of maneuvering against succeeding waves of planes. The destroyer *Isokaze* closed in from astern, apparently intending to take survivors off the stricken *Yahagi*, but she was hit by one or two bombs that set her afire and put her out of action. The *Suzutsuki* was hit and crippled, but somehow survived and limped back to Sasebo, a naval base near Nagasaki.

The *Yamato*'s port list was corrected through counterflooding, but fires continued to spread through the after regions of the ship. The firefighting and damage control teams had been decimated in the attacks, so the fires were never brought under control, and they were still advancing as the second wave of American planes arrived over the task force. On the bridge, Admiral Ito stood silently, his arms folded over his chest, as stretcher-bearers loaded bullet-riddled bodies onto litters and carried them away. As a result of the fires, casualties, and damage, command and control between the bridge and the various crew departments and stations was beginning to break down.

In a second wave of attacks, beginning about forty minutes after the first, the *Yamato* took five or six more torpedo hits on her port side, and at least one to starboard. Another exploded against her stern, destroying her rudder post and depriving her of steering. SB2C dive-bombers rained heavy armor-piercing shells down along her topside works, while swarms of low-flying Hellcats and Corsairs strafed her remaining antiaircraft batteries. Yoshida recalled "incessant explosions, blinding flashes of light, thunderous noises, and crushing weights of blast pressure."[63] The destroyers *Asashimo* and *Kasumi* were badly mauled, and would either sink or be scuttled. The immobilized *Yahagi* caught four more torpedoes and seven or eight more bombs. Captain Hara, looking fore and aft, judged that his ship was nearly finished. Whitewater towers erupted as torpedoes exploded against the hull. Bomb blasts ejected debris and bodies into the air. Rivets begin popping out of the steel deck plates, and the bridge begin pulsating under his feet. "Our dying ship quaked with the detonations," wrote Hara. "The explosions finally stopped but the list continued as waves washed blood pools from the deck and dismembered bodies fell rolling into the sea."[64]

The *Yamato* rode low in the water, her lower regions flooded and her port list increasing to 18 degrees. Her upper works were a shambles—smashed, blackened, and burning. Some of the crew began to panic. The skipper came on the loudspeaker and ordered, "All hands to work to trim ship!" But the damage control parties had suffered heavy losses, and the bridge was finding it difficult to maintain contact with stations below. Fires and flooding had prevented the crew from sealing off stricken compartments on the port side. Damage to the pumps and valves had thwarted efforts to counterflood into the *Yamato*'s starboard "pumping-in" rooms. The executive officer told the skipper, "Correction of listing hopeless!"[65]

Recognizing that his ship was in imminent danger of capsize, Captain Aruga took the deliberate and cold-blooded decision to flood the starboard engine and boiler rooms. A warning buzzer was sounded, and a frantic telephone call warned the crew to evacuate, but there was not enough time. The "black gang," hundreds of men who maintained the ship's engines, were trapped in their compartments and drowned at their posts. Ensign

Yoshida called it "a thankless end to all their days of toil in the scorching heat and deafening noise of their laborious duty."[66]

When the *Yorktown*'s air group arrived at 1:45 p.m., the *Yamato* was listing visibly and her speed had fallen to under 10 knots. Her gunnery defenses had been crippled by the prior attacks; only a few of her weapons were still functioning, and it was no longer possible to move ammunition up from the magazines. Once again, with plenty of time to plan and execute their attacks, the Avengers timed their torpedo runs with the strafing and diving assaults of the Helldivers and Hellcats. The Japanese officers on the bridge watched with helpless admiration for the skill and bravery of their foes. As torpedoes tore into the stricken battleship's hull, Captain Aruga shouted, "Hold on, men! Hold on, men!"[67] But the loudspeaker system was

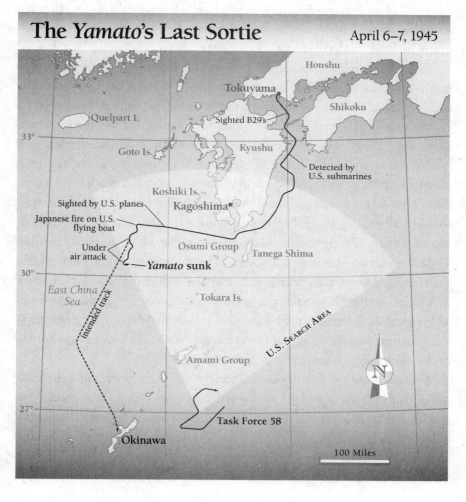

The *Yamato*'s Last Sortie

April 6–7, 1945

no longer working, so only those in earshot could hear him. The *Yamato*'s list increased to 35 degrees, and then to 45 degrees, which exposed the bilge keel on the starboard side, leaving the unarmored and vulnerable underside of the ship to the mercy of the last torpedo-armed Avengers.

All power was lost, and the skipper began preparations to order abandon ship. Without internal communications, many on the lower decks probably never received the order to leave their posts. Admiral Ito shook hands with his surviving staff officers, and then retreated to his sea cabin. He was never seen again.

About a mile astern, dive-bombers plummeted down on the immobilized *Yahagi*. Hara gritted his teeth and muttered, "All right, you Yankee devils, finish us off!"[68] At 2:06 p.m., he shouted to his crew to abandon ship. F6F Hellcats were roaring overhead as he leapt into the sea. Hara was sucked under by whirlpools, but his life vest pulled him back to the surface, where he held on to debris with a number of other oil-covered castaways.

The *Yamato* rolled steadily, almost onto her beam ends. So much smoke was overhead that the day had darkened, as if it were twilight instead of midday. Ensign Yoshida, clinging to the bridge structure, later recorded his impressions of the terrible scene: "The horizon seemed to take on a mad new angle. Dark waves splattered and reached for us as the stricken ship healed to the incredible list of 80 degrees." Looking aft, he saw the great 30-foot-long "Sun and Rays" battle flag dipping toward the ocean. A young sailor gripped the bottom of the staff, evidently determined to go down with the ship. From deep in the hull came rumbles, tremors, and the crash of falling machinery. On the bridge, Captain Aruga lashed himself to a binnacle. The navigator and his assistant had tied themselves tightly together, and "as the ship rolled over they merely stared at the onrushing waves."[69] Admiral Ito's chief of staff shouted at the younger officers to save themselves, and when some of the young men were slow to leave the ship, he began physically striking and shoving them into the sea. As waves crashed against the bridge deck, many lost their grip and were swept away.

Yoshida swam through congealed bunker oil. As the great ship began sliding under, whirlpools and eddies formed in the sea around her, and he was sucked under. From beneath the surface, he saw a flash of light and "a gigantic pillar of flame shot high into the dark sky."[70] The *Yamato*'s main magazine had detonated. Yoshida broke the surface, then was pulled down again, and surfaced again, to find himself treading water among debris and other swimmers.

The cloud that rose above the *Yamato* was more than a thousand feet in diameter, and it ascended to 20,000 feet above sea level. The explosion was seen in Kagoshima, 125 miles away. When the cloud lifted, the *Yamato* was no longer there. Just 23 officers and 246 enlisted men survived; the ship had taken nearly 3,000 souls with her into the abyss. Three remaining undamaged Japanese destroyers circulated among the swimmers and hauled them aboard.

More than 4,000 Japanese sailors had perished in this largely symbolic expedition. The Americans had won their victory at a cost of just ten planes and twelve airmen.

While the strike was away, Task Force 58 was attacked by about one hundred kamikazes. Most were shot down, but one hit the battleship *Maryland*—the "Fighting Mary's" second such ordeal of the war—and another dove through a low cloud ceiling to strike the flight deck of the *Hancock*. Raging fires were brought under control within forty-five minutes, and the *Hancock* was able to land her own planes when they returned. But the attack killed sixty-four and wounded seventy-one of her crew. Most of the casualties were trapped below decks, where they were burned, blown up, or succumbed to fatal smoke inhalation.

ACCORDING TO THE INVASION PLAN issued by General Buckner, the marines of the III Amphibious Corps would charge across Okinawa, bisecting the island and taking control of the east coast, and then turn north to occupy and pacify the middle and northern part of the island. They would take the smaller island of Ie Shima, off the Motobu Peninsula, by amphibious assault. Whatever enemy forces held out in the hilly, forested, far north of Okinawa could be sealed off and isolated. Meanwhile, the army divisions of XXIV Corps would drive into the forbidding hills and ridges to the south, seize the prefectural capital of Naha and its harbor, and overrun the enemy's fortified lines around Mount Shuri. The entire operation was expected to take forty-five to sixty days.

With few Japanese troops standing in their way, the marines made unexpectedly speedy progress in the early days of the campaign. Advance patrols crossed to the east coast of Okinawa on the afternoon of Love Day plus one (the day after the invasion). That move bisected the island, effectively isolating Japanese troop detachments in the north from the main bulk of their army to the south. The "Old Breed" 1st Marine Division, and three regiments of the 6th Marine Division—the newest and (to this day) the highest numbered division of the Marine Corps—pushed up the eastern and western shore roads into the narrow northeast isthmus known as the "Ishikawa Neck." Opposition was negligible, virtually nonexistent. The climate was splendid and the scenery gorgeous. According to Sterling Mace of the 5th Marines, "The ocean was a lilting shade of azur, the sandy beaches were unsullied and crystalline white, and beautiful Okinawan horses ran wild, close to the water, having been abandoned by their masters."[71] Inland, beyond the dunes, they found a quilted landscape of wheat fields, canefields, pastures, and rice paddies demarcated by narrow dirt lanes and burbling brooks. Rolling hills were terraced for cultivation, and studded with ancient stone tombs. The spring wildflowers were in bloom, and the hilltops were capped with dense stands of pine trees that gave off a sweet, pungent scent. Every half a mile or so, the marines passed through a miniature hamlet made up of squat, close-built stone houses with thatched roofs. Okinawa, wrote Private Gene Sledge, was "as pretty as a pastoral painting."[72]

Much of the civilian population had either moved south with the Japanese army or been evacuated to Japan. Here and there, on the road or in villages, the Americans encountered a group of civilians. Nearly all were women and children, with a few elderly men; there were hardly any young Okinawan males to be found anywhere in the zones occupied by the invasion forces. Most appeared to be poor farmers and peasants, dressed in sackcloth trousers or plain cotton robes; many were barefoot and dirty, and all appeared malnourished. The older people were petrified. Many bowed deep at the waist, cringing as if expecting to be struck. But the children, responding to the warm smiles of the Americans, were quick to lose their fear. With wide eyes and open hands, they advanced to receive the alms offered by the conquerors—candy, chewing gum, and C-rations. "The children were nearly all cute and bright-faced," wrote Sledge. "They had round faces and dark eyes. The little boys usually had close-cropped hair, and the little girls had their shiny jet black locks bobbed in the Japanese children's style of the period. The children won our hearts."[73] Watching these sociable exchanges in stupefied relief, the adults lost their fear. Contrary to what the Japanese army propagandists had told them, the invaders were not ogres or demons. Okinawans were not, after all, to be raped, tortured, mutilated, and murdered. Indeed, the Americans had shipped in provisions to feed the civilian

Nihonbashi district of Tokyo, with the Sumida River in background. This photograph was taken shortly after the March 10, 1945, firebombing. *Chuo City Peaceful Prayer Virtual Museum, Tokyo, Japan.*

A typical scene in Tokyo's Shitamachi district on March 10, 1945.

The beachhead at Okinawa, early April 1945. Amphibious LSTs and LSMs unload equipment and vehicles onto the beach, while LVTs and tanks advance inland across a quilted landscape. Japanese forces did not oppose the initial landing. *National Archives.*

Chiran Airfield, southern Kyushu, April 12, 1945. Labor service maidens wave cherry blossom branches to a departing kamikaze.

USS *Bunker Hill*, Admiral Marc Mitscher's Task Force 58 flagship, after being hit by two kamikazes off Okinawa on May 11, 1945. *National Archives.*

A propaganda leaflet produced by the U.S. Office of War Information (OWI), depicting Chester Nimitz and Douglas MacArthur choking off the sea route that carried oil from the East Indies to the Japanese home islands. Millions of propaganda leaflets were scattered across Japan and Japanese-occupied territories in 1944–1945. *Office of War Information files, Hoover Institution Archives.*

Japanese prisoner in a POW stockade on Okinawa. *National Archives.*

President Harry S. Truman, Secretary of State James Byrnes, and Fleet Admiral William Leahy during the Potsdam Conference, July 16, 1945. Hours later, they learned that the TRINITY nuclear test had succeeded. *Harry S. Truman Library.*

The second atomic bomb detonates over Nagasaki on August 9, 1945. *National Archives.*

Urakami Valley, Nagasaki, September 1945. In the background on a hill to the left are the ruins of Urakami Cathedral, which had been the largest Roman Catholic church in Japan. *National Archives*.

Japanese prisoners of war in a stockade on Guam listen to the Emperor Hirohito's surrender broadcast, August 15, 1945. *U.S. Navy photograph, now in the collections of the National Archives.*

A Japanese prisoner of war on Guam, after listening to Hirohito's surrender broadcast, August 15, 1945. *U.S. Navy photograph, now in the collections of the National Archives.*

Allied prisoners of war at the Aomori Prison Camp, near Yokohama, Japan, as they are rescued on August 29, 1945. *National Archives*.

Halsey and Admiral John S. McCain on board the *Missouri* in Tokyo Bay, shortly before the surrender ceremony on September 2, 1945. McCain departed for the United States immediately after the ceremony. Four days later, at home in Coronado, California, he died of a heart attack. *Naval History and Heritage Command*.

Spectators, sailors, and journalists crowd the decks of the *Missouri* on the morning of September 2, 1945. *National Archives.*

The Japanese surrender delegation awaits the appearance of General MacArthur. Standing in the front rank are Foreign Minister Mamoru Shigemitsu (in top hat and frock coat) and General Yoshijiro Umezu, Chief of the Army General Staff. Toshikazu Kase, an aide to Shigemitsu, later recalled: "A million eyes seemed to beat on us with the million shafts of a rattling storm of arrows barbed with fire. . . . Never had I realized that staring eyes could hurt so much." *National Archives*.

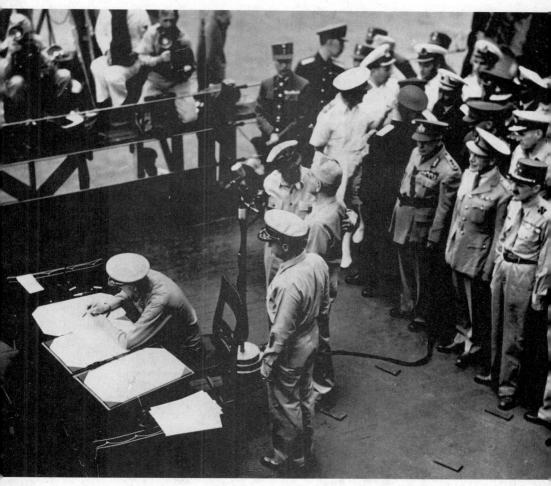

Admiral Nimitz signs the Instrument of Surrender on behalf of the United States. Standing directly behind him, MacArthur and Halsey enjoy the moment while Forrest Sherman looks on. Allied signatories stand in ranks to the right; the outboard press riser is seen at top of frame. *National Archives*.

An American sailor rides a bicycle in Tokyo, using a traditional Japanese parasol for shade. Circa September–October 1945. *National Archives.*

5th Marine Division cemetery on Iwo Jima, March 1945, with Mount Suribachi in the background. *U.S. Navy photograph, now in the collections of the National Archives.*

The aircraft carrier *Saratoga* (CV-3) serving as a troop transport during Operation MAGIC CARPET, September 1945. She brought home a total of 29,204 Pacific War veterans, more than any other ship. *U.S. Navy photograph, originally published in* All Hands *magazine, October 1945.*

population, and intended to return them to their homes and villages as soon as it was safe to do so. Forty-eight hours after Love Day, civilian refugees were waving or saluting as American jeeps and tanks passed in column, and infantrymen were reaching out to tousle the hair of passing children.

For the marines, the first month on Okinawa was a tranquil interlude. They heard booming artillery far to the south, but for the moment that was the army's problem. Some of the new "replacement" marines chided the veterans, suggesting that their accounts of the horrors of Pacific island combat must have been exaggerated. Making camp each evening, they dug foxholes and set up perimeters as they had been trained. The mortarmen registered their weapons on the places they deemed most likely as routes of Japanese night infiltration attacks. Okinawan soil was soft clay loam, which yielded easily before their picks and portable entrenching shovels. Compared to the rocky coral ground of Peleliu, the easy digging was a mercy. The nights were cool, and the men were grateful for their wool-lined field jackets.

Artillery and mortar platoons commandeered local horses to carry their weapons and ammunition. Marines were seen riding the animals, bareback. Some stripped off their uniforms and bathed in the local streams. According to the journalist Ernie Pyle, traveling with the 6th Marine Division, a "few dozen dirty and unshaved marines" scavenged pink and blue Japanese kimonos out of the wreckage of smashed houses, and wore them while washing their uniforms.[74] Another adopted a little white goat as his pet. An eighteen-year-old marine told Bob Sherrod that he hoped to run into enemy troops soon, because "I'm tired of carrying all this ammunition."[75]

To the south, meanwhile, the army was heavily engaged. Probing south from the Hagushi beachhead, General John Hodges's XXIV Corps ran into entrenched Japanese positions in the hilly country north of Naha. The 96th Infantry Division was stopped by artillery, mortars, and tenacious enemy infantry counterattacks on a terrain feature they called the Kakazu Ridge. After four days of hard fighting between April 4 and 8, XXIV Corps had suffered more than 1,500 casualties. The Americans were forced to dig in, and the situation threatened to deteriorate into a protracted and bloody stalemate. The great natural fortress of the Shuri Line loomed ahead. It could not be outflanked, nor even approached except by exposed routes covered by well-aimed artillery and mortars. Those who had fought on the Western Front during the First World War felt an unnerving sense of déjà vu. The Japanese had chosen their ground well, and they had a shrewd plan to defend it. They did not launch profligate and futile *banzai* charges. To a greater degree than in previous battles, their infantry attacks were well synchronized with their artillery and mortar barrages. They had made clever use of reverse-slope firing positions and fortifications, putting their guns out of reach of U.S. artillery and tanks. Their artillerists were more sparing in their use of ammunition than the better-supplied Americans, but they were making every shell count.

Colonel Yahara, the Thirty-Second Army's operations officer, had envisioned waging a battle of attrition, bleeding the American forces and buying time for their colleagues in the homeland to strengthen their defenses. But General Ushijima's higher-ups pressured him to counterattack with all his might, with the aim of recapturing the Yontan and Kadena airfields. The Imperial General Headquarters in Tokyo and the Tenth Area Army in Formosa sent a stream of radio dispatches urging him to push the invaders back to the beach. The Combined Fleet chief of staff, Admiral Kusaka, radioed his Thirty-Second Army counterpart, General Cho, asking that the two airfields be wrested back from the Americans.[76] On April 2, when General Yoshijirō Umezu briefed the emperor, Hirohito expressed concern about the public repercussions of losing Okinawa, asking, "Why isn't the army fighting back?"[77]

Concerned for Ushijima's reputation, General Cho insisted that the Thirty-Second Army must launch a counterattack. Yahara called the proposal "completely irresponsible," warning that Japanese troops would be mowed down as soon as they left their fortified lines. But the pressure from Tokyo and Formosa could not be ignored, and the mood in the command bunker was strongly in favor of an attack. After hearing Cho's and Yahara's contending arguments, Ushijima approved plans for a surprise night attack on April 12. A brigade drawn from the Sixty-Second and Twenty-Fourth Divisions would sally out from their lines after dark, to penetrate American entrenched positions below Kakazu Ridge.

The attack began at midnight on April 12. After hours of savage combat, including desperate fighting at hand-to-hand, the Japanese withdrew, but then renewed their attacks on the two following nights. The American army took losses, but stopped the attacks and hurled the Japanese back. The experience seemed to vindicate the views of Colonel Yahara—whatever the advantages of night infiltration attacks, the American advantages in artillery and firepower would inflict disproportionate losses on Japanese troops whenever they left their caves and entrenchments. General Ushijima cancelled the operation on the morning of April 13, but the impulse to attack was in the marrow of the Japanese army's bones, and the Cho-Yahara debate would be reprised later in the campaign.

AFTER THE BIG KAMIKAZE RAIDS OF APRIL 6, U.S. intelligence analysts judged that the enemy's aircraft reserves must be so depleted that they could not mount another attack on such a scale, at least not in the near term. But that appraisal was too optimistic. The Japanese were preparing to hurl thousands of planes at the Allied fleet. April 6 was only the first of ten *Kikusui* "floating chrysanthemum" operations—and in between these major massed aerial attacks, the Japanese would launch smaller raids nearly every day of the Okinawa campaign. The attacking aircraft included a sundry assortment of obsolete models that the Americans had not seen for years, but also plenty of the newer-type bombers and fighters. Conventional dive-bombing and torpedo attacks were combined with kamikazes and even *Oka* rocket-propelled manned suicide missiles. Total Japanese aerial sorties during the campaign would eventually surpass 3,700, and the attackers would hit more than 200 Allied ships, killing more than 4,900 naval officers and bluejackets.

Japanese air commanders had allowed themselves to believe that the April 6 attacks had dealt a shattering blow to the Allied fleet. In his diary, Admiral Ugaki recorded that a reconnaissance plane had counted 150 columns of black smoke, and that "the sea around Okinawa had thus turned into a scene of carnage." Listening in on the American fighter control circuits, the Japanese had taken satisfaction in the "hurried confusion" of the enemy's airmen. On April 6, Ugaki concluded that "it was almost certain that we destroyed four carriers."[78] After a fuller assessment, drawing upon observations by the Thirty-Second Army on Okinawa, the Imperial Headquarters accepted estimates that thirty-five American ships had been hit and twenty-two had sunk.[79] This exaggerated tally persuaded the high command that the massed suicide attacks held the potential to overpower and scatter the enemy fleet, perhaps even to force the Americans to abandon Okinawa. On April 9, Admiral Toyoda ordered air reinforcements from bases across Japan to stage into Kyushu airfields, in preparation for *Kikusui* No. 2.

For Task Force 58, operating in a 60-square-mile defensive zone north-

east of Okinawa, the daily routines were an exhausting struggle. The force
had been at sea for nearly a month, without respite, constantly fighting off
hair-raising aerial and kamikaze assaults. More than one-third of its aircraft
carriers had been mauled in these attacks, often with appalling loss of life.
The days and nights passed in a nightmarish blur. Nervous strain, at every
level of the command chain, became a vital concern. It was necessary to
rotate ships out of the theater, back to Guam, Ulithi, or Leyte Gulf—partly
for repairs, upkeep, and reprovisioning, but also to provide a short break for
the crews. The fleet surgeons warned that symptoms of pilot fatigue were
rife. Jocko Clark's Task Group 58.1 staff, for the sake of the admiral's mental
health, did not show him the overnight messages until he had completed
his morning ablutions and eaten a quiet breakfast.[80] Marine fighters flew
into Yontan Field on April 8, but for various reasons the land-based air units
could not assume primary responsibility for protecting the island and fleet
until much later in the campaign. "The fleet that came to stay" was forced
to stick it out, making good its nickname.

As the campaign wore on, the Americans learned important lessons in
the unforgiving school of daily aerial combat. The Japanese constantly tried
new tactics, forcing the defenders to adjust. When reconnaissance planes
began approaching at very high altitudes, the Americans stacked "high
CAP" at 35,000 feet. The Hellcat and Corsair pilots circled at that lofty
height, their cockpits as cold as igloos, breathing canned oxygen through
their masks. Remaining on station required deft flying, because the westerly
winds at that altitude often surpassed 150 knots. Radar was a godsend at
Okinawa—even more than in previous campaigns—but the systems then
in use did not always provide accurate estimates of the altitude of incoming
planes, and as the range closed they often lost contact.

As a countermeasure, the Americans deployed radar picket destroyers at
sixteen "stations" on the outskirts of the island and the fleet patrol area. The
busiest picket stations were patrolled by a pair of destroyers, with two to four
amphibious gunboats to provide supporting antiaircraft fire. They maintained
continuous radar, sound, and visual searches for enemy planes and submarines. During the days, a strong combat air patrol orbited overhead. Fighter
director officers (FDOs) were established on board the destroyer pickets
themselves, to direct the orbiting fighters. The specialized dialogue between
the FDOs and the CAP, laden with jargon and codenames, was broadcast
on the Inter-Fighter Director (IFD) net, and played through loudspeakers on

ships throughout the fleet. This gave officers and sailors a means to track the progress of incoming air raiders even before they could be seen in the sky above. "The IFD net was at once our salvation and our entertainment," said an antiaircraft gunnery officer on one of the battleships off Okinawa. "It prepared us to defend ourselves by following the progress of approaching enemies and, of course, under the circumstances it was perfectly fascinating."[81]

The cold reality, which no admiral was willing to admit out loud, was that the picket ships were not just an early-warning radar "tripwire." They were a decoy force whose purpose was to divert the attention of a certain percentage of the incoming enemy planes. Destroyers and gunboats (LCSs and LCIs) were less valuable than the larger warships to the south, or the heavily laden troopships and transports off the beachhead. They were expendable, and their crews knew it. Throughout the long campaign, the picket vessels bore the brunt of the kamikazes' wrath. The CAP over the picket stations was often spotty, especially in thick weather or after sunset. Unlike the carrier fighters, the suicide pilots did not have to worry about navigating back to their bases in darkness. Often, the little picket ships had only their helms and their antiaircraft guns to protect them. And even if a strong CAP was overhead to intercept the Japanese raids, the radar scopes could not distinguish friend from foe. Kamikazes might break out of an aerial melee at any moment, diving suddenly on the ships below. When a picket destroyer was targeted by more than one diver simultaneously, the fire control officers had to divide their fire, and accuracy suffered accordingly.

Gradually, with experience, the picket destroyer skippers learned to maneuver more effectively against attacks. They rang up maximum speed for every action, to improve the ship's nimbleness. They steered to keep the diving planes on the beam, so that the greatest possible volume of antiaircraft fire could be trained on the target. A picket ship that was hit once—or even suffered a single damaging near-miss—was likely to lose a portion of her speed and maneuverability. One or more of her antiaircraft batteries might be silenced—the weapons put out of action or the gun crews killed—rendering her more vulnerable to any kamikaze that followed. This problem was disastrously illustrated by the ordeal of the *Laffey* at Radar Picket Station No. 1 on April 16, when the 2,200-ton destroyer was attacked by twenty-two Japanese planes in eighty minutes. Struck by four bombs and six kamikazes, the *Laffey* lost thirty-two killed and seventy-one wounded, nearly one-third of her crew.

In ten massed *Kikusui* attacks between April 6 and June 22, the attacking planes simply overwhelmed the Allied defenses by weight of numbers. Enemy planes might circle their targets at 5 or 6 miles, beyond effective range of the antiaircraft guns, and then attack simultaneously from all directions, forcing individual antiaircraft batteries to fire almost at random as the attacking planes swarmed in. For the entire period of the Okinawa campaign, fifteen radar picket vessels were sunk and fifty damaged, amounting to nearly one in every three vessels that served on the stations during the period. Total crew casualties on the radar pickets alone (not including the rest of the fleet) were 1,348 killed and 1,586 wounded.[82]

Admiral Turner sent Admiral Nimitz a series of twenty-eight photographs of picket ships damaged by kamikazes. One image after another depicted grievously mangled destroyers and gunboats, with gaping holes torn in the decks, smashed and charred superstructures, gun turrets hanging over the side, and molten steel drooping seaward. In a covering letter, Turner wrote: "These will give you an idea of what our boys are going through. How they ever get their ships back is a mystery; but they are cheerful and do everything they can to keep their ships up here instead of being sent to the rear areas. Morale seems very high, even among our radar picket vessels who well realize what they are up against as do all of us, and they are willing to fight it out on this line."[83]

Again and again, Mitscher sent carrier task groups north to raid Japanese airfields on Kyushu. They bombed the runways, shot down defending fighters, and strafed whatever parked aircraft they could find. But the Americans never managed to stifle the Japanese air threat at its source; they could not simply throw the "big blue blanket" over Kyushu, as they had done on Luzon. Kyushu was too large, with too many airfields, too widely scattered, and the antiaircraft defenses were much more formidable than on Luzon. Ugaki's Fifth Air Fleet could also disperse planes to airfields on nearby Shikoku, or southern Honshu. From his headquarters on Guam, Admiral Nimitz exercised his provisional authority to call upon the services of the Twentieth Air Force, and hundreds of B-29s dropped high-explosive "iron bombs" on Kyushu and Shikoku's airfields on seventeen different days in April and May 1945. But these raids could never put the Fifth Air Fleet out of business; Kanoya and its many satellite airfields remained a cornucopia of kamikazes. The Japanese planes were kept dispersed, hidden under camouflage netting or brush, and moved into takeoff position under cover of the predawn darkness. Craters in the runways were quickly filled in by teams of laborers working with basic tools and equipment, including wheelbarrows, baskets, shovels, and hand-pulled rollers. The carrier bombers and Superfortresses dropped delayed-action bombs, fused to detonate hours after the U.S. planes had departed—but no matter how many workers were killed by these blasts, the Japanese never lacked manpower to replace their losses.

These operations were never popular with the USAAF generals, who objected to diverting the B-29s from their ongoing strategic bombing mission against Japanese cities and aircraft plants. But when General LeMay complained to Nimitz, the CINCPAC firmly told him to keep flying the bombing raids. The argument was bucked up the chain of command to the JCS, which backed Nimitz. The Superforts flew more than 1,600 bombing sorties against Kyushu and Shikoku airfields between April 8 and May 11, when they were finally released from this unwanted duty. In his memoir, LeMay argued that the mission had been misbegotten, and was not worth the effort: "The B-29 was not a tactical bomber and never pretended to be. No matter how we socked away at those airdromes, we could not reduce the kamikaze threat to zero. In some proportion it was always there."[84]

West of Okinawa, in the crowded coastal waters off Naha and the Hagushi beachhead, the sea was littered with flotsam and jetsam. Crews of the transport and amphibious fleet watched vigilantly for suicide speedboats, "midget" submarines, and even swimmers wearing explosive belts. After the destroyer *Charles J. Badger* was hit by a mine dropped by a speedboat before dawn on April 9, sentries with flashlights and Tommy guns were posted on all ships. Taking no chances, they tended to fire upon any debris that drifted within range. The fleet supported the Tenth Army with naval call fire and night-long illumination over the battlefields north of Shuri and Naha. The "no-man's-land" between the American and Japanese lines was kept brightly lit by starshells, every night, from dusk to dawn. The troops ashore were grateful for this service, and credited it with reducing the threat of night infiltration attacks.

Whenever the voices on the IFD net reported "bogeys" approaching the picket lines, an alarm buzzer rang through the ship, a bugler played a bugle call through the loudspeakers, and the crew went to general quarters. The captain set "Condition Zed," requiring that all watertight doors and hatches be slammed shut and dogged down. The bombardment ships of Admiral

Deyo's Task Force 54 fell into a defensive circular formation, like covered wagons on the old western frontier. The chemical smoke generators began emitting a thick, bluish-gray miasma that drifted on the breeze and appeared to cling to the sea. The gunners and fire directors scanned the skies and listened to the radio dialog between the FDO and the fighter pilots. The gunners in the "firing line" on each ship, manning antiaircraft weapons ranging in size from 5-inch down to 20mm, kept their barrels pointed skyward and their eyes peeled.

The most deadly and versatile antiaircraft gun of this period was the mid-ranged 40mm Bofors, which fired a 2-pound projectile with a muzzle velocity of 2,890 feet per second and a cyclic rate of 160 rpm per barrel, and held a flat trajectory to a range of nearly two miles. The Bofors could hit a steeply diving kamikaze when it was still more than a mile away, and the 40mm rounds would begin to take the plane apart—sawing off its wings, tearing away chunks of the fuselage, shattering the windshield and canopy, shooting away the propeller. The engine and frame, being the heaviest and sturdiest portions of the airplane, might continue forward for a brief time—even after the rest of the plane was gone—until finally nosing down into the ocean. Lieutenant Robert Wallace, an antiaircraft gunnery officer on the *Idaho*, concluded of the Bofors gun: "No kamikaze could get past even a single quad-40 if its people knew what they were doing."[85]

The full potential of the larger 5-inch/38 caliber gun was realized with the introduction of the VT (variable time) fuse, also known as the "influence" or "proximity" fuse, which placed a small short-ranged Doppler radar directly into the shell itself. This technological marvel solved the problem of detonating a shell in close proximity to a small, rapidly moving target—the enemy airplane—rather than below or behind it.[86] To witnesses, the successful performance of a 5-inch VT-fused shell was a spectacular sight. If the target aircraft was a bomber, the shell usually set off the bomb that the plane carried. Rather than bursting into flames and diving toward the ocean, the enemy plane simply disintegrated in midair, leaving nothing but a puff of black smoke.

On April 12, a clear, fresh day with almost unlimited visibility, Admiral Ugaki ordered the second "floating chrysanthemums" operation, consisting of 185 kamikazes accompanied by 150 fighters and 45 torpedo planes. The action began shortly after 11:00 a.m., when 129 planes took off from southern Kyushu airfields. Two hours later, the radar scopes of the two destroyers and four LCS(L)s (gunboats) at Radar Picket Station No. 1 (nicknamed "coffin corner") lit up, and thirty Aichi dive-bombers fell upon the *Purdy* and *Cassin Young*. The two destroyers erected a wall of antiaircraft fire, and about a dozen flaming planes splashed down into the sea around them. Both destroyers and one of the gunboats were hit and badly damaged in the ensuing fracas. The *Purdy*'s skipper remarked in his action report, "The prospects of a long and illustrious career for a destroyer assigned to radar picket station duty is below average expectancy. That duty is extremely hazardous, very tiring, and entirely unenjoyable."[87]

Later that afternoon, in the waters west of Okinawa known as "kamikaze gulch," Admiral Deyo's Task Force 54 warships were assaulted by a swarm of planes. At 1:26 p.m., the call came over the IFD net: "Exbrook. Exbrook. [Attention all ships.] Conductor says, 'Flash Red, Control Green [shoot approaching planes on sight].' "[88] Three torpedo planes approached in a high-speed wavetop attack, hopping over the screening vessels and aiming for the battleships at the heart of the formation. One, riddled with 40mm fire, struck the port side of the destroyer *Zellars* and exploded in a ball of fire, killing twenty-nine of her crew. The battleship *Tennessee* was rushed by five more low-flying attackers that came through the smoke thrown off by the *Zellars*. They went down one by one, hit by the converging tracers of the *Tennessee*'s and *Idaho*'s 40mm and 20mm fire. A few minutes later, another descended out of the sky in a well-timed gliding attack on the *Tennessee*, and was shot down directly ahead of the ship. An Aichi dive-bomber on the port bow zoomed in directly toward the superstructure. It struck one of the 40mm quads, killing the entire crew and sending burning gasoline across the deck. Its 250-pound bomb pierced the deck and exploded in the berthing areas for the warrant officers. The *Tennessee* suffered casualties of 23 killed and 106 wounded, including dozens of men who suffered hideous burns.

Two Nakajima "Kate" torpedo planes now began a run at the *Idaho*, attacking on her port quarter. A 5-inch VT shell triggered the first Nakajima's bomb, destroying the aircraft so comprehensively that no wreckage or debris was seen falling into the ocean. The second Kate kept coming, momentarily shielded by the smoke from its destroyed twin. A 20mm mount finally stopped that plane at point-blank range, perhaps as near as 20 feet from the *Idaho*'s port quarter. Its bomb detonated, hurling wreckage and shrapnel over the deck, flooding eight of the ship's torpedo blisters, and injuring a dozen men. From his station forward of the *Idaho*'s superstructure,

Lieutenant Wallace thought the plane must have hit the ship. "A bomb exploding so close to you does not make a booming sound, as heard in the movies," he observed; "It makes a crackling sound, like lightning."[89]

Intermittent fights continued until dusk. Task Force 58 was spared any hits or damaging misses, and its fighters returned with claims of 151 Japanese planes shot down.[90]

THE MORNING AFTER THIS UNPRECEDENTED ASSAULT upon the fleet, devastating news was distributed to every ship and station via an "ALNAV"—a message to the entire navy—from Secretary Forrestal in Washington. President Franklin Delano Roosevelt was dead. He had succumbed to a massive cerebral hemorrhage in Warm Springs, Georgia. On the battleship *Tennessee*, still recovering from the kamikaze hit she had taken the previous day, the ship's loudspeakers announced: "Attention! Attention, all hands! President Roosevelt is dead. Repeat, our Supreme Commander, President Roosevelt, is dead."[91]

The news was greeted with shock, grief, and apprehension about the future course of the war. Younger men had no memory of a time when FDR had not been president of the United States. A sailor on an attack transport off Hagushi recalled: "Few of us spoke, or even looked at each other. We drifted apart, seeming instinctively to seek solitude. Many prayed. Many shed tears."[92] *New Yorker* correspondent John Lardner was at a marine regimental command post on Okinawa when the news arrived by telephone. Lardner observed that many marines were "nonplussed and unable to put their thoughts into words; others were shocked into stillness and went about their work in a sort of walking reverie. . . . I had never seen any news have an effect quite like this one."[93]

John A. Roosevelt, Franklin and Eleanor's sixth and youngest child, was a staff supply officer on the *Hornet*. Admiral Jocko Clark went down to Lieutenant Roosevelt's stateroom and broke the news. Clark offered to send Roosevelt home for his father's funeral, but the lieutenant declined, saying: "My place is here."[94]

By order of Secretary Forrestal, all ships held special memorial services on Sunday, April 15. In a typical ceremony, five minutes' silence was observed by the ship's company, and three volleys of rifle fire marked the late president's passing.

Harry Truman was FDR's third vice president since 1933. Many Americans did not even recognize his name. William Dunn, the CBS radio correspondent in MacArthur's Manila headquarters, sheepishly admitted that he could not remember the name of the sitting vice president. Upon hearing the news of FDR's death, "I held the dubious distinction of being an American reporter who didn't know who was at the helm of his great nation!"[95] Gene Sledge recorded that he and his fellow marines were "curious and a bit apprehensive" about Truman: "We surely didn't want someone in the White House who would prolong [the war] one day longer than necessary."[96]

By contrast, the mood in the Japanese Thirty-Second Army command bunker was euphoric. According to Colonel Yahara, "Many seemed convinced that we would now surely win the war!"[97] Some conjectured that the ground attack on Okinawa and the massed *Kikusui* kamikaze attacks of April 12 must have triggered the stroke that killed FDR. A Japanese propaganda leaflet aimed at American forces on the island asserted that seven of every ten U.S. aircraft carriers had been sunk or damaged, and that the fleet had suffered 150,000 casualties. "Not only the late president but anyone else would die in the excess of worry to hear of such an annihilative damage. The dreadful loss that led your late leader to death will make you orphans on this island. The Japanese special attack corps will sink your vessels to the last destroyer. You will witness it realized in the near future."[98]

The same day that the news of FDR's death was cabled around the world, momentous political developments were announced in Tokyo. Prime Minister Koiso and most of his cabinet had been ousted from power. Kantaro Suzuki, a seventy-seven-year-old retired admiral and senior figure in the imperial court, had been appointed the new prime minister. Five of six members of the Supreme War Direction Council (the "Big Six") had been replaced; the sole survivor was Admiral Yonai, known to be a leader of the peace party. Admiral Ugaki wrote in his diary, probably ironically, that the recent massed kamikaze attack and ground offensive on Okinawa "thus overthrew the cabinet and killed Roosevelt, creating various reactions."[99]

Chapter Fourteen

DETERMINED TO BREAK THE STALEMATE ON THE NAHA-SHURI-YONABARU line, General Buckner approved plans for a renewed ground offensive. Three army divisions—from west to east, the 7th, the 96th, and the 27th—would attack together in a line abreast, with the aim of winning control of the Kakazu Ridge, the Nishibaru Ridge, and the Tanabaru Escarpment. At dawn on April 19, the U.S. artillery and naval guns opened the largest barrage of the campaign. Tenth Army artillery fired 19,000 rounds on the Japanese lines for forty minutes. The guns of six battleships, six cruisers, and eight destroyers rained high-explosive projectiles down on assigned targets. Marine and naval carrier planes added bombs and rockets. The spectacle mesmerized all who witnessed it, but the bombardment was mostly sound and fury. Japanese troops had remained safely hunkered down in their caves and bunkers, well protected by natural limestone, and they surged back up to the surface as soon as it lifted. Brigadier General Joseph Sheetz, commanding the 24th Corps Artillery, judged that no more than one Japanese soldier had been killed for every one hundred artillery shells hurled against their lines.[1]

The 27th Division attacked up Kakazu Ridge with thirty Sherman tanks backed by infantry. As the tanks reached the steeper section of the slope, Japanese artillery and mortars suddenly buried them under a murderous fire. Several machines were hit and disabled by 47mm antitank guns. As the barrage lifted, hundreds of screaming Japanese soldiers charged down the ridge. They drove the American infantry back and attacked the tanks with grenades and 22-pound satchel charges. Twenty-two Shermans were destroyed; it was the single worst one-day slaughter of American tanks in the Pacific War. To the west, the 7th Infantry Division was caught in the open under artillery and mortar fire that had been preregistered to hit the lower slopes. The 96th Division attacked the Tanabaru-Nishibaru ridgeline, at the heart of the zone defended by Japan's Sixty-Second Division. Two advanced platoons that gained the ridgeline were pinned down by fire from higher ground, and could do nothing but withdraw with heavy losses. In the April 19 attack, Americans had gained no permanent advantage on any tactically important ridge in the area, and had been driven back almost to their starting lines, at a cost of 720 dead, wounded, and missing.

Buckner and his subordinates began to understand that a long, hard, bloody battle lay ahead. The enemy's line of fortifications was well constructed, and it crossed the island from coast to coast. The terrain offered scant prospects for flanking or field maneuvers, and many sections were too steep and broken to accommodate tanks. According to the army's official history of the battle, the land was "utterly without pattern; it was a confusion of little, mesa-like hilltops, deep draws, rounded clay hills, gentle green valleys, bare and ragged coral ridges, lumpy mounds of earth, narrow ravines and sloping finger ridges extending downward from the hill masses."[2] For the Americans, control of the air and superior firepower were valuable advantages, but they were not decisive. The dilemma was similar to what the marines had faced on Iwo Jima, but on a larger scale. The Americans would have to use brute force, advancing uphill into some of the most onerous terrain in the Pacific.

The failed attack of April 19 was followed by five days of intense ground fighting all up and down the line. With bitter experience, the American infantrymen were learning how to attack the redoubtable Japanese fortifications. Mapping the battlefield down to every last boulder, cave, and pillbox, they discovered blind spots or "dead zones" between the Japanese firing ports. With closer timing of infantry movements with artillery barrages, advance patrols managed to infiltrate into those zones while the Japanese were still emerging from cover. If the squads could surround a pillbox or cave opening, or climb on top of it, the Japanese occupants would be blinded. As they emerged from their covered positions, they were cut down. It was slow, bloody, treacherous work, involving flamethrowers, grenades, satchel charges, small arms, bayonets, and even knives and bare hands. General Buckner referred to these tactics as the "blowtorch and corkscrew" method. The Japanese called it the "cavalry charge" or "horse-riding" attack.

Naval gunfire and air support were valuable on Okinawa, but they never superseded the bravery, initiative, and grit of individual infantry units. In the end, the soldiers and marines had to dig their enemies out of the ground and kill them. There was no other way. Rarely could they gain an advantage through flanking maneuvers. On the constricted terrain around the Shuri ridges, each battalion was wedged into a densely populated section of the line—on average, a thousand troops for every 600 yards—and the only way to hit the enemy was by frontal assault. They might briefly seize control of the top of a facing ridge, but then be driven back by heavy artillery fire from positions farther south, or by Japanese infantry counterattacks in superior force. That was a recurring pattern on Okinawa: the high ground often changed hands, in a succession of attacks and counterattacks, sometimes as many as a dozen times. American and Japanese dead were splayed side by side on the battlefield. All foliage had been blasted or burned away from the once-verdant landscape, and the zones between the opposing lines were a scarred and denuded wasteland. Artillery and mortar shells fell relentlessly, shaking the walls of the trenches and foxholes. Japanese infiltration attacks were a nightly horror. More than on any previous Pacific battlefield, infantrymen suffered psychotic breaks, and had to be evacuated as "psycho" cases. The war correspondent John Lardner saw a soldier led away from the front line by two medical corpsmen. He was uninjured, but wide-eyed and shrieking: "They'll get every one of you! They'll get every one of you!"[3]

On the Motobu Peninsula, which protruded from the coast of northwest Okinawa, the 6th Marine Division had gradually hunted down and destroyed two battalions of Japanese troops. Hard fighting was required in the rugged, thickly wooded high ground at the center of the peninsula, and even after the marines had secured control, they required a lengthy process of mopping up. Three regiments of the 77th Infantry Division had landed on Ie Shima, a small island just off the western cape of the Motobu Peninsula. Reconnaissance flights had failed to determine the extent of Japanese troop strength on the island, and the army ran into unexpectedly stiff resistance on a terrain feature they called "Bloody Ridge." Five days were needed to quell resistance on Ie Shima. The Americans suffered 258 killed and 879 wounded; virtually the entire garrison of 4,700 Japanese troops was wiped out.

The fierce scrap on Ie Shima also claimed the life of Ernie Pyle, the famed and much-loved war correspondent, whom the GIs had nicknamed "the Soldier's Friend."[4] During past campaigns in Africa, Italy, northern Europe, and the Pacific, Pyle had often exposed himself to serious danger while marching and living with troops in the field. The Ie Shima operation was to be his last combat assignment of the war; he had already been assigned a seat on a C-54 transport for return to the United States. On April 18, Pyle was riding with a battalion commander in the back of a jeep, on a tour of the front lines. As the vehicle slowed at a crossroad, a Japanese machine gun opened fire. The weapon had been concealed in a patch of thick brush, a few feet from the side of the road. The driver and passengers leapt out of the vehicle and took cover in a ditch on the opposite side of the road. None had been hit by that first burst, but Pyle made the mistake of raising his head to have a look. He was hit in the left temple, just below his helmet, and died instantly. Later, soldiers erected a wooden sign: "On this spot, the 77th Infantry Division lost a buddy, Ernie Pyle, 18 April, 1945."[5]

On April 30, General Buckner ordered the marines into the center and western sections of the Shuri Line. Heading south on May 1, marines on trucks passed through tent cities, supply dumps, and road construction sites where bulldozers and earthmoving equipment were reshaping the landscape. Marching north, the other way, were the bloodied veterans of the 27th Division, whom the 1st Marine Division would be replacing in the line. "Tragic expressions revealed where they had been," wrote Gene Sledge. "They were dead beat, dirty and grisly, hollow-eyed and tight-faced. I hadn't seen such faces since Peleliu." One passing soldier told Sledge what to expect: "It's hell up there, Marine."[6]

As they approached the front, the din of battle grew steadily louder, and the rustic, rolling landscape gave way to a gray, pitted wasteland. On the higher parts of the ridge, artillery had exposed the ivory-colored coral escarpments, where the rock was chipped and blasted by artillery shells. Corporal William Manchester, gazing ahead from a rise at the top of a hill, thought the scene looked "hideous, but it was also strangely familiar, resembling, I then realized, photographs of 1914–1918. This, I thought, is what Verdun and Passchendaele must have looked like. The two great armies, squatting opposite one another in mud and smoke, were locked together in unimaginable agony. There was no room for a flanking operation; the Pacific Ocean lay to the east and the East China Sea to the west."[7]

IN THE JAPANESE THIRTY-SECOND ARMY COMMAND BUNKER, deep below
Shuri Castle, the rain of U.S. artillery shells and bombs was little more
than a nuisance. The blasts were comfortably muffled, as if they were a
long way away. But the bunker was clammy and stifling, and smoke sometimes drifted down the ventilation shafts, sending everyone scrambling for
their masks. On April 29, Lieutenant General Cho summoned the staff
and divisional commanders to a conference. Cho was in favor of launching
another counterattack, but on a scale many times larger than the abortive
operation of April 12. As usual, Colonel Yahara took the other side of the
argument; he was for continuing the defensive attrition tactics that had
bled the American forces for three weeks. Yahara observed that the enemy's
advance toward Shuri had been held to a pace of about 100 meters per
day. To send the Japanese troops out of their secure fortifications, to expose
them to the enemy's vast array of artillery, naval firepower, and air power,
would be "reckless and would lead to certain defeat."[8] But Cho's desire to
seize the initiative resonated with the division and field commanders, who
foresaw that Yahara's defensive tactics must lead eventually to total defeat.

After hearing the views of all his subordinates, General Ushijima ruled
in favor of the attack. It was scheduled for predawn on May 4. The final
order urged: "Display a combined strength. Each soldier will kill at least one
American devil."[9]

The operation commenced with the heaviest Japanese mortar and artillery barrage of the entire battle, expending 13,000 rounds in the first three
hours. Small commando patrols crept out of the Japanese caves to attempt
to infiltrate behind American lines. The Japanese Twenty-Seventh Tank
Regiment brought its light and medium tanks forward, intending to launch
them into the center of the XXIV Corps front, near the boundary between
the U.S. 7th and 77th Divisions. Japanese amphibious striking forces set
out in boats from beaches south of Naha and Yonabaru. Early progress
seemed encouraging. The Thirty-Second Regiment captured a hill east
of Maeda village, and the Twenty-Second Regiment advanced to a ridge
north of Onaga, driving two American machine-gun crews from their positions. Three companies of the U.S. 184th Regiment were outflanked and
isolated on the rocky ridgetop features they had named the Chimney Crag
and the Roulette Wheel. By noon, however, the forward momentum of

the Japanese attack was petering out. Counterbattery fire and airstrikes destroyed more than fifty Japanese artillery pieces, and most of the others were pulled back into caves for cover. Some of the Japanese tanks lost their way, and were forced to pull back; others were disabled or destroyed by U.S. artillery or aircraft. The amphibious attacks failed on both the east and west coasts; most of the boats were destroyed before any of the troops could get ashore, with losses of five hundred to eight hundred troops and nearly all of the landing craft.

By the end of May 5, Ushijima acknowledged the failure of the offensive, and recalled all attacking units to their earlier positions. The Japanese had lost at least 6,000 troops, and the Twenty-Seventh Tank Regiment had only six remaining medium tanks. The Japanese artillery battalions had lost many guns and also had expended a great deal of their remaining ammunition. In a tearful encounter in the Shuri bunker, Ushijima told Colonel Yahara that he had been right, and pledged to stick to defensive attrition tactics for the remainder of the battle on Okinawa. However, as Colonel Yahara said, "There was no miracle medicine to heal the critical wounds of the May 4 debacle."[10] A feeling of despair spread through the Japanese ranks.

The two U.S. Army divisions had suffered 335 casualties on May 4, and another 379 casualties on May 5. But the balance of power along the line had shifted, and the Americans moved immediately to exploit their advantage. General Buckner informed his division and corps commanders that he expected to break through to Shuri in another two weeks. The 1st Marines attacked Hill 60, a main feature at the western end of the Japanese line. The summit changed hands twice in fierce fighting between May 6 and 9, when the marines finally consolidated their hold on the hill. To their left, the 5th Marines attacked with tanks and infantry into confused terrain south of the town of Awacha. The 184th Infantry (7th Division) opened a new offensive on Gaja Ridge and Conical Hill, and made surprisingly rapid progress on May 7 and 8. At the center of the U.S. lines, the 77th Division advanced down Route 5, overcoming fanatical Japanese resistance on every hill and ridge. By May 11, the Tenth Army had control of a line running through Maeda, Kochi, and Awacha, with secure supply lines running back to the Hagushi beachhead. But the menacing citadel of Shuri Castle still loomed to the south, and more hard fighting would be needed to take it.

ON APRIL 14, THE IMPERIAL GENERAL HEADQUARTERS in Tokyo had announced that air attacks on the Allied fleet off Okinawa had sunk or crippled 326 ships. Among the "fully confirmed" sinkings were six aircraft carriers, seven battleships, thirty-four cruisers, forty-eight destroyers, and various auxiliary vessels. According to the official communiqué, the true figures were thought to be even higher—but out of an abundance of caution, in order to avoid haste and error, unconfirmed claims were being withheld pending "further checkup."[11] A week later, Radio Tokyo reported that the enemy had lost half of the 1,400 ships he had brought to Okinawa, including four hundred sunk, with casualties of no fewer than 800,000! These shocking losses, the announcer declared, had driven the Americans "into the black depths of confusion and agony."[12]

The reports made Tokyo's earlier flights of hyperbole seem picayune by comparison. Ugaki's second-in-command, Admiral Toshiyuki Yokoi, later explained that air commanders in Kyushu felt pressure from down the ranks to certify the grossly exaggerated claims. When Yokoi cast doubt on one such report, a kamikaze squadron commander told him: "If the results achieved are going to be so underestimated, there is no justification for the deaths of my men. If headquarters will not acknowledge these achievements at full value, I must commit hara-kiri [suicide] as an expression of my disapproval and by way of apology."[13]

Yet it seems that leaders in Tokyo really did believe that the kamikazes might be winning the fight for Okinawa. The Naval General Staff estimated that the U.S. fleet was in "an unstable condition and the chance of winning now stands fifty-fifty."[14] IGHQ ordered more Kikusui operations, in hopes of scoring a knockout blow. Time was of the essence; the suicide planes must strike quickly, before the amphibious fleet had unloaded the bulk of its cargo and retired to Ulithi or Leyte. A steady stream of replacement airplanes and pilots flew south from Honshu, into the Fifth Air Fleet's staging bases in Kyushu.[15]

At Kanoya Air Base, the kamikaze pilots lived in the finest barracks on the base. Their quarters stood on the bank of a burbling stream that meandered through a verdant bamboo forest and a meadow dotted with wild roses. Living in the shadow of imminent death, they strolled contemplatively through these pastoral surroundings. They wrote letters and poetry. Local citizens brought them gifts, including sake, liquor, and food that could hardly be spared in those famished times. Farmers donated eggs, chickens, pigs, and even cattle to be slaughtered for their last feasts. Teenaged girls of the local labor service corps looked after their laundry, cooking, and house-keeping. These "labor service maidens" became emotionally bonded to the kamikaze pilots—in a chaste sense, it seems—revering them as "the older brothers," and calling themselves "the younger sisters." Before a mission, the maidens worked all night to decorate the kamikaze planes with cherry blos-soms, and left cloth dolls and origami figures in the cockpits. They attended the send-off ceremonies on the flight line, tearfully waving cherry blossom boughs or Rising Sun flags to the departing aircraft. They collected the pilots' hair and fingernail clippings and mailed them to the families with letters of gratitude.

In the early days of the kamikaze corps, there had never been a short-age of volunteers. But in the spring of 1945, air commanders noted a shift in attitudes among the new crop of suicide pilots. Many had been "asked" to volunteer in circumstances that made it impossible to refuse. According to a naval staff officer, "there developed a pressure, not entirely artificial, which encouraged 'volunteering,' and it is understandable that this change in cir-cumstance would effect a change in the attitude of the men concerned." He added that many of the new arrivals "appeared to be disturbed by their situation."[16] An entire class of flight cadets at an army training base in Mito was asked by the commanding officer to volunteer for suicide assignments. "I don't even remember telling my feet to move," a cadet later said. "It was like a strong gust of wind whooshed up from behind the ranks and blew everyone forward a step, almost in perfect unison."[17]

About half of the kamikaze pilots of 1945 had been drawn from the ranks of university students. Many were cosmopolitan intellectuals who had been exposed to foreign ideas and influences, including Western philosophy and literature. These traits had not endeared them to their officers and NCOs in military training camps. Many young scholars had been singled out for spe-cial abuse, including vicious beatings—leaving them with feelings of con-tempt and loathing for military authority, and for the tyrannical regime that held the nation's fate in its grip. In diaries and letters, many of these future kamikazes identified themselves as political liberals and democrats. Some found much to admire in the American model of society and government. Others harbored radical, utopian, pacifist, or even Marxist views.

Tadao Hayashi, for example, had been drafted out of Kyoto University.

In his writings, Hayashi disavowed the war aims of the imperialist regime; he even held that Japan's defeat was both necessary and desirable. Yet he was determined to die for his country: "The situation is tense indeed. But for me, it is all right for Japan to be destroyed. . . . Historical necessity led to the crisis of our people. We rise to defend our people in the land we love."[18] Hayashi died at age twenty-four, less than three weeks before the end of the war. Hachiro Sasaki, drafted out of Tokyo Imperial University, believed that Japan had been hopelessly corrupted by capitalism, and that its pending defeat would give way to revolution. This learned young communist died in a suicide mission off Okinawa on April 14, 1945, aged twenty-two. He left behind a personal library that included works of history, science, philosophy, economics, and literature in German, English, French, Russian, Italian, and Latin.[19] Ichizo Hayashi, from Fukuoka, Kyushu, was a devout Christian who carried a bible on his final flight, along with a copy of Kierkegaard's *Sickness Unto Death* and a photograph of his mother. "I will put your photo right on my chest," he wrote to her, in a last letter from Kanoya. "I shall be sure to sink an enemy vessel. When you hear over the radio of our success in sinking their vessels, please remember that one of them is the vessel I plunged into. I will have peace of mind, knowing that mother is watching me and praying for me."[20] Ensign Hayashi, aged twenty-three, died in the second *Kikusui* operation on April 12, 1945.

Some did not want to go. Gestures of defiance, overt and covert, became more common as the conflict wore on. Admiral Yokoi recalled attitudes ranging "from the despair of sheep headed for the slaughter to open expressions of contempt for their superior officers."[21] On the night before embarking on a last mission, the kamikaze squadrons held riotous bacchanals, guzzling sake and vandalizing their furnishings. A witness recounted one such scene: "The whole place turned to mayhem. Some broke hanging light bulbs with their swords. Some lifted chairs to break the windows and tore white tablecloths. A mixture of military songs and curses filled the air. While some shouted and raged, others cried aloud. It was their last night of life."[22] After taking off, mutinous pilots sometimes flew low over the quarters of their superior officers, as if to crash or strafe them. If they went on to fulfill their mission, the offense could not be punished.

Increasingly, in the later phases of the Okinawa campaign, kamikaze planes turned back and returned to land at their bases. The pilots reported baffling engine malfunctions, or claimed that they had been unable to locate enemy ships. Others ditched their planes at sea, near islands between Kyushu and Okinawa, hoping to get ashore and survive until the end of the war. Pilots were known to sneak out to the flight line in darkness, on the night before a scheduled departure, and sabotage their own planes. They might simply unscrew the gas cap, intending to run low on fuel, an excuse to turn back. After returning to base nine consecutive times, one pilot (a graduate of Waseda University) was executed by firing squad. In another infamous case, a kamikaze dove his plane into a railroad embankment near his family's neighborhood in Kagoshima, apparently choosing to die close to home.

Southern Kyushu was in full spring bloom. For hours each afternoon, Admiral Ugaki hunted pheasants through the hills and countryside around his headquarters at Kanoya. On April 13, he noted that the wheat was "pretty high" and the trees were "vividly green."[23] The cherry blossoms were at the height of their grandeur. Local civilians had planted vacant lots with potatoes and vegetables, and the admiral was pleased to see these fresh plantings thrive. He noted that the wheat had "grown to full length with its ears all pointing upward like spearheads as if calling the whole nation to arms."[24] When the spring hunting season ended on April 21, Ugaki turned in his hunting license and placed his shotgun in storage. He told his diary that he did not expect to be alive when the shooting season resumed in the fall.[25]

The Kyushu airfields came under near-daily attack by B-29s and U.S. carrier planes. Hellcats and Corsairs flew low over the airfields, strafing parked planes and ground crews. Superfortresses soared high overhead, dropping sticks of 1,000-pound high-explosive bombs to fall across the heart of the runways. Some bombs exploded instantly, while others—armed with delayed-action fuses—buried themselves in the asphalt and lay doggo. The main runways at Kanoya were decorated with small red flags marking the locations of timed bombs that had not yet blown. Admiral Ugaki considered them "quite troublesome. . . . They can't be disposed of as duds too soon, for some are timed with as long as a 72-hour fuse."[26]

At Chiran Airfield on Kagoshima Bay, the labor service maidens were put to work repairing the runways. They shoveled dirt and gravel into the bomb craters, until their palms blistered and their backs ached. One day in early May, their work was interrupted by an air-raid siren, and they ran to the trenches by the side of the runway. A file of F6F Hellcats flew low over the field, strafing parked planes and ground installations. "The Americans flew so low you could see their pink faces and blue eyes and those big, square, white-framed goggles they wore," said Reiko Torihama. "We hated to admit it, but we admired their cockiness, flying in so low like that. I'm still not sure if they were either very brave or just thought so little of us that there was nothing to be afraid of."[27]

On the morning of a scheduled kamikaze attack, the ground crews, the local headquarters staffs, and the labor service maidens attended an elegiac send-off ceremony on the flight line. The pilots, acclaimed as "divine eagles who will attack and not return," wore white scarves and rising sun headbands. Some had shaved all of their body hair for the occasion. With their unit commander, they raised their cups in a last toast. Then they climbed into their cockpits, which had been scrubbed clean and decorated by the maidens, started their engines, and taxied out to the runway. One by one they took off, and then banked south for the two-hour flight to the enemy fleet off Okinawa. They flew low over the rice terraces, wheat fields, and hills of southern Kyushu. "We'd go outside and wave flags, or just our hands," a local woman recalled. "One plane, perhaps the leader's, would fly low and dip its wings in greeting. We cried and cried. We knew that would be the last we saw of them. We'd wave frantically until they disappeared, then we'd pray for them."[28]

FOR CREWMEN ON THE WARSHIPS OFF OKINAWA, the days and nights passed in a mind-numbing cycle of attacks and false alarms. Whenever the divine wind began to blow, the ear-splitting buzzer alarms sounded, calling men to their battle stations. The smoke generators exuded an opaque chemical haze, the 5-inch antiaircraft guns began firing with deep, repeating blasts (*boom! boom! boom!*), and dark flak bursts dirtied the sky. When fired at a low trajectory, flak posed a lethal hazard to neighboring ships, and friendly fire claimed untold hundreds of casualties over the course of the Okinawa campaign. The seemingly endless blast concussions made by the guns wore the sailors down and set them on edge. But no matter how much 5-inch, 40mm, and 20mm fire the gunners threw up, there was always more ammunition waiting in the storeships at Kerama Retto—so they kept firing, without concern for thrift. Off the Hagushi beachhead, the volume of antiaircraft fire was incredible. One witness recalled watching a battleship at night, under air attack, as her batteries spat out an uninterrupted stream of incandescent tracer fire: "I never saw so much fire and tracers coming from one place in my entire life. . . . It just made a big cone up there, and the cone would move around. Then you'd see a plane light up at the tip of the cone and go down, and the cone would just keep moving. It was a spectacular sight."[29]

Blasted, scorched, and crippled ships crowded into the repair anchorage at Kerama Retto, which the Americans had nicknamed "Busted Ship Bay." Kelly Turner's earlier decision to seize the archipelago had been handsomely vindicated. If the fleet had not possessed a protected anchorage so close to Okinawa, many more of the stricken ships would have had to be scuttled. As it was, repair ships and floating drydocks could handle minor repairs, and the more badly damaged ships could be patched up and dispatched to Ulithi or even to Pearl Harbor under their own steam. Between April 6 and June 22, more than two hundred Allied ships and support vessels were hit by kamikazes or conventional bombing attacks, or damaged by near misses—but only thirty-six were sunk or scuttled.

The stress of prolonged operations was wearing on the navy crews, but the Fifth Fleet boss remained as stoic and unflappable as ever. Raymond Spruance had been forced out of his first flagship, the *Indianapolis*, by a kamikaze attack on March 31, before the assault troops had even set foot on Okinawa. His second flagship, the old battleship *New Mexico*, fought off near-daily aerial attacks throughout April and May. Yet the slender, deeply tanned four-star admiral appeared no worse for wear. As usual, he took his daily exercise by pacing around the forecastle for hours each day, and slept soundly even while the *New Mexico*'s guns blazed through the night. David Willcutts, the Fifth Fleet naval surgeon, recalled an incident toward the end of April 1945. Admiral Spruance was on the quarterdeck with several other officers, watching a swarm of Japanese planes approach from the northwest. A lone kamikaze commenced a steep diving attack on the *New Mexico*. The other officers withdrew and took cover, but Spruance remained at the rail, erect and unflinching, with his binoculars trained on the charging plane. The 40mm batteries finally destroyed the kamikaze, which "disintegrated and plunged into the sea, really a matter of feet from the *New Mexico*."

Dr. Willcutts ventured to reprimand the chief for exposing himself unnecessarily. Spruance replied: "If you were a good Presbyterian you would know that there is no danger unless your number is up."[30]

As always, the destroyers and gunboats at the fifteen outlying radar picket stations got the worst of it. After three or four days of continuous duty at one of these "windy corners," the crews began to show signs of acute fatigue. They remained at battle stations day and night, eating sandwiches, hard-boiled eggs, and coffee distributed from the galleys. "The strain became almost intolerable," recalled the skipper of an LCS(L) gunboat. "We were gaunt and filthy, red-eyed and stinking. The ship was a mess, with empty shell casings everywhere. My face was pockmarked with particles of burned gunpowder, since one Oerlikon antiaircraft gun fired as close as three yards from my battle station. We prayed for bad weather, which was about the only thing that slowed down the stream of Japanese planes."[31] A sailor on another gunboat wrote that the entire crew was at "a breaking point." Nerves were brittle, and shipmates snarled at one another over petty annoyances. When someone dropped a heavy wrench on the deck, "I jumped like I had been jolted with high-voltage electricity."[32]

A typically desperate action was fought at Radar Picket Station No. 10 on May 3, 1945. It was sunset, just after the Hellcats and Corsairs of the CAP had departed to return to their carriers. The destroyers *Aaron Ward* and *Little*, accompanied by four gunboats, were attacked by about fifty Japanese planes. The *Aaron Ward* was hit by seven kamikazes. She was badly flooded, to a near-sinking condition, and fierce fires spread through her lower decks. Forty-five of her crew were killed, forty-nine injured.[33] After a long, gallant firefighting and salvage effort, the stricken ship was towed into Kerama Retto. Meanwhile, the *Little* was targeted by at least eighteen suicide planes, and hit by four, including one that made a near-vertical dive and crashed her after-torpedo mount. The penetrating impact broke the *Little*'s keel, and her main decks were awash within two minutes. A member of the crew, emerging on deck, was shocked by the carnage: "Officers walked briskly about the decks silently drawing gray blankets over still warm and bleeding bodies . . . in many respects the dead were the luckiest of us all. They neither had to abandon nor to remember."[34] Just twelve minutes after the first kamikaze had hit her, the *Little* was gone. Thirty of her crew were dead, seventy-nine injured.

Task Force 58 kept station to the east of Okinawa, constantly patrolling in an area of about 60 square miles. Admiral Mitscher had hoped to be released from the duty to protect the amphibious fleet and the island by the end of April, if not earlier—but the army and marine air units were unable to assume this responsibility until the last week of May. The delay was caused by a combination of factors. Airfield development on Okinawa lagged behind schedule, because the terrain was soft and wet, and grew more so as the spring rains began falling in May. As on Leyte, the island lacked ample sources of coral rock to be used in paving the airfields. The Japanese-built airfields at Yontan and Kadena were rough and muddy, and at night they were lighted by burning pits of gasoline and kerosene dug along the margins of the runways. The pilots and ground crews were quartered in tents that had been shredded by falling flak fragments.

On the night of May 24, the Japanese staged a daring commando raid on Yontan. Five Japanese bombers arrived suddenly, at low altitude, with wheels down, and attempted to land on the field. Four were shot down before they could land, but the fifth actually landed and taxied to a stop near the parking hardstands. A dozen Japanese commandos poured out of the airplane and spread out among the parked U.S. aircraft, destroying them with grenades and satchel charges. Nine American planes were destroyed, and more than two dozen damaged. Marine guards began firing wildly, including at each other, and many were injured or killed by friendly fire. The Japanese blew up a fuel dump, destroying 70,000 gallons of aviation fuel. The firefight continued all night, until the last Japanese commando was hunted down and killed after dawn. Colonel Ronald D. Salmon, a marine aviation officer at the base, described the situation as "pretty grim . . . one of the most exciting nights I've seen in any war."[35]

Individual task groups were diverted north repeatedly to raid Kyushu, but the bulk of Task Force 58 remained pinned to the beachhead, with its mobility sharply restricted. The daily pattern became predictable, and predictability was dangerous. Mitscher grumbled that his task force had become "a high-speed stationary target for the Japanese air force."[36] Most nights, small groups of enemy patrol planes came out to snoop the fleet, dropping flares, and sometimes attacked with bombs or torpedoes. The intruders were tracked on radar, and night fighters were vectored out to intercept them. Larger raids occurred during the day, often in the late morning or early afternoon. Most Japanese planes were intercepted and shot down by the CAP, usually at least 30 miles from the heart of the task groups, but it was not uncommon for a few to get through the outer screen to make diving runs on the carriers. These were always high-tension affairs for the crews of the ships. Everything happened quickly, and no one could predict when a plane would slip through the storm of antiaircraft fire to crash a ship. Men below, especially, were unnerved by these raids—and with good reason, because fatalities were disproportionately high on the lower decks, where crewmen could easily be trapped by fire or suffocated by smoke.

The tedious routine seemed unending. Humor provided some relief. After several consecutive days of harrowing attacks, Admiral Jocko Clark signaled his task group: "See Hebrews 13, Verse 8." On ships throughout the group, bibles were opened and the verse read aloud: "Jesus Christ, the same yesterday, today, and forever."[37]

Men became irritable and short-tempered. It was an open secret, throughout the fleet, that many sailors were imbibing high-proof "torpedo juice" purloined from the weapons shacks on the hangar decks. All crewmen were told to apply an anti–flash burn ointment that left an oily white sheen on their faces and arms, but many detested the feel and odor of the stuff. The young pilots of the replacement squadrons now learned the meaning of pilot fatigue, and the flight surgeons warned that they must soon be relieved, or operational accidents would rise sharply. Orders and announcements over the loudspeakers urged all to stay alert, so that they could stay alive. On one carrier, someone scrawled a message on a blackboard in a fighter squadron ready room: "Keep alert—remember your poor scared pals on the ship!"[38] On another, a plan of the day stated: "It is fully realized that our present operations have been tiring and difficult, but let's not lose our sense of proportion." All crewmen were urged to "guard against the hasty flow of ill-chosen words that not only cheapens you, but causes you to lose the friendship of a shipmate. . . . a sour disposition, like sour garbage, should be ground up and thrown overboard."[39]

On the morning of May 11, 1945, Admiral Mitscher's flagship *Bunker Hill* was the victim of one of the most horrific kamikaze strikes of the war. Two Mitsubishi Zeros took advantage of a low cloud ceiling over the task force, dropping through solid overcast before the gunners could react. The first approached the carrier's starboard quarter in a shallow dive, releasing its 550-pound bomb just before crashing the flight deck aft of the No. 3 elevator, where it ploughed into a squadron of thirty-four fueled-up Hellcats. The bomb ripped through three decks before exiting the hull and exploding close aboard. The second plane came down in a nearly vertical dive, with speed probably surpassing 500 knots, and pierced the flight deck at the base of the island. As in all such disasters, the most catastrophic damage was caused by secondary explosions and fires as the *Bunker Hill*'s own ordnance and fuel ignited. Hundreds of sailors were killed without any chance of escape—either in the blasts, or in the fires, or through asphyxiation. Hundreds more were forced off the flight deck to the catwalks and galleries, where they awaited rescue or simply leapt into the sea on their own initiative. Fires raged and a column of black smoke ascended to a height of 1,000 feet. The journalist Phelps Adams, stationed on the nearby *Enterprise*, described the burning carrier:

> The entire rear end of the ship was burning with uncontrollable fury. It looked very much like the newsreel shots of a blazing oil well, only worse—for this fire was feeding on highly refined gasoline and live ammunition. Greasy black smoke rose in a huge column from the ship's stern, shot through with angry tongues of cherry-red flame. Blinding white flashes appeared continuously as ready ammunition in the burning planes or in the gun galleries was touched off. Every few minutes the whole column of smoke would be swallowed in a great burst of flame as another belly tank exploded or as the blaze reached another pool of gasoline flowing from the broken aviation fuel lines on the hangar deck below.
>
> For more than an hour there was no visible abatement in the fury of the flames. They would seem to be dying down slightly as hundreds of thousands of gallons of water and chemicals were poured on them, only to burst forth more hungrily than ever as some new explosion occurred within the stricken ship.[40]

Among the dead were three officers and ten enlisted men of the Task Force 58 staff.[41] Admiral Mitscher had personally lost many good friends in the air group and the ship's crew. At three that afternoon, he left the still-burning *Bunker Hill* with sixty surviving members of his staff, transferring to the *Enterprise*. As Mitscher came aboard, wrote Adams, "He looked tired and old and just plain mad. His deeply lined face was more than weather-beaten—it looked like an example of erosion in the dust-bowl country—but his eyes flashed fire and vengeance."[42]

After an eight-hour fight to quell the flames and repair the damage, the *Bunker Hill* was a pitiful sight, much like her sister the *Franklin* six weeks earlier. She had lost 389 killed and 264 wounded. The abnormally high ratio of dead to wounded was explained by circumstances—the victims had been belowdecks when the planes struck, and succumbed to smoke inhalation before they could climb the ladders. While excavating the ready room of the carrier's fighter squadron, VF-84, salvage teams found the bodies of twenty-two pilots piled in the hatchway, where they had been trying to escape when their compartment filled with smoke.

The *Bunker Hill's* engine rooms and power plant were largely intact, and she was able to retire to Ulithi Atoll at nearly 20 knots. On May 12, she buried more than three hundred of her crew at sea. The gutted carrier was patched up at Ulithi and made the transpacific passage under her own steam. When the war ended three months later, she was under repair at Bremerton Naval Shipyard in Puget Sound.

Mitscher's new flagship *Enterprise* was hit by a kamikaze three days later, forcing the admiral to shift his flag yet again, to the *Randolph*—which was herself no stranger to kamikaze attacks. Mitscher remarked to his operations officer, James Flatley, "Jimmy, tell my task group commanders that if the Japs keep this up they're going to grow hair on my head yet."[43]

One day after the *Bunker Hill's* ordeal, Admiral Spruance's flagship *New Mexico* caught it. The battleship was returning toward Hagushi Bay from Kerama Retto, where she had replenished her ammunition. It was a cool, calm day. At 5:00 p.m., two low-flying Japanese planes approached "up sun," from astern. A 5-inch shell scored a direct hit on the lead plane, and it crashed about a quarter of a mile from the *New Mexico's* port quarter. The second flew through and around the flak and crashed the starboard side of the ship, just abaft the foremast. Its bomb detonated on the gun deck, and the plane's wreckage buried itself in the funnel, tearing a 30-foot hole in the thin steel skin of the smokestack. The explosion ruptured an aviation gasoline storage tank, and fires engulfed the superstructure. Ready service ammunition of the 40mm and 20mm batteries fell through the battle bars into the stack, and began detonating. But damage control parties had hoses working in less than sixty seconds, and soon brought the fires under control. All were extinguished within an hour.

At first, Admiral Spruance could not be found, and his staff feared that he may have been killed. Rear Admiral Arthur C. Davis, the chief of staff, and Charles F. Barber, flag lieutenant, left the mess deck together and hurried up to the flag bridge. Spruance was not there. Eventually they found him on the second deck, manning a fire hose with other members of the crew. He was uninjured and, as always, unperturbed. Lieutenant Barber recalled: "Admiral Spruance, as he often did, took his time and finished what he was doing."[44] An hour after the attack, when the *New Mexico's* damage had been contained, he told his staff that he did not see any reason to transfer his flag again: "I believe that we can remain on station, complete repairs, and carry on."[45]

The *New Mexico* had suffered 177 casualties, including 55 dead. The bomb had blown a "ghastly huge crater" in the stack, but the ship was otherwise seaworthy.[46] The next morning, Spruance wrote to Carl Moore, his former chief of staff: "I had just started for the bridge when the AA batteries opened up, so I remained under cover while going forward on the second deck, and we were hit before I got very far, which was fortunate for me as the two routes to the bridge led right through the area where the plane and bomb hit." As usual, the Fifth Fleet chief was clinical in his appraisal: "The suicide plane is a very effective weapon, which we must not underestimate. I do not believe anyone who has not been around within its area of operations can realize its potentialities against ships."[47]

MAY 8, 1945, BROUGHT NEWS of the unconditional surrender of Nazi Germany. The warships off Okinawa commemorated this historic occasion by launching one of the most awesome and sustained naval bombardments of the Pacific War. But for men in the trenches, V-E Day was met with shrugs and grimaces. The event seemed barely relevant to their own predicament. If V-E Day meant that troops and airplanes would be redeployed from Europe, it was to be welcomed. But they angrily spurned suggestions that it should be celebrated. As a marine fighting on Okinawa observed, the news "didn't change the position of our lines, or the texture of the mud, the tint of this sky, or the amount of ammunition each of us carried in our ponchos." Another agreed: "Nazi Germany might as well have been on the moon."[48]

Three days later, on May 11, the Tenth Army renewed its offensive with a coordinated assault by two mixed corps—on the west, III Amphibious Corps, consisting of the 1st and 6th Marine Divisions; in the east, XXIV Corps, including the 77th and 96th Infantry Divisions, with the 7th Division in reserve. On the far right and left flanks, the army and marines would push south along the coasts, while keeping up strong pressure on the entire defensive system around Shuri Castle. This opened the most intense and desperate phase of ground combat on this or any other island of the Pacific

War. The soldiers and marines advanced against well-fortified Japanese positions in nondescript and previously nameless hills and ridges, which the Americans named as they drew their maps: the Chocolate Drop, Flat Top Hill, Tombstone Ridge, Conical Hill, Wana Ridge, Wana Draw, and Sugarloaf Hill. Six weeks earlier, this had been a peaceful, green, cultivated region, a landscape of rolling hills and terraced hillsides, with vistas overlooking the brilliant blue sea. Now it was a colorless waste, denuded of vegetation, strewn with dead men and caked in mud.

The opposing armies advanced and retreated, attacking and counterattacking, surging up and down slopes, over tank traps and minefields, into the teeth of machine-gun fire, seizing summits and then being driven back, until the Japanese and American dead accumulated on the ground, scattered promiscuously together. Sky-splitting artillery and mortar barrages preceded each new thrust, while the Sherman tanks rumbled in idle, hatches open, their drivers waiting for the signal to advance. Mortarmen and howitzer crews were assigned "fire missions," with coordinates and range cards, and instructions concerning how many rounds they should fire, and what kind, and for how long. The infantry drew ammunition, filled their canteens, and got their equipment squared away—and then tensed in their foxholes and trenches, heads down, awaiting the signal from their officers and sergeants to move out. The bombardment swelled to a crescendo, with the naval guns offshore adding their immense firepower to that of the field artillery, and nothing could be heard but an indistinguishable roar. Last came the phosphorus mortar rounds, to draw a curtain of smoke across the enemy's sightlines. At a signal, the tank engines slammed into gear with an audible thud, the treads bit into the mud, and the infantrymen stood and advanced in a low crouching jog, keeping five paces between themselves and the men ahead and behind. Their objectives were the blind corners between the Japanese firing positions, where they could flank the pillboxes and cave entrances. Out of the smoke the enemy's rifle and machine-gun fire whined, popped, and snapped around their ears, and they knew now that they were playing the law of averages, with life and death a matter of blind luck. Mortar shells fell among them. When the smoke was thick, the Japanese "nambu" light machine guns fired in quick, two- or three-round bursts to conserve ammunition: "*Tat tat . . . tat tat tat . . . tat tat.*" But the moment the smoke cleared, and the Japanese gunners could see a target, they held their fingers down and swept the field of fire. If a man to the left or right went down, his friends kept moving. "You look at it but you keep going," a marine recalled. "You don't stop, because he's dead."[49]

Rarely was there any chance of a flanking maneuver; the ground attacks were straight ahead. Each forward advance drew punishing fire from many different kinds of weapons, from seemingly unassailable positions. In an attack on Wana Draw on May 15, Japanese 47mm antitank fire destroyed several Shermans right away, and the others were forced back. If the tanks could make no progress against such defenses, what could the simple infantrymen hope to achieve? At times, they despaired of making any progress at all. The rattle of machine guns and popping of rifle fire rarely abated, and beneath it was the throaty roaring, whining, and blasting of artillery and mortars. There seemed too great a volume of steel in the air for any kind of attack to be anything other than suicidal. And yet the orders were blunt, and the pressure intense: they must break the back of the Japanese defenses, and they must do so quickly. They could do nothing but hammer away at the enemy line. Gradually, through costly trial and error, they refined new tactics. Often, innovations were developed by junior officers and NCOs on the line, who suddenly realized how an enemy position might be taken, and took local initiative. The Japanese use of reverse-slope entrenchments was shrewd and effective, but it could be countered with accurate and precisely timed use of mortar fire. Bit by bit, in fits and starts, the American mortarmen found the range. Mortars could be lobbed over the peaks of the hills and ridges, to land directly among the trenches and cave openings. If a barrage was timed with a feigned ground attack, the mortars would hit home just as the Japanese soldiers were emerging from their protected underground positions to repel the Americans. Many were killed, and others withdrew, allowing the American infantry squads to launch their "blowtorch and corkscrew" attacks while their enemies were still under the ground, blinded, at a tactical disadvantage.

Beginning on May 21, a ten-day deluge of slashing rains turned the battlefield into a sea of mud. Soldiers and marines huddled under their ponchos, soaking and miserable. Their foxholes began to fill in with water, and they bailed with their helmets. Men attempted to salvage ammunition boxes to create a wooden floor at the bottom of their flooded entrenchments. The skin on their hands and fingers was wrinkled and pellucid. Their feet, never dry, developed open sores, and became slimy to the touch—and when they pulled off their boots, they found small clumps of dead flesh clinging to their wet socks. When they read letters from home, they were obliged to read quickly, before the ink was smeared and blotted out by the rain. When they opened their ration cans, the can filled with rainwater and turned their food into a cold soup. Jeeps and trucks sank to their axles, immobilized. Even tanks and tracked vehicles were unable to advance. Ammunition, provisions, and 5-gallon water cans had to be muscled up to the lines by hand, through knee-deep mud, in driving rain, over fields swept by Japanese fire.

Under relentless, pounding rains, visibility was sometimes cut to 10 feet. Occasionally, the Americans caught a glimpse of their enemy—small, stocky men with brown uniforms and wide-rimmed helmets, moving quickly and efficiently over the ruined terrain. No-man's-land was kept illuminated all night long by the use of starshells and parachute flares. The Americans were on constant guard against night infantry attacks, by small parties of stealthy infiltrators or by company-sized bayonet charges, with the attackers shouting "*Nippon Banzai!*" Japanese soldiers were known to wear captured American helmets and uniforms and to walk nonchalantly into the American lines, where they would suddenly open fire. On Okinawa, the enemy could be coming from any direction, at any time. From the Japanese lines, of course—but they could also approach from the flanks, or from behind, via tunnels or bypassed positions. The American infantrymen even cast wary glances at the sky whenever an aircraft engine was heard, because they had been warned to watch for paratroopers.

Corpses were strewn across the battlefield, and the stomach-churning stench of putrefying flesh was pervasive and inescapable. On the front lines, it was impossible to remove the dead without exposing burial crews to deadly fire. If corpses were buried where they lay, mortar and artillery blasts exhumed them in violent upheavals and scattered them in fragments across the battlefield. Continued explosions mashed the exposed remains into fragments of bone and flesh, until nothing remained but streaks of red in the mud. The problem of sanitation was worse than on any other Pacific battlefield. William Manchester observed, "If you put more than a quarter million men in a line for three weeks, with no facilities for the disposal of human waste, you are going to confront a disgusting problem. We were fighting and sleeping in one vast cesspool."[50] Plump, writhing white maggots lived among them in the muck. When a man fell and then stood again, he found maggots squirming on his dungarees and cartridge belt, or tumbling out of his pockets. A fellow marine would scrape them off with the edge of a knife. For Gene Sledge, the maggots were very nearly the last straw: "Having to wallow in war's putrefaction was almost more than the toughest of us could bear."[51] Seven months earlier, on Peleliu, he had been certain that he and his fellow marines were suffering through the worst combat conditions imaginable. But now, "I existed from moment to moment, sometimes thinking death would have been preferable. We were in the depths of the abyss, the ultimate horror of war. During the fighting around the Urmurbrogal Pocket on Peleliu, I had been depressed by the wastage of human lives. But in the mud and driving rain before Shuri, we were surrounded by maggots and decay. Men struggled and fought and bled in an environment so degrading I believed we had been flung into hell's own cesspool."[52]

On the western end of the line, the 6th Marine Division battered away at the terrain feature they called "Sugarloaf Hill," which the Japanese called "Amekudai." A ridge of coral rock and volcanic ash, about 300 yards long and 100 feet high, was flanked by two other hills, Half Moon and Horseshoe, in an arrowhead configuration. Sheer escarpments had been excavated and honeycombed with tunnels and firing apertures. The arrangement of the terrain ensured that the Japanese always had multiple, overlapping fields of fire on all approaches. Both sides understood that this part of the line was critical; if the Americans broke through, they would have a clear lane to flank and envelop Shuri Castle. The Japanese commanders, with a direct line of sight to the battle from their observation posts at Shuri, responded to each new U.S. thrust by pouring reinforcements into the area. The Americans pulverized Sugarloaf with barrages of artillery, rockets, napalm, smoke grenades, and naval gunfire. For ten consecutive days, the 6th Marine Division attacked the complex with tanks and infantry. Again and again, the marines gained a tenuous foothold atop Sugarloaf, only to be forced to withdraw by fierce Japanese artillery barrages and infantry charges. Finally, on May 26, the Americans seized the position and held it, beating back repeated furious counterattacks.

Colonel Yahara believed that if the Japanese artillerists had enjoyed greater reserves of ammunition, they might have held the marines off indefinitely. As it was, the defenders "were unyielding and fought so intrepidly [that] the battle at Amekudai lasted much longer than expected. Even after Amekudai was captured by the enemy, it was so unbelievable to our troops that they continued to fight."[53]

The stalemate began to give way as the eastern and western ends of the Japanese lines buckled, and soldiers and marines advanced down the coasts. This double envelopment threatened to isolate the main defensive strongholds at the center of the Japanese lines. Having turned the Japanese flank at Sugarloaf, the marines cleared the southern coastal road across the Asato River and entered the desolated city of Naha. From that position, the marines now had an open route to the Kokuba Hills, which would lead into the Shuri defensive system. To the east, 96th Division seized the eastern shoulder of Conical Hill, which rose 476 feet above the coastal plain around Yonabaru, and Japanese positions overlooking Nakagusuku Bay became untenable. Tactical withdrawals followed, and the Japanese forces fell back by about half a mile to a new line immediately north of Shuri.

General Ushijima was now persuaded that his forces could no longer hold the coast-to-coast line that they had held for a month. The flanks, east and west, were caving in under the enemy's relentless onslaught. The entire Japanese line had been pushed back by about half a mile, and Ushijima had no more infantry reserves to replace his losses. His forces still held the concentric fortifications around Shuri, but the Americans were poised to launch a crushing pincer attack from two directions. As Colonel Yahara later wrote, "Overall, the situation appeared stable, but in reality, after May 28, it was comparable to a patient in the final stage of tuberculosis. He may look normal, but his chest cavities are hollow."[54]

During the heavy rains of late May, the Thirty-Second Army command bunker had become even more fetid and miserable. The flooding was so bad that "brooks flowed in the tunnels," and all hands were put to work raising the beds and furniture.[55] American artillery shells had seemingly pinpointed the mouth of their cave, and fell thickly around the entrance at all hours, so that leaving the bunker for any reason was a risky proposition. In urgent radio cables to Tokyo, General Ushijima notified the Imperial Headquarters that his position was about to be overrun. He asked for another round of kamikaze attacks on the fleet offshore, hoping against evidence that the U.S. ground forces could be starved of ammunition and supplies. IGHQ told Ushijima to hold the line as long as possible, and prolong the battle in order to buy time for the homeland to prepare its defenses.

Colonel Yahara, who had been right in the past, proposed a tactical withdrawal to the Kiyan Peninsula, at the southern point of Okinawa, where subterranean positions had already been prepared in high rocky terrain that would stop the American tanks. The move south would not alter the result of the Battle for Okinawa—the Thirty-Second Army was going to be destroyed, and all the Japanese commanders knew it—but it might extend the duration of the fight and claim a higher toll of dead and wounded Americans. The idea was opposed by several of the division and brigade commanders. The Sixty-Second Division chief of staff noted that thousands of men had died defending Shuri, and their comrades wanted to die on the same ground. There were thousands of wounded men in the tunnels, who would have to be left behind. The civilian governor of Okinawa was concerned about the fate of civilians in the Shuri area; many would try to follow the army south, and they would be caught in the crossfire, or fall into the enemy's hands.

After hearing the contending arguments, Ushijima decided in favor of the southern retreat. "Some of our fighting strength is left," he said, "and we are getting strong support from the islanders. With these we will fight to the southernmost hill, to the last square inch of land, and to the last man."[56]

The Japanese commanders employed deception and guile to conceal their withdrawal. Designated frontline units staged "demonstration" attacks on the American lines, while the bulk of the army left their positions at night and moved south, either in vehicles or on foot. The Japanese Sixty-Second Division withdrew on the night of May 24–25, while rearguard units staged fierce attacks on the U.S. 77th Infantry Division. The Japanese Twenty-Fourth Division pulled back three nights later, and the Forty-Fourth Independent Mixed Brigade on May 31. Each retreating soldier carried as much ammunition and provisions as he could manage, about 130 pounds per man. Most of the wounded were left behind; many were killed by receiving a drink of milk laced with potassium cyanide.

The top commanders of the Thirty-Second Army pulled out of their Shuri bunker on May 27, leaving the command cave in cohorts. General Ushijima struck out alone, on foot, walking down a rocky trail in darkness. Staff officers, attempting to keep up with him, stumbled and fell, bruising themselves badly. The route was strewn with dead Japanese soldiers and Okinawan civilians, many of whom had been putrefying in the open air for a long time. The officers climbed into the back of a truck and rode along on the darkened roads, without headlights, passing long columns of retreating Japanese troops and immense crowds of civilian refugees.

The Americans did not recognize what was happening until the bulk of Japanese forces had escaped to new defensive positions in the Kiyan

Peninsula. Inclement weather had worked to the benefit of the Japanese, as rain, mists, and overcast concealed their movements even in daylight. Through gaps in the clouds, U.S. pilots occasionally caught glimpses of large numbers of Japanese streaming south, but they assumed they were all civilians. For American commanders who had battered against the seemingly impregnable lines around Shuri Castle, it seemed inconceivable that the Japanese army would voluntarily yield this prized fortress. Even the in-house intelligence sections of the army corps and division commands judged that the Japanese were planning to make their final stand on those heights.

The American pincer now closed on the weakened Shuri complex. The fight was long and bitter, even against the depleted Japanese rearguard forces left behind to cover the Thirty-Second Army's withdrawal. Bucketing rains cut visibility to 10 feet. Vehicles could not climb the washed-out roads to the top of the ridge, making resupply difficult. Low-flying U.S. planes air-dropped provisions and ammunition into zones marked by flares and smoke pots. Finally, on May 29, advance units of the 1st Marine Division entered Shuri Castle—or the ruins of the castle's ancient stone masonry—while elements of the 77th Division took the adjoining town. The sacrificial Japanese rearguard offered ferocious resistance right up to the end, and perished to the last man.

ADMIRAL HALSEY RETURNED to take command of the fleet, relieving Spruance, at midnight on May 27. The next day, McCain relieved Mitscher in command of the fast carrier striking force. The Fifth Fleet reverted to its designation as the Third Fleet; Task Force 58 was again Task Force 38. The *New Jersey* was being refitted, so Halsey and his Dirty Tricksters now rode in her sister, the battleship *Missouri*.

The command turnover had occurred a month earlier than planned. The reason, never publicized, was that Nimitz and King wanted their "first team" of Spruance, Mitscher, and Turner in command during the OLYMPIC landings in Kyushu the following November. To maintain the five-month rotating command cycle, it was necessary to bring Halsey and McCain back early.[57]

For the moment, Task Force 38 continued to cover the amphibious fleet off Okinawa, and its planes flew close air support missions over the island. The fighting ashore was well in hand, and kamikaze attacks were smaller and less frequent, but the threat remained. The carrier groups were weary after more than two months of intense daily operations. One group, Admiral Ted Sherman's 38.3, was sent down to Leyte Gulf for a period of rest and reprovisioning. Arthur Radford's Task Group 38.4 was sent north to launch another round of fighter sweeps against airbases on Kyushu. Jocko Clark's Group 38.1 (in which Halsey's new flagship operated in the inner screen) stuck close to Okinawa and provided combat air patrol over the island.

The first of June brought the first indications of a typhoon brewing in the south, near the Palaus. Weather Central at Guam tracked the north-bound "tropical disturbance," collecting and aggregating weather reports by ships, submarines, and long-range patrol planes. The reports were scattered and often contradictory, offering a confused picture. But on June 4, third anniversary of the Battle of Midway, there were worrisome reports of a full-scale typhoon heading directly for the waters off eastern Okinawa, the Third Fleet's current location.

As usual, the storm's track could not be predicted with perfect accuracy, but no one had forgotten the previous December's disaster. Aircraft were recalled to the carriers and struck down in the hangar decks, where they were secured with double and triple lashings. The destroyers were hastily refueled. After conferring with his staff and weather forecasters, Halsey chose to put his two task groups on an east-southeast course of 110 degrees, estimating that it would put them well clear of the storm, with a margin of "sea room" away from Okinawa. But subsequent reports suggested that the storm had taken a more northerly course, and was traveling faster than previously supposed. Barometric pressure was sinking and the skies were turning ugly. Halsey ordered a course change to the northwest. His idea was to cross ahead of the storm, skirting across the projected track to its more docile western semicircle. But the typhoon seemed to have a malevolent purpose of its own, as if it were deliberately chasing the Third Fleet. Those who had been with the fleet six months earlier felt a sinister sensation of déjà vu.

Clark's Task Group 38.1 got the worst of it. In the early hours of June 5, radar scopes in his flagship *Hornet* detected a tight circular "eye" of the storm, the hallmark of a powerful typhoon, bearing directly down on them.[58] The *Hornet* was bucking like a destroyer in the steep seas. The smaller ships were in danger of being swamped. At 4:20 a.m., Clark contacted McCain on the short-range voice radio and asked permission to turn south, so that his ships could run before the storm. McCain bucked the question up to Halsey, and the reply was delayed by twenty minutes. During the interval, Clark ordered all ships to heave-to and steer into the waves as best they could. At 4:40 a.m., when McCain's affirmative response was received on the flag bridge of the *Hornet*, it was too late to act. Clark's ships were pinned down in the shrieking maelstrom.

As the first purple glow of dawn appeared on the eastern horizon, a "mountain of water" broke over the bow of the *Hornet*. "Gad!" said Roy L. Johnson, the ship's executive officer, "it must have been ten times as high as a house, and the impact of all of that, when it came down on the flight deck, carried away everything. The edges of the flight deck were bent down; all the antennae were gone; all the catwalks and some airplanes were over the side. We were in bad shape."[59]

As conditions gradually abated, it became clear that the entire task group had suffered a cruel beating. No ships were lost, but nearly all reported significant damage, including all four carriers in Group 38.1. The forward corners of the flight decks of the *Hornet* and the *Bennington* had folded over, like place markers in a book. About 100 feet of the bow of the heavy cruiser *Pittsburgh* had been torn completely off the ship. The *Pittsburgh*'s sister *Baltimore*—the ship that had carried FDR to Hawaii the previous year—was also heavily battered, although she stayed together and was later repaired in drydock. Total aircraft losses were 233 swept overboard, 36 damaged beyond repair and jettisoned, and 23 more badly damaged. Six men had been lost at sea; four others were severely injured.

As the storm blew over, Halsey ordered another round of strikes on Kyushu. The *Hornet* was in no shape to launch planes, but Clark was determined to try. An F4U Corsair trying a deck run on the shortened flight deck nosed straight down into the sea and sank with its pilot. The folded-over flight deck created too much air turbulence. The crew broke out blowtorches and attempted to cut away as much of the damaged portion on the deck as possible, but after working through the rest of the day and night, the blowtorch teams had only cut away a small portion of the damaged steel. At Clark's prodding—even though he was not the captain of the ship—the *Hornet* managed to launch planes off the stern. This remarkable carnival trick had never been attempted on an *Essex*-class aircraft carrier. The engines were reversed and "sternway" was made into the wind. The ship's engineer fretted over excessive strain on the engines. But for two days, the *Hornet* conducted flight operations in this manner, launching planes directly over the fantail and recovering them over the damaged bow.

On June 10, General Kenney's Fifth Air Force was ready to assume full responsibility for the air defenses at Okinawa, and the Third Fleet was released to pull back to Leyte Gulf for a badly needed period of repairs, reprovisioning, and rest. The fleet was exhausted, and the storm-mauling only exacerbated the situation. After his flagship *Yorktown* dropped anchor in San Pedro Bay, Admiral Radford fell into his bunk and slept almost twenty-four hours straight.[60] Admiral Sherman's Task Group 38.3 had been at sea for seventy-nine days, engaging in combat during fifty-two of those days—a navy record.[61]

Having blundered into a second typhoon in six months, Halsey knew that his command was hanging by a thread. He lost no time in laying the groundwork for his defense. Weather reporting, he told Nimitz, had been abysmal. Reports of the storm's position and track had literally been all over the map: "The early estimates of the storm's location covered an area of 34,000 square miles. The reports were also greatly delayed."[62] A court of inquiry was convened in the wardroom of the *New Mexico*. It was chaired by Admiral John Hoover, the same gimlet-eyed seaman who had chaired the court that had blamed Halsey for the December typhoon. Task group commanders Clark and Radford gave harshly critical testimony. Radford, a future chairman of the JCS, judged that "Admiral Halsey was completely responsible and, in this instance, culpably negligent." He suggested that both Halsey and McCain, having just returned to the fleet after a long stateside leave, were too proud to take advice from their more experienced subordinates. Acknowledging the poor state of weather reporting, Radford said that basic seamanship should have guided the two admirals to better decisions: "Why [Halsey] tried so hard to get all three task groups together remains a mystery to me; the individual groups could have done much better on their own. My group would have escaped the storm by remaining where we were."[63]

The court of inquiry recommended that "serious consideration" be given to relieving both Halsey and McCain of their commands, and reassigning them to other duties. The ultimate decision was left to higher-ups. King evidently did give serious consideration to relieving both admirals, and Secretary Forrestal said he would back the decision. In the end, however, it was decided to keep Halsey on, while recalling McCain to Washington to serve as deputy chief of the Veterans Administration. (The war ended before McCain was relieved, and the admiral died of a heart attack before he could assume his new post.)

In this case, it is likely that Halsey's status as a popular hero had saved his command. Throughout that summer of 1945, his image and his smash-mouth oratory were featured prominently in the American press. The very same week that the court of inquiry rendered its verdict, Halsey's leering face appeared on the cover of *Time* magazine, under his trademark slogan: "Kill Japs, Kill Japs, and Then Kill More Japs."[64]

As THE TENTH ARMY PURSUED the retreating Japanese down the island, its progress was hindered by continuing rain and muddy roads. Even tanks and tracked vehicles were mired in the brown quagmires, and many had to be abandoned. The supply problem was partly solved by landing supplies on the coasts, and partly by air drops. Samuel Hynes flew dozens of supply runs over "what seemed the ruins of an ancient, peaceful world—tiny fields and old stone walls, deep, narrow lanes lined with gnarled old trees, a heap of stones where a house had been, all very close under our wings, everything clearly visible, even in the rain."[65]

The roads leading south were an open-air morgue, strewn with dead Japanese and Okinawans. American infantrymen were put on clearance details, dragging the corpses off the roads, to clear a way for the trucks and tanks. Thomas McKinney of the 6th Marine Division recalled finding the bodies of wounded Japanese soldiers who had tried to crawl south after their retreating army. "We found, I don't know, hundreds of them with arms and legs off, laying out there, and it was obvious that they had tried to crawl. The stumps of their legs and all were still bandaged but covered with mud and everything else. They crawled through it. They had tried it. They were bound and determined to go. They died along the way."[66]

The Thirty-Second Army would make its last stand on a line bisecting the Kiyan Peninsula, a tongue of rugged tableland and coral escarpments at the southernmost point of Okinawa. The main line of defense ran through the Yuza-Dake and Yaeju-Dake ridge systems. This final corner of contested territory on Okinawa took in about eleven square miles.

The retreat from Shuri had been deftly executed. By the time the Americans had discovered the move, it was too late to exploit the opportunity to destroy the retreating columns while they were out in the open. Nevertheless, the Thirty-Second Army was badly weakened, and its retreat to Kiyan was only going to postpone defeat by another two or three weeks, if that. On June 4, after collecting reports from division and regimental commanders, the headquarters staff concluded that the army's remaining troop strength was approximately 30,000, down from 40,000 two weeks earlier. Some of the most elite veteran units had been lost in rearguard actions on the Shuri line. The largest remaining organized force was the Japanese Twenty-Fourth Division, with 12,000 troops in its ranks. But fighting efficiency was greatly reduced by the loss of heavy weaponry, ammunition, and other supplies.

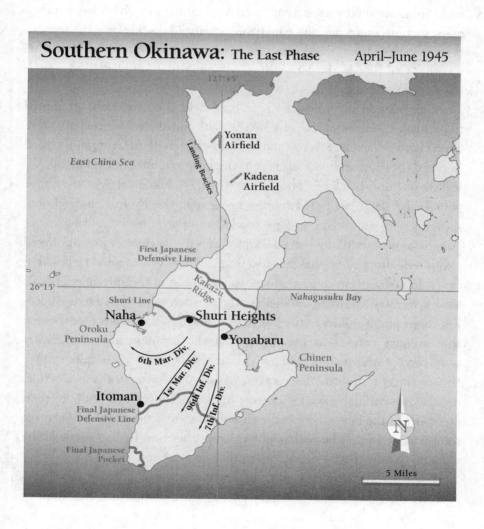

Southern Okinawa: The Last Phase   April–June 1945

On June 6, four American divisions (two army, two marine) launched probing attacks along the principal strong points on the Yaeju-Dake and Yuza-Dake escarpments. Field artillery blasted away coral rock outcroppings to clear lanes for the tanks of the 713th Armored Flamethrower Battalion, which threw jets of fire into the mouths of the natural limestone caves in the area. The Americans made rapid progress on the eastern part of the line, where the terrain was a bit more friendly, capturing a terrain feature called "Hill 95" on the night of June 11. Japanese resistance was scattered, and largely disorganized, but a lot of Americans would give their lives in this last stage of the fight for Okinawa. As the army and marines closed the ring around the enemy's shrinking perimeter, small Japanese squads launched night infiltration attacks and *banzai* charges. Snipers on the ridges claimed many victims, and when the Americans advanced quickly over the terrain, their casualties from friendly mortar and artillery fire increased. Worst hit was the "Old Breed," the 1st Marine Division, which suffered 1,150 casualties in the week from June 11 to June 18.

More than on any previous Pacific battlefield, the Americans attempted to persuade their enemies to give up the fight. Surrender inducements were aimed both at Japanese troops and at Okinawan civilians. Aircraft dropped hundreds of thousands of leaflets into the Japanese lines, including 30,000 leaflets on June 12 alone. The Tenth Army Psychological Warfare Office published a daily Japanese-language newspaper, the *Ryukyu Shuho*. Loudspeakers were mounted on jeeps, trucks, and patrol boats, and Japanese-American *nisei* translators issued scripted appeals. Portable battery-powered radios were dropped by parachute, so that U.S. broadcasts could be heard in caves. In comparison to past efforts, the leaflets and the surrender appeals were better written, more intelligible, and more closely tailored to the peculiar cultural sensitivities of the Japanese. All emphasized a few core themes: that military defeat was inevitable, that the Japanese militarist leaders were corrupt and incompetent, and that the Japanese must rally to save their country from total destruction.[67] The word "surrender" was carefully avoided; instead, Japanese forces were invited to "come over and join their comrades as the best way out of their hopeless predicament." The Japanese soldier was told that he had fought valiantly, but now he had "done all he can and that he will be needed when the war is over."[68]

These appeals were more effective than at any prior phase of the Pacific War. In the last stages of the fight on the Kiyan Peninsula, thousands of

Japanese soldiers emerged from the caves with their hands held above their heads. Most remarkably—and scandalously, in the traditional Japanese view—entire units surrendered while under the organized command of their own officers. The process tended to snowball—as more Japanese crossed into the American lines, more were willing to follow their example. Many brave American *nisei*—including men whose parents, siblings, wives, and children had been interned in camps at home—volunteered to descend alone into caves, where they engaged enemy soldiers in face-to-face negotiations. Some captured Japanese were even willing to assist in inducing their former comrades to surrender, by returning to the caves or bunkers where they knew them to be hiding. In all, some 11,000 prisoners of war were taken on Okinawa, including more than 7,000 regular Japanese soldiers. The prisoner of war enclosures grew steadily to accommodate this influx. An American lieutenant marveled that "one needed a jeep to go from one end of a POW stockade to another."[69]

Tens of thousands of Okinawan civilians had retreated south with the Japanese army, terrified by an enemy they had been taught to regard as demonic. There were perhaps 100,000 civilians in the southern part of the island, near the zone of combat—more than three civilians for each Japanese soldier on the battlefield. Never before, except perhaps in the battle for Manila, had a major Pacific War battlefield been so crowded with civilians. The Japanese army often evicted civilians from the caves, turning them out into the open to be exposed to artillery barrages. They took their food; they forced Okinawan mothers with crying infants to leave the caves, or to kill their own children, or they killed the infants themselves. Men, women, and children died in artillery strikes, naval bombardments, aerial bombing, the crossfire of machine guns, flamethrowers, and other infantry field weapons. By prior order of the Japanese army, any civilian caught speaking a language other than Japanese could be executed as a spy. But many older Okinawans did not know Japanese, and paid the price for it. An Okinawan remarked that the Japanese army treated the civilians as sacrificial pawns—"like go pieces, in a game of go."[70]

As the U.S. forces pressed south, they encountered long columns of refugees coming the other way—pathetic cavalcades of desperate, starving, filthy people, women with children strapped to their backs, bundles of clothing or other possessions on their shoulders. Many chewed stalks of sugarcane. Some were wounded, crawling on their hands and knees. Kikuko

Miyagi, a sixteen-year-old Okinawan student, recalled the awful scenes: "Tens of thousands of people moving like ants. Civilians. Grandfathers, grandmothers, mothers with children on their backs, scurrying along, covered in mud. When children were injured, they were left along the roadside. Just thrown away. Those children could tell we were students. They'd call out, '*Nei, nei!*' and try to cling to us. That's Okinawan dialect for 'Older Sister!' It was so pitiable. I still hear those cries today."[71]

Many Okinawan civilians were shot as they approached American military positions. American sentries had orders to shoot them all, especially at night, when it was difficult to distinguish military personnel from civilians. Flares and starshells lit up the crowds coming north, toward the American lines. In a few cases, Japanese army forces had even pushed the Okinawan civilians in front of them, forcing them to advance as a kind of human shield. In order to prevent needless deaths, leaflets were distributed widely over the islands, with drawings and notices in simple Japanese and Okinawan: "Keep away from aircraft! Keep away from the roads! Don't go near ammunition dumps! Keep away from military positions! Even if, by accident, you overlook any of the warnings set forth above, you may meet with a sad fate."[72] Norris Buchter, with the 6th Marine Division, recalled that many Japanese soldiers dressed like civilians, some even trying to disguise themselves as women, to slip through the lines by hiding among the civilian population. "Unfortunately, then, we had to shoot them. That's when a lot of the poor Okinawans got killed. They were victims of war. We felt bad about having to do it, but we were protecting our own life."[73] John Garcia, a private in the 7th Infantry Division, shot a dark figure as it approached across a field at night. At dawn, he went forward and found "a woman there and a baby tied to her back. The bullet had gone through her and out the baby's back. That still bothers me, that hounds me. I still feel I committed murder. You see a figure in the dark, it's stooped over. You don't know if it's a soldier or a civilian."[74] But Charles Miller, with the 6th Marine Division, said that many of his fellow marines shot Okinawan civilians more or less indiscriminately. "Guys would say, 'There goes a slant-eyed chink, pow, pow. . . . There goes a slant-eyed pig, pow, pow.' We were not the most charming people in the world."[75]

At the same time, many American marines and soldiers took significant personal risks to save civilians. Lieutenant Lewis Thomas, an officer in the navy medical corps, was posted near the town of Nago, in northern Okinawa. The medical facility was guarded by a company of marines. A trip-wire had been set up across the road. One dark night, flares revealed a large crowd of civilians coming up the road. A marine sentry radioed: "Hold your fire. Civilians." Then he climbed over his bank of sandbags and ran forward, into the darkness. A few minutes later he returned, escorting a group of old men, women, and children. "I don't suppose anyone recorded this act, but if we had had the authority, we would have voted him a gold medal," recalled Lieutenant Thomas. "As it was, we clapped our hands and cheered and told him he was a great Marine."[76]

The final Thirty-Second Army command cave was so crowded with soldiers and civilian refugees that not even General Ushijima had a private space to himself. The staff officers were obliged to sleep in shifts in the few bunks that remained, or they stretched out on the ground in dirty passageways. The interior cavities of the limestone caves were fetid and damp. Water dripped from stalactites. The soldiers in the caves included hundreds of stragglers who had become detached from their units. Many were catatonic, staring blankly, wandering aimlessly through the caves, speaking only in monosyllables. U.S. aircraft dropped napalm bombs along the ridge overhead, and personnel in the upper portions of the cave system succumbed to fire or smoke inhalation. Patrol boats off the coast continued to fire constantly into the mouths of the caves, until they started coming down, slab by slab. One Japanese recalled, "When the big bombs and shells exploded on the Mabuni cliff, our entire cave shook as in a great earthquake."[77]

General Ushijima spent his last days alone, at a small desk, reading books and writing letters of commendation by candlelight. He sometimes fanned himself with a handheld paper fan. General Cho, in a cave next door, smoked a large pipe and read books. On Monday, June 18, General Ushijima sent a last message to all commands. He thanked his "beloved soldiers" for having done their duty. From that point on, all were to obey their local commanding officer's orders. General Cho added a postscript instructing, "Do not suffer the shame of being taken prisoner. You will live for eternity."[78] Remaining stragglers were told to attempt to exfiltrate the American lines and to get to the northern part of the island, where small detachments of the Japanese army remained in the hills, and to wage a guerilla war.

The commanders could hear the surrender appeals, transmitted through loudspeakers on patrol boats offshore, urging the Okinawan civilians to surrender. Some of the die-hard officers dismissed these appeals, saying,

"Americans always talk nonsense."[79] But many civilians and even servicemen could be seen swimming out to the boats off the coast. On June 18,
the staff received a surrender appeal from General Buckner, addressed
directly to General Ushijima: "The forces under your command have fought
bravely and well, and your infantry tactics have merited the respect of your
opponents. . . . Like myself, you are an infantry general long schooled and
practiced in infantry warfare. . . . I believe, therefore, that you understand
as clearly as I, that the destruction of all Japanese resistance on the island
is merely a matter of days."[80] The message evoked hearty laughter. Ushijima
remarked wryly: "The enemy has made me an expert on infantry warfare."[81]

Three days later, Ushijima radioed a farewell message to Tokyo. Then he
invited his staff to a final banquet. The last remaining bottles of sake and
liquor were opened, and the men drank a round of valedictory toasts. Then
Ushijima and Cho left the cave and sat on a narrow ledge overlooking the
East China Sea. Ushijima was dressed in a full-dress uniform, General Cho
in a white kimono. At 4:10 a.m. on June 22, they plunged daggers into their
midsections, and were immediately beheaded by subordinate officers wielding samurai swords.

According to Masahide Ota, the Americans subsequently found the
grave of General Ushijima. Ota found an American knife struck into the
grave marker, and read rude messages scrawled in English.[82]

Some 15,000 Japanese troops remained in the caves along the southern
coast, and it would take some time to root them all out. Small unit fighting would continue through July, but organized resistance was essentially
finished, and there was no longer a "front line" on Okinawa. Caves were
systematically scoured with flamethrowers and sealed off with demolitions;
thousands of Japanese troops and civilians were entombed. During the last
eight days of the battle, after the collapse of organized resistance, an estimated 8,975 Japanese soldiers were killed, and thousands of Japanese prisoners were taken. Many others took their own lives.

Kikuko Miyagi, the sixteen-year-old student, hid in a cave for more than
two weeks. On June 17, it was blown up, probably by an American hand
grenade. Kikuko was uninjured, but many of her fellow students were mortally wounded:

I smelled blood. I thought instantly, "They've just been hit!" We
lived in darkness and sensed everything by smell. From below I heard

my classmates' voices, "I don't have a leg!" "My hand's gone!" At my teacher's urging, I descended into a sea of blood. Nurses, soldiers, students killed instantly or severely injured, among them a friend of mine, Katsuko-san, with a wound in her thigh. "Quick, Teacher, quick," she was crying. "It hurts!" I was struck dumb. There was no medicine left, and near me a senior student was desperately trying to push her intestines back into her stomach. "I won't make it," she whispered, "so please take care of other people first." Then she stopped breathing.[83]

Kikuko and a few other uninjured girls managed to escape the cave. They climbed down a cliff to a rocky beach. They were badly dehydrated, their hair crawling with lice, their fingernails overgrown, their bodies thick with fleas, and their skin covered with filth. They were emaciated to the point of starvation, and their skin itched constantly. She and the other girls promised one another: "If I'm unable to move, or you're disabled, I'll give you cyanide." They kept one hand grenade each, "like a talisman."[84]

On the beaches, they found a crowd numbering in the tens of thousands, including Japanese soldiers and Okinawan civilians. American patrol boats were just offshore, and Japanese-American speakers were issuing surrender appeals through loudspeakers: "Those who can swim, swim out! We'll save you. Those who can't swim, walk towards Minatogawa! Walk by day. Don't travel by night. We have food! We will rescue you!"

But the girls did not trust the voices. "From the time we'd been children, we'd only been educated to hate them," said Kikuko. "They would strip the girls naked and do with them whatever they wanted, then run over them with tanks. We really believed that. . . . We didn't answer that voice, but continued our flight. We were simply too terrified of being stripped naked. That's what a girl fears most, isn't it?"[85] She was shocked to see a Japanese soldier raise his hands and begin wading out into the sea. Another Japanese soldier shot him in the back.

Four days later, she was captured. She had lost consciousness, and awoke in a daze to find an American soldier poking her with a gun and gesturing for her to stand. She assumed she was about to be killed or assaulted, when to her surprise she saw other civilians being treated by American combat medics. Their wounds were being bandaged and they were being given saline injections. "Until that moment I could think of the Americans only as devils and demons. I was simply frozen. I couldn't believe what I saw."[86]

As THEY RETURNED TO THEIR BIVOUAC areas and rest camps around Hagushi
Bay, combat-weary American infantrymen scarcely recognized Okinawa.
The earthmoving, engineering, and construction teams had reshaped the
landscape. The 640-square-mile island was to serve as the primary staging
base for the largest amphibious operation in history—the prospective invasion of Kyushu (Operation OLYMPIC), scheduled for November 1, 1945. B-24s,
B-17s, and army fighters of the Eighth Air Force were already arriving from
pacified Europe. At Yontan, near the invasion beach, a 7,000-foot airstrip
was in operation by June 17. The roadbuilders would build 1,400 miles of
new paved roads, including two four-lane highways running north-south
along the length of the island, and several more from coast to coast. To span
rivers and to replace destroyed bridges, the engineers used "bailey bridges"—
portable, prefabricated steel truss bridges that had been developed by the
British. The roads around the major airfields and supply complexes were
jammed with traffic of all kinds—trucks, jeeps, trailers, and horse-drawn
carts. Soldiers were directing traffic. Near Kadena airfield, the traffic was
so heavy that a traffic circle was established at a major intersection. Dozens
of bulldozers leveled entire hills and filled in ravines and streambeds. The
ports at Okinawa were expanded with jetties, wharves, and dredging barges.
By June, they were unloading more cargo per month than the port of New
York handled in a typical peacetime month. An official history of the navy's
base-building program offered a compilation of eyepopping statistics: "By
the close of 1945, naval facilities on Okinawa covered 20,000 acres, and
included 4,180 lineal feet of wharves, 712,000 square feet of general covered
storage, 11,778,000 square feet of open storage, 193,000 cubic feet of cold
storage, as well as storage for 8,820,000 gallons of aviation gasoline, 30,000
barrels of diesel oil, 50,000 barrels of fuel oil, 13,000 square feet for ammunition. Aviation repair shops covered 324,100 square feet and general repair
shops, 91,000 square feet. Hospital space amounted to 338,000 square feet,
and quarters 4,755,000 square feet."[87] A Seabee put it more succinctly: "Our
development of Okinawa was to be comparable to the total development of
Rhode Island from virgin forest land."[88]

The farther one traveled from the front lines, the more one found the
rancor of interservice rivalries—ranging from mild raillery to noxious accusations, shouting matches, and fistfights. Bored marines trained Okinawan
children to approach the army camps and declare: "General MacArthur

eats shit!" (The children had been taught that this meant: "Give me a cigarette.")[89] But the Seabees, uniquely, were liked and admired by all of their sister services. Sergeant John Vollinger and another marine went into a Seabee camp on Okinawa to see if they could scrounge up a bar of soap. While there, they were surprised to find a professional shoemaker. Vollinger showed the man his boot, which had a nail protruding from the heel. "He took a look at the heel and said 'Give me the other one.' With that he removed both heels and put on new ones. He then asked us if we had eaten yet, and when we assured him we would survive until we got back to the battery, he said, 'Come with me.' He took us to the C.P.O. mess hall and we had an unbelievable meal of fried oysters which some enterprising Seabees had gathered from the reef."[90]

No matter how one measured it, Okinawa had been a singularly harrowing battle. American casualties (including naval, air, and ground) were the highest for any amphibious fight in the Pacific—49,151, including 12,520 killed or missing and 36,361 wounded. The Tenth Army had 7,613 killed and about 31,000 wounded. Among the dead was General Buckner, killed by an artillery strike on June 18, the highest-ranking U.S. military officer lost to enemy fire in World War II. An additional 26,000 troops were cited as "nonbattle" casualties, a category that included those who fell ill as a result of diseases, but also those who were pulled off the line as a result of "combat neurosis" or "fatigue."[91] As one American military analyst has observed, "The Okinawa battle was unusual in that it exhibited the stasis and lethality of World War I fronts even though it employed the full range of mobile World War II weapons: tanks, aircraft, radios, and trucks."[92] The American tanks had vitiated some of the advantages conferred by the Japanese cave defenses. But no progress could be made against the toughest fortifications on the Shuri line except by the valor, initiative, and perseverance of individual infantry squads, who were willing to advance into heavy fire and engage their enemies at hand-to-hand range.

The navy had suffered its worst beating of the Pacific War, with 368 ships damaged and thirty-six sunk, including fifteen amphibious ships and twelve destroyers. The navy had lost 4,907 officers and sailors killed in action, most in kamikaze attacks. The number of naval personnel killed during the Okinawa campaign exceeded the figures for either the army or the marines— although the combined losses in the ground campaign were higher.

The Japanese army had been outnumbered by two to one on the ground, and had been heavily overmatched in the categories of artillery firepower, naval firepower, and airpower. But General Ushijima's forces had held out for nearly twelve weeks, inflicting heavy casualties on their enemies. Despite steady pressure from Tokyo and Formosa to launch tactically foolish counterattacks, the army had largely stuck to its original plan of a stubborn yardby-yard terrain defense. In the end, as intended, nearly the entire army was lost, amounting to nearly 90,000 combatant and service troops killed, and 11,000 captured.

Caught in the gears of the grinding battle, Okinawa's civilians had suffered almost unimaginably. They had been killed in the crossfire, killed by bombing and artillery, accidentally or deliberately; they had starved, or died of diseases. As on Saipan almost a year before, Japanese propaganda had warned that a fate worse than death awaited any civilian captured by American forces—and as on Saipan, many terrified civilians took their lives and those of their loved ones. Since many were entombed in caves, and their bodies never counted, the precise number of civilian casualties can only be estimated. According to the Okinawan prefectural government, 94,000 Okinawan civilians died during the battle; and of these, 59,939 perished in June 1945, after the Japanese army's retreat from Shuri.[93]

For the victors, possession of the island conferred tremendous strategic advantages. The island provided a staging area and springboard for the prospective invasion of Japan, less than 400 miles from the targeted invasion beaches in southern Kyushu. It provided airbases within easy range of Japan for American bombers and fighters, and protected anchorages for the fleet and amphibious forces. Admiral Spruance had foreseen all of these advantages a year earlier, when he had argued in favor of capturing Okinawa. For the Japanese, the loss of Okinawa only confirmed what their leaders already knew—that the war was lost, and that their enemy possessed the means and the will to invade and conquer their homeland.

Chapter Fifteen

IN THE EARLY WEEKS OF TRUMAN'S PRESIDENCY, A REMARK WAS OFTEN heard repeated in the White House press room: "Franklin D. Roosevelt was for the people. Harry S. Truman is of the people." Even on his feet, the spare midwesterner seemed smaller than his wheelchair-bound predecessor. He appeared awkward and self-conscious in his new role. When a band played "Hail to the Chief," Truman did not know the protocol, and could not decide what to do with his hands. Salute? Stand at attention with hands at his side? Shake hands with visitors? The first time it happened, he tried to do all three. A reporter assigned to write a "color story" about the new president told his editor: "This man's color lies in his utter lack of color. He's Mr. Average. You see him on your bus or streetcar. He sits next to you at the drugstore soda fountain. There must be millions like him."[1]

The morning after Truman was sworn in, he arrived early at the White House. He had expected a morning briefing with his senior military aides. But a message had evidently miscarried, for they had not received the word and were nowhere to be found. For more than an hour the new president waited, "somewhat impatiently," until a flustered secretary tracked down Admiral Leahy, the White House chief of staff, and Vice Admiral Wilson Brown, the senior White House naval aide. They collected their briefing papers and hurried to the Oval Office, where they found the new president seated behind FDR's mahogany desk, still covered with his predecessor's collection of sundry trinkets and gadgets.

The two admirals, standing to attention, began summarizing the latest issues before the Joint Chiefs of Staff. Truman interrupted: "For God's sake, sit down! You make me nervous! Come around here in the light where I can get a good look at you." Leahy and Brown pulled up chairs. Truman studied their faces, Brown recalled, "without the least trace of self-consciousness about the fact that we were also examining him."[2]

In the course of their discussion, and in a larger meeting with the Joint Chiefs at eleven o'clock, it became painfully clear that Truman was not up to speed. He had not been adequately briefed on the state of the war, either in Europe or the Pacific, and he knew little about the latest moves in the global geostrategic chess match that was being played against the Soviet Union. The new president possessed a commendable work ethic, and he read top-secret reports and memoranda until his eyes smarted from the strain. In his diary, he wrote of long "hectic days" in the "Great White Jail," his nickname for the White House.[3] At times he seemed defensive about the gaps in his knowledge, even in private meetings with his inner circle of advisers and military chiefs. Some noted Truman's reluctance to ask questions, for fear of appearing ignorant, even when he plainly needed more information. When a course of action was proposed, Truman often replied that he had already been thinking along the same lines, as if trying to avoid the impression that he was merely doing as he was told.

Historians have concluded that Truman grew into the role of commander in chief, and eventually proved more than equal to the job. But in the spring and summer of 1945, the growing pains were evident—and the decisions he must confront during those early weeks were among the most important of his presidency.

In his diary, Bill Leahy expressed concern about the "staggering burdens of war and peace that [Truman] must carry." Privately, according to Leahy's son, the admiral regarded his new boss as a "bush-leaguer." He had been accustomed to speaking his mind to Roosevelt, knowing that the late president was "captain of the team" and might accept or reject his advice according to his own judgment. But Truman did not yet possess the confidence or independence to buck his advisers. Truman was in their hands, Leahy told another aide, which meant that everyone who advised the president bore heavy responsibility, and must be absolutely sure they were right.[4]

In his diary and his subsequent memoir, Leahy betrayed no sense of responsibility or culpability for the new president's relative ignorance. One is struck by this lack of self-awareness in a Washington statesman otherwise respected for his wisdom and good judgment. Whatever he knew or did not know about the state of FDR's declining health, Leahy had been at the late president's elbow for most of the last year of his life. He certainly knew enough to anticipate that Truman might be thrust into the role of commander in chief at any moment. Leahy was the White House chief of staff and the chairman of the JCS. What steps did he take to ensure that the vice president was properly briefed? Who else had that duty, if not himself? No adequate explanation has ever been provided for this breakdown in the basic procedures of sound constitutional government.

Leahy had been personally close to FDR, he told Truman, and was "distressed" by his death. He was inclined to retire from the navy and from his position as White House chief of staff. But Truman needed him for the sake of continuity, if nothing else, and asked him to stay on the job to help him "pick up the strands of the business of the war." After Truman gave assurances that he would adhere to the same decision-making procedures used by FDR, Leahy agreed to remain on the job for at least a few more months.[5] It turned out that he served another four years, to the end of Truman's first term in office.

Even now, at this late stage of the campaign, basic questions of military strategy and foreign policy in the Pacific remained unresolved. Would an invasion of Japan be necessary, or would the intensifying blockade and bombing campaign be enough to force surrender? Should the Allies land on the coast of China? Did they still need or want Russia in the war? How strong was the "peace party" in the Japanese ruling circle, and could it be strengthened? Must the late FDR's doctrine of unconditional surrender be unbendingly applied? Did Hirohito wield the power and influence to put an end to the war—and if so, should the Allies signal that he could keep his throne? These were immensely complex questions, without obvious answers. The ordinary mechanisms of military planning were blended with high considerations of international politics. Defeating Japan was only the most immediate problem. Looming ahead was the creation of a new postwar order in Asia, with its implications for the territorial ambitions of Stalin, the red menace in China, and the status of former British, French, and Dutch colonies.

At a State-War-Navy meeting on May 1, Jim Forrestal told his two colleagues that it was time to "make a thorough study of our political objectives in the Far East." Given Stalin's recent backsliding on the political independence of Eastern Europe, they should be wary of Soviet ambitions in the Far East. Forrestal asked: "Do we desire a counterweight to that influence?

And should it be China or should it be Japan?" If the latter, the United States must have a plan to rebuild Japan's economic power and regional standing. In subsequent meetings, the cabinet considered the future status of Korea, Hong Kong, Indochina (Vietnam), and Manchuria. Entries in Forrestal's diary leave the impression that these questions were being confronted for the first time. At another State-War-Navy meeting on May 29, the three secretaries considered whether Truman should release a statement clarifying the meaning of unconditional surrender, and perhaps addressing the postwar status of Japan's imperial dynasty. The question was tabled by unanimous agreement, because "the time was not appropriate for [the president] to make such a pronouncement."[6]

Leading figures in the navy and the Army Air Forces roughly agreed on one point: that an invasion of Japan was unnecessary and should be avoided. They stressed the cumulative effect of the air-sea blockade, which promised to cut off virtually all remaining maritime traffic into Japan. Without this last dribble of imported oil, raw materials, and food, the Japanese economy would seize up and its people would starve. Concurrently, the destructive intensity of the aerial bombing campaign would surge to new heights. Hundreds of newly commissioned B-29 Superfortresses were flying into the theater from the United States, and thousands of bombers and fighters of the Eighth Air Force were redeploying from Europe. The Third Fleet was preparing a six-week rampage in enemy waters, which promised the largest carrier airstrikes in history against Japanese cities, seaports, and the road and rail network.

While these punishing blows took effect, some argued in favor of landing troops on the Asian mainland. Lieutenant General Albert C. Wedemeyer, U.S. Army commander in China, wrote that "establishment of a lodgment on the coast would of course electrify the Chinese and cause them to redouble their efforts to gain land contact and thus open communications."[7] Admirals Nimitz and Spruance advocated seizing the Chusan Islands group, southeast of Shanghai, and the nearby Ningpo peninsula, on the southern side of the Yangtze river estuary. Their objective was to establish a bridgehead into China, throw a lifeline to Chiang Kai-shek, and provide more time (said one of Nimitz's top planners) to "build more airfields and just bomb Japan to its knees."[8] This prospective "Operation LONG-TOM" won the provisional backing of the JCS, and was assigned a tentative launch date of August 1945.

MacArthur argued for a direct invasion of Japan at the earliest possible date. Pecking away at the coast of China, he said, would only waste time, lives, and treasure. The Japanese could not be defeated by blockade and bombing alone, he said—and he pointed to the example of their German allies, who had refused to surrender even after their cities had been reduced to rubble. "The strongest military element of Japan is the Army which must be defeated before our success is assured. This can only be done by the use of large ground forces. . . . Just as is the case with Germany, we must defeat Japan's Army and for that purpose our strategy must devise ways and means to bring our ground forces into contact with his at decisive points."[9] From his headquarters in Manila, MacArthur told Marshall that he could take Kyushu with forces already in the Pacific. If it became necessary to invade Honshu and capture Tokyo, he would require reinforcements from Europe and the United States.[10]

Operation DOWNFALL, as it was codenamed, aimed at conquering and pacifying Japan within eighteen months of the final defeat of Germany. An early version of the plan, developed by the JCS planning staff in Washington, was presented to FDR and Churchill in February 1945 at the Argonaut Conference on Malta. DOWNFALL consisted of two phases: an invasion of southern Kyushu in late 1945 (OLYMPIC), to be followed by an invasion of Honshu in the spring of 1946 (CORONET). Each of these great amphibious assaults, especially CORONET, would dwarf the previous year's invasion of Normandy. DOWNFALL would require the combined strength of all branches of the military services and all forces within both MacArthur's and Nimitz's theaters, with a supporting role by British and other Allied forces. The assault on Kyushu would be handled by the veteran Sixth Army under General Krueger, veteran of the Philippines campaign. His forces would include two reinforced army corps plus a third comprised of three marine divisions; they would land simultaneously at Miyazaki on the east coast, Ariake Bay to the south, and Kushikino on the west coast. The decisive second-phase CORONET would be aimed at the heavily populated and industrialized region of the Kanto Plain. It would be spearheaded by the Eighth Army under General Eichelberger, whose forces would land on beaches at the north end of Sagami Bay. The CORONET assault would involve no fewer than twenty-five divisions, with additional reinforcements to be brought into action as needed. If an overpowering pincer attack on Tokyo did not force a surrender, Allied forces would occupy the capital—and then fan out from that hub, attacking in every direction, wiping out organized resistance in one province after another, until the entire nation lay prostrate and subjugated.

The initial timetable, fixed by the JCS in late March 1945, envisioned an OLYMPIC landing on December 1, 1945, followed by a CORONET landing on March 1, 1946. On Nimitz's recommendation, considering the risks to the fleet posed by winter storms, the target date for OLYMPIC was moved forward to November 1, 1945.[11]

For the moment, the JCS left the perennially quarrelsome issue of command unity unresolved. Like all amphibious invasions, DOWNFALL would require sustained and intricate cooperation between the air, ground, and naval forces. But in the spring of 1945, the various internecine frictions and rivalries in the Pacific were growing worse, not better. Personal communi-

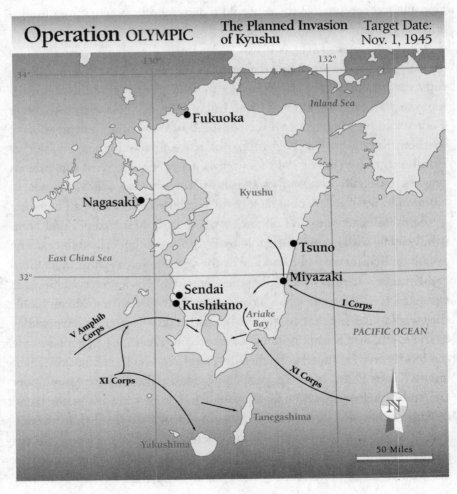

cations between the two theater commanders were frosty on a good day. In April, each man invited the other to visit his respective headquarters in Manila and Guam; both invitations were regretfully declined.[12] General Richardson, the senior army officer in Nimitz's theater, asked to travel to the Philippines to confer with MacArthur. Nimitz withheld permission, explaining that he wanted first to settle the ongoing negotiations.[13] A week later, Nimitz swallowed his pride and flew to Manila, where he was briefed on MacArthur's draft plan for DOWNFALL. The SWPA commander proposed to take command of Okinawa and other islands in the Ryukyus, and all land-based air forces in the Pacific. Nimitz balked. He flew back to Guam and put his staff to work on an independent navy plan for the amphibious phase of DOWNFALL, intending only to "consult" with MacArthur as necessary.[14]

Nimitz kept a framed photograph of MacArthur prominently displayed in his office in Guam. Visitors naturally assumed that it was a gesture of respect. When the Pacific fleet intelligence officer, Ed Layton, asked why the photograph was there, Nimitz smiled and replied, "Layton, I'll tell you. It's to remind me not to be a horse's ass."[15]

On April 13, General Sutherland, MacArthur's right hand, traveled to Guam and proposed a basic reorganization of the Pacific theater commands. The multiservice theater command, he said, had been shown to be an unworkable "shibboleth." MacArthur wanted command of all army forces throughout the Pacific, including garrisons on islands under Nimitz's command. Nimitz was welcome to take command of the Seventh Fleet, which had been under MacArthur's command for the past three years. Each service would assume administrative and logistical responsibility for its own forces, regardless of their locations. After the Okinawa operation, added Sutherland, "no army troops would be allowed to serve under an admiral."[16]

MacArthur's proposal amounted to an amicable divorce between the army and navy, but it would require complex administrative reassignments that would absorb staff attention during preparations for the largest operation of the war. The issue could only be decided by the Joint Chiefs of Staff. As Leahy later observed, "The problem of command in the Pacific was one of those situations that would not remain quiet despite successive 'settlements' made."[17] Judging that it was the only way to avert an open break between the army and navy, the chiefs issued the necessary directives. MacArthur took the new title "Commander in Chief, United States Army Forces in the Pacific," or COMAFPAC. In an "eyes only" message to MacArthur, General

George Marshall referred to "a great deal of most unfortunate rumor and talk in this country" about the army-navy feud, and asked the new COMAFPAC to "do your best to suppress such critical comments in subordinate echelons and I will do the same here with a heavy hand."[18]

No sooner was that issue resolved, however, than a new quarrel broke out over the command setup for DOWNFALL. Nimitz wanted to keep the model that his commanders had employed since Operation GALVANIC in November 1943, in which the invasion force was landed under naval command, and the ground general took control of his forces only upon setting up his headquarters ashore.[19] MacArthur not only rejected this proposal but refused to discuss it further, insisting that it be sent up to the JCS for a ruling. He took special umbrage at the suggestion that the fleet commander, during the passage to the invasion beaches and the initial landing phase, should control "all publicity, including army as well as navy elements."[20]

In Washington, the issue seemed headed toward stalemate. Marshall bluntly told King that they were "apparently in complete disagreement" about the command structure for DOWNFALL, and insisted that the JCS immediately choose "a commander with the primary responsibility for this campaign."[21] The threat was implicit. If the question could not be settled in the next JCS conference, it would have to be appealed to the president of the United States. As the two Pacific offensives converged on Japan, it was growing harder to sustain the case for two autonomous theater commanders. MacArthur was senior to Nimitz, and he was unrivaled in public popularity and stature. FDR had been a dyed-in-the-wool navy man, but Truman was a veteran of the army. Recognizing the weakness of his position, King retreated. The JCS issued a directive assigning "primary responsibility" for DOWNFALL to MacArthur, with the face-saving proviso that Nimitz or his designated fleet commander would have broad leeway, if not autonomy, during the amphibious phase of the operation.[22] Operation LONGTOM, the proposed landing on the China coast, was scrapped.

ADMIRAL BARON KANTARO SUZUKI, the prime minister who assumed power in April 1945, was a decrepit old man of seventy-seven years, hard of hearing and prone to nod off in meetings. Long retired from the navy, he had served for nearly a decade as a grand chamberlain of the imperial court, and was personally close to Hirohito. During the aborted army *coup d'état* of

February 1936, he had been shot and nearly killed. Privately, there seems to have been an understanding between Suzuki and the emperor that the new government must find a way to end the war, even if it meant acquiescing to harsh Allied demands. When the time was ripe, it was agreed, the emperor would be invited to issue a "sacred decree" to end the war.

At the same time, every figure in the leadership was cognizant of the threat of military uprisings, assassinations, and even civil war. If the government was overthrown, there would be no chance of opening talks with the Allies, and Japan would be completely destroyed. In a sense, the peace party's struggle to end the war was a conspiracy that had to be kept secret long enough for it to succeed. That Suzuki had narrowly survived an earlier assassination attempt only made the point more poignant. As Richard B. Frank writes in *Downfall*, his study of the end of the Pacific War, "The recognition of deadly threats from within is a key to understanding the motivations of some of the tiny handful of men controlling Japan's destiny."[23]

The reshuffled cabinet represented an attempt to integrate the various ruling factions, which were stalemated on fundamental questions of war and peace. Admiral Yonai, the furtive peacemaker, was retained as navy minister. General Korechika Anami was brought in as army minister, a move that placated Hideki Tojo and other hardliners of the army's ascendant "control" faction. Admiral Soemu Toyoda, the former commander in chief of the Combined Fleet, was made chief of the Naval General Staff, in which capacity he would join the hardline "fight on" caucus with Anami and army chief of staff Yoshijirō Umezu. Shigenori Togo, a former ambassador to the Soviet Union, was appointed foreign minister. Togo accepted the post only after receiving assurances that he would be free to pursue a plan to extract Japan from the war within one year.

The main decision-making body of the government remained the six-headed Supreme War Direction Council (SWDC), of which all the aforementioned were members. But a new and important change was now introduced: SWDC conferences would be limited to the six principals, without aides or lower-ranking officers in the room. The "Big Six" would confer behind closed doors, with the Marquis Koichi Kido (the Lord Keeper of the Privy Seal) and the emperor to make eight. And it was these eight men—influenced by perhaps ten or fifteen more—who would grapple toward a consensus in the closing weeks of the Pacific War.

Consensus was their elusive goal. Nothing could be done unless and until it was established. To describe their painstaking ritual of group decision-making, the Japanese used an expression derived from ancient gardening practices: *nemawashi*. What it meant, literally, was the process of extracting the roots of a mature tree from the soil before it was transplanted to a new location. Each individual root had to be dug out of the ground. It was a meticulous and delicate job that required time and care. If it was done badly, the tree might die. *Nemawashi* explained why a formidable statesman like Admiral Yonai, a former prime minister who had led a secret peace faction since joining the government in 1944, could not bring himself to speak plainly to his colleagues. Even after the defeat of Nazi Germany, when the inevitability of Japan's defeat was no longer in doubt, Yonai found that "it was difficult for me, or I think for anyone else, to broach the subject of war conclusion to anyone." He spoke to Suzuki only in an "abstract way," remarking that "I don't think we can continue with this much longer."[24]

The same institutional defects that had produced Japan's irrational decision to launch the war in 1941 now prevented a rational decision to end it. There was no real locus of responsibility or accountability in Tokyo. Power was dispersed in piecemeal fashion across various military staffs and bureaucracies. Army and navy leaders were figureheads who could be manipulated, deposed, replaced, or even killed by younger officers down the ranks. A sudden turn from war toward peace would require the compliance of many widely scattered interests and players, including officers in the middle ranks of both services. A stubborn lack of consensus, combined with the chronic threat of revolt, explained what the U.S. Strategic Bombing Survey called the "unusual time-lapse between the top civilian political decision to accept defeat and the final capitulation."[25]

At Yonai's suggestion, Suzuki had ordered the SWDC staff secretary to prepare a survey of Japan's overall economic and strategic position. The secret report, entitled "Survey of National Resources as of 1–10 June 1945," was presented on June 6. The conclusions were spelled out with culturally atypical directness—not only was defeat inevitable, but the national economy was headed toward a crackup, and the Japanese people were losing faith in their leaders. Statistics told the story of shipping losses, production declines, depletion of oil stocks, disruption in rail transportation, and a worsening food situation. With the pending loss of Okinawa, sea communications with the Asian mainland would be severed, and entire industries would have to suspend operations. Shortages of consumer goods would cause skyrocketing inflation, and the food situation would reach the point of crisis by the end of 1945, with the "appearance of starvation conditions in the isolated sections of the nation." As for the military situation, all remaining warplanes would be deployed as kamikazes, but critical shortages in aviation gasoline loomed. Even assuming that the suicide planes and submarines managed to sink one-fourth of the U.S. invasion fleet, "it would be difficult to defeat American plans through annihilation on the sea." The report detailed the overwhelming power of American fleets and air forces, and warned that "about one-half of the approximately 60 divisions assigned to the Western European Theater of Operations have been redeployed against Japan."[26]

Admiral Toyoda, one of three hardliners on the Big Six, later told American interrogators that the statistics proved that Japan's war-making potential was in precipitous decline. And yet, he said, no one in the room summoned the courage to propose that Japan accept defeat on Allied terms. "When a large number of people are present like that, it is difficult for any one member to say that we should so entreat," said Toyoda, "so the decision was that something must be done to continue this war."[27] The roots would have to be dug out of the ground, one by one. More time was needed. Caught between competing impulses to seek peace or go on fighting, the SWDC moved to do both. The council unanimously adopted a two-track "fundamental policy." The army and navy would mobilize forces for an all-out defense of the homeland. The foreign ministry would ask the Soviet Union to initiate and mediate peace negotiations with the Allies. On June 8, Hirohito gave this plan his official sanction, as he always did when his advisers were unanimous.

"Ketsu-go," the operational plan to repel an Allied invasion of the homeland, was circulated the same week the Suzuki government came to power. It involved a climactic, spasmodic effort to pour substantially all of the nation's remaining military and economic resources into countering an invasion. Ketsu called for a massive troop buildup, to be accomplished through the mobilization of new and reserve army divisions; the deployment of forces to the regions considered most likely as points of invasion; the construction of coastal fortifications behind the expected invasion beaches; and an unprecedentedly large kamikaze assault on the Allied fleet. The plan correctly anticipated that the invasion would occur before the end of the calendar year 1945. The Japanese were also right in assuming that the first landing would come in southern Kyushu, to be followed in the spring of 1946 by a larger invasion of the Kanto Plain and the Greater Tokyo region.

As recently as January 1945, there had been only eleven fully mobilized army divisions in Japan. In April and May, as U.S. forces overran Okinawa, the Imperial Japanese Army began transferring units from Korea and Manchuria, and mobilized new and reserve divisions at home. By July 1945, a two-stage mobilization had brought the total to thirty frontline fighting divisions, twenty-four coastal defense divisions, twenty-three independent mixed brigades, two armored divisions, seven tank brigades, and three infantry brigades.[28] At the same time, Japanese forces were transferred to Kyushu, where the next Allied thrust was expected. By the end of July there were fifteen divisions, seven independent mixed brigades, three independent tank brigades, and two coastal defense units on the island, with total troop strength surpassing 800,000. Due to shortages and declining munitions production, not all of these units were properly armed or equipped. Despite a prodigious attempt to stockpile ammunition in caves and bunkers impervious to bombing or bombardment, it was expected that many Japanese frontline units in Kyushu would run low on ammunition if the campaign lasted beyond a few weeks.

At the same time, Tokyo stepped up efforts to organize, arm, and train civilian militias. All men between the ages of fifteen and sixty, and all women between the ages of seventeen and forty, were drafted into these local fighting organizations, whose enlistment roles officially topped 25 million. Many were equipped with nothing better than spears or household weapons. Every citizen-fighter was exhorted to kill at least one barbarian invader before dying in turn. These preparations proceeded under the new national slogan: "The Glorious Death of the 100 Million."[29]

After early June 1945 the Japanese air forces largely abandoned their attempts to defend against American raids, husbanding their remaining planes for the final battle. In July, about 9,000 aircraft were in reserve throughout the home islands; virtually all, including trainer aircraft, would be deployed as kamikazes against the U.S. invasion fleet. The aircraft industry was assigned to turn out another 2,500 planes for this purpose by the end of September. Pilot training had been so curtailed that many of the prospective kamikaze flyers could do nothing but take off and perform basic aerial maneuvers. Given the depletion of avgas reserves, most would remain grounded until the day they took off to fly their last mission.

American bombing raids and fighter sweeps continued to target Japanese airfields, and great numbers of planes were destroyed on the ground. But there was only so much the Americans could do to counter the kamikaze threat. Some of the enemy "airplanes" they destroyed on the ground were actually mockups made of plywood, while the real machines were dispersed and well hidden. American bombs punched craters in airstrips, but the kamikazes only had to take off—they did not intend to return or to land at all—and therefore they could operate from primitive dirt airstrips that were quickly and cheaply repaired. In attacking an invasion fleet off Kyushu, the kamikazes would enjoy two tactical advantages that they had not possessed during the Okinawa campaign. First, it was a short flight; and second, the attackers would fly from various airfields around the island, which meant that they would approach the invasion fleet from different directions simultaneously. The Japanese navy was also pouring major efforts into producing suicide submarines and speedboats, as well as suicide gliders to be launched from mountain peaks. The plan aimed to destroy one-fourth of the U.S. invasion fleet. Even if that estimate was out of reach, as it almost certainly was, the kamikazes could realistically hope to draw more blood off Kyushu than they had off Okinawa.

Even as they poured troop reinforcements into Kyushu, the Japanese could not discount the possibility that the initial attack would come on Honshu near Tokyo—or even somewhere farther afield, such as northern Honshu or Shikoku. Plan Ketsu provided contingency plans for troop movements to meet the invaders wherever they might land. Coastal sea lifts and rail transportation would be provided whenever possible. But given the ongoing disruption of transportation systems, combined with the myriad problems of a looming energy crisis, ground force mobility would be limited. If necessary, reinforcements would march across the country on foot, as in the ancient days of the samurai. If the Americans bypassed Kyushu and landed on the Kanto Plain, according to the IGHQ's estimate, sixty-five days would be needed to move reinforcements from Kyushu to Nagoya, and an additional ten days to deploy them on the battlefield. If it took two-and-a-half months to get those reinforcements into action, it was doubtful whether they could arrive in time to save the capital.[30]

The situation might grow so dire that the headquarters could not maintain its communications with outlying regions. Anticipating the erosion of basic command-and-control functions, the army was reorganized into quasi-autonomous regional commands—the First, Second, and Third Armies, with responsibility for north, central, and southern Japan, respectively. Civil administration was decentralized, with more local autonomy granted to prefectural governments, so that they could deal with local crises brought about by food shortages and disrupted transportation. The growing assault of the B-29s, the loss of sea communications even in the Inland Sea and the Sea of Japan, the threatened breakdown of the electrical power grid, the depletion of remaining fuel stocks, and the specter of famine—given these calamitous trends, it was not clear whether the Japanese would be capable of mounting a centrally organized defense of their homeland.

The second "track" pursued by the Suzuki government, a bid for peace talks, was coordinated through Togo and the foreign ministry. Tentative peace feelers had been sent out through diplomats and private citizens in neutral European capitals, and through the Catholic Church. Allied intelligence had tracked and reported on these various cloak-and-dagger capers, correctly inferring that they did not have the full and undivided backing of the Japanese regime.[*] Hopes for a truce in China led nowhere, as did plans to ask Chiang Kai-shek's Nationalist regime to mediate broader peace talks with the Allies.

Moscow remained the focus of Tokyo's diplomacy. Japan was willing to surrender most (perhaps all) of the territory and commercial privileges it had won in the Russo-Japanese War forty years earlier. In return, it hoped to obtain oil and other needed raw materials from Siberia, and to retain the status of an independent "buffer state" in East Asia, balancing the interests of the USSR and the Anglo-American powers. With the backing of the SWDC, including the hardline faction, the Japanese government formally asked the Kremlin for assistance in arranging a truce and a negotiated peace with the Allies. These entreaties were conveyed simultaneously through the Japanese ambassador in Moscow and the Soviet ambassador in Tokyo. The Japanese asked the Russians to receive a special diplomatic

---

[*] Future CIA director Allen Dulles, posted to Bern, Switzerland as an agent of the OSS, was in indirect contact with representatives of the Japanese government. The fascinating details were declassified in 1993. See "OSS Memoranda for the President, January–July, 1945," accessed September 7, 2018, https://www.cia.gov/library/center-for-the-study-of-intelligence. When queried directly by JCS chairman William Leahy, Dulles denied knowledge of any such contacts. Leahy, *I Was There*, p. 384.

envoy in Moscow—Fumimaro Konoye, the royal prince and former prime minister who had been ousted from power in 1941.

The Russians listened to these plaintive entreaties and offered no encouraging reply, but did not reject them outright. Vyacheslav Molotov, Stalin's commissar of foreign affairs, seemed to drag his feet. He was often unavailable; meetings were postponed, rescheduled, and then postponed again. Molotov asked Japanese ambassador Naotake Sato to provide more concrete proposals. The USSR would reply to the Japanese requests, he told Sato, after he and Stalin had returned from the Allied conference in Potsdam, Germany (July 17–August 2, 1945). The Japanese did not yet know or suspect that the Russians had already pledged to join the war against Japan. At Yalta, Stalin had fixed the date of the Soviet attack for three months after the fall of Germany. The Soviet dictator led the Japanese along with inconclusive diplomatic exchanges, intending only to buy time for his forces to redeploy from Europe. Throughout June and July, Russian troops, tanks, and artillery were traveling east by rail and massing on the Manchurian border. The point of Stalin's characteristically devious game was to get his country into the last phase of the war against Japan, thus gobbling up territory on the cheap.

In an SWDC meeting of June 18, Hirohito gave the clearest signal yet that he was with the peace faction, stating, "I desire that concrete plans to end the war, unhampered by existing policy, be speedily studied and that efforts be made to implement them."[31] He wanted to know the timing of Prince Konoye's mission to Moscow. Konoye later told American interrogators that he received "direct and secret instructions from the Emperor to secure peace at any price, notwithstanding its severity." According to the SWDC staff secretary, Suzuki and Togo secretly agreed that if the Kremlin refused to mediate peace talks, they would appeal directly to the United States for terms.[32]

But the factions in Tokyo had agreed on nothing beyond a vague appeal to the USSR. Nothing more concrete or conciliatory would be tolerated by the army. The regime's public policy was to fight to the bitter last, while its diplomatic activities were kept secret. Prime Minister Suzuki's public statements remained as spirited and bellicose as ever. The very idea of surrender was anathema; even the peacemakers were working on the assumption that some kind of bargain could be struck. Privately, some in the ruling circle recognized that Japan would be forced to give up its entire overseas empire, but others expected to retain territories the nation had controlled in earlier decades, including Korea and Formosa. The army high command was willing and even eager to pull out of China and southeast Asia—but they intended to withdraw their troops under Japanese command, not to surrender and be disarmed. As for allowing an Allied occupation force on Japanese soil without a fight, any Japanese leader who proposed such a disgraceful idea was asking for a bullet between the eyes. Even now, in the summer of 1945, the men who ruled Japan were slow to recognize that they could not simply turn the hands of the clock back to 1941, or 1937, or 1931, or even 1905. They wanted peace, but they could not yet face up to the stark reality of their total defeat.

FOR AMERICAN SUBMARINES on patrol in the western Pacific, the spring of 1945 was a season of famine. They found few Japanese ships of any kind. "Gone were the fat, loot-laden convoys that tried to blast their way back to the Empire," wrote Vice Admiral Charlie Lockwood, the Pacific submarine commander. "Vanished were the huge transports, piled high with munitions and packed to the rails with enemy troops, headed southward from the enemy's homeland."[33] Sinking scores plummeted. In April, nineteen submarines managed to sink just eighteen enemy cargo ships of combined 66,352 tons, and ten warships of 13,651 tons. In May, the score declined to fifteen merchantmen of 30,194 tons and five warships of 4,484 tons.[34] Most of the few remaining targets were found in the domain of Admiral Fife's Subic Bay command—in the Java Sea, the Gulf of Siam, and close inshore along the coast of Indochina. Increasingly, U.S. submarines preyed upon the dilapidated little trawlers, junks, and sampans that were always found teeming in those waters. Most were innocently laden with noncontraband cargoes such as rice, grain, fish, coffee, sugar, or salt, and manned by Chinese, Thai, or Malayan crews. But they were plying the coastal trade between ports in Japanese-occupied territories, and that was enough to doom them. In a July 1945 patrol off the east coast of Malaya, the submarine *Blenny* sank sixty-three small craft with her deck guns. In most cases, but not all, skipper William Hazard gave the crews a warning before opening fire, allowing them to evacuate their vessels and take to their rafts and lifeboats.

As solitary commerce-raiding cruises became less productive, the submarine fleet had to devote itself to new missions involving closer cooperation with other Allied forces. During the Iwo Jima and Okinawa campaigns, submarines acted in versatile roles—to scout the Japanese coast, sink enemy picket boats, and provide early warning of kamikaze strikes. They scouted and charted enemy minefields, and laid mines themselves in channels traversed by enemy shipping.[35] Supporting technologies advanced by giant steps. By the spring of 1945, U.S. subs were equipped with new sonar and radar systems that made them considerably more deadly as hunters, and new radio transceivers enabled them to send and receive communications even while submerged. Lockwood and LeMay, whose respective headquarters were now neighbors on Guam, collaborated personally to improve recovery rates for downed Superfortress aircrews. By February 1945, at least four submarines were stationed directly along the flight line of each B-29 bombing mission. They called themselves the "Lifeguard League." Procedures improved continuously, though never at a pace to satisfy either Lockwood or LeMay. By June, Lifeguard League submarine crews were coordinating directly by radio with the aircrews of the navy "Dumbos"—search and rescue patrol planes—as they patrolled overhead.[36]

Japan's last remaining viable sea link to Asia was through the Sea of Japan, the "back door" between the enemy's home islands and its vital territories of Korea and Manchuria. No American submarine had attempted to penetrate that largely enclosed marginal sea since the destruction of Mush Morton's *Wahoo* in September 1943. In the interim, the Japanese had upgraded and fortified their antisubmarine defenses in the three main entrance and exit routes. The narrow northern lanes at La Perouse and Tsugaru Straits were heavily patrolled by aircraft and small craft and guarded by coastal artillery. Tsushima Strait, between Kyushu and Korea, was 40 miles wide, but a powerful warm current ran north through it, and it was one of the most heavily mined seaways in the world. Lockwood had taken an interest in new frequency-modulated (FM) sonar systems that might enable a submarine to thread the Tsushima mine barrier, and by 1945 the technology had matured enough that it seemed worth the obvious risks. After conducting tests in dummy minefields off Pearl Harbor, Lockwood sold the idea to King and Nimitz. The operation was dubbed BARNEY.

On June 4, 1945, a nine-submarine wolfpack crept into Tsushima Strait. They entered in three groups of three, each taking a slightly different route through a four-layered mine barrier. They stayed deep, below 150 feet, with their FM sonar sets tilted upward to "see" the locations of floating mines.

As each boat snuck through the forest of steel mine cables, eluding the faint, ghostlike images depicted on the FM sonar scopes, the seconds passed like minutes, and minutes like hours. The *Flying Fish* remained submerged for sixteen hours, near the limit of her battery's endurance, while her crew panted and sweated in the oxygen-deprived confines of her hull.[37] On the *Tinosa*, a mine cable scraped along the length of the outer hull, making a noise that every man on her crew could identify with hideous clarity. Would it pull the mine down and blow the boat apart? One sailor recorded in his diary that the tension aboard the *Tinosa* was so severe that "if you dropped a penny on the deck, people would be on the ceiling."[38]

All nine made it safely through to "Hirohito's private bathtub," where they commenced a three-week rampage, sinking a total of twenty-eight ships for 54,784 tons.[39] With its maritime economy teetering on the brink of collapse, Japan could not afford to lose those ships. The *Bonefish* was destroyed in Toyama Bay on June 19 by the Japanese frigate *Okinawa* and a flotilla of smaller patrol craft. The remaining eight survived and escaped the enclosed sea by dashing through La Perouse Strait, the same northern passage where the *Wahoo* had met her end two years earlier. Their tactic was to stick together and remain on the surface, using their surface guns to fight off any Japanese destroyers or patrol craft that tried to stop them. But a welcome heavy fog concealed their daring high-speed surface run on June 24, and they encountered no opposition. They returned directly to Pearl Harbor, arriving on July 4. The *Bonefish* and her crew were mourned, but twenty-eight sinkings were deemed an acceptable result. Lockwood had hoped for more, but Operation BARNEY had productively capped the remarkable wartime career of the Pacific submarine fleet.

After flying hundreds of tactical missions over Kyushu, in support of the invasion of Okinawa, LeMay's B-29s resumed their strategic bombing campaign against Japanese cities and industries. Growing armadas of Superfortresses returned again and again to hit the aircraft plants in greater Tokyo and Nagoya, and the remaining industrial areas of Osaka, Kawasaki, Kobe, and Yokohama. Faced with raw materials shortages and crippling airstrikes, the Japanese largely abandoned any hope of replacing their aircraft losses. Indiscriminate firebombing of the urban centers continued and intensified. On April 13, northwest Tokyo was hit by 327 Superforts carrying a mix of incendiaries and 500-pound general-purpose bombs. The citizens had learned to run away, rather than stay and fight the fires, so the casualty figures were lower than during the great March 9–10 raid. Otherwise, the results on the ground were much the same: 11 square miles of the city burned to the ground. Two days later, another major strike hit Kawasaki, south of Tokyo, and destroyed much of the city. Tokyo was largely burned out by that time, but the Superfortresses returned to the capital several more times. A five-hundred-plane daylight raid targeted the southern and central downtown districts on May 24. Two nights later, when some of the fires of the May 24 raid were still burning, another massive attack dropped 3,252 tons of M-77 bombs into Ginza and Hibiya, upscale downtown commercial and residential neighborhoods bordering upon the Imperial Palace.

After seven major incendiary raids, there was not much of Tokyo left to bomb. Half of the great metropolis, about 57 square miles, lay in ashes. The population had declined by about 50 percent, and homeless refugees would continue their exodus until the end of the war.

In late March, the 313th Bombardment Wing began laying mines in Japanese harbors and inland waterways, a campaign aptly called Operation STARVATION. LeMay initially resisted taking on this new mission, regarding it as yet another exasperating diversion from his main strategic bombing program—but aerial minelaying ultimately proved to be one of the single most productive uses of the B-29s. In an initial weeklong blitz, the planes dropped hundreds of mines into Shimonoseki Strait, the channel between Kyushu and Honshu. Surprised by this sudden rain of mines into a vital shipping chokepoint, the Japanese lacked effective countermeasures. The Americans dropped a variety of different mine types—acoustic, magnetic, and pressure-triggered devices—that sank to various depths. Japanese minesweepers were overwhelmed, lacking the equipment or know-how to locate more than a fraction of the mines. Some were equipped with diabolically clever arming devices, including timed delays and counters that did not activate the warhead until a specified number of ships had passed over. The pressure mine, triggered by fluctuations in water pressure caused by a passing ship, could not be detected at all by the minesweepers. The Japanese called it "the Unsweepable."[40]

In April and May, the 313th Wing Superforts mined all major waterways in the Inland Sea, the Kure-Hiroshima anchorages, the naval base at Sasebo, the ports of Tokyo, Nagoya, Kobe, and Osaka, the Bungo Suido Strait, and the major ports on the Sea of Japan. When minesweepers began making progress in clearing Shimonoseki Strait, waves of B-29s rained thousands of new mines into it. The assault effectively shut down this vital western gateway to Japan's Inland Sea. In growing desperation, Japanese merchant sea captains tried to force the minefields, hoping and praying for good luck. Many ships vanished in gigantic towers of whitewater.

Operation STARVATION eventually sowed more than 12,000 mines into Japanese waters. Though it spanned only the last five months of the Pacific War, the campaign sank or otherwise disabled 1,250,000 tons of shipping, accounting for 9.3 percent of all Japanese shipping losses during the war. The missions were usually flown at night, over areas that were not strongly defended by antiaircraft batteries. In 1,529 aerial minelaying sorties, only fifteen B-29s failed to return, representing a loss rate of less than 1 percent. USSBS analysts concluded that the deadly campaign should have been launched earlier and laid on with greater weight: "Minelaying has been the most economical in both men and material of all types of warfare against shipping."[41]

The Twentieth Air Force was growing rapidly as reinforcements flew in from China and the United States. By July it was brought up to five wings, totaling more than 1,000 B-29s, with total personnel (including flight crews, administrative personnel, and ground support units) of 83,000. The 58th Bombardment Wing, which redeployed from China and India following the dissolution of the 20th Bomber Command, set up shop on West Field, Tinian. The newly activated 315th Bombardment Wing operated from the just-completed Northwest Field on Guam. Equipped with the new AN/ APQ-7 Eagle radar system, the 315th Wing Superforts executed a series of pinpoint strikes on Japan's largest oil refineries, storage complexes, and pipelines. Using radar alone, the specially trained aircrews could hit their targets with deadly precision, even when bombing through impenetrable cloud cover. During the last six weeks of the Pacific War, maximum effort bombing missions—huge strikes involving six hundred or seven hundred Superfortresses—hit Japan two to three times a week. The pilot Charles Phillips wrote of those late-war missions: "We could pick any city and burn it to the ground at will, in good weather or bad, visually or by radar."[42]

Performance and maintenance metrics improved by leaps and bounds. The average engine life of the once-troublesome Wright R-3350 engines was tripled, from 250 hours to 750 hours. Mission abort rates fell to under 10 percent. P-51 Mustangs joined up with the northbound B-29s from their newly expanded airbases on Iwo Jima. They easily massacred the Japanese fighters that rose to intercept the incoming formations, scoring a cumulative shootdown ratio of approximately eight to one. After mid-June, Japanese interceptors were rarely seen by the American aircrews. B-29 loss rates fell to under 1 percent per mission. By the end of the war, as LeMay was fond of saying, it was statistically safer to fly a bombing mission over Japan than to fly a training mission at home.

On July 1, the Third Fleet was back at sea, radio silent, northbound for Japan. An armada of 105 ships, including seventeen aircraft carriers and eight battleships, was arrayed in three task groups. By a fair margin, it was the most powerful naval striking force ever assembled in history. Its mission was to operate against the Japanese home islands, launching airstrikes along the coasts of Honshu and Hokkaido, hitting cities, factories, dockyards, and shipping and transportation facilities. It would strike "virgin" targets in Japan's northern regions, which lay beyond the range of the B-29s. And it would attempt to finish off the last vestiges of the Japanese fleet, at anchor in Tokyo Bay and the Inland Sea. Admiral Halsey and his force would be at sea for several weeks, rearming and refueling from logistics ships and tankers that would meet him at predetermined times and coordinates, and then returning again and again to strike the home islands with unprecedented fury.

On July 10, before dawn, the fleet maneuvered into a launch point about 170 miles southeast of Tokyo. The initial fighter sweep caught the Japanese completely by surprise. In a long and busy day of air operations over greater Tokyo, the carrier planes dropped 454 tons of bombs and fired 1,648 rockets on industrial facilities, dockyards, bridges, power stations, and airfields. No Japanese fighters rose to offer resistance. Antiaircraft fire claimed ten U.S. planes; five more were lost to operational accidents.[43]

Vanishing into the Pacific void, the fleet raced north, and then doubled back to descend suddenly upon northern Honshu and southern Hokkaido, which had never yet been struck by enemy bombing raids. Barnstorming over the region's many harbors, carrier planes dropped bombs and fired rockets into ships at anchor, returning with claims of twenty-four ships destroyed and many more damaged. They destroyed planes on the ground, parked wingtip to wingtip alongside remote northern airstrips; they hit and destroyed ammunition dumps, buildings, radio stations, factories, and ware-

houses. Others targeted the rail infrastructure, tearing up railyards, destroying bridges, and smashing locomotives and boxcars. Honshu and Hokkaido
were linked by a cross-channel rail ferry system. The carrier airmen sank
four rail ferries and hit several more, which were forced to run aground.
This single day's work cut coal shipments from Hokkaido to Honshu by
about 50 percent.[44] It was poor flying weather, wet and cloudy with poor
visibility, and many of the strikes were cancelled; but Task Force 38 still
managed to complete 871 sorties before nightfall.[45] According to Admiral
Radford, "Aerial opposition was practically nil."[46]

July 15 brought a new milestone in the war: the first naval bombardment
of the enemy's homeland. A battleship-cruiser-destroyer force maneuvered
into the offing near Kamaishi, site of a major steelworks, and opened fire at
dawn. For two hours, 16-inch shells fired by the *South Dakota*, *Indiana*, and
Massachusetts laid waste to the foundry and coke ovens. The following day,
another surface force hit the Nihon Steel Company and the Wanishi Iron-
works at Muroran, Hokkaido. The *Missouri* joined the bombardment group
off Muroran, giving Halsey a front-row seat to a "magnificent spectacle."[47]
Fires spread into nearby Kushiro, burning about twenty city blocks to the
ground. According to Mick Carney, they saw no enemy aircraft at all, and
counterfire from shore batteries was weak and intermittent. He concluded
that the Japanese must be nearly finished: "We moved the battleships right
in there to bombardment range any place along the coast that we felt like it,
and there was no ability to resist effectively. So it was pretty apparent that
we were flogging a dead horse."[48]

In those last weeks of the war, the Japanese were doing little or no offshore scouting. U.S. submarines and carrier planes had sunk most of their
coastal picket vessels. They had few remaining patrol planes or pilots. "They
would send out one airplane to scout the fleet, and we would shoot him
down," recalled Arthur R. Hawkins, a Hellcat pilot with VF-31 on the *Belleau Wood*. "Then they would do it again the next day. They sent him out;
if he didn't come back, they knew the fleet was out there."[49] Finding that
they could operate with impunity even within sight of the Japanese coast,
the Americans did not bother to conceal their location. "There just wasn't
anything to shoot at," said Hawkins. "They weren't in the air. We were on
bombing strikes, and we would go in, drop our bombs, and just sit around
and shoot them on the ground."[50]

On the sixteenth, Task Force 38 withdrew to the east and rendezvoused with its fueling and logistics group. Sidling up alongside the fleet oilers, the great fleet drank 379,157 barrels of fuel. Simultaneously, 6,369 tons of ammunition and 1,635 tons of supplies and provisions were transferred from the storeships into the fleet's storerooms and magazines. The entire process was completed in about eighteen hours. Admiral Radford did not exaggerate when he called it "the greatest logistic feat ever performed on the high seas."[51]

Charging back toward Honshu on July 17, Task Force 38 planes swooped down on Tokyo Bay and the naval base at Yokosuka. They ganged up on the battleship *Nagato*, at anchor in the bay. At the outset of the war, and during the attack on Pearl Harbor, she had been the flagship of Admiral Isoroku Yamamoto. Now she was reduced to a blackened, smoking, listing wreck. Other U.S. planes strafed and bombed airfields throughout the region, destroying would-be future kamikazes on the ground. Battleships and cruisers moved in close to the shoreline to bombard the Mito-Hitachi area. Falling in with the British Pacific Fleet under Vice Admiral Bernard Rawlings, the whole enormous force launched coordinated airstrikes against major ports in the eastern part of the Inland Sea. They paid special attention to the remaining units of the Japanese fleet anchored off Kure Naval Base.

The Japanese navy was immobilized, and no longer presented a threat to the Allies, but the airmen were determined to pay off this final installment of a forty-four-month-old debt. "Remember Pearl Harbor" was chalked on the fleet's ready room blackboards. "Call this what you will," said Mick Carney, "it was a deep-seated feeling in the minds of all of us, that the ignominy of Pearl Harbor would never be wiped off the slate until they had been repaid in full, and until they were utterly destroyed."[52] In a *coup de grâce* on July 26, carrier planes pulverized two dozen Japanese warships riding at anchor, effectively wiping out the last remnants of Japanese naval power. "By sunset that evening," wrote Halsey, "the Japanese navy had ceased to exist."[53]

During those late-war operations, Halsey regularly spoke to war correspondents assigned to ride with the Third Fleet, serving up his familiar threats to impose a vengeful peace on the Japanese. Asked about conditions for a Japanese surrender, he said that Hirohito should "pay for impersonating God."[54] He pledged to seize the emperor's white horse as a trophy of war. In an interview for *Collier's* magazine, Halsey said that Japan was "not fit to live in a civilized world," and suggested that one Japanese officer should be

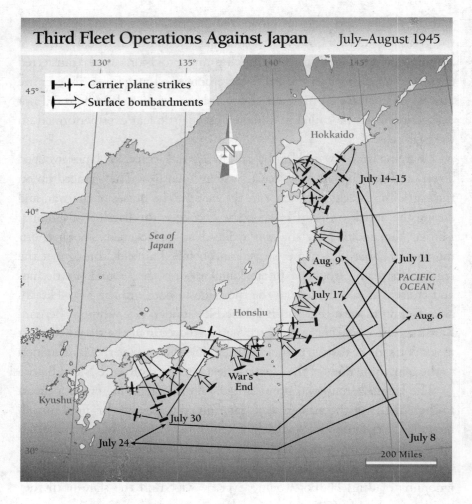

Third Fleet Operations Against Japan   July–August 1945

executed for every American prisoner of war who died in captivity.[55] On July 23, his catchphrase "Kill More Japs" appeared under his face on the cover of *Time* magazine.[56] Halsey was annoyed by the prohibition against bombing the Imperial Palace in Tokyo. The Third Fleet commander, according to Carney, had little time for the "pantywaist idea" that Hirohito might be useful to the Allies in a postwar role: "The thing to do, as we saw it, was to go get him, get Number 1 and knock him off."[57]

Halsey's pugnacious tirades played well in the American press, but they contradicted and undermined the themes of Allied propaganda. A week after Halsey's return to the Pacific, an analysis published by the Office of War Information (OWI) warned:

The downward trend in Japanese morale may take a long or a short time before it reaches a point that makes possible the termination of the war. The military pressure brought to bear will be the principal controlling factor, but of major significance will be the degree to which most of the Japanese continue to believe that the Allies intend:

    a. To kill, torture or enslave the Japanese people;

    b. To destroy the Japanese way of life with its Emperor and related values.[58]

Throughout that summer, Halsey's own carrier planes were dropping millions of leaflets over Japan. The documents encouraged Japanese civilians to look forward to a peaceful, prosperous, and just future after the war. "The United States do not want to hurt you or your families," one such leaflet stated. "The United States do not want your country. What the United States wants is an end to aggression and peace throughout the world."[59]

With a coordinated effort by the State Department, the military, and the OWI, the Americans had finally crafted a coherent strategy for "Psyops," or psychological operations against Japan. An OWI leaflet-producing operation on Guam employed hundreds of civilians and printing machinery on the scale of a major newspaper. Fresh from the presses, the documents were loaded into 500-pound casings that were triggered to open 4,000 feet above the ground. By these means, one leaflet "bomb" could cover an entire city. According to OWI's estimates, 63 million leaflets were dropped on Japan in the last three months of the war.[60]

A few major themes were emphasized in all propaganda leaflets: Japan's military defeat was inevitable; the militarist regime was feckless, deceitful, and self-serving; peace would improve the lives of the Japanese people. A fundamental tenet of all Allied propaganda was to avoid mentioning the emperor at all, but to aim all criticism at the "military clique." Nazi Germany, Japan's major ally, had suffered total defeat. Now Japan was alone, and would bear the full brunt of Allied power. "Japan now faces a crisis, in which the full strength of the Allied nations will soon be concentrated against her," a typical leaflet stated: "Does she not feel lonely?"[61] The documents were often decorated with favorite Japanese motifs, such as Mount Fuji or cherry blossoms in bloom. The dialect used in early leaflets was rather stiff and formal—"too highbrow for practical effect," as one analyst put it.[62] But as Japanese-American *nisei* and other language experts brought their expertise to bear on the problem, the prose grew more fluid and straightforward. In some cases, Japanese prisoners of war assisted in drafting or editing the messages. Elmer Davis, the OWI chief, wrote that all propaganda messages repeated three overarching themes—"that we are coming, that we are going to win, and that in the long run everybody will be better off because we won."[63]

Added to the leaflet campaign were 100,000-watt shortwave radio transmissions from Hawaii and California, later amplified by a 50,000-watt clear channel radio tower erected on the northern coast of Saipan. The OWI broadcasts were repetitive, often echoing the same messages printed on the leaflets, and postwar research revealed that very few Japanese had heard them at all. The most effective propaganda broadcasts were aimed directly at the Japanese leadership, most notably the "Zacharias broadcasts" of June and July 1945.

Ellis Zacharias was a naval intelligence officer who had lived and studied in Japan in the 1920s, and spoke the language fluently. He was a friend and colleague of Edwin Layton, the Pacific Fleet intelligence officer, and Joseph Rochefort, who had led the code-breaking unit at Pearl Harbor that had won the Battle of Midway. Zacharias believed that the ruling group in Tokyo might be susceptible to a direct appeal to end the war. He proposed a series of broadcasts modifying or at least clarifying the meaning of the "unconditional surrender" doctrine. After many weeks of discussion, a series of broadcast scripts was approved by the State Department, the OWI, and the Joint Chiefs. Zacharias made his initial radio broadcast on May 8, 1945—VE-Day. They followed at weekly intervals, until the first week of August: fourteen broadcasts in all. In each, Zacharias repeated that "unconditional surrender" applied only to "the form in which hostilities are terminated," and did not constitute an intention to subjugate or enslave Japan. He quoted other Allied statements, such as the Atlantic Charter and the Cairo Declaration, which guaranteed universal human rights and the principle of self-determination. Japan had come to a fork in the road, said Zacharias, and the nation faced a categorical choice: "One is the virtual destruction of Japan followed by a dictated peace. The other is unconditional surrender with its attendant benefits as laid down by the Atlantic Charter."[64]

Zacharias's fourth broadcast brought forth a direct reply from Dr. Isamu Inouye, who identified himself as an official government spokesman. It came by way of a shortwave radio broadcast from Tokyo. The text was stilted, cagey, and noncommittal. But the tone was moderate, and it did not reject the suggestion of a peace settlement: "Japan would be ready to discuss peace terms," said Inouye, "provided there were certain changes in the unconditional surrender formula."[65]

PHYSICISTS HAD KNOWN for four decades that vast stores of energy were locked up inside the atom. In the years immediately prior to the Second World War, experiments had shown that a rare isotope of uranium, U-235, had the property of being highly "fissionable," meaning that its neutrons could penetrate the positive electrical barrier of the nucleus, a process that liberated "free" energy. Nuclear fission offered great promise as a source of cheap, limitless electrical power. But the momentous discovery also pointed to a more ominous scenario—that under certain conditions not found in nature, a mass of pure U-235 could be manipulated to trigger a chain reaction that would release a spectacular burst of energy, an explosion equivalent to about 20,000 tons of TNT. Nonscientists struggled to comprehend what the physicists were talking about, and most were instinctively skeptical. But an impressive consensus was found among leading scientists in the field. They warned that the theoretical basis for an atomic "superbomb" was sound, and the daunting challenges involved in building it could be overcome, probably within a few years, with a sufficient investment of funding, expertise, and industrial-scale engineering.

Humanity would certainly be safer without possessing this terrible power, but no one trusted Adolf Hitler to agree. Germany was thought to possess the requisite scientific competence to build an atomic bomb, and Allied intelligence warned that the Nazis had taken steps to secure the needed materials. Through their conquests, the Germans controlled a "heavy water" plant in Norway, and had access to uranium ore deposits in Czechoslovakia and the Belgian Congo. If Hitler should obtain a nuclear weapon, there would be no effective countermeasure; the Nazi dictator could use it to impose his will on the world, even if his armies were vanquished in conventional military terms. The sole defense would be to possess the same monstrosity, with the credible threat to retaliate in kind.

British research into the field they called "Tube Alloys" had advanced to a certain point in 1941, when the United States entered the war. Churchill and Roosevelt had agreed to combine national efforts, and to carry on the work in the mainland United States. On December 28, 1942, FDR signed an order to commence major industrial construction. Colonel Leslie R. Groves, an army engineer who had overseen the completion of the Pentagon, was placed in charge of the secret project. It was assigned a first-priority AAA rating, which empowered Groves to lay claim to funds, resources, and personnel without having to explain to anyone what he was doing. If it was necessary to identify the program—to fill in a blank on a requisition form, for example—Groves instructed his clerks to write "Manhattan Engineer District," a sleight of hand inspired by the fact that no part of the project was in New York.

To fund this "Manhattan Project," Stimson and Marshall began by raiding the accounts of various conventional weapons development programs. But when the time came to build huge and expensive isotope separation plants in Tennessee and Washington state, the secretary and the army chief of staff knew they needed congressional authority. They went up to Capitol Hill and sat down with House and Senate leaders. Stimson spoke vaguely about an abstruse science that he did not really understand—but neither did the congressmen, he added, so what was the point of going over the details? The War Department needed $600 million right away, and would need more soon. For the sake of secrecy, there should be no details on the appropriation line, and the rank-and-file members of Congress should be told nothing at all. As Marshall remembered it, Stimson told the legislators that they "would have to take his word for it and my word for it that it was of vital importance that we get this additional money and that it was of equally vital importance that not a word be breathed of what the thing really was."[66] They wanted a blank check for a project whose details were also left blank, and they got it. The total cost of the Manhattan Project eventually grew to $2 billion.

Berkeley physicist J. Robert Oppenheimer managed the project's brain center, which gathered the specialists and scientists together in a remote and heavily guarded compound at Los Alamos, New Mexico. The site was an arid mesa between rocky canyons, nestled between the Jemez Mountains to the west and the Sangre de Cristo Range to the east. The roads, unpaved and muddy during the spring rains, were heavily traveled by jeeps and army trucks. Research and development work was conducted in the Technical Area, a fenced-in complex of offices and laboratories the size of four city blocks. In an outer perimeter was the residential district, a community of cookie-cutter prefabricated apartment houses, laundries, mess halls, schools, and a movie theater. Los Alamos grew steadily throughout the war, to a peak population of about 5,800—a mountain village of wayward and willful geniuses, whose scientists, mathematicians, and engineers included some of the most renowned figures in their respective fields. Despite the heavy security presence—fences, watchtowers, checkpoints, dogs on leashes, soldiers with fixed bayonets—Los Alamos was a young and vibrant civilian community, where pregnant wives pushed strollers along sidewalks and gangs of children roamed among the white clapboard buildings. Many residents had fled Europe to escape the rampaging armies of the Third Reich, giving their presence here a dimension of karmic justice.

The first problem confronted by the designers was to separate the two main isotopes of uranium, acquiring a pure "critical mass" of the lighter and rarer isotope U-235. At the outset, no one could say precisely what that critical mass might be. Estimates ranged from a low of about one pound to a high of about 200 pounds. If the figure was at the lower end of that range, the bomb might be feasible; if at the higher, it might lie beyond the industrial engineering resources of any nation, at least within the expected duration of the war. In that sense, the Manhattan Project was undertaken with full knowledge that it might fail. The substance U-235 had never been isolated in pure form, except in submicroscopic quantities. There were several possible means of enriching larger amounts: the leading candidates were gaseous, chemical, and thermal diffusion. A fourth possibility, whose discovery was a major breakthrough, was to convert U-238 into plutonium, a new and extremely fissionable element which could then be more easily separated from the residual uranium. In each case, however, there was no easy means to attain the weapons-grade purity needed for an atomic bomb. There were no shortcuts. All of the proposed enrichment processes required industrial engineering on a monumental scale.

Having received a blank check from the U.S. taxpayer, the project directors decided to pursue all routes simultaneously. A complex of uranium enrichment plants was established on a 56,000-acre site in Oak Ridge, Tennessee. The site was chosen in part for its isolation, in part because the energy-hungry uranium "calutrons" could draw upon the power capacity of the nearby Tennessee Valley Authority. The plutonium operation was built at the Hanford Engineer Works near Richland, Washington. This was remote sagebrush country northwest of the Columbia River, which provided a plentiful supply of water to cool the reactors. The scale of the construction was gargantuan even by Manhattan Project standards; more than 1,200 buildings were built at the Hanford site, and during the construction phase the population of the secretive camp surpassed 60,000, making it the fourth most populous city in the state.[67]

The second hurdle faced by the scientists at Los Alamos was to bring two separated portions of fissile material together almost instantaneously, forming a critical mass that would initiate a self-sustaining chain reaction. The two halves had to be slammed together at high velocity, or the chain reaction might sputter out before the entire mass was merged, producing a much smaller blast, or none at all. The trigger mechanism, with the fissile material, had to be housed in a metal casing small enough to be carried and dropped by an airplane. The original idea was to fire the subcritical halves at one another using conventional explosives in the form of a "double gun." But in July 1944, the scientists discovered that plutonium was so spontaneously fissionable that a simple gun-type mechanism would produce a weak "fizzle" rather than a full-scale nuclear blast. The proposed solution was to create a symmetrical implosion shockwave using an intricate system of lenses. Work on this project lagged, and some of the scientists assigned to it actually despaired of solving the problem. After fits and starts, with theoretical contributions by the Hungarian mathematician John Von Neumann and the practical engineering work of Russian-born chemist George Kistiakowsky, a functional implosion trigger was made ready in the spring of 1945.

By that time, sufficient quantities of weapons-grade fissionable uranium and plutonium were finally being produced at Oak Ridge and Hanford. Oppenheimer and his team were confident that they could deliver three bombs—one uranium and two plutonium—by the middle of the year. Because the implosion mechanism entailed a risk of failure, they planned to test the first plutonium bomb in July 1945. (Confident that the simpler gun-type trigger in the uranium bomb would work as designed, they did not believe it needed advance testing.) By sheer quirk of fate, therefore, the first atomic bombs would become available after the defeat of Germany but before the defeat of Japan.

Before succeeding to the presidency, Truman had been only faintly aware of the Manhattan Project. In 1943, when he was still a senator from Missouri, his select committee to investigate waste and corruption in the war industries (the "Truman Committee") had demanded information about the mysterious plants under construction in Tennessee and Washington. Secretary Stimson had warned him off, referring only to a top-secret weapons program involving a new field of science, and Truman had gamely agreed to inquire no further. As vice president he had been told nothing more, in conformity with the strict need-to-know stricture enforced upon the project. On his first day as president in April 1945, Truman received a short verbal briefing from Stimson about the secret drive to build "a new explosive of almost unbelievable destructive power." Later that afternoon, Truman learned more from James F. Byrnes, the former war mobilization tsar who would soon be appointed secretary of state. In his memoir, Truman wrote that he was "puzzled" by these thumbnail sketches of a bomb that might have the power to "destroy the whole world."[68] On April 25, he received a formal soup-to-nuts briefing from Stimson and Groves (since promoted to major general), who answered all of the president's many questions about the project.

To advise on the issues presented by atomic weapons and energy, its use in the war and the postwar period, Truman established a committee of senior political, industrial, and scientific figures. Its ad hoc character was reflected in its name: the "Interim Committee." More formal agencies would be created later; for now, however, the limitations of secrecy allowed only for a small panel whose members were already "read in." Stimson was appointed chairman, and Byrnes was among its members; others included Vannevar Bush, James Conant, Karl Compton, Ralph Bard (Forrestal's deputy at the Navy Department), and William Clayton, an assistant secretary of state. A scientific advisory panel was added as a subcommittee; Robert Oppenheimer and Enrico Fermi were among its members.

In introductory remarks at the first meeting of the Interim Committee, Stimson urged his colleagues to think broadly about the issues before them: "While the advances in the field to date had been fostered by the needs of war, it was important to realize that the implications of the project went far beyond the needs of the present war."[69] Meeting for two consecutive days on May 31 and June 1, 1945, the committee agreed that the new bomb should be used against Japan "as soon as possible."[70] Formal recommendations to the president were deferred to a later date, but the minutes reflected a collective view that "we could not give the Japanese any warning; that we could not concentrate on a civilian area; but that we should seek to make a profound psychological impression on as many of the inhabitants as possible." Dr. Conant suggested, and Stimson agreed, that the "most desirable target would be a vital war plant employing a large number of workers and closely surrounded by workers' houses."[71] Selection of targets was referred to a target committee, whose members included General Groves and several Manhattan Project scientists.

The welter of major policy decisions taken by American leaders between May and August 1945 were among the most complex in the nation's history. Purely military strategy was amalgamated into high considerations of foreign policy; all minds, including those of senior generals and admirals, were turning toward the postwar order. The president's men were absorbed in the day-in, day-out skirmishes with Stalin over the Yalta accords, the occupation and reconstruction of Germany, the political claims of Charles de Gaulle in France, and the charter of the United Nations. They were just beginning to think about the future of Asia, the status of former Japanese territories, the fate of British colonies, the red insurgency in China, the future of Japan under Allied occupation, and the still-uncertain matter of whether Japan's overseas armies would lay down arms if ordered to do so by Tokyo, or if they would have to be beaten in the field even after the home islands were subjugated. Major decisions were confronted under pressure of time and events. They were rendered by a tiny circle of civilian and military officials whose numbers were limited by secrecy, and who had been carrying a staggering workload for years. In some cases, by their own accounts, the president's men were feeling the strain of prolonged physical and mental fatigue. Far-reaching decisions were made "on the road," while they were at the Allied conference in Potsdam, Germany. Their neophyte commander in chief had not been well prepared for the job, and he had not been doing it long enough to acquire his predecessor's expertise, self-assurance, and finesse.

In considering whether to leave Hirohito on his throne, U.S. policymakers were of two minds. Joseph C. Grew, the last prewar ambassador to Tokyo, who now served as undersecretary of state, was sensitive to American public opinion, which demanded that the emperor be held accountable as a war criminal. He took a hawkish tone in his public statements, as when he told a radio audience that negotiating terms of surrender with Japan would be to "temporize with murder and to negotiate with treachery embodied in human flesh."[72] Grew was wary of diplomatic exchanges that might draw the Allies into protracted negotiations. But he privately argued that Hirohito must play a role in the war's final act, because he alone possessed the power to compel all his forces at home and overseas to lay down arms. An imperial rescript issued by the *Showa* emperor, Grew told a journalist friend, was "the one thing that might do the trick and it might save the lives of tens of thousands of our own fighting men."[73]

In deliberations preceding the issuance of the Potsdam Declaration, most of the leading American players (including Truman) favored signaling to the Japanese that their imperial house would survive unconditional surrender. In JCS and cabinet meetings in June, a consensus seemed to gel that it would serve the interests of the United States and the Allies to retain the emperor as a partner or puppet. But the precise wording of such a statement always evoked dissent. All were sensitive to the charge that they were subverting their late commander in chief's doctrine of unconditional surrender. In answer to seemingly ad hoc objections, they repeatedly struck all references to the emperor or his dynasty from American and Allied public statements. That did not change until the second week of August 1945, following the bombings of Hiroshima and Nagasaki but before the final Japanese surrender, when the Americans implicitly promised to leave Hirohito alone. In the end, as Grew put it ruefully, the United States "demanded unconditional surrender, then dropped the bomb and accepted conditional surrender."[74]

Meeting with the president in the Oval Office on June 18, Secretaries Stimson and Forrestal and the four Joint Chiefs reviewed their overall strategy against Japan. The blockade of the home islands was underway and would intensify, and all could hope that a surrender might precede the invasion of Kyushu, or at least the invasion of Honshu the following spring. In either case, however, planning and logistical moves had to be taken immediately to prepare for a landing on November 1. Marshall argued that Operation OLYMPIC was "essential to a strategy of strangulation" because it would have the effect of tightening the air-sea blockade while at the same time providing the logistical backstop for the decisive CORONET invasion of the Kanto Plain. Admiral King, speaking for the navy, agreed that it was important to proceed with all contingent preparations for OLYMPIC and CORONET. However, he believed that "the defeat of Japan could be accomplished by sea-air power, without the necessity of invasion."[75] Leahy continued to argue that an invasion of Japan was neither necessary nor desirable, but he did not object to preparing contingency plans. Truman approved the DOWNFALL plans and signed orders to transfer the necessary forces from Europe and the United States.

One of the knottiest questions that summer was the desirability of Soviet participation in the East Asian war. FDR had gone to great lengths to secure Stalin's promise to join the war against Japan; in 1943 and 1944, it had probably been the highest U.S. priority in diplomacy with Moscow. But by June 1945, as it became clear that communism and democracy must wage a long global contest in the decades ahead, many in the U.S. camp questioned whether the Russians were needed or even wanted in the war against Japan. Soviet entry into the war was more likely to force Japan to surrender, but it would also allow the Red Army to seize strategic territory from which it would not be easily dislodged. A larger Soviet footprint in East Asia threatened to enhance communist influence throughout the region. MacArthur later declared that he was "astonished" to learn that a deal had been struck to bring the Soviet Union into the war: "From my viewpoint, any intervention by Russia during 1945 was not required."[76] King and Eisenhower each separately advised the president to offer no concessions or inducements to secure Russia's participation.[77] Newly sworn Secretary of State James F. Byrnes had earlier favored inviting the Soviets into the war; now he wanted to keep them out. Byrnes distrusted the Russians, based on their treacherous conduct in Eastern Europe; and he did not think they were needed, because he expected the atomic bomb to force a quick Japanese surrender.[78] Byrnes's assistant Walter Brown recorded in his diary: "JFB still hoping for time, after atomic bomb Japan will surrender and Russia will not get in so much on the kill, thereby being in a position to press for claims against China."[79]

Truman was not pleased about traveling to Potsdam, and he would have liked to give the conference a miss. But the JCS and cabinet was unanimous in agreeing that the president's presence was necessary. On the train from Washington to Newport News, Virginia, where he would embark upon the cruiser *Augusta* for the eight-day transatlantic passage, Truman wrote his wife to say that he was "as blue as indigo about going."[80] Leading his entourage were Admiral Leahy, Secretary Byrnes, and a large deputation of military and civilian aides. (Byrnes had managed to keep his rival, Henry Stimson, off the ship; Stimson flew to Europe and joined the party in Potsdam.) The *Augusta* arrived at Antwerp on July 15. Truman and his party traveled in a forty-car motorcade to an airfield near Brussels, and then flew over the war-scarred wastelands of the fallen German Reich to Potsdam, a historic seat of Prussian kings, south of Berlin.

The Potsdam Conference would deal mainly with European questions, unresolved in the Yalta talks earlier that year, including German-Polish-Soviet borders, reparations, occupation zones in Germany, and Turkish sovereignty over the Dardanelles. The final push against Japan, and the arrangements that would prevail in postwar Asia, were addressed only between the seams of the main conference agenda, largely in informal sessions among the principals. Churchill traveled to Potsdam, but during the second week of the conference he was replaced by a new prime minister, Clement Attlee, whose Labour Party had won a landslide victory in Britain's first national election since 1939.

Potsdam being in the Russian zone of occupation, Stalin served as the conference host. Formal meetings were held in the opulent halls of the Cecilienhof Palace, a former royal prince's residence. Dignitaries of the several powers were quartered at grand houses in Babelsberg, a nearby town, from which the residents had been summarily expelled at gunpoint. Truman and his party moved into a three-story stucco house on Kaiserstrasse, which the Americans called the "Little White House." Listening devices had been placed throughout the house, and the service staff included several Soviet NKVD agents.

Stalin, arriving a day late, first met Truman at the Little White House at noon on July 17. The two leaders shook hands with a cheerful flourish, grinning broadly and baring their teeth at each other. Stalin summarized his government's ongoing negotiations with the Chinese, aimed at securing an agreement that would establish borders and conditions for the pending Soviet attack on Manchuria. Truman was noncommittal, a posture that may have disappointed Stalin; the Soviet leader had hoped that the U.S. president would issue a formal request for the USSR's participation in the East Asian war, providing a pretense for the Russians to abrogate their neutrality pact with Japan. But Truman and his government had no intention of providing that satisfaction, because it was now clear that they had soured on the prospective Soviet entry into the war. Winston Churchill noticed this new attitude and remarked upon it in a note to Sir Anthony Eden, the British foreign secretary: "It is quite clear that the United States do not at the present time desire Russian participation in the war against Japan."[81]

THE SITE CHOSEN FOR TRINITY, the first nuclear test, was a desolate plain deep in the New Mexico desert, about 200 miles south of Los Alamos. The bomb would be detonated atop a 100-foot steel tower, at the coordinates designated "Ground Zero." A control bunker built of heavy timbers covered by earth was located 6 miles from the tower; the base camp was 10 miles away. The test was scheduled for dawn on July 16, 1945.

As the clock ticked down to "Zero-Hour," the desert was dark and chilly. The beam of a searchlight, positioned near the tower, sliced through the low overcast. At Sandy Ridge, an observation site south of the base camp, scientists, journalists, and visitors drank coffee from thermoses and stamped their feet to keep warm. Passing around a pair of binoculars, they took turns studying the distant floodlit tower. An army sergeant read out instructions by the light of a flashlight. When the two-minute count-down began, he said, the observers should lie down on the ground, faces turned away from the tower. After the blast, they could turn and look at the cloud above the tower, but to avoid injuring their eyes they should not gaze directly at the fireball. For those determined to look directly at the explosion, plates of welding glass were handed out; they were instructed to hold them in front of their faces and to peer through them. They should wear long sleeves and trousers to protect their skin. Bottles of suntan lotion were passed around in the inky darkness, and people smeared it on their exposed faces and hands. They should remain prone until the shockwave had passed over: "The hazard from blast is reduced by lying down on the ground in such a manner that flying rocks, glass and other objects do not intervene between the source of blast and the individual."[82] Automobile windows should be left open.

A siren would indicate when it was safe to rise from the ground. At that point, all personnel whose duties did not require them to remain in the area should return to base camp immediately and board the waiting buses. The zone would be evacuated until radiation measurements were taken.

At an earlier stage of the Manhattan Project, physicists had debated the risk that the blast might be much larger than predicted by their calcula-tions. Some had worried that it would ignite the nitrogen in Earth's atmo-sphere, perhaps even annihilate the planet. Subsequent calculations had seemed to rule out that scenario. But Enrico Fermi, who was at the observa-tion post at Sandy Ridge that night, had a predilection for gallows humor.

He offered to take wagers on the odds that the bomb would set fire to the atmosphere, and if so, whether it would destroy the State of New Mexico or the entire world. Either way, his colleagues might have retorted, no one would collect winnings.

At the control bunker, Oppenheimer and Groves presided over a technical and communications staff of about twenty. The small, enclosed space was cluttered with electronic equipment and radios. They were concerned about the weather. Flashes of lightning were seen in the overcast, and scattered showers had been reported to the south. A meteorology team was in radio contact with specially equipped B-29 weather reconnaissance planes overhead. If the wind was blowing too hard in the wrong direction, there was a risk of deadly fallout traveling 300 miles east to descend over Amarillo, Texas. But an hour before dawn, conditions were deemed suitable for the test.

At zero minus twenty minutes, the first of several red warning flares went up at Ground Zero. All remaining personnel at the steel tower left by jeep for the bunker. The time intervals were announced by an impassive voice on the radio net. In the bunker, men crouched over their instrument panels. Tension escalated; time seemed to slow down. Dr. Conant said he "never imagined seconds could be so long."[83] Oppenheimer did not speak, and did not even seem to breathe; he held on to a wooden post to steady himself as he gazed through the bunker's nearly opaque blue-tinted windows. At zero minus ten seconds, a green flare shot up and descended slowly through the clouds above Ground Zero. The final ten seconds seemed to last an eternity. Whatever they thought of the bomb as a military weapon, the scientists had dedicated years of their lives to building it; they had staked the prestige of modern physics upon it; they had convinced Uncle Sam to divert rivers of the taxpayers' money to pay for it. Whatever their religious beliefs, or lack thereof, an observer noted: "It can safely be said that most of those present were praying and praying harder than they had ever prayed before."[84]

At 5:30 a.m., the countdown reached zero and the voice on the loudspeaker said, "Now." A pinprick of searing white light expanded almost instantly to become a small sun, half a mile in diameter, and the predawn darkness vanished in a cosmic flash, as blinding as a photographer's flashbulb. For a moment, the desert was lit to the horizon by a noonlike brightness, until most of the light was suddenly sucked back into the vortex of the blast, or so it appeared to the witnesses. Ascending, the great orb seemed to liquefy and dissolve into boiling neon colors, a mesmerizing kaleidoscope of gold, green, orange, blue, gray, and purple. Elongating vertically into the shape of a column, it rose through the cloud ceiling and climbed to 10,000 feet, 20,000 feet, 30,000 feet. A mushroom cloud formed at the top, at an altitude later estimated at 41,000 feet, while the base remained a surging, seething, churning mass of gas, smoke, and dust, as bright as burning magnesium but more colorful. For 40 miles in every direction, the New Mexico wilderness was bathed in a violet light that illuminated every hill, ridge, and gulch with searing clarity.

At the bunker, the observation posts, and the base camp, men rose to their feet and embraced, slapped backs, shook hands, shouted in glee, and laughed and danced like children. The tension on Oppenheimer's face dissolved and was replaced by an expression of grateful relief. Dr. Kistiakowsky, designer of the plutonium implosion trigger that had just proven itself to work, threw his arms around Oppenheimer and shouted in triumph. Someone said to General Groves: "The war is over." Groves replied, "Yes, after we drop two bombs on Japan."[85]

At Sandy Ridge, most observers ignored the instruction to lie down while awaiting the arrival of the shockwave. Forty-five seconds after the explosion, the phantasmagoric tableau remained silent—they felt heat on their faces but had heard no noise at all. Finally the sound fell upon them, a sustained, awesome, guttural rumble with a gust of warm air and a tremble in the earth underfoot. The reverberations merged into waves of sound that rose and fell for a long time before subsiding. Some found the blast wave gentle or even anticlimactic after the spectacular visual effects they had witnessed. That was undoubtedly true, but only because they were a long way from Ground Zero.

After their first flush of triumph, the observers became more subdued and reflective. Ernest O. Lawrence recalled "hushed murmuring bordering on reverence."[86] To Kistiakowsky, the atomic blast was "the nearest thing to doomsday that one could possibly imagine. I am sure that at the end of the world—in the last millisecond of the earth's existence—the last man will see what we have just seen."[87] As they boarded their vehicles to clear out of the area, the sun peeked over the eastern horizon. Philip Morrison noticed that the sensation of heat on his face was the same as that produced by the earlier explosion. On that morning, he said, "we had two sunrises."[88]

The light had been seen in communities as far away as Santa Fe to the north, Silver City to the west, and El Paso to the south. In Albuquerque, 175 miles north of Ground Zero, early-rising civilians had stopped and wondered at the flash of light on the southern horizon. According to a story in the local press, a blind girl in the city had cried out, "What was that?"[89] To discourage inconvenient questions, Groves arranged to have the commanding officer of the Alamogordo Air Base announce that an ammunition depot had blown up.[90]

In the days following the test, a few brave souls returned to the TRINITY site to investigate the results. Their portable Geiger counters cried out so loudly and insistently that they switched them off. To limit their exposure to radiation, a ten-minute rule was applied: each individual could visit the site only once, and could remain for only ten minutes. A mile from Ground Zero, the desert brush was blackened and flattened, facing away from the blast site; closer in, it was entirely burned away. Where the tower had once stood was a bowl of pulverized earth at the bottom of a shallow crater, 1,200 feet in diameter. The ground was glassy and smooth, with greenish streaks running through it; the sand had literally been turned to glass.

A faint rust-red blotch stained the ground at the center of the crater. Investigators determined that it was vaporized ferrous oxide, which had condensed and fused with the silicon in the sand—or in other words, the last trace of the ten-story steel tower that had held the TRINITY bomb.

THE FIRST REPORT ARRIVED IN POTSDAM later that day, at 7:30 p.m. local time. A War Department aide telegrammed Stimson: "Operated on this morning. Diagnosis not yet completed but results seem satisfactory and already exceeded expectations."[91] Stimson walked over to the "Little White House" to deliver the news to Truman and Byrnes, who were delighted. The cryptic first telegram was followed by several more, all inscribed in similarly cagey terms. A long and detailed report from Groves arrived by courier on July 21. The force of the explosion had equaled between 15,000 and 20,000 tons of TNT, which was at the higher end of the range of predictions. Groves had once boasted that the Pentagon (his earlier creation) was invulnerable to aerial bombing; he now withdrew that claim.

Stimson read the entire text to Truman and Byrnes. The war secretary recorded in his diary that the president was "tremendously pepped up and spoke to me of it again and again when I saw him."[92] Churchill noted that

Truman's newfound pep was on display the next morning in negotiations with Stalin, when he "stood up to the Russians in a most emphatic and decisive manner, telling them as to certain demands that they absolutely could not have, and that the United States was entirely against them."[93]

After discussing it with his advisers, Truman decided to let Stalin know of the TRINITY test, though only in the most general terms. He approached the Soviet dictator on the evening of July 24, and told him (through an interpreter) that the United States had developed a "new weapon of unusual destructive force." Stalin seemed unmoved, remarking casually that he hoped the Americans would make good use of it against Japan. Truman wondered whether the other man had grasped the significance of what he had been told. He did not know or suspect that Soviet espionage had successfully penetrated the Manhattan Project, and that the Russians were already well informed about the bomb.

American cryptanalysts had long since broken the codes used by the Japanese government to communicate with its diplomats in foreign capitals. This message traffic, codenamed MAGIC, was summarized and analyzed in top-secret memoranda distributed to senior American civilian and military officials. By this means, U.S. leaders were fully aware of Tokyo's bid to persuade the Soviet government to mediate an armistice with the Allies. The spirited exchanges between Foreign Minister Shigenori Togo and Ambassador-in-Moscow Naotake Sato made for lively and fascinating reading. The tenor of Togo's "extremely urgent" cables to Sato revealed his sense of desperation. On July 11, he urged the ambassador to act with "all haste" in petitioning the Kremlin. The following day, Togo added that Sato should convey to Foreign Commissar Molotov that "His Majesty" personally hoped "to restore peace with all possible speed."[94] In a comment accompanying this intercept, U.S. intelligence analysts noted that it offered the first tangible evidence that Hirohito was behind these diplomatic appeals to Moscow.

Sato's length of service in the diplomatic corps made him senior to Togo, and he had previously served as foreign minister (in 1937). As such, he was not at all cowed by the current head of the ministry, and did not hesitate to express his own magnificently blunt opinions about these desperate eleventh-hour overtures. Sato informed Togo that the Kremlin would never be enticed by the vague petitions he had been instructed to make. Being "extremely realistic," the Russians would not be moved by anything short of concrete proposals to end the war on terms that the Allies might deem acceptable. "If the Japanese empire is really faced with the necessity of ending the war," he lectured the foreign minister on July 12, "we must first of all make up our minds to do so."[95] Truer words had never been written, but Togo could act only according to the halfhearted consensus agreed to by the SWDC. Any proposal including specific peace terms would divide the ruling group and cause the Suzuki government to fall.

In his subsequent cables to Tokyo, Sato urged the government to recognize that the war was already lost, which meant that Japan had "no alternative but unconditional surrender or its equivalent." The sole condition that might tempt the Allies, he judged, would be "maintenance of our national structure," meaning an assurance to leave Hirohito on his throne.[96] But Togo only reiterated his prior instructions to petition the Kremlin for assistance in arranging a truce. Peace was urgent, he wrote, but "on the other hand it is difficult to decide on concrete peace terms here at home all at once."[97] Sato could read the meaning between those lines: the regime was hopelessly divided, and the intransigent militarists abhorred any terms resembling unconditional surrender. Togo's hands were tied, and so were Sato's.

As the second week of the Potsdam Conference got underway, the Americans confronted pressing decisions about the Pacific endgame. Preparations for DOWNFALL were underway with a scheduled invasion date of November 1. Intelligence sources had detected a buildup of Japanese troop strength on Kyushu. The Americans had become wary of Russian participation in the war, but they knew they could do nothing to keep their erstwhile communist allies out of it, and the Red Army would be prepared to invade Manchuria by mid-August at the latest. According to General Groves, two atomic bombs would be ready for use against Japan within the next two weeks. Some had raised objections on moral grounds against using the weapons without providing an explicit prior warning, or using them against cities instead of military targets. Petitions had been submitted by various groups of Manhattan Project scientists. Ralph Bard, undersecretary of the navy and a member of the Interim Committee, favored a preliminary warning. He wrote Stimson: "The position of the United States as a great humanitarian nation and the fair play attitude of our people generally is responsible in the main for this feeling."[98]

But the prevailing assumption in the Interim Committee, its subcommittees, and the cabinet had always been that the bombs would be used against Japan. Proposals for a demonstration or a warning were considered and rejected, chiefly because they seemed unlikely to lead to surrender. Admitting that opinions among Manhattan Project scientists were varied, the Scientific Panel (Oppenheimer, Conant, Lawrence, and Fermi) concluded: "We can propose no technical demonstration likely to bring an end to the war; we see no acceptable alternative to direct military use."[99]

The Target Committee had produced a final list of four cities: Hiroshima, Nagasaki, Kokura, and Niigata. The four were selected because they had not yet been leveled by conventional bombing, and thus promised to give the fullest and most dramatic expression to the bomb's power. Stimson had struck Kyoto off an earlier list. Reasoning that the ancient capital's historical and cultural significance made it unique, Stimson worried that destroying it would arouse the hatred of future generations of Japanese. (The war secretary was obliged to nix Kyoto twice: evidently, Groves really wanted to hit the city.) Hiroshima and Kokura were home to important military bases, depots, or arsenals; Nagasaki and Niigata were identified only as important shipping and industrial centers. By order to the Twentieth Air Force, those four cities had been set aside—preserved, quarantined, left intact, spared the fury of LeMay's incendiaries, so that the atomic bombs could destroy them at one stroke. Although radar targeting was now reliable, the bombs were to be dropped in clear weather, so that the explosions could be seen and photographed from the air: "The four targets give a very high probability of one being open even if the weather varies . . . as they are considerably separated."[100]

The Allies had agreed in principle that a final warning would be issued to Japan. Issuing this declaration from Potsdam, amidst the ruins of Nazi Germany, would lend symbolic power to the ultimatum—emphasizing that Japan was now without allies, and would soon share the same fate. But the precise wording of the declaration was the subject of prolonged and intricate debate. In several previous statements, including the Atlantic Charter, the Cairo Declaration, and the United Nations Charter (signed in San Francisco a month earlier), the Allies had already set forth their war aims and their vision for the postwar international order. The question now arose: Should these be repeated and amplified? To what extent should the Allies spell out intentions for the occupation of Japan? Several leading figures in the American camp, including Stimson and Grew, favored giving an assurance that the imperial dynasty could continue as a constitutional monarchy. They reasoned that such an assurance might empower the peace faction in Tokyo, perhaps bringing the emperor directly into the decision. Moreover, they added, the Allies were going to need Hirohito to enforce the surrender and to serve as a consenting vassal. Others, notably Secretary of State Byrnes, objected that any such pledge would compromise the doctrine of unconditional surrender, and might be read by the Japanese as a sign of irresolution.

On July 17, as the draft "Three-Party Statement" circulated through the Allied governments, the Joint Chiefs of Staff organization recommended edits in a cable from Washington. The draft had stated that the Japanese people would choose their own government, and "This may include a constitutional monarchy under the present dynasty if it be shown to the complete satisfaction of the world that such a government never again will aspire to aggression." On the recommendation of the JSSC—the internal JCS "think tank"—the chiefs recommended deleting that sentence entirely. Two reasons were offered: first, because the reference to the "present dynasty" might be misconstrued as an intention to depose Hirohito in favor of his son; and second, because the provision might discourage "radical elements in Japan" by suggesting that the Allies intended to maintain the system of "Emperor worship."[101] The reasoning was not persuasive on either count. The first objection called for a clarification of the wording, not wholesale deletion; the second made little sense at all, because "radical elements in Japan" had no power to influence the decision to surrender. Nevertheless, the proposed deletion was accepted by Truman and his advisers in Potsdam, apparently without much discussion or debate. Both Leahy and Marshall seem to have supported the deletion without objection, although both had earlier favored clarifying the emperor's postwar status.

On July 24, Stimson made a last-ditch attempt to reinsert a provision offering to retain the Japanese monarchy. According to a diary entry he made later that day, Stimson met with Truman and "spoke of the importance which I attributed to the reassurance of the Japanese on the continuance of their dynasty and I had felt that the insertion of that in the formal warning was important and might be just the thing that would make or mar their acceptance."[102] Truman declined on practical grounds, explaining that a draft of the declaration had already been sent to Chiang Kai-shek for his signature. Stimson accepted that reasoning, but he recommended that

Truman be prepared to offer verbal assurances through diplomatic channels if and when direct talks were opened with the Japanese government.

Meanwhile, orders to carry out the atomic attacks were being written and distributed in Washington. A special B-29 air group based on Tinian had trained to drop the atomic bombs, and was ready to perform their mission. Various components of the weapons were being transferred to the Marianas by air and sea. General Carl Spaatz, recently named overall commander of USAAF Strategic Air Forces in the Pacific, was in Washington. On July 25, he reported to the War Department and conferred with Marshall's deputy, General Thomas T. Handy, the acting army chief of staff in Marshall's absence. Spaatz had received verbal orders to drop the two bombs, but he told Handy that he needed a "piece of paper" spelling out the order. Handy drafted and signed an order directing the Twentieth Air Force to deliver the "first special bomb as soon as weather will permit visual bombing after about 3 August 1945 on one of the targets: Hiroshima, Kokura, Niigata and Nagasaki." Additional bombs would be dropped on the same list of target cities "as soon as made ready by the project staff."[103] A final clause added that the directive had been issued "by direction and with the approval" of Secretary Stimson and General Marshall. That was the only written order pertaining to the use of atomic bombs against Japan.

At the "Little White House" in Potsdam, on that same date (July 25), Truman met alone with his secretary of war—and if the president's diary is to be believed, his verbal instructions to Stimson could not be reconciled with the orders just issued in Washington:

I have told the Sec. Of War, Mr. Stimson to use it so that military objectives and soldiers and sailors are the target and not women and children. Even if the Japs are savages, ruthless, merciless and fanatic, we as the leader of the world for the common welfare cannot drop this terrible bomb on the old Capitol or the new [i.e., Kyoto or Tokyo].

He & I are in accord. The target will be a purely military one and we will issue a warning statement asking the Japs to surrender and save lives. I'm sure they will not do that, but we will have given them the chance.[104]

But Handy's order, written under Stimson's authority, was in line with the instructions he had already received from Potsdam. It was based upon the recommendations of the Interim Committee and its subcommittees, as approved by the cabinet and the president. The bombs would be dropped as they were made ready, and as weather conditions permitted, on the four Japanese cities selected by the Target Committee. The order made no mention of warnings, military objectives, or sparing women and children. The cities had not been chosen for their military character, and the military installations therein were not specified as aiming points for the bombs. They were chosen because they fulfilled the three conditions specified by the Target Committee—namely, that they were "large urban area[s] of more than three miles diameter," which were "capable of being damaged effectively by a blast," and were "likely to be unattacked by next August."[105]

Truman's diary entry of July 25 remains an inexplicable curiosity. Perhaps he felt sudden qualms, and soothed them with therapeutic delusions. He might have sensed that future historians and biographers were reading over his shoulder, and hoped to be commended as a man of delicate conscience. If so, the entry was a feckless gesture, serving only to leave the impression that the diary was not a faithful record of Truman's inner thoughts. His famous homespun motto—"The buck stops here"—was printed on a sign featured prominently on his desk in the Oval Office. After the first atomic bomb detonated over the center of the seventh largest city in Japan, the non-buck-passing commander in chief would identify Hiroshima as an "important Japanese Army base," which was true in the same sense that San Diego was an important American naval base. In his memoirs, published in 1955, Truman took responsibility for the decision to use the atomic bombs—but even then, in retirement, a decade after the fact, he could not bring himself to acknowledge that cities had been targeted. Reproducing in full the July 25, 1945, directive signed by General Handy, Truman added: "With this order, the wheels were set in motion for the first use of an atomic weapon against a military target. I had made the decision. I also instructed Stimson that the order would stand unless I notified him that the Japanese reply to our ultimatum was acceptable."[106]

On July 26, the Potsdam Declaration was released to the global press by the governments of the United States, Great Britain, and China. It demanded the immediate and unconditional surrender of Japanese armed forces, and warned that refusal would result in the "utter devastation" of the Japanese homeland: "Following are our terms. We will not deviate from them. There are no alternatives. We shall brook no delay."[107] Japan would never again be permitted to embark on a career of foreign conquest. The influence of the militarist caste would be completely and permanently eliminated. War crimes would be prosecuted in international tribunals. All foreign territories would be given up, and Japanese sovereignty would be forever limited to the home islands. Its forces overseas would be disarmed and permitted to return home in peace. The Allies would occupy "points in Japanese territory" for as long as necessary to ensure that the "self-willed militaristic advisers" were ousted and the military demobilized. Industry would be permitted to recover, and the economy would have access to international trade. Contrary to the propaganda disseminated by the Japanese regime, said the statement, "We do not intend that the Japanese shall be enslaved as a race or destroyed as a nation," and a peaceful and responsible government would be instituted "in accordance with the freely expressed will of the Japanese people."

The declaration was received in Tokyo shortly after dawn on July 27, via shortwave radio broadcast from San Francisco. As the text of this "Three-Party Statement" was translated and circulated through the ministry offices, Japanese leaders fixated on the fact that it was signed by the U.S., British, and Chinese leaders, but not by Stalin. Upon this thin reed they placed great hopes. They knew Stalin and Molotov were in Potsdam, in close touch with the Americans and British, and yet the USSR had not backed the ultimatum. Did that mean the Soviets were willing to step in as a mediator?

Foreign Minister Togo acted quickly to head off a preemptive rejection of the declaration. In a private meeting with the emperor, he said that the statement "leaves room for further study of the concrete terms," and "we plan to find out what these concrete terms are through the Soviet Union."[108] In an emergency meeting of the SWDC later that morning, Togo told his colleagues that the declaration could be interpreted as a softening of prior demands, and might plausibly be represented as a face-saving "conditional" surrender. Although it contained no reference to the Imperial House, the reference to the "freely expressed will of the Japanese people" gave hope that the emperor could be retained. He warned that rejecting the declaration outright might bring catastrophic consequences, and recommended withholding any official reaction until his diplomats could sound out the

Russians. Further discussion produced a shaky accord. While awaiting the Russian response to Japan's prior entreaties, the government would express no view on the Potsdam Declaration. The newspapers would be directed to downplay it.

The following afternoon, at four o'clock on July 28, the aged Prime Minister Kantaro Suzuki held a press conference carried over the radio. It was no easy task to explain the temporizing policy negotiated by the two factions of the Big Six. Suzuki could say nothing of the overtures in Moscow, which were secret; and he could not imply that the declaration provided an opening for peace talks, because the hardliners would rise up in protest. In an apparently off-the-cuff remark, he told the press that the government intended to "*mokusatsu*" the Potsdam Declaration. This idiomatic Japanese expression translated literally as "to kill with silence," but could also be translated as to "ignore," "reject," or "take no notice of." Under the circumstances, "*mokusatsu*" might be seen as an attempt to steer a middle course between accepting and rejecting the ultimatum—in other words, "no comment."

If that was Suzuki's purpose, he failed badly. The phrase was ambiguous even in Japanese, let alone in English translation. Without clear contrary guidance from the government, the Japanese press reported that the prime minister had rejected the declaration with a contemptuous flourish. On the twenty-ninth, the *Yomiuri Shinbun* led with the headline: "Laughable Surrender Conditions to Japan."[109] By then it was too late for Suzuki to walk his comments back. In a subsequent meeting of the SWDC, the three hardliners agreed that it was unacceptable for the government to take an equivocal position on the Potsdam Declaration. Peacemakers Togo and Yonai argued that nothing more should be said, but the prime minister agreed to issue a clarification. At a press conference that morning, Suzuki said: "I think that the joint statement is a rehash of the Cairo declaration. The government does not think that it has serious value. We can only ignore it. We will do our utmost to complete the war to the bitter end."[110]

At first the American translators had puzzled over "*mokusatsu*" and debated the possible shades of meaning or emphasis. But this second statement sent a much clearer signal. Truman offered his own pungent translation: "They told me to go to hell, words to that effect."[111] The old Japan hands in Washington noted that Suzuki had carefully avoided rejecting the ultimatum outright. They inferred that he was talking to potential insurrectionists in the army, rather than to the governments that had issued the ultimatum. In the following days, radio eavesdroppers picked up army and diplomatic communications suggesting that some in Tokyo were ready to surrender on the basis of the Potsdam Declaration. But those intelligence tidbits only confirmed what American leaders already knew— that the Japanese ruling group was deadlocked, and the hardline "fight on" faction remained strong enough to arrest any move toward surrender.

A secure cable from the "Little White House" instructed General Groves to launch the first atomic bombing mission no sooner than August 2, 1945, the final day of the Potsdam Conference. Truman wanted to be away and at sea when the first nuclear weapon was dropped.[112]

That same week, the conventional bombing assault on the Japanese homeland was reaching an unprecedented scale. The results on the ground went far beyond anything that had been done in Europe—or indeed, anywhere else in the history of warfare. In the heart of major cities, one could gaze to the horizon in any direction and see nothing but fields of ash and hillocks of rubble, with a few blackened chimneys or steel girders standing here and there. The largest air raid of the war occurred on August 1, 1945, when 853 B-29s dropped more 6,486 tons of incendiaries, precision bombs, and aerial mines on cities and waterways throughout western Japan. By that date, the Japanese civilian death toll had probably run well into the hundreds of thousands.

If the war had lasted any longer than it did, the scale and ferocity of the conventional bombing campaign would have risen to inconceivable new heights. Hundreds of bombers and fighters of all types, U.S. and British, were redeploying from Europe; at the same time, new airplanes were being turned out of American aviation plants, and freshly trained aircrews were flying them into newly constructed airfields on nearby Okinawa. At the height of the bombing campaign, between May and August 1945, a monthly average of 34,402 tons of high-explosive and incendiary bombs were dropped on Japan.[113] According to USAAF chief Hap Arnold, the monthly total would have reached 100,000 tons in September 1945, and then risen steadily month by month. By early 1946, if the Japanese were still fighting, eighty USAAF combat groups would be operating against Japan, a total of about 4,000 bombers. In January 1946, they would drop 170,000 tons of bombs on Japan, surpassing in one month the cumulative tonnage actually dropped on the country during the entire Pacific War. By March

1946, the anticipated date of the CORONET landings on the Tokyo Plain, the monthly bombing figure would surpass 200,000 tons.[114] The rain of devastation would cripple the nation's internal transportation infrastructure, shutting down the economy and leading to mass famine in urban regions. "Another six months and Japan would have been beaten back into the dark ages," said Curtis LeMay, "which practically was the case anyhow."[115]

In those last weeks of the war, the Twentieth Air Force began waging a new and devastating form of psychological warfare. The Superforts began "calling their shots"—that is, dropping leaflets over cities to be hit, warning the population to evacuate, and then returning one or two days later to destroy them. On July 27, for example—the same day the Potsdam Declaration was received in Japan—60,000 warning leaflets were dropped on eleven cities. Six of those eleven were hit the following day. The ploy was repeated again on August 1 and a third time on August 4. In each case, the warnings were made good. The Japanese government and news media attempted to suppress the warnings, but the news spread widely by word of mouth, and panic swept through the leafleted cities. Refugees clogged the roads and trains as entire urban populations tried to flee to the country. Munitions industries were paralyzed for lack of workers. After the war, the USSBS concluded that the "shot-calling" leaflets had been "one of the most spectacular moves in psychological warfare."[116] They had dramatized the powerlessness of Japan's military and air forces, convincing many ordinary Japanese that defeat was inevitable. The USSBS concluded that approximately half the Japanese population had either seen one of the leaflets or had heard about their contents by word of mouth.

At the same time, the warnings were appreciated by many Japanese as gestures of consideration and sympathy. A woman in Nagaoka credited the leaflets with saving her life. Her own government had refused to pass on the vital news that the city had been listed as a target, she said—but "I believed the Americans were honest and good people in letting us know in advance of impending raids." She fled, and three days later Nagaoka was firebombed. A factory worker in Akita shared the sentiment. "They were not barbarians," he said of the men flying the great silver bombers overhead. "They gave us notice. They said to evacuate."[117]

Chapter Sixteen

Tinian, the once-verdant tropical island south of Saipan, was now the largest airbase in the world. Nearly half of its 39 square miles had been paved over to accommodate airfields for B-29s and fighters. North and West Fields included eight great runways for Superfortresses, each almost two miles long and the width of a ten-lane highway. They were connected to parking aprons, hardstands, and fuel storage farms by 11 miles of taxiways. Most of a long ridge had been leveled to supply the coral rock for this vastness of pavement and asphalt. From the air, a witness recounted, Tinian resembled "a giant aircraft carrier, its deck loaded with bombers."[1] Others were reminded of Manhattan, an island comparable in size, which was likewise paved over. Tinian's road network, like that of Manhattan, was laid out in a grid pattern. Its two major north-south roads were called Broadway and Eighth Avenue; east-west "cross streets" included Wall Street, Forty-Second Street, and 110th Street. An undeveloped livestock reserve in the middle of the island was called "Central Park."

At the intersection of Eighth Avenue and 125th Street, near the isolated northern end of North Field, a guardhouse marked the entry gate to the 509th Composite Group, a mysterious and secretive B-29 unit whose compound was double-fenced and patrolled by armed sentries. The 509th was self-contained—meaning that it had its own separate ground support, logistics, communications, security, and administrative organizations. It did not interact at all with the 313th Bombardment Wing, to which it technically belonged. Bold red and black signs warned unauthorized personnel to stay away from the perimeter. Even the 313th Wing commander, Brigadier General James Davies, did not know the purpose of these enigmatic Superforts that ostensibly fell within his chain of command. When Davies tried to visit the compound, he was turned away at gunpoint.

The sole mission of the 509th Composite Group was to drop the atomic bombs. Paul W. Tibbets Jr., a twenty-nine-year-old lieutenant colonel, led the group. Tibbets had been provided with virtually unlimited resources to fulfill his mission. He had the power to requisition materials, equipment, or personnel as he chose, and he built his team by lifting entire B-29 squadrons out of other air groups, without explanation. In December 1944, the 509th had set up shop at Wendover Army Airfield in Utah—a bleak, arid airbase wedged between the Utah salt flats and the Nevada border. The aircrews and ground support personnel were told that they must never breathe a word of what they were doing to anyone. Those who asked too many questions, even internally, would be sacked. All personnel were kept on a strict need-to-know basis, but the pilots and bombardiers were told that they must train to drop a 9,000-pound "special bomb," which for the sake of security they called "the gadget."[2]

An aircraft that dropped the new bomb was required to fly at least 8 miles away from the point at which the device was set to detonate. It would have forty seconds to complete the maneuver. That required a hard-banking 155-degree turn, during which the pilot would dive steeply to pick up speed. Tactical analysis of Japanese fighter defenses led Tibbets to conclude that they should remove most of the armament from the planes, and rely on speed and altitude to thwart interception. The 509th Composite Group would also have to oversee major alterations to the B-29, because the new bomb would not fit into the aircraft's standard bomb bay. The group trained at Wendover using "pumpkin bombs," which mimicked the size, weight, and ballistics profile of the uranium and plutonium weapons, named "Little Boy" and "Fat Man," respectively. In training runs, the B-29s aimed these dummy weapons at a 300-foot circle painted on the ground, and then executed the evasive maneuvers.

Immediately upon completion of the TRINITY test, the major components of the two bombs were transported to Tinian. Crates containing the "gun-type" trigger for Little Boy, and half of the bomb's uranium U-235 core, were flown to San Francisco and loaded onto the cruiser *Indianapolis*. The ship made an uneventful passage to a pier in Tinian, arriving on July 26. The crates were transferred to an assembly building at the 509th compound, staffed by a specialized team of Manhattan Project scientists and technicians. The remaining portion of the uranium, packed in two crates, was flown across the Pacific in a C-54. By August 1, all of the bomb components were on Tinian and ready for assembly.

Having discharged her mysterious cargo, the *Indianapolis* sailed for Leyte Gulf. Her passage was cut short on July 30, when the ship was struck by two torpedoes fired by Japanese submarine *I-58*. She sank in twelve minutes. Her distress messages were not received, and her absence was not noted until three days later. A fourth day passed before rescue vessels arrived on the scene. About 900 of her crew of 1,200 had abandoned ship as she went down, but few lifeboats had been launched, so the men were left treading water or clinging to debris. During their four-day ordeal, adrift in the open sea, about six hundred perished as a result of exposure, dehydration, saltwater poisoning, drowning, or shark attacks. Only 317 of the crew survived. The *Indianapolis*, Admiral Raymond Spruance's former Fifth Fleet flagship, was the last major American warship lost in the Second World War.

Although B-29 operations had grown safer since the pioneering days of 1944, crashes on takeoff were still common. Fuel-laden planes were heavier on takeoff than at any other point in a mission. Burnt-out hulks of crashed Superforts lined the margins of the runways of the various Twentieth Air Force airfields. On August 4, two days before the Hiroshima mission, four B-29s crashed on takeoff at airfields throughout the Marianas. The accidents dramatized the necessity of leaving the atomic bombs unassembled until the planes carrying them were safely aloft. That meant sending assembly teams up with the aircrews.

Colonel Tibbets would pilot the B-29 that would drop the uranium bomb. Model number B-29–45-MO was better known as the *Enola Gay*; Tibbets had named the aircraft for his mother, Enola Gay Tibbets. Two 509th Superforts would fly in company with the *Enola Gay* as observers, and would drop various measuring instruments. Three more would fly ahead to reconnoiter the weather over the target.

August 6 began with a midnight briefing in a heavily guarded Quonset hut, and a prayer by the chaplain. The aircrews of the *Enola Gay* and the other planes boarded canvas-covered trucks lined with benches to be driven to the airfield. They passed through numerous checkpoints en route. Arriving at the hardstand, the airmen found an unexpected scene. The *Enola Gay* was surrounded by a crowd numbering in the hundreds—VIPs, ground crews, soldiers, and a large deputation of the press. The big airplane was brightly lit by klieg lights. Motion picture cameras were mounted on portable risers. Lightbulbs flashed. Witnesses were reminded of a Broadway premiere or a Hollywood film opening.

Tibbets and his crew posed in front of their plane for a formal photograph. "Okay," Tibbets said at 2:20 a.m., "let's get to work." The crew climbed aboard the plane, waved again, and then closed the hatch. Before starting the engines, Tibbets stuck his grinning face out of the left-seat cockpit window and waved one last time for the cameras. Below the window was stenciled, in black letters, his mother's name: *Enola Gay.*

The crowd moved back as the great engines fired up. The long propellers began spinning, the engines roared, and the airplanes taxied to the edges of Runways A and B. The *Enola Gay*, showing no running lights, started its takeoff run at 2:45. With a 5-ton atomic bomb and a full load of fuel, the strike plane required nearly the entire length of runway to get off the ground. *The Great Artiste*, the instrument plane, took off exactly two minutes later on Runway B, followed two minutes later by the second observer plane, *Necessary Evil*. The three planes banked north and began climbing.

With the *Enola Gay* safely aloft, Captain William S. "Deak" Parsons of the navy, the chief weaponeer, climbed back into the bomb bay and started the intricate process of arming Little Boy. The weapon was 10 feet long and 2.5 feet in diameter; it weighed 9,800 pounds. Parsons inserted the explosive charges into the gun device. He would return several hours later to connect the priming lines.

At 5:45 a.m., the crew caught sight of Iwo Jima, with Mount Suribachi clear in the morning sun. *The Great Artiste* slipped into formation, just 30 feet off the *Enola Gay*'s right wing; the *Necessary Evil* joined up to the lead plane's left. Two hours north of Iwo Jima, the three planes began a slow climb to 9,000 feet. Several of the crewmen, with no duties to perform, caught a few hours of sleep.

The three weather planes, *Straight Flush, Jabit III,* and *Full House,* had taken off earlier and flown ahead to reconnoiter the weather over Hiroshima and the secondary targets, Kokura and Nagasaki. The *Enola Gay* radioman copied a coded message from *Straight Flush*, circling above Hiroshima: "Cloud cover less than three tenths at all altitudes. Advice: Bomb primary." The crew pulled on their flak suits and strapped into their parachutes. Tibbets pressurized the cabin and the *Enola Gay* resumed its gradual climb, finally leveling off at 32,700 feet. The plane crossed the south coast of Shikoku at 8:50 a.m. No Japanese fighters were in the air, and no antiair-craft fire was seen.

Captain Parsons and his assistant returned to the bomb bay and com-pleted their arming checklist. They removed the safety devices, screwed in the live breech plugs, connected the firing line, and installed the armor plate over these mechanisms. Little Boy was now fully armed. They removed and secured the catwalk and left the bomb bay. They would not return.

Tibbets and his copilot (Robert Lewis) looked down through the *Enola Gay*'s greenhouse nose at the familiar coastal contours and islands of the Inland Sea. It was a bright, clear morning, with only sparse and scattered cloud cover. They flew directly over the lobster-shaped island of Etajima, site of the Japanese Naval Academy. The port and city of Kure passed below and to their right. Ahead, the densely populated fan-shaped delta of Hiroshima came into view. It was a broad, flat city intercut by diverging tidal estuaries of the Ota River, bordered by the Inland Sea on one side and green ridges on three others. Tibbets made his final turn onto 272 degrees magnetic course. Through a gap in the clouds, he and his copilot had a clear view of their aiming point—the large T-shaped Aioi Bridge, spanning the Ota just north of Nakajima Island. The *Enola Gay* and its escorts were at 31,600 feet, almost 6 miles above the city. At 8:05 a.m. (Hiroshima time), the navigator announced, "10 minutes to the AP."

At 8:14 a.m., one minute before the drop, Tibbets ordered: "On glasses." Each member of the crew put on his protective dark polarized welder's gog-gles. The bombardier, Thomas Ferebee, checked the Norden bombsight and confirmed that the aiming point was "inside," meaning that the plane was directly on target. A radio warning signal was sent to the two observation planes. At 8:15 a.m., the *Enola Gay*'s bomb bay doors opened, and Little Boy's restraining hook was retracted back into its slot. Ferebee told Tib-bets, "Bomb away"—but the pilot would have known it anyway, because the plane was suddenly 5 tons lighter, and it lurched upward accordingly. Tibbets banked to the right.

Charles Sweeney, piloting *The Great Artiste* just off the *Enola Gay*'s right wing, watched the 10-foot cylinder as it fell from the strike plane. He thought, "It's too late now. There are no strings or cables attached. We can't get it back, whether it works or not."[3] Little Boy wobbled or "porpoised" slightly, then steadied on its course, like a missile. It took a steeper trajectory and shrank quickly from sight. It would fall for forty-three seconds to 1,800 feet over the Aioi Bridge, its detonation point.

The Great Artiste released its instrument canisters, which would collect measurements and transmit them back to the plane by radio. Then Sweeney banked sharply to the left, putting his B-29 into the 155-degree diving turn that he and the other 509th pilots had practiced for nine months. The *Enola Gay* was turning in a similar arc to the right. Tests in Wendover had shown that the Superfortresses could withstand such a turn without undue risk of structural damage.[4]

Both Tibbets and Sweeney watched their instruments carefully during the turn. Both had trouble reading the panels through the welder's goggles, so they pushed them up to their foreheads. *The Great Artiste* was flying away from the epicenter, but the interior of the airplane was suddenly suffused with a blinding silver-bluish light, and Sweeney noted that the sky ahead was bleached to a bright white hue. He instinctively shut his eyes, but felt a sensation of light filling his head. At the same time, he noted a peculiar taste in his mouth, like lead. (This was ozone, caused by gamma rays.) On the *Necessary Evil*, now 15 miles from the blast, one crew member found the light in the cabin so bright that he could have read the fine print in his pocket bible even through the dark goggles.

Tibbets noticed the metallic taste and the flash at the same time. "I got the brilliance," he said later. "I tasted it. Yeah, I could taste it. It tasted like lead. And this was because of the fillings in my teeth. So that's radiation, see. So I got this lead taste in my mouth and that was a big relief—I knew she had blown."[5] His copilot, Robert Lewis, turned back in his seat to look. He shouted wildly, striking Tibbets on the shoulder: "Look at that! Look at that! Look at that!" Lewis later wrote in his log of the mission, "My god, what have we done?"[6]

About a minute later, the *Enola Gay* was hit by the first shockwave. The plane's aluminum skin made a sharp, cracking retort, as if someone had swung a very large sledgehammer at the fuselage from outside. The aircraft jerked and trembled, but held together. Tibbets estimated that the hit was equivalent in force to about two-and-one-half Gs. This first shockwave was followed quickly by a second, moderately less violent—it was an echo of the first, having struck the ground and rebounded upward.

Not having witnessed the TRINITY test, the airmen were unprepared for the sight they beheld as the planes turned back toward the epicenter to take photographs. Sergeant Abe Spitzer, a radio operator on *The Great Artiste*, thought it looked as if "the sun fell out of the sky and was on the ground."[7] It was an awesome and terrible sight, a fireball ascending with many different shades of purple and amber, amidst a boiling mass of dust and flaming gases. A dirty gray mushroom cloud was forming at the top of a great pillar of smoke. The pillar had already climbed higher than the altitude of the airplanes, so the airmen looked *up* at the mushroom. No part of Hiroshima remained visible from the air, except the ends of a few of the longer piers on the waterfront. The green ridges to the north and west stood above the devastation, but the carpet of smoke and dust was spreading inland along the meandering paths of the river valleys. "Down below all you could see was a black, boiling nest," Tibbets said. "I didn't think about what was going on down on the ground—you need to be objective about this. I didn't order the bomb to be dropped, but I had a mission to do."[8]

The *Enola Gay* and *The Great Artiste* circled Hiroshima three times, ascending gradually in a corkscrew pattern, while the crewmen continued to gape in awe at the unspeakable devastation below. For a long time, no one spoke. The high-speed cameras in the instrument plane snapped hundreds of photos, and the technicians reported that they had made an excellent record. Captain Parsons radioed a coded message back to Tinian, reporting that the blast had been successful and the B-29s were returning to base.

Joe Stiborik, a member of the *Enola Gay*'s crew, later recalled that everyone aboard remained almost completely silent during the long flight home. "I was dumbfounded," he said. "It was just too much to express in words, I guess. We were all in a kind of state of shock. I think the foremost thing in all our minds was that this thing was going to bring an end to the war, and we tried to look at it that way."[9]

THROUGHOUT THE SUMMER, dark rumors had circulated through the city. The Americans were said to be preparing some awful fate for Hiroshima. Why else would the city have been left untouched by bombs, when nearly every other city in the region, including Kure, Iwakuni, and Tokuyama, had been devastated? Two air raid sirens had sounded during the night of August 5–6. Some had risen dutifully and gone to their bomb shelters, but many others had slept through the alarms.

Early that morning, the coastal radar net had detected the weather reconnaissance B-29s that had preceded the *Enola Gay*. Air raid sirens had churned, summoning the city's residents to their shelters. An all-clear signal had sounded at 8:00 a.m. Members of the air raid volunteer corps, including many school-age children, were being dismissed from their duties.

It was a clear, hot, still summer morning, with barely a cloud in the sky. The streets were crowded with morning rush hour traffic, including pedestrians, bicycles, rickshaws, horse carts, automobiles, and streetcars. When the *Enola Gay* and its two escorts droned in from the south, they could be seen clearly from the ground. Witnesses spotted a cluster of parachutes blossoming at high altitude. They were the instrument canisters dropped by *The Great Artiste*.

Little Boy exploded at 8:16 a.m., 1,870 feet above the ground, only 550 feet wide of its aiming point. The nuclear chain reaction it triggered created a core temperature of about 1 million degrees Celsius, igniting the air around it to a diameter of nearly a kilometer. The fireball engulfed the center of the city, vaporizing about 20,000 people on the ground. Thermal and ionizing radiation killed virtually all people within a kilometer of the surface of the fireball, burning them to death or rupturing their internal organs. Farther out, in successive concentric circles around the epicenter, people were exposed to gamma rays, neutron radiation, flash burns, the blast wave, and firestorms. The initial shockwave raced away from the epicenter at greater than the speed of sound, some 984 miles per hour. Streetcars were lifted from their tracks and scattered like toys. Clothing was torn from bodies. Nearly all wooden buildings within 2.3 kilometers were completely leveled, and about half of all such buildings to a radius of 3.2 kilometers. Later, investigators found the shadows of people caught within the inner radius around the hypocenter. They had been vaporized, but their bodies had left faint silhouettes on the pavement or on nearby walls.

Like the aircrews of the B-29s overhead, surviving witnesses on the ground remembered the flash (*pika*) and the taste of ozone in the mouth. Dr. Michihiko Hachiya was sitting at home when his living room filled with a bright white light. In the moment before his house collapsed, the doctor wondered whether someone had lit a magnesium flare just outside his windows. Yoshido Matsushige, a photographer for the Hiroshima daily paper, recalled a "brilliant flash of immaculate white, like the igniting of the magnesium we used to use for taking photographs."[10] Father Johannes Siemes, a

German Jesuit priest and a professor of modern philosophy at Tokyo's Catholic University, had been evacuated from the capital to the Novitiate of the Society of Jesus in Nagatsuke, a suburb of Hiroshima. He was sitting in his spartan bedroom, about a mile from the epicenter, when the room was suddenly filled with a "garish light which resembles the magnesium light used in photography, and I am conscious of a wave of heat."[11]

Moments later came a great tearing sound, a sudden collapse of ceilings and walls, and a sensation of falling or sliding into an abyss. Dr. Hachiya's house was filled with swirling dust. He could see only a wooden pillar, leaning askew, and then noted that the roof was caving in. He had been wearing underwear, but a moment after the flash he was completely naked, though he had not noticed the garments being ripped away. Like many others, the doctor first assumed that a conventional bomb had fallen directly on his house. He shouted to his wife, "It's a 500-ton bomb!"[12]

Those caught in the open were lifted off their feet and carried through the air. Michiko Yamaoka, a fifteen-year-old girl on her way to her job at the telephone exchange, was looking up at the planes overhead when the bomb exploded. "You can't really say it washed over me," she recalled years later. "It's hard to describe. I simply fainted. I remember my body floating in the air. That was probably the blast, but I don't know how far I was blown."[13] Fragments of glass and wooden splinters tore into flesh. Eiko Taoka, a twenty-one-year-old mother carrying her infant son, was on a streetcar approaching the center of the city when the car was filled with "a strange smell and sound." She looked down and saw that a shard of glass had pierced her child's head. He was bleeding, but did not comprehend what had happened, and did not seem to be suffering any pain. He looked up at his mother and smiled through the blood on his face.[14] Hatsuyo Nakamura, another young mother, worked frantically to dig her children out of the wreckage of their home. Her five-year-old daughter was shrieking in pain. "There's no time now to say whether it hurts or not," she replied, and yanked the girl free. She was cut and bruised, but otherwise uninjured.[15] Futaba Kitayama, a thirty-three-year-old woman serving on a firebreak demolition team, was buried under the remains of a home that she had been working to pull down. Extracting herself from the wreckage, she noted that she was bleeding. There were embers in her hair, and shards of glass had torn into her flesh. She found a towel and began wiping blood from her face. "To my horror, I found that the skin on my face had come off in the towel. Oh! The skin on my hands, on my arms, came off too. From elbow to fingertips, all the skin on my right arm had come loose and was hanging grotesquely. The skin of my left hand fell off too, the five fingers, like a glove."[16]

The smoke and dust hung so thick over the city that the sun was blotted out, and it was as dark as night. Nakamura's daughter kept asking questions as they ran from the wreckage of their home: "Why is it night already? Why did our house fall down? What happened?"[17] A procession of refugees— a tide of human wretchedness and misery—was fleeing before the fires, headed away from the epicenter, or pressing down to the river banks. They moved jerkily, with arms held away from their bodies; many had lost most of their skin, and were avoiding the painful friction of their arms rubbing against their torsos. Many were naked, and seemingly unaware of their nakedness—and many were also barefoot, because their shoes had lodged in the burning asphalt and been wrenched off. Their faces were hideously blackened and swollen, and their hair singed and frizzy. Those trapped beneath wreckage called out to passersby, begging for assistance or a drink of water. Everywhere, the plaintive mantra was heard: "*Mizu, mizu, mizu!*"[18] (Water, water, water!)

When she regained consciousness, Yamaoka realized that she was badly burned. "My clothes were burnt and so was my skin. I was in rags. I had braided my hair, but now it was like a lion's mane. There were people, barely breathing, trying to push their intestines back in. People with their legs wrenched off. Without heads. Or with faces burned and swollen out of shape."[19] Yoshido Matsushige had taken his camera out to the street, intending to take photographs for his newspaper, but at first he could not bring himself to record the ghastly scenes. "People's bodies were all swollen up," he said. "Their skin, burst open, was hanging down in rags. Their faces were burnt black. I put my hand on my camera, but it was such a hellish apparition that I couldn't press the shutter."[20]

Fires spread, mounted in strength, and merged into fast-moving firestorms. They advanced quickly over the devastated landscape, consuming wreckage and engulfing refugees on foot. In this respect, the aftermath of the Hiroshima bombing was similar to the earlier incendiary raids on Tokyo and other cities. Many who might otherwise have survived died by the inhalation of dust, ash, and smoke. The flames whipped up powerful whirlwinds, like tornadoes, and sections of roofing, doors, tatami mats, and various other debris were lifted and carried away. The odor of burning flesh settled like a pall over the city. According to Matsushige, "the fat of the bodies was bubbling up and sputtering as it burned. That was the only time I've seen humans roasting."[21]

Instinct drove people toward the bridges and riverbanks, either to soothe their wounds or to take a drink of water. They ran down the stone embankment steps to the narrow, muddy banks, where they found impossibly large crowds of refugees. As in the firebombed cities, the rivers became mass graves. Futaba Kitayama, badly injured, made a beeline for the nearby Tsurumi Bridge—but when she looked down into the water, she drew back in horror. "People by the hundreds were flailing in the river. I couldn't tell if they were men or women; they were all in the same state: their faces were puffy and ashen, their hair tangled, they held their hands raised and, groaning with pain, threw themselves into the water. I had a violent impulse to do so myself, because of the pain burning through my whole body. But I can't swim and I held back."[22] The decision probably saved her life. Many others leapt from the bridges, onto the heads of others—or they climbed down to the banks and waded into the water, pushing the floating dead aside. Hiroshima was an alluvial plain, and the rivers were tidal estuaries: the water was brackish, and not potable. Those who drank it vomited it back up, and blood was often intermixed in their vomit.

About two hours after the explosion came the black rain: freakishly large and heavy drops, the size of marbles, black and sticky in color and consistency. Caused by condensation that had absorbed rising ash and dust, the black raindrops were large enough to cause pain when they fell upon refugees, and they stained their skin with dark blotches that would not wash away. The black rain was very cold, and some of those who were caught out under it began to shiver. Though the survivors would not know it until later, this sinister rainfall was contaminated with radiation.

Those in the city saw the flash but did not notice the boom. Those who lived farther out on the outskirts saw the flash and then afterward heard the boom. The Japanese in Hiroshima spoke of a *pika*, meaning a flash, and a *don*, meaning a very loud sound. Thus, the nuclear explosion was called the *pikadon*, the flash-boom.[23]

At the Jesuit novitiate in Nagatsuke, the priests did what they could to assist the walking wounded who streamed up the valley from the city. Their chapel and library served as emergency medical wards, but they were soon so crowded with patients that no more could be admitted. The priests laid tatami mats out on the grass. One had studied medicine before taking holy orders, and he instructed the others in providing basic first aid. But the novitiate's supply of bandages and medicines soon gave out. They cleaned the wounds as best they could, and then applied cooking oil to the burns as a salve.

Later that afternoon, the priests learned that two of their fellow Jesuits had been at the Parish House in the city and were badly injured. They had taken refuge in Asano Park, on the Enko River (near the remains of Hiroshima Castle and the Second Army headquarters). Father Siemes and several of his colleagues collected two stretchers and headed into the city. It was difficult to make headway against the tide of refugees coming the other way. The devastation worsened as they drew closer to the city center. "Where the city stood," Siemes later said, "there is a gigantic burned-out scar." Injured people cried out to them. The priests did what they could, picking out a single wounded child here or there, but they could not help everyone, and were forced to turn a deaf ear to many pathetic entreaties. The scene in Asano Park was terrible. Tens of thousands were camped on the grounds. A firestorm had uprooted large trees and deposited them across the paths, so that one had to pick one's way through seemingly endless numbers of hideously wounded men, women, and children. The rescue party found their fellow priests and loaded them onto the stretchers. They returned to Nagatsuke at dawn the following morning. Their round-trip journey had taken twelve hours.

The Red Cross Hospital, adjacent to Asano Park, was partly collapsed and gutted by fire, but still the surviving doctors and nurses remained on their feet, and the wards were filled with an estimated 10,000 horribly burned and wounded patients. Little could be done for the worst burn cases. If the doctors even tried to remove their clothing, the skin peeled off with it. Signs of radiation poisoning were seen even on August 6; they would grow more distinct in the following weeks and months. Victims bled through the skin, gums, and eyes; they vomited blood, or expelled bloody diarrhea; their hair came out in clumps. Many patients in the hospital received nothing but a dab of iodine on their wounds. One man confronted a doctor at the hospital, asking why the medical staff were doing nothing for the immense crowds in Asano Park. The doctor replied: "In an emergency like this, the first task is to help as many as possible—to save as many lives as possible.

There is no hope for the heavily wounded. They will die. We can't bother with them."[24]

For the Hiroshima survivors, time was distorted. In the city, throughout nearly all of August 6, the sky remained dark until late afternoon. Most clocks and watches had been destroyed. Dr. Hachiya remembered wondering whether it was day or night. "Time had no meaning," he said. "What I had experienced might have been crowded into a moment or been endured through the monotony of eternity." Knowing nothing of the concept of an atomic bomb, they wondered what had happened. Had the Americans somehow sprayed the entire city with an invisible gasoline mist, and then ignited it? On the morning of the seventh, the air was clearer, and the citizens of Hiroshima got their first glimpse of the ugly scar that marked the place where their city had once stood. Here and there, a few sections of ferrous-concrete walls or steel girders remained standing. The green mountains to the north and east, and the Inland Sea to the south, seemed closer and more vivid than ever before. The flattened city had cleared the views: "How small Hiroshima was with its houses gone."[25]

Among the survivors, few expressed anger. The predominant mood was one of passivity and fatalism. Many shrugged and remarked, "*Shikata Ga Nai*."[26] The expression was common in wartime Japan: "It can't be helped." The disaster had occurred, and now it would run its course. Some would live, others would die, and the war would go on until those in power said it was over.

TRUMAN RECEIVED THE NEWS while crossing the Atlantic in the *Augusta*. He was seated on a bench at a long table in the enlisted men's mess, shoulder to shoulder with members of the crew, eating his lunch off a steel tray. A military aide begged pardon and handed him a high-priority radio telegram from Washington. It told him that the first special bomb had been dropped on Hiroshima under ideal weather conditions, with results seemingly better than those of the New Mexico test. Truman beamed, shook hands with the aide, and exclaimed, "This is the greatest thing in history."[27] Ten minutes later came a second report, directly from Secretary Stimson, estimating that the blast had equaled 20,000 tons of TNT. Truman stood and read it aloud to the crowded mess deck. The assembled sailors clapped and cheered. The president then went up to the wardroom and repeated his announcement for the ship's officers, who likewise applauded. Lieutenant Rigdon said that the crew was cheered by "a hope that the Pacific war might come to a speedier end."[28]

By prearrangement, the White House issued a statement announcing that the United States had dropped the world's first atomic bomb on Hiroshima, "an important Japanese Army base."[29] Truman met briefly with the traveling pool of press correspondents, but he could tell them little that was not included in the formal announcement. He then read portions of the statement for a newsreel crew. The film was made in his stateroom in "flag country" on the *Augusta*. Wearing a light tan summer suit with red tie, the president sat at a desk facing the camera, a round porthole visible behind him. "It is an atomic bomb," he said. "It is a harnessing of the basic power of the universe. The force from which the sun draws its power has been loosed against those who brought war to the Far East." He explained that the United States, with assistance from Great Britain, had assembled the leading scientists and built the immense industrial plants required for this enterprise, at a cost of more than $2 billion. More details about the project would be released by the War Department, he said. As for the Japanese, the Potsdam Declaration had given the Japanese a fair opportunity to avoid this awful fate, but leaders in Tokyo had promptly rejected that ultimatum, and therefore: "If they do not now accept our terms they may expect a rain of ruin from the air, the like of which has never been seen on this earth."[30]

IN TOKYO, NEWS OF THE CATASTROPHE in Hiroshima arrived in fits and starts. At 8:30 a.m., fifteen minutes after the explosion, the Kure Navy Yard reported that the neighboring city had been struck by "a new weapon of unprecedented destructiveness."[31] An hour and a half later, an airbase 80 miles outside Hiroshima reported that "a violent, large, special type bomb, giving the appearance of magnesium," had exploded in a blinding flash, and the blast wave had flattened everything within a 2-mile radius. Tellingly, IGHQ in Tokyo received no word at all from the Second Army headquarters in Hiroshima; all radio and landline communications links were down. A radio correspondent who had been 8 miles outside the city managed to relay a verbal report by telephone to the Domei News Agency in Tokyo at 11:20 a.m. He said the city had been completely annihilated by a bomb or bombs dropped by just one or two B-29s.[32]

At first the army leaders and technical authorities expressed doubt that the Americans could have built such a weapon. Admiral Toyoda, who had been fully briefed on Japan's failed nuclear program, judged that even if the enemy had assembled enough fissile material for a bomb, they had probably built only one. And even if they had more than one, the number could not be more than two or three, so they would not have enough to destroy the entire country from the air. (On that score, he was right.) Civil defense authorities moved to suppress panicked rumors, and falsely reported that all Hiroshimans who had been in their underground bomb shelters had escaped without injury.[33]

Before dawn the next day, news monitors in Tokyo picked up the text of President Truman's announcements reporting that an atomic bomb had been dropped on Hiroshima, and the peace party began maneuvering to force the issue of surrender. Foreign Minister Togo met with the emperor at the Imperial Palace that morning. Hirohito declared that the war must end, and asked Togo to convey his wishes for immediate peace to the prime minister. After briefing the emperor that afternoon, Marquis Kido recorded in his diary that he had been gravely concerned and had asked many questions. But in a meeting of the SWDC that day, the hardline faction played for time, arguing that no action should be taken until an investigation could determine what precisely had happened to Hiroshima. Anami said that the army's technical advisers were skeptical of the existence of an atomic bomb, but that an investigatory mission had been sent to Hiroshima to learn the facts. At a meeting of the newly formed "Atomic Bomb Countermeasure Committee," representatives of the Technical Board said they doubted that the Americans could have built such a bomb, or if they had, they could not have transported such an unstable device across the Pacific. They speculated that Hiroshima had been hit by a "new type [of] bomb with special equipment, but its content is unknown." The press was authorized only to say that Hiroshima had been hit by a new type of weapon, but no mention of atomic bombs was made in Japanese newspapers until the eighth.

The investigative team, seven military officers and scientists, flew into the city on the morning of August 7. The group included Yoshio Nishina, Japan's leading nuclear scientist, who had led its abortive atomic bomb program. As they circled above the devastated city, Nishina said he knew at a glance that "nothing but an atomic bomb could have done such damage."[34] His Geiger counter confirmed it. As their plane taxied to a stop at the airfield, they were met by an officer who was himself a rather vivid example of what the bomb could accomplish. The man had been exposed to flash burns, but he had been facing in a perpendicular direction to the epicenter, so one-half of his face was completely burned, and the other unharmed. He told the investigators, "Everything which is exposed gets burned, but anything which is covered even only slightly can escape burns. Therefore it cannot be said that there are no countermeasures."[35] The next day, the team submitted its report to the Imperial General Headquarters, concluding that there was no possible doubt that Hiroshima had been hit by an atomic bomb.[36]

In Tokyo, on August 8, Prime Minister Suzuki summoned the Big Six to another meeting of the SWDC, but was informed that certain members could not attend because they had been detained by other duties. A full forty-eight hours after the first atomic bomb had been dropped, no change in Japanese policy was even possible, because the ruling council did not have a quorum. Instead, the government renewed its urgent petitions to Moscow. The Japanese government was still ignorant of Soviet preparations for an attack on Manchuria. Togo cabled Ambassador Sato, asking whether the Russians had given any indications of an answer. Replying a few hours later, Sato said that Foreign Commissar Molotov had finally agreed to receive him that day at 5:00 p.m., Moscow time.

According to Hisatsune Sakomizu, the chief cabinet secretary, the entire capital was now on tenterhooks, hoping for some encouraging signal from the Russians that might offer salvation in the form of a diplomatic exit to the war.[37]

Sato was on time to the minute for his appointment at Molotov's office in the Kremlin. As the Japanese ambassador commenced his formal greetings, Molotov cut him off and invited him to take a seat, adding that he had a formal statement he wished to read. Molotov took a page out of a folder on his desk and began reading the Soviet declaration of war against Japan, pausing at intervals for the translator. He stated that his government was acting in response to the request of the Allied governments of the United States, Great Britain, and China, which had invited the Soviets to join in the Potsdam Declaration. (That was false.) The USSR was acting to "bring peace nearer, free the people from further sacrifice and suffering and give the Japanese people the possibility of avoiding the dangers and destruction suffered by Germany after her refusal to capitulate unconditionally."[38] The

Soviet Union would consider itself at war with Japan on the following day, August 9, 1945. Molotov did not offer any justification or rationale for abrogating the Soviet-Japanese Neutrality Pact, which was scheduled to expire the following year.

With genteel sarcasm, Sato thanked Molotov for his diligent labors in the cause of peace. The ambassador received a copy of the document and was shown the door. It had not occurred to him to ask precisely what time zone should be used in calculating the starting hour for pending hostilities. Sato may have assumed that Molotov meant August 9 in Moscow— that is, the following morning. But the Russians had considered the timing carefully. Five o'clock in Moscow was eleven o'clock in the Trans-Baikal (UTC+10) time zone. At midnight, one hour later, it would be August 9, 1945 on the Siberian-Manchurian border. At that hour, to the minute, Soviet warplanes would take off and Soviet tanks would begin rolling.

Working in closely guarded secrecy for the past several months, the Soviets had prepared one of the largest and most overpowering ground offensives in history. Assembly areas were set up well behind the border, and senior field commanders had traveled into the region incognito, wearing uniforms of junior officers. Troops, tanks, field artillery, and other war matériel had been moved east on the Trans-Siberian railroad, with continuous round-trips of some 136,000 rail cars. Since the fall of Germany three months earlier, Red Army strength in the region had more than doubled, to about eighty-nine divisions.[39] Japanese intelligence had failed to detect any sign of these vast preparations and troop movements.

Russian plans called for a simultaneous three-pronged attack on Manchuria from the north, east, and west across a front more than 2,600 miles long. A new Far East and Transbaikal regional theater command was set up under the leadership of Marshal Aleksandr Vasilevsky, who would direct the overall campaign from a fully staffed headquarters. The western attack on the Transbaikal Front would require Red Army forces under Marshal R. Y. Malinovsky to cross arduous desert and mountain terrain, the Gobi Desert and the Altai Mountains, and to penetrate quickly into the heart of Manchuria to seize Mukden (now Shenyang). From the east, the First Far Eastern Front, commanded by Marshal K. A. Meretskov, would cross the Lesser Khingan mountain range and seize the city of Changchun, and then pour into northern Korea. The Second Far Eastern Front would provide support to the two wings while advancing into Manchuria from the north. The total number of Red Army troops involved in the operation was about 1.5 million, more than double the number of Japanese troops in the region—and the Soviet troops were mechanized. The Red Army, bloodied and victorious on the Eastern Front, was at its peak strength and efficiency—manned by veterans at all ranks, lavishly equipped, and superbly led. As one American military analyst has written: "Soviet plans were as innovative as any in the war. Superb execution of those plans produced victory in only two weeks of combat."[40]

Although the Soviet plan was called the "Manchurian Strategic Offensive Operation," it included auxiliary operations to occupy northern Korea, the southern half of Sakhalin Island, and the Kurile Islands. An amphibious landing in the Kuriles would commence one day after Japan's surrender on August 15, and Red Army forces would quickly seize the rest of the chain, with offensive operations continuing even after Soviet representatives had accepted the Japanese instrument of surrender aboard the battleship *Missouri* in Tokyo Bay on September 2, 1945. Stalin had also directed that contingency plans be drawn up to seize Hokkaido. If the Japanese surrender had been delayed by even a few weeks, Japan's northern island might have passed forty-five years on the other side of the Iron Curtain.

By the time Moscow's declaration of war was known in Tokyo, the Red Army was already charging into Manchuria. By dawn on August 9, the army ministry and the Imperial General Headquarters were already teeming with bleary-eyed officers. Many had anticipated the Soviet attack, but few had suspected that a large offensive could be launched so soon after the defeat of Germany. A staff study published a month earlier had estimated that a major Russian offensive in East Asia could not be mounted until February 1946, at the earliest. Therefore, according to Lieutenant General Torashirō Kawabe, the deputy army chief of staff, the sudden assault "was a great shock when it actually came."[41] At IGHQ, senior officers had discussed the possibility that the Russians might demand, as the price of Soviet neutrality and diplomatic assistance in ending the war, a withdrawal of all Japanese troops from the Asian mainland. Many had argued that the Japanese should accede to such a request, if it came—a measure of the Japanese high command's consciousness of its weakness in the region.

As reports came in from Manchuria, it was soon clear that the Red Army was attacking on three fronts simultaneously, with huge armored and mechanized columns. The army that had overpowered the German *Wehrmacht* now appeared to be turning its full fury on the depleted Kwantung Army. Japanese soldiers fought with their customary tenacity and courage, but they were overmatched in every respect: troop numbers, tanks, air power, logistics, and mobility. As the Russians poured into the combat zone, they committed mass civilian atrocities on a scale and ferocity that matched those committed against German civilians earlier that year. Hundreds of thousands of Japanese soldiers were taken prisoner by the Russians, many to be held as forced laborers in Siberia for years after the close of hostilities.

Prime Minister Suzuki called Sumihisa Ikeda, chief of the cabinet planning bureau, and asked, "Is the Kwantung Army capable of repulsing the Soviet army?"

Ikeda replied, "The Kwantung Army is hopeless." The once-elite army had been stripped of its best troops, equipment, and munitions to reinforce Formosa, the homeland, and other Pacific battlefields. Now it was merely a "hollow shell" of its former self.

Suzuki let out a deep sigh at these words. "Is the Kwantung Army that weak?" he asked. "Then the game is up."

"The greater the delay in making the final decision, the worse the situation will be for us," said Ikeda.

To which Suzuki replied, "Absolutely correct."[42]

Stalin's perfidy in August 1945 was another chapter in a sequence of international betrayals, beginning with the Molotov-Ribbentrop Neutrality Pact of 1939, and the ruthless partition of Poland between the Nazis and Soviets. That insidious covenant had ended with Hitler's surprise invasion of Russia in June 1941. In the same spirit, Moscow's faithless pantomime of diplomacy with Tokyo between June and August 1945 provided cover for Stalin's pending abrogation of the Soviet-Japanese Neutrality Pact. The Russian declaration of war, delivered to the Japanese precisely one hour before the planned attack in Manchuria, could be seen as an indirect repayment of the treachery embodied in Japan's strike on Pearl Harbor in 1941, which was likewise planned and prepared under cover of diplomatic talks.

In Tokyo's view, the immediate military emergency posed by the Soviet attack was only half the story, and not necessarily the most important half. The peace-seeking faction had placed all of its diplomatic eggs into one basket. Moscow's sudden declaration of war extinguished their last hope of a negotiated armistice that would preserve some vestige of Japanese sovereignty. Now, the timing of Japan's surrender would have consequences for the Soviet role in the postwar occupation. Sumihisa Ikeda had observed in his conversation with Prime Minister Suzuki, "The greater the delay in making the final decision, the worse the situation will be for us." He meant that the Japanese now faced a quandary in which the longer they took to acknowledge the necessity of surrender, the greater the risk that the Soviet Union would claim a role in governing Japan. Many in the regime feared the growth of communist influence in Japan even more than the prospect of surrendering to the Western democracies.

Huddling with his senior staff at the foreign ministry, Togo said that he would recommend immediate acceptance of the Potsdam Declaration with no conditions, but with an accompanying unilateral declaration that the peace "shall not have any influence on the position of the imperial house."[43] In meetings with Suzuki and Yonai, Togo won their advance support for this approach. Yonai remarked to a colleague at the navy ministry that the bombing of Hiroshima and the Soviet entry into the war were in a sense a "godsend," because they had created a crisis that might be used to break the deadlock on the SWDC, and because they provided the army with a face-saving way to accept defeat.[44]

WHILE THE SOVIET ATTACK was getting underway, the second atomic bomb was being prepared at the 509th Composite Group compound on Tinian, in a cinderblock warehouse off the flight line. "Fat Man" was a big bomb, worthy of its name. It was squat and wide around the middle, shaped like an egg—or as mission commander Charles Sweeney observed, an oversized decorative squash. The weapon weighed more than 5 tons. Painted bright yellow, it had two acronyms stenciled on its nose: "FM1" and "JANCFU." They stood for "Fat Man 1" and "Joint Army-Navy-Civilian Foul-up."

Technicians and scientists had used great care in handling the 11-pound plutonium core. It was an ordinary-looking substance, but it was warm to the touch, as if it were a living organism. In the warehouse, the pieces of plutonium were fitted into the assigned casings. The implosion device contained 5,300 pounds of Composition B and Baratol—which made Fat Man, even in conventional terms, one of the largest bombs ever carried on an airplane. Installing the lensing system was a delicate task, and the specialists took their time. When the mechanism was assembled, the steel plates were bolted shut, and the green safety plugs were inserted into the outer sockets.

Once the strike plane was safely aloft and at altitude, the weaponeer would remove these and replace them with the red plugs, at which point the bomb would be fully armed.

On the afternoon of August 8, Fat Man was rolled out of the windowless, air-conditioned, green cinderblock warehouse on a handcart pulled by three men. They bolted the tailfin assembly to the rear section, then moved the bomb to a specially constructed concrete loading pit. The strike plane, *Bockscar*, was backed over the pit. Its bomb doors opened. With great care, the men hoisted the bomb into the plane and secured it. It was a snug fit.

Originally, Colonel Tibbets had planned to lead this second mission and fly the strike plane, as he had on the Hiroshima mission three days earlier. Instead, for unknown reasons, he decided not to go, and assigned the job to Sweeney. Some were surprised by the decision. Sweeney, a twenty-five-year-old army major from North Quincy, Massachusetts, was known as a naturally gifted pilot, probably the second-best pilot in the 509th Composite Group after Tibbets himself. (Before joining the 509th, Sweeney had been assigned to train General Curtis LeMay to fly the B-29.) He had piloted *The Great Artiste*, the instrument plane, on the Hiroshima mission three days earlier. However, Sweeney had not flown over Germany and had limited experience flying in combat.

The primary target for the mission was Kokura, an ancient castle town and industrial city near the northern tip of Kyushu, facing the Shimonoseki Strait. The secondary target was Nagasaki, a major seaport and shipbuilding center on the island's west coast.

Most of the aircrew on the three planes had flown the Hiroshima mission. Some later said that they were surprised that a second atomic bomb was to be dropped. They had hoped that one would be enough to end the war. Radioman Abe Spitzer of *The Great Artiste* recorded his sense of dismay: "There was no need for more missions, more bombs, more fear and more dying. Good God, any fool could see that."[45]

In operational terms, the mission to drop the bomb on Hiroshima had been flawless. From the beginning, by contrast, the Nagasaki flight was marred by various snafus and mishaps that nearly caused the mission to fail. The cheeky acronym JANCFU would prove all too prescient. There were technical problems with the bomb, fuel system problems on the strike plane, a missed rendezvous, tumultuous weather, garbled radio transmissions, a near collision, and abysmal visibility over both the primary and secondary targets. These problems were exacerbated by poor judgments by Sweeney and an ambiguous command relationship with the mission's chief weaponeer. At various points during the *Bockscar*'s nineteen-hour odyssey, many of the crew apparently despaired of surviving, assuming that their airplane was going to crash or ditch at sea—and the commanders on Tinian were left wondering whether the strike plane with its precious cargo had already gone down. *Bockscar* survived only by making a wild emergency landing on Okinawa, engines running on fumes, where it nearly took out a row of parked B-24s. Many of these issues did not come to light until decades later. When they did, acrimonious charges were exchanged in print between various participants, including Tibbets and Sweeney.

Sweeney's regular plane was *The Great Artiste*, which he had flown as instrument plane for the Hiroshima mission. Originally, he was to drop Fat Man from that plane, and *Bockscar* would serve as instrument plane. But that would involve a time-consuming transfer of instruments from one plane to another, which would tax the ground crews. Instead, it was decided that Sweeney and his aircrew would simply fly the *Bockscar* as strike plane, while Captain Frederick C. Bock and his crew would transfer into *The Great Artiste*. William Laurence, a *New York Times* correspondent assigned to fly as a passenger in the instrument plane, was never informed of this switch, and his widely read account reported that *The Great Artiste* had dropped the bomb on Nagasaki. This error was subsequently repeated in many histories after the war.

The trouble started before the *Bockscar* even left the ground. At 2:15 a.m. on August 9, as the crew was going through the preflight checklist, the flight engineer discovered that a fuel pump was not working. It needed a new solenoid, a job that would require several hours. The mission would have to be postponed. According to Tibbets, the reserve fuel served mainly as ballast, to balance the weight of the bomb. He did not believe that it would be needed. By Sweeney's account, Tibbets told him to make the call, and Sweeney announced that they would go.[46] The bad pump meant that the mission would have a lower fuel budget, and it would have to be managed accordingly.

At 3:40 a.m., as *Bockscar* taxied to the takeoff line, the weather to the north was dodgy. Squalls of rain had been passing through since shortly after midnight, and flashes of lightning were seen on the northern horizon. Stormy weather was forecast along the flight route. At 77 tons, *Bockscar* was 30 percent heavier than the maximum weight recommended by Boeing. With four engines straining at 2,600 rpm, Sweeney lowered the flaps, pushed the throttle forward, and released the brakes. The heavy plane made a long takeoff run, requiring all the asphalt the runway had to give, and the mighty airplane with its mighty bomb left the ground only about 200 feet before crossing the rocky drop to the beach. Sweeney kept the plane level to give it speed and lift, and then commenced the long, slow climb to altitude.

Few stars were visible as they droned north at 17,000 feet. The temperature outside was 30 degrees below zero. The planes were tossed sickeningly during their long flight to the rendezvous point south of Kyushu. Aboard *The Great Artiste,* Laurence noticed an uncanny luminous blue plasma forming around the spinning propellers, "as though we were riding the whirlwind through space on a chariot of blue fire." When he wondered aloud about it, Captain Bock explained that it was St. Elmo's fire. A few minutes after five o'clock, a purple glow on the horizon to starboard announced the first blush of dawn. Climbing to the rendezvous altitude of 30,000 feet, the cotton-ball cumulus layer fell away below. "At that height the vast ocean below and the sky above seem to merge into one great sphere," Laurence wrote. "I was on the inside of that firmament, riding above the giant mountains of white cumulus clouds."[47]

In *Bockscar,* there was no elaborate process to arm Fat Man, as there had been with Little Boy on the previous mission. The plutonium implosion lensing system was so complex that it had to be set up prior to the bomb's being loaded onto the plane. Therefore, Captain Frederick L. Ashworth of the navy, the mission's chief weaponeer, only had to climb into the *Bockscar*'s bomb bay, remove the green safety plugs, and insert the red live plugs. Now the weapon was armed. For redundancy it had no fewer than eight fuses, which could be triggered by radio, radar, altitude, or contact with the ground. For all the careful preparations on Tinian, however, something was amiss. At about seven, Ashworth and his assistant noted a blinking red light that should not have been on. The light began blinking faster. For a moment they panicked, believing that the bomb might be on the verge of detonating in flight, with unfavorable consequences for the *Bockscar* and its crew. Working quickly, with adrenaline surging, they unrolled the bomb's blueprints and studied the circuitry. Then they removed the outer casing and examined the switches. Bizarrely, given the care apparently practiced by the technicians on the ground, two had been set in the wrong positions.

They reset the switches, and the warning light went out. The two men replaced the casing, and did not breathe a word of what had happened until decades later.[48]

Bockscar arrived at the rendezvous over Yakushima at 7:45 a.m. They were at 30,000 feet. They had been flying for five hours. Within a few minutes, *The Great Artiste* joined up on the strike plane's right wing. But there was no sign of the camera plane, *The Big Stink.* Another twenty minutes passed, with the two planes circling and burning fuel. Fuel consumption was high in the thin air at that altitude, about 500 gallons per hour. Far below, they caught glimpses of Yakushima through the clouds—a round island, green and rugged, with steep mountains and plunging gorges. Sweeney made the controversial decision to keep waiting. Another twenty-five minutes went by; still no sign of the missing plane. Later, it was discovered that *The Big Stink* was at 39,000 feet, the wrong altitude.

Finally, after forty-five minutes of circling and burning fuel, Sweeney decided to turn north and fly to Kokura, the primary target. Now the sun was well above the horizon. *Bockscar* and *The Great Artiste* flew the entire length of Kyushu, south to north, over some of the largest kamikaze airbases in Japan. The two planes kept radio silence, but the pilot of the wayward camera plane called to Tinian. According to the various accounts, he asked: "Has Sweeney aborted?" and "Is *Bockscar* down?" This query was garbled, but a fragmentary radio transmission was received on Tinian, and interpreted as "*Bockscar* down." For the next several hours, commanders on Tinian believed that the plane and the bomb may have been lost at sea.

As the two Superfortresses arrived over Kokura, the city was shrouded in smoke and haze. Peering down through the Plexiglas nose section, the crew could identify certain landmarks—but the Kokura Arsenal, the designated aiming point, was obscured. Fires were burning in nearby Yawata, which had been hit by a conventional bombing raid the previous day, and brown smoke had drifted over Kokura. Additional smoke was created by a tar-burning operation at a local steel foundry—a civil defense measure intended to obscure visibility from the air.[49] The city's antiaircraft batteries opened fire on the *Bockscar* and *The Great Artiste* shortly after their arrival. At first, the flak bursts were low, but they crept steadily higher as the two planes circled at 30,000 feet. The 509th Composite Group had been ordered to use visual bombing, meaning that the bombardier was to identify the aiming point through his Norden bombsight before releasing the weapon. Sweeney banked around three times, making three successive bomb runs. Each time the bombardier stated that he could not see the aiming point. The antiaircraft bursts were creeping steadily closer.

Sweeney and Bock climbed to 31,000 feet, and then to 32,000 feet. The radioman intercepted Japanese chatter on the frequency used by the local fighter command, which meant that they could expect unwanted company. The aircrews watched the fuel needles in consternation—they knew they were cutting it close. Tension rose in the cockpits of both airplanes. Many of the airmen, according to their later accounts, thought the mission was likely to fail, possibly with the loss of both planes.

Incredibly, there did not appear to be clear contingency plans for this situation. Although poor visibility was a notorious problem over Japan, they

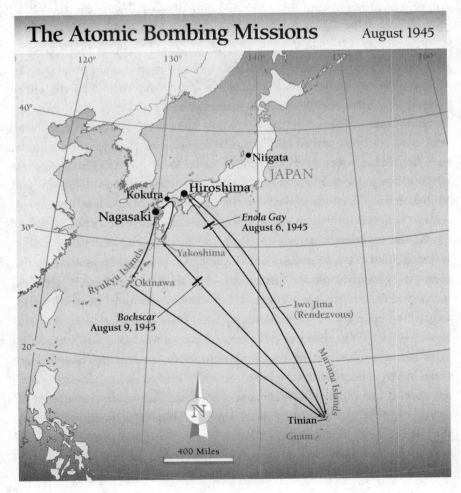

The Atomic Bombing Missions August 1945

did not have authority to employ radar bombing. Given that pinpoint accuracy was hardly needed for an atomic bomb, the oversight seems inexplicable.

After an hour over Kokura, Sweeney decided to divert to the secondary target. He banked south and asked his navigator for a course heading to Nagasaki. While making the turn, according to Captain Ashworth, the *Bockscar* and *The Great Artiste* nearly collided. Then Sweeney's elbow inadvertently brushed the cockpit selector button which switched the intercom function to the command transmit function. A routine query intended for his own crew was transmitted from the airplane, thus breaking radio silence. The pilot of the missing camera plane, *The Big Stink*, received this transmission and immediately replied, "Chuck? Is that you, Chuck? Where the hell are you?"[50] Sweeney did not reply, knowing that the Japanese were undoubtedly listening in on these wayward transmissions. He also knew that the *Bockscar* lacked the fuel to attempt a rendezvous with the missing plane.

It took only twenty minutes to complete the 100-mile flight to Nagasaki. *Bockscar* arrived over the city at 11:50 a.m., more than two hours later than the planned drop time. The airplane had been in the air for more than eight hours, and its fuel reserve was near the point of no return. Looking down, Sweeney and his copilots saw with dismay that Nagasaki was fairly socked in, with "80 to 90% cumulus clouds at 6,000 to 8,000 feet."[51] The plane did not have fuel for more than a single bomb run, but the bombardier could not see the aiming point, the Mitsubishi Steel and Arms Works. In desperation, Sweeney said that he would authorize a radar drop on his own authority. The alternative was to dump the bomb into the ocean. But as the *Bockscar* entered the bomb run, the bombardier suddenly shouted that he had a visual fix: "I got it! I got it!" Forty-five seconds later, Fat Man fell from *Bockscar's* bomb bay, and Sweeney banked hard to the right to evade. *The Great Artiste* followed.

Again, as at Hiroshima three days earlier, a burst of blinding silver light flooded the interiors of the two planes, and the sky was blanched white. Two successive shockwaves, stronger than those over Hiroshima, smacked the planes and caused them to shimmy and groan. One aircrewman said that he thought *Bockscar* would be torn apart.

Looking down, observers saw a sphere of purple-pink light burst through the cloud ceiling, like an air bubble breaking the surface of a body of water. William Laurence, watching from a window in *The Great Artiste*, was awestruck. The sphere merged into an ascending column of dirty brown smoke and ash, and "we watched it shoot upward like a meteor coming from the earth instead of from outer space, becoming ever more alive as it climbed skyward through the white clouds. It was no longer smoke, or dust, or even a cloud of fire. It was a living thing, a new species of being, born right before our incredulous eyes."[52] As the column rose higher than the altitude of the two planes, a frothing white mushroom cloud formed at the top. Below, Nagasaki had vanished in a churning cauldron of smoke, dust, ash, and fire. Gazing down through the Plexiglas panels beneath his feet, Sweeney said: "All we could see was a blanket of thick, dirty, brownish smoke with fires breaking through sporadically."[53]

The two planes circled the explosion, snapping photos and rolling cameras. As the mushroom cap spread, it appeared that *Bockscar* might be too close, and would be engulfed by the cloud. A member of the crew shouted: "The mushroom cloud is coming toward us!"[54] Sweeney executed a second sharp right turn, away from the explosion. For a few breathless minutes the aircrewmen watched the expanding cloud in dread. The *Bockscar* cleared the hazard, but the maneuver burned additional fuel that could hardly be spared.

FAT MAN HAD DETONATED about 1,800 feet above the Urakami Valley, a northern district of Nagasaki comprising densely built neighborhoods of traditional Japanese wooden homes, a Christian cathedral, schools and colleges, and two Mitsubishi industrial plants. The bomb was about three-quarters of a mile off target, northwest of the planned aiming point, but it still managed to do the job it had been intended to do. Exploding at the midpoint between the Mitsubishi Steel and Arms Works in the south, and the Mitsubishi-Urakami Ordnance Works in the north, the bomb demolished both factories.

Because the local press had not yet reported that an atomic bomb had hit Hiroshima, many residents were not prepared for the possibility that one or two B-29s could destroy a city. When the two planes winged in from the north at high altitude, some ignored the air raid sirens and remained where they were standing, watching the intruders as they soared overhead. As in Hiroshima, the bomb detonated in a blinding cosmic ball of light, and anyone caught in the open within about half a mile of the hypocenter was vaporized instantly. The horrors of Nagasaki faithfully replicated those in Hiroshima three days earlier. Those who had taken shelter emerged afterward to find a dystopian hellscape, the sun blotted out and fires advancing, the terrain reshaped and unrecognizable. As in Hiroshima, the cloud of dust and smoke overhead eclipsed the sun, and the scene was suffused in a macabre reddish glow. The region around ground zero was made up mostly of smaller wooden dwellings of traditional Japanese architecture, and they had been almost entirely flattened, vaporized, or burned away. Across the landscape, corrugated tin panels and steel girders, twisted and blackened, stood among endless hillocks of wreckage. Houses directly below the epicenter were smashed directly downward, into the ground, their roof tiles merging into the mud and debris. At Nagasaki Medical College, half a mile from ground zero, all the campus's wooden buildings were razed, and all persons inside were killed. In the concrete buildings, the walls provided enough shelter that about six of every ten occupants survived, though many suffered dreadful wounds. A teenaged girl cried out to her classmates, as they made their way from their bomb shelter back toward their school, "Weren't there houses here when we came to the shelter?"[55]

The wounded were strewn along the roadways, trapped beneath wreckage, some limping and some crawling, some naked or nearly so—the blast wave having torn away their clothing—many immobilized and begging for water ("*Mizu, mizu, mizu!*"). Some were burned so badly that they lacked recognizable facial features, with blood-matted hair and skin hanging from their bodies in ribbons; lacerations so deep that bones showed through the torn flesh; holding their arms out from the bodies to avoid the painful friction that would result from burned and abraded skin rubbing against burned and abraded skin. The procession of refugees on the road south of ground zero reminded one witness of a "march of ants."[56] As in Hiroshima, survivors instinctively headed for the river—in this instance, the Urakami River. Thousands clustered along its banks and plunged into its water, hoping to soothe their wounds or take a drink. Soon the river was a great floating mortuary, and the ebb tide carried the mass of bodies down to the harbor and out to sea.

About an hour after the blast came the same hideous rain that had fallen on Hiroshima—strangely large globules of sticky black paste, hard and heavy enough to cause physical pain as it fell on people caught out in the open. The black rain convinced many survivors that the day of judgment was upon them. Some speculated they had arrived in *jigoku*, the Buddhist hell.

Fat Man had fallen only half a mile from Urakami Cathedral, the largest and most famous church in Japan. The great stone edifice was almost completely leveled; only a few partial walls and one of the two bell towers stood among the rubble. The surrounding residential district was wiped out. For four centuries, since the arrival of the first Spanish and Portuguese Jesuit missionaries, the coastal region around Nagasaki had been a beachhead for Japanese Christianity. Since about 1700, the Urakami Valley had been the epicenter of this small but resilient community of faith, which had survived repeated campaigns of persecution, often by worshipping in secret. An estimated 10,000 Japanese Christians died in the atomic blast, or succumbed to their wounds soon afterward. Noting that Nagasaki's great Shinto shrine (*Suwa-Jinja*) was unharmed, some Japanese argued that divine providence must explain the disparity. They mused that the ancient Shinto deities were stronger than the foreigners' alien god.

Unlike Hiroshima, which occupied a flat alluvial plain, Nagasaki was divided by hills and ridges. The uneven terrain shielded outlying districts of the city from the worst effects of the bomb. A steep ridgeline west of Urakami Valley absorbed most of the blast wave and radiation and largely spared the rest of Nagasaki. The hills facing ground zero were scorched, with most of the structures and vegetation burned away, giving them the appearance (said one witness) of a "premature autumn."[57] But on the other side of the ridge, one found another world, where the grass and trees were still green and most of the buildings appeared undamaged.

As surveyors collected data from both atomic bomb sites, it was soon clear that the Nagasaki bomb had packed a bigger punch. Fat Man's yield was about 30 percent greater than Little Boy's, and the bowl-shaped topography of the Urakami Valley had amplified the force of the explosion. The second bomb had done considerably more damage to comparable structures at a comparable distance from the hypocenter.[58]

As in Hiroshima, precise casualty figures were hard to pin down. It is believed that 40,000 to 75,000 residents of Nagasaki were killed on August 9 or shortly thereafter, with another 70,000 dead by the end of 1945.

LOW ON FUEL, THE TWO B-29s had no hope of flying back to Tinian. The nearest friendly airfield was on Okinawa, a flight of 460 miles. Sweeney did not believe that he had the fuel to make it, but he would try to coax every last mile of forward progress out of every last gallon of gas. Start-ing at 30,000 feet, the *Bockscar* had plenty of altitude to give up. Sweeney throttled the engines back to 1,800 rpm, from their normal cruising setting of 2,000 rpm. Then he throttled back to 1,600 rpm, which was below the engine specifications. It would place a lot of strain on the engines, poten-tially damaging them. But if the *Bockscar* ran out of fuel before reaching Okinawa, the health of the engines would be moot. Assuming that they would be forced to ditch at sea, Captain Ashworth told the crew to put on their life jackets.

Sixty miles north of Okinawa, with the fuel needles bouncing on empty, the radioman tried to hail the control tower at Yontan Airfield. There was no response. He tried every possible frequency; still no response. Sweeney put out a "mayday" call. He throttled the engines back to a virtual glide. As the airfield came into view ahead, Sweeney could see fighters and bombers in the landing circle. There was a lot of air traffic, but for some reason the control tower was not responding. The *Bockscar* did not have fuel to fly a landing pattern. Sweeney intended to simply aim for the end of the runway and attempt a virtual deadstick landing. But did the airfield know he was coming? "I want any goddamn tower on Okinawa!" Sweeney shouted to the radioman. He repeated the mayday call. Then he told the crew to fire flares from the overhead hatch. A crewman asked, which flares? "Fire every god-damn flare we have on board!"[59]

The copilot opened the hatch and fired eight flares. Each one communi-cated a specific message, telling the control tower (for example) that *Bocks-car* was on fire, out of fuel, and had wounded men aboard. But in this case the flares were only for one purpose, to get the airfield's attention, and in this respect they succeeded. As the *Bockscar* made its final approach, the traffic cleared. The right outboard engine coughed, sputtered, and cut out. Sweeney said, "I was now barreling in straight ahead, like a runaway freight train."[60] He kept his airspeed up and aimed for the midpoint of the runway. *Bockscar* struck the pavement hard, bounced 25 feet in the air, and then settled back down. The left outboard engine quit. Airspeed was too high, about 140 miles per hour. The airplane began veering left, toward a hard-stand lined with parked B-24s. Sweeney activated the reversible propellers—a feature found only on the 509th Composite Group planes—and stood on the emergency brakes. The *Bockscar* veered back onto the centerline of the runway and finally came to a stop. As it rolled onto the taxiway, a third engine cut out. Sweeney cut the fourth and braked. He slumped back in his seat, exhausted. A tow truck would have to bring the plane the rest of the way. *Bockscar* had 7 gallons of fuel left in its tanks.

The Eighth Air Force commander, General James Doolittle, had watched the wild landing. He had been sure the plane would crash. Afterward Sweeney reported to his office and explained what his mission had been. Neither man missed the significance—they were, in a sense, bookends. Doolittle had led the first air raid on the Japanese homeland, in April 1942; Sweeney had just dropped the bomb that would effectively mark the end of the war.

After eating a meal in the mess hall, the *Bockscar*'s crew reboarded their plane, now refueled, for the five-hour run to Tinian. At 10:30 p.m., the airplane landed on Runway A at North Field. The mission had lasted nineteen hours. There was no welcoming party, no press, no celebrations at all. Sweeney was interrogated by Tibbets and LeMay, who concluded that he had made several bad judgments and had nearly botched the mission. They debated whether to haul him before a court of inquiry. But in the end, they decided to leave it alone. Insofar as the world knew, the Nagasaki mission had succeeded, and they preferred to keep it that way. The harrowing details of the *Bockscar*'s near-demise were not made public until decades later.

In Tokyo, in a long meeting of the SWDC that morning, the Big Six found themselves evenly divided along their familiar three-to-three lines. Notably, even the three hardliners conceded that the war must end, and they agreed "in principle" to Foreign Minister Togo's proposal to initiate truce negotiations with the Allies. But they insisted upon attaching several conditions. General Anami vowed that neither he nor the army would abide an unconditional surrender. He referred to the looming threat of anarchy and even civil war, which could have been interpreted as a threat. He was backed, as usual, by General Umezu and Admiral Toyoda.

In the midst of their deliberations, at 11:30 a.m., the council was informed that Nagasaki had been hit by another atomic bomb. But the ominous news did nothing to resolve their impasse.

After three hours of vexed debate, the two factions were deadlocked between a "one-condition" and a "four-condition" response to the Potsdam Declaration. All six men agreed that the Allies must consent to retain the emperor and the imperial house. The peacemakers Togo, Suzuki, and Yonai argued that this should be the sole condition; any additional demands, they warned, would be tantamount to a rejection of the Potsdam Declaration, and the war would continue until Japan was destroyed. But the hardliners held out for three additional conditions. First, that there be no foreign occupation of Japanese soil; second, that Japanese forces overseas would be withdrawn and demobilized under the command of their own officers; and third, that the Japanese would conduct their own war crimes prosecutions.

In an emergency meeting of the full cabinet that afternoon, Admiral Yonai stated baldly that Japan had no chance of repelling an Allied invasion on Japanese soil. Anami countered that the army was confident of inflicting heavy losses on the Allies as they stormed ashore, and such a blow might at least bring about the conditions for a more favorable peace. Anami added, "We will find a way to escape an impossible situation with *gyokusai* [fight to the death] by 100 million people."[61] Several civilian ministers emphasized the impossibility of fighting on, citing the woeful state of transportation, shipping, fuel reserves, the economy, and agriculture. The home minister, whose portfolio included law enforcement, warned of a breakdown in civil order if the public learned that surrender negotiations were underway. That evening at 8:00 p.m., the views of all ministers not on the SWDC were recorded. Six backed Togo's "one-condition" response, four voted to support the belligerent "four-condition" response, and the others offered intermediate views or pledged to support the prime minister's decision.

Under normal circumstances, the impasse might have been resolved in good time. The customary methods of *nemawashi* ("digging around the roots for a consensus") were underway. The most eventful discussions of this momentous day occurred in private one-on-one meetings in the ministries and at the Imperial Palace. Prime Minister Suzuki and Marquis Kido each had several private audiences with Hirohito, keeping him closely informed of the status of the debate in the SWDC and the cabinet. Several members of the *jushin* (the "senior statesmen," comprising all former Japanese prime ministers) met with Kido. Former foreign minister Mamoru Shigemitsu, who had a close rapport with Kido, was fetched from his country home in Nikko to lobby for Togo's position. Several members of the royal family were active throughout the afternoon. Prince Takamatsu, the emperor's younger brother, at first backed the four-condition response—but he was gradually persuaded by the peace party's reasoning, and by the end of the day he was firmly behind the one-condition response.[62]

A second echelon of civilian officials, working behind the scenes with the peacemakers in the cabinet, maneuvered to orchestrate a "sacred decision" for surrender. Chief cabinet secretary Sakomizu collected the signatures of the Big Six on a document consenting to a formal imperial conference at the palace. Evidently, Sakomizu led the SWDC hardliners to believe that they would simply be presenting their views to Hirohito. Had they suspected that the emperor would rule directly to break the stalemate, they could have withheld their signatures and the meeting would not have been possible.

The historic late-night conference convened just before midnight in a cramped and stifling air raid shelter in the basement of the palace. The members of the council, wearing formal suits or dress uniforms and white gloves, sat in rigid wooden chairs under electric lights. The emperor, dressed in a uniform, sat facing them. Behind him was a gilded gold screen. Sakomizu read the Potsdam Declaration aloud. Drafts of two prospective responses—the peace party's one-condition acceptance and the hardliners' four-condition acceptance—were distributed to all participants.

Speaking first and with great force, Togo recited the arguments he had been advancing since early that morning. There was no other realistic course, he said, but to accept the Potsdam Declaration with the sole proviso that the emperor's status be preserved. To add a litany of other conditions would be tantamount to a flat rejection of the Allied terms. Talks would break off before they had begun, and Japan would face the revolting options of suffering complete destruction or (with even greater loss of face) consenting to unconditional surrender after all. Anami replied with indignant bluster, insisting that the Japanese army was not yet defeated and would enjoy considerable tactical advantages in a battle for the homeland. The army should be allowed to beat the invader back; in the wake of such a battle, the government would possess the leverage to obtain better terms at the bargaining table. Speaking softly, Yonai supported Togo's view. The two chiefs of staff, Umezu and Toyoda, said they agreed with Anami, though neither seemed to possess Anami's conviction. Marquis Kido and Baron Kiichirō Hiranuma, the Privy Council president, sided with the advocates of the one-condition acceptance. The debate continued for two hours, until everyone in the room had spoken. Suzuki withheld his opinion, perhaps because he wanted to present himself as an honest broker, and he knew what was going to happen next.

At two in the morning, the aged prime minister rose to his feet and faced his colleagues. "Gentlemen," he intoned, "we have spent hours in deliberation without coming to a decision and yet agreement is not in sight. You are fully aware that we cannot afford to waste even a minute at this juncture." He turned to face the throne. "I propose, therefore, to seek the imperial guidance and substitute it for the decision of this conference."[63]

There was no constitutional precedent for this maneuver, and it seems to have stunned the hardliners. With rare exceptions, Hirohito had refrained from breaking deadlocks in his cabinets. The last time he had exercised this dubious authority was in February 1936, during an aborted army *coup d'état*. Anami and his allies could have raised a point-of-order objection on the spot, and forced the conference to adjourn before the emperor could voice his opinion. But to do so would have required a show of defiance in the man-god's presence. It would also have caused the government to fall, exacerbating the national crisis. Perhaps, in the moment, they were too dumbfounded to speak up. Or perhaps, as some have speculated, the hardliners actually *wanted* the emperor to rule for surrender, because they knew that no realistic alternative existed, and felt that only a firm imperial decision would compel their rebellious subordinates to fall in line.

After an emotional silence, Hirohito spoke in a low voice. "I agree with the first opinion as expressed by the foreign minister," he said. He was deeply saddened by the sacrifice of so many brave and loyal soldiers and sailors, and the suffering of the Japanese people under aerial bombardment. But the sole alternative to accepting the Allied terms was national annihilation, as well as prolonged suffering throughout Asia and the world. As for the army's proposed decisive battle in the homeland, the emperor bluntly stated that he had lost confidence in his military commanders, because past experience had established "that there has always been a discrepancy between plans and performance."[64] The time had come, said Hirohito, to "bear the unbearable"—a reference to the Meiji emperor's verdict on the Tripartite Intervention of 1895, when Russia, Germany, and France had pressured Japan to rewrite the peace treaty ending the first Sino-Japanese war. His grandfather's remark was a fitting precedent for Japan's current agony. Once again, a mortifying loss of face must be endured for the sake of national survival.

Suzuki then said, "The Imperial decision has been expressed. This should be the conclusion of the conference."[65] Hirohito stood and left the chamber. There was no dissent. The single-condition document was signed by every member of the SWDC, including Anami, Umezu, and Toyoda. Suzuki summoned the full cabinet to another emergency meeting, where the ministers ratified the decision unanimously. Togo's foreign ministry began drafting a formal surrender note to be conveyed to U.S. Secretary of State James Byrnes through the neutral European capitals of Bern and Stockholm. It was transmitted at seven o'clock that morning, Tokyo time. Japan would accept the Potsdam Declaration, it said, "with the understanding that the said declaration does not comprise any demand which prejudices the prerogatives of His Majesty as a Sovereign Ruler."[66]

Having slept not at all, General Anami returned to the grand white art deco–style army ministry at Ichigaya. He summoned his section chiefs and staff to a briefing at 9:00 a.m. In a muted, solemn voice he told of the emperor's decision. The counteroffer was on its way to the Allies, he said, and depending on the response, the army would either fight on or accept the Potsdam terms with the proviso that the kokutai would be retained. This shocking news was met by a rumble of angry murmurs. One young officer leapt to his feet and asked, "Is the Army Minister actually considering surrender?" Anami responded by smashing a table with his swagger stick. The army must remain unified and disciplined during this crisis, he said: "I have no excuse to offer for the fact that peace has been decided upon. However, those of you who are dissatisfied and wish to stave it off will have to do it over my dead body."[67] That last remark was no mere figure of speech, and every man in the room knew it.

In acquiescing to the Potsdam terms, Hirohito had calculated that he must sacrifice the army and navy in order to save the core essence of the kokutai (the emperor-centered "polity" or political structure). In its future postwar incarnation, the kokutai would be stripped of its traditional military carapace. What remained would be a more purely religious model based upon State Shinto and the continuity of the imperial ancestral line. In a postwar account, the emperor explained that he had feared for the safety of the Ise and Atsuta Shrines. If an invasion force should come ashore in Ise Bay and capture the two holy places, the enemy would gain control of the imperial regalia—the three sacred objects or treasures of Shinto—in which case, "it would be difficult to preserve the national polity."[68] This religious belief may well have roused Hirohito and other leading figures in the royal family and the imperial household. If the military had to be sacrificed to protect the ancient Shinto traditions, so be it. Pursuant to the emperor's sacred decision, the army and navy would be not only disarmed and demobilized but actually extirpated. Its leaders would be hauled before international war crimes tribunals, probably to be imprisoned or hanged.

But that was not the worst of it. Most galling to the army leaders was the knowledge that the emperor had plainly stated that he no longer believed their promises. General Umezu, in despair, told General Kawabe that "since very long ago, the emperor had already lost all hope about the results of military operations. He has lost all faith in the military."[69] In a long, anguished entry in his diary, Kawabe lamented this humiliating state of affairs, but admitted that the emperor's criticism was a "picture of reality." It was true that the army had no real hope of repelling the impending invasion of the homeland, and the generals had refused to face up to Japan's hopeless predicament. Kawabe wrote: "I was bound by the feeling, 'I do not want to surrender. I do not want to admit I am defeated, even in the face of death.' With that feeling I only directed the final operations in this war."[70]

The chastened Kawabe pledged to do his utmost to persuade the rank-and-file of the army to acquiesce in the emperor's decision. But it was not clear that discipline could be maintained. During the final five days of the Pacific War, the political situation in Tokyo was explosive. Mid-ranking officers in the army and even the navy maneuvered to scuttle the peace talks, and laid the groundwork for a general revolt and *coup d'état*. The contending hawks and doves vied to disseminate their views through the domestic and even the international news media. Officials at the foreign ministry arranged to have an international wire announcement (in English) radioed by the Domei News Agency, under the headline "Japan Accepts Potsdam Proclamation."[71] Furious army officers then attempted to seize Domei's shortwave broadcasting equipment. On the evening of August 10, the army ministry released, in Anami's name, a rousing message exhorting the troops to "fight the sacred war to defend to the last this land of the gods. Even though we have to eat grass and chew dirt and lay in the field we must fight to the bitter end, ever firm in our belief that we shall find life and death."[72] Privately, Anami informed overseas army headquarters that truce negotiations were underway, but until they bore fruit, the troops must fight on "even in the face of complete annihilation."[73]

Plotters drew up lists of names. Cabinet officials who were known to have supported the peace party would be arrested or assassinated. The surrender was teetering on a knife's edge. There was talk of occupying the imperial palace and declaring martial law, perhaps even taking the emperor into "protective custody." A bomb was thrown over the front gate of Foreign Minister Togo's official residence. Meanwhile, the peacemakers knowingly risked their lives to bring the war to an end. Hisatsune Sakomizu was preparing a draft imperial rescript for the emperor's seal, and Kido was planning an unprecedented broadcast by the emperor announcing the end of the war. And yet, at the end of the day on August 11, no word had been received from the Allied governments. Should the one condition be rejected, Japan would fight on to its own utter destruction. The diplomat Toshikazu Kase later wrote of those tense days: "The clock ticking out each second seemed to be spelling out the suspended doom of the empire now about to crumble."[74]

THE JAPANESE NOTE ARRIVED in Washington by several routes. First, the American codebreakers intercepted and broke the message between Tokyo and Bern, and rushed it up the chain of command. The Domei shortwave radio message arranged by Japanese diplomats arrived in the small hours of the morning of August 10. (This message made headlines in the United States and throughout the world, and counterbalanced the toxic impression given by Anami's more bellicose statement to the army.) Later that afternoon, the formal message was received in the U.S. State Department via the Swiss Embassy.

Secretary Stimson received word as he was being driven to an airfield to board a plane that would take him to the Adirondack lakes region of upstate New York, where he would enjoy a well-earned summer vacation. The car turned around and took him back to the War Department. As he read the Japanese note asking for assurances regarding the emperor, Stimson reflected, "It is curious that this was the very single point that I feared would make trouble."[75] In his diary, he wrote that political demands in America to punish the emperor were now a threat to the hope of a bloodless victory over Japan. A clear majority of the American people wanted Hirohito held accountable for his role in the war. In a Gallup poll conducted in May 1945, 33 percent of Americans favored the execution of the emperor; 11 percent said that he should be imprisoned, and 9 percent said that he should be exiled. Stimson remarked that such views were found even in higher circles of government, "mostly by people who know no more about Japan than has been given them by Gilbert and Sullivan's 'Mikado.'"[76]

Truman summoned his military chiefs and state-war-navy secretaries to the White House. They convened in the Oval Office at nine o'clock. The arguments were largely a recap of the debates that had occurred three weeks earlier in Potsdam. Secretary of State Byrnes was concerned that accepting the note would amount to a retreat from the ultimatum for unconditional surrender: "I cannot understand why now we should go further [toward conciliation] than we were willing to go at Potsdam when we had no atomic bomb, and Russia was not in the war." He warned of political consequences for Truman. Accepting the Japanese condition, he said, would mean "the crucifixion of the president."[77]

Leahy and Stimson were ready to accept the Japanese condition on its face. Retaining the emperor, said Leahy, was a small price to pay for a quick end to the war. "I had no feelings about little Hirohito, but was convinced that it would be necessary to use him in effecting the surrender."[78] Stimson agreed, adding that time was running against the Allies, because the Soviet footprint in Asia was expanding by the hour. The Red Army's onslaught dictated that the Americans take a more pragmatic approach to these last rounds of negotiations, said Stimson, because "it was a great importance to get the homeland into our hands before the Russians could put in any substantial claim to occupy and help rule it."[79] The more territory the Russians swallowed on the northern borders of China, the more assistance Moscow might later provide to Mao Zedong's communist guerillas in the nascent Chinese Civil War. Russian ambitions in Korea were a growing concern; there was even talk of putting a U.S. amphibious force ashore in Inchon. The Soviets were openly demanding a role in the occupation of Japan, perhaps by adopting a multinational occupation authority, as in Germany. The future of Asia, it could be said without exaggeration, depended on the fastest possible resolution of the standoff between Tokyo and Washington.

A brainstorm by Jim Forrestal solved the impasse. The Allies need not accept or reject the Japanese proviso at all, he said; they could simply make an "affirmative statement" setting out their views on the emperor's subordinate status. Such a statement would ignore the Japanese condition while implicitly reassuring the Japanese that Hirohito would be left on his throne.[80] The suggestion was adopted. The key passage of Byrnes's reply stated: "From the moment of surrender the authority of the Emperor and the Japanese Government to rule the state shall be subject to the Supreme Commander of the Allied powers, who will take such steps as he deems proper to effectuate the surrender terms." As for the future form of the Japanese government, it would be established "by the freely expressed will of the Japanese people."[81] The singular term "Supreme Commander" was chosen deliberately, to emphasize that the occupation would be run by a single officer rather than by an Allied coalition. On that same day, President Truman confirmed the decision that everyone had expected for months: Douglas MacArthur would serve as supreme commander for the Allied powers (SCAP) in occupied Japan.

Stimson and Forrestal recommended a moratorium on bombing while negotiations proceeded. Stimson cited a "growing feeling of apprehension and misgiving" among the American people about the atomic bomb. Truman agreed to order a halt to the atomic bombings—in any case, the third weapon would not be ready until later in the month—but he ruled that the conventional bombing campaign would continue "at its present intensity" until Japan finally capitulated.[82]

Thanks to the shortwave radio broadcast arranged by the doves in Tokyo, the world now knew that Japan had sued for peace. While the cabinet and military chiefs were huddled with the president, a crowd gathered outside the White House gates, and a clamor of jubilant shouting and car horns was heard from Pennsylvania Avenue. Radio news bulletins carried stories of similar public celebrations in cities across the United States. In territories throughout the Pacific, servicemen fired their weapons into the sky. Allied warships sounded their whistles and let fly with starshells, flares, tracer fire, and antiaircraft rounds. In Hagushi Anchorage off Okinawa, the air was so thick with celebratory flak that several sailors were killed.[83] The marine flyer Sam Hynes remembered it as a "hysterical, frightening night, a purging of war's emotions."[84] Those ashore with an instinct for self-preservation retreated to their foxholes or trenches. The local naval base commander signaled the fleet: "All firing of antiaircraft weapons for celebrative purposes will be discontinued on receipt this msg."[85]

The Third Fleet was off northern Japan, where it had been hitting targets throughout the region. On the *Yorktown*, the captain announced the news over the loudspeaker system, and "cheers rose from the blackness on the flight deck where crews were respotting planes."[86] On the *Missouri*, Halsey and his staff were watching a technicolor musical starring the synchronized swimming star Esther Williams. A communications officer approached from behind and whispered the news into Carney's and Halsey's ears. Halsey waved him away, saying: "Let's just watch the picture."[87] Having received no orders to cease offensive operations, the mighty fleet continued south toward Tokyo, where it was scheduled to launch another big strike on August 12.

BYRNES'S REPLY WAS BROADCAST to Tokyo by a commercial radio station in San Francisco. It was received before dawn on August 12. Arriving early to his office at the foreign ministry, Togo mulled it over with his deputies. It was not ideal, they agreed, but it could be worse. The emperor would become a subordinate partner to the occupying force. Under a somewhat labored interpretation of the clause, it might be understood as a pledge not to arrest, depose, or otherwise molest Hirohito or his family. The translators attempted to take the sting out of the Byrnes note, softening the English phrase "subject to" to a Japanese phrase meaning "under the restriction of."

In the various power centers of Tokyo—the IGHQ, the ministries, the Imperial Palace—Japanese leaders pored over the note and debated its meaning and merits. August 12 was a long and chaotic day. Some who had been steadfast members of the peace camp now entertained doubts, and vacillated. Baron Kiichirō Hiranuma, a reactionary former prime minister, argued that accepting the American terms would obliterate the *kokutai*. He did not like the stipulation that the government would be determined by the "freely expressed will" of the Japanese people, which he regarded as an invitation to "subversive activities calculated to overthrow monarchical government."[88] Briefly, on the morning of the twelfth, it appeared that Prime Minister Suzuki and Navy Minister Yonai, who had been Togo's only dependable allies on the Big Six, would be swayed by these objections. In a meeting of the SWDC that morning, and in a later meeting of the full cabinet, the familiar deadlocks reemerged. Several ministers wanted to ask the United States for a "clarification" of the terms concerning the emperor. Togo countered that any such response risked a rupture in negotiations, in which case Japan would be destroyed. He implied that he would resign rather than send another temporizing note to Washington.

In the period between the first surrender offer on August 10 and the final capitulation on August 15, the tone of the Japanese newspapers was vacillating and uncertain. The acceptance of the Potsdam terms had been broadcast to overseas audiences in English, but the same report did not appear in the NHK domestic broadcasts. Anami's fight-to-the-finish message, which had been on the airwaves only one hour after the surrender offer, was prominently featured in both print and radio reports on August 10 and 11.

The army ministry at Ichigaya was a volcano. Rebellion was brewing among the younger radical officers. They spoke openly of a *coup d'état*. Among the firebrands, plans were afoot to take control of the Imperial Guards and seal off the imperial compound. They would arrest or assassinate the doves in the cabinet, declare a military dictatorship, occupy the foreign ministry, and seize control of all radio stations. Meanwhile, a stream of telegrams arrived from senior army commanders overseas, urging against surrender. General Yasuji Okamura, supreme commander of the China Expeditionary Army, said that it was unthinkable that his undefeated forces would surrender to their inferior Chinese foes.[89] Army hotheads tried to release a statement over the forged signatures of the high command, calling for an intensification of the war on all fronts. Alerted to the ruse, the Cabinet Information Board intercepted and suppressed the document before it was released to the press.

Lieutenant Colonel Masahiko Takeshita, brother-in-law to Army Minister Anami, pitched plans for a rebellion to Anami, Umezu, Kawabe, and other senior army figures. The leaders listened and equivocated, neither accepting nor rejecting the proposals. The tepid response encouraged the rebel leaders to proceed in the hope that they could later win the support of the high command. Anami, grasping at straws, asked the foreign minister whether any hope remained of recruiting the Soviet government to mediate with the Allies. (It was now three days since the Red Army had attacked, and it was already deep into Manchuria.) General Kawabe had little sympathy for the plotters, concluding that "more harm will be done than good to kick and struggle at this point."[90] He was evidently still somewhat dazed by the revelation that the emperor had lost faith in the army.

Prime Minister Suzuki told a subordinate that there was no time to lose, because of the rapid advances of the Red Army. "If we miss today, the Soviet Union will take not only Manchuria, Korea, Karafuto [South Sakhalin], but also Hokkaido. This would destroy the foundations of Japan. We must end the war when we can deal with the United States."[91]

The army and navy chiefs of staff, General Umezu and Admiral Toyoda, took the extraordinary step of submitting a joint letter to the emperor. Acceptance of the surrender terms spelled out in the Byrnes note, they warned, "may lead to a situation that cannot be controlled. . . . It is very awful to say this, but this means that it will reduce this imperial nation to a vassal status that we should never accept."[92]

To address themselves directly to the throne in such a manner was a scandalous breach of protocol, and would have ended their careers in ordinary circumstances. By imposing his will on the government, however, Hirohito had already abrogated an even more important protocol. A furious Yonai hauled Toyoda into his office and upbraided him. But it is an open question whether the two chiefs were really determined to avert surrender, or whether they were only "going through the motions," as Tsuyoshi Hasegawa has suggested, to "allay the dissatisfaction of radical officers."[93] The Umezu-Toyoda note stipulated that "we hereafter will reach a complete agreement of our opinions with the government and then we will ask for your majesty's decision."[94] The final clause signaled that they would obey the emperor's final command, whatever it might be.

The emperor was steadfast. Having rendered his opinion on August 9, he now acted to bring the curtain down on the last act of the Pacific War. In a series of private conferences at the palace, he informed Kido, Suzuki, Togo, the *jushin*, the royal princes, and other members of the ruling circle that he found the Byrnes note acceptable and did not wish to extend negotiations.

But the cabinet was divided, so another "sacred decision" was necessary. As news of the emperor's views circulated through the ruling circle, the possibility of chaos seemed very real. At any moment the government could fall, which would make surrender impossible. If Anami resigned, as seemed likely, the army could then refuse to name another army minister and no succeeding cabinet could even be formed. Before Hirohito could issue an imperial rescript ending the war, the countersignatures of all cabinet ministers were needed. If even one minister should refrain from signing the document, a mass resignation of the government would have followed. In other words, it was not enough to have the emperor decide for surrender; it was necessary that the entire government, including the army, fall in line behind Hirohito's decision. As evening fell on August 13, that scenario seemed unachievable.

Nothing could save the possibility of surrender except concerted action on behalf of the peace party, working together with the emperor. The formal Byrnes note was expected at any time. (The news had been received by radio broadcast, but the formal note would not be delivered to the foreign ministry via the Swiss legation until the morning of August 14.) But the two chiefs of staff declined to sign a document authorizing the prime minister to convene an imperial conference. This presented a procedural obstacle. Finally, on the morning of the fourteenth, Suzuki acted to circumvent this problem by prevailing upon the emperor to call a conference on his own authority.

Finally, by these means, the full cabinet was summoned to the Imperial Palace at 10 a.m., where they crowded into the cramped basement bomb shelter. They waited stiffly until 10:50 a.m., when the emperor entered and took his seat. He wore a military uniform and white gloves. Prime Minister Suzuki stood and summarized the arguments for and against accepting the Byrnes note, and told the emperor that despite long efforts, the cabinet had failed to obtain a consensus. Suzuki then asked the three hardliners to summarize their view. Umezu, Anami, and Toyoda each spoke briefly. They wanted to ask the Americans for a more definite guarantee of the emperor's status, and if the answer was deficient, to fight on to the end. Suzuki then turned directly to the emperor and asked for his decision.

To no one's surprise, Hirohito made his second and conclusive intervention into the broken decision-making machinery of the militarist regime. In comparison to the scene three days earlier, his remarks this morning were firm, direct, and to the point. The emperor spoke directly to the three holdouts. "It seems to me that there is no other opinion to support your side," he said. "I shall explain mine. I hope all of you will agree with my opinion. My opinion is the same as the one I expressed the other night. The American answer seems to me acceptable."[95] The Byrnes note provided sufficient guarantee for the continuation of his imperial line. Several ministers were now sobbing openly. Hirohito instructed the military leaders to do their utmost to maintain discipline in the ranks. The emperor asked his cabinet to draft an imperial rescript announcing the surrender, and said he was willing to read it over the air in a national radio broadcast. When the emperor had finished speaking, Suzuki stood and apologized for the cabinet's failure to obtain a consensus.

There was no open dissent. Every member of the cabinet affixed his signature to the decision—including Anami, Umezu, and Toyoda—and the cabinet secretary began work on the rescript. The rest of the afternoon was consumed in forming a consensus around the wording of the rescript. The foreign ministry cabled a note in Togo's name to Switzerland and Sweden, for transmittal to the Allied governments. It accepted the Potsdam Declaration on the basis of Byrnes's note.

Throughout the day, army insurgents were mulling about in the grand entrance hall and the basement of the army ministry at Ichigaya. Even after the emperor had settled the question, they continued to plot a military takeover. No action was taken to arrest them, and the plotters openly lobbied and even threatened the army brass. Vice Admiral Onishi, recently appointed vice chief of the Naval General Staff, was the highest-ranking figure among the would-be rebels. In vain, he attempted to persuade his colleagues that surrender was unthinkable. Often, he was reduced to tears as he urged his case. He said that the only honorable way forward was to use suicide tactics on a mass scale. He appealed to Yonai, who sternly rebuked him; to Umezu, who gave him no hope, and to Anami, who seemed personally sympathetic but refused to commit himself. Onishi directly lobbied every leading figure in the military and the government, and even several princes of the royal family.

An hour after the emperor's final decision, rebel officers attempted to distribute a counterfeit order from the IGHQ to army commands overseas, calling for a new offensive against the United States, Britain, the Soviet Union, and China. General Umezu's loyalists managed to intercept this message before it was broadcast over commercial radio. That was fortunate, as it might have sent a misleading impression to the Allies.

Umezu was a rock, and wielded his authority to enforce discipline. He disseminated a slogan to convince the army to lay down arms: "Obey the Imperial Will without fail."[96] But Anami appeared to waver. He polled the various players in the army ranks, leaving some with the impression that he might be tempted to join a plot. The major regional army headquarters in the capital, the Eastern Army, would have to back the revolt if it was to have any chance of succeeding. But the Eastern Army would not support the contemplated *coup d'état* unless directly ordered to do so by the army minister. The order would have to be in writing, and signed by Anami himself. But Anami was unwilling to put his signature on a document that contradicted the emperor's clear will, to say nothing of the several other documents that Anami had already signed.

The Japanese refer to the attempted *coup d'état* on the last night of the Second World War as the "Kyūjō Incident." Ringleaders Kenji Hatanaka and Jirō Shiizaki, officers at the army ministry, led a battalion of rebels into the Imperial Palace. Lying brazenly, Hatanaka and Shiizaki told the commander of the Second Imperial Guard Regiment that the top brass had ordered the palace sealed off from the outside. The guards, believing that a broader revolt was afoot, agreed to comply with their instructions pending the arrival of the Eastern Army. But Lieutenant General Takeshi Mori, commander of the guards, smelled a rat. Refusing to join the plot, he was shot dead in cold blood. The confederates then forged an order in General Mori's name and sealed it with Mori's official stamp. The document instructed the Imperial Guards to occupy the palace, seal off communications with anyone outside the moats, and "protect" the emperor against unspecified threats.

In the palace itself, the imperial stenographer was putting the finishing brushstrokes on the Imperial Rescript on Surrender. The emperor's seal was fixed to the document, making it official. Shortly before midnight, Hirohito entered a soundproof bunker under the palace, where a team of NHK technicians had set up recording equipment. The emperor read the surrender rescript into a microphone. The recording was four minutes and forty-five seconds long; the English translation, broadcast overseas the same day, totaled just 652 words. Only one take was needed. The technicians transferred the recording onto two vinyl records, which were pressed on the spot and deposited in a safe under the palace.

With the Imperial Guards behind them, the coup leaders occupied the palace and cut the phone lines. Persuaded that the Eastern Army was on its way, the guards closed the gates and cut off all automobile and foot traffic into and out of the walled compound. The rebels searched the catacombs under the palace, arresting and interrogating staff members at the points of bayonets. They searched for Marquis Kido, the lord privy seal, but could not find him. They also failed to find the phonograph recordings. With an air raid blackout in progress, the lights were doused and the searchers had to use flashlights. The search parties did not know the layout of the underground labyrinth of passageways and bunkers, and found it difficult to interpret the archaic signs marking the locations of various rooms.

Meanwhile, other coconspirators spread out through Tokyo and Yokohama. The aged Prime Minister Suzuki, who had survived an assassination attempt nine years earlier, was warned moments before his would-be killers arrived. He exited by a side door and took refuge in a neighbor's house. In frustration, the intruders machine-gunned his office and set it afire. Rebels went to Anami's official residence and attempted to convince the army minister to join their coup. When Anami refused, they did not bother to assassinate him; he already intended to take his own life by ritual disembowelment. Baron Kiichirō Hiranuma's home was also invaded; like Suzuki, he escaped shortly before the arrival of the rebels. Other detachments occupied the major radio stations, intending to intercept the emperor's surrender recording before it could be broadcast to the nation.

As dawn approached, Hatanaka and Shiizaki realized that their options were limited. No general or admiral had committed to support the revolt. Even Admiral Onishi, who had been the most passionate advocate of fighting to the end, had given up the cause and was preparing to take the samurai's way out. General Shizuichi Tanaka, commander of the Eastern Army, was determined to put the rebellion down. A full division of well-equipped troops surrounded the Imperial compound and sealed off the bridges spanning the moat. The exhausted ringleaders, outgunned and outmaneuvered, knew that their bid had failed. At 8:00 a.m. they gave themselves up. Hatanaka begged to be permitted to broadcast a ten-minute appeal over the radio, but was refused. He and Shiizaki were not arrested, perhaps because it was understood that they would take their own lives. For the next several hours, the two men roamed around Tokyo, distributing leaflets explaining what they had done and why. Shortly before the emperor's broadcast went on the air, both shot themselves.

Without the support of the military leadership, the rebellion had been stillborn. If either Anami or Umezu had backed it, they might have convinced Tanaka to join them. If all three had supported it, it is difficult to see how it could have failed. But the officers at the top of the command ladder obeyed the emperor, and they acted to maintain discipline down the ranks. Whatever trials and hardships defeat might bring, they judged that it was necessary to remain united as a nation.

The army fanatics had tried to bully the entire nation into fighting a final battle to the death of all—national *gyokusai*—as so many Japanese soldiers had fought on innumerable Pacific islands. But the people of Japan did not want such a fight. Nor did the civilian ministers, the royal family, the court, the *jushin*, or the emperor. In the end, not even the top ranks of the army leadership wanted it. In the days to follow, between the surrender and the arrival of occupation troops, there were scattered flare-ups, in Tokyo and on military bases around the country, typically involving groups of mid-ranking officers who occupied public installations or distributed leaflets claiming that the emperor's broadcast had been faked. But no senior military or civilian official joined in attempting to reverse the emperor's sacred decision.

AT 7:00 P.M. THAT EVENING, an NHK radio announcer instructed all Japanese to be near a radio at noon the following day: "At noon tomorrow, August 15, an important broadcast will be made. This will be an unprecedented broadcast and the 100 million subjects must listen honestly and solemnly without fail."[97] Subsequent bulletins added that the broadcast would include "the Jeweled Sound of His Imperial Highness."[98] In order to ensure that every citizen could hear it, electrical power would be provided to neighborhoods that would normally be blacked out. In anticipation of the momentous broadcast, all musical programming ceased at 10:00 p.m. on the fourteenth. It would not resume until after the emperor had been heard.

As the coup attempt was in its last throes, one of the two vinyl phonographs was delivered to NHK, Japan's national broadcasting corporation. An hour before the scheduled broadcast, the record was in the hands of the broadcast engineers. Troops of the Eastern Army had taken control of the streets around NHK headquarters. Both the coup plotters and the authorities knew that once the emperor's voice went across the airwaves, there would be no turning back, and no revolt could possibly succeed.

Throughout Japan, on the morning of August 15, citizens spoke to one another in low voices, speculating over the meaning of the forthcoming broadcast. Some had heard that foreign monarchs often spoke on the radio, but no such thing had ever occurred in Japan. Very few Japanese had ever heard the name Hirohito; the emperor was known simply as "*tenno*." How could they even imagine the "jeweled sound" (*gyokuon*) of the man-god's voice? A small bank run began in certain regions, as rumors spread that the banks would stop honoring withdrawals. Some suspected that the end of the war was at hand, but many others assumed that the broadcast would be for the purpose of declaring war on Russia. Perhaps the emperor would exhort his subjects to fight to the end. Beginning at dawn, air raid sirens wailed almost continuously, and waves of U.S. carrier planes appeared over Tokyo—Halsey's Third Fleet had launched one of its largest strikes of the war. "As before, we had no way of knowing how things really stood," recalled Michio Takeyama. "We knew only what we saw and heard within our own narrow radius. In fear amid the chaos, we could only conjecture and surmise from the rumors, yet we could tell from the newspapers that something was afoot."[99]

In outlying rural communities, there might be only one radio in a village, so the entire community gathered in an outdoor space—a street, a park, a school playground. In the cities, neighborhood associations connected radios to loudspeakers. Friends and neighbors gathered in private homes. Many workers came home so that they could listen to the broadcast with their families. In factories, in offices, in schools, in military barracks, the Japanese gathered around the radios, solemn and reverent, with heads bowed and hats in hand. Some knelt, murmuring timorously: "Please let us hear." The NHK transmitted dead air, punctuated occasionally by solemn announcements confirming that the special broadcast would begin at noon.

At 11:59 a.m., air raid sirens churned briefly, and then fell silent. The audiences listened with breathless intensity. The streets fell dead silent. In many places, the summer cicadas warbled loudly, and people cocked their heads to hear. At the NHK studios in Tokyo, a technician dropped the needle on the phonograph, and then stood and bowed his head.

A voice came across the airwaves. It was faint, reedy, and tremulous. Many found it difficult to follow amid a hiss of static. It began, "To Our good and loyal subjects."

> After pondering deeply the general trends of the world and the actual conditions obtaining in Our Empire today, We have decided to effect a settlement of the present situation by resorting to an extraordinary measure.
>
> We have ordered Our Government to communicate to the Governments of the United States, Great Britain, China and the Soviet Union that Our Empire accepts the provisions of their Joint Declaration.[100]

The language was archaic, an obscure dialect of the ancient Japanese imperial court. Even highly educated Japanese found the speech cryptic and perplexing; those who had received less schooling were completely baffled. Akio Morita, a young navy lieutenant and future cofounder of the Sony Corporation, found the language difficult to comprehend. But he knew it was the emperor as soon as he heard the voice, "and even though we couldn't follow the words exactly, we knew what the message was, what he was telling us, and we were frightened and yet relieved."[101] To naval aviator Takeshi Maeda, "it seemed like the cicadas stopped making noise momentarily."[102] The emperor continued:

> Despite the best that has been done by everyone—the gallant fighting of the military and naval forces, the diligence and assiduity of Our servants of the State, and the devoted service of Our one hundred million people—the war situation has developed not necessarily to Japan's advantage, while the general trends of the world have all turned against her interest. Moreover, the enemy has begun to employ a new and most cruel bomb, the power of which to do damage is, indeed, incalculable, taking the toll of many innocent lives. Should We continue to fight, not only would it result in an ultimate collapse and obliteration of the Japanese nation, but also it would lead to the total extinction of human civilization.[103]

The phrase "not necessarily to Japan's advantage" has been lampooned as an understatement. A previous draft had more accurately stated that "the war situation went daily from bad to worse."[104] The army ministry had insisted on softening that language. The point had been debated at length by the cabinet on the afternoon of August 14. Even in the throes of defeat, the army was determined to take some of the sting out of its humiliation.

In the United States and Allied nations, where translations of the message were published the following day, many were angered by a tone they regarded as self-righteous and even defiant. Hirohito had suggested that Japan's motives in waging war had been pure and just, for "self-preservation and the stabilization of East Asia," and that it had never been Japan's purpose to "infringe on the sovereignty of other Nations or to embark on territorial aggrandizement." In the emperor's telling, his decision to surrender was a gallant gesture of self-abnegation and altruism.

At the conclusion of the broadcast, many Japanese were dumbstruck and tearful. They bowed deeply to their neighbors, then returned wordlessly to their homes. A few gathered and whispered to one another. Those who had understood more of the archaic dialect translated for their neighbors. In private musings, in conversations or in diary entries, many Japanese expressed deep concern for the emperor's feelings. They felt collectively responsible for having caused him sorrow and anxiety. Many were moved by the clear indication of "His Majesty's compassion."[105] Navy maintenance officer Hachiro Miyashita found that he could not eat, could not speak, and could not concentrate on his work. He passed the day in a catatonic stupor. Elsewhere, there were outbursts of anger. One man said that he and his neighbors felt "the horror of being defeated"—but even worse, they shared "the inexpressible horror of being the citizens of a defeated country."[106] A fifth grader who had been evacuated to the country made the mistake of telling his classmates: "Now that the war is over, we'll be able to go home." Several other boys set upon him and beat him, shouting: "You traitor! We swore we would do all we could here until the day of victory!"[107] Parents who had lost sons in the war were furious that their sacrifice had been rendered meaningless. If ending the war was so easy, if the emperor wielded the power to simply call it off, why hadn't he acted earlier? "Your Majesty," one said, "because of this my sons have all died in vain, a dog's death."[108]

Dr. Michihiko Hachiya in Hiroshima had been working for nine consecutive days to care for those injured by the atomic bomb. After listening to the emperor's broadcast, many of the patients in his ward burst out in anger. They shouted: "How can we lose the war! . . . Only a coward would back out now! . . . I would rather die than be defeated! . . . What have we been suffering for? . . . Those who died can't go to heaven in peace now!" Dr. Hachiya noted that many who had expressed defeatist sentiments after the bombing now demanded that the fight should go on, as if they could not make sense of their terrible burns and the loss of loved ones unless the entire nation immolated itself in a final battle. "The one word—surrender—had produced a greater shock than the bombing of our city," the doctor wrote in his diary. "The more I thought, the more wretched and miserable I became."[109]

But the emperor had expressed his will, and there was no opposing him. Most public anger was turned against the government and the military leadership. Some decried the leaders who had prevailed upon the emperor to surrender; others condemned the same leaders for having plunged Japan into a reckless and catastrophic war. Many were fearful, assuming that they were to be enslaved by the Allied victors. Shaking their heads, they simply repeated the inconceivable fact, again and again, in a daze: "We've been defeated." And they asked one another, with wide eyes, "Now that we have been defeated, what will happen?"[110] No one knew, but it was easy to imagine the worst, especially for those who had some inkling of how Japanese forces had behaved in China, Malaya, the Philippines, and elsewhere. Yet many others felt a dawning sense of relief. The air raids would finally end. They would not have to fight off an invading barbarian army with kitchen cleavers and bamboo spears. Perhaps the government would reopen the bathhouses, and they could all wash off the accumulated filth. Even on the night of August 15, the first night of the peace, air raid regulations were relaxed and electric lights were left on after dark. People took down their blackout shades. Hisako Yoskizawa, a secretary living in Tokyo, wondered how her neighbors were taking the momentous news, and concluded that "an unmistakable brightness in their faces told the story."[111]

On military bases, discipline broke down. Soldiers refused to take orders. Young hotheads vowed: "We'll behead the evil subordinates of the Emperor!"[112] Those posted overseas felt a keen desire to get home, to protect their families against the incoming army of occupation; they planned to desert the military as soon as they reached Japanese soil. Enlisted men who had been physically abused by their officers took the opportunity to exact revenge. One soldier who had expressed defeatist sentiments recalled: "I cheered that I had been right, and I was hit by an officer. I hit him back."[113] A nurse at an army hospital in Tochigi Prefecture watched several officers crying "Forgive me, forgive me!" while being beaten by their own men.[114]

In a calmer frame of mind, Japanese servicemen considered whether it was their duty to kill themselves. Many did not relish the thought of returning home in defeat after so many others had given their lives. They did not expect to be greeted warmly by their neighbors, perhaps not even by their families, because they would be "bearing the dishonor of defeat."[115] Shoji Tsuchida, a kamikaze pilot stationed at Tachiarai Airbase, had expected to fly his last mission on the same day as the emperor's broadcast. He wrote in his diary, "I feel the evanescence of the fate of defeat. The eyes of locals seem to be appealing to us for something, but the truth is that we have been stained with the stigma of defeat."[116] At Imperial Headquarters in Tokyo, officers were divided over whether or not they should comply with the surrender order, launch a guerilla resistance movement in the mountains, or kill themselves. Many vowed to fight, or die by their own hands, but one young lieutenant remarked, "Dying is the easier thing to do. Consider living under the ugly enemy. It will be harrowing and painful. . . . It will not be easy to live through the dark ages and to transmit our culture to the next age. But if this is not done, there will not be an age when the Japanese people are truly awakened."[117] Some who had given up all hope of surviving the war now realized with a surge of elation that they been granted a second life. The emperor's statement had clearly absolved them of responsibility for the nation's defeat, and had summoned them to the work of rebuilding a peaceful Japan. To defy surrender would dishonor his will and subvert his authority. The rescript had included this stern injunction, an echo of Meiji's Imperial Rescript to Soldiers and Sailors: "Beware most strictly of any outbursts of emotion that may engender needless complications, and of any fraternal contention and strife that may create confusion, lead you astray and cause you to lose the confidence of the world."[118]

In the end, with surprisingly few exceptions, the great majority of Japanese officers and enlisted men of all ranks chose to live. "I thought of committing suicide, but was unable to go through with it," a soldier in southern Kyushu later admitted. "'I'll be reborn seven times and attack America,' I vowed. With this, I permitted myself to continue living."[119]

GENERAL ANAMI WAS ONE OF THE EXCEPTIONS. He did not hear Hirohito's broadcast; he spared himself that mortification by taking the samurai's way out in the early morning hours of August 15. He had been up all night, drinking sake and entertaining visitors, refusing to give any support to the attempted military *coup d'état* that was unfolding at the Imperial Palace. At dawn, the well-sodden general composed his traditional "poem upon departing the world." With a few brushstrokes, Anami kept it simple:

> *Not even a half word*
> *To be left behind*
> *For benevolence has been bestowed upon me by His Imperial*
> *   Majesty the Emperor.*[120]

Then he plunged a short steel blade into his own abdomen, up to the hilt, and carved through his viscera, left to right. The blade severed the descending aorta, causing massive hemorrhaging into the abdominal cavity. He died slowly, painfully—and in the traditional Japanese view, honorably.

One night later, Admiral Onishi performed the same gory ritual, thrusting the knife into his belly and carving out his own bowels. Many officers came to visit him in his death throes, but he refused their offers to put him out of his misery. It took him fifteen hours to bleed out. Lying in a pool of his own blood, this most warlike of hardliners told the young officers who visited him that they must obey the emperor and follow his instructions to strive for the peace of the world.

General Shizuichi Tanaka, who had played a crucial role in putting down the August 14–15 rebellion, shot himself on August 24, the day the first advance detachments of U.S. occupiers set foot on Japanese soil. General Hajime Sugiyama, who had preceded Anami as army minister, shot himself on September 12; his wife, Keiko, killed herself a day later.

General Tojo, the "little Mussolini" who had led his nation into a disastrous war, tried and failed to take his own life on September 11, 1945. As U.S. troops knocked on his front door, intending to arrest him as a war criminal, Tojo peeked out of a second story window. Realizing that he was cornered, he retreated into his study and shot himself in the chest. The wound was serious but not mortal. His captors rushed him to a hospital, where surgeons sewed up the wound and replaced his lost blood through an intravenous feed. The failed suicide was considered by Tojo's countrymen as the crowning ignominy of his odious career. He made a full recovery, only to be convicted of war crimes and hanged in 1948.

FROM HIS FIFTH AIR FLEET headquarters in Kyushu, Admiral Matome Ugaki had at first refused to believe the "hateful news" that the emperor had decided for surrender. After receiving confirmation by telephone from the Combined Fleet command bunker in Hiyoshi, he wrote in his diary that the leaders in Tokyo were "nothing but selfish weaklings who don't think seriously about the future of the nation and only seek immediate benefits."[121] On the morning of August 15, he received orders to suspend attacks on enemy forces. The Fifth Air Fleet staff stood to attention while listening to the emperor's noon broadcast. Ugaki did not understand all of it, but he understood enough to know that the war was over. "I've never been filled with so much trepidation. As one of the officers the throne trusted, I met this sad day. I've never been so ashamed of myself. Alas!"[122]

Since assuming command in Kyushu, Ugaki had sent thousands of young kamikaze flyers to their deaths. Now he resolved to follow them. He consigned his personal diary—fifteen leather-bound volumes of fastidious brush-stroke calligraphy—to the safekeeping of his Naval Academy Class of 1912 association.

The Ugaki diary remains one of the most significant documentary records of the Pacific War. It covers the entire period of the war, beginning in the weeks leading up to the attack on Pearl Harbor, when Ugaki was chief of staff to Admiral Isoroku Yamamoto; it continues through the vicissitudes of Coral Sea, Midway, and Guadalcanal, to the aerial assassination of Yamamoto in April 1943. In 1944, Ugaki had commanded the Japanese navy's main battleship division, including the superships *Yamato* and *Musashi*, during the battles of the Philippine Sea and Leyte Gulf; and in 1945, as commander Fifth Air Fleet, he had been in charge of the largest kamikaze campaign of the war. Throughout it all, Ugaki had committed his private daily thoughts to his diary.

Determined to be off before a formal ceasefire order arrived from Tokyo, Ugaki moved quickly. In his last entry, he wrote, "I myself have made up my mind to serve this country even after death takes my body from this earth." In defeat, Japan would face a long crucible, and he hoped that all Japanese would "display the traditional spirit of this nation more than ever, do their best to rehabilitate this country, and finally revenge this defeat in the future."[123]

At 4:00 p.m., after drinking a final farewell toast of sake with the headquarters staff, Admiral Ugaki was driven the short distance to Oita Airfield. Eleven D4Y *Suisei* dive-bombers were lined up on the flight line. Twenty-two pilots and aircrewmen stood in ranks. All wore Rising Sun headbands. Orders had been given for a flight of five planes, but all of the aircrewmen wanted to fly the mission.

Ugaki asked, "Will all of you go with me?"

They shouted, with right hands raised: "Yes, sir!"

Ugaki removed his rank insignia. He wore a green uniform, white gloves, and a traditional samurai short sword that had been a gift of Isoroku Yamamoto. In a photograph taken just before he boarded his plane, Ugaki gazed straight back into the camera. He appeared serene and determined, with the barest hint of a Mona Lisa smile.

He climbed onto the wing of the lead plane and slid into the rear cockpit. The radioman-navigator, who normally occupied that seat, begged to be permitted to come aboard. Ugaki assented, and the young man wedged himself into the space just forward of the admiral's knees.

As the eleven planes taxied to the end of the runway, Ugaki's white gloved hand was seen waving from the cockpit. The planes took off and droned away to the south. Three later returned and landed, their crews reporting "engine problems."

At 7:24 p.m., Ugaki's plane radioed back to base. The attack group was proceeding to ram the "arrogant American ships" off the coast of Okinawa. No more was heard from them.[124]

According to U.S. Navy reports, a handful of enemy planes had attempted diving attacks on transports anchored off Ie Shima Island, off the coast of Okinawa. All were shot down by antiaircraft fire, and no American vessels were hit or damaged. The next morning, the crew of a tank landing ship (*LST-926*) found wreckage of Japanese warplanes in the shallows off the island. The bodies were extracted from the wreckage and buried on the beach.

Back at the Fifth Air Fleet barracks in Kyushu, an orderly collected Ugaki's personal belongings, intending to send them on to his next of kin. He found a handwritten note, evidently written earlier that day. It read: "Having a dream, I will go up into the sky."[125]

Epilogue

It's utterly impossible for me to build my life on a foundation of chaos, suffering and death. I see the world being slowly transformed into a wilderness; I hear the approaching thunder that, one day, will destroy us too. I feel the suffering of millions. And yet, when I look up at the sky, I somehow feel that everything will change for the better, that this cruelty will end, that peace and tranquility will return once more.
—ANNE FRANK, DIARY ENTRY OF JULY 15, 1944

ON THE EVENING OF AUGUST 14, THE WHITE HOUSE PRESS CORPS WAS invited into the Oval Office. President Truman was seated behind his desk, with his cabinet secretaries, military chiefs, and aides standing behind him. Their beaming faces told the tale. The president came directly to the point. The Japanese government had accepted the terms of the Potsdam Declaration, and therefore, the Second World War was over. The reporters rushed back to the press room, and moments later the news was on the wires. Soon a boisterous crowd gathered outside the White House gates. Admiral Leahy noted in his diary: "A noisy celebration is going on in the city with all motor cars sounding their horns, and great crowds of shouting people milling in the streets and bringing traffic to a standstill. The radio is bearing forth news of the celebration in cities from Los Angeles to Boston, in all of which the populace seems to be celebrating the war's end with noise in crowded streets." Leahy did not approve. He felt that the occasion called for calm, thoughtful, dignified reflection, "but the proletariat considers noise appropriate and the greatest number of people in democracies must have their way."[1]

They *did* have their way, in cities across the country, throughout the rest of that long summer evening and into the following day. Crowds poured into public squares, hands held up in triumph, mugging for the cameras, servicemen and civilians, men and women, black and white, victorious citizens abandoning themselves to a riotous bacchanal. In downtown business districts, the air was filled with scraps of torn-up paper thrown from high windows—makeshift ticker-tape—and toilet paper rolls trailing long tissue-streamers. The police stepped back and let it happen, declining to stop any but the most outrageous crimes against people or property. Bottles were passed from stranger to stranger. Automobiles inched forward, blocked by surging mobs, and people clambered onto the roofs and hoods, converting every passing vehicle into an impromptu parade float. In New York, a crowd of 60,000 poured into Times Square, where the electronic billboard on the angled building between Broadway and 7th Avenue was flashing: "Japs Surrender!" A *Life* magazine photographer snapped an iconic photo of a sailor kissing a nurse. Hal Buell, a navy lieutenant who had flown a dive-bomber for three years in the Pacific, found himself trapped in a packed mass of delirious New Yorkers, and because he was wearing his uniform he was "patted, pawed, kissed, and cheered." He accepted a bottle of beer from a woman who shouted into his ear: "The war is over and my son is alive!" Buell and a fellow officer staggered through Manhattan that night, from one bar to the next, and no one let them pay for a drink.[2]

In Los Angeles, a citizen remembered, "The celebrating was unbelievable. People were dancing in the streets, all of the stores were closed, and everybody joined in the celebration. Some streets were blocked off completely. You could only drive at a snail's pace, if at all."[3] In Portland, Oregon, a woman recalled, "the hotel where we were staying just fell apart. There was no room service, no phone operators. Everybody was just running around out in the streets. It was chaos, just total chaos. A lot of people drinking, staggering around."[4] Patricia Livermore, who was visiting San Diego, wandered around the city and got caught up in the celebrations: "Any girl that was at the Horton Plaza in downtown San Diego got kissed and thrown in the Plaza fountain. I got thrown in about ten times." Livermore and her friends were staying at the Pickwick Hotel. The local liquor stores had sold out their entire inventory, but the hotel bellhop hustled up a few bottles at markup prices. From their room on a high floor, they filled condoms with water and threw them from the window at the crowd below. "It was all we could use," she explained, "because we couldn't find any balloons."[5]

In Hawaii, where the territory passed much of the war under martial law, blackout regulations were merrily ignored and Honolulu bars stayed open all night. A packed mass of whitehats celebrated on Hotel Street. Crowds began hauling coils of barbed wire away from the beaches. Some climbed the Aloha Tower and began tearing down the camouflage nets. The MPs, shore patrol, police, and national guardsmen either stood aside or joined the fun.

In downtown San Francisco, V-J Day celebrations took a darker turn. As darkness fell, drunken civilians and servicemen battled police on Market Street. The mob smashed storefront windows, overturned cars, and preyed upon innocent citizens. Thirty streetcars were disabled or destroyed. According to the *San Francisco Chronicle*, "Windows are crashing from Sixth to Third streets. The police and shore patrol are unable to and not trying to stop it. There is barely five minutes without the clatter of plate glass punctuating a steady roar of voices and the explosions of firecrackers."[6] Overwhelmed by numbers, pelted by bricks and bottles, the police retreated. Two hours later, reinforced by MPs and shore patrolmen, they advanced up Market Street together in a line abreast, swinging their batons. Much of the mob scattered along side streets. Those who stood their ground were beaten, arrested, and thrown into paddy wagons. Eleven people were killed and about a thousand injured.[7] This "Victory Riot," as the hometown newspapers called it, was the deadliest in San Francisco's history. But the mayhem received almost no national press coverage and was quickly forgotten.

At sea south of Japan, the Third Fleet received Nimitz's ceasefire order at 6:14 a.m. on August 15—west of the International Date Line, and thus one day ahead of the United States. Before dawn that morning, Task Force 38 had launched hundreds of warplanes to hit Tokyo—and the first wave was already over the Japanese capital, dropping bombs and firing rockets. The American airmen found Japanese fighter resistance unexpectedly fierce, calling it "the most determined air opposition since the Okinawa operation."[8] Seven U.S. aircraft went down in air combat on the morning of V-J Day, and another two were lost to accidents. The others turned for home, and were back aboard their carriers by eleven o'clock.

At noon, the *Missouri* sounded her whistle and siren for one full minute.

Her battle flags and admiral's four-star flag were broken out at the main. Halsey ordered a signal run up: "Well Done." He told the carriers to stow their attack planes on their hangar decks, so that the flight decks could be reserved for defensive fighter operations. The combat air patrol was reinforced. Halsey was not convinced that the peace would stick—and even if the Japanese government really meant to surrender, there was every reason to expect kamikaze attacks by defiant pilots. In a message that prompted hearty laughter throughout the fleet, he ordered the Hellcat and Corsair pilots to "investigate and shoot down all snoopers—not vindictively, but in a friendly sort of way."[9]

Halsey's wariness was well-founded. Twenty minutes later, radar scopes detected inbound bogeys. The combat air patrol and picket destroyers shot down eight Japanese warplanes during the next several hours. The last, at 2:45 p.m. on V-J Day, drew the final curtain on the Third Fleet's war: the fleet did not fire another shot in anger.

General MacArthur, as supreme commander for the Allied powers (SCAP), lost no time in asserting his authority. His headquarters in Manila began broadcasting directly to Tokyo on several frequencies, issuing instructions regarding communications, disarmament, release of Allied prisoners, a formal surrender agreement, and the forthcoming arrival of occupation forces. He directed that a "competent representative," authorized by the emperor, should fly into Manila to confer on these matters.

No one could say whether the rank and file of the Japanese army and navy would obey the emperor's surrender edict. The first occupation units might have to fight their way into Japan after all—or short of that, they might find critical installations sabotaged or booby-trapped. The troops would have to be prepared for all contingencies, but they would also have to pour into the defeated nation quickly, so that a critical mass of strength could be obtained. The great movement of forces would involve every branch of the service—army, navy, marines, and the Army Air Forces, staging from both MacArthur's and Nimitz's theaters. The needed ground forces were scattered across Okinawa, the Marianas, and the Philippines, where they had been preparing for the Operation OLYMPIC landings on Kyushu. The Third Fleet, still at sea off Japan, was assigned to enter and secure Tokyo Bay, including Yokosuka Naval Base. Because of the press of time, the Yokosuka landing force would have to be assembled using marines and bluejackets already at sea with the fleet. Without knowing the state of the facilities ashore, they would have to be accompanied by electricians, carpenters, plumbers, police, doctors, interpreters, and—Mick Carney recalled—"all the 101 other things that go to make up the daily life in a civilized community, in this case superimposed by military authority."[10]

The 11th Airborne Division would fly into Atsugi Airbase, southwest of Tokyo, in a massive airlift beginning on August 26. The Army Air Transport Command planned to send 300 C-54 transports into Atsugi per day, the largest airlift of the war—but the big four-engine planes would be landing at an airbase that had suffered months of heavy aerial bombing, and most of the ground installations had been reduced to rubble. The logistical challenge was stupendous. The paratroopers would be flying into an airfield that was, as of V-J Day, a hotbed of militarist sedition and rebellion. Immediately following Hirohito's broadcast, Japanese airmen at Atsugi had vowed to climb into their planes and launch suicide attacks against the U.S. fleet. Officers who attempted to restore discipline were attacked and beaten. "The airbase was pandemonium itself," recalled Saburo Sakai. "Many of the pilots were blind drunk, shouting and cursing wildly."[11] In the capital, meanwhile, rebellious army units seized Ueno Hill and Atago Hill near the city center, and urged the rest of the army to join their revolt.[12] Demonstrations and mass suicides took place on the plaza outside the Imperial Palace. Admiral Yonai was deeply worried that military discipline would break down, and that Japan would descend into chaos. He finally managed to put down the mutiny at Atsugi by persuading Prince Takamatsu, the emperor's brother, to visit the base in person. Yonai also mobilized naval base troops at nearby Yokosuka and sent them in to occupy Atsugi, where they removed the propellers from the aircraft. "During my long career as Navy Minister," Yonai later said, "I probably never worried so much as I did during the period from the 14th to about the 23rd of that month."[13]

During the same week, however, it was becoming clear that the Japanese government, including the top echelon of the military, was committed to surrender in good faith. Radio messages between Tokyo and Manila were brisk, clear, and courteous in tone. The Japanese readily submitted to MacArthur's instructions, often requesting clarification in such a way as to confirm that they were committed to full and rigorous compliance. On August 17, two days after his more famous surrender broadcast, Hirohito issued a second Imperial Rescript in the form of a direct order to the armed forces, instructing them to "comply with our intention" and to "maintain a solid unity and strict discipline in your movements."[14] Prince Naruhiko Higashikuni, appointed that day as interim prime minister, declared that "no action or words in violation of His Imperial Majesty's instructions is to be permitted any one of his subjects."[15] Members of the imperial family were dispatched to bases and headquarters all across Asia, acting as personal representatives of Hirohito, to ensure that all overseas Japanese armies laid down arms. When Tokyo requested safe conduct for the aircraft transporting these emissaries, MacArthur quickly assented.[16]

In obedience to MacArthur's instructions, a Japanese truce delegation flew to Manila on August 19. It was headed by General Kawabe, Umezu's deputy on the army's imperial headquarters staff. A conference at Manila City Hall was formal but civil. The Americans gave detailed instructions concerning the disarming of warplanes and warships, the securing of ordnance and weapons, the evacuation of Allied prisoners, the establishment of navigational lights and buoys, and the clearing of mines.[17] The Japanese asked for permission to muster and disarm their own troops, especially in Tokyo. The situation was potentially volatile, they said—but with a bit more time they could get their recalcitrant hotheads under control. The Americans were firm, but willing to show a certain degree of flexibility. They agreed to a forty-eight-hour delay in the landings at both Yokosuka and Atsugi. A Japanese participant said that he was impressed by the bearing of the victors, finding them stern but fair, "neither arrogant nor mocking."[18]

On August 27, a major portion of the Third Fleet anchored in Sagami Bay, a shallow indentation on the coast of Honshu, southwest of Tokyo Bay. The fleet included battleships, cruisers, and destroyers—but not aircraft carriers, which had all been left at sea, where they could provide air cover while remaining less exposed to counterattack. The *Missouri* anchored off the Miura Peninsula, near the historic coastal town of Kamakura. Mount Fuji loomed to the west, just 40 miles away. At sunset, from the fleet's vantage point, the sun was aligned directly behind Fuji, so that the sinking red orb appeared to descend directly into the black stratocone's caldera. Admiral Halsey and the rest of the Dirty Tricks Department crowded out onto the *Missouri*'s flag bridge veranda to watch the breathtaking spectacle, and summoned the ship's photographers to record it.[19] After the sun sank out of sight, according to an officer on the nearby battleship *Idaho*, Mount Fuji "cast forth the bright red bars of light so prominently seen on Japanese maritime flags. We knew we had come to the right place."[20]

At dawn the next morning, a squadron of minesweepers began the peril-ous work of clearing mines from the entrance to Tokyo Bay. With the assis-tance of Japanese harbor pilots, a safe channel was charted and buoyed. An anchorage was cleared in the southwest quadrant of the bay, including the zones around the Yokosuka and Yokohama waterfronts and the river estu-aries that led up to Tokyo. The *Missouri* anchored in ten fathoms of water, about four miles off Yokosuka, with her accompanying cruisers and destroy-ers arrayed around her. Nearby were three other battleships, including the *South Dakota*, now serving as flagship for Admiral Nimitz, who had flown in from Guam the previous day.

From here the Americans could gaze in any direction, all around the compass rose, and see nothing but Japanese territory. The sensation was exhilarating but also unnerving. Some believed that the surrender had been a sham, and that the Japanese intended a treacherous attack. The fleet remained on hair-trigger alert, with the crews at general quarters and the naval guns trained on targets ashore.

For the carrier air groups, the first days of peace were as busy as any they had experienced during the war. Between August 16 and September 2, Task Force 38 pilots flew a total of 7,726 sorties, more than in any comparable period of the war.[21] Carrier planes dropped leaflets on Allied POW camps, urging the prisoners to remain in the vicinity of their camps until Allied personnel could reach them. "The end is near," one such leaflet stated. "Do not be disheartened. We are thinking of you. Plans are underway to assist you at the earliest possible moment."[22] Relief parcels containing food, cloth-ing, medicine, and cigarettes were dropped by parachute. In Tokyo Bay, a number of prisoners actually made their way to the waterfront and began shouting and signaling to U.S. patrol vessels. Nimitz authorized a rescue mission. Small craft went up the estuaries and embarked prisoners from camps closer to Tokyo. The infamous Omori 8 Camp, on an artificial island off Yokohama, was completely liberated on August 29. By the end of that day, more than seven hundred Allied prisoners had been evacuated to the hospital ship *Benevolence*, at anchor in the bay. The half-starved men ate heartily and put on weight at a fantastic rate, often 4 or 5 pounds per day.

The 4th Marine Regimental Combat Team went ashore at Yokosuka on August 30. They landed in full combat gear, as if expecting a fight—but they encountered no hostile troops and no evidence of trickery. On a ware-house they found painted, in English, "Three cheers for the United States

Navy and Army!"[23] The base was largely deserted, and the few Japanese servicemen who remained were anxious to avoid trouble. By nightfall, 10,000 marines and naval personnel were safely ashore. The Japanese base commander, Vice Admiral Michitaro Tozuka, was polite and compliant.[24] Mick Carney, to whom Tozuka surrendered with a deep bow, found the situation disorienting, even alarming: "Little kids in the street made the V sign at us. How do you interpret this thing?" He found the friendly attitude of the Japanese "scarier than if we'd found a sullen or resistant attitude. . . . The thing was weird."[25]

Bomb damage was evident everywhere at Yokosuka, and many of the facilities were filthy. A marine officer recalled, "They had evidently given up; the floors in the barracks had not been scrubbed in months, they were

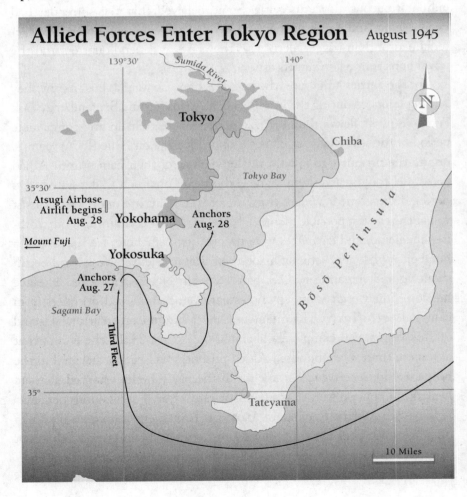

Allied Forces Enter Tokyo Region August 1945

half an inch or an inch deep in mud. The facilities were in terrible conditions. The cesspools were emptied daily and the waste matter carried away in wooden carts and oversized buckets, all of which leaked. We had swarms of flies in the streets, in the barracks, in the mess halls, and it took us several months to renovate the sewage system to clean up this place. I was worried about the health of the men."[26] When Admiral Halsey went ashore later that afternoon, he found the officers' club "overrun with rats of an extraordinary size and character."[27] The bunks in the barracks at Yokosuka were generally too short for the Americans, so cots and hammocks were brought in from the fleet. The Seabees went to work immediately, constructing galleys and mess halls, repairing the electrical grid and telephone network, repaving the roads, and applying layers of asphalt to the Japanese airstrips. In the weeks ahead, they would build chapels, cold storage units, baseball diamonds, gyms, water chlorination plants, and hot water showers.

The airlift into Atsugi commenced on August 28, when advance elements of the 11th Airborne Division landed in the first C-54 transports. They were greeted cordially by the Japanese staff, with salutes and handshakes, and escorted to barracks recently occupied by kamikaze pilots, which had been carefully cleaned and prepared for their arrival. They were offered a fresh-cooked meal served in the mess hall. By August 30, more than three hundred C-54 Skymasters were shuttling continuously between Okinawa and Atsugi, a flight of 980 miles. They landed at Atsugi at the rate of about twenty per hour, or one every three minutes. Task Force 38 carrier planes provided fighter escort along the route.

MacArthur arrived on August 30. It was a clear, sunny day, with superb visibility all along the south coast of Honshu. During the five-hour flight from Okinawa in his C-54 *Bataan*, the general alternated between pacing the aisle and visiting the cockpit. When Mount Fuji appeared in the cockpit windshield, more than 100 miles ahead, he buckled in to the right-side pilot seat and remained there for the remainder of the flight. The *Bataan* flew over the waist of the Miura Peninsula, low enough that the great bronze Buddha at Kamakura could be seen from the windows. Then it made a wide turn over Tokyo Bay, providing a fine view of the Third Fleet at anchor. Descending, the plane flew over verdant farmland and rice paddies. Crossing the boundary of the airbase, MacArthur and his pilot could see the bombed-out remains of hangars and ground installations, and Japanese planes whose propellers had been removed. The *Bataan* touched down at exactly 2:00 p.m., and taxied behind a guide jeep to a parking area, where a large contingent of officers, soldiers, and war correspondents were gathered.

Before debarking, MacArthur instructed all officers on the plane to remove their sidearms and leave them on the plane. The weapons were useless, he said, because there were "fifteen fully armed Jap divisions within ten miles of us. If they decided to start anything, those toy cannon of ours wouldn't do any good."[28] MacArthur would not carry a sidearm for his entire six-year stint in occupied Japan. General Kenney, MacArthur's air commander, said that he realized only in retrospect that the gesture was a masterstroke of psychology, because "it made a tremendous impression on the Japs to see us walking around in their country unarmed and simply with utter disregard of danger from the nation of 70 million people we had defeated. To them it meant that there was no doubt about it. They had lost."[29]

The Japanese had assembled about fifty cars and buses of various makes, colors, and vintages, many retrofitted to run on charcoal. This fleet of jalopies, which would carry MacArthur and his party to the New Grand Hotel in downtown Yokohama, was led by a rattletrap red fire truck that started up with a loud backfire. CBS radio correspondent Bill Dunn judged that "not one of the dilapidated, battered, and wheezing charcoal burners" looked capable of making the 18-mile journey.[30] MacArthur climbed into the back of a Lincoln sedan, and the motorcade set out on pockmarked roads through a landscape of well-tended rice plots and small wooden houses. Thousands of armed Japanese troops lined the roadway, at intervals of about two meters, facing outward with their backs to the road in the "present arms" position. This, the Americans learned, was a gesture of respect. Some civilian farmworkers looked up curiously at the passing cars, and a few even waved, but most kept their eyes down.

As they entered the outskirts of Yokohama, the Americans saw at ground level the results of their firebombing campaign. Fields of ash alternated with heaps of debris, with nothing left standing except stone chimneys and the gutted remains of concrete office blocks. Indigent civilians were seen foraging among the ruins. Many were living in makeshift huts and lean-tos made of lumber, piping, and corrugated metal. Downtown Yokohama was better preserved, but it was a ghost town. "Shop windows were boarded up, blinds were drawn, and many of the sidewalks were deserted," Courtney Whitney recalled. "Down empty streets we were taken to the New Grand Hotel, where we would stay until MacArthur made his formal entry into Tokyo."[31]

As MacArthur's car pulled up in front of the hotel, the manager and staff were waiting on the front steps to greet him. They appeared genuinely happy to receive him, as if they were conscious of a great honor. Bowing deeply, gesturing the way forward with open palms, the manager escorted MacArthur to the elevator, and up to his suite, the best in the hotel. The furnishings were old and threadbare, but the rooms were clean. An hour later, the general came back down to the dining room, where he was served a steak dinner. His aides fretted about the risk of poison, but MacArthur serenely replied, "No one can live forever," and cut into his meat.[32] The hotel manager later thanked MacArthur for his trust, adding that he and his staff were "honored beyond belief."[33]

The dining room was crowded with Allied officers and war correspondents, who were arriving from Atsugi in a constant stream. Somehow the kitchen was able to turn out enough food to feed them all. The supply of steaks gave out, leaving nothing on the menu but fish sautéed in oil. MacArthur urged his officers to eat the fish even if it was not particularly appetizing, as a show of good faith to the staff, because "this was doubtless the only food they had to offer us."[34]

Later, in the hotel lobby, MacArthur was reunited with General Jonathan M. Wainwright, who had been left behind as commanding officer on Corregidor in March 1942, and had surrendered the island to the Japanese in May 1942. Wainwright had been held at a camp in Manchuria, along with other senior officers including British general A. E. Percival, who had surrendered Singapore in February 1942. Both officers were down to skin and bones, and their appearance greatly angered the Allies. For the entire war, Wainwright had wondered whether he had disgraced himself by surrendering Corregidor—and indeed, for a time, MacArthur had told subordinates that he blamed Wainwright for failing to fight to the end. Now, however, all was forgiven. MacArthur embraced his old subordinate and said, "Why, Jim, your old corps is yours when you want it."[35]

Bucketing rains fell on August 31 and September 1. MacArthur and his staff moved into their new temporary headquarters at the Custom House, a large stone building three blocks from the hotel, near the Yokohama waterfront. The airlift into Atsugi continued without pause, and occupation troops poured into the country. By September 2, American sentries had set up checkpoints and guardhouses at intersections around the hotel and waterfront. Elements of the 11th Airborne Division moved up to the outskirts of Tokyo, but stopped at the south bank of the Tama River, where they could see Japanese troops encamped on the opposite bank. The Japanese authorities had petitioned MacArthur to delay the American entrance into the capital by another week, in order to provide sufficient time to disarm the troops in the area, and he had agreed.[36]

Meanwhile, military dignitaries and journalists continued to fly into Atsugi. The shortage of vehicles called for carpooling, but the pecking order of rank came into play as senior officers brusquely commandeered waiting cars. On the 18-mile route between Atsugi and the hotel at Yokohama, dozens of cars and charcoal-burning buses were broken down and stranded by the roadside. After interminable delays, buses sometimes arrived to collect stranded passengers, and generals and admirals tried to keep their dignity while sitting on suitcases in the aisles of these crowded vehicles. While transferring to one such bus, Russian general Kuzma Derevyanko was seen in his shirtsleeves, hauling baggage, and taking special care with his personal supply of vodka.[37]

According to General Robert C. Richardson, who flew into Atsugi on August 31, "The roads were terrible, all greatly pitted and very narrow. The road led through green countryside, highly cultivated, and some villages, all of which were extremely flimsy and poverty-stricken. Bedraggled humanity—men and women—straggled along the sides of these terrible roads."[38] He found Yokohama to be a "city of the dead—no life, no shops, no motion—only an occasional trolley or 'El' train."[39]

The formal signing of the Instrument of Surrender would take place aboard the Third Fleet flagship *Missouri*, the ship christened by President Truman's daughter and named for his native state. The crew of the 45,000-ton battleship had holystoned the decks until the teak showed through the gray fireproof paint, polished the brass fittings until they shone like mirrors, and slapped fresh paint over streaks of oil and patches of rust. The ceremony was planned down to the minute, with strict adherence to naval and diplomatic etiquette. It would take place on the starboard side of the galley deck, a small, triangular veranda wedged against the towering steel barbette of a forward 16-inch gun turret. Each participant was assigned a specific place to stand, marked on the deck. As visitors and war correspondents came aboard, they would be guided to their assigned spots by sailors acting as escorts.[40]

The second of September was an unseasonably cool day with a gray, overcast sky. Senior officers and signatories, American and Allied, began coming aboard shortly after seven o'clock in the morning. Destroyers came alongside the *Missouri*'s port side and the visitors boarded via a gangway. The ship's band played the national anthems of the several Allied nations. As Admiral Nimitz came aboard, Halsey's four-star pennant was hauled down from the masthead, and Nimitz's five stars were broken out. General Wainwright, who had never seen an *Iowa*-class battleship, gazed up at the towering superstructure in open-mouthed awe. "I simply could not believe that anything could be so huge, so studded with guns," he later wrote. "Its guns looked like the bristles of a gigantic hedgehog."[41]

MacArthur and his party were brought out to the *Missouri* aboard a destroyer, the *Buchanan*. The supreme Allied commander went up the starboard forward gangway, where he was greeted by Nimitz and Halsey. As he stepped aboard, a second five-star triangular flag was unfurled at the masthead, at exactly the same height as Nimitz's pennant. This arrangement was unprecedented. Naval protocol dictated that only one pennant should fly on a warship at any time—for the senior admiral on board—but this was an unprecedented day, and no one wanted to risk offending MacArthur's thin-skinned staff.

Nimitz and Halsey escorted him back to Halsey's cabin, where the trio shared a moment of private conversation. Mick Carney noticed that MacArthur was friendly and familiar with Halsey, whom he addressed as "Bull," but somewhat colder and more formal toward Nimitz.[42] MacArthur disappeared into Halsey's private washroom and remained there for some time. Dusty Rhoades noted in his diary, "I could hear him retching, and I asked him if he wanted me to get a doctor. He replied that he would be all right in a moment."[43] Minutes later he stepped out onto the balcony overlooking the galley deck. Photographers saw him and shouted, asking that he look toward them. MacArthur struck a pose and said, "All right, boys, shoot this one."[44]

The ceremony would be covered by an enormous press delegation, numbering 225 correspondents and 75 photographers from around the world, including a Japanese motion picture crew from the Domei News Agency. A temporary press riser had been constructed outboard of the starboard rail, and this platform was crowded with reporters and photographers. Unruly newsmen jostled their colleagues, hoping for a better position, even to the point of pushing and shoving. A Russian newspaperman wanted to stand directly behind General Derevyanko, who would sign the Instrument of Surrender on behalf of the Soviet Union. When instructed to move, he refused, explaining that he had special instructions from Moscow. Captain Stuart S. Murray summoned two brawny marines, who grasped the man by either arm and dragged him to his assigned spot, two decks higher. Several of the American officers and foreign dignitaries were amused by this little contretemps—including General Derevyanko, who chortled happily and exclaimed, "Wonderful, wonderful, wonderful."[45]

As the participants took their places, one correspondent noted that there were more three- and four-star American generals and admirals standing on the little veranda deck than the United States had ever commissioned prior to the Second World War. Many of the navy's leading figures of the Pacific War were present, including Turner, McCain, Lockwood, Radford, Bogan, Towers, the two Shermans, and the two Spragues—but notably lacking Spruance and Mitscher, whom Nimitz had asked to stay away, in case a well-timed kamikaze attack should decapitate the high command at one stroke. The Marine Corps was represented by Lieutenant General Geiger and two brigadiers. Representing the U.S. Army and USAAF, standing in ranks with their backs to the great 16-inch gun turret, was a khaki phalanx whose first row included Generals Krueger, Eichelberger, Kenney, Spaatz, Stilwell, and Richardson. General Sutherland, MacArthur's deputy, stood with the emaciated former POWs Wainwright and Percival, who would stand directly behind MacArthur as he signed the surrender document. The podgy white-clad Admiral C. E. L. Helfrich was the signatory for the Netherlands; General Hsu Yung-Chang, wearing an olive uniform with black shoulder strap, represented China; General Jacques LeClerc, with a toothbrush moustache and high cylindrical *kepi* hat, would sign for France. Admiral Sir Bruce Fraser, whose schoolboyish summer uniform included white shorts, white shoes, and white socks pulled up to his knees, represented the United Kingdom. Other signatories represented Canada, Australia, and New Zealand.

At the center of the deck, a table from the *Missouri*'s enlisted men's mess deck was covered with a plain green baize cloth. Two copies of the Instrument of Surrender had been placed on the table, with a quantity of black fountain pens.

The Japanese delegation included eleven civilians and military officers led by General Yoshijirō Umezu, representing the Imperial General Staff, and Foreign Minister Mamoru Shigemitsu, who had returned to that office (succeeding Togo) the day after the surrender. Their names had been kept secret in Japan, lest they be targeted for assassination. Arriving at the Yokohama docks, they passed through several U.S. military checkpoints before boarding an American destroyer, the *Lansdowne*. After a long, slow passage into the heart of the U.S. fleet, during which time the American crew told them nothing, the Japanese delegates were transferred into a motor launch to be taken to the *Missouri*. As they approached the great battleship, they looked up and saw rows of American sailors lining the rails, gazing down at them in stony silence. The Japanese came aboard at the starboard gangway, one by one, under the hard gaze of a row of armed marines. General Umezu and the other Japanese officers saluted, but the Americans did not reciprocate. Foreign Minister Shigemitsu, who had lost a leg in a bombing attack in Shanghai many years earlier, walked on a wooden prosthetic leg with the help of a cane. It was a long, slow climb up the swaying gangway, but the limping old diplomat evoked no sympathy among the crew. One American said that he could hear "the thump of his artificial limb on each rung of the gangway ladder as he struggled up over the side of the *Missouri*," and a war correspondent noted that Shigemitsu's labored effort was watched "with savage satisfaction."[46]

On the veranda deck, the eleven Japanese arranged themselves in three rows and waited at stiff attention. Shigemitsu, leaning on his cane at the head of the delegation, was dressed in traditional formal diplomatic attire—a black frock coat, striped trousers, white gloves, and a tall silk hat. General Umezu, to his left, wore an olive uniform with gold braid and a row of ribbons on his chest. Both kept their eyes down. Toshikazu Kase, an aide to Shigemitsu, looked up and noticed that every square inch of space on every deck, turret, and rail was teeming with spectators. Sailors were even hanging from platforms and cables on the *Missouri*'s masts. Glancing at the battleship's smokestack, Kase saw rows of small Rising Sun flags, each representing a Japanese plane destroyed by the ship's antiaircraft guns. On a bulkhead by the captain's cabin, prominently displayed in a glass case, was the thirty-one-star American flag that Commodore Matthew Perry's "Black Ships" had flown ninety-two years earlier, when they had anchored in these same waters.

Camera shutters clicked, but no one spoke. The Japanese stood waiting for four minutes, but the interval seemed an eternity. "A million eyes seemed to beat on us with the million shafts of a rattling storm of arrows barbed with fire," wrote Kase. "I felt them sink into my body with a sharp physical pain. Never had I realized that staring eyes could hurt so much."[47]

Promptly at nine o'clock, the *Missouri's* gunnery officer cupped his hands around his mouth and shouted, "Attention, all hands!" MacArthur stepped out on deck, followed by Nimitz and Halsey. The three walked briskly to the space behind the green baize-covered table. All wore plain khaki uniforms without ties. A war correspondent noticed that MacArthur's uniform was well-worn: "The cuffs of the trousers were frayed and the shirt, open at the throat, was obviously worn. The breast was completely bare of ribbons and medals and the circlet of five silver stars pinned to his collar was all there was to distinguish this uniform from that of any unranked GI."[48] The well-worn, unadorned khaki made a striking contrast to the colorful finery worn by several of the Allied signatories who stood behind him.

MacArthur stepped up to the battery of microphones. After a pause, he began speaking in a measured, stentorian tone:

> We are gathered here, representative of the major warring powers, to
> conclude a solemn agreement whereby peace may be restored. The
> issues, involving divergent ideals and ideologies, have been determined
> on the battlefields of the world and hence are not for our discussion or
> debate. Nor is it for us here to meet, representing as we do a majority
> of the peoples of the earth, in a spirit of distrust, malice or hatred. But
> rather it is for us, both victors and vanquished, to rise to that higher
> dignity which alone benefits the sacred purposes we are about to serve,
> committing all our people unreservedly to faithful compliance with
> the understanding they are here formally to assume.[49]

The supreme commander spoke clearly, but he was obviously moved. His hands shook with emotion as he read from the handwritten notes he had prepared.[50] MacArthur gestured to the documents on the table and said: "The representatives of the Imperial Japanese Government and of the Imperial Japanese Staff will now come forward and sign."

In a hushed silence, Shigemitsu shuffled forward and lowered himself into the chair at the table. Kase stood by his side. The foreign minister removed his hat and gloves and placed them on the table. A moment of confusion followed, as he studied the two copies of the surrender agreement, unsure of where to sign. Shigemitsu read English perfectly, so there did not appear to be any reason for the delay. Halsey suspected that he was stalling, and suppressed the urge to slap the foreign minister and shout "Sign, damn you! Sign!"[51] Finally MacArthur turned to Sutherland and said tersely, "Sutherland, show him where to sign."[52]

Sutherland put his finger down on the line over the foreign minister's name. Shigemitsu glanced up at Kase, who checked his watch and said that it was 9:04. With a few strokes of the pen, the foreign minister signed his name in kanji and added the time. With that, the Second World War was formally ended.

When Shigemitsu had stood and returned to his spot, General Umezu came forward briskly, avoiding eye contact with MacArthur or any other Allied officer. He did not take a seat. Removing a pen from his breast pocket, he leaned over the table and signed, then returned quickly to his place and stood at attention, eyes still downcast. A witness noted that another Japanese officer, standing behind Umezu, was in tears.

MacArthur gestured Wainwright and Percival forward, then took a seat at the table. He took six fountain pens from his pocket and placed them on the table. He began writing his name, then stopped, turned to Wainwright, and gave him the pen. He picked up another pen, wrote several more letters, then turned and handed it to Percival. He finished his signature using the four remaining pens, which he would offer as gifts to various recipients in the United States. A reporter noted that MacArthur's hand shook with emotion as he signed.[53]

Admiral Nimitz then signed on behalf of the United States. He also seemed tense and emotional, and later told a friend, "I shook so with excitement I could hardly sign my name."[54]

One by one, the Allied signatories came forward to add their signatures: China, the United Kingdom, the Soviet Union, Australia, Canada, France, the Netherlands, and New Zealand.

MacArthur then returned to the microphone and said, "Let us pray that peace be now restored to the world and that God will preserve it always. These proceedings are closed."

As MacArthur and the other senior Allied officers adjourned to Halsey's cabin for coffee and cinnamon rolls, Foreign Minister Shigemitsu and Toshikazu Kase stepped forward to inspect the Japanese copy of the surrender document. They noted that one of the signatories, L. Moore

Cosgrave of Canada, had signed on the wrong line. Three other Allied representatives, following Cosgrave, had each signed one line down, so that their signatures did not match the printed names under the signature lines. General Sutherland and several other American officers huddled with Shigemitsu and Kase as they examined the document. Finally, Sutherland sat down, took up a pen, drew lines through the printed names of the Allied representatives and wrote the correct names beneath the errant signatures. Sutherland later said that the document was slightly blemished by these edits, but he suspected that "very few people would ever see it anyway, since it probably would be buried in the deepest recesses of their most secret archives."[55]

As the Japanese descended the gangway to the waiting motor launch, the drone of aircraft engines was heard in the south. They looked up as the drone gradually ascended to a roar. A hundred B-29s thundered overhead at low altitude, under the cloud ceiling, in precisely spaced formation. Then came an armada of 450 carrier planes, Hellcats, and Corsairs, from Task Force 38. They approached from the east, crossing the track of the B-29s at right angles, and continued over Yokohama and Tokyo. The carrier planes were stacked from about 200 to 400 feet, nearly masthead altitude, lower than the Superforts.

The flyover lasted for a full thirty minutes. The engines of the low-flying warplanes were so loud that men on the deck of the *Missouri* had to raise their voices to make themselves heard. Mick Carney called it "a terrific show, awe-inspiring," and added that the massed aerial parade "would certainly have given pause to anybody that wanted to start anything again."[56]

U.S. AND ALLIED FORCES poured into the defeated nation. Fourteen major designated occupation zones ranged from southern Kyushu to the northern island of Hokkaido, including all urban and industrial regions, all military and naval bases, and all the major strategic waterways and ports of entry along the coasts. In most regions, a vanguard force went in by airlift, secured an airfield capable of receiving cargo planes on a regular schedule, and then linked up with a nearby seaport where supplies and additional troops could be brought in by sea. Three days after the ceremony on the *Missouri*, heavily armored advance patrols of the 1st Cavalry Division and XI Corps entered Tokyo, securing the main roads and bridges in preparation for the arrival of major occupation forces on September 8. By the end of September 1945, the U.S. Eighth Army had a total of 232,379 troops in central and northern Japan, including all of the greater Tokyo region and the Kanto Plain, and the U.S. Sixth Army had commenced airlifting troops into the Osaka-Kyoto-Kobe area, the remainder of southern Honshu, and the island of Shikoku. The Sixth Army headquarters force landed at Wakayama, at the mouth of Osaka Bay, and set up shop in Kyoto two days later. Two marine divisions, the 2nd and the 5th, landed at Sasebo and Nagasaki in Kyushu, and moved overland to occupy ports and cities throughout the big southern island. At the high tide of the occupation, more than 700,000 Allied troops would be stationed in Japan.[57]

In many outlying areas, there was little more than a token occupation force, which could have been overrun quickly if recalcitrant extremists in the Japanese military had chosen to fight. A report produced by General MacArthur's headquarters called the occupation "a great, though calculated, military gamble."[58] The Americans wagered that the emperor's will and authority would cast a psychological spell over the Japanese people, and especially the rank and file of the army and navy, which were not yet disarmed. The gamble paid off in spectacular fashion. Across the length and breadth of the populous country, not a single shot was fired at Allied occupation troops. The shift from war to peace was jarring in its suddenness and totality. Three or four weeks earlier, the Japanese people had been preparing to meet the invaders with bamboo spears and kitchen knives. Now they bowed and grinned and welcomed the newcomers as honored guests.

U.S. Army Sergeant Richard Leonard went ashore at Wakayama on September 11. His platoon made an assault landing from Higgins boats. As they strode up the beach, weapons at the ready, unarmed Japanese civilians welcomed them with warm smiles, and vendors offered trinkets and souvenirs for sale. The sailor James Fahey of the cruiser *Montpelier* went ashore at nearby Kobe the following day, and explored the area on foot with a few shipmates. The Japanese stared at them in curiosity, but without fear or hostility. A group of women standing in line for sweet potatoes were amused by the freakish height—to their eyes—of the American sailors. "We laughed along with them," Fahey wrote in his diary. "Everyone had a good time. They were very friendly."[59]

Separately, both the occupation forces and the Japanese had been warned against fraternizing with one another. But the prohibition seems to have been widely ignored on both sides. A young Japanese man invited Fahey and another sailor to visit his home and meet his family. Fahey described the visit: "They had a very nice place. I could see that they came from a good class of people. In one room there was a large fancy table and a radio in the corner. They also had a picture of Emperor Hirohito, hanging on the wall. To them he is their God. Before we left we shook hands and waved goodbye." As a veteran of many ferocious naval battles and kamikaze attacks, Fahey was surprised to find that ordinary Japanese were honest and hardworking, "no different from the people in any other part of the world."[60] Sergeant Leonard agreed. In a letter to his fiancée, he observed that the "average Jap doesn't give a damn about 'ruling the world' any more than you or I do. He's just an ordinary joker who went to war because he was told to, and he did the job the way he was told."[61] During the war Leonard had hated the Japanese—hated them all—but now he found the feeling dissolving like a half-remembered dream:

> I'm pretty skeptical by nature, but who am I supposed to hate? Can I hate the boy who ran alongside my train window for 50 yards to pay me for a pack of cigarettes that I had sold him just before the train left the station? Can I hate the old man who took us to his home for dinner and made us accept his family heirlooms for souvenirs? Can I hate the kids that run up and throw their arms around me in the street? Or a Jap truck driver who went miles out of his way to drive me home one night? Or the little girl (about 4) who ran up to me and gave me her one and only doll for a present? My answer is that I can't.[62]

For the Japanese, likewise, the discovery that most Americans were instinctively decent and courteous came as a great relief. Fear had gripped the communities scheduled to receive the first advance units of occupation troops. Civilians still under the influence of wartime propaganda—or perhaps with some inkling of how Japanese forces had behaved overseas—had assumed they would suffer brutality, pillage, massacres, and rape.[63] Many women and girls fled to remote mountain villages. Others stayed off the streets, hiding themselves, or disguised themselves as boys, or smeared coal on their faces in the hope of making themselves ugly. Some even carried a sharp blade, intending to take their own lives by severing a vital artery. As American soldiers first arrived in Miyagi, north of Tokyo, a group of evacuated schoolchildren hid in their dormitory and peeked through a hole they had poked in a paper screen. They did not expect to see human beings. "It occurred to us, 'They must have horns!'" one recalled. "We had images of glaring demons with horns sprouting from their heads. We were disappointed, of course. No horns at all."[64] Some of the boys went out and returned in triumph with chocolate bars.

Small acts of kindness were noted by the Japanese. On streetcars, Americans often gave up their seats to pregnant women or the elderly, a custom that had not been common in Japan. It was noted that American officers and enlisted men were on relatively easy terms, and that officers and NCOs did not strike their subordinates. American GIs were instinctively generous with children, who soon learned that begging from the newcomers was a profitable enterprise. They picked up snippets of English: "Gibu me candy," and "Gibu me chocolate."[65] A Japanese woman told a USSBS surveyor: "During rain, American vehicles try not to splash mud on the pedestrians and I appreciate this."[66] A man pulling a wagon on a narrow street in Tokyo was blocked by an American truck coming in the opposite direction. "They stopped the truck and lifted my small wagon to the other side of their truck," the man recounted. "Smiling, they said goodbye to me and left. Tears came to my eyes. Yes, they are very much human, aren't they? It was funny, but I started to pull my wagon with strength that I did not experience before."[67]

The Japanese had assumed, as a matter of course, that they would be required to feed the occupying army. In foreign territories occupied by the Japanese, it had been a standard practice to requisition food from conquered populations. But since farm production had been badly disrupted by the war, and the occupiers could be expected to eat heartily, mass starvation seemed inevitable. After the surrender, officials of the Agricultural Ministry and the Economics Board warned that domestic food production would fall far short of minimum requirements for the coming winter. But on August 18, MacArthur's headquarters announced that the occupation forces would ship in their own provisions.[68] Indeed, the occupiers would often provide food relief to local civilians, much of it in unofficial or ad hoc gestures of charity. At Yokosuka Naval Base, shortly after the surrender, the Americans provided "twenty truck-loads of flour, rolled oats, canned goods, and rice" for local civilians, and the next day, another eleven trucks arrived with "medical supplies, blankets, tea, and other goods."[69] At an army barracks south of Tokyo, small, hungry faces pressed against the wire enclosure. Flouting regulations, the soldiers fed the children. Word spread, and more appeared, until queues of women and children formed at the gate each morning, and soldiers passed out canned C-rations from a gunny sack while their commanding officer looked the other way.

In one Tokyo neighborhood, the Americans passed out cans of Sterno, but the function and purpose of the portable cooking canisters did not penetrate the language barrier. Recipients opened the cans and tried to eat the fuel. Spitting it out in disgust, they exclaimed that the Americans had tried to poison them. The theory gained credence when a neighbor who read a little English noted that the word "poison" actually appeared on the can. The confusion was finally cleared up by a Japanese-American woman. "How awed they were to see me strike a match to it!" she said. "Fuel was scarce, and when the people understood the use of the Sterno they were grateful to have it."[70]

The occupation was not uniformly friendly and law-abiding. The old hatreds died hard. Many of the soldiers and marines in the occupation forces were veterans of savage battles on Pacific islands. Some found the apparent kindliness of their recent enemies to be bizarre and unnerving, and refused to trust it. The emaciated condition of liberated POWs aroused their fury. Crimes were committed by American and Allied troops in Japan, including robbery, rape, and murder. But the statistics for such crimes are elusive, as the occupying authorities did not allow the newspapers to report them, and did not keep detailed records of their internal military judicial processes. (The subject has received little attention in histories of the occupation, and there is little to be found in American archives.) In hopes of limiting incidents of sexual violence, the Japanese government had established a "Recreation Amusement Association," and recruited thousands of lower-class Japanese women to work as prostitutes in brothels near Yokosuka and other bases. For a time, U.S. authorities tolerated these establishments, and even allowed military doctors to examine the women (as had been done in Hawaii and other locations).[71]

Many Japanese were scandalized and offended by the sight of Japanese women in the company of occupation troops. The "pan-pan girls," as they were called, were young Japanese women who wore bright red lipstick, nylon stockings and high-heeled shoes, and were often seen riding with American servicemen on jeeps and trucks. During the hardscrabble early years of the occupation, they obviously ate and lived better than many of their fellow citizens.

According to General Eichelberger, there was only one case of "concerted resistance" to his Eighth Army troops. In Yamata, a community between Yokohama and Tokyo, a vigilante group banded together to keep Allied troops out of Yamata during their off-duty periods. Two Americans were abducted and beaten. Eichelberger ordered a show of force, and "armored vehicles in battle array cruised the streets of Yamata for several hours." The perpetrators were arrested and imprisoned.[72]

But such incidents were seen as the exception, rather than the rule, by both the occupiers and the Japanese. By and large, the Japanese embraced defeat and made the most of it. The existing agencies of Japanese government continued to function under the supervision of MacArthur's headquarters. Japanese military forces accepted the authority of the occupiers, generally with no outward manifestations of hostility or resentment. Military officers cooperated willingly in demobilizing their own forces and destroying remaining warplanes, ordnance, and weaponry. Professional relations were cordial. Captain Tameichi Hara recalled that when he surrendered a suicide speedboat base in Kyushu to a U.S. Navy captain on September 23, "The American captain astonished me by behaving more like a friend than a conqueror."[73] Exceptions were rare. That same day, in nearby Nagasaki harbor, the captain of a Japanese coastal defense vessel "acted in an insolent and provocative manner" to an American naval delegation. When the incident was reported, the offender was arrested and dismissed from the Japanese navy, confirming that the authorities were determined to enforce cooperation.[74] The early stages of the occupation proceeded so smoothly that General MacArthur announced, less than a month after the *Missouri* ceremony, that the total number of Allied troops in Japan would be reduced to 200,000 by July 1946.[75]

The surprise and relief felt by the Japanese, upon learning that their former enemies were largely decent and honorable, was accompanied by another sensation. With a sudden rush, ordinary Japanese understood how thoroughly deceived they had been by their own leaders. The propaganda was still ringing in their ears—they could hardly forget it—but it all seemed demented in retrospect. The Potsdam Declaration had insisted: "There must be eliminated for all time the authority and influence of those who have deceived and misled the people of Japan into embarking on world conquest," and the country must be rid of "irresponsible militarism."[76] The Japanese people would fulfill that condition on their own, regardless of the policies of their postwar government. The wartime military leadership was held in widespread contempt. These attitudes had been prevalent even before the surrender, though never uttered publicly for fear of repression. Now they came to the surface—a potent, instinctive, deeply felt hatred of war, and for those who had plunged Japan into it. "I abhor military men," said Shigeo Hatanaka, in a typical opinion. "I consider them a separate race of humanity because of education. Military men put on ceremonial uniforms for special occasions. Theirs is childish, simple-minded thinking."[77] As Japanese soldiers were repatriated from overseas, many ordinary civilians learned for the first time of the extent of Japanese war crimes. One young girl overheard soldiers speaking callously of the atrocities they had committed in China, and laughing about the number of women they had raped. She was horrified at the thought that she had supported the war: "Now I couldn't bear it."[78] As Gwen Terasaki observed, "Looking now at themselves more carefully than they had ever done in their history, the Japanese perceived not only the fanaticism of the militarists but also their own great ignorance in having trusted them. The people's disillusionment penetrated to the marrow."[79]

LOOKING BACK ON THE WAR THEY HAD JUST LOST, Japanese leaders marveled at their own stupidity. Asked to name the turning point of the Pacific War, Admiral Yonai replied: "To be very frank, I think that the turning point was the start. I felt from the very beginning that there was no chance of success. . . . I think to this day that it was not a proper plan in view of the situation, our national war strength."[80] Similar views were expressed by many of the Japanese leaders interrogated by the U.S. Strategic Bombing Survey in the fall of 1945. Their fateful decision to attack the United States and the Allies in December 1941 had been founded upon a catalog of faulty assumptions. They had assumed that the war could be won quickly, averting a prolonged war of attrition in which American economic power would become decisive. They had assumed that Nazi Germany was unbeatable in Europe, and would break Britain and Russia to its yoke; that sea routes linking Japan to its oil supply in the East Indies could be secured against submarine and air attacks; and that the main U.S. naval fleet would charge into the western Pacific to be met and annihilated in a single decisive sea battle, reprising the Imperial Navy's triumph at the Battle of Tsushima in 1905.

From childhood, the Japanese had been taught that they were a unique race, guided by a divine emperor, watched over by their ancient gods, with a sacred destiny to rule Asia. Indulging shallow stereotypes about American culture and democracy, the Japanese miscalculated the temper and character of their enemy. They assumed that Americans lacked the stomach to fight a long, bloody war on the opposite side of the world. They assumed that their enemies had grown soft and decadent by easy living, and were hopelessly infatuated by popular entertainment. The Americans were a mongrel people, a nation of immigrants, without unity or higher purpose, enfeebled by racial, ethnic, class, and ideological infighting. Women had the vote, and therefore wielded influence in politics—and they would resist sending their sons and husbands to fight on distant foreign shores. The size and strength of the U.S. economy would count for nothing if it could not be mobilized for war, and the capitalist oligarchs would not consent to retool their lucrative industries. The strike on Pearl Harbor was intended to shock and demoralize the American public, so that they would react to the disaster by pressuring Washington to make peace. "We thought that we could easily tackle them," a leading Japanese officer later admitted, "a race so steeped in material comfort and absorbed in the pursuit of pleasure was spiritually degenerate."[81]

If all of these premises had been right, Japan would have won the Pacific War, and might even be the dominant power in the region today. If even some had been right, Japan might have escaped the conflict with its sovereignty intact, and perhaps some remnant of its overseas empire. But as it turned out, all of these assumptions, in some degree, were wrong. In a sense, as Admiral Yonai and others grasped, the outcome of the Pacific War had been foreordained from the start, and Japan's defeat was plainly foreseeable even in December 1941. Worse, defeat was actually foreseen and even predicted by some of the men who had acquiesced in the fateful decision to launch the unwinnable war in the first place. Above all, the Pacific War was the product of a political failure in Tokyo—a failure of catastrophic proportions, one of the worst in the annals of any government or any nation.

During the Meiji era of the nineteenth century, when Japan's samurai elite had first set out to modernize and industrialize their isolated and backward country, they had understood that they must secure foreign imports of oil and other commodities that did not exist in their home islands. Foreign trade had met that imperative, especially trade with the

United States, Britain, the Netherlands, and the Asian territories and colonies they controlled. With full awareness of those basic economic conditions, so vital to the national interest, the military-dominated Japanese regime of 1940 had committed itself to an alliance with two European fascist states, Germany and Italy, that were not major exporters of oil and other raw materials, and that were at war (or soon to be at war) with the nations that *did* export such products to Japan. In other words, Tokyo set out to make enemies of its primary trading partners, while making allies of nations that could do nothing to make good the inevitable shortfalls, leading to an entirely foreseeable economic and energy crisis. As trade sanctions cut off imports of oil and other materials, the regime compounded its error by attacking a nation (the United States) that was locally weak and unprepared for war, but which possessed at least ten times Japan's latent industrial-military strength.

The Meiji Constitution had reserved a privileged position for the army and navy, placing them in a direct advisory relationship with the throne. The emperor, in turn, was granted broad powers to command the armed forces, but by the 1930s, this authority had been truncated by legal precedents. (One can only speculate whether a stronger personality than Hirohito might have steered the ship of state into calmer waters.) Both branches of the military wielded hegemonic power over their own budgets and policies, but also over the civilian administration of the state. No cabinet could be formed and no prime minister appointed without the consent of both the army and navy, and that consent could be withdrawn at any time, causing the government to fall. But no mechanism existed to resolve disputes between the two services, and nothing could be done unless army and navy leaders were in accord. Decisions in the inner circle of power were shaped by the need for consensus, which was most readily achieved by serving the parochial interests of both military services simultaneously. This feature of the Japanese regime became more costly in the 1930s, as the rivalry between the army and navy grew more bitter, and the services grappled for advantage in the competition for funds and critical raw materials. Major foreign and defense policies were formulated with an eye toward budgetary goals.

For decades, the navy had designated the United States as its "hypothetical enemy" for planning purposes—not because it really wanted or expected to fight the Americans, but because that scenario provided leverage in budget negotiations. The navy's war planning envisioned a "southern advance" to the East Indies, chiefly because such a plan justified a large fleet buildup. As the crisis approached in 1940 and 1941, the Tokyo admirals did not really want to fight in the Pacific, but they were unwilling to say so outright for fear that the army would win the contest for control of funding and materials. In any case, the admirals were not necessarily the most important players in the navy. Events and decisions were increasingly driven by elite middle-echelon officers on the general staff or at the navy ministry, who were recklessly committed to take Japan to war. These younger war hawks, commanders and captains, fabricated estimates and statistics to buttress the case for war, and pressured their superiors to accept them at face value. Well-reasoned objections were shouted down, literally. When the rear admiral in charge of war mobilization warned that Japan's shipbuilding capacity was too limited to support a war with the United States, a captain cried: "Such an estimate makes it impossible to go to war!"[82] The navy brass was somehow unable to withstand "pressures bordering on intimidation" from unruly firebrands down the ranks.[83] The admirals were swept along in a riptide of fatalism, magical thinking, and hot-blooded belligerence. "Many people knew at the very beginning it was very unwise to make war against Anglo-Saxons," said Admiral Nomura, the last prewar ambassador to the United States, "but the situation being as it was, they were very compelled to go to war."[84] Admiral Shigeru Fukudome later mused that the entire process of deciding for war was "very strange." He recalled: "When we were discussing tete-a-tete, we [navy leaders] were all for avoiding war, but when we held a conference the conclusion always moved step by step in the direction of war."[85]

In arguing against the Pacific War, Admiral Isoroku Yamamoto had repeatedly pressed this point upon his colleagues. There was no foreseeable scenario in which Japan could conquer and subjugate the United States, he warned—but it was at least *possible* that the United States could conquer and subjugate Japan. As a gambler, Yamamoto grasped that the risk-reward tradeoff was lopsided. Before 1941, the Japanese had achieved a singular feat among Asian nations—they had safeguarded their independence and political autonomy against the encroachments of Western imperialism. In choosing war against the United States, the Japanese placed their most cherished asset on the block—their independence and autonomy—to be wagered against the doubtful future rewards of conquest and empire in China, Southeast Asia, and the Pacific islands.

The war had opened with a Japanese sea-air-amphibious *Blitzkrieg* that blindsided the U.S. battle fleet in Pearl Harbor, wiped out American air-power in the Philippines, wiped out British airpower in Malaya, sank two British battleships operating at sea in full combat readiness, overran the U.S. territories of Wake Island and Guam, obliterated an Allied fleet in the Java Sea, drove the British out of Hong Kong and Burma, trapped MacArthur's forces in a doomed siege on Bataan, captured 75,000 British troops in Singapore, and laid waste to the Australian town of Darwin. This series of spectacular victories appeared to vindicate the assumptions that had led the Japanese to war, silencing the skeptics and undercutting the case for an early bid to end the war through diplomacy. The Japanese had proved a far more formidable enemy than the West had supposed, but the astonish-ing success of this initial offensive owed as much to the local weakness of the Allies as to the prowess of Japanese arms. In Japan, the early victories were lavishly feted and publicized, but the subsequent reversals at Coral Sea and Midway were carefully concealed from the public, and indeed from all but an inner circle of military leaders. In the Solomons campaign of 1942, Japanese naval airpower suffered badly and never really recovered; its ship-ping losses were severe and irreplaceable, and the Japanese army lost almost 30,000 troops on Guadalcanal. Japanese naval operations were often inflex-ible and predictable, exposing a lack of adaptability that the Americans moved to exploit. It was a problem that many line officers had recognized and tried to address, but the rigid command culture of the Imperial Navy was deeply entrenched. Three centuries earlier, the venerated samurai phi-losopher Miyamoto Musashi had extolled the virtues of adaptability, which he called "mountain and sea changing."

"Mountain and sea" means that it is bad to do the same thing over and over again. You may have to repeat something once, but it shouldn't be done a third time. When you try something on an adversary, if it doesn't work the first time, you won't get any benefit out of rushing to do it again. Change your tactics abruptly, doing something completely different. If that still doesn't work, then try something else.

Thus the science of the art of war involves the presence of mind to "act as the sea when the enemy is like a mountain, and act as a moun-tain when the enemy is like a sea." This requires careful reflection.[86]

By the end of 1942, the industrial-military might of the U.S. economy was beginning to bear on the conflict. The South Pacific counteroffensive, beginning in the Solomons and continuing up the chain of islands to the northwest, bypassed the strongest Japanese positions and leapt past Rabaul in February 1944. According to one Japanese intelligence officer's estimate, the Allied offensive bypassed seventeen Japanese-held islands, leaving 160,000 troops to their rear. None of the bypassed garrisons could be fully evacuated, so they were simply left suspended in limbo, with no further role in the war, and about one-fourth subsequently died of starvation or tropical diseases.[87] The Japanese had no good answer for this bypassing strategy, which they hated but understood and respected. A second, parallel offensive to the north, driving west through the Micronesian archipelagoes of the central Pacific, was more decisive. The U.S. naval victory at the Battle of the Philippine Sea (June 19–20, 1944) led to the final and irreversible defeat of Japan's carrier airpower, and the conquest of Saipan and Guam provided airfields from which the newly deployed B-29 Superfortress could hit Tokyo and the Kanto Plain. These events, in June and July 1944, ensured Japan's eventual strategic defeat no matter what the outcome of successive battles.

If the Pacific War had been a game of chess, played between grandmasters, there would have been no endgame. With the outcome no longer in doubt, neither grandmaster would have felt the need to play to the end. Foreseeing that his king was soon to be checkmated, the Japanese player would have laid it down on the board and shaken hands with his opponent. But this was war, not a board game, and conditions in Japan did not allow for the possibility of a negotiated truce until long after defeat had become inevitable. Another 1.5 million Japanese servicemen and civilians were to be sacrificed, like so many pawns, before the checkmate in August 1945. Those 1.5 million deaths, in the final year of the conflict, represented nearly one-half of the total Japanese killed in the wars of Asia and the Pacific from 1937 to 1945.[88]

Even in this final year of the war, however, Japanese military forces showed great valor and audacity, with occasional flashes of brilliance. The army largely abandoned its costly practice of launching massed bayonet charges against disciplined, well-armed, and entrenched Allied troops. On Peleliu, Iwo Jima, and Okinawa, especially, the Japanese army revealed its proficiency in the use of ingenious subterranean or "honeycomb" defensive fortifications, largely vitiating U.S. advantages in artillery and airpower. The Japanese navy managed to produce a few new fighter plane models that were capable of contending with the American Hellcat, Corsair, and Lightning, when handled by their remaining elite veteran aces—just not in sufficient numbers to reverse the overall tide of the war. When in a magnanimous mood, Allied aviation experts were willing to concede that the Japanese firm Kawanishi had designed and built the best reconnaissance seaplanes in the world. The kamikazes were a singularly Japanese phenomenon, arising in a unique cultural context. But in tactical terms, the suicide plane was like a weapon from the future, allowing the Japanese to deploy guided missiles at a time when no other combatant possessed such weapons, or effective measures to counter them.

In defeat, the Japanese were exhausted, weary of war, apprehensive of the future, and still largely preoccupied with survival. The obvious threat of political repression was gone, but otherwise, life after the war was largely similar to life during the war. None could foresee the "economic miracle" that would lift Japan to prosperity and economic power in the 1970s and 1980s. Corruption was endemic, as officers of the army and navy purloined surplus military assets and sold them on the black market. As returning servicemen poured into Japan through the seaports, a great reverse tide of civilian refugees who had left the cities in 1944 and 1945—an estimated 10 million people, or one in every seven Japanese—was flowing back into the stricken cities. "Our everyday life too is filled with difficulty and unforeseen events," wrote Michio Takeyama in his diary, in the fall of 1945. "We can't establish a routine. A day-to-day, hand-to-mouth existence has to be the fundamental style of life."[89]

Memories of the war faded, and a culture of silence and forgetting took root in postwar Japan. In 1947, a Japanese journalist wrote that the year 1942 seemed as if it were thirty years in the past.[90] In the cities, the rubble was carted away and new buildings rose from the ashes, and many younger people never learned that their entire neighborhoods had once been burned off the map. Little rooms or alcoves in houses served as private shrines where families remembered their dead husbands, fathers, or sons. A small altar was topped with photographs, letters from overseas, burning incense, and—for those who received cremated remains—a wooden ossuary box. But those were strictly private rituals. Hitoshi Inoue undoubtedly spoke for many of his fellow Pacific War veterans when he wrote that he did not want to dredge up the hateful old memories. When the time came for him to search his soul about it, Inoue would do so alone, in private reflection. He did not believe the reckoning should be public, or collective, and certainly it was not to be discussed openly or taught in schools: "Don't we all have things, whether many or few, that we don't want to recall? We don't want people to pick at our old wounds."[91] In an interview given in the 1980s, an elderly resident of Tokyo said that he had tried to forget the war, but a traumatic memory occasionally resurfaced—as when he was walking in the Ginza, and "suddenly I see a place and think, 'I clung to this wall and hid myself here during the bombing.'"[92]

To the extent that they remembered the war at all, many Japanese remembered it as a tragedy that had befallen Japan, rather than as a monstrous evil that their nation had deliberately set in motion. Questions of accountability and self-reflection were largely banished from the public square. Many Japanese considered the issue of war crimes to have been resolved by the International Military Tribunal Far East, which conducted the Tokyo War Crimes Trials, and by the treaties ending the war and reestablishing Japanese sovereignty. With the conviction of the Class A, B, and C war criminals in postwar justice tribunals, the Japanese people would be taught to believe that the perpetrators had been brought to justice, absolving the public of any responsibility for the war. To this day, when assessing the question of responsibility for the war and its tribulations, many Japanese tend toward legalistic responses, dwelling on official acts and statements of governments, or treaty law. A popular view in Japan holds that the nation's cause was fundamentally just, that war crimes committed by Japanese forces were deplorable but no worse than those committed by other nations, and that Japan's defeat was a worthy sacrifice because it liberated Asia from Western colonialism. Some on the Japanese right still argue that Japan had no choice but to wage war, as a matter of national survival, in order to break the "encirclement" of Allied powers. In August 1945, when the emperor's "jeweled voice" went over the airwaves, the national about-face occurred with jarring abruptness. Artists, writers, and scholars who had supported the ideology of the wartime regime buried their past work in file cabinets, or burned it, and started anew. Teachers who had taught ultranationalist and militarist values announced to their classrooms: "From now on it is an age of democracy."[93] Students were instructed to open their textbooks and tear out offending pages, or blot out offending passages with ink. Many children relished the novelty of defacing the textbooks that they had previously been taught to revere.[94] The Duralumin that had been used in manufacturing airplanes was bundled off the black market and sold to industrial firms retooling to produce consumer goods. The swords were beaten into ploughshares, but in this case it was Mitsubishi Zeros beaten into dustpans and kitchen crockery.[95]

During the postwar occupation, many of MacArthur's policies reinforced and abetted the collective amnesia of the Japanese. By order of the supreme commander, there was no concerted public effort to preserve the history or memory of the war—no monuments, no references in school textbooks, no national museum. The decision to leave Hirohito on his throne, as a national symbol and object of reverence (if no longer worship), created a sense of continuity. Exonerating the emperor seemed a small price to pay to ease the occupation and to erect a bulwark against communism in Asia. Criticism of the emperor was strictly taboo in postwar Japan—the "chrysanthemum taboo," as it was called—and polite Japanese opinion accepted that he had been a figurehead manipulated by a conspiracy of militarists. The *Showa* era, which remained the basis of the Japanese calendar throughout his reign, continued to the emperor's death in 1989.

Just ninety-two years had passed since Commodore Matthew Perry's "Black Ships" had anchored in Tokyo Bay and forced the Japanese people, against their will, to reckon with the outside world. Ninety-two years: less than a century; the span of one long human life. In 1945, the oldest Japanese could still summon early childhood memories of life in the Tokugawa Shogunate, when the nation was ruled by samurai who wore suits of lacquered armor and fought with swords and spears. During that span of time the Japanese people had experienced a wrenching acceleration of historical change. They had modernized and industrialized at a headlong pace, rising to become one of the most formidable naval and military powers in the world, and inflicted humiliating defeats on several of the leading nations of the West. Falling under the sway of fanatical militarists, they had poured their armies and fleets out across Asia and the Pacific, spreading misery across the region and making themselves infamous in the eyes of their neighbors. That misadventure had ended in total defeat. What would the future bring? How would Japan fare, while tucked under the eagle's wing? No one could know in 1945, and perhaps the answers would not come into focus until another ninety-two years had elapsed.

FROM THE ALEUTIANS TO NEW GUINEA, from the atolls of Micronesia to the green jungles of the Philippines, in one remote Pacific island group after another—the Solomons, the Gilberts, the Admiralties, the Marshalls, the Bismarcks, the Palaus, the East Indies, the Marianas, the Ryukyus, the Bonins, the Volcanoes—the invasion beaches were pulverized and misshapen. Rusting and bullet-riddled landing craft lay awash in the shallows or half buried in the sand. A few paces inland, at the tree line, palm logs lay broken, blackened, splintered, and scattered across the ground like fallen matchsticks. Gun emplacements and blockhouses lay demolished under broken slabs of concrete, with steel reinforcing rods twisted and splayed. Rats, snakes, and lizards were living in abandoned rifle pits and pillboxes. Infantrymen's litter was strewn among the underbrush and piled in the bottom of ravines: ration cans, spent casings, blood bottles, ammunition boxes, rucksacks, canteens, stretchers, shovels, every imaginable kind of junk—some of it to be collected by cleanup details, some to be claimed as souvenirs, some to be salvaged by natives, and some to buried by time, like archeological artifacts.

In the hot, fecund islands of the South Pacific, the jungle would swiftly reassert its hegemony. In a year or less, vines began crawling over the rusting remains of abandoned bulldozers, tanks, and guns. Eventually, fresh vegetation would completely swallow these relics of war. Wrecked and gutted airplanes were scattered around the margins of abandoned airstrips— tilted, upside down, wings and tails torn off and piled in unruly heaps, with paint and tail markings gradually fading in the sun. In lagoons and anchorages one found hundreds of rusting, oil-streaked, salt-caked hulks: transports, oil tankers, auxiliary ships, and mobile drydocks that were not designed for a long life, and were worth little or nothing on secondary markets. Some would be salvaged for their scrap metal value; others would be towed out to the ocean and scuttled; others would simply be abandoned at anchor. Some of those in the Marshall Islands would serve as targets for nuclear weapons tests.

Military cemeteries were found on many islands—long, symmetrical rows of white crosses, interspersed here and there with a Star of David. Helmets or keepsakes had been left resting on the ground by some of the markers. On the larger battlefields, where casualties had arrived too quickly for the burial details to keep up, the dead had sometimes been committed to communal graves, in long trenches hastily dug by bulldozers, marked by a single placard with the date of interment. Dog tags had been collected and—if possible—the location of each body recorded. Most American soldiers and marines buried on Pacific battlefields would be exhumed and transported to another final resting place, according to the stated wishes of their next of kin: either a permanent military cemetery overseas, a national cemetery in the United States, or a private cemetery in the dead man's hometown. Of the 279,867 American war dead worldwide, families requested the repatriation to the United States of 171,539 remains.[96] Most of the others were also exhumed and transferred, at least once and sometimes twice, to a large permanent cemetery on foreign soil.

Like every other aspect of the American military experience in the Second World War, these exhumation operations were monumental in scale. The task fell to the Graves Registration Service (GRS) of the U.S. Army's quartermaster's office, which employed 18,000 military and civilian personnel at its peak. When opening a battlefield grave, the GRS workers wore masks and heavy rubber or leather gloves that came up to the elbows. Using poles with stiff sheet metal flaps at the bottom, like giant kitchen spatulas, they pried the remains out of the earth and rolled them onto open canvas body bags. The bags were zipped shut and lifted to the surface by ropes. This system was found to be most efficient, and also best for morale, because it saved the workers on the exhumation details "from having decayed flesh and liquefied remains spilled on them."[97] At the end of each working day, each man burned his clothing and drew a new uniform for the following day. On Okinawa, the American graves were very large and also rather poorly marked, so that it was often necessary to open several graves in order to locate a single individual. In one case, according to the GRS, "84 graves were opened in order to locate an unknown."[98] Not surprisingly, personnel on the exhumation details suffered high rates of the syndrome that would later be called post-traumatic stress disorder.

According to one authoritative estimate, total American combat deaths in the Pacific were 111,606, a figure that included 31,157 officers and enlisted men of the U.S. Navy. Most of the latter would sleep forever in Davy Jones' Locker, beyond the reach of the exhumation details, with no grave marker but an eternally monotonous blue seascape.[99]

The living just wanted to get home, the sooner the better. And their families wanted them home. In Washington, demonstrators gathered each morning outside the White House gates, demanding the return of their husbands, sons, and fathers. Letters poured into Congress. Some Americans wanted an immediate cessation of the draft—but others, including those still in uniform, lobbied for an extension of the peacetime draft, so that replacement troops could be shipped overseas, allowing the veterans to come home more quickly.[100] In view of emerging threats in East Asia—the territorial ambitions of the Russians, the gains of Mao's communist guerrillas in China, the looming power vacuum in Korea as Japanese forces left the peninsula—American military leaders warned against a precipitate drawdown that would destabilize the region. But the citizen-soldiers, citizen-sailors, citizen-marines, and citizen-airmen had completed the job they had been sent to do, as they saw it, and they were impatient to get on with their lives. As a junior naval officer in the Pacific put it: "We saw no reason why we should not, each of us, return to the States not only immediately, but also before anyone else."[101]

A rigid formula determined the order of priority for discharge. Servicemen with the highest number of "points" were the first to ship out. Points were allocated for a range of variables, including age, length of service, time overseas, number of days in combat, and the number and type of decorations a man had received. Additional points were assigned to married men, and still more to fathers, with a certain number for each dependent child. Samuel Hynes wrote that it was "a good enough system, and nobody complained. We just calculated our scores, figured the order of departure, and waited."[102] But the first men to ship out were inevitably the older, more seasoned veterans, including many of the noncommissioned officers. Their sudden departure deprived the fighting forces of leadership and experience at every rank. Field and task force commanders resisted letting go of their most experienced veterans, and exploited loopholes to keep them in service. Regulations permitted local commanders to impose a "freeze" on discharges of certain key personnel for reasons of military necessity. But such freezes were unpopular and aroused protests in Washington. Admiral King moved to restrict the practice, distributing an order to all naval ships and stations in September 1945: "Commanding Officers shall immediately reconsider the cases of all personnel who meet the required point scores and are being retained on the basis of 'military necessity.' Continued retention of such personnel shall be based only upon a literal and realistic interpretation of the term 'military necessity.'"[103]

Admiral Radford, commanding a carrier task group in the Pacific, was concerned that the rushed demobilization would leave the U.S. military in a "shambles," and that the Soviets might attempt to exploit the situation. In Washington, Navy Secretary Jim Forrestal warned President Truman that if the demobilization continued at its headlong pace, "neither the army nor the navy will have sufficient trained men to be able to operate efficiently."[104] General George C. Marshall remarked to Samuel Eliot Morison: "It was not a demobilization; it was a rout."[105]

Even those who accumulated the required points could not be sure of a quick trip home. Most of the rank and file were obliged to wait, sometimes for weeks, to be assigned a berth on an eastbound ship. Washington had assumed that the Pacific War would continue for at least nine months after the collapse of Germany, and Japan's sudden capitulation had thrown its demobilization plans into turmoil. Much of the needed shipping had already been committed to the Atlantic. Hundreds of Douglas C-54 and C-47 transports were flying regular routes between Tokyo, Guam, Okinawa, Luzon, Hawaii, and California—but the seats were reserved for generals, admirals, war correspondents, well-connected junior officers, and important civilians. Throughout the Pacific, transit barracks accommodated crowds of idled servicemen. At Yokosuka, eight hundred cots were set up in an airplane hangar, and men stood in long lines to receive sheets, pillowcases, and blankets. They would live together in that cavernous space—soldiers, sailors, marines, and airmen—until orders came through to board a departing ship. At the piers, frustrated men attempted to sneak aboard ships without orders, and some succeeded. According to a marine officer, most of these stowaways were never disciplined, and simply "got away with it."[106]

In the chaos of demobilization, corruption was rife. Charles McCandless, a Seabee officer, was told by a chief yeoman in Manila that a hundred other men were due to receive their discharge papers, so McCandless would have to wait. "I asked him if a hundred dollars, American, would help. He said that a hundred and fifty dollars would get the orders the next day and I should come back in the morning." McCandless paid the bribe and obtained the needed documents. Later that day, he paid another $100 to someone in the transport command for a berth on a departing ship.[107]

In an operation designated MAGIC CARPET, the War Shipping Administration hastily converted 546 Liberty and Victory ships to provide sealift for returning veterans.[108] Tiered wooden bunks, some stacked as many as nine high, were erected in airless, filthy cargo holds. Homeward-bound naval vessels, including battleships, aircraft carriers, and LSTs, were pressed into service as provisional troop transports. Carriers transferred their airplanes ashore and installed tiered bunks in their hangars. Every returning ship carried troops—some in the hundreds, and others in the thousands. In San Francisco, the most frequent port of entry for returning Pacific War veterans, ferries sounded their fog horns, fire boats shot high-arching streams of water into the sky, and citizens cheered from the pedestrian walkways of the Golden Gate Bridge. At the piers along the Embarcadero, the veterans marched down the gangways, perhaps to be greeted by a brass band and a volunteer contingent of beaming Navy League ladies serving coffee and cookies. These gestures were appreciated by all, but the men who lived east of the Rocky Mountains found themselves in another exasperating limbo, stranded for lack of eastbound transportation. Barracks, airfields, commercial airports, and railway stations were crowded with idle servicemen waiting for a seat. The navy had warned families against traveling to California in hopes of meeting their returning sons or husbands, citing a "critical housing shortage in West Coast ports."[109] Some tried to telephone their families in the east, but in 1945 it was no easy task to place a call across the continent, requiring a fistful of coins and delicate negotiations with a live switchboard operator.

Describing the melancholy atmosphere at a transit barracks in San Diego, a marine compared it to "a locker room after a game, a game that you've lost."[110] Men parted ways with the friends they had lived with and fought with for years. "Goodbyes were said with mixed feelings, not much sentiment or emotion," said the marine John Vollinger. "We had made it 'home alive in forty-five' and could hardly believe it."[111]

Moving the great mass of demobilizing soldiers and sailors east across the country taxed the passenger-hauling capacity of the railways. Obsolete rail cars were hauled out of stockyards and returned to temporary service, including coal-burning locomotives and ancient wooden passenger cars from the days of the Old West. Servicemen departing San Francisco boarded one of the huge Southern Pacific rail ferries and crossed the bay to the end of the Oakland Mole. Nearby, at the Oakland Terminal, flag-draped caskets were lifted from cargo ships in slings, and loaded into U.S. Army Transportation Corps "mortuary" railway cars.[112] The mortuary cars were added to the end of some of the same civilian passenger trains that brought the living veterans home.

The transcontinental journey was long and uncomfortable. Every train was loaded to capacity, with servicemen and civilians sitting on their luggage in the aisles or lying on the overhead luggage racks. From San Francisco to Chicago was a journey of three days. Babies wailed. The lights flickered out. The bathrooms grew filthy and unsanitary. The cars were fetid and stifling, but when the windows were opened, recalled a sailor, they "let in as much in the way of coal smoke, cinders, small stones, and birds' feathers as they did air."[113] Troop trains were equipped with stoves, food, and cooking utensils, but the provisions often gave out and the men went hungry. At stations along the way, they debarked to stretch their legs and buy a hot dog or a sandwich, but as they stepped down onto the platforms, an officer told them that any man who was not back aboard when the train left the station "would be considered AWOL and subject to courts-martial."[114]

Having won the war and returned to their home soil, the veterans' tolerance for military authority was running short. On many trains, discipline began to disintegrate. Louis Auchincloss, a navy lieutenant and future novelist, was placed in command of a troop train from Portland, Oregon to New York City. A generous quantity of liquor had been smuggled on board. Lieutenant Auchincloss insisted on patrolling the cars and confiscating the illicit bottles, until a delegation of chief petty officers politely warned that "if I continued to inspect the train, it was only a matter of time before I was knocked over the head with a bottle." He wisely accepted their recommendation to leave discipline in their hands. For the rest of the transcontinental journey, Auchincloss remained sequestered in his private cabin, reading Edward Gibbon's *The Decline and Fall of the Roman Empire*.

As the trains arrived in the east, many veterans felt a powerful temptation to simply go home. But if they did not first obtain a legal discharge, they could be declared AWOL and face a general court-martial. "Everyone wanted to go home," wrote Admiral Jocko Clark. "Many of our young enlisted men simply left without permission. The war was over. Navy regulations meant nothing." A young sailor brought up on charges of desertion told Clark: "I wanted to see my mother."[115] Hoping to avoid a general epidemic of desertion, the navy scrambled to set up temporary regional separation centers in gymnasiums and public meeting halls. Some sailors were invited to reenlist. All were informed of their rights and benefits under the Servicemen's Readjustment Act—the "GI Bill." Those who mustered out received their discharge papers and a train or bus ticket home.

The first wave of returning veterans, arriving from Europe in the summer of 1945, were welcomed with speeches, bunting, brass bands, and parades. On the West Coast, the early waves of returning servicemen received a similarly rapturous welcome. But most Pacific War veterans came home in the fall of 1945 or the spring of 1946, and by that time the bloom was off the rose. The American people were eager to forget the war, and there was no great novelty in seeing a young man in uniform. The wartime control measures that had kept inflation in check were collapsing under the weight of public opinion and political pressure. Unions demanded pay raises and launched nationwide strikes in most basic industries, including automobiles, steel, coal, and railroads. Veterans returned to a roaring economy, instead of the expected postwar depression, and that was a welcome surprise. But many found it difficult to transition back into the civilian workforce. They were perplexed by workplace politics and the rat race. Jobs seemed senseless and boring, lacking the unifying purpose they had known in war. They found themselves missing the elemental companionship of their old frontline units. Veterans found it difficult to replace the personal bonds forged by war, even with their own wives, parents, siblings, friends, and children. According to Private Gene Sledge of the 1st Marine Division, "all the good life and luxury didn't seem to take the place of old friendships forged in combat."[116]

Many young veterans went back to college or enrolled in vocational training programs, but others lived on a government stipend paid under the "52–20 program" of the GI Bill. Uncle Sam paid a weekly stipend of $20 to veterans, for up to a year, to subsidize their transition back into the civilian economy. To collect the check, they had to visit an unemployment insurance office each week and tell a story about their ongoing efforts to find a job. Many young veterans were content to take a year off in the "52–20 Club," whiling away their time in neighborhood bars, playing poker and craps, and "doing everything we can to forget."[117] George Niland, veteran of the 6th Marine Division, went out drinking with his fellow veterans every night. Returning home at one in the morning, he was confronted by his father, a Boston firefighter. "Listen, you bum," the elder Niland told the younger, "you either go to work or go to college, but you're not going to continue coming in here."[118] Niland moved out, and soon afterwards found a job. Another 6th Division veteran, Bill Pierce, bought a motorcycle and rode around the country with some other nomadic bikers. His parents dubbed him "bum of the year," but Pierce finally went to college, also on the government's dime. He considered it "another horrible experience to a combat marine, sitting there learning English, poetry, business, arithmetic . . . drove me batty!"[119]

The humorist Bob Yoder noted that women had grown accustomed to looking after themselves and earning a living; they had acquired certain skills and a self-sufficiency that were likely to upend relations between the sexes. Watching a group of female mechanics working on an automobile, Yoder reflected: "The fact of the matter is, they are learning more about the anatomy of automobiles than their husbands even pretend to know." He joked: "A little light brain-work may be all that is in store for men. It is a prospect the adult male will face bravely. We are too pretty to work anyway."[120] But the dilemma was a real one, as many couples learned after the war. Shirley Hackett, who had lived on her own, and supported herself by working on the assembly line in a ball bearings factory, found it difficult to adjust to the domestic role that her husband expected her to perform. "I remember changing tires on cars, taking care of the motor myself, yet he treated me as if I were insane to think that I could do these things."[121]

Government-sponsored public service announcements urged women to leave their jobs, to yield them up to demobilizing veterans. Some left dutifully, because they were willing and even eager to resume their customary roles in the home. Others resisted, and were let go or demoted. PSAs and advertising campaigns depicted an idyllic, blissful domestic life, in kitchens equipped with modern, time-saving appliances, with machines that would perform the drudgery of housework without fuss or bother. When her husband returned from the war, said the magazines and film shorts, she should defer to his authority. The home must be his refuge, and he must be in charge. "After the war, fashions changed drastically," said Frankie Cooper, who had worked as a crane operator in a steel mill. "You were supposed to become a feminine person. We laid aside our slacks, our checkered shirts, and we went in for ostrich feathers, ruffles, high-heeled shoes. All this was part of the propaganda in magazines and newspapers to put a woman back in her 'rightful place' in the home. Go back now, forget all you've learned, be feminine. Go home and make your bread, raise your children. Forget you had them in a nursery and you were out there in pants."[122] Dellie Hahne, whose husband was a sergeant in the Army Air Forces, had conjured up an elaborate fantasy about their future after the war. Much of it was inspired by stories she had read in *Good Housekeeping* magazine. In her fantasy, she and her husband lived in a three-bedroom house in the suburbs, "and I got up at seven every morning and fixed my husband's breakfast, and in my head I had a schedule of keeping the house. I'd do my ironing at eleven-thirty, and I would scrub the kitchen floor at two in the afternoon, and at the end of the day dinner would be on the table and I would be changed into a lovely cocktail dress and meet my husband at the door with martinis." But the man Hahne had married was not the husband depicted in the pages of *Good Housekeeping.* He was more like a character in a country music song. "I got a drunk and a gambler and a guy who loved to show me the lipstick on his handkerchiefs—and it wasn't my lipstick. So I thought, how in the hell am I going to be an American housewife if I don't have the guy?"[123] Frankie Cooper, the former crane operator, remained married for three years after the war. Then she left her husband and returned to the workforce as a schoolteacher. "I was not the same person I had been when I married him," she explained. "I realized that I had grown. I could take care of myself. I did not need to go from my father's house to my husband's house. . . . My husband would have been happy if I had gone back to the kind of girl I was when he married me—a little homebody there on the farm, in the kitchen, straining the milk. But I wasn't that person anymore. I tried it for three years, but it just didn't work out. All at once I took a good look at myself, and I said no. No, you're just not going to do it. You're not going back where you started from."[124] As legions of social historians have observed, the Second World War was a slingshot for second-wave feminism.

Many couples had married in haste in 1942 and 1943, just as young men were shipping off to the war, and had never really grown to know one another. When reunited, they regarded each other with shyness and apprehension. If they were lucky, they might find that they were well suited to each other, and lived long and happy lives together. Many others recognized quickly that they had erred, and they divorced. Those in the latter category caused an unprecedented spike in the divorce rate. In 1946, there were more than 4.3 divorces and annulments per 1,000 persons—the highest rate recorded up to that year, which would not be surpassed until the mid-1970s.[125]

The medical profession had not yet developed effective treatments for the condition known as "battle neurosis" or "combat stress reaction." Doctors ruefully admitted that their medical manuals and hospitals offered no such thing as "soul surgery." Powerful social and cultural stigmas inhibited discussion of such disorders. Many veterans were reluctant to acknowledge that they needed help. As a rule, they did not choose to talk about what they had seen and done in the war. They did not have a name for what afflicted them; some called it the "demons of war." James Covert observed of his older brother: "He and his friends were carrying a lot of feelings that I was not able to understand as a thirteen-year-old. At that age I could not really comprehend the kind of experiences he had endured in the war."[126] Many veterans felt a constant, gnawing anxiety, and were disturbed by nightmares and sleeplessness. They struggled to suppress or forget the ghoulish sights, sounds, and smells they had experienced in combat. Many suffered flash-backs, sleeping or waking, triggered by loud noises or bright lights: they might be triggered by a dropped object, a car backfiring, or an aircraft pass-ing low overhead. Traumatic events from the past suddenly intruded upon the present, as if they had been caught in a time warp. Flashbacks might bring a sudden recollection of sights or sounds from the worst moments of combat; they might also arrive in the form of a sudden onslaught of grief, of sadness for the friends they had left behind, or even for the suffering of the enemy. They awoke in the small hours of the morning, hearts pounding and sheets soaked with sweat. Former sailors complained that a house was too quiet for sleeping. They had grown accustomed to the low throbbing of a ship's engine, like a heartbeat. As one navy veteran said: "It was so quiet I couldn't sleep. I couldn't hear, or feel, the vibrations of the diesel electric engines. It was just impossible to sleep."[127] They found it difficult to trust others, and felt a terrible and inconsolable loneliness even when surrounded by friends or loved ones. They had bouts of uncontrollable shaking and weeping, and suffered from a physical muscular tension that led, over time, to chronic physical pain and fatigue. They found it difficult to concentrate on complex tasks. Many were drained by their interactions with others, and sought solitude. They avoided situations that were likely to trigger a resur-gence of harrowing memories, and were often intolerant of crowds. Many found it difficult to plan for the future, to make important decisions. Some were alienated from their wives and families, but others developed a pattern of unhealthy and excessive emotional dependence, to a childlike degree. They experienced sudden, uncontrollable surges of anger, and lashed out in violence at their wives or children. They felt a yawning sense of hopeless-ness about the future, a sense of meaninglessness, an existential emptiness, and an inability to experience joy, even in activities that had once provided pleasure. Some entertained thoughts of suicide, and some proceeded to act upon those thoughts.

Marjorie Cartwright, a West Virginian who had spent the war in San Francisco, waiting for her sailor husband to be mustered out of the navy, found it very difficult to reconnect with the young man she had married. "When my husband returned from the navy, he was unable to adjust to civilian life. He couldn't cope. When he joined the service, he was like most young men, a happy-go-lucky person. He came out very disillusioned, very bitter. The doctor said he had gone through too much trauma." He had fought in the South Pacific, in several of the battles around Guadalcanal. His ship had been sunk, and many of his shipmates had died. Cartwright recalled: "When he came home he had terrible nightmares. It made it difficult for him to go to sleep at night. He said, 'Every time I close my eyes I see my buddies being killed around me.' He had one horrifying experience when one of his best friends had his head blown off right in front of him and fell into his arms."[128] He began drinking heavily. "My husband couldn't deal with his feelings, so he sat around and drank and brooded. The men rehashed their war experiences to each other, of course, but he felt he couldn't talk to me, that I wouldn't understand, and I don't think I could have, because I haven't been through what he had." The doctors wanted to place him in an institution, but he refused. After seven years, they divorced. "I didn't know what else I could do," said Cartwright. "Staying with him wasn't helping him or changing him. I realized that I had to do something for myself, because I couldn't do anything to save my husband."[129]

Approximately 900,000 African Americans had served in uniform. They came home with the confidence and expectations of men entitled to the full rights and privileges of citizenship. But for many, shedding the uniform meant resuming the dubious status they had held as civilians. In the American South, especially, in a culture that valued military service, former black soldiers represented a peculiar challenge to the regime of racial oppression. Like all soldiers, they had been trained to stand up straight, with chins up, shoulders back, and chests forward, with parade-ground posture and bearing. Many had acquired advanced training in hand-to-hand combat, and in the handling of weapons. They were men, after all; but now they returned to a place where they were called "boys" by other adults, and where a black man who held his head high was condemned as "uppity." In certain rural precincts of the South, where lynching and other forms of extrajudicial violence remained common, black men who had served their country in uniform were specifically targeted. In several notorious cases of late 1945 and 1946, white mobs or police officers abducted, beat, whipped, or murdered black veterans who, in the words of one Alabaman, "must not expect or demand any change in their status from that which existed before they went overseas."[130] Even in the ostensibly more enlightened North, black veterans were systematically denied the full benefits of the GI Bill. Mainstream colleges would not admit them, at least not in great numbers, and historically black colleges could not expand rapidly enough to accommodate the sudden upsurge in demand. Vanishingly few home loans were extended to black veterans.

For all of that, World War II was a catalyst for the civil rights movement. The war and the economic opportunity it offered touched off a surge in migration out of the American South, to the North, the Midwest, and the West Coast. In all regions, blacks migrated into cities—driven off the land by farm mechanization, and lured into cities by high-wage jobs—so that in the space of one generation, the demographic profile of African Americans crossed the scale from predominantly rural to predominantly urban. By 1945, blacks held about 8 percent of all war industry jobs, a proportion close to the percentage of blacks in the national population. Seven hundred thousand African Americans left the South during the war, and the exodus continued unabated in the postwar years. In the decade of the 1940s, some 339,000 blacks moved to the western half of the country. Large African American enclaves were created in such places as Los Angeles and Oakland. Sybil Lewis migrated from her hometown of Sapulpa, Oklahoma to Los Angeles, where she worked as a riveter in a Douglas aircraft plant. She recalled: "Had it not been for the war I don't think blacks would be in the position they are now. The war and defense work gave black people opportunities to work on jobs they never had before. It gave them the opportunity to do things they had never experienced before. They made more money and began to experience a different lifestyle. Their expectations changed. Money will do that. You could sense that they would no longer be satisfied with the way they had lived before."[131] Had the war not been fought, Lewis assumed that she would have ended up as a schoolteacher in rural Oklahoma, "but the impact of the war changed my life, gave me an opportunity to leave my small town and discover there was another way of life."[132]

LACKING THE REQUISITE POINTS FOR DISCHARGE, hundreds of thousands of young Americans remained marooned in the Pacific. Many would pass their third or fourth consecutive Christmas under the blinding tropical sun. That December, Bing Crosby's ballad "I'll Be Home for Christmas" played in heavy rotation on the Armed Forces Radio Service (AFRS)—but now, more than ever before, the melancholy refrain seemed to mock their dilemma: "If only in my dreams." With diminished responsibilities, men worked at a peacetime pace, giving only the minimum effort required to complete their assigned duties. Discipline gave way to cynicism. An attitude of lethargy spread through the camps and barracks. Men whiled away their hours of leisure playing cards or sunbathing. Black market liquor flowed freely, much of it produced in illicit stills. Everyone knew exactly how many discharge points he had accumulated, and how many more he needed for a ticket home. Having won the war, the servicemen had been told that they must now "win the peace." But as a navy lieutenant observed, "none of us gave a good goddamn about 'winning the peace.' We just wanted to go home."[133]

Pilots continued to fly routine search patrols. Some were dispatched on missions to drop leaflets on islands still occupied by the Japanese, or they were assigned to actually land on such islands and to accept the surrender of Japanese garrisons. Operational accidents were less common than in wartime, but they continued with distressing regularity. All felt a special pity for those who died in plane crashes after the Japanese surrender. Aviators who had fought like lions in air combat now resented flying missions in dicey weather, and remonstrated angrily with their commanding officers. Flying through a nighttime storm over the East China Sea, the veteran dive-bomber pilot Samuel Hynes felt a new kind of fear, different from anything he had experienced in combat. He was outraged to have been placed in that treacherous situation, with the war won, "alone and half-blind with lightning and blackness," risking his life "on a pointless exercise in the dark."[134]

Fifty thousand marines of the III Amphibious Corps, including most of the 1st and the 6th Marine Divisions, were sent into northeastern China in an operation codenamed BELEAGUER. Their mission was to stabilize the region, and to supervise the surrender, disarmament, and repatriation of Japanese troops and foreign nationals. Many marines who had survived the horrors of Peleliu and Okinawa were caught up in these operations, and did not return to the United States until the spring of 1946. Their brothers in the 3rd Marine Division remained in Guam, as a potential reserve force. To fill up their idle hours, officers on Guam organized a voluntary "school," in which any marine who had special knowledge or skills in any field taught his fellow marines. Classes were offered in woodworking, geology, auto repair, Latin, watercolor painting, and dozens of other subjects. Majors and colonels attended classes taught by privates and corporals. One marine had participated in an "aquacade"—a synchronized swimming cabaret—in New York. The division still had an ample supply of dynamite on hand. They used it to blast out a huge pool in a coastal reef, rigged up lights and music, and put on a show involving two hundred marines swimming in formation. "So the division became completely and totally occupied," said Colonel Robert E. Hogaboom, "and we had absolutely none of these problems that occurred in some other units . . . this [attitude of] 'Let's go home, let's get out of here' did not affect our division, because we had everybody working at something."[135]

For most young veterans, the moment had not yet come to reflect on the war or its meaning, or the ways in which the experience had shaped them. It had been an ordeal, an unpleasant detour from their conventional life plans, a liminal phase between adolescence and manhood. History and fate had thrown the war into the path of their generation, and so they—rather than their fellow citizens in other age cohorts—had been obliged to fight and win it. During the war, they had been living only for the future, for the return of peace, and their return to the United States, when their authentic lives would begin. They had been on the right side of the conflict, and took justifiable pride in having vanquished fascism and Japanese military imperialism, but they did not look to the future with a great sense of optimism. Many assumed, as a matter of course, that the world would fight more such wars in the future. Most had applauded the use of atomic bombs against Japan, but when they took time to reflect on the implications of nuclear power, they feared for the future of global civilization. Norman Mailer, an army sergeant and incipient novelist, shared his thoughts in a letter to his wife: "There will be another war, if not in twenty years, then in fifty, and if half of mankind survives, then what of the next war—I believe that to survive, the world cities of tomorrow will be built a mile beneath the earth."[136] Even the optimists kept their expectations in check. Douglas Edward Leach, a navy lieutenant, said that the end of the war brought "a satisfying sense of peace restored—in microcosm the world as it was meant to be—not perfect, but livable and potentially happy."[137]

There was virtue in forgetting, as well as in remembering. Veterans insisted upon remembering and honoring those who had paid the ultimate price—but with that exception, in 1945 and 1946, they were not much interested in talking about the war, and civilians were not much interested in hearing about it. Their attention was directed to the future, not to the past. Ben Bradlee, who had served in destroyers in the Pacific, and would become editor-in-chief of the *Washington Post*, wrote that the postwar zeitgeist had left little space for wartime reminiscences. "In 1946, who cared what you did in the war? I thought that the people who sat around and talked about their war were terrible bores." Only gradually, with time and perspective, did he begin to understand how formative an experience the war had been, for himself and his entire generation. "It may sound trite to modern ears, but those really were years when you could get involved in something beyond yourself—something that connected you to your times in ways that no longer seem so natural, or expected."[138] James Michener, a thirty-seven-year-old naval officer who had served in rear-area bases in the South Pacific, was one of the exceptions. Even in the fall of 1945, he was thinking about "what the great Pacific adventure meant in human terms." As he began work on the novel that would eventually be published as *Tales of the South Pacific*, Michener knew that his fellow veterans would show little interest in such a book in 1946, or even in 1947, and few publishing houses would see a market for it. But after three or four more years had passed, and their memories of boredom, homesickness, terror, suffering, and grief began to fade, veterans would look back on their shared experience with curiosity and interest. "Clearly, almost clinically, I concluded that if you ordered all the young men of a generation to climb Mount Everest, you would expect the climb to have a major significance in their lives. And while they were climbing the damned mountain they would bitch like hell and condemn the assignment, but years later, as they looked back, they'd see it as the supreme adventure it was and they'd want to read about it to reexperience it."[139]

December 1945 was the peak month for Operation MAGIC CARPET. In harbors and lagoons throughout the Pacific, sailors worked to patch up their ships, hoping to make them seaworthy enough to be cleared for the homeward passage. Troops crammed into any ship that could take them home. When the escort carrier *Fanshaw Bay* returned that fall, it carried thousands of soldiers and marines who slept in tiered bunks on the hangar deck. The pilots, aircrewmen, and airedales of the carrier's air group, Composite

Squadron Ten (VC-10), were largely idled, because most of their planes had been put ashore to make room for the passengers. Like the soldiers and marines, they loafed on the flight deck, playing cards or dice, or reading, or just sitting in the sun. At night, the ship turned on its running lights, a peacetime procedure that they still found unfamiliar and unnerving. In daily practice exercises, the antiaircraft gun crews went through a panto-mime of loading and aiming their weapons, but they did not fire with live ammunition. The ship was crowded and uncomfortable, but no one com-plained. They were headed home, and that was all that mattered.

One evening, the VC-10 commander, Edward J. Huxtable Jr., watched the sun sink into the ship's wake, "and it was one of the most beautiful sunsets I had ever seen with the purples, never had I seen such purples, and the dark hues that were in the sky as in an Arizona sunset." But few of the other veterans on the *Fanshaw Bay* were paying attention. They had seen a thousand Pacific sunsets, and the spectacle no longer drew their interest. If they looked anywhere on the sea horizon, they looked forward, to the east, toward home. And one of the other VC-10 pilots, standing nearby on the flight deck, remarked to Huxtable: "You know, Captain, these fellows don't know it yet, but this experience will have been the greatest experience of their lives."[140]

NOTES

Prologue

1. FDR Press Conference #676, August 30, 1940, p. 2.
2. Smith, *Thank You, Mr. President*, p. 22.
3. For example, FDR Press Conference #389, August 9, 1937, pp. 5, 17; and #523, February 3, 1939, p. 8.
4. White, *FDR and the Press*, p. 31; FDR Press Conference #389, August 9, 1937, p. 23; and #915, August 31, 1943, p. 7.
5. FDR Press Conference #523, February 3, 1939, pp. 6–8.
6. Tully, *F.D.R.: My Boss*, p. 87.
7. Arthur Krock in *New York Times*, October 8, 1940, quoted in White, *FDR and the Press*, p. 122.
8. Rodgers, ed., *The Impossible* H. L. *Mencken*, pp. liv–lv.
9. Reilly and Slocum, *Reilly of the White House*, p. 91.
10. FDR Press Conference #790, December 9, 1941, pp. 1–2.
11. Ibid., pp. 6–9.
12. Fireside Chat No. 19, "On the Declaration of War with Japan," Radio Address from Washington, December 9, 1941, FDR Library.
13. *Whaley-Eaton American Letter*, December 26, 1942, quoted in Parker, *A Priceless Advantage*, p. 70.
14. FDR, Statement to the Press, December 16, 1941, quoted in Price, "Governmental Censorship in War-Time," *American Political Science Review* 36, No. 5, October 1942, p. 841.
15. Address by Byron Price to American Society of Newspaper Editors, April 16, 1942, reprinted in Summers, ed., *Wartime Censorship of Press and Radio*, p. 30.
16. "Defense Shake-Up," *New York Times*, December 18, 1941.
17. "Washington News on Fighting Scant," *New York Times*, December 10, 1941.
18. McCarten, "General MacArthur: Fact and Legend," *American Mercury*, Vol. 58, No. 241, January 1944.
19. Davis, *The U.S. Army and the Media in the 20th Century*, p. 51.
20. "We Shall Do Our Best, General MacArthur States," *New York Times*, December 12, 1941.

21. "Keep Flag Flying, MacArthur Orders," *New York Times*, December 16, 1941.

22. "MacArthur Glide Is New Dance," *New York Times*, March 16, 1942.

23. "MacArthur Works On Birthday," *New York Times*, January 27, 1942.

24. *Philadelphia Record*, January 27, 1942, quoted in Borneman, *MacArthur at War*, p. 125.

25. *New York Times*, February 13, 1942, p. 17.

26. Eisenhower, *Crusade in Europe*, p. 18.

27. Ibid., p. 22.

28. Dwight D. Eisenhower diary, February 23, 1942, in Ferrell, ed., *The Eisenhower Diaries*, p. 49.

29. Dwight D. Eisenhower diary, February 23, 1942, in ibid., p. 49.

30. Buell, *Master of Sea Power*, p. 249.

31. Perry, *"Dear Bart,"* p. 79.

32. Forrestal quoted in Buell, *Master of Sea Power*, p. 253.

33. Forrestal recounted the quote in a letter to Carl Vinson dated August 30, 1944. Millis, ed., *The Forrestal Diaries*, p. 9.

34. *Basic Field Manual, Regulations for Correspondents Accompanying U.S. Army Forces in the Field*, War Department, January 21, 1942, p. 4.

35. Dunn, *Pacific Microphone*, p. 149.

36. Driscoll, *Pacific Victory 1945*, p. 226.

37. Ibid.

38. Liebling, "The A.P. Surrender," *New Yorker*, May 12, 1945.

39. Ewing, "Nimitz: Reflections on Pearl Harbor," pp. 1–2.

40. Sherrod, *On to Westward*, p. 234.

41. "Girding of Pacific Speeded by Nimitz," *New York Times*, January 31, 1942.

42. Robert Bostwick Carney, oral history, CCOH Naval History Project, Vol. 1, No. 539, p. 362.

43. Waldo Drake, oral history, in *Recollections of Fleet Admiral Chester W. Nimitz*, p. 19.

44. Casey, *Torpedo Junction*, p. 234.

45. Waldo Drake, oral history, in *Recollections of Fleet Admiral Chester W. Nimitz*, p. 14.

46. Casey, *Torpedo Junction*, p. 278.

47. Brinkley, *Washington Goes to War*, pp. 190–91.

48. Davis and Price, *War Information and Censorship*, p. 13.

49. Ritchie, *Reporting from Washington*, p. 62.

50. Brinkley, *Washington Goes to War*, p. 190.

51. Current, *Secretary Stimson*, p. 201.

52. Burlingame, *Don't Let Them Scare You*, p. 195.

53. Healy and Catledge, *A Lifetime on Deadline*, p. 109.

54. "Navy Had Word of Jap Plan to Strike at Sea," *Chicago Sunday Tribune*, June 7, 1942, p. 1.

55. Tom Dyer, one of Joe Rochefort's lieutenants at Station Hypo, observed that the Japanese adopted a new coding edition the same week as the Battle of Midway, too early to have been prompted by the *Tribune* story. Thomas H. Dyer, oral history, pp. 270–71.

56. Glen Perry to Edmond Barnett, October 22, 1942; full text of letter in Perry, *Dear Bart*, p. 70.

57. Navy Department communiqué No. 88, June 12, 1942.

58. Navy Department communiqué No. 107, August 17, 1942.

59. Hanson Baldwin, oral history, p. 359.

60. Burlingame, *Don't Let Them Scare You*, p. 201.

61. Navy Department communiqué No. 147, October 12, 1942.

62. Navy Department communiqué No. 149, October 13, 1942.

63. Navy Department communiqué No. 168, October 26, 1942.

64. Navy Department communiqué No. 169, October 26, 1942.

65. Navy Department communiqué No. 175, October 31, 1942.

66. CINCPAC to COMINCH, November 1, 1942, in CINCPAC Gray Book, Book 2, p. 970.

67. Perry, *Dear Bart*, p. 84.

68. Glen Perry's memorandum to editors, November 1, 1942, in Perry, *Dear Bart*, p. 85.

69. Phelps H. Adams quoted in Buell, *Master of Sea Power*, pp. 260–61.

70. Glen Perry's memorandum to editors, November 7, 1942, Perry, *Dear Bart*, p. 91.

71. Phelps H. Adams quoted in Buell, *Master of Sea Power*, p. 261.

72. Glen Perry's memorandum to editors, November 30, 1942, Perry, *Dear Bart*, p. 107.

73. Robert L. Eichelberger to Emma Eichelberger, undated, in Luvaas, ed., *Dear Miss Em*, pp. 64–65.

74. Luvaas, ed., *Dear Miss Em*, p. 65.

75. Ibid.

76. SWPA Communiqué No. 326, March 4, 1943; SWPA Communiqué No. 329, March 7, 1943; RG, RG-4, Reel 611, MacArthur Memorial Archives.

77. Press release, SWPA headquarters, April 14, 1943, RG-4, Reel 611, MacArthur Memorial Archives.

78. MacArthur to Chief of Staff, War Department, September 7, 1943, RG-4, Reel 593, MacArthur Memorial Archives.

79. LeGrande Diller, oral history, September 26, 1982, MacArthur Memorial Archives, p. 13.

80. William Manchester notes MacArthur's paranoid tendency to use the pronouns "they" and "them" to refer to nameless Washington enemies in *American Caesar*, p. 273.

81. Robert L. Eichelberger to Emma Eichelberger, January 29, 1944, in Luvaas, ed., *Dear Miss Em*, pp. 90–91.

82. James, *The Years of MacArthur*, Vol. 2, pp. 280–81.

83. Robert L. Eichelberger to Emma Eichelberger, June 13, 1943, in Luvaas, ed., *Dear Miss Em*, p. 71.

84. Meijer, *Arthur Vandenberg*, p. 218.

85. This according to Faubion Bowers, an interpreter and loyal aide-de-camp, in "The Late General MacArthur," in Leary, ed., *MacArthur and the American Century*, p. 254.

86. "Eichelberger Dictations," November 12, 1953, in Luvaas, ed., *Dear Miss Em*, p. 77.

87. Arthur Vandenberg, "Why I Am for MacArthur," *Collier's Weekly*, February 12, 1944, p. 14.

88. James, *The Years of MacArthur*, Vol. 2, p. 423.

89. Clapper described the exchange to Captain John L. McCrea, former White House naval aide, in January 1944. McCrea, *Captain McCrea's War*, p. 210. The following month, Clapper was killed while reporting on the FLINTLOCK landings in the Marshall Islands. He was riding as a passenger in a navy bomber when it collided with another U.S. plane.

90. John McCarten, "General MacArthur: Fact and Legend," *American Mercury*, Vol. 58, No. 241, January 1944.

91. Ibid.

92. MacArthur to Marshall, cable in the clear, March 11, 1944, RG-4, MacArthur correspondence files, MacArthur Memorial Archives.

93. Robert L. Eichelberger to Emma Eichelberger, January 28, 1944, in Luvaas, ed., *Dear Miss Em*, p. 90.

94. James, *The Years of MacArthur*, Vol. 2, p. 435.

95. Ibid., p. 436.

96. MacArthur, *Reminiscences*, p. 185.

97. Press release, SWPA headquarters, Statement of Douglas MacArthur, April 30, 1944, RG-4, Reel 611, MacArthur Memorial Archives.

98. "Dewey Refuses to Say Directly That Roosevelt Withheld Pacific Supplies," *Courier-Journal* (Louisville, KY), September 15, 1944, p. 6.

Chapter One

1. Press and radio conference No. 961, July 11, 1944, FDR Library.

2. FDR to Stephen T. Early, October 24, 1944, in Stephen T. Early Papers, "Memoranda, FDR, 1944," Box 24, FDR Library.

3. Smith, "Thank You, Mr. President!," *Life* magazine, August 19, 1946, p. 49.

4. William D. Hassett diary, March 6, 1944, in Hassett, *Off the Record with FDR*, p. 239.

5. Evans, *The Hidden Campaign*, p. 52.

6. White House daily log, July 16, 1944, FDR Library.

7. Rigdon, *White House Sailor*, p. 19.

8. William D. Leahy diary, July 21, 1944, p. 61, William D. Leahy Papers, LCMD.

9. "JCS to CINCPOA and CINCSOWESPAC," March 12, 1944, FDR Map Room Papers, Box 182.

10. Hayes, *The History of the Joint Chiefs of Staff in World War II*, p. 503.

11. MacArthur to Sutherland, March 8, 1943, RG-30, Reel 1007, Signal Corps No. Q4371, MacArthur Memorial Archives.

12. Marshall to General Douglas MacArthur, June 24, 1944, Radio No. WAR-55718, George C. Marshall Papers, Pentagon Office Collection, Selected Materials, George C. Marshall Research Library, Lexington, Virginia.

13. MacArthur to Marshall, Radio No. CX-13891, June 18, 1944, in Marshall, *The Papers of George Catlett Marshall*, ed. Bland and Stevens.

14. The documentary evidence was discovered and published by Carol M. Petillo in 1979. Petillo, "Douglas MacArthur and Manuel Quezon." Paul P. Rogers, a clerk on MacArthur's staff, witnessed conversations involving Quezon, MacArthur, and Sutherland on Corregidor and typed out the order. Rogers, *The Good Years: MacArthur and Sutherland*, pp. 165–66.

15. Dwight D. Eisenhower diary, June 20, 1942, in *The Eisenhower Diaries*, p. 63.

16. Press conference, April 17, 1944, in Perry, *Dear Bart*, p. 270.

17. Barbey, *MacArthur's Amphibious Navy*, p. 183.

18. Charles J. Moore, oral history, p. 1063.

19. Interview with Raymond A. Spruance by Philippe de Baussel for Paris *Match*, July 6, 1965, p. 21, Raymond A. Spruance Papers, MS Collection 12, Box 1, Folder 1.

20. Spruance to Professor E. B. Potter, March 28, 1960, p. 1, Raymond A. Spruance Papers, Collection 707, Box 3, NHHC Archives.

21. Robert Bostwick Carney, oral history, CCOH Naval History Project, p. 435.

22. Ibid.

23. Ibid., p. 438.

24. John Henry Towers diary, July 20, 1944, John H. Towers Papers, LCMD.

25. Robert Bostwick Carney, oral history, CCOH Naval History Project, p. 440.

26. Buell, *Master of Sea Power*, p. 467.

27. CINCPOA to COMINCH, July 24, 1944, in CINCPAC Gray Book, Book 5, p. 2334.

28. "Notes, 1950–1952," pp. 5–6, Ernest J. King Papers, LCMD.

29. John Henry Towers diary, July 26, 1944, John H. Towers Papers, LCMD.

30. Robert C. Richardson Jr. diary, July 27, 1944, Robert C. Richardson Jr. Papers, Hoover Institution Archives.

31. Whelton Rhoades diary, July 26, 1944, in Rhoades, *Flying MacArthur to Victory*, p. 257.

32. Ibid., p. 258.

33. John Henry Towers diary, July 26, 1944, John H. Towers Papers, LCMD. Note that Whelton Rhoades mistook Towers for Nimitz, and erroneously recorded in

his diary that the CINCPAC had met the plane. Rhoades diary, July 26, 1944, in Rhoades, *Flying MacArthur to Victory*, p. 258.

34. Rosenman, *Working With Roosevelt*, pp. 456–57. General Richardson took his car from the *Baltimore* to Fort Shafter to fetch MacArthur, so the two generals would likely have returned together. Robert C. Richardson Jr. diary, July 27, 1944. The open touring car was certainly present in the Navy Yard on July 26, because the film footage shows that FDR and Leahy left in it. "FDR's Tour of Inspection to the Pacific July–Aug, 1944," 16mm film footage, MP71-8:63–64, Motion Pictures Collection, FDR Library.

35. Sommers, *Combat Carriers and My Brushes with History*, pp. 97–99.

36. Faubion Bowers, "The Late General MacArthur," in Leary, ed., *MacArthur and the American Century*, p. 254.

37. Leahy, *I Was There*, p. 250.

38. "FDR's Tour of Inspection to the Pacific July–Aug, 1944," 16mm film footage, MP71-8:63–64, Motion Pictures Collection, FDR Library.

39. Ibid.

40. Sommers, *Combat Carriers and My Brushes with History*, pp. 97–99.

41. William D. Leahy diary, July 26, 1944, William D. Leahy Papers, LCMD.

42. Robert C. Richardson Jr. diary, July 27, 1944, Richardson Papers, Hoover Institution Archives.

43. Ibid.

44. FDR Press Conference #962, July 29, 1944, FDR Library.

45. Reilly and Slocum, *Reilly of the White House*, p. 191.

46. Rigdon, *White House Sailor*, p. 116.

47. McIntire, *White House Physician*, p. 199.

48. James, *The Years of MacArthur*, Vol. 2, p. 529.

49. Whelton Rhoades diary, July 29, 1944, in Rhoades, *Flying MacArthur to Victory*, pp. 260–61.

50. Robert L. Eichelberger to Emma Eichelberger, September 12, 1944, in Luvaas, ed., *Dear Miss Em*, pp. 155–56.

51. "Presidential Conference in Hawaii," 35mm film footage, FDR2757-28-2 and FDR2757-28-3, Motion Pictures Collection, FDR Library.

52. Ibid.

53. Blaik, *The Red Blaik Story*, pp. 501–2; Eichelberger and MacKaye, *Our Jungle Road to Tokyo*, p. 165.

54. Faubion Bowers, "The Late General MacArthur," in Leary, ed., *MacArthur and the American Century*, p. 254.

55. Blaik, *The Red Blaik Story*, p. 500; MacArthur, *Reminiscences*, p. 172.

56. Robert C. Richardson Jr. diary, January 19, 1945, Richardson Papers, Hoover Institution Archives.

57. MacArthur, *Reminiscences*, pp. 197–98.

58. Morison, *History of United States Naval Operations in World War II*, Vol. 12, *Leyte*, p. 9.

59. Robert C. Richardson Jr. diary, July 28, 1944, Richardson Papers, Hoover Institution Archives.
60. Leahy, *I Was There*, p. 251.
61. Robert C. Richardson Jr. diary, July 28, 1944, Richardson Papers, Hoover Institution Archives.
62. Drea, *In the Service of the Emperor*, p. 129.
63. MacArthur, *Reminiscences*, p. 198.
64. Robert C. Richardson Jr. diary, July 28, 1944, Richardson Papers, Hoover Institution Archives.
65. Nimitz et al., *The Great Sea War*, pp. 370–73.
66. William D. Leahy diary, July 28, 1944, William D. Leahy Papers, LCMD.
67. MacArthur, *Reminiscences*, pp. 197–98.
68. Robert L. Eichelberger to Emma Eichelberger, September 12, 1944, in Luvaas, ed., *Dear Miss Em*, pp. 155–56.
69. Hayes, *The History of the Joint Chiefs of Staff in World War II*, p. 92.
70. Emphasis in the original. "Notes, 1950–1952," p. 3, Ernest J. King Papers.
71. Whitney, *MacArthur: His Rendezvous with History*, p. 125.
72. D. Clayton James offers this theory in his otherwise excellent multivolume biography, *The Years of MacArthur*. Many others have followed the trail he blazed.
73. McIntire, *White House Physician*, p. 200.
74. Manchester, *American Caesar*, p. 370.
75. Whelton Rhoades diary, July 29, 1944, in Rhoades, *Flying MacArthur to Victory*, pp. 260–61.
76. Howard G. Bruenn, M.D., "Clinical Notes," in Evans, *The Hidden Campaign*, Appendix B, p. 149.
77. William D. Leahy diary, July 29, 1944; White House daily log, July 29, 1944; "Presidential Conference in Hawaii," 35mm film footage, FDR 2757-28-2 and FDR 2757-28-3, Motion Pictures Collection, FDR Library.
78. FDR daily log, July 29, 1944, FDR Library; also "Presidential Conference in Hawaii—July 1944," 35mm film footage, FDR 2757-28-4, Motion Pictures Collection, FDR Library.
79. White House daily log, July 29, 1944, FDR Library.
80. "Presidential Conference in Hawaii—July 1944," 35mm film footage, FDR 2757-28-4, Motion Pictures Collection, FDR Library.
81. McIntire, *White House Physician*, p. 11.
82. Ibid., p. 13.
83. Rosenman quoted in Dallek, *Franklin D. Roosevelt*, p. 568.
84. "Presidential Conference in Hawaii—July 1944," 35mm film footage, FDR 2757-28-4, Motion Pictures Collection, FDR Library.
85. Press Conference #962, July 29, 1944, FDR Library.
86. Ibid.
87. William D. Leahy diary, July 29, 1944, William D. Leahy Papers, LCMD.
88. Letter, FDR to MacArthur, August 9, 1944, FDR Library.

89. Press Conference #962, July 29, 1944, FDR Library.

90. "JCS to CINCPOA and CINCSOWESPAC," March 12, 1944, FDR Map Room Papers, Box 182.

91. Whelton Rhoades diary, July 29, 1944, in Rhoades, *Flying MacArthur to Victory*, pp. 260–61.

92. Joint Staff Planners, Washington, to Staff Planners of CINCPOA, CINCSWPA, July 27, 1944, CINCPAC Gray Book, Book 5, p. 2336.

93. Hayes, *The History of the Joint Chiefs of Staff in World War II*, p. 612.

94. Leahy memorandum to JCS, "Discussion of Pacific Strategy," September 5, 1944. Includes summary of past meetings. Inserted into William D. Leahy diary after entry for August 3, 1944, William D. Leahy Papers, LCMD.

95. Charles J. Moore, oral history, p. 1073.

96. Ibid.

97. CINCPOA to COMINCH, August 18, 1944, CINCPAC Gray Book, Book 5, p. 2342.

98. John Henry Towers diary, July 20, 1944, John H. Towers Papers, LCMD.

99. Graves B. Erskine, oral history, CCOH Marine Corps Project, p. 379.

100. Joint Chiefs of Staff to Nimitz, MacArthur, September 9, 1944, CINCPAC Gray Book, Book 5, p. 2350.

101. Robert L. Eichelberger to Emma Eichelberger, September 12, 1944, in Luvaas, ed., *Dear Miss Em*, pp. 155–56.

102. Letter, FDR to MacArthur, September 15, 1944, FDR Library.

103. Geographic codenames have been replaced with corresponding place-names. MacArthur to Chief of Staff, War Department, September 21, 1944, CINCPAC Gray Book, Book 5, pp. 2362–63.

104. John Henry Towers diary, September 26, 1944, John H. Towers Papers, LCMD.

105. Admiral Raymond A. Spruance, interview in Paris *Match*, July 6, 1965, p. 21, Spruance Papers, Naval War College Archives.

106. Ibid.

107. "Notes, 1950–1952," p. 7, Ernest J. King Papers.

Chapter Two

1. De Seversky, "Victory Through Air Power!," *American Mercury*, February 1942, Vol. 54, pp. 135–54.

2. Mitscher to Captain Luis De Florez, quoted in Taylor, *The Magnificent Mitscher*, pp. 188–89.

3. MacWhorter and Stout, *The First Hellcat Ace*, p. 70.

4. Commander James C. Shaw, USN, "Fast Carrier Operations, 1941–1945," in the introduction to Morison, *History of United States Naval Operations in World War II*, vol. 7, *Aleutians, Gilberts, and Marshalls*, p. xxxii.

5. David S. McCampbell account in Wooldridge, ed., *Carrier Warfare in the Pacific*, p. 212.

6. Arleigh Burke, oral history, p. 5, RG-38, World War II Oral Histories and Interviews, 1942–1946, Box 4, NARA.

7. Olson, *Tales from a Tin Can*, p. 195.

8. Hugh Melrose account, in Olson, *Tales from a Tin Can*, p. 196.

9. J. Bryan III diary, February 13, 1945, in Bryan, *Aircraft Carrier*, p. 21.

10. Two different war correspondents noted a resemblance between Spruance and Rogers. "Our Unsung Admiral," by Frank D. Morris, *Collier's Weekly*, January 1, 1944, p. 48; Fletcher Pratt, "Spruance: Picture of the Admiral," *Harper's Magazine*, August 1946, p. 144.

11. Buell, *The Quiet Warrior*, p. 185.

12. Ibid., p. 212.

13. Ibid., p. 258.

14. Charles F. Barber, Interview by Evelyn M. Cherpak, March 1, 1996, Naval War College Archives.

15. Buell, *The Quiet Warrior*, p. 269.

16. Charles J. Moore, oral history, p. 838.

17. "Our Unsung Admiral," by Frank D. Morris, *Collier's Weekly*, January 1, 1944, p. 17.

18. Charles J. Moore, oral history, p. 839.

19. Moore to his wife on July 1, 1944, quoted in Charles J. Moore, oral history, p. 1047.

20. Spruance to E. M. Eller, July 22, 1966, Raymond A. Spruance Papers, MS Collection 12, Box 2, Folder 7.

21. Buell, *The Quiet Warrior*, p. 329.

22. Robert Bostwick Carney, oral history, p. 382.

23. Comments on E. B. Potter's book, Spruance Papers, NHHC Archives, Collection 707, Box 3, p. 9.

24. For example, a September 1944 broadcast referred to the activities of "Vice Admiral Halsey's Third Fleet," "Admiral Spruance's Fifth Fleet," and "Vice Admiral Kinkaid's Seventh Fleet." "Digest of Japanese Broadcasts, September 20, 1944," p. 3, NARA Records of Japanese Navy and Related Documents, Digest: Japanese Radio Broadcasts, Box 22.

25. Spruance to Potter, December 1, 1944, pp. 2–3, Spruance Papers, NHHC Archives, Collection 707, Box 3.

26. Radford, *From Pearl Harbor to Vietnam*, notes for chapters 1–4, p. 453.

27. Trumbull, "All Out with Halsey!," *New York Times Magazine*, December 6, 1942, p. 1.

28. "Halsey Predicts Victory This Year," *New York Times*, January 3, 1943.

29. Halsey to Capt. Gene Markey, January 24, 1945, Halsey Papers, LCMD.

30. "Interview with Admiral C. J. Moore," by John T. Mason, November 28, 1966, p. 4, Papers of Raymond Spruance, Series 188, Box 3, NHHC Archive.

31. Sherrod, *On to Westward*, p. 239.

32. Reynolds, *The Fast Carriers*, p. 238.

33. Buell, *Dauntless Helldivers*, p. 327.

34. Ibid., pp. 327–28.

35. The Bonins (Muko, Chichi, and Haha Jima) and the Volcano Islands (Iwo Jima and its neighbors) were geographically distinct, with differing terrain, topography, and climate, but U.S. commanders often referred to them all as "the Bonins," and this narrative sometimes follows that convention.

36. Third Fleet War Diary, September 2, 1944, in NARA, RG 38, World War II War Diaries, Box 30; CINCPAC Gray Book, Book 5, p. 2055, entry for September 3, 1944.

37. CTG 38.4 to Com3rdFlt, CTF 38, September 3, 1944, CINCPAC Gray Book, Book 5, p. 2226.

38. Third Fleet War Diary, August 24, 1944.

39. Solberg, *Decision and Dissent*, p. 23.

40. Third Fleet War Diary, August 31, 1944.

41. Ibid., entries for June 18 & July 7, 1944; NARA, RG 38, World War II War Diaries, Box 30.

42. Robert Bostwick Carney, oral history, p. 383.

43. Solberg, *Decision and Dissent*, pp. 22–23.

44. Nimitz-Halsey letters, August–December 1944, in Halsey Papers/LCMD.

45. Third Fleet War Diary, September 11, 1944.

46. Ibid., September 8, 1944.

47. Ibid., September 9, 1944.

48. Ibid.

49. COM3RDFLT to CTF 38, September 9, 1944, CINCPAC Gray Book, Book 5, p. 2351.

50. St. John, *Leyte Calling*, p. 168.

51. Buell, *Dauntless Helldivers*, p. 332.

52. Davis, *Sinking the Rising Sun*, pp. 226–27.

53. Ibid., p. 228.

54. Okumiya, Horikoshi, and Caidin, *Zero!*, pp. 242–43.

55. COM3RDFLT to CINCPOA, September 14, 1944, CINCPAC Gray Book, Book 5, pp. 2229–30.

56. Halsey, *Admiral Halsey's Story*, p. 200.

57. COM3RDFLT to CINCPOA, CINCSWPA, COMINCH, Message 130300, September 1944, RG-4, MacArthur correspondence files, MacArthur Memorial Archives.

58. CINCPAC to COM3RDFLT, Info etc., September 13, 1944, CINCPAC Gray Book, Book 5, p. 2353.

59. CINCPOA to COMINCH, Sept 14, 1944, CINCPAC Gray Book, Book 5, p. 2356.

60. Ibid.

61. Barbey, *MacArthur's Amphibious Navy*, p. 227; and MacArthur to Joint Chiefs of Staff, September 15, 1944, RG-4, MacArthur correspondence files, MacArthur Memorial Archives.

62. Joint Chiefs of Staff to Nimitz, MacArthur, Info Halsey, September 15, 1944, CINCPAC Gray Book, Book 5, p. 2357.

63. Third Fleet War Diary, September 14, 1944.

64. "Message on the State of the Union," January 6, 1945, FDR Library.

Chapter Three

1. Sledge, *With the Old Breed*, p. 32.

2. Ibid., pp. 35–36.

3. Burgin and Marvel, *Islands of the Damned*, p. 120.

4. Donigan, "Peleliu: The Forgotten Battle."

5. Mason, *"We Will Stand By You,"* p. 216.

6. Donigan, "Peleliu: The Forgotten Battle."

7. Ibid.

8. Mace and Allen, *Battleground Pacific*, p. 28.

9. Hunt, *Coral Comes High*, p. 36.

10. Ibid., p. 37.

11. Sledge, *With the Old Breed*, p. 56.

12. Lea and Greeley, *The Two Thousand Yard Stare*, p. 176.

13. Hunt, *Coral Comes High*, p. 71.

14. Lea and Greeley, *The Two Thousand Yard Stare*, p. 177.

15. Ibid., pp. 177–78.

16. Ibid., p. 182.

17. Gayle, *Bloody Beaches*, p. 13.

18. Mason, *"We Will Stand By You,"* p. 221.

19. Hunt, *Coral Comes High*, p. 137.

20. Ibid., p. 124.

21. Ibid., p. 103.

22. Burgin and Marvel, *Islands of the Damned*, p. 132.

23. Ibid., p. 133.

24. Sledge, *With the Old Breed*, p. 79.

25. Ibid., p. 80.

26. Ronald D. Salmon, oral history, p. 86.

27. Mace and Allen, *Battleground Pacific*, p. 64.

28. Lea and Greeley, *The Two Thousand Yard Stare*, p. 189.

29. CTF 38 to COM3RDFLT Info CINCPAC, September 7, 1944, CINCPAC Gray Book, Book 5, p. 2227.

30. Mace and Allen, *Battleground Pacific*, p. 92.

31. Third Fleet Diary, October 5, 1944.

32. McCandless, *A Flash of Green*, pp. 164, 166.

33. Sledge, *With the Old Breed*, p. 103.

34. Mace and Allen, *Battleground Pacific*, p. 103.

35. War Diary, September 22, 1944 (Oahu date), CINCPAC Gray Book, Book 5, p. 2079.
36. "Operation Report, 81st Infantry Division, Capture of Ulithi Atoll," April 13, 1945, p. 29, FDR Map Room Files, Box 193, FDR Library.
37. Hunt, *Coral Comes High*, p. 91.
38. Burgin and Marvel, *Islands of the Damned*, p. 152.
39. "Operation Report, 81st Infantry Division, Capture of Ulithi Atoll," April 13, 1945, p. 113, FDR Map Room Files, Box 193, FDR Library.
40. Ronald D. Salmon, oral history, p. 89.
41. Sledge, *With the Old Breed*, p. 121.
42. Ibid., p. 143.
43. Ibid., p. 123.
44. Ibid., p. 148.
45. Ibid., p. 120.
46. Ibid., pp. 152–53.
47. Ibid., p. 150.
48. "CTF 57 to CINCPOA Info CTG 57.14," November 6, 1944, Enclosure (A), CINCPAC Gray Book, Vol. 5, p. 2282.
49. Donigan, "Peleliu: The Forgotten Battle."
50. "Operation Report, 81st Infantry Division, Capture of Ulithi Atoll," April 13, 1945, p. 111, FDR Map Room Files, Box 193, FDR Library.
51. Ibid., p. 24.
52. Wees, *King-Doctor of Ulithi*, p. 36.
53. "Operation Report, 81st Infantry Division, Capture of Ulithi Atoll," April 13, 1945, pp. 28–29, FDR Map Room Files, Box 193, FDR Library.
54. McCandless, *A Flash of Green*, pp. 170–71.
55. Third Fleet Diary, October 2, 1944, CINCPAC Gray Book, October 5, 1944, Book 5, p. 2093; Task Group 38.3 Diary, October 5, 1944.
56. Task Group 38.3 Diary, October 7, 1944.
57. Third Fleet Diary, October 8, 1944.
58. Robert Bostwick Carney, oral history, p. 392.
59. COM3RDFLT to CINCPOA, etc., October 13, 1944, in CINCPAC Gray Book, Book 5, p. 2239.
60. Task Group 38.3 Diary, October 11, 1944.
61. Fukudome, "The Air Battle Off Taiwan," in Evans, ed., *The Japanese Navy in World War II*, p. 346.
62. USSBS, *Interrogations of Japanese Officials*, Nav No. 115, USSBS No. 503, Vice Admiral Shigeru Fukudome, IJN.
63. Fukudome, "The Air Battle Off Taiwan," in Evans, ed., *The Japanese Navy in World War II*, p. 338.
64. Robert Bostwick Carney, oral history, p. 398.
65. Third Fleet Diary, October 12, 1944.

66. Solberg, *Decision and Dissent*, p. 58.

67. Third Fleet Diary, October 12, 1944; Matome Ugaki diary, October 13, 1944, in Ugaki, *Fading Victory*, p. 470.

68. Third Fleet Diary, October 13, 1944; Task Group 38.3 Diary, October 13, 1944.

69. Kent Lee account in Wooldridge, ed., *Carrier Warfare in the Pacific*, p. 227.

70. Davis, *Sinking the Rising Sun*, p. 250.

71. Ibid., p. 252.

72. War Diary, October 12, 1944 (Oahu date), CINCPAC Gray Book, Book 5, p. 2097.

73. Task Group 38.3 Diary, October 13, 1944.

74. Davis, *Sinking the Rising Sun*, p. 257.

75. Third Fleet Diary, October 14, 1944.

76. Task Group 38.3 Diary, October 14, 1944.

77. William Ransom account in Kuehn et al., *Eyewitness Pacific Theater*, p. 203.

78. "Running Estimate," October 14, 1944 (Oahu date), CINCPAC Gray Book, Book 5, p. 2099.

79. Halsey, *Admiral Halsey's Story*, p. 207.

80. "Digest of Japanese Broadcasts," October 15, 1944, p. 2.

81. Ibid., October 14, 1944, p. 2.

82. "Digest of Japanese Broadcasts," October 14, 1944, cited in memo dated October 20, 1944, p. 1.

83. "Digest of Japanese Broadcasts," October 17, 1944, p. 2.

84. Halsey, *Admiral Halsey's Story*, p. 206.

85. Fukudome, "The Air Battle Off Taiwan," in Evans, ed., *The Japanese Navy in World War II*, p. 352.

86. "Digest of Japanese Broadcasts," October 15, 1944, p. 7, and October 16, 1944, p. 2.

87. Carney, oral history, p. 399.

88. CINCPAC to COMFAIRWING, October 15, 1944; CINCPAC Gray Book, Book 5, p. 2240.

89. Third Fleet Diary, October 15, 1944.

90. Captain Inglis of the *Birmingham*, quoted in Morison, *History of United States Naval Operations in WWII*, Vol. 12, *Leyte*, p. 103.

91. Morison, *History of United States Naval Operations*, Vol. 12, *Leyte*, p. 96.

92. Third Fleet Diary, October 17, 1944.

Chapter Four

1. Michio Takeyama essay in Minear, ed., *The Scars of War*, p. 35.

2. Ibid.

3. Havens, *Valley of Darkness*, p. 131.

4. Ibid., p. 94.

5. Kiyoshi Kiyosawa diary, July 24, 1944, Kiyosawa, *A Diary of Darkness*, p. 232.

6. Tsunejiro Tamura diary, January 16, 1945; Yamashita, ed., *Leaves from an Autumn of Emergencies*, p. 113.

7. Havens, *Valley of Darkness*, p. 96.

8. An anonymous woman's remark, recorded in Kiyoshi Kiyosawa diary, July 22, 1944, Kiyosawa, *A Diary of Darkness*, p. 230.

9. Taetora Ogata, president of the Board of Information, September 1944, quoted in USSBS, *The Effects of Strategic Bombing on Japanese Morale*, p. 124.

10. "Digest of Japanese Broadcasts, October 13, 1944," p. 3.

11. Uichiro Kawachi, oral history, in Cook and Cook, eds., *Japan at War*, p. 218.

12. Kiyoshi Kiyosawa diary, October 20, 1944, Kiyosawa, *A Diary of Darkness*, p. 267.

13. "Digest of Japanese Broadcasts," October 16, 1944, p. 1.

14. Ibid., October 17, 1944, p. 3, and October 18, 1944, p. 1.

15. Fukudome, "The Air Battle Off Taiwan," in Evans, ed., *The Japanese Navy in World War II*, p. 354.

16. Matome Ugaki diary, October 14, 1944, Ugaki, *Fading Victory*, p. 474.

17. Kenryo Sato, "Dai Toa War Memoir" (unpublished manuscript), pp. 7–9, John Toland Papers, FDR Library, Series 1, Box 16.

18. Kawachi, oral history, in Cook and Cook, eds., *Japan at War*, p. 218.

19. "Digest of Japanese Broadcasts, October 20, 1944," p. 7.

20. Auer, ed., *From Marco Polo Bridge to Pearl Harbor*, p. 176.

21. USSBS, *Interrogations of Japanese Officials*, Nav No. 76, USSBS No. 379, Admiral Mitsumasa Yonai, IJN.

22. Hirohito "Soliloquy," translation in Irokawa, *The Age of Hirohito*, p. 92.

23. Auer, ed., *From Marco Polo Bridge to Pearl Harbor*, p. 178.

24. USSBS, *Interrogations of Japanese Officials*, Nav No. 90, USSBS No. 429, Admiral Kichisaburo Nomura, IJN.

25. "Digest of Japanese Broadcasts, August 25, 1944," p. 2.

26. Premier Kuniaki Koiso, in speech to Diet, September 8, 1944; Tolischus, *Through Japanese Eyes*, p. 156.

27. "Digest of Japanese Broadcasts, August 19, 1944," p. 5.

28. *Chibu Nihon Shinbun*, July 26, 1944, quoted in Kiyoshi Kiyosawa diary, same date, in Kiyosawa, *A Diary of Darkness*, p. 233.

29. Report entitled "Current Conditions of the Empire's Strength," dated July 1944, quoted in Havens, *Valley of Darkness*, p. 131.

30. For example, see USSBS interrogations of Kurita (No. 47), Nomura (No. 429), and Ozawa (No. 227). Kurita: "We had believed that General MacArthur would come from the south to [the Philippines]." Nomura: "There was much talk by one of your Generals that he would recapture the Philippines. . . . Therefore, it was our opinion that you had to go there." Ozawa: "The original *Sho* Operation was very general, that the Philippines were to be defended," and "the American invasion could take place sometime in the middle of October."

31. USSBS, *Interrogations of Japanese Officials*, Nav No. 55, USSBS no. 227, Vice Admiral Jisaburo Ozawa.

32. Verbatim [sic]. Kenryo Sato, "Dai Toa War Memoir" (unpublished manuscript), pp. 7–9, John Toland Papers, FDR Library, Series 1, Box 16.

33. Kenryo Sato, "Dai Toa War Memoir" (unpublished manuscript), pp. 7–9, John Toland Papers, FDR Library, Series 1, Box 16.

34. Ibid.

35. USSBS, *Interrogations of Japanese Officials*, Nav No. 64, USSBS No. 258, Rear Admiral Toshitane Takata, IJN, attached successively to the Staff of the Third Fleet, the Combined Fleet, and the Naval General Staff.

36. Ito and Pineau, *The End of the Imperial Japanese Navy*, pp. 125–26.

37. USSBS, *Interrogations of Japanese Officials*, Nav No. 64, USSBS No. 258, Rear Admiral Toshitane Takata, IJN.

38. USSBS, *Interrogations of Japanese Officials*, Nav No. 9, USSBS No. 47, Vice Admiral Takeo Kurita.

39. USSBS, *Interrogations of Japanese Officials*, Nav No. 55, USSBS No. 227, Vice Admiral Jisaburo Ozawa, IJN. Also see *Interrogation of Rear Admiral Chiaki Matsuda*, IJN, Nav No. 69, USSBS No. 345: "My opinion at that time was that after all the plan of the operation was insufficient to check your advance; however, under the circumstances, I thought it was the best plan. I thought it would be the last engagement for me and counted on death in the action."

40. Sakai, with Caidin and Saito, *Samurai!*, p. 221.

41. Ibid., p. 220.

42. Naoji Kozu, oral history, in Cook and Cook, eds., *Japan at War*, p. 315.

43. USSBS, *Interrogations of Japanese Officials*, Nav No. 12, USSBS No. 62, Captain Rikibei Inoguchi.

44. Ibid.

45. USSBS, *Interrogations of Japanese Officials*, Nav No. 75, USSBS No. 378, Admiral Soemu Toyoda.

46. Ibid.

47. USSBS, *Interrogations of Japanese Officials*, Nav No. 55, USSBS No. 227, Vice Admiral Jisaburo Ozawa, IJN.

48. Inoguchi et al., *The Divine Wind*, p. 25.

49. Auer, ed., *From Marco Polo Bridge to Pearl Harbor*, p. 236.

50. "Digest of Japanese Broadcasts, October 6, 1944," p. 2.

51. Goro Sugimoto, quoted in Victoria, *Zen at War*, p. 123.

52. Dr. Reiho Masunaga in *Chugai Nippon*, May–June 1945, quoted in Victoria, *Zen at War*, p. 139.

53. *Thirty-Six Strategies* cited in Cleary, *The Japanese Art of War*, p. 91.

54. Inoguchi et al., *The Divine Wind*, p. 61.

55. USSBS, *Interrogations of Japanese Officials*, Nav No. 12, USSBS No. 62, Captain Rikibei Inoguchi.

56. Auer, ed., *From Marco Polo Bridge to Pearl Harbor*, p. 165.
57. Inoguchi et al., *The Divine Wind*, p. 7.
58. USSBS, *Interrogations of Japanese Officials*, Nav No. 12, USSBS No. 62, Captain Rikibei Inoguchi.
59. Hastings, *Retribution*, pp. 166–67.
60. Inoguchi et al., *The Divine Wind*, p. 11.
61. Ibid., p. 27.
62. Statement read over Radio Tokyo, 4:30 p.m., October 15, 1944, in "Digest of Japanese Broadcasts," October 15, 1944, p. 3.
63. USSBS, *Interrogations of Japanese Officials*, Nav No. 98, Lieutenant General Torashirō Kawabe, November 30, 1945.
64. Matome Ugaki diary, October 21, 1944, Ugaki, *Fading Victory*, p. 485.

Chapter Five

1. Edward J. Huxtable, Composite Squadron Ten, recollections and notes, p. 5.
2. Thomas C. Kinkaid, oral history, p. 301.
3. "Joint Chiefs of Staff to MacArthur, Nimitz," October 3, 1944, #2255, in CINCPAC Gray Book, Book 5, p. 2378.
4. "MacArthur to COM3RDFLT," October 21, 1944, #2240, in CINCPAC Gray Book, Book 5, p. 2389.
5. Carney, oral history, pp. 396–97.
6. Marsden, *Attack Transport*, p. 120.
7. Log of Captain Ray Tarbuck, U.S. Navy, entry for October 19, 1944, 0958, quoted in Barbey, *MacArthur's Amphibious Navy*, p. 245.
8. Entry for 1400; Third Amphibious Force War Diary, October 20, 1944, p. 6, in NARA, RG 38, World War II War Diaries, Box 177.
9. Dickinson, "MacArthur Fulfills Pledge to Return," in Stenbuck, ed., *Typewriter Battalion. Dramatic Frontline Dispatches from World War II*, p. 239.
10. Romulo, *I See the Philippines Rise*, p. 90.
11. Ibid., p. 91.
12. Ibid., p. 92.
13. Boquet, *The Philippine Archipelago*, p. 100.
14. USSBS, *Interrogations of Japanese Officials*, Nav No. 79, USSBS No. 390, Commander Shigeru Nishino, IJN.
15. USSBS, *Interrogations of Japanese Officials*, Nav No. 9, USSBS No. 47, Vice Admiral Takao Kurita.
16. USS *Darter* (SS-227) War Patrol Report No. 4, November 5, 1944, accessed August 12, 2017, https://issuu.com/hnsa/docs.
17. "Running Estimate" entry dated October 22, 1944, in CINCPAC Gray Book, Book 5, p. 2106.
18. Solberg, *Decision and Dissent*, p. 77.

19. USS *Darter* (SS-227) War Patrol Report No. 4, November 5, 1944, accessed August 12, 2017, https://issuu.com/hnsa/docs.

20. Thomas, *Sea of Thunder*, p. 190.

21. USS *Dace* (SS-247) War Patrol Report No. 5, November 6, 1944, Enclosure (A), p. 34, accessed August 12, 2017, https://issuu.com/hnsa/docs.

22. USS *Dace* (SS-247) War Patrol Report No. 5, November 6, 1944, Enclosure (A), p. 37, accessed August 12, 2017, https://issuu.com/hnsa/docs.

23. Matome Ugaki diary, October 23, 1944, Ugaki, *Fading Victory*, p. 487.

24. Solberg, *Decision and Dissent*, p. 99.

25. Tully, *Battle of Surigao Strait*, p. 68.

26. Halsey, *Admiral Halsey's Story*, p. 211.

27. Yoshimura, *Battleship Musashi*, p. 159.

28. Astor, *Wings of Gold*, p. 361.

29. Solberg, *Decision and Dissent*, p. 105.

30. TG 38.3 War Diary, October 24, 1944.

31. David S. McCampbell account, in Wooldridge, ed., *Carrier Warfare in the Pacific*, p. 212.

32. Woodward, *The Battle for Leyte Gulf*, p. 52.

33. David S. McCampbell account, in Wooldridge, ed., *Carrier Warfare in the Pacific*, p. 212.

34. War Damage Report No. 62, U.S.S. *Princeton* (CVL-23), Loss in Action Off Luzon, 24 October 1944, accessed September 6, 2017, https://www.history.navy.mil/research/library.

35. Peggy Hull Deuell, "Death of Carriers Described," in *Reporting World War II*, Part One, p. 549.

36. War Damage Report No. 62, U.S.S. *Princeton* (CVL-23), Loss in Action Off Luzon, 24 October 1944, accessed September 6, 2017, https://www.history.navy.mil/research/library.

37. John Sheehan, oral history, in Petty, ed., *Voices from the Pacific War*, p. 108.

38. Peggy Hull Deuell, "Death of Carriers Described," in *Reporting World War II*, p. 550.

39. Excerpts from *Birmingham* war diary, quoted in Morison, *History of United States Naval Operations in World War II*, Vol. 12, *Leyte*, p. 181.

40. Lee Robinson, oral history, in Petty, ed., *Voices from the Pacific War*, p. 239.

41. USSBS, *Interrogations of Japanese Officials*, Nav No. 115, USSBS No. 503, Vice Admiral Shigeru, Fukudome, IJN.

42. Jack Lawton, oral history, in Springer, *Inferno*, p. 134.

43. Robert Freligh, email to author, February 11, 2018.

44. Jack Lawton, oral history, in Springer, *Inferno*, p. 134.

45. Robert Freligh, email to author, February 11, 2018.

46. USSBS, *Interrogations of Japanese Officials*, Nav No. 83, USSBS No. 407, Captain Kenkichi Kato, IJN (Executive Officer, *Musashi*, when sunk at Leyte Gulf).

47. USSBS, *Interrogations of Japanese Officials*, Nav No. 9, USSBS No. 47, Vice Admiral Takeo Kurita.

48. Ito, *The End of the Imperial Japanese Navy*, p. 106. Ugaki approved of the westward turn, remarking in his diary: "I noticed that it would be more advantageous for tomorrow's fighting if we could deceive the enemy by turning back once before evening." Matome Ugaki diary, October 24, 1944, Ugaki, *Fading Victory*, p. 490.

49. Ito, *The End of the Imperial Japanese Navy*, p. 108.

50. Ibid.

51. USSBS, *Interrogations of Japanese Officials*, Nav No. 9, USSBS No. 47, Vice Admiral Takeo Kurita.

52. Thomas, *Sea of Thunder*, p. 223.

53. Haruo Tohmatsu, email to H. P. Willmott, December 3, 2003, quoted in Willmott, *The Battle of Leyte Gulf*, p. 132.

54. USSBS, *Interrogations of Japanese Officials*, Nav No. 64, USSBS No. 258, Rear Admiral Toshitane Takata, IJN, attached successively to the Staff of the Third Fleet, the Combined Fleet, and the Naval General Staff.

55. Ito, *The End of the Imperial Japanese Navy*, p. 111.

56. Matome Ugaki diary, October 24, 1944, Ugaki, *Fading Victory*, p. 490.

57. Asada, *From Mahan to Pearl Harbor*, p. 206.

58. Matome Ugaki diary, October 24, 1944; Ugaki, *Fading Victory*, p. 491.

59. Com 3rd Fleet to CINCPAC, 26 October 1944 (251317); NARA, RG 38, "CNO Zero-Zero Files," Box 4, "CINCPOA Dispatches, October 1944."

60. Third Fleet action report, Serial 0088, October 23–26, 1944, p. 3; Halsey Papers, Box 35, "Action Reports, Third Fleet, October 23–26, 1944," LCMD.

61. "COM3RDFLEET to ALL TFC'S 3RD FLEET, ALL TGC'S OF TF 38 Info COMINCH, CINCPAC," Oct 24, 1944, 0612; in CINCPAC Gray Book, Book 5, p. 2242.

62. Halsey, *Admiral Halsey's Story*, p. 214.

63. Third Fleet action report, Serial 0088, October 23–26, 1944, p. 3; Halsey Papers, Box 35, "Action Reports, Third Fleet, October 23–26, 1944," LCMD.

64. Third Fleet action report, Serial 0088, October 23–26, 1944, p. 3; Halsey Papers, Box 35, "Action Reports, Third Fleet, October 23–26, 1944," LCMD.

65. Solberg, a direct eyewitness, names Doug Moulton, Harold Stassen, and Rollo Wilson, in Solberg, *Decision and Dissent*, p. 117.

66. Thomas, *Sea of Thunder*, p. 226.

67. COM3RDFLT to CTF 77, etc. (241124), in CINCPAC Gray Book, Book 5, p. 2243.

68. Gerald F. Bogan, oral history, p. 109.

69. Ibid.

70. Ibid., p. 113.

71. Conveyed by a member of Lee's staff to Samuel Eliot Morison in a letter dated March 6, 1950, Morison, *History of United States Naval Operations in World War II*, Vol. 12, *Leyte*, p. 195n34.

72. Cutler, *The Battle of Leyte Gulf*, p. 208.
73. Prados, *Storm Over Leyte*, p. 224.
74. Thomas, *Sea of Thunder*, p. 231.
75. Robert Bostwick Carney, oral history, p. 407.
76. Halsey to Nimitz, October 6, 1944, LCMD, Halsey Papers, Box 15.
77. Radford, *From Pearl Harbor to Vietnam*, p. 40.
78. Reynolds, *The Fast Carriers*, p. 258.
79. Roland Smoot, oral history, quoted in Adams, *Witness to Power*, p. 347.
80. Commander Task Force 77 to COMINCH, "Preliminary Action Report of Engagements in Leyte Gulf and Off Samar Island on 25 October 1944," Serial 002335, November 18, 1944, FDR Library, FDR Map Room files, Box 186, enclosure: Dispatches, p. 19.
81. Action Report, USS *West Virginia*, "Action in Battle of Surigao Straits 25 October 1944," Serial 0538, November 1, 1944. Comments by Captain Herbert V. Wiley.
82. Commander Task Force 77 to COMINCH, "Preliminary Action Report of Engagements in Leyte Gulf and Off Samar Island on 25 October 1944," Serial 002335, November 18, 1944, FDR Library, FDR Map Room files, Box 186, p. 7.
83. Woodward, *The Battle for Leyte Gulf*, p. 89.
84. Tully, *Battle of Surigao Strait*, p. 84.
85. Action Report, USS *West Virginia*, "Action in Battle of Surigao Straits 25 October 1944," Serial 0538, November 1, 1944.

Chapter Six

1. Tomoo Tanaka quoted in Tully, *Battle of Surigao Strait*, p. 47.
2. Yasuo Kato quoted in ibid., p. 47.
3. Shigeru Nishino quoted in Ito, *The End of the Imperial Japanese Navy*, p. 116.
4. Bob Clarkin quoted in Sears, "Wooden Boats at War: Surigao Strait," *World War II Magazine*, Vol. 28, Issue No. 5, February 2014.
5. "Lone PT Attacked Japanese Fleet," *New York Times*, November 14, 1944.
6. Action Report, USS *West Virginia*, "Action in Battle of Surigao Straits 25 October 1944," Serial 0538, November 1, 1944.
7. Bates, U.S. Naval War College Battle Evaluation Group Report, *The Battle for Leyte Gulf*, Vol. 5, "Battle of Surigao Strait," p. 322.
8. USSBS, *Interrogations of Japanese Officials*, Nav No. 79, USSBS No. 390, Commander Shigeru Nishino, IJN.
9. Tully, *Battle of Surigao Strait*, p. 158.
10. Bates, U.S. Naval War College Battle Evaluation Group Report, *The Battle for Leyte Gulf*, Vol. 5, "Battle of Surigao Strait," p. 328.
11. Ibid., p. 395.
12. USSBS, *Interrogations of Japanese Officials*. Nav No. 79, USSBS No. 390, Commander Shigeru Nishino, IJN.
13. Tully, *Battle of Surigao Strait*, p. 185.

14. Ibid., p. 186.

15. Ibid., p. 188.

16. Smoot quoted in Morison, *History of United States Naval Operations in World War II*, Vol. 12, *Leyte*, p. 228.

17. Action Report, USS *West Virginia*, "Action in Battle of Surigao Straits 25 October 1944," Serial 0538, November 1, 1944. Comments by Captain Herbert V. Wiley.

18. Comments by commanding officer of the *Denver*, "Battle Experience: Battle of Leyte Gulf, Information Bulletin No. 22," U.S. Navy Department, March 1, 1945, p. [78–20].

19. James L. Holloway III, "Second Salvo at Surigao Strait," *Naval History* 24, No. 5, October 2010.

20. Tully, *Battle of Surigao Strait*, p. 194.

21. Comments by commanding officer of the *Daly*, "Battle Experience: Battle of Leyte Gulf, Information Bulletin No. 22," U.S. Navy Department, March 1, 1945, p. [78–24].

22. Tully, *Battle of Surigao Strait*, p. 212.

23. USSBS, *Interrogations of Japanese Officials*, Nav. No. 79, USSBS No. 390, Commander Shigeru Nishino, IJN, November 18, 1945.

24. Ibid.

25. Action Report, USS *West Virginia*, "Action in Battle of Surigao Straits 25 October 1944."

26. Bates, *The Battle for Leyte Gulf, October 1944*, Vol. 5, "Battle of Surigao Strait," p. 329.

27. Prados, *Storm Over Leyte*, p. 25.

28. Tully, *Battle of Surigao Strait*, p. 227.

29. Morison, *History of United States Naval Operations in World War II*, Vol. 12, *Leyte*, p. 240.

30. Comments by commanding officer of the *Denver*, "Battle Experience: Battle of Leyte Gulf, Information Bulletin No. 22," U.S. Navy Department, March 1, 1945, p. [78–20].

31. Tully, *Battle of Surigao Strait*, p. 239.

32. Morison, *History of United States Naval Operations in World War II*, Vol. 12, *Leyte*, p. 238.

33. James L. Holloway III, "Second Salvo at Surigao Strait," *Naval History* 24, No. 5, October 2010.

34. USSBS, *Interrogations of Japanese Officials*, Nav No. 41, USSBS No. 170, Commander Tonosuke Otani, IJN, Operations Officer on the Staff of C-in-C Second Fleet.

35. Koyanagi, "The Battle of Leyte Gulf," in Evans, ed., *The Japanese Navy in World War II*, p. 369.

36. Sprague, "The Japs Had Us on the Ropes," *American Magazine*, Vol. 139, No. 4, April 1945, p. 40.

37. Michael Bak Jr., oral history, pp. 154–55.

38. Koyanagi, "The Battle of Leyte Gulf," in Evans, ed., *The Japanese Navy in World War II*, p. 367.

39. *Yamato* action report, quoted in Lundgren, *The World Wonder'd*, p. 21.

40. Sprague, "The Japs Had Us on the Ropes," p. 40.

41. *White Plains* (CVE-66) action report, quoted in Lundgren, *The World Wonder'd*, p. 29.

42. Ibid., p. 31.

43. Ibid., p. 35.

44. Huxtable, "Composite Squadron Ten, recollections," p. 7.

45. Ibid., p. 9.

46. Captain Sugiura of the *Haguro*, quoted in Lundgren, *The World Wonder'd*, p. 57.

47. Morison, *History of United States Naval Operations in World War II*, Vol. 12, *Leyte*, p. 253.

48. Robert C. Hagen, as told to Sidney Shalett, "We Asked for the Jap Fleet—and Got It," *Saturday Evening Post*, May 26, 1945, accessed August 14, 2018, http://www.bosamar.com/pages/hagen_story.

49. Ibid.

50. Ibid.

51. Sprague, "The Japs Had Us on the Ropes," p. 40.

52. CTF 77 to COM3RDFLT, October 24, 1944, CINCPAC Gray Book, Book 5, p. 2246.

53. Halsey, "The Battle for Leyte Gulf," *Naval Institute Proceedings*, May 1952, Vol. 78/5/591.

54. Task Group 38.3 War Diary, October 25, 1944 entry.

55. Weil quoted in Buell, *Dauntless Helldivers*, p. 348.

56. Davis, *Sinking the Rising Sun*, pp. 275–76.

57. Ibid., p. 276.

58. USSBS, *Interrogations of Japanese Officials*, Nav No. 36, USSBS No. 150, Captain Toshikazu Ohmae, IJN.

59. Task Group 38.3 War Diary, October 25, 1944 entry.

60. CTF 77 to COM3RDFLT, CTF 34, in CINCPAC Gray Book, Book 5, p. 2246.

61. Halsey, "The Battle for Leyte Gulf," *Naval Institute Proceedings*, May 1952, Vol. 78/5/591.

62. Solberg, *Decision and Dissent*, p. 152.

63. CTF 77 to COM3RDFLT, CTF 34, in CINCPAC Gray Book, Book 5, p. 2246.

64. COM3RDFLT to CTG 38.1, in ibid.

65. CINCPAC Gray Book, Book 5, pp. 2246–47.

66. CTF 77 to COM3rdFLT, in ibid., p. 2247.

67. COM3rdFLT to CTG 38.1 info ALL TFC'S AND TGC'S 3rd Fleet, CTF 77, Com7thFlt, in CINCPAC Gray Book, Book 5, p. 2247.

68. CTF 77 to COM3RDFLT, in CINCPAC Gray Book, Book 5, p. 2246.

69. Charles M. Fox Jr., oral history, March 17, 1970, in *Recollections of Fleet Admiral Chester W. Nimitz*, pp. 2–3.

70. COM3RDFLT to CTF 77, in CINCPAC Gray Book, Book 5, p. 2250.

71. James Fife, oral history, CCOH Naval History Project, Vol. 2, No. 452, p. 400. According to Halsey's May 1952 article in *Proceedings*, Kinkaid radioed in plain language at 10:00: "WHERE IS LEE. SEND LEE." This despairing *cri de coeur* has been quoted frequently, but no such message appears in the CINCPAC Gray Book, and since Halsey's article loosely paraphrases several other messages, it may not be verbatim.

72. Lieutenant John Marshall quoted in Wukovits, *Admiral "Bull" Halsey*, p. 196.

73. Joseph J. Clark, oral history, p. 501.

74. Bernard Austin, oral history, p. 514.

75. Chester W. Nimitz, "Some Thoughts to Live By."

76. Bernard Austin, oral history, p. 513.

77. CINCPAC to COM3RDFLT Info COMINCH, CTF 77, in CINCPAC Gray Book, Book 5, p. 2250. Austin claims to have dictated it to a yeoman; Hedding says he watched Sherman write it. Bernard Austin, oral history, p. 514; Truman J. Hedding, oral history, pp. 97–98.

78. Potter and Nimitz, eds., *The Great Sea War*, pp. 389–90n.

79. Charles M. Fox Jr., oral history, March 17, 1970, in *Recollections of Fleet Admiral Chester W. Nimitz*, p. 3. Fox's superior officer, Ham Dow, confirmed the details in a 1959 letter: Leonard J. Dow, RADM, U.S. Navy (ret.) to E. B. Potter, January 6, 1959. "Leyte, correspondence regarding, 1958–1959," Halsey Papers.

80. Halsey, *Admiral Halsey's Story*, p. 220.

81. Drury and Clavin, *Halsey's Typhoon*, p. 49.

82. Thomas, *Sea of Thunder*, p. 300.

83. Charles M. Fox Jr., oral history, March 17, 1970, in *Recollections of Fleet Admiral Chester W. Nimitz*, p. 4.

84. Halsey to E. B. Potter, December 12, 1958, "Leyte, correspondence regarding, 1958–1959," Halsey Papers.

85. Potter, *Nimitz*, p. 593 (Nimitz's remark to the author quoted in his source notes for chapter 20).

86. Potter, *Bull Halsey*, p. 304.

87. COM3RDFLT to CTF 77 Info COM7THFLT in CINCPAC Gray Book, Book 5, p. 2250.

88. Report by Lieutenant Maurice Fred Green, Survivor of the *Hoel*, accessed October 2017, http://ussjohnston-hoel.com/6199.html.

89. Commanding officer, U.S.S. *Hoel*, "Combined Action Report and Report of Loss of U.S.S. *Hoel* (DD 533) on 25 October, 1944."

90. Matome Ugaki diary, October 25, 1944, Ugaki, *Fading Victory*, p. 493.

91. Report by Lieutenant Maurice Fred Green, Survivor of the *Hoel*, accessed October 2017, http://ussjohnston-hoel.com/6199.html.

92. Ibid.

93. Matome Ugaki diary, October 25, 1944, Ugaki, *Fading Victory*, p. 495.

94. Report by Glenn H. Parkin, Survivor of the *Hoel*, accessed October 2017, http://ussjohnston-hoel.com/6253.html.

95. Michael Bak Jr., oral history, p. 155.

96. Ibid., p. 156.

97. Robert M. Deal, personal account, USS *Johnston* Veterans Association pamphlet, p. 70.

98. "Action Report—surface engagement off Samar, P.I., 25 October 1944," USS *Johnston*, DD557/A16-3, Serial 04, November 14, 1944, submitted by "Senior Surviving Officer."

99. Robert C. Hagen, as told to Sidney Shalett, "We Asked for the Jap Fleet–and Got It." *Saturday Evening Post*, May 26, 1945.

100. Tadashi Okuno letter to the *Asahi Shinbun*, published in Gibney, ed., *Senso*, pp. 136–37.

101. USSBS, *Interrogations of Japanese Officials*, Nav No. 9, USSBS No. 47, Vice Admiral Takeo Kurita.

102. Koyanagi, "The Battle of Leyte Gulf," in Evans, ed., *The Japanese Navy in World War II*, p. 368.

103. Sprague, "The Japs Had Us on the Ropes," *American Magazine*, Vol. 139, No. 4, April 1945, p. 40.

104. CTF 77 to COM3RDFLT, etc., 250146 and 250231, CINCPAC Gray Book, Book 5, p. 2250.

105. Robert Bostwick Carney, oral history, p. 409.

106. Task Group 38.3 War Diary, October 25, 1944.

107. Ibid.

108. USSBS, *Interrogations of Japanese Officials*, Nav No. 55, USSBS No. 227, Vice Admiral Jisaburo Ozawa.

109. COM3RDFLT to CINCPAC Info etc., October 25, 1944 (251226), CINCPAC Gray Book, Book 5, p. 2256.

110. COM3RDFLT to CINCPAC, 26 October 1944 (251317). NARA, RG 38, "CNO Zero-Zero Files," Box 4, "CINCPOA Dispatches, October 1944."

111. C. Vann Woodward quoted in Shenk, ed., *Authors at Sea*, p. 232.

112. USSBS, *Interrogations of Japanese Officials*, Nav No. 9, USSBS No. 47, Vice Admiral Takeo Kurita.

113. Ibid.

114. Ibid.

115. Interrogator's notes in ibid.

116. USSBS, *Interrogations of Japanese Officials*, Nav No. 9, USSBS No. 47, Vice Admiral Takeo Kurita.

117. USSBS, *Interrogations of Japanese Officials*, Nav No. 35, USSBS No. 149, Rear Admiral Tomiji Koyanagi, IJN.

118. Ibid.; Nav No. 41, USSBS No. 170, Commander Tonosuke Otani, IJN; Matome Ugaki diary, October 25, 1944, Ugaki, *Fading Victory*, pp. 496–97.

119. Hara, *Japanese Destroyer Captain*, p. 256.

120. Ito, *The End of the Imperial Japanese Navy*, p. 100.

121. Koyanagi, "The Battle of Leyte Gulf," in Evans, ed., *The Japanese Navy in World War II*, p. 377.

122. Radford later served as chairman of the Joint Chiefs of Staff, 1953–1957. Radford, *From Pearl Harbor to Vietnam*, p. 30.

123. Halsey, *Admiral Halsey's Story*, p. 128.

124. Charles J. Moore, oral history, p. 1032.

125. Morison, *History of United States Naval Operations in World War II*, Vol. 12, *Leyte*, p. 58.

126. Third Fleet action report, Serial 0088, October 23–26, 1944, p. 5; Halsey Papers, Box 35, "Action Reports, Third Fleet, October 23–26, 1944," LCMD.

127. Truman J. Hedding, oral history, p. 101.

128. Third Fleet action report, Serial 0088, October 23–26, 1944, pp. 4–5, Halsey Papers, Box 35, "Action Reports, Third Fleet, October 23–26, 1944," LCMD.

129. Ibid.

130. MacArthur, *Reminiscences*, pp. 227–28.

131. Halsey to Nimitz, November 4, 1944, LCMD, Halsey Papers, Box 15.

132. COM3RDFLT to CINCPAC Info etc., October 25, 1944 (251226), CINCPAC Gray Book, Book 5, p. 2256.

133. Merrill, *A Sailor's Admiral*, p. 169.

134. "Admiral Halsey Reports," British Pathé newsreel archive, URN: 74239, Film ID: 2121.

135. USSBS, *Interrogations of Japanese Officials*, Nav No. 55, USSBS No. 227, Vice Admiral Jisaburo Ozawa, IJN.

136. Halsey, "The Battle for Leyte Gulf," *Naval Institute Proceedings*, May 1952, Vol. 78/5/591.

137. "Statement to the author, April 9, 1953," in Taylor, *The Magnificent Mitscher*, p. 265.

138. Letters between Halsey and Morison, and Halsey and Ralph E. Wilson, January–February 1951, in Halsey Papers, "Correspondence Files."

139. Halsey to officers, November 14, 1958, "Leyte, correspondence regarding, 1958–1959," Halsey Papers.

140. Carney to Halsey, November 14, 1958, "Leyte, correspondence regarding, 1958–1959," Halsey Papers.

141. Halsey to Prof. E. B. Potter, July 27, 1959, "The Battle of Leyte Gulf, Halsey's comments," Halsey Papers.

142. Halsey and Bryant, *Admiral Halsey's Story*, Author's Foreword, p. 1.

143. Halsey to Charlie Belknap, March 24, 1949, Halsey Papers, Box 7.

Chapter Seven

1. Wylie, "Reflections on the War in the Pacific," Naval Institute *Proceedings.*
2. USSBS, *The War Against Japanese Transportation*, pp. 32–33.
3. USSBS, *The War Against Japanese Transportation*, p. 2.
4. USSBS, *Summary Report, Pacific War*, p. 11; USSBS, *The Effects of Strategic Bombing on Japan's War Economy*, p. 176, Table C-G9.
5. USSBS, *Summary Report, Pacific War*, p. 13.
6. Robert Bostwick Carney, oral history, p. 386.
7. Halsey to Nimitz, September 28, 1944, Halsey Papers.
8. Nimitz to Halsey, October 8, 1944, Halsey Papers.
9. MacArthur radiogram to Marshall, February 2, 1944, p. 1; RG-4, Records of Headquarters, U.S. Army Forces Pacific (USAFPAC), 1942–1947, MacArthur Memorial Archives.
10. Hansell, *The Strategic Air War Against Germany and Japan*, p. 173.
11. John W. Clary, "Wartime Diary," accessed January 3, 2018, http://www.warfish .com/gaz_clary.html.
12. Beach, *Submarine!*, p. 59.
13. "Recorded interview, Commander Dudley W. Morton," September 9, 1943, Sub-Pac headquarters, Pearl Harbor. NARA, RG 38: World War II Oral Histories, Interviews and Statements, Box 20.
14. "U.S.S. *Wahoo*, Report of Fourth War Patrol," entry for March 17, 1943, *U.S.S. Wahoo (SS-238), American Submarine Patrol Reports*, p. 69.
15. "Recorded interview, Commander Dudley W. Morton," September 9, 1943, Sub-Pac headquarters, Pearl Harbor. NARA, RG 38: World War II Oral Histories, Interviews and Statements, Box 20.
16. John W. Clary MoMM1c, "Wartime Diary."
17. "U.S.S. *Wahoo*, Report of Fourth War Patrol," entry for March 25, 1943, *U.S.S. Wahoo (SS-238), American Submarine Patrol Reports*, p. 75.
18. Ibid.
19. "Recorded interview, Commander Dudley W. Morton," September 9, 1943, Sub-Pac headquarters, Pearl Harbor. NARA, RG 38, World War II Oral Histories, Interviews and Statements, Box 20.
20. "Recorded interview, Commander Dudley W. Morton," September 9, 1943, SubPac headquarters, Pearl Harbor, and *Wahoo* patrol report, March 22, 1943. NARA, RG 38: World War II Oral Histories, Interviews and Statements, Box 20.
21. "U.S.S. *Wahoo*, Report of Fourth War Patrol," entry for March 25, 1943, *U.S.S. Wahoo (SS-238), American Submarine Patrol Reports*, p. 76.
22. Beach, "Culpable Negligence," in Sears, *Eyewitness to World War II* (first published December 1980 in *American Heritage*), p. 74.
23. Blair, *Silent Victory*, p. 402.
24. Ibid., p. 403.

25. "U.S.S. *Wahoo*, Report of War Patrol Number Six," Item (O): "Health and Habitability," *U.S.S. Wahoo (SS-238), American Submarine Patrol Reports*, p. 138.

26. "Recorded interview, Commander Dudley W. Morton," September 9, 1943, SubPac headquarters, Pearl Harbor. NARA, RG 38: World War II Oral Histories, Interviews and Statements, Box 20.

27. USSBS, *The War Against Japanese Transportation*, Appendix A, p. 114.

28. CINCPAC to COMINCH, 7 November 1944, "Operations in Pacific Ocean Areas, June 1944: Part VI, Pacific Fleet Submarines," p. 18, Map Room Files, USN Action Reports, Box 183, FDR Library.

29. USSBS, *The War Against Japanese Transportation*, Appendix A, p. 114.

30. CINCPAC to CNO, "Operations in the Pacific Ocean Areas, August 1945," Serial: 034296, December 10, 1945.

31. Tillman, *Whirlwind*, p. 34.

32. Phillips Jr., *Rain of Fire*, p. 17.

33. Sweeney, *War's End*, p. 56.

34. LeMay and Kantor, *Mission with LeMay*, p. 321.

35. Ibid., p. 322.

36. Craven and Cate, eds., *The Army Air Forces in World War II*, Vol. 5, p. 546.

37. Hansell quoted in LeMay and Yenne, *Superfortress*, p. 96.

38. Hansell, *The Strategic Air War Against Germany and Japan: A Memoir*, p. 175.

39. Letter written by Charles L. Phillips Jr., quoted in Phillips Jr., *Rain of Fire*, p. 32.

40. November 4, 1944 entry, CINCPAC Gray Book, Book 5, p. 2125.

41. Marshall Chester diary, November 18–26, 1944, in Brawley, Dixon, and Trefalt, eds., *Competing Voices from the Pacific War*, p. 128.

42. NARA, RG 38, "CNO Zero-Zero Files," Box 60, Folder 21 labeled "Gen. Spaatz," entry dated November 23, 1944, in CINCPAC Gray Book, Book 5, p. 2149.

43. Hansell quoted in LeMay and Yenne, *Superfortress*, p. 101.

44. Submarine Division 102, "First Endorsement to CO *Archerfish* Conf. Ltr. SS311/16-3, Serial 013-44 dated December 15, 1944," p. 1, Item 3, appended to "U.S.S. *Archerfish*, Report of Fifth War Patrol," December 15, 1944. NARA, RG 38: U.S. Submarine War Patrol Reports, 1941–1945.

45. U.S.S. *Archerfish*, "Report of Fifth War Patrol," SS311/16-3, Serial 013–44, December 15, 1944, enclosure (A), entry for November 26, 1944, p. 7.

46. Enright and Ryan, *Sea Assault*, p. 46.

47. U.S.S. *Archerfish*, "Report of Fifth War Patrol," SS311/16-3, Serial 013–44, December 15, 1944, enclosure (A), entry for November 28, 1944, p. 8.

48. Oshima Morinari letter to the *Asahi Shinbun*, in Gibney, ed., *Senso*, p. 49.

49. Enright, *Sea Assault*, p. 95.

50. Ibid.

51. Ibid., p. 103.

52. Ibid., p. 114.

53. U.S.S. *Archerfish*, "Report of Fifth War Patrol," SS311/16-3, Serial 013–44, December 15, 1944, enclosure (A), entry for November 28, 1944, p. 9.

54. U.S.S. *Archerfish*, "Report of Fifth War Patrol," SS311/16-3, Serial 013–44, December 15, 1944, enclosure (A), entry for November 29, 1944, p. 9.

55. Enright, *Sea Assault*, p. 178.

56. Ibid., p. 183.

57. Ibid., p. 184.

58. Ibid., p. 185.

59. Ibid.

60. Ibid., pp. 186–87.

61. U.S.S. *Archerfish*, "Report of Fifth War Patrol," SS311/16-3, Serial 013–44, December 15, 1944, enclosure (A), entry for November 29, 1944, p. 10.

62. Enright, *Sea Assault*, p. 201.

63. Ibid., pp. 245–46.

Chapter Eight

1. Evans, *Wartime Sea Stories*, p. 94.

2. St. John, *Leyte Calling*, p. 195.

3. James Orvill Raines to Ray Ellen Raines, December 4, 1944, in Raines and McBride, eds., *Good Night Officially*, p. 156.

4. Commander Third Amphibious Force, CTF 79, "Report of Leyte Operation," November 13, 1944, enclosure (E).

5. Commander Third Amphibious Force, CTF 79, "Report of Leyte Operation," November 13, 1944, p. 4.

6. Eichelberger and MacKaye, *Our Jungle Road to Tokyo*, p. 170.

7. General Yoshiharu Tomochika, "The True Facts of the Leyte Operation," John Toland Papers, Box 12, FDR Library, p. 6.

8. USSBS, *Interrogations of Japanese Officials*, Nav No. 115, USSBS No. 503, Vice Admiral Shigeru Fukudome.

9. General Yoshiharu Tomochika, "The True Facts of the Leyte Operation," John Toland Papers, Box 12, FDR Library, p. 13.

10. Third Fleet War Diary, October 28, 1944.

11. COM3RDFLT to CTF 77, Info etc. (251230), CINCPAC Gray Book, Book 5, p. 2256.

12. CTF 77 to COM3RDFLT, Info etc. (260316), CINCPAC Gray Book, Book 5, p. 2258.

13. Halsey, *Admiral Halsey's Story*, p. 234.

14. COM3RDFLT to CINCSOWESPAC, Info etc. (261235), CINCPAC Gray Book, Book 5, p. 2395.

15. CINCPAC to COM3RDFLT, Info COMINCH, COMSERVPAC (261812), CINCPAC Gray Book, Book 5, p. 2395.

16. Ibid.

17. James S. Russell, oral history, p. 44.

18. Ibid.

19. Radio Tokyo broadcast, October 26, 1944, in Tolischus, *Through Japanese Eyes*, p. 157.

20. Kiyoshi Kiyosawa diary, November 14, 1944: "The army and navy competitively are loudly proclaiming special attack forces," in Kiyosawa, *A Diary of Darkness*, p. 281.

21. Imperial Japanese Navy Directive No. 482, 29 October 1944. NARA, RG 38: "Records of Japanese Navy and Related Documents," Box 42.

22. *Mainichi Shinbun*, November 1, 1944, quoted in Shillony, *Politics and Culture in Wartime Japan*, p. 97.

23. Koiso quoted in Morris, *The Nobility of Failure*, p. 300.

24. USSBS, *Interrogations of Japanese Officials*, Nav No. 115, USSBS No. 503, Vice Admiral Shigeru Fukudome.

25. Inoguchi et al., *The Divine Wind*, p. 58.

26. Lieutenant Commander Iyozo Fujita Account, in Werneth, ed., *Beyond Pearl Harbor*, p. 243.

27. Naoji Kozu, oral history, in Cook and Cook, eds., *Japan at War*, p. 315.

28. Morris, *The Nobility of Failure*, p. 296.

29. Inoguchi et al., *The Divine Wind*, p. 71.

30. Ibid., p. 72.

31. USSBS, *Interrogations of Japanese Officials*, Nav No. 115, USSBS No. 503, Vice Admiral Shigeru Fukudome.

32. USSBS, *Interrogations of Japanese Officials*, Nav No. 12, USSBS No. 62, Captain Rikibei Inoguchi; Inoguchi et al., *The Divine Wind*, p. 73.

33. Report of Captain Charlie Nelson, USNR, accessed February 16, 2018, http://destroyerhistory.org/fletcherclass.

34. Third Fleet War Diary, November 1, 1944, p. 1.

35. Third Fleet War Diary, October 27, 1944, p. 44.

36. Krueger, *From Down Under to Nippon*, p. 350.

37. CTF 77 to CINCSWPA, November 1, 1944, RS-4, MacArthur Memorial Archives, Third Fleet War Diary, November 1, 1944, p. 2.

38. Task Group 38.3 War Diary, November 5, p. 8; Third Fleet War Diary, November 1944, p. 5.

39. James Orvill Raines to Ray Ellen Raines, November 24, 1944, in Raines and McBride, eds., *Good Night Officially*, p. 139.

40. Sherrod, *On to Westward*, p. 290.

41. Buell, *The Quiet Warrior*, p. 344.

42. John Thach account, in Wooldridge, ed., *Carrier Warfare in the Pacific*, p. 265.

43. COM2NDCARTASKFORPAC to COMINCH, etc., October 23, 1944, in CINC PAC Gray Book, Book 5, p. 2391.

44. Ibid.

45. Sherrod, *On to Westward*, p. 245.

46. Reynolds, *On the Warpath in the Pacific*, p. 223.

47. Nimitz to Halsey, October 22, 1944, Halsey Papers, Box 15; Third Fleet War Diary, November 29, 1944, p. 27.

48. "COM3RDFLT to CINCPAC Info, etc.," November 28, 1944, CINCPAC Gray Book, Book 5, p. 2292.

49. CINCPAC Report, "Operations in the Pacific Ocean Areas During the Month of December 1944," June 25, 1945, p. 7.

50. John Thach account, in Wooldridge, ed., *Carrier Warfare in the Pacific*, p. 266.

51. Ibid., p. 268.

52. Halsey, *Admiral Halsey's Story*, p. 232.

53. Task Group 38.3 War Diary, November 25, 1944, pp. 31–32.

54. James J. Fahey diary, November 27, 1944, in Fahey, *Pacific War Diary 1942–1945*, p. 229.

55. Ibid.

56. Ibid., p. 230.

57. Ibid., p. 234.

58. U.S.S. *Maryland* Cruise Book, U.S. Navy Library, Washington Navy Yard, Washington, DC, pp. 31–32.

59. Memorandum to MacArthur, "Our Present Situation—Leyte Gulf, Mindoro, Lingayen Gulf," November 30, 1944, RS-4, MacArthur Memorial Archives.

60. Arthur H. McCollum, oral history, Vol. 1, pp. 527–29.

61. Eichelberger and MacKaye, *Our Jungle Road to Tokyo*, p. 170.

62. Press Release, General Headquarters, Southwest Pacific Area, November 3, 1944.

63. Arthur H. McCollum, oral history, Vol. 1, pp. 527–29.

64. MacArthur, *Reminiscences*, p. 232.

65. Task Group 38.3 War Diary, November 11, 1944, p. 16.

66. General Yoshiharu Tomochika, "The True Facts of the Leyte Operation," John Toland Papers, Box 12, FDR Library, p. 20.

67. Eugene George Anderson, "Nightmare in Ormoc Bay," *Sea Combat* magazine, accessed October 14, 2018, http://www.dd-692.com/nightmare.htm.

68. CINCPAC Report, "Operations in the Pacific Ocean Areas During the Month of December 1944," June 25, 1945, p. 40.

69. General Yoshiharu Tomochika, "The True Facts of the Leyte Operation," John Toland Papers, Box 12, FDR Library, p. 25.

70. Ibid., p. 21.

71. Huie, *From Omaha to Okinawa*, p. 211.

72. CTF 77 to CINCSWPA, December 7, 1944, CINCPAC Gray Book, Book 5, p. 2298.

73. MacArthur, *Reminiscences*, p. 233.

74. Third Fleet War Diary, December 1, 1944, p. 2.

75. Naval Debriefing, December 12, 1944: Captain Philip G. Beck, U.S. Naval Reserve, USS *Mississinewa*, NARA RG 38, Records of the Office of the Chief of Naval Operations, World War Oral Histories and Interviews," 1942–1946, Box 2, p. 2; Task Group 38.3 War Diary, November 20, p. 27.

76. Sherman, *Combat Command*, p. 272.

77. Third Fleet War Diary, November 14, 1944, p. 14.

78. Steven Jurika Jr. account, in Wooldridge, ed., *Carrier Warfare in the Pacific*, p. 251.

79. Third Fleet War Diary, December 11, 1944, p. 9.

80. Halsey, *Admiral Halsey's Story*, p. 236.

81. Third Fleet War Diary, December 14–16, 1944; CINCPAC Report, "Operations in the Pacific Ocean Areas During the Month of December 1944," June 25, 1945, p. 9.

82. CINCPAC Report, "Operations in the Pacific Ocean Areas During the Month of December 1944," June 25, 1945, p. 39.

83. J. Bryan III diary, February 24, 1945, in Bryan, *Aircraft Carrier*, p. 39.

84. Third Fleet War Diary, December 17, 1944, p. 17.

85. Radford, *From Pearl Harbor to Vietnam*, p. 32.

86. Robert Bostwick Carney, oral history, p. 418.

87. Third Fleet War Diary, December 17, 1944, p. 23.

88. Robert Bostwick Carney, oral history, p. 417.

89. CINCPAC Report, "Operations in the Pacific Ocean Areas During the Month of December 1944," June 25, 1945, p. 13.

90. Third Fleet War Diary, December 18, 1944, p. 27.

91. Ibid., p. 30.

92. Ibid., p. 31; CINCPAC Report, "Operations in the Pacific Ocean Areas During the Month of December 1944," June 25, 1945, p. 13.

93. Third Fleet War Diary, December 18, 1944, p. 31.

94. CINCPAC Report, "Operations in the Pacific Ocean Areas During the Month of December 1944," June 25, 1945, Annex B, "The December Typhoon," p. 75.

95. Robert Bostwick Carney, oral history, p. 418.

96. Radford, *From Pearl Harbor to Vietnam*, p. 34.

97. CINCPAC Report, "Operations in the Pacific Ocean Areas During the Month of December 1944," June 25, 1945, Annex B, "The December Typhoon," p. 82.

98. Ibid.

99. Joseph Conrad, "Typhoon," accessed December 14, 2017, http://www.gutenberg.org/files/1142/.

100. Olson, *Tales from a Tin Can*, pp. 226–27.

101. CINCPAC Report, "Operations in the Pacific Ocean Areas During the Month of December 1944," June 25, 1945, Annex B, "The December Typhoon," p. 73.

102. Ibid., p. 75.

103. Radford, *From Pearl Harbor to Vietnam*, p. 36.

104. CINCPAC Report, "Operations in the Pacific Ocean Areas During the Month of December 1944," June 25, 1945, Annex B, "The December Typhoon," p. 73.

105. Third Fleet War Diary, December 20, 1944, p. 37.
106. Third Fleet War Diary, December 19, 1944, p. 36.
107. CINCPAC Report, "Operations in the Pacific Ocean Areas During the Month of December 1944," June 25, 1945, Annex B, "The December Typhoon," p. 85.
108. COM3RDFLT to CINCPAC, December 19, 1944, in CINCPAC Gray Book, Book 5, p. 2462; ibid., p. 13.
109. Third Fleet War Diary, December 24, 1944, p. 41.
110. Halsey, *Admiral Halsey's Story*, p. 241.
111. Gerald F. Bogan, oral history, p. 126.
112. Truman J. Hedding, oral history, p. 103.
113. Ibid., p. 105.
114. Third Fleet War Diary, December 28, 1944, p. 42.
115. Truman J. Hedding, oral history, p. 104.
116. Nimitz, "Pacific Fleet Confidential Letter 14CL–45," February 13, 1945, "Damage in Typhoon, Lessons of," CINCPAC File A2-11 L11-1.

Chapter Nine

1. James Orvill Raines to Ray Ellen Raines, September 16, 1944, Raines and McBride, eds., *Good Night Officially*, p. 74.
2. Sledge, *With the Old Breed*, p. 266.
3. Willard Waller, "Why Veterans Are Bitter," *American Mercury*, August 1945, p. 147.
4. Ibid.
5. "Boos" for the flag are recalled by Walter R. Evans. He also describes the attitudes of his shipmates on the repair ship *Vestal* toward "Hollywood phonyism." Evans, *Wartime Sea Stories*, p. 38.
6. Hunt, *Coral Comes High*, p. 21.
7. U.S. Commerce Department, *Historical Statistics of the United States*, Chapter F, "National Income and Wealth," Series F 1–5. In current prices, $99.7 billion in 1940, rising to $210.1 billion in 1944; in 1958 prices, $227.2 billion in 1940, rising to $361.3 billion in 1944.
8. The latter figure comes to $31.66 billion in 1940 terms. U.S. Commerce Department, *Historical Statistics of the United States*, Series F 540–551, "National Saving, by Major Saver Groups, in Current Prices, 1897 to 1945."
9. Blum, *V Was For Victory*, p. 98.
10. John Kenneth Galbraith, oral history; Terkel, ed., *"The Good War,"* p. 323.
11. Winkler, *Home Front U.S.A.*, p. 45.
12. Marjorie Cartwright, oral history, in Harris, Mitchell, and Schechter, eds., *The Homefront*, pp. 190–91.
13. U.S. Commerce Department, *Historical Statistics of the United States*, Series N1–29, "Value of New Private and Public Construction Put in Place: 1915 to 1970."

14. Lerner, *Public Journal*, pp. 28–29.

15. Baime, *The Arsenal of Democracy*, p. 247.

16. Don McFadden, oral history, Terkel, ed., *"The Good War,"* p. 148.

17. Perret, *Days of Sadness, Years of Triumph*, p. 315.

18. Reid, *The Brazen Age*, p. 8.

19. "Navy Officer Says Teamsters Hit Him," *New York Times*, October 3, 1944, p. 15.

20. Ibid.

21. "Dickins v. International Brotherhood, Etc., 171 F.2d 21 (D.C. Cir. 1948)," October 18, 1948, United States Court of Appeals District of Columbia Circuit.

22. Blum, *V Was For Victory*, p. 297.

23. The "Mead Report" quoted in Cooke, *The American Home Front*, p. 300.

24. Perret, *Days of Sadness, Years of Triumph*, p. 399.

25. Peggy Terry, oral history, Terkel, ed., *"The Good War,"* p. 112.

26. Eisenhower to FDR, March 31, 1945, FDR Library.

27. King/Marshall letter to FDR, January 1945, excerpted in "Letters on the Pressing Manpower Problem," *New York Times*, January 18, 1945.

28. "Curfew Used to Teach 'War Awareness' Lesson," *New York Times*, February 25, 1945, p. 67.

29. Yoder, *There's No Front Like Home*, p. 115.

30. Hunt, *Coral Comes High*, p. 21.

31. Elliot Johnson account, in Harris, Mitchell, and Schechter, eds., *The Homefront*, p. 198.

32. Marjorie Cartwright account, in Harris, Mitchell, and Schechter, eds., *The Homefront*, pp. 190–91.

33. U.S. Navy Department, "Annual Report, Fiscal Year 1944, Secretary of the Navy James Forrestal to the President of the United States," p. 15, Hopkins Papers, Group 24, FDR Library.

34. Reynolds, *The Fast Carriers*, p. 324.

35. Delaney, "Corpus Christi: University of the Air," *Naval History* 27, no. 3, June 2013, p. 37.

36. Davis, *Sinking the Rising Sun*, p. 42.

37. Smyth, *Sea Stories*, p. 39.

38. Buell, *Dauntless Helldivers*, p. 26.

39. Davis, *Sinking the Rising Sun*, p. 72.

40. Portz, "Aviation Training and Expansion," *Naval Aviation News*, July–August 1990, p. 24.

41. Baker, *Growing Up*, p. 216.

42. Davis, *Sinking the Rising Sun*, p. 61.

43. Ibid., p. 67.

44. Hynes, *Flights of Passage*, p. 69.

45. Smyth, *Sea Stories*, p. 48.

46. Buell, *Dauntless Helldivers*, p. 39

47. MacWhorter and Stout, *The First Hellcat Ace*, p. 134.

48. Vernon, *Hostile Sky*, p. 99.
49. Davis, *Sinking the Rising Sun*, p. 44.
50. Hynes, *Flights of Passage*, p. 60.
51. Lieutenant William A. Bell, "Under the Nips' Nose," pp. 12–13.
52. Third Fleet War Diary, January 7, 1945, p. 8.
53. Halsey, *Admiral Halsey's Story*, p. 195.
54. Third Fleet War Diary, January 11, 1945, p. 11.
55. William A. Bell Diary, January 12, 1945, p. 7.
56. Halsey, *Admiral Halsey's Story*, p. 198.
57. Lieutenant William A. Bell, "Under the Nips' Nose," p. 24.
58. Ibid., p. 23.
59. Sherman, *Combat Command*, p. 279; Clark and Reynolds, *Carrier Admiral*, p. 196.
60. Third Fleet War Diary, January 19, 1945, p. 18.
61. Ibid., p. 21.
62. William A. Bell Diary, January 21, 1945, pp. 17–18.

Chapter Ten

1. A 30 percent loss rate is estimated by Rikihei Inoguchi in *The Divine Wind*, p. 87.
2. Ibid., p. 88.
3. Marsden, *Attack Transport*, p. 153.
4. MacArthur, *Reminiscences*, p. 240.
5. James Orvill Raines to Ray Ellen Raines, January 15, 1945, Raines and McBride, eds., *Good Night Officially*, p. 204.
6. Marsden, *Attack Transport*, p. 155.
7. MacArthur, *Reminiscences*, p. 241.
8. Herman, *Douglas MacArthur: American Warrior*, p. 570.
9. Krueger, *From Down Under to Nippon*, p. 228.
10. Japanese Monograph 114, "Philippine Area Naval Operations, Part IV," January–August 1945, pp. 30–31.
11. GHQ, SWPA, Communique No. 1027, January 29, 1945, quoted in *Reports of General MacArthur*, vol. 1, p. 270.
12. Smith, *United States Army in WWII, The War in the Pacific*, p. 219.
13. Dunn, *Pacific Microphone*, p. 279.
14. Carl Mydans, "My God, It's Carl Mydans!," *Life*, February 19, 1945, in *Reporting World War II, Part Two*, p. 607.
15. Dunn, *Pacific Microphone*, p. 293.
16. Robin Prising quoted in Scott, *Rampage*, p. 188.
17. Carl Mydans, "My God, It's Carl Mydans!," *Life*, February 19, 1945, in *Reporting World War II, Part Two*, p. 616.
18. MacArthur, *Reminiscences*, p. 247.
19. Bill Dunn's CBS Radio Broadcast, February 4, 1945, quoted in Scott, *Rampage*, p. 170.

20. Scott, *Rampage*, p. 198.

21. Sworn Affidavit of Hobert D. Mason of the 112th Medical Battalion, "Report on Destruction of Manila and Japanese Atrocities, February 1945," U.S. Army Forces, Southwest Pacific Area, Military Intelligence Section, Bonner Fellers Papers, Box 2, Hoover Institution Archives.

22. Sworn affidavit, Major David V. Binkley, U.S. Army, "Report on Destruction of Manila and Japanese Atrocities, February 1945," U.S. Army Forces, Southwest Pacific Area, Military Intelligence Section, Bonner Fellers Papers, Box 2, Hoover Institution Archives.

23. MacArthur, *Reminiscences*, p. 248.

24. Borneman, *MacArthur At War*, p. 467.

25. Eichelberger and MacKaye, *Our Jungle Road to Tokyo*, p. 176.

26. Scott, *Rampage*, p. 205.

27. Japanese Monograph 114, "Philippine Area Naval Operations, Part IV," January–August 1945, "Battle of Manila, First Phase," p. 12.

28. "Directions Concerning Combat by Shimbu Group Headquarters," in "Documents and Orders Captured in the Field," accessed October 11, 2018, http://battleofmanila.org.

29. "Report on Destruction of Manila and Japanese Atrocities, February 1945," p. 1, U.S. Army Forces, Southwest Pacific Area, Military Intelligence Section, Bonner Fellers Papers, Box 2, Hoover Institution Archives.

30. Japanese Monograph 114, "Philippine Area Naval Operations, Part IV," January–August 1945, p. 15.

31. Scott, *Rampage*, p. 248.

32. H. O. Eaton Jr., "Assault Tactics Employed as Exemplified by the Battle of Manila, A Report by XIV Corps."

33. Scott, *Rampage*, p. 317.

34. Ibid., p. 350.

35. Dunn, *Pacific Microphone*, p. 313.

36. Captured diary, unknown soldier of Ninth Shipping Engineer Regiment, Japanese Army, "Report on Destruction of Manila and Japanese Atrocities, February 1945," U.S. Army Forces, Southwest Pacific Area, Military Intelligence Section, Bonner Fellers Papers, Box 2, Hoover Institution Archives.

37. Ibid., p. 4.

38. Ibid., p. 3.

39. Sworn affidavits of Father Francis J. Cosgrave and Major David V. Binkley, U.S. Army Forces, "Report on Destruction of Manila and Japanese Atrocities, February 1945," in ibid.

40. Sworn affidavit, Dr. Walter K. Funkel, "Report on Destruction of Manila and Japanese Atrocities, February 1945," U.S. Army Forces, Southwest Pacific Area, Military Intelligence Section. Bonner Fellers Papers, Box 2, Hoover Institution Archives.

41. Scott, *Rampage*, p. 25.
42. Ibid., p. 263.
43. Ibid., p. 309.
44. Admiral Sanji Iwabuchi to Shimbu Group headquarters, Japanese Monograph 114, "Philippine Area Naval Operations, Part IV," January–August 1945, pp. 18–19.
45. Admiral Sanji Iwabuchi to C-in-C, Southwest Area Fleet at Baguio, Japanese Monograph 114, "Philippine Area Naval Operations, Part IV," January–August 1945, p. 18.
46. McEnery, *The XIV Corps Battle for Manila, February 1945*, p. 98.
47. "Intramuros a City of Utter Horror," George E. Jones, *New York Times*, February 25, 1945, p. 25.
48. Quoted in Friend, *The Blue-Eyed Enemy*, p. 205.
49. H. O. Eaton Jr., "Assault Tactics Employed as Exemplified by the Battle of Manila, A Report by XIV Corps."
50. MacArthur, *Reminiscences*, p. 247.
51. Ibid., p. 252.
52. Ibid., pp. 251–52, and newsreel footage, "Ceremony at Malacañang Palace," February 27, 1945, accessed July 20, 2018, http://www.criticalpast.com/video/65675037789_Sergio-Osmena_General-MacArthur_Commonwealth-Government_legislature.
53. MacArthur, *Reminiscences*, p. 250.
54. Romulo, *I See the Philippines Rise*, p. 223.
55. "Report on Destruction of Manila and Japanese Atrocities, February 1945," p. 1, U.S. Army Forces, Southwest Pacific Area, Military Intelligence Section, Bonner Fellers Papers, Box 2, Hoover Institution Archives.
56. "Imperial Rescript to Soldiers and Sailors (1882)," p. 227, in Allinson, ed., *The Columbia Guide to Modern Japanese History*.
57. Scott, *Rampage*, p. 265.
58. "Digest of Japanese Broadcasts," March 9, 1945, p. 2.
59. Takamaro Nishihara letter to the *Asahi Shinbun*, in Gibney, ed., *Senso*, p. 157.
60. Kiyofumi Kojima, oral history, in Cook and Cook, eds., *Japan at War*, p. 376.
61. Ibid., p. 378.
62. MacArthur, *Reminiscences*, p. 261.
63. Reported in 1964 by the Japan Ministry of Health and Welfare, cited by Cook and Cook, eds., *Japan at War*, p. 373.

Chapter Eleven

1. Kakehashi and Murray, *So Sad to Fall in Battle*, p. 18.
2. Sakai, Caidin, and Saito, *Samurai!*, p. 235.
3. Kakehashi and Murray, *So Sad to Fall in Battle*, p. 66.

4. Major Yoshitaka Horie, unpublished manuscript, "Iwo Jima," John Toland Papers, Series 1: *The Rising Sun*, Box 6, p. 78.

5. Major Yoshitaka Horie, unpublished manuscript, "Iwo Jima," John Toland Papers, Series 1: *The Rising Sun*, Box 6, p. 63.

6. Private Shuji Ishii quoted in Kakehashi, *So Sad to Fall in Battle*, p. 66.

7. King and Ryan, *A Tomb Called Iwo Jima*, p. 30.

8. Kakehashi and Murray, *So Sad to Fall in Battle*, p. 68.

9. Letters quoted in Kakehashi and Murray, *So Sad to Fall in Battle*, p. 93.

10. Major Yoshitaka Horie, unpublished manuscript, "Iwo Jima," John Toland Papers, Series 1: Box 6, p. 78.

11. Japanese soldier's diary, entry dated February 18, 1945, in Dixon, Brawley, and Trefalt, eds., *Competing Voices from the Pacific War*, p. 140.

12. Fields quoted in Alexander, *Closing In*, p. 31.

13. Kakehashi and Murray, *So Sad to Fall in Battle*, p. 39.

14. Tsuruji Akikuisa quoted in King and Ryan, *A Tomb Called Iwo Jima*, p. 111.

15. Toshiharu Takahashi quoted in Kakehashi and Murray, *So Sad to Fall in Battle*, pp. 101–2.

16. Bruce and Leonard, *Crommelin's Thunderbirds*, p. 30.

17. Buell, *The Quiet Warrior*, p. 356.

18. "Air Combat Notes for Pilots," Enclosure (C) of Action Report, Commander Task Force 58, Operations of February 10 to March 1, 1945, Serial 0045, pp. 2–3.

19. Roy W. Bruce quoted in Bruce and Leonard, *Crommelin's Thunderbirds*, p. 35.

20. "Areological Summary for Action Report," Enclosure (G) of Action Report, Commander Task Force 58, February 10 to March 1, 1945, Serial 0045.

21. J. Bryan III diary, February 16, 1945, Bryan, *Aircraft Carrier*, p. 10.

22. McWhorter, *The First Hellcat Ace*, p. 152.

23. Bruce and Leonard, *Crommelin's Thunderbirds*, p. 52.

24. Fifth Fleet War Diary, February 17, 1945, p. 2.

25. Ensign John Morris quoted in Bruce and Leonard, *Crommelin's Thunderbirds*, p. 51.

26. Sheftall, *Blossoms in the Wind*, p. 180.

27. "Air Combat Notes for Pilots," Enclosure (C) of Action Report, Commander Task Force 58, February 10 to March 1, 1945, Serial 0045, p. 3.

28. Action Report, Commander Task Force 58, February 10 to March 1, 1945, Serial 0045, March 13, 1945, p. 25.

29. William W. Buchanan, oral history, pp. 78–79.

30. Sherrod, *On to Westward*, p. 169.

31. Lieutenant Ronald D. Thomas, unpublished written account, PC # 2718, p. 16, U.S. Marine Corps Archive, Quantico, Virginia.

32. Smith, *Coral and Brass*, p. 214.

33. Charles F. Barber, Interview by Evelyn M. Cherpak, March 1, 1996, p. 18, Naval War College Archives.

34. Sherrod, *On to Westward*, p. 154.

35. Elton N. Shrode, unpublished written account, Coll. 3736, p. 15, U.S. Marine Corps Archive, Quantico, Virginia.

36. Lieutenant Ronald D. Thomas, unpublished written account, PC # 2718, p. 16, U.S. Marine Corps Archive.

37. Vernon E. Megee, oral history, p. 34.

38. Corporal Edward Hartman quoted in Alexander, *Closing In*, p. 12.

39. Sherrod, *On to Westward*, p. 170.

40. Smith, *Coral and Brass*, p. 224.

41. Lieutenant Colonel Justice M. Chambers quoted in Alexander, *Closing In*, p. 14.

42. Sherrod, *On to Westward*, p. 176.

43. Smith, *Coral and Brass*, p. 225.

44. King and Ryan, *A Tomb Called Iwo Jima*, p. 122.

45. James Orvill Raines to Ray Ellen Raines, February 22, 1945, in Raines and McBride, eds., *Good Night Officially*, p. 238.

46. Sherrod, *On to Westward*, p. 192.

47. Major Yoshitaka Horie, unpublished manuscript, "Iwo Jima," John Toland Papers, Series 1: *The Rising Sun*, Box 6.

48. Lieutenant Ronald D. Thomas, unpublished written account, PC # 2718, p. 18, U.S. Marine Corps Archive.

49. Leo D. Hermle, oral history, p. 86.

50. Smith and Finch, *Coral and Brass*, p. 227.

51. Ibid., p. 228.

52. Forrestal diary, February 23, 1945, in Millis, ed., *The Forrestal Diaries*, p. 30.

53. Sherrod, *On to Westward*, p. 192.

54. Smith and Finch, *Coral and Brass*, p. 230.

55. Joseph L. Stewart, oral history, pp. 39–40.

56. John Lardner, "D-Day, Iwo Jima," *New Yorker*, March 17, 1945, p. 48.

57. Sherrod, *On to Westward*, p. 196.

58. Ted Allenby, oral history, Terkel, ed., *"The Good War,"* p. 181.

59. Elton N. Shrode, unpublished written account, Coll. 3736, p. 16, U.S. Marine Corps Archive.

60. Edward A. Craig, oral history, p. 142.

61. Elton N. Shrode, unpublished written account, Coll. 3736, p. 19, U.S. Marine Corps Archive.

62. Sherrod, *On to Westward*, p. 182.

63. Bradley, *Flags of Our Fathers*, p. 268.

64. James Orvill Raines to Ray Ellen Raines, February 22, 1945, in Raines and McBride, eds., *Good Night Officially*, pp. 239–40.

65. Vernon E. Megee, oral history, p. 37.

66. Ibid., p. 46.

67. Sherrod, *On to Westward*, p. 195.

68. King and Ryan, *A Tomb Called Iwo Jima*, p. 131.

69. Kakehashi and Murray, *So Sad to Fall in Battle*, p. 156.

70. Elton N. Shrode, unpublished written account, Coll. 3736, p. 16, U.S. Marine Corps Archive.

71. *Experiences in Battle of the Medical Department of the Navy*, Navmed P-SOS1, U.S. Department of the Navy, 1953, p. 95.

72. Sherrod, *On to Westward*, p. 187.

73. Ibid., p. 219.

74. *Experiences in Battle of the Medical Department of the Navy*, 1953, p. 101.

75. Griffin, *Out of Carnage*, p. 13.

76. Sherrod, *On to Westward*, p. 188.

77. Ibid., p. 213.

78. Smith and Finch, *Coral and Brass*, p. 238.

79. Kakehashi and Murray, *So Sad to Fall in Battle*, p. 165.

80. Major Yoshitaka Horie, unpublished manuscript, "Iwo Jima," John Toland Papers, Box 6, p. 93.

81. Kakehashi and Murray, *So Sad to Fall in Battle*, p. xviii.

82. Ibid., p. xx.

83. Major Yoshitaka Horie, unpublished manuscript, "Iwo Jima," John Toland Papers, Box 6, p. 99.

84. Bartley, *Iwo Jima: Amphibious Epic*, p. 192.

85. Miller, *It's Tomorrow Out Here*, p. 180.

86. Galer quoted in Alexander, *Closing In*, p. 49.

87. Alexander, *Closing In*, p. 49.

88. Smith and Finch, *Coral and Brass*, p. 15.

89. Sherrod, *On to Westward*, p. 235.

90. Quoted in *San Bernardino Sun*, Vol. 51, February 28, 1945, p. 1.

91. William W. Buchanan, oral history, p. 79.

Chapter Twelve

1. Arnold signed Marshall COMGENAAFPOA to Richardson for Harmon Info CINCPOA, December 7, 1944, CINCPAC Gray Book, Book 5, p. 2444.

2. "Those Who Witnessed Series—How Civilians Viewed the War," NHK television documentary, accessed January 4, 2019, https://www.youtube.com/watch?v=lHJH2UzYrLw; Okumiya, Horikoshi, and Caiden, *Zero!*, p. 257.

3. "War History of the 5th Air Fleet," February 10, 1945, to August 19, 1945, Library of Congress, Japanese Monograph Series, No. 86.

4. Sakai, Caidin, and Saito, *Samurai!*, p. 264.

5. John Ciardi, oral history, Terkel, ed., *"The Good War,"* pp. 201–2.

6. Ibid., p. 201.

7. Sherrod, *On to Westward*, p. 152.

8. Hansell, *The Strategic Air War Against Germany and Japan*, p. 217.
9. Ibid., p. 215.
10. Matsuo Kato quoted in *Time-Life* Books, *Japan at War*, p. 157.
11. Yamashita, *Daily Life in Wartime Japan*, p. 100.
12. Michio Takeyama essay in Minear, ed., *The Scars of War*, p. 62.
13. Kiyoshi Kiyosawa diary, January 2, 1945, Kiyosawa, *A Diary of Darkness*, p. 300.
14. "Let There Be a People of 100 Million Heroes," *Mainichi Shinbun*, January 2, 1945, quoted in Kiyosawa, *A Diary of Darkness*, p. 300.
15. *Asahi Shinbun* headlines on January 15 & 16, 1945, quoted in Kiyosawa, *A Diary of Darkness*, p. 307.
16. Sakai, Caidin, and Saito, *Samurai!*, p. 243.
17. Kiyoshi Kiyosawa diary, March 29, 1945, Kiyosawa, *A Diary of Darkness*, p. 339.
18. USSBS, *The Effects of Strategic Bombing on Japanese Morale*, p. 1.
19. Ibid., p. 26.
20. Havens, *Valley of Darkness*, p. 158.
21. Quoted in Cook and Cook, eds., *Japan at War*, p. 337.
22. Quoted in *Time-Life* Books, *Japan at War*, p. 44.
23. Statement, Cabinet Board of Information, December 22, 1943, quoted in USSBS, *The Effects of Strategic Bombing on Japanese Morale*, p. 73n1.
24. Havens, *Valley of Darkness*, p. 162; "Digest of Japanese Broadcasts," October 6, 1944, p. 2.
25. Havens, *Valley of Darkness*, p. 165.
26. Yamashita, *Daily Life in Wartime Japan*, p. 122.
27. Koiso address to Japanese National Diet, quoted in "Digest of Japanese Broadcasts," September 8, 1944, p. 4.
28. Cook and Cook, eds., *Japan at War*, p. 173.
29. Hideo Sato, oral history, Cook and Cook, eds., *Japan at War*, p. 236.
30. "Digest of Japanese Broadcasts," October 4, 1944 memo cited in broadcast of October 11, 1944, p. 3.
31. Mihoko Nakane, diary entries, April–June 1945, Yamashita, ed., *Leaves from an Autumn of Emergencies*, pp. 268–305.
32. Naokata Sasaki, oral history, Cook and Cook, eds., *Japan at War*, p. 468.
33. Hideo Sato, oral history, Cook and Cook, eds., *Japan at War*, p. 237.
34. Mihoko Nakane diary, June 17, 1945, Yamashita, ed., *Leaves from an Autumn of Emergencies*, p. 289.
35. War Diary, Guam Island Commander, March 1945 summary, pp. 5–9, NARA, RG-38: Records of the Office of the Chief of Naval Operations, World War II War Diaries, Box 53.
36. Pyle, *Last Chapter*, p. 19.
37. Welfare Office Monthly Report, pp. 2–6, in War Diary, Guam Island Commander, March 1945, NARA, RG-38: Records of the Office of the Chief of Naval Operations, World War II War Diaries, Box 53.

38. Dos Passos, *Tour of Duty*, p. 73.
39. Ibid.
40. War Diary, Guam Island Commander, March 1945, p. 4, NARA, RG-38: Records of the Office of the Chief of Naval Operations, World War II War Diaries, Box 53.
41. LeMay and Kantor, *Mission with LeMay*, pp. 340–42.
42. Truman J. Hedding, oral history, p. 108; Lamar, "I Saw Stars," p. 12.
43. LeMay and Yenne, *Superfortress*, p. 110.
44. LeMay and Kantor, *Mission with LeMay*, p. 342.
45. Ibid., pp. 341–42.
46. Message 221837, Arnold (signed Marshall) to Richardson, Harmon, and Nimitz, December 22, 1944, in CINCPAC Gray Book, Book 5, p. 2471.
47. CINCPOA PEARL to COMGENPOA, COMGENAAFPOA, DEPCOM 20THAF, etc., March 28, 1945, CINCPAC Gray Book, Book 6, green pages, p. 2808.
48. Edwards to King, November 14, 1944; NARA, RG 38, "CNO Zero-Zero Files," Box 60, Folder 21, labeled "General Spaatz."
49. Straubel, *Air Force Diary*, p. 450.
50. McKelway and Gopnik, *Reporting at Wit's End*, p. 177.
51. LeMay and Kantor, *Mission with LeMay*, p. 349.
52. Selden, "A Forgotten Holocaust," *Asia–Pacific Journal*, Vol. 5, Issue 5, May 2, 2007.
53. Ralph, "Improvised Destruction," *War in History*, Vol. 13, No. 4, October 2006, p. 498.
54. Tanaka, Tanaka, and Young, *Bombing Civilians: A Twentieth-Century History*, p. 81.
55. Parker, *The Second World War: A Short History*, p. 170.
56. LeMay and Yenne, *Superfortress*, p. 125.
57. Ibid., p. 122.
58. McKelway and Gopnik, *Reporting at Wit's End*, p. 185.
59. LeMay and Kantor, *Mission with LeMay*, p. 312.
60. Ibid., pp. 351–52.
61. Ibid., p. 349.
62. Fedman and Karacas, "A Cartographic Fade to Black," *Journal of Historical Geography*, Vol. 38, Issue 3, July 2012, pp. 306–28.
63. Caidin, *A Torch to the Enemy*, p. 75.
64. Phillips, *Rain of Fire*, p. 37.
65. Pyle, *Last Chapter*, p. 29.
66. LeMay and Yenne, *Superfortress*, p. 122.
67. Phillips, *Rain of Fire*, p. 48.
68. McKelway and Gopnik, *Reporting at Wit's End*, p. 192.
69. Phillips, *Rain of Fire*, p. 41.

70. Ibid., p. 42.
71. Ibid., p. 37.
72. Caidin, *A Torch to the Enemy*, p. 120.
73. Phillips, *Rain of Fire*, p. 44.
74. "Deadly WWII U.S. firebombing raids on Japanese cities largely ignored."
75. Caidin, *A Torch to the Enemy*, p. 111.
76. Auer, ed., *From Marco Polo Bridge to Pearl Harbor*, pp. 196–97.
77. Kazuyo Funato, oral history, Cook and Cook, eds., *Japan at War*, p. 346.
78. Michiko Okubo letter to the *Asahi Shinbun*, Gibney, ed., *Senso*, pp. 207–8.
79. Isamu Kase quoted in "Deadly WWII U.S. firebombing raids on Japanese cities largely ignored."
80. Hiroyasu Kobayashi, oral history, Cook and Cook, eds., *Japan at War*, p. 351.
81. Ibid., p. 352.
82. Kazuyo Funato, oral history, Cook and Cook, eds., *Japan at War*, p. 347.
83. Tomoko Shinoda letter to the *Asahi Shinbun*, Gibney, ed., *Senso*, p. 205.
84. Ibid.
85. Caidin, *A Torch to the Enemy*, p. 141.
86. Sumi Ogawa letter to the *Asahi Shinbun*, Gibney, ed., *Senso*, p. 204.
87. "Deadly WWII U.S. firebombing raids on Japanese cities largely ignored."
88. Caidin, *A Torch to the Enemy*, p. 143.
89. Auer, ed., *From Marco Polo Bridge to Pearl Harbor*, p. 195.
90. USSBS, *The Effects of Strategic Bombing on Japanese Morale*, p. 37.
91. *Asahi Shinbun* quoted in Cook and Cook, eds., *Japan at War*, pp. 340–42.
92. McKelway and Gopnik, *Reporting at Wit's End*, p. 190.
93. Caidin, *A Torch to the Enemy*, p. 78.
94. McKelway and Gopnik, *Reporting at Wit's End*, p. 194.
95. Phillips, *Rain of Fire*, p. 45.
96. LeMay and Kantor, *Mission with LeMay*, p. 354.
97. Caidin, *A Torch to the Enemy*, p. 154.
98. LeMay and Kantor, *Mission with LeMay*, p. 368.
99. USSBS, *The Effects of Strategic Bombing on Japanese Morale*, p. 123.
100. Naruo Shirai letter to the *Asahi Shinbun*, Gibney, ed., *Senso*, p. 206.

Chapter Thirteen

1. Clark and Reynolds, *Carrier Admiral*, p. 213; USS *Randolph*, CV-15, "Action Report, Attack by Enemy Plane at Ulithi, 11–12 March 1945," CV-15 A6-3 Serial: 004; Fifth Fleet War Diary, March 11, 1945, p. 10; CO *Randolph* to Com5thFlt, March 14, 1945, CINCPAC Gray Book, Book 6, green pages, p. 2793.
2. 5th Air Fleet War Diary (Japanese Monograph No. 86), entry dated March 11, 1945, p. 18.
3. Clark and Reynolds, *Carrier Admiral*, pp. 213–14.

4. Commander Task Force 58 to CINCPAC, Report of Operations of Task Force 58 in support of landings at Okinawa, 14 March Through 28 May, 1945, A16-3 Serial: 00222, 18 June 1945.

5. Combined Fleet Telegram Order No. 564-B, reproduced in Ugaki, *Fading Victory*, p. 553.

6. IGHQ Navy Directive No. 510, dated March 1, 1945, p. 157, NARA, RG 38, Imperial Gen. HQ Navy Directives, in "Records of Japanese Navy & Related Documents," Vol. 2, No. 316, Box 42.

7. 5th Air Fleet War Diary (Japanese Monograph No. 86) entry dated March 18, 1945, p. 23; Ugaki, *Fading Victory*, p. 527.

8. Commander Task Force 58 to CINCPAC, "Report of Operations of Task Force 58 in Support of Landings at Okinawa, 14 March through 28 May, 1945," A16-3 Serial: 00222, 18 June 1945.

9. Ibid.

10. Commander Joe Taylor, Executive Officer, "Narrative of Action 19 March 1945," Enclosure C, USS *Franklin* (CV-13) Action Report, Serial 00212, 11 April 1945, FDR Library Map Room, Box 191.

11. Radford and Jurika, *From Pearl Harbor to Vietnam*, p. 46.

12. J. Bryan III diary, March 19, 1945, Bryan, *Aircraft Carrier*, p. 78.

13. Commander Fifth Fleet War Diary, March 19, 1945, p. 18.

14. Potter and Nimitz, *The Great Sea War*, p. 449.

15. COM5THFLT to CINCPAC, March 21, 1945, CINCPAC Gray Book, Book 6, green pages, p. 2797.

16. J. Bryan III diary, April 2, 1945, Bryan, *Aircraft Carrier*, p. 105.

17. Dyer, *The Amphibians Came to Conquer*, p. 1078.

18. CTF 58 to CTF 51, March 25, 1945, CINCPAC Gray Book, Book 6, green pages, p. 2801.

19. Charles F. Barber, oral history, p. 6, Interview by Evelyn M. Cherpak, March 1, 1996, U.S. Naval War College Archives.

20. Michael Bak Jr., oral history, U.S. Naval Institute, 1988, p. 192.

21. Mace and Allen, *Battleground Pacific*, p. 223.

22. Sledge, *With the Old Breed*, p. 179.

23. Ibid., p. 185.

24. Dyer, *The Amphibians Came to Conquer*, p. 1094.

25. Morison, *History of United States Naval Operations in World War II*, Vol. 14, *Victory in the Pacific*, p. 149.

26. U.S. Department of Defense, Department of the Army, Center of Military History, *Ryukyus: The U.S. Army Campaigns of World War II*, p. 11.

27. Sledge, *With the Old Breed*, p. 187.

28. Lardner, "Suicides and Bushwhackers," *New Yorker*, May 19, 1945, p. 32.

29. CTF 51 [Turner] to COM5THFLT [Spruance], April 1, 1945, CINCPAC Gray Book, Book 6, green pages, pp. 2810–11.

30. Yahara, *The Battle for Okinawa*, p. xi.
31. Ibid., p. 8.
32. Ibid., p. 46.
33. Huber, *Japan's Battle of Okinawa, April–June 1945*, p. 12.
34. *Okinawa Shinpo*, January 27, 1945, quoted in Auer, ed., *From Marco Polo Bridge to Pearl Harbor*, p. 163.
35. IGHQ Navy Directive No. 510, March 1, 1945, p. 143. NARA, RG 38, Imperial Gen. HQ Navy Directives, in "Records of Japanese Navy & Related Documents," Vol. 2, No. 316, Box 42.
36. "Outline of Army and Navy Operations," January 19, 1945, NARA, RG 38, Imperial Gen. HQ Navy Directives, in "Records of Japanese Navy & Related Documents," Vol. 2, No. 316, Box 42.
37. IGHQ Navy Directive No. 510, dated March 1, 1945, p. 157, NARA, RG 38, Imperial Gen. HQ Navy Directives, in "Records of Japanese Navy & Related Documents," Vol. 2, No. 316, Box 42.
38. 5th Air Fleet War Diary, Japanese Monograph No. 86, entry dated March 17, 1945, p. 22.
39. Matome Ugaki diary, March 21, 1945, Ugaki, *Fading Victory*, pp. 559–60.
40. 5th Air Fleet War Diary (Japanese Monograph No. 86), entry dated March 22, 1945, p. 28.
41. Ibid., entry dated April 4, 1945, p. 42.
42. Matome Ugaki diary, March 11, 1945, Ugaki, *Fading Victory*, p. 550.
43. J. Bryan III diary, April 4, 1945, Bryan, *Aircraft Carrier*, p. 110.
44. Michael Bak Jr., oral history, pp. 193–94.
45. Walker, *Ninety Day Wonder*, pp. 109–10.
46. Clark and Reynolds, *Carrier Admiral*, p. 224.
47. Sherrod, *On to Westward*, p. 292.
48. Commander Task Force 58 to CINCPAC, Report of Operations of Task Force 58 in support of landings at Okinawa, 14 March Through 28 May, 1945. A16-3 Serial: 00222, 18 June 1945.
49. CTF 58 to ATFC5THFLT Info CINCPAC, April 7, 1945, CINCPAC Gray Book, Book 6, green pages, p. 2823.
50. Reynolds, *On the Warpath in the Pacific*, p. 413.
51. Admiral Keizo Komura, commander of the fleet's destroyer squadron, quoted in Hara, Saito, and Pineau, *Japanese Destroyer Captain*, p. 261.
52. Hara, Saito, and Pineau, *Japanese Destroyer Captain*, p. 262.
53. Yoshida and Minear, *Requiem for Battleship Yamato*, p. 8.
54. Ibid., p. 24.
55. Yoshida, "The Sinking of the *Yamato*," in Evans, ed., *The Japanese Navy in World War II*, p. 482.
56. Yoshida, "The Sinking of the *Yamato*," p. 484.
57. Astor, *Wings of Gold*, p. 402.

58. J. Bryan III diary, April 7, 1945, Bryan, *Aircraft Carrier*, p. 118.

59. Astor, *Wings of Gold*, p. 405.

60. Yoshida, "The Sinking of the *Yamato*," p. 485.

61. Ibid.

62. Hara, Saito, and Pineau, *Japanese Destroyer Captain*, p. 278.

63. Yoshida, "The Sinking of the *Yamato*," p. 486.

64. Hara, Saito, and Pineau, *Japanese Destroyer Captain*, p. 280.

65. Yoshida, "The Sinking of the *Yamato*," p. 492.

66. Ibid., p. 488.

67. Ibid., p. 492.

68. Hara, Saito, and Pineau, *Japanese Destroyer Captain*, p. 282.

69. Yoshida, "The Sinking of the *Yamato*," p. 494

70. Yoshida and Minear, *Requiem for Battleship Yamato*, p. 118.

71. Mace and Allen, *Battleground Pacific*, p. 235.

72. Sledge, *With the Old Breed*, p. 197.

73. Ibid., pp. 192–93.

74. Pyle, *Last Chapter*, p. 89.

75. Sherrod, *On to Westward*, p. 285.

76. Reported in Admiral Ugaki's diary on April 1, 1945, Ugaki, *Fading Victory*, p. 571.

77. Auer, ed., *From Marco Polo Bridge to Pearl Harbor*, p. 161.

78. Matome Ugaki diary, Friday, April 6, 1945, Ugaki, *Fading Victory*, pp. 572–73.

79. 5th Air Fleet War Diary, April 6, 1945, pp. 45–46.

80. Clark and Reynolds, *Carrier Admiral*, p. 227.

81. Wallace, *From Dam Neck to Okinawa*, p. 36.

82. Appendix 1, "Ships Damaged or Sunk on Radar Picket Duty," in Rielly, *Kamikazes, Corsairs, and Picket Ships*, pp. 351–53.

83. Wallace, *From Dam Neck to Okinawa*, pp. 35–36.

84. LeMay and Kantor, *Mission with LeMay*, p. 372.

85. Wallace, *From Dam Neck to Okinawa*, p. 9.

86. Rowland and Boyd, *U.S. Navy Bureau of Ordnance in World War II*, Bureau of Ordnance, Department of the Navy, Washington, DC, 1953, pp. 270–74.

87. USS *Purdy* Serial 024 Action Report 20 April 1945, p. 28, quoted in Rielly, *Kamikazes, Corsairs, and Picket Ships*, p. 134.

88. Wallace, *From Dam Neck to Okinawa*, p. 38.

89. Ibid., p. 40.

90. Commander Task Force 58 to CINCPAC, Report of Operations of Task Force 58 in support of landings at Okinawa, 14 March Through 28 May, 1945, A16-3 Serial: 00222, 18 June 1945, p. 12.

91. Morison, *History of United States Naval Operations in World War II*, Vol. 14, *Victory in the Pacific*, p. 231.

92. Ibid.

93. Lardner, "Suicides and Bushwhackers," *New Yorker*, May 19, 1945, p. 32.

94. Reynolds, *On the Warpath in the Pacific*, p. 415.

95. Dunn, *Pacific Microphone*, p. 319.

96. Sledge, *With the Old Breed*, p. 201.

97. Yahara, *The Battle for Okinawa*, p. 45.

98. Quoted in Rielly, *Kamikazes, Corsairs, and Picket Ships*, p. 151.

99. Matome Ugaki diary, Friday, April 13, 1945, Ugaki, *Fading Victory*, p. 584.

Chapter Fourteen

1. Appleman, *Okinawa: The Last Battle*, p. 194.

2. Appleman, *Okinawa: The Last Battle*, p. 187.

3. Lardner, "Suicides and Bushwhackers," *New Yorker*, May 19, 1945, p. 32.

4. Leckie, *Okinawa*, p. 125.

5. Appleman, *Okinawa: The Last Battle*, p. 163.

6. Sledge, *With the Old Breed*, p. 205.

7. Manchester, *Goodbye, Darkness*, p. 360.

8. Huber, *Japan's Battle of Okinawa, April–June 1945*, p. 83.

9. Appleman et al., *Okinawa: The Last Battle*, p. 286.

10. Yahara, *The Battle for Okinawa*, p. 42.

11. "Tokyo, Domei, in English, to China and South Seas," Digest of Japanese Broadcasts, April 14, 1945, p. 1.

12. "Tokyo, Domei, in English, to America," Digest of Japanese Broadcasts, April 20, 1945, p. 2.

13. Toshiyuki Yokoi, "Kamikazes in the Okinawa Campaign," in Evans, ed., *The Japanese Navy in World War II*, p. 469.

14. Matome Ugaki diary, April 9, 1945, Ugaki, *Fading Victory*, p. 578.

15. 5th Air Fleet War Diary (Japanese Monograph No. 86), entry dated April 18, 1945, p. 59.

16. Inoguchi et al., *The Divine Wind*, p. 141.

17. Iwao Fukagawa quoted in Sheftall, *Blossoms in the Wind*, p. 214.

18. Ohnuki-Tierney, *Kamikaze Diaries*, p. 88.

19. Ibid., p. 69.

20. Ibid., p. 175.

21. Toshiyuki Yokoi, "Kamikazes in the Okinawa Campaign," in Evans, ed., *The Japanese Navy in World War II*, p. 468.

22. Letter from Takeo Kasuga to Shozo Umezawa, June 21, 1945, quoted in Ohnuki-Tierney, *Kamikaze Diaries*, p. 10.

23. Matome Ugaki diary, April 13, 1945, Ugaki, *Fading Victory*, p. 584.

24. Ibid., p. 595.

25. Matome Ugaki diary, April 21, 1945, Ugaki, *Fading Victory*, p. 594.

26. Matome Ugaki diary, April 29, 1945, Ugaki, *Fading Victory*, p. 600.

27. Reiko Torihama quoted in Sheftall, *Blossoms in the Wind*, p. 287.

28. Shigeko Araki, oral history, Cook and Cook, eds., *Japan at War*, p. 320.

29. Chief Ship's Clerk (W-2) C. S. King, oral history, in Wooldridge, ed., *Carrier Warfare in the Pacific*, p. 282.

30. Dr. David Willcutts, "Reminiscences of Admiral Spruance," p. 6, Manuscript Item 297, U.S. Naval War College Archives.

31. H. D. Chickering, commanding officer of LCS(L) *51*, quoted in Rielly, *Kamikazes, Corsairs, and Picket Ships*, p. 346.

32. Charles Thomas, crewman on the LCS(L) *35*, quoted in Rielly, *Kamikazes, Corsairs, and Picket Ships*, p. 10.

33. "CO USS *Aaron Ward* comments," in Secret Information Bulletin No. 24: "Battle Experience: Radar Pickets and Methods of Combating Suicide Attacks Off Okinawa, March–May 1945," July 20, 1945, p. 81-41.

34. Fenoglio, Y3C, "This I Remember," accessed April 21, 2019, https://dd803.org/crew/stories-from-the-crew/melvin-fenoglio-account.

35. Ronald D. Salmon, oral history, p. 110; John C. Munn, oral history, p. 81.

36. Reynolds, *On the Warpath in the Pacific*, p. 419.

37. Ibid, p. 417.

38. Pyle, *Last Chapter*, p. 83.

39. J. Bryan III diary, April 11, 1945, Bryan, *Aircraft Carrier*, p. 121.

40. Phelps Adams, "Attack on Carrier *Bunker Hill*," *New York Sun*, June 28, 1945, article reprinted in *Reporting World War II*, Part 2, p. 757.

41. Commander Task Force 58 to CINCPAC, Report of Operations of Task Force 58 in support of landings at Okinawa, 14 March Through 28 May, 1945, A16-3 Serial: 00222, 18 June 1945, p. 14.

42. Phelps Adams, "Attack on Carrier *Bunker Hill*," *New York Sun*, June 28, 1945; article reprinted in *Reporting World War II*, Part 2, p. 759.

43. Marc Mitscher quoted in Reynolds, *On the Warpath in the Pacific*, p. 417.

44. Charles F. Barber, Interview by Evelyn M. Cherpak, March 1, 1996, p. 27, Naval War College Archives.

45. Dr. David Willcutts, "Reminiscences of Admiral Spruance," p. 8, Manuscript Item 297, Naval War College Archives.

46. A "ghastly huge crater" is Dr. Willcutts's description. Willcutts, "Reminiscences of Admiral Spruance," p. 8, Manuscript Item 297, Naval War College Archives.

47. Letter, Raymond Spruance to Charles J. Moore, May 13, 1945, NHHC Archives, Raymond Spruance Papers, Coll/707, Box 1.

48. Mace and Allen, *Battleground Pacific*, p. 293; Sledge, *With the Old Breed*, p. 223.

49. Bill Pierce quoted in James Holland, "The Battle for Okinawa: One Marine's Story," *BBC History Magazine* and *BBC World Histories Magazine*, accessed May 2, 2019, https://www.historyextra.com/period/second-world-war/the-battle-for-okinawa-one-marines-story/.

50. William Manchester, "The Bloodiest Battle of All," *New York Times*, June 14, 1987.

51. Sledge, *With the Old Breed*, p. 278.

52. Ibid., p. 253.

53. Yahara, *The Battle for Okinawa*, p. 59.

54. Ibid., p. 67.

55. Ibid., p. 83.

56. Ushijima quoted in Auer, ed., *From Marco Polo Bridge to Pearl Harbor*, p. 162.

57. Nimitz: "It is my view that in OLYMPIC the country will be best served if Spruance controls the amphibious phases which require meticulous planning while Halsey is employed in offensive covering operations. . . . Thus each will be employed in the field in which he is best qualified." CINCPAC to COMINCH, Message 0226, April 5, 1945, in CINCPAC Gray Book, Book 6, p. 3078. King replied: "I agree with your view that this command should be Fifth Fleet team of Spruance and Turner." Message 1921, April 9, 1945, in CINCPAC Gray Book, Book 6, p. 3079.

58. Third Fleet War Diary, June 4, 1945, p. 7.

59. Roy L. Johnson account, Wooldridge, ed., *Carrier Warfare in the Pacific*, pp. 245–46.

60. Radford, *From Pearl Harbor to Vietnam*, p. 60.

61. Sherman, *Combat Command*, p. 308.

62. Third Fleet War Diary, June 4, 1945, p. 7.

63. Radford, *From Pearl Harbor to Vietnam*, p. 60.

64. *Time* magazine, July 23, 1945.

65. Hynes, *Flights of Passage*, p. 236.

66. Thomas McKinney quoted in Lacey, *Stay Off the Skyline*, p. 86.

67. "Japanese Radio Plan," pp. 1–2, "Weekly Plan for Psychological Warfare, April 28, 1945." Office of Military Secretary to Commander Chief, U.S. Army Forces in the Pacific, Hoover Institution Archives, Bonner Fellers Papers.

68. Appendix, "Inducement to Surrender of Japanese Forces," Combined Chiefs of Staff, Anglo-American Outline Plan for Psychological Warfare Against Japan, Reference A, CCS-539 Series, p. 10, Hoover Institution Archives, Bonner Fellers Papers.

69. Frank B. Gibney's commentary in Yahara, *The Battle for Okinawa*, p. 199.

70. Masahide Ota quoted in Lacey, *Stay Off the Skyline*, p. 61.

71. Kikuko Miyagi, oral history, Cook and Cook, eds., *Japan at War*, pp. 357–58.

72. The leaflet is reproduced in Yahara, *The Battle for Okinawa*, illustrations insert after p. 70.

73. Norris Buchter quoted in Lacey, *Stay Off the Skyline*, p. 67.

74. John Garcia, oral history, Terkel, ed., *"The Good War,"* p. 23.

75. Charles Miller quoted in Lacey, *Stay Off the Skyline*, p. 73.

76. Lewis Thomas account in Shenk, ed., *Authors at Sea*, pp. 241–42.

77. Yahara, *The Battle for Okinawa*, p. 135.

78. Ibid., p. 137.

79. Ibid., p. 136.

80. Quoted in Appleman, et al., *Okinawa: The Last Battle*, p. 463.

81. Yahara, *The Battle for Okinawa*, p. 136.

82. Masahide Ota, oral history, Cook and Cook, eds., *Japan at War*, p. 369.

83. Kikuko Miyagi, oral history, Cook and Cook, eds., *Japan at War*, p. 358.

84. Ibid., p. 360.

85. Ibid.

86. Ibid., p. 362.

87. *Building the Navy's Bases in World War II*, p. 410, Department of the Navy, Bureau of Yards and Docks.

88. Huie, *From Omaha to Okinawa*, p. 214.

89. Hynes, *Flights of Passage*, p. 209.

90. "The World War II Memoirs of John Vollinger," http://www.janesoceania.com/ww2_johann_memoirs/index.htm.

91. Morison, *History of United States Naval Operations in World War II*, Vol. 14, *Victory in the Pacific*, p. 282.

92. Huber, *Japan's Battle of Okinawa, April–June 1945*, p. 122.

93. Auer, ed., *From Marco Polo Bridge to Pearl Harbor*, p. 162.

Chapter Fifteen

1. Smith, *Thank You, Mr. President*, p. 218.

2. Brown, "Aide to Four Presidents," *American Heritage*, February 1955, Vol. 6, Issue 2.

3. Truman diary, June 1, 1945.

4. William D. Leahy diary, April 12, 1945, William D. Leahy Papers, LCMD; Adams, *Witness to Power*, p. 283.

5. Leahy, *I Was There*, p. 347.

6. Forrestal diary, entries dated May 1, 12, & 29, 1945, Millis, ed., *The Forrestal Diaries*, pp. 52–66.

7. Wedemeyer to Marshall, May 1, 1945, CINCPAC Gray Book, Book 6, p. 3220.

8. Truman J. Hedding, oral history, p. 109.

9. Statement Released to the Press, SWPA Headquarters, February 16, 1944; RG-4, Reel 612, MacArthur Memorial Archives.

10. MacArthur to Marshall, April 21, 1945, #1920, CINCPAC Gray Book, Book 6, p. 3212.

11. CINCPAC to COMINCH, #0230, April 5, 1945, CINCPAC Gray Book, Book 6, p. 3073.

12. Messages between Nimitz and MacArthur, April 7–8, 1945, CINCPAC Gray Book, Book 6, pp. 3077–78.

13. Robert C. Richardson Jr. diary, April 10, 1945, Richardson Papers, Hoover Institution Archives.

14. Nimitz to King, May 17, 1945, CINCPAC Gray Book, Book 6, p. 3229.

15. Layton, *"And I Was There,"* p. 484.

16. Nimitz to King, April 13, #2346, CINCPAC Gray Book, Book 6, p. 3203.

17. Leahy, *I Was There*, p. 370.

18. Marshall to MacArthur, April 4, 1945, War Department #63196; RG-30, Reel 1007, radio files, MacArthur Memorial Archives.

19. Nimitz to MacArthur, May 26, 1945, #0552, CINCPAC Gray Book, Book 6, p. 3233.

20. MacArthur to Nimitz, May 25, 1945, #1102, CINCPAC Gray Book, Book 6, pp. 3141–42.

21. Marshall to King, memorandum dated May 22, 1945, NARA, RG 38, "CNO Zero-Zero Files," Box 60, Folder 20.

22. MacArthur, *Reminiscences*, p. 261.

23. Frank, *Downfall*, p. 98.

24. USSBS, *Interrogations of Japanese Officials*, Nav No. 76, USSBS No. 379, Admiral Mitsumasa Yonai, IJN.

25. USSBS, *Japan's Struggle to End the War*, p. 5.

26. Ibid., p. 20.

27. USSBS, *Interrogations of Japanese Officials*, Nav No. 75, USSBS No. 378, Admiral Soemu Toyoda.

28. *Reports of General MacArthur, The Campaigns of MacArthur in the Pacific*, Vol. 1, p. 402.

29. Shillony, *Politics and Culture in Wartime Japan*, p. 82.

30. *Reports of General MacArthur, The Campaigns of MacArthur in the Pacific*, Vol. 1, p. 403.

31. Kort, ed., *The Columbia Guide to Hiroshima and the Bomb*, p. 64.

32. USSBS, *Japan's Struggle to End the War*, p. 13.

33. Lockwood and Adamson, *Hellcats of the Sea*, p. 40.

34. Joint Army-Navy Assessment Committee (JANAC) scores cited in Lockwood, *Sink 'Em All*, pp. 274–75, 285–86.

35. James Fife, oral history, CCOH Naval History Project, No. 452, Vol. 2, p. 415.

36. Lockwood, *Sink 'Em All*, pp. 249–50.

37. Russell, *Hell Above, Deep Water Below*, p. 103.

38. Smith, "Payback: Nine American Subs Avenge a Legend's Death," *World War II Magazine*, 10/24/2016, accessed August 22, 2018, http://www.historynet.com/uss-wahoo-vengeance.html.

39. Blair, *Silent Victory*, p. 863.

40. Ostrander, "Chaos at Shimonoseki," *Naval Institute Proceedings*, Vol. 73, No. 532, June 1947, p. 652.

41. USSBS, *The Offensive Mine Laying Campaign Against Japan*, p. 2.

42. Phillips, *Rain of Fire*, p. 99.

43. Third Fleet War Diary, July 10, 1945.

44. Morison, *History of United States Naval Operations in World War II*, Vol. 14, *Victory in the Pacific*, p. 312.

45. Third Fleet War Diary, July 14, 1945.

46. Radford, *From Pearl Harbor to Vietnam*, p. 62.

47. Halsey, *Admiral Halsey's Story*, p. 257.

48. Robert Bostwick Carney, oral history, CCOH Naval History Project, No. 539, Vol. 1, p. 442.

49. Arthur R. Hawkins account, in Wooldridge, ed., *Carrier Warfare in the Pacific*, p. 273.

50. Ibid.

51. Radford, *From Pearl Harbor to Vietnam*, p. 62.

52. Robert Bostwick Carney, oral history, CCOH Naval History Project, No. 539, Vol. 1, p. 465.

53. Sherman, *Combat Command*, p. 312.

54. "Halsey Ridicules Japanese Power," *New York Times*, June 4, 1945.

55. Wukovits, *Admiral "Bull" Halsey*, p. 232.

56. *Time* magazine, Vol. 46, No. 4, July 23, 1945.

57. Robert Bostwick Carney, oral history, CCOH Naval History Project, No. 539, Vol. 1, pp. 443–44.

58. Office of War Information, Bureau of Overseas Intelligence, Special Report No. 5, "Current Psychological and Social Tensions in Japan," June 1, 1945, p. 5, Hoover Institution Archives, Office of War Information, Box 3, "Reports on Japan, 1945."

59. Leaflet 36J6, Leaflet File No. 2, Box 2, Bonner Fellers Papers, Hoover Archives.

60. Williams, "Paths to Peace: The Information War in the Pacific, 1945," p. 4, Center for the Study of Intelligence, CIA, accessed November 4, 2018, https://www.cia.gov/library.

61. Leaflet entitled "What Can Be Done Against Overwhelming Odds?," Leaflet File No. 2, Box 2, Bonner Fellers Papers, Hoover Archives.

62. "The Reaction of Japanese to Psychological Warfare," p. 6, Annex 26, Report of SWPA Headquarters, "Psychological Effect of Leaflets," RG-4, MacArthur Archives.

63. Davis and Price, *War Information and Censorship*, p. 20.

64. *Foreign Relations of the United States: Diplomatic Papers, The Conference of Berlin (The Potsdam Conference)*, 1945, Vol. 2, 740.00119 PW/7–2245: Telegram No. 1243, The Acting Secretary of State to the Secretary of State, July 22, 1945.

65. Zacharias, *Secret Missions*, p. 358.

66. Interview with George C. Marshall, by Forrest C. Pogue Jr., February 11, 1957, George C. Marshall Foundation Collections.

67. Smyth, *Atomic Energy for Military Purposes*, p. 146.

68. Truman, *Year of Decisions*, pp. 10–11.

69. "Notes of the Interim Committee Meeting," Thursday, 31 May 1945, accessed September 2, 2018, https://www.trumanlibrary.org/whistlestop/study_collections/bomb.

70. Kort, ed., *The Columbia Guide to Hiroshima and the Bomb*, p. 51.

71. "Notes of the Interim Committee Meeting," Thursday, 31 May 1945, accessed

September 2, 2018, https://www.trumanlibrary.org/whistlestop/study_collections/bomb.

72. "Address Before the Cleveland Public Affairs Council," February 5, 1943, in Grew, *Turbulent Era*, Vol. 2, p. 1398.

73. Joseph C. Grew to Randall Gould, ed., *Shanghai Evening Post and Mercury*, April 14, 1945, in Grew, *Turbulent Era*, Vol. 2, p. 1420.

74. Grew, *Turbulent Era*, Vol. 2, p. 1424.

75. King and Whitehill, *Fleet Admiral King*, p. 598.

76. MacArthur, *Reminiscences*, p. 261.

77. King and Whitehill, *Fleet Admiral King*, p. 598; Forrestal diary, entry dated July 28, 1945, and additional references to a 1947 conversation with Eisenhower, undated, Millis, ed., *The Forrestal Diaries*, p. 78.

78. Byrnes, *Speaking Frankly*, p. 210.

79. Walter Brown diary quoted in Hasegawa, *Racing the Enemy*, p. 158.

80. Hasegawa, *Racing the Enemy*, p. 130.

81. Churchill to Eden, July 23, 1945, meeting "minute," in Alperovitz and Tree, *The Decision to Use the Atomic Bomb*, p. 271.

82. Trinity Test observer instructions quoted in Laurence, *Dawn Over Zero*, p. 7.

83. No. 1305, Commanding General, Manhattan District Project (Groves) to the Secretary of War (Stimson), 18 July 1945, p. 1367, *Foreign Relations of the United States: Diplomatic Papers, The Conference of Berlin (The Potsdam Conference), 1945*, Vol. 2.

84. Brigadier General Thomas F. Farrell quoted in No. 1305, Commanding General, Manhattan District Project (Groves) to the Secretary of War (Stimson), 18 July 1945, p. 1365, *Foreign Relations of the United States*, Vol. 2.

85. Kort, ed., *The Columbia Guide to Hiroshima and the Bomb*, p. 25.

86. No. 1305, Commanding General, Manhattan District Project (Groves) to the Secretary of War (Stimson), 18 July 1945, Encl. 4, "Thoughts by E. O. Lawrence," p. 1369, *Foreign Relations of the United States*, Vol. 2.

87. Kistiakowsky quoted in Laurence, *Dawn Over Zero*, p. 10.

88. Kort, ed., *The Columbia Guide to Hiroshima and the Bomb*, p. 25.

89. H. D. Smyth, *Atomic Energy for Military Purposes*, Appendix 6: War Department Release on New Mexico Test, July 16, 1945, p. 250.

90. No. 1305, Commanding General, Manhattan District Project (Groves) to the Secretary of War (Stimson), 18 July 1945, Encl. 3, p. 1368, *Foreign Relations of the United States*, Vol. 2.

91. No. 1303, Acting Chairman of the Interim Committee (Harrison) to the Secretary of War (Stimson), 16 July 1945, *Foreign Relations of the United States*, Vol. 2.

92. Stimson diary, July 21, 1945, accessed September 23, 2018, www.doug-long.com/stimson8.htm.

93. Stimson diary, July 22, 1945, Kort, ed., *The Columbia Guide to Hiroshima and the Bomb*, pp. 222–23.

94. MAGIC Diplomatic Summaries Nos. 1204 & 1205, July 12–13, 1945, Kort, ed., *The Columbia Guide to Hiroshima and the Bomb*, pp. 278–79.

95. MAGIC Diplomatic Summary No. 1206, July 14, 1945, Kort, ed., *The Columbia Guide to Hiroshima and the Bomb*, p. 282.

96. MAGIC Diplomatic Summaries Nos. 1208 & 1212, July 16–20, 1945, Kort, ed., *The Columbia Guide to Hiroshima and the Bomb*, pp. 282–84.

97. MAGIC Diplomatic Intercept No. 1225, August 2, 1945, Kort, ed., *The Columbia Guide to Hiroshima and the Bomb*, p. 287.

98. Ralph Bard, "Memorandum on the Use of S-1 Bomb," June 17, 1945, Kort, ed., *The Columbia Guide to Hiroshima and the Bomb*, p. 209.

99. The Scientific Panel, Interim Committee, "Recommendation on the Immediate Use of Nuclear Weapons," June 16, 1945, Kort, ed., *The Columbia Guide to Hiroshima and the Bomb*, p. 201.

100. Memorandum for General Arnold, July 24, 1945, Document B18, Kort, ed., *The Columbia Guide to Hiroshima and the Bomb*, p. 258.

101. Joint Chiefs of Staff, Memorandum to the President, July 17, 1945, Document B17, Kort, ed., *The Columbia Guide to Hiroshima and the Bomb*, p. 257.

102. Henry L. Stimson diary, July 24, 1945, Stoff et al., eds., *The Manhattan Project*, p. 214.

103. U.S. National Archives, Record Group 77, Records of the Office of the Chief of Engineers, Manhattan Engineer District, TS Manhattan Project File '42 to '46, Folder 5B, "Directives, Memos, Etc. to and from C/S, S/W, etc."

104. Truman diary, June 25, 1945.

105. Memorandum from Major J. A. Derry and Dr. N. F. Ramsey to General L. R. Groves, May 10–11, 1945, accessed September 14, 2018, https://www.atomicheritage.org/key-documents/target-committee-recommendations.

106. Truman, *Year of Decision*, p. 421.

107. Document A45, "The Potsdam Declaration," July 26, 1945, Kort, ed., *The Columbia Guide to Hiroshima and the Bomb*, p. 226.

108. Hasegawa, *Racing the Enemy*, p. 166.

109. *Yomiuri Shinbun* headline quoted in Hasegawa, *Racing the Enemy*, p. 167.

110. Suzuki quoted in *Yomiuri Shinbun* account, Hasegawa, *Racing the Enemy*, pp. 167–68.

111. Ferrell, *Harry S. Truman*, p. 215.

112. Sourced to assistant naval aide George Elsey: Adams, *Witness to Power*, p. 298.

113. LeMay and Yenne, *Superfortress*, pp. 159–60.

114. Arnold to Marshall, Joint Chiefs of Staff, June 17, 1945, RG-30, Reel 1007, MacArthur Memorial Archives.

115. LeMay quoted in Caidin, *A Torch to the Enemy*, p. 157.

116. USSBS, *The Effects of Strategic Bombing on Japanese Morale*, p. 132.

117. Ibid.

Chapter Sixteen

1. Phillip Morrison quoted in Rhodes, *The Making of the Atomic Bomb*, p. 681.
2. Kort, ed., *The Columbia Guide to Hiroshima and the Bomb*, p. 49.
3. Sweeney, *War's End*, Foreword, p. i.
4. Groves, *Now It Can Be Told*, p. 318.
5. Julian Ryall, "Hiroshima Bomber Tasted Lead After Nuclear Blast, Rediscovered Enola Gay Recordings Reveal," *The Telegraph* (UK), August 6, 2018.
6. Kort, ed., *The Columbia Guide to Hiroshima and the Bomb*, p. 4; Interview with crew of Enola Gay, October 1962, Unknown Collections: 509th Composite Group, https://www.manhattanprojectvoices.org/oral-histories/atomic-bombers.
7. Merle and Spitzer, *We Dropped the A-Bomb*, Introduction, p. 1.
8. Kelly, ed., *The Manhattan Project*, p. 330.
9. Stiborik quoted in Patricia Benoit, "From Czechoslovakia to Life in Central Texas," *Temple Daily Telegram*, August 23, 2015.
10. Yoshido Matsushige, oral history, Cook and Cook, eds., *Japan at War*, p. 391.
11. "Chapter 25 – Eyewitness Account," Hiroshima, August 6, 1945, by Father John A. Siemes, Avalon Project, Yale Law School, Lillian Goldman Law Library, http://avalon.law.yale.edu.
12. Hachiya and Wells, *Hiroshima Diary*, p. 2.
13. Michiko Yamaoka, oral history, Cook and Cook, eds., *Japan at War*, p. 385.
14. Eiko Taoka, "Testimony of Hatchobori Streetcar Survivors," The Atomic Archive, http://www.atomicarchive.com/Docs/Hibakusha/Hatchobori.shtml.
15. Hersey, *Hiroshima*, p. 19.
16. Futaba Kitayama quoted in Robert Guillain, "I Thought My Last Hour Had Come," *The Atlantic*, August 1980.
17. Hersey, *Hiroshima*, p. 19.
18. Ibid., p. 31.
19. Michiko Yamaoka, oral history, Cook and Cook, eds., *Japan at War*, p. 385.
20. Yoshido Matsushige, oral history, Cook and Cook, eds., *Japan at War*, p. 392.
21. Ibid., p. 393.
22. Futaba Kitayama quoted in Robert Guillain, "I Thought My Last Hour Had Come," *The Atlantic*, August 1980.
23. Frank, *Downfall*, p. 265.
24. Hersey, *Hiroshima*, p. 50.
25. Hachiya and Wells, *Hiroshima Diary*, p. 8.
26. Hersey, *Hiroshima*, p. 89.
27. Lieutenant William M. Rigdon, USN, "Log: President's Trip to the Berlin Conference," August 6, 1945, p. 50, Leahy, *I Was There*, pp. 432–33.
28. Ibid.
29. Truman's Statement on the Bombing of Hiroshima, August 6, 1945, Kort, ed., *The Columbia Guide to Hiroshima and the Bomb*, p. 230.
30. Ibid.

31. Hasegawa, *Racing the Enemy*, p. 184.

32. The Pacific War Research Society, *The Day Man Lost*, p. 270.

33. Frank, *Downfall*, p. 269.

34. Kort, ed., *The Columbia Guide to Hiroshima and the Bomb*, p. 26.

35. Frank, *Downfall*, p. 270.

36. The Pacific War Research Society, *The Day Man Lost*, p. 293.

37. USSBS Interrogation No. 609, Hisatsune Sakomizu, December 11, 1945, Kort, *The Columbia Guide to Hiroshima and the Bomb*, p. 361.

38. "Soviet Declaration of War on Japan," August 8, 1945, Avalon Project, Yale Law School Lillian Goldman Law Library, http://avalon.law.yale.edu/wwii/s4.asp.

39. Lieutenant Colonel David M. Glantz, *August Storm: The Soviet 1945 Strategic Offensive in Manchuria*, pp. 1–2, Leavenworth Papers, Combat Studies Institute, U.S. Army Command and General Staff College, Fort Leavenworth, Kansas, February 1983.

40. Glantz, *August Storm*, p. xiv.

41. Document G9, Miscellaneous Statements of Japanese Officials, Document No. 52608: Lieutenant General Torashirō Kawabe, November 21, 1949, in Kort, ed., *The Columbia Guide to Hiroshima and the Bomb*, p. 382.

42. Document G7, Miscellaneous Statements of Japanese Officials, Document No. 54479: Statement of Sumihisa Ikeda, December 23, 1949, in Kort, ed., *The Columbia Guide to Hiroshima and the Bomb*, p. 379.

43. Hasegawa, *Racing the Enemy*, p. 197.

44. Auer, ed., *From Marco Polo Bridge to Pearl Harbor*, p. 201.

45. Merle and Spitzer, *We Dropped the A-Bomb*, p. 123.

46. Sweeney, *War's End*, p. 204; Paul Tibbets, oral history, accessed November 7, 2018, https://www.manhattanprojectvoices.org/oral-histories/general-paul-tibbets.

47. William L. Laurence, "Atomic Bombing of Nagasaki Told by Flight Member," *New York Times*, September 9, 1945.

48. According to Ellen Bradbury, "What happened does not seem to have appeared in any official histories, but Ashworth swore to me it was true," in Bradbury and Blakeslee, "The Harrowing Story of the Nagasaki Bombing Mission," *Bulletin of the Atomic Scientists*, August 4, 2015.

49. Alex Wellerstein, "Nagasaki: The Last Bomb," *New Yorker*, August 7, 2015.

50. Sweeney, *War's End*, p. 215.

51. Ibid., p. 216.

52. William L. Laurence, "Atomic Bombing of Nagasaki Told by Flight Member," *New York Times*, September 9, 1945.

53. Sweeney, *War's End*, p. 219.

54. Bradbury and Blakeslee, "The Harrowing Story of the Nagasaki Bombing Mission."

55. William L. Leary and Michie Hattori Bernstein, "Eyewitness to the Nagasaki Atomic Bomb," *World War II* magazine, July/August 2005, http://www.historynet.com/michie-hattori-eyewitness-to-the-nagasaki-atomic-bomb-blast.htm.

56. Shizuko Nagae eyewitness account, as told to her daughter, Masako Waba, "A Survivor's Harrowing Account of Nagasaki Bombing," *CBC News*, May 26, 2016, https://www.cbc.ca/news/world/nagasaki-atomic-bomb-survivor-transcript-1.3601606.

57. "The Atomic Bombings of Hiroshima and Nagasaki," p. 11, Report by the Manhattan Engineer District, June 29, 1946, http://www.atomicarchive.com/Docs/MED/med_chp9.shtml.

58. "The Atomic Bombings of Hiroshima and Nagasaki," p. 11.

59. Sweeney, *War's End*, p. 225.

60. Ibid.

61. Auer, ed., *From Marco Polo Bridge to Pearl Harbor*, p. 253.

62. Document D14, diary entries of Marquis Koichi Kido, in Kort, ed., *The Columbia Guide to Hiroshima and the Bomb*, p. 307.

63. Here Kase paraphrases. In the account given by Sakomizu to the USSBS, Suzuki's wording is slightly different, but the meaning is identical. Kase, *Journey to the Missouri*, p. 234; USSBS, *Japan's Struggle to End the War*, p. 8.

64. Document E1, Emperor Hirohito's Surrender Decision, August 10, 1945, in Kort, ed., *The Columbia Guide to Hiroshima and the Bomb*, p. 323.

65. USSBS, *Japan's Struggle to End the War*, p. 9.

66. Document 412, "The Secretary of State to the Swiss Chargé (Grässli), Washington, August 11, 1945," in U.S. Department of State, *Foreign Relations of the United States: The British Commonwealth*, Vol. 6, p. 627.

67. Document G11, Miscellaneous Statements of Japanese Officials, Document No. 50025A, Lieutenant Colonel Masahiko Takeshita, June 11, 1949, in Kort, ed., *The Columbia Guide to Hiroshima and the Bomb*, pp. 383–84.

68. Emperor's "Monologue," quoted in Irokawa, *The Age of Hirohito*, p. 125.

69. Auer, ed., *From Marco Polo Bridge to Pearl Harbor*, p. 201.

70. Torashirō Kawabe diary, August 10, 1945, in Kort, ed., *The Columbia Guide to Hiroshima and the Bomb*, p. 313.

71. Hasegawa, *Racing the Enemy*, p. 217.

72. Document D9, Army Minister Korechika Anami Broadcast: "Instruction to the Troops," August 10, 1945, in Kort, ed., *The Columbia Guide to Hiroshima and the Bomb*, p. 300.

73. Document D10, Army General Staff Telegram, August 11, 1945, in Kort, ed., *The Columbia Guide to Hiroshima and the Bomb*, p. 301.

74. Kase, *Journey to the Missouri*, p. 240.

75. Stimson diary, August 10, 1945, quoted in Alperovitz and Tree, *The Decision to Use the Atomic Bomb*, p. 489.

76. Stimson diary, August 10, 1945, quoted in Janssens, *'What Future for Japan?': U.S. Wartime Planning for the Postwar Era, 1942–1945*, p. 318.

77. Hasegawa, *Racing the Enemy*, p. 220.

78. Leahy, *I Was There*, p. 434.

79. Hasegawa, *Racing the Enemy*, p. 220.

80. Forrestal diary, August 10, 1945, Millis, ed., *The Forrestal Diaries*, p. 83.

81. *Foreign Relations of the United States*, The British Commonwealth, Vol. 6, pp. 631–32.

82. Forrestal diary, August 10, 1945, Millis, ed., *The Forrestal Diaries*, pp. 83–84.

83. James J. Fahey diary, August 10, 1945, Fahey, *Pacific War Diary, 1942–1945*, p. 375.

84. Hynes, *Flights of Passage*, p. 254.

85. Wallace, *From Dam Neck to Okinawa*, p. 54.

86. Radford, *From Pearl Harbor to Vietnam*, p. 64.

87. Robert Bostwick Carney, oral history, CCOH Naval History Project, Vol. 1, No. 539, p. 447.

88. Kase, *Journey to the Missouri*, pp. 243–44.

89. Documents C-17, C-18, C-19, Magic Diplomatic Intercept Numbers 1236–1238, August 13–15, 1945, in Kort, ed., *The Columbia Guide to Hiroshima and the Bomb*, pp. 289–90.

90. Hasegawa, *Racing the Enemy*, p. 228.

91. Ibid., p. 237.

92. Document D12, Toyoda and Umezu Report to the Emperor, August 12, 1945, in Kort, ed., *The Columbia Guide to Hiroshima and the Bomb*, pp. 302–3.

93. Hasegawa, *Racing the Enemy*, p. 229.

94. Document D12, Toyoda and Umezu Report to the Emperor, August 12, 1945, in Kort, ed., *The Columbia Guide to Hiroshima and the Bomb*, pp. 302–3.

95. USSBS, *Japan's Struggle to End the War*, p. 9.

96. Wray et al., *Bridging the Atomic Divide*, p. 159.

97. "Digest of Japanese Broadcasts," August 14, 1945, pp. 2–3.

98. Yamashita, *Daily Life in Wartime Japan*, p. 175.

99. Takeyama and Minear, eds., *The Scars of War*, p. 50.

100. "Master Recording of Hirohito's War-End Speech Released in Digital Form," *The Japan Times*, August 1, 2015 (includes English translation of the surrender rescript as it appeared in the newspaper on August 15, 1945).

101. Morita, Reingold, and Shimomura, *Made in Japan*, p. 34.

102. Takeshi Maeda account in Werneth, ed., *Beyond Pearl Harbor*, p. 126.

103. "Master Recording of Hirohito's War-End Speech."

104. Kase, *Journey to the Missouri*, p. 256.

105. Yamashita, *Daily Life in Wartime Japan*, p. 177.

106. Ibid., p. 179.

107. Iwamoto Akira letter to the *Asahi Shinbun*, in Gibney, ed., *Senso*, p. 258.

108. Irokawa, *The Age of Hirohito*, p. 35.

109. Dr. Michihiko Hachiya diary, August 15, 1945, in Hachiya and Wells, *Hiroshima Diary*, p. 83.

110. Yamashita, *Daily Life in Wartime Japan*, p. 179.

111. Hisako Yoskizawa diary, August 15, 1945, Yamashita, ed., *Leaves from an Autumn of Emergencies*, p. 217.

112. Sadao Mogami, oral history, in Cook and Cook, eds., *Japan at War*, p. 456.
113. Haruyoshi Kagawa letter to the *Asahi Shinbun*, Gibney, ed., *Senso*, p. 50.
114. Michi Fukuda letter to the *Asahi Shinbun*, Gibney, ed., *Senso*, p. 42.
115. Yamashita, *Daily Life in Wartime Japan*, p. 187.
116. Ibid., p. 186.
117. Ibid., p. 184.
118. "Master Recording of Hirohito's War-End Speech."
119. Hideo Yamaguchi letter to the *Asahi Shinbun*, in Gibney, ed., *Senso*, p. 273.
120. "Digest of Japanese Broadcasts," August 15, 1945, p. 16.
121. Matome Ugaki diary, August 11, 1945, Ugaki, *Fading Victory*, p. 659.
122. Ibid., p. 664.
123. Ibid.
124. Ugaki, *Fading Victory*, p. 666.
125. Ibid.

Epilogue

1. William D. Leahy diary, August 14, 1945, Leahy Papers, LCMD.
2. Buell, *Dauntless Helldivers*, p. 307.
3. Sylvia Summers, oral history, Richardson and Stillwell, *Reflections of Pearl Harbor*, p. 98.
4. Barbara De Nike, oral history, Harris, Mitchell, and Schechter, eds., *The Homefront*, p. 213.
5. Patricia Livermore, oral history, Harris, Mitchell, and Schechter, eds., *The Homefront*, p. 212.
6. Stanton Delaplane, "Victory Riot," *San Francisco Chronicle Reader*, p. 198.
7. Carl Nolte, "The Dark Side of V-J Day," *San Francisco Chronicle*, August 15, 2005.
8. Third Fleet War Diary, August 15, 1945; CINCPAC to CNO, "Operations in the Pacific Ocean Areas, August 1945," Serial: 034296, December 10, 1945.
9. Halsey, *Admiral Halsey's Story*, p. 272.
10. Robert Bostwick Carney, oral history, CCOH Naval History Project, No. 539, Vol. 1, p. 449.
11. Sakai, Caidin, and Saito, *Samurai!*, p. 269.
12. Kase, *Journey to the Missouri*, p. 262; USSBS *Interrogations of Japanese Officials*, Nav No. 90, USSBS No. 429, Admiral Kichisaburo Nomura, IJN.
13. USSBS *Interrogations of Japanese Officials*, Nav No. 76, USSBS No. 379, Admiral Mitsumasa Yonai, IJN.
14. Imperial Rescript of August 17, 1945, in Kort, ed., *The Columbia Guide to Hiroshima and the Bomb*, p. 334.
15. "Speech of Prince Higashi-Kuni to the Japanese People Upon Becoming Premier," August 17, 1945, accessed June 4, 2019, http://www.ibiblio.org/pha/policy/1945/1945-08-17c.html.

16. "Exchange of Messages Between General MacArthur and Japanese General Headquarters on Manila Meeting," August 15–19, 1945, *United States Department of State Bulletin*, accessed June 7, 2019, http://www.ibiblio.org/pha/policy/1945/1945-08-15b.html.

17. "General MacArthur's Instructions to Japanese on Occupation Landings," reprinted in *New York Times*, August 23, 1945.

18. Radford, *From Pearl Harbor to Vietnam*, p. 67.

19. Robert Bostwick Carney, oral history, CCOH Naval History Project, No. 539, Vol. 1, p. 451.

20. Wallace, *From Dam Neck to Okinawa*, p. 55.

21. CINCPAC to CNO, "Operations in the Pacific Ocean Areas, August 1945," Serial: 034296, December 10, 1945.

22. Hoover Institution Archives, U.S. Office of War Information, Psychological Warfare Division, "Leaflets," Box 2.

23. Wheeler, *Dragon in the Dust*, p. xxiv.

24. Roland Smoot, oral history, p. 192.

25. Robert Bostwick Carney, oral history, CCOH Naval History Project, No. 539, Vol. 1, pp. 452–53.

26. John C. Munn, oral history, p. 86.

27. Halsey, *Admiral Halsey's Story*, p. 280.

28. Kenney, *General Kenney Reports*, p. 575.

29. Ibid.

30. Dunn, *Pacific Microphone*, p. 351.

31. Courtney Whitney, "Lifting Up a Beaten People," *Life* magazine, August 22, 1955, p. 90.

32. Courtney Whitney's recollections, quoted in MacArthur, *Reminiscences*, p. 271.

33. Manchester, *American Caesar*, p. 447.

34. Whelton Rhoades diary, August 30, 1945, Rhoades, *Flying MacArthur to Victory*, p. 448.

35. MacArthur, *Reminiscences*, p. 272.

36. CINCPAC to CNO, "Operations in the Pacific Ocean Areas, August 1945," Serial: 034296, December 10, 1945.

37. Whelton Rhoades diary, August 31, 1945, Rhoades, *Flying MacArthur to Victory*, p. 450.

38. Robert C. Richardson Jr. diary, August 31, 1945.

39. Ibid.

40. Stuart S. Murray, oral history, "A Harried Host in the *Missouri*," in Mason, ed., *The Pacific War Remembered*, p. 350.

41. Jonathan M. Wainwright, *General Wainwright's Story*, pp. 279–80.

42. Robert Bostwick Carney, oral history, CCOH Naval History Project, Vol. 1, No. 539, pp. 472–73.

43. Whelton Rhoades diary, September 2, 1945, Rhoades, *Flying MacArthur to Victory*, p. 452.

44. Robert Bostwick Carney, oral history, CCOH Naval History Project, No. 539, Vol. 1, pp. 472–73.

45. Stuart S. Murray oral history, "A Harried Host in the *Missouri*," in Mason, ed., *The Pacific War Remembered*, p. 355.

46. Lamar, "I Saw Stars," p. 22; Manchester, *American Caesar*, p. 451.

47. Kase, *Journey to the Missouri*, p. 7.

48. Dunn, *Pacific Microphone*, pp. 360–61.

49. MacArthur, *Reminiscences*, p. 275.

50. Halsey and Richardson each separately noted that MacArthur's hands shook. Halsey, *Admiral Halsey's Story*, p. 523; Robert C. Richardson Jr. diary, September 2, 1945.

51. Halsey, *Admiral Halsey's Story*, p. 524.

52. Kenney, *General Kenney Reports*, p. 577.

53. Associated Press, "Tokyo Aides Weep as General Signs," September 2, 1945.

54. Lilly, *Nimitz at Ease*, p. 303.

55. Whelton Rhoades diary, September 2, 1945, Rhoades, *Flying MacArthur to Victory*, p. 454.

56. Robert Bostwick Carney, oral history, CCOH Naval History Project, Vol. 1, No. 539, p. 472.

57. *Reports of General MacArthur*, Vol. 1 Supplement, pp. 32–45.

58. *Reports of General MacArthur*, Vol. 1, p. 452.

59. James J. Fahey diary, October 22, 1945, Fahey, *Pacific War Diary, 1942–1945*, p. 400.

60. Ibid.

61. Richard Leonard to Arlene Bahr, November 3, 1945, in Carroll, ed., *War Letters*, p. 318.

62. Ibid., pp. 318–19.

63. For example, a USSBS survey conducted in late 1945 found that two-thirds of Japanese had expected "brutality, enslavement, tyranny, starvation, subservience." USSBS, *The Effects of Strategic Bombing on Japanese Morale*, p. 155n7.

64. Naokata Sasaki, oral history, in Cook and Cook, eds., *Japan at War*, p. 469.

65. Radike, *Across the Dark Islands*, p. 258.

66. USSBS, *The Effects of Strategic Bombing on Japanese Morale*, p. 155.

67. Ibid.

68. *Reports of General MacArthur*, Vol. 1 Supplement, p. 23.

69. Ibid., p. 49.

70. Terasaki, *Bridge to the Sun*, p. 200.

71. Charles F. Barber, Interview by Evelyn M. Cherpak, March 1, 1996, U.S. Naval War College Archives.

72. Eichelberger and MacKaye, *Our Jungle Road to Tokyo*, p. 255.

73. Hara, Saito, and Pineau, *Japanese Destroyer Captain*, Foreword, p. x.

74. Morison, *History of United States Naval Operations in World War II*, Vol. 15, *Supplement and General Index*, p. 9.

75. *Reports of General MacArthur*, Vol. 1 Supplement, p. 47.

76. Document A45, "The Potsdam Declaration," July 26, 1945, in Kort, ed., *The Columbia Guide to Hiroshima and the Bomb*, p. 227.

77. Shigeo Hatanaka, oral history, in Cook and Cook, eds., *Japan at War*, p. 227.

78. Junko Ozaki letter to the *Asahi Shinbun*, in Gibney, ed., *Senso*, p. 75.

79. Terasaki, *Bridge to the Sun*, p. 233.

80. USSBS *Interrogations of Japanese Officials*, Nav No. 76, USSBS No. 379, Admiral Mitsumasa Yonai, IJN.

81. Chihaya Masataka quoted in Asada, *From Mahan to Pearl Harbor*, p. 292.

82. Asada, *From Mahan to Pearl Harbor*, p. 289.

83. Ibid.

84. USSBS *Interrogations of Japanese Officials*, Nav No. 90, USSBS No. 429, Admiral Kichisaburo, Nomura, IJN.

85. Asada, *From Mahan to Pearl Harbor*, p. 292.

86. "Fire Scroll," *Book of Five Spheres*, quoted in Cleary, *The Japanese Art of War*, p. 84.

87. Eizo Hori, statistics cited in Auer, ed., *From Marco Polo Bridge to Pearl Harbor*, p. 148.

88. According to the Japanese Health, Labor, and Welfare Ministry, 3.1 million Japanese were killed in the Asian and Pacific wars of 1937 to 1945. The figure included 2.3 million military deaths and 800,000 civilian deaths. Of the latter, an estimated 500,000 were killed in Japan, and 300,000 overseas. Auer, ed., *From Marco Polo Bridge to Pearl Harbor*, p. 242.

89. Michio Takeyama quoted in Takeyama and Minear, eds., *The Scars of War*, p. 68.

90. Goldstein and Dillon, eds., *The Pacific War Papers*, p. 67.

91. Hitoshi Inoue letter to *Asahi Shinbun*, in Gibney, ed., *Senso*, p. 80.

92. Uichiro Kawachi, oral history, in Cook and Cook, eds., *Japan at War*, p. 214.

93. Kazuo Ikezaki letter to *Asahi Shinbun*, in Gibney, ed., *Senso*, p. 301.

94. Fusako Kawamura letter to *Asahi Shinbun*, in Gibney, ed., *Senso*, p. 279.

95. Yukio Hashimoto letter to *Asahi Shinbun*, in Gibney, ed., *Senso*, p. 181.

96. Murrie and Petersen, "Last Train Home," *American History*, February 2018. Adapted with permission from *Railroad History*, Spring–Summer 2015.

97. Steere, *The Graves Registration Service in World War II*, p. 405.

98. Ibid., p. 426.

99. Most of those who perished at sea to causes other than combat, including accidents and illnesses, were also buried at sea. Globally, the navy reported 25,664 non-combat deaths during WWII. Naval History and Heritage Command (NHHC) website, accessed August 4, 2019, https://www.history.navy.mil/research/library/online-reading-room/title-list-alphabetically/u/us-navy-personnel-in-world-war-ii-service-and-casualty-statistics.html.

100. For example, the soldier and future novelist Norman Mailer wrote: "A good part

of me approves anything which will shorten the war, and get me home sooner, and this is often antagonistic to older more basic principles. For instance I hope the peacetime draft is passed because if it's not, there may be an agonizingly slow demobilization." Letter to Beatrice Mailer, August 8, 1945, "In the Ring: Life and Letters," *New Yorker*, October 6, 2008, pp. 51–52.

101. Lee, *To the War*, p. 163.
102. Hynes, *Flights of Passage*, p. 257.
103. Radford, *From Pearl Harbor to Vietnam*, p. 70.
104. James Forrestal diary, October 16, 1945, Millis, ed., *The Forrestal Diaries*, p. 102.
105. Morison, *History of United States Naval Operations in World War II*, Vol. 15, *Supplement and General Index*, p. 17.
106. John C. Munn, oral history, p. 91.
107. McCandless, *A Flash of Green*, p. 219.
108. Morison, *History of United States Naval Operations in World War II*, Vol. 15, *Supplement and General* Index, p. 13.
109. "Plan of the Day," Sunday, September 2, 1945, USS *Missouri*, p. 2, "Notes," accessed May 21, 2019, http://www.bb63vets.com/docs/DOC_6.pdf.
110. Hynes, *Flights of Passage*, p. 266.
111. "The World War II Memoirs of John Vollinger," http://www.janesoceania.com/ ww2_johann_memoirs/index.htm.
112. Murrie and Petersen, "Last Train Home," *American History*, February 2018. Adapted with permission from *Railroad History*, Spring–Summer 2015.
113. Beaver, *Sailor from Oklahoma*, p. 226.
114. "The World War II Memoirs of John Vollinger," http://www.janesoceania.com/ ww2_johann_memoirs/index.htm.
115. Clark and Reynolds, *Carrier Admiral*, p. 245.
116. Sledge, *With the Old Breed*, p. 266.
117. Mace and Allen, *Battleground Pacific*, p. 327.
118. George Niland, oral history, in Lacey, *Stay Off the Skyline*, p. 189.
119. William Pierce, oral history, in Lacey, *Stay Off the Skyline*, p. 193.
120. Yoder, *There's No Front Like Home*, pp. 108, 112.
121. Shirley Hackett, oral history, in Harris, Mitchell, and Schechter, eds., *The Homefront*, p. 231.
122. Frankie Cooper, oral history, in Harris, Mitchell, and Schechter, eds., *The Homefront*, p. 249.
123. Dellie Hahne, oral history, in Harris, Mitchell, and Schechter, eds., *The Homefront*, p. 228.
124. Frankie Cooper, oral history, in Harris, Mitchell, and Schechter, eds., *The Homefront*, p. 249.
125. Randal S. Olson, "144 Years of Marriage and Divorce in One Chart," June 15, 2015, accessed June 2, 2019, www.randalolson.com. Data from Centers for Disease Control (CDC)/National Center for Health Statistics (NCHS).

126. James Covert, oral history, in Harris, Mitchell, and Schechter, eds., *The Homefront*, p. 223.

127. Marshall Ralph Doak, *My Years in the Navy*, http://www.historycentral.com/Navy/Doak.

128. Marjorie Cartwright, oral history, in Harris, Mitchell, and Schechter, eds., *The Homefront*, p. 226.

129. Ibid., p. 228.

130. Caro, *Master of the Senate*, p. 196.

131. Sybil Lewis, oral history, in Harris, Mitchell, and Schechter, eds., *The Homefront*, p. 251.

132. Ibid., p. 252.

133. Lee, *To the War*, p. 164.

134. Hynes, *Flights of Passage*, p. 255.

135. Robert E. Hogaboom, oral history, Marine Corps Project, No. 813, Vol. 1, p. 235.

136. Norman Mailer to Beatrice Mailer, August 8, 1945, "In the Ring: Life and Letters," in *New Yorker*, October 6, 2008, pp. 51–52.

137. Leach, *Now Hear This*, p. 175.

138. Ben Bradlee, "A Return," *New Yorker*, October 2, 2006.

139. Michener, *The World Is My Home*, p. 265.

140. Edward J. Huxtable, commanding officer, Composite Squadron Ten, 1943–1945, "Some Recollections," pp. 27–28, Huxtable Papers, Hoover Institution Archives.

BIBLIOGRAPHY

Archival Collections

Archives and Special Collections, Library of the Marine Corps,
Quantico, Virginia (USMC Archives)

Fifth Amphibious Corps files
Elton N. Shrode, unpublished written account, Coll. 3736
Holland M. Smith Collection
Ronald D. Thomas, unpublished written account, PC No. 2718
Arthur Vandegrift Collection

Hoover Institution Library & Archives, Stanford University, Palo Alto, California

Bonner Fellers Papers
Edward J. Huxtable, "Composite Squadron Ten, Recollections and Notes"
William Neufeld Papers, 1942–1960
Robert Charlwood Richardson Jr. Papers
U.S. Office of War Information (OWI), Psychological Warfare Division Files

Library of Congress, Manuscript Division, Washington, DC (LCMD)

William Frederick Halsey Jr. Papers
Ernest J. King Papers
William D. Leahy Papers
Samuel Eliot Morison Papers
John Henry Towers Papers

MacArthur Memorial Archives, Norfolk, Virginia

LeGrande A. Diller, oral history, recorded September 26, 1982
Papers of Lieutenant General Richard K. Sutherland (RG-30)
General Douglas MacArthur's Private Correspondence, 1848–1964
Radio Message files, 1941–1951
Records of Headquarters, U.S. Army Forces Pacific (USAFPAC), 1942–1947 (RG-4)

National Archives and Records Administration, College Park, Maryland (NARA)

Digests of Japanese Radio Broadcasts
Office Files of the Chief of Naval Operations ("CNO Zero-Zero Files")
Records of Japanese Navy and Related Documents
Records of the Office of the Chief of Engineers, Manhattan Engineer District (RG-77)
Records of the Office of the Chief of Naval Operations, 1875–2006 (RG-38)
World War II Action and Operational Reports
World War II Oral Histories and Interviews
World War II War Diaries

Naval Historical Collection, Naval War College, Newport, Rhode Island

Charles F. Barber, "Reminiscences of Admiral Raymond A. Spruance"
Thomas B. Buell Collection
Raymond A. Spruance Papers
David Willcutts, "Reminiscences of Admiral Spruance"
World War II Battle Evaluation Group Project ("Bates Reports")

Operational Archives Branch, Naval History and Heritage Command Archives, Washington, DC (NHHC)

Japanese Monographs (U.S. Army, Far East Command, Military History Section)
Samuel Eliot Morison Papers
Raymond A. Spruance Papers
Richmond K. Turner Papers

Franklin D. Roosevelt Library, Hyde Park, New York

"FDR Day by Day," White House Daily Log
FDR Safe Files
Stephen T. Early Papers
Harry L. Hopkins Papers
Motion Pictures Collection
The President's Secretary's File, 1933–1945
Press Conferences of President Franklin D. Roosevelt, 1933–1945
John Toland Papers, 1949–1991
White House Map Room Papers, 1941–1945

Oral History Collections

The Columbia Center for Oral History (CCOH), Columbia University, New York, NY

John J. Ballentine   William W. Buchanan
Robert Blake   Robert Bostwick Carney

Joseph J. Clark
Edward A. Craig
Donald Duncan
Graves B. Erskine
James Fife
Leo D. Hermle
Harry W. Hill
Robert E. Hogaboom
John Hoover
Louis R. Jones
Thomas C. Kinkaid
John C. McQueen

Vernon E. Megee
Charles J. Moore
John C. Munn
Ralph C. Parker
Dewitt Peck
James S. Russell
Ronald D. Salmon
Joseph L. Stewart
Edward W. Snedeker
Felix B. Stump
Henry Williams

Oral History Program, U.S. Naval Institute, Annapolis, Maryland, 1969–2005

George W. Anderson Jr.
Bernard L. Austin
Paul H. Backus
Michael Bak Jr.
Hanson W. Baldwin
Bernhard H. Bieri
Gerald F. Bogan
Roger L. Bond
Thomas B. Buell
Arleigh A. Burke
Slade D. Cutter
James H. Doolittle
Thomas H. Dyer
Harry D. Felt
Noel Gayler
Truman J. Hedding
Stephen Jurika Jr.
Cecil S. King Jr.
Edwin T. Layton

Fitzhugh Lee
Kent L. Lee
David McCampbell
Arthur H. McCollum
John L. McCrea
George H. Miller
Henry L. Miller
Catherine Freeman Nimitz et al.,
   *Recollections of Fleet Admiral Chester
   W. Nimitz*
James D. Ramage
Herbert D. Riley
Joseph J. Rochefort
William J. Sebald
Roland N. Smoot
Arthur D. Struble
Ray Tarbuck
John S. Thach

Government and Military Publications, Official Histories, Unpublished Diaries, Lectures, and Correspondence

Alexander, Joseph H. *Closing in: Marines in the Seizure of Iwo Jima.* History and Museums Division, Headquarters, U.S. Marine Corps, 1994.
Appleman, Roy Edgar. *Okinawa: The Last Battle.* The Department of the Army, 1948.
Bartley, Whitman S. *Iwo Jima: Amphibious Epic.* Historical Branch, G-3 Division, Headquarters, U.S. Marine Corps, 1954.

Bates, Richard W. *The Battle for Leyte Gulf, October 1944: Strategical and Tactical Analysis. Vol. 5. "Battle of Surigao Strait."* U.S. Naval War College Battle Evaluation Group Report, prepared for Bureau of Naval Personnel, 1958.

Bell, William A. Diary, December 1944 to January 1945.

Bell, William A. "Under the Nips' Nose," unpublished manuscript.

Boyd, William B., and Buford Rowland. *U.S. Navy Bureau of Ordnance in World War II.* Bureau of Ordnance, Department of the Navy, Washington, DC, 1953.

Carter, Worrall Reed. *Beans, Bullets, and Black Oil: The Story of Fleet Logistics Afloat in the Pacific During World War II.* Washington: Department of the Navy, 1953.

Clary, John W. "Wartime Diary." Accessed January 3, 2018. http://www.warfish.com/gaz_clary.html.

Commander in Chief, U.S. Pacific Fleet. "CINCPAC Grey Book: Running Estimate of the Situation for the Pacific War." Naval Historical Center, Washington, DC.

Craven, Wesley Frank, and James Lea Cate, eds. *The Army Air Forces in World War II. Vol. 5. The Pacific: Matterhorn to Nagasaki: June 1944 to August 1945.* University of Chicago Press, 1948.

Davis, Elmer, and Byron Price. *War Information and Censorship.* American Council on Public Affairs, 1944.

Deal, Robert M. Personal account. *USS Johnston* Veterans Association pamphlet.

Donigan, Henry J. *Peleliu: The Forgotten Battle. Marine Corps Gazette,* September 1994. Accessed October 19, 2017. https://www.sofmag.com/fury-in-the-pacific-battle-of-peleliu-battle-of-angaur-world-war-ii/.

Dyer, George C. *The Amphibians Came to Conquer: The Story of Admiral Richmond Kelly Turner.* Washington: U.S. Dept. of the Navy, U.S. Govt. Print. Off., 1972.

Fenoglio, Melvin. "This I Remember." Accessed April 21, 2019. https://dd803.org/crew/stories-from-the-crew/melvin-fenoglio-account.

Gayle, Gordon D. *Bloody Beaches: The Marines at Peleliu.* Diane Publishing, 1996.

Genda, Minoru. "Tactical Planning in the Imperial Japanese Navy." Lecture delivered at the U.S. Naval War College, March 7, 1969.

Glantz, David M. *August Storm: The Soviet 1945 Strategic Offensive in Manchuria.* Leavenworth Papers, Combat Studies Institute, U.S. Army Command and General Staff College, Fort Leavenworth, Kansas, 1983.

Green, Maurice Fred. *Report by Lieutenant Maurice Fred Green, Survivor of the Hoel.* Accessed October 2017. http://ussjohnston-hoel.com/6199.html.

Hansell, Haywood S. *The Strategic Air War Against Germany and Japan: A Memoir.* Office of Air Force History, U.S. Air Force, 1986.

Hayes, Grace P. *The History of the Joint Chiefs of Staff in World War II: The War Against Japan.* Historical Section, Joint Chiefs of Staff, 1953.

Heimdahl, William C., and Edward J. Marolda, eds. *Guide to United States Naval Administrative Histories of World War II.* Washington: Naval History Division, Dept. of the Navy, 1976.

Japanese Defense of Cities as Exemplified by the Battle of Manila, A Report by XIV Corps. Published by A. C. of S., G-2, Headquarters Sixth Army, July 1, 1945.

Joint Army Navy Assessment Committee (JANAC). *Japanese Naval and Merchant Shipping Losses During World War II by All Causes.* Washington: Government Printing Office, 1947.

Koda, Yoji, Vice Admiral, JMSDF (ret.). "Doctrine and Strategy of IJN." Lecture with slides delivered at the U.S. Naval War College, January 6, 2011.

Matloff, Maurice, and Edwin M. Snell. *Strategic Planning for Coalition Warfare 1941–1942.* Washington: Office of the Chief of Military History, Dept. of the Army, 1953–59.

McDaniel, J. T., ed. *U.S.S. Tang (SS-306): American Submarine War Patrol Reports.* Riverdale, GA: Riverdale Books, 2005.

——. *U.S.S. Wahoo (SS-238): American Submarine War Patrol Reports.* Riverdale, GA: Riverdale Books, 2005.

McEnery, Kevin T. *The XIV Corps Battle for Manila, February 1945.* U.S. Army, Fort Leavenworth, KS, 1993.

Nelson, Charlie. "Report of Captain Charlie Nelson, USNR." http://destroyerhistory .org/fletcherclass.

Parker, Frederick D. *A Priceless Advantage: U.S. Navy Communications Intelligence and the Battles of Coral Sea, Midway, and the Aleutians.* Series IV: World War II, Vol. 5, 2017. Center for Cryptologic History, National Security Agency, Washington.

Price, Byron. *A Report on the Office of Censorship.* United States Government Printing Office, Washington, 1945.

Reports of General MacArthur: The Campaigns of MacArthur in the Pacific. U.S. Army General Staff of G.H.Q., 1966.

Rigdon, William. "Log of the President's Trip to the Berlin Conference," July 6 to August 7, 1945. Washington: Office of the President, 1945.

Ryukyus: The U.S. Army Campaigns of World War II. U.S. Department of Defense, Department of the Army, Center of Military History, 2014.

Sato, Kenryo. "Dai Toa War Memoir" (unpublished manuscript). John Toland Papers, FDR Library, Hyde Park, New York.

Schwartz, Joseph L. *Experiences in Battle of the Medical Department of the Navy.* U.S. Department of the Navy, 1953.

Shaw, Nalty, et al. *History of U.S. Marine Corps Operations in World War II: Central Pacific Drive.* Historical Branch, G-3 Division, Headquarters, U.S. Marine Corps, 1958.

Smith, Robert Ross. *Triumph in the Philippines.* Office of the Chief of Military History, Department of the Army, 1963.

Smyth, H. D. *Atomic Energy for Military Purposes.* Princeton University Press, 1945.

Steere, Edward. *The Graves Registration Service in World War II.* Q.M.C. Historical Studies No. 21. Washington: Historical Section, Office of the Quartermaster General, General Printing Office, 1951.

Stimson, Henry L. *Henry Lewis Stimson Diaries.* Manuscripts and Archives, Yale University Library, New Haven, Connecticut.

U.S. Army, Far East Command. *5th Air Fleet Operations, February–August 1945.* Japanese Operational Monograph Series, No. 86. Tokyo: Military History Section, Special Staff, General Headquarters, Far East Command, published in English translation, March 14, 1962.

U.S. Army, Far East Command. *The Imperial Japanese Navy in World War II: A Graphic Presentation of the Japanese Naval Organization and List of Combatant and Non-Combatant Vessels Lost or Damaged in the War.* Japanese Operational Monograph Series, No. 116. Tokyo: Military History Section, Special Staff, General Headquarters, Far East Command, 1952.

U.S. Civilian Production Administration. *Industrial Mobilization for War: History of the War Production Board and Predecessor Agencies, 1940–1945.* Washington: U.S. Govt. Print. Off., 1947.

U.S. Department of Commerce, Bureau of the Census. *Historical Statistics of the United States, Colonial Times to 1970.* Washington: U.S. Govt. Print. Off., 1975.

U.S. Department of State. *Foreign Relations of the United States: Diplomatic Papers. The Conference of Berlin (the Potsdam Conference) 1945.* U.S. Govt. Print. Off., 1960.

U.S. Department of the Navy. *Building the Navy's Bases in World War II: History of the Bureau of Yards and Docks and the Civil Engineer Corps, 1940–1946.* Washington: U.S. Govt. Print. Off., 1947.

U.S. Department of the Navy. Secret Information Bulletin No. 24: "Battle Experience: Radar Pickets and Methods of Combating Suicide Attacks Off Okinawa, March–May 1945," July 20, 1945.

U.S. Department of War. *Basic Field Manual: Regulations for Correspondents Accompanying U.S. Army Forces in the Field.* Washington: U.S. Govt. Print. Off., 1942.

U.S. Office of Naval Operations. *U.S. Naval Aviation in the Pacific.* Washington: U.S. Govt. Print. Off., 1947.

U.S. Strategic Bombing Survey (USSBS). *Air Campaigns of the Pacific War.* Washington: U.S. Strategic Bombing Survey, Military Analysis Division, 1947.

———. *The Campaigns of the Pacific War.* Washington: U.S. Strategic Bombing Survey (Pacific), Naval Analysis Division, 1946.

———. *Effects of Air Attack on Japanese Urban Economy (Summary Report).* 1947.

———. *Effects of Atomic Bombs on Hiroshima & Nagasaki.* 1946.

———. *The Effects of Bombing on Health and Medical Services in Japan.* 1947.

———. *The Effects of Strategic Bombing on Japanese Morale.* 1947.

———. *The Effects of Strategic Bombing on Japan's War Economy.* 1946.

———. *Effects of the Incendiary Bomb Attacks on Japan (a Report on Eight Cities).* 1947.

———. *Interrogations of Japanese Officials.* 2 vols. 1947.

———. *Japanese Air Power.* 1946.

———. *Japanese Merchant Shipping.* 1946.

———. *Japanese War Production Industries.* 1946.

———. *Japan's Struggle to End the War.* 1946.

———. *The Offensive Mine Laying Campaign Against Japan.* 1946.

———. *A Report on Physical Damage in Japan (Summary Report).* 1947.

————. *The Strategic Air Operations of Very Heavy Bombardment in the War Against Japan (Twentieth Air Force)*. 1947.

————. *Summary Report (Pacific War)*. 1946.

————. *The War Against Japanese Transportation, 1941–45*. 1947.

Vollinger, John. "The World War II Memoirs of John Vollinger." http://www .janesoceania.com/ww2_johann_memoirs.

The War Reports of General of the Army George C. Marshall, Chief of Staff, General of the Army H. H. Arnold, Commanding General, Army Air Forces [and] Fleet Admiral Ernest J. King, Commander-in-Chief, United States Fleet and Chief of Naval Operations. Philadelphia: Lippincott, 1947.

Wolfson Collection of Decorative and Propaganda Arts. The Wolfsonian Library, Miami Beach, Florida.

Books

Adams, Henry Hitch. *Witness to Power: The Life of Fleet Admiral William D. Leahy*. Naval Institute Press, 1985.

Agawa, Hiroyuki. *The Reluctant Admiral: Yamamoto and the Imperial Navy*. Kodansha International, 1979.

Albion, Robert G. *Makers of Naval Policy, 1798–1947*. Naval Institute Press, 1980.

Allinson, Gary D., ed. *The Columbia Guide to Modern Japanese History*. New York: Columbia University Press, 1999.

Alperovitz, Gar, and Sanho Tree. *The Decision to Use the Atomic Bomb*. New York: Harper Collins, 1996.

Arnold, Henry Harley. *Global Mission*. 1st ed. New York: Harper, 1949.

Asada, Sadao. *From Mahan to Pearl Harbor: The Imperial Japanese Navy and the United States*. Naval Institute Press, 2006.

Astor, Gerald. *Wings of Gold: The U.S. Naval Air Campaign in World War II*. Presidio Press/Ballantine Books, 2004.

Auer, James E., ed. *From Marco Polo Bridge to Pearl Harbor: Who Was Responsible?* Yomiuri Shinbunsha, 2010.

Badgley, John. *Frigate Men: Life on Coast Guard Frigate U.S.S. Bisbee, PF-46, During World War II*. New Vintage Press, 2007.

Baime, A. J. *The Arsenal of Democracy: FDR, Detroit, and an Epic Quest to Arm an America at War*. Mariner Books, Houghton Mifflin Harcourt, 2015.

Baker, Russell. *Growing Up*. Congdon & Weed, 1982.

Barbey, Daniel E. *MacArthur's Amphibious Navy: Seventh Amphibious Force Operations, 1943–1945*. Naval Institute Press, 1971.

Beach, Edward L. *Submarine!* Pocket Star Books, 2004.

Beaver, Floyd. *Sailor from Oklahoma: One Man's Two-Ocean War*. Naval Institute Press, 2009.

Becton, F. J., et al. *The Ship That Would Not Die*. Pictorial Histories Publ. Co., 1993.

Belote, James H., and William M. Belote. *Titans of the Seas: The Development and Operations of Japanese and American Carrier Task Forces During World War II*. New York: Harper & Row, 1975.

Benedict, Ruth. *The Chrysanthemum and the Sword: Patterns of Japanese Culture*. Tokyo: Charles E. Tuttle Co., 1954.

Bix, Herbert P. *Hirohito and the Making of Modern Japan*. New York: HarperCollins, 2000.

Black, Conrad. *Franklin Delano Roosevelt: Champion of Freedom*. New York: Public Affairs, 2003.

Blaik, Earl H. *The Red Blaik Story*. Arlington House, 1974.

Blair, Clay. *Silent Victory: The U.S. Submarine War Against Japan*. 1st ed. Philadelphia: Lippincott, 1975.

Blum, John Morton. *V Was for Victory: Politics and American Culture During World War II*. Harcourt Brace, 1977.

Boquet, Yves. *The Philippine Archipelago*. Springer, 2017.

Borneman, Walter R. *MacArthur at War: World War II in the Pacific*. Back Bay Books, 2017.

Bradlee, Benjamin C. *A Good Life: Newspapering and Other Adventures*. Simon & Schuster, 1995.

Bradley, James. *Flags of Our Fathers: Heroes of Iwo Jima*. Bantam, 2000.

———. *Flyboys: A True Story of Courage*. Little, Brown, 2006.

Bridgland, Tony. *Waves of Hate: Naval Atrocities of the Second World War*. Leo Cooper, 2002.

Brinkley, David. *Washington Goes to War: The Extraordinary Story of the Transformation of a City and a Nation*. New York: Alfred A. Knopf, 1988.

Bruce, Roy W., and Charles R. Leonard. *Crommelin's Thunderbirds: Air Group 12 Strikes the Heart of Japan*. Naval Institute Press, 1994.

Bruning, John R. *Ship Strike Pacific*. Zenith Press, 2005.

Bryan, J. III. *Aircraft Carrier*. Ballantine Books, 1954.

Budiansky, Stephen. *Battle of Wits: The Complete Story of Codebreaking in World War II*. Free Press, 2000.

Buell, Harold L. *Dauntless Helldivers: A Dive-bomber Pilot's Epic Story of the Carrier Battles*. New York: Orion, 1991.

Buell, Thomas B. *Master of Sea Power: A Biography of Fleet Admiral Ernest J. King*. Little, Brown, 1980.

———. *The Quiet Warrior: A Biography of Admiral Raymond A. Spruance*. Naval Institute Press, 1987.

Buhite, Russell D., and David W. Levy, eds. *FDR's Fireside Chats*. Penguin Books, 1992.

Burgin, R. V., and Bill Marvel. *Islands of the Damned: A Marine at War in the Pacific*. NAL Caliber, 2011.

Burlingame, Roger. *Don't Let Them Scare You: The Life and Times of Elmer Davis*. Greenwood Press, 1974.

Burns, James MacGregor. *Roosevelt: The Soldier of Freedom*. Harcourt Brace Jovanovich, 1970.

Buruma, Ian. *Inventing Japan, 1853–1964*. Modern Library, 2003.

Byrnes, James F. *Speaking Frankly*. Greenwood Press, 1974.

Caidin, Martin. *A Torch to the Enemy: The Fire Raid on Tokyo*. Bantam Books, 1992.

Calhoun, C. Raymond. *Tin Can Sailor: Life Aboard the USS Sterett, 1939–1945*. Naval Institute Press, 1993.

Calvert, James F. *Silent Running: My Years on a World War II Attack Submarine*. Castle, 2008.

Caro, Robert A. *Master of the Senate: The Years of Lyndon Johnson, Vol. 3*. Random House, 2003.

Carroll, Andrew, ed. *War Letters: Extraordinary Correspondence from American Wars*. Scribner, 2001.

Casey, Robert J. *Battle Below*. Bobbs-Merrill, 1945.

———. *Torpedo Junction*. London: Jarrolds, 1944.

Childs, Marquis W. *I Write from Washington*. Harper, 1942.

Clark, J. J., and Clark G. Reynolds. *Carrier Admiral*. New York: D. McKay, 1967.

Cleary, Thomas. *The Japanese Art of War: Understanding the Culture of Strategy*. Boston: Shambhala Classics, 2005.

Coffey, Thomas M. *Hap: The Story of the U.S. Air Force and the Man Who Built It, General Henry H. "Hap" Arnold*. Viking Press, 1982.

Coletta, Paolo E. *Admiral Marc A. Mitscher and U.S. Naval Aviation: Bald Eagle*. Edwin Mellen Press, 1997.

Colman, Penny. *Rosie the Riveter: Women Working on the Home Front in World War II*. Crown Publishers, 1995.

Conant, Jennet. *Tuxedo Park: A Wall Street Tycoon and the Secret Palace of Science That Changed the Course of World War II*. Thorndike, 2002.

Conrad, Joseph, and Cedric Thomas Watts. *Typhoon and Other Tales*. Oxford University Press, 2008.

Cook, Haruko Taya, and Theodore F. Cook, eds. *Japan at War: An Oral History*. The New Press, 1992.

Cooke, Alistair. *The American Home Front, 1941–1942*. Atlantic Monthly Press, 2006.

Cooper, Page. *Navy Nurse*. New York: Whittlesey House, McGraw-Hill, 1946.

Crew, Thomas E. *Combat Loaded: Across the Pacific on the USS Tate*. Texas A & M University Press, 2007.

Current, Richard Nelson. *Secretary Stimson: A Study in Statecraft*. Rutgers University Press, 1954.

Cutler, Thomas J. *The Battle of Leyte Gulf, 23–26 October, 1944*. Naval Institute Press, 2001.

Dallek, Robert. *Franklin D. Roosevelt: A Political Life*. Viking, 2017.

———. *Franklin D. Roosevelt and American Foreign Policy, 1932–1945*. Oxford University Press, 1995.

Davidson, Joel R. *The Unsinkable Fleet: The Politics of U.S. Navy Expansion in World War II*. Naval Institute Press, 1996.

Davis, Kenneth S. *FDR: The War President, 1940–1943: A History*. Random House, 2000.

Davis, Robert T. *The U.S. Army and the Media in the 20th Century*. Combat Studies Inst. Press, 2009.

Davis, William E. *Sinking the Rising Sun: Dog Fighting & Dive Bombing in World War II: A Navy Fighter Pilot's Story*. Zenith Press, 2007.

Deacon, Richard. *Kempei Tai: The Japanese Secret Service Then and Now*. Tokyo: Charles E. Tuttle Co., 1982.

DeRose, James F. *Unrestricted Warfare: How a New Breed of Officers Led the Submarine Force to Victory in World War II*. Castle Books, 2006.

Dixon, Chris, Sean Brawley, and Beatrice Trefalt, eds. *Competing Voices from the Pacific War: Fighting Words*. Santa Barbara, CA: Greenwood/ABC-CLIO, 2009.

Dos Passos, John. *Tour of Duty*. Greenwood Press, 1974.

Dower, John W. *Cultures of War: Pearl Harbor, Hiroshima, 9–11, Iraq*. W. W. Norton, 2010.

———. *Japan In War and Peace: Selected Essays*. New Press; distributed by W. W. Norton, 1993.

———. *War Without Mercy: Race and Power in the Pacific War*. Pantheon Books, 1986.

Drea, Edward J. *In the Service of the Emperor: Essays on the Imperial Japanese Army*. University of Nebraska Press, 2003.

Driscoll, Joseph. *Pacific Victory 1945*. Lippincott, 1944.

Drury, Bob, and Thomas Clavin. *Halsey's Typhoon: The True Story of a Fighting Admiral, an Epic Storm, and an Untold Rescue*. Atlantic Monthly Press, 2007.

Dull, Paul S. *A Battle History of the Imperial Japanese Navy, 1941–1945*. Naval Institute Press, 1978.

Dunn, William J. *Pacific Microphone*. Texas A & M Univ. Press, 1988.

Edgerton, Robert B. *Warriors of the Rising Sun: A History of the Japanese Military*. W. W. Norton, 1997.

Eichelberger, Robert L., and Milton MacKaye. *Our Jungle Road to Tokyo*. The Viking Press, 1950.

Eisenhower, Dwight D. *Crusade in Europe*. The Easton Press, 2001.

Eisenhower, Dwight D. *The Eisenhower Diaries*, ed. Robert Hugh Ferrell. The Easton Press, 1989.

Ellis, John. *World War II, a Statistical Survey: The Essential Facts and Figures for All the Combatants*. New York: Facts on File, 1995.

Elphick, Peter. *Liberty: The Ships That Won the War*. Naval Institute Press, 2001.

Enright, Joseph F., and James W. Ryan. *Sea Assault: The Sinking of Japan's Secret Supership*. St. Martin's Paperbacks, 2000.

Evans, David, and Mark Peattie. *Kaigun: Strategy, Tactics, and Technology in the Imperial Japanese Navy, 1887–1941*. Naval Institute Press, 1997.

Evans, David C., ed. *The Japanese Navy in World War II: In the Words of Former Japanese Naval Officers*. Naval Institute Press, 1993.

Evans, Hugh E. *The Hidden Campaign: FDR's Health and the 1944 Election*. Routledge, 2016.

Evans, Walter R. *Wartime Sea Stories: Life Aboard Ships, 1942–1945*. IUniverse, 2006.

Ewing, Steve. *Thach Weave: The Life of Jimmie Thach*. Naval Institute Press, 2004.

Fahey, James J. *Pacific War Diary, 1942–1945*. Houghton, 1963.

Feifer, George. *Tennozan: The Battle of Okinawa and the Atomic Bomb*. Ticknor & Fields, 1992.

Feis, Herbert. *From Trust to Terror: The Onset of the Cold War, 1945–1950*. W. W. Norton, 1970.

Ferrell, Robert H. *Harry S. Truman*. CQ Press, 2003.

———. *Harry S. Truman and the Bomb: A Documentary History*. High Plains Pub. Co., 1996.

Fisher, Clayton E. *Hooked: Tales & Adventures of a Tailhook Warrior*. Denver, CO: Outskirts, 2009.

Forrestal, James. *The Forrestal Diaries*, ed. Walter Millis. The Viking Press, 1951.

Frank, Richard B. *Downfall: The End of the Imperial Japanese Empire*. Penguin Books, 2001.

Friend, Theodore. *The Blue-Eyed Enemy: Japan Against the West in Java and Luzon, 1942–1945*. Princeton University Press, 2014.

Fujitani, Takashi, et al. *Perilous Memories: The Asia-Pacific Wars*. Duke University Press, 2001.

Fussell, Paul. *Wartime: Understanding and Behavior in the Second World War*. Oxford University Press, 1989.

Gadbois, Robert O. *Hellcat Tales: A U.S. Navy Fighter Pilot in World War II*. Merriam Press, 2011.

Galantin, I. J. *Take Her Deep! A Submarine Against Japan in World War II*. Naval Institute Press, 2007.

Garvey, John. *San Francisco in World War II*. Arcadia Pub., 2007.

Giangreco, D. M. *Hell to Pay: Operation Downfall and the Invasion of Japan, 1945–47*. Naval Institute Press, 2017.

Gibney, Frank, ed. *Senso: The Japanese Remember the Pacific War*. Armonk, NY: M. E. Sharpe, 1995.

Gilbert, Alton. *A Leader Born: The Life of Admiral John Sidney McCain, Pacific Carrier Commander*. Philadelphia: Casemate, 2006.

Gluck, Carol. *Japan's Modern Myths: Ideology in the Late Meiji Period*. Princeton Univ. Press, 1985.

Gluck, Carol, and Stephen R. Graubard, eds. *Showa: The Japan of Hirohito*. W. W. Norton, 1992.

Glusman, John A. *Conduct Under Fire: Four American Doctors and Their Fight for Life as Prisoners of the Japanese 1941–1945*. Penguin Books, 2006.

Goldstein, Donald M., and Kathryn V. Dillon. *The Pacific War Papers: Japanese Documents of World War II*. Washington, DC: Potomac Books, 2006.

Goodwin, Doris Kearns. *No Ordinary Time: Franklin and Eleanor Roosevelt: The Home Front in World War II*. Simon & Schuster, 1994.

Grew, Joseph C. *Turbulent Era: A Diplomatic Record of Forty Years: 1904–1945*. Ayer Co. Pub., 1952.

Grider, George, and Lydel Sims. *War Fish*. Ballantine Books, 1973.

Griffin, Alexander R. *Out of Carnage*. Howell, Soskin, 1945.

Groves, Leslie Richard. *Now It Can Be Told: The Story of the Manhattan Project*. Harper & Row, 1962.

Hachiya, Michihiko, and Warner Wells. *Hiroshima Diary: The Journal of a Japanese Physician, August 6–September 30, 1945: Fifty Years Later*. University of North Carolina Press, 1995.

Halsey, William F., and J. Bryan III. *Admiral Halsey's Story*. Whittlesey House, 1947.

Hammel, Eric, ed. *Aces Against Japan: The American Aces Speak*. Pocket Books, 1992.

Hara, Tameichi, Fred Saito, and Roger Pineau. *Japanese Destroyer Captain: Pearl Harbor, Guadalcanal, Midway—The Great Naval Battles As Seen Through Japanese Eyes*. Naval Institute Press, 2007.

Harper, John A. *Paddles! The Foibles and Finesse of One World War II Landing Signal Officer*. Schiffer Publishing, 2000.

Harries, Meirion, and Susie Harries. *Soldiers of the Sun: The Rise and Fall of the Imperial Japanese Army*. Random House, 1991.

Harris, Brayton. *Admiral Nimitz: The Commander of the Pacific Ocean Theater*. Palgrave Macmillan, 2012.

Harris, Mark Jonathan, Franklin D. Mitchell, and Steven J. Schechter, eds. *The Homefront: America During World War II*. Putnam, 1984.

Hasegawa, Tsuyoshi. *Racing the Enemy: Stalin, Truman, and the Surrender of Japan*. Belknap Press of Harvard University Press, 2006.

Hassett, William D. *Off the Record with F.D.R., 1942–1945*. Academy Chicago Publishers, 2001.

Hastings, Max. *Retribution: The Battle for Japan, 1944–45*. Vintage, 2009.

Havens, Thomas R. H. *Valley of Darkness: The Japanese People and World War Two*. University Press of America, 1986.

Healy, George W., and Turner Catledge. *A Lifetime on Deadline: Self-Portrait of a Southern Journalist*. Pelican, 1976.

Henderson, Bruce B. *Down to the Sea: An Epic Story of Naval Disaster and Heroism in World War II*. HarperCollins, 2008.

Herman, Arthur. *Douglas MacArthur: American Warrior*. Random House, 2017.

Hersey, John. *Hiroshima*. Pendulum Press, 1978.

Higa, Tomiko. *The Girl with the White Flag*. Dell Pub., 1991.

Hoehling, A. A. *The Fighting Liberty Ships: A Memoir*. Naval Institute Press, 1996.

Holmes, W. J. *Double-Edged Secrets: U.S. Naval Intelligence Operations in the Pacific During World War II*. Naval Institute Press, 1979.

Hoopes, Townsend, and Douglas Brinkley. *Driven Patriot: The Life and Times of James Forrestal*. Naval Institute Press, 2000.

Hornfischer, James D. *The Last Stand of the Tin Can Sailors*. Bantam Books, 2005.

———. *The Fleet at Flood Tide: America at Total War in the Pacific, 1944–1945*. Bantam Books, 2017.

Hoyt, Edwin Palmer. *How They Won the War in the Pacific: Nimitz and his Admirals*. Weybright and Talley, 1970.

Huber, Thomas M. *Japan's Battle of Okinawa, April–June 1945*. University Press of the Pacific, 2005.

Hughes, Thomas Alexander. *Admiral Bill Halsey: A Naval Life*. Harvard University Press, 2016.

Huie, William Bradford. *Can Do! The Story of the Seabees*. E. P. Dutton, 1944.

———. *From Omaha to Okinawa: The Story of the Seabees*. E. P. Dutton & Company, Inc., 1945.

Hull, McAllister H., et al. *Rider of the Pale Horse: A Memoir of Los Alamos and Beyond*. University of New Mexico Press, 2015.

Hunt, George P. *Coral Comes High*. Harper, 1946.

Hynes, Samuel L. *Flights of Passage: Reflections of a World War II Aviator*. Naval Institute Press, 1988.

Inoguchi, Rikihei, and Tadashi Nakajima. *The Divine Wind: Japan's Kamikaze Force in World War II*. Translated by Roger Pineau. Naval Institute Press, 1994.

Irokawa, Daikichi. *The Age of Hirohito: In Search of Modern Japan*. The Free Press, 1995.

Itō, Masanori. *The End of the Imperial Japanese Navy*, trans. Roger Pineau. Jove, 1986.

Jackson, Robert H. *That Man: An Insider's Portrait of Franklin D. Roosevelt*. Oxford University Press, 2004.

Jackson, Steve. *Lucky Lady: The World War II Heroics of the USS Santa Fe and Franklin*. Carroll & Graf Pub., 2004.

James, Dorris Clayton. *The Years of MacArthur*. Vol. 1, 1880–1941; Vol. 2, 1941–1945. Houghton Mifflin, 1970.

Janssens, Ruud. *"What Future for Japan?": U.S. Wartime Planning for the Postwar Era, 1942–1945*. Rodopi, 1995.

Jeffries, John W. *Wartime America: The World War II Home Front*. Ivan R. Dee, 1998.

Jernigan, Emory J. *Tin Can Man*. Vandamere Press, 1993.

Johnston, Stanley. *Queen of the Flat-Tops: The U.S.S. Lexington and the Coral Sea Battle*. E. P. Dutton, 1942.

Josephy, Alvin M. *The Long and the Short and the Tall: The Story of a Marine Combat Unit in the Pacific*. Burford Books, 2000.

Kakehashi, Kumiko, and Giles Murray. *So Sad to Fall in Battle: An Account of War Based on General Tadamichi Kuribayashi's Letters from Iwo Jima*. Translated by Giles Murray. Presidio Press/Ballantine Books, 2007.

Kase, Toshikazu. *Journey to the Missouri*. Yale University Press, 1950.

Kawahara, Toshiaki. *Hirohito and His Times: A Japanese Perspective*. Tokyo: Kodansha International, 1990.

Keene, Donald. *So Lovely a Country Will Never Perish: Wartime Diaries of Japanese Writers*. Columbia University Press, 2010.

Keith, Don. *Undersea Warrior: The World War II Story of "Mush" Morton and the USS Wahoo*. Dutton Caliber, 2012.

Kelly, Cynthia C., ed. *The Manhattan Project: The Birth of the Atomic Bomb in the Words of Its Creators, Eyewitnesses, and Historians*. Black Dog & Leventhal, 2017.

Kennedy, David M. *The American People in World War II: Freedom from Fear, Part Two*. Oxford University Press, 2003.

Kenney, George C. *General Kenney Reports: A Personal History of the Pacific War*. Duell, Sloan, and Pearce, 1949.

Kershaw, Alex. *Escape from the Deep: The Epic Story of a Legendary Submarine and Her Courageous Crew*. Da Capo, 2009.

Kido, Kōichi. *The Diary of Marquis Kido, 1931–45: Selected Translations into English*. Frederick, MD: University Publications of America, 1984.

King, Dan. *The Last Zero Fighter: Firsthand Accounts from WWII Japanese Naval Pilots*. Pacific Press, 2016.

King, Dan, and Linda Ryan. *A Tomb Called Iwo Jima: Firsthand Accounts from Japanese Survivors*. CreateSpace Independent Publishing Platform, 2015.

King, Ernest J., and Walter Muir Whitehill. *Fleet Admiral King: A Naval Record*. W. W. Norton, 1952.

Kiyosawa, Kiyoshi. *A Diary of Darkness: The Wartime Diary of Kiyosawa Kiyoshi*. Translated by Eugene Soviak and Kamiyama Tamie. Princeton University Press, 1999.

Kort, Michael, ed. *The Columbia Guide to Hiroshima and the Bomb*. Columbia University Press, 2007.

Krueger, Walter. *From Down Under to Nippon: The Story of Sixth Army in World War II*. Battery Classics, 1989.

Kuehn, John T., et al. *Eyewitness Pacific Theater: Firsthand Accounts of the War in the Pacific from Pearl Harbor to the Atomic Bombs*. Sterling, 2008.

Lacey, Laura Homan. *Stay off the Skyline: A Personal History of the 6th Marine Division*. Potomac Books, 2007.

Lane, Frederic Chapin. *Ships for Victory: A History of Shipbuilding under the U.S. Maritime Commission in World War II*. Johns Hopkins Univ. Press, 2001.

Laurence, William L. *Dawn Over Zero: The Story of the Atomic Bomb*. Greenwood Press, 1972.

Lawson, Robert. *U.S. Navy Dive and Torpedo Bombers of World War II*. Zenith Press, 2001.

Lawson, Robert, and Barrett Tillman. *U.S. Navy Air Combat, 1939–46*. Osceola, WI: MBI Publishing, 2000.

Layton, Edwin T., with Roger Pineau and John Costello. *"And I Was There": Pearl Harbor and Midway—Breaking the Secrets*. William Morrow, 1985.

Lea, Tom, and Brendan M. Greeley. *The Two Thousand Yard Stare: Tom Lea's World War II*. Texas A & M University Press, 2008.

Leach, Douglas Edward. *Now Hear This: The Memoir of a Junior Naval Officer in the Great Pacific War.* Kent, OH: Kent State Univ. Press, 1987.

Leahy, William D. *I Was There.* Whittlesey, 1950.

Leary, William M. *MacArthur and the American Century: A Reader.* University of Nebraska Press, 2003.

Leckie, Robert. *Okinawa: The Last Battle of World War II.* Penguin, 1996.

Lee, Clark. *They Call It the Pacific: An Eye-Witness Story of Our War Against Japan From Bataan to the Solomons.* Viking Press, 1943.

Lee, Robert Edson. *To the War.* Alfred A. Knopf, 1968.

LeMay, Curtis E., and MacKinlay Kantor. *Mission with LeMay.* Doubleday, 1965.

LeMay, Curtis E., and Bill Yenne. *Superfortress: The Boeing B-29 and American Airpower in World War II.* Westholme Publishing, 2007.

Lerner, Max. *Public Journal: Marginal Notes on Wartime America.* Viking Press, 1945.

Lilly, Capt. Michael A., USN (Ret). *Nimitz at Ease.* Stairway Press, 2019.

Lingeman, Richard. *Don't You Know There's a War On? The American Home Front, 1941–45.* G. P. Putnam's Sons, 1970.

Litoff, Judy Barrett, and David C. Smith, eds. *American Women in a World at War: Contemporary Accounts from World War II.* Wilmington, DE: Scholarly Resources, 1997.

———. *Since You Went Away: World War II Letters from American Women on the Home Front.* Oxford University Press, 1991.

Lockwood, Charles A. *Sink 'Em All.* Bantam Books, 1951.

Lockwood, Charles A., and Hans Christian Adamson. *Hellcats of the Sea: Operation Barney and the Mission to the Sea of Japan.* Chilton Co., 1955.

Lotchin, Roger W. *The Bad City in the Good War: San Francisco, Los Angeles, Oakland and San Diego.* Bloomington: Indiana Univ. Press, 2003.

Lott, Arnold S. *Brave Ship, Brave Men.* Naval Institute Press, 1994.

Lucas, Jim Griffing. *Combat Correspondent.* New York: Reynal & Hitchcock, 1944.

Lundgren, Robert. *The World Wonder'd: What Really Happened off Samar.* Nimble Books, 2014.

Luvaas, Jay, ed. *Dear Miss Em: General Eichelberger's War in the Pacific, 1942–1945.* Greenwood Press, 1972.

MacArthur, Douglas. *Reminiscences.* 1st ed. McGraw-Hill, 1964.

Mace, Sterling, and Nick Allen. *Battleground Pacific: A Marine Rifleman's Combat Odyssey in K/3/5.* St. Martin's Griffin, 2013.

McWhorter, Hamilton, and Jay A. Stout. *The First Hellcat Ace.* Pacifica Military History, 2000.

Mahan, A. T., and Allan F. Westcott. *Mahan on Naval Warfare: Selections from the Writing of Rear Admiral Alfred T. Mahan.* Dover Publications, 1999.

Mair, Michael. *Kaiten: Japan's Secret Manned Suicide Submarine and the First American Ship It Sank in WWII.* Penguin Group US, 2015.

Manchester, William Raymond. *American Caesar: Douglas MacArthur, 1880–1964.* Little, Brown, 1978.

———. *Goodbye, Darkness: A Memoir of the Pacific War.* Little, Brown, 1980.

Marsden, Lawrence A. *Attack Transport: The Story of the U.S.S. Doyen.* University of Michigan Press, 1946.

Marshall, George Catlett. *The Papers of George Catlett Marshall,* ed. Larry I. Bland and Sharon R. Stevens. Johns Hopkins Univ. Press, 2003.

Mason, John T., ed. *The Pacific War Remembered: An Oral History Collection.* Naval Institute Press, 1986.

Mason, Theodore C. *Battleship Sailor.* Naval Institute Press, 1982.

———. *Rendezvous with Destiny: A Sailor's War.* Naval Institute Press, 1997.

———. *"We Will Stand by You": Serving in the Pawnee, 1942–1945.* Naval Institute Press, 1996.

McCandless, Charles S. *A Flash of Green: Memories of World War II.* Authors Press, 2019.

McCrea, John L., et al. *Captain McCrea's War: The World War II Memoir of Franklin D. Roosevelt's Naval Aide and USS Iowa's First Commanding Officer.* Skyhorse Publishing, 2016.

McCullough, David. *Truman.* Simon & Schuster, 1992.

McIntire, Vice-Admiral Ross T. *White House Physician.* G. P. Putnam's Sons, 1946.

McKelway, St. Clair, and Adam Gopnik. *Reporting at Wit's End: Tales from The New Yorker.* Bloomsbury USA, 2010.

Meijer, Hendrik. *Arthur Vandenberg: The Man in the Middle of the American Century.* University of Chicago Press, 2019.

Melton, Buckner F. *Sea Cobra: Admiral Halsey's Task Force and the Great Pacific Typhoon.* Lyons Press, 2007.

Mencken, H. L., and Marion Elizabeth Rodgers. *The Impossible H. L. Mencken: A Selection of His Best Newspaper Stories.* Doubleday, 1991.

Mendenhall, Corwin. *Submarine Diary.* Naval Institute Press, 1995.

Merrill, James M. *A Sailor's Admiral: A Biography of William F. Halsey.* 1st American ed. Crowell, 1976.

Michener, James A. *The World Is My Home.* Random House, 1992.

Miller, Edward S. *War Plan Orange: The U.S. Strategy to Defeat Japan, 1897–1945.* Naval Institute Press, 1991.

Miller, Max. *It's Tomorrow Out Here.* Whittlesey House, 1945.

Miller, Merle, and Abe Spitzer. *We Dropped the A-Bomb.* T. Y. Crowell Co., 1946.

Monroe-Jones, Edward, and Michael Green. *The Silent Service in World War II: The Story of the U.S. Navy Submarine Force in the Words of the Men Who Lived It.* Casemate, 2012.

Morison, Samuel Eliot. *History of United States Naval Operations in World War II.* Vol. 7. *Aleutians, Gilberts and Marshalls, June 1942–April 1944;* Vol. 8. *New Guinea and the Marianas, 1944;* Vol. 12. *Leyte, June 1944–January 1945;* Vol. 13. *The Liberation of the Philippines, 1944–1945;* Vol. 14. *Victory in the Pacific;* Vol. 15. *Supplement and General Index.* Little, Brown, 1947–1962.

Morita, Akio, Edwin M. Reingold, and Mitsuko Shimomura. *Made in Japan: Akio Morita and Sony*. Dutton Books, 1986.

Morris, Ivan. *The Nobility of Failure: Tragic Heroes in the History of Japan*. Tokyo: Charles E. Tuttle Co., 1982.

Newcomb, Richard F. *Iwo Jima*. Holt, Rinehart and Winston, 1965.

Naitō, Hatsuho. *Thunder Gods: The Kamikaze Pilots Tell Their Story*. Dell Pub., 1990.

Nitobe, Inazo. *Bushido: The Soul of Japan*. Tokyo: Charles E. Tuttle Co., 1969.

O'Donnell, Patrick K, ed. *Into the Rising Sun: In Their Own Words, World War II's Pacific Veterans*. Free Press, 2010.

Ohnuki-Tierney, Emiko. *Kamikaze Diaries: Reflections of Japanese Student Soldiers*. University of Chicago Press, 2007.

O'Kane, Richard H. *Clear the Bridge!: The War Patrols of the U.S.S. Tang*. Chicago: Rand McNally, 1977.

———. *Wahoo: The Patrols of America's Most Famous World War II Submarine*. Novato, CA: Presidio Press, 1987.

Okumiya, Masatake, Jiro Horikoshi, and Martin Caidin. *Zero!* E. P. Dutton, 1956.

Oliver, Douglas L. *Oceania: The Native Cultures of Australia and the Pacific Islands*. Univ. of Hawaii Press, 1989.

Olson, Michael Keith. *Tales from a Tin Can: The USS Dale from Pearl Harbor to Tokyo Bay*. St. Paul: Zenith Press, 2007.

Overy, Richard James. *Why the Allies Won*. Random House, 1995.

The Pacific War Research Society. *The Day Man Lost: Hiroshima, 6 August 1945*. Kodansha International, 1972.

———. *Japan's Longest Day*. Kodansha International, 1973.

Parker, Robert Alexander Clarke. *The Second World War: A Short History*. W. Ross MacDonald School Resource Services Library, 2011.

Perret, Geoffrey. *Days of Sadness, Years of Triumph: The American People, 1939–1945*. University of Wisconsin Press, 1985.

Perry, Glen C. H. *"Dear Bart": Washington Views of World War II*. Greenwood Press, 1982.

Perry, Mark. *The Most Dangerous Man in America: The Making of Douglas MacArthur*. Basic Books, 2014.

Petty, Bruce M., ed. *Voices from the Pacific War: Bluejackets Remember*. Naval Institute Press, 2004.

Phillips, Charles L. *Rain of Fire: B-29s over Japan, 1945*. Paragon Agency, 2002.

Potter, E. B. *Bull Halsey*. Naval Institute Press, 1985.

———. *Nimitz*. Naval Institute Press, 1976.

Potter, E. B., and Chester W. Nimitz. *The Great Sea War: The Story of Naval Action in World War II*. Englewood Cliffs, NJ: Prentice-Hall, 1960.

Prados, John. *Storm over Leyte: The Philippine Invasion and the Destruction of the Japanese Navy*. New American Library, 2016.

Pyle, Ernie. *Last Chapter*. Henry Holt, 1946.

Radford, Arthur William, and Stephen Jurika. *From Pearl Harbor to Vietnam: The Memoirs of Admiral Arthur W. Radford*. Hoover Institution Press, 1980.

Radike, Floyd W. *Across the Dark Islands: The War in the Pacific*. Presidio Press/Ballantine, 2003.

Raines, James Orvill, and William M. McBride. *Good Night Officially: The Pacific War Letters of a Destroyer Sailor: The Letters of Yeoman James Orvill Raines*. Westview, 1994.

Reid, David. *The Brazen Age: New York City and the American Empire: Politics, Art, and Bohemia*. Pantheon Books, 2016.

Reilly, Michael F., and William J. Slocum. *Reilly of the White House*. Simon & Schuster, 1947.

Reischauer, E. O. *The Japanese*. Charles E. Tuttle Co., 1977.

Reporting World War II. Part One: American Journalism 1938–1944; Part Two: American Journalism 1944–1946. New York: Literary Classics of the United States, 1995.

Reynolds, Clark G. *Admiral John H. Towers: Struggle for Naval Air Supremacy*. Naval Institute Press, 1992.

———. *The Fast Carriers: The Forging of an Air Navy*. Naval Institute Press, 2015.

———. *On the Warpath in the Pacific: Admiral Jocko Clark and the Fast Carriers*. Naval Institute Press, 2005.

Rhoades, Weldon E. *Flying MacArthur to Victory*. Texas A & M University Press, 1987.

Rhodes, Richard. *The Making of the Atomic Bomb*. Simon & Schuster, 1987.

Richardson, K. D., and Paul Stillwell. *Reflections of Pearl Harbor: An Oral History of December 7, 1941*. Greenwood Publishing Group, 2005.

Rielly, Robin L. *Kamikazes, Corsairs and Picket Ships: Okinawa 1945*. Casemate, 2010.

Rigdon, William McKinley. *White House Sailor*. Doubleday, 1962.

Ritchie, Donald A. *Reporting from Washington: The History of the Washington Press Corps*. Oxford University Press, 2006.

Robinson, C. Snelling. *200,000 Miles Aboard the Destroyer Cotton*. Kent State University Press, 2000.

Roeder, George H. *The Censored War: American Visual Experience During World War II*. Yale University Press, 1995.

Rogers, Paul P. *The Good Years: MacArthur and Sutherland*. Praeger, 1990.

Romulo, Carlos P. *I See the Philippines Rise*. AMS Press, 1975.

Rosenau, James N. *The Roosevelt Treasury*. 1st ed. Garden City, NY: Doubleday, 1951.

Rosenman, Samuel Irving. *Working with Roosevelt*. Harper, 1952.

Ruhe, William J. *War in the Boats: My World War II Submarine Battles*. Brassey's, 2005.

Russell, Dale. *Hell Above, Deep Water Below*. Tillamook, OR: Bayocean Enterprises, 1995.

Russell, Ronald W. *No Right to Win: A Continuing Dialogue with Veterans of the Battle of Midway*. New York: iUniverse, Inc., 2006.

Rynn, Midori Yamanouchi., and Joseph L. Quinn. *Listen to the Voices from the Sea: Writings of the Fallen Japanese Students*. University of Scranton Press, 2000.

Sakai, Saburo, with Martin Caidin and Fred Saito. *Samurai!* E. P. Dutton, 1956.

Sakaida, Henry. *Imperial Japanese Navy Aces, 1937–45*. Osprey Aerospace, 1998.

Sawyer, L. A., and W. H. Mitchell. *The Liberty Ships: The History of the Emergency Type Cargo Ships Constructed in the United States During the Second World War*. Lloyds of London Press, 1985.

Schaller, Michael. *Douglas MacArthur: The Far Eastern General*. Oxford University Press, 1989.

Schratz, Paul R. *Submarine Commander: A Story of World War II and Korea*. Pocket Books, 1990.

Schultz, Robert, and James Shell. *We Were Pirates: A Torpedoman's Pacific War*. Naval Institute Press, 2009.

Scott, James. *Rampage: MacArthur, Yamashita, and the Battle of Manila*. W. W. Norton, 2018.

———. *The War Below: The Story of Three Submarines That Battled Japan*. Simon & Schuster, 2014.

Sears, David. *At War with the Wind: The Epic Struggle with Japan's World War II Suicide Bombers*. Citadel, 2009.

Sears, Stephen W. *Eyewitness to World War II: The Best of American Heritage*. Houghton Mifflin, 1991.

Sheftall, Mordecai G. *Blossoms in the Wind: Human Legacies of the Kamikaze*. NAL Caliber, 2006.

Shenk, Robert, ed. *Authors at Sea: Modern American Writers Remember Their Naval Service*. Naval Institute Press, 1997.

Sherman, Frederick C. *Combat Command: The American Aircraft Carriers in the Pacific War*. Dutton, 1950.

Sherrod, Robert. *On to Westward: War in the Central Pacific*. Duell, Sloan and Pearce, 1945.

Sherwood, Robert E. *Roosevelt and Hopkins: An Intimate History*. Harper & Brothers, 1948.

Shillony, Ben-Ami. *Politics and Culture in Wartime Japan*. Oxford: Clarendon Press, 1981.

Skulski, Janusz. *The Battleship Yamato*. Naval Institute Press, 1988.

Sledge, E. B. *With the Old Breed: At Peleliu and Okinawa*. Presidio Press, 1990.

Sloan, Bill. *Brotherhood of Heroes: The Marines at Peleliu, 1944: The Bloodiest Battle of the Pacific War*. Simon & Schuster, 2006.

———. *The Ultimate Battle: Okinawa 1945—The Last Epic Struggle of World War II*. Simon & Schuster, 2009.

Smith, Holland M., and Percy Finch. *Coral and Brass*. Scribner, 1949.

Smith, Merriman. *Thank You, Mr. President: A White House Notebook*. Harper & Brothers, 1946.

Smith, Peter C. *Kamikaze: To Die for the Emperor*. Pen & Sword Aviation, 2014.

Smith, Rex Alan, and Gerald A. Meehl. *Pacific War Stories: In the Words of Those Who Survived*. Abbeville Press, 2011.

Smyth, Robert T. *Sea Stories*. iUniverse, 2004.

Solberg, Carl. *Decision and Dissent: With Halsey at Leyte Gulf.* Naval Institute Press, 1995.

Sommers, Sam. *Combat Carriers and My Brushes with History: World War II, 1939–1946.* Montgomery, AL: Black Belt, 1997.

Spector, Ronald H. *Eagle Against the Sun: The American War with Japan.* Free Press, 1984.

Springer, Joseph A. *Inferno: The Epic Life and Death Struggle of the USS Franklin in World War II.* Voyageur Press, 2011.

Stafford, Edward Peary. *The Big E: The Story of the USS Enterprise.* Random House, 1962.

Starr, Kevin. *Embattled Dreams: California in War and Peace, 1940–1950.* Oxford University Press, 2002.

Stenbuck, Jack, ed. *Typewriter Battalion: Dramatic Frontline Dispatches from World War II.* W. Morrow, 1995.

Sterling, Forest. *Wake of the Wahoo.* Riverside, CA: R. A. Cline Publishing, 1999.

Stillwell, Paul, ed. *Air Raid, Pearl Harbor! Recollections of a Day of Infamy.* Naval Institute Press, 1981.

———. *Carrier War: Aviation Art of World War II.* Barnes & Noble, 2007.

Stimson, Henry L., and McGeorge Bundy. *On Active Service in Peace and War.* Harper & Brothers, 1947.

St. John, John F. *Leyte Calling.* The Vanguard Press, 1945.

Stoff, Michael B., et al. *The Manhattan Project: A Documentary Introduction to the Atomic Age.* McGraw-Hill, 2000.

Stoler, Mark A. *Allies and Adversaries: The Joint Chiefs of Staff, the Grand Alliance, and U.S. Strategy in World War II.* Chapel Hill: University of North Carolina Press, 2000.

Straubel, James H. *Air Force Diary: 111 Stories from the Official Service Journal of the USAAF.* Simon & Schuster, 1947.

Sturma, Michael. *Surface and Destroy: The Submarine Gun War in the Pacific.* University Press of Kentucky, 2012.

Summers, Robert E., ed. *Wartime Censorship of Press and Radio.* H. W. Wilson Co., 1942.

Sweeney, Charles W. *War's End: An Eyewitness Account of America's Last Atomic Mission.* Avon Books, 1997.

Takeyama, Michio. *The Scars of War: Tokyo During World War II: The Writings of Takeyama Michio,* ed. Richard H. Minear. Lanham, MD: Rowman & Littlefield, 2007.

Tamayama, Kazuo, and John Nunneley. *Tales by Japanese Soldiers.* Cassell, 2001.

Tanaka, Toshiyuki, Yuki Tanaka, and Marilyn Blatt Young. *Bombing Civilians: A Twentieth-Century History.* New Press, 2010.

Tanaka, Yuki. *Hidden Horrors: Japanese War Crimes in World War II.* Routledge, 2019.

Taylor, Theodore. *The Magnificent Mitscher.* Naval Institute Press, 1991.

Terasaki, Gwen. *Bridge to the Sun*. Rock Creek Books, 2009.

Terkel, Studs, ed. *"The Good War": An Oral History of World War II*. New Press, 1984.

Thomas, Evan. *Sea of Thunder: Four Commanders and the Last Great Naval Campaign, 1941–1945*. The Easton Press, 2008.

Tillman, Barrett. *Whirlwind: The Air War Against Japan, 1942–1945*. Simon & Schuster, 2011.

Time-Life Books. *Japan at War / World War II*. Time-Life Books, 1980.

Toland, John. *The Rising Sun: The Decline and Fall of the Japanese Empire, 1936–1945*. Random House, 1970.

Tolischus, Otto David. *Through Japanese Eyes*. Reynal & Hitchcock, 1945.

Townsend, Hoppes, and Douglas Brinkley. *Driven Patriot: The Life and Times of James Forrestal*. Knopf, 1994.

Truman, Harry S. *Year of Decisions*. Doubleday, 1955.

Tully, Anthony P. *Battle of Surigao Strait*. Indiana University Press, 2014.

Tully, Grace. *F.D.R.: My Boss*. Charles Scribner's Sons, 1949.

Tuohy, Bill. *The Bravest Man: Richard O'Kane and the Amazing Submarine Adventures of the USS Tang*. Sutton, 2001.

Ugaki, Matome. *Fading Victory: The Diary of Admiral Matome Ugaki, 1941–1945*. Translated by Masataka Chihaya. University of Pittsburgh Press, 1991.

Vernon, James W. *Hostile Sky: A Hellcat Flyer in World War II*. Naval Institute Press, 2014.

Veronico, Nick. *World War II Shipyards by the Bay*. Arcadia, 2007.

Victoria, Brian Daizen. *Zen at War*. Weatherhill, 1997.

Wainwright, Jonathan M. *General Wainwright's Story*. Doubleday, 1946.

Walker, Lewis Midgley. *Ninety Day Wonder*. Harlo Press, 1989.

Wallace, Robert F. *From Dam Neck to Okinawa: A Memoir of Antiaircraft Training in World War II*. Washington: Naval Historical Center, Department of the Navy, 2001.

Wees, Marshall Paul, and Francis Beauchesne Thornton. *King-Doctor of Ulithi: The True Story of the Wartime Experiences of Marshall Paul Wees*. Macmillan, 1952.

Weinberg, Gerhard L. *A World at Arms: A Global History of World War II*. Cambridge University Press, 1994.

Weller, George, and Anthony Weller, ed. *First into Nagasaki: The Censored Eyewitness Dispatches on Post-Atomic Japan and Its Prisoners of War*. Three Rivers Press, 2007.

———. *Weller's War: A Legendary Foreign Correspondent's Saga of World War II on Five Continents*. Three Rivers Press, 2010.

Werneth, Ron, ed. *Beyond Pearl Harbor: The Untold Stories of Japan's Naval Airmen*. Atglen, PA: Schiffer Pub., 2008.

Wheeler, Post. *Dragon in the Dust*. Marcel Rodd Co., 1946.

White, Graham J. *FDR and the Press*. Univ. of Chicago Press, 1979.

Whitney, Courtney. *MacArthur: His Rendezvous with History*. Greenwood Press, 1977.

Willmott, H. P. *The Battle of Leyte Gulf: The Last Fleet Action*. Indiana University Press, 2005.

Winkler, Allan M. *Home Front U.S.A.: America During World War II*. Arlington Heights, IL: Harlan Davidson, 1986.

Woodward, C. Vann. *The Battle for Leyte Gulf*. Ballantine Books, 1957.

Wooldridge, E. T., ed. *Carrier Warfare in the Pacific: An Oral History Collection*. Smithsonian Institute Press, 1993.

Wray, Harry, et al. *Bridging the Atomic Divide: Debating Japan–US Attitudes on Hiroshima and Nagasaki*. Lexington Books, 2019.

Wukovits, John F. *Admiral "Bull" Halsey: The Life and Wars of the Navy's Most Controversial Commander*. Palgrave Macmillan, 2010.

Yahara, Hiromichi. *The Battle for Okinawa*. John Wiley & Sons, 1995.

Yamashita, Samuel Hideo. *Daily Life in Wartime Japan, 1940–1945*. University Press of Kansas, 2016.

———, ed. *Leaves from an Autumn of Emergencies: Selections from the Wartime Diaries of Ordinary Japanese*. Honolulu: University of Hawaii Press, 2005.

Yoder, Robert M. *There's No Front like Home*. Hardpress Publishing, 2012.

Yokota, Yutaka. *Suicide Submarine!* Ballantine Books, 1962.

Yoshida, Mitsuru, and Richard H. Minear. *Requiem for Battleship Yamato*. Naval Institute Press, 1999.

Yoshimura, Akira. *Battleship Musashi: The Making and Sinking of the World's Biggest Battleship*. Translated by Vincent Murphy. Kodansha International, 1999.

———. *Zero Fighter*. Westport, CT: Praeger, 1996.

Zacharias, Ellis M. *Secret Missions: The Story of an Intelligence Officer*. Naval Institute Press, 2003.

Zich, Arthur, and the Editors of Time-Life Books. *The Rising Sun*. Alexandria, VA: Time-Life Books, 1977.

Articles

Anderson, George. "Nightmare in Ormoc Bay." *Sea Combat*. Accessed October 14, 2018. http://www.dd-692.com/nightmare.htm.

Associated Press, "Deadly WWII U.S. firebombing raids on Japanese cities largely ignored." https://www.japantimes.co.jp/news/2015/03/10.

———. "Tokyo Aides Weep as General Signs." September 2, 1945.

Bennett, Henry Stanley. "The Impact of Invasion and Occupation on the Civilians of Okinawa." *Naval Institute Proceedings*, Vol. 72, No. 516, February 1946.

Benoit, Patricia. "From Czechoslovakia to Life in Central Texas." *Temple Daily Telegram*, August 23, 2015.

Bradbury, Ellen, and Sandra Blakeslee. "The Harrowing Story of the Nagasaki Bombing Mission." *Bulletin of the Atomic Scientists*, August 4, 2015.

Ben Bradlee. "A Return." *The New Yorker*, October 2, 2006.

Brown, Wilson. "Aide to Four Presidents." *American Heritage*, February 1955.

Cosgrove, Ben. "V-J Day, 1945: A Nation Lets Loose." *Life*, August 1, 2014.

Davis, Captain H. F. D. "Building Major Combatant Ships in World War II." *Naval Institute Proceedings*, Vol. 73, No. 531, May 1947.

Delaney, Norman C. "Corpus Christi, University of the Air." *Naval History*, Vol. 27, No. 3, June 2013.

Delaplane, Stanton. "Victory Riot." In Hogan, William, and William German, eds. *The San Francisco Chronicle Reader*. McGraw-Hill Book Co., 1962.

De Seversky, Alexander P. "Victory Through Air Power!" *The American Mercury*, Vol. 54, February 1942.

"Dewey Refuses to Say Directly That Roosevelt Withheld Pacific Supplies." *The Courier-Journal* (Louisville, KY), September 15, 1944.

Eckelmeyer, Edward H. Jr. "The Story of the Self-Sealing Tank." *Naval Institute Proceedings*, Vol. 78, No. 4, May 1952.

Eller, Ernest M. "Swords into Plowshares: Some of Fleet Admiral Nimitz's Contributions to Peace." Fredericksburg, TX: Admiral Nimitz Foundation, 1986.

Ewing, William H. "Nimitz: Reflections on Pearl Harbor." Fredericksburg, TX: Admiral Nimitz Foundation, 1985.

Fedman, David, and Cary Karacas, "A Cartographic Fade to Black: Mapping the Destruction of Urban Japan During World War II." *Journal of Historical Geography*, Vol. 38, Issue 3, July 2012.

"General MacArthur's Instructions to Japanese on Occupation Landings." Reprinted in *New York Times*, August 23, 1945.

Goldsmith, Raymond W. "The Power of Victory: Munitions Output in World War II." *Military Affairs*, 10, No. 1, Spring 1946.

Guillain, Robert. "I Thought My Last Hour Had Come." *The Atlantic*, August 1980.

Hagen, Robert C., as told to Sidney Shalett. "We Asked for the Jap Fleet—and Got It." *The Saturday Evening Post*, May 26, 1945.

Halsey, Ashley Jr. "The CVL's Success Story." *Naval Institute Proceedings*, Vol. 72, No. 518, April 1946.

Halsey, William F. Jr. "The Battle for Leyte Gulf." *Naval Institute Proceedings*, Vol. 78/5/591, May 1952.

Hammer, Captain D. Harry. "Organized Confusion: Building the Base." *Naval Institute Proceedings*, Vol. 73, No. 530, April 1947.

Heinl, R. D. Jr. "Naval Gunfire: Scourge of the Beaches." *Naval Institute Proceedings*, Vol. 78, No. 4, May 1952.

Herbig, Katherine L. "American Strategic Deception in the Pacific: 1942–1944." In *Strategic and Operational Deception in the Second World War*, ed. Michael I. Handel, 260–300. London: Cass, 1987.

Hessler, William H. "The Carrier Task Force in World War II." *Naval Institute Proceedings*, Vol. 71, No. 513, November 1945.

Holland, James. "The Battle for Okinawa: One Marine's Story." *BBC History Magazine* and *BBC World Histories Magazine*. Accessed May 2, 2019. https://www.historyextra.com/period/second-world-war/the-battle-for-okinawa-one-marines-story/.

Holloway, James L. III. "Second Salvo at Surigao Strait." *Naval History*, Vol. 24, No. 5, October 2010.

Hunt, Richard C. Drum. "Typhoons in the North Pacific." *Naval Institute Proceedings*, Vol. 72, No. 519, May 1946.

Jones, George E. "Intramuros a City of Utter Horror." *New York Times*, February 25, 1945.

Lamar, H. Arthur. "I Saw Stars." Fredericksburg, TX: The Admiral Nimitz Foundation, 1985.

Lardner, John. "D-Day, Iwo Jima." *The New Yorker*, March 17, 1945.

———. "Suicides and Bushwhackers." *The New Yorker*, May 19, 1945.

Laurence, William L. "Atomic Bombing of Nagasaki Told by Flight Member." *New York Times*, September 9, 1945.

Leary, William L., and Michie Hattori Bernstein. "Eyewitness to the Nagasaki Atomic Bomb." *World War II*, July/August 2005.

Liebling, A. J. "The A.P. Surrender." *The New Yorker*, May 12, 1945.

Mailer, Norman. "In the Ring: Life and Letters." *The New Yorker*, October 6, 2008.

Manchester, William. "The Bloodiest Battle of All." *New York Times*, June 14, 1987.

"Master Recording of Hirohito's War-End Speech Released in Digital Form." *The Japan Times*, August 1, 2015. (Includes English translation of the surrender rescript as it appeared in the newspaper on August 15, 1945.)

McCarten, John. "General MacArthur: Fact and Legend." *The American Mercury*, Vol. 58, No. 241, January 1944.

Morris, Frank D. "Our Unsung Admiral." *Collier's Weekly*, January 1, 1944.

Murrie, James I., and Naomi Jeffery Petersen. "Last Train Home." *American History*, February 2018. Adapted with permission from *Railroad History*, Spring–Summer 2015.

Mydans, Carl. "My God, It's Carl Mydans!" *Life*, February 19, 1945.

Nimitz, Chester W. "Some Thoughts to Live By." The Admiral Nimitz Foundation, Fredericksburg, TX, 1971.

Nolte, Carl. "The Dark Side of V-J Day." *San Francisco Chronicle*, August 15, 2005.

Ostrander, Colin. "Chaos at Shimonoseki." *Naval Institute Proceedings*, Vol. 73, No. 532, June 1947.

Petillo, Carol M. "Douglas MacArthur and Manuel Quezon: A Note on an Imperial Bond." *Pacific Historical Review*, Vol. 48, No. 1, Feb. 1979.

Portz, Matthew H. "Aviation Training and Expansion." *Naval Aviation News*, July–August 1990.

———. "Why Primary Flight Training?" *Naval Institute Proceedings*, Vol. 70, No. 496, June 1944.

Pratt, Fletcher. "Spruance: Picture of the Admiral." *Harper's Magazine*, August 1946.

Price, Bryon. "Governmental Censorship in War-Time." *The American Political Science Review*, Vol. 36, No. 5, October 1942.

Ralph, William W. "Improvised Destruction: Arnold, LeMay, and the Firebombing of Japan." *War in History*, Vol. 13, No. 4, October 2006.

Ryall, Julian. "Hiroshima Bomber Tasted Lead After Nuclear Blast, Rediscovered Enola Gay Recordings Reveal." *The Telegraph* (UK), August 6, 2018.

Say, Harold Bradley. "They Pioneered a Channel to Tokyo." *Naval Institute Proceedings*, Vol. 71, No. 513, November 1945.

Sears, David. "Wooden Boats at War: Surigao Strait." *World War II*, Vol. 28, issue No. 5, February 2014.

Selden, Mark. "A Forgotten Holocaust: U.S. Bombing Strategy, the Destruction of Japanese Cities and the American Way of War from World War II to Iraq." *Asia-Pacific Journal*, Vol. 5, No. 5, May 2, 2007.

Siemes, John A. "Eyewitness Account, Hiroshima, August 6, 1945," by Avalon Project, Yale Law School, Lillian Goldman Law Library. http://avalon.law.yale.edu.

Smith, Merriman. "Thank You, Mr. President!" *Life*, August 19, 1946.

Smith, Steven Trent. "Payback: Nine American Subs Avenge a Legend's Death." *World War II* Magazine, October 24, 2016.

Sprague, Rear Admiral C. A. F., U.S.N. "The Japs Had Us on the Ropes." *The American Magazine*, Vol. 139, No. 4, April 1945.

Taoka, Eiko. "Testimony of Hatchobori Streetcar Survivors." *The Atomic Archive*. http://www.atomicarchive.com/Docs/Hibakusha/Hatchobori.shtml.

Trumbull, Robert. "All Out with Halsey!" *New York Times Magazine*, December 6, 1942.

Vandenberg, Arthur. "Why I Am for MacArthur." *Collier's Weekly*, February 12, 1944.

Vogel, Bertram. "Japan's Homeland Aerial Defense." *Naval Institute Proceedings*, Vol. 74, No. 540, February 1948.

Waba, Masako. "A Survivor's Harrowing Account of Nagasaki Bombing." *CBC News*, May 26, 2016. https://www.cbc.ca/news/world/nagasaki-atomic-bomb-survivor-transcript-1.3601606.

Waller, Willard. "Why Veterans Are Bitter." *The American Mercury*, August 1945.

Wellerstein, Alex. "Nagasaki: The Last Bomb." *The New Yorker*, August 7, 2015.

Whitney, Courtney. "Lifting Up a Beaten People." *Life*, August 22, 1955, p. 90.

Williams, Josette H. "Paths to Peace: The Information War in the Pacific, 1945." Center for the Study of Intelligence, CIA. Accessed November 4, 2018. https://www.cia.gov/library.

Williams, R. E. "You Can't Beat 'Em If You Can't Sink 'Em." *Naval Institute Proceedings*, Vol. 72, No. 517, March 1946.

Wylie, J. C. "Reflections on the War in the Pacific." *Naval Institute Proceedings*, Vol. 78, No. 4, May 1952.

INDEX

Page numbers followed by *m* indicate maps.